"A very important guide. Gives a very clear, very factual picture. I must admit that I carry and use the book like a bible and refer to it often. Thank you *Billboard* and thank you Joel."

Hy Lit
Program Director
WSNI RADIO, Philadelphia

"For a number of years I have used a review of music from a specific year as a specialty on my radio show. In those years I've been nicknamed 'The Professor' for my history lessons on music. One of my choice sources for information has been Joel Whitburn's books. Thanks."

Scott Muni
WNEW-FM, New York

"There's nothing else like it — only Joel Whitburn could accurately track 9,311 records of the rock era. *The Billboard Book of Top 40 Hits* is worth its weight in solid gold!"

Arnie "Woo Woo" Ginsburg
WXKS-FM, Boston

"Don't stay home without it!"

Bruce Bradley
WYNY-FM, New York

"Hit records have changed the way we dress, dance, talk, and even perceive ourselves. They make us happy, sad, or just help us to pass the time. Music *is* the message, and with this book Joel has given us a firm platform to catalog those messages and memories."

Jack Armstrong
KFRC, San Francisco

"A valuable reference for oldies but goodies — we wouldn't leave home without it!"

Art Laboe
Los Angeles radio personality
President, Original Sound
Record Co., Hollywood

"Very informative — takes the guesswork out of pop music."

Joe Niagara
WPEN, Philadelphia

"*The Billboard Book of Top 40 Hits* is an invaluable aid to anyone interested in pop music."

Dick Biondi
WNMB-FM, North Myrtle Beach
South Carolina

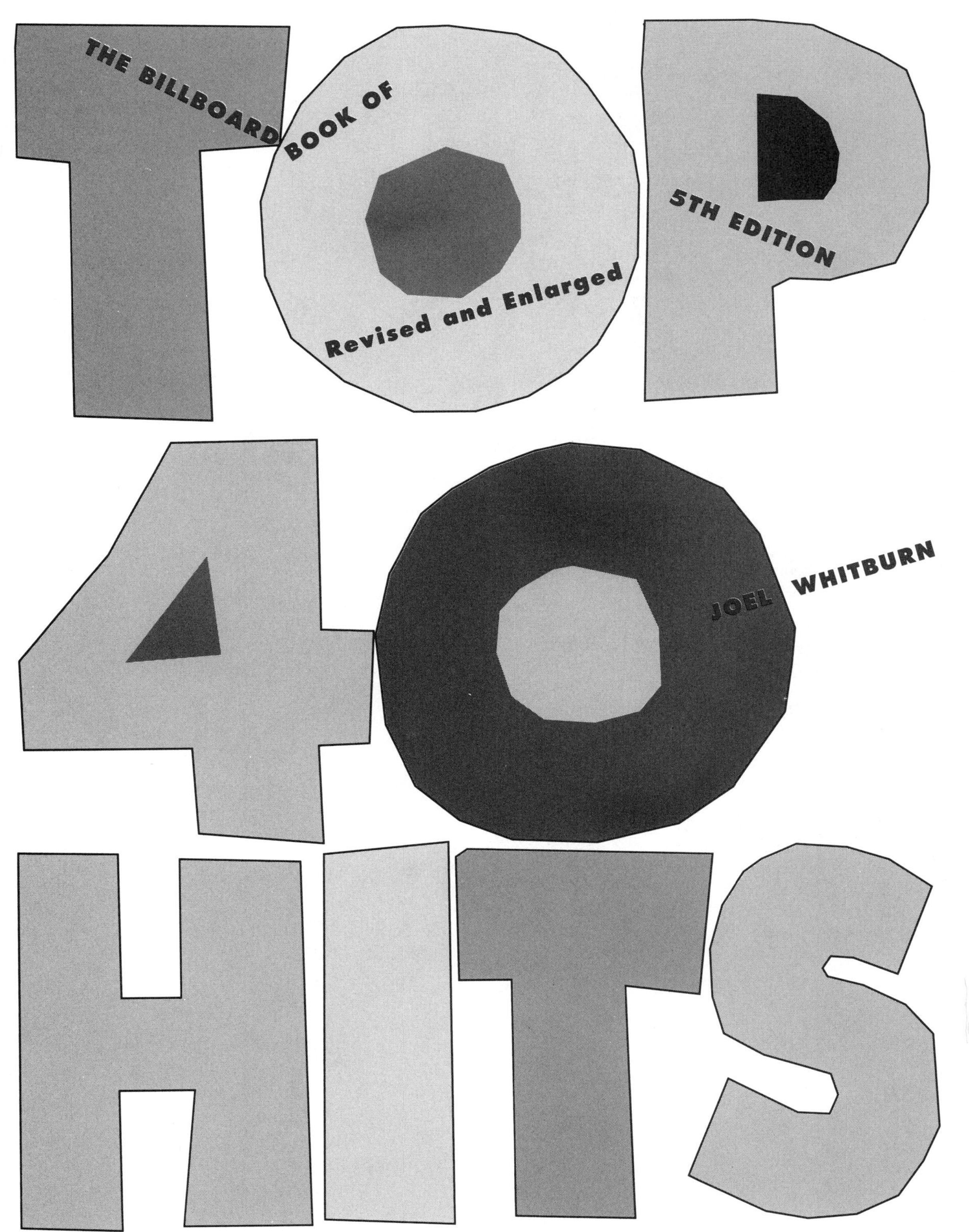

BILLBOARD BOOKS
An imprint of Watson-Guptill Publications/New York

Edited by Fred Weiler
Photo captions by Dave DiMartino
Picture sleeves selected from Joel Whitburn's personal collection
Photography by Malcolm Hjerstedt of Munroe Studios, Inc.
Chart typesetting by Quantum Imaging, Inc.
Book and cover design by Bob Fillie
Graphic production by Marybeth Tregarthen

First published 1992 by Billboard Publications, Inc.
1515 Broadway, New York, NY 10036.

ISBN 8230-8280-6

Library of Congress Cataloging-in-Publication Data

Whitburn, Joel.
The Billboard book of top 40 hits / Joel Whitburn. — 5th ed.
p. cm.
ISBN 0-8230-8280-6 : $19.95
1. Popular music—United States—Discography. 2. Popular music—United States—Statistics. I. Billboard. II. Title. III. Title: Billboard book of top forty hits. IV. Title: Top 40 hits.
ML156242P6W44 1992
016.78164'026'6—dc20 91-45488
CIP
MN

Manufactured in the United States of America

First printing, 1992

2 3 4 5 6 7 8/99 98 97 96 95 94 93

This book is dedicated to my three favorite ladies: my wife, Fran; my daughter, Kim; and my mother, Ruth. I can't imagine three more caring, understanding, and helpful persons in all of the world, who have, at one time or another, shared and tolerated my lifetime passion for music.

The author wishes to give thanks to
the staff of Record Research:

Bill Hathaway
Kim Whitburn
Brent Olynick
Kim Gaarder
Joanne Wagner
Troy Kluess
Fran Whitburn
Ruth Whitburn
Joyce Riehl
Brian Niese
Jeanne Olynick
Oscar Vidotto

CONTENTS

INTRODUCTION
by Shadoe Stevens

I've been in love with hit records ever since I was a little boy growing up in Jamestown, North Dakota. My uncle gave me a wireless broadcast kit; I put it together and started my own radio station at the age of 10. I covered the town. And what did I play? Hits, of course—the records I heard on real radio stations.

I didn't really find out about the *Billboard* charts until my first professional job as "The World's Youngest Disc Jockey." Since then, I've known what every DJ knows: there's nothing like the pop charts, and it ain't a hit till *Billboard* says it's a hit.

Since I started hosting ABC Radio Network's *American Top 40*, I've learned that Joel Whitburn's books are an integral part of the facts and figures we DJs reel off with deceptive ease on every weekly show. With Record Research volumes on pop, country, R&B, Top 10 charts, and albums, Joel's got all the bases covered.

So whether you're counting down along with *AT40*, just tuned to the radio, or listening to your own music collection, you'll want *Top 40 Hits* right by your side. Look up one song and it may lead to an artist's entire Top 40 output—or maybe to other versions of the same song. The photos of picture sleeves show how styles have changed, along with the music and the format, in this day and age of cassette and CD singles. And the back of this book is a real brain-boggler—the all-time record holders in a cross-section of categories.

For the pop radio pro or the fun-minded fan, *Top 40 Hits* is a treasure trove of hit facts, tune trivia, and a whole lot more. All you have to do is flip your fingers through it!

SHADOE STEVENS
American Top 40

AUTHOR'S NOTE

Did Fats Domino or Pat Boone have more hits on *Billboard*'s Hot 100? Who charted higher with their 1955 versions of "Unchained Melody"—Les Baxter, Al Hibbler, or Roy Hamilton? How many weeks was Bill Doggett's "Honky Tonk" on the pop charts?

These are the kind of questions I asked myself in the early 1960s as I began to devote more time to my record-collecting hobby. I wanted answers, but no books existed that chronicled a record's chart life. So the only way to satisfy my curiosity was to follow, week by week, each title up and down the pop charts.

I pulled out my old issues of *Billboard* and put them to use. On 3" x 5" index cards, I kept track of my favorite pop artists' charted titles, debut dates, peak positions, weeks on the chart, etc., and set out to collect each of these titles. Soon I was making up index cards for every charted artist, but as I started compiling these statistics, I didn't know anyone else who shared my enthusiasm for the charts.

At the urging of a few DJ friends, I decided to transcribe the research from my index cards into book form. In 1970, the history of the rock era on the *Billboard* charts was available, for the first time, in a slim volume simply titled *Record Research*. The growing interest in my book indicated that others besides disc jockeys were keeping a keen eye on the charts. Five more versions of what came to known as *Top Pop Singles* followed, with each new edition featuring more artist and title information than the previous one. In 1983, Billboard Books published a spinoff of *Top Pop Singles*, *The Billboard Book of Top 40 Hits*. *Top 40 Hits* is already in its fifth edition—a testimony to the enormously popular appeal of the pop charts.

I am deeply grateful to *Billboard* magazine for the honor of compiling and publishing the results of each week's record race. It is an honor to be associated with my favorite magazine of the last four decades. I also applaud my fellow chart devotees, who eagerly anticipate each new issue of *Billboard* magazine.

JOEL WHITBURN

DAVID SANBORN
SAN SEBASTIAN STRINGS
SALSOUL ORCHESTRA
BUFFY SAINTE MARIE
SADE
S
SPARKS
SOUTHSIDE JOHNNY

JOEL WHITBURN: CHARTING HIS OWN COURSE

It was in 1970 that Joel Whitburn published the book bound to become a business.

The book—*Top Pop Records*—was a natural outgrowth of Joel's love of records and his penchant for filling file cards with *Billboard* chart data on each record he owned, the better to control his swelling collection.

This slim, 104-page volume—listing every single to ever appear on *Billboard*'s Pop music charts from 1955–1969—was soon a big hit with the record and radio industries. And Record Research, Inc. was born.

Since then, few, if any, individuals have taken the charts to heart quite like Joel Whitburn. In addition to *The Billboard Book of Top 40 Hits*, "the world's foremost chart authority" has compiled well over thirty other books detailing the history and development of charted music from 1890 to the present.

Today, Joel's team of Record Researchers delves deeper into *Billboard*'s charts than ever before, pouring out a steady stream of chart reference books widely noted for their detail, diversity, and painstaking accuracy. These books, currently used worldwide by collectors, disc jockeys, program directors, musicologists, artists and others, cover musical genres ranging from pop to country to R&B and beyond.

As the largest privately-held record collection in the world, Joel's vast music library completely fills an environmentally-controlled underground vault adjacent to his Menomonee Falls, Wisconsin home. Here you'll find all the 80,000+ titles that ever appeared on *Billboard*'s "Hot 100" and "Top Pop Albums" charts, along with a good share of the records that made *Billboard*'s other charts.

And here, too, you'll find Joel Whitburn, collector extraordinaire, for whom charting a record's rise and fall has never lost its excitement or intrigue.

RESEARCHING THE CHARTS

The majority of the research within this book was compiled from *Billboard* magazine's Hot 100 chart. The Hot 100 made its debut on August 4, 1958, and has long been regarded as the definitive weekly ranking of America's most popular singles in sales and radio airplay.

The pop chart research for this book began with the January 1, 1955 issue of *Billboard*. At this time, *Billboard* was publishing the forerunners to the Hot 100 chart. These charts appeared in the magazine weekly and each focused on specific areas of the music trade. The most obvious antecedent of the Hot 100 was the Top 100 chart, which *Billboard* debuted in November of 1955. By October of 1958, all of these charts were discontinued in favor of the all-encompassing Hot 100.

The following *Billboard* pop charts were researched for this book:

Chart Title	Dates Researched	# of Positions
Best Sellers In Stores	1/1/55-10/13/58 (chart ended)	25-50
Most Played By Jockeys	1/1/55-7/28/58 (chart ended)	20-25
Most Played In Juke Boxes	1/1/55-6/17/57 (chart ended)	20
Top 100	11/12/55-7/28/58 (chart ended)	100
Hot 100	8/4/58-7/27/91	100

A chart-by-chart breakdown of the highest position a record attained on any of the above 1955-1958 *Billboard* Pop charts is listed below the title. However, if a record hit only the Top 100 or Hot 100, no chart information is shown below that title. Keep in mind that records which peaked at positions 51-100 could only have charted on the Top 100 or Hot 100.

pre If a record enters a newly published chart well after the record's peak chart performance, the word **pre** is shown after the position. Had the chart been published earlier, the record would, most likely, have scored higher on that chart.

end If a record had not yet peaked on a chart that was terminated, the word **end** is shown after the position. Had the chart continued, the still-climbing record would probably have reached a higher position.

A record's *date* is *Billboard*'s actual issue date from the chart on which it first reached the Top 40. It is not the "week-ending" date which *Billboard* published on their various charts. The issue and week-ending dates were different until January 13, 1962, when *Billboard* began using one date system for both the issue and the charts inside.

The record's *highest position* (**POS**) is taken from the chart on which it achieved its highest ranking.

The record's *weeks charted* in the Top 40 (**WKS**) and weeks at positions No. 1 or No. 2 are taken from the chart on which it achieved its highest total.

Directly under nearly every artist name are brief notes about the artist or group. Directly under some song titles are brief notes that may be of special interest, such as a record that may have first charted on the Hot 100 at an earlier date, but did not reach the Top 40, or one that may feature a famous singer providing background vocals. If the song is featured in a Broadway musical or film, the title of the show is given under the record title. You will note the occasional use of POS in both title and artist trivia, which simply stands for "position."

DON'T BE CRUEL/HOUND DOG

For 11 consecutive weeks (August 18, 1956 through October 27, 1956) on the Best Sellers charts, and for 11 consecutive weeks (September 1, 1956 through November 10, 1956) on the Juke Box charts, the biggest two-sided single in history held down the #1 spot. During this period, both charts combined two-sided hits into a single listing on the charts. In both cases, "Hound Dog" debuted as the top side, with "Don't Be Cruel" listed later as the top side. Both sides were enormously strong, and it's logical to assume that each would have held the #1 spot for at least eight to nine weeks had they been released as separate singles. However, as a powerhouse dual single, and with *Billboard* alternating the side shown first, their combined total stay at #1 makes it the biggest charted single of the rock era.

1989-1991 CASSETTE SINGLES

Nearly all of the singles that hit *Billboard*'s pop charts from 1955 through 1988 were commercially available on vinyl 45 rpm; a handful were exclusively available as vinyl 12-inch singles which is indicated in their title trivia. From 1989 through 1991, most Top 40 singles were still available on vinyl; however, some were available only on cassette. The "#" symbol listed to the immediate right of the label number indicates which 1989, 1990, and 1991 singles were commercially released on cassette only and not vinyl. Unless there is a cassette-only symbol or a trivia note indicating that a title is exclusively available on 12-inch or maxi-cassette single, all label numbers listed in the book are for vinyl 7-inch singles.

THE ARTISTS

HOW TO USE THIS SECTION

This section lists, alphabetically by artist name, every single release to make the Top 40 on *Billboard*'s pop singles chart from January 1, 1955 through July 27, 1991.

Each artist's Top 40 hits are listed in chronological order. A sequential number is shown in front of each song title to indicate that artist's number of Top 40 hits. All Top 10 hits are highlighted in dark type.

Columnar headings show the following data:

DATE: Date record debuted in the Top 40

POS: Record's highest charted position (highlighted in bold type)

WKS: Total weeks charted in the Top 40

LABEL & NO.: Original record label and number

Other data and symbols:

(1) Number in parentheses to the right of a No. 1 or No. 2 peak position is the total weeks the record held that position
\+ Indicates record peaked in the year after it first charted (symbol shown next to date)
● RIAA certified gold record (million seller)
▲ RIAA certified platinum record (two-million seller)
Commercially available only as a cassette single (shown only for 1989, 1990, and 1991 singles)
/ Divides a two-sided hit. Complete chart data (date, peak position, etc.) is shown for both sides if each side achieved its own peak position. If a title was shown only as the B-side, then only the weeks it was shown as a "tagalong" are listed.

The Record Industry Association of America began certifying gold records in 1958 and platinum records in 1976. Prior to these dates, there are most certainly some hits that would have qualified as gold or platinum records. Also, some record labels have never requested RIAA certification for their hits. As of January 1, 1989, the RIAA lowered the certification for gold singles to the sale of 500,000 units and platinum to one million units.

Letter(s) in brackets after titles indicate:

[I] instrumental recording
[N] novelty recording
[C] comedy recording
[S] spoken recording
[F] foreign language recording
[X] Christmas recording
[R] re-entry, reissue, remix or re-recording of a previous hit by that artist

See RESEARCHING THE CHARTS for an explanation of the chart names listed below records titles from 1955-1958.

DATE	POS	WKS	ARTIST—RECORD TITLE	LABEL & NO.
			A	
			ABBA	
			Pop quartet formed in Stockholm, Sweden in 1970, using their first initials as an acronym. Consisted of Anni-Frid "Frida" Lyngstad and Agnetha Faltskog (vocals), Bjorn Ulvaeus (guitar) and Benny Andersson (keyboards). Benny and Bjorn recorded together in 1966. Bjorn and Agnetha married in 1971, divorced in 1979. Benny and Frida married in 1978, divorced in 1981. Disbanded in the early 1980s.	
6/22/74	**6**	12	**1. Waterloo**	Atlantic 3035
10/12/74	**27**	4	2. Honey, Honey	Atlantic 3209
10/11/75	**15**	8	3. SOS	Atlantic 3265
3/27/76	**15**	8	4. I Do, I Do, I Do, I Do, I Do	Atlantic 3310
6/19/76	**32**	4	5. Mamma Mia	Atlantic 3315
9/25/76	**13**	11	6. Fernando	Atlantic 3346
1/22/77	**1**(1)	15	● **7. Dancing Queen**	Atlantic 3372
6/04/77	**14**	10	8. Knowing Me, Knowing You	Atlantic 3387
1/28/78	**12**	9	9. The Name Of The Game	Atlantic 3449
5/06/78	**3**	14	● **10. Take A Chance On Me**	Atlantic 3457
6/09/79	**19**	10	11. Does Your Mother Know	Atlantic 3574
12/08/79+	**29**	6	12. Chiquitita	Atlantic 3629
12/27/80+	**8**	16	**13. The Winner Takes It All**	Atlantic 3776
2/06/82	**27**	8	14. When All Is Said And Done all of above written and produced by Benny & Bjorn	Atlantic 3889
			ABBOTT, Gregory	
			Soul singer/songwriter from New York. At age eight, member of St. Patrick's Cathedral Choir. Psychology major at Boston University and Stanford; taught English at Berkeley.	
11/08/86+	**1**(1)	16	**1. Shake You Down**	Columbia 06191
			ABC	
			Electro-pop group from Sheffield, England. Formed as Vice Versa with Stephen Singleton and Mark White. Lead singer Martin Fry joined in 1980, group renamed ABC. Singleton left group in 1985.	
10/30/82+	**18**	13	1. The Look Of Love (Part One)	Mercury 76168
2/26/83	**25**	8	2. Poison Arrow	Mercury 810340
9/28/85	**9**	11	**3. Be Near Me**	Mercury 880626
2/15/86	**20**	7	4. (How To Be A) Millionaire	Mercury 884382
8/01/87	**5**	12	**5. When Smokey Sings** a tribute to Smokey Robinson	Mercury 888604
			ABDUL, Paula	
			Los Angeles singer/choreographer born on 6/19/62 of Brazilian and French Canadian parentage. While still a teen, was the choreographer and member of the Los Angeles Lakers cheerleaders. Choreographed Janet Jackson's *Control* album and videos, and "The Tracy Ullman Show."	
12/24/88+	**1**(3)	16	▲ **1. Straight Up**	Virgin 99256
4/01/89	**1**(2)	14	● **2. Forever Your Girl**	Virgin 99230
7/08/89	**1**(1)	15	● **3. Cold Hearted**	Virgin 99196
10/07/89	**3**	14	**4. (It's Just) The Way That You Love Me** [R]	Virgin 99282

DATE	POS	WKS	ARTIST—RECORD TITLE	LABEL & NO.
			originally charted in 1988 (POS 88)	
1/06/90	1(3)	14	● **5. Opposites Attract**	Virgin 99158
			PAULA ABDUL with THE WILD PAIR	
			rap by Derrick Delite from The Soul Purpose	
5/11/91	1(5)	15	● **6. Rush, Rush**	Virgin 98828
7/20/91	1(1)	13	**7. The Promise Of A New Day**	Virgin 98752
			AC/DC	
			Hard-rock band formed in Sydney, Australia in 1974. Consisted of brothers Angus and Malcolm Young (guitars), Ron Belford "Bon" Scott (lead singer), Phil Rudd (drums) and Mark Evans (bass). Cliff Williams replaced Evans in 1977. Bon Scott died on 2/19/80 (age 33) from alcohol abuse and was replaced by Brian Johnson. Simon Wright replaced Rudd in 1985. Wright joined Dio in 1989, replaced by Chris Slade of The Firm. Angus and Malcolm are the younger brothers of George Young of The Easybeats.	
10/25/80	**35**	3	1. You Shook Me All Night Long	Atlantic 3761
2/07/81	**37**	5	2. Back In Black	Atlantic 3787
1/26/91	**23**	5	3. Moneytalks	Atco 98881
			ACE	
			Pub-rock quintet from Sheffield, England led by vocalist Paul Carrack. Disbanded in 1977. Carrack joined Squeeze in 1981, then Mike + The Mechanics in 1985.	
4/05/75	**3**	11	**1. How Long**	Anchor 21000
			ACE, Johnny	
			R&B vocalist/pianist/organist/composer. Born John Marshall Alexander, Jr. on 6/09/29 in Memphis. Worked with the B.B. King band, then formed The Beale Streeters with Bobby Bland and Earl Forrest before going solo. Killed playing Russian Roulette backstage at the City Auditorium in Houston on 12/24/54.	
2/19/55	**17**	9	1. Pledging My Love	Duke 136
			Best Seller #17 / Juke Box #17 / Jockey #19	
			with Johnny Board's Orchestra	
			ACKLIN, Barbara	
			R&B singer/songwriter born on 2/28/44 in Chicago. Cousin to Monk Higgins, who produced her first sessions for Special Agent in 1966 (as Barbara Allen).	
8/10/68	**15**	8	1. Love Makes A Woman	Brunswick 55379
			ADAM & THE ANTS — see ANT, Adam	
			ADAMS, Bryan	
			Born on 11/05/59 in Kingston, Ontario. Rock singer/songwriter/guitarist based in Vancouver, Canada. Lead singer of Sweeney Todd in 1976. Teamed with Jim Vallance in 1977 in songwriting partnership. Cameo appearance in the film *Pink Cadillac*.	
4/16/83	**10**	11	**1. Straight From The Heart**	A&M 2536
6/25/83	**15**	8	2. Cuts Like A Knife	A&M 2553
10/01/83	**24**	6	3. This Time	A&M 2574
11/24/84+	**6**	12	**4. Run To You**	A&M 2686
2/23/85	**11**	10	5. Somebody	A&M 2701
4/27/85	1(2)	14	**6. Heaven**	A&M 2729
7/13/85	**5**	12	**7. Summer Of '69**	A&M 2739
9/28/85	**13**	9	8. One Night Love Affair	A&M 2770
12/07/85+	**15**	9	9. It's Only Love	A&M 2791
			BRYAN ADAMS/TINA TURNER	

DATE	POS	WKS	ARTIST—RECORD TITLE	LABEL & NO.
4/11/87	**6**	10	**10. Heat Of The Night**	A&M 2921
7/04/87	**26**	6	11. Hearts On Fire	A&M 2948
9/12/87	**32**	5	12. Victim Of Love	A&M 2964
7/06/91	**1**(7)	17	▲ **13. (Everything I Do) I Do It For You**	A&M 1567
			from the film *Robin Hood: Prince of Thieves*	
			ADAMS, Johnny	
			Born Lathan John Adams on 1/05/32 in New Orleans. Soul singer nicknamed "The Tan Canary." First recorded on the Ric label in 1959.	
7/26/69	**28**	4	1. Reconsider Me	SSS Int'l. 770
			ADAMS, Oleta	
			Native of Yakima, Washington. Discovered by Tears For Fears in Kansas City; backing singer on their *Seeds Of Love* LP and tour.	
2/09/91	**5**	10	**1. Get Here**	Fontana 878476
			ADDERLEY, "Cannonball"	
			Born Julian Edwin Adderley on 9/15/28 in Tampa. Nickname derived from "cannibal" — in tribute to his love of eating. Alto saxophonist/leader of own jazz combo. Died on 8/08/75 in Gary, Indiana.	
1/28/67	**11**	8	1. Mercy, Mercy, Mercy [I]	Capitol 5798
			ADDRISI BROTHERS, The	
			Pop singing/songwriting duo: Dick and Don Addrisi. Don died of cancer on 11/13/84 (age 45).	
2/26/72	**25**	7	1. We've Got To Get It On Again	Columbia 45521
5/14/77	**20**	8	2. Slow Dancin' Don't Turn Me On	Buddah 566
			AD LIBS, The	
			Newark, New Jersey quintet: Mary Ann Thomas (lead singer), Hugh Harris, Danny Austin, Norman Donegan and Dave Watt.	
2/06/65	**8**	7	**1. The Boy From New York City**	Blue Cat 102
			ADVENTURES OF STEVIE V	
			Dance outfit assembled by Stevie Vincent, a native of Bedfordshire, England. Includes singer Melodie Washington and multi-instrumentalist Mick Walsh.	
8/25/90	**25**	8	1. Dirty Cash (Money Talks)	Mercury 875802#
			AEROSMITH	
			Hard-rock band formed in Sunapee, New Hampshire in 1970. Consisted of Steven Tyler (lead singer; b: Steven Tallarico), Joe Perry and Brad Whitford (guitars), Tom Hamilton (bass) and Joey Kramer (drums). Perry left for own Joe Perry Project in 1979; replaced by Jimmy Crespo. Whitford left in 1981; replaced by Rick Dufay. Original band reunited in April 1984.	
7/12/75	**36**	3	1. Sweet Emotion	Columbia 10155
2/14/76	**6**	11	**2. Dream On** **[R]**	Columbia 10278
			originally charted in 1973 (POS 59)	
6/26/76	**21**	10	3. Last Child	Columbia 10359
12/18/76+	**10**	11	**4. Walk This Way**	Columbia 10449
			revived in 1986 (with Tyler & Perry) as a "rap" hit by Run-D.M.C.	
5/07/77	**38**	2	5. Back In The Saddle	Columbia 10516
9/02/78	**23**	7	6. Come Together	Columbia 10802
11/14/87	**14**	10	7. Dude (Looks Like A Lady)	Geffen 28240
2/27/88	**3**	15	**8. Angel**	Geffen 28249
7/09/88	**17**	8	9. Rag Doll	Geffen 27915
9/16/89	**5**	11	● **10. Love In An Elevator**	Geffen 22845

DATE	POS	WKS	ARTIST—RECORD TITLE	LABEL & NO.
12/16/89+	**4**	13	**11. Janie's Got A Gun**	Geffen 22727#
3/31/90	**9**	10	**12. What It Takes**	Geffen 19944
7/21/90	**22**	7	13. The Other Side	Geffen 19927
			AFTERNOON DELIGHTS, The	
			Female studio vocal quartet from Boston.	
9/12/81	**33**	5	1. General Hospi-Tale [N] parody of TV's "General Hospital"	MCA 51148
			AFTER 7	
			Indianapolis vocal trio: Keith Mitchell with brothers Kevon and Melvin Edmonds. Keith is the cousin of L.A. Reid. Kevon and Melvin are the brothers of Babyface.	
4/28/90	**7**	13	● **1. Ready or Not**	Virgin 98995
8/25/90	**6**	15	● **2. Can't Stop**	Virgin 98961
1/26/91	**19**	5	3. Heat Of The Moment [R] originally charted in 1989 (POS 74); above 3 written and produced by L.A. Reid and Babyface	Virgin 99204
7/06/91	**24**	5	4. Nights Like This from the film *The Five Heartbeats*	Virgin 98798#
			AFTER THE FIRE	
			English band led by guitarist Andy Piercy.	
3/05/83	**5**	14	**1. Der Kommissar** Kommissar: a Russian government official	Epic 03559
			A-HA	
			Trio formed in Oslo, Norway: Morten Harket (vocals), Pal Waaktaar (guitar) and Mags Furuholem (keyboards).	
8/24/85	**1**(1)	15	**1. Take On Me**	Warner 29011
1/11/86	**20**	8	2. The Sun Always Shines On T.V.	Warner 28846
			AIR SUPPLY	
			Melbourne, Australia duo: Russell Hitchcock (born on 6/15/49 in Melbourne) and Graham Russell (born on 6/01/50 in Nottingham, England). Disbanded in 1988. Both members recorded solo. Reunited in 1991.	
3/08/80	**3**	17	**1. Lost In Love**	Arista 0479
7/19/80	**2**(4)	17	● **2. All Out Of Love**	Arista 0520
11/15/80+	**5**	17	**3. Every Woman In The World**	Arista 0564
5/23/81	**1**(1)	14	● **4. The One That You Love**	Arista 0604
10/03/81	**5**	15	**5. Here I Am (Just When I Thought I Was Over You)**	Arista 0626
1/09/82	**5**	15	**6. Sweet Dreams**	Arista 0655
6/26/82	**5**	13	**7. Even The Nights Are Better**	Arista 0692
10/23/82	**38**	2	8. Young Love	Arista 1005
12/25/82+	**38**	5	9. Two Less Lonely People In The World	Arista 1004
8/13/83	**2**(3)	17	● **10. Making Love Out Of Nothing At All**	Arista 9056
6/08/85	**19**	10	11. Just As I Am	Arista 9353
			AKENS, Jewel	
			Black male vocalist/producer born in Houston in 1940.	
2/06/65	**3**	12	**1. The Birds And The Bees**	Era 3141

DATE	POS	WKS	ARTIST—RECORD TITLE	LABEL & NO.
			ALABAMA	
			Country quartet from Fort Payne, Alabama: Randy Owen (vocals, guitar), Jeff Cook (keyboards, fiddle), Teddy Gentry (bass, vocals) and Mark Herndon (drums, vocals). Randy, Jeff and Teddy are cousins.	
7/25/81	**20**	8	1. Feels So Right	RCA 12236
1/16/82	**15**	10	2. Love In The First Degree	RCA 12288
6/05/82	**18**	8	3. Take Me Down	RCA 13210
6/04/83	**38**	3	4. The Closer You Get	RCA 13524
			all of above titles hit #1 on *Billboard*'s country charts	
			ALBERT, Morris	
			Brazilian singer/songwriter born Morris Albert Kaisermann.	
8/23/75	**6**	16	● **1. Feelings**	RCA 10279
			AL B. SURE!	
			Black singer born Al Brown in Boston and raised in Mt. Vernon, New York.	
5/14/88	**7**	13	**1. Nite And Day**	Warner 28192
4/07/90	**31**	4	2. The Secret Garden (Sweet Seduction Suite)	Qwest 19992
			QUINCY JONES/AL B. SURE!/JAMES INGRAM/EL DeBARGE/BARRY WHITE	
			ALEXANDER, Arthur	
			Born on 5/10/40 in Florence, Alabama. Teamed with Rick Hall in studio work at Muscle Shoals. First recorded for Judd in 1960.	
3/31/62	**24**	6	1. You Better Move On	Dot 16309
			ALIAS	
			Rock quintet formed in Los Angeles by former Sheriff bandmates Freddy Curci (vocals) and Steve DeMarchi (guitar), and Roger Fisher (ex-guitarist of Heart).	
9/29/90	**2**(1)	15	**1. More Than Words Can Say**	EMI 50324#
2/02/91	**13**	9	2. Waiting For Love	EMI 50337#
			ALIVE AND KICKING	
			New York City-based, five-man, one-woman, pop-rock group led by singers Pepe Cardona and Sandy Toder.	
7/04/70	**7**	10	**1. Tighter, Tighter**	Roulette 7078
			ALLAN, Davie/The Arrows	
			Davie began as a session guitarist for Mike Curb in Los Angeles. Also see Max Frost And The Troopers.	
9/09/67	**37**	3	1. Blue's Theme [I]	Tower 295
			from the film *The Wild Angels*	
			ALLEN, Deborah	
			Born Deborah Lynn Thurmond on 9/30/53 in Memphis. Country singer/songwriter.	
12/24/83+	**26**	7	1. Baby I Lied	RCA 13600
			ALLEN, Donna	
			Soul singer born in Key West and raised in Tampa. Former cheerleader for the Tampa Bay Buccaneers.	
3/28/87	**21**	9	1. Serious	21 Records 99497

DATE	POS	WKS	ARTIST—RECORD TITLE	LABEL & NO.
			ALLEN, Rex	
			Born on 12/31/20 in Wilcox, Arizona. Singer/guitarist/actor. Starred in 35 western films in the 1950s. Narrator for over 80 Disney films during the 1960s and 1970s.	
10/06/62	**17**	4	1. Don't Go Near The Indians	Mercury 71997
			ALLEN, Steve	
			Born on 12/26/21 in New York City. Comedian/actor/composer/author. In 1954, became the first host of TV's "Tonight Show." Played title role in 1956 film *The Benny Goodman Story.* Hosted own variety and talk shows, 1956-80. Married to actress Jayne Meadows.	
12/03/55	**35**	2	1. Autumn Leaves [I] **STEVE ALLEN with GEORGE CATES**	Coral 61485
			ALLISON, Gene	
			R&B singer born on 8/29/34 in Nashville. First recorded for Calvert in 1956.	
3/10/58	**36**	1	1. You Can Make It If You Try Best Seller #36 / Top 100 #37	Vee-Jay 256
			ALLMAN, Gregg	
			Keyboardist/vocalist born on 12/08/47 in Nashville and raised in Daytona Beach, Florida. In 1965, Greg and brother Duane formed the Allman Joys which evolved into the Allman Brothers Band by 1969. Married to Cher from 1975-77.	
1/19/74	**19**	8	1. Midnight Rider	Capricorn 0035
			ALLMAN BROTHERS BAND, The	
			Southern-rock band formed in Macon, Georgia in 1969. Consisted of brothers Duane (lead guitar) and Gregg Allman (keyboards), Dickey Betts (guitar), Berry Oakley (bass), and the drum duo of Butch Trucks and Jai Johnny Johanson (pronounced: Jay Johnny Johnson). Duane and Gregg known earlier as the Allman Joys and Hour Glass. Duane was the top session guitarist at Muscle Shoals studio; he was killed in a motorcycle crash on 10/29/71 (age 24). Oakley died in another cycle accident on 11/11/72 (age 24); he was replaced by Lamar Williams. Chuck Leavell (keyboards) added in 1972. Group split up in 1976. Gregg formed the Gregg Allman Band. Betts formed Great Southern. Leavell, Williams and Johanson formed the fusion-rock band Sea Level. Allman and Betts reunited with a new Allman Brothers' lineup in 1978. Disbanded in 1981. Allman, Betts, Trucks and Johanson regrouped with Warren Haynes (guitar), Allen Woody (bass) and Johnny Neel (keyboards) in 1989. Neel left in 1990.	
9/08/73	**2**(1)	13	**1. Ramblin Man**	Capricorn 0027
4/07/79	**29**	5	2. Crazy Love	Capricorn 0320
9/19/81	**39**	2	3. Straight From The Heart	Arista 0618
			ALPERT, Herb/The Tijuana Brass	
			Herb was born on 3/31/35 in Los Angeles. Producer/composer/trumpeter/bandleader. Played trumpet since age eight. A&R for Keen Records. Produced first Jan & Dean session. Wrote "Wonderful World" hit for Sam Cooke. Formed A&M Records with Jerry Moss in 1962. Used studio musicians until early 1965, then formed own band.	
11/10/62	**6**	11	**1. The Lonely Bull** **[I]** **THE TIJUANA BRASS featuring HERB ALPERT** crowd noises dubbed in from bullring in Tijuana, Mexico	A&M 703
			HERB ALPERT & THE TIJUANA BRASS:	
10/16/65	**7**	13	**2. Taste Of Honey** **[I]**	A&M 775
1/22/66	**11**	7	3. Zorba The Greek/ [I] from the film of the same title	
2/05/66	**38**	2	4. Tijuana Taxi [I]	A&M 787
4/09/66	**24**	5	5. What Now My Love/ [I]	

DATE	POS	WKS	ARTIST—RECORD TITLE		LABEL & NO.
4/09/66	**27**	4	6. Spanish Flea	[I]	A&M 792
			theme song from TV's "The Dating Game"		
7/09/66	**18**	6	7. The Work Song	[I]	A&M 805
9/17/66	**28**	4	8. Flamingo	[I]	A&M 813
12/03/66	**19**	6	9. Mame		A&M 823
			from the Broadway show *Mame*		
4/01/67	**37**	2	10. Wade In The Water	[I]	A&M 840
4/29/67	**27**	6	11. Casino Royale	[I]	A&M 850
			from the film of the same title		
7/22/67	**32**	3	12. The Happening	[I]	A&M 860
9/30/67	**35**	3	13. A Banda	[I]	A&M 870
			HERB ALPERT:		
5/25/68	**1**(4)	12	● **14. This Guy's In Love With You**		A&M 929
8/25/79	**1**(2)	15	● **15. Rise**	**[I]**	A&M 2151
12/22/79+	**30**	6	16. Rotation	[I]	A&M 2202
7/31/82	**37**	4	17. Route 101	[I]	A&M 2422
5/02/87	**5**	12	**18. Diamonds**		A&M 2929
			vocals by Janet Jackson and Lisa Keith		
8/29/87	**35**	3	19. Making Love In The Rain		A&M 2949
			vocal by Lisa Keith		
			AMAZING RHYTHM ACES, The		
			Memphis country-rock group: Russell Smith (lead vocals, guitar), Barry "Byrd" Burton (guitar, dobro), Billy Earhart III (keyboards), Jeff Davis (bass) and Butch McDade (drums). Disbanded in 1980.		
7/26/75	**14**	9	1. Third Rate Romance		ABC 12078
			AMBOY DUKES, The		
			Detroit rock group led by Ted Nugent.		
7/27/68	**16**	7	1. Journey To The Center Of The Mind		Mainstream 684
			AMBROSIA		
			Los Angeles-based pop group: David Pack and Joe Puerta (lead singers), Burleigh Drummond and Christopher North. North left in 1977.		
7/19/75	**17**	8	1. Holdin' On To Yesterday		20th Century 2207
4/02/77	**39**	2	2. Magical Mystery Tour		20th Century 2327
			from the film *All This & World War II*		
9/30/78	**3**	14	**3. How Much I Feel**		Warner 8640
4/19/80	**3**	14	**4. Biggest Part Of Me**		Warner 49225
8/02/80	**13**	10	5. You're The Only Woman (You & I)		Warner 49508
			AMERICA		
			Trio formed in London in 1969. Consisted of Americans Dan Peek, Gerry Beckley and Englishman Dewey Bunnell. All played guitars. Met at U.S. Air Force base. Members of Daze in 1970. Moved to the U.S. in February 1972. Won the 1972 Best New Artist Grammy Award. Peek left in 1976 and became a popular Contemporary Christian artist.		
3/04/72	**1**(3)	12	● **1. A Horse With No Name**		Warner 7555
5/27/72	**9**	9	**2. I Need You**		Warner 7580
11/04/72	**8**	9	**3. Ventura Highway**		Warner 7641
2/24/73	**35**	2	4. Don't Cross The River		Warner 7670
9/21/74	**4**	11	**5. Tin Man**		Warner 7839
1/18/75	**5**	10	**6. Lonely People**		Warner 8048

DATE	POS	WKS	ARTIST—RECORD TITLE	LABEL & NO.
4/26/75	**1(1)**	12	**7. Sister Golden Hair**	Warner 8086
8/16/75	**20**	7	8. Daisy Jane	Warner 8118
6/12/76	**23**	6	9. Today's The Day above 5 produced by George Martin (Beatles' producer)	Warner 8212
8/21/82	**8**	15	**10. You Can Do Magic**	Capitol 5142
7/16/83	**33**	6	11. The Border	Capitol 5236
			AMERICAN BREED, The	
			Interracial rock quartet from Cicero, Illinois led by Gary Loizzo. Drummer Andre Fisher was later a member of Rufus.	
7/08/67	**24**	4	1. Step Out Of Your Mind	Acta 804
12/16/67+	**5**	12	• **2. Bend Me, Shape Me**	Acta 811
3/16/68	**39**	3	3. Green Light	Acta 821
			AMES, Ed	
			One of The Ames Brothers. Played the Indian "Mingo" on the "Daniel Boone" TV series.	
2/11/67	**8**	10	**1. My Cup Runneth Over** from the musical *I Do, I Do*	RCA 9002
12/30/67+	**19**	4	2. Who Will Answer?	RCA 9400
			AMES BROTHERS, The	
			Vocal group from Malden, Massachusetts formed in 1947. Family name Urick. Consisted of Ed (b: 7/09/27), Gene (b: 2/13/25), Joe (b: 5/03/24) and Vic (b: 5/20/26, d: 1/23/78). Own TV series in 1955. Ed recorded solo and acted on Broadway and TV.	
11/20/54+	**3**	15	**1. The Naughty Lady Of Shady Lane** Best Seller #3 / Jockey #3 / Juke Box #3	RCA 5897
9/24/55	**11**	11	2. My Bonnie Lassie Best Seller #11 / Top 100 #11 / Jockey #14 / Juke Box #16	RCA 6208
3/24/56	**35**	3	3. Forever Darling from the film of the same title	RCA 6400
5/19/56	**11**	20	4. It Only Hurts For A Little While Juke Box #11 / Top 100 #15 / Jockey #15 / Best Seller #16	RCA 6481
7/22/57	**5**	16	**5. Tammy** Jockey #5 / Best Seller #24 / Top 100 #29 from the film *Tammy and the Bachelor*	RCA 6930
10/07/57	**5**	14	**6. Melodie D'Amour** Jockey #5 / Best Seller #12 / Top 100 #12	RCA 7046
3/31/58	**23**	2	7. A Very Precious Love Jockey #23 / Top 100 #65 from the film *Marjorie Morningstar*	RCA 7167
9/29/58	**17**	10	8. Pussy Cat Hot 100 #17 / Best Seller #20 end	RCA 7315
1/19/59	**37**	4	9. Red River Rose orchestra directed by Hugo Winterhalter on all of above (except #5)	RCA 7413
2/22/60	**38**	2	10. China Doll	RCA 7655
			ANDERSON, Bill	
			Born James William Anderson III on 11/01/37 in Columbia, South Carolina. Country singer/songwriter/ actor. Hosted Nashville Network's TV game show "Fandango." Member of the "Grand Ole Opry" since 1961. Known as "Whispering Bill."	
5/11/63	**8**	11	**1. Still**	Decca 31458

DATE	POS	WKS	ARTIST—RECORD TITLE	LABEL & NO.
			ANDERSON, Carl — see LORING, Gloria	
			ANDERSON, Lynn	
			Born on 9/26/47 in Grand Forks, North Dakota; raised in Sacramento. Country singer; daughter of Liz Anderson. An accomplished equestrian, she was the California Horse Show Queen in 1966.	
12/19/70+	**3**	14	● **1. Rose Garden**	Columbia 45252
			ANDREWS, Lee/The Hearts	
			Lee was born Arthur Lee Andrew Thompson in Goldsboro, North Carolina. Moved to Philadelphia at age two. Formed vocal group The Hearts in 1952. First recorded for Rainbow in 1954. Group on Chess included Thomas "Butch" Curry, Ted Weems, Roy and Wendell Calhoun.	
12/09/57	**20**	10	1. Tear Drops Best Seller #20 / Top 100 #20 / Jockey #21	Chess 1675
6/16/58	**33**	1	2. Try The Impossible Best Seller #33 / Top 100 #33 first released on Casino 452 in 1958	United Art. 123
			ANGELS, The	
			Female pop trio from Orange, New Jersey. Formed as the Starlets with sisters Phyllis "Jiggs" & Barbara Allbut, and Linda Jansen (lead singer). Jansen was replaced by Peggy Santiglia in 1962. Disbanded in 1967.	
12/04/61+	**14**	7	1. 'Til	Caprice 107
4/07/62	**38**	1	2. Cry Baby Cry	Caprice 112
8/10/63	**1**(3)	12	**3. My Boyfriend's Back**	Smash 1834
11/09/63	**25**	5	4. I Adore Him	Smash 1854
			ANIMALS, The	
			Formed in Newcastle, England in 1958 as the Alan Price Combo. Consisted of Eric Burdon (vocals), Alan Price (keyboards), Bryan "Chas" Chandler (bass), Hilton Valentine (guitar) and John Steel (drums). Price left in May 1965, replaced by Dave Rowberry. Steel left in 1966, replaced by Barry Jenkins. Group disbanded in July 1968. After a period with War, Burdon and the other originals reunited in 1983.	
8/15/64	**1**(3)	10	**1. The House Of The Rising Sun**	MGM 13264
10/17/64	**19**	6	2. I'm Crying	MGM 13274
3/06/65	**15**	6	3. Don't Let Me Be Misunderstood	MGM 13311
5/29/65	**32**	4	4. Bring It On Home To Me	MGM 13339
9/04/65	**13**	8	5. We Gotta Get Out Of This Place	MGM 13382
12/04/65+	**23**	8	6. It's My Life	MGM 13414
4/02/66	**34**	1	7. Inside-Looking Out	MGM 13468
6/04/66	**12**	8	8. Don't Bring Me Down	MGM 13514
			ERIC BURDON & THE ANIMALS:	
10/01/66	**10**	7	**9. See See Rider** #14 hit for Ma Rainey in 1925	MGM 13582
12/31/66	**29**	4	10. Help Me Girl	MGM 13636
4/22/67	**15**	6	11. When I Was Young	MGM 13721
8/19/67	**9**	8	**12. San Franciscan Nights**	MGM 13769
12/30/67+	**15**	6	13. Monterey	MGM 13868
6/22/68	**14**	10	14. Sky Pilot (Part One)	MGM 13939

DATE	POS	WKS	ARTIST—RECORD TITLE	LABEL & NO.
			ANIMOTION	
			Techno-pop quintet led by Astrid Plane and Bill Wadhams. Four of five members replaced in 1988, including Plane and Wadhams. New vocalists are Paul Engemann (formerly of Device) and actress/dancer Cynthia Rhodes (appeared in the films *Staying Alive* and *Dirty Dancing*; married Richard Marx on 1/08/89). Plane married group's founding bassist, Charles Ottavio, on 10/13/90.	
3/02/85	**6**	14	**1. Obsession**	Mercury 880266
7/27/85	**39**	1	2. Let Him Go	Mercury 880737
3/11/89	**9**	11	**3. Room To Move** from the film *My Stepmother Is An Alien*	Polydor 871418
			ANKA, Paul	
			Born on 7/30/41 in Ottawa, Canada. Performer since age 12. Father financed first recording, "I Confess," on RPM 472 in 1956. Wrote "My Way" for Frank Sinatra, "She's A Lady" for Tom Jones. Also wrote theme for TV's "Tonight Show." Own variety show in 1973. Longtime popular entertainer in Las Vegas.	
7/29/57	**1**(1)	18	**1. Diana** Best Seller #1 / Top 100 #2 / Jockey #2	ABC-Para. 9831
2/03/58	**7**	11	**2. You Are My Destiny** Top 100 #7 / Best Seller #9 / Jockey #9	ABC-Para. 9880
4/28/58	**15**	10	3. Crazy Love/ Best Seller #15 / Top 100 #19	
4/28/58	**16**	10	4. Let The Bells Keep Ringing Best Seller #16 / Jockey #18 / Top 100 #30	ABC-Para. 9907
12/15/58+	**29**	5	5. The Teen Commandments [S] **PAUL ANKA-GEO. HAMILTON IV-JOHNNY NASH** inspirational talk from the above 3 ABC-Paramount artists	ABC-Para. 9974
1/05/59	**15**	13	6. (All of a Sudden) My Heart Sings	ABC-Para. 9987
4/20/59	**33**	3	7. I Miss You So	ABC-Para. 10011
6/08/59	**1**(4)	14	**8. Lonely Boy** from the film *Girl's Town*	ABC-Para. 10022
9/14/59	**2**(3)	14	**9. Put Your Head On My Shoulder** all of above arranged and conducted by Don Costa	ABC-Para. 10040
11/30/59	**4**	12	**10. It's Time To Cry**	ABC-Para. 10064
3/07/60	**2**(2)	11	**11. Puppy Love**	ABC-Para. 10082
6/06/60	**8**	9	**12. My Home Town**	ABC-Para. 10106
8/22/60	**23**	6	13. Hello Young Lovers/	
9/12/60	**40**	1	14. I Love You In The Same Old Way	ABC-Para. 10132
10/10/60	**11**	7	15. Summer's Gone	ABC-Para. 10147
2/06/61	**16**	5	16. The Story Of My Love	ABC-Para. 10168
3/27/61	**13**	8	17. Tonight My Love, Tonight	ABC-Para. 10194
6/12/61	**10**	7	**18. Dance On Little Girl**	ABC-Para. 10220
9/11/61	**35**	1	19. Kissin' On The Phone	ABC-Para. 10239
3/17/62	**12**	9	20. Love Me Warm And Tender	RCA 7977
6/16/62	**13**	7	21. A Steel Guitar And A Glass Of Wine	RCA 8030
11/24/62	**19**	5	22. Eso Beso (That Kiss!)	RCA 8097
2/09/63	**26**	4	23. Love (Makes The World Go 'Round)	RCA 8115
5/25/63	**39**	1	24. Remember Diana	RCA 8170
2/01/69	**27**	6	25. Goodnight My Love	RCA 9648

DATE	POS	WKS	ARTIST—RECORD TITLE	LABEL & NO.
			PAUL ANKA with ODIA COATES:	
7/27/74	**1**(3)	11	● **26. (You're) Having My Baby**	United Art. 454
11/30/74+	**7**	11	**27. One Man Woman/One Woman Man**	United Art. 569
4/05/75	**8**	10	**28. I Don't Like To Sleep Alone**	United Art. 615
8/16/75	**15**	8	29. (I Believe) There's Nothing Stronger Than Our Love	United Art. 685
			PAUL ANKA:	
11/29/75+	**7**	12	**30. Times Of Your Life**	United Art. 737
5/01/76	**33**	3	31. Anytime (I'll Be There)	United Art. 789
11/18/78	**35**	3	32. This Is Love	RCA 11395
9/03/83	**40**	2	33. Hold Me 'Til The Mornin' Comes	Columbia 03897
			ANNETTE with THE AFTERBEATS	
			Born Annette Funicello on 10/22/42 in Utica, New York. Became a Mouseketeer in 1955. Acted in several teen films in the early 1960s. Co-starred with Frankie Avalon in the 1987 film *Back To The Beach.*	
2/02/59	**7**	9	**1. Tall Paul**	Disneyland 118
12/14/59+	**20**	10	2. First Name Initial	Vista 349
3/07/60	**10**	8	**3. O Dio Mio**	Vista 354
			ANNETTE	
6/20/60	**36**	3	4. Train Of Love written by Paul Anka	Vista 359
9/05/60	**11**	9	5. Pineapple Princess	Vista 362
			ANN-MARGRET	
			Actress Ann-Margret Olsson. Born on 4/28/41 in Stockholm, Sweden. Moved to Wilmette, Illinois in 1946.	
8/21/61	**17**	6	1. I Just Don't Understand	RCA 7894
			ANOTHER BAD CREATION	
			Pre-teen vocal quintet managed and produced by Michael Bivins of Bell Biv DeVoe and New Edition. Made up of Atlanta natives: Chris Sellers, Dave Shelton, Romell Chapman, with brothers Marliss & Demetrius Pugh.	
2/02/91	**9**	15	● **1. Iesha** backing rap by Michael Bivins	Motown 2070#
5/18/91	**10**	10	**2. Playground**	Motown 2088#
			ANT, Adam	
			Born Stuart Goddard on 11/03/54 in London. Formed romantic-punk group Adam & The Ants in 1976. Ant headed new lineup in 1980. Original members Matthew Ashman and Dave Barbarossa founded Bow Wow Wow. Ant went solo in 1982. Appeared in the films *World Gone Wild* and *Slam Dance*, and the TV show "The Equalizer."	
12/11/82+	**12**	14	1. Goody Two Shoes	Epic 03367
4/07/90	**17**	8	2. Room At The Top	MCA 53679
			ANTHONY, Ray	
			Trumpeter/bandleader. Born Raymond Antonini on 1/20/22 in Bentleyville, Pennsylvania and raised in Cleveland. Joined Al Donahue in 1939, then with Glenn Miller and Jimmy Dorsey from 1940-42. Led U.S. Army band. Own band in 1946. Own TV series in the '50s. Appeared in the film *Daddy Long Legs* with Fred Astaire in 1955. Wrote "Bunny Hop." Married for a time to actress Mamie Van Doren.	
1/22/55	**19**	4	1. Melody Of Love **FRANK SINATRA AND RAY ANTHONY** Jockey #19	Capitol 3018

DATE	POS	WKS	ARTIST—RECORD TITLE	LABEL & NO.
1/19/59	**8**	13	**2. Peter Gunn** [I] title song from the hit TV series	Capitol 4041
			ANTON, Susan — see KNOBLOCK, Fred	
			APOLLO 100	
			English studio band featuring keyboardist Tom Parker.	
1/22/72	**6**	10	**1. Joy** [I] adaptation of Bach's *Jesu, Joy of Man's Desiring*	Mega 0050
			APPLEJACKS, The	
			Dave Appell, leader of studio band from Philadelphia.	
10/06/58	**16**	9	1. Mexican Hat Rock [I] Hot 100 #16 / Best Seller #29 end	Cameo 149
1/12/59	**38**	3	2. Rocka-Conga	Cameo 155
			APRIL WINE	
			Rock quintet from Montreal: Myles Goodwyn (lead singer, guitar), Brian Greenway (guitar), Steve Lang (bass), Gary Moffet (guitar) and Jerry Mercer (drums). Lang, Moffet and Mercer replaced by Daniel Barbe (keyboards), Jean Pellerin (bass) and Marty Simon (drums) in 1985.	
4/29/72	**32**	5	1. You Could Have Been A Lady	Big Tree 133
4/14/79	**34**	4	2. Roller	Capitol 4660
3/14/81	**21**	7	3. Just Between You And Me	Capitol 4975
			AQUATONES, The	
			Group formed in Valley Stream, Long Island, New York in 1957. Consisted of Lynn Nixon and Larry Vannata (lead singers), David Goddard and Eugene McCarthy.	
5/05/58	**21**	8	1. You Top 100 #21 / Best Seller #24	Fargo 1001
			ARBORS, The	
			Formed at the University of Michigan in Ann Arbor by two pairs of brothers: Edward and Fred Farran, and Scott and Tom Herrick.	
4/05/69	**20**	3	1. The Letter	Date 1638
			ARCADIA	
			English group featuring Duran Duran's Simon LeBon, Nick Rhodes and Roger Taylor.	
11/02/85	**6**	12	**1. Election Day** narration by Grace Jones	Capitol 5501
3/01/86	**33**	3	2. Goodbye Is Forever	Capitol 5542
			ARCHIES, The	
			Studio group created by Don Kirshner; based on the Saturday morning cartoon television series. Ron Dante (b: Carmine Granito on 8/22/45 in Staten Island, New York) was lead vocalist. All tunes written and produced by Jeff Barry.	
11/02/68	**22**	8	1. Bang-Shang-A-Lang	Calendar 1006
8/16/69	**1**(4)	18	● **2. Sugar, Sugar**	Calendar 1008
12/20/69+	**10**	10	● **3. Jingle Jangle**	Kirshner 5002
3/28/70	**40**	2	4. Who's Your Baby?	Kirshner 5003
			ARDEN, Toni	
			Vocalist from New York City. Real name: Antoinette Aroizzone. Sang with Al Trace in 1945 and Joe Reichman in 1946.	
6/02/58	**13**	11	1. Padre	Decca 30628

DATE	POS	WKS	ARTIST—RECORD TITLE	LABEL & NO.
			Jockey #13 / Top 100 #18 / Best Seller #19	
			ARGENT	
			British rock quartet. Consisted of ex-Zombies member Rod Argent (vocals, keyboards), Jim Rodford (bass; Argent's cousin), Robert Henrit (drums) and Russ Ballard (guitar; later a successful songwriter).	
7/08/72	**5**	11	**1. Hold Your Head Up**	Epic 10852
			ARMS, Russell	
			One of the regulars on TV's "Your Hit Parade."	
2/02/57	**22**	8	1. Cinco Robles (Five Oaks) Best Seller #22 / Top 100 #23 / Jockey #23 with Pete King and orchestra	Era 1026
			ARMSTRONG, Louis	
			Born Daniel Louis Armstrong in New Orleans on 8/04/01 (not 7/04/1900, as Armstrong claimed). Nickname: "Satchmo." Joined Joe "King" Oliver in Chicago in 1922. By 1929, had become the most widely known black musician in the world. Influenced dozens of singers and trumpet players, both black and white. Numerous appearances on radio, TV and in films. Won Lifetime Achievement Grammy in 1972. Died on 7/06/71 in New York. Inducted into the Rock and Roll Hall of Fame in 1990 as a forefather of rock music.	
2/25/56	**20**	7	1. A Theme From The Threepenny Opera (Mack The Knife) **LOUIS ARMSTRONG AND THE ALL STARS**	Columbia 40587
12/15/56	**29**	1	2. Blueberry Hill **LOUIS ARMSTRONG AND GORDON JENKINS** recorded in 1949	Decca 30091
2/29/64	**1**(1)	19	**3. Hello, Dolly!** **LOUIS ARMSTRONG AND THE ALL STARS** title song from the Broadway musical	Kapp 573
3/19/88	**32**	3	4. What A Wonderful World [R] from the film *Good Morning, Vietnam*; originally hit "Easy Listening" chart in 1967 and "Bubbled Under" in 1968 on ABC 10982	A&M 3010
			ARNOLD, Eddy	
			Born Richard Edward Arnold on 5/15/18 near Henderson, Tennessee. Became popular on Nashville's "Grand Ole Opry" as a singer with Pee Wee King (1940-43). Nicknamed "The Tennessee Plowboy" on all RCA recordings through 1954. Elected to the Country Music Hall of Fame in 1966. CMA award: Entertainer of the Year - 1967. Ranked as the #1 artist in *Joel Whitburn's Top Country Singles 1944-1988* book.	
12/01/56	**22**	1	1. I Wouldn't Know Where To Begin Jockey #22 / Top 100 #64	RCA 6699
11/13/65	**6**	10	**2. Make The World Go Away**	RCA 8679
3/12/66	**36**	5	3. I Want To Go With You	RCA 8749
6/18/66	**40**	1	4. The Last Word In Lonesome Is Me all of above produced by Chet Atkins	RCA 8818
			ARROWS, The — see ALLAN, Davie	
			ARTISTS UNITED AGAINST APARTHEID	
			Benefit group of 49 superstar artists formed to protest the South African apartheid government; proceeds went to political prisoners in South Africa.	
12/07/85	**38**	3	1. Sun City	Manhattan 50017

DATE	POS	WKS	ARTIST—RECORD TITLE	LABEL & NO.
			ART OF NOISE, The	
			British techno-pop trio: Anne Dudley (keyboards), J.J. Jeczalik (keyboards, programmer) and Gary Langan (engineer). All three were part of Trevor Horn's production team in the early 1980s. Worked with ABC, Frankie Goes To Hollywood and others. Disbanded in mid-1990.	
9/20/86	**34**	4	1. Paranoimia **THE ART OF NOISE with MAX HEADROOM** Max Headroom is a British "computer-generated" celebrity	China 43002
12/24/88+	**31**	6	2. Kiss **THE ART OF NOISE featuring TOM JONES**	China 871038
			ASHFORD & SIMPSON	
			Husband-and-wife R&B vocal/songwriting duo: Nickolas Ashford (b: 5/04/42, Fairfield, South Carolina) and Valerie Simpson (b: 8/26/46, New York City). Team wrote for Chuck Jackson and Maxine Brown. Joined staff at Motown and wrote and produced for many of the label's top stars. Valerie recorded solo in 1972.	
10/13/79	**36**	2	1. Found A Cure	Warner 8870
1/05/85	**12**	11	2. Solid	Capitol 5397
			ASHTON, GARDNER & DYKE	
			British pop trio: Tony Ashton, Kim Gardner and Roy Dyke.	
8/07/71	**40**	1	1. Resurrection Shuffle	Capitol 3060
			ASIA	
			British rock supergroup: guitarist Steve Howe (Yes), drummer Carl Palmer (Emerson, Lake & Palmer), keyboardist Geoff Downes (Buggles, Yes) and vocalist/bassist John Wetton (King Crimson, Uriah Heep, Roxy Music). Howe replaced by Mandy Meyer (Krokus) in 1985. Meyer replaced in 1990 by Oakland, California native Pat Thrall (Automatic Man, Pat Travers Band).	
5/01/82	**4**	12	**1. Heat Of The Moment**	Geffen 50040
8/14/82	**17**	8	2. Only Time Will Tell	Geffen 29970
8/06/83	**10**	11	**3. Don't Cry**	Geffen 29571
11/12/83	**34**	5	4. The Smile Has Left Your Eyes	Geffen 29475
			ASSEMBLED MULTITUDE, The	
			Philadelphia-based studio group arranged and conducted by Tom Sellers (d: 3/09/88 in a fire in his hometown of Wayne, Pennsylvania at age 39).	
8/01/70	**16**	7	1. Overture From Tommy (A Rock Opera) [I]	Atlantic 2737
			ASSOCIATION, The	
			Group formed in Los Angeles in 1965. Consisted of Terry Kirkman (plays 23 wind, reed and percussion instruments), Gary "Jules" Alexander (guitar), Brian Cole (bass), Jim Yester (guitar), Ted Bluechel, Jr. (drums) and Russ Giguere (percussion). Larry Ramos, Jr. joined in early 1968. Cole died on 8/02/73 of a heroin overdose.	
6/25/66	**7**	8	**1. Along Comes Mary**	Valiant 741
9/03/66	**1**(3)	12	● **2. Cherish**	Valiant 747
12/17/66	**35**	3	3. Pandora's Golden Heebie Jeebies	Valiant 755
6/03/67	**1**(4)	13	● **4. Windy**	Warner 7041
9/09/67	**2**(2)	11	● **5. Never My Love** written by The Addrisi Brothers	Warner 7074
2/10/68	**10**	8	**6. Everything That Touches You**	Warner 7163
6/22/68	**39**	2	7. Time For Livin'	Warner 7195

DATE	POS	WKS	ARTIST—RECORD TITLE	LABEL & NO.
			ASTLEY, Rick	
			Pop singer/guitarist born on 2/06/66 in Warrington and raised in Manchester, England.	
1/23/88	**1**(2)	14	● **1. Never Gonna Give You Up**	RCA 5347
4/30/88	**1**(1)	12	**2. Together Forever**	RCA 8319
8/06/88	**10**	10	**3. It Would Take A Strong Strong Man**	RCA 8663
1/07/89	**6**	10	**4. She Wants To Dance With Me**	RCA 8838
5/27/89	**38**	1	5. Giving Up On Love	RCA 8872
3/09/91	**7**	12	**6. Cry For Help**	RCA 2774
			ATLANTA RHYTHM SECTION	
			Group formed of musicians from Studio One, Doraville, Georgia in 1971. Consisted of Rodney Justo (vocals), Barry Bailey and J.R. Cobb (guitars), Paul Goddard (bass), Dean Daughtry (keyboards) and Robert Nix (drums). Cobb, Daughtry and band manager Buddy Buie had been with the Classics IV, others had been with Roy Orbison. Justo left after first album, replaced by Ronnie Hammond.	
11/09/74	**35**	2	1. Doraville	Polydor 14248
2/26/77	**7**	14	**2. So In To You**	Polydor 14373
3/25/78	**7**	12	**3. Imaginary Lover**	Polydor 14459
7/08/78	**14**	7	4. I'm Not Gonna Let It Bother Me Tonight	Polydor 14484
6/16/79	**19**	9	5. Do It Or Die	Polydor 14568
9/08/79	**17**	8	6. Spooky	Polydor 2001
10/10/81	**29**	4	7. Alien	Columbia 02471
			ATLANTIC STARR	
			Originally an eight-man, one-woman soul band formed in 1976 in White Plains, New York. Lead singers: brothers Wayne & David Lewis, and Sharon Bryant. In 1984, reduced to a quintet; Barbara Weathers replaced Bryant. Porscha Martin replaced Weathers in 1989.	
5/15/82	**38**	3	1. Circles	A&M 2392
1/25/86	**3**	14	**2. Secret Lovers**	A&M 2788
4/25/87	**1**(1)	14	**3. Always**	Warner 28455
			AUSTIN, Patti	
			Patti was born on 8/10/48 in New York City. Backup work in New York. God-daughter of Quincy Jones. Made Harlem's Apollo Theatre debut at age four. In 1988 film *Tucker.*	
12/04/82+	**1**(2)	18	● **1. Baby, Come To Me** **PATTI AUSTIN with JAMES INGRAM**	Qwest 50036
			AUSTIN, Sil	
			Born Sylvester Austin in 1929 in Donellon, Florida. R&B tenor saxophonist. Played with the Tiny Bradshaw Band before forming own group.	
11/24/56	**17**	7	1. Slow Walk [I] Juke Box #17 / Top 100 #19 / Best Seller #20	Mercury 70963
			AUTOGRAPH	
			Los Angeles-based rock quintet led by vocalist Steve Plunkett.	
2/23/85	**29**	5	1. Turn Up The Radio	RCA 13953

DATE	POS	WKS	ARTIST—RECORD TITLE	LABEL & NO.
			AVALON, Frankie	
			Born Francis Avallone on 9/18/39 in Philadelphia. Teen idol managed by Bob Marcucci. Worked in bands in Atlantic City, New Jersey in 1953. Radio and TV with Paul Whiteman, mid-1950s. Singer/trumpet player with Rocco & His Saints in 1957 which included Bobby Rydell. Co-starred in many films with Annette. Appeared in films *Disc Jockey Jamboree* (1957), *Guns of the Timberland* (1960), *The Carpetbaggers* (1962) and *Back to the Beach* (1987).	
1/27/58	**7**	11	**1. Dede Dinah**	Chancellor 1011
			Top 100 #7 / Best Seller #9 / Jockey #24	
7/28/58	**9**	12	**2. Ginger Bread**	Chancellor 1021
			Hot 100 #9 / Best Seller #11 backing vocals by The Four Dates	
11/17/58	**15**	10	3. I'll Wait For You	Chancellor 1026
2/23/59	**1**(5)	14	**4. Venus**	Chancellor 1031
6/01/59	**8**	10	**5. Bobby Sox To Stockings/**	
6/15/59	**10**	9	**6. A Boy Without A Girl**	Chancellor 1036
9/14/59	**7**	11	**7. Just Ask Your Heart**	Chancellor 1040
12/07/59	**1**(1)	12	**8. Why/**	
1/04/60	**39**	1	9. Swingin' On A Rainbow	Chancellor 1045
3/28/60	**22**	6	10. Don't Throw Away All Those Teardrops	Chancellor 1048
8/01/60	**32**	4	11. Where Are You	Chancellor 1052
			all of above arranged and conducted by Peter De Angelis	
10/17/60	**26**	7	12. Togetherness	Chancellor 1056
5/05/62	**26**	4	13. You Are Mine	Chancellor 1107
			AVANT-GARDE, The	
10/26/68	**40**	1	1. Naturally Stoned	Columbia 44590
			written by game show host Chuck Woolery	
			AVERAGE WHITE BAND	
			Vocal/instrumental group formed in Scotland in 1972. Consisted of Alan Gorrie (vocal, bass), Hamish Stuart (vocal, guitar), Onnie McIntyre (vocal, guitar), Malcolm Duncan (saxophone), Roger Ball (keyboards, saxophone) and Robbie McIntosh (drums). McIntosh died of drug poisoning on 9/23/74, replaced by Steve Ferrone.	
			AWB:	
12/21/74+	**1**(1)	13	● **1. Pick Up The Pieces** [I]	Atlantic 3229
4/26/75	**10**	12	**2. Cut The Cake**	Atlantic 3261
9/27/75	**39**	2	3. If I Ever Lose This Heaven	Atlantic 3285
12/20/75	**33**	3	4. School Boy Crush	Atlantic 3304
			AVERAGE WHITE BAND:	
10/16/76	**40**	1	5. Queen Of My Soul	Atlantic 3354
			B	
			BABYFACE	
			Vocalist/instrumentalist Kenneth Edmonds, formerly with Manchild and The Deele. Brother of Kevon and Melvin Edmonds of After 7. Prolific writing/production duo with L.A. Reid of The Deele.	
9/09/89	**7**	10	**1. It's No Crime**	Solar 68966

DATE	POS	WKS	ARTIST—RECORD TITLE	LABEL & NO.
12/23/89+	**14**	9	2. Tender Lover	Solar 74003
3/17/90	**6**	11	**3. Whip Appeal**	Solar 74007
7/21/90	**30**	5	4. My Kinda Girl	Solar 74515
			BABYS, The	
			British rock group: John Waite (vocals), Walt Stocker, Mike Corby and Tony Brock. By 1980, keyboardist Jonathan Cain (later of Journey) had replaced Corby and bassist Ricky Phillips joined group. In 1989, Waite formed Bad English with Phillips and Cain.	
10/29/77	**13**	11	1. Isn't It Time	Chrysalis 2173
2/03/79	**13**	10	2. Every Time I Think Of You	Chrysalis 2279
3/08/80	**33**	3	3. Back On My Feet Again	Chrysalis 2398
			BACHELORS, The	
			Trio from Dublin, Ireland: brothers Declan & Con Cluskey with John Stokes. Formed as a harmonica instrumental trio known as the Harmonichords.	
5/16/64	**10**	8	**1. Diane** #2 hit for the Nat Shilkret Orchestra in 1928	London 9639
8/01/64	**33**	2	2. I Believe #2 hit for Frankie Laine in 1953	London 9672
1/30/65	**27**	4	3. No Arms Can Ever Hold You	London 9724
7/03/65	**15**	7	4. Marie written by Irving Berlin in 1928	London 9762
11/06/65	**32**	3	5. Chapel In The Moonlight	London 9793
5/14/66	**38**	2	6. Love Me With All Of Your Heart	London 9828
			BACHMAN-TURNER OVERDRIVE	
			Hard-rock group formed in Vancouver, Canada in 1972. Brothers Randy (vocals, guitar), Tim (guitar) and Robbie Bachman (drums) with C. Fred Turner (vocals, bass). Originally known as Brave Belt. Randy had been in The Guess Who and recorded solo. Tim left in 1973, replaced by Blair Thornton. Randy left in 1977. Randy and Tim regrouped with C.F. Turner in 1984.	
3/23/74	**23**	9	1. Let It Ride	Mercury 73457
6/29/74	**12**	10	2. Takin' Care Of Business	Mercury 73487
10/05/74	**1**(1)	12	● **3. You Ain't Seen Nothing Yet**	Mercury 73622
2/01/75	**14**	7	4. Roll On Down The Highway	Mercury 73656
6/07/75	**21**	7	5. Hey You	Mercury 73683
2/28/76	**33**	3	6. Take It Like A Man	Mercury 73766
			BACKUS, Jim — see BAKUS	
			BAD COMPANY	
			British band: Paul Rodgers (vocals), Mick Ralphs (guitar), Simon Kirke (drums) and Boz Burrell (bass). Rodgers and Kirke from Free; Ralphs from Mott The Hoople; and Burrell from King Crimson. Disbanded in 1982. Rodgers was a member of the supergroup The Firm (1984-86) and The Law (since 1991). Rodgers and Burrell reunited group with new vocalist Brian Howe in 1988.	
8/31/74	**5**	11	**1. Can't Get Enough**	Swan Song 70015
2/08/75	**19**	6	2. Movin' On	Swan Song 70101
5/31/75	**36**	2	3. Good Lovin' Gone Bad	Swan Song 70103
7/26/75	**10**	11	**4. Feel Like Makin' Love**	Swan Song 70106
4/24/76	**20**	7	5. Young Blood	Swan Song 70108
4/14/79	**13**	12	● 6. Rock 'N' Roll Fantasy	Swan Song 70119

DATE	POS	WKS	ARTIST—RECORD TITLE	LABEL & NO.
1/26/91	**16**	8	7. If You Needed Somebody	Atco 98914#
			BAD ENGLISH	
			Rock supergroup: John Waite (vocals), Ricky Phillips (bass), Jonathan Cain (keyboards), Neal Schon (guitar) and Deen Castronovo (drums). Waite, Phillips and Cain were members of The Babys. Cain and Schon were members of Journey.	
9/30/89	**1**(2)	15	● **1. When I See You Smile**	Epic 69082
1/20/90	**5**	11	**2. Price Of Love**	Epic 73094
7/14/90	**21**	8	3. Possession	Epic 73398
			BADFINGER	
			Welsh quartet originally known as The Iveys. Leader Pete Ham (b: 4/27/47) committed suicide on 4/23/75. Group disbanded from 1975-78. Bassist Tom Evans committed suicide on 11/23/83 (age 36). Yes keyboardist Tony Kaye was a member from 1978 until group disbanded in 1982.	
3/07/70	**7**	11	**1. Come And Get It**	Apple 1815
			written by Paul McCartney; from the film *The Magic Christian*	
11/21/70	**8**	9	**2. No Matter What**	Apple 1822
12/18/71+	**4**	12	● **3. Day After Day**	Apple 1841
			produced by George Harrison	
4/08/72	**14**	7	4. Baby Blue	Apple 1844
			produced by Todd Rundgren	
			BAEZ, Joan	
			Folk song stylist born in New York City on 1/09/41. Became a political activist while attending Boston University in the late 1950s.	
8/28/71	**3**	13	● **1. The Night They Drove Old Dixie Down**	Vanguard 35138
			written by Robbie Robertson (leader of The Band)	
11/08/75	**35**	2	2. Diamonds And Rust	A&M 1737
			BAILEY, Philip	
			Born on 5/08/51 in Denver. Percussionist/co-lead vocalist with Earth, Wind & Fire since 1971.	
12/08/84+	**2**(2)	16	● **1. Easy Lover**	Columbia 04679
			PHILIP BAILEY with PHIL COLLINS	
			BAKER, Anita	
			Soul singer born in Memphis on 12/20/57 and raised in Detroit. Female lead singer of Chapter 8 from 1976-84.	
9/13/86	**8**	11	**1. Sweet Love**	Elektra 69557
2/07/87	**37**	2	2. Caught Up In The Rapture	Elektra 69511
10/22/88	**3**	15	**3. Giving You The Best That I Got**	Elektra 69371
2/04/89	**14**	11	4. Just Because	Elektra 69327
			BAKER, George, Selection	
			Baker is Johannes Bouwens (b: 12/09/44). Vocalist/guitarist/keyboardist of Dutch group.	
4/11/70	**21**	10	1. Little Green Bag	Colossus 112
1/10/76	**26**	5	2. Paloma Blanca	Warner 8115

DATE	POS	WKS	ARTIST—RECORD TITLE	LABEL & NO.
			BAKER, LaVern	
			Born Delores Williams on 11/11/29 in Chicago. Recorded as "Little Miss Share Cropper" and "Bea Baker." After working with the Todd Rhodes Orchestra, 1952-53, toured Europe, solo. Returned to work for Atlantic Records and became one of the most popular female R&B singers in the early rock era. Backing group: The Gliders. Inducted into the Rock and Roll Hall of Fame in 1991.	
1/15/55	**14**	11	1. Tweedlee Dee **LaVERN BAKER AND THE GLIDERS** Juke Box #14 / Best Seller #22	Atlantic 1047
10/13/56	**22**	2	2. I Can't Love You Enough Jockey #22 / Top 100 #48	Atlantic 1104
12/29/56+	**17**	14	3. Jim Dandy **LaVERN BAKER AND THE GLIDERS** Best Seller #17 / Jockey #20 / Top 100 #22	Atlantic 1116
12/28/58+	**6**	15	**4. I Cried A Tear**	Atlantic 2007
6/01/59	**33**	2	5. I Waited Too Long written by Neil Sedaka	Atlantic 2021
5/01/61	**37**	3	6. Saved	Atlantic 2099
1/05/63	**34**	3	7. See See Rider	Atlantic 2167
			BAKUS, Jim, AND FRIEND	
			Jim Backus was born on 2/25/13 in Cleveland. Actor, starred in dozens of films. Played Thurston Howell III on TV's "Gilligan's Island." Also famous as the voice of Mr. Magoo in the cartoon series Label misspelloed last name as Bakus. Died of pneumonia on 7/03/89.	
7/21/58	**40**	2	1. Delicious! [N] Best Seller #40 / Top 100 #42	Jubilee 5330
			BALANCE	
			New York City-based rock trio led by Illinois native Peppy Castro (founder of the Blues Magoos).	
8/15/81	**22**	9	1. Breaking Away	Portrait 02177
			BALIN, Marty	
			Born on 1/30/43 in Cincinnati. Co-founder of Jefferson Airplane/Jefferson Starship/KBC.	
6/13/81	**8**	13	**1. Hearts**	EMI America 8084
10/10/81	**27**	5	2. Atlanta Lady (Something About Your Love)	EMI America 8093
			BALL, Kenny, and His Jazzmen	
			Born on 5/22/30 in Ilford, England. Leader of English Dixieland jazz band formed in 1958.	
2/17/62	**2**(1)	12	**1. Midnight In Moscow** [I] original Russian title: "Padmeskoveeye Vietchera"	Kapp 442
			BALLARD, Hank/The Midnighters	
			R&B vocal group from Detroit, formed in 1952 as The Royals: Henry Booth, Charles Sutton, Lawson Smith and Sonny Woods. In late 1953, Henry "Hank" Ballard (b: 11/18/36, Detroit) replaced Smith and became lead singer. Name changed to Midnighters in 1954. Had the original recording of "The Twist," written by Ballard, who is still active as a solo artist. After group disbanded in 1965, re-formed with Frank Stadford, Walter Miller and Wesley Hargrove. Worked in the James Brown Revue. Ballard inducted into the Rock and Roll Hall of Fame in 1990.	
7/18/60	**7**	13	**1. Finger Poppin' Time**	King 5341
8/29/60	**28**	6	2. The Twist	King 5171

DATE	POS	WKS	ARTIST—RECORD TITLE	LABEL & NO.
			B-side of Hank's first Hot 100 hit "Teardrops On Your Letter" (1959)	
10/17/60	**6**	11	**3. Let's Go, Let's Go, Let's Go**	King 5400
1/16/61	**23**	4	4. The Hoochi Coochi Coo	King 5430
3/20/61	**39**	1	5. Let's Go Again (Where We Went Last Night)	King 5459
5/01/61	**33**	3	6. The Continental Walk	King 5491
7/17/61	**26**	4	7. The Switch-A-Roo	King 5510
			BALLOON FARM, The	
			New York flower-pop quintet. A Hugo & Luigi production.	
3/16/68	**37**	4	1. A Question Of Temperature	Laurie 3405
			BALTIMORA	
			Baltimora is Jimmy McShane; born in Londonderry, Northern Ireland.	
1/11/86	**13**	10	1. Tarzan Boy	Manhattan 50018
			BANANARAMA	
			Female trio from London: Sarah Dallin, Keren Woodward and Siobhan Fahey. Group name is combination of the children's show "The Banana Splits" and the Roxy Music song "Pyjamarama." Fahey married Dave Stewart (Eurythmics) on 8/01/87; left group in early 1988, replaced by Jacqui O'Sullivan (who left in mid 1991).	
8/11/84	**9**	11	**1. Cruel Summer**	London 810127
7/19/86	**1**(1)	12	**2. Venus**	London 886056
8/15/87	**4**	12	**3. I Heard A Rumour**	London 886165
			BAND, The	
			Formed in Woodstock, New York in 1967: Robbie Robertson (guitar), Levon Helm (drums), Rick Danko (bass), Richard Manuel and Garth Hudson (keyboards). All from Canada (except Helm from Arkansas) and all were with Ronnie Hawkins' Hawks. Recorded extensively with Bob Dylan. Disbanded on Thanksgiving Day in 1976. Manuel committed suicide on 3/04/86 (age 42).	
11/29/69+	**25**	7	1. Up On Cripple Creek	Capitol 2635
10/14/72	**34**	6	2. Don't Do It	Capitol 3433
			BAND AID	
			A benefit recording to assist famine relief in Ethiopia. All-star group organized by Bob Geldof of The Boomtown Rats.	
1/05/85	**13**	4	● 1. Do They Know It's Christmas? [X]	Columbia 04749
			with Paul Young, Boy George & Jon Moss (Culture Club), George Michael, Sting, Phil Collins, Duran Duran, Bananarama, Spandau Ballet, Paul Weller (Style Council), Boomtown Rats, and members Kool & The Gang, U2, Ultravox, Status Quo and Heaven 17	
			BANGLES	
			Female rock quartet formed in Los Angeles in January 1981. Consisted of sisters Vicki (lead guitar) & Debbi Peterson (drums), Michael Steele (bass) and Susanna Hoffs (guitar). Originally named The Bangs. Steele was previously in The Runaways. Hoffs starred in the 1987 film *The Allnighter*. Disbanded in October 1989. Hoffs recorded solo in 1991.	
2/22/86	**2**(1)	14	**1. Manic Monday**	Columbia 05757
			written by Prince under the pseudonym "Christopher"	
6/14/86	**29**	5	2. If She Knew What She Wants	Columbia 05886
11/01/86	**1**(4)	15	● **3. Walk Like An Egyptian**	Columbia 06257
3/14/87	**11**	9	4. Walking Down Your Street	Columbia 06674
12/05/87+	**2**(1)	14	**5. Hazy Shade Of Winter**	Def Jam 07630

DATE	POS	WKS	ARTIST—RECORD TITLE	LABEL & NO.
			from the film *Less Than Zero*	
11/12/88+	**5**	12	**6. In Your Room**	Columbia 08090
2/11/89	**1**(1)	14	● **7. Eternal Flame**	Columbia 68533
6/03/89	**30**	5	8. Be With You	Columbia 68744
			BANKS, Darrell	
			Born Darrell Eubanks in 1938 in Buffalo. Soul singer. Killed by a gunshot wound in Detroit, March 1970.	
9/10/66	**27**	4	1. Open The Door To Your Heart	Revilot 201
			BARBER, Chris, Jazz Band	
			Trombonist/leader Barber was born on 4/17/30 in Welwyn Garden City, England. Dixieland-styled band, formed in 1949, included Monty Sunshine on clarinet.	
2/02/59	**5**	10	**1. Petite Fleur (Little Flower)** **[I]**	Laurie 3022
			written in 1952 by jazz great Sidney Bechet	
			BARBOUR, Keith	
			Singer/songwriter; formerly with The New Christy Minstrels. Married to TV actress Deidre Hall ("Our House" and "Days of Our Lives") from 1971-78.	
11/01/69	**40**	2	1. Echo Park	Epic 10486
			BARBUSTERS, The — see JETT, Joan	
			BARCLAY, Eddie	
			Head of the French recording company Compagnie Phonographique Francaise and own Barclay label. Born on 1/26/21 in Paris.	
7/16/55	**18**	1	1. The Bandit (O'Cangaceiro) [I]	Tico 249
			Juke Box #18	
			BARDEUX	
			Los Angeles female dance duo: Stacy "Acacia" Smith and Jazz (replaced by Melanie Taylor in 1989).	
5/28/88	**36**	3	1. When We Kiss	Synthicide 75018
			BARE, Bobby	
			Born Robert Joseph Bare on 4/07/35 in Ironton, Ohio. Prominent country singer/songwriter/guitarist. Drafted by the Army in 1958; left a demo tape of "The All American Boy" with Fraternity Records. The song was released erroneously as by Bill Parsons. Wrote songs for the film *Teenage Millionaire* and acted in the film *A Distant Trumpet* in 1964. Own TV series in the mid-1980s.	
12/28/58+	**2**(1)	13	**1. The All American Boy** **[N]**	Fraternity 835
			BILL PARSONS	
8/18/62	**23**	7	2. Shame On Me	RCA 8032
6/29/63	**16**	9	3. Detroit City	RCA 8183
10/26/63	**10**	7	**4. 500 Miles Away From Home**	RCA 8238
3/07/64	**33**	2	5. Miller's Cave	RCA 8294
			BAR-KAYS	
			R&B vocal/instrumental combo: Jimmy King (guitar), Ronnie Caldwell (organ), James Alexander (bass), Carl Cunningham (drums), Phalon Jones (saxophone) and Ben Cauley (trumpet). Formed by Al Jackson, drummer with Booker T & The MG's. The plane crash that killed Otis Redding (12/10/67) also claimed the lives of all the Bar-Kays except Alexander (not on the plane) & Cauley (survived the crash). Alexander re-formed the band. Appeared in the film *Wattstax*; much session work at Stax. Alexander's son Phalon began solo career in 1990.	
7/01/67	**17**	9	1. Soul Finger [I]	Volt 148

DATE	POS	WKS	ARTIST—RECORD TITLE	LABEL & NO.
12/04/76+	**23**	8	2. Shake Your Rump To The Funk	Mercury 73833
			BARNUM, H.B.	
			Born on 7/15/36 in Houston. Member of The Dyna-Sores.	
2/06/61	**35**	1	1. Lost Love [I]	Eldo 111
			BARRETTO, Ray	
			Percussionist born in Brooklyn in April 1939. With Tito Puente and Herbie Mann before forming his own group Charanga Moderna.	
5/11/63	**17**	7	1. El Watusi [F-N]	Tico 419
			BARRY, Joe	
			Singer/guitarist born Joe Barrios in Cut Off, Louisiana.	
5/29/61	**24**	5	1. I'm A Fool To Care first released on JIN 144 in 1961	Smash 1702
			BARRY, Len	
			Born Leonard Borisoff on 12/06/42 in Philadelphia. In The Dovells from 1957-63.	
10/23/65	**2**(1)	10	**1. 1-2-3**	Decca 31827
1/22/66	**27**	5	2. Like A Baby	Decca 31889
4/09/66	**26**	5	3. Somewhere from *West Side Story*	Decca 31923
			BARRY AND THE TAMERLANES	
			California pop trio led by Barry DeVorzon and arranged by Perry Botkin, Jr. Songwriters Terry Smith and Bodie Chandler were The Tamerlanes. DeVorzon founded the Valiant label and began his ongoing prolific songwriting career in the mid-1950s.	
11/16/63	**21**	5	1. I Wonder What She's Doing Tonight	Valiant 6034
			BARTLEY, Chris	
			Soul singer/guitarist born on 4/17/49 in New York City. Sang with the Soulful Inspirations and own group, the Mindbenders, in the mid-1960s.	
8/19/67	**32**	2	1. The Sweetest Thing This Side Of Heaven written and produced by Van McCoy	Vando 101
			BASIA	
			Britain-based, female pop-jazz singer/composer Basia Trzetrzelewska (pronounced: Basha Tshetshelevska). Raised in Jaworzno, Poland. Former vocalist of the group Matt Bianco.	
9/24/88	**26**	7	1. Time And Tide	Epic 07730
5/12/90	**29**	4	2. Cruising For Bruising	Epic 73239#
			BASIE, Count	
			Born William Basie on 8/21/04 in Red Bank, New Jersey; died on 4/26/84. World-renowned jazz, big-band- leader/pianist/organist. Learned music and piano from mother, organ from Fats Waller. First recorded with own band in 1937 for Decca. Appeared in many films and toured into the '70s. Won the Grammy's Trustees Award in 1981.	
2/04/56	**28**	3	1. April In Paris [I] written in 1932; Grammy Hall of Fame Award winner in 1985	Clef 89162
			BASIL, Toni	
			Los Angeles-based vocalist/dancer/choreographer/actress/video director born in 1950. Worked on the TV shows "Shindig" and "Hullabaloo." Choreographed the film *American Grafitti*. Appeared in the film *Easy Rider* and others.	
10/09/82	**1**(1)	18	▲ **1. Mickey**	Chrysalis 2638

DATE	POS	WKS	ARTIST—RECORD TITLE	LABEL & NO.
			BASS, Fontella	
			Born on 7/03/40 in St. Louis. Soul vocalist/pianist/organist. Mother was a member of Clara Ward Gospel Troupe. Sang in church choirs; with Oliver Sain Band, St. Louis; with Little Milton blues show to 1964. Married to trumpet player Lester Bowie.	
3/27/65	**33**	3	1. Don't Mess Up A Good Thing **FONTELLA BASS & BOBBY McCLURE**	Checker 1097
10/23/65	**4**	10	**2. Rescue Me**	Checker 1120
1/29/66	**37**	1	3. Recovery	Checker 1131
			BASSEY, Shirley	
			Born on 1/08/37 in Cardiff, Wales. Soul songstress.	
2/27/65	**8**	8	**1. Goldfinger** from the James Bond film; with John Barry's orchestra	United Art. 790
			BAXTER, Les	
			Born on 3/14/22 in Mexia, Texas. Orchestra leader/arranger. Began as a conductor on radio shows in the 1930s. Member of Mel Torme's vocal group, the Mel-Tones. Musical arranger for Capitol Records (Nat King Cole, Margaret Whiting and others) in the 1950s. Composed over 100 film scores.	
4/09/55	**1**(2)	21	**1. Unchained Melody** Jockey #1 / Best Seller #2 / Juke Box #3 from the film *Unchained*	Capitol 3055
8/13/55	**5**	12	**2. Wake The Town And Tell The People** Jockey #5 / Juke Box #8 / Best Seller #10 / Top 100 #24 pre vocals by The Notables	Capitol 3120
2/18/56	**1**(6)	20	**3. The Poor People Of Paris** **[I]** Top 100 #1(6) / Jockey #1(6) / Best Seller #1(4) / Juke Box #1(3)	Capitol 3336
			BAY CITY ROLLERS	
			Formed in 1967 in Edinburgh, Scotland as the Saxons. Original members: brothers Alan & Derek Longmuir, Les McKeoun (lead singer), Eric Faulkner and Stuart "Woody" Wood.	
11/08/75+	**1**(1)	12	● **1. Saturday Night**	Arista 0149
2/14/76	**9**	11	**2. Money Honey**	Arista 0170
5/22/76	**28**	4	3. Rock And Roll Love Letter	Arista 0185
9/18/76	**12**	12	4. I Only Want To Be With You	Arista 0205
6/25/77	**10**	12	**5. You Made Me Believe In Magic**	Arista 0256
11/19/77+	**24**	9	6. The Way I Feel Tonight	Arista 0272
			BAZUKA	
			Instrumental studio group assembled by producer Tony Camillo.	
6/07/75	**10**	11	**1. Dynomite - Part I** **[I]** **TONY CAMILLO'S BAZUKA**	A&M 1666
			B. BUMBLE & THE STINGERS	
			Los Angeles sessionmen Plas Johnson, Rene Hall, Earl Palmer and Al Hassan comprised recording group with Ernie Freeman playing piano on first two recordings and pianist Lincoln Mayorga on "Nut Rocker." Pianist R.C. Gamble toured as B. Bumble.	
4/24/61	**21**	5	1. Bumble Boogie [I] adaptation of Rimsky-Korsakov's *Flight Of The Bumble Bee*	Rendezvous 140
3/31/62	**23**	7	2. Nut Rocker [I] adapted from Tchaikovsky's *The Nutcracker*	Rendezvous 166

DATE	POS	WKS	ARTIST—RECORD TITLE	LABEL & NO.
			BEACH BOYS, The	
			Group formed in Hawthorne, California in 1961. Consisted of brothers Brian (keyboards, bass), Carl (guitar), and Dennis Wilson (drums); their cousin Mike Love (lead vocals, saxophone), and Al Jardine (guitar). Known in high school as Kenny & The Cadets, Carl & The Passions, then The Pendletones. First recorded for X/Candix in 1961. Jardine replaced by David Marks from March 1962 to March 1963. Brian quit touring with group in December 1964, replaced briefly by Glen Campbell until Bruce Johnston (of Bruce & Terry) joined permanently in April 1965. Johnston and Campbell also recorded in the studio band Sagittarius in 1967. Brian continued to write for and produce group, returned to stage in 1983. Daryl Dragon (of Captain & Tennille) was a keyboardist in their stage band. Dennis Wilson drowned on 12/28/83 (age 39). Lineup of Carl, Brian, Mike, Alan and Bruce continues to perform today. Carnie and Wendy Wilson, daughters of Brian Wilson, are members of Wilson Phillips. Group was inducted into the Rock and Roll Hall of Fame in 1988.	
9/15/62	**14**	10	1. Surfin' Safari	Capitol 4777
4/13/63	**3**	13	**2. Surfin' U.S.A./**	
5/25/63	**23**	8	3. Shut Down	Capitol 4932
8/17/63	**7**	11	**4. Surfer Girl/**	
9/07/63	**15**	7	5. Little Deuce Coupe	Capitol 5009
11/23/63	**6**	8	**6. Be True To Your School/** featuring cheerleading by The Honeys, and the march "On Wisconsin"	
11/30/63	**23**	6	7. In My Room	Capitol 5069
2/22/64	**5**	9	**8. Fun, Fun, Fun**	Capitol 5118
6/06/64	**1**(2)	13	• **9. I Get Around/**	
6/27/64	**24**	6	10. Don't Worry Baby	Capitol 5174
9/19/64	**9**	8	**11. When I Grow Up (To Be A Man)**	Capitol 5245
11/21/64	**8**	8	**12. Dance, Dance, Dance**	Capitol 5306
3/13/65	**12**	7	13. Do You Wanna Dance?	Capitol 5372
5/01/65	**1**(2)	11	**14. Help Me, Rhonda**	Capitol 5395
8/07/65	**3**	9	**15. California Girls**	Capitol 5464
12/11/65+	**20**	5	16. The Little Girl I Once Knew	Capitol 5540
1/15/66	**2**(2)	9	**17. Barbara Ann** featuring vocals by Dean Torrence (of Jan & Dean)	Capitol 5561
4/09/66	**3**	10	**18. Sloop John B** originally a folk song originating from the West Indies in 1927	Capitol 5602
8/20/66	**8**	7	**19. Wouldn't It Be Nice/**	
9/17/66	**39**	2	20. God Only Knows	Capitol 5706
10/29/66	**1**(1)	12	• **21. Good Vibrations**	Capitol 5676
8/12/67	**12**	5	22. Heroes And Villains	Brother 1001
11/18/67	**31**	4	23. Wild Honey	Capitol 2028
1/13/68	**19**	6	24. Darlin'	Capitol 2068
8/17/68	**20**	7	25. Do It Again	Capitol 2239
4/05/69	**24**	6	26. I Can Hear Music	Capitol 2432
9/28/74	**36**	1	27. Surfin' U.S.A. [R] song now credited as by Chuck Berry ("Sweet Little Sixteen")	Capitol 3924
6/19/76	**5**	13	**28. Rock And Roll Music**	Brother 1354
9/18/76	**29**	4	29. It's O.K.	Brother 1368
6/09/79	**40**	1	30. Good Timin'	Caribou 9029
8/15/81	**12**	11	31. The Beach Boys Medley	Capitol 5030

DATE	POS	WKS	ARTIST—RECORD TITLE	LABEL & NO.
			Good Vibrations/Help Me Rhonda/I Get Around/Shut Down/ Surfin' Safari/Barbara Ann/Surfin' USA/Fun, Fun, Fun	
12/19/81+	**18**	8	32. Come Go With Me	Caribou 02633
6/08/85	**26**	7	33. Getcha Back	Caribou 04913
8/08/87	**12**	11	34. Wipeout **FAT BOYS AND THE BEACH BOYS**	Tin Pan 885960
9/24/88	**1**(1)	15	▲ **35. Kokomo** from the film *Cocktail*	Elektra 69385
			BEASTIE BOYS	
			New York white rap trio formed in 1981, consisting of King Ad-Rock (Adam Horovitz, son of playwright Israel Horovitz), MCA (Adam Yauch) and Mike D (Michael Diamond). Horovitz starred in the film *Lost Angels* in 1988. Their DJ, Dr. Dre, became host of "Yo! MTV Raps."	
1/24/87	**7**	10	**1. (You Gotta) Fight For Your Right (To Party!)**	Def Jam 06595
8/26/89	**36**	2	2. Hey Ladies	Capitol 44454
			BEATLES, The	
			The world's #1 rock group was formed in Liverpool, England in the late 1950s. Known in early forms as The Quarrymen, Johnny & the Moondogs, The Rainbows, and the Silver Beatles. Named The Beatles in 1960. Originally consisted of John Lennon, Paul McCartney, George Harrison (guitars), Stu Sutcliffe (bass) and Pete Best (drums). Sutcliffe left in April 1961 (died on 4/10/62 of a brain hemorrhage); McCartney moved to bass. Best replaced by Ringo Starr in August 1962. Group managed by Brian Epstein (died on 8/27/67 of sleeping-pill overdose) and produced by George Martin. First U.S. tour in February 1964. Won the 1964 Best New Artist Grammy Award. Group starred in films *A Hard Day's Night* (1964), *Help* (1965) and *Magical Mystery Tour* (1967); voices of *Yellow Submarine* cartoon (1968). Own Apple label in 1968. McCartney publicly anounced group's dissolution on 4/10/70. Won the Grammy's Trustees Award in 1972. Inducted into the Rock and Roll Hall of Fame in 1988.	
1/25/64	**1**(7)	14	● **1. I Want To Hold Your Hand/**	
1/25/64	**14**	8	2. I Saw Her Standing There	Capitol 5112
2/01/64	**1**(2)	14	**3. She Loves You**	Swan 4152
2/22/64	**3**	10	**4. Please Please Me** recorded November 1962	Vee-Jay 581
3/07/64	**26**	2	5. My Bonnie **THE BEATLES with TONY SHERIDAN**	MGM 13213
3/21/64	**2**(4)	9	**6. Twist And Shout**	Tollie 9001
3/28/64	**1**(5)	9	● **7. Can't Buy Me Love**	Capitol 5150
4/11/64	**2**(1)	9	**8. Do You Want To Know A Secret/**	
4/25/64	**35**	3	9. Thank You Girl	Vee-Jay 587
5/02/64	**1**(1)	11	**10. Love Me Do/**	
5/16/64	**10**	7	**11. P.S. I Love You** above 2 recorded September 1962 (with Andy White on drums, Ringo on tambourine)	Tollie 9008
7/18/64	**1**(2)	12	● **12. A Hard Day's Night**	Capitol 5222
8/01/64	**19**	7	13. Ain't She Sweet recorded May 1961 (Pete Best, Lennon, McCartney, Harrison)	Atco 6308
8/08/64	**12**	7	14. And I Love Her	Capitol 5235
8/15/64	**25**	5	15. I'll Cry Instead 12, 14 & 15: from the film *A Hard Day's Night*	Capitol 5234
9/19/64	**17**	5	16. Matchbox/ written by Carl ("Blue Suede Shoes") Perkins	
9/26/64	**25**	4	17. Slow Down	Capitol 5255

ABC emerged from the industrial town of Sheffield, England, during the heyday of punk and new-wave rock, sharing a name with a Jackson 5 hit and a hit song title—1982's "The Look Of Love"—with Dusty Springfield. Which may be why no one thought it odd that their 1987 hit "When Smokey Sings" was a tribute to Smokey Robinson.

Paula Abdul helped Janet Jackson's career take off in 1986 by choreographing the singer's videos, then took off all by herself. Her debut album *Forever Your Girl*—which contains the hits "Straight Up" and "Opposites Attract"—is the largest-selling album in Virgin Records' history.

Bryan Adams' massive 1991 hit "(Everything I Do) I Do It For You" from the soundtrack to *Robin Hood: Prince of Thieves* was certified triple platinum and scored as the biggest single ever for A&M Records.

Air Supply defined the sound of soft pop in the early 80s with seven consecutive Top 5 hits on Arista from 1980's "Lost In Love" to 1982's "Even The Nights Are Better." Though Graham Russell would later record under his own name, by 1991 the Australian duo was recording again for Giant Records.

Al B. Sure!, born an otherwise unpunctuated Al Brown, first cracked the Top 10 with 1988's "Nite And Day" and attracted a vocal young female following. Recognizing that they had a hot commodity on their hands, Warner Bros. shipped to DJs a special version of his next album, 1990's *Private Times . . . And The Whole 9!*, in a package resembling a fully lockable diary.

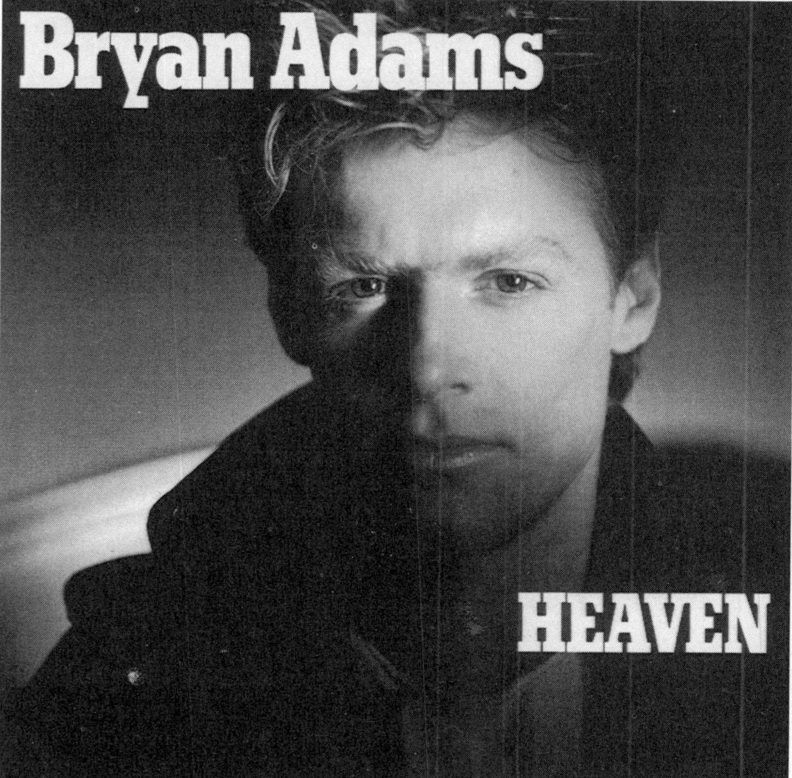

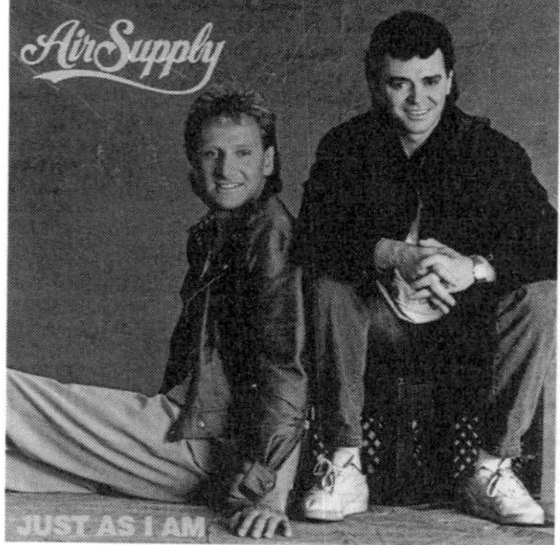

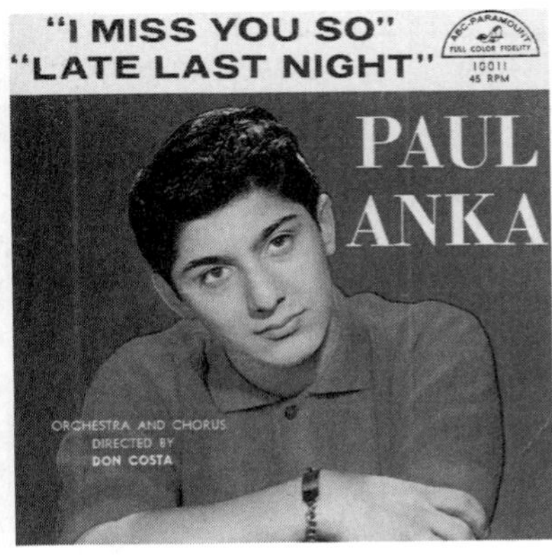

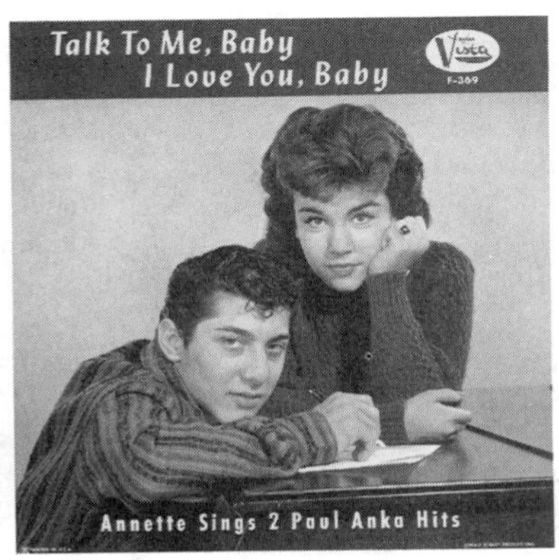

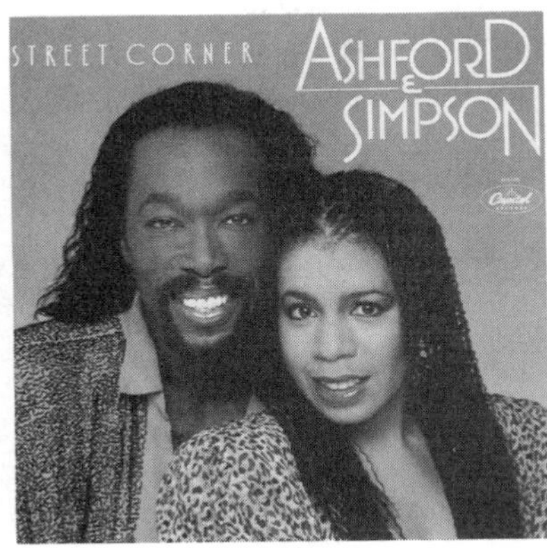

Paul Anka's last hit as a teen sensation was 1960's "My Home Town," yet his first to be certified gold came 14 years later. "(You're) Having My Baby," performed with the late Odia Coates, stayed at the No. 1 slot for three weeks in 1974—undoubtedly to the chagrin of feminists who questioned the song's lyrical slant.

Annette (Funicello) scored five top-40 hits, with 1959's "Tall Paul" peaking at No. 7. Yet an entire generation knows her less for her recording career than for her dual roles as perky Mouseketeer and Frankie Avalon's co-star in the *Beach Party* films. She and Avalon reprised their roles in 1987's *Back to the Beach*.

Ann-Margret's sole appearance in the Top 40 came via her 1961 single "I Just Don't Understand," but the versatile actress/singer/dancer—who some call the "original" Paula Abdul—was also prominent on the 1963 soundtrack to the film *Bye Bye Birdie.*

Ashford & Simpson's own recording career blossomed in the mid-70s, but the married couple are still best known for songs they wrote for others—including "Ain't No Mountain High Enough," "Ain't Nothing Like The Real Thing" and "You're All I Need To Get By."

Frankie Avalon's run of Top 10 singles in the early 60s peaked with the dual No. 1's "Venus" and "Why." One of many young talents to then emerge from Philadelphia, Avalon was later paired with another—Fabian—in an unusual greatest-hits package issued by MCA in 1985.

DATE	POS	WKS	ARTIST—RECORD TITLE	LABEL & NO.
			written by Larry ("Short Fat Fannie") Williams	
12/05/64	**1**(3)	11	● **18. I Feel Fine/**	
12/12/64	**4**	8	**19. She's A Woman**	Capitol 5327
2/27/65	**1**(2)	9	● **20. Eight Days A Week/**	
3/20/65	**39**	1	21. I Don't Want To Spoil The Party	Capitol 5371
5/01/65	**1**(1)	9	**22. Ticket To Ride**	Capitol 5407
8/14/65	**1**(3)	12	● **23. Help!**	Capitol 5476
			above 2 from the film *Help* (originally *Eight Arms to Hold You*)	
10/02/65	**1**(4)	9	● **24. Yesterday**	Capitol 5498
			more than 2500 recorded versions of this song; the first 5-million performance song (25,000 hours of U.S. radio and TV play)	
12/18/65+	**1**(3)	11	● **25. We Can Work It Out/**	
12/25/65+	**5**	8	**26. Day Tripper**	Capitol 5555
3/05/66	**3**	9	● **27. Nowhere Man**	Capitol 5587
6/11/66	**1**(2)	10	● **28. Paperback Writer/**	
6/25/66	**23**	5	29. Rain	Capitol 5651
8/27/66	**2**(1)	8	● **30. Yellow Submarine/**	
			title song of The Beatles' animated film, released in 1968	
9/10/66	**11**	6	31. Eleanor Rigby	Capitol 5715
3/04/67	**1**(1)	9	● **32. Penny Lane/**	
3/11/67	**8**	7	**33. Strawberry Fields Forever**	Capitol 5810
7/29/67	**1**(1)	9	● **34. All You Need Is Love/**	
8/12/67	**34**	2	35. Baby You're A Rich Man	Capitol 5964
12/09/67	**1**(3)	10	● **36. Hello Goodbye**	Capitol 2056
3/23/68	**4**	10	● **37. Lady Madonna**	Capitol 2138
9/14/68	**1**(9)	19	● **38. Hey Jude/**	
9/14/68	**12**	11	39. Revolution	Apple 2276
5/10/69	**1**(5)	12	● **40. Get Back/**	
			THE BEATLES with BILLY PRESTON	
5/10/69	**35**	3	41. Don't Let Me Down	Apple 2490
			THE BEATLES with BILLY PRESTON	
6/21/69	**8**	8	● **42. The Ballad Of John And Yoko**	Apple 2531
10/18/69	**1**(1)	16	● **43. Come Together/**	
10/18/69	**3**	16	● **44. Something**	Apple 2654
3/21/70	**1**(2)	13	● **45. Let It Be**	Apple 2764
5/23/70	**1**(2)	10	**46. The Long And Winding Road**	Apple 2832
			above 2 from the documentary film *Let It Be*	
6/19/76	**7**	11	**47. Got To Get You Into My Life**	Capitol 4274
			from the 1966 album *Revolver*	
4/10/82	**12**	8	48. The Beatles' Movie Medley	Capitol 5107
			Magical Mystery Tour/All You Need Is Love/You've Got To Hide Your Love Away/I Should Have Known Better/A Hard Day's Night/Ticket To Ride/Get Back	
8/30/86	**23**	7	49. Twist And Shout [R]	Capitol 5624
			revived through inclusion in films *Ferris Bueller's Day Off* and *Back to School*	
			BEAU, Toby — see TOBY	

DATE	POS	WKS	ARTIST—RECORD TITLE	LABEL & NO.
			BEAU BRUMMELS, The	
			Formed in 1964 in San Francisco. Led by Sal Valentino (b: Sal Spaminato on 9/08/42, San Francisco; vocals) and Ron Elliott (b: 10/21/43, Haddsburg, California; guitar).	
1/30/65	**15**	8	1. Laugh, Laugh	Autumn 8
5/08/65	**8**	9	**2. Just A Little**	Autumn 10
8/28/65	**38**	1	3. You Tell Me Why	Autumn 16
			BECK, Jeff, Group	
			Veteran guitarist (b: 6/24/44 in Surrey, England). With The Yardbirds from 1964-66. Rod Stewart and Ron Wood were members of the Jeff Beck Group from 1967-69. Member of supergroup The Honeydrippers.	
8/30/69	**36**	2	1. Goo Goo Barabajagal (Love Is Hot) **DONOVAN with THE JEFF BECK GROUP**	Epic 10510
			BECKHAM, Bob	
			Stratford, Oklahoma pop-country singer. Moved to Nashville in 1959.	
10/12/59	**32**	10	1. Just As Much As Ever	Decca 30861
2/29/60	**36**	1	2. Crazy Arms	Decca 31029
			BEE GEES	
			Trio of brothers from Manchester, England: Barry (b: 9/01/47) and twins Robin and Maurice Gibb (b: 12/22/49). First performed December 1955. To Australia in 1958, performed as the Gibbs, later as BG's, finally the Bee Gees. First recorded for Leedon/Festival in 1963. Returned to England in February 1967, with guitarist Vince Melouney and drummer Colin Peterson. Toured Europe and the U.S. in 1968. Melouney left in December 1968; Robin left for solo career in 1969. When Peterson left in August 1969, Barry and Maurice went solo. After eight months, the brothers reunited. Composed soundtracks of *Saturday Night Fever* and *Staying Alive.* Acted in film *Sgt. Pepper's Lonely Hearts Club Band.* Youngest brother Andy Gibb was a successful solo singer (d: 3/10/88).	
6/10/67	**14**	5	1. New York Mining Disaster 1941 (Have You Seen My Wife, Mr. Jones)	Atco 6487
7/29/67	**17**	7	2. To Love Somebody	Atco 6503
10/21/67	**16**	5	3. Holiday	Atco 6521
11/25/67	**11**	6	4. (The Lights Went Out In) Massachusetts	Atco 6532
2/10/68	**15**	8	5. Words	Atco 6548
9/07/68	**8**	10	**6. I've Gotta Get A Message To You**	Atco 6603
1/04/69	**6**	9	**7. I Started A Joke**	Atco 6639
4/12/69	**37**	3	8. First Of May	Atco 6657
12/26/70+	**3**	10	● **9. Lonely Days**	Atco 6795
7/03/71	**1**(4)	14	● **10. How Can You Mend A Broken Heart**	Atco 6824
2/05/72	**16**	7	11. My World	Atco 6871
8/26/72	**16**	7	12. Run To Me	Atco 6896
12/02/72	**34**	4	13. Alive	Atco 6909
6/28/75	**1**(2)	12	● **14. Jive Talkin'**	RSO 510
10/18/75	**7**	13	**15. Nights On Broadway**	RSO 515
1/17/76	**12**	12	16. Fanny (Be Tender With My Love)	RSO 519
7/17/76	**1**(1)	12	● **17. You Should Be Dancing**	RSO 853
10/02/76	**3**	16	● **18. Love So Right**	RSO 859
1/29/77	**12**	9	19. Boogie Child	RSO 867
8/13/77	**26**	5	20. Edge Of The Universe	RSO 880
10/08/77	**1**(3)	26	● **21. How Deep Is Your Love**	RSO 882

DATE	POS	WKS	ARTIST—RECORD TITLE	LABEL & NO.
12/24/77+	1(4)	22	▲ **22. Stayin' Alive**	RSO 885
2/11/78	1(8)	18	▲ **23. Night Fever**	RSO 889
			above 3 from the film *Saturday Night Fever*	
11/18/78+	1(2)	17	▲ **24. Too Much Heaven**	RSO 913
2/10/79	1(2)	13	▲ **25. Tragedy**	RSO 918
4/21/79	1(1)	13	• **26. Love You Inside Out**	RSO 925
10/10/81	**30**	4	27. He's A Liar	RSO 1066
5/28/83	**24**	6	28. The Woman In You	RSO 813173
			from the film *Staying Alive*	
8/12/89	**7**	10	**29. One**	Warner 22899
			BEGINNING OF THE END, The	
			Bahamas quartet consisting of brothers Raphael "Ray" (organ), Liroy "Roy" (guitar) and Frank "Bud" Munnings (drums), with Fred Henfield (bass).	
6/05/71	**15**	10	1. Funky Nassau-Part I	Alston 4595
			BELAFONTE, Harry	
			Born Harold George Belafonte, Jr. on 3/01/27 in Harlem. Actor in American Negro Theater, Drama Workshop, mid-1940s. Started career as a "straight pop" singer. Recorded for Jubilee Records in 1949, shortly afterward began specializing in folk music. Rode the crest of the calypso craze to worldwide stardom. Starred in eight films from 1953-74. Replaced Danny Kaye in 1987 as UNICEF goodwill ambassador. Father of actress Shari Belafonte.	
11/24/56+	**14**	16	1. Jamaica Farewell	RCA 6663
			Jockey #14 / Best Seller #17 / Top 100 #17 / Juke Box #17	
12/29/56	**12**	3	2. Mary's Boy Child [X]	RCA 6735
			Best Seller #12 / Jockey #12 / Top 100 #15	
1/12/57	**5**	17	**3. Banana Boat (Day-O)**	RCA 6771
			Best Seller #5 / Top 100 #5 / Jockey #5 / Juke Box #5	
3/23/57	**11**	10	4. Mama Look At Bubu	RCA 6830
			Best Seller #11 / Top 100 #13 / Jockey #14 / Juke Box #18	
7/08/57	**25**	3	5. Cocoanut Woman /	
			Best Seller #25 / Top 100 #48	
7/08/57	**30**	3	6. Island In The Sun	RCA 6885
			Best Seller #30 / Top 100 #42 from the film (starring Belafonte) of the same title	
			BELL, Archie/The Drells	
			Born on 9/01/44 in Henderson, Texas. Lead singer of the Drells, R&B vocal group from Leo Smith Junior High School in Houston. First recorded for Ovid in 1967. Recorded "Tighten Up" with group consisting of Bell, Huey "Billy" Butler, Joe Cross and James Wise. Bell was in U.S. Army at time of hit. Later recordings consisted of Bell, Wise, Lee Bell and Willie Parnell. Still active in "beach music" scene.	
4/13/68	1(2)	13	• **1. Tighten Up**	Atlantic 2478
8/03/68	**9**	8	**2. I Can't Stop Dancing**	Atlantic 2534
1/04/69	**21**	8	3. There's Gonna Be A Showdown	Atlantic 2583
			BELL, Benny	
			Jewish risque songwriter from New York City.	
4/19/75	**30**	4	1. Shaving Cream [N]	Vanguard 35183
			vocal by Paul Wynn; originally released in 1946	

DATE	POS	WKS	ARTIST—RECORD TITLE	LABEL & NO.
			BELL, Madeline	
			In cast of *Black Nativity*, toured England in the mid-1960s and remained there. Formed group Blue Mink, 1969-73. Commercial jingle singer since then.	
3/09/68	**26**	5	1. I'm Gonna Make You Love Me	Philips 40517
			BELL, Vincent	
			Veteran studio guitarist. Born Vincent Gambella. Leader of the Ramrods. Also see Ferrante & Teicher.	
4/25/70	**31**	5	1. Airport Love Theme (Gwen And Vern) [I] from the film *Airport*	Decca 32659
			BELL, William	
			Born William Yarborough on 7/16/39 in Memphis. R&B singer.	
3/12/77	**10**	9	● **1. Tryin' To Love Two**	Mercury 73839
			BELLAMY BROTHERS	
			Country duo from Darby, Florida: brothers Howard (b: 2/02/46; guitar) and David Bellamy (b: 9/16/50; guitar, keyboards). Made their professional debut in 1958. David wrote "Spiders And Snakes" hit for Jim Stafford. Moved to Los Angeles in 1973.	
3/06/76	**1**(1)	12	**1. Let Your Love Flow**	Warner 8169
7/14/79	**39**	2	2. If I Said You Have A Beautiful Body Would You Hold It Against Me	Warner 8790
			BELL & JAMES	
			R&B duo of Leroy Bell and Casey James. Began as songwriting team for Bell's uncle, producer Thom Bell.	
3/10/79	**15**	8	● 1. Livin' It Up (Friday Night)	A&M 2069
			Trio of New Edition members: Ricky Bell, Michael Bivins and Ronnie DeVoe.	
4/14/90	**3**	17	▲ **1. Poison**	MCA 53772
7/21/90	**3**	16	**2. Do Me!**	MCA 79045
11/10/90	**26**	5	3. B.B.D. (I Thought It Was Me)?	MCA 53897
			BELLE STARS, The	
			English female band formed as The Bodysnatchers in 1981. Changed name to The Belle Stars in 1983. Features Jennie McKeown (vocals) and Sarah-Jane Owen (guitar).	
4/01/89	**14**	10	1. Iko Iko from the film *Rain Man*; earlier version featured on their 1983 LP *The Belle Stars*	Capitol 44343
			BELL NOTES, The	
			Quintet from Long Island, New York: Carl Bonura (sax), Ray Ceroni (guitar), Lenny Giamblavo (bass), Peter Kane (piano) and John Casey (drums).	
2/09/59	**6**	11	**1. I've Had It**	Time 1004
			BELLS, The	
			Canadian quintet; lead singers Jacki Ralph and Cliff Edwards.	
3/27/71	**7**	11	● **1. Stay Awhile**	Polydor 15023
			BELLUS, Tony	
			Born Anthony Bellusci on 4/17/36 in Chicago. Pop singer/accordionist. First recorded for Shi-Fi in 1958.	
6/29/59	**25**	11	1. Robbin' The Cradle	NRC 023

DATE	POS	WKS	ARTIST—RECORD TITLE	LABEL & NO.
			BELMONTS, The	
			Angelo D'Aleo, Fred Milano and Carlo Mastrangelo. Sang with Dion from 1957-60. Named after Belmont Avenue in the Bronx. Frank Lyndon replaced Mastrangelo in May 1962.	
6/19/61	**18**	6	1. Tell Me Why	Sabrina 500
			first released on Surprise 1000 in 1961	
8/25/62	**28**	8	2. Come On Little Angel	Sabina 505
			BELVIN, Jesse	
			Born Jessie Lorenzo Belvin on 12/15/32 in San Antonio, Texas. Jesse and his wife were killed in an auto accident on 2/06/60. Recorded with Marvin Phillips as "Jesse & Marvin." A pivotal figure in the development of the R&B sound on the West Coast. Co-wrote "Earth Angel" with Curtis Williams of The Penguins. Also see The Shields.	
4/13/59	**31**	9	1. Guess Who	RCA 7469
			written by Jesse's wife, Jo Anne Belvin	
			BENATAR, Pat	
			Born Patricia Andrzejewski in Lindenhurst, Long Island, New York in 1952. Married her producer/guitarist Neil Giraldo on 2/20/82. Acted in the film *Union City* and the 1989 ABC afterschool TV special "Torn Between Two Fathers."	
2/09/80	**23**	10	1. Heartbreaker	Chrysalis 2395
5/17/80	**27**	6	2. We Live For Love	Chrysalis 2419
10/18/80	**9**	15	● **3. Hit Me With Your Best Shot**	Chrysalis 2464
1/31/81	**18**	10	4. Treat Me Right	Chrysalis 2487
8/01/81	**17**	9	5. Fire And Ice	Chrysalis 2529
10/31/81	**38**	2	6. Promises In The Dark	Chrysalis 2555
11/06/82	**13**	10	7. Shadows Of The Night	Chrysalis 2647
3/05/83	**20**	7	8. Little Too Late	Chrysalis 03536
5/21/83	**39**	3	9. Looking For A Stranger	Chrysalis 42688
10/15/83	**5**	14	● **10. Love Is A Battlefield**	Chrysalis 42732
11/03/84+	**5**	14	**11. We Belong**	Chrysalis 42826
2/09/85	**36**	3	12. Ooh Ooh Song	Chrysalis 42843
7/27/85	**10**	11	**13. Invincible**	Chrysalis 42877
			theme from the film *Legend of Billie Jean*	
12/14/85+	**28**	7	14. Sex As A Weapon	Chrysalis 42927
7/30/88	**19**	8	15. All Fired Up	Chrysalis 43268
			BENNETT, Boyd/His Rockets	
			Boyd was born in Muscle Shoals, Alabama on 12/07/24. Attended high school in Tennessee and formed first band there. Later became a DJ in Kentucky.	
7/09/55	**5**	17	**1. Seventeen**	King 1470
			Best Seller #5 / Juke Box #8 / Jockey #9 / Top 100 #28 pre	
11/12/55	**39**	1	2. My Boy - Flat Top	King 1494
			vocals on above 2 by Big Moe	
			BENNETT, Joe/The Sparkletones	
			Teenage band from Spartanburg, South Carolina. Consisted of Joe Bennett (vocals, guitar), Howard Childress (guitar), Wayne Arthur (bass) and Irving Denton (drums).	
9/23/57	**17**	9	1. Black Slacks	ABC-Para. 9837
			Top 100 #17 / Best Seller #18 / Jockey #21	

DATE	POS	WKS	ARTIST—RECORD TITLE	LABEL & NO.
			BENNETT, Tony	
			Born Anthony Dominick Benedetto on 8/13/25 in Queens, New York. Jazz/ballad vocalist. Worked local clubs while in high school, sang in U.S. Army bands. Audition record of "Boulevard Of Broken Dreams" earned a Columbia contract in 1950. Appeared in the film *The Oscar.*	
5/05/56	**16**	11	1. Can You Find It In Your Heart Best Seller #16 / Juke Box #18 / Top 100 #19 / Jockey #20	Columbia 40667
8/18/56	**11**	7	2. From The Candy Store On The Corner To The Chapel On The Hill/ Jockey #11 / Top 100 #33; female vocal by Lois Winter	
10/06/56	**38**	2	3. Happiness Street (Corner Sunshine Square)	Columbia 40726
11/17/56	**18**	4	4. The Autumn Waltz Jockey #18 / Top 100 #41	Columbia 40770
8/12/57	**9**	14	**5. In The Middle Of An Island** Best Seller #9 / Top 100 #9 / Jockey #13	Columbia 40965
11/18/57	**22**	1	6. Ca, C'est L'amour Jockey #22 / Top 100 #96; from the film *Les Girls*	Columbia 41032
6/30/58	**23**	1	7. Young And Warm And Wonderful Jockey #23 / Best Seller #42 / Top 100 #57	Columbia 41172
9/22/58	**20**	8	8. Firefly Hot 100 #20 / Best Seller #45 end	Columbia 41237
9/29/62	**19**	10	9. I Left My Heart In San Francisco	Columbia 42332
2/16/63	**14**	10	10. I Wanna Be Around	Columbia 42634
6/01/63	**18**	6	11. The Good Life	Columbia 42779
10/31/64	**33**	6	12. Who Can I Turn To (When Nobody Needs Me) from the musical *The Roar of the Greasepaint*	Columbia 43141
3/20/65	**34**	4	13. If I Ruled The World from the musical *Pickwick*; with The Will Bronson Chorus	Columbia 43220
			BENSON, George	
			Born on 3/22/43 in Pittsburgh. R&B-jazz guitarist. Played guitar from age eight. Played in Brother Jack McDuff's trio in 1963. House musician at CTI Records to early '70s. Influenced by Wes Montgomery.	
7/17/76	**10**	11	**1. This Masquerade** written by Leon Russell	Warner 8209
9/03/77	**24**	7	2. The Greatest Love Of All from the film *The Greatest*	Arista 0251
4/22/78	**7**	10	**3. On Broadway**	Warner 8542
3/24/79	**18**	8	4. Love Ballad	Warner 8759
8/02/80	**4**	14	**5. Give Me The Night**	Warner 49505
11/21/81+	**5**	16	**6. Turn Your Love Around**	Warner 49846
8/27/83	**30**	6	7. Lady Love Me (One More Time)	Warner 29563
			BENSON, Jo Jo — see SCOTT, Peggy	
			BENTON, Brook	
			R&B singer/songwriter. Born Benjamin Franklin Peay on 9/19/31 in Camden, South Carolina; died on 4/09/88 of complications from spinal meningitis. In The Camden Jubilee Singers. To New York in 1948, joined Bill Langford's Langfordaires. With Jerusalem Stars in 1951. First recorded under own name for Okeh in 1953. Wrote "Looking Back," "A Lover's Question," "The Stroll," "It's Just A Matter Of Time" and "Endlessly."	
2/09/59	**3**	14	**1. It's Just A Matter Of Time**	Mercury 71394
5/04/59	**12**	9	2. Endlessly/	

DATE	POS	WKS	ARTIST—RECORD TITLE	LABEL & NO.
6/08/59	38	1	3. So Close	Mercury 71443
8/03/59	16	9	4. Thank You Pretty Baby	Mercury 71478
10/26/59	6	13	**5. So Many Ways**	Mercury 71512
2/08/60	5	12	**6. Baby (You've Got What It Takes)** DINAH WASHINGTON & BROOK BENTON	Mercury 71565
5/09/60	37	1	7. The Ties That Bind	Mercury 71566
6/06/60	7	10	**8. A Rockin' Good Way (To Mess Around And Fall In Love)** DINAH WASHINGTON & BROOK BENTON	Mercury 71629
8/22/60	7	13	**9. Kiddio/**	
8/29/60	16	10	10. The Same One	Mercury 71652
11/21/60	24	7	11. Fools Rush In (Where Angels Fear To Tread)	Mercury 71722
2/27/61	11	9	12. Think Twice/	
3/20/61	28	1	13. For My Baby	Mercury 71774
6/05/61	2(3)	12	**14. The Boll Weevil Song** [N]	Mercury 71820
9/04/61	20	4	15. Frankie And Johnny	Mercury 71859
12/18/61+	15	5	16. Revenge	Mercury 71903
1/27/62	19	5	17. Shadrack written in 1931 as "Shadrack Meshack, Abednigo"	Mercury 71912
9/15/62	13	6	18. Lie To Me	Mercury 72024
12/08/62+	3	10	**19. Hotel Happiness**	Mercury 72055
4/06/63	28	4	20. I Got What I Wanted	Mercury 72099
7/13/63	22	4	21. My True Confession	Mercury 72135
10/05/63	32	5	22. Two Tickets To Paradise	Mercury 72177
2/15/64	35	3	23. Going Going Gone	Mercury 72230
1/31/70	4	12	● **24. Rainy Night In Georgia** written by Tony Joe White	Cotillion 44057
			BERLIN	
			Los Angeles electro-pop group. Went from a sextet to a trio in 1985 featuring Terri Nunn (vocals), John Crawford (bass) and Rob Brill (drums). Nunn left in 1987.	
4/07/84	23	8	1. No More Words	Geffen 29360
7/19/86	1(1)	13	**2. Take My Breath Away** love theme from the film *Top Gun*	Columbia 05903
			BERNARD, Rod	
			Born on 8/12/40 in Opelousas, Louisiana. R&B singer/guitarist. On local radio since age 10. DJ for KSLO in 1957. First recorded for Carl in 1957. Program director for KVOL-Lafayette, Louisiana in the '60s.	
3/23/59	20	9	1. This Should Go On Forever first released on JIN 105 in 1958	Argo 5327
			BERNSTEIN, Elmer	
			Born on 4/04/22 in New York City. Composer/conductor for over 60 movie soundtracks.	
4/07/56	16	9	1. Main Title From "The Man With The Golden Arm" [I] Best Seller #16 / Top 100 #32 from the movie of the same title; featuring Shelly Manne, drums	Decca 29869

DATE	POS	WKS	ARTIST—RECORD TITLE	LABEL & NO.
			BERRY, Chuck	
			Born Charles Edward Anderson Berry on 10/18/26 in San Jose, California. Grew up in St. Louis. Muddy Waters introduced Chuck to Leonard Chess (Chess Records) in Chicago. First recording, "Maybellene," was an instant success. Appeared in the film *Rock, Rock, Rock* in 1956, and several others. Won Lifetime Achievement Grammy in 1984. Inducted into the Rock and Roll Hall of Fame in 1986. Film documentary/ concert tribute to Chuck, *Hail! Hail! Rock 'N' Roll*, released in 1987. Acclaimed as one of rock and roll's most influential artists.	
8/20/55	**5**	11	**1. Maybellene** Best Seller #5 / Juke Box #6 / Jockey #13 / Top 100 #42 pre Grammy Hall of Fame Award winner in 1988	Chess 1604
6/30/56	**29**	1	2. Roll Over Beethoven Grammy Hall of Fame Award winner in 1989	Chess 1626
4/20/57	**3**	15	**3. School Day** Best Seller #3 / Top 100 #5 / Jockey #6 / Juke Box #7	Chess 1653
11/11/57	**8**	13	**4. Rock & Roll Music** Top 100 #8 / Best Seller #9	Chess 1671
2/24/58	**2**(3)	11	**5. Sweet Little Sixteen** Best Seller #2 / Top 100 #2 / Jockey #5	Chess 1683
5/05/58	**8**	11	**6. Johnny B. Goode** Top 100 #8 / Best Seller #9 / Jockey #16	Chess 1691
9/15/58	**18**	5	7. Carol Hot 100 #18 / Best Seller #29	Chess 1700
4/20/59	**32**	7	8. Almost Grown	Chess 1722
7/13/59	**37**	1	9. Back In The U.S.A.	Chess 1729
4/04/64	**23**	5	10. Nadine (Is It You?)	Chess 1883
6/13/64	**10**	7	**11. No Particular Place To Go**	Chess 1898
8/22/64	**14**	5	12. You Never Can Tell	Chess 1906
9/09/72	**1**(2)	12	● **13. My Ding-A-Ling** [N]	Chess 2131
1/06/73	**27**	7	14. Reelin' & Rockin' above 2 recorded live in Manchester, England; "Reelin' " was originally the B-side of "Sweet Little Sixteen"	Chess 2136
			B-52'S, The	
			Formed in 1977 in Athens, Georgia as a new wave dance band. Guitarist Keith Strickland with vocalists Kate Pierson, Fred Schneider, Cindy Wilson and her brother Ricky Wilson (drums; died of AIDS on 10/12/85). B-52 is slang for the bouffant hairstyle worn by Kate and Cindy.	
9/30/89	**3**	17	● **1. Love Shack**	Reprise 22817
1/20/90	**3**	13	● **2. Roam**	Reprise 22667
5/19/90	**30**	4	3. Deadbeat Club	Reprise 19938
			BIG BOPPER	
			Born Jiles Perry Richardson on 10/24/30 in Sabine Pass, Texas. DJ at KTRM in Beaumont, Texas. Wrote "Running Bear" for Johnny Preston. Died with Buddy Holly and Ritchie Valens in the 2/03/59 plane crash.	
8/04/58	**6**	22	**1. Chantilly Lace** [N] Hot 100 #6 / Best Seller #13 end first released on "D" 1008 in 1958	Mercury 71343
12/22/58	**38**	1	2. Big Bopper's Wedding [N]	Mercury 71375

DATE	POS	WKS	ARTIST—RECORD TITLE	LABEL & NO.
			BIG BROTHER AND THE HOLDING COMPANY	
			Formed in San Francisco in 1965. Janis Joplin joined as lead singer in 1966. Other members: Peter Albin (bass), James Gurley (guitar), Sam Andrew (guitar) and David Getz (drums). Sensation at the Monterey Pop Festival in 1967. Disbanded in 1972.	
9/28/68	**12**	8	1. Piece Of My Heart	Columbia 44626
			BIG COUNTRY	
			Rock quartet formed in Dunfermline, Scotland: Stuart Adamson (vocals, guitar), Bruce Watson (guitar), Tony Butler (bass) and Mark Brzezicki (drums).	
11/12/83	**17**	9	1. In A Big Country	Mercury 814467
			BILK, Mr. Acker	
			Clarinetist/composer. Born Bernard Stanley Bilk on 1/28/29 in Somerset, England.	
4/07/62	1(1)	15	● **1. Stranger On The Shore** [I]	Atco 6217
			BILLY & LILLIE	
			Vocal duo of Billy Ford (b: 3/09/25, Bloomfield, New Jersey) and Lillie Bryant (b: 2/14/40, Newburg, New York). Backing group: Billy Ford and the Thunderbirds.	
1/13/58	**9**	10	**1. La Dee Dah** Top 100 #9 / Best Seller #10 / Jockey #23	Swan 4002
1/05/59	**14**	8	2. Lucky Ladybug	Swan 4020
			BILLY & THE BEATERS — see VERA, Billy	
			BILLY JOE & THE CHECKMATES	
			Born Louis Bideu on 3/21/19 in El Paso, Texas. Worked as a comedian. Hosted own local *Lew Bedell Show* in New York. Dubbed himself Billy Joe Hunter in the early 1960s.	
2/17/62	**10**	7	**1. Percolator** [I]	Dore 620
			BINGOBOYS featuring PRINCESSA	
			Dance trio of DJs from Vienna, Austria: Klaus Biedermann, Paul Pfab and Helmut Wolfgruber. Princessa is a female rapper from New York.	
3/16/91	**25**	6	1. How To Dance samples Chic's "Dance, Dance, Dance" and Sylvester's "Dance (Disco Heat)"	Atlantic 87756#
			BISHOP, Elvin	
			Born on 10/21/42 in Tulsa, Oklahoma. Lead guitarist with The Paul Butterfield Blues Band (1965-68).	
4/03/76	**3**	12	● **1. Fooled Around And Fell In Love** lead vocal by Mickey Thomas (of Starship)	Capricorn 0252
			BISHOP, Stephen	
			Pop-rock singer/songwriter born in 1951 in San Diego. Wrote movie theme for *The China Syndrome*. Cameo role as the "Charming Guy With Guitar" in *National Lampoon's Animal House*.	
1/22/77	**22**	7	1. Save It For A Rainy Day guitar solo: Eric Clapton; background vocal by Chaka Khan	ABC 12232
7/23/77	**11**	15	2. On And On	ABC 12260
10/28/78	**32**	5	3. Everybody Needs Love	ABC 12406
4/02/83	**25**	8	4. It Might Be You theme from the film *Tootsie*	Warner 29791

DATE	POS	WKS	ARTIST—RECORD TITLE	LABEL & NO.
			BIZ MARKIE	
			Rapper born in Harlem on 4/08/64. Real name: Marcel Hall.	
2/10/90	**9**	11	▲ **1. Just A Friend**	Cold Chill. 22784
			BLACK('S), Bill, Combo	
			Bill was born on 9/17/26 in Memphis; died of a brain tumor on 10/21/65. Bass guitarist. Session work in Memphis; backed Elvis Presley (with Scotty Moore, guitar; D.J. Fontana, drums) on most of his early records. Formed own band in 1959. Labeled as "The Untouchable Sound."	
12/21/59+	**17**	8	1. Smokie — Part 2 [I]	Hi 2018
3/21/60	**9**	11	**2. White Silver Sands [I]**	Hi 2021
7/04/60	**18**	8	3. Josephine [I] #3 hit for Wayne King's Orchestra in 1937	Hi 2022
10/03/60	**11**	9	4. Don't Be Cruel [I] Bill played bass on Elvis Presley's original hit	Hi 2026
12/12/60	**16**	7	5. Blue Tango [I] #1 hit for Leroy Anderson in 1952	Hi 2027
3/06/61	**20**	4	6. Hearts Of Stone [I]	Hi 2028
6/26/61	**25**	4	7. Ole Buttermilk Sky [I] written and popularized in 1946 by Hoagy Carmichael	Hi 2036
1/20/62	**26**	4	8. Twist-Her [I]	Hi 2042
			BLACK, Cilla	
			Born Priscilla White on 5/27/43 in Liverpool, England.	
7/25/64	**26**	4	1. You're My World	Capitol 5196
			BLACK, Jeanne	
			Born Gloria Jeanne Black on 10/25/37 in Pomona, California. Appearances on local TV show, "Hometown Jamboree." Discovered by Cliffie Stone.	
5/02/60	**4**	10	**1. He'll Have To Stay** answer song to Jim Reeves' "He'll Have To Go"	Capitol 4368
			BLACK BOX	
			Male Italian dance trio of producer Daniele Davoli and musicians Mirko Limoni and Valerio Semplici. Videos feature French model Katrin Quinol as lead singer; however, Martha Wash (Weather Girls) is the uncredited lead vocalist.	
9/01/90	**8**	12	**1. Everybody Everybody**	RCA 2628#
1/19/91	**23**	4	2. I Don't Know Anybody Else	RCA 2735#
4/27/91	**8**	12	**3. Strike It Up**	RCA 2794#
			BLACKBYRDS, The	
			Soul group founded in 1973 by Donald Byrd while teaching at Howard University in Washington, D.C.	
3/15/75	**6**	12	**1. Walking In Rhythm**	Fantasy 736
4/17/76	**19**	6	2. Happy Music	Fantasy 762
			BLACK CROWES, The	
			Hard-rock quintet from Atlanta led by brothers Chris (vocals) and Rich (guitar) Robinson. Includes Jeff Cease, Steve Gorman and Johnny Colt.	
4/20/91	**30**	7	1. She Talks To Angels	Def Amer. 19403
7/20/91	**26**	6	2. Hard To Handle [R] originally charted on 10/27/90 (POS 45)	Def Amer. 19245

DATE	POS	WKS	ARTIST—RECORD TITLE	LABEL & NO.
			BLACKFOOT	
			Rick "Rattlesnake" Medlocke, lead singer of band from Jacksonville, Florida.	
8/04/79	**26**	6	1. Highway Song	Atco 7104
12/22/79	**38**	4	2. Train, Train	Atco 7207
			BLACK OAK ARKANSAS	
			Southern-rock sextet led by Jim "Dandy" Mangrum (vocals). Group named after their hometown.	
1/26/74	**25**	6	1. Jim Dandy female singer: Ruby Starr	Atco 6948
			BLANCHARD, Jack, & MISTY MORGAN	
			Husband-and-wife country duo. Both born in Buffalo. Jack (b: 5/08/42) plays saxophone and keyboards. Misty (b: 5/23/45) plays keyboards. Met and married while working in Florida.	
3/28/70	**23**	8	1. Tennessee Bird Walk [N]	Wayside 010
			BLAND, Billy	
			Born on 4/05/32 in Wilmington, North Carolina. R&B singer; formed group, the Four Bees, in 1954. First recorded solo for Old Town in 1955.	
3/28/60	**7**	13	**1. Let The Little Girl Dance**	Old Town 1076
			BLAND, Bobby	
			Born Robert Calvin Bland on 1/27/30 in Rosemark, Tennessee. Nicknamed "Blue." Sang in gospel group The Miniatures in Memphis, late '40s. Member of the Beale Streeters which included Johnny Ace, B.B. King, Rosco Gordon, Earl Forest and Willie Nix in 1949. Driver and valet for B.B. King; appeared in the Johnny Ace Revue, early '50s. First recorded in 1952 for the Modern label. Toured with B.B. King into the '80s.	
1/20/62	**28**	3	1. Turn On Your Love Light	Duke 344
2/02/63	**22**	7	2. Call On Me/	
2/09/63	**33**	5	3. That's The Way Love Is	Duke 360
3/28/64	**20**	6	4. Ain't Nothing You Can Do	Duke 375
			BLANE, Marcie	
			Born on 5/21/44 in Brooklyn, New York.	
11/10/62	**3**	13	**1. Bobby's Girl**	Seville 120
			BLEYER, Archie	
			Born on 6/12/09 in Corona, New York. Arranger/music director for the TV show "Arthur Godfrey and His Friends" from 1949-54. Founded Cadence Records. Married Chordettes member Janet Ertel in 1954. Died on 3/20/89 of Parkinson's disease.	
12/04/54+	**17**	6	1. The Naughty Lady Of Shady Lane Jockey #17 / Juke Box #20 / Best Seller #26	Cadence 1254
			BLONDIE	
			New York City techno-pop sextet formed in 1975. Consisted of Debbie Harry (lead singer), Chris Stein, Frank Infante, Jimmy Destri, Gary Valentine and Clem Burke. Harry had been in the folk-rock group Wind In The Willows. Did solo work from 1980; appeared in several films. Disbanded in 1983.	
3/17/79	**1**(1)	14	● **1. Heart Of Glass**	Chrysalis 2295
6/30/79	**24**	7	2. One Way Or Another	Chrysalis 2336
11/03/79	**27**	6	3. Dreaming	Chrysalis 2379
3/08/80	**1**(6)	19	● **4. Call Me** theme from the film *American Gigolo*	Chrysalis 2414
6/21/80	**39**	3	5. Atomic	Chrysalis 2410

DATE	POS	WKS	ARTIST—RECORD TITLE	LABEL & NO.
11/29/80+	**1**(1)	17	● **6. The Tide Is High**	Chrysalis 2465
2/14/81	**1**(2)	14	● **7. Rapture**	Chrysalis 2485
6/26/82	**37**	3	8. Island Of Lost Souls	Chrysalis 2603
			all of above produced by Mike Chapman (except #4: Giorgio Moroder)	
			BLOODROCK	
			Rock group from Fort Worth, Texas — Jim Rutledge, lead vocals. Rutledge headed own production company in the 1970s; produced Meri Wilson's "Telephone Man."	
2/27/71	**36**	2	1. D.O.A.	Capitol 3009
			BLOODSTONE	
			Soul group from Kansas City, Missouri. Formed in 1962 as the Sinceres. Consisted of Charles McCormick, Willis Draffen, Charles Love, Henry Williams and Roger Durham (d: 1973).	
6/09/73	**10**	12	● **1. Natural High**	London 1046
4/06/74	**34**	4	2. Outside Woman	London 1052
			BLOOD, SWEAT & TEARS	
			Pop-jazz group formed by Al Kooper (The Royal Teens, The Blues Project) in 1968. Nucleus consisted of Kooper (keyboards), Steve Katz (guitar; The Blues Project), Bobby Colomby (drums) and Jim Fielder (bass). Kooper replaced by lead singer David Clayton-Thomas in 1969. Clayton-Thomas replaced by Jerry Fisher in 1972. Katz left in 1973. Clayton-Thomas rejoined in 1974. Colomby later worked as a television music reporter and an executive with Epic, Capitol, EMI and CBS.	
3/15/69	**2**(3)	11	● **1. You've Made Me So Very Happy**	Columbia 44776
6/07/69	**2**(3)	12	● **2. Spinning Wheel**	Columbia 44871
10/25/69	**2**(1)	12	● **3. And When I Die**	Columbia 45008
			written by Laura Nyro	
8/15/70	**14**	6	4. Hi-De-Ho	Columbia 45204
10/10/70	**29**	6	5. Lucretia Mac Evil	Columbia 45235
8/14/71	**32**	5	6. Go Down Gamblin'	Columbia 45427
			BLOOM, Bobby	
			Singer/songwriter, much session work in the '60s. Died from an accidental shooting on 2/28/74.	
10/17/70	**8**	11	**1. Montego Bay**	L&R/MGM 157
			BLOW MONKEYS, The	
			British quartet led by Dr. Robert (Robert Howard). Includes: Mick Anker, Neville Henry and Tony Kiley.	
6/14/86	**14**	10	1. Digging Your Scene	RCA 14325
			BLUE-BELLES, The — see STARLETS	
			BLUE CHEER	
			San Francisco hard-rock group led by Dickie Peterson (vocals, bass).	
3/23/68	**14**	10	1. Summertime Blues	Philips 40516
			BLUE HAZE	
			British male group.	
12/23/72+	**27**	7	1. Smoke Gets In Your Eyes	A&M 1357
			#1 hit for Paul Whiteman in 1934	

DATE	POS	WKS	ARTIST—RECORD TITLE	LABEL & NO.
			BLUE JAYS, The	
			R&B group from Los Angeles — Leon Peels, lead singer.	
9/04/61	**31**	4	1. Lover's Island	Milestone 2008
			BLUE MAGIC	
			Soul vocal group from Philadelphia. Consisted of Theodore Mills (lead vocals), Vernon Sawyer, Wendell Sawyer, Keith Beaton and Richard Pratt.	
6/08/74	**8**	15	● **1. Sideshow**	Atco 6961
11/23/74	**36**	2	2. Three Ring Circus	Atco 7004
			BLUE OYSTER CULT	
			Hard-rock quintet formed in Long Island, New York in 1970: Donald "Buck Dharma" Roeser (guitar), Eric Bloom (vocal), Allen Lanier (keyboards), and brothers Joe (bass) and Albert (drums) Bouchard.	
9/04/76	**12**	14	1. (Don't Fear) The Reaper	Columbia 10384
10/03/81	**40**	3	2. Burnin' For You	Columbia 02415
			BLUE RIDGE RANGERS, The — see FOGERTY, John	
			BLUES BROTHERS	
			Joliet "Jake" (John Belushi; b: 1/24/49, Wheaton, Illinois; d: 3/05/82) and Elwood Blues (Dan Aykroyd; b: 7/01/52, Ottawa, Ontario); originally created for TV's "Saturday Night Live."	
1/06/79	**14**	9	1. Soul Man	Atlantic 3545
3/31/79	**37**	3	2. Rubber Biscuit [N]	Atlantic 3564
6/21/80	**18**	8	3. Gimme Some Lovin' from the soundtrack *The Blues Brothers*	Atlantic 3666
1/31/81	**39**	2	4. Who's Making Love	Atlantic 3785
			BLUES IMAGE	
			Tampa, Florida rock quintet led by Mike Pinera, a featured guitarist with Iron Butterfly in 1970.	
5/23/70	**4**	12	● **1. Ride Captain Ride**	Atco 6746
			BLUES MAGOOS	
			Bronx, New York psychedelic rock quintet led by singer/guitarist Peppy Castro (real name: Emil Thielhelm). Originally known as the Bloos Magoos. Castro later became lead singer of Balance.	
1/07/67	**5**	10	**1. (We Ain't Got) Nothin' Yet**	Mercury 72622
			BLUE STARS	
			Four-man, four-woman, pop-jazz group from Paris, led by Blossom Dearie, former big band vocalist born 4/28/26 in East Durham, New York.	
2/04/56	**16**	7	1. Lullaby Of Birdland [F] Jockey #16 / Best Seller #20 / Top 100 #20 arranged by Michel Legrand; composed by George Shearing	Mercury 70742
			BLUE SWEDE	
			Swedish pop sextet — Bjorn Skifs, lead singer.	
3/02/74	**1**(1)	14	● **1. Hooked On A Feeling**	EMI 3627
9/07/74	**7**	8	**2. Never My Love**	EMI 3938
			BOBBETTES, The	
			Female doo-wop quintet (ages 11-13 in '57) from New York City. Consisted of sisters Emma and Janice Pought, Laura Webb, Helen Gathers and Reather Dixon. Originally called the Harlem Queens.	
8/12/57	**6**	14	**1. Mr. Lee**	Atlantic 1144

DATE	POS	WKS	ARTIST—RECORD TITLE	LABEL & NO.
			Top 100 #6 / Jockey #6 / Best Seller #7 song inspired by group's 5th grade teacher	
			BOB B. SOXX/The Blue Jeans	
			Bobby Sheen with Darlene Love and Fanita James (both formerly with The Blossoms). Love and James later replaced by Gloria Jones and Carolyn Willis.	
12/08/62+	**8**	9	**1. Zip-A-Dee Doo-Dah**	Philles 107
			from the 1947 Academy Award-winning film *Song of the South*	
3/23/63	**38**	3	2. Why Do Lovers Break Each Other's Heart?	Philles 110
			BOLTON, Michael	
			Born Michael Bolotin on 2/26/54 in New Haven, Connecticut. Lead singer of Blackjack in the late '70s. Began recording as Michael Bolton in 1983.	
11/07/87	**19**	10	1. That's What Love Is All About	Columbia 7322
2/13/88	**11**	10	2. (Sittin' On) The Dock Of The Bay	Columbia 07680
8/12/89	**17**	7	3. Soul Provider	Columbia 68909
11/25/89+	**1**(3)	16	**4. How Am I Supposed To Live Without You**	Columbia 73017
3/17/90	**3**	12	**5. How Can We Be Lovers**	Columbia 73318
6/09/90	**7**	11	**6. When I'm Back On My Feet Again**	Columbia 73342
10/06/90	**36**	2	7. Georgia On My Mind	Columbia 73490
			sax solo by Kenny G on single version, Michael Brecker on album version; tune written in 1930 by Hoagy Carmichael	
4/20/91	**4**	13	**8. Love Is A Wonderful Thing**	Columbia 73719
7/27/91	**7**	13	**9. Time, Love And Tenderness**	Columbia 73889
			BOND, Johnny	
			Born Cyrus Whitfield Bond on 6/01/15 in Enville, Oklahoma; died of a heart attack on 6/12/78. Country singer/songwriter/actor/author; worked on radio from age 19. Appeared with Jimmy Wakely in 1937 and joined "Gene Autry's Melody Ranch" in 1940. Appeared in over 50 movies.	
8/22/60	**26**	7	1. Hot Rod Lincoln [N]	Republic 2005
			BONDS, Gary U.S.	
			Born Gary Anderson on 6/06/39 in Jacksonville, Florida. To Norfolk, Virginia in the mid-1950s. Signed to Legrand by Frank Guida. Wrote "Friend Don't Take Her," hit for Johnny Paycheck in 1972.	
			U.S. BONDS:	
10/31/60	**6**	11	**1. New Orleans**	Legrand 1003
6/05/61	**1**(2)	12	**2. Quarter To Three**	Legrand 1008
			music taken from "A Night With Daddy G" (Church Street Five)	
			GARY U.S. BONDS:	
7/31/61	**5**	9	**3. School Is Out**	Legrand 1009
11/06/61	**28**	2	4. School Is In	Legrand 1012
1/13/62	**9**	11	**5. Dear Lady Twist**	Legrand 1015
4/07/62	**9**	9	**6. Twist, Twist Senora**	Legrand 1018
7/07/62	**27**	4	7. Seven Day Weekend	Legrand 1019
			from the film *It's Trad-Dad*	
5/02/81	**11**	13	8. This Little Girl	EMI America 8079
7/10/82	**21**	9	9. Out Of Work	EMI America 8117
			above 2 produced by Bruce Springsteen and Miami Steve Van Zandt	

DATE	POS	WKS	ARTIST—RECORD TITLE	LABEL & NO.
			BONEY M	
			Vocal group assembled in Germany by producer/composer Frank Farian. Farian created the Far Corporation in 1986 and Milli Vanilli in 1988.	
7/22/78	**30**	6	1. Rivers Of Babylon	Sire 1027
			BON JOVI	
			New Jersey hard-rock quintet consisting of Jon Bon Jovi (actual spelling: Bongiovi; lead vocals), Richie Sambora (guitar), Dave Bryan (keyboards), Alec John Such (bass) and Tico Torres (drums).	
4/21/84	**39**	1	1. Runaway	Mercury 818309
10/11/86	**1**(1)	14	**2. You Give Love A Bad Name**	Mercury 884953
1/10/87	**1**(4)	13	**3. Livin' On A Prayer**	Mercury 888184
4/25/87	**7**	12	**4. Wanted Dead Or Alive**	Mercury 888467
10/01/88	**1**(2)	12	**5. Bad Medicine**	Mercury 870657
12/17/88+	**3**	13	**6. Born To Be My Baby**	Mercury 872156
3/18/89	**1**(1)	13	**7. I'll Be There For You**	Mercury 872564
6/17/89	**7**	11	**8. Lay Your Hands On Me**	Mercury 874452
10/28/89	**9**	12	**9. Living In Sin**	Mercury 876070
			JON BON JOVI:	
7/28/90	**1**(1)	14	▲ **10. Blaze Of Glory**	Mercury 875896
			with Jeff Beck and Aldo Nova (guitars) and Randy Jackson (bass)	
11/10/90	**12**	11	11. Miracle	Mercury 878392
			above 2 from *Young Guns II* soundtrack	
			BONNIE LOU	
			Born Bonnie Lou Kath on 10/27/24 in Bloomington, Illinois. Worked on radio KMBC-Kansas City and WLW-Cincinnati. On "Midwestern Hayride" for over 20 years.	
11/26/55	**14**	3	1. Daddy-O	King 4835
			Juke Box #14 / Best Seller #25 / Top 100 #28	
			BONNIE SISTERS	
			Pat, Jean and Sylvia Bonnie from New York City. All were nurses at Bellevue Hospital.	
2/25/56	**18**	3	1. Cry Baby	Rainbow 328
			Best Seller #18 / Top 100 #35	
			BONOFF, Karla	
			Singer/songwriter/pianist. Born on 12/27/52 in Los Angeles.	
6/05/82	**19**	12	1. Personally	Columbia 02805
			BOOKER T. & THE MG'S	
			Band formed by sessionmen from Stax Records, Memphis, in 1962. Consisted of Booker T. Jones (b: 11/12/44, Memphis), keyboards; Steve Cropper (b: 10/21/42, Ozark Mountains, Missouri.), guitar; Donald "Duck" Dunn (b: 11/24/41, Memphis), bass; and Al Jackson, Jr. (b: 11/27/34, Memphis; murdered in 1975), drums. MG stands for Memphis Group. Group disbanded in 1971, and reorganized for a short time in 1973. Jones produced Willie Nelson's *Stardust* album. Cropper and Dunn joined the Blues Brothers.	
9/01/62	**3**	12	● **1. Green Onions** **[I]**	Stax 127
5/20/67	**37**	3	2. Hip Hug-Her [I]	Stax 211
9/02/67	**21**	7	3. Groovin' [I]	Stax 224
8/03/68	**17**	7	4. Soul-Limbo [I]	Stax 0001
12/28/68+	**9**	11	**5. Hang 'Em High** **[I]**	Stax 0013

DATE	POS	WKS	ARTIST—RECORD TITLE	LABEL & NO.
			from the film of the same title	
4/05/69	**6**	10	**6. Time Is Tight** [I]	Stax 0028
			from the film *Uptight*	
7/05/69	**37**	3	7. Mrs. Robinson [I]	Stax 0037
			from the film *The Graduate*	
			BOONE, Daniel	
			English singer/songwriter. Real name: Peter Lee Stirling.	
8/05/72	**15**	11	1. Beautiful Sunday	Mercury 73281
			BOONE, Debby	
			Born on 9/22/56 in Hackensack, New Jersey. Third daughter of Pat and Shirley Boone and granddaughter of Red Foley. Worked with the Boone Family from 1969, sang with sisters in the Boones' gospel quartet. Went solo in 1977. Winner of three Grammys including Best New Artist of 1977. Popular Contemporary Christian artist. Married Gabriel Ferrer, the son of Rosemary Clooney and Jose Ferrer, in 1982.	
9/17/77	**1**(10)	21	▲ **1. You Light Up My Life**	Warner 8455
			theme from the movie of the same title	
			BOONE, Pat	
			Born Charles Eugene Boone on 6/01/34 in Jacksonville, Florida. To Tennessee in 1936. Direct descendant of Daniel Boone. Married Red Foley's daughter, Shirley, on 11/07/53. Won on "Ted Mack's Amateur Hour" and "Arthur Godfrey's Talent Scouts" in 1954. First recorded for Republic Records in 1954. Graduated from New York's Columbia University in 1958. Hosted own TV show, "The Pat Boone-Chevy Showroom" from 1957-60. Appeared in 15 films. Toured with wife and daughters Cherry, Linda Lee, Deborah Anne and Laura Gene in the mid-1960s. Recording artist Nick Todd is his younger brother. Pat's trademark: white buck shoes.	
4/02/55	**16**	12	1. Two Hearts	Dot 15338
			Best Seller #16 / Juke Box #16 #8 R&B hit for The Charms in 1955	
7/09/55	**1**(2)	20	**2. Ain't That A Shame**	Dot 15377
			Juke Box #1 / Best Seller #2 / Jockey #2 / Top 100 #21 pre	
10/29/55	**7**	10	**3. At My Front Door (Crazy Little Mama)/**	
			Top 100 #7 / Juke Box #7 / Best Seller #8 / Jockey #10	
11/19/55	**26**	5	4. No Other Arms (No Arms Can Ever Hold You)	Dot 15422
12/24/55+	**19**	5	5. Gee Whittakers!	Dot 15435
			Juke Box #19 / Top 100 #27 #14 R&B hit for The Five Keys in 1956	
2/04/56	**4**	18	**6. I'll Be Home/**	
			Jockey #4 / Juke Box #4 / Top 100 #5 / Best Seller #6 #5 R&B hit for The Flamingos in 1956	
2/04/56	**12**	10	7. Tutti' Frutti	Dot 15443
			Top 100 #12 / Juke Box #13 / Best Seller #15 / Jockey #15	
4/28/56	**8**	9	**8. Long Tall Sally**	Dot 15457
			Juke Box #8 / Top 100 #18 / Best Seller #23 / Jockey #23	
6/09/56	**1**(4)	19	**9. I Almost Lost My Mind**	Dot 15472
			Juke Box #1(4) / Top 100 #1(2) / Best Seller #2 / Jockey #2 #1 R&B hit for Ivory Joe Hunter in 1950	
9/22/56	**5**	17	**10. Friendly Persuasion (Thee I Love)/**	
			Jockey #5 / Top 100 #8 / Juke Box #8 / Best Seller #9 from the Gary Cooper film *Friendly Persuasion*	
9/29/56	**10**	7	**11. Chains Of Love**	Dot 15490
			Juke Box #10 / Best Seller #15 / Top 100 #20 #2 R&B hit for Joe Turner in 1951	
12/22/56+	**1**(1)	19	**12. Don't Forbid Me/**	

DATE	POS	WKS	ARTIST—RECORD TITLE	LABEL & NO.
			Top 100 #1(1) / Juke Box #1(1) / Jockey #2 / Best Seller #3	
1/26/57	**37**	2	13. Anastasia from the Ingrid Bergman film *Anastasia*	Dot 15521
3/23/57	**5**	13	**14. Why Baby Why/** Best Seller #5 / Top 100 #6 / Jockey #7 / Juke Box #7	
3/23/57	**27**	5	15. I'm Waiting Just For You #2 R&B hit for Lucky Millinder in 1951	Dot 15545
5/13/57	**1**(7)	24	**16. Love Letters In The Sand/** Jockey #1(7) / Best Seller #1(5) / Top 100 #1(5) / Juke Box #2 end	
5/20/57	**14**	13	17. Bernardine Jockey #14 / Top 100 #23 above 2 from the film *Bernardine*	Dot 15570
8/12/57	**6**	14	**18. Remember You're Mine/** Jockey #6 / Best Seller #10 / Top 100 #20	
8/19/57	**14**	11	19. There's A Gold Mine In The Sky Best Seller #14 / Jockey #20 / Top 100 #28	Dot 15602
10/28/57	**1**(6)	19	**20. April Love** Jockey #1(6) / Best Seller #1(2) / Top 100 #1(1) from the film of the same title starring Pat Boone & Shirley Jones	Dot 15660
2/17/58	**4**	15	**21. A Wonderful Time Up There/** Best Seller #4 / Jockey #7 / Top 100 #10	
2/17/58	**4**	15	**22. It's Too Soon To Know** Best Seller #4 / Jockey #11 / Top 100 #13	Dot 15690
5/12/58	**5**	12	**23. Sugar Moon** Jockey #5 / Best Seller #10 / Top 100 #11	Dot 15750
7/14/58	**7**	10	**24. If Dreams Came True/** Jockey #7 / Best Seller #11 / Hot 100 #12	
8/04/58	**39**	1	25. That's How Much I Love You	Dot 15785
9/22/58	**23**	4	26. For My Good Fortune/ Hot 100 #23 / Best Seller #29	
10/06/58	**21**	2	27. Gee, But It's Lonely Best Seller #21 / Hot 100 #31 written by Phil Everly	Dot 15825
11/17/58	**34**	5	28. I'll Remember Tonight from the film *Mardi Gras*	Dot 15840
1/26/59	**21**	8	29. With The Wind And The Rain In Your Hair top 5 hit in 1940 for both Bob Crosby and Kay Kyser	Dot 15888
4/06/59	**23**	7	30. For A Penny	Dot 15914
6/29/59	**17**	6	31. Twixt Twelve And Twenty	Dot 15955
9/28/59	**29**	4	32. Fools Hall Of Fame	Dot 15982
3/07/60	**18**	7	33. (Welcome) New Lovers	Dot 16048
5/22/61	**1**(1)	12	**34. Moody River**	Dot 16209
9/04/61	**19**	5	35. Big Cold Wind	Dot 16244
12/25/61+	**35**	3	36. Johnny Will	Dot 16284
2/24/62	**32**	3	37. I'll See You In My Dreams 4 versions of this tune hit the top 10 in 1925	Dot 16312
6/30/62	**6**	10	**38. Speedy Gonzales** **[N]** female voice: Robin Ward	Dot 16368

DATE	POS	WKS	ARTIST—RECORD TITLE	LABEL & NO.
			BOSTON	
			Rock group from Boston, spearheaded by Tom Scholz (guitars and keyboards) and Brad Delp (lead vocals). Originally a quintet, group also included Barry Goudreau (guitar), Fran Sheehan (bass) and Sib Hashian (drums). Goudreau formed Orion The Hunter. After a long absence from the charts, Boston returned in 1986 as a duo: Scholz and Delp. Delp and Groudreau led RTZ in 1991.	
10/16/76	**5**	14	**1. More Than A Feeling**	Epic 50266
2/12/77	**22**	6	2. Long Time	Epic 50329
6/18/77	**38**	2	3. Peace Of Mind	Epic 50381
8/26/78	**4**	10	**4. Don't Look Back**	Epic 50590
12/23/78+	**31**	5	5. A Man I'll Never Be	Epic 50638
10/04/86	**1**(2)	12	**6. Amanda**	MCA 52756
12/27/86+	**9**	10	**7. We're Ready**	MCA 52985
3/28/87	**20**	5	8. Can'tcha Say (You Believe In Me)/Still In Love	MCA 53029
			BOTKIN, Perry Jr. — see DeVORZON, Barry	
			BOURGEOIS, Brent	
			Former member of Bourgeois Tagg. Born in New Orleans, raised in New Jersey and Dallas.	
6/09/90	**32**	3	1. Dare To Fall In Love	Charisma 98971#
			BOURGEOIS TAGG	
			West Coast rock quintet formed in 1984 and led by Brent Bourgeois and Larry Tagg.	
12/05/87	**38**	2	1. I Don't Mind At All produced by Todd Rundgren	Island 99409
			BOWEN, Jimmy	
			Born on 11/30/37 in Santa Rita, New Mexico. Formed The Rhythm Orchids at West Texas State University with Buddy Knox, Don Lanier and Dave "Dicky Doo" Alldred. Jimmy became a producer and top record executive on the West Coast. In 1977, moved to Nashville. In 1984, became president of MCA Records in Nashville (renamed Universal Records in 1988).	
3/09/57	**14**	12	1. I'm Stickin' With You **JIMMY BOWEN with THE RHYTHM ORCHIDS** Top 100 #14 / Juke Box #15 / Best Seller #16 / Jockey #20 originally on Triple-D 798 (B-side: "Party Doll" by Buddy Knox)	Roulette 4001
			BOWIE, David	
			Born David Robert Jones on 1/08/47 in London. First recorded as David Jones & the King Bees, Lower Third, Manish Boys in 1963. Brought highly theatrical values to rock through work with Lindsay Kemp Mime Troupe. Periods of reclusiveness heightened his appeal. Films *The Man Who Fell to Earth* (1976), *Labyrinth*, *Absolute Beginners* (1986) and others. In Broadway play *The Elephant Man* (1980). Formed the group Tin Machine in 1988.	
2/24/73	**15**	10	1. Space Oddity first released on Mercury 72949 in 1969	RCA 0876
4/19/75	**28**	4	2. Young Americans	RCA 10152
8/02/75	**1**(2)	14	● **3. Fame** backing vocal by John Lennon	RCA 10320
1/10/76	**10**	16	**4. Golden Years**	RCA 10441
12/05/81+	**29**	8	5. Under Pressure **QUEEN & DAVID BOWIE**	Elektra 47235
4/09/83	**1**(1)	14	● **6. Let's Dance** features guitarist Stevie Ray Vaughan	EMI America 8158

DATE	POS	WKS	ARTIST—RECORD TITLE	LABEL & NO.
7/09/83	**10**	11	**7. China Girl**	EMI America 8165
10/01/83	**14**	9	8. Modern Love	EMI America 8177
9/29/84	**8**	10	**9. Blue Jean**	EMI America 8231
3/09/85	**32**	4	10. This Is Not America **DAVID BOWIE/PAT METHENY GROUP** theme from the film *The Falcon and the Snowman*	EMI America 8251
9/07/85	**7**	9	**11. Dancing In The Street** **MICK JAGGER/DAVID BOWIE** from the Live-Aid concert	EMI America 8288
4/25/87	**21**	7	12. Day-In Day-Out	EMI America 8380
9/05/87	**27**	5	13. Never Let Me Down	EMI Amer. 43031
			BOX TOPS, The	
			Pop-rock group formed in Memphis in 1966. Included Alex Chilton (b: 12/28/50, Memphis; lead singer, guitar, bass, harmonica), Bill Cunningham (b: 1/23/50, Memphis; keyboards) and Gary Talley (b: 8/17/47, Memphis; guitar, bass). Reorganized after first hit to include Tom Boggs, drums; and Rick Allen, organ. Disbanded in 1970. Chilton later formed the precursor new-wave pop band Big Star. Cunningham is the brother of B.B. Cunningham of The Hombres.	
8/26/67	**1**(4)	13	● **1. The Letter**	Mala 565
12/02/67	**24**	5	2. Neon Rainbow	Mala 580
3/16/68	**2**(2)	12	● **3. Cry Like A Baby**	Mala 593
6/08/68	**26**	6	4. Choo Choo Train	Mala 12005
10/12/68	**37**	1	5. I Met Her In Church	Mala 12017
2/08/69	**28**	9	6. Sweet Cream Ladies, Forward March	Mala 12035
8/23/69	**18**	7	7. Soul Deep	Mala 12040
			BOYCE, Tommy, & BOBBY HART	
			Songwriting/singing/production duo. Boyce was born on 9/29/44 in Charlottesville, Virginia and Hart was born in 1944 in Phoenix.	
8/05/67	**39**	2	1. Out & About	A&M 858
1/20/68	**8**	9	**2. I Wonder What She's Doing Tonite**	A&M 893
8/03/68	**27**	6	3. Alice Long (You're Still My Favorite Girlfriend)	A&M 948
			BOY GEORGE	
			Born George O'Dowd on 6/14/61 in Bexleyheath, England. Former lead singer of Culture Club. Previously known as Lieutenant Lush, a backing singer with Bow Wow Wow.	
2/20/88	**40**	1	1. Live My Life from the film *Hiding Out*	Virgin 99390
			BOY MEETS GIRL	
			Seattle songwriting/recording duo: Shannon Rubicam and George Merrill. Wrote Whitney Houston's hits "How Will I Know" and "I Wanna Dance With Somebody." Married in 1988.	
5/25/85	**39**	1	1. Oh Girl	A&M 2713
10/15/88	**5**	16	**2. Waiting For A Star To Fall**	RCA 8691
			BOYS, The	
			Quartet of brothers, ages 9-14 in 1988, from Northridge, California: Khiry (lead), Hakeem, Tajh and Bilal Samad. All are members of performing gymnastic troupes.	
1/14/89	**13**	9	1. Dial My Heart	Motown 53301
9/08/90	**29**	8	2. Crazy	Motown 924

DATE	POS	WKS	ARTIST—RECORD TITLE	LABEL & NO.
			BOYS CLUB	
			Duo formed in Minneapolis: vocalists Joe Pasquale and Gene Hunt (real name: Eugene Wolfgramm, formerly with his family group, The Jets).	
11/19/88+	**8**	12	**1. I Remember Holding You**	MCA 53430
			BOYS DON'T CRY	
			British quintet — Nick Richards, lead singer.	
5/17/86	**12**	9	1. I Wanna Be A Cowboy	Profile 5084
			BOYZ II MEN	
			R&B vocal quartet formed in 1988 at Philadelphia's High School of Creative and Performing Arts: Wanya Morris (age 17 in 1991), Michael McCary, Shawn Stockman and Nathan Morris.	
7/06/91	**3**	18	**1. Motownphilly**	Motown 2090
			BRADLEY, Jan	
			Born Addie Bradley on 7/06/43 in Byhalia, Mississippi and raised in Robbins, Illinois. Soul singer. First recorded for Formal in 1961. Became a social worker in 1976.	
2/02/63	**14**	9	1. Mama Didn't Lie first released on Formal 1044 in 1962	Chess 1845
			BRADLEY, Owen, Quintet	
			Born on 10/21/15 in Westmoreland, Tennessee. Bandleader/producer/organist/combo leader. Country A&R director for Decca from 1958-68. Vice president of MCA from 1968. Elected to the Country Music Hall of Fame in 1974.	
7/29/57	**18**	4	1. White Silver Sands Jockey #18 / Top 100 #68 vocals by the Anita Kerr Quartet	Decca 30363
			BRAM TCHAIKOVSKY	
			Rock quartet led by Bram (real name: Peter Bramall, earlier with The Motors). Formed in Lincolnshire, England.	
8/18/79	**37**	3	1. Girl Of My Dreams	Polydor 14575
			BRANIGAN, Laura	
			Born on 7/03/57 in Brewster, New York. Former backing vocalist with Leonard Cohen. Acted in the TV show "CHiPS" and in the 1984 film *Mugsy's Girl*.	
9/04/82	**2**(3)	22	● **1. Gloria**	Atlantic 4048
4/02/83	**7**	13	**2. Solitaire**	Atlantic 89868
8/13/83	**12**	12	3. How Am I Supposed To Live Without You	Atlantic 89805
5/05/84	**4**	15	**4. Self Control**	Atlantic 89676
8/25/84	**20**	8	5. The Lucky One from the TV program *An Uncommon Love*	Atlantic 89636
9/07/85	**40**	2	6. Spanish Eddie	Atlantic 89531
11/28/87+	**26**	9	7. Power Of Love	Atlantic 89191
			BRASS CONSTRUCTION	
			Nine-man, multi-ethnic disco ensemble. Formed in Brooklyn in 1968 as Dynamic Soul by Guyana-born vocalist Randy Muller. Randy also produced the band Skyy.	
5/08/76	**14**	9	1. Movin' [I]	United Art. 775

DATE	POS	WKS	ARTIST—RECORD TITLE	LABEL & NO.
			BRASS RING, The	
			New York studio band headed by Phil Bodner (producer/arranger/sax/clarinet).	
4/16/66	**32**	4	1. The Phoenix Love Theme [I]	Dunhill 4023
			from the film *The Flight of the Phoenix*	
3/04/67	**36**	2	2. The Dis-Advantages Of You [I]	Dunhill 4065
			melody taken from a Benson & Hedges cigarette jingle	
			BRAT PACK, The	
			Male vocal duo from New Jersey: Patrick J. Donovan and Ray-Ray Frazier. Donovan was a member of gospel artist CeCe Roger's stage band.	
3/17/90	**36**	3	1. You're The Only Woman	Vendetta 1447
			#13 hit for Ambrosia in 1980	
			BRAUN, Bob	
			Born Robert Earl Brown on 4/20/29 in Ludlow, Kentucky. Hosted TV show in Cincinnati.	
8/18/62	**26**	4	1. Till Death Do Us Part [S]	Decca 31355
			BREAD	
			Formed in Los Angeles in 1969. Consisted of leader David Gates (vocals, guitar, keyboards), James Griffin (guitar), Robb Royer (guitar) and Jim Gordon (drums). Originally called Pleasure Faire. Griffin and Royer co-wrote award-winning "For All We Know" with Fred Karlin in 1969. Mike Botts replaced Gordon after first album. Royer replaced by Larry Knechtel (top sessionman, member of Duane Eddy's Rebels) in 1971. Disbanded in 1973, reunited briefly in 1976. All songs written and produced by David Gates.	
7/11/70	**1**(1)	13	● **1. Make It With You**	Elektra 45686
10/10/70	**10**	9	**2. It Don't Matter To Me**	Elektra 45701
1/30/71	**28**	4	3. Let Your Love Go	Elektra 45711
4/03/71	**4**	11	**4. If**	Elektra 45720
8/14/71	**37**	2	5. Mother Freedom	Elektra 45740
11/06/71	**3**	10	● **6. Baby I'm-A Want You**	Elektra 45751
2/05/72	**5**	11	**7. Everything I Own**	Elektra 45765
5/06/72	**15**	8	8. Diary	Elektra 45784
8/05/72	**11**	9	9. The Guitar Man	Elektra 45803
11/18/72	**15**	8	10. Sweet Surrender	Elektra 45818
2/17/73	**15**	8	11. Aubrey	Elektra 45832
12/04/76+	**9**	13	**12. Lost Without Your Love**	Elektra 45365
			BREAKFAST CLUB	
			New York-based dance/pop quartet. Madonna was with the group for a short time in the early '80s. Member Steve Bray co-produced Madonna's *True Blue* album.	
4/11/87	**7**	11	**1. Right On Track**	MCA 52954
			BREATHE	
			Band from suburban London: David Glasper (vocals), Ian "Spike" Spice, Marcus Lillington and Michael Delahunty (who left in 1988).	
6/11/88	**2**(2)	16	**1. Hands To Heaven**	A&M 2991
10/01/88	**3**	16	**2. How Can I Fall?**	A&M 1224
1/28/89	**10**	10	**3. Don't Tell Me Lies**	A&M 1267
9/15/90	**21**	8	4. Say A Prayer	A&M 1519#
1/05/91	**34**	3	5. Does She Love That Man?	A&M 1535#
			BREATHE featuring DAVID GLASPER	

DATE	POS	WKS	ARTIST—RECORD TITLE	LABEL & NO.
			BREMERS, Beverly	
			Chicago-born actress/singer.	
1/22/72	**15**	10	1. Don't Say You Don't Remember	Scepter 12315
7/22/72	**40**	2	2. We're Free	Scepter 12348
			BRENDA & THE TABULATIONS	
			R&B group from Philadelphia, formed in 1966, with Brenda Payton, Jerry Jones, Eddie Jackson and Maurice Coates. Bernard Murphy was added in 1969. Reorganized in 1970 with vocalists Brenda Payton, Pat Mercer and Deborah Martin.	
3/25/67	**20**	6	1. Dry Your Eyes	Dionn 500
5/01/71	**23**	9	2. Right On The Tip Of My Tongue	Top & Bottom 407
			BRENNAN, Walter	
			Beloved character actor born on 7/25/1894 in Swampscott, Massachusetts. Died on 9/21/74. First film role in 1924. Three-time Oscar winner. Played Grandpa on "The Real McCoys" TV series.	
5/30/60	**30**	3	1. Dutchman's Gold [S] **WALTER BRENNAN with BILLY VAUGHN**	Dot 16066
4/21/62	**5**	9	**2. Old Rivers [S]**	Liberty 55436
12/01/62	**38**	1	3. Mama Sang A Song [S] above 2 with The Johnny Mann Singers	Liberty 55508
			BREWER, Teresa	
			Born Theresa Breuer on 5/07/31 in Toledo, Ohio. Debuted on "Major Bowes Amateur Hour" at age five, toured with show until age 12. Appeared on "Pick & Pat" radio show. First recorded for London in 1949. In the film *Those Red Heads from Seattle* (1953).	
12/18/54+	**6**	12	**1. Let Me Go, Lover!** **TERESA BREWER with THE LANCERS** Juke Box #6 / Jockey #7 / Best Seller #8	Coral 61315
3/19/55	**17**	3	2. Pledging My Love Jockey #17 / Juke Box #18 / Best Seller #30	Coral 61362
6/04/55	**20**	1	3. Silver Dollar Juke Box #20 orchestra directed by Jack Pleis on above 3	Coral 61394
7/30/55	**15**	4	4. The Banjo's Back In Town Juke Box #15	Coral 61448
3/03/56	**5**	17	**5. A Tear Fell/** Juke Box #5 / Top 100 #7 / Best Seller #9 / Jockey #9	
3/10/56	**17**	10	6. Bo Weevil Top 100 #17 / Jockey #20	Coral 61590
6/16/56	**7**	16	**7. A Sweet Old Fashioned Girl** Juke Box #7 / Top 100 #9 / Jockey #11 / Best Seller #12	Coral 61636
11/17/56	**21**	8	8. Mutual Admiration Society Top 100 #21 / Best Seller #24 / Jockey #24 from the musical *Happy Hunting*	Coral 61737
4/27/57	**13**	9	9. Empty Arms Juke Box #13 / Top 100 #18 / Jockey #19 / Best Seller #23	Coral 61805
11/11/57	**8**	11	**10. You Send Me** Jockey #8 / Best Seller #27 / Top 100 #31	Coral 61898
10/20/58	**38**	1	11. The Hula Hoop Song	Coral 62033
4/06/59	**40**	1	12. Heavenly Lover	Coral 62084
9/12/60	**31**	6	13. Anymore 4-13: orchestra directed by Dick Jacobs	Coral 62219

DATE	POS	WKS	ARTIST—RECORD TITLE	LABEL & NO.
			BREWER & SHIPLEY	
			Folk-rock duo formed in Los Angeles: Mike Brewer and Tom Shipley.	
3/13/71	**10**	10	**1. One Toke Over The Line**	Kama Sutra 516
			BRICK	
			Disco-jazz group formed in Atlanta in 1972. Consisted of Jimmy Brown (vocals), Ray Ransom, Donald Nevins, Reggie Hargis and Eddie Irons. Session work in the early 1970s.	
11/20/76+	**3**	15	**1. Dazz**	Bang 727
10/01/77	**18**	10	2. Dusic	Bang 734
			BRICKELL, Edie/New Bohemians	
			Vocalist Brickell (pronounced: BREE-kell) joined the Dallas-based band in 1985. Varying personnel since then. Brickell was born in Oak Cliff, Texas; her father, Eddie, is a pro bowler.	
1/14/89	**7**	10	**1. What I Am**	Geffen 27696
			BRIDGES, Alicia	
			Atlanta-based disco singer/songwriter; originally from Lawndale, North Carolina.	
9/09/78	**5**	19	• **1. I Love The Nightlife (Disco 'Round)**	Polydor 14483
			BRIGGS, Lillian	
			Pop singer/trombonist from Philadelphia. Discovered by Alan Freed while working in Joy Cayler's All-Girl Orchestra in New York City.	
9/17/55	**18**	3	1. I Want You To Be My Baby Jockey #18 / Juke Box #19 / Best Seller #23 / Top 100 #53 pre	Epic 9115
			BRIGHTER SIDE OF DARKNESS	
			R&B group formed at Calumet High School, Chicago in 1971; featuring 12-year-old lead singer Darryl Lamont, Ralph Eskridge, Randolph Murph and Larry Washington.	
1/06/73	**16**	8	• 1. Love Jones	20th Century 2002
			BRILEY, Martin	
			British session musician/songwriter. Moved to New York City in 1977.	
7/16/83	**36**	3	1. The Salt In My Tears	Mercury 812165
			BRISTOL, Johnny	
			Soul vocalist/composer/producer from Morgantown, North Carolina. Teamed with Jackie Beaver, recorded as Johnny & Jackie for Tri-Phi, 1961. Teamed with Harvey Fuqua as Motown producers until 1973.	
7/20/74	**8**	13	**1. Hang On In There Baby**	MGM 14715
			BROOD, Herman	
			Leader of rock band from the Netherlands. Born on 11/05/46 in Zwolle, Holland.	
9/01/79	**35**	3	1. Saturdaynight	Ariola 7754
			BROOKLYN BRIDGE	
			Long Island, New York outfit led by vocalist Johnny Maestro (of The Crests). The Del-Satins, a vocal quartet led by Maestro, and The Rhythm Method, a seven-piece band, united as Brooklyn Bridge in 1967.	
1/04/69	**3**	10	• **1. Worst That Could Happen**	Buddah 75
			BROOKLYN DREAMS	
			New York trio: Joe "Bean" Esposito, Eddie Hokenson and Bruce Sudano (Donna Summer's husband).	
1/20/79	**4**	14	• **1. Heaven Knows**	Casablanca 959

DATE	POS	WKS	ARTIST—RECORD TITLE	LABEL & NO.
			DONNA SUMMER with BROOKLYN DREAMS	
			BROOKS, Donnie	
			Born John Faircloth in Dallas; raised in Ventura, California. Early recording names: Johnny Faire, Dick Bush and Johnny Jordan.	
7/11/60	**7**	15	**1. Mission Bell**	Era 3018
12/26/60	**31**	3	2. Doll House	Era 3028
			BROTHER BEYOND	
			British pop quartet: Nathan Moore (vocals), David White, Carl Fysh and Steve Alexander.	
8/11/90	**27**	4	1. The Girl I Used To Know	EMI 50287#
			BROTHERHOOD OF MAN, The	
			British studio group featuring Tony Burrows, Johnny Goddison and Sunny (female singer). Burrows was lead singer of Edison Lighthouse, First Class, The Pipkins and White Plains. 1976 hit featured new members.	
5/23/70	**13**	10	1. United We Stand	Deram 85059
6/19/76	**27**	4	2. Save Your Kisses For Me	Pye 71066
			BROTHERS FOUR, The	
			Folk-pop quartet: Dick Foley, Bob Flick, John Paine and Mike Kirkland. Formed while Phi Gamma Delta fraternity brothers at the University of Washington.	
3/21/60	**2**(4)	15	**1. Greenfields**	Columbia 41571
4/24/61	**32**	3	2. Frogg [N] new version of tune written back in 1580 as "Frog Went A Courtin' "	Columbia 41958
			BROTHERS JOHNSON, The	
			Los Angeles R&B-funk duo of brothers George (b: 5/17/53) and Louis Johnson (b: 4/13/55). Own band, the Johnson Three + 1, with brother Tommy and cousin Alex Weir. With Billy Preston's band to 1975.	
5/22/76	**3**	12	● **1. I'll Be Good To You**	A&M 1806
9/18/76	**30**	6	2. Get The Funk Out Ma Face	A&M 1851
7/30/77	**5**	13	● **3. Strawberry Letter 23**	A&M 1949
4/12/80	**7**	13	**4. Stomp!**	A&M 2216
			BROWN('S), Al, Tunetoppers Featuring Cookie Brown	
			Born in Fairmont, West Virginia in 1930. Tunetoppers formed in 1953.	
5/02/60	**23**	5	1. The Madison	Amy 804
			BROWN, Arthur, The Crazy World Of	
			Born Arthur Wilton on 6/24/44 in Whitby, England. Theatrical rock singer. Band included drummer Carl Palmer, later of Emerson, Lake & Palmer.	
9/21/68	**2**(1)	11	● **1. Fire**	Atlantic 2556
			BROWN, Bobby	
			Born on 2/05/69 in Boston. Former member of the teen R&B-pop group New Edition. Had a bit part in the film *Ghostbusters II*.	
8/20/88	**8**	14	● **1. Don't Be Cruel**	MCA 53327
11/12/88+	**1**(1)	15	● **2. My Prerogative**	MCA 53383
1/28/89	**3**	11	**3. Roni**	MCA 53463
4/15/89	**3**	13	● **4. Every Little Step**	MCA 53618
7/01/89	**2**(3)	13	▲ **5. On Our Own** from the film *Ghostbusters II*	MCA 53662

Bachman-Turner Overdrive's all-time greatest hit was "You Ain't Seen Nothing Yet," which reached No. 1 in 1974. The band was one of several for Canadian guitarist Randy Bachman, who also recorded with the Guess Who, Brave Belt, and Ironhorse, among other groups.

Bad Company scored their first top-5 hit in 1974 with "Can't Get Enough," a song brought to the newly-formed group by former Mott The Hoople guitarist Mick Ralphs. Perceived as a "supergroup" at the time—other members included Paul Rodgers and Simon Kirke from Free and Boz Burrell from King Crimson—Bad Company continues today with only one original member.

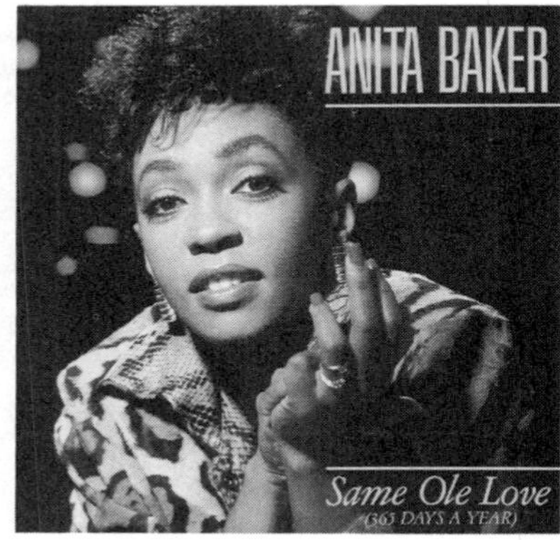

Joan Baez's longstanding desire to reach listeners everywhere was no doubt satisfied when her 1975 hit "Diamonds And Rust" was covered—quite loudly—by heavy-metal group Judas Priest.

Anita Baker's 1988 hit "Giving You The Best That I Got," which reached No. 3, helped push her album of the same name to the No. 1 slot for four weeks. Baker's first solo album, recorded for another label, was reissued by Elektra in late 1991.

Bananarama's first appearance on record in the U.S. came as special guests on the 1982 debut album by Chrysalis group Fun Boy Three; the latter group returned the favor by appearing on Bananarama's "Really Saying Something," from their first album.

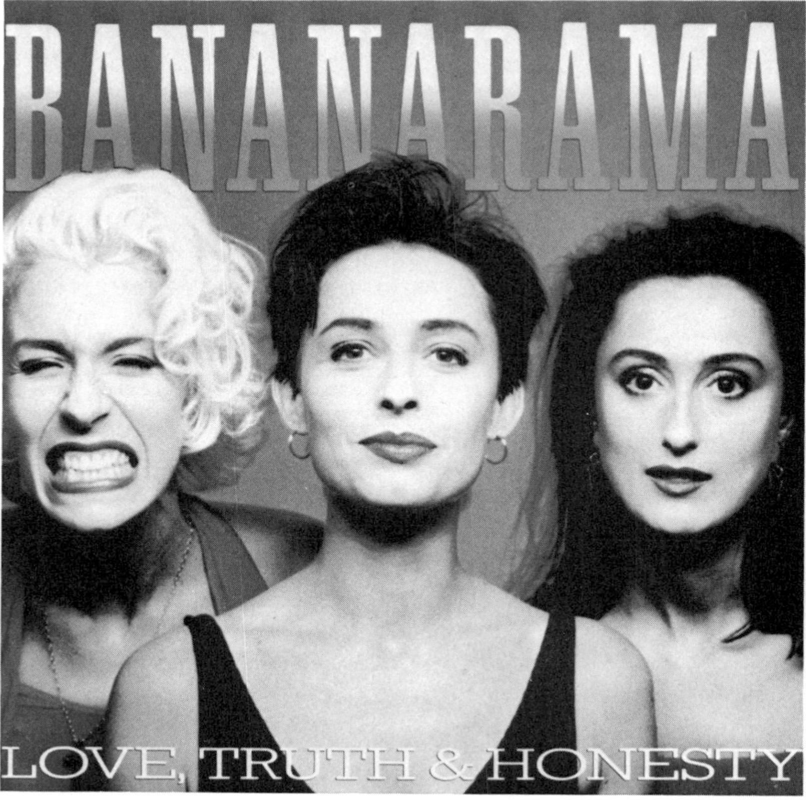

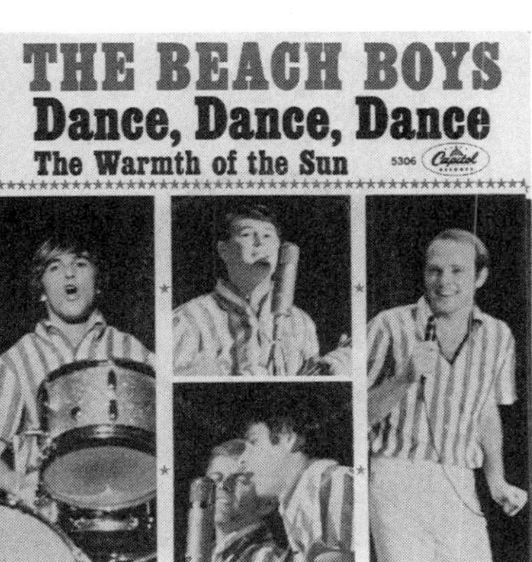

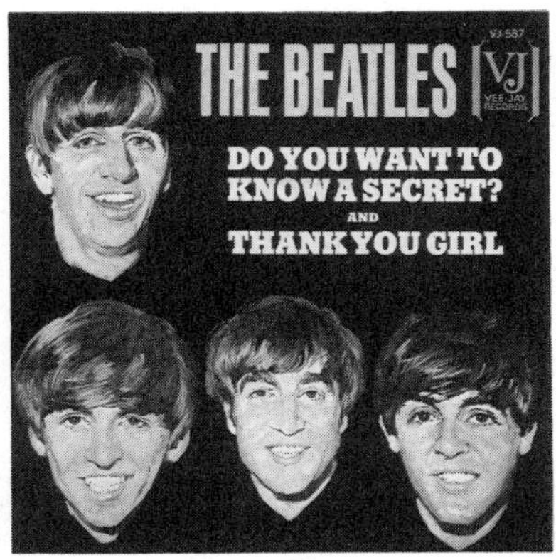

The Beach Boys have sustained a remarkably long career in the music business—as the 24-year span between their first (1964's "I Get Around") and most recent (1988's "Kokomo") No. 1 singles amply illustrates.

The Beatles enjoyed 20 No. 1 hits between 1964-1970—and had the No. 1 song in the nation for 59 various weeks during that period. That, among other things, helped make them the No. 1 artist of the 60s.

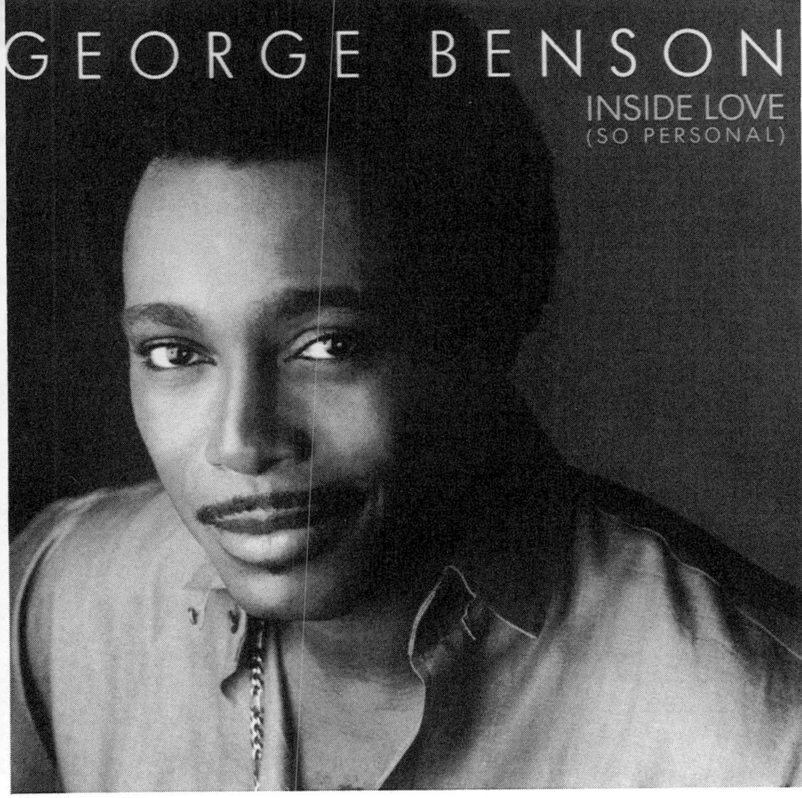

George Benson's second hit to reach the Top 40 came from the film *The Greatest*, starring Muhammed Ali. The song, which reached No. 24 in 1977, was "The Greatest Love Of All"—later redone and taken to the top by 80s superstar Whitney Houston.

Brook Benton & Dinah Washington had joint success in 1960 with "Baby (You've Got What It Takes)" and "A Rockin' Good Way (To Mess Around And Fall In Love)," which reached the No. 5 and No. 7 slots, respectively. Now both deceased, the artists recorded for Mercury and have been subjects of highly-regarded reissues from that label.

Chuck Berry's role as the founding father of rock is disputed by few. Compared to earlier hits such as "Johnny B. Goode" and "Maybellene," however, the worthiness of his sole No. 1 record—1972's novelty track "My Ding-A-Ling"—is open to debate.

DATE	POS	WKS	ARTIST—RECORD TITLE	LABEL & NO.
9/16/89	**7**	11	• **6. Rock Wit'cha**	MCA 53652
5/26/90	**1**(2)	0	• **7. She Ain't Worth It**	MCA 79047
			GLENN MEDEIROS featuring BOBBY BROWN	
			BROWN, Boots/His Blockbusters	
			Boots was born Milton "Shorty" Rogers on 4/14/24 in Lee, Massachusetts. Great jazz trumpeter/bandleader.	
9/15/58	**23**	3	1. Cerveza [I]	RCA 7269
			Best Seller #23 / Hot 100 #62	
			BROWN, Buster	
			R&B vocalist/harmonica player, born on 8/15/11 in Cordele, Georgia. Died on 1/31/76.	
3/28/60	**38**	3	1. Fannie Mae	Fire 1008
			BROWN, Chuck/The Soul Searchers	
			Washington, D.C.-based, nine-member group.	
3/17/79	**34**	5	• 1. Bustin' Loose Part 1	Source 40967
			BROWN, James	
			Born on 5/03/28 in Macon, Georgia. Raised in Augusta. Formed own vocal group, the Famous Flames. Cut a demo record of own composition "Please Please Please" in November 1955, at radio station WIBB in Macon. Signed to King/Federal Records in January 1956 and re-recorded the song. Cameo appearances in films *The Blues Brothers* and *Rocky IV*. One of the originators of "Soul" music, variously billed on Polydor hits as "Soul I," "The Creator," "The Godfather of Soul," "The Hit Man" and "Minister of New New Super Heavy Funk." His backing group, The JB's, featured various personnel, including Nat Kendrick, Bootsy Collins, Maceo Parker and Fred Wesley. Inducted into the Rock and Roll Hall of Fame in 1986. On 12/15/88, received a six-year prison sentence after leading police on an interstate car chase; released from prison on 2/27/91. Ranked as the #1 artist in *Joel Whitburn's Top R&B Singles 1942-1988* book.	
5/30/60	**33**	2	1. Think	Federal 12370
4/03/61	**40**	2	2. Bewildered	King 5442
5/19/62	**35**	4	3. Night Train	King 5614
5/18/63	**18**	7	4. Prisoner Of Love	King 5739
			#1 hit for Perry Como in 1946	
2/15/64	**23**	7	5. Oh Baby Don't You Weep (Part 1)	King 5842
9/12/64	**24**	5	6. Out Of Sight	Smash 1919
			JAMES BROWN AND HIS ORCHESTRA	
8/07/65	**8**	9	**7. Papa's Got A Brand New Bag Part I**	King 5999
11/20/65	**3**	10	**8. I Got You (I Feel Good)**	King 6015
5/07/66	**8**	8	**9. It's A Man's Man's Man's World**	King 6035
1/28/67	**29**	4	10. Bring It Up	King 6071
8/12/67	**7**	8	**11. Cold Sweat - Part 1**	King 6110
11/25/67	**40**	1	12. Get It Together (Part 1)	King 6122
12/30/67+	**28**	5	13. I Can't Stand Myself (When You Touch Me)/	
2/17/68	**36**	4	14. There Was A Time	King 6144
3/23/68	**6**	10	**15. I Got The Feelin'**	King 6155
6/01/68	**14**	7	16. Licking Stick - Licking Stick (Part 1)	King 6166
			all of above on King labeled as: **JAMES BROWN & THE FAMOUS FLAMES**	
9/14/68	**10**	10	**17. Say It Loud - I'm Black And I'm Proud (Part 1)**	King 6187
12/07/68	**31**	2	18. Goodbye My Love	King 6198

DATE	POS	WKS	ARTIST—RECORD TITLE		LABEL & NO.
2/08/69	**15**	7	19. Give It Up Or Turnit A Loose		King 6213
4/19/69	**20**	6	20. I Don't Want Nobody To Give Me Nothing (Open Up The Door, I'll Get It Myself)		King 6224
6/21/69	**11**	10	21. Mother Popcorn (You Got To Have A Mother For Me) Part 1		King 6245
6/28/69	**30**	5	22. The Popcorn	[I]	King 6240
9/27/69	**37**	2	23. World (Part 1)		King 6258
11/01/69	**21**	5	24. Let A Man Come In And Do The Popcorn Part One		King 6255
12/13/69+	**24**	8	25. Ain't It Funky Now (Part 1)	[I]	King 6280
1/24/70	**40**	2	26. Part Two (Let A Man Come In And Do The Popcorn)		King 6275
2/28/70	**32**	6	27. It's A New Day (Part 1) & (Part 2)		King 6292
5/23/70	**32**	2	28. Brother Rapp (Part 1) & (Part 2)		King 6310
8/01/70	**15**	7	29. Get Up I Feel Like Being Like A Sex Machine (Part 1)		King 6318
10/17/70	**13**	8	30. Super Bad (Part 1 & Part 2)		King 6329
1/16/71	**34**	5	31. Get Up, Get Into It, Get Involved Pt. 1		King 6347
3/13/71	**29**	6	32. Soul Power Pt. 1		King 6368
6/26/71	**35**	3	33. Escape-ism (Part 1)	[S]	People 2500
7/17/71	**15**	9	34. Hot Pants Pt. 1 (She Got To Use What She Got To Get What She Wants)		People 2501
9/11/71	**22**	6	35. Make It Funky (Part 1)		Polydor 14088
12/04/71	**35**	3	36. I'm A Greedy Man - Part I		Polydor 14100
2/26/72	**27**	4	37. Talking Loud And Saying Nothing - Part I		Polydor 14109
4/01/72	**40**	2	38. King Heroin	[S]	Polydor 14116
9/09/72	**18**	8	● 39. Get On The Good Foot-Part 1		Polydor 14139
2/10/73	**27**	4	40. I Got Ants In My Pants - Part 1 (and i want to dance)		Polydor 14162
4/13/74	**26**	9	● 41. The Payback - Part 1		Polydor 14223
8/03/74	**29**	4	42. My Thang		Polydor 14244
9/21/74	**31**	3	43. Papa Don't Take No Mess Part I		Polydor 14255
1/11/86	**4**	11	**44. Living In America** from the film *Rocky IV*		Scotti Br. 05682
			BROWN, Maxine Born in Kingstree, South Carolina. With gospel groups Manhattans and Royaltones in New York City in the late 1950s.		
1/30/61	**19**	6	1. All In My Mind		Nomar 103
4/24/61	**25**	5	2. Funny		Nomar 106
12/05/64+	**24**	7	3. Oh No Not My Baby		Wand 162
			BROWN, Nappy Born Napoleon Brown Culp on 10/12/29 in Charlotte, North Carolina. R&B-gospel singer.		
4/30/55	**25**	4	1. Don't Be Angry Best Seller #25		Savoy 1155
			BROWN, Peter Soul vocalist/keyboardist/producer, born on 7/11/53 in Blue Island, Illinois.		
10/08/77	**18**	8	1. Do Ya Wanna Get Funky With Me		Drive 6258

DATE	POS	WKS	ARTIST—RECORD TITLE	LABEL & NO.
			background vocals by Wildflower	
5/06/78	**8**	14	**2. Dance With Me**	Drive 6269
			PETER BROWN with BETTY WRIGHT	
			BROWN, Polly	
			White soul singer. Lead vocalist of the British groups Pickettywitch and Sweet Dreams.	
2/08/75	**16**	7	1. Up In A Puff Of Smoke	GTO 1002
			BROWN, Roy	
			R&B vocalist/pianist. Born on 9/10/25 in New Orleans. One of the originators of the New Orleans R&B sound. Wrote "Good Rocking Tonight." Died of a heart attack on 5/25/81 in Los Angeles.	
7/01/57	**29**	1	1. Let The Four Winds Blow	Imperial 5439
			Best Seller #29 / Top 100 #38	
			BROWN, Ruth	
			Born on 1/30/28 in Portsmouth, Virginia as Ruth Weston. Married singer/trumpeter Jimmy Brown in 1945. In late 1946, sang for one month with Lucky Millinder's band, then fired. Later heard by Duke Ellington, who alerted Herb Abramson of the then-new Atlantic Records. Abramson signed her to a contract. Became Atlantic Records' top-selling artist of the 1950s. Married for a time to Willis Jackson. In later years, had acting roles in the TV shows "Hello, Larry" and "Checking In", plus several Broadway and Las Vegas musicals. Appeared in the films *Under the Rainbow* (1981) and *Hairspray* (1988). Starred in the 1988 musical *Black and Blue*.	
3/02/57	**25**	5	1. Lucky Lips	Atlantic 1125
			Best Seller #25 / Jockey #25 / Top 100 #26	
10/13/58	**24**	2	2. This Little Girl's Gone Rockin'	Atlantic 1197
			sax solo: King Curtis	
			BROWN, Shirley	
			Born on 1/06/47 in West Memphis, Arkansas and raised in East St. Louis. Soul vocalist.	
11/23/74	**22**	6	1. Woman To Woman	Truth 3206
			BROWNE, Jackson	
			Born on 10/09/48 in Heidelberg, Germany. Vocalist/guitarist/pianist/composer. To Los Angeles in 1951. With Tim Buckley and Nico in 1967 in New York City. Returned to Los Angeles, concentrated on songwriting. His songs were recorded by Linda Ronstadt, Tom Rush, Joe Cocker, The Byrds, Johnny Rivers, Bonnie Raitt, and many others. Worked with the Eagles. Produced Warren Zevon's first album. Wife Phyllis committed suicide on 3/25/76. Activist against nuclear power.	
4/08/72	**8**	9	**1. Doctor My Eyes**	Asylum 11004
2/19/77	**23**	6	2. Here Come Those Tears Again	Asylum 45379
3/04/78	**11**	12	3. Running On Empty	Asylum 45460
7/08/78	**20**	7	4. Stay/	
		7	5. The Load-Out	Asylum 45485
			originally issued with "Rosie" as the B-side	
7/26/80	**19**	10	6. Boulevard	Asylum 47003
10/18/80	**22**	5	7. That Girl Could Sing	Asylum 47036
8/21/82	**7**	12	**8. Somebody's Baby**	Asylum 69982
			from the soundtrack *Fast Times At Ridgemont High*	
7/16/83	**13**	12	9. Lawyers In Love	Asylum 69826
10/22/83	**25**	7	10. Tender Is The Night	Asylum 69791
11/23/85+	**18**	12	11. You're A Friend Of Mine	Columbia 05660

DATE	POS	WKS	ARTIST—RECORD TITLE	LABEL & NO.
			CLARENCE CLEMONS And JACKSON BROWNE includes vocals by actress Daryl Hannah (Browne's then-girlfriend)	
3/29/86	**30**	5	12. For America	Asylum 69566
			BROWNS, The	
			Family trio: Jim Ed Brown (b: 4/01/34, Sparkman, Arkansas) and his sisters Maxine (b: 4/27/32, Sampti, Louisiana) and Bonnie (b: 7/31/37, Sparkman, Arkansas).	
8/03/59	**1**(4)	14	**1. The Three Bells**	RCA 7555
11/23/59	**13**	9	2. Scarlet Ribbons (For Her Hair)	RCA 7614
3/28/60	**5**	12	**3. The Old Lamplighter**	RCA 7700
			THE BROWNS featuring JIM EDWARD BROWN #1 hit for Sammy Kaye's Orchestra in 1946	
			BROWNSVILLE STATION	
			Rock trio from Ann Arbor, Michigan: Cub Koda (guitar), Michael Lutz (vocals) and Henry Weck (drums). Koda writes a column for the record collector's magazine, *Goldmine*.	
12/08/73+	**3**	13	● **1. Smokin' In The Boy's Room**	Big Tree 16011
10/05/74	**31**	3	2. Kings Of The Party	Big Tree 16001
			BRUBECK, Dave, Quartet	
			Born David Warren on 12/06/20 in Concord, California. Leader of jazz quartet consisting of Brubeck (piano), Paul Desmond (alto sax), Joe Morello (drums) and Eugene Wright (bass). One of America's all-time most popular jazz groups on college campuses.	
9/25/61	**25**	7	1. Take Five [I]	Columbia 41479
			BRYANT, Anita	
			Born on 3/25/40 in Barnsdale, Oklahoma. As Miss Oklahoma, she was second runner-up to Miss America in 1958.	
7/27/59	**30**	7	1. Till There Was You	Carlton 512
			from the Broadway musical *The Music Man*	
5/02/60	**5**	12	**2. Paper Roses**	Carlton 528
8/08/60	**10**	9	**3. In My Little Corner Of The World**	Carlton 530
12/26/60+	**18**	6	4. Wonderland By Night	Carlton 537
			BRYANT, Ray, Combo	
			Ray was born Raphael Bryant on 12/24/31 in Philadelphia. R&B-jazz pianist/bandleader. Uncle of jazz guitarist Kevin Eubanks.	
5/09/60	**30**	4	1. The Madison Time - Part I [S-I]	Columbia 41628
			dance calls: Eddie Morrison (died on 2/28/87 in Chicago)	
			BRYANT, Sharon	
			Lead singer of Atlantic Starr from 1976-84. Native of White Plains, New York. Married Rick Gallwey (former percussionist with the group Change) in 1984.	
9/30/89	**34**	4	1. Let Go	Wing 871722
			BRYSON, Peabo	
			Born Robert Peabo Bryson on 4/13/51 in Greenville, South Carolina. R&B singer/producer. First solo recording for Bang in 1970.	
9/03/83	**16**	15	1. Tonight, I Celebrate My Love	Capitol 5242
			PEABO BRYSON/ROBERTA FLACK	
6/30/84	**10**	13	**2. If Ever You're In My Arms Again**	Elektra 69728

DATE	POS	WKS	ARTIST—RECORD TITLE	LABEL & NO.
			B.T. EXPRESS	
			Brooklyn, New York disco outfit earlier known as Brooklyn Trucking Express. Keyboardist Michael Jones, who joined group at age 15, later recorded solo as techno-funk musician Kashif.	
10/05/74	**2**(2)	14	● **1. Do It ('Til You're Satisfied)**	Roadshow 12395
2/08/75	**4**	11	● **2. Express** **[I]**	Roadshow 7001
9/06/75	**40**	2	3. Give It What You Got/	
9/13/75	**31**	4	4. Peace Pipe	Roadshow 7003
			BUBBLE PUPPY, The	
			Psychedelic rock band from Houston. Later recorded as Demian.	
3/15/69	**14**	7	1. Hot Smoke & Sasafrass	Int. Artists 128
			BUCHANAN and GOODMAN	
			Bill Buchanan and Richard "Dickie" Goodman conceived the idea of a radio show being interrupted by reports of flying saucers in 1956. Segments of popular records were spliced into the dialogue. The record was heard by Alan Freed and he played it on his WINS-New York radio show. A national hit resulted and the "break-in" record was born. Buchanan left the music business in 1959. Also see Dickie Goodman.	
8/11/56	**3**	10	**1. The Flying Saucer (Parts 1 & 2)** **[N]** Best Seller #3 / Top 100 #7 / Jockey #9 / Juke Box #9 originally titled "Back To Earth" on Luniverse 101	Luniverse 101
7/29/57	**18**	8	2. Flying Saucer The 2nd [N] Best Seller #18 / Top 100 #19	Luniverse 105
12/30/57	**32**	2	3. Santa And The Satellite (Parts I & II) [X-N] Top 100 #32 / Best Seller #36 narration by disc jockey Paul Sherman	Luniverse 107
			BUCHANAN BROTHERS	
			Producers Terry Cashman, Gene Pistilli and Tommy West.	
5/31/69	**22**	7	1. Medicine Man (Part I)	Event 3302
			BUCKINGHAM, Lindsey	
			Born on 10/03/47 in Palo Alto, California. Guitarist/vocalist. Lindsey, along with Stevie Nicks, joined Fleetwood Mac in 1975. Lindsey left Fleetwood Mac in 1987.	
11/07/81+	**9**	14	**1. Trouble**	Asylum 47223
8/25/84	**23**	9	2. Go Insane	Elektra 69714
			BUCKINGHAMS, The	
			Chicago rock quintet: Dennis Tufano (lead singer), Carl Giammarese, Nick Fortune, Jon Paulos and Dennis Miccoli. Martin Grebb replaced Miccoli in 1967. Paulos died of a drug overdose on 3/26/80 (age 32).	
1/21/67	**1**(2)	10	**1. Kind Of A Drag**	U.S.A. 860
4/08/67	**6**	10	**2. Don't You Care**	Columbia 44053
7/01/67	**5**	10	**3. Mercy, Mercy, Mercy**	Columbia 44182
9/30/67	**12**	7	4. Hey Baby (They're Playing Our Song)	Columbia 44254
12/23/67+	**11**	10	5. Susan	Columbia 44378
			BUCKNER & GARCIA	
			Atlanta-based duo: Jerry Buckner and Gary Garcia.	
1/30/82	**9**	14	● **1. Pac-Man Fever** **[N]** inspired by the all-time #1 video game "Pac-Man"; originally released on BGO 1001 in 1981	Columbia 02673

DATE	POS	WKS	ARTIST—RECORD TITLE	LABEL & NO.
			BUFFALO SPRINGFIELD, The	
			Superstar group formed in Los Angeles in 1966: Stephen Stills, Neil Young, Richie Furay, Dewey Martin and Bruce Palmer (replaced by Jim Messina after first two albums). Disbanded in 1968. Stills and Young formed Crosby, Stills, Nash & Young. Furray and Messina formed Poco.	
2/18/67	**7**	11	**1. For What It's Worth (Stop, Hey What's That Sound)**	Atco 6459
			BUFFETT, Jimmy	
			Born on 12/25/46 in Mobile, Alabama. Has BS degree in history and journalism from the University of Southern Mississippi. After working in New Orleans, moved to Nashville in 1969. Settled in Key West in 1971. Owns a store called Margaritaville and has his own line of tropical clothing.	
6/29/74	**30**	5	1. Come Monday	Dunhill 4385
5/07/77	**8**	15	**2. Margaritaville**	ABC 12254
10/22/77	**37**	3	3. Changes In Latitudes, Changes In Attitudes	ABC 12305
5/27/78	**32**	4	4. Cheeseburger In Paradise [N]	ABC 12358
10/20/79	**35**	3	5. Fins	MCA 41109
			BUGGLES, The	
			English duo: Geoff Downes and Trevor Horne (both joined group Yes in 1980). Downes became a member of Asia in 1981.	
12/15/79	**40**	1	1. Video Killed The Radio Star the premiere video on MTV's first show (8/01/81)	Island 49114
			BULL & THE MATADORS	
			Three-man group from St. Louis: JaMell "Bull" Parks (b: 6/07/45), Milton Hardy and James Otis Love.	
11/16/68	**39**	1	1. The Funky Judge	Toddlin' Town 108
			BULLET	
			London-based duo of former Atomic Rooster members: John Cann (vocals) and Paul Hammond (drums).	
12/25/71+	**28**	5	1. White Lies, Blue Eyes	Big Tree 123
			BUOYS, The	
			Rock quintet from northeastern Pennsylvania led by vocalist Bill Kelly. Included Fran Brozena, Jerry Hludzik, Carl Siracuse and Chris Hanlon. Rupert Holmes was their composer/arranger.	
4/17/71	**17**	8	1. Timothy written by Rupert Holmes	Scepter 12275
			BURDON, Eric/WAR	
			Eric was born on 5/11/41 in Newcastle-On-Tyne, England. After leaving The Animals, Eric teamed up with the funk band War for two albums. Starred in the 1982 film *Comeback*.	
7/11/70	**3**	13	• **1. Spill The Wine**	MGM 14118
			BURKE, Solomon	
			Born in 1936 in Philadelphia. Preached and broadcast from own church, "Solomon's Temple," in Philadelphia from 1945-55 as the "Wonder Boy Preacher." Church was founded for him by his grandmother. First recorded for Apollo in 1954. Left music to attend mortuary school, returned in 1960.	
11/13/61	**24**	7	1. Just Out Of Reach (Of My Two Open Arms)	Atlantic 2114
5/25/63	**37**	2	2. If You Need Me	Atlantic 2185
5/23/64	**33**	4	3. Goodbye Baby (Baby Goodbye)	Atlantic 2226
4/03/65	**22**	5	4. Got To Get You Off My Mind	Atlantic 2276
7/03/65	**28**	5	5. Tonight's The Night	Atlantic 2288

DATE	POS	WKS	ARTIST—RECORD TITLE	LABEL & NO.
			BURNETTE, Dorsey	
			Born on 12/28/32 in Memphis; died of a heart attack on 8/19/79 in Canoga Park, California. Older brother of Johnny Burnette, father of Billy Burnette.	
2/22/60	**23**	9	1. (There Was A) Tall Oak Tree	Era 3012
			BURNETTE, Johnny	
			Born on 3/25/34 in Memphis; died on 8/01/64 in a boating accident on Clear Lake in California. Johnny, brother Dorsey and Paul Burlison formed the Johnny Burnette Rock 'N Roll Trio, 1953-57. Father of Rocky Burnette.	
8/15/60	**11**	11	1. Dreamin'	Liberty 55258
11/21/60	**8**	11	**2. You're Sixteen**	Liberty 55285
2/20/61	**17**	6	3. Little Boy Sad	Liberty 55298
11/06/61	**18**	4	4. God, Country And My Baby	Liberty 55379
			BURNETTE, Rocky	
			Born on 6/12/53 in Memphis. Son of Johnny Burnette, nephew of Dorsey Burnette and uncle of Billy Burnette (of Fleetwood Mac).	
6/07/80	**8**	12	**1. Tired Of Toein' The Line**	EMI America 8043
			BUSCH, Lou	
			Born on 7/18/10 in Louisville; died on 9/19/79. Pianist/orchestra leader. Also recorded as Joe "Fingers" Carr.	
3/24/56	**35**	2	1. 11th Hour Melody	Capitol 3349
6/16/56	**19**	10	2. Portuguese Washerwomen [I] **JOE "FINGERS" CARR** Jockey #19 / Best Seller #25 / Top 100 #25	Capitol 3418
			BUSH, Kate	
			Born on 7/30/58 in Bexley, Kent, England. Signed to EMI at age 16.	
11/09/85	**30**	4	1. Running Up That Hill	EMI America 8285
			BUSTERS, The	
			Western Massachusetts rock group. Originally known as the Northern Lights, recorded "Typhoid" which was released as "Bust Out" by The Busters. Members Jack Baker (sax) and Fran Parda (drums) put together new touring group known as The Busters.	
9/28/63	**25**	5	1. Bust Out [I]	Arlen 735
			BUTLER, Jerry	
			Born on 12/08/39 in Sunflower, Mississippi. Older brother of Billy Butler. Sang in the Northern Jubilee Gospel Singers, with Curtis Mayfield. Later with the Quails. In 1957, Butler and Mayfield joined the Roosters with Sam Gooden and brothers Arthur & Richard Brooks. Changed name to The Impressions in 1957. Left for solo career in autumn of 1958. Dubbed "The Ice Man."	
6/16/58	**11**	9	1. For Your Precious Love **JERRY BUTLER AND THE IMPRESSIONS** Best Seller #11 / Top 100 #11 / Jockey #25 released first on Falcon, then on Abner 1013 (also on Vee-Jay 280 in 1958)	Falcon 1013
11/07/60	**7**	13	**2. He Will Break Your Heart**	Vee-Jay 354
4/03/61	**27**	4	3. Find Another Girl	Vee-Jay 375
8/07/61	**25**	4	4. I'm A Telling You	Vee-Jay 390
10/30/61	**11**	11	5. Moon River from the film *Breakfast at Tiffany's*	Vee-Jay 405
8/18/62	**20**	4	6. Make It Easy On Yourself	Vee-Jay 451
12/28/63+	**31**	5	7. Need To Belong	Vee-Jay 567

DATE	POS	WKS	ARTIST—RECORD TITLE	LABEL & NO.
9/19/64	**5**	11	**8. Let It Be Me** BETTY EVERETT & JERRY BUTLER	Vee-Jay 613
11/25/67	**38**	2	9. Mr. Dream Merchant	Mercury 72721
6/08/68	**20**	9	10. Never Give You Up	Mercury 72798
10/05/68	**16**	8	11. Hey, Western Union Man	Mercury 72850
1/18/69	**39**	2	12. Are You Happy	Mercury 72876
3/08/69	**4**	12	● **13. Only The Strong Survive**	Mercury 72898
6/21/69	**24**	7	14. Moody Woman	Mercury 72929
9/06/69	**20**	9	15. What's The Use Of Breaking Up	Mercury 72960
2/05/72	**21**	10	● 16. Ain't Understanding Mellow JERRY BUTLER AND BRENDA LEE EAGER	Mercury 73255
			BUTLER, Jonathan Born in Capetown, South Africa. Soul guitarist/singer/songwriter. Migrated to London, 1984 (at age 21).	
8/15/87	**27**	5	1. Lies	Jive 1038
			BYRD, Charlie Born on 9/16/25 in Chuckatuch, Virginia. Jazz and classical guitar virtuoso.	
10/27/62	**15**	10	1. Desafinado [I] STAN GETZ/CHARLIE BYRD	Verve 10323
			BYRDS, The Folk-rock group formed in Los Angeles in 1964. Consisted of James "Roger" McGuinn, (12-string guitar), David Crosby (guitar), Gene Clark (percussion), Chris Hillman (bass) and Mike Clarke (drums). McGuinn, who changed his name to Roger in 1968, had been with Bobby Darin and The Chad Mitchell Trio. Clark had been with The New Christy Minstrels. All except Clarke had folk music background. First recorded as the Beefeaters for Elektra in 1964. Also recorded as the Jet Set. Professional debut in March 1965. Clark left after "Eight Miles High." Crosby left in late 1967 to form Crosby, Stills & Nash. Re-formed in 1968 with McGuinn, Hillman, Kevin Kelly (drums) and Gram Parsons (guitar). Hillman and Parsons left that same year to form the Flying Burrito Brothers. McGuinn again re-formed with Clarence White (guitar), John York (bass) and Gene Parsons (drums). Reunions with original members in 1973 and 1979. Gram Parsons died on 9/19/73 (age 26) of a heroin overdose. McGuinn, Clark and Hillman later recorded as a trio. In 1986, Hillman formed popular country group, The Desert Rose Band. McGuinn, Crosby and Hillman reunited on stage on 2/24/90 for a Roy Orbison tribute. Clark died on 5/24/91 (age 46) of natural causes. Group inducted into the Rock and Roll Hall of Fame in 1991.	
6/05/65	**1**(1)	10	**1. Mr. Tambourine Man**	Columbia 43271
8/21/65	**40**	1	2. All I Really Want To Do	Columbia 43332
11/06/65	**1**(3)	11	**3. Turn! Turn! Turn! (To Everything There Is A Season)** lyrics adapted by Pete Seeger from the Book of Ecclesiastes	Columbia 43424
4/30/66	**14**	6	4. Eight Miles High	Columbia 43578
10/22/66	**36**	2	5. Mr. Spaceman	Columbia 43766
2/18/67	**29**	3	6. So You Want To Be A Rock 'N' Roll Star	Columbia 43987
4/29/67	**30**	3	7. My Back Pages 1, 2, 7: written by Bob Dylan	Columbia 44054
			BYRNES, Edward Born Edward Breitenberger on 7/30/33 in New York City. Best known as Kookie on TV's "77 Sunset Strip."	
4/27/59	**4**	11	**1. Kookie, Kookie (Lend Me Your Comb)** [N] EDWARD BYRNES AND CONNIE STEVENS	Warner 5047

DATE	POS	WKS	ARTIST—RECORD TITLE	LABEL & NO.
			C	
			CADETS, The	
			Los Angeles R&B quintet: Aaron Collins (lead singer), Ted Taylor, William "Dub" Jones (bass man for The Coasters), Willie Davis and Lloyd McCraw. Also recorded as The Jacks on RPM with Davis as lead. Collins and Davis later joined The Flares. Collins' sisters, Betty and Rosie, recorded as The Teen Queens.	
7/21/56	**15**	7	1. Stranded In The Jungle [N]	Modern 994
			Best Seller #15 / Jockey #16 / Juke Box #16 / Top 100 #18	
			CADILLACS, The	
			R&B vocal group formed at P.S. 139 in Harlem in 1953 as the Carnations. The first R&B vocal group to extensively use choreography in their stage routines. Lead vocalist Earl "Speedoo" Carroll left in 1958 to join The Coasters.	
2/04/56	**17**	5	1. Speedoo	Josie 785
			Best Seller #17 / Top 100 #30 song's title is Earl Carroll's nickname	
1/12/59	**28**	3	2. Peek-A-Boo	Josie 846
			CAFFERTY, John/The Beaver Brown Band	
			Rock sextet from Narrangansett, Rhode Island. Wrote and recorded the music for the soundtrack of *Eddie and the Cruisers.* Band, led by singer/guitarist Cafferty, includes Bob Cotoia, Gary Gramolini, Kenny Jo Silva, Pat Lupo and Michael Antunes.	
9/15/84	**7**	11	**1. On The Dark Side [R]**	Scotti Br. 04594
			originally charted on 10/08/83 (POS 64)	
12/08/84+	**31**	7	2. Tender Years [R]	Scotti Br. 04682
			originally charted on 1/28/84 (POS 78); above 2 from the film *Eddie and the Cruisers*	
6/01/85	**22**	8	3. Tough All Over	Scotti Br. 04891
8/31/85	**18**	8	4. C-I-T-Y	Scotti Br. 05452
			CAIN, Tane	
			Wife of Jonathan Cain (of The Babys, Journey and Bad English).	
9/18/82	**37**	3	1. Holdin' On	RCA 13287
			CAIOLA, Al	
			Born on 9/07/20 in Jersey City, New Jersey. Guitarist/composer/bandleader. First recorded for Savoy in 1955. Prolific studio work.	
1/16/61	**35**	4	1. The Magnificent Seven [I]	United Art. 261
			from the film of the same title	
5/01/61	**19**	5	2. Bonanza [I]	United Art. 302
			theme from the TV series of the same title	
			CALDWELL, Bobby	
			Born on 8/15/51 in New York City. Vocalist/composer/multi-instrumentalist. Wrote tracks for "New Mickey Mouse Club" TV show and commercials.	
2/03/79	**9**	12	**1. What You Won't Do For Love**	Clouds 11
			CALE, J.J.	
			Born John J. Cale on 12/05/38 in Oklahoma City. Singer/songwriter/guitarist. Wrote Eric Clapton's "After Midnight" and "Cocaine."	
3/11/72	**22**	8	1. Crazy Mama	Shelter 7314

DATE	POS	WKS	ARTIST—RECORD TITLE	LABEL & NO.
			CALLOWAY	
			Brother duo of Reggie and Cino-Vincent Calloway from Cincinnati. Both founded Midnight Star.	
3/10/90	**2**(1)	15	● **1. I Wanna Be Rich**	Solar 74005
			CAMEO	
			New York City soul-funk group, formed in 1974 as The New York City Players by Larry "Mr. B" Blackmon (drums) and Gregory "Straps" Johnson (keyboards). Vocals by Wayne Cooper and Tomi "Tee" Jenkins. By 1985, group pared down to a trio of Blackmon, Jenkins and Nathan Leftenant.	
10/04/86	**6**	14	**1. Word Up**	Atl. Art. 884933
2/14/87	**21**	7	2. Candy	Atl. Art. 888193
			CAMILLO, Tony — see BAZUKA	
			CAMPBELL, Glen	
			Born on 4/22/36 in Billstown, Arkansas. Vocalist/guitarist/composer. With his uncle Dick Bills' band, 1954-58. To Los Angeles; recorded with The Champs in 1960. Became prolific studio musician; with The Beach Boys in 1965 and Sagittarius in 1967. Own TV show "The Glen Campbell Goodtime Hour," 1968-72. In films *True Grit*, *Norwood* and *Strange Homecoming*.	
11/25/67	**26**	7	1. By The Time I Get To Phoenix	Capitol 2015
5/25/68	**36**	2	2. I Wanna Live	Capitol 2146
8/03/68	**32**	3	3. Dreams Of The Everyday Housewife	Capitol 2224
11/02/68	**39**	1	4. Gentle On My Mind [R] originally charted in 1967 (POS 62)	Capitol 5939
11/16/68+	**3**	13	● **5. Wichita Lineman**	Capitol 2302
3/08/69	**36**	1	6. Let It Be Me **BOBBIE GENTRY & GLEN CAMPBELL**	Capitol 2387
3/15/69	**4**	10	● **7. Galveston**	Capitol 2428
5/17/69	**26**	5	8. Where's The Playground Susie	Capitol 2494
8/23/69	**35**	2	9. True Grit from the John Wayne movie of the same title	Capitol 2573
11/01/69	**23**	7	10. Try A Little Kindness	Capitol 2659
1/31/70	**19**	7	11. Honey Come Back 1, 5, 7, 8, 11: written by Jimmy Webb	Capitol 2718
3/14/70	**27**	6	12. All I Have To Do Is Dream **BOBBIE GENTRY & GLEN CAMPBELL**	Capitol 2745
5/09/70	**40**	2	13. Oh Happy Day	Capitol 2787
9/26/70	**10**	9	**14. It's Only Make Believe**	Capitol 2905
3/27/71	**31**	4	15. Dream Baby (How Long Must I Dream)	Capitol 3062
6/21/75	**1**(2)	18	● **16. Rhinestone Cowboy**	Capitol 4095
11/22/75+	**11**	11	17. Country Boy (You Got Your Feet In L.A.)	Capitol 4155
4/17/76	**27**	5	18. Don't Pull Your Love/Then You Can Tell Me Goodbye	Capitol 4245
3/05/77	**1**(1)	15	● **19. Southern Nights**	Capitol 4376
8/13/77	**39**	2	20. Sunflower written by Neil Diamond	Capitol 4445
12/09/78	**38**	2	21. Can You Fool	Capitol 4584

DATE	POS	WKS	ARTIST—RECORD TITLE	LABEL & NO.
			CAMPBELL, Jo Ann	
			Born on 7/20/38 in Jacksonville, Florida. First recorded for El Dorado in 1957. In the films *Johnny Melody, Go Johnny Go* and *Hey, Let's Twist.* Married country singer Troy Seals (cousin of Dan Seals) in the early 1960s; recorded together as Jo Ann & Troy in 1964.	
9/08/62	**38**	3	1. (I'm The Girl On) Wolverton Mountain	Cameo 223
			CAMPBELL, Tevin	
			Texas native born in 1978. Won role in 1988 for the TV show "Wally & The Valentines." Discovered by Quincy Jones. Appeared in the film *Graffiti Bridge*.	
2/09/91	**12**	13	● 1. Round And Round written and produced by Prince	Paisley P. 21740
			C & C MUSIC FACTORY	
			Production duo of Tennesseean David Cole and New Yorker Robert Clivilles. Vocalists include Freedom Williams and Deborah Cooper (Fatback, Change). Martha Wash (Two Tons O' Fun, The Weather Girls) is the actual vocalist of "Gonna Make You Sweat," lip-synched in video by Liberian-born Zelma Davis.	
12/15/90+	**1**(2)	17	▲ **1. Gonna Make You Sweat (Everybody Dance Now)** featuring Freedom Williams	Columbia 73604
3/23/91	**3**	14	● **2. Here We Go** **C & C MUSIC FACTORY PRESENTS FREEDOM WILLIAMS AND ZELMA DAVIS**	Columbia 73690
7/27/91	**4**	12	● **3. Things That Make You Go Hmmmm . . .** **C & C MUSIC FACTORY featuring Freedom Williams**	Columbia 73687
			CANDYMAN	
			Rapper from Los Angeles born on 6/25/68. Backing rapper/dancer with Tone-Loc.	
10/13/90	**9**	12	▲ **1. Knockin' Boots** samples The Young Rascals' "Groovin' " and Rose Royce's "Ooh Boy"	Epic 73450
			CANNED HEAT	
			Blues-rock band formed in Los Angeles in 1966. Consisted of Bob "The Bear" Hite (vocals, harmonica), Alan "Blind Owl" Wilson (guitar, harmonica, vocals), Henry Vestine (guitar), Larry Taylor (bass) and Frank Cook (drums). Cook replaced by Fito de la Parra in 1968. Vestine replaced by Harvey Mandel in 1969. Wilson died of a drug overdose on 9/03/70 (age 27). Hite died of a drug-related heart attack on 4/06/81 (age 36).	
9/07/68	**16**	7	1. On The Road Again	Liberty 56038
12/21/68+	**11**	9	2. Going Up The Country	Liberty 56077
11/07/70	**26**	6	3. Let's Work Together	Liberty 56151
			CANNIBAL AND THE HEADHUNTERS	
			Four Mexican-American youths based in Los Angeles; led by Frankie "Cannibal" Garcia.	
4/17/65	**30**	6	1. Land Of 1000 Dances	Rampart 642
			CANNON, Ace	
			Born on 5/05/34 in Grenada, Mississippi. Saxophonist since age 10. Worked with Bill Black's Combo.	
1/27/62	**17**	10	1. Tuff [I]	Hi 2040
5/19/62	**36**	1	2. Blues (Stay Away From Me) [I]	Hi 2051

DATE	POS	WKS	ARTIST—RECORD TITLE	LABEL & NO.
			CANNON, Freddy	
			Born Frederick Picariello on 12/04/39 in Lynn, Massachusetts. Local work with own band, Freddy Karmon & The Hurricanes. Nickname "Boom Boom" came from big bass drum-sound on his records. Band arrangements by Frank Slay on all Swan recordings.	
5/25/59	**6**	10	**1. Tallahassee Lassie** song written by Freddy's mother	Swan 4031
12/07/59+	**3**	11	**2. Way Down Yonder In New Orleans** jazz song written in 1922	Swan 4043
3/07/60	**34**	3	3. Chattanooga Shoe Shine Boy #1 hit for Red Foley in 1950	Swan 4050
5/30/60	**28**	4	4. Jump Over	Swan 4053
9/04/61	**35**	1	5. Transistor Sister	Swan 4078
5/26/62	**3**	12	**6. Palisades Park** written by Chuck Barris (host of "The Gong Show")	Swan 4106
2/15/64	**16**	6	7. Abigail Beecher all of above produced by Frank Slay	Warner 5409
8/28/65	**13**	6	8. Action from the TV show "Where the Action Is"	Warner 5645
			CAPALDI, Jim	
			Born on 8/24/44 in Evesham, England. Drummer with Traffic, 1967-74.	
5/28/83	**28**	5	1. That's Love	Atlantic 89849
			CAPITOLS, The	
			R&B vocal trio from Detroit. Consisted of lead singer Sam George (murdered on 3/17/82 [age 39]), "Donald Norman" Storball and "Richard Mitchell" McDougall.	
5/21/66	**7**	11	**1. Cool Jerk**	Karen 1524
			CAPRIS, The	
			Italian vocal group from Queens, New York, formed in 1958. Consisted of Nick Santamaria (lead), Vinny Narcardo (baritone), Mike Mincelli (1st tenor), Frank Reina (2nd tenor) and John Cassese (bass). Group disbanded in 1959, re-formed when song "There's A Moon Out Tonight" was reissued on Lost Nite in 1960 and became a hit in 1961.	
1/23/61	**3**	10	**1. There's A Moon Out Tonight** originally released on Planet 1010 in 1959	Old Town 1094
			CAPTAIN & TENNILLE	
			Daryl "The Captain" Dragon (b: 8/27/42, Los Angeles) and his wife, Toni Tennille (b: 5/08/43, Montgomery, Alabama). Dragon is the son of noted conductor Carmen Dragon. Keyboardist with The Beach Boys, nicknamed the "Captain" by Mike Love. Duo had own TV show on ABC from 1976-77.	
5/24/75	**1**(4)	16	● **1. Love Will Keep Us Together**	A&M 1672
10/04/75	**4**	14	● **2. The Way I Want To Touch You** first released on Butterscotch Castle 001, then on Joyce 101, then on A&M 1624, all in 1974	A&M 1725
2/07/76	**3**	13	● **3. Lonely Night (Angel Face)**	A&M 1782
5/08/76	**4**	12	● **4. Shop Around**	A&M 1817
10/09/76	**4**	15	● **5. Muskrat Love**	A&M 1870
4/02/77	**13**	8	6. Can't Stop Dancin' written by Ray Stevens	A&M 1912
9/09/78	**10**	14	**7. You Never Done It Like That** 1, 3, 7: written by Neil Sedaka	A&M 2063
1/27/79	**40**	1	8. You Need A Woman Tonight	A&M 2106

DATE	POS	WKS	ARTIST—RECORD TITLE	LABEL & NO.
11/10/79+	**1**(1)	22	● **9. Do That To Me One More Time**	Casablanca 2215
			CARA, Irene	
			Vocalist/actress/dancer/pianist. Born on 3/18/59 in New York City. Professional debut at age seven. Won Obie Award for *The Me Nobody Knows* in 1970. Much TV work, including "Electric Company" and *Roots 2*; in films *Fame*, *D.C. Cab* and *The Cotton Club*.	
7/26/80	**4**	12	**1. Fame**	RSO 1034
9/27/80	**19**	9	2. Out Here On My Own above 2 from the film *Fame*	RSO 1048
4/16/83	**1**(6)	20	● **3. Flashdance...What A Feeling** from the film *Flashdance*	Casabl. 811440
11/05/83	**13**	10	4. Why Me?	Geffen 29464
1/28/84	**37**	3	5. The Dream (Hold On To Your Dream) from the film *D.C. Cab*	Geffen 29396
4/14/84	**8**	11	**6. Breakdance**	Geffen 29328
			CARAVELLES, The	
			English duo: Andrea Simpson and Lois Wilkinson.	
11/23/63	**3**	10	**1. You Don't Have To Be A Baby To Cry**	Smash 1852
			CAREFREES, The	
			British group.	
4/11/64	**39**	1	1. We Love You Beatles [N]	London Int. 10614
			CAREY, Mariah	
			Born on 3/27/70 of Irish and Black/Venezuelan parentage. Her mother is Patricia Carey, former singer with the New York City Opera. Mariah sang backup for Brenda K. Starr. Won the 1990 Best New Artist Grammy Award.	
6/16/90	**1**(4)	17	● **1. Vision Of Love**	Columbia 73348
9/29/90	**1**(3)	18	● **2. Love Takes Time**	Columbia 73455
1/19/91	**1**(2)	15	● **3. Someday**	Columbia 73561
4/13/91	**1**(2)	14	**4. I Don't Wanna Cry**	Columbia 73743
			CAREY, Tony	
			Born on 10/16/53; raised in America. Settled in Germany in 1978. Ex-keyboardist with Rainbow and lead singer of Planet P.	
3/31/84	**22**	8	1. A Fine Fine Day	MCA 52343
7/14/84	**33**	2	2. The First Day Of Summer	MCA 52388
			CARGILL, Henson	
			Born on 2/05/41 in Oklahoma City. Country singer.	
1/20/68	**25**	7	1. Skip A Rope	Monument 1041
			CARLISLE, Belinda	
			Born on 8/17/58 in Hollywood. Lead singer of the Go-Go's, 1978-84. Married to Morgan Mason, son of late actor James Mason.	
6/21/86	**3**	14	**1. Mad About You**	I.R.S. 52815
10/10/87	**1**(1)	15	**2. Heaven Is A Place On Earth**	MCA 53181
1/23/88	**2**(1)	13	**3. I Get Weak**	MCA 53242
5/07/88	**7**	10	**4. Circle In The Sand**	MCA 53308
10/28/89	**11**	10	5. Leave A Light On	MCA 53706
2/17/90	**30**	5	6. Summer Rain	MCA 53783

DATE	POS	WKS	ARTIST—RECORD TITLE	LABEL & NO.
			CARLTON, Carl	
			Soul singer. Born in 1952 in Detroit. Singing since age nine. First recorded for Lando Records in 1964.	
10/12/74	**6**	10	**1. Everlasting Love**	Back Beat 27001
9/26/81	**22**	7	● 2. She's A Bad Mama Jama (She's Built, She's Stacked)	20th Century 2488
			CARMEN, Eric	
			Born on 8/11/49 in Cleveland. Classical training at Cleveland Institute of Music from early years to mid-teens. Lead singer of the Raspberries from 1970-74.	
1/17/76	**2**(3)	14	● **1. All By Myself**	Arista 0165
5/22/76	**11**	10	2. Never Gonna Fall In Love Again	Arista 0184
9/18/76	**34**	3	3. Sunrise	Arista 0200
9/24/77	**23**	8	4. She Did It	Arista 0266
10/28/78	**19**	7	5. Change Of Heart	Arista 0354
2/09/85	**35**	4	6. I Wanna Hear It From Your Lips	Geffen 29118
12/12/87+	**4**	16	**7. Hungry Eyes** from the film *Dirty Dancing*	RCA 5315
6/18/88	**3**	13	**8. Make Me Lose Control**	Arista 9686
			CARNES, Kim	
			Vocalist/pianist/composer. Born on 7/20/45 in Los Angeles. Member of The New Christy Minstrels with husband/co-writer Dave Ellingson and Kenny Rogers, late 1960s. Wrote for and performed in commercials.	
8/05/78	**36**	3	1. You're A Part Of Me **GENE COTTON with KIM CARNES**	Ariola 7704
4/12/80	**4**	14	**2. Don't Fall In Love With A Dreamer** **KENNY ROGERS with KIM CARNES**	United Art. 1345
6/14/80	**10**	15	**3. More Love**	EMI America 8045
4/11/81	**1**(9)	20	● **4. Bette Davis Eyes** written by Jackie DeShannon and Donna Weiss	EMI America 8077
8/29/81	**28**	6	5. Draw Of The Cards	EMI America 8087
9/11/82	**29**	6	6. Voyeur	EMI America 8127
12/25/82+	**36**	4	7. Does It Make You Remember	EMI America 8147
11/26/83	**40**	2	8. Invisible Hands	EMI America 8181
10/13/84	**15**	9	9. What About Me? **KENNY ROGERS with KIM CARNES AND JAMES INGRAM**	RCA 13899
6/01/85	**15**	9	10. Crazy In The Night (Barking At Airplanes)	EMI America 8267
			CAROSONE, Renato	
			Male vocalist from Naples, Italy.	
5/12/58	**18**	9	1. Torero [F] Jockey #18 / Top 100 #19 / Best Sellers #20	Capitol 71080

DATE	POS	WKS	ARTIST—RECORD TITLE	LABEL & NO.
			CARPENTERS	
			Richard Carpenter (b: 10/15/46) and sister Karen (b: 3/02/50; d: 2/04/83 of heart failure due to anorexia). From New Haven, Connecticut. Richard played piano from age nine. To Downey, California in 1963. Karen played drums in group with Richard and bass player Wes Jacobs in 1965. The trio recorded for RCA in 1966. After a period with the band Spectrum, the Carpenters recorded as a duo for A&M in 1969. Won the 1970 Best New Artist Grammy Award. Hosts of the TV variety show "Make Your Own Kind of Music" in 1971. 1988 TV movie *The Karen Carpenter Story* was based on Karen's life.	
6/27/70	**1**(4)	15	• **1. (They Long To Be) Close To You**	A&M 1183
10/03/70	**2**(4)	14	• **2. We've Only Just Begun**	A&M 1217
2/13/71	**3**	12	• **3. For All We Know** from the film *Lovers and Other Strangers*	A&M 1243
5/22/71	**2**(2)	11	• **4. Rainy Days And Mondays**	A&M 1260
9/11/71	**2**(2)	12	• **5. Superstar** written by Leon Russell and Bonnie Bramlett	A&M 1289
1/22/72	**2**(2)	11	• **6. Hurting Each Other**	A&M 1322
5/13/72	**12**	8	7. It's Going To Take Some Time written by Carole King	A&M 1351
7/22/72	**7**	9	**8. Goodbye To Love**	A&M 1367
3/10/73	**3**	11	• **9. Sing**	A&M 1413
6/16/73	**2**(1)	12	• **10. Yesterday Once More**	A&M 1446
10/20/73	**1**(2)	16	• **11. Top Of The World**	A&M 1468
4/27/74	**11**	9	12. I Won't Last A Day Without You 2, 4, 12: written by Paul Williams and Roger Nichols	A&M 1521
12/07/74+	**1**(1)	12	• **13. Please Mr. Postman**	A&M 1646
4/12/75	**4**	9	**14. Only Yesterday**	A&M 1677
8/16/75	**17**	7	15. Solitaire written by Neil Sedaka	A&M 1721
3/13/76	**12**	8	16. There's A Kind Of Hush (All Over The World)	A&M 1800
7/04/76	**25**	5	17. I Need To Be In Love	A&M 1828
6/18/77	**35**	3	18. All You Get From Love Is A Love Song	A&M 1940
11/05/77	**32**	4	19. Calling Occupants Of Interplanetary Craft (The Recognized Anthem of World Contact Day)	A&M 1978
7/04/81	**16**	8	20. Touch Me When We're Dancing	A&M 2344
			CARR, Cathy	
			Songstress from the Bronx, New York. Born on 6/28/36; died in November 1988.	
4/07/56	**2**(1)	18	**1. Ivory Tower** Juke Box #2 / Top 100 #6 / Best Seller #7 / Jockey #9	Fraternity 734
			CARR, Joe "Fingers" — see BUSCH, Lou	
			CARR, Valerie	
			Black vocalist born in 1936 in New York.	
6/09/58	**19**	2	1. When The Boys Talk About The Girls Jockey #19 / Top 100 #84	Roulette 4066
			CARR, Vikki	
			Born Florencia Martinez Cardona on 7/19/41 in El Paso, Texas. Regular on TV's "Ray Anthony Show," 1962.	
9/30/67	**3**	11	**1. It Must Be Him**	Liberty 55986

DATE	POS	WKS	ARTIST—RECORD TITLE	LABEL & NO.
1/27/68	**34**	1	2. The Lesson	Liberty 56012
6/28/69	**35**	4	3. With Pen In Hand	Liberty 56092
			CARRACK, Paul	
			Born on 4/22/51 in Sheffield, England. Lead singer of Ace (1973-76), Squeeze (1981) and Mike + The Mechanics (since 1985). Keyboardist with Roxy Music (1978-80).	
10/30/82	**37**	2	1. I Need You	Epic 03146
12/19/87+	**9**	13	**2. Don't Shed A Tear**	Chrysalis 43164
4/23/88	**28**	5	3. One Good Reason	Chrysalis 43204
11/25/89	**31**	4	4. I Live By The Groove	Chrysalis 23427
			CARRADINE, Keith	
			Born on 8/08/49 in San Mateo, California. Leading actor in dozens of films including *Pretty Baby*, *The Long Riders*, *The Moderns* and others. Son of actor John Carradine; half-brother of David Carradine.	
6/12/76	**17**	12	1. I'm Easy from the movie *Nashville* (which Keith appeared in)	ABC 12117
			CARROLL, David	
			Born Nook Schrier on 10/15/13 in Chicago. Arranger/conductor since 1951 for many top Mercury artists.	
1/08/55	**8**	17	**1. Melody Of Love** [I] Jockey #8 / Best Seller #9 / Juke Box #12 narrative (Paul Tremaine) version on Mercury 70521	Mercury 70516
12/17/55	**20**	1	2. It's Almost Tomorrow Jockey #20 / Top 100 #34 vocal: Jack Halloran Singers	Mercury 70717
			CARS, The	
			Rock group formed in Boston in 1976. Consisted of Ric Ocasek (lead vocals, guitar), Elliot Easton (guitar), Greg Hawkes (keyboards), Benjamin Orr (bass, vocals) and David Robinson (drums; formerly with the Modern Lovers). Ocasek, Orr and Hawkes had been in trio in the early 1970s. Group named by Robinson, got start at the Rat Club in Boston. All songs written by Ocasek. Disbanded in 1988.	
8/12/78	**27**	7	1. Just What I Needed	Elektra 45491
12/09/78	**35**	5	2. My Best Friend's Girl	Elektra 45537
7/28/79	**14**	9	3. Let's Go	Elektra 46063
10/11/80	**37**	3	4. Touch And Go	Elektra 47039
12/12/81+	**4**	17	**5. Shake It Up**	Elektra 47250
3/24/84	**7**	11	**6. You Might Think**	Elektra 69744
5/26/84	**12**	11	7. Magic	Elektra 69724
8/11/84	**3**	14	**8. Drive**	Elektra 69706
11/10/84	**20**	10	9. Hello Again	Elektra 69681
3/09/85	**33**	5	10. Why Can't I Have You	Elektra 69657
11/16/85+	**7**	12	**11. Tonight She Comes**	Elektra 69589
3/08/86	**32**	4	12. I'm Not The One	Elektra 69569
9/12/87	**17**	9	13. You Are The Girl	Elektra 69446
			CARSON, Kit	
			Real name: Liza Morrow. Orchestra conducted by Dick Hyman. Former band vocalist with George Paxton.	
12/31/55+	**11**	11	1. Band Of Gold Jockey #11 / Top 100 #17	Capitol 3283

DATE	POS	WKS	ARTIST—RECORD TITLE	LABEL & NO.
			CARSON, Mindy	
			Born on 7/16/27 in New York City. Sang with Paul Whiteman in the 1940s.	
8/27/55	**13**	8	1. Wake The Town And Tell The People Jockey #13 / Juke Box #13 / Best Seller #20 / Top 100 #33 pre	Columbia 40537
1/05/57	**34**	2	2. Since I Met You Baby	Columbia 40789
			CARTER, Carlene — see ORRALL, Robert Ellis	
			CARTER, Clarence	
			Born in 1936 in Montgomery, Alabama. R&B vocalist/guitarist. Blind since age one; self-taught on guitar at age 11. Teamed with vocalist/pianist Calvin Scott as Clarence & Calvin, recorded for Fairlane in the early 1960s. Carter went solo in 1966. Married for a time to Candi Staton.	
8/17/68	**6**	11	• **1. Slip Away**	Atlantic 2508
11/30/68+	**13**	11	• 2. Too Weak To Fight	Atlantic 2569
3/29/69	**31**	5	3. Snatching It Back	Atlantic 2605
8/01/70	**4**	12	• **4. Patches**	Atlantic 2748
			CARTER, June — see CASH, Johnny	
			CARTER, Mel	
			Born on 4/22/39 in Cincinnati. Soul vocalist/actor. Sang on local radio from age four; with Lionel Hampton on stage show at age nine. With Paul Gayten, Jimmy Scott bands. Joined Raspberry Singers gospel group in the early '50s. With his mother's gospel group, The Carvetts, in the mid-1950s. Named Top Gospel Tenor in 1957. Recorded in late '50s for Tri-State, Arwin, then Mercury. With Gospel Pearls in the early '60s. Acted on TV's "Quincy," "Sanford and Son," "Marcus Welby, MD" and "Magnum P.I."	
7/24/65	**8**	11	**1. Hold Me, Thrill Me, Kiss Me**	Imperial 66113
11/27/65	**38**	2	2. (All Of A Sudden) My Heart Sings	Imperial 66138
5/21/66	**32**	2	3. Band Of Gold	Imperial 66165
			CASCADES, The	
			Group from San Diego consisting of John Gummoe (lead vocals), Eddie Snyder, David Stevens, David Wilson and David Zabo.	
1/26/63	**3**	13	**1. Rhythm Of The Rain**	Valiant 6026
			CASH, Alvin/The Crawlers	
			Alvin was born on 2/15/39 in St. Louis. Singer/dancer. Formed song/dance troupe, The Crawlers, in 1960, with brothers Robert, Arthur and George (ages eight to 10). They never sang on any of Alvin's hits. Alvin moved to Chicago in 1963. First recorded for Mar-V-Lus in 1964. Cut "Twine Time" with backing band the Nightlighters from Louisville, who changed their name to the Registers.	
1/30/65	**14**	7	1. Twine Time [I]	Mar-V-Lus 6002
			CASH, Johnny	
			Born on 2/26/32 in Kingsland, Arkansas. To Dyess, Arkansas at age three. Brother Roy led the Dixie Rhythm Ramblers band in late 1940s. In U.S. Air Force, 1950-54. Formed trio with Luther Perkins (guitar) and Marshall Grant (bass) in 1955. First recorded for Sun in 1955. On "Louisiana Hayride" and "Grand Ole Opry" in 1957. Own TV show for ABC from 1969-71. Worked with June Carter from 1961, married her in March 1968. Ranks within the top three male vocalists of the country charts. Daughter Rosanne Cash and stepdaughter Carlene Carter currently enjoying successful singing careers. Elected to the Country Music Hall of Fame in 1980. Won Grammy's Legends Award in 1990.	
10/20/56	**17**	11	1. I Walk The Line Best Seller #17 / Juke Box #17 / Top 100 #19 / Jockey #25	Sun 241
2/10/58	**14**	13	2. Ballad Of A Teenage Queen	Sun 283

DATE	POS	WKS	ARTIST—RECORD TITLE	LABEL & NO.
			Jockey #14 / Best Seller #16 / Top 100 #16	
6/09/58	**11**	13	3. Guess Things Happen That Way	Sun 295
			Best Seller #11 / Top 100 #11 / Jockey #18	
9/01/58	**24**	6	4. The Ways Of A Woman In Love	Sun 302
			Hot 100 #24 / Best Seller #26	
11/10/58	**38**	1	5. All Over Again	Columbia 41251
2/02/59	**32**	6	6. Don't Take Your Guns To Town	Columbia 41313
6/22/63	**17**	10	7. Ring Of Fire	Columbia 42788
3/14/64	**35**	3	8. Understand Your Man	Columbia 42964
6/29/68	**32**	6	9. Folsom Prison Blues	Columbia 44513
			original version released in 1956 on Sun 232	
8/02/69	**2**(3)	11	● **10. A Boy Named Sue** [N]	Columbia 44944
			recorded live at San Quentin prison	
2/21/70	**36**	2	11. If I Were A Carpenter	Columbia 45064
			JOHNNY CASH & JUNE CARTER	
4/25/70	**19**	6	12. What Is Truth	Columbia 45134
5/15/76	**29**	3	13. One Piece At A Time [N]	Columbia 10321
			JOHNNY CASH & THE TENNESSEE THREE	
			CASH, Rosanne	
			Born on 5/24/55 in Memphis, daughter of Johnny Cash and Vivian Liberto. Raised by her mother in California, then moved to Nashville after high school graduation. Worked in the Johnny Cash Road Show. Married Rodney Crowell in 1979.	
6/13/81	**22**	7	1. Seven Year Ache	Columbia 11426
			CASHMAN & WEST	
			Duo of record producers/songwriters/singers Dennis "Terry Cashman" Minogue (b: 7/05/41) and Thomas "Tommy West" Picardo, Jr. (b: 8/17/42). Also see Buchanan Brothers.	
10/21/72	**27**	7	1. American City Suite	Dunhill 4324
			Sweet City Song/All Around The Town/A Friend Is Dying	
			CASINOS, The	
			Nine-man group from Cincinnati formed by Gene Hughes (lead singer).	
1/28/67	**6**	10	**1. Then You Can Tell Me Goodbye**	Fraternity 977
			CASSIDY, David	
			Son of actor Jack Cassidy and actress Evelyn Ward, born on 4/12/50 in New York City. Played Keith Partridge, the lead singer of TV's "The Partridge Family." Married for a time to actress Kay Lenz.	
11/13/71	**9**	11	● **1. Cherish**	Bell 45150
3/25/72	**37**	2	2. Could It Be Forever	Bell 45187
6/10/72	**25**	5	3. How Can I Be Sure	Bell 45220
10/14/72	**38**	2	4. Rock Me Baby	Bell 45260
10/27/90	**27**	5	5. Lyin' To Myself	Enigma 75084#
			CASSIDY, Shaun	
			Born on 9/27/59 in Los Angeles. Son of actor Jack Cassidy and actress Shirley Jones. Played Joe Hardy on TV's "The Hardy Boys." Shaun and David Cassidy are half-brothers. Cast member of the TV soap "General Hospital" in 1987.	
6/04/77	**1**(1)	12	● **1. Da Doo Ron Ron**	Warner 8365
8/20/77	**3**	15	● **2. That's Rock 'N' Roll**	Warner 8423
11/26/77+	**7**	12	● **3. Hey Deanie**	Warner 8488

DATE	POS	WKS	ARTIST—RECORD TITLE	LABEL & NO.
			above 2 written by Eric Carmen	
4/22/78	**31**	5	4. Do You Believe In Magic	Warner 8533
			CASTAWAYS, The	
			Teen quintet formed in Richfield, Minnesota. Nucleus of group: Denny Craswell (drums), Dick Roby (bass) and Roy Hensley (guitar). Craswell later joined Crow.	
9/18/65	**12**	9	1. Liar, Liar	Soma 1433
			CASTELLS, The	
			Santa Rosa, California quartet: Bob Ussery, Tom Hicks, Joe Kelly and Chuck Girard.	
7/03/61	**20**	7	1. Sacred	Era 3048
5/26/62	**21**	5	2. So This Is Love	Era 3073
			CASTLEMAN, Boomer	
			Owen "Boomer" Clarke of The Lewis & Clarke Expedition. Originally from Farmers Branch, Texas.	
5/31/75	**33**	3	1. Judy Mae	Mums 6038
			CASTOR, Jimmy	
			R&B singer/saxophonist/composer/arranger. Born on 6/02/43 in New York City. Formed the Jimmy Castor Bunch in 1972, with Gerry Thomas (keyboards), Doug Gibson (bass), Harry Jensen (guitar), Lenny Fridie, Jr. (congas) and Bobby Manigault (drums).	
2/04/67	**31**	3	1. Hey, Leroy, Your Mama's Callin' You [I]	Smash 2069
			THE JIMMY CASTOR BUNCH:	
5/27/72	**6**	10	● **2. Troglodyte (Cave Man) [N]**	RCA 1029
3/22/75	**16**	8	3. The Bertha Butt Boogie-Part 1 [N]	Atlantic 3232
			CATE BROS.	
			Duo of twins Ernie (vocals, piano) and Earl Cate (guitar), born on 12/26/42 in Fayetteville, Arkansas.	
4/17/76	**24**	8	1. Union Man	Asylum 45294
			CATES, George	
			Born on 10/19/11 in New York City. Arranger for Bing Crosby, Teresa Brewer, The Andrews Sisters and others. Musical director of TV's "Lawrence Welk Show" for 25 years.	
12/03/55	**35**	2	1. Autumn Leaves [I]	Coral 61485
			STEVE ALLEN with GEORGE CATES	
4/21/56	**4**	19	**2. Moonglow And Theme From "Picnic" [I]**	Coral 61618
			Top 100 #4 / Jockey #4 / Best Seller #5 / Juke Box #7 featuring The Stan Wrightsman Quartet; from the film *Picnic*	
			CATHY JEAN/The Roommates	
			Cathy was born on 9/08/45 in Brooklyn. The Roommates were a male teen-age vocal quartet from Queens, New York.	
3/06/61	**12**	10	1. Please Love Me Forever	Valmor 007
			CAT MOTHER AND THE ALL NIGHT NEWS BOYS	
			New York rock quintet produced by Jimi Hendrix.	
7/12/69	**21**	6	1. Good Old Rock 'N Roll	Polydor 14002
			Sweet Little Sixteen/Long Tall Sally/Chantilly Lace/Whole Lotta Shakin' Goin On/Blue Suede Shoes/Party Doll	

DATE	POS	WKS	ARTIST—RECORD TITLE	LABEL & NO.
			CAVALIERE, Felix	
			Born on 11/29/43 in Pelham, New York. Lead singer of The Rascals after a stint with Joey Dee's band.	
4/12/80	**36**	3	1. Only A Lonely Heart Sees	Epic 50829
			C COMPANY featuring TERRY NELSON	
5/01/71	**37**	3	● 1. Battle Hymn Of Lt. Calley [S]	Plantation 73
			Calley: U.S. Army officer court-martialed for the massacre of civilians at My Lai, Vietnam	
			CELEBRATION featuring MIKE LOVE	
			Mike is The Beach Boys' lead singer.	
6/03/78	**28**	4	1. Almost Summer	MCA 40891
			from the film of the same title	
			CERRONE	
			Composer/producer/drummer. Born Jean-Marc Cerrone in France in 1952.	
3/26/77	**36**	3	1. Love In 'C' Minor - Pt. I [I]	Cotillion 44215
			CETERA, Peter	
			Born on 9/13/44 in Chicago. Lead singer/bass guitarist of Chicago for their first 17 albums.	
6/21/86	**1**(2)	14	**1. Glory Of Love**	Full Moon 28662
			theme from the film *The Karate Kid Part II*	
10/11/86	**1**(1)	15	**2. The Next Time I Fall**	Full Moon 28597
			PETER CETERA W/AMY GRANT	
8/06/88	**4**	13	**3. One Good Woman**	Full Moon 27824
4/01/89	**6**	11	● **4. After All**	Geffen 27529
			CHER AND PETER CETERA	
			love theme from the film *Chances Are*	
			CHAD & JEREMY	
			Folk-rock duo formed in the early 1960s: Chad Stuart (b: 12/10/43, England) and Jeremy Clyde (b: 3/22/44, England). Broke up in 1967. Re-formed briefly in 1982.	
			CHAD STUART AND JEREMY CLYDE:	
6/13/64	**21**	6	1. Yesterday's Gone	World Art. 1021
9/19/64	**7**	9	**2. A Summer Song**	World Art. 1027
			CHAD & JEREMY:	
12/12/64+	**15**	8	3. Willow Weep For Me	World Art. 1034
3/13/65	**23**	5	4. If I Loved You	World Art. 1041
			from the musical *Carousel*	
5/29/65	**17**	6	5. Before And After	Columbia 43277
8/28/65	**35**	3	6. I Don't Wanna Lose You Baby	Columbia 43339
8/13/66	**30**	2	7. Distant Shores	Columbia 43682
			CHAIRMEN OF THE BOARD	
			Soul vocal group formed in Detroit in 1969. Consisted of General Norman Johnson, Danny Woods, Harrison Kennedy and Eddie Curtis. First recorded for Invictus in 1969. Johnson was leader of The Showmen from 1961-67; wrote "Patches," hit for Clarence Carter. Johnson went solo in 1976.	
2/07/70	**3**	12	● **1. Give Me Just A Little More Time**	Invictus 9074
6/06/70	**38**	2	2. (You've Got Me) Dangling On A String	Invictus 9078
9/12/70	**38**	2	3. Everything's Tuesday	Invictus 9079
			CHAIRMAN OF THE BOARD	

DATE	POS	WKS	ARTIST—RECORD TITLE	LABEL & NO.
12/12/70+	**13**	9	4. Pay To The Piper	Invictus 9081
			CHAKACHAS, The	
			Belgian sextet led by Gaston Boogaerts (b: 7/31/21).	
2/19/72	**8**	10	● **1. Jungle Fever** [I]	Polydor 15030
			CHAMBERLAIN, Richard	
			Born on 3/31/35 in Los Angeles. Leading film, theater and TV actor. Played lead role in TV's "Dr. Kildare," 1961-66.	
6/23/62	**10**	10	**1. Theme From Dr. Kildare (Three Stars Will Shine Tonight)**	MGM 13075
10/27/62	**21**	5	2. Love Me Tender	MGM 13097
3/09/63	**14**	7	3. All I Have To Do Is Dream	MGM 13121
			CHAMBERS BROTHERS, The	
			Four Mississippi-born brothers: George (bass), Willie (guitar), Lester (harmonica) and Joe Chambers (guitar). Formed as a gospel group in Los Angeles in 1954. Drummer Brian Keenan added in 1965.	
9/14/68	**11**	9	1. Time Has Come Today	Columbia 44414
12/21/68	**37**	2	2. I Can't Turn You Loose written by Otis Redding	Columbia 44679
			CHAMPAIGN	
			Interracial sextet from Champaign, Illinois — Pauli Carman and Rena Jones, lead singers.	
3/28/81	**12**	13	1. How 'Bout Us	Columbia 11433
5/14/83	**23**	9	2. Try Again	Columbia 03563
			CHAMPS, The	
			Instrumental combo from Los Angeles. Named after Gene Autry's horse, Champ. Originally consisted of studio musicians Dave Burgess (rhythm guitar), Buddy Bruce (lead guitar), Danny Flores (sax; later changed name to Chuck Rio), Cliff Hils (bass) and Gene Alden (drums). Shortly after "Tequila" became a hit, Bruce and Hils were replaced by Dale Norris and Joe Burnas. Eight months after recording "Tequila," Flores and Alden left and were replaced by Jimmy Seals (sax) and Dash Crofts (drums). Other personnel changes followed and in 1960 guitarist Glen Campbell spent some time in the group.	
3/03/58	**1**(5)	16	**1. Tequila** [I] Best Seller #1(5) / Top 100 #1(5) / Jockey #1(2)	Challenge 1016
6/02/58	**30**	5	2. El Rancho Rock [I] Top 100 #30 / Best Seller #31 based on the 1934 tune "El Rancho Grande"	Challenge 59007
2/08/60	**30**	5	3. Too Much Tequila [I]	Challenge 59063
7/14/62	**40**	1	4. Limbo Rock [I]	Challenge 9131
			CHANDLER, Gene	
			R&B singer/producer. Born Eugene Dixon on 7/06/37 in Chicago. Formed the Gaytones at Englewood High School in 1955. Joined The Dukays vocal group in 1957. U.S. Army, Germany, 1957-60. Rejoined The Dukays in 1960; they first recorded for Nat in 1961. Group then recorded "Duke Of Earl" for Vee-Jay. Due to contract conflicts with Nat, Dixon left the group, changed his name to Gene Chandler and promoted "Duke Of Earl." Own label, Mr. Chand, 1969-73.	
1/27/62	**1**(3)	11	**1. Duke Of Earl**	Vee-Jay 416
8/01/64	**19**	7	2. Just Be True	Constellation 130
11/14/64	**39**	1	3. Bless Our Love	Constellation 136
1/16/65	**40**	1	4. What Now	Constellation 141

DATE	POS	WKS	ARTIST—RECORD TITLE	LABEL & NO.
5/22/65	**18**	6	5. Nothing Can Stop Me 2, 4, 5: written by Curtis Mayfield	Constellation 149
8/08/70	**12**	11	● 6. Groovy Situation	Mercury 73083
			CHANGE European-American studio group formed by Italian producer Jacques Fred Petrus.	
7/19/80	**40**	1	1. A Lover's Holiday	RFC 49208
			CHANNEL, Bruce Born on 11/28/40 in Jacksonville, Texas. Appeared on "Louisiana Hayride" in 1958.	
2/10/62	**1**(3)	12	**1. Hey! Baby** harmonica player: Delbert McClinton; first released on Le Cam 953 in 1961	Smash 1731
			CHANSON Studio disco band. Lead vocals by James Jamerson Jr. and David Williams.	
12/16/78+	**21**	9	1. Don't Hold Back	Ariola 7717
			CHANTAY'S Teenage surf-rock quintet from Santa Ana, California: Bob Spickard (lead guitar), Brian Carman (rhythm guitar), Rob Marshall (piano), Warren Waters (bass) and Bob Welsh (drums).	
4/06/63	**4**	11	**1. Pipeline** [I] first released on Downey 104 in 1962	Dot 16440
			CHANTELS, The Vocal group from the Bronx. Formed in high school, with lead Arlene Smith, Sonia Goring, Rene Minus, Jackie Landry and Lois Harris. Group name taken from that of a rival school, St. Francis de Chantelle. Auditioned for Richard Barrett, who became their manager and obtained a contract with Gone/End Records.	
1/27/58	**15**	12	1. Maybe Top 100 #15 / Best Seller #16	End 1005
4/07/58	**39**	3	2. Every Night (I Pray) Best Seller #39 / Top 100 #40	End 1015
9/11/61	**14**	8	3. Look In My Eyes	Carlton 555
12/11/61	**29**	3	4. Well. I Told You answer song to Ray Charles' "Hit The Road Jack"	Carlton 564
			CHAPIN, Harry Folk-rock balladeer. Born on 12/07/42 in New York City. Died in an auto accident on 7/16/81.	
4/22/72	**24**	9	1. Taxi	Elektra 45770
3/16/74	**36**	2	2. WOLD	Elektra 45874
11/02/74	**1**(1)	12	● **3. Cat's In The Cradle**	Elektra 45203
11/22/80	**23**	7	4. Sequel sequel to 1972's "Taxi"	Boardwalk 5700
			CHAPMAN, Tracy Boston-based singer/songwriter. Born in Cleveland. Graduated from Tufts University in 1986 with an anthropology degree. Won the 1988 Best New Artist Grammy Award.	
7/16/88	**6**	12	**1. Fast Car**	Elektra 69412

DATE	POS	WKS	ARTIST—RECORD TITLE	LABEL & NO.
			CHARLENE	
			Charlene Duncan (nee: D'Angelo). Born on 6/01/50 in Hollywood.	
3/27/82	**3**	14	**1. I've Never Been To Me** **[R]**	Motown 1611
			originally charted in 1977 (POS 97)	
			CHARLES, Jimmy	
			Born in 1942 in Paterson, New Jersey. R&B singer. Won Apollo Amateur Contest in 1958.	
9/05/60	**5**	11	**1. A Million To One**	Promo 1002
			vocal backing by The Revelletts	
			CHARLES, Ray	
			Born Ray Charles Robinson on 9/23/30 in Albany, Georgia. To Greenville, Florida while still an infant. Partially blind at age five, completely blind at seven (glaucoma). Studied classical piano and clarinet at State School for Deaf and Blind Children, St. Augustine, Florida, 1937-45. With local Florida bands; moved to Seattle in 1948. Formed the McSon Trio (also known as the Maxim Trio and the Maxine Trio) with Gossady McGhee (guitar) and Milton Garred (bass). First recordings were very much in the King Cole Trio style. Formed own band in 1954. The 1950s female vocal group, The Cookies, became his backing group The Raeletts. Inducted into the Rock and Roll Hall of Fame in 1986. Recipient of the Grammy Lifetime Achievement Award in 1987. Popular performer with many TV and film appearances.	
11/25/57	**34**	1	1. Swanee River Rock (Talkin' 'Bout That River)	Atlantic 1154
			Best Seller #34 / Top 100 #42 based on Stephen Foster's "Old Folks At Home"	
7/20/59	**6**	11	**2. What'd I Say (Part I)**	Atlantic 2031
12/14/59	**40**	1	3. I'm Movin' On	Atlantic 2043
8/08/60	**40**	1	4. Sticks And Stones	ABC-Para. 10118
10/10/60	**1**(1)	10	**5. Georgia On My Mind**	ABC-Para. 10135
			#10 hit for Frankie Trumbauer in 1931	
12/12/60	**28**	5	6. Ruby	ABC-Para. 10164
			there were 6 top 30 versions of this tune in 1953	
3/27/61	**8**	9	**7. One Mint Julep** **[I]**	Impulse 200
9/18/61	**1**(2)	11	**8. Hit The Road Jack**	ABC-Para. 10244
12/04/61+	**9**	10	**9. Unchain My Heart**	ABC-Para. 10266
4/21/62	**20**	4	10. Hide 'Nor Hair	ABC-Para. 10314
5/19/62	**1**(5)	14	• **11. I Can't Stop Loving You**	ABC-Para. 10330
8/04/62	**2**(1)	9	**12. You Don't Know Me**	ABC-Para. 10345
12/01/62	**7**	9	**13. You Are My Sunshine/**	
12/08/62	**29**	5	14. Your Cheating Heart	ABC-Para. 10375
			#1 country hit for Hank Williams in 1953	
3/16/63	**20**	4	15. Don't Set Me Free	ABC-Para. 10405
4/27/63	**8**	8	**16. Take These Chains From My Heart**	ABC-Para. 10435
7/06/63	**21**	5	17. No One/	
7/06/63	**29**	4	18. Without Love (There Is Nothing)	ABC-Para. 10453
9/14/63	**4**	11	**19. Busted**	ABC-Para. 10481
12/21/63+	**20**	7	20. That Lucky Old Sun	ABC-Para. 10509
			#1 hit for Frankie Laine in 1949	
3/21/64	**38**	2	21. My Heart Cries For You/	
			there were 9 top 30 versions of this tune in 1951	
3/21/64	**39**	1	22. Baby, Don't You Cry	ABC-Para. 10530
1/15/66	**6**	9	**23. Crying Time**	ABC-Para. 10739

DATE	POS	WKS	ARTIST—RECORD TITLE	LABEL & NO.
4/16/66	**19**	5	24. Together Again above 2 written by Buck Owens	ABC-Para. 10785
6/25/66	**31**	4	25. Let's Go Get Stoned	ABC 10808
10/01/66	**32**	2	26. I Chose To Sing The Blues 4, 8, 9, 13, 15, 17, 23, 25, 26: backing vocals by The Raelets featuring Margie Hendrix	ABC 10840
6/10/67	**15**	9	27. Here We Go Again	ABC 10938
9/23/67	**33**	3	28. In The Heat Of The Night from the Sidney Poitier film of the same title	ABC 10970
12/02/67	**25**	3	29. Yesterday	ABC 11009
7/20/68	**35**	3	30. Eleanor Rigby	ABC/TRC 11090
4/17/71	**36**	4	31. Don't Change On Me	ABC/TRC 11291
5/15/71	**36**	2	32. Booty Butt [I] **THE RAY CHARLES ORCHESTRA**	Tangerine 1015
12/16/89+	**18**	8	33. I'll Be Good To You **QUINCY JONES featuring RAY CHARLES AND CHAKA KHAN**	Qwest 22697
			CHARLES, Ray, Singers Born Charles Raymond Offenberg on 9/13/18 in Chicago. Arranger/conductor for many TV shows including the "Perry Como Show," "Glen Campbell Goodtime Hour" and "Sha-Na-Na." Winner of two Emmys.	
5/02/64	**3**	12	**1. Love Me With All Your Heart (Cuando Calienta El Sol)**	Command 4046
7/25/64	**29**	4	2. Al-Di-La	Command 4049
12/19/64+	**32**	5	3. One More Time	Command 4057
			CHARLES, Sonny Former lead singer of The Checkmates, Ltd., an integrated quintet from Ft. Wayne, Indiana. Consisted of Sonny, Bobby Stevens, Harvey Trees, Bill Van Buskirk and Marvin Smith.	
1/22/83	**40**	2	1. Put It In A Magazine	Highrise 2001
5/31/69	**13**	10	2. Black Pearl **SONNY CHARLES AND THE CHECKMATES, LTD.**	A&M 1053
			CHARLIE British rock quintet led by Terry Thomas (vocals, guitar).	
8/06/83	**38**	2	1. It's Inevitable	Mirage 99862
			CHARMS, The R&B vocal group from Cincinnati consisting of Otis Williams, Richard Parker, Donald Peak, Joe Penn and Rolland Bradley. Group first recorded for Rockin' in 1953. Otis later recorded country music.	
11/27/54+	**15**	15	1. Hearts Of Stone Best Seller #15 / Juke Box #15 / Jockey #20	DeLuxe 6062
1/15/55	**26**	3	2. Ling, Ting, Tong Best Seller #26	DeLuxe 6076
4/14/56	**11**	15	3. Ivory Tower **OTIS WILLIAMS AND HIS CHARMS** Jockey #11 / Top 100 #12 / Best Seller #13 / Juke Box #19	DeLuxe 6093
			CHARTBUSTERS, The Washington, D.C. rock quartet.	
8/15/64	**33**	3	1. She's The One	Mutual 502

The B-52s, a colorful group emerging from Athens, Ga. in the late 70s, experienced a career resurgence in 1989 with their *Cosmic Thing* album. After hitting with the album's two Top 5 singles—"Love Shack" and "Roam," which both reached No. 3—lead vocalist Kate Pierson prominently appeared on singles by both R.E.M. and Iggy Pop.

Biz Markie, a rapper uninhibited enough to pose with his finger up his nose on an album cover, saw surprising top-40 success with his 1990 hit "Just A Friend," on the Warner Bros.-distributed Cold Chillin' label.

Michael Bolton's ascendancy to stardom in the late 80s was long in coming; prior to scoring with No. 1 adult-contemporary hits such as "How Am I Supposed To Live Without You," he sang with hard-rock group Blackjack in the 70s and as solo artist Michael Bolotin. Long out of print, that material was, predictably, later reissued by Bolton's former labels.

Bon Jovi's huge popular success in the late 80s resulted in solo albums by singer Jon Bon Jovi and band guitarist Richie Sambora, as well as a new record label—Jambco—with which Bon Jovi reintroduced performer Billy Falcon.

David Bowie's illustrious past as a singles artist—thought by the general public to have begun in the early 70s with "Space Oddity"—was comprehensively documented by Rhino Records in 1991. Called *Early On (1964-1966)*, the set contains 17 tracks Bowie recorded with his early groups the Manish Boys, the King Bees, the Buzz, and the Lower Third.

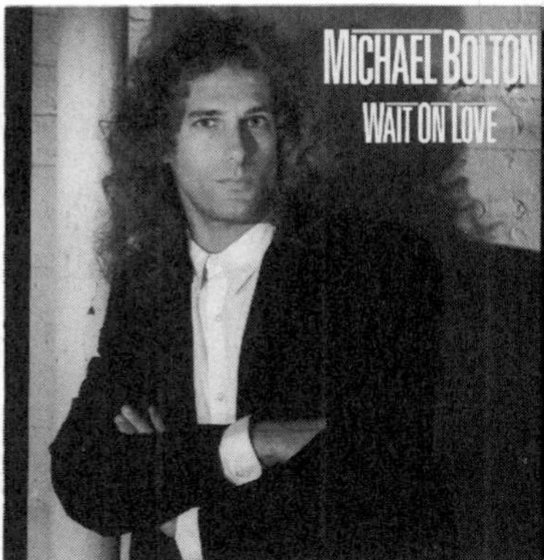

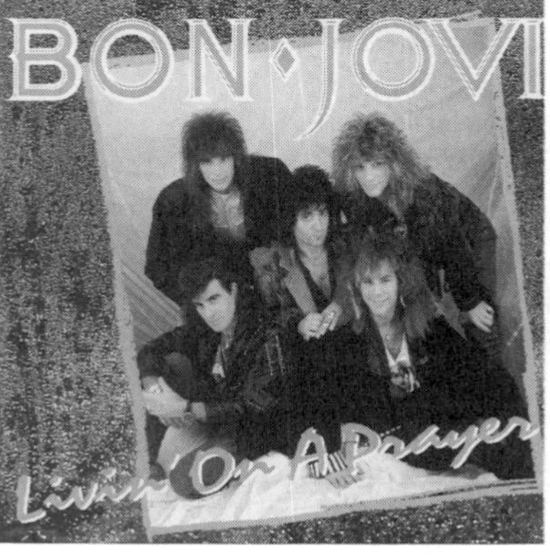

The Boys gave the newly-revived Motown one of its first platinum albums with 1989's *Messages from the Boys*. Like another famous group formerly on Motown—the Jackson 5—the act consists of several young brothers who can sing.

Walter Brennan may have played Grandpa Amos McCoy on TV's "The Real McCoys," but true fans know he excelled as an early 60s hitmaker. His all-time classic "Old Rivers" reached No. 5 in 1962, and voice impersonators everywhere were ecstatic.

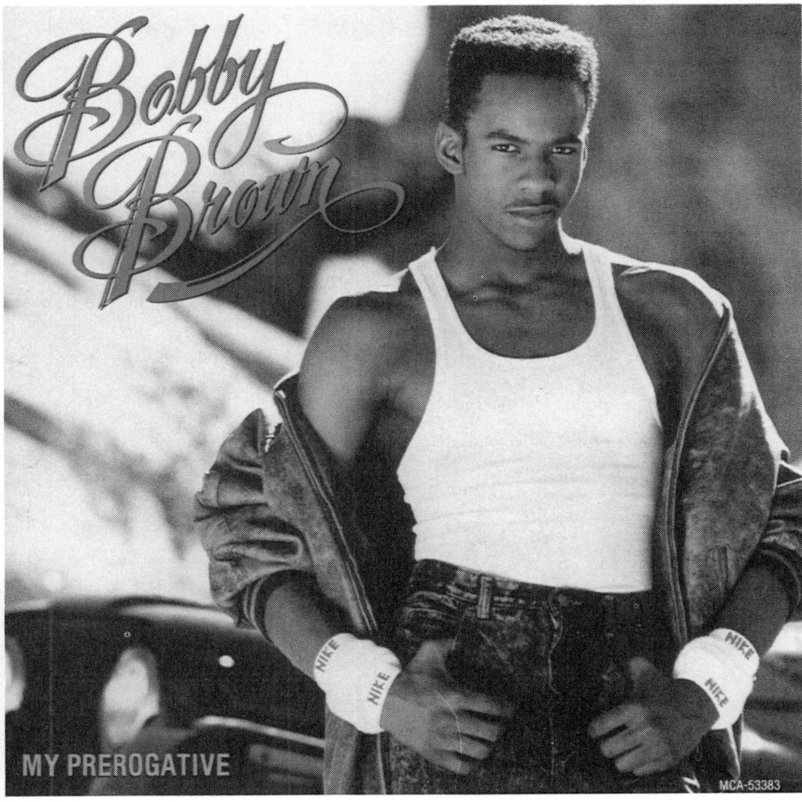

Bobby Brown's solo success outside his group New Edition resulted in one of the industry's very first remix albums. One year after 1988's *Don't Be Cruel* came *Dance! . . . Ya Know It*, containing new versions of previously-released hits like "My Prerogative" and "Roni."

James Brown's staggering career as the Godfather of Soul has one ironic downside: despite scoring dozens of top-40 hits since 1960's "Think," the closest he's ever come to having a No. 1 pop hit was with 1965's "I Got You (I Feel Good)," which only reached No. 3.

The Dave Brubeck Quartet did the unthinkable and put jazz in the Top 40. "Take Five" took the No. 25 slot in 1961 and was the best-selling pianist's sole brush with top-40 fame.

Sharon Bryant was a founding member of Atlantic Starr and enjoyed one top-40 hit with them—1982's "Circles" on A&M—before leaving the group to establish her own solo career. Her "Let Go" single hit the Top 40 in October 1989.

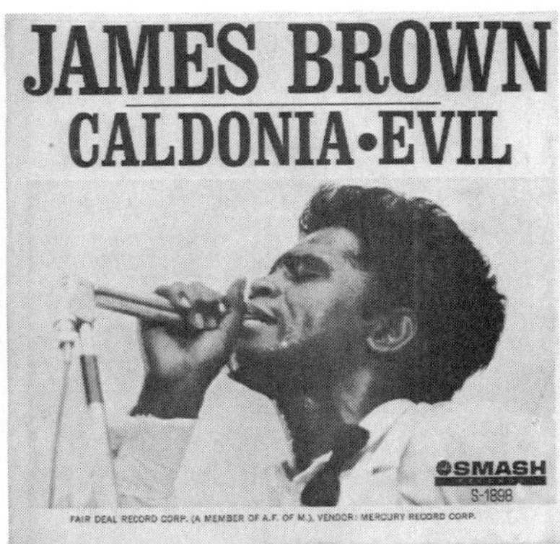

DATE	POS	WKS	ARTIST—RECORD TITLE	LABEL & NO.
			CHASE	
			Jazz-rock band organized by trumpeter Bill Chase (formerly with Woody Herman and Stan Kenton). Chase and three other members were killed in a plane crash on 8/09/74.	
6/26/71	**24**	8	1. Get It On	Epic 10738
			CHEAP TRICK	
			Rock quartet from Rockford, Illinois consisting of Rick Nielsen (guitar), Bun E. Carlos (real name: Brad Carlson; drums), Robin Zander (vocals) and Tom Petersson (bass; replaced by Jon Brant in 1980). Founded by Nielsen and Petersson, former members of Nazz. Petersson returned in 1988 (replacing Brant).	
5/26/79	**7**	13	• **1. I Want You To Want Me**	Epic 50680
9/15/79	**35**	3	2. Ain't That A Shame	Epic 50743
10/27/79	**26**	5	3. Dream Police	Epic 50774
1/19/80	**32**	3	4. Voices	Epic 50814
5/21/88	**1**(2)	14	**5. The Flame**	Epic 07745
8/20/88	**4**	12	**6. Don't Be Cruel**	Epic 07965
12/17/88	**33**	5	7. Ghost Town	Epic 08097
8/18/90	**12**	7	8. Can't Stop Fallin' Into Love	Epic 73444
			CHECKER, Chubby	
			Born Ernest Evans on 10/03/41 in Philadelphia. Did impersonations of famous singers. First recorded for Parkway in 1959. Cover version of Hank Ballard's "The Twist" started worldwide dance craze. On 4/12/64, married Miss World 1962, Dutch-born Catharina Lodders ("Loddy Lo" written for her).	
6/15/59	**38**	2	1. The Class [N] imitations of Fats Domino, The Coasters, Elvis, and The Chipmunks	Parkway 804
8/08/60	**1**(1)	15	**2. The Twist**	Parkway 811
10/31/60	**14**	9	3. The Hucklebuck written in 1949; #5 hit for Tommy Dorsey; #10 for Frank Sinatra	Parkway 813
1/30/61	**1**(3)	14	**4. Pony Time**	Parkway 818
5/01/61	**24**	4	5. Dance The Mess Around	Parkway 822
7/03/61	**8**	15	**6. Let's Twist Again** originally charted for 9 weeks; re-entered on 11/20/61 (POS 22)	Parkway 824
10/02/61	**7**	11	**7. The Fly**	Parkway 830
11/20/61+	**1**(2)	18	**8. The Twist** **[R]** except for Bing Crosby's "White Christmas", "The Twist" is the only song in history to re-enter charts and return to #1 position	Parkway 811
12/25/61	**21**	3	9. Jingle Bell Rock [X] **BOBBY RYDELL/CHUBBY CHECKER**	Cameo 205
3/10/62	**3**	12	**10. Slow Twistin'** female vocal: Dee Dee Sharp	Parkway 835
7/07/62	**12**	7	11. Dancin' Party	Parkway 842
9/29/62	**2**(2)	17	**12. Limbo Rock/**	
9/29/62	**10**	9	**13. Popeye The Hitchhiker**	Parkway 849
2/23/63	**20**	8	14. Let's Limbo Some More/	
3/23/63	**15**	7	15. Twenty Miles	Parkway 862
6/01/63	**12**	7	16. Birdland	Parkway 873
8/03/63	**25**	5	17. Twist It Up	Parkway 879
11/23/63	**12**	9	18. Loddy Lo/	
1/11/64	**17**	8	19. Hooka Tooka	Parkway 890

DATE	POS	WKS	ARTIST—RECORD TITLE	LABEL & NO.
4/04/64	**23**	5	20. Hey, Bobba Needle	Parkway 907
7/11/64	**40**	1	21. Lazy Elsie Molly	Parkway 920
5/22/65	**40**	1	22. Let's Do The Freddie many of above Checker hits written by Kal Mann and Dave Appell	Parkway 949
7/09/88	**16**	8	23. The Twist (Yo, Twist!) [R] **FAT BOYS with CHUBBY CHECKER**	Tin Pan 887571
			CHECKMATES, LTD., The — see CHARLES, Sonny	
			CHEECH & CHONG Comedians Richard "Cheech" Marin (b: 7/13/46, Watts, California) and Thomas Chong (b: 5/24/38, Edmonton, Alberta, Canada). Starred in movies since 1980. Chong, the father of actress Rae Dawn Chong, was the guitarist of Bobby Taylor's Vancouvers.	
9/29/73	**15**	7	1. Basketball Jones Featuring Tyrone Shoelaces [N] parody of "Love Jones" by Brighter Side Of Darkness	Ode 66038
12/29/73+	**24**	5	2. Sister Mary Elephant (Shudd-Up!) [C]	Ode 66041
8/31/74	**9**	8	**3. Earache My Eye Featuring Alice Bowie [C]**	Ode 66102
			CHEERS, The Vocal trio from Los Angeles consisting of TV actor Bert Convy (died on 7/15/91 of a brain tumor), Gil Garfield and Sue Allen.	
9/24/55	**6**	11	**1. Black Denim Trousers** Best Seller #6 / Jockey #6 / Top 100 #13 / Juke Box #20 orchestra and chorus directed by Les Baxter	Capitol 3219
			CHER Born Cherilyn LaPierre on 5/20/46 in El Centro, California. Worked as backup singer for Phil Spector. Recorded as "Bonnie Jo Mason" and "Cherilyn" in 1964. Recorded with Sonny Bono as "Caesar & Cleo" in 1963, then as Sonny & Cher from 1965-73. Married to Bono from 1963-74. Married to Gregg Allman from 1975-77. Own TV series with Bono from 1971-77. Member of the group Black Rose in 1980. Acclaimed film actress (won Best Actress Oscar in 1987 for *Moonstruck*).	
8/07/65	**15**	6	1. All I Really Want To Do	Imperial 66114
11/06/65	**25**	3	2. Where Do You Go	Imperial 66136
3/26/66	**2**(1)	9	**3. Bang Bang (My Baby Shot Me Down)**	Imperial 66160
8/20/66	**32**	3	4. Alfie from the film of the same title	Imperial 66192
11/18/67	**9**	9	**5. You Better Sit Down Kids** all of above produced by Sonny Bono	Imperial 66261
10/02/71	**1**(2)	14	● **6. Gypsys, Tramps & Thieves**	Kapp 2146
2/12/72	**7**	10	**7. The Way Of Love**	Kapp 2158
6/03/72	**22**	6	8. Living In A House Divided	Kapp 2171
9/01/73	**1**(2)	14	● **9. Half-Breed**	MCA 40102
2/02/74	**1**(1)	12	● **10. Dark Lady**	MCA 40161
6/15/74	**27**	4	11. Train Of Thought	MCA 40245
3/17/79	**8**	11	● **12. Take Me Home**	Casablanca 965
1/16/88	**10**	12	**13. I Found Someone**	Geffen 28191
4/30/88	**14**	9	14. We All Sleep Alone co-written and co-produced by Jon Bon Jovi	Geffen 27986
4/01/89	**6**	11	● **15. After All**	Geffen 27529

DATE	POS	WKS	ARTIST—RECORD TITLE	LABEL & NO.
			CHER and PETER CETERA	
			love theme from the film *Chances Are*	
8/05/89	**3**	14	● **16. If I Could Turn Back Time**	Geffen 22886
11/18/89	**8**	11	**17. Just Like Jesse James**	Geffen 22844
3/24/90	**20**	6	18. Heart Of Stone	Geffen 19953
1/19/91	**33**	2	19. The Shoop Shoop Song (It's In His Kiss)	Geffen 19659
			from the film *Mermaids*; produced by Peter Asher	
6/29/91	**17**	9	20. Love And Understanding	Geffen 19023
			CHERI	
			Canadian duo: Rosalind Milligan Hunt and Lyn Cullerier.	
6/05/82	**39**	2	1. Murphy's Law [N]	Venture 149
			CHERRELLE	
			Born Cheryl Norton in Los Angeles. Soul vocalist/drummer. Cousin of vocalist Pebbles. Moved to Detroit in 1979. Discovered by Michael Henderson.	
3/29/86	**26**	6	1. Saturday Love	Tabu 05767
3/05/88	**28**	6	2. Never Knew Love Like This	Tabu 07646
			CHERRY, Don	
			Born on 1/11/24 in Wichita Falls, Texas. Studied voice after the service in mid-1940s. Vocalist with Jan Garber band in the late '40s. Accomplished professional golfer.	
12/10/55+	**4**	18	**1. Band Of Gold**	Columbia 40597
			Jockey #4 / Best Seller #5 / Top 100 #5 / Juke Box #5	
4/14/56	**29**	6	2. Wild Cherry	Columbia 40665
8/11/56	**22**	6	3. Ghost Town	Columbia 40705
			Jockey #22 / Top 100 #26	
			orchestra and chorus directed by Ray Conniff on above 3	
			CHERRY, Neneh	
			London-based singer. Born on 8/10/64 in Stockholm, of Swedish and West African parentage and raised in New York City. Stepdaughter of jazz trumpeter Don Cherry.	
5/06/89	**3**	14	● **1. Buffalo Stance**	Virgin 99231
			from the film *Slaves of New York*	
8/19/89	**8**	8	**2. Kisses On The Wind**	Virgin 99183
			CHIC	
			Disco group formed in New York City by producers Bernard Edwards (bass) and Nile Rodgers (guitar). Vocalists: Norma Jean Wright (replaced by Alfa Anderson) and Luci Martin; drums: Tony Thompson. Wright began solo career in 1978; recorded as Norma Jean. Edwards recorded with the studio group Roundtree in 1978. Rodgers joined The Honeydrippers in 1984. Thompson joined the Power Station in 1985 and Edwards became their producer.	
12/10/77+	**6**	17	● **1. Dance, Dance, Dance (Yowsah, Yowsah, Yowsah)**	Atlantic 3435
6/17/78	**38**	1	2. Everybody Dance	Atlantic 3469
11/18/78	**1**(6)	19	▲ **3. Le Freak**	Atlantic 3519
3/10/79	**7**	12	● **4. I Want Your Love**	Atlantic 3557
7/07/79	**1**(1)	14	● **5. Good Times**	Atlantic 3584

DATE	POS	WKS	ARTIST—RECORD TITLE	LABEL & NO.
			CHICAGO	
			Jazz-oriented rock group formed in Chicago in 1967. Consisted of Robert Lamm (keyboards), James Pankow (trombone), Lee Loughnane (trumpet), Terry Kath (guitar; d: 1/23/78 playing Russian Roulette [age 31]), Walt Parazaider (reeds), Peter Cetera (bass) and Danny Seraphine (drums). Originally called The Big Thing, later Chicago Transit Authority. To Los Angeles in the late '60s. Kath replaced by Donnie Dacus (left in 1979). Bill Champlin (keyboards) joined in 1982. Cetera left in 1985, replaced by Jason Scheff. Seraphine left in 1989, guitarist DaWayne Bailey added.	
4/25/70	**9**	11	**1. Make Me Smile**	Columbia 45127
8/01/70	**4**	11	**2. 25 Or 6 To 4**	Columbia 45194
11/21/70+	**7**	11	**3. Does Anybody Really Know What Time It Is?**	Columbia 45264
3/06/71	**20**	6	4. Free	Columbia 45331
5/29/71	**35**	4	5. Lowdown	Columbia 45370
7/10/71	**7**	11	**6. Beginnings/**	
		11	7. Colour My World originally the B-side of "Make Me Smile"	Columbia 45417
10/30/71	**24**	6	8. Questions 67 And 68 [R] originally charted in 1969 (POS 71)	Columbia 45467
8/12/72	**3**	10	• **9. Saturday In The Park**	Columbia 45657
11/18/72	**24**	6	10. Dialogue (Part I & II)	Columbia 45717
7/07/73	**10**	12	**11. Feelin' Stronger Every Day**	Columbia 45880
10/20/73	**4**	14	• **12. Just You 'N' Me**	Columbia 45933
4/06/74	**9**	12	**13. (I've Been) Searchin' So Long**	Columbia 46020
7/13/74	**6**	8	**14. Call On Me**	Columbia 46062
10/26/74	**11**	10	15. Wishing You Were Here backing vocals by The Beach Boys	Columbia 10049
3/08/75	**13**	7	16. Harry Truman	Columbia 10092
5/10/75	**5**	7	**17. Old Days**	Columbia 10131
7/17/76	**32**	4	18. Another Rainy Day In New York City	Columbia 10360
8/21/76	**1**(2)	17	• **19. If You Leave Me Now**	Columbia 10390
10/15/77	**4**	12	**20. Baby, What A Big Surprise** all of above produced by James Wilkin Guercio	Columbia 10620
10/28/78	**14**	8	21. Alive Again	Columbia 10845
1/13/79	**14**	9	22. No Tell Lover	Columbia 10879
6/26/82	**1**(2)	18	• **23. Hard To Say I'm Sorry** from the film *Summer Lovers*	Full Moon 29979
10/23/82	**22**	8	24. Love Me Tomorrow	Full Moon 29911
5/12/84	**16**	10	25. Stay The Night	Full Moon 29306
8/25/84	**3**	15	**26. Hard Habit To Break**	Full Moon 29214
12/01/84+	**3**	14	**27. You're The Inspiration**	Full Moon 29126
3/09/85	**14**	10	28. Along Comes A Woman	Full Moon 29082
12/27/86+	**3**	13	**29. Will You Still Love Me?**	Full Moon 28512
4/25/87	**17**	8	30. If She Would Have Been Faithful . . .	Warner 28424
7/02/88	**3**	13	**31. I Don't Wanna Live Without Your Love**	Reprise 27855
10/15/88	**1**(2)	16	• **32. Look Away**	Reprise 27766
2/04/89	**10**	10	**33. You're Not Alone**	Reprise 27757
12/23/89+	**5**	12	**34. What Kind Of Man Would I Be?**	Reprise 22741
3/09/91	**39**	2	35. Chasin' The Wind	Reprise 19466

DATE	POS	WKS	ARTIST—RECORD TITLE	LABEL & NO.
			CHICAGO LOOP, The	
			Chicago band featuring guitarist Stefan Grossman.	
11/26/66	**37**	3	1. (When She Needs Good Lovin') She Comes To Me	DynoVoice 226
			CHIFFONS, The	
			Black female vocal group from the Bronx. Formed while high school classmates; worked as backup singers in 1960. Consisted of Judy Craig, Barbara Lee, Patricia Bennett and Sylvia Peterson. Also recorded as The Four Pennies on the Rust label.	
3/09/63	**1**(4)	12	**1. He's So Fine**	Laurie 3152
6/08/63	**5**	9	**2. One Fine Day**	Laurie 3179
10/19/63	**40**	1	3. A Love So Fine	Laurie 3195
1/04/64	**36**	1	4. I Have A Boyfriend	Laurie 3212
5/28/66	**10**	7	**5. Sweet Talkin' Guy**	Laurie 3340
			CHILD, Jane	
			Toronto native. Member of the Children's Chorus of the Canadian Opera Company at age 12. Studied piano at the Royal Conservatory of Music.	
3/03/90	**2**(3)	14	● **1. Don't Wanna Fall In Love**	Warner 19933
			CHI-LITES, The	
			R&B vocal group from Chicago. Consisted of Eugene Record (lead vocals), Robert "Squirrel" Lester (tenor), Marshall Thompson (baritone) and Creadel "Red" Jones (bass). First recorded as the Hi-Lites on Daran in 1963. Eugene Record went solo in 1976.	
5/08/71	**26**	6	1. (For God's Sake) Give More Power To The People	Brunswick 55450
10/30/71	**3**	13	**2. Have You Seen Her**	Brunswick 55462
4/15/72	**1**(1)	14	**3. Oh Girl**	Brunswick 55471
3/24/73	**33**	5	4. A Letter To Myself	Brunswick 55491
9/01/73	**30**	5	5. Stoned Out Of My Mind	Brunswick 55500
			CHILLIWACK	
			Canadian rock group led by Bill Henderson (vocals).	
10/31/81	**22**	11	1. My Girl (Gone, Gone, Gone)	Millennium 11813
2/27/82	**33**	3	2. I Believe	Millennium 13102
			CHIMES, The	
			Brooklyn-based vocal quintet led by Leonard Cocco.	
1/16/61	**11**	6	1. Once In Awhile #1 hit for Tommy Dorsey in 1937	Tag 444
5/15/61	**38**	1	2. I'm In The Mood For Love #1 hit for Little Jack Little in 1935	Tag 445
			CHIPMUNKS, The	
			Characters created by Ross Bagdasarian ("David Seville") who named Alvin, Simon and Theodore after Liberty executives Alvin Bennett, Simon Waronker and Theodore Keep. The Chipmunks starred in own prime-time animated TV show in the early 1960s and a Saturday morning cartoon series in the mid-1980s. Bagdasarian died on 1/16/72 (age 52). His son, Ross Jr., resurrected the act in 1980.	
			THE CHIPMUNKS with DAVID SEVILLE:	
12/08/58	**1**(4)	11	**1. The Chipmunk Song** **[X-N]**	Liberty 55168
			DAVID SEVILLE AND THE CHIPMUNKS:	
2/23/59	**3**	9	**2. Alvin's Harmonica** **[N]**	Liberty 55179
7/13/59	**16**	6	3. Ragtime Cowboy Joe [N] #1 hit for Bob Roberts in 1912	Liberty 55200

DATE	POS	WKS	ARTIST—RECORD TITLE	LABEL & NO.
3/07/60	**33**	2	4. Alvin's Orchestra [N]	Liberty 55233
12/26/60	**21**	1	5. Rudolph The Red Nosed Reindeer [X-N]	Liberty 55289
1/06/62	**39**	1	6. The Chipmunk Song [X-R]	Liberty 55250
3/31/62	**40**	1	7. The Alvin Twist [N]	Liberty 55424
12/29/62	**40**	1	8. The Chipmunk Song [X-R]	Liberty 55250
			CHORDETTES, The	
			Female vocal group from Sheboygan, Wisconsin formed in 1946. Consisted of Janet Ertel (nee: Buschman; bass), her sister-in-law Carol Buschman (baritone), Lynn Evans (lead singer; replaced Dorothy Schwartz [nee: Hummitzsch], 1953) and Margie Needham (tenor; replaced Jinny Lockard, 1953). With Arthur Godfrey from 1949-53. Ertel married Cadence owner Archie Bleyer in 1954; her daughter Jackie was married to Phil Everly. Janet died of cancer on 11/22/88.	
3/10/56	**14**	9	1. Eddie My Love Jockey #14 / Best Seller #17 / Top 100 #18	Cadence 1284
6/02/56	**5**	17	**2. Born To Be With You** Top 100 #5 / Jockey #5 / Juke Box #5 / Best Seller #7	Cadence 1291
10/13/56	**16**	10	3. Lay Down Your Arms Top 100 #16 / Juke Box #16 / Best Seller #18 / Jockey #20	Cadence 1299
9/16/57	**8**	8	**4. Just Between You And Me** Jockey #8 / Best Seller #15 / Top 100 #19	Cadence 1330
3/10/58	**2**(2)	12	**5. Lollipop** Best Seller #2 / Top 100 #2 / Jockey #2	Cadence 1345
5/26/58	**17**	7	6. Zorro Top 100 #17 / Best Seller #18 / Jockey #22	Cadence 1349
3/30/59	**27**	4	7. No Other Arms, No Other Lips	Cadence 1361
7/03/61	**13**	8	8. Never On Sunday	Cadence 1402
			CHRISTIAN, Chris	
			Guitarist/songwriter/producer. With trio Cotton, Lloyd & Christian.	
11/14/81	**37**	3	1. I Want You, I Need You	Boardwalk 126
			CHRISTIE	
			English trio: Jeff Christie, Vic Elms and Mike Blakely (brother of Alan Blakely of The Tremeloes).	
10/24/70	**23**	8	1. Yellow River	Epic 10626
			CHRISTIE, Lou	
			Born Lugee Sacco on 2/19/43 in Glen Willard, Pennsylvania. Joined vocal group the Classics; first recorded for Starr in 1960. Started long association with songwriter Twyla Herbert. Recorded as Lugee & The Lions for Robbee in 1961.	
2/16/63	**24**	6	1. The Gypsy Cried	Roulette 4457
4/27/63	**6**	10	**2. Two Faces Have I**	Roulette 4481
1/22/66	**1**(1)	10	● **3. Lightnin' Strikes**	MGM 13412
4/23/66	**16**	4	4. Rhapsody In The Rain	MGM 13473
9/13/69	**10**	9	**5. I'm Gonna Make You Mine**	Buddah 116
			CHRISTOPHER, Gavin	
			Chicago-born soul singer/composer/producer. His sister is singer Shawn Christopher.	
7/12/86	**22**	7	1. One Step Closer To You	Manhattan 50028

DATE	POS	WKS	ARTIST—RECORD TITLE	LABEL & NO.
			CHURCH, Eugene/The Fellows	
			Los Angeles native. Born on 1/23/38. Recorded with Jesse Belvin as The Cliques.	
2/23/59	**36**	2	1. Pretty Girls Everywhere backing vocals by Bobby Day	Class 235
			CHURCH, The	
			Australian folk-rock quartet: Steve Kilbey (vocals), Peter Koppes, Marty Willson-Piper & Richard Ploog.	
5/28/88	**24**	5	1. Under The Milky Way	Arista 9673
			CINDERELLA	
			Pennsylvania-based, heavy-metal band consisting of Tom Keifer (vocals, guitar), Jeff LaBar (guitar), Eric Brittingham (bass) and Fred Coury (drums).	
1/17/87	**13**	8	1. Nobody's Fool	Mercury 884851
10/01/88	**12**	11	2. Don't Know What You Got (Till It's Gone)	Mercury 870644
2/25/89	**36**	2	3. The Last Mile	Mercury 872148
5/20/89	**20**	7	4. Coming Home	Mercury 872982
1/26/91	**36**	2	5. Shelter Me	Mercury 878700
			CITY BOY	
			British rock sextet — Lol Mason, lead singer.	
9/09/78	**27**	6	1. 5.7.0.5.	Mercury 73999
			C.J. & CO.	
			Detroit group assembled by Dennis Coffey. Included Cornelius Brown Jr., Curtis Durden, Joni Tolbert, Connie Durden and Charles Clark.	
7/09/77	**36**	2	1. Devil's Gun	Westbound 55400
			CLANTON, Jimmy	
			Born on 9/02/40 in Baton Rouge, Louisiana. Played in local bands, discovered by Ace Records while making a demo at Cosimo Matassa's studio in New Orleans. Recorded with famous New Orleans sessionmen, including Huey "Piano" Smith, Earl King (guitar) and Lee Allen (tenor sax). Toured with Dick Clark's Caravan of Stars. Starred in film *Go, Johnny, Go!*, 1959. DJ in Lancaster, Pennsylvania from 1972-76.	
7/21/58	**4**	15	**1. Just A Dream** **JIMMY CLANTON AND HIS ROCKETS** Hot 100 #4 / Best Seller #4	Ace 546
11/17/58	**25**	5	2. A Letter To An Angel/	
12/01/58	**38**	2	3. A Part Of Me	Ace 551
8/17/59	**33**	6	4. My Own True Love melody is "Tara's Theme" from *Gone With the Wind*	Ace 567
12/21/59+	**5**	11	**5. Go, Jimmy, Go**	Ace 575
5/30/60	**22**	6	6. Another Sleepless Night	Ace 585
9/01/62	**7**	10	**7. Venus In Blue Jeans** above 2 written by Neil Sedaka	Ace 8001

DATE	POS	WKS	ARTIST—RECORD TITLE	LABEL & NO.
			CLAPTON, Eric	
			Prolific rock-blues guitarist/vocalist. Born on 3/30/45 in Ripley, England. With The Roosters in 1963, The Yardbirds, 1963-65, and John Mayall's Bluesbreakers, 1965-66. Formed Cream with Jack Bruce and Ginger Baker in 1966. Formed Blind Faith in 1968; worked with John Lennon's Plastic Ono Band, and Delaney & Bonnie. Formed Derek and The Dominos in 1970. After two years of reclusion (1971-72), Clapton performed his comeback concert at London's Rainbow Theatre in January 1973. Began actively recording and touring again in 1974. Eric's four-year-old son killed on 3/20/91 in a 53-floor fall in New York City.	
11/14/70	**18**	8	1. After Midnight	Atco 6784
6/17/72	**10**	10	**2. Layla** [R] **DEREK AND THE DOMINOS** originally charted in 1971 (POS 51); 1971 version: 2:43; 1972 version: 7:10	Atco 6809
8/03/74	**1**(1)	10	• **3. I Shot The Sheriff** written by Bob Marley	RSO 409
11/23/74	**26**	5	4. Willie And The Hand Jive	RSO 503
11/13/76	**24**	6	5. Hello Old Friend	RSO 861
2/04/78	**3**	17	• **6. Lay Down Sally**	RSO 886
6/10/78	**16**	7	7. Wonderful Tonight	RSO 895
			ERIC CLAPTON AND HIS BAND:	
11/25/78+	**9**	11	**8. Promises/**	
3/24/79	**40**	2	9. Watch Out For Lucy	RSO 910
7/26/80	**30**	5	10. Tulsa Time/	
		5	11. Cocaine	RSO 1039
3/14/81	**10**	12	**12. I Can't Stand It**	RSO 1060
			ERIC CLAPTON:	
2/19/83	**18**	10	13. I've Got A Rock N' Roll Heart	Duck 29780
3/30/85	**26**	6	14. Forever Man	Duck 29081
			CLARK, Claudine	
			Born on 4/26/41 in Macon, Georgia. Moved to Philadelphia when very young. First recorded for Herald in 1958. Also recorded for Swan as Joy Dawn.	
7/21/62	**5**	10	**1. Party Lights**	Chancellor 1113
			CLARK, Dave, Five	
			Dave formed the rock group in Tottenham, England in 1960. Consisted of Clark (drums), Mike Smith (lead vocals, keyboards), Lenny Davidson (guitar), Dennis Payton (sax) and Rick Huxley (bass). First recorded for Ember/Pye in 1962. On "The Ed Sullivan Show" in March 1964. In the film *Having a Wild Weekend* in 1965. Disbanded in 1973. Clark had been a stuntman in films; formed group to raise money for his soccer team, the Tottenham Hotspurs. Clark wrote the 1986 London stage musical *Time*.	
3/07/64	**6**	11	**1. Glad All Over**	Epic 9656
4/11/64	**4**	10	**2. Bits And Pieces**	Epic 9671
5/09/64	**11**	9	3. Do You Love Me	Epic 9678
6/20/64	**4**	9	**4. Can't You See That She's Mine**	Epic 9692
8/08/64	**3**	9	**5. Because**	Epic 9704
10/17/64	**15**	6	6. Everybody Knows (I Still Love You)	Epic 9722
12/05/64+	**14**	9	7. Any Way You Want It	Epic 9739
2/27/65	**14**	6	8. Come Home	Epic 9763
5/08/65	**23**	5	9. Reelin' And Rockin'	Epic 9786
7/10/65	**7**	8	**10. I Like It Like That**	Epic 9811

DATE	POS	WKS	ARTIST—RECORD TITLE	LABEL & NO.
9/04/65	**4**	9	**11. Catch Us If You Can** from the film *Having a Wild Weekend*	Epic 9833
11/20/65	**1**(1)	11	**12. Over And Over**	Epic 9863
2/19/66	**18**	5	13. At The Scene	Epic 9882
4/23/66	**12**	5	14. Try Too Hard	Epic 10004
7/02/66	**28**	4	15. Please Tell Me Why	Epic 10031
4/15/67	**7**	7	**16. You Got What It Takes**	Epic 10144
7/01/67	**35**	2	17. You Must Have Been A Beautiful Baby	Epic 10179
			CLARK, Dee	
			Born Delecta Clark on 11/07/38 in Blytheville, Arkansas. To Chicago in 1941. In Hambone Kids with Sammy McGrier and Ronny Strong; first recorded for Okeh in 1952. Joined R&B vocal group the Goldentones in 1953. Group became the Kool Gents; billed as The Delegates for Vee-Jay recording in 1956. First solo recording for Falcon in 1957. Died on 12/07/90 of a heart attack.	
1/12/59	**21**	6	1. Nobody But You	Abner 1019
5/25/59	**18**	9	2. Just Keep It Up	Abner 1026
9/14/59	**20**	9	3. Hey Little Girl	Abner 1029
1/04/60	**33**	5	4. How About That	Abner 1032
3/06/61	**34**	4	5. Your Friends	Vee-Jay 372
5/22/61	**2**(1)	12	**6. Raindrops**	Vee-Jay 383
			CLARK, Petula	
			Born on 11/15/32 in Epsom, England. Singer/actress. On radio at age nine; own show "Pet's Parlour" at age 11. TV series in England in 1950. First U.S. record release for Coral in 1951. Appeared in over 20 British films from 1944-57; revived her film career in the late 1960s, starring in *Finian's Rainbow* and *Goodbye Mr. Chips.*	
1/02/65	**1**(2)	13	● **1. Downtown**	Warner 5494
4/03/65	**3**	9	**2. I Know A Place**	Warner 5612
7/31/65	**22**	5	3. You'd Better Come Home	Warner 5643
10/30/65	**21**	4	4. Round Every Corner	Warner 5661
1/15/66	**1**(2)	9	**5. My Love**	Warner 5684
4/02/66	**11**	7	6. A Sign Of The Times	Warner 5802
7/30/66	**9**	7	**7. I Couldn't Live Without Your Love**	Warner 5835
10/29/66	**21**	6	8. Who Am I	Warner 5863
12/31/66+	**16**	7	9. Color My World all of above written and produced by Tony Hatch	Warner 5882
3/18/67	**3**	9	**10. This Is My Song** from the Charlie Chaplin film *A Countess from Hong Kong*	Warner 7002
6/17/67	**5**	7	**11. Don't Sleep In The Subway**	Warner 7049
9/16/67	**26**	4	12. The Cat In The Window (The Bird In The Sky)	Warner 7073
12/30/67	**31**	2	13. The Other Man's Grass Is Always Greener	Warner 7097
3/02/68	**15**	9	14. Kiss Me Goodbye	Warner 7170
8/24/68	**37**	1	15. Don't Give Up	Warner 7216
			CLARK, Roy	
			Born on 4/15/33 in Meherrin, Virginia. Superb guitar, banjo and fiddle player. With the TV series "Hee Haw" from the first show in 1969.	
7/12/69	**19**	6	1. Yesterday, When I Was Young	Dot 17246

DATE	POS	WKS	ARTIST—RECORD TITLE	LABEL & NO.
			CLARK, Sanford	
			Born in 1935 in Tulsa, Oklahoma. Moved to Phoenix in his teens.	
8/11/56	**7**	15	**1. The Fool** Best Seller #7 / Juke Box #7 / Top 100 #9 / Jockey #16 first released on MCI 1003 in 1956 featuring Al Casey, guitar	Dot 15481
			CLARKE, Stanley	
			Born on 6/30/51 in Philadelphia. Bassist/violinist/cellist. With Chick Corea in Return To Forever in 1973. Much session work, solo debut in 1974. Member of Animal Logic in 1989.	
6/13/81	**19**	9	1. Sweet Baby **STANLEY CLARKE/GEORGE DUKE**	Epic 01052
			CLARKE, Tony	
			Soul singer/songwriter. Born in New York City and raised in Detroit. Acted in film *They Call Me Mr. Tibbs*. Died in Detroit in 1970.	
5/08/65	**31**	2	1. The Entertainer	Chess 1924
			CLASH, The	
			Eclectic new-wave rock group formed in London in 1976. Consisted of Joe Strummer (vocals, lyricist), Mick Jones (guitar), Paul Simonon (bass) and Topper Headon (drums). Political activists, they wrote songs protesting racism and oppression. Headon left in May 1983; replaced by Peter Howard. Jones (not to be confused with Mick Jones of Foreigner) left band in 1984 to form Big Audio Dynamite. Strummer disbanded The Clash in early 1986. Strummer appeared in the 1987 film *Straight to Hell*.	
4/26/80	**23**	7	1. Train In Vain (Stand By Me)	Epic 50851
11/13/82+	**8**	15	**2. Rock The Casbah**	Epic 03245
			CLASSICS, The	
			White vocal quartet from Brooklyn, formed in 1958. Consisted of Emil Stucchio (lead), Johnny Gambale, Tony Victor and Jamie Troy.	
7/20/63	**20**	5	1. Till Then #8 pop hit for The Mills Brothers in 1944	Musicnote 1116
			CLASSICS IV	
			Quintet formed in Jacksonville, Florida. Consisted of Dennis Yost (vocals), J.R. Cobb (lead guitar), Wally Eaton (rhythm guitar), Joe Wilson (bass; replaced by Dean Daughtry) and Kim Venable (drums). Cobb, Daughtry and producer Buddy Buie joined the Atlanta Rhythm Section in 1974.	
1/13/68	**3**	12	**1. Spooky**	Imperial 66259
			CLASSICS IV featuring DENNIS YOST:	
11/16/68	**5**	12	● **2. Stormy**	Imperial 66328
2/22/69	**2**(1)	10	**3. Traces**	Imperial 66352
5/31/69	**19**	7	4. Everyday With You Girl	Imperial 66378
			DENNIS YOST AND THE CLASSICS IV:	
12/09/72	**39**	3	5. What Am I Crying For?	MGM South 7002
			CLAY, Judy	
			Real name: Judy Guion. Vocalist from New York City. In backup group with Cissy Houston, Dionne and Dee Dee Warwick, for Don Covay, Wilson Pickett and many others.	
3/23/68	**36**	1	1. Country Girl - City Man **BILLY VERA & JUDY CLAY**	Atlantic 2480

DATE	POS	WKS	ARTIST—RECORD TITLE	LABEL & NO.
			CLAY, Tom	
			Working as a substitute DJ at KGBS-Los Angeles when he created this recording.	
7/24/71	8	7	**1. What The World Needs Now Is Love/Abraham, Martin and John** vocal accompaniment by The Blackberries	[S] Mowest 5002
			CLEFTONES, The	
			Doo-wop group from Queens, New York, formed at Jamaica High School in 1955. Consisted of Herbie Cox (lead), Charlie James (first tenor), Berman Patterson (second tenor), William McClain (baritone) and Warren Corbin (bass). Originally called the Silvertones.	
6/19/61	**18**	4	1. Heart And Soul	Gee 1064
			CLEMONS, Clarence	
			Born on 1/11/42 in Norfolk, Virginia. Saxophonist in Bruce Springsteen's E Street Band, 1973-89.	
11/23/85+	**18**	12	1. You're A Friend Of Mine **CLARENCE CLEMONS AND JACKSON BROWNE** includes vocals by actress Daryl Hannah (Browne's then-girlfriend)	Columbia 05660
			CLIFF, Jimmy	
			Born James Chambers in 1948. Jamaican reggae singer/composer. Starred in films *The Harder They Come* (1975) and *Club Paradise* (1986).	
12/27/69+	**25**	7	1. Wonderful World, Beautiful People	A&M 1146
			CLIFFORD, Buzz	
			Born Reese Francis Clifford III on 10/08/42 in Berwyn, Illinois.	
1/30/61	6	10	**1. Baby Sittin' Boogie** [N] babies' voices are by the children (boy & girl) of the producer	Columbia 41876
			CLIFFORD, Mike	
			Born on 11/06/43 in Los Angeles. In the 1970s Broadway production of *Grease*.	
10/13/62	**12**	8	1. Close To Cathy	United Art. 489
			CLIMAX	
			Los Angeles-based quintet — Sonny Geraci, lead singer (formerly with The Outsiders).	
1/22/72	3	12	● **1. Precious And Few** originally released on Carousel 30055	Rocky Road 30055
			CLIMAX BLUES BAND	
			Blues-rock band formed in Stafford, England. Nucleus consisted of Colin Cooper (sax, vocals), Peter Haycock (guitar, vocals), Derek Holt (bass) and John Cuffley (drums).	
3/26/77	3	14	**1. Couldn't Get It Right**	Sire 736
4/04/81	**12**	17	2. I Love You	Warner 49669
			CLIMIE FISHER	
			U.K.-based duo: Simon Climie (vocals) and Rob Fisher (keyboards). Fisher was a member of Naked Eyes. Chrysalis songwriter Climie wrote Pat Benatar's "Invincible" and "I Knew You Were Waiting (For Me)" by Aretha Franklin and George Michael.	
7/02/88	**23**	6	1. Love Changes (Everything)	Capitol 44137

DATE	POS	WKS	ARTIST—RECORD TITLE	LABEL & NO.
			CLINE, Patsy	
			Born Virginia Patterson Hensley on 9/08/32 in Winchester, Virginia. Killed in a plane crash with Cowboy Copas and Hawkshaw Hawkins on 3/05/63 near Camden, Tennesee. Elected to the Country Music Hall of Fame in 1973. Jessica Lange played Patsy in the 1985 biographical film *Sweet Dreams*.	
3/02/57	**12**	11	1. Walkin' After Midnight Juke Box #12 / Top 100 #17 / Best Seller #21 / Jockey #22	Decca 30221
7/24/61	**12**	10	2. I Fall To Pieces	Decca 31205
11/06/61	**9**	7	**3. Crazy** written by Willie Nelson	Decca 31317
2/24/62	**14**	8	4. She's Got You	Decca 31354
			CLIQUE, The	
			Pop-rock quintet from Texas.	
9/27/69	**22**	7	1. Sugar On Sunday written by Tommy James	White Whale 323
			CLOONEY, Rosemary	
			Born on 5/23/28 in Maysville, Kentucky. One of the most popular singers of the 1950s, Rosemary and sister Betty sang with the Tony Pastor band in the late '40s before her solo career was launched. Rosemary was featured in *White Christmas* and several other '50s movies. After a period of personal difficulties, she re-emerged in the late '70s as a successful jazz and ballad singer. Married for a time to actor Jose Ferrer; their son Gabriel married Debby Boone.	
3/17/56	**20**	1	1. Memories Of You **THE BENNY GOODMAN TRIO with ROSEMARY CLOONEY** Juke Box #20 / Top 100 #52 from the film *The Benny Goodman Story*	Columbia 40616
4/13/57	**10**	9	**2. Mangos** Jockey #10 / Best Seller #23 / Top 100 #25	Columbia 40835
			CLOVERS, The	
			R&B group from Washington, D.C. By 1949, personnel lineup included John "Buddy" Bailey (lead), Matthew McQuater, Harold Lucas, Harold Winely and Bill Harris. Bailey entered the Army in 1952, replaced by Billy Mitchell. Upon Bailey's return, Mitchell stayed in the group. Group had 13 consecutive top 10 R&B hits from 1951-54. Harris died of pancreatic cancer on 12/10/88 (age 63). A Clovers unit with Lucas is still performing.	
7/28/56	**30**	3	1. Love, Love, Love	Atlantic 1094
11/02/59	**23**	5	2. Love Potion No. 9	United Art. 180
			CLUB NOUVEAU	
			Sacramento-based, dance-disco group formed and fronted by Jay King (producer/owner of King Jay Records; produced the Timex Social Club). Early lineup: vocalists Valerie Watson and Samuelle Prater with Denzil Foster and Thomas McElroy. Prater, Foster and McElroy left in 1988, replaced by David Agent and Kevin Irving. Agent left in 1989.	
2/21/87	**1**(2)	12	● **1. Lean On Me** King Jay/Warner 7" sold 600,000 units; Tommy Boy 12" sold 400,000	Warner 28430
7/18/87	**39**	1	2. Why You Treat Me So Bad	Warner 28360

DATE	POS	WKS	ARTIST—RECORD TITLE	LABEL & NO.
			COASTERS, The	
			R&B group formed in Los Angeles in late 1955 from elements of the Robins. Originally consisted of Carl Gardner (ex-Robins; lead), Leon Hughes (tenor), Billy Guy (baritone lead), Bobby Nunn (ex-Robins; bass) and Adolph Jacobs (guitar). Noted for serio-comic recordings, primarily of Leiber & Stoller songs. Cornelius Gunter (early member of The Flairs, brother of Shirley Gunter) joined in 1957, left in 1961. Will "Dub" Jones (ex-Cadets) replaced Nunn in late 1958 and is heard on "Charlie Brown" and "Along Came Jones." Earl "Speedoo" Carroll (ex-Cadillacs) joined group in 1961. Bobby Nunn died of a heart attack on 11/05/86 (age 61). Gunter was shot to death on 2/26/90 (age 51). Today there are two or three "Coasters" groups still working, some of which contain one or two original members. Inducted into the Rock and Roll Hall of Fame in 1987.	
5/20/57	**3**	22	**1. Searchin'/** Best Seller #3 / Top 100 #5 / Jockey #6 / Juke Box #10 end	
5/20/57	**8**	11	**2. Young Blood** Top 100 #8 / Jockey #10 / Juke Box #12 / Best Seller #14	Atco 6087
6/09/58	**1**(1)	15	**3. Yakety Yak** Top 100 #1 / Best Seller #2 / Jockey #2	Atco 6116
2/09/59	**2**(3)	12	**4. Charlie Brown** [N]	Atco 6132
6/01/59	**9**	8	**5. Along Came Jones** [N]	Atco 6141
9/07/59	**7**	11	**6. Poison Ivy/**	
9/21/59	**38**	1	7. I'm A Hog For You	Atco 6146
1/25/60	**36**	1	8. Run Red Run	Atco 6153
2/27/61	**37**	2	9. Wait A Minute written by Bobby Darin	Atco 6186
5/29/61	**23**	6	10. Little Egypt (Ying-Yang) [N] all of above (except #9) written by Leiber and Stoller	Atco 6192
			COATES, Odia — see ANKA, Paul	
			COCHRAN, Eddie	
			Influential rock and roll singer/guitarist. Born Edward Ray Cochrane on 10/03/38 in Oklahoma City, Oklahoma and raised in Albert Lea, Minnesota. Moved to Bell Gardens, California in 1953. Teamed with Hank Cochran (no relation) as the Cochran Brothers; first recorded as country act for Ekko Records in 1954. Appeared in films *The Girl Can't Help It, Untamed Youth* and *Go, Johnny, Go!*. Killed in a car accident in Chippenham, Wiltshire, England on 4/17/60. Accident also injured Gene Vincent. Inducted into the Rock and Roll Hall of Fame in 1987.	
3/30/57	**18**	8	1. Sittin' In The Balcony Top 100 #18 / Jockey #18 / Juke Box #20 / Best Seller #22	Liberty 55056
8/25/58	**8**	12	**2. Summertime Blues** Hot 100 #8 / Best Seller #13 end	Liberty 55144
1/05/59	**35**	1	3. C'mon Everybody	Liberty 55166
			COCKBURN, Bruce	
			Cockburn (pronounced: Co-burn) was born on 5/27/45 in Canada. Singer/songwriter.	
5/03/80	**21**	9	1. Wondering Where The Lions Are	Millennium 11786
			COCKER, Joe	
			Born John Robert Cocker on 5/20/44 in Sheffield, England. Own skiffle band, the Cavaliers, late 1950s, later reorganized as Vance Arnold & The Avengers. Assembled the Grease Band in the mid-1960s. Performed at Woodstock in 1969. Successful tour with 43-piece revue, Mad Dogs & Englishmen, in 1970. Notable spastic stage antics were based on Ray Charles' movements at the piano.	
1/10/70	**30**	7	1. She Came In Through The Bathroom Window	A&M 1147

DATE	POS	WKS	ARTIST—RECORD TITLE	LABEL & NO.
			written by John Lennon and Paul McCartney	
5/09/70	**7**	9	**2. The Letter**	A&M 1174
			with Leon Russell & The Shelter People	
10/24/70	**11**	7	3. Cry Me A River	A&M 1200
			recorded live at Fillmore East, New York on 3/27/70	
6/19/71	**22**	6	4. High Time We Went	A&M 1258
1/29/72	**33**	5	5. Feeling Alright [R]	A&M 1063
			originally charted in 1969 (POS 69)	
10/07/72	**27**	5	6. Midnight Rider	A&M 1370
			JOE COCKER AND THE CHRIS STAINTON BAND	
2/15/75	**5**	10	**7. You Are So Beautiful**	A&M 1641
			co-written by Billy Preston	
10/02/82	**1**(3)	15	▲ **8. Up Where We Belong**	Island 99996
			JOE COCKER AND JENNIFER WARNES	
			love theme from the film *An Officer and a Gentleman*	
12/02/89+	**11**	11	9. When The Night Comes	Capitol 44437#
			COCK ROBIN	
			Los Angeles pop quartet — Peter Kingsbery and Anna LaCazio, vocals.	
8/17/85	**35**	3	1. When Your Heart Is Weak	Columbia 04875
			COFFEY, Dennis/The Detroit Guitar Band	
			Detroit native Coffey was a session guitarist for The Temptations, The Jackson 5 and others. Coffey later formed C.J. & Co.	
11/13/71+	**6**	15	● **1. Scorpio** [I]	Sussex 226
3/11/72	**18**	8	2. Taurus [I]	Sussex 233
			COHN, Marc	
			Cleveland-born singer/songwriter. Formed a 14-piece band in New York, the Supreme Court, which was discovered by Carly Simon and played at Caroline Kennedy's wedding.	
5/25/91	**13**	10	1. Walking In Memphis	Atlantic 87747#
			COLE, Cozy	
			Born William Randolph Cole on 10/17/09 in East Orange, New Jersey; died of cancer on 1/29/81. Lead drummer for many swing bands, including Benny Carter, Willie Bryant, Cab Calloway and Louis Armstrong.	
9/29/58	**3**	14	**1. Topsy II/** [I]	
			Hot 100 #3 / Best Seller #10 end	
10/27/58	**27**	3	2. Topsy I [I]	Love 5004
			Hot 100 #27 / Best Seller #45	
12/28/58	**36**	1	3. Turvy II [I]	Love 5014
			COLE, Jude	
			Native of East Moline, Illinois. Male guitarist/vocalist of Moon Martin's band. Touring guitarist with Billy Thorpe, Del Shannon and Dwight Twilley.	
5/05/90	**16**	10	1. Baby, It's Tonight	Reprise 19869
9/22/90	**32**	4	2. Time For Letting Go	Reprise 19743
			COLE, Natalie	
			Born on 2/06/50 in Los Angeles. Daughter of Nat "King" Cole. Professional debut at age 11. Married for a time to her producer, Marvin Yancey, Jr. Later married Andre Fischer, former drummer of Rufus and producer for Brenda Russell, Michael Franks and Andrea Crouch. Natalie won the 1975 Best New Artist Grammy Award. Hosted own syndicated variety TV show "Big Break" in 1990.	
10/04/75	**6**	11	**1. This Will Be**	Capitol 4109

DATE	POS	WKS	ARTIST—RECORD TITLE	LABEL & NO.
2/28/76	**32**	5	2. Inseparable	Capitol 4193
6/26/76	**25**	7	3. Sophisticated Lady (She's A Different Lady)	Capitol 4259
2/26/77	**5**	14	● **4. I've Got Love On My Mind**	Capitol 4360
2/11/78	**10**	15	● **5. Our Love**	Capitol 4509
8/09/80	**21**	9	6. Someone That I Used To Love	Capitol 4869
8/22/87	**13**	10	7. Jump Start	Manhattan 50073
12/19/87+	**13**	11	8. I Live For Your Love	Manhattan 50094
3/19/88	**5**	12	**9. Pink Cadillac** written and recorded by Bruce Springsteen in 1984 (B-side of his pop hit "Dancing In The Dark")	EMI-Man. 50117
5/13/89	**7**	13	**10. Miss You Like Crazy**	EMI 50185
3/31/90	**34**	3	11. Wild Women Do from the film *Pretty Woman*	EMI 50275#
7/27/91	**14**	10	● 12. Unforgettable **NATALIE COLE with NAT "KING" COLE** Nat King Cole's vocals dubbed in from his original 1951 hit	Elektra 64875

COLE, Nat "King"

Born Nathaniel Adams Coles on 3/17/17 in Montgomery, Alabama and raised in Chicago. Died of lung cancer on 2/15/65 in Santa Monica, California. Own band, the Royal Dukes, at age 17. First recorded in 1936 in band led by brother Eddie. Toured with "Shuffle Along" musical revue, resided in Los Angeles. Formed King Cole Trio in 1939: Nat (piano), Oscar Moore (guitar; later joined brother's group, Johnny Moore's Three Blazers) and Wesley Prince (bass; replaced several years later by Johnny Miller). Long series of top-selling records led to his solo career in 1950. In films *St. Louis Blues*, *Cat Ballou*, and many other film and TV appearances. Stopped performing in 1964 due to ill health. Daughter Natalie is also a recording star. Won Lifetime Achievement Grammy in 1990.

DATE	POS	WKS	ARTIST—RECORD TITLE	LABEL & NO.
3/05/55	**7**	16	**1. Darling Je Vous Aime Beaucoup/** Jockey #7 / Best Seller #10 / Juke Box #14	
3/05/55	**23**	13	2. The Sand And The Sea Best Seller #23	Capitol 3027
5/07/55	**2**(1)	20	**3. A Blossom Fell/** Best Seller #2 / Juke Box #2 / Jockey #3	
5/21/55	**8**	10	**4. If I May** **NAT "KING" COLE AND THE FOUR KNIGHTS** Jockey #8	Capitol 3095
7/16/55	**24**	2	5. My One Sin Best Seller #24	Capitol 3136
10/22/55	**13**	8	6. Forgive My Heart/ Best Seller #13 / Top 100 #21	
10/22/55	**13**	8	7. Someone You Love Best Seller #13 / Jockey #19 / Top 100 #21	Capitol 3234
3/03/56	**18**	3	8. Ask Me Jockey #18 / Top 100 #25	Capitol 3328
4/21/56	**21**	6	9. Too Young To Go Steady Jockey #21 / Top 100 #31 from the musical *Strip for Action*	Capitol 3390
7/21/56	**16**	12	10. That's All There Is To That **NAT "KING" COLE AND THE FOUR KNIGHTS** Juke Box #16 / Best Seller #17 / Top 100 #18 / Jockey #18	Capitol 3456
11/03/56	**11**	10	11. Night Lights/ Jockey #11 / Top 100 #16 / Best Seller #17	
11/10/56	**25**	2	12. To The Ends Of The Earth	Capitol 3551

DATE	POS	WKS	ARTIST—RECORD TITLE	LABEL & NO.
			Best Seller #25 / Jockey #25 / Top 100 #39	
2/23/57	**18**	5	13. Ballerina Jockey #18 / Top 100 #36 orchestra on all of above conducted by Nelson Riddle	Capitol 3619
7/01/57	**6**	18	**14. Send For Me/** Best Seller #6 / Top 100 #7 / Jockey #9	
8/05/57	**21**	1	15. My Personal Possession **NAT "KING" COLE AND THE FOUR KNIGHTS** Jockey #21 / Top 100 #63	Capitol 3737
10/21/57	**30**	4	16. With You On My Mind Best Seller #30 / Top 100 #33	Capitol 3782
2/24/58	**33**	3	17. Angel Smile Best Seller #33 / Top 100 #35	Capitol 3860
4/14/58	**5**	16	**18. Looking Back** Best Seller #5 / Top 100 #5 / Jockey #9	Capitol 3939
7/28/58	**38**	2	19. Come Closer To Me Best Seller #38 / Top 100 #41	Capitol 4004
2/15/60	**30**	3	20. Time And The River	Capitol 4325
8/18/62	**2**(2)	13	**21. Ramblin' Rose**	Capitol 4804
12/01/62	**13**	8	22. Dear Lonely Hearts	Capitol 4870
5/25/63	**6**	9	**23. Those Lazy-Hazy-Crazy Days Of Summer**	Capitol 4965
9/28/63	**12**	9	24. That Sunday, That Summer	Capitol 5027
5/16/64	**22**	6	25. I Don't Want To Be Hurt Anymore	Capitol 5155
10/24/64	**34**	4	26. I Don't Want To See Tomorrow	Capitol 5261
			COLLINS, Dave And Ansil	
			Jamaican duo. By 1983, known as Clint Eastwood & General Saint.	
7/03/71	**22**	8	1. Double Barrel	Big Tree 115
			COLLINS, Dorothy	
			Born Marjorie Chandler on 11/18/26 in Windsor, Ontario. Star of TV's "Your Hit Parade." Married orchestra leader Raymond Scott.	
12/03/55	**16**	2	1. My Boy-Flat Top Juke Box #16 / Top 100 #22	Coral 61510
2/11/56	**17**	2	2. Seven Days Juke Box #17 / Top 100 #25	Coral 61562
			COLLINS, Judy	
			Contemporary folk singer/songwriter. Born on 5/01/39 in Seattle and raised in Denver.	
11/23/68	**8**	9	**1. Both Sides Now** written by Joni Mitchell	Elektra 45639
1/09/71	**15**	11	2. Amazing Grace recorded at St. Paul's Chapel, Columbia University; song attributed to hymn writer Rev. John Newton, 1779	Elektra 45709
3/17/73	**32**	5	3. Cook With Honey	Elektra 45831
7/26/75	**36**	3	4. Send In The Clowns from the Broadway musical *A Little Night Music*	Elektra 45253
10/15/77	**19**	8	5. Send In The Clowns [R]	Elektra 45253

DATE	POS	WKS	ARTIST—RECORD TITLE	LABEL & NO.
			COLLINS, Phil	
			Born on 1/30/51 in London. Stage actor as a young child; played the Artful Dodger in the London production of *Oliver.* With group Flaming Youth in 1969. Joined Genesis as their drummer in 1970, became lead singer in 1975. Also with jazz-rock group Brand X. First solo album in 1981. Starred in the 1988 film *Buster.*	
4/11/81	**19**	9	1. I Missed Again	Atlantic 3790
7/11/81	**19**	8	2. In The Air Tonight "Bubbled Under" in 1984 due to play on TV's "Miami Vice"	Atlantic 3824
11/27/82+	**10**	16	**3. You Can't Hurry Love**	Atlantic 89933
3/26/83	**39**	3	4. I Don't Care Anymore	Atlantic 89877
3/10/84	**1**(3)	16	● **5. Against All Odds (Take A Look At Me Now)** title song from the film *Against All Odds*	Atlantic 89700
12/08/84+	**2**(2)	16	● **6. Easy Lover** **PHILIP BAILEY with PHIL COLLINS**	Columbia 04679
2/23/85	**1**(2)	12	● **7. One More Night**	Atlantic 89588
5/11/85	**1**(1)	14	● **8. Sussudio**	Atlantic 89560
7/27/85	**4**	13	**9. Don't Lose My Number**	Atlantic 89536
10/12/85	**1**(1)	16	**10. Separate Lives** **PHIL COLLINS AND MARILYN MARTIN** love theme from the film *White Nights*	Atlantic 89498
3/29/86	**7**	11	**11. Take Me Home**	Atlantic 89472
9/17/88	**1**(2)	13	● **12. Groovy Kind Of Love**	Atlantic 89017
11/26/88+	**1**(2)	13	**13. Two Hearts** above 2 from the film *Buster*	Atlantic 88980
11/11/89	**1**(4)	14	● **14. Another Day In Paradise** backing vocal by David Crosby	Atlantic 88774
2/17/90	**3**	11	**15. I Wish It Would Rain Down**	Atlantic 88738
5/05/90	**4**	13	**16. Do You Remember?**	Atlantic 87955
8/18/90	**4**	12	**17. Something Happened On The Way To Heaven**	Atlantic 87885
12/08/90+	**23**	7	18. Hang In Long Enough	Atlantic 87800
			COLLINS, Tyler	
			Female singer born in Harlem and raised in Detroit.	
6/02/90	**6**	13	**1. Girls Nite Out**	RCA 2630
			COLOR ME BADD	
			New York City-based dance vocal quartet of 21-year-olds: Bryan Abrams, Sam Watters, Mark Calderon and Kevin Thornton. Formed while in high school in Oklahoma City.	
4/27/91	**2**(4)	16	▲ **1. I Wanna Sex You Up**	Giant 19382
			COLTER, Jessi	
			Born Miriam Johnson on 5/25/47 in Phoenix. Country singer/songwriter. Married to Duane Eddy from 1962-68. Married Waylon Jennings in October 1969.	
4/26/75	**4**	14	**1. I'm Not Lisa**	Capitol 4009
			COLTRANE, Chi	
			Born on 11/16/48 in Racine, Wisconsin. Female vocalist/pianist. Chi pronounced: shy.	
9/30/72	**17**	9	1. Thunder And Lightning	Columbia 45640

DATE	POS	WKS	ARTIST—RECORD TITLE	LABEL & NO.
			COMMANDER CODY AND HIS LOST PLANET AIRMEN	
			Group formed while Cody (George Frayne) attended the University of Michigan. To San Francisco in 1968.	
4/15/72	**9**	11	**1. Hot Rod Lincoln** [N]	Paramount 0146
			COMMODORES	
			Formed in Tuskegee, Alabama in 1970. Consisted of Lionel Richie (vocals, saxophone), William King (trumpet), Thomas McClary (guitar), Milan Williams (keyboards), Ronald LaPread (bass) and Walter "Clyde" Orange (drums). First recorded for Motown in 1972. In film *Thank God It's Friday*. Richie began solo work in 1981, left in 1982.	
7/06/74	**22**	6	1. Machine Gun [I]	Motown 1307
6/28/75	**19**	7	2. Slippery When Wet	Motown 1338
2/14/76	**5**	14	**3. Sweet Love**	Motown 1381
10/09/76	**7**	11	**4. Just To Be Close To You**	Motown 1402
2/19/77	**39**	1	5. Fancy Dancer	Motown 1408
6/25/77	**4**	13	**6. Easy**	Motown 1418
9/17/77	**5**	11	**7. Brick House**	Motown 1425
1/14/78	**24**	7	8. Too Hot Ta Trot	Motown 1432
7/08/78	**1**(2)	16	**9. Three Times A Lady**	Motown 1443
11/04/78	**38**	2	10. Flying High	Motown 1452
8/18/79	**4**	12	**11. Sail On**	Motown 1466
10/13/79	**1**(1)	15	**12. Still**	Motown 1474
1/26/80	**25**	6	13. Wonderland	Motown 1479
7/12/80	**20**	11	14. Old-Fashion Love	Motown 1489
7/11/81	**8**	15	**15. Lady (You Bring Me Up)**	Motown 1514
10/10/81	**4**	15	**16. Oh No** Lionel Richie's last song as lead singer	Motown 1527
3/02/85	**3**	13	**17. Nightshift** a tribute to Marvin Gaye and Jackie Wilson	Motown 1773
			COMMUNARDS	
			British duo consisting of Bronski Beat vocalist Jimmy Somerville & multi-instrumentalist Richard Coles.	
3/07/87	**40**	1	1. Don't Leave Me This Way backing vocal by Sara Jane Morris	MCA 52928
			COMO, Perry	
			Born Pierino Como on 5/18/12 in Canonsburg, Pennsylvania. Owned barbershop in hometown. With Freddy Carlone band in 1933; with Ted Weems, 1936-1942. In the films *Something for the Boys*, *Doll Face*, *If I'm Lucky* and *Words and Music*, 1944-48. Own "Supper Club" radio series to late 1940s. Television shows (15 minutes) from 1948-55. Host of hourly TV shows from 1955-63. Winner of five Emmys.	
2/05/55	**2**(3)	14	**1. Ko Ko Mo (I Love You So)** Jockey #2 / Best Seller #4 / Juke Box #5	RCA 5994
			PERRY COMO AND JAYE P. MORGAN:	
6/11/55	**12**	5	2. Chee Chee-Oo-Chee (Sang the Little Bird) / Jockey #12 / Juke Box #14 / Best Seller #24	
6/25/55	**18**	1	3. Two Lost Souls Jockey #18; from the Broadway musical *Damn Yankees*	RCA 6137

DATE	POS	WKS	ARTIST—RECORD TITLE	LABEL & NO.
			PERRY COMO:	
8/13/55	**5**	14	**4. Tina Marie/** Jockey #5 / Best Seller #6 / Juke Box #8 / Top 100 #12 pre	
8/20/55	**20**	1	5. Fooled Jockey #20	RCA 6192
11/19/55+	**11**	11	6. All At Once You Love Her Jockey #11 / Top 100 #24 from the Broadway musical *Pipe Dream*	RCA 6294
3/10/56	**1**(1)	20	**7. Hot Diggity (Dog Ziggity Boom)/** Jockey #1 / Best Seller #2 / Top 100 #2 / Juke Box #2	
3/10/56	**10**	10	**8. Juke Box Baby** Top 100 #10 / Jockey #11	RCA 6427
6/16/56	**4**	14	**9. More/** Best Seller #4 / Juke Box #6 / Jockey #8 / Top 100 #9	
6/23/56	**8**	12	**10. Glendora** Jockey #8 / Top 100 #14	RCA 6554
8/25/56	**18**	3	11. Somebody Up There Likes Me Juke Box #18 / Jockey #22 / Top 100 #26 from the film of the same title	RCA 6590
3/02/57	**1**(2)	19	**12. Round And Round** Jockey #1(2) / Best Seller #1(1) / Top 100 #1(1) / Juke Box #3	RCA 6815
5/27/57	**13**	7	13. The Girl With The Golden Braids Jockey #13 / Top 100 #15 / Best Seller #26	RCA 6904
10/14/57	**12**	14	14. Just Born (To Be Your Baby)/ Best Seller #12 / Jockey #13 / Top 100 #19	
10/21/57	**18**	8	15. Ivy Rose Jockey #18 / Top 100 #32	RCA 7050
1/13/58	**1**(1)	16	● **16. Catch A Falling Star/** Jockey #1 / Best Seller #3 / Top 100 #9	
1/20/58	**4**	12	**17. Magic Moments** Jockey #4 / Top 100 #27 / Best Seller #42	RCA 7128
4/21/58	**6**	11	**18. Kewpie Doll/** Jockey #6 / Best Seller #12 / Top 100 #12	
5/05/58	**19**	1	19. Dance Only With Me Jockey #19 from the Broadway musical *Say Darling*	RCA 7202
8/04/58	**28**	6	20. Moon Talk Best Seller #28 / Hot 100 #29	RCA 7274
11/17/58	**33**	2	21. Love Makes The World Go 'Round	RCA 7353
3/23/59	**29**	3	22. Tomboy	RCA 7464
2/22/60	**22**	6	23. Delaware [N]	RCA 7670
4/28/62	**23**	6	24. Caterina	RCA 8004
7/20/63	**39**	1	25. (I Love You) Don't You Forget It orchestra on all of above conducted by Mitchell Ayres; backing vocals by The Ray Charles Singers on most all of above	RCA 8186
5/01/65	**25**	6	26. Dream On Little Dreamer backing vocals by The Anita Kerr Quartet	RCA 8533
5/31/69	**38**	1	27. Seattle from the TV series "Here Come the Brides"	RCA 9722
12/05/70+	**10**	13	**28. It's Impossible**	RCA 0387
5/19/73	**29**	8	29. And I Love You So written by Don McLean	RCA 0906

DATE	POS	WKS	ARTIST—RECORD TITLE	LABEL & NO.
			COMPANY B	
			Miami-based, dance-disco trio founded and produced by Foxy leader Ish Ledesma. Consisted of Lori L, Lezlee Livrano and Susan Johnson.	
5/09/87	**21**	8	1. Fascinated	Atlantic 89294
			CONCRETE BLONDE	
			Los Angeles alternative rock group formed in 1982 by female lead singer Johnette Napolitano and bassist James Mankey. Originally known as Dream 6, renamed by Michael Stipe of R.E.M. Other members included Harry Rushakoff, Alan Block (1989) and Paul Thompson (1990).	
10/06/90	**19**	8	1. Joey	I.R.S. 73014#
			CON FUNK SHUN	
			Soul band formed as Project Soul in Vallejo, California in 1968 by high school classmates Mike Cooper (lead vocals, guitar) and Louis McCall (drums). Moved to Memphis in 1972, changed name to Con Funk Shun.	
1/21/78	**23**	6	1. Ffun	Mercury 73959
2/28/81	**40**	1	2. Too Tight	Mercury 76089
			CONLEY, Arthur	
			Soul singer, born on 1/04/46 in Atlanta. Discovered by Otis Redding in 1965. First recorded for NRC as Arthur & The Corvets.	
4/01/67	**2**(1)	11	● **1. Sweet Soul Music** originally written by Sam Cooke as "Yeah Man"	Atco 6463
7/01/67	**31**	3	2. Shake, Rattle & Roll	Atco 6494
4/06/68	**14**	9	3. Funky Street	Atco 6563
			CONNIFF, Ray	
			Born on 11/06/16 in Attleboro, Massachusetts. Trombonist/arranger with Bunny Berigan, Bob Crosby, Harry James, Vaughn Monroe and Artie Shaw bands. Long string of hit albums beginning in 1957.	
7/09/66	**9**	9	**1. Somewhere, My Love** **RAY CONNIFF AND THE SINGERS** Lara's Theme from the film *Dr. Zhivago*	Columbia 43626
			CONNOR, Chris	
			Born on 11/08/27 in Kansas City, Missouri. Female jazz-styled singer; with Stan Kenton from 1952-53.	
2/16/57	**34**	3	1. I Miss You So	Atlantic 1105
			CONNORS, Norman	
			Born on 3/01/48 in Philadelphia. Jazz drummer with Archie Shepp, John Coltrane, Pharoah Sanders and others. Own group on Buddah in 1972.	
10/02/76	**27**	10	1. You Are My Starship vocal by Michael Henderson	Buddah 542
			CONTI, Bill	
			Born on 4/13/42 in Providence, Rhode Island. Composer/conductor for the first three *Rocky* films.	
5/07/77	**1**(1)	13	● **1. Gonna Fly Now** [I] theme from the film *Rocky*	United Art. 940
			CONTOURS, The	
			R&B vocal group formed in Detroit: Billy Gordon, Billy Hoggs, Joe Billingslea, Sylvester Potts, Huey Davis (guitar) and Hubert Johnson (d: 7/11/81). Dennis Edwards, a member in 1967, joined The Temptations in 1968. Gordon was married to Georgeanna Tillman of The Marvelettes. Johnson was the cousin of Jackie Wilson.	
9/22/62	**3**	11	**1. Do You Love Me**	Gordy 7005

DATE	POS	WKS	ARTIST—RECORD TITLE	LABEL & NO.
7/02/88	**11**	8	2. Do You Love Me [R] featured in the film *Dirty Dancing*	Motown Yest. 448
			COOKE, Sam	
			Born on 1/02/31 in Clarksdale, Mississippi and raised in Chicago. Died from a gunshot wound on 12/11/64 in Los Angeles. Son of a Baptist minister. Sang in choir from age six. Joined the gospel group, the Highway Q.C.'s. Lead singer of the Soul Stirrers from 1950-56. First recorded secular songs in 1956 as "Dale Cook" on Specialty. String of hits on Keen label led to contract with RCA. Nephew is singer R.B. Greaves. Shot by female motel manager under mysterious circumstances. Inducted into the Rock and Roll Hall of Fame in 1986. Revered as the definitive soul singer.	
10/28/57	**1**(3)	17	**1. You Send Me** Top 100 #1(3) / Best Seller #1(2) / Jockey #1(1) written by Sam's brother, Charles "L.C." Cooke	Keen 34013
12/23/57+	**18**	10	2. I'll Come Running Back To You Best Seller #18 / Top 100 #22	Specialty 619
1/06/58	**17**	7	3. (I Love You) For Sentimental Reasons Best Seller #17 / Top #43	Keen 4002
3/24/58	**26**	5	4. Lonely Island/ Best Seller #26 / Top 100 #39	
3/24/58	**27**	5	5. You Were Made For Me Best Seller #27 / Top 100 #39	Keen 4009
9/08/58	**22**	6	6. Win Your Love For Me Best Seller #22 / Hot 100 #33	Keen 2006
12/15/58	**26**	7	7. Love You Most Of All	Keen 2008
3/30/59	**31**	5	8. Everybody Likes To Cha Cha Cha	Keen 2018
7/06/59	**28**	4	9. Only Sixteen	Keen 2022
5/23/60	**12**	11	10. Wonderful World	Keen 2112
8/29/60	**2**(2)	13	**11. Chain Gang**	RCA 7783
12/19/60	**29**	4	12. Sad Mood	RCA 7816
3/20/61	**31**	4	13. That's It-I Quit-I'm Movin' On	RCA 7853
6/26/61	**17**	9	14. Cupid	RCA 7883
2/17/62	**9**	13	**15. Twistin' The Night Away**	RCA 7983
6/16/62	**17**	9	16. Having A Party/	
8/04/62	**13**	5	17. Bring It On Home To Me backing vocal by Lou Rawls	RCA 8036
10/20/62	**12**	8	18. Nothing Can Change This Love	RCA 8088
2/02/63	**13**	8	19. Send Me Some Lovin'	RCA 8129
5/04/63	**10**	9	**20. Another Saturday Night**	RCA 8164
8/17/63	**14**	7	21. Frankie And Johnny	RCA 8215
11/09/63	**11**	8	22. Little Red Rooster	RCA 8247
2/15/64	**11**	7	23. Good News	RCA 8299
6/27/64	**11**	7	24. Good Times/	
7/04/64	**35**	4	25. Tennessee Waltz Hugo & Luigi produced all of above RCA recordings	RCA 8368
10/24/64	**31**	4	26. Cousin Of Mine	RCA 8426
1/16/65	**7**	9	**27. Shake/**	
2/13/65	**31**	4	28. A Change Is Gonna Come	RCA 8486
8/28/65	**32**	3	29. Sugar Dumpling	RCA 8631

DATE	POS	WKS	ARTIST—RECORD TITLE	LABEL & NO.
			COOKIES, The	
			R&B vocal trio from New York with varying membership. Backup work for Neil Sedaka, Carole King, and Little Eva. One member, Ethel "Earl-Jean" McCrea, later went solo. The 1950s lineup of The Cookies became Ray Charles' vocal backing trio, The Raeletts.	
12/01/62	**17**	8	1. Chains	Dimension 1002
3/23/63	**7**	9	**2. Don't Say Nothin' Bad (About My Baby)**	Dimension 1008
1/18/64	**33**	4	3. Girls Grow Up Faster Than Boys	Dimension 1020
			COOLEY, Eddie/The Dimples	
			Eddie, a New York songwriter, wrote "Fever" (hit for Little Willie John, Peggy Lee and The McCoys). The Dimples were a female trio.	
11/24/56	**20**	8	1. Priscilla Best Seller #20 / Juke Box #20 / Top 100 #26	Royal Roost 621
			COOLIDGE, Rita	
			Born on 5/01/44 in Nashville. Had own group, R.C. and the Moonpies, at Florida State University. Moved to Los Angeles in the late '60s. Did backup work for Delaney & Bonnie, Leon Russell, Joe Cocker and Eric Clapton. With Kris Kristofferson from 1971, married to him from 1973-80. Known as "The Delta Lady," for whom Leon Russell wrote the song of the same name.	
6/11/77	**2**(1)	17	● **1. (Your Love Has Lifted Me) Higher And Higher**	A&M 1922
10/15/77	**7**	13	● **2. We're All Alone** written by Boz Scaggs	A&M 1965
2/04/78	**20**	7	3. The Way You Do The Things You Do	A&M 2004
7/29/78	**25**	6	4. You	A&M 2058
1/05/80	**38**	2	5. I'd Rather Leave While I'm In Love	A&M 2199
8/06/83	**36**	4	6. All Time High from the James Bond film *Octopussy*	A&M 2551
			COOPER, Alice	
			Born Vincent Furnier on 2/04/48 in Detroit. Formed rock group in Phoenix in 1965; changed name to Alice Cooper in 1966. To Los Angeles in 1968, then to Detroit in 1969. Alice is known primarily for his bizarre stage antics. Appeared in the 1987 film *Prince of Darkness.*	
3/20/71	**21**	8	1. Eighteen	Warner 7449
6/24/72	**7**	10	**2. School's Out**	Warner 7596
10/21/72	**26**	6	3. Elected	Warner 7631
3/10/73	**35**	3	4. Hello Hurray	Warner 7673
5/12/73	**25**	8	5. No More Mr. Nice Guy	Warner 7691
5/03/75	**12**	11	6. Only Women	Atlantic 3254
10/30/76+	**12**	14	● 7. I Never Cry	Warner 8228
6/11/77	**9**	13	**8. You And Me**	Warner 8349
11/11/78	**12**	11	9. How You Gonna See Me Now	Warner 8695
7/05/80	**40**	1	10. Clones (We're All)	Warner 49204
10/14/89	**7**	10	● **11. Poison**	Epic 68958
			COOPER, Les/The Soul Rockers	
			Lee was born on 3/15/31 in Norfolk, Virginia. Pianist/singer/arranger/leader.	
11/17/62+	**22**	11	1. Wiggle Wobble [I] tenor sax solo: Joe Grier (former lead singer of The Charts)	Everlast 5019

DATE	POS	WKS	ARTIST—RECORD TITLE	LABEL & NO.
			COPELAND, Ken	
			Texas native born in 1937. Currently is a televangelist with own Kenneth Copeland Ministries, based in Fort Worth, Texas. Also records Inspirational albums.	
4/20/57	**12**	8	1. Pledge Of Love	Imperial 5432
			Jockey #12 / Top 100 #17 / Best Seller #23 first released on LIN 5007 in 1957	
			COREY, Jill	
			Born Norma Jean Speranza on 9/30/35. Married major league baseball player Don Hoak.	
2/02/57	**21**	5	1. I Love My Baby (My Baby Loves Me)	Columbia 40794
			Jockey #21 / Top 100 #28	
8/05/57	**11**	9	2. Love Me To Pieces	Columbia 40955
			Best Seller #11 / Jockey #11 / Top 100 #18 from the CBS-TV show "Studio One Summer Theatre"	
			CORINA	
			Manhattan-born, Bronx-raised dance singer. Placed second in the Miss Puerto Rico pageant in 1983.	
6/22/91	6	13	**1. Temptation**	Atco 98775#
			CORNELIUS BROTHERS & SISTER ROSE	
			Family group from Dania, Florida. Consisted of Edward, Carter and Rose. Billie Jo was added in 1973. All 15 Cornelius children play instruments or sing. Carter currently lives in Florida as Gideon Israel, the leader of a Muslim religious sect.	
5/15/71	3	13	● **1. Treat Her Like A Lady**	United Art. 50721
			first released on Platinum 105 in 1970	
6/17/72	2(2)	11	● **2. Too Late To Turn Back Now**	United Art. 50910
9/23/72	**23**	7	3. Don't Ever Be Lonely (A Poor Little Fool Like Me)	United Art. 50954
2/03/73	**37**	2	4. I'm Never Gonna Be Alone Anymore	United Art. 50996
			CORNELL, Don	
			Popular singer/guitarist who worked from the late 1930s with many bands, but achieved greatest success with Sammy Kaye ("It Isn't Fair") from 1947-50.	
5/14/55	**14**	6	1. Most Of All	Coral 61393
			Jockey #14 / Best Seller #20	
9/10/55	7	13	**2. The Bible Tells Me So/**	
			Best Seller #7 / Juke Box #8 / Jockey #18 / Top 100 #31 pre written by Roy Rogers' wife, Dale Evans	
11/05/55	**26**	3	3. Love Is A Many-Splendored Thing	Coral 61467
			from the film of the same title	
11/12/55	**25**	1	4. Young Abe Lincoln	Coral 61521
			CORSAIRS featuring JAY "BIRD" UZZELL	
			R&B vocal quartet from La Grange, North Carolina, consisting of brothers Jay "Bird" (lead singer), James and Moses Uzzell, with cousin George Wooten.	
1/27/62	**12**	10	1. Smoky Places	Tuff 1808

DATE	POS	WKS	ARTIST—RECORD TITLE	LABEL & NO.
			CORTEZ, Dave "Baby"	
			Born David Cortez Clowney on 8/13/38 in Detroit. Black keyboardist/composer. Played organ and sang with vocal group The Pearls from 1955-57, and also with the Valentines, which included Richard Barrett and Ronnie Bright (of "Mr. Bass Man" fame), from 1956-57. Frequent session work in New York. First recorded (as David Clooney) for Ember in 1956.	
3/30/59	**1**(1)	14	**1. The Happy Organ** [I]	Clock 1009
8/11/62	**10**	9	**2. Rinky Dink** [I]	Chess 1829
			COSBY, Bill	
			Born on 7/12/38 in Philadelphia. Top comedian who has appeared in nightclubs, on film and on TV. His first seven comedy albums were all million sellers. Played Alexander Scott on TV series "I Spy." Star of the highly-rated NBC-TV series "The Cosby Show." Winner of five Emmys and nine Grammys.	
9/16/67	**4**	8	**1. Little Ole Man (Uptight-Everything's Alright)** [N]	Warner 7072
			COSTA, Don	
			Born on 6/10/25 in Boston; died on 1/19/83. Arranger for Vaughn Monroe, Frank Sinatra, Vic Damone, The Ames Brothers and many more. A&R director of ABC-Paramount Records, then for United Artists Records.	
6/27/60	**27**	4	1. Theme From "The Unforgiven" (The Need For Love) [I] from the Burt Lancaster and Deborah Kerr film *The Unforgiven*	United Art. 221
8/29/60	**19**	14	2. Never On Sunday [I] from the film of the same title; originally charted for 11 weeks; re-entered on 5/14/61 (POS 37)	United Art. 234
			COSTELLO, Elvis	
			Born Declan McManus in Liverpool, England on 8/25/54. Changed name to Elvis Costello in 1976. Formed backing band The Attractions in 1977. Appeared in the 1987 film *Straight to Hell*. Married Cait O'Riordan, former bassist with The Pogues, on 5/16/86. Leading eclectic rock singer.	
10/15/83	**36**	2	1. Everyday I Write The Book **ELVIS COSTELLO & THE ATTRACTIONS**	Columbia 04045
5/27/89	**19**	6	2. Veronica written by Paul McCartney and Elvis Costello	Warner 22981
			COTTON, Gene	
			Born in Columbus, Ohio. Attended Ohio State University. Recording since 1972.	
1/22/77	**33**	3	1. You've Got Me Runnin'	ABC 12227
3/04/78	**23**	7	2. Before My Heart Finds Out	Ariola 7675
8/05/78	**36**	3	3. You're A Part Of Me **GENE COTTON with KIM CARNES**	Ariola 7704
11/11/78	**40**	2	4. Like A Sunday In Salem (The Amos & Andy Song) originally released as the B-side of #2 above	Ariola 7723
			COUGAR, John — see MELLENCAMP	
			COUNT FIVE	
			Psychedelic garage rock quintet of teenagers from San Jose, California — Kenn Ellner, lead singer.	
9/24/66	**5**	9	**1. Psychotic Reaction**	Double Shot 104

Peabo Bryson was initially signed as a session singer and songwriter to Atlanta-based Bang Records in 1975, but the label liked what they heard and launched him as a solo artist. Since then, he's enjoyed some of his biggest hits singing duets with partners like Roberta Flack, Natalie Cole, Regina Belle, and Melissa Manchester.

The Buckinghams had a string of top-10 hits in 1967—including "Kind Of A Drag," "Don't You Care," and "Mercy, Mercy, Mercy"—and unknowingly launched a musical movement. Both Blood, Sweat & Tears and Chicago followed the group's lead and, with the help of producer James William Guercio, soon added horns to pop and created "jazz-rock."

Cameo, a long-lived funk group centered around drummer Larry Blackmon, had a major crossover hit with 1986's "Word Up!" The single went to No. 6 and gave the group its first platinum album.

Freddy Cannon's last hit to reach the Top 40 was one most American teens could hear every day on television. "Action," which reached No. 13, was the theme song to Dick Clark's ABC-TV series "Where the Action Is."

The Carefrees were just one of a seeming flood of artists to cash in on Beatlemania. Their sole hit, "We Love You Beatles," reached No. 39 in April 1964—the same week the Fab Four managed to fill the Top 10 with five hits of their own.

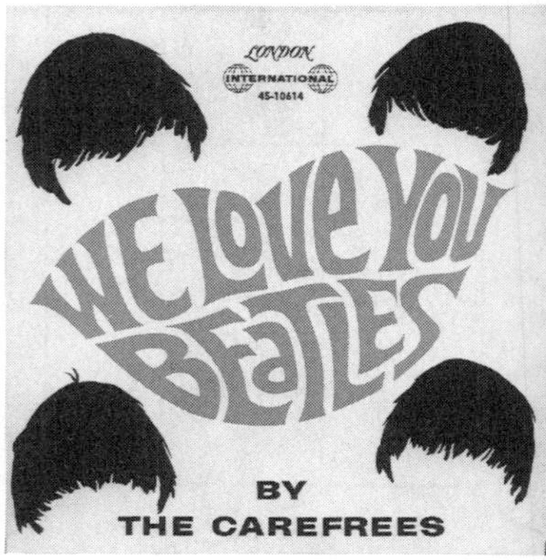

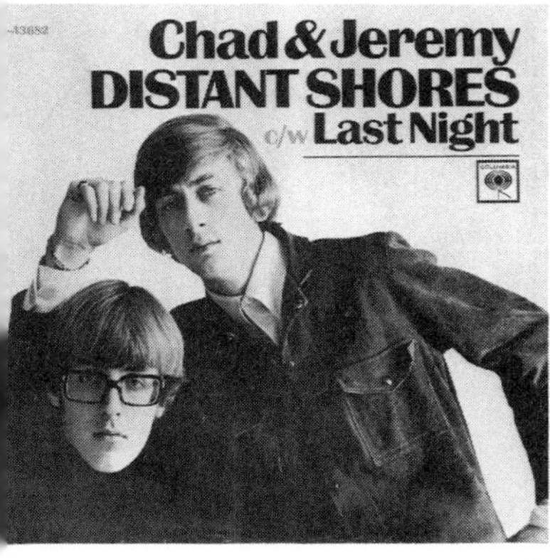

Chad & Jeremy were often confused with similar British Invasion duo Peter & Gordon, who also featured a bespectacled singer. Of their seven singles to reach the Top 40, only one entered the Top 10; Peter & Gordon managed three out of 10.

Tracy Chapman, who won the 1988 Best New Artist Grammy, suprised many when her folkish sounds enjoyed platinum sales. Her single "Fast Car" rapidly accelerated up the charts to a peak position of No. 6 the same year.

Chubby Checker's entire career seems inextricably linked with his waistline. A surprising number of people still don't see his name as a purposeful pun on Fats Domino's; his last hit, a new version of his early 60s song "The Twist," came via a 1988 duet with the Fat Boys.

Cheech & Chong were apparently more offensive in restrospect—judging from Warner Bros.' decision to sticker eight of the comedy duo's albums with parental guidance warnings upon reissuing them on CD in 1991.

Neneh Cherry's two top-10 hits of 1989—"Buffalo Stance" and "Kisses On The Wind"—were a far cry from the music of her famed stepfather, jazz trumpeter Don Cherry. Her former group, England's Rip Rig & Panic, also had a jazzy name—in their case, derived from an album by saxophonist Rahsaan Roland Kirk.

The Chipmunks, with their impressive array of hits in the late 50s and early 60s, may be viewed as the Godfathers of cartoon pop by future generations who've accepted records by such acts as the Simpsons and M.C. Skat Kat.

DATE	POS	WKS	ARTIST—RECORD TITLE	LABEL & NO.
			COVAY, Don	
			Born in March 1938 in Orangeburg, South Carolina. R&B singer/songwriter. Member of the Rainbows in 1955. Recorded as "Pretty Boy" with Little Richard's band for Atlantic in 1957. Formed group, The Goodtimers, in 1960.	
10/03/64	**35**	5	1. Mercy, Mercy	Rosemart 801
			DON COVAY & THE GOODTIMERS	
8/11/73	**29**	5	2. I Was Checkin' Out She Was Checkin' In	Mercury 73385
			COVEN	
			Pop quintet featuring the voice of Jinx Dawson.	
10/30/71	**26**	6	1. One Tin Soldier, The Legend of Billy Jack	Warner 7509
			from the Tom Laughlin movie *Billy Jack*	
			COVER GIRLS, The	
			New York City-based female vocal dance trio: Louise "Angel" Sabater, Caroline Jackson and Sunshine Wright (replaced by Margo Urban in 1989).	
1/30/88	**27**	8	1. Because Of You	Fever 1914
5/21/88	**40**	1	2. Promise Me	Fever 1917
10/21/89	**38**	2	3. My Heart Skips A Beat	Capitol 44436#
1/13/90	**8**	11	**4. We Can't Go Wrong**	Capitol 44498#
			COWBOY CHURCH SUNDAY SCHOOL, The	
			Lead vocal by adult singer Carol Sue. At 45 rpm, recording sounds like a child's voice.	
1/01/55	**8**	21	**1. Open Up Your Heart (And Let The Sunshine In) [N]**	Decca 29367
			Best Seller #8 / Jockey #18 / Juke Box #19	
			COWSILLS, The	
			Family pop group from Newport, Rhode Island. Consisted of five brothers (Bill, Bob, Paul, Barry and John), with their little sister (Susan) and mother (Barbara, d: 1/31/85 [age 56]). Bob, Paul, John and Susan reunited for touring in 1990.	
10/21/67	**2**(2)	12	● **1. The Rain, The Park & Other Things**	MGM 13810
2/03/68	**21**	6	2. We Can Fly	MGM 13886
6/22/68	**10**	9	**3. Indian Lake**	MGM 13944
3/29/69	**2**(2)	13	● **4. Hair**	MGM 14026
			from the rock musical *Hair*	
			CRABBY APPLETON	
			West Coast rock quintet led by Michael Fennelly.	
6/27/70	**36**	5	1. Go Back	Elektra 45687
			CRADDOCK, Billy "Crash"	
			Country-rock singer. Born on 6/16/39 in Greensboro, North Carolina. First recorded for Colonial in 1957. Nickname "Crash" came from his stock car racing hobby.	
7/27/74	**16**	9	1. Rub It In	ABC 12013
12/28/74+	**33**	2	2. Ruby, Baby	ABC 12036
			CRAMER, Floyd	
			Nashville's top session pianist. Born on 10/27/33 in Samti, Louisiana and raised in Huttig, Arkansas. Played piano from age five. Moved to Nashville in 1955. Toured with Elvis Presley, Johnny Cash, Perry Como and Chet Atkins.	
10/31/60	**2**(4)	15	**1. Last Date** [I]	RCA 7775
3/13/61	**4**	11	**2. On The Rebound** [I]	RCA 7840
6/26/61	**8**	8	**3. San Antonio Rose** [I]	RCA 7893

DATE	POS	WKS	ARTIST—RECORD TITLE	LABEL & NO.
			written by Bob Wills in 1938	
2/24/62	**36**	2	4. Chattanooga Choo Choo [I]	RCA 7978
			#1 hit for Glenn Miller in 1941	
			CRANE, Les	
			TV talkshow host from San Francisco.	
10/23/71	**8**	10	**1. Desiderata** **[S]**	Warner 7520
			originally a piece of prose, written in 1906 by Max Ehrmann	
			CRAWFORD, Johnny	
			Born on 3/26/46 in Los Angeles. One of the original Mouseketeers. Played Chuck Connor's son (Mark McCain) in the TV series "The Rifleman," 1958-63.	
6/02/62	**8**	9	**1. Cindy's Birthday**	Del-Fi 4178
8/25/62	**14**	6	2. Your Nose Is Gonna Grow	Del-Fi 4181
11/24/62	**12**	7	3. Rumors	Del-Fi 4188
1/26/63	**29**	4	4. Proud	Del-Fi 4193
			CRAWFORD, Randy — see CRUSADERS, The	
			CRAY, Robert, Band	
			Born on 8/01/53 in Columbus, Georgia. Blues guitarist/vocalist. Played bass with fictional band, Otis Day & The Knights, in the film *Animal House.* Band formed in 1974 as backing tour group for Albert Collins.	
3/21/87	**22**	6	1. Smoking Gun	Mercury 888343
			CRAZY ELEPHANT	
			Bubblegum studio concoction of producers Jerry Kasenetz and Jeff Katz. Ex-Cadillac member Robert Spencer on lead vocals. Touring group formed later.	
4/05/69	**12**	8	1. Gimme Gimme Good Lovin'	Bell 763
			first released on Sphere Sound 77005 in 1968	
			CRAZY OTTO	
			German pianist Fritz Schulz-Reichel. Born on 7/04/12.	
2/26/55	**19**	5	1. Glad Rag Doll/ [I]	
			Best Seller #19	
2/26/55	**21**	3	2. Smiles [I]	Decca 29403
			Best Seller #21	
			CREAM	
			British supergroup: Eric Clapton (guitar), Ginger Baker (drums) and Jack Bruce (bass).	
2/24/68	**5**	12	● **1. Sunshine Of Your Love**	Atco 6544
			originally charted for 2 weeks (POS 36); re-entered on 7/06/68	
10/19/68	**6**	9	**2. White Room**	Atco 6617
2/08/69	**28**	6	3. Crossroads	Atco 6646
			CREEDENCE CLEARWATER REVIVAL	
			Rock group formed while members attended high school at El Cerrito, California. Consisted of John Fogerty (vocals, guitar), brother Tom Fogerty (guitar), Stu Cook (keyboards, bass) and Doug Clifford (drums). First recorded as the Blue Velvets for the Orchestra label in 1959. Recorded as the Golliwogs for Fantasy in 1964. Tom Fogerty left for a solo career in 1971 and group disbanded in October 1972. Tom Fogerty died on 9/06/90 (age 48) of respiratory failure.	
9/28/68	**11**	9	● 1. Suzie Q. (Part One)	Fantasy 616
2/08/69	**2**(3)	12	▲ **2. Proud Mary**	Fantasy 619

DATE	POS	WKS	ARTIST—RECORD TITLE	LABEL & NO.
5/17/69	**2(1)**	12	▲ **3. Bad Moon Rising**	Fantasy 622
8/09/69	**2(1)**	11	● **4. Green River/**	
8/09/69	**30**	7	5. Commotion	Fantasy 625
11/08/69	**3**	13	▲ **6. Down On The Corner/**	
11/08/69	**14**	13	7. Fortunate Son	Fantasy 634
2/07/70	**2(2)**	9	▲ **8. Travelin' Band/**	
		9	9. Who'll Stop The Rain	Fantasy 637
5/02/70	**4**	10	● **10. Up Around The Bend**	Fantasy 641
8/15/70	**2(1)**	12	▲ **11. Lookin' Out My Back Door**	Fantasy 645
2/06/71	**8**	9	● **12. Have You Ever Seen The Rain** 2-12: written, produced and arranged by John Fogerty	Fantasy 655
7/24/71	**6**	8	● **13. Sweet Hitch-Hiker**	Fantasy 665
5/20/72	**25**	5	14. Someday Never Comes	Fantasy 676
			CRENSHAW, Marshall	
			Singer/songwriter/guitarist from Detroit. Played John Lennon in the road show of *Beatlemania* in 1976. Appeared in film *Peggy Sue Got Married* and portrayed Buddy Holly in the 1987 film *La Bamba*.	
8/14/82	**36**	4	1. Someday, Someway	Warner 29974
			CRESCENDOS, The	
			Vocal group from Nashville. Formed as The Spades in high school with George Lanuis (lead singer), his cousin James Lanuis, Ken Brigham, Tom Fortner and Jim Hall.	
1/20/58	**5**	14	**1. Oh Julie** Top 100 #5 / Best Seller #6 / Jockey #7 female voice: Janice Green	Nasco 6005
			CRESTS, The	
			Formed as a black quartet in 1955 at a Manhattan junior high school, consisting of Brooklyn-born white singer Johnny Mastrangelo (Maestro; shown as Mastro on all The Crests' hits; joined as lead singer in 1956), Harold Torres, Talmadge Gough, J.T. Carter and Patricia Van Dross. Van Dross left group in 1958. Mastrangelo left for solo work as Johnny Maestro in 1960, replaced by James Ancrum. Maestro later formed Brooklyn Bridge.	
12/22/58+	**2(2)**	14	**1. 16 Candles**	Coed 506
4/13/59	**28**	7	2. Six Nights A Week	Coed 509
9/14/59	**22**	9	3. The Angels Listened In	Coed 515
4/04/60	**14**	8	4. Step By Step	Coed 525
7/18/60	**20**	8	5. Trouble In Paradise	Coed 531
			CREW-CUTS, The	
			Vocal group from Toronto formed in 1952. Consisted of John Perkins (lead), his brother Ray Perkins (bass), Pat Barrett (tenor) and Rudi Maugeri (baritone). First called the Canadaires, changed name in 1954. Maugeri did vocal arrangements for the group. Disbanded in 1963.	
1/29/55	**3**	13	**1. Earth Angel/** Jockey #3 / Juke Box #8 / Best Seller #8	
1/29/55	**6**	14	**2. Ko Ko Mo (I Love You So)** Juke Box #6 / Best Seller #10 / Jockey #11	Mercury 70529
4/30/55	**14**	8	3. Don't Be Angry Best Seller #14 / Jockey #14 / Juke Box #19	Mercury 70597
6/25/55	**16**	7	4. A Story Untold Best Seller #16	Mercury 70634
8/27/55	**10**	8	**5. Gum Drop**	Mercury 70668

DATE	POS	WKS	ARTIST—RECORD TITLE	LABEL & NO.
			Best Seller #10 / Jockey #14 / Juke Box #20 / Top 100 #80 pre	
12/17/55+	**11**	15	6. Angels In The Sky /	
			Best Seller #11 / Top 100 #13 / Juke Box #13 / Jockey #16	
1/07/56	**31**	8	7. Mostly Martha	Mercury 70741
2/18/56	**18**	5	8. Seven Days	Mercury 70782
			Jockey #18 / Top 100 #20	
1/26/57	**17**	3	9. Young Love	Mercury 71022
			Jockey #17 / Juke Box #17 / Top 100 #24 orchestra conducted by David Carroll on all of above	
			CREWE, Bob	
			Born on 11/12/37 in Newark, New Jersey. Wrote many hit songs beginning with "Silhouettes" in 1957. One of the top producers of the 1960s; worked with The 4 Seasons. Head of several labels, publishing and production companies. Assembled The Bob Crewe Generation, an aggregation of studio musicians.	
1/21/67	**15**	7	1. Music To Watch Girls By [I]	DynoVoice 229
			tune used in a Diet Pepsi commercial	
			CRICKETS, The — see HOLLY, Buddy	
			CRITTERS, The	
			New Jersey quintet led by Don Ciccone, who later joined The 4 Seasons.	
9/03/66	**17**	8	1. Mr. Dieingly Sad	Kapp 769
8/05/67	**39**	3	2. Don't Let The Rain Fall Down On Me	Kapp 838
			CROCE, Jim	
			Born on 1/10/43 in Philadelphia; killed in plane crash on 9/20/73 in Natchitoches, Louisiana. Vocalist/ guitarist/composer. Recorded with wife Ingrid for Capitol in 1968. Lead guitarist on his hits, Maury Muehleisen, was killed in the same crash.	
7/22/72	**8**	10	**1. You Don't Mess Around With Jim**	ABC 11328
11/04/72	**17**	8	2. Operator (That's Not the Way it Feels)	ABC 11335
3/17/73	**37**	3	3. One Less Set Of Footsteps	ABC 11346
6/02/73	**1**(2)	16	● **4. Bad, Bad Leroy Brown**	ABC 11359
10/13/73	**10**	13	**5. I Got A Name**	ABC 11389
			from the film *The Last American Hero*	
12/01/73	**1**(2)	12	● **6. Time In A Bottle**	ABC 11405
3/16/74	**9**	11	**7. I'll Have To Say I Love You In A Song**	ABC 11424
6/29/74	**32**	6	8. Workin' At The Car Wash Blues	ABC 11447
			CROSBY, Bing	
			One of the most popular entertainers of the 20th century's first 50 years. Harry Lillis Crosby was born on 5/02/01 (or 04) in Tacoma, Washington. He and singing partner Al Rinker were hired in 1926 by Paul Whiteman; with Harry Barris they became the Rhythm Boys and gained an increasing following. The trio split from Whiteman in 1930, and Bing sang briefly with Gus Arnheim's band. It was his early-1931 smash with Arnheim, "I Surrender, Dear," which earned Bing a CBS radio contract and launched an unsurpassed solo career. Over the next three decades the resonant Crosby baritone and breezy persona sold more than 300 million records and was featured in over 50 movies (won Academy Award for *Going My Way*, 1944). Crosby died of a heart attack on 10/14/77 on a golf course near Madrid, Spain. Won the Lifetime Achievement Grammy in 1962. Ranked as the #1 artist in *Joel Whitburn's Pop Memories 1890-1954* book.	
12/31/55	**7**	2	**1. White Christmas [X-R]**	Decca 23778

DATE	POS	WKS	ARTIST—RECORD TITLE	LABEL & NO.
			Jockey #7 / Top 100 #18 with the Ken Darby Singers and John Scott Trotter's Orchestra; originally hit #1 in December 1942; made pop charts for 20 Christmas seasons; the best-selling single of all time	
10/06/56	**3**	22	**2. True Love** **BING CROSBY AND GRACE KELLY** (died in an auto accident, 9/14/82) Jockey #3 / Top 100 #4 / Best Seller #5 / Juke Box #6	Capitol 3507
10/21/57	**25**	1	3. Around The World Best Seller #25 / Top 100 #54 from Michael Todd's film *Around The World in Eighty Days*; B-side is Victor Young's hit instrumental version	Decca 30262
12/23/57	**34**	2	4. White Christmas [X-R] Top 100 #34 / Best Seller #36	Decca 23778
12/19/60	**26**	2	5. White Christmas [X-R]	Decca 23778
12/18/61	**12**	3	6. White Christmas [X-R]	Decca 23778
12/29/62	**38**	1	7. White Christmas [X-R]	Decca 23778
			CROSBY, David	
			Born David Van Cortland on 8/14/41 in Los Angeles. Vocalist/guitarist with The Byrds from 1964-68 and later Crosby, Stills & Nash. Frequent troubles with the law due to drug charges.	
6/10/72	**36**	4	1. Immigration Man **GRAHAM NASH & DAVID CROSBY**	Atlantic 2873
			CROSBY, STILLS & NASH	
			Trio from Laurel Canyon, California, formed in 1968. Consisted of David Crosby (b: 8/14/41, Los Angeles; guitar), Stephen Stills (b: 1/03/45, Dallas; guitar, keyboards, bass) and Graham Nash (b: 1942, Lancashire, England; guitar). Crosby had been in The Byrds, Stills had been in Buffalo Springfield, and Nash was with The Hollies. Won the 1969 Best New Artist Grammy Award. Neil Young (b: 11/12/45, Toronto; guitar), formerly with Buffalo Springfield, joined group in 1969, left in 1974. Reunion in 1988.	
8/02/69	**28**	6	1. Marrakesh Express	Atlantic 2652
10/25/69	**21**	9	2. Suite: Judy Blue Eyes written by Stephen Stills for Judy Collins	Atlantic 2676
			CROSBY, STILLS, NASH & YOUNG:	
4/04/70	**11**	10	3. Woodstock written by Joni Mitchell about festival in New York, August 1969	Atlantic 2723
6/20/70	**16**	9	4. Teach Your Children	Atlantic 2735
7/11/70	**14**	7	5. Ohio written by Young after four students killed at Kent State Univ.	Atlantic 2740
10/10/70	**30**	6	6. Our House	Atlantic 2760
			CROSBY, STILLS & NASH:	
7/02/77	**7**	12	**7. Just A Song Before I Go**	Atlantic 3401
7/03/82	**9**	12	**8. Wasted On The Way**	Atlantic 4058
10/09/82	**18**	9	9. Southern Cross	Atlantic 89969
			CROSS, Christopher	
			Born Christopher Geppert on 5/03/51 in San Antonio, Texas. Formed own group with Rob Meurer (keyboards), Andy Salmon (bass) and Tommy Taylor (drums) in 1973. Won the 1980 Best New Artist Grammy Award.	
3/01/80	**2**(4)	17	**1. Ride Like The Wind** backing vocal by Michael McDonald	Warner 49184
7/05/80	**1**(1)	13	**2. Sailing**	Warner 49507
10/25/80	**15**	12	3. Never Be The Same	Warner 49580

DATE	POS	WKS	ARTIST—RECORD TITLE	LABEL & NO.
4/25/81	**20**	7	4. Say You'll Be Mine	Warner 49705
8/29/81	**1**(3)	17	● **5. Arthur's Theme (Best That You Can Do)**	Warner 49787
			from the Dudley Moore movie *Arthur*	
1/22/83	**12**	13	6. All Right	Warner 29843
5/21/83	**33**	5	7. No Time For Talk	Warner 29662
12/24/83+	**9**	11	**8. Think Of Laura**	Warner 29658
			popularized through play on TV's "General Hospital"; all of above produced by Michael Omartian	
			CROSS COUNTRY	
			Jay Siegel, Mitch and Phil Margo; all formerly with The Tokens.	
9/22/73	**30**	4	1. In The Midnight Hour	Atco 6934
			CROW	
			Rock-blues quintet from Minneapolis — Dave Wagner, lead singer. Drummer Denny Craswell was a member of The Castaways.	
11/29/69+	**19**	10	1. Evil Woman Don't Play Your Games With Me	Amaret 112
			CROWDED HOUSE	
			New Zealand/Australian trio founded by former Split Enz members Neil Finn (vocals, guitar, piano) and Paul Hester (drums), with Nick Seymour (bass). Neil's brother, Tim Finn (also of Split Enz) joined the band in 1991.	
2/21/87	**2**(1)	15	**1. Don't Dream It's Over**	Capitol 5614
5/30/87	**7**	11	**2. Something So Strong**	Capitol 5695
			CROWELL, Rodney	
			Born on 8/07/50 in Houston. Country singer/songwriter/guitarist. Married Rosanne Cash in 1979. Wrote the Dirt Band's "American Dream" and many other country hits.	
6/28/80	**37**	2	1. Ashes By Now	Warner 49224
			CRUSADERS, The	
			Instrumental jazz-oriented group formed in Houston. 1979 lineup: Joe Sample (keyboards), Wilton Felder (reeds) and Nesbert "Stix" Hooper (drums). Sample and Felder reunited with a new lineup in 1991.	
10/27/79	**36**	3	1. Street Life	MCA 41054
			vocal by Randy Crawford	
			CRYSTALS, The	
			Female vocal group from Brooklyn. Consisted of Barbara Alston, Lala Brooks, Dee Dee Kennibrew, Mary Thomas and Patricia Wright. Discovered by producer Phil Spector.	
12/11/61+	**20**	7	1. There's No Other (Like My Baby)	Philles 100
4/28/62	**13**	8	2. Uptown	Philles 102
10/06/62	**1**(2)	12	**3. He's A Rebel**	Philles 106
			written by Gene Pitney	
1/19/63	**11**	8	4. He's Sure The Boy I Love	Philles 109
			above 2 are actually by Darlene Love (lead) & The Blossoms	
5/11/63	**3**	10	**5. Da Doo Ron Ron (When He Walked Me Home)**	Philles 112
8/31/63	**6**	9	**6. Then He Kissed Me**	Philles 115
			CUFF LINKS, The	
			Group is actually the overdubbed voices of Ron Dante (The Archies).	
10/04/69	**9**	9	**1. Tracy**	Decca 32533

DATE	POS	WKS	ARTIST—RECORD TITLE	LABEL & NO.
			CULTURE CLUB	
			Formed in London in 1981. Consisted of George "Boy George" O'Dowd (b: 6/14/61; vocals), Roy Hay (guitar, keyboards), Michael Craig (bass) and Jon Moss (drums). Designer Sue Clowes originated distinctive costuming for the group. Won the 1983 Best New Artist Grammy Award. Boy George went solo in 1987.	
1/15/83	**2**(3)	18	**1. Do You Really Want To Hurt Me**	Epic 03368
4/30/83	**2**(2)	13	**2. Time (Clock Of The Heart)**	Epic 03796
7/16/83	**9**	12	**3. I'll Tumble 4 Ya**	Epic 03912
10/29/83	**10**	12	**4. Church Of The Poison Mind**	Epic 04144
12/10/83+	**1**(3)	16	● **5. Karma Chameleon**	Virgin 04221
3/03/84	**5**	12	**6. Miss Me Blind** backing vocal by Jermaine Stewart	Virgin 04388
5/19/84	**13**	8	7. It's A Miracle	Virgin 04457
10/20/84	**17**	7	8. The War Song	Virgin 04638
1/12/85	**33**	5	9. Mistake No. 3	Virgin 04727
4/19/86	**12**	10	10. Move Away	Virgin 05847
			CUMMINGS, Burton	
			Born on 12/31/47 in Winnipeg, Canada. Lead singer of The Guess Who.	
11/06/76+	**10**	15	● **1. Stand Tall**	Portrait 70001
10/24/81	**37**	2	2. You Saved My Soul	Alfa 7008
			CURB, Mike, Congregation	
			Mike was born on 12/24/44 in Savannah, Georgia. Pop music mogul and politician. President of MGM Records, 1969-73. Elected lieutenant governor of California in 1978. Formed own company, Curb Records.	
2/27/71	**34**	4	1. Burning Bridges from the film *Kelly's Heroes*	MGM 14151
			CURE, The	
			British techno-rock group led by Robert Smith (b: 4/21/59; vocals, guitar). Producer and early member Phil Thornalley joined Johnny Hates Jazz as lead singer in 1989. Co-founder/keyboardist Laurence Tolhurst left by 1990.	
1/09/88	**40**	1	1. Just Like Heaven	Elektra 69443
8/26/89	**2**(1)	12	**2. Love Song**	Elektra 69280
			CURTIS, King — see KING CURTIS	
			CUTTING CREW	
			British rock group led by singer Nick Van Eede, with Kevin Scott MacMichael (guitar; from Canada), Colin Farley (bass) and Martin Beedle (drums).	
3/21/87	**1**(2)	13	**1. (I Just) Died In Your Arms**	Virgin 99481
7/18/87	**38**	2	2. One For The Mockingbird	Virgin 99464
10/03/87	**9**	11	**3. I've Been In Love Before**	Virgin 99425
			CYMARRON	
			Male pop vocal trio formed in Memphis: Richard Mainegra, Rick Yancey and Sherrill Parks.	
7/17/71	**17**	7	1. Rings	Entrance 7500
			CYMBAL, Johnny	
			Singer/songwriter/producer born on 2/03/45 in Ochitree, Scotland. Moved to Goderich, Ontario in 1952. Moved to Cleveland in 1960. Also recorded as Derek.	
3/16/63	**16**	8	1. Mr. Bass Man [N]	Kapp 503

DATE	POS	WKS	ARTIST—RECORD TITLE	LABEL & NO.
			bass singer: Ronnie Bright (member of the Valentines)	
			CYRKLE, The	
			Pop group formed while attending Lafayette College in Easton, Pennsylvania. Signed to Columbia Records and managed by The Beatles' Brian Epstein. Featured vocalists Don Dannemann and Tom Dawes.	
6/04/66	**2**(1)	11	**1. Red Rubber Ball**	Columbia 43589
			written by Paul Simon and Bruce Woodley (of The Seekers)	
8/27/66	**16**	5	2. Turn-Down Day	Columbia 43729
			D	
			DADDY DEWDROP	
			Cleveland singer Richard Monda.	
4/10/71	**9**	11	**1. Chick-A-Boom (Don't Ya Jes' Love It)** [N]	Sunflower 105
			DADDY-O'S, The	
			Produced by guitarist Billy Mure.	
6/23/58	**39**	3	1. Got A Match? [I]	Cabot 122
			Best Seller #39 / Top 100 #40	
			DALE, Alan	
			Born Aldo Sigiamundi on 7/09/25 in Brooklyn. Baritone singer formerly with Carmen Cavallaro. Hosted his own TV show in 1951.	
4/30/55	**14**	7	1. Cherry Pink (And Apple Blossom White)	Coral 61373
			Juke Box #14 / Jockey #19 / Best Seller #27 from the film *Underwater!*	
7/02/55	**10**	7	**2. Sweet And Gentle**	Coral 61435
			Jockey #10 / Best Seller #12 / Juke Box #14 orchestra directed by Dick Jacobs on above 2	
			DALE & GRACE	
			Vocal duo: Dale Houston (of Ferriday, Louisiana) and Grace Broussard (of Prairieville, Louisiana).	
10/26/63	**1**(2)	12	**1. I'm Leaving It Up To You**	Montel 921
2/08/64	**8**	7	**2. Stop And Think It Over**	Montel 922
			above 2 first released on Michelle 921 and 923, respectively	
			DALTREY, Roger	
			Born on 3/01/44 in London. Formed band the Detours, which later became The Who. Roger was The Who's lead singer and starred in the films *Tommy*, *Lisztomania*, *The Legacy* and *McVicar*.	
10/25/80	**20**	8	1. Without Your Love	Polydor 2121
			from the *McVicar* soundtrack	
			DAMIAN, Michael	
			Danny Romalotti on TV's "The Young & The Restless." In cast since 1981 (age 17) when discovered by show's producers while performing on "American Bandstand."	
4/08/89	**1**(1)	13	● **1. Rock On**	Cypress 1420
			from the film *Dream a Little Dream*	
7/29/89	**31**	4	2. Cover Of Love	Cypress 1430
12/23/89+	**24**	9	3. Was It Nothing At All	Cypress 1451#

DATE	POS	WKS	ARTIST—RECORD TITLE	LABEL & NO.
			DAMN YANKEES	
			Superstar rock group: guitarist Ted Nugent (Amboy Dukes), bassist/vocalist Jack Blades (Night Ranger), guitarist/vocalist Tommy Shaw (Styx) and drummer Michael Cartellone.	
11/03/90+	**3**	18	● **1. High Enough**	Warner 19595
			DAMON('S), Liz, Orient Express	
			Liz is the leader of the three-woman, six-man vocal/instrumental group from Hawaii.	
1/30/71	**33**	3	1. 1900 Yesterday	White Whale 368
			DAMONE, Vic	
			Born Vito Farinola on 6/12/28 in Brooklyn. Vic is among the most popular of postwar ballad singers. Appeared in several movies and hosted own TV series (1956-57). Married actress Diahann Carroll on 1/03/87.	
6/02/56	**4**	16	**1. On The Street Where You Live** Jockey #4 / Best Seller #8 / Top 100 #8 / Juke Box #13 from the Broadway musical *My Fair Lady*	Columbia 40654
9/30/57	**16**	4	2. An Affair To Remember (Our Love Affair) Jockey #16 / Top 100 #35 from the Cary Grant movie *An Affair to Remember*	Columbia 40945
5/22/65	**30**	4	3. You Were Only Fooling (While I Was Falling In Love)	Warner 5616
			DANA, Vic	
			Born on 8/26/42 in Buffalo, New York. Moved to California as a teen.	
4/25/64	**27**	5	1. Shangri-La	Dolton 92
3/06/65	**10**	8	**2. Red Roses For A Blue Lady**	Dolton 304
6/04/66	**30**	4	3. I Love You Drops	Dolton 319
			DANCER, PRANCER AND NERVOUS	
12/28/59	**34**	1	1. The Happy Reindeer [X-N]	Capitol 4300
			DANIELS, Charlie, Band	
			Daniels (b: 10/28/36, Wilmington, North Carolina; vocals, guitar, fiddle) formed band in Nashville in 1971. Included Tom Crain (guitar), Joe "Taz" DiGregorio (keyboards), Charles Hayward (bass) and James W. Marshall (drums). Daniels led the Jaguars from 1958-67. Went solo in 1968 and worked as a session musician in Nashville. Played on Bob Dylan's *Nashville Skyline* hit album. In the film *Urban Cowboy*.	
7/21/73	**9**	9	**1. Uneasy Rider** **[N]** CHARLIE DANIELS	Kama Sutra 576
3/15/75	**29**	3	2. The South's Gonna Do It	Kama Sutra 598
7/21/79	**3**	12	▲ **3. The Devil Went Down To Georgia**	Epic 50700
6/28/80	**11**	8	4. In America	Epic 50888
9/27/80	**31**	4	5. The Legend Of Wooley Swamp	Epic 50921
4/17/82	**22**	8	6. Still In Saigon	Epic 02828
			DANLEERS, The	
			R&B quintet from Brooklyn — Jimmy Weston, lead singer. Group was named after their manager, Danny Webb, who wrote "One Summer Night."	
6/30/58	**7**	10	**1. One Summer Night** Jockey #7 / Best Seller #14 / Top 100 #16 originally released on AMP-3 2115 as by The Dandleers	Mercury 71322

DATE	POS	WKS	ARTIST—RECORD TITLE	LABEL & NO.
			DANNY & THE JUNIORS	
			Formed while at high school in Philadelphia in 1955 as the Juvenairs, with Danny Rapp (b: 5/10/41; lead), David White (first tenor), Frank Maffei (second tenor) and Joe Terranova (baritone). White later joined The Spokesmen. Danny Rapp committed suicide on 4/08/83.	
12/09/57+	**1**(7)	18	**1. At The Hop**	ABC-Para. 9871
			Top 100 #1(7) / Best Seller #1(5) / Jockey #1(3) song originally written as "Do The Bop"; first released on Singular 711 in 1957	
3/10/58	**19**	7	2. Rock And Roll Is Here To Stay	ABC-Para. 9888
			Best Seller #19 / Top 100 #19	
7/21/58	**39**	1	3. Dottie	ABC-Para. 9926
			Best Seller #39 / Top 100 #41	
10/10/60	**27**	3	4. Twistin' U.S.A.	Swan 4060
			DANNY WILSON	
			Trio from Dundee, Scotland: brothers Gary (lead vocals, guitar) and Kit Clark (keyboards, percussion), with Ged Grimes (bass). Group takes its name from a mid-1950s Frank Sinatra film. Disbanded in 1990.	
8/01/87	**23**	8	1. Mary's Prayer	Virgin 99465
			DANTE AND THE EVERGREENS	
			Born Donald Drowty on 9/08/41, lead singer of pop quartet from Los Angeles. Included Bill Young, future record producer Tony Moon and future Beverly Hills lawyer Frank D. Rosenthal.	
6/13/60	**15**	8	1. Alley-Oop [N]	Madison 130
			D'ARBY, Terence Trent	
			England-based, soul-pop singer, born on 3/15/62 in New York City. Last name originally spelled Darby. Was a member of U.S. Army boxing team.	
2/27/88	**1**(1)	15	**1. Wishing Well**	Columbia 07675
6/18/88	**4**	13	**2. Sign Your Name**	Columbia 07911
10/08/88	**30**	5	3. Dance Little Sister (Part One)	Columbia 08023
			DARIN, Bobby	
			Vocalist/pianist/guitarist/drummer. Born Walden Robert Cassotto on 5/14/36 in the Bronx; died of heart failure on 12/20/73 in Los Angeles. First recorded in 1956 with The Jaybirds (Decca). First appeared on TV in March 1956 on "The Tommy Dorsey Show." Won the 1959 Best New Artist Grammy Award. Married to actress Sandra Dee from 1960-67. Nominated for an Oscar for his performance in the film *Captain Newman, MD*, 1963. Formed own record company, Direction. Inducted into the Rock and Roll Hall of Fame in 1990.	
6/30/58	**3**	13	**1. Splish Splash**	Atco 6117
			Hot 100 #3 / Best Seller #4 / Jockey #5 end	
8/11/58	**24**	5	2. Early In The Morning	Atco 6121
			THE RINKY-DINKS Hot 100 #24 / Best Seller #24 originally issued on Brunswick 55073 as by the Ding Dongs (to conceal Darin's identity; he was under contract at Atco)	
10/27/58	**9**	14	**3. Queen Of The Hop**	Atco 6127
2/23/59	**38**	2	4. Plain Jane	Atco 6133
5/04/59	**2**(1)	13	**5. Dream Lover**	Atco 6140
9/07/59	**1**(9)	22	**6. Mack The Knife**	Atco 6147
			written in 1928 as "Moritat" or "Theme From The Threepenny Opera"	
1/25/60	**6**	11	**7. Beyond The Sea**	Atco 6158
			#26 hit for Benny Goodman in 1948	

DATE	POS	WKS	ARTIST—RECORD TITLE	LABEL & NO.
4/04/60	**21**	6	8. Clementine written in 1884 as "Oh, My Darling Clementine"	Atco 6161
6/20/60	**19**	5	9. Won't You Come Home Bill Bailey #1 hit for Arthur Collins in 1902	Atco 6167
10/17/60	**20**	8	10. Artificial Flowers from the musical *Tenderloin*	Atco 6179
2/20/61	**14**	7	11. Lazy River #19 hit for Hoagy Carmichael in 1932	Atco 6188
7/10/61	**40**	1	12. Nature Boy #1 hit for Nat King Cole in 1948	Atco 6196
9/11/61	**5**	9	**13. You Must Have Been A Beautiful Baby** #1 hit for Bing Crosby in 1938	Atco 6206
1/13/62	**15**	8	14. Irresistible You /	
1/20/62	**30**	5	15. Multiplication from film *Come September* co-starring Bobby Darin and Sandra Dee	Atco 6214
4/14/62	**24**	5	16. What'd I Say (Part 1)	Atco 6221
7/21/62	**3**	9	**17. Things**	Atco 6229
10/27/62	**32**	3	18. If A Man Answers from the film of the same title (again with Darin & Dee)	Capitol 4837
2/02/63	**3**	12	**19. You're The Reason I'm Living**	Capitol 4897
5/25/63	**10**	7	**20. 18 Yellow Roses**	Capitol 4970
10/08/66	**8**	9	**21. If I Were A Carpenter**	Atlantic 2350
2/11/67	**32**	3	22. Lovin' You	Atlantic 2376
			DARREN, James Born James William Ercolani on 10/03/36 in Philadelphia. Singer/actor, studied acting in New York City. Moved to Hollywood in 1955. In films *Rumble on the Docks, The Brothers Rico, Operation Mad Ball, Gunman's Walk, The Guns of Navarone, Because They're Young* and *Let No Man Write My Epitaph.* Played Moondoggie, Gidget's boyfriend, in *Gidget, Gidget Goes Hawaiian* and *Gidget Goes to Rome.* In "The Time Tunnel" TV series from 1966-67.	
11/06/61	**3**	12	**1. Goodbye Cruel World**	Colpix 609
2/17/62	**6**	8	**2. Her Royal Majesty**	Colpix 622
5/05/62	**11**	7	3. Conscience	Colpix 630
8/04/62	**39**	1	4. Mary's Little Lamb	Colpix 644
2/18/67	**35**	2	5. All from the film *Run for Your Wife*	Warner 5874
			DARTELLS, The Oxnard, California band consisting of Doug Phillips (vocals, bass), Dick Burns, Corky Wilkie, Rich Peil, Randy Ray and Gary Peeler.	
4/27/63	**11**	9	1. Hot Pastrami first released on Arlen 509 in 1962	Dot 16453
			DAVID & DAVID Los Angeles duo: David Baerwald and David Ricketts.	
11/15/86	**37**	3	1. Welcome To The Boomtown	A&M 2857

DATE	POS	WKS	ARTIST—RECORD TITLE	LABEL & NO.
			DAVID & JONATHAN	
			Songwriting/producing/vocal duo from Bristol, England: Roger Greenaway (David) and Roger Cook (Jonathan). Both later were production team for White Plains. Cook founded Blue Mink.	
1/29/66	**18**	5	1. Michelle written by Lennon/McCartney; produced by George Martin	Capitol 5563
			DAVIS, Mac	
			Born on 1/21/42 in Lubbock, Texas. Vocalist/guitarist/composer. Worked as a regional rep for Vee-Jay and Liberty Records. Wrote "In The Ghetto," "Don't Cry Daddy," hits for Elvis Presley. Host of own musical variety TV series from 1974-76. Appearances in several films, including *North Dallas Forty* in 1979.	
8/05/72	**1**(3)	13	● **1. Baby Don't Get Hooked On Me**	Columbia 45618
5/25/74	**11**	14	2. One Hell Of A Woman	Columbia 46004
9/07/74	**9**	10	**3. Stop And Smell The Roses**	Columbia 10018
12/21/74+	**15**	8	4. Rock N' Roll (I Gave You The Best Years Of My Life)	Columbia 10070
			DAVIS, Paul	
			Born on 4/21/48 in Meridian, Mississippi. Singer/songwriter/producer. Appeared as "Peter" on the 1970 concept LP *Jesus Christ Superstar*.	
12/07/74+	**23**	8	1. Ride 'Em Cowboy	Bang 712
9/11/76	**35**	3	2. Superstar tribute: Elton John, Stevie Wonder, Linda Ronstadt, Joni Mitchell	Bang 726
10/29/77+	**7**	25	**3. I Go Crazy**	Bang 733
10/07/78	**17**	13	4. Sweet Life	Bang 738
4/12/80	**23**	6	5. Do Right	Bang 4808
11/28/81+	**11**	13	6. Cool Night	Arista 0645
3/20/82	**6**	13	**7. '65 Love Affair**	Arista 0661
8/28/82	**40**	2	8. Love Or Let Me Be Lonely	Arista 0697
			DAVIS, Sammy, Jr.	
			Born on 12/08/25 in New York City; died of throat cancer on 5/16/90. Vocalist/dancer/actor of Broadway, film and TV. With family dance act, the Will Mastin Trio, in the early 1940s.	
5/28/55	**12**	12	1. Love Me Or Leave Me/ Best Seller #12 / Jockey #20 from the film of the same title	
6/04/55	**9**	11	**2. Something's Gotta Give** Best Seller #9 / Juke Box #16 / Jockey #20 from the film *Daddy Long Legs*	Decca 29484
7/02/55	**13**	6	3. That Old Black Magic Jockey #13 / Best Seller #16 / Juke Box #18 #1 hit for Glenn Miller in 1943	Decca 29541
10/06/62	**17**	10	4. What Kind Of Fool Am I from the musical *Stop the World-I Want to Get Off*	Reprise 20048
2/01/64	**17**	9	5. The Shelter Of Your Arms	Reprise 20216
6/24/67	**37**	4	6. Don't Blame The Children [S]	Reprise 0566
1/18/69	**11**	11	7. I've Gotta Be Me from the Broadway musical *Golden Rainbow*	Reprise 0779
4/15/72	**1**(3)	16	● **8. The Candy Man** from the film *Willy Wonka and the Chocolate Factory*	MGM 14320

DATE	POS	WKS	ARTIST—RECORD TITLE	LABEL & NO.
			DAVIS, Skeeter	
			Country singer. Born Mary Penick on 12/30/31 in Dry Ridge, Kentucky. Recorded with friend Betty Davis as the Davis Sisters, until Betty was killed in a car accident on 8/02/53. Formerly married to TV's "Nashville Now" host, Ralph Emery. Later married Joey Spampinato, the bassist of jazz-rock band NRBQ.	
9/05/60	**39**	1	1. (I Can't Help You) I'm Falling Too answer song to Hank Locklin's "Please Help Me, I'm Falling"	RCA 7767
1/16/61	**26**	2	2. My Last Date (With You) answer song to Floyd Cramer's "Last Date"	RCA 7825
2/16/63	**2**(1)	13	**3. The End Of The World**	RCA 8098
9/21/63	**7**	11	**4. I Can't Stay Mad At You**	RCA 8219
			DAVIS, Spencer, Group	
			Davis was born on 7/14/41. Vocalist/rhythm guitarist. Formed his R&B-styled rock group in Birmingham, England in 1963. Featured Steve Winwood (lead vocals, lead guitar, keyboards), his brother Muff Winwood (bass) and Pete York (drums). Steve Winwood left in 1967 to form the group Traffic; later, a successful solo artist. Muff became senior director of A&R at CBS Records, U.K.	
1/28/67	**7**	9	**1. Gimme Some Lovin'**	United Art. 50108
4/08/67	**10**	7	**2. I'm A Man**	United Art. 50144
			DAVIS, Tyrone	
			Soul singer. Born on 5/04/38 in Greenville, Mississippi and raised in Saginaw, Michigan. To Chicago in 1959. Worked as valet/chauffeur for Freddy King until 1962. Working local clubs when discovered by Harold Burrage. First recorded for Four Brothers in 1965 as Tyrone The Wonder Boy. His younger sister, Jean Davis, was a member of the group Facts Of Life.	
1/04/69	**5**	11	● **1. Can I Change My Mind**	Dakar 602
4/12/69	**34**	2	2. Is It Something You've Got	Dakar 605
4/04/70	**3**	11	● **3. Turn Back The Hands Of Time**	Dakar 616
8/25/73	**32**	3	4. There It Is	Dakar 4523
10/30/76	**38**	4	5. Give It Up (Turn It Loose)	Columbia 10388
			DAWN	
			Vocal trio formed in New York City: Tony Orlando (b: 4/03/44, New York City), Telma Hopkins (b: 10/28/48, Louisville) and Joyce Vincent (b: 12/14/46, Detroit). Orlando had recorded solo from 1961-63; Hopkins and Vincent had been backup singers. Orlando was manager for April-Blackwood Music at the time of their first hit. Own TV show from 1974-76. All of their hits produced by Hank Medress (The Tokens) and Dave Appell. Hopkins in TV series "Bosom Buddies," "Gimme A Break" and "Family Matters."	
8/29/70	**3**	13	● **1. Candida**	Bell 903
12/05/70+	**1**(3)	16	● **2. Knock Three Times**	Bell 938
4/10/71	**25**	5	3. I Play And Sing	Bell 970
7/10/71	**33**	6	4. Summer Sand	Bell 45107
			DAWN featuring TONY ORLANDO:	
11/13/71	**39**	1	5. What Are You Doing Sunday	Bell 45141
3/17/73	**1**(4)	17	● **6. Tie A Yellow Ribbon Round The Ole Oak Tree**	Bell 45318
7/28/73	**3**	13	● **7. Say, Has Anybody Seen My Sweet Gypsy Rose**	Bell 45374
			TONY ORLANDO & DAWN:	
12/01/73	**27**	7	8. Who's In The Strawberry Patch With Sally	Bell 45424
9/07/74	**7**	9	**9. Steppin' Out (Gonna Boogie Tonight)**	Bell 45601
1/11/75	**11**	8	10. Look In My Eyes Pretty Woman	Bell 45620

DATE	POS	WKS	ARTIST—RECORD TITLE	LABEL & NO.
3/29/75	**1**(3)	10	● **11. He Don't Love You (Like I Love You)**	Elektra 45240
7/12/75	**14**	6	12. Mornin' Beautiful	Elektra 45260
9/20/75	**34**	3	13. You're All I Need To Get By	Elektra 45275
2/21/76	**22**	6	14. Cupid	Elektra 45302
			DAY, Bobby	
			R&B singer. Born Robert Byrd on 7/01/30 in Ft. Worth, Texas; died on 7/15/90 of cancer. To Watts, Los Angeles in 1948. Formed the Hollywood Flames in 1950. Group also recorded as The Flames in 1950. Wrote "Little Bitty Pretty One."	
8/04/58	**2**(2)	19	**1. Rock-in Robin** Hot 100 #2 / Best Seller #4 end	Class 229
			DAY, Doris	
			Born Doris Kappelhoff on 4/03/22 in Cincinnati. Doris sang briefly with Bob Crosby in 1940 and shortly thereafter became a major star with the Les Brown band ("Sentimental Journey"). Her great solo recording success was soon transcended by Hollywood as Doris became the #1 box office star of the late '50s and early '60s. Star of own popular TV series from 1968-73. Her son, Terry Melcher, was a member of the Rip Chords and Bruce & Terry, and a prolific producer (The Beach Boys).	
7/23/55	**13**	9	1. I'll Never Stop Loving You Jockey #13 / Best Seller #15 / Top 100 #93 pre from the film *Love Me or Leave Me*	Columbia 40505
7/07/56	**2**(3)	22	**2. Whatever Will Be, Will Be (Que Sera, Sera)** Top 100 #2 / Jockey #2 / Best Seller #3 / Juke Box #3 from the film *The Man Who Knew Too Much*	Columbia 40704
7/21/58	**6**	12	**3. Everybody Loves A Lover** Jockey #6 end / Hot 100 #14 / Best Seller #17	Columbia 41195
			DAY, Morris	
			Leader of Minneapolis funk group The Time (formerly Prince's backing band). Born in Springfield, Illinois and raised in Minneapolis. Acted in the films *Purple Rain, The Adventures of Ford Fairlane* and *Graffiti Bridge*.	
3/26/88	**23**	6	1. Fishnet	Warner 28201
			DAYNE, Taylor	
			Real name: Leslie Wonderman. Female singer from Long Island, New York.	
11/14/87+	**7**	15	● **1. Tell It To My Heart**	Arista 9612
3/12/88	**7**	11	**2. Prove Your Love**	Arista 9676
7/23/88	**3**	16	● **3. I'll Always Love You**	Arista 9700
11/26/88+	**2**(1)	13	**4. Don't Rush Me**	Arista 9722
11/04/89	**5**	13	**5. With Every Beat Of My Heart**	Arista 9895
2/03/90	**1**(1)	15	● **6. Love Will Lead You Back**	Arista 9938
5/19/90	**4**	12	**7. I'll Be Your Shelter**	Arista 2005
8/18/90	**12**	10	8. Heart Of Stone	Arista 2057
			DAZZ BAND	
			Cleveland ultrafunk band, formerly Kinsman Dazz. "Dazz" means "danceable jazz."	
5/15/82	**5**	16	**1. Let It Whip**	Motown 1609
			DEAD OR ALIVE	
			Disco outfit formed in Liverpool, England by lead singer Pete Burns (b: 8/05/59). Wayne Hussey (later a member of Sisters Of Mercy and Mission) was an early member.	
6/29/85	**11**	11	1. You Spin Me Round (Like A Record)	Epic 04894

DATE	POS	WKS	ARTIST—RECORD TITLE	LABEL & NO.
1/31/87	**15**	9	2. Brand New Lover	Epic 06374
			DEAL, Bill/The Rhondels	
			Eight-man, brassy-rock band from New York City.	
3/15/69	**39**	1	1. May I	Heritage 803
5/31/69	**35**	3	2. I've Been Hurt	Heritage 812
9/13/69	**23**	5	3. What Kind Of Fool Do You Think I Am	Heritage 817
			DEAN, Jimmy	
			Born on 8/10/28 in Plainview, Texas. Vocalist/pianist/guitarist/composer. With Tennessee Haymakers in Washington, D.C. in 1948. Own Texas Wildcats in 1952. Recorded for Four Star in 1952. Own CBS-TV series, 1957-58; ABC-TV series, 1963-66.	
1/06/58+	**32**	1	1. Little Sandy Sleighfoot [X-N] Top 100 #32 / Best Seller #37	Columbia 41025
10/09/61	**1**(5)	13	• **2. Big Bad John** **[S]**	Columbia 42175
1/20/62	**24**	3	3. Dear Ivan [S] background music: "Battle Hymn Of The Republic"	Columbia 42259
2/10/62	**22**	5	4. The Cajun Queen/ [S]	
2/10/62	**26**	5	5. To A Sleeping Beauty [S] background music: "Memories"; soliloquy first recorded by Jackie Gleason in 1957 (Capitol EP-871)	Columbia 42282
4/14/62	**8**	9	**6. P.T. 109** based on the sinking of John F. Kennedy's torpedo boat in 1943	Columbia 42338
10/06/62	**29**	5	7. Little Black Book	Columbia 42529
5/22/76	**35**	2	• 8. I.O.U. [S] Jimmy Dean's ode of thanks to his mother	Casino 052
			DEAN AND JEAN	
			Welton Young and Brenda Lee Jones from Dayton, Ohio.	
12/14/63+	**35**	2	1. Tra La La La Suzy	Rust 5067
3/21/64	**32**	3	2. Hey Jean, Hey Dean	Rust 5075
			DeBARGE/EL DeBARGE	
			Family group from Grand Rapids, Michigan. Consisted of lead vocalist Eldra (b: 6/04/61; keyboards), Mark (trumpet, saxophone), James (keyboards), Randy (bass) and Bunny DeBarge (vocals). Brothers Bobby and Tommy were in Switch. James was briefly married to Janet Jackson in 1984.	
			DeBARGE:	
3/26/83	**31**	6	1. I Like It	Gordy 1645
5/28/83	**17**	10	2. All This Love	Gordy 1660
11/26/83+	**18**	11	3. Time Will Reveal	Gordy 1705
3/09/85	**3**	14	**4. Rhythm Of The Night** from the Berry Gordy film *The Last Dragon*	Gordy 1770
6/22/85	**6**	12	**5. Who's Holding Donna Now**	Gordy 1793
			EL DeBARGE:	
5/17/86	**3**	13	**6. Who's Johnny** theme from the film *Short Circuit*	Gordy 1842
4/07/90	**31**	4	7. The Secret Garden (Sweet Seduction Suite) **QUINCY JONES/AL B. SURE!/JAMES INGRAM/ EL DeBARGE/BARRY WHITE**	Qwest 19992

DATE	POS	WKS	ARTIST—RECORD TITLE	LABEL & NO.
			DeBARGE, Chico	
			DeBarge sibling, but not a member of the group DeBarge.	
12/27/86+	**21**	11	1. Talk To Me	Motown 1858
			DeBURGH, Chris	
			British pop-rock singer. Born Christopher John Davidson on 10/15/48 in Argentina of Irish parentage.	
6/11/83	**34**	4	1. Don't Pay The Ferryman	A&M 2511
4/04/87	**3**	14	**2. The Lady In Red**	A&M 2848
			DeCASTRO SISTERS, The	
			Peggy, Babette and Cherie DeCastro; raised on their father's sugar plantation in Cuba.	
5/07/55	**17**	4	1. Boom Boom Boomerang Juke Box #17 / Best Seller #24 bass voice: Thurl Ravenscroft	Abbott 3003
			DEE, Joey/The Starliters	
			Born Joseph DiNicola on 6/11/40 in Passaic, New Jersey. In September 1960, Joey & The Starlighters became the house band at the Peppermint Lounge, New York City. After 1964, group included three members who later formed The Young Rascals, plus guitarist Jimi Hendrix. In films *Hey, Let's Twist* and *Two Tickets to Paris*.	
12/04/61+	**1**(3)	14	**1. Peppermint Twist - Part I** inspired by New York City's Peppermint Lounge club	Roulette 4401
3/03/62	**20**	4	2. Hey, Let's Twist	Roulette 4408
3/31/62	**6**	9	**3. Shout - Part I** above 2 from the film *Hey, Let's Twist!* starring Dee	Roulette 4416
9/15/62	**18**	6	4. What Kind Of Love Is This from the film *Two Tickets to Paris*; written by Johnny Nash	Roulette 4438
6/01/63	**36**	1	5. Hot Pastrami With Mashed Potatoes - Part I	Roulette 4488
			DEE, Johnny — see LOUDERMILK, John D.	
			DEE, Kiki	
			Born Pauline Matthews on 3/06/47 in Yorkshire, England.	
10/19/74	**12**	10	1. I've Got The Music In Me **THE KIKI DEE BAND**	Rocket 40293
7/17/76	**1**(4)	15	● **2. Don't Go Breaking My Heart** **ELTON JOHN AND KIKI DEE**	Rocket 40585
			DEE, Lenny	
			Organist, born in the 1920s in Illinois and raised in Florida. Discovered by Red Foley.	
2/12/55	**19**	15	1. Plantation Boogie [I] Juke Box #19 / Best Seller #23	Decca 29360
			DEE, Tommy	
			Born Thomas Donaldson on 7/15/36 in Vicker, Virginia. Disc jockey at KFXM-San Bernadino at time of only hit; first recorded by Eddie Cochran. Currently a producer/promoter/record company exec. in Nashville.	
4/13/59	**11**	8	1. Three Stars [S] a tribute to Buddy Holly, Ritchie Valens and The Big Bopper; narration by Tommy Dee; vocals by Carol Kay and the Teen-Aires	Crest 1057

DATE	POS	WKS	ARTIST—RECORD TITLE	LABEL & NO.
			DEEE-LITE	
			New York-based dance trio: Super DJ Dmitry (from Kiev, Soviet Union), Jungle DJ Towa Towa (from Tokyo, Japan) and vocalist Lady Miss Kier (Kier Kirby from Youngstown, Ohio). Group's name inspired by the tune "It's De-lovely" from the 1936 Cole Porter musical *Red, Hot & Blue.*	
10/20/90	**4**	13	● **1. Groove Is In The Heart**	Elektra 64934#
			features backing vocals by Bootsy Collins and rap by Q-Tip of A Tribe Called Quest	
			DEELE, The	
			R&B funk sextet from Cincinnati, led by Darnell "Dee" Bristol. Included the songwriting/production team of Mark "L.A. Reid" Rooney and Kenneth "Babyface" Edmonds. Reid (cousin of Keith Mitchell of After 7 and son of The Exciters' Herb Rooney and Brenda Reid) married Pebbles in 1989. Former member of Manchild, Edmonds (brother of After 7's Kevon and Melvin Edmonds) began solo career as Babyface in 1989.	
4/02/88	**10**	12	**1. Two Occasions**	Solar 70015
			DEEP PURPLE	
			British hard-rock band: Ritchie Blackmore (guitar), Rod Evans (vocals), Jon Lord (keyboards), Ian Paice (drums) and Nicky Simper (bass). Evans and Simper left in 1969, replaced by Ian Gillan and Roger Glover. Gillan and Glover left in late 1973. New members included David Coverdale and Tommy Bolin (ex-James Gang; d: 1976). Blackmore left to form Rainbow (which Glover later joined). Coverdale, Lord and Paice formed Whitesnake. Blackmore, Gillan, Lord and Paice reunited in 1984. Gillan left in 1989 to form Garth Rockett & The Moonshiners. 1990 lineup featured former Rainbow vocalist Joe Lynn Turner, with Blackmore, Lord, Paice and Glover.	
8/24/68	**4**	9	**1. Hush**	Tetragramm. 1503
12/07/68	**38**	3	2. Kentucky Woman	Tetragramm. 1508
6/16/73	**4**	12	● **3. Smoke On The Water**	Warner 7710
			DEES, Rick, And His Cast Of Idiots	
			Rick was born Rigdon Osmond Dees III in Memphis in 1950. DJ working at WMPS-Memphis when he conceived idea for "Disco Duck." Currently one of America's top radio DJs. Host of TV's "Solid Gold" (1984) and his own late-night talk show "Into The Night."	
9/04/76	**1**(1)	16	▲ **1. Disco Duck (Part 1)** [N]	RSO 857
			DEF LEPPARD	
			Hard-rock quintet formed in Sheffield, England in 1977: Joe Elliott (lead singer), Pete Willis & Steve Clark (lead guitars), Rick Savage (bass) and Rick Allen (drums; lost his left arm in an auto accident on New Year's Eve in 1984). Phil Collen replaced Pete Willis in late 1982. Clark died on 1/08/91 (age 30) of alcohol-related respiratory failure. Band continued to record as a quartet.	
4/16/83	**12**	9	1. Photograph	Mercury 811215
7/09/83	**16**	9	2. Rock Of Ages	Mercury 812604
10/08/83	**28**	5	3. Foolin'	Mercury 814178
11/21/87	**19**	9	4. Animal	Mercury 888832
2/13/88	**10**	10	**5. Hysteria**	Mercury 870004
5/21/88	**2**(1)	15	**6. Pour Some Sugar On Me**	Mercury 870298
8/20/88	**1**(1)	13	**7. Love Bites**	Mercury 870402
12/03/88+	**3**	12	**8. Armageddon It**	Mercury 870692
3/18/89	**12**	9	9. Rocket	Mercury 872614

DATE	POS	WKS	ARTIST—RECORD TITLE	LABEL & NO.
			DeFRANCO FAMILY featuring TONY DeFRANCO	
			Family group from Ontario: Tony (age 13 in 1973), Merlina (16), Nino (17), Marisa (18) and Benny (19).	
9/29/73	**3**	14	● **1. Heartbeat - It's A Lovebeat**	20th Century 2030
1/26/74	**32**	4	2. Abra-Ca-Dabra	20th Century 2070
5/25/74	**18**	6	3. Save The Last Dance For Me	20th Century 2088
			DeJOHN SISTERS	
			Julie (b: 3/18/31) and Dux (b: 1/21/33) DeGiovanni from Chester, Pennsylvania.	
12/25/54+	**6**	13	**1. (My Baby Don't Love Me) No More** Jockey #6 / Best Seller #8 / Juke Box #11	Epic 9085
			DEKKER, Desmond/The Aces	
			Born Desmond Dacris on 7/16/41 in Kingston, Jamaica. Reggae's first successful artist.	
6/07/69	**9**	7	**1. Israelites**	Uni 55129
			del AMITRI	
			Rock quartet from Glasgow, Scotland led by vocalist Justin Currie and guitarist Iain Harvie.	
6/30/90	**35**	3	1. Kiss This Thing Goodbye	A&M 1485#
			DELANEY & BONNIE	
			Delaney Bramlett (b: 7/01/39, Acton, Illinois) and wife Bonnie Lynn Bramlett (b: 11/08/44, Pontotoc County, Mississippi). Friends — backing artists included, at various times, Leon Russell, Rita Coolidge, Dave Mason, Eric Clapton, Duane Allman and many others.	
6/26/71	**13**	10	1. Never Ending Song Of Love DELANEY & BONNIE AND FRIENDS	Atco 6804
10/09/71	**20**	7	2. Only You Know And I Know	Atco 6838
			DE LA SOUL	
			Psychedelic rap trio from Amityville, Long Island, New York: Posdnous (Kelvin Mercer), Trugoy the Dove (David Jolicoeur) and P.A. Pasemaster Mase (Vincent Mason, Jr.).	
7/22/89	**34**	3	● 1. Me Myself And I	Tommy B. 7926#
			DELEGATES, The	
			A Dickie Goodman-type recording, featuring DJ Bob DeCarlo.	
11/04/72	**8**	6	**1. Convention '72** [N] featuring bits of some of the top pop hits of 1972	Mainstream 5525
			DELFONICS, The	
			Soul group from Philadelphia. Formed in 1965 as the Four Gents. Consisted of William and Wilbert Hart, Ritchie Daniels and Randy Cain. First recorded for Moon Shot in 1967. Daniels left for the service in 1968, group continued as a trio. Cain was replaced by Major Harris in 1971. Harris went solo in 1974.	
2/24/68	**4**	12	**1. La - La - Means I Love You**	Philly Groove 150
10/05/68	**35**	4	2. Break Your Promise	Philly Groove 152
1/25/69	**35**	1	3. Ready Or Not Here I Come (Can't Hide From Love)	Philly Groove 154
10/04/69	**40**	2	4. You Got Yours And I'll Get Mine	Philly Groove 157
2/07/70	**10**	10	● **5. Didn't I (Blow Your Mind This Time)**	Philly Groove 161
7/25/70	**40**	1	6. Trying To Make A Fool Of Me	Philly Groove 162

DATE	POS	WKS	ARTIST—RECORD TITLE	LABEL & NO.
			all of above produced by Thom Bell	
			DELIVERANCE Soundtrack — see WEISSBERG, Steve	
			DELLS, The	
			R&B vocal group formed at Thornton Township High School in Harvey, Illinois: Johnny Funches (lead), Marvin Junior (baritone lead), Verne Allison (tenor), Mickey McGill (baritone) and Chuck Barksdale (bass). First recorded as the El-Rays for Chess in 1953. Signed with Vee-Jay in 1955. Group remained intact into the 1980s, with the exception of Funches, who was replaced by Johnny Carter (ex-Flamingos) in 1960.	
2/17/68	**20**	7	1. There Is	Cadet 5590
7/20/68	**10**	10	**2. Stay In My Corner** [R] originally a #23 R&B hit on Vee-Jay 674 in 1965	Cadet 5612
11/02/68	**18**	5	3. Always Together	Cadet 5621
2/08/69	**38**	2	4. Does Anybody Know I'm Here	Cadet 5631
6/21/69	**22**	6	5. I Can Sing A Rainbow/Love Is Blue	Cadet 5641
8/23/69	**10**	10	**6. Oh, What A Night** [R] originally a #4 R&B hit on Vee-Jay 204 in 1956	Cadet 5649
9/18/71	**30**	6	7. The Love We Had (Stays On My Mind)	Cadet 5683
6/23/73	**34**	2	● 8. Give Your Baby A Standing Ovation	Cadet 5696
			DELL-VIKINGS, The	
			Interracial R&B-rock group formed at the Air Force Serviceman's Club in Pittsburgh in 1955. Consisted of Norman Wright, Corinthian "Kripp" Johnson, Donald "Gus" Backus, David Lerchey and Clarence Quick. Backus and Lerchey are white, others black. First recorded for Fee Bee and Luniverse labels, then Dot. After discharge from the Air Force, Johnson formed new Dell-Vikings for the Dot label with Chuck Jackson, who went on to a successful solo career. Backus and the other members formed new Del Vikings group for Mercury in 1957. Johnson died on 6/22/90 (age 57) of prostate cancer.	
3/02/57	**4**	22	**1. Come Go With Me** Best Seller #4 / Top 100 #5 / Jockey #6 / Juke Box #6 first released on Fee Bee 205 in 1956	Dot 15538
7/15/57	**9**	13	**2. Whispering Bells** Top 100 #9 / Best Seller #10 / Jockey #19 first released on Fee Bee 214 in 1956	Dot 15592
7/15/57	**12**	1	3. Cool Shake **DEL VIKINGS** Jockey #12 / Top 100 #46	Mercury 71132
			DEMENSIONS, The	
			Vocal group from the Bronx: Phil Del Giudice (lead), Lenny Dell, Howard Margolin and Marisa Martelli.	
8/08/60	**16**	9	1. Over The Rainbow first sung by Judy Garland in the movie *The Wizard of Oz*	Mohawk 116
			DENNIS, Cathy	
			Former lead singer of D-Mob. Born in 1970 in Norwich, England.	
12/08/90+	**9**	12	**1. Just Another Dream**	Polydor 877962
3/23/91	**2(2)**	14	**2. Touch Me (All Night Long)** #70 R&B hit for Wish featuring Fonda Rae in 1985	Polydor 879466
7/27/91	**8**	13	**3. Too Many Walls**	Polydor 867134

DATE	POS	WKS	ARTIST—RECORD TITLE	LABEL & NO.
			DENNY, Martin, The Exotic Sounds Of	
			Denny was born on 4/10/11 in New York City. Composer/arranger/pianist. Originated the "Exotic Sounds" in Hawaii, featuring Julius Wechter (Baja Marimba Band) on vibes and marimba.	
4/27/59	**4**	13	**1. Quiet Village** [I]	Liberty 55162
			written by Les Baxter	
11/16/59	**28**	2	2. The Enchanted Sea [I]	Liberty 55212
			DENVER, John	
			Born John Henry Deutschendorf on 12/31/43 in Roswell, New Mexico. To Los Angeles in 1964. With the Chad Mitchell Trio from 1965-68. Wrote "Leaving On A Jet Plane." Starred in the 1978 film *Oh, God.* Won an Emmy in 1975 for the TV special "An Evening with John Denver."	
6/26/71	**2**(1)	14	● **1. Take Me Home, Country Roads**	RCA 0445
			backing vocals by Fat City (Bill Danoff & Taffy Nivert, later of Starland Vocal Band)	
1/06/73	**9**	12	**2. Rocky Mountain High**	RCA 0829
2/16/74	**1**(1)	13	● **3. Sunshine On My Shoulders**	RCA 0213
6/15/74	**1**(2)	11	● **4. Annie's Song**	RCA 0295
			written by Denver for his wife Ann Martell (married 1967-83)	
10/05/74	**5**	10	● **5. Back Home Again**	RCA 10065
1/11/75	**13**	8	6. Sweet Surrender	RCA 10148
4/05/75	**1**(1)	15	● **7. Thank God I'm A Country Boy**	RCA 10239
			above 2 recorded live at Universal City Amphitheater, California	
8/30/75	**1**(1)	13	● **8. I'm Sorry/**	
10/11/75	**2**(4)	7	**9. Calypso**	RCA 10353
			dedicated to Jacques Cousteau and his ship "Calypso"	
12/13/75+	**13**	9	10. Fly Away	RCA 10517
			backing vocals by Olivia Newton-John	
3/20/76	**29**	4	11. Looking For Space	RCA 10586
10/02/76	**36**	2	12. Like A Sad Song	RCA 10774
4/30/77	**32**	3	13. My Sweet Lady	RCA 10911
			also the B-side of "Thank God I'm A Country Boy"; all of above produced by Milton Okun	
9/05/81	**36**	4	14. Some Days Are Diamonds (Some Days Are Stone)	RCA 12246
4/24/82	**31**	5	15. Shanghai Breezes	RCA 13071
			DEODATO	
			Born Eumir Deodato Almeida on 6/21/42 in Rio de Janeiro, Brazil. Keyboardist/composer/producer/ arranger. Kool & The Gang's producer from 1979-82.	
2/17/73	**2**(1)	10	**1. Also Sprach Zarathustra (2001)** [I]	CTI 12
			theme from the film *2001: A Space Odyssey*, written by classical composer Richard Strauss in 1896	
			DEPECHE MODE	
			All-synthesized band formed in Basildon, England consisting of David Gahan (vocals), Martin Gore, Vince Clarke and Andy Fletcher. Clarke left in 1982 (formed Yaz, then Erasure), replaced by Alan Wilder. Group name is French for "fast fashion." Gore recorded solo in 1989.	
6/22/85	**13**	10	1. People Are People	Sire 29221
2/10/90	**28**	6	● 2. Personal Jesus	Sire 19941#
5/26/90	**8**	12	● **3. Enjoy The Silence**	Sire 19885
9/01/90	**15**	9	4. Policy Of Truth	Sire 19842

DATE	POS	WKS	ARTIST—RECORD TITLE	LABEL & NO.
			DEREK	
			Derek is singer Johnny Cymbal and producer George Tobin.	
11/23/68+	**11**	11	1. Cinnamon	Bang 558
			DEREK AND THE DOMINOS — see CLAPTON, Eric	
			DERRINGER, Rick	
			Born Richard Zehringer on 8/05/47 in Celina, Ohio. Lead singer/guitarist of The McCoys. Performed on and produced sessions for both Edgar and Johnny Winter's bands; also a producer for "Weird Al" Yankovic.	
3/02/74	**23**	6	1. Rock And Roll, Hoochie Koo	Blue Sky 2751
			DeSARIO, Teri	
			Singer/songwriter from Miami.	
12/22/79+	**2**(2)	16	● **1. Yes, I'm Ready** TERI DeSARIO with K.C.	Casablanca 2227
			DeSHANNON, Jackie	
			Born Sharon Myers on 8/21/44 in Hazel, Kentucky. Vocalist/composer. On radio at age six. First recorded (as Sherry Lee Myers) for Glenn in 1959. To Los Angeles in 1960. Attained prominence as a prolific songwriter (over 600 to date). Co-writer of mega-pop hit "Bette Davis Eyes." Toured with The Beatles for 26 concerts in 1964. In the films *Surf Party, C'mon Let's Live a Little* and *Hide and Seek*. Married composer/film scorer (*Ghostbusters II, Twins, Kindergarten Cop*) Randy Edelman.	
6/19/65	**7**	9	**1. What The World Needs Now Is Love**	Imperial 66110
7/26/69	**4**	10	● **2. Put A Little Love In Your Heart**	Imperial 66385
12/06/69	**40**	1	3. Love Will Find A Way	Imperial 66419
			DESMOND, Johnny	
			Born Giovanni Desimons on 11/14/20 in Detroit; died on 9/06/85. Sang with Bob Crosby, Gene Krupa and Glenn Miller's military band. Featured on the "Breakfast Club" radio show throughout the 1950s.	
3/26/55	**6**	11	**1. Play Me Hearts And Flowers (I Wanna Cry)** Jockey #6 / Juke Box #11 / Best Seller #16	Coral 61379
8/13/55	**3**	16	**2. The Yellow Rose Of Texas** Jockey #3 / Juke Box #4 / Best Seller #6 / Top 100 #16 pre	Coral 61476
12/03/55	**17**	1	3. Sixteen Tons Jockey #17 / Top 100 #50 orchestra on above 2 directed by Dick Jacobs	Coral 61529
			DETERGENTS, The	
			Trio from New York: Ron Dante (of Archies, Cuff Links), Tommy Wynn and Danny Jordan.	
12/19/64+	**19**	6	1. Leader Of The Laundromat [N] parody of The Shangri-Las' "Leader Of The Pack"	Roulette 4590
			DETROIT EMERALDS	
			Group formed in Little Rock, Arkansas by the Tilmon brothers: Abrim (d: 1982, heart attack), Ivory, Cleophus and Raymond. In 1970, group reduced to trio of: Abrim, Ivory and friend James Mitchell.	
2/19/72	**36**	4	1. You Want It, You Got It	Westbound 192
7/29/72	**24**	7	2. Baby Let Me Take You (In My Arms)	Westbound 203

DATE	POS	WKS	ARTIST—RECORD TITLE	LABEL & NO.
			DeVAUGHN, William	
			R&B vocalist/songwriter/guitarist from Washington, D.C. Worked for the federal government.	
5/18/74	**4**	10	● **1. Be Thankful For What You Got**	Roxbury 0236
			DEVICE	
			Los Angeles-based, pop-rock trio: Paul Engemann (lead singer), Holly Knight (keyboards, bass) and Gene Black (guitar). Engemann joined Animotion in 1988.	
8/02/86	**35**	4	1. Hanging On A Heart Attack	Chrysalis 42996
			DEVO	
			Robotic rock group formed in Akron, Ohio, consisting of brothers Mark and Bob Mothersbaugh, brothers Jerry and Bob Casale, and Alan Myers. David Kendrick replaced Myers by 1988. Mark and Jerry met while both were art students at Kent State.	
10/04/80	**14**	15	● 1. Whip It	Warner 49550
			DeVORZON, Barry, and Perry Botkin, Jr.	
			Songwriting/producing/arranging duo based in California. Barry was born on 7/31/34 in New York City. Founded Valiant Records (The Cascades were on this label). Leader of Barry & The Tamerlanes. Began prolific songwriting career in the mid-1950s. Perry was born on 4/16/33 in New York City. Son of orchestra leader Perry Botkin, Sr.	
10/02/76	**8**	16	● **1. Nadia's Theme (The Young And The Restless)** [I] originally written as "Cotton's Dream" for the film *Bless the Beasts & Children*, then used as the theme song for TV's "The Young and the Restless," and finally as the music for then Romanian olympic gymnast Nadia Comaneci	A&M 1856
			DEVOTIONS, The	
			Vocal quintet formed in New York City in 1960: Ray Sanchez (bass, lead), Bob Weisbrod, Bob Hovorka and Frank and Joe Pardo. Broke up in 1964 before their first hit.	
4/04/64	**36**	1	1. Rip Van Winkle [N] first released on Delta 101 and then on Roulette 4406 in 1962	Roulette 4541
			DEXYS MIDNIGHT RUNNERS	
			Kevin Rowland (b: 8/17/53, Wolverhampton, England), leader of eight-piece Birmingham, England band.	
2/26/83	**1**(1)	14	**1. Come On Eileen**	Mercury 76189
			DeYOUNG, Cliff	
			Born on 2/12/46 in Los Angeles. Actor in many films (*Harry & Tonto*, *Protocol*, *F/X*, *Glory* and others) and several made-for-TV movies (*Sunshine*, among them).	
2/16/74	**17**	8	1. My Sweet Lady written by John Denver; from the TV soundtrack "Sunshine"	MCA 40156
			DeYOUNG, Dennis	
			Born on 2/18/47 in Chicago. Lead singer/keyboardist of Styx.	
9/22/84	**10**	12	**1. Desert Moon**	A&M 2666
			DIAMOND, Leo	
			Born on 6/29/15 in New York City; died in Los Angeles on 9/15/66. Arranger/lead harmonica player for The Borrah Minevitch Harmonica Rascals, 1930-46.	
2/19/55	**30**	1	1. Melody Of Love [I] Best Seller #30	RCA 5973

DATE	POS	WKS	ARTIST—RECORD TITLE	LABEL & NO.
			DIAMOND, Neil	
			Born on 1/24/41 in Brooklyn. Vocalist/guitarist/prolific composer. With Roadrunners folk group, 1954-56. Worked as song-plugger/staff writer in New York City. Wrote for "The Monkees" TV show. First recorded for Duel in 1961. Wrote score for the film *Jonathan Livingston Seagull.* Starred in and composed the music for *The Jazz Singer* in 1980.	
9/10/66	**6**	9	**1. Cherry, Cherry**	Bang 528
11/26/66	**16**	6	2. I Got The Feelin' (Oh No No)	Bang 536
2/11/67	**18**	5	3. You Got To Me	Bang 540
4/29/67	**10**	8	**4. Girl, You'll Be A Woman Soon**	Bang 542
8/05/67	**13**	7	5. I Thank The Lord For The Night Time	Bang 547
10/28/67	**22**	6	6. Kentucky Woman	Bang 551
3/29/69	**22**	7	7. Brother Love's Travelling Salvation Show	Uni 55109
7/12/69	**4**	12	• **8. Sweet Caroline (Good Times Never Seemed So Good)**	Uni 55136
11/15/69	**6**	12	• **9. Holly Holy**	Uni 55175
3/21/70	**24**	8	10. Shilo	Bang 575
5/16/70	**30**	4	11. Soolaimon (African Trilogy II)	Uni 55224
8/15/70	**21**	7	12. Solitary Man [R] re-entry of Neil's first hit (POS 55, 1966)	Bang 578
8/29/70	**1**(1)	14	• **13. Cracklin' Rosie**	Uni 55250
11/21/70	**20**	9	14. He Ain't Heavy...He's My Brother	Uni 55264
12/05/70	**36**	5	15. Do It	Bang 580
4/03/71	**4**	8	**16. I Am...I Said**	Uni 55278
11/27/71	**14**	7	17. Stones	Uni 55310
5/13/72	**1**(1)	12	• **18. Song Sung Blue**	Uni 55326
9/02/72	**11**	7	19. Play Me	Uni 55346
11/25/72	**17**	8	20. Walk On Water	Uni 55352
4/21/73	**31**	4	21. "Cherry Cherry" from Hot August Night [R] live version of Neil's 1966 hit (from *Hot August Night* LP)	MCA 40017
11/24/73	**34**	3	22. Be from the film *Jonathan Livingston Seagull*	Columbia 45942
10/19/74	**5**	10	**23. Longfellow Serenade**	Columbia 10043
3/01/75	**34**	2	24. I've Been This Way Before	Columbia 10084
6/26/76	**11**	8	25. If You Know What I Mean	Columbia 10366
12/24/77+	**16**	9	26. Desiree	Columbia 10657
11/04/78	**1**(2)	15	• **27. You Don't Bring Me Flowers** **BARBRA** (Streisand) & **NEIL**	Columbia 10840
2/17/79	**20**	6	28. Forever In Blue Jeans	Columbia 10897
1/19/80	**17**	10	29. September Morn'	Columbia 11175
11/01/80+	**2**(3)	17	**30. Love On The Rocks**	Capitol 4939
1/31/81	**6**	12	**31. Hello Again**	Capitol 4960
5/02/81	**8**	13	**32. America** above 3 from the film *The Jazz Singer* starring Diamond	Capitol 4994
11/14/81+	**11**	12	33. Yesterday's Songs	Columbia 02604
3/06/82	**27**	5	34. On The Way To The Sky	Columbia 02712
6/19/82	**35**	4	35. Be Mine Tonight	Columbia 02928
10/02/82	**5**	11	**36. Heartlight** inspired by the film *E.T.*	Columbia 03219

DATE	POS	WKS	ARTIST—RECORD TITLE	LABEL & NO.
2/19/83	**35**	4	37. I'm Alive all of above (except #14) composed by Diamond	Columbia 03503
			DIAMONDS, The	
			Vocal group from Toronto formed in 1953. Consisted of Dave Somerville (lead), Ted Kowalski (tenor), Phil Leavitt (baritone) and Bill Reed (bass). Recorded for Coral in 1955. Debuted on Mercury in January 1956. Michael Douglas replaced Leavitt in early 1958. Reed and Kowalski replaced in 1959 by Evan Fisher and John Felten (killed in a plane crash in 1982). Frequent personnel changes. Dave teamed with Four Preps' co-founder, Bruce Belland, as a duo from 1962-69. Bob Duncan (lead) joined in 1978 and re-formed the group, after Felten's death, with new lineup. Group hit the country charts in 1987.	
3/17/56	**12**	11	1. Why Do Fools Fall In Love Jockey #12 / Top 100 #16 / Best Seller #18 / Juke Box #19	Mercury 70790
5/12/56	**14**	11	2. The Church Bells May Ring Best Seller #14 / Juke Box #15 / Jockey #17 / Top 100 #20	Mercury 70835
7/28/56	**30**	2	3. Love, Love, Love	Mercury 70889
9/29/56	**34**	1	4. Soft Summer Breeze/	
9/29/56	**35**	2	5. Ka-Ding-Dong	Mercury 70934
3/16/57	**2**(8)	21	**6. Little Darlin'** Best Seller #2 / Top 100 #2 / Jockey #2 / Juke Box #2 original version by Maurice Williams' group, The Gladiolas	Mercury 71060
7/15/57	**13**	2	7. Words Of Love Jockey #13 / Top 100 #76 written by Buddy Holly	Mercury 71128
9/30/57	**16**	1	8. Zip Zip Jockey #16 / Top 100 # 45	Mercury 71165
11/04/57	**10**	8	**9. Silhouettes** Jockey #10 / Top 100 #60	Mercury 71197
1/06/58	**4**	14	**10. The Stroll** Jockey #4 / Top 100 #5 / Best Seller #7 orchestra arrangements on all of above by David Carroll	Mercury 71242
5/19/58	**37**	1	11. High Sign Best Seller #37 / Top 100 #38	Mercury 71291
7/28/58	**16**	1	12. Kathy-O Jockey #16 end / Best Seller #41 / Hot 100 #45 ballad from the Patty McCormack movie of the same title	Mercury 71330
11/17/58	**29**	6	13. Walking Along	Mercury 71366
2/09/59	**18**	10	14. She Say (Oom Dooby Doom)	Mercury 71404
8/07/61	**22**	4	15. One Summer Night	Mercury 71831
			DIBANGO, Manu	
			Jazz-R&B saxophonist/pianist. Born in 1934 in Cameroon, Africa.	
7/21/73	**35**	3	1. Soul Makossa [I]	Atlantic 2971
			DICK AND DEEDEE	
			Dick St. John Gosting and Deedee Sperling. Formed duo while students in high school at Santa Monica.	
8/28/61	**2**(2)	10	**1. The Mountain's High** first released on Lama 7778 in 1961	Liberty 55350
5/12/62	**22**	5	2. Tell Me first released on Lama 7783 in 1961	Liberty 55412
4/06/63	**17**	6	3. Young And In Love	Warner 5342
12/21/63+	**27**	4	4. Turn Around	Warner 5396

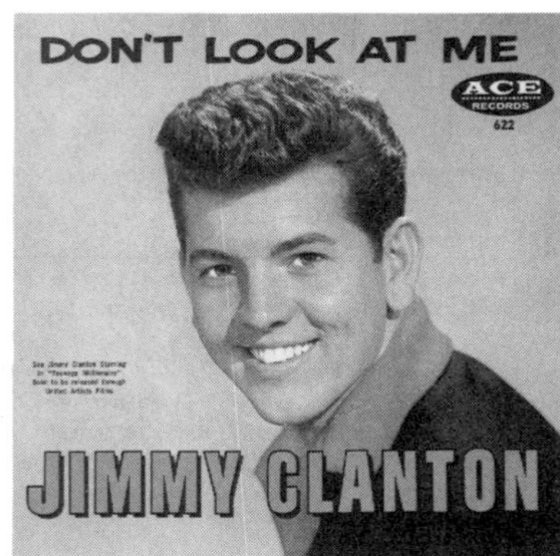

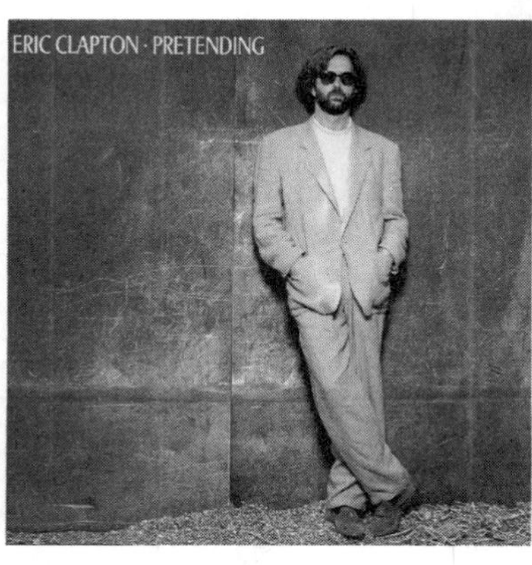

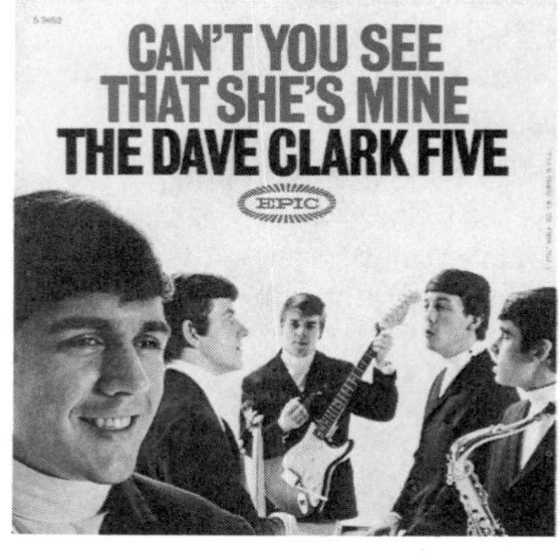

Cinderella brought some hard rocking back into the single charts in the late 80s with "Nobody's Fool" and "Don't Know What You Got (Till It's Gone)," tracks that reached Nos. 13 and 12, respectively. Many oldtimers begrudgingly respected them for their success despite their seemingly non-heavy-metal bandname.

Jimmy Clanton's last hit "Venus In Blue Jeans" had other female company in the Top 10 when it reached No. 7 in October 1962: the 4 Seasons' "Sherry" and Nat King Cole's "Ramblin Rose."

Eric Clapton's critical high-standing as a preeminent guitarist has not kept him out of the Top 10. Since "I Shot The Sheriff," which topped the chart in 1974, the former Yardbird and Cream member has had three other major hits: 1978's "Lay Down Sally" and "Promises," and 1981's "I Can't Stand It."

The Dave Clark Five's many hits—they had 12 in the Top 40 between 1964–1965 and early on were considered the Beatles' only serious competion—are presently unavailable to American consumers and highly sought-after by collectors.

Natalie Cole's career surged once again with her 1991 *Unforgettable* album, a tribute to her famous father, Nat King Cole. Just as country singer Hank Williams, Jr. sang a studio-concocted duet with his late father on 1989's "There's A Tear In My Beer," the two Coles sang together on the album's title track.

Nat King Cole's name was regularly heard in record stores in 1991, due not only to the album made in his honor by daughter Natalie, but to a flood of popular CD reissues from his former label, Capitol.

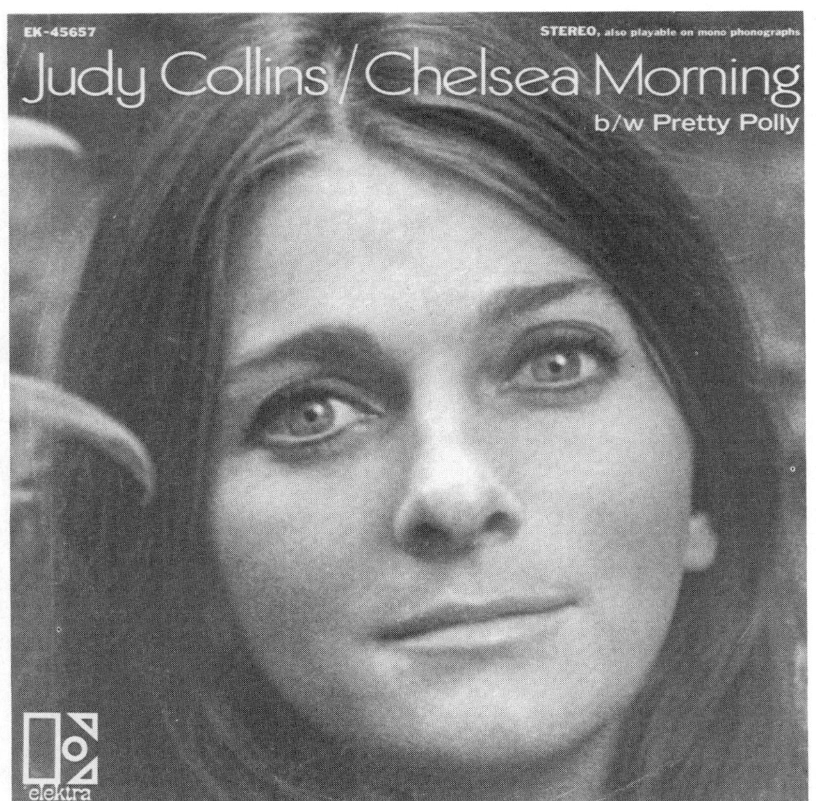

Judy Collins had five top-40 hits between 1968-1977, with Stephen Sondheim's memorable "Send In The Clowns" scoring both in 1975 and two years later. The distinguished singer, who recorded for Elektra for most of her lengthy career, surprised many when she moved to Sony Music in the early 90s.

Phil Collins may be a hitmaker now, but his first recorded exposure on these shores—on a 1969 Uni album by group Flaming Youth—went unnoticed by very many.

Sam Cooke's last top-40 hit, 1965's "Sugar Dumpling," peaked at No. 29—the same week that the Beatles' "Help," Bob Dylan's "Like A Rolling Stone," and the Beach Boys' "California Girls" were battling for (and respectively won) the chart's top three slots.

The Cover Girls typified the appeal of female-sung dance pop in the late 80s with 1988's "Because Of You," which peaked at No. 27. Well into the video age, the attractive trio was very accurately named.

The Cowboy Church Sunday School's "Open Up Your Heart (And Let The Sunshine In)" was one of the first examples of studio trickery. The track, which reached No. 8 in 1955, sounded as if it were sung by a child—but was in fact a woman's voice, speeded up.

Billy "Crash" Craddock's country stylings were deemed sufficiently pop enough to cross over to the Hot 100 in 1974 with two tracks—"Rub It In," which climbed to No. 16, and "Ruby, Baby," which peaked at 33.

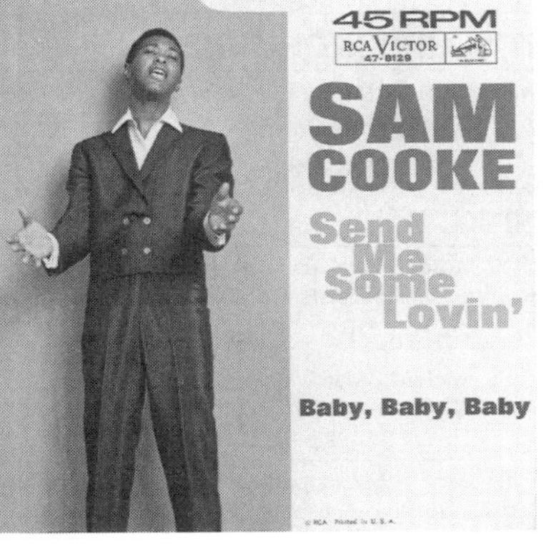

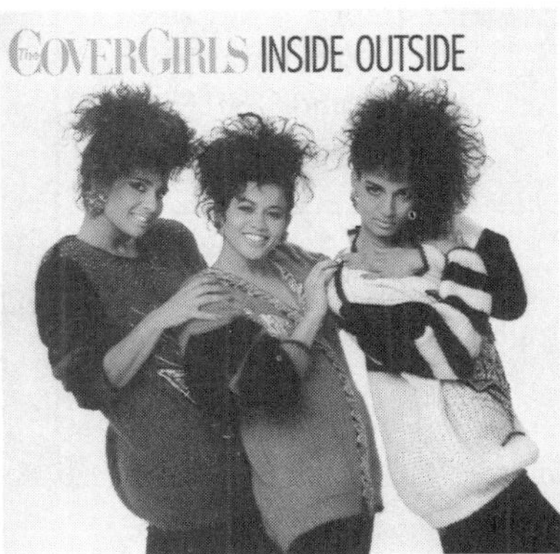

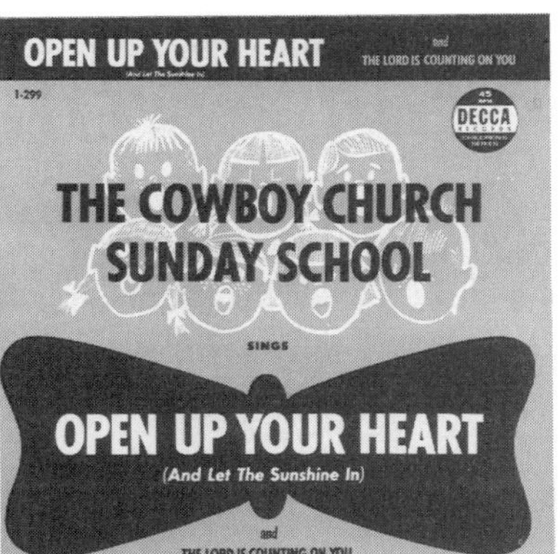

DATE	POS	WKS	ARTIST—RECORD TITLE	LABEL & NO.
12/12/64+	**13**	10	5. Thou Shalt Not Steal	Warner 5482
			DICKENS, "Little" Jimmy	
			Born on 12/19/20 in Bolt, West Virginia. Country singer who stands only 4'11" tall.	
11/13/65	**15**	5	1. May The Bird Of Paradise Fly Up Your Nose [N]	Columbia 43388
			DICKY DOO AND THE DON'TS	
			Vocal group founded by Gerry Granahan in Brooklyn. Group named after the nickname of Dick Clark's son, Dicky Doo. Group featured Harvey Davis (bass), Ray Gangi (guitar), Al Ways (sax) and Dave Alldred (ex-drummer of the Rhythm Orchids).	
2/17/58	**28**	6	1. Click-Clack Top 100 #28 / Best Seller #29	Swan 4001
5/12/58	**40**	1	2. Nee Nee Na Na Na Na Nu Nu [I] Top 100 #40 / Best Seller #42	Swan 4006
			DIDDLEY, Bo	
			Unique and influential R&B-rock & roll guitarist/vocalist. Born Otha Ellas Bates McDaniel on 12/30/28 in McComb, Mississippi. Adopted as an infant by his mother's cousin, Mrs. Gussie McDaniel. Moved to Chicago at age seven. Began recording in 1955 with the Chess/Checker label. Name "bo diddley" is a one-stringed African guitar. His first record was a two-sided #1 hit on the R&B charts, "Bo Diddley"/"I'm A Man." Inducted into the Rock and Roll Hall of Fame in 1987.	
10/05/59	**20**	7	1. Say Man [N] Bo trades insults with maracas player, Jerome Green	Checker 931
			DIESEL	
			Rock quartet from Holland featuring singer/guitarist Rob Vunderink.	
10/17/81	**25**	6	1. Sausalito Summernight	Regency 7339
			DIGITAL UNDERGROUND	
			Rap-funk crew based in Northern California. Features vocalists Humpty-Hump and Money-B. Appeared in the 1991 film *Nothing But Trouble.*	
4/14/90	**11**	14	▲ 1. The Humpty Dance	Tommy B. 7944#
			DINNING, Mark	
			Born on 8/17/33 in Drury, Oklahoma; died of a heart attack on 3/22/86. Brother of the Dinning Sisters vocal trio. First recorded for MGM in 1957.	
1/04/60	**1**(2)	14	**1. Teen Angel** written by Mark's sister, Jeannie	MGM 12845
			DINO	
			Las Vegas-based singer/songwriter/producer. Born Dino Esposito on 7/20/63 in Encino, California and raised in Hawaii and Connecticut. Former DJ/music director at KCEP in Las Vegas.	
6/24/89	**7**	14	● **1. I Like It**	4th & B'way 7483
10/14/89	**23**	6	2. Sunshine	4th & B'way 7489
9/01/90	**6**	10	**3. Romeo**	Island 878012
12/22/90+	**31**	5	4. Gentle lead female vocal by Delona Tanner	Island 878472#
			DINO, Kenny	
			Native of Hicksville, Long Island, New York. Born on 9/12/39.	
12/04/61	**24**	6	1. Your Ma Said You Cried In Your Sleep Last Night	Musicor 1013

DATE	POS	WKS	ARTIST—RECORD TITLE	LABEL & NO.
			DINO, Paul	
			Born Paul Dino Bertuccini, Jr on 3/02/35 in Philadelphia. Married for a time to Justine Correlli, a regular on TV's "American Bandstand."	
4/10/61	**38**	1	1. Ginnie Bell	Promo 2180
			DINO, DESI & BILLY	
			Dino (Dean Martin's son, Dean Martin, Jr.), Desi (Lucille Ball and Desi Arnaz's son, Desiderio Arnaz IV) & Billy (a schoolmate from Beverly Hills, William Hinsche.) Dino (formerly married to Olympic skater Dorothy Hamill) was killed on 3/21/87 (age 35) when his Air National Guard jet crashed.	
7/24/65	**17**	7	1. I'm A Fool	Reprise 0367
10/16/65	**25**	5	2. Not The Lovin' Kind	Reprise 0401
			DION	
			Born Dion DiMucci on 7/18/39 in the Bronx. First recorded as Dion & The Timberlanes on Mohawk in 1957. Formed vocal group, Dion & The Belmonts, in the Bronx in 1958. Consisted of Dion (lead), Angelo D'Aleo (b: 2/03/40; first tenor), Fred Milano (b: 8/22/39; second tenor) and Carlo Mastrangelo (b: 10/05/38; bass). Named for Belmont Avenue in the Bronx. Angelo was in the Navy in 1959 and missed some recording and picture sessions. Dion went solo in 1960. Moved to Miami in 1968. Brief reunion with the Belmonts in 1967 and 1972, periodically since then. Also records contemporary Christian songs. Inducted into the Rock and Roll Hall of Fame in 1989.	
			DION AND THE BELMONTS:	
5/26/58	**22**	10	1. I Wonder Why Top 100 #22 / Best Seller #24	Laurie 3013
9/15/58	**19**	8	2. No One Knows Best Seller #19 end / Hot 100 #24 #1 hit for Hal Kemp & His Orchestra in 1937	Laurie 3015
1/05/59	**40**	1	3. Don't Pity Me	Laurie 3021
4/27/59	**5**	13	**4. A Teenager In Love**	Laurie 3027
1/11/60	**3**	11	**5. Where Or When** #1 hit for Hal Kemp & His Orchestra in 1937	Laurie 3044
5/16/60	**30**	2	6. When You Wish Upon A Star from the film *Pinocchio*; #1 hit for Glenn Miller in 1940	Laurie 3052
8/15/60	**38**	1	7. In The Still Of The Night the Cole Porter classic; #3 hit for Tommy Dorsey in 1937	Laurie 3059
			DION:	
11/14/60	**12**	11	8. Lonely Teenager	Laurie 3070
10/02/61	**1**(2)	12	**9. Runaround Sue**	Laurie 3110
12/18/61+	**2**(1)	13	**10. The Wanderer/**	
12/18/61	**36**	1	11. The Majestic	Laurie 3115
5/05/62	**3**	9	**12. Lovers Who Wander**	Laurie 3123
7/21/62	**8**	8	**13. Little Diane**	Laurie 3134
11/24/62	**10**	9	**14. Love Came To Me**	Laurie 3145
1/26/63	**2**(3)	11	**15. Ruby Baby**	Columbia 42662
3/30/63	**21**	6	16. Sandy	Laurie 3153
5/04/63	**21**	6	17. This Little Girl	Columbia 42776
7/27/63	**31**	3	18. Be Careful Of Stones That You Throw	Columbia 42810
			DION DI MUCI:	
9/28/63	**6**	8	**19. Donna The Prima Donna**	Columbia 42852
11/23/63	**6**	9	**20. Drip Drop**	Columbia 42917

DATE	POS	WKS	ARTIST—RECORD TITLE	LABEL & NO.
			DION:	
11/02/68	**4**	12	• **21. Abraham, Martin And John** a tribute to Lincoln, King and Kennedy	Laurie 3464
			DION, Celine	
			French Canadian singer. Born on 3/30/68 in Charlemagne, Quebec. Popular in France and Canada since her teen years.	
1/05/91	**4**	15	**1. Where Does My Heart Beat Now**	Epic 73536
6/01/91	**35**	1	2. (If There Was) Any Other Way	Epic 73665
			DIRE STRAITS	
			Rock group formed in London by songwriter/producer Mark Knopfler (lead vocals, lead guitar) and his brother David Knopfler (guitar), with John Illsley (bass) and Pick Withers (drums). David left in late 1979, replaced by Hal Lindes (who left in 1985). Added keyboardist Alan Clark in 1982. Terry Williams replaced drummer Pick Withers in 1983. Guitarist Guy Fletcher added in 1984. Mark and Guy also worked with The Notting Hillbillies in 1990.	
2/17/79	**4**	12	**1. Sultans Of Swing**	Warner 8736
8/10/85	**1**(3)	13	**2. Money For Nothing** written by Sting and Mark Knopfler	Warner 28950
11/16/85+	**7**	15	**3. Walk Of Life**	Warner 28878
3/22/86	**19**	7	4. So Far Away	Warner 28789
			DIRKSEN, Senator Everett McKinley	
			U.S. senator from Illinois, 1950-69. Born in Pekin, Illinois in 1896; died on 9/07/69 (age 73).	
1/07/67	**29**	3	1. Gallant Men [S]	Capitol 5805
			DIRT BAND, The — see NITTY GRITTY DIRT BAND	
			DISCO TEX & THE SEX-O-LETTES	
			Disco studio group assembled by producer Bob Crewe. Featuring lead voice Sir Monti Rock III (real name: Joseph Montanez, Jr.), owner of a chain of hairdressing salons.	
12/28/74+	**10**	9	**1. Get Dancin'**	Chelsea 3004
5/17/75	**23**	5	2. I Wanna Dance Wit' Choo (Doo Dat Dance), Part 1	Chelsea 3015
			DIVINYLS	
			Vocalist Christina Amphlett and guitarist Mark McEntee formed Australian rock group in 1981. Bassist Rick Grossman joined the Hoodoo Gurus in 1989.	
3/30/91	**4**	12	**1. I Touch Myself**	Virgin 98873
			DIXIEBELLES, The	
			Black female trio from Memphis: Shirley Thomas, Mary Hunt and Mildred Pratcher. Backed by pianist Jerry Smith (of Cornbread And Jerry).	
10/26/63	**9**	8	**1. (Down At) Papa Joe's**	Sound Stage 2507
2/08/64	**15**	5	2. Southtown, U.S.A.	Sound Stage 2517
			DIXIE CUPS, The	
			Black female trio from New Orleans: Barbara Ann Hawkins (b: 10/23/43), her sister Rosa Lee Hawkins (b: 9/24/44) and their cousin Joan Marie Johnson. Discovered by singer/producer Joe Jones.	
5/16/64	**1**(3)	11	**1. Chapel Of Love**	Red Bird 001
8/01/64	**12**	7	2. People Say	Red Bird 006

DATE	POS	WKS	ARTIST—RECORD TITLE	LABEL & NO.
11/21/64	**39**	1	3. You Should Have Seen The Way He Looked At Me	Red Bird 012
5/01/65	**20**	5	4. Iko Iko	Red Bird 024
			D.J. JAZZY JEFF & THE FRESH PRINCE	
			Philadelphia rap duo: D.J. Jeff Townes and rapper Will Smith. Smith stars in the TV sitcom "Fresh Prince of Bel Aire."	
6/18/88	**12**	10	● 1. Parents Just Don't Understand	Jive 1099
8/20/88	**15**	9	2. A Nightmare On My Street	Jive 1124
6/29/91	**4**	13	▲ **3. Summertime**	Jive 1465#
			samples Kool & The Gang's "Summer Madness"	
			D-MOB	
			British dance outfit headed by producer/mixer Danny D. Lead vocalist Cathy Dennis went solo in 1991.	
1/27/90	**10**	12	**1. C'mon And Get My Love**	FFRR 886798#
			from the film *She-Devil*	
			D.N.A. — see VEGA, Suzanne	
			DOBKINS, Carl, Jr.	
			Born Carl Edward Dobkins on 1/13/41 in Cincinnati. "Junior" added to last name when Carl started singing at age 16. First recorded for Fraternity in 1958. Left music, mid-1960s.	
6/01/59	**3**	16	**1. My Heart Is An Open Book**	Decca 30803
1/18/60	**25**	8	2. Lucky Devil	Decca 31020
			DR. BUZZARD'S ORIGINAL "SAVANNAH" BAND	
			New York City 1930s-styled disco group formed by brothers Stony Browder and August Darnell (real name: Thomas August Darnell Browder), with Cory Daye, lead singer. Darnell left in 1980 to form Kid Creole & The Coconuts.	
12/11/76+	**27**	8	1. Whispering/Cherchez La Femme/Se Si Bon	RCA 10827
			DR. HOOK	
			Group formed in New Jersey in 1968. Fronted by Ray Sawyer (Dr. Hook — because of eye patch) and Dennis Locorriere. Appeared in and performed the music for the film *Who Is Harry Kellerman and Why Is He Saying Those Terrible Things About Me?* starring Dustin Hoffman.	
			DR. HOOK AND THE MEDICINE SHOW:	
5/06/72	**5**	10	● **1. Sylvia's Mother**	Columbia 45562
2/03/73	**6**	11	● **2. The Cover Of "Rolling Stone"** [N]	Columbia 45732
			DR. HOOK:	
2/07/76	**6**	14	● **3. Only Sixteen**	Capitol 4171
7/31/76	**11**	14	4. A Little Bit More	Capitol 4280
10/14/78+	**6**	16	● **5. Sharing The Night Together**	Capitol 4621
6/02/79	**6**	16	● **6. When You're In Love With A Beautiful Woman**	Capitol 4705
11/03/79+	**12**	14	7. Better Love Next Time	Capitol 4785
3/15/80	**5**	15	● **8. Sexy Eyes**	Capitol 4831
11/29/80	**34**	6	9. Girls Can Get It	Casablanca 2314
3/27/82	**25**	6	10. Baby Makes Her Blue Jeans Talk	Casablanca 2347

DATE	POS	WKS	ARTIST—RECORD TITLE	LABEL & NO.
			DR. JOHN	
			Born Malcolm "Mac" Rebennack on 11/21/40 in New Orleans. Pioneer "swamp rock"-styled instrumentalist.	
5/12/73	**9**	13	**1. Right Place Wrong Time**	Atco 6914
			DOGGETT, Bill	
			Born on 2/16/16 in Philadelphia. Leading jazz-R&B organist/pianist. Formed own band in 1938, recorded with the Jimmy Mundy Band in 1939. With the Ink Spots, Illinois Jacquet, Lucky Millinder, Louis Jordan, Ella Fitzgerald, Louis Armstrong, Coleman Hawkins and many others. Formed own combo in 1952. Still active into the '90s with a touring combo.	
8/25/56	**2**(3)	22	**1. Honky Tonk (Parts 1 & 2)** **[I]**	King 4950
			Best Seller #2 / Top 100 #2 / Juke Box #2 / Jockey #6 saxophone: Clifford Scott	
12/15/56+	**26**	5	2. Slow Walk [I]	King 5000
12/02/57	**35**	1	3. Soft [I]	King 5080
			Best Seller #35 / Top 100 #51	
			DOLBY, Thomas	
			Born Thomas Morgan Dolby Robertson of British parentage on 10/14/58 in Cairo, Egypt. Master of computer-generated music and self-directed videos. Keyboardist of Bruce Woolley & The Camera Club, and the Lene Lovich band (1979-80). Film *Howard the Duck* featured Dolby's music under moniker Dolby's Cube. Married to actress Kathleen Beller (Kirby Colby of TV's "Dynasty").	
3/19/83	**5**	15	**1. She Blinded Me With Science**	Capitol 5204
			DOMINO, Fats	
			Born Antoine Domino on 2/26/28 in New Orleans. Classic New Orleans R&B piano-playing vocalist; heavily influenced by Fats Waller and Albert Ammons. Joined the Dave Bartholomew Band, mid-1940s. Signed to Imperial record label in 1949. His first recording "The Fat Man" reportedly was a million-seller. Heard on many sessions cut by other R&B artists, including Lloyd Price and Joe Turner. In films *Shake, Rattle and Roll*, *Jamboree*, *The Big Beat* and *The Girl Can't Help It*. Teamed with co-writer Dave Bartholomew on majority of his hits. Lives in New Orleans with wife Rosemary and eight children. Frequently appears in Las Vegas. Inducted into the Rock and Roll Hall of Fame in 1986. Winner of Grammy's Hall of Fame (1987) and Lifetime Achievement (1987) Awards.	
7/16/55	**10**	13	**1. Ain't That A Shame**	Imperial 5348
			Juke Box #10 / Best Seller #16 / Top 100 #86 pre originally titled as "Ain't It A Shame"	
4/07/56	**35**	1	2. Bo Weevil	Imperial 5375
5/05/56	**3**	18	**3. I'm In Love Again/**	
			Juke Box #3 / Best Seller #4 / Top 100 # 5 / Jockey #6	
5/05/56	**19**	13	4. My Blue Heaven	Imperial 5386
			Juke Box #19 / Top 100 #21 #1 hit for both Gene Austin and Paul Whiteman in 1927	
7/28/56	**14**	8	5. When My Dreamboat Comes Home	Imperial 5396
			Juke Box #14 / Best Seller #21 / Top 100 #22 #3 hit for Guy Lombardo in 1937	
10/13/56+	**2**(3)	21	**6. Blueberry Hill**	Imperial 5407
			Juke Box #2 / Best Seller #3 / Top 100 #4 / Jockey #7 Grammy Hall Of Fame Award winner in 1987; #1 hit for Glenn Miller in 1940	
1/12/57	**5**	12	**7. Blue Monday**	Imperial 5417
			Juke Box #5 / Best Seller #9 / Top 100 #9 / Jockey #9 from the film *The Girl Can't Help It*	
3/09/57	**4**	14	**8. I'm Walkin'**	Imperial 5428

DATE	POS	WKS	ARTIST—RECORD TITLE	LABEL & NO.
			Jockey #4 / Best Seller #5 / Top 100 #5 / Juke Box #5	
5/27/57	**8**	13	**9. Valley Of Tears/**	
			Best Seller #8 / Top 100 #13 / Jockey #13	
6/24/57	**6**	6	**10. It's You I Love**	Imperial 5442
			Best Seller #6 / Top 100 #22	
8/26/57	**29**	2	11. When I See You	Imperial 5454
			Best Seller #29 / Top 100 #36	
10/21/57	**23**	6	12. Wait And See	Imperial 5467
			Best Seller #23 / Top 100 #27 from the film *Jamboree*	
12/23/57+	**26**	9	13. The Big Beat/	
			Best Seller #26 / Top 100 #36 from the film of the same title	
12/30/57+	**32**	8	14. I Want You To Know	Imperial 5477
			Best Seller #32 / Top 100 #48	
5/05/58	**22**	7	15. Sick And Tired	Imperial 5515
			Best Seller #22 / Top 100 #30	
12/01/58+	**6**	12	**16. Whole Lotta Loving**	Imperial 5553
5/25/59	**16**	7	17. I'm Ready	Imperial 5585
8/10/59	**8**	10	**18. I Want To Walk You Home/**	
8/10/59	**17**	9	19. I'm Gonna Be A Wheel Some Day	Imperial 5606
11/09/59	**8**	10	**20. Be My Guest/**	
11/09/59	**33**	2	21. I've Been Around	Imperial 5629
2/15/60	**25**	5	22. Country Boy	Imperial 5645
7/04/60	**6**	11	**23. Walking To New Orleans/**	
7/18/60	**21**	7	24. Don't Come Knockin'	Imperial 5675
9/12/60	**15**	9	25. Three Nights A Week	Imperial 5687
11/14/60	**14**	11	26. My Girl Josephine/	
12/05/60	**38**	3	27. Natural Born Lover	Imperial 5704
2/06/61	**22**	6	28. What A Price/	
2/13/61	**33**	4	29. Ain't That Just Like A Woman	Imperial 5723
			#17 hit for Louis Jordan in 1946	
4/03/61	**32**	2	30. Fell In Love On Monday/	
4/17/61	**32**	2	31. Shu Rah	Imperial 5734
6/19/61	**23**	5	32. It Keeps Rainin'	Imperial 5753
7/31/61	**15**	6	33. Let The Four Winds Blow	Imperial 5764
10/23/61	**22**	4	34. What A Party	Imperial 5779
12/25/61+	**30**	3	35. Jambalaya (On The Bayou)	Imperial 5796
			#1 country hit for Hank Williams in 1952	
3/17/62	**22**	5	36. You Win Again	Imperial 5816
			#10 country hit for Hank Williams in 1952	
10/26/63	**35**	2	37. Red Sails In The Sunset	ABC-Para. 10484
			#1 hit for both Bing Crosby and Guy Lombardo in 1935	
			DONALDSON, Bo/The Heywoods	
			Cincinnati septet. Regulars on Dick Clark's "Action '73" TV show.	
5/11/74	**1**(2)	12	● **1. Billy, Don't Be A Hero**	ABC 11435
8/24/74	**15**	7	2. Who Do You Think You Are	ABC 12006
12/14/74	**39**	1	3. The Heartbreak Kid	ABC 12039

DATE	POS	WKS	ARTIST—RECORD TITLE	LABEL & NO.
			DON & JUAN	
			Black vocal duo from New York City: Roland Trone (d: 1983) and Claude Johnson of The Genies.	
2/24/62	**7**	9	**1. What's Your Name**	Big Top 3079
			DONEGAN, Lonnie/His Skiffle Group	
			Lonnie was born Anthony Donegan on 4/29/31 in Glasgow, Scotland. Britain's "King of Skiffle." Member of Chris Barber's Jazz Band in 1954.	
3/31/56	**8**	11	**1. Rock Island Line**	London 1650
			Best Seller #8 / Top 100 #10 / Jockey #10 / Juke Box #13	
8/14/61	**5**	9	**2. Does Your Chewing Gum Lose Its Flavor (On The Bedpost Over Night)**	[N] Dot 15911
			#9 hit in 1924 for Ernest Hare & Billy Jones as "Does The Spearmint Lose Its Flavor On The Bedpost Overnight?"; originally released on Dot 15911 in March 1959	
			DONNER, Ral	
			Born on 2/10/43 in Chicago; died of cancer on 4/06/84. Narrator for the film *This Is Elvis.*	
5/01/61	**19**	8	1. Girl Of My Best Friend	Gone 5102
			recorded by Elvis in 1960 on his *Elvis Is Back!* LP	
7/24/61	**4**	9	**2. You Don't Know What You've Got (Until You Lose It)**	Gone 5108
11/13/61	**39**	1	3. Please Don't Go	Gone 5114
2/03/62	**18**	4	4. She's Everything (I Wanted You To Be)	Gone 5121
			DONNIE AND THE DREAMERS	
			Donnie is Louis Burgio. Italian-American vocal quartet from New York City.	
6/12/61	**35**	3	1. Count Every Star	Whale 500
			#4 hit for Ray Anthony's band in 1950	
			DONOVAN	
			Born Donovan Phillip Leitch on 2/10/46 near Glasgow, Scotland. Singer/songwriter/guitarist. To London at age 10. Worked Newport Folk Festival in 1965. Wrote score for film *If It's Tuesday This Must Be Belgium.* In films *The Pied Piper of Hamlin* (1972) and *Brother Sun, Sister Moon* (1973). In retirement from 1974-81. Father of actress Ione Skye (*Say Anything*).	
6/12/65	**23**	5	1. Catch The Wind	Hickory 1309
8/13/66	**1**(1)	10	**2. Sunshine Superman**	Epic 10045
11/19/66	**2**(3)	10	• **3. Mellow Yellow**	Epic 10098
			whispering vocals: Paul McCartney	
2/25/67	**19**	5	4. Epistle To Dippy	Epic 10127
8/26/67	**11**	6	5. There Is A Mountain	Epic 10212
12/09/67	**23**	5	6. Wear Your Love Like Heaven	Epic 10253
3/30/68	**26**	5	7. Jennifer Juniper	Epic 10300
6/29/68	**5**	10	**8. Hurdy Gurdy Man**	Epic 10345
10/19/68	**33**	4	9. Lalena	Epic 10393
3/01/69	**35**	2	10. To Susan On The West Coast Waiting/	
4/26/69	**7**	10	**11. Atlantis**	Epic 10434
8/30/69	**36**	2	12. Goo Goo Barabajagal (Love Is Hot)	Epic 10510
			DONOVAN with THE JEFF BECK GROUP	
			all of above written by Donovan	

DATE	POS	WKS	ARTIST—RECORD TITLE	LABEL & NO.
			DOOBIE BROTHERS, The	
			Rock/R&B-styled group formed in San Jose, California in 1970: Pat Simmons (vocals, guitar), Tom Johnston (lead vocals, guitar, keyboards), John Hartman (percussion) and Dave Shogren (bass). First recorded for Warner in 1971. Many personnel changes. Michael McDonald (lead vocals, keyboards) joined in 1975. Johnston left in 1978. Tom Johnston wrote majority of hits from 1972-75; Michael McDonald from 1976-83. Disbanded in 1983. Re-formed in early 1988 with Johnston, Simmons, Hartman, Tiran Porter (bass), Mike Hossack (drums) and Bobby LaKind (percussion).	
9/23/72	**11**	10	1. Listen To The Music	Warner 7619
2/17/73	**35**	2	2. Jesus Is Just Alright	Warner 7661
5/26/73	**8**	11	**3. Long Train Runnin'**	Warner 7698
9/15/73	**15**	8	4. China Grove	Warner 7728
6/01/74	**32**	2	5. Another Park, Another Sunday	Warner 7795
1/11/75	**1**(1)	12	● **6. Black Water**	Warner 8062
			originally the B-side of Warner 7795	
5/17/75	**11**	9	7. Take Me In Your Arms (Rock Me)	Warner 8092
8/30/75	**40**	1	8. Sweet Maxine	Warner 8126
5/15/76	**13**	8	9. Takin' It To The Streets	Warner 8196
1/22/77	**37**	2	10. It Keeps You Runnin'	Warner 8282
2/10/79	**1**(1)	14	● **11. What A Fool Believes**	Warner 8725
5/19/79	**14**	9	12. Minute By Minute	Warner 8828
9/15/79	**25**	6	13. Dependin' On You	Warner 49029
9/06/80	**5**	11	**14. Real Love**	Warner 49503
12/06/80+	**24**	7	15. One Step Closer	Warner 49622
			all of above produced by Ted Templeman	
6/03/89	**9**	9	**16. The Doctor**	Capitol 44376
			DOORS, The	
			Rock group formed in Los Angeles in 1965. Consisted of Jim Morrison (b: 12/08/43, Melbourne, Florida; d: 7/03/71, Paris; lead singer), Ray Manzarek (keyboards), Robby Krieger (guitar) and John Densmore (drums). Controversial onstage performances by Morrison caused several arrests and cancellations. Morrison left group on 12/12/70. In film *A Feast of Friends*. Group disbanded in 1973. 1991 film based on their career, *The Doors*, stars Val Kilmer as Morrison.	
6/24/67	**1**(3)	14	● **1. Light My Fire**	Elektra 45615
10/07/67	**12**	7	2. People Are Strange	Elektra 45621
12/30/67+	**25**	4	3. Love Me Two Times	Elektra 45624
5/04/68	**39**	3	4. The Unknown Soldier	Elektra 45628
7/13/68	**1**(2)	11	● **5. Hello, I Love You**	Elektra 45635
1/04/69	**3**	12	● **6. Touch Me**	Elektra 45646
4/24/71	**11**	9	7. Love Her Madly	Elektra 45726
7/24/71	**14**	9	8. Riders On The Storm	Elektra 45738
			DORE, Charlie	
			British female vocalist.	
3/22/80	**13**	10	1. Pilot Of The Airwaves	Island 49166
			DORMAN, Harold	
			Born on 12/23/26 in Drew and raised in Sledge, Mississippi. To Memphis in 1955; recorded for Sun in 1957. Suffered two strokes in 1984.	
4/18/60	**21**	9	1. Mountain Of Love	Rita 1003

DATE	POS	WKS	ARTIST—RECORD TITLE	LABEL & NO.
			DORSEY, Jimmy	
			Born on 2/29/04 in Shenandoah, Pennsylvania. Died of cancer on 6/12/57. Esteemed alto sax and clarinet soloist/bandleader, beginning in 1935. Recorded with his brother Tommy in the Dorsey Brothers Orchestra, 1928-35 and 1953-56.	
4/13/57	**2**(4)	26	**1. So Rare** Top 100 #2 / Jockey #2 / Best Seller #3 / Juke Box #6 end featuring Jimmy on sax; #1 hit for Guy Lombardo in 1937	Fraternity 755
9/09/57	**21**	2	2. June Night Jockey #21 / Best Seller #27 / Top 100 #39 cut 5 days after Jimmy's death, under the direction of Lee Castle (d: 11/16/90) and featuring Dick Stabile on sax; #2 hit for Ted Lewis in 1924	Fraternity 777
			DORSEY, Lee	
			Born Irving Lee Dorsey on 12/24/24 in New Orleans. Moved to Portland, Oregon at age 10. Prizefighter in early '50s as "Kid Chocolate." Major hits produced by Allen Toussaint and Marshall Sehorn. Lee died of emphysema in New Orleans on 12/01/86.	
9/25/61	**7**	10	**1. Ya Ya**	Fury 1053
1/20/62	**27**	5	2. Do-Re-Mi	Fury 1056
7/31/65	**28**	4	3. Ride Your Pony	Amy 927
8/13/66	**8**	9	**4. Working In The Coal Mine**	Amy 958
11/19/66	**23**	5	5. Holy Cow	Amy 965
			DORSEY, Tommy	
			Born on 11/19/05 in Mahanoy Plane, Pennsylvania; choked to death on 11/26/56. Esteemed trombonist and bandleader beginning in 1935. Tommy and brother Jimmy recorded together as the Dorsey Brothers Orchestra from 1928-35, reunited, 1953-56. Hosted musical variety TV show from 1954-56. Warren Covington fronted band after Tommy's death.	
9/15/58	**7**	14	**1. Tea For Two Cha Cha** [I] **THE TOMMY DORSEY ORCHESTRA STARRING WARREN COVINGTON** Hot 100 #7 / Best Seller #8 end #1 hit for Marion Harris in 1925	Decca 30704
			DOUBLE	
			Swiss pop duo (pronounced: doo-BLAY) of Kurt Maloo and Felix Haug. Both were in jazz trio Ping Pong.	
8/09/86	**16**	9	1. The Captain Of Her Heart	A&M 2838
			DOUGLAS, Carl	
			Born in Jamaica, West Indies and raised in California. Studied engineering in the U.S. and in England.	
11/09/74	**1**(2)	12	● **1. Kung Fu Fighting**	20th Century 2140
			DOUGLAS, Carol	
			Born on 4/07/48 in Brooklyn. Worked on commercials. Member of The Chantels vocal group in the early '70s.	
12/21/74+	**11**	11	1. Doctor's Orders	Midland I. 10113
			DOUGLAS, Mike	
			Born Michael Dowd, Jr. in Chicago on 8/11/25. Longtime syndicated TV talkshow host (1961-80). Singer with Kay Kyser's band, 1945-50 (vocalist on Kyser's #1 hit "Ole Buttermilk Sky" in 1946).	
1/08/66	**6**	7	**1. The Men In My Little Girl's Life**	Epic 9876

DATE	POS	WKS	ARTIST—RECORD TITLE	LABEL & NO.
			DOVE, Ronnie	
			Born on 9/07/40 in Herndon, Virginia. Discovered while singing in Baltimore. Nearly all of Ronnie's hits were produced by Phil Kahl (vice president of Diamond Records).	
9/26/64	**40**	1	1. Say You	Diamond 167
11/14/64	**14**	7	2. Right Or Wrong	Diamond 173
4/10/65	**14**	7	3. One Kiss For Old Times' Sake	Diamond 179
6/26/65	**16**	6	4. A Little Bit Of Heaven	Diamond 184
9/18/65	**21**	5	5. I'll Make All Your Dreams Come True	Diamond 188
11/27/65	**25**	4	6. Kiss Away	Diamond 191
			above 4 arranged by Ray Stevens	
2/05/66	**18**	7	7. When Liking Turns To Loving	Diamond 195
5/07/66	**20**	5	8. Let's Start All Over Again	Diamond 198
7/09/66	**27**	4	9. Happy Summer Days	Diamond 205
9/24/66	**22**	5	10. I Really Don't Want To Know	Diamond 208
12/10/66	**18**	6	11. Cry	Diamond 214
			DOVELLS, The	
			Vocal group formed at Overbrook High School in Philadelphia. Originally called the Brooktones. Consisted of Leonard Borisoff ("Len Barry"), Arnie Silver, Jerry Gross ("Jerry Summers"), Mike Freda ("Mike Dennis") and Jim Meeley ("Danny Brooks"). Brooks left in 1962. Barry left in late 1963 and recorded solo. Group continued as a trio. Recorded as The Magistrates for MGM in 1968.	
9/18/61	**2**(2)	14	**1. Bristol Stomp**	Parkway 827
			Bristol: town near Philadelphia	
3/03/62	**37**	2	2. Do The New Continental	Parkway 833
6/23/62	**27**	5	3. Bristol Twistin' Annie	Parkway 838
9/15/62	**25**	7	4. Hully Gully Baby	Parkway 845
5/11/63	**3**	11	**5. You Can't Sit Down**	Parkway 867
			DOWELL, Joe	
			Born on 1/23/40 in Bloomington, Indiana. Signed to Mercury's Smash label by Shelby Singleton, Jr.	
7/17/61	**1**(1)	12	**1. Wooden Heart**	Smash 1708
			based on the German folk song "Muss I Denn"; originally sung by Elvis Presley in the film *G.I. Blues*	
7/28/62	**23**	4	2. Little Red Rented Rowboat	Smash 1759
			DOZIER, Lamont	
			Born on 6/16/41 in Detroit. R&B singer/songwriter/producer. Recorded as Lamont Anthony for Anna in 1961. With the brothers Brian and Eddie Holland in highly successful songwriting/production team for Motown. Trio left Motown in 1968 and formed own Invictus/Hot Wax label. Inducted into the Rock and Roll Hall of Fame in 1990.	
2/16/74	**15**	9	1. Trying To Hold On To My Woman	ABC 11407
7/06/74	**26**	6	2. Fish Ain't Bitin'	ABC 11438
			DRAKE, Charlie	
			Born on 6/19/25 in London.	
2/17/62	**21**	6	1. My Boomerang Won't Come Back [N]	United Art. 398

DATE	POS	WKS	ARTIST—RECORD TITLE	LABEL & NO.
			DRAKE, Pete, And His Talking Steel Guitar	
			Pete was born on 10/08/32 in Atlanta; died on 7/29/88. Was Nashville's top steel guitar sessionman.	
4/11/64	**25**	5	1. Forever	Smash 1867
			DRAMATICS, The	
			Soul group from Detroit. First recorded for Wingate as the Dynamics, 1966. Members in 1971: Ron Banks (lead singer), William Howard, Larry Demps, Willie Ford and Elbert Wilkins. Howard and Wilkins replaced by L.J. Reynolds and Lenny Mayes in 1973. Reynolds, formerly of Chocolate Syrup, began solo career in 1981. Banks recorded solo in 1983. Drummer Carl Smalls was a member of Undisputed Truth and Sweat Band.	
7/31/71	**9**	11	**1. Whatcha See Is Whatcha Get**	Volt 4058
3/04/72	**5**	11	**2. In The Rain**	Volt 4075
			DRAPER, Rusty	
			Born Farrell H. Draper in Kirksville, Missouri. Began career at the age of 12, singing and playing guitar over the radio in Tulsa, Oklahoma.	
8/20/55	**18**	4	1. Seventeen Best Seller #18 / Top 100 #88 pre	Mercury 70651
10/01/55	**3**	16	**2. The Shifting, Whispering Sands** Juke Box #3 / Best Seller #6 / Top 100 #7 / Jockey #14	Mercury 70696
12/31/55+	**11**	12	3. Are You Satisfied? Best Seller #11 / Juke Box #11 / Top 100 #12	Mercury 70757
9/22/56	**20**	8	4. In The Middle Of The House [N] Top 100 #20 / Jockey #24 backing vocals on above 3 by the Jack Halloran Singers; orchestra conducted on all of above by David Carroll	Mercury 70921
5/27/57	**6**	12	**5. Freight Train** Jockey #6 / Top 100 #11 / Best Seller #17	Mercury 71102
			DREAM ACADEMY, The	
			English trio: Nick Laird-Clowes (guitar, vocals), Gilbert Gabriel (keyboards) & Kate St. John (vocals).	
1/11/86	**7**	11	**1. Life In A Northern Town**	Warner 28841
5/31/86	**36**	3	2. The Love Parade	Reprise 28750
			DREAMLOVERS, The	
			Black vocal quintet formed while in high school in Philadelphia. Backup vocal group for most of Chubby Checker's hits. Named after Bobby Darin's hit record.	
8/28/61	**10**	6	**1. When We Get Married**	Heritage 102
			DREAM WEAVERS, The	
			Two-woman, one-man vocal trio from Miami led by Wade Buff.	
11/12/55+	**7**	21	**1. It's Almost Tomorrow** Juke Box #7 / Best Seller #8 / Top 100 #8 / Jockey #10	Decca 29683
5/19/56	**33**	1	2. A Little Love Can Go A Long, Long Way **THE DREAM WEAVERS featuring WADE BUFF** from the Goodyear TV Playhouse Production "Joey"	Decca 29905

DATE	POS	WKS	ARTIST—RECORD TITLE	LABEL & NO.
			DRIFTERS, The	
			Vocal group formed to showcase lead singer Clyde McPhatter on Atlantic in 1953. Included Gerhart and Andrew Thrasher, Bill Pinkney and McPhatter (who went solo in 1955). Group continued with various lead singers until 1958. In 1958, manager George Treadwell disbanded the group and brought in The Five Crowns and renamed them The Drifters. The majority of The Drifters' pop hits were sung by three different lead singers: Ben E. King (1959-60), Rudy Lewis (1961-63) and Johnny Moore (1957, 1964-66). Rudy died of a heart attack in the summer of 1964. Many personnel changes throughout career and several groups have used the name in later years. Inducted into the Rock and Roll Hall of Fame in 1988.	
6/29/59	**2**(1)	14	**1. There Goes My Baby**	Atlantic 2025
11/02/59	**15**	9	2. Dance With Me/	
11/23/59	**33**	5	3. (If You Cry) True Love, True Love	Atlantic 2040
3/14/60	**16**	6	4. This Magic Moment	Atlantic 2050
9/19/60	**1**(3)	14	**5. Save The Last Dance For Me**	Atlantic 2071
12/31/60+	**17**	7	6. I Count The Tears	Atlantic 2087
			Ben E. King, lead singer on all of above (except #3)	
4/10/61	**32**	6	7. Some Kind Of Wonderful	Atlantic 2096
6/26/61	**14**	8	8. Please Stay	Atlantic 2105
9/25/61	**16**	9	9. Sweets For My Sweet	Atlantic 2117
3/24/62	**28**	4	10. When My Little Girl Is Smiling	Atlantic 2134
12/29/62+	**5**	11	**11. Up On The Roof**	Atlantic 2162
4/06/63	**9**	8	**12. On Broadway**	Atlantic 2182
			above 6: Rudy Lewis, lead singer	
10/05/63	**25**	5	13. I'll Take You Home	Atlantic 2201
7/11/64	**4**	12	**14. Under The Boardwalk**	Atlantic 2237
10/10/64	**33**	5	15. I've Got Sand In My Shoes	Atlantic 2253
11/28/64	**18**	7	16. Saturday Night At The Movies	Atlantic 2260
			above 4: Johnny Moore, lead singer	
			DRUSKY, Roy	
			Born on 6/22/30 in Atlanta. Country singer/guitarist; leader of own band, The Loners. In films *The Golden Guitar* and *Forty-Acre Feud*.	
6/26/61	**35**	1	1. Three Hearts In A Tangle	Decca 31193
			DUALS	
			Black instrumental duo from Los Angeles: Henry Bellinger and Johnny Lageman.	
10/02/61	**25**	6	1. Stick Shift [I]	Sue 745
			first released on Star Revue 1031 in 1961	
			DUBS, The	
			R&B quintet — Richard Blandon, lead singer.	
11/18/57	**23**	8	1. Could This Be Magic	Gone 5011
			Best Seller #23 / Top 100 #24	
			DUDLEY, Dave	
			Born David Pedruska on 5/03/28 in Spencer, Wisconsin. Country singer/guitarist/songwriter.	
7/20/63	**32**	4	1. Six Days On The Road	Golden Wing 3020

DATE	POS	WKS	ARTIST—RECORD TITLE	LABEL & NO.
			DUKE, George	
			Born on 1/12/46 in San Rafael, California. Top jazz-rock keyboardist. Played with Jean-Luc Ponty, the Mothers of Invention, and Cannonball Adderley's band.	
6/13/81	**19**	9	1. Sweet Baby STANLEY CLARKE/GEORGE DUKE	Epic 01052
			DUKE, Patty	
			Born Anna Marie Duke on 12/14/46 in Elmhurst, New York. Actress. Married actor John Astin. Won an Oscar for her performance in film *The Miracle Worker* (1962). Starred in TV series "The Patty Duke Show" (1963-65), "It Takes Two" (1982-83) and "Hail to the Chief" (1985). Winner of three Emmys.	
7/17/65	**8**	8	**1. Don't Just Stand There**	United Art. 875
10/30/65	**22**	4	2. Say Something Funny	United Art. 915
			DULFER, Candy — see STEWART, David A.	
			DUNDAS, David	
			Oxford, England-born singer/actor/commercial jingle writer.	
11/27/76+	**17**	13	1. Jeans On originally a jingle in England for Brutus Jeans	Chrysalis 2094
			DUPREE, Robbie	
			Singer/songwriter. Born Robert Dupuis in Brooklyn in 1947.	
5/03/80	**6**	15	**1. Steal Away**	Elektra 46621
8/09/80	**15**	12	2. Hot Rod Hearts	Elektra 47005
			DUPREES, The	
			Italian-American vocal quintet from Jersey City: Joseph ("Joey Vann") Canzano (lead singer), Mike Arnone, Tom Bialablow, John Salvato and Joe Santollo. Joey Vann died on 2/28/84 (age 40).	
8/25/62	**7**	9	**1. You Belong To Me** #1 hit for Jo Stafford in 1952	Coed 569
11/10/62	**13**	6	2. My Own True Love Tara's Theme from *Gone with the Wind*	Coed 571
9/14/63	**37**	3	3. Why Don't You Believe Me #1 hit for Joni James in 1952	Coed 584
11/30/63	**18**	6	4. Have You Heard #4 hit for Joni James in 1953	Coed 585
			DURAN DURAN	
			Synth-pop-dance band formed in Birmingham, England in 1980. Consisted of Simon LeBon (b: 10/27/58; vocals), Andy Taylor (b: 2/16/61; guitar), Nick Rhodes (b: 6/08/62; keyboards), John Taylor (b: 6/20/60; bass) and Roger Taylor (b: 4/26/60; drums). None of the Taylors are related. Group named after a villain in the Jane Fonda film *Barbarella.* In 1984, Andy and Roger left group. In 1985, Andy and John recorded with supergroup The Power Station; Simon, Nick and Roger recorded as Arcadia. Duran Duran reduced to a trio in 1986 of Simon, Nick and John. Expanded to a quintet in 1990 with the addition of Warren Cuccurullo (ex-guitarist of Missing Persons) and Sterling Campbell.	
1/22/83	**3**	16	**1. Hungry Like The Wolf** also released on Capitol/Harvest 5134	Harvest 5195
4/09/83	**14**	9	2. Rio also released on Harvest 5175	Capitol 5215
6/18/83	**4**	12	**3. Is There Something I Should Know**	Capitol 5233
11/19/83	**3**	12	**4. Union Of The Snake**	Capitol 5290

DATE	POS	WKS	ARTIST—RECORD TITLE	LABEL & NO.
1/28/84	**10**	10	**5. New Moon On Monday**	Capitol 5309
4/28/84	**1**(2)	15	**6. The Reflex**	Capitol 5345
11/03/84	**2**(4)	14	**7. The Wild Boys**	Capitol 5417
2/16/85	**16**	8	8. Save A Prayer	Capitol 5438
5/25/85	**1**(2)	13	**9. A View To A Kill** from the James Bond film of the same title	Capitol 5475
11/15/86+	**2**(1)	13	**10. Notorious**	Capitol 5648
3/14/87	**39**	1	11. Skin Trade	Capitol 5670
			DURANDURAN:	
10/22/88	**4**	13	**12. I Don't Want Your Love**	Capitol 44237
1/21/89	**22**	6	13. All She Wants Is	Capitol 44287
			DYKE AND THE BLAZERS	
			Band led by Arlester "Dyke" Christian (b: 1943, Brooklyn). With O'Jays' backing band, the Blazers, in the mid-1960s. Dyke was shot to death in 1971.	
7/05/69	**35**	3	1. We Got More Soul	Original Sound 86
11/01/69	**36**	1	2. Let A Woman Be A Woman - Let A Man Be A Man	Original Sound 89
			DYLAN, Bob	
			Born Robert Allen Zimmerman on 5/24/41 in Duluth, Minnesota. Singer/songwriter/guitarist/harmonica player. Took stage name from poet Dylan Thomas. To New York City in December 1960. Worked Greenwich Village folk clubs. Signed to Columbia Records in October 1961. Innovator of folk-rock style. Motorcycle crash on 7/29/66 led to short retirement. Films *Don't Look Back* (1965), *Eat the Document* (1969) and *Pat Garrett and Billy the Kid* (1973). Made film *Renaldo and Clara* (1978). Newly-found Christian faith reflected in his recordings of 1979. Co-starred with Fiona in the 1987 film *Hearts of Fire.* Member of the supergroup Traveling Wilburys. Inducted into the Rock and Roll Hall of Fame in 1988. Won Grammy's Lifetime Achievement Award in 1991.	
5/15/65	**39**	1	1. Subterranean Homesick Blues	Columbia 43242
8/14/65	**2**(2)	9	**2. Like A Rolling Stone**	Columbia 43346
10/09/65	**7**	7	**3. Positively 4th Street**	Columbia 43389
4/23/66	**2**(1)	9	**4. Rainy Day Women #12 & 35**	Columbia 43592
7/16/66	**20**	4	5. I Want You	Columbia 43683
10/01/66	**33**	3	6. Just Like A Woman	Columbia 43792
8/02/69	**7**	11	**7. Lay Lady Lay**	Columbia 44926
12/25/71+	**33**	4	8. George Jackson	Columbia 45516
9/29/73	**12**	11	9. Knockin' On Heaven's Door	Columbia 45913
3/29/75	**31**	3	10. Tangled Up In Blue	Columbia 10106
1/03/76	**33**	3	11. Hurricane (Part I) dedicated to boxer Rubin Carter, a convicted murderer	Columbia 10245
10/06/79	**24**	6	12. Gotta Serve Somebody all of above written by Dylan	Columbia 11072
			DYSON, Ronnie	
			Soul singer. Born on 6/05/50 in Washington, D.C. and raised in Brooklyn. Leading role in the Broadway musical *Hair.* In the film *Putney Swope.* Died on 11/10/90 of heart failure complicated by chronic lung disease.	
7/25/70	**8**	9	**1. (If You Let Me Make Love To You Then) Why Can't I Touch You?** from the off-Broadway musical *Salvation*	Columbia 45110

DATE	POS	WKS	ARTIST—RECORD TITLE	LABEL & NO.
4/07/73	**28**	4	2. One Man Band (Plays All Alone)	Columbia 45776
			E	
			EAGLES	
			Formed in Los Angeles in 1971. Consisted of Glenn Frey (vocals, guitar), Bernie Leadon (guitar), Randy Meisner (bass) and Don Henley (drums). Meisner founded Poco, Leadon had been in the Flying Burrito Brothers and Frey and Henley were with Linda Ronstadt. Debut album recorded in England in 1972. Don Felder (guitar) added in 1975. Leadon replaced by Joe Walsh in 1975. Meisner replaced by Timothy B. Schmit in 1977. Frey and Henley were the only members to play on all recordings. Disbanded in 1982.	
6/24/72	**12**	8	1. Take It Easy	Asylum 11005
9/30/72	**9**	10	**2. Witchy Woman**	Asylum 11008
2/03/73	**22**	6	3. Peaceful Easy Feeling	Asylum 11013
6/22/74	**32**	3	4. Already Gone	Asylum 11036
12/28/74+	**1**(1)	14	**5. Best Of My Love**	Asylum 45218
6/14/75	**1**(1)	14	**6. One Of These Nights**	Asylum 45257
9/27/75	**2**(2)	11	**7. Lyin' Eyes**	Asylum 45279
1/17/76	**4**	14	**8. Take It To The Limit**	Asylum 45293
12/25/76+	**1**(1)	13	• **9. New Kid In Town**	Asylum 45373
3/12/77	**1**(1)	15	• **10. Hotel California**	Asylum 45386
5/28/77	**11**	8	11. Life In The Fast Lane	Asylum 45403
12/23/78	**18**	5	12. Please Come Home For Christmas [X]	Asylum 45555
10/13/79	**1**(1)	13	• **13. Heartache Tonight**	Asylum 46545
12/08/79+	**8**	12	**14. The Long Run**	Asylum 46569
3/01/80	**8**	12	**15. I Can't Tell You Why**	Asylum 46608
1/10/81	**21**	7	16. Seven Bridges Road	Asylum 47100
			EARL-JEAN	
			Earl-Jean McCrea of The Cookies.	
8/08/64	**38**	1	1. I'm Into Somethin' Good	Colpix 729
			EARLS, The	
			White vocal quartet from the Bronx: Larry "Chance" Figueiredo, Bob Del Din, Eddie Harder and Jack Wray.	
1/12/63	**24**	4	1. Remember Then	Old Town 1130
			EARTH, WIND & FIRE	
			Los Angeles-based R&B group formed by Chicago-bred producer/songwriter/vocalist/percussionist/kalimba player Maurice White. In 1969, White, former session drummer for Chess Records and member of The Ramsey Lewis Trio, formed the Salty Peppers; recorded for Capitol. Maurice's brother Verdine White was the group's bassist. Eighteen months later, the brothers hired a new band and recorded as Earth, Wind & Fire — named for the three elements of Maurice's astrological sign. Co-lead singer Philip Bailey joined as lead singer in 1971. Group generally contained eight to 10 members, with frequent personnel shuffling. Appeared in the films *That's the Way of the World* (1975) and *Sgt. Pepper's Lonely Hearts Club Band* (1978). Elaborate stage shows featured an array of magic acts and pyrotechnics. Group members Philip Bailey, Wade Flemons, Ronnie Laws and Maurice White had solo hits.	
4/27/74	**29**	7	1. Mighty Mighty	Columbia 46007

DATE	POS	WKS	ARTIST—RECORD TITLE	LABEL & NO.
10/12/74	**33**	2	2. Devotion	Columbia 10026
3/22/75	**1**(1)	14	● **3. Shining Star**	Columbia 10090
7/26/75	**12**	11	4. That's The Way Of The World	Columbia 10172
12/13/75+	**5**	12	● **5. Sing A Song**	Columbia 10251
4/24/76	**39**	2	6. Can't Hide Love	Columbia 10309
8/14/76	**12**	12	● 7. Getaway	Columbia 10373
12/11/76+	**21**	10	8. Saturday Nite	Columbia 10439
11/26/77+	**13**	13	9. Serpentine Fire	Columbia 10625
4/01/78	**32**	5	10. Fantasy	Columbia 10688
8/05/78	**9**	9	● **11. Got To Get You Into My Life**	Columbia 10796
12/16/78+	**8**	11	● **12. September**	ARC 10854
5/26/79	**6**	12	● **13. Boogie Wonderland** **EARTH, WIND & FIRE with THE EMOTIONS**	ARC 10956
7/28/79	**2**(2)	13	● **14. After The Love Has Gone**	ARC 11033
10/31/81	**3**	16	● **15. Let's Groove**	ARC 02536
2/12/83	**17**	10	16. Fall In Love With Me	Columbia 03375
			EASTON, Sheena Born on 4/27/59 in Glasgow, Scotland. Real last name is Orr. Vocalist/actress. Portrayed a singer in the 1980 BBC-TV documentary *The Big Time*. Won the 1981 Best New Artist Grammy Award. Portrayed Sonny Crockett's wife in five episodes of TV's "Miami Vice."	
2/28/81	**1**(2)	15	● **1. Morning Train (Nine To Five)**	EMI America 8071
6/06/81	**18**	9	2. Modern Girl	EMI America 8080
8/22/81	**4**	14	**3. For Your Eyes Only** from the James Bond film of the same title	Liberty 1418
12/19/81+	**15**	12	4. You Could Have Been With Me	EMI America 8101
5/08/82	**30**	6	5. When He Shines	EMI America 8113
1/29/83	**6**	15	**6. We've Got Tonight** **KENNY ROGERS AND SHEENA EASTON**	Liberty 1492
9/10/83	**9**	14	**7. Telefone (Long Distance Love Affair)**	EMI America 8172
2/11/84	**25**	6	8. Almost Over You	EMI America 8186
9/22/84	**7**	15	**9. Strut**	EMI America 8227
1/19/85	**9**	9	**10. Sugar Walls** written and produced by Prince (as Alexander Nevermind)	EMI America 8253
11/30/85	**29**	4	11. Do It For Love	EMI America 8295
12/24/88+	**2**(1)	14	**12. The Lover In Me**	MCA 53416
12/02/89	**36**	0	13. The Arms Of Orion **PRINCE with SHEENA EASTON**	Warner 22757
4/20/91	**19**	9	14. What Comes Naturally	MCA 53742#
			EASYBEATS, The Rock quintet formed in Australia in 1965. Moved to England in 1966. Vocalist Steven Wright and drummer Gordon Fleet were English. Bassist Dick Diamonde and guitarist Harry Vanda were Dutch. Guitarist George Young (the older brother of AC/DC's Angus and Malcolm Young) was from Scotland. Young and Vanda later formed Flash & The Pan.	
4/22/67	**16**	8	1. Friday On My Mind	United Art. 50106
			EASY RIDERS, The — see GILKYSON, Terry, and LAINE, Frankie	

DATE	POS	WKS	ARTIST—RECORD TITLE		LABEL & NO.
			ECHOES, The		
			Brooklyn trio: Tommy Duffy, Harry Doyle and Tom Morrissey.		
3/27/61	**12**	9	1. Baby Blue		Seg-way 103
			first released on SRG 101 in 1960		
			EDDY, Duane		
			Born on 4/26/38 in Corning, New York. Began playing guitar at age five. At age 13, moved to Tucson, then to Coolidge, Arizona. To Phoenix in 1955, and then began long association with producer/songwriter Lee Hazlewood. Eddy's backing band, The Rebels, included three top sessionmen: Larry Knechtel on piano (later with Bread) and Jim Horn and Steve Douglas on sax. Films *Because They're Young, A Thunder of Drums, The Wild Westerners, The Savage Seven* and *Kona Coast.* Married to Jessi Colter from 1962-68. Duane originated the "twangy" guitar sound and is the all-time #1 rock and roll instrumentalist. Currently resides in the Nashville area.		
7/07/58	**6**	12	**1. Rebel-'Rouser**	**[I]**	Jamie 1104
			Best Seller #6 / Top 100 #6 / Jockey #14 end handclaps and rebel yells by The Rivingtons		
9/15/58	**27**	5	2. Ramrod	[I]	Jamie 1109
			Best Seller #27 / Hot 100 #28		
11/17/58	**15**	9	3. Cannonball	[I]	Jamie 1111
2/02/59	**23**	8	4. The Lonely One	[I]	Jamie 1117
4/20/59	**30**	2	5. "Yep!"	[I]	Jamie 1122
6/29/59	**9**	11	**6. Forty Miles Of Bad Road**	**[I]**	Jamie 1126
10/26/59	**37**	3	7. Some Kind-A Earthquake	[I]	Jamie 1130
1/11/60	**26**	5	8. Bonnie Came Back	[I]	Jamie 1144
			traditional Scottish tune "My Bonnie Lies Over The Ocean"		
6/06/60	**4**	12	**9. Because They're Young**	**[I]**	Jamie 1156
			from the film of the same title		
10/31/60	**27**	4	10. Peter Gunn	[I]	Jamie 1168
			new version with The Art Of Noise charted in 1986 (POS 50)		
1/16/61	**18**	7	11. "Pepe"	[I]	Jamie 1175
			from the film of the same title		
4/17/61	**39**	1	12. Theme From Dixie	[I]	Jamie 1183
			classic Civil War song, written in 1860 by blackface composer Daniel Emmett; vocals by the Anita Kerr Singers & The Jordanaires		
8/11/62	**33**	3	13. The Ballad Of Paladin	[I]	RCA 8047
			theme from the TV series "Have Gun-Will Travel"		
11/03/62	**12**	10	14. (Dance With The) Guitar Man		RCA 8087
2/23/63	**28**	5	15. Boss Guitar		RCA 8131
			above 2: female vocal backing by The Rebelettes (The Blossoms)		
			EDISON LIGHTHOUSE		
			British studio group featuring lead singer Tony Burrows (also of The Brotherhood Of Man, First Class, The Pipkins and White Plains).		
2/28/70	**5**	12	• **1. Love Grows (Where My Rosemary Goes)**		Bell 858
			EDMUNDS, Dave		
			Born on 4/15/44 in Cardiff, Wales. Singer/songwriter/guitarist/producer. Formed Love Sculpture in 1967. Formed rockabilly band Rockpile in 1976. Produced for Shakin' Stevens, Brinsley Schwarz and Stray Cats.		
1/16/71	**4**	9	**1. I Hear You Knocking**		MAM 3601
			#2 R&B hit for Smiley Lewis in 1955		
7/30/83	**39**	1	2. Slipping Away		Columbia 03877

DATE	POS	WKS	ARTIST—RECORD TITLE	LABEL & NO.
			written and produced by Jeff Lynne (ELO)	
			EDSELS, The	
			R&B quintet from Youngstown, Ohio featuring George Jones, Jr. (lead) and Marshall Sewell (bass).	
6/05/61	**21**	5	1. Rama Lama Ding Dong	Twin 700
			originally released on Dub 2843 in 1958 as "Lama Rama Ding Dong"	
			EDWARD BEAR	
			Trio from Toronto — Larry Evoy, lead singer. Took name from a character in *Winnie the Pooh.*	
1/27/73	**3**	12	● **1. Last Song**	Capitol 3452
5/26/73	**37**	2	2. Close Your Eyes	Capitol 3581
			EDWARDS, Bobby	
			Real name: Robert Moncrief. Country singer from Anniston, Alabama.	
10/16/61	**11**	9	1. You're The Reason	Crest 1075
			backing vocals by The Four Young Men	
			EDWARDS, Jonathan	
			Born on 7/28/46 in Minnesota. Formed bluegrass band Sugar Creek in 1965.	
12/04/71+	**4**	12	● **1. Sunshine**	Capricorn 8021
			EDWARDS, Tommy	
			Born on 2/17/22 in Richmond, Virginia; died on 10/23/69. R&B singer/pianist/songwriter. Performing since age nine. First recorded for Top in 1949.	
8/25/58	**1**(6)	19	**1. It's All In The Game** **[R]**	MGM 12688
			Hot 100 #1(6) / Best Seller #1(3) end written by U.S. Vice President Charles Dawes in 1912	
11/17/58	**15**	9	2. Love Is All We Need	MGM 12722
3/02/59	**11**	8	3. Please Mr. Sun/ [R]	
3/23/59	**27**	4	4. The Morning Side Of The Mountain [R]	MGM 12757
			1, 3, 4: new versions of Edwards' 1951-52 charted hits	
6/08/59	**26**	4	5. My Melancholy Baby	MGM 12794
			#9 hit for Walter Van Brunt in 1915	
6/06/60	**18**	7	6. I Really Don't Want To Know	MGM 12890
			#11 hit for Les Paul & Mary Ford in 1954	
			EGAN, Walter	
			Born on 7/12/48 in Jamaica, New York.	
7/01/78	**8**	13	● **1. Magnet And Steel**	Columbia 10719
			8TH DAY, The	
			Five-man, three-woman group of session musicians from Detroit.	
6/05/71	**11**	10	● 1. She's Not Just Another Woman	Invictus 9087
10/16/71	**28**	6	2. You've Got To Crawl (Before You Walk)	Invictus 9098
			ELBERT, Donnie	
			Vocalist/multi-instrumentalist, born on 5/25/36 in New Orleans; died on 1/26/89. First recorded for DeLuxe in 1957. A&R director for Polygram Records, Canada, in the mid-1980s.	
11/20/71	**15**	8	1. Where Did Our Love Go	All Platinum 2330
2/12/72	**22**	6	2. I Can't Help Myself (Sugar Pie, Honey Bunch)	Avco 4587

DATE	POS	WKS	ARTIST—RECORD TITLE	LABEL & NO.
			EL CHICANO	
			Mexican-American band formed in Los Angeles as the VIP's in 1965, featuring Jerry Salas (lead vocals).	
5/02/70	**28**	5	1. Viva Tirado - Part I [I]	Kapp 2085
			first released on Gordo 703 in 1970	
12/22/73	**40**	1	2. Tell Her She's Lovely	MCA 40104
			EL DORADOS, The	
			Chicago R&B quintet featuring Pirkle Lee Moses, Jr., lead singer.	
10/15/55	**17**	6	1. At My Front Door	Vee-Jay 147
			Best Seller #17 / Top 100 #35	
			ELECTRIC INDIAN, The	
			Instrumental group assembled from top Philadelphia studio musicians. Some members later joined MFSB.	
8/23/69	**16**	8	1. Keem-O-Sabe [I]	United Art. 50563
			first released on Marmaduke 4001 in 1969	
			ELECTRIC LIGHT ORCHESTRA	
			Orchestral rock band formed in Birmingham, England in 1971, by Roy Wood, Bev Bevans and Jeff Lynne of The Move. Wood left after their first album, leaving Lynne as the group's leader. Much personnel shuffling from then on. From a group size of eight in 1971, the 1986 ELO consisted of three members: Lynne (vocals, guitar, keyboards), Bevans (drums) and Richard Tandy (keyboards). Lynne is a member of the supergroup Traveling Wilburys.	
1/25/75	**9**	10	**1. Can't Get It Out Of My Head**	United Art. 573
12/13/75+	**10**	12	**2. Evil Woman**	United Art. 729
4/10/76	**14**	9	3. Strange Magic	United Art. 770
11/13/76+	**13**	14	4. Livin' Thing	United Art. 888
3/05/77	**24**	6	5. Do Ya [R]	United Art. 939
			new version of their first hit (as The Move - POS 93 in 1972)	
7/09/77	**7**	16	● **6. Telephone Line**	United Art. 1000
12/10/77+	**13**	10	7. Turn To Stone	Jet 1099
3/11/78	**17**	12	8. Sweet Talkin' Woman	Jet 1145
7/29/78	**35**	3	9. Mr. Blue Sky	Jet 5050
6/02/79	**8**	11	**10. Shine A Little Love**	Jet 5057
8/11/79	**4**	11	● **11. Don't Bring Me Down**	Jet 5060
11/17/79	**37**	2	12. Confusion	Jet 5064
1/26/80	**39**	2	13. Last Train To London	Jet 5067
6/14/80	**16**	8	● 14. I'm Alive	MCA 41246
8/16/80	**13**	9	15. All Over The World	MCA 41289
8/30/80	**8**	10	**16. Xanadu**	MCA 41285
			OLIVIA NEWTON-JOHN/ELECTRIC LIGHT ORCHESTRA	
			above 3 from the film *Xanadu*	
			ELO:	
8/08/81	**10**	13	**17. Hold On Tight**	Jet 02408
11/28/81	**38**	2	18. Twilight	Jet 02559
7/09/83	**19**	9	19. Rock 'N' Roll Is King	Jet 03964
			ELECTRIC LIGHT ORCHESTRA:	
3/01/86	**18**	7	20. Calling America	CBS Assoc. 05766
			all of above written (except #5) and produced by Jeff Lynne	

DATE	POS	WKS	ARTIST—RECORD TITLE	LABEL & NO.
			ELECTRIC PRUNES, The	
			Seattle psychedelic rock quintet — James Lowe, lead singer.	
1/21/67	**11**	8	1. I Had Too Much To Dream (Last Night)	Reprise 0532
4/22/67	**27**	5	2. Get Me To The World On Time	Reprise 0564
			ELECTRONIC	
			Collaboration between Manchester, England natives Bernard Sumner (vocalist of New Order) and Johnny Marr (guitarist of The Smiths and The The). Outside contributors include Neil Tennant (of Pet Shop Boys) on backing vocals, Anne Dudley (of The Art Of Noise) on strings and David Palmer on drums.	
5/19/90	**38**	2	1. Getting Away With It originally available as an import on Factory 257	Warner 19880
			ELEGANTS, The	
			White vocal group formed in Staten Island, New York in 1957: Vito Picone (lead singer), Arthur Venosa, Frank Tardogna, Carmen Romano and James Moschella. All were veterans of other groups.	
7/28/58	**1**(1)	16	**1. Little Star** Hot 100 #1 / Best Seller #2 tune adapted from Mozart's (age 5) "Twinkle Twinkle Little Star"	Apt 25005
			ELGART, Larry/His Manhattan Swing Orchestra	
			Larry was born on 3/20/22 in New London, Connecticut. Alto saxman in brother Les' band and his own band.	
7/03/82	**31**	5	1. Hooked On Swing [I] In The Mood/Cherokee/American Patrol/Sing, Sing, Sing/Don't Be That Way/Little Brown Jug/Opus #1/Zing Went The Strings Of My Heart/String Of Pearls	RCA 13219
			ELLEDGE, Jimmy	
			Born on 1/08/43 in Nashville. Discovered by Chet Atkins.	
12/25/61+	**22**	7	1. Funny How Time Slips Away written by Willie Nelson; produced by Chet Atkins	RCA 7946
			ELLIMAN, Yvonne	
			Born on 12/29/51 in Honolulu. Portrayed Mary Magdalene on the concept LP and in the rock opera and film *Jesus Christ Superstar*. Joined with Eric Clapton during his 1974 comeback tour.	
5/22/71	**28**	6	1. I Don't Know How To Love Him from the rock opera *Jesus Christ Superstar*	Decca 32785
11/06/76	**14**	12	2. Love Me	RSO 858
4/16/77	**15**	9	3. Hello Stranger	RSO 871
2/25/78	**1**(1)	16	● **4. If I Can't Have You** from the film *Saturday Night Fever*	RSO 884
12/01/79	**34**	3	5. Love Pains	RSO 1007
			ELLIS, Shirley	
			Born in 1941 in the Bronx. Soul singer/songwriter. Was in the group The Metronomes.	
12/07/63+	**8**	10	**1. The Nitty Gritty**	Congress 202
1/09/65	**3**	10	**2. The Name Game**	Congress 230
4/03/65	**8**	7	**3. The Clapping Song (Clap Pat Clap Slap)** above 3 written by Shirley's manager & husband, Lincoln Chase	Congress 234

DATE	POS	WKS	ARTIST—RECORD TITLE	LABEL & NO.
			EMERSON, LAKE & PALMER	
			English classical-oriented rock trio formed in 1969. Consisted of Keith Emerson (with The Nice; keyboards), Greg Lake (King Crimson; vocals, bass, guitars) and Carl Palmer (Atomic Rooster, Crazy World of Arthur Brown; drums). Group split up in 1979, with Palmer joining supergroup Asia. Emerson and Lake re-grouped in 1986 with new drummer Cozy Powell. Palmer returned in 1987, replacing Powell who joined Black Sabbath in 1990.	
10/21/72	**39**	2	1. From The Beginning	Cotillion 44158
			EMF	
			Dance-punk band from Forest of Dean, England: James Atkin (vocals), Ian Dench, Mark Decloedt, Zac Foley and Derry Brownson. EMF stands for the name of New Order groupies called the Epson Mad Funkers.	
5/11/91	**1**(1)	16	● **1. Unbelievable**	EMI 50350#
			EMOTIONS, The	
			Black female trio from Chicago, consisting of sisters Wanda (lead), Sheila and Jeanette Hutchinson. First worked as a child gospel group called the Heavenly Sunbeams. Left gospel, became The Emotions in 1968. Jeanette replaced by cousin Theresa Davis in 1970, and later by sister Pamela. Jeanette returned to group in 1978.	
7/19/69	**39**	1	1. So I Can Love You	Volt 4010
7/02/77	**1**(5)	17	● **2. Best Of My Love**	Columbia 10544
5/26/79	**6**	12	● **3. Boogie Wonderland** EARTH, WIND & FIRE with THE EMOTIONS	ARC 10956
			ENCHANTMENT	
			Soul quintet from Detroit formed in 1966. Did soundtrack for the film *Deliver Us from Evil.*	
3/05/77	**25**	5	1. Gloria	United Art. 912
3/11/78	**33**	4	2. It's You That I Need	Roadshow 1124
			ENGLAND DAN & JOHN FORD COLEY	
			Pop duo from Austin, Texas: Dan Seals (b: 2/08/48) and Coley (b: 10/13/48). In the late '60s, both were members of Southwest F.O.B. Dan, the brother of Jim Seals of Seals & Crofts, charted solo pop hits and is currently a top country artist.	
7/10/76	**2**(2)	17	● **1. I'd Really Love To See You Tonight**	Big Tree 16069
10/30/76	**10**	12	**2. Nights Are Forever Without You**	Big Tree 16079
6/18/77	**21**	8	3. It's Sad To Belong	Big Tree 16088
11/05/77	**23**	6	4. Gone Too Far	Big Tree 16102
3/11/78	**9**	8	**5. We'll Never Have To Say Goodbye Again**	Big Tree 16110
4/07/79	**10**	10	**6. Love Is The Answer** written by Todd Rundgren	Big Tree 16131
			ENGLISH CONGREGATION, The	
			British group — Brian Keith, lead vocals.	
2/19/72	**29**	5	1. Softly Whispering I Love You	Atco 6865
			ENIGMA	
			Enigma is producer Michael Cretu. Born on 5/18/57 in Bucharest, Romania. Moved to Germany in 1975. Worked with Vangelis and The Art Of Noise. Featured vocalist is Cretu's wife, Sandra.	
3/02/91	**5**	11	● **1. Sadeness Part 1** [F] features traditional Gregorian chants backed by a dance rhythm; sadeness (pronounced: sadness) refers to 18th-century French author/libertine the Marquis de Sade	Charisma 98864#

DATE	POS	WKS	ARTIST—RECORD TITLE	LABEL & NO.
			EN VOGUE	
			Black female vocal quartet from the San Francisco Bay area. Formed by the production team of Denzil Foster and Thomas McElroy. Consists of Dawn Robinson, Terry Ellis, Cindy Herron and Maxine Jones.	
5/12/90	**2**(1)	17	▲ **1. Hold On**	Atlantic 87984
10/13/90	**38**	1	2. Lies	Atlantic 87893
			ENYA	
			Born Eithne Ni Bhraonain in Donegal, Ireland. From 1980-82, she was a member of her siblings' folk-rock group Clannad.	
3/11/89	**24**	8	1. Orinoco Flow (Sail Away) Orinoco is a river in South America	Geffen 27633
			EPPS, Preston	
			Bongo player born in 1931 in Oakland. Discovered by Original Sound owner, Art Laboe.	
6/01/59	**14**	9	1. Bongo Rock [I]	Original Sound 4
			EQUALS, The	
			Interracial British-Jamaican quintet led by Eddy Grant (guitar) and Derv Gordon (vocals).	
9/28/68	**32**	6	1. Baby, Come Back	RCA 9583
			ERASURE	
			British techno-soul duo of composer/producer/multi-instrumentalist Vince Clark and lyricist/vocalist Andy Bell. Clark was a member of Depeche Mode and Yaz.	
9/10/88	**12**	11	1. Chains Of Love	Sire 27844
1/21/89	**14**	9	2. A Little Respect	Sire 27738
			ERIC B. & RAKIM — see WATLEY, Jody	
			ERNIE — see HENSON, Jim	
			ERUPTION	
			London-based, techno-funk quintet of Jamaican natives featuring lead singers Precious Wilson and Lintel.	
6/10/78	**18**	6	1. I Can't Stand The Rain	Ariola 7686
			ESCAPE CLUB, The	
			London-based rock quartet formed in 1983: Trevor Steel (vocals), John Holliday (guitar), Johnnie Christo (bass) and Milan Zekavica (drums).	
9/17/88	**1**(1)	16	● **1. Wild, Wild West**	Atlantic 89048
1/21/89	**28**	5	2. Shake For The Sheik	Atlantic 88983
6/29/91	**8**	14	**3. I'll Be There** produced by Peter Wolf	Atlantic 87683#
			ESQUIRES, The	
			Soul quintet from Milwaukee formed at North Division High School in 1957 by Gilbert (lead singer), Alvis and Betty Moorer (left in 1965). Joined by Sam Pace in 1961, Shawn Taylor in 1965, and Millard Edwards in 1967.	
9/16/67	**11**	10	1. Get On Up	Bunky 7750
12/16/67	**22**	5	2. And Get Away	Bunky 7752
			ESSEX, David	
			Born David Cook on 7/23/47 in London. Portrayed Christ in the London production of *Godspell.* Star of British films since 1970.	
1/12/74	**5**	14	● **1. Rock On**	Columbia 45940

DATE	POS	WKS	ARTIST—RECORD TITLE	LABEL & NO.
			ESSEX, The	
			R&B quintet formed by members of U.S. Marine Corps at Camp LeJeune, North Carolina in 1962. Consisted of Anita Humes (lead), Walter Vickers, Rodney Taylor, Billie Hill and Rudolph Johnson.	
6/22/63	**1**(2)	10	**1. Easier Said Than Done**	Roulette 4494
9/14/63	**12**	6	2. A Walkin' Miracle	Roulette 4515
			ESTEFAN, Gloria/Miami Sound Machine	
			Latin American-flavored pop music band based in Miami, led by singer Gloria Estefan with her husband, percussionist Emilio Estefan, Jr. Band formed in 1975. Gloria (b: Gloria Fajardo, 12/01/57) came to Miami from Cuba in 1960. Emilio emigrated in 1965. On March 20, 1990, both were involved in a serious crash involving their tour bus, in which Gloria suffered a broken vertebra but fully recovered within a year.	
			MIAMI SOUND MACHINE:	
11/23/85+	**10**	16	● **1. Conga**	Epic 05457
3/29/86	**8**	12	● **2. Bad Boy**	Epic 05805
7/26/86	**5**	13	**3. Words Get In The Way**	Epic 06120
12/13/86+	**25**	8	4. Falling In Love (Uh-Oh)	Epic 06352
			GLORIA ESTEFAN AND MIAMI SOUND MACHINE:	
6/13/87	**5**	12	**5. Rhythm Is Gonna Get You**	Epic 07059
10/24/87	**36**	2	6. Betcha Say That	Epic 07371
1/16/88	**6**	11	**7. Can't Stay Away From You**	Epic 07641
3/26/88	**1**(2)	14	● **8. Anything For You**	Epic 07759
6/25/88	**3**	13	**9. 1-2-3**	Epic 07921
			GLORIA ESTEFAN:	
7/22/89	**1**(1)	13	● **10. Don't Wanna Lose You**	Epic 68959
10/21/89	**11**	8	11. Get On Your Feet	Epic 69064
1/13/90	**6**	11	**12. Here We Are**	Epic 73084
2/02/91	**1**(2)	14	**13. Coming Out Of The Dark**	Epic 73666
			ESTUS, Deon	
			Detroit-born black bassist. Formerly with George Michael, Wham!, Marvin Gaye and Brainstorm.	
3/11/89	**5**	11	**1. Heaven Help Me** DEON ESTUS with GEORGE MICHAEL	Mika 871538
			E.U.	
			E.U.: Experience Unlimited. Ten-member male group from Washington, D.C. Gregory "Sugar Bear" Elliott, lead vocals, bass.	
5/14/88	**35**	4	1. Da'Butt from the film *School Daze*	EMI-Man. 50115
			EUROPE	
			Swedish rock quintet: Joey Tempest (vocals), Kee Marcello (guitar), John Leven (bass), Mic Michaeli (keyboards) and Ian Haugland (drums).	
2/21/87	**8**	9	**1. The Final Countdown** featured in the film *Rocky IV*	Epic 06416
6/06/87	**30**	4	2. Rock The Night	Epic 07091
8/22/87	**3**	12	**3. Carrie**	Epic 07282
9/24/88	**31**	4	4. Superstitious	Epic 07979

DATE	POS	WKS	ARTIST—RECORD TITLE	LABEL & NO.
			EURYTHMICS	
			Synth/pop duo: Annie Lennox (b: 12/25/54, Aberdeen, Scotland; vocals, keyboards, flute, composer) and David Stewart (b: 9/09/52, England; keyboards, guitar, synthesizer, composer). Both had been in the Tourists from 1977-80. First album recorded in Cologne, Germany, with drummer Clem Burke (formerly of Blondie). Stewart married Siobhan Fahey of Bananarama on 8/01/87. Lennox appeared in TV film *The Room*.	
6/18/83	**1**(1)	17	● **1. Sweet Dreams (Are Made of This)**	RCA 13533
10/15/83	**23**	6	2. Love Is A Stranger	RCA 13618
2/04/84	**4**	14	**3. Here Comes The Rain Again**	RCA 13725
5/19/84	**21**	7	4. Who's That Girl?	RCA 13800
8/11/84	**29**	5	5. Right By Your Side	RCA 13695
5/11/85	**5**	13	**6. Would I Lie To You?**	RCA 14078
8/17/85	**22**	7	7. There Must Be An Angel (Playing With My Heart)	RCA 14160
11/02/85	**18**	8	8. Sisters Are Doin' It For Themselves **EURYTHMICS AND ARETHA FRANKLIN**	RCA 14214
8/30/86	**14**	9	9. Missionary Man	RCA 14414
11/04/89	**40**	1	10. Don't Ask Me Why	Arista 9880
			EVANS, Paul	
			Born on 3/05/38 in New York City. First recorded for RCA in 1957. Wrote hits "When" for the Kalin Twins, "Roses Are Red (My Love)" for Bobby Vinton, "I Gotta Know" and "The Next Step Is Love" for Elvis Presley. Wrote the score for the Broadway show *Loot* and the film *Live Young*.	
10/05/59	**9**	11	**1. Seven Little Girls Sitting In The Back Seat** with the Curls (female backing duo: Sue Singleton and Sue Terry)	Guaranteed 200
2/15/60	**16**	7	2. Midnite Special	Guaranteed 205
5/30/60	**10**	8	**3. Happy-Go-Lucky-Me**	Guaranteed 208
			EVERETT, Betty	
			Born on 11/23/39 in Greenwood, Mississippi. Vocalist/pianist. Performed in gospel choirs. To Chicago in the late 1950s. First recorded for Cobra in 1958. Toured England in the mid-1960s.	
3/21/64	**6**	10	**1. The Shoop Shoop Song (It's In His Kiss)**	Vee-Jay 585
9/19/64	**5**	11	**2. Let It Be Me** **BETTY EVERETT & JERRY BUTLER**	Vee-Jay 613
2/15/69	**26**	6	3. There'll Come A Time	Uni 55100
			EVERLY BROTHERS, The	
			Donald (real name: Isaac Donald) was born on 2/01/37 in Brownie, Kentucky; Philip on 1/19/39 in Chicago. Vocal duo/guitarists/songwriters. Parents were folk and country singers. Don (beginning at age eight) and Phil (age six) sang with parents through high school. Invited to Nashville by Chet Atkins and first recorded there for Columbia in 1955. Signed to Archie Bleyer's Cadence Records in 1957. Phil married for a time to the daughter of Janet Bleyer (Chordettes). Duo split up in July 1973 and reunited in September 1983. Inducted into the Rock and Roll Hall of Fame in 1986. Don's daughter Erin was married for a short time to Axl Rose of Guns N' Roses in 1990.	
5/27/57	**2**(4)	22	**1. Bye Bye Love** Best Seller #2 / Top 100 #2 / Jockey #2 / Juke Box #9 end	Cadence 1315
9/30/57	**1**(4)	20	**2. Wake Up Little Susie** Jockey #1(4) / Top 100 #1(2) / Best Seller #1(1)	Cadence 1337
2/17/58	**26**	3	3. This Little Girl Of Mine Best Seller #26 / Top 100 #28 #9 R&B hit for Ray Charles in 1955	Cadence 1342

Johnny Crawford may be remembered as a child actor who appeared on early TV shows "The Rifleman" and "The MIckey Mouse Club"—but to those who heard his 1962 hit "Your Nose Is Gonna Grow," Crawford's fame may come for actually singing the lyric "the boogeyman will get you."

Robert Cray's status among blues fans is forever assured for the singer's putting the bluesy "Smoking Gun" into the pop charts in 1987. The young bluesman's first album, 1980's hard-to-find *Who's Been Talkin'*, was reissued by Tomato Records in late 1991.

Bing Crosby's achievements are indeed vast, but some suspect his presence in the record collections of David Bowie fans—the pair sang "Little Drummer Boy" together on a mid-70s Crosby TV special, and RCA issued it—may be among the strangest.

Bobby Darin's diverse recording career is ably represented by two separate CDs issued by Atlantic in late 1991. One collects his pop hits for the label (such as 1966's "If I Were A Carpenter"); the other features standards like 1960's "Beyond The Sea."

Taylor Dayne, born Leslie Wonderman, come out singing with her Arista debut album *Tell It to My Heart*. The 1988 set contained all four of her Top 10 singles, including "Prove Your Love," "I'll Always Love You," "Don't Rush Me," and the title track.

Deep Purple's international reputation as a premiere hard-rock band may obscure their humble pop origins. The group's first two singles, issued here in 1968 on Tetragrammaton, were covers of songs by Joe South ("Hush") and Neil Diamond ("Kentucky Woman").

ROBERT CRAY

SMOKING GUN

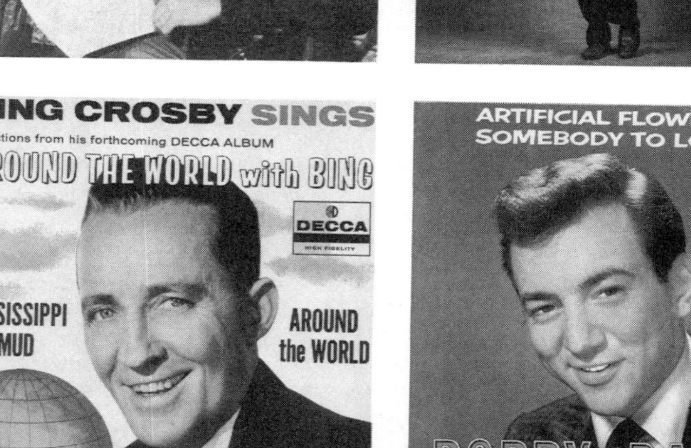

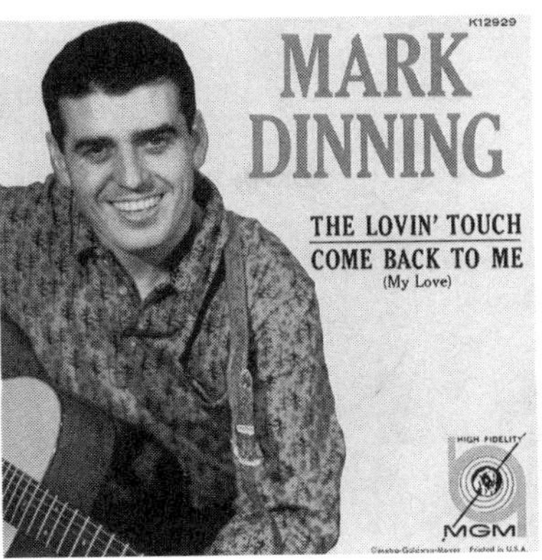

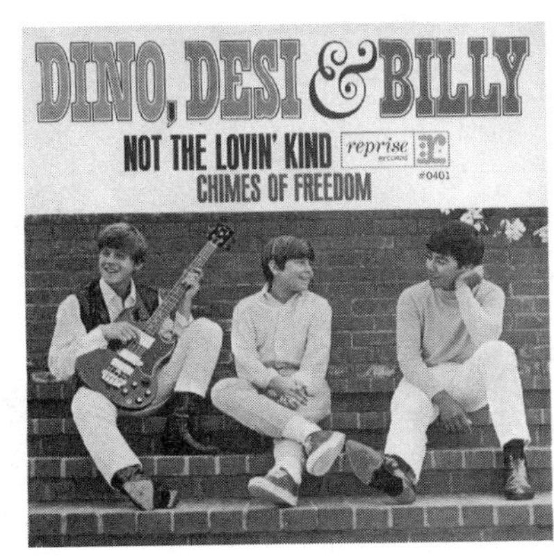

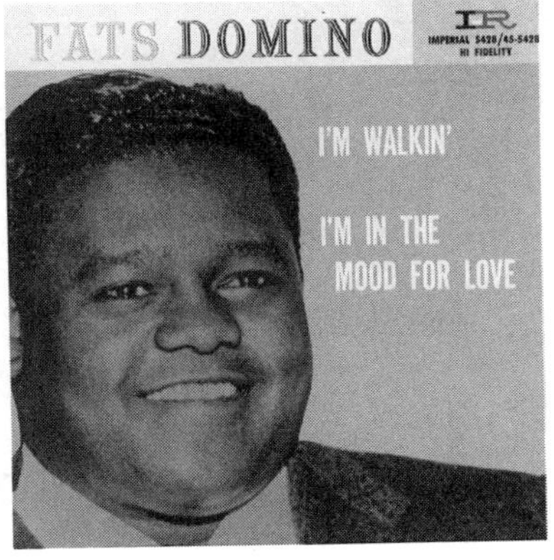

Neil Diamond's most recent No. 1 song, 1978's "You Don't Bring Me Flowers," was a duet with Barbra Streisand that had a bizarre origin. A disc jockey noticed that each artist's separate version was recorded in the same key—so he spliced together a version of his own that set phones ringing and kept Columbia busy catching up.

Mark Dinning's "Teen Angel," which held the No. 1 slot for two weeks in 1960, was the start of a slew of "teenage death" songs that included J. Frank Wilson & the Cavaliers' "Last Kiss," Dickey Lee's "Patches," and many more.

Dino, Desi & Billy's two 1965 hits—"I'm A Fool" and "Not The Lovin' Kind"—came about, some say, because of the industry connections of famous fathers Dean Martin and Desi Arnaz. But 25 years later, they now seem forebears of hitmakers Wilson Phillips, Nelson, and Julian Lennon.

Dion & the Belmonts scored only two top-10 hits, but Dion alone—with such hits as 1961's "Runaround Sue" and "The Wanderer'—managed nine. His last, 1968's "Abraham, Martin And John," went gold and peaked at No. 4.

D.J. Jazzy Jeff & the Fresh Prince were among the very first rappers to cross over to pop with "Parents Just Don't Understand" in 1988. So commercial was rapper Will Smith, in fact, that he soon starred in his own NBC-TV series, "Fresh Prince of Bel Air."

Fats Domino's enormous contributions to pop were lovingly compiled by EMI Records in 1991 and issued on *They Call Me the Fat Man*—a 4-CD set containing 100 of his classic recordings for the Imperial label.

DATE	POS	WKS	ARTIST—RECORD TITLE	LABEL & NO.
4/28/58	1(5)	16	**4. All I Have To Do Is Dream/** Jockey #1(5) / Best Seller #1(4) / Top 100 #1(3)	
5/12/58	30	2	5. Claudette written by Roy Orbison	Cadence 1348
8/11/58	1(1)	15	**6. Bird Dog/** Best Seller #1 / Hot 100 #2	
8/18/58	10	11	**7. Devoted To You**	Cadence 1350
11/24/58	2(1)	11	**8. Problems/**	
12/15/58	40	1	9. Love Of My Life	Cadence 1355
4/20/59	16	8	10. Take A Message To Mary/	
4/20/59	22	6	11. Poor Jenny	Cadence 1364
8/24/59	4	13	**12. ('Til) I Kissed You**	Cadence 1369
1/25/60	7	11	**13. Let It Be Me**	Cadence 1376
5/02/60	1(5)	13	**14. Cathy's Clown**	Warner 5151
6/27/60	8	9	**15. When Will I Be Loved**	Cadence 1380
9/12/60	7	10	**16. So Sad (To Watch Good Love Go Bad)/**	
9/12/60	21	7	17. Lucille	Warner 5163
11/28/60	22	4	18. Like Strangers 1, 2, 4, 6-11, 18: written by Boudleaux and Felice Bryant	Cadence 1388
2/13/61	7	10	**19. Walk Right Back/**	
2/13/61	8	9	**20. Ebony Eyes**	Warner 5199
6/12/61	27	3	21. Temptation #3 hit for Bing Crosby in 1934	Warner 5220
10/09/61	20	6	22. Don't Blame Me #6 hit for Ethel Waters in 1933; released as 7" E.P. with "Muskrat," "Walk Right Back" & "Lucille"	Warner 5501 & 2
2/03/62	6	9	**23. Crying In The Rain**	Warner 5250
6/02/62	9	7	**24. That's Old Fashioned (That's The Way Love Should Be)**	Warner 5273
12/05/64	31	2	25. Gone, Gone, Gone	Warner 5478
7/08/67	40	2	26. Bowling Green	Warner 7020
			EVERY MOTHERS' SON	
			Quintet formed in Greenwich Village, led by brothers Dennis and Lary Larden.	
5/27/67	6	12	**1. Come On Down To My Boat**	MGM 13733
			EXCITERS, The	
			R&B vocal quartet from Jamaica, New York: Herb Rooney, wife Brenda Reid, Carol Johnson & Lillian Walker.	
12/15/62+	4	10	**1. Tell Him**	United Art. 544
			EXILE	
			Band formed in Lexington, Kentucky in 1963 as The Exiles — J.P. Pennington, lead singer. Toured with Dick Clark in 1965. Changed name to Exile in 1973. Pennington left band in early 1989, replaced by Paul Martin. A top country act since 1983.	
8/05/78	1(4)	17	● **1. Kiss You All Over**	Warner 8589
2/03/79	40	1	2. You Thrill Me	Warner 8711

DATE	POS	WKS	ARTIST—RECORD TITLE	LABEL & NO.
			EXPOSE	
			Miami-based, vocal dance trio assembled by producer/songwriter Lewis Martinee. Consists of Miamian Ann Curless, Los Angeles native Jeanette Jurado and Italian-born, New York-raised Gioia Bruno.	
2/14/87	**5**	12	**1. Come Go With Me**	Arista 9555
5/30/87	**5**	11	**2. Point Of No Return** [R]	Arista 9579
			new version of their 1985 Dance/Disco hit on Arista 9326	
9/05/87	**7**	13	**3. Let Me Be The One**	Arista 9617
12/05/87+	**1**(1)	16	**4. Seasons Change**	Arista 9640
6/03/89	**8**	11	● **5. What You Don't Know**	Arista 9836
9/02/89	**10**	12	**6. When I Looked At Him**	Arista 9868
12/23/89+	**9**	11	**7. Tell Me Why**	Arista 9916
4/14/90	**17**	9	8. Your Baby Never Looked Good In Blue	Arista 2011
			EXTREME	
			Boston metal-funk band: Gary Cherone (vocals), Nuno Bettencourt, Pat Badger and Paul Geary.	
4/13/91	**1**(1)	17	● **1. More Than Words**	A&M 1552#
			EYE TO EYE	
			Pop duo: vocalist Deborah Berg from Seattle and pianist Julian Marshall (of Marshall Hain) from England.	
7/17/82	**37**	3	1. Nice Girls	Warner 50050
			F	
			FABARES, Shelley	
			Born Michele Fabares on 1/19/44 in Santa Monica, California. Niece of actress Nanette Fabray. Starred with Elvis in three of his movies. Best known as Mary Stone on "The Donna Reed Show." Married record producer Lou Adler in 1964. Cast member of several TV series since 1972, among them "One Day at a Time" (1981-84) and "Coach."	
3/17/62	**1**(2)	13	**1. Johnny Angel**	Colpix 621
6/30/62	**21**	6	2. Johnny Loves Me	Colpix 636
			FABIAN	
			Born Fabiano Forte on 2/06/43 in Philadelphia. Discovered at age 14 (because of his good looks and intriguing name) by a chance meeting with Bob Marcucci, owner of Chancellor Records. Began acting career in 1959 with the film *Hound Dog Man.*	
2/02/59	**31**	3	1. I'm A Man	Chancellor 1029
4/06/59	**9**	11	**2. Turn Me Loose**	Chancellor 1033
6/22/59	**3**	10	**3. Tiger**	Chancellor 1037
9/28/59	**29**	3	4. Come On And Get Me	Chancellor 1041
11/30/59	**9**	11	**5. Hound Dog Man/**	
12/07/59	**12**	9	6. This Friendly World	Chancellor 1044
			above 2 from the film *Hound Dog Man* (starring Fabian)	
3/14/60	**31**	3	7. About This Thing Called Love/	
			all of above produced by Peter de Angelis	
3/14/60	**39**	2	8. String Along	Chancellor 1047

DATE	POS	WKS	ARTIST—RECORD TITLE	LABEL & NO.
			FABRIC, Bent, and His Piano	
			Born Bent Fabricius-Bjerre on 12/07/24 in Copenhagen. Head of Metronome Records in Denmark.	
8/25/62	**7**	12	**1. Alley Cat** **[I]**	Atco 6226
			FABULOUS THUNDERBIRDS, The	
			Austin, Texas rock and roll group: Kim Wilson (lead singer), Jimmie Vaughan (guitar; older brother of Stevie Ray Vaughan), Preston Hubbard (bass) and Fran Christina (drums). Vaughan appeared in the 1989 film *Great Balls of Fire* and recorded in The Vaughan Brothers in 1990. Disbanded in June 1990. Reorganized in 1991 with Wilson, Hubbard, Christina and guitarists Duke Robillard and Kid Bangham.	
5/24/86	**10**	10	**1. Tuff Enuff**	CBS Assoc. 05838
			FACENDA, Tommy	
			Born on 11/10/39 in Norfolk, Virginia. Backup vocals with Gene Vincent from 1957-58. Nicknamed "Bubba." Discovered by Frank Guida, who wrote Facenda's hit and discovered Gary U.S. Bonds. First recorded for Nasco in 1958. Later became a firefighter in Virginia.	
11/09/59	**28**	3	1. High School U.S.A. [N] first released as "High School U.S.A. Virginia" on Legrand 1001; Atlantic then released 28 different versions of this record, each mentioning the names of high schools in various areas	Atlantic 51 to 78
			FACES	
			With the departure of lead singer Steve Marriott who formed Humble Pie, the British group Small Faces added, in 1969, former Jeff Beck Group members: Rod Stewart (vocals) and Ron Wood (bass, joined The Rolling Stones in 1976). Other members were Ian McLagen, Kenney Jones (joined The Who in 1978, formed The Law in 1991) and Ronnie Lane (left in 1973, replaced by ex-Free bassist Tetsu Yamauchi). Disbanded in late 1975.	
11/27/71	**24**	6	1. (I Know) I'm Losing You **ROD STEWART with FACES**	Mercury 73244
1/15/72	**17**	8	2. Stay With Me	Warner 7545
			FACE TO FACE	
			Boston-based rock quintet. Group appeared as backing band in the film *Streets of Fire* for which lead singer Laurie Sargent recorded actress Diane Lane's vocals.	
7/21/84	**38**	3	1. 10-9-8	Epic 04430
			FACTS OF LIFE	
			Soul trio formed by Millie Jackson, originally known as The Gospel Truth: Jean Davis (younger sister of Tyrone Davis), Keith William (formerly with the Imperials and Flamingos) and Chuck Carter.	
4/09/77	**31**	4	1. Sometimes produced by Millie Jackson	Kayvette 5128
			FAGEN, Donald	
			Born on 1/10/48 in Passaic, New Jersey. Backup keyboardist/vocalist with Jay & The Americans. At New York's Bard College, formed band with Walter Becker and drummer-turned-actor Chevy Chase. Fagen and Becker formed Steely Dan in 1972.	
10/30/82	**26**	7	1. I.G.Y. (What A Beautiful World) I.G.Y.: International Geophysical Year (Jul '57-Dec '58)	Warner 29900
			FAIRCHILD, Barbara	
			Born on 11/12/50 in Knobel, Arkansas. Country singer/songwriter.	
5/12/73	**32**	5	1. Teddy Bear Song	Columbia 45743

DATE	POS	WKS	ARTIST—RECORD TITLE	LABEL & NO.
			FAITH, Adam	
			Born Terence Nelhams on 6/23/40 in London. Actor in films and television. Produced Roger Daltrey's first solo album. Managed Leo Sayer.	
2/20/65	**31**	2	1. It's Alright with backing band The Roulettes	Amy 913
			FAITH, Percy	
			Born on 4/07/08 in Toronto; died of cancer on 2/09/76. Orchestra leader. Moved to the United States in 1940. Joined Columbia Records in 1950 as conductor/arranger for their leading singers (Tony Bennett, Doris Day, Rosemary Clooney, Johnny Mathis and others).	
1/25/60	**1**(9)	17	● **1. The Theme From "A Summer Place"** [I] from the film *A Summer Place*	Columbia 41490
6/27/60	**35**	1	2. Theme For Young Lovers [I]	Columbia 41655
			FAITHFULL, Marianne	
			Born on 12/29/46 in Hampstead, London. Discovered by Rolling Stones' manager, Andrew Loog Oldham. Involved in a long, tumultuous relationship with Mick Jagger. Acted in several stage and screen productions. Married British art gallery owner John Dunbar, Vibrators bassist Ben Brierly and American playwright Giorgio Dellaterza.	
12/19/64+	**22**	6	1. As Tears Go By	London 9697
3/27/65	**26**	5	2. Come And Stay With Me	London 9731
6/26/65	**32**	5	3. This Little Bird	London 9759
9/04/65	**24**	5	4. Summer Nights	London 9780
			FAITH NO MORE	
			San Francisco rock quintet: Michael "Vlad Dracula" Patton (vocals), Jim Martin, Roddy Bottum, Billy Gould and Mike Bordin.	
7/14/90	**9**	13	● **1. Epic**	Slash 19813
			FALCO	
			Falco (Johann Holzel) was born on 2/19/57 in Vienna, Austria.	
2/22/86	**1**(3)	13	**1. Rock Me Amadeus**	A&M 2821
5/17/86	**18**	8	2. Vienna Calling	A&M 2832
			FALCONS, The	
			Detroit R&B group: Eddie Floyd (lead vocals; replaced in 1961 by Wilson Pickett), Bonny "Mack" Rice, Joe Stubbs (brother of the Four Tops' Levi Stubbs), Willie Schofield and Lance Finnie.	
6/08/59	**17**	10	1. You're So Fine Joe Stubbs, lead singer	Unart 2013
			FALTERMEYER, Harold	
			West German keyboardist/songwriter/arranger/producer. Arranged and played keyboards on the film scores of *Midnight Express* and *American Gigolo*.	
4/13/85	**3**	12	**1. Axel F** [I] from the film *Beverly Hills Cop*; Eddie Murphy played Axel Foley	MCA 52536
			FALTSKOG, Agnetha	
			Pronounced: Ag-nyet-ta Felts-kogue. Born on 4/05/50 in Sweden. Member of Abba.	
10/08/83	**29**	5	1. Can't Shake Loose	Polydor 815230

DATE	POS	WKS	ARTIST—RECORD TITLE	LABEL & NO.
			FAME, Georgie	
			Born Clive Powell on 6/26/43 in Lancashire, England. Began as a pianist with Billy Fury's backup group The Blue Flames.	
2/27/65	**21**	6	1. Yeh, Yeh with The Blue Flames	Imperial 66086
3/02/68	**7**	12	**2. The Ballad Of Bonnie And Clyde**	Epic 10283
			FANCY	
			English rock quartet — Helen Court, lead singer.	
8/03/74	**14**	8	1. Wild Thing	Big Tree 15004
11/16/74	**19**	4	2. Touch Me	Big Tree 16026
			FANNY	
			Female rock quartet from California: vocalists/sisters June and Jean Millington, with Alice DeBuhr and Nickey Barclay. Jean and Alice left in 1974, replaced by Brie Brandt-Howard and Patti Quatro (sister of Suzi Quatro).	
11/06/71	**40**	1	1. Charity Ball	Reprise 1033
3/15/75	**29**	4	2. Butter Boy	Casablanca 814
			FANTASTIC JOHNNY C	
			Born Johnny Corley on 4/28/43 in Greenwood, South Carolina. Produced and managed by Jesse James.	
11/04/67	**7**	12	**1. Boogaloo Down Broadway**	Phil-L.A. 305
8/10/68	**34**	2	2. Hitch It To The Horse	Phil-L.A. 315
			FARDON, Don	
			Born Don Maughn in Coventry, England. Lead singer of English group The Sorrows.	
9/21/68	**20**	6	1. (The Lament Of The Cherokee) Indian Reservation	GNP Cresc. 405
			FARGO, Donna	
			Born Yvonne Vaughan on 11/10/49 in Mt. Airy, North Carolina. Recorded for Ramco in 1969. Worked as a high school teacher until June 1972. Donna was stricken with multiple sclerosis in 1979. Has own music publishing company.	
7/08/72	**11**	10	● 1. The Happiest Girl In The Whole U.S.A.	Dot 17409
11/11/72+	**5**	14	● **2. Funny Face**	Dot 17429
			FASTER PUSSYCAT	
			Los Angeles-based, hard-rock quintet led by vocalist Taime Downe. Name taken from the 1962 action film *Faster Pussycat! Kill! Kill!*	
4/21/90	**28**	6	1. House Of Pain	Elektra 64995
			FAT BOYS	
			Brooklyn-born rap trio: Darren "The Human Beat Box" Robinson, Mark "Prince Markie Dee" Morales and Damon "Kool Rock-ski" Wimbley. Combined weight of over 750 pounds. Appeared in the 1987 film *Disorderlies*.	
8/08/87	**12**	11	1. Wipeout **FAT BOYS and THE BEACH BOYS**	Tin Pan 885960
7/09/88	**16**	8	2. The Twist (Yo, Twist!) **FAT BOYS with CHUBBY CHECKER**	Tin Pan 887571
			FATHER M.C.	
			Rapper Timothy Brown, raised in Brooklyn and Queens.	
2/16/91	**20**	8	● 1. I'll Do 4 U backing tune sampled from "Got To Be Real" by Cheryl Lynn	Uptown 53914#

DATE	POS	WKS	ARTIST—RECORD TITLE	LABEL & NO.
			FELICIANO, Jose	
			Born on 9/08/45 in Puerto Rico; raised in New York City. Blind since birth. Virtuoso acoustic guitarist. Composed score for TV's "Chico & The Man." Won the 1968 Best New Artist Grammy Award.	
8/03/68	**3**	11	**1. Light My Fire**	RCA 9550
10/26/68	**25**	7	2. Hi-Heel Sneakers	RCA 9641
			FENDER, Freddy	
			Born Baldemar Huerta on 6/04/37 in San Benito, Texas. Mexican-American singer/guitarist. First recorded in Spanish under his real name for Falcon in 1956. In the film *The Milagro Beanfield War.* Joined the Texas Tornados in 1990.	
3/08/75	**1**(1)	15	● **1. Before The Next Teardrop Falls**	ABC/Dot 17540
7/19/75	**8**	14	● **2. Wasted Days And Wasted Nights** originally recorded by Fender on the Duncan label in 1959	ABC/Dot 17558
11/08/75	**20**	6	3. Secret Love #1 hit for Doris Day in 1954	ABC/Dot 17585
3/20/76	**32**	4	4. You'll Lose A Good Thing	ABC/Dot 17607
			FENDERMEN, The	
			Duo of Phil Humphrey (from Stoughton, Wisconsin) and Jim Sundquist (from Niagara, Wisconsin); both were born on 11/26/37. Formed at the University of Wisconsin-Madison.	
6/13/60	**5**	13	**1. Mule Skinner Blues** written in 1931 by country great Jimmie Rodgers; originally released on Cuca 1003 in 1959	Soma 1137
			FERGUSON, Jay	
			Born on 5/10/43 in San Fernando Valley, California. Before going solo, Jay formed and led the groups Spirit and Jo Jo Gunne.	
1/28/78	**9**	12	**1. Thunder Island**	Asylum 45444
6/09/79	**31**	4	2. Shakedown Cruise	Asylum 46041
			FERGUSON, Johnny	
			Born on 3/22/37 in Nashville. Worked as a DJ in the late 1950s.	
4/18/60	**27**	3	1. Angela Jones	MGM 12855
			FERGUSON, Maynard	
			Jazz trumpeter. Born on 5/04/28 in Verdun, Quebec, Canada. Moved to the U.S. in 1949. Played for Charlie Barnet and then Stan Kenton's Band (1950-56).	
5/28/77	**28**	6	1. Gonna Fly Now (Theme From "Rocky") [I] from the film *Rocky*	Columbia 10468
			FERKO STRING BAND	
			Philadelphia string band directed by William Connors. String bands parade annually in Philadelphia's famed New Year's Day Mummers Parade. Also see Nu Tornados.	
6/18/55	**14**	6	1. Alabama Jubilee [I] Juke Box #14 / Best Seller #18 #2 hit for Arthur Collins & Byron Harlan in 1915	Media 1010
			FERRANTE & TEICHER	
			Piano duo: Arthur Ferrante (b: 9/07/21, New York City) and Louis Teicher (b: 8/24/24, Wilkes-Barre, Pennsylvania). Met as children while attending Manhattan's performing arts academy the Juilliard School.	
8/08/60	**10**	15	**1. Theme From The Apartment** [I]	United Art. 231

DATE	POS	WKS	ARTIST—RECORD TITLE	LABEL & NO.
			from the Billy Wilder film *The Apartment*; tune originally entitled "Jealous Lover"	
11/28/60+	**2**(1)	18	**2. Exodus** [I]	United Art. 274
			theme from the Otto Preminger film of the same title	
4/17/61	**37**	1	3. Love Theme From One Eyed Jacks [I]	United Art. 300
			from the Marlon Brando film *One Eyed Jacks*	
11/13/61	**8**	8	**4. Tonight** [I]	United Art. 373
			from the film *West Side Story*	
11/29/69+	**10**	11	**5. Midnight Cowboy** [I]	United Art. 50554
			from the Jon Voight/Dustin Hoffman film of the same title; featuring the "water sound" guitar of Vincent Bell	
			FERRY, Bryan	
			Born on 9/26/45 in County Durham, England. Lead singer of Roxy Music.	
4/16/88	**31**	3	1. Kiss And Tell	Reprise 28117
			from the film *Bright Lights, Big City*	
			FIELDS, Ernie	
			Born on 8/26/05 in Nacogdoches, Texas. Trombonist/pianist/bandleader/arranger.	
10/12/59	**4**	14	**1. In The Mood** [I]	Rendezvous 110
			#1 hit for Glenn Miller in 1940	
			FIESTAS, The	
			R&B vocal group from Newark, New Jersey: Tommy Bullock (lead), Eddie Morris (tenor), Sam Ingalls (baritone) and Preston Lane (bass).	
4/27/59	**11**	11	1. So Fine	Old Town 1062
			5TH DIMENSION, The	
			Los Angeles-based vocal group formed in 1966: Marilyn McCoo, Florence LaRue, Billy Davis, Jr., Lamont McLemore and Ron Townson. McLemore and McCoo had been in the Hi-Fi's; Townson and Davis had been with groups in St. Louis. First called the Versatiles. Davis and McCoo were married in 1969 and recorded as a duo since 1976.	
2/04/67	**16**	7	1. Go Where You Wanna Go	Soul City 753
6/17/67	**7**	10	**2. Up-Up And Away**	Soul City 756
			above 2 produced by Johnny Rivers (Soul City is his own label)	
12/09/67	**34**	1	3. Paper Cup	Soul City 760
2/24/68	**29**	5	4. Carpet Man	Soul City 762
6/22/68	**3**	12	▲ **5. Stoned Soul Picnic**	Soul City 766
10/26/68	**13**	6	6. Sweet Blindness	Soul City 768
1/11/69	**25**	6	7. California Soul	Soul City 770
3/15/69	**1**(6)	16	▲ **8. Aquarius/Let The Sunshine In**	Soul City 772
			from the Broadway rock musical *Hair*	
8/09/69	**20**	7	9. Workin' On A Groovy Thing	Soul City 776
			written by Neil Sedaka (also #12 below)	
10/04/69	**1**(3)	14	▲ **10. Wedding Bell Blues**	Soul City 779
1/24/70	**21**	6	11. Blowing Away	Soul City 780
5/02/70	**24**	5	12. Puppet Man	Bell 880
6/27/70	**27**	5	13. Save The Country	Bell 895
			5, 6, 10, 11, 13: written by Laura Nyro	
11/21/70	**2**(2)	15	▲ **14. One Less Bell To Answer**	Bell 940
3/13/71	**19**	8	15. Love's Lines, Angles And Rhymes	Bell 965
10/02/71	**12**	9	16. Never My Love	Bell 45134

DATE	POS	WKS	ARTIST—RECORD TITLE	LABEL & NO.
1/29/72	**37**	3	17. Together Let's Find Love	Bell 45170
4/22/72	**8**	13	▲ **18. (Last Night) I Didn't Get To Sleep At All**	Bell 45195
9/30/72	**10**	12	**19. If I Could Reach You**	Bell 45261
2/10/73	**32**	4	20. Living Together, Growing Together 3-20: produced by Bones Howe; from the film *Lost Horizon*	Bell 45310
			FIFTH ESTATE, The	
			Studio group assembled by producers Steve and Bill Jerome.	
6/10/67	**11**	6	1. Ding Dong! The Witch Is Dead song originally appeared in the 1939 film *The Wizard of Oz*	Jubilee 5573
			FINE YOUNG CANNIBALS	
			Pop trio from Birmingham, England: Roland Gift (vocals) and English Beat members David Steele (bass) and Andy Cox (guitar). Group appeared in the film *Tin Men*; Gift was in the films *Sammy and Rosie Get Laid* and *Scandal.*	
2/25/89	**1**(1)	14	• **1. She Drives Me Crazy**	I.R.S. 53483
5/20/89	**1**(1)	13	**2. Good Thing** from the 1987 film *Tin Men*	I.R.S. 53639
8/26/89	**11**	8	3. Don't Look Back	I.R.S. 53695
			FINNEGAN, Larry	
			Born John Lawrence Finneran on 8/10/38 in New York City. Moved to Sweden in 1966; headed own record company. To Switzerland in 1967 and back to the U.S. in 1970. Died of a brain tumor on 7/22/73.	
3/31/62	**11**	8	1. Dear One	Old Town 1113
			FIORILLO, Elisa	
			Los Angeles-based vocalist raised in Philadelphia. Commercial jingle singer as a child. Winner on TV's "Star Search." Signed with Chrysalis in 1985 at age 15.	
8/15/87	**16**	8	1. Who Found Who **JELLYBEAN/ELISA FIORILLO**	Chrysalis 43120
12/08/90+	**27**	6	2. On The Way Up	Chrysalis 23497#
			FIREBALLS, The	
			Rock and roll band formed while high schoolers in Raton, New Mexico: George Tomsco (b: 4/24/40, lead guitar), Dan Trammell (b: 7/14/40, rhythm guitar), Eric Budd (b: 10/23/38, drums), Stan Lark (b: 7/27/40, bass) and Chuck Tharp (b: 2/03/41, vocalist). First recorded for Kapp in 1958. Trammell left group in 1959. Doug Roberts (d: 11/18/81) replaced Budd in 1962. Tharp quit group in 1960 and was replaced by Jimmy Gilmer (lead vocals, piano). Gilmer was introduced to The Fireballs by their record producer Norman Petty at his famed Clovis, New Mexico studio.	
10/26/59	**39**	2	1. Torquay [I]	Top Rank 2008
2/01/60	**24**	6	2. Bulldog [I]	Top Rank 2026
8/07/61	**27**	3	3. Quite A Party [I]	Warwick 644
			JIMMY GILMER AND THE FIREBALLS:	
9/28/63	**1**(5)	13	• **4. Sugar Shack**	Dot 16487
1/04/64	**15**	8	5. Daisy Petal Pickin'	Dot 16539
			THE FIREBALLS:	
1/27/68	**9**	10	**6. Bottle Of Wine**	Atco 6491

DATE	POS	WKS	ARTIST—RECORD TITLE	LABEL & NO.
			FIREFALL	
			Mellow rock group formed in Boulder, Colorado. Original lineup: Rick Roberts (lead singer), Larry Burnett (guitar), Jack Bartley (lead guitar), Mark Andes (bass; formerly with Spirit and Jo Jo Gunne) and Mike Clarke (drums). David Muse (keyboards) joined in 1977. Andes joined Heart in 1980.	
9/25/76	**9**	15	**1. You Are The Woman**	Atlantic 3335
4/30/77	**34**	3	2. Cinderella	Atlantic 3392
9/17/77	**11**	12	3. Just Remember I Love You	Atlantic 3420
10/28/78	**11**	10	4. Strange Way	Atlantic 3518
5/10/80	**35**	3	5. Headed For A Fall	Atlantic 3657
2/28/81	**37**	3	6. Staying With It lead vocals by Lisa Nemzo and Rick Roberts	Atlantic 3791
			FIREFLIES	
			White doo-wop quartet formed by Gerry Granahan and featuring Ritchie Adams, lead singer.	
9/28/59	**21**	10	1. You Were Mine	Ribbon 6901
			FIREHOUSE	
			Hard-rock quartet from North Carolina: C.J. Snare (vocals), Bill Leverty, Perry Richardson and Michael Foster.	
4/20/91	**19**	10	1. Don't Treat Me Bad	Epic 73676
			FIRM, The	
			British supergroup: Jimmy Page (Led Zeppelin, The Honeydrippers; guitar), Paul Rodgers (Free, Bad Company; vocals), Chris Slade (Manfred Mann; drums) and Tony Franklin (keyboards). Disbanded in 1986. Franklin joined Blue Murder in 1989. Slade joined AC/DC in 1990. Rodgers joined The Law in 1991.	
3/16/85	**28**	6	1. Radioactive	Atlantic 89586
			FIRST CHOICE	
			Female soul trio from Philadelphia, formed as the Debronettes. Consisted of Rochelle Fleming, Annette Guest and Joyce Jones.	
4/28/73	**28**	5	1. Armed And Extremely Dangerous	Philly Groove 175
			FIRST CLASS	
			British studio quartet: Tony Burrows (vocals), John Carter, Del John and Chas Mills. Burrows was the vocalist on hits by The Brotherhood Of Man, Edison Lighthouse, The Pipkins and White Plains.	
8/17/74	**4**	11	**1. Beach Baby**	UK 49022
			FIRST EDITION, The — see ROGERS, Kenny	
			FISCHER, Lisa	
			Native of Fort Greene, Brooklyn, New York. Session singer with Billy Ocean, Melba Moore and others. Touring vocalist with Luther Vandross.	
6/01/91	**11**	8	1. How Can I Ease The Pain	Elektra 64897#
			FISHER, Eddie	
			Born Edwin Jack Fisher on 8/10/28 in Philadelphia. Radio work while still in high school. At Copacabana night club in New York at age 17. With Buddy Morrow and Charlie Ventura in 1946. On Eddie Cantor's radio show in 1949. In the Armed Forces Special Services, 1952-53. Married Debbie Reynolds in 1955. Other marriages to Elizabeth Taylor and Connie Stevens. Daughter with Debbie is actress Carrie Fisher (b: 1956). Daughter with Connie is singer Tricia Leigh Fisher. Own "Coke Time" 15-minute TV series, 1953-57. In films *All About Eve* (1950), *Bundle of Joy* (1956) and *Butterfield 8* (1960). Eddie was the #1 idol of bobbysoxers during the early 1950's.	
3/05/55	**16**	2	1. A Man Chases A Girl (Until She Catches Him)/	

DATE	POS	WKS	ARTIST—RECORD TITLE	LABEL & NO.
			Jockey #16 / Juke Box #20 / Best Seller #27 from the film *There's No Business Like Show Business*	
4/02/55	**20**	1	2. (I'm Always Hearing) Wedding Bells Juke Box #20	RCA 6015
5/14/55	**6**	13	**3. Heart** Jockey #6 / Juke Box #13 / Best Seller #15 from the Broadway musical *Damn Yankees*	RCA 6097
8/27/55	**11**	8	4. Song Of The Dreamer Juke Box #11 / Best Seller #16 / Jockey #16 / Top 100 #43 pre	RCA 6196
12/24/55+	**7**	16	**5. Dungaree Doll/** Top 100 #7 / Juke Box #7 / Best Seller #8 / Jockey #9	
12/31/55	**20**	1	6. Everybody's Got A Home But Me Jockey #20 / Top 100 #41 from the Broadway musical *Pipe Dream*	RCA 6337
6/30/56	**18**	7	7. On The Street Where You Live Juke Box #18 / Top 100 #28 from the Broadway musical *My Fair Lady*	RCA 6529
10/20/56	**10**	17	**8. Cindy, Oh Cindy** Best Seller #10 / Top 100 #10 / Jockey #10 / Juke Box #10	RCA 6677
			FISHER, Miss Toni	
			Born in Los Angeles in 1931.	
11/23/59	**3**	14	**1. The Big Hurt**	Signet 275
7/14/62	**37**	1	2. West Of The Wall **TONI FISHER**	Big Top 3097
			FITZGERALD, Ella	
			The most honored jazz singer of all time. Born on 4/25/18 in Newport News, Virginia. Discovered after winning on the "Harlem Amateur Hour" in 1934, she was hired by Chick Webb and in 1938 created a popular sensation with "A-Tisket, A-Tasket." Following Chick's death in 1939, Ella took over the band for three years. Appeared in several films. Won the Lifetime Achievement Grammy in 1967. Winner of the Down Beat poll as top female vocalist more than 20 times and winner of 12 Grammys, she remains among the undisputed royalty of 20th century popular music.	
5/30/60	**27**	7	1. Mack The Knife live recording with the Paul Smith Quartet written in 1928 as "Moritat" or "Theme From The Threepenny Opera"	Verve 10209
			FIVE AMERICANS, The	
			Dallas-based quintet, originally from Oklahoma, led by vocalist Michael Rabon. Keyboardist John Durrill wrote Cher's "Dark Lady" and "I Saw A Man And He Danced With His Wife." Member Jimmy Wright married Robin of Jon & Robin & The In Crowd.	
2/12/66	**26**	5	1. I See The Light first released on Abnak 109 in 1965	HBR 454
3/18/67	**5**	9	**2. Western Union**	Abnak 118
6/17/67	**36**	2	3. Sound Of Love	Abnak 120
9/16/67	**36**	1	4. Zip Code	Abnak 123
			FIVE BLOBS, The	
			Studio production — vocals by Bernie Nee.	
11/03/58	**33**	3	1. The Blob from the film of the same title (written by Burt Bacharach)	Columbia 41250
			FIVE FLIGHTS UP	
10/03/70	**37**	5	1. Do What You Wanna Do	T-A 202

DATE	POS	WKS	ARTIST—RECORD TITLE	LABEL & NO.
			FIVE KEYS, The	
			R&B quintet originally formed as the Sentimental Four in Newport News, Virginia, late 1940s. Consisted of two sets of brothers: Rudy & Bernie West and Ripley & Raphael Ingram. In 1949, added Maryland Pierce and changed group name to The Five Keys. Dickie Smith replaced Raphael Ingram. Smith replaced by Ramon Loper in 1953. Rudy West sings lead on the ballads, Maryland Pierce lead on the rhythm tunes.	
12/25/54+	**28**	2	1. Ling, Ting, Tong Best Seller #28	Capitol 2945
10/06/56	**23**	6	2. Out Of Sight, Out Of Mind Best Seller #23 / Top 100 #27	Capitol 3502
1/12/57	**35**	2	3. Wisdom Of A Fool	Capitol 3597
			FIVE MAN ELECTRICAL BAND	
			Ontario, Canada rock group — Les Emmerson, lead singer.	
7/10/71	**3**	12	● **1. Signs**	Lionel 3213
10/30/71	**26**	6	2. Absolutely Right	Lionel 3220
			FIVE SATINS, The	
			R&B group from New Haven, Connecticut. Consisted of Fred Parris (lead), Al Denby, Jim Freeman, Eddie Martin and Jessie Murphy (piano). Parris was stationed in the Army in Japan when "In The Still Of The Nite" charted, and the group re-formed with Bill Baker as lead singer. Parris returned in January 1958, replacing Baker.	
9/29/56	**24**	6	1. In The Still Of The Nite Best Seller #24 / Top 100 #29 written by Fred Parris and recorded in a New Haven church basement; originally released on Standard 200; record reportedly has sold multi-millions	Ember 1005
8/12/57	**25**	8	2. To The Aisle Best Seller #25 / Top 100 #25	Ember 1019
			FIVE STAIRSTEPS, The	
			Soul group from Chicago, consisting of brothers Clarence, Jr., James, Kenneth and Dennis Burke with their sister Aloha. Later joined by their five-year-old brother Cubie. Managed by their father and produced by Curtis Mayfield; later became The Invisible Man's Band.	
6/20/70	**8**	11	● **1. O-o-h Child**	Buddah 165
			5000 VOLTS	
11/15/75	**26**	5	1. I'm On Fire	Philips 40801
			FIXX, The	
			London-based, techno-pop group: Cy Curnin (lead singer, piano), Jamie West-Oram (guitars), Rupert Greenall (keyboards), Adam Woods (drums) and Dan K. Brown (bass).	
7/09/83	**20**	8	1. Saved By Zero	MCA 52213
9/10/83	**4**	13	**2. One Thing Leads To Another**	MCA 52264
12/17/83+	**32**	7	3. The Sign Of Fire	MCA 52316
9/08/84	**15**	8	4. Are We Ourselves?	MCA 52444
6/28/86	**19**	6	5. Secret Separation	MCA 52832
5/04/91	**35**	3	6. How Much Is Enough	Impact 54028#

DATE	POS	WKS	ARTIST—RECORD TITLE	LABEL & NO.
			FLACK, Roberta	
			Born on 2/10/39 in Asheville, North Carolina and raised in Arlington, Virginia. Played piano from an early age. Music scholarship to Howard University at age 15; classmate of Donny Hathaway (soul singer born on 10/01/45 in Chicago). Discovered by jazz musician Les McCann. Signed to Atlantic in 1969.	
7/03/71	**29**	9	1. You've Got A Friend **ROBERTA FLACK & DONNY HATHAWAY**	Atlantic 2808
3/25/72	**1**(6)	15	● **2. The First Time Ever I Saw Your Face** popularized because of inclusion in the film *Play Misty for Me*	Atlantic 2864
6/24/72	**5**	11	● **3. Where Is The Love** **ROBERTA FLACK & DONNY HATHAWAY**	Atlantic 2879
2/03/73	**1**(5)	13	● **4. Killing Me Softly With His Song**	Atlantic 2940
10/13/73	**30**	5	5. Jesse	Atlantic 2982
7/06/74	**1**(1)	13	● **6. Feel Like Makin' Love**	Atlantic 3025
3/18/78	**2**(2)	14	● **7. The Closer I Get To You** **ROBERTA FLACK & DONNY HATHAWAY**	Atlantic 3463
6/24/78	**24**	5	8. If Ever I See You Again	Atlantic 3483
4/17/82	**13**	11	9. Making Love from the film of the same title	Atlantic 4005
9/03/83	**16**	15	10. Tonight, I Celebrate My Love **PEABO BRYSON/ROBERTA FLACK**	Capitol 5242
			FLAMING EMBER, The	
			White soul-rock group from Detroit formed as the Flaming Embers: Joe Sladich (guitar), Bill Ellis (piano), Jim Bugnel (bass) and Jerry Plunk (drums).	
11/15/69	**26**	6	1. Mind, Body and Soul	Hot Wax 6902
6/20/70	**24**	10	2. Westbound #9	Hot Wax 7003
11/28/70	**34**	6	3. I'm Not My Brothers Keeper	Hot Wax 7006
			FLAMINGOS, The	
			R&B group formed in Chicago in 1952. Consisted of cousins Zeke & Jake Carey and cousins Paul Wilson & Johnny Carter, with lead singer Sollie McElroy. First recorded for Chance Records in 1953. In 1954, Sollie departed and was replaced by Nate Nelson. Tommy Hunt and Terry Johnson joined in July 1956, replacing Army-bound Zeke Carey and Johnny Carter. Carey returned in 1958 and group signed with End Records. Nelson joined The Platters in 1966; died of a heart attack on 6/01/84 (age 52).	
6/08/59	**11**	11	1. I Only Have Eyes For You #2 hit for Ben Selvin in 1934	End 1046
5/23/60	**30**	3	2. Nobody Loves Me Like You written by Sam Cooke	End 1068
			FLARES, The	
			Los Angeles-based R&B quintet, featuring lead singer Aaron Collins of The Cadets/The Jacks.	
10/09/61	**25**	9	1. Foot Stomping - Part 1 B-side is an instrumental version by The Ramrocks	Felsted 8624
			FLASH	
			English rock quartet led by Peter Banks (guitar) and Colin Carter (vocals).	
7/29/72	**29**	6	1. Small Beginnings	Capitol 3345

DATE	POS	WKS	ARTIST—RECORD TITLE	LABEL & NO.
			FLASH CADILLAC & THE CONTINENTAL KIDS	
			Fifties-styled act formed by six students at the University of Colorado. Appeared as the prom band in the film *American Graffiti*. Flash is lead singer Samuel McFadden.	
10/02/76	**29**	6	1. Did You Boogie (With Your Baby) with spoken interludes by Wolfman Jack	Private S. 45079
			FLEETWOOD MAC	
			Formed as a British blues band in 1967 by ex-John Mayall's Bluesbreakers Peter Green (guitar), Mick Fleetwood (drums) and John McVie (bass), along with guitarist Jeremy Spencer. Many lineup changes followed as group headed toward rock superstardom. Green and Spencer left in 1970. Christine McVie (keyboards) joined in August 1970. Bob Welch (guitar) joined in April 1971, stayed through 1974. Group relocated to California in 1974, whereupon Lindsey Buckingham (guitar) and Stevie Nicks (vocals) joined in January 1975. Buckingham left in summer of 1987. Guitarists/vocalists Billy Burnette (son of Dorsey Burnette) and Rick Vito joined in July 1987. Christine McVie and Nicks quit touring with the band at the end of 1990.	
12/13/75+	**20**	7	1. Over My Head	Reprise 1339
4/10/76	**11**	11	2. Rhiannon (Will You Ever Win)	Reprise 1345
7/31/76	**11**	13	3. Say You Love Me	Reprise 1356
1/22/77	**10**	11	**4. Go Your Own Way**	Warner 8304
4/30/77	**1**(1)	13	● **5. Dreams**	Warner 8371
7/23/77	**3**	14	**6. Don't Stop**	Warner 8413
10/29/77	**9**	10	**7. You Make Loving Fun**	Warner 8483
10/13/79	**8**	10	**8. Tusk** with U.S.C. Trojan Marching Band, recorded live at Dodger Stadium	Warner 49077
12/22/79+	**7**	11	**9. Sara**	Warner 49150
3/29/80	**20**	7	10. Think About Me	Warner 49196
6/19/82	**4**	15	**11. Hold Me**	Warner 29966
9/25/82	**12**	8	12. Gypsy	Warner 29918
12/11/82+	**22**	8	13. Love In Store	Warner 29848
4/11/87	**5**	11	**14. Big Love**	Warner 28398
7/04/87	**19**	8	15. Seven Wonders	Warner 28317
9/12/87	**4**	13	**16. Little Lies**	Warner 28291
12/26/87+	**14**	10	17. Everywhere	Warner 28143
4/28/90	**33**	4	18. Save Me	Warner 19866
			FLEETWOODS, The	
			Trio formed while in high school in Olympia, Washington in 1958: Gary Troxel (b: 11/28/39), Gretchen Christopher (b: 2/29/40) and Barbara Ellis (b: 2/20/40).	
3/16/59	**1**(4)	12	**1. Come Softly To Me** also released on Liberty 55188 in 1959	Dolphin 1
6/22/59	**39**	1	2. Graduation's Here	Dolton 3
9/14/59	**1**(1)	17	**3. Mr. Blue**	Dolton 5
2/29/60	**28**	3	4. Outside My Window	Dolton 15
6/27/60	**23**	4	5. Runaround	Dolton 22
5/08/61	**10**	8	**6. Tragedy**	Dolton 40
10/02/61	**30**	4	7. (He's) The Great Impostor	Dolton 45
11/24/62	**36**	2	8. Lovers By Night, Strangers By Day	Dolton 62
7/13/63	**32**	4	9. Goodnight My Love	Dolton 75

DATE	POS	WKS	ARTIST—RECORD TITLE	LABEL & NO.
			FLINT, Shelby	
			Singer/songwriter from North Hollywood, California.	
2/06/61	**22**	5	1. Angel On My Shoulder	Valiant 6001
			FLIRTATIONS, The	
			Group consisted of Shirley and Earnestine Pearce from South Carolina, and Viola Billups from Alabama. The Pearce sisters had been in the Gypsies from 1962-65.	
5/24/69	**34**	2	1. Nothing But A Heartache	Deram 85038
			FLOATERS, The	
			Detroit soul group: Charles Clarke (lead), Larry Cunningham and brothers Paul & Ralph Mitchell.	
7/30/77	**2**(2)	11	● **1. Float On**	ABC 12284
			FLOCK OF SEAGULLS, A	
			British techno-rock group led by vocalist Mike Score.	
9/04/82	**9**	10	**1. I Ran (So Far Away)**	Jive 102
1/08/83	**30**	7	2. Space Age Love Song	Jive 2003
6/11/83	**26**	7	3. Wishing (If I Had A Photograph Of You)	Jive 2006
			FLOOD, Dick	
			Born on 11/13/32 in Philadelphia. Singer/songwriter.	
9/14/59	**23**	4	1. The Three Bells (The Jimmy Brown Story)	Monument 408
			FLOYD, Eddie	
			Born on 6/25/35 in Montgomery, Alabama and raised in Detroit. Original member of The Falcons, 1955-63. Eddie's uncle, Robert West, founded the Lu Pine record label.	
11/19/66	**28**	6	1. Knock On Wood	Stax 194
9/07/68	**40**	2	2. I've Never Found A Girl (To Love Me Like You Do)	Stax 0002
11/16/68	**17**	9	3. Bring It On Home To Me	Stax 0012
			FLOYD, King	
12/12/70+	**6**	13	● **1. Groove Me**	Chimneyville 435
4/03/71	**29**	7	2. Baby Let Me Kiss You	Chimneyville 437
			FLYING MACHINE, The	
			Studio project of British songwriters/producers Tony Macauley and Geoff Stevens. Touring group featured Tony Newman as lead vocalist.	
10/18/69	**5**	12	● **1. Smile A Little Smile For Me**	Congress 6000
			FOCUS	
			Dutch progressive-rock quartet led by guitar virtuoso Jan Akkerman and flutist Thijs van Leer.	
4/21/73	**9**	11	**1. Hocus Pocus** [I]	Sire 704
			FOGELBERG, Dan	
			Born on 8/13/51 in Peoria, Illinois. Vocalist/composer. Worked as a folk singer in Los Angeles. With Van Morrison in the early '70s. Session work in Nashville.	
3/01/75	**31**	3	1. Part Of The Plan	Epic 50055
11/04/78	**24**	7	2. The Power Of Gold DAN FOGELBERG/TIM WEISBERG	Full Moon 50606
1/19/80	**2**(2)	13	**3. Longer**	Full Moon 50824

DATE	POS	WKS	ARTIST—RECORD TITLE	LABEL & NO.
4/19/80	**21**	6	4. Heart Hotels	Full Moon 50862
12/27/80+	**9**	13	**5. Same Old Lang Syne**	Full Moon 50961
9/19/81	**7**	10	**6. Hard To Say**	Full Moon 02488
12/19/81+	**9**	16	**7. Leader Of The Band**	Full Moon 02647
4/24/82	**18**	8	8. Run For The Roses	Full Moon 02821
11/13/82	**23**	9	9. Missing You	Full Moon 03289
3/05/83	**29**	6	10. Make Love Stay	Full Moon 03525
2/11/84	**13**	10	11. The Language Of Love	Full Moon 04314
			FOGERTY, John	
			Born on 5/28/45 in Berkeley, California. Multi-instrumentalist. With his brother Tom in the Blue Velvets in 1959. Group became the Golliwogs and recorded for Fantasy in 1964. Renamed Creedence Clearwater Revival in 1967. Wrote "Proud Mary," "Have You Ever Seen The Rain," "Bad Moon Rising," "Lookin' Out My Back Door" and many others. Went solo in 1972 and recorded as The Blue Ridge Rangers.	
			THE BLUE RIDGE RANGERS:	
1/06/73	**16**	10	1. Jambalaya (On the Bayou)	Fantasy 689
5/19/73	**37**	2	2. Hearts Of Stone	Fantasy 700
			JOHN FOGERTY:	
10/04/75	**27**	6	3. Rockin' All Over The World	Asylum 45274
1/19/85	**10**	9	**4. The Old Man Down The Road**	Warner 29100
4/06/85	**20**	6	5. Rock And Roll Girls	Warner 29053
			FOGHAT	
			British rock quartet: Lonesome Dave Peverett (vocals, guitar; formerly with Savoy Brown), Rod Price (guitar), Tony Stevens (bass) and Roger Earl (drums). Settled in New York City in 1975, many bass player changes since. Price replaced by Erik Cartwright in 1981.	
1/10/76	**20**	12	1. Slow Ride	Bearsville 0306
12/25/76+	**34**	4	2. Drivin' Wheel	Bearsville 0313
10/15/77	**33**	3	3. I Just Want To Make Love To You [R] live version of their 1972 hit (POS 83)	Bearsville 0319
6/24/78	**36**	2	4. Stone Blue	Bearsville 0325
12/08/79+	**23**	10	5. Third Time Lucky (First Time I Was A Fool)	Bearsville 49125
			FONTANA, Wayne — see MINDBENDERS, The	
			FONTANE SISTERS, The	
			Trio from New Milford, New Jersey: sisters Marge, Bea and Geri, whose family name is Rosse. With Perry Como on radio, TV and recordings from 1945-54.	
12/11/54+	**1**(3)	20	**1. Hearts Of Stone** Juke Box #1(3) / Best Seller #1(1) / Jockey #2	Dot 15265
2/26/55	**13**	8	2. Rock Love Juke Box #13 / Best Seller #19	Dot 15333
6/04/55	**13**	6	3. Rollin' Stone Juke Box #13	Dot 15370
8/20/55	**3**	15	**4. Seventeen** Juke Box #3 / Best Seller #6 / Jockey #7 / Top 100 #15 pre	Dot 15386
11/26/55	**11**	11	5. Daddy-O Top 100 #11 / Juke Box #11 / Best Seller #13 / Jockey #18	Dot 15428
12/31/55	**36**	1	6. Nuttin' For Christmas [X-N]	Dot 15434
3/17/56	**11**	11	7. Eddie My Love	Dot 15450

DATE	POS	WKS	ARTIST—RECORD TITLE	LABEL & NO.
			Juke Box #11 / Top 100 #12 / Jockey #13 / Best Seller #15	
7/14/56	**38**	1	8. I'm In Love Again	Dot 15462
1/12/57	**13**	10	9. The Banana Boat Song Jockey #13 / Juke Box #14 / Top 100 #22	Dot 15527
4/28/58	**12**	9	10. Chanson d'Amour (Song Of Love) Jockey #12 / Top 100 #68 orchestra directed by Billy Vaughn on all of above	Dot 15736
			FORBERT, Steve Born in 1955 in Meridian, Mississippi. Moved to New York City in 1976.	
1/05/80	**11**	12	1. Romeo's Tune	Nemperor 7525
			FORCE M.D.'S Staten Island-based, soul-rap quintet. Originally called Dr. Rock & The M.C.'s.	
3/01/86	**10**	11	**1. Tender Love** from the film *Krush Groove*	Warner 28818
			FORD, Frankie Born Frank Guzzo on 8/04/39 in Gretna, Louisiana. Appeared with Sophie Tucker, Ted Lewis and Carmen Miranda at local shows at an early age. Appeared in the film *American Hot Wax*.	
3/09/59	**14**	12	1. Sea Cruise with Huey "Piano" Smith & The Clowns	Ace 554
			FORD, Lita Born in London. Lead guitarist of Los Angeles-based female rock group The Runaways, at age 15, in 1975.	
5/14/88	**12**	10	1. Kiss Me Deadly	RCA 6866
4/22/89	**8**	12	● **2. Close My Eyes Forever** **LITA FORD with OZZY OSBOURNE**	RCA 8899
			FORD, "Tennessee" Ernie Born Ernest Jennings Ford on 2/13/19 in Bristol, Tennessee; died on 10/17/91 of liver complications. Began career as a DJ. Host of musical variety TV shows, 1955-65. America's favorite hymn singer.	
3/19/55	**5**	17	**1. Ballad Of Davy Crockett** Juke Box #5 / Best Seller #6 / Jockey #7 from the Walt Disney film *Davy Crockett*	Capitol 3058
11/12/55	**1**(8)	19	**2. Sixteen Tons** Juke Box #1(8) / Best Seller #1(7) / Top 100 #1(6) / Jockey #1(6)	Capitol 3262
3/10/56	**17**	1	3. That's All Jockey #17 / Top 100 #44	Capitol 3343
9/23/57	**23**	1	4. In The Middle Of An Island Jockey #23 / Top 100 #56	Capitol 3762
			FOREIGNER British-American rock group formed in New York City in 1976. Consisted of Mick Jones (guitar), Lou Gramm (vocals), Ian McDonald (guitar, keyboards), Ed Gagliardi (bass), Al Greenwood (keyboards) and Dennis Elliott (drums). Gagliardi, Gramm and Greenwood are from New York. Most of material written by Jones (ex-Spooky Tooth) and Gramm. Rick Wills (formerly with Roxy Music and Small Faces) replaced Gagliardi in 1979. Greenwood and McDonald (ex-King Crimson) left in 1980. Gram left in 1991 to form Shadow King; replaced by Johnny Edwards. Jones not to be confused with Mick Jones of The Clash and Big Audio Dynamite.	
4/23/77	**4**	13	**1. Feels Like The First Time**	Atlantic 3394
8/13/77	**6**	15	**2. Cold As Ice**	Atlantic 3410

DATE	POS	WKS	ARTIST—RECORD TITLE	LABEL & NO.
1/14/78	**20**	8	3. Long, Long Way From Home	Atlantic 3439
7/08/78	**3**	14	• **4. Hot Blooded**	Atlantic 3488
9/30/78	**2**(2)	12	• **5. Double Vision**	Atlantic 3514
1/20/79	**15**	8	6. Blue Morning, Blue Day	Atlantic 3543
9/22/79	**12**	9	7. Dirty White Boy	Atlantic 3618
11/24/79	**14**	9	8. Head Games	Atlantic 3633
7/11/81	**4**	17	**9. Urgent** sax solo: Jr. Walker	Atlantic 3831
10/17/81	**2**(10)	19	• **10. Waiting For A Girl Like You**	Atlantic 3868
3/06/82	**26**	6	11. Juke Box Hero	Atlantic 4017
6/05/82	**26**	6	12. Break It Up	Atlantic 4044
12/15/84+	**1**(2)	16	• **13. I Want To Know What Love Is** vocal backing: New Jersey Mass Choir and Jennifer Holliday	Atlantic 89596
3/23/85	**12**	10	14. That Was Yesterday	Atlantic 89571
12/26/87+	**6**	12	**15. Say You Will**	Atlantic 89169
4/09/88	**5**	11	**16. I Don't Want To Live Without You**	Atlantic 89101
			FORTUNES, The	
			English pop quintet led by guitarists/vocalists Glen Dale (Garforth) and Barry Pritchard. Dale left in July 1966, replaced by Scotsman Shel MacRae.	
9/11/65	**7**	8	**1. You've Got Your Troubles**	Press 9773
11/27/65	**27**	4	2. Here It Comes Again	Press 9798
6/19/71	**15**	9	3. Here Comes That Rainy Day Feeling Again	Capitol 3086
			FOSTER, David	
			Keyboardist/composer/arranger born in Victoria, British Columbia. Member of the groups Skylark and Attitudes. Wrote hits for Chicago, Barbra Streisand and others.	
10/05/85	**15**	10	1. Love Theme From St. Elmo's Fire [I] from the film *St. Elmo's Fire*	Atlantic 89528
			FOUNDATIONS, The	
			British interracial R&B-pop group. Lead singer Clem Curtis (from Trinidad) replaced by Colin Young (West Indies) in 1968. Disbanded in 1970.	
1/13/68	**11**	10	1. Baby, Now That I've Found You	Uni 55038
1/18/69	**3**	13	• **2. Build Me Up Buttercup**	Uni 55101
			FOUR ACES featuring AL ALBERTS	
			Vocal group from Chester, Pennsylvania: Al Alberts (lead singer), Dave Mahoney (tenor), Sol Vaccaro (baritone) and Lou Silvestri (bass). Worked Ye Olde Mill near Philadelphia, late 1940s. First recorded for Victoria in 1951.	
1/15/55	**3**	21	**1. Melody Of Love** Juke Box #3 / Jockey #9 / Best Seller #11	Decca 29395
5/28/55	**13**	6	2. Heart Jockey #13 / Juke Box #20 / Best Seller #23 from the Broadway musical *Damn Yankees*	Decca 29476
8/27/55	**1**(6)	21	**3. Love Is A Many-Splendored Thing** Jockey #1(6) / Top 100 #1(3) / Juke Box #1(3) / Best Seller #1(2) from the William Holden/Jennifer Jones film of the same title	Decca 29625
12/03/55	**14**	12	4. A Woman In Love Jockey #14 / Top 100 #19 / Best Seller #20 from the film *Guys and Dolls*	Decca 29725
8/04/56	**22**	5	5. I Only Know I Love You Jockey #22 / Top 100 #35	Decca 29989

DATE	POS	WKS	ARTIST—RECORD TITLE	LABEL & NO.
10/20/56	**20**	2	6. You Can't Run Away From It Jockey #20 / Top 100 #70 from the film of the same title; orchestra directed by Jack Pleis on all of above	Decca 30041
			FOUR COINS, The	
			Vocal group of Greek descent from Canonsburg, Pennsylvania: George Mantalis, George Gregorakis, and brothers Michael & George Mahramas. In film *Disc Jockey Jamboree*.	
1/15/55	**28**	1	1. I Love You Madly Best Seller #28	Epic 9082
12/10/55	**22**	8	2. Memories Of You Best Seller #22 / Top 10 #28 from the film *The Benny Goodman Story*	Epic 9129
6/17/57	**11**	14	3. Shangri-La Jockey #11 / Best Seller #22 / Top 100 #23	Epic 9213
10/14/57	**28**	4	4. My One Sin Best Seller #28 / Top 100 #29	Epic 9229
11/17/58	**21**	8	5. The World Outside introduced in 1942 film *Suicide Squadron* as "Warsaw Concerto"	Epic 9295
			FOUR ESQUIRES, The	
			Formed group at Boston University: Bill Courtney, Frank Mahoney, Bob Golden and Wally Gold.	
12/16/57	**25**	1	1. Love Me Forever Jockey #25 / Best Seller #44 / Top 100 #51	Paris 509
11/03/58	**21**	6	2. Hideaway	Paris 520
			FOUR FRESHMEN, The	
			Jazz-styled vocal and instrumental group formed in 1948 while at Arthur Jordan Conservatory of Music in Indianapolis. Consisted of brothers Ross and Don Barbour, their cousin Bob Flanigan and Ken Errair.	
6/09/56	**17**	7	1. Graduation Day Jockey #17 / Best Seller #25 / Top 100 #27	Capitol 3410
			FOUR JACKS AND A JILL	
			South African quintet; Jill is Glenys Lynne (lead singer).	
5/18/68	**18**	7	1. Master Jack	RCA 9473
			FOUR KNIGHTS, The — see COLE, Nat "King"	
			FOUR LADS, The	
			Vocal group from Toronto: Bernie Toorish (lead tenor), Jimmie Arnold (second tenor), Frankie Busseri (baritone) and Connie Codarini (bass). Sang in choir at St. Michael's Cathedral in Toronto. Worked local hotels and clubs. Worked Le Ruban Bleu in New York City. Signed as backup singers by Columbia in 1950. Backed Johnnie Ray on his #1 hit "Cry."	
9/03/55	**2**(6)	25	**1. Moments To Remember** Jockey #2 / Best Seller #3 / Top 100 #3 / Juke Box #4	Columbia 40539
1/28/56	**2**(4)	19	**2. No, Not Much!** Jockey #2 / Top 100 #3 / Best Seller #4 / Juke Box #4	Columbia 40629
4/28/56	**3**	18	**3. Standing On The Corner/** Best Seller #3 / Top 100 #3 / Jockey #3 / Juke Box #3 from the Broadway musical *The Most Happy Fella*	
4/28/56	**22**	12	4. My Little Angel Best Seller #22 / Jockey #24 / Top 100 #30	Columbia 40674
9/15/56	**16**	6	5. A House With Love In It/	

DATE	POS	WKS	ARTIST—RECORD TITLE	LABEL & NO.
			Best Seller #16 / Jockey #20 / Top 100 #23	
9/15/56	**17**	6	6. The Bus Stop Song (A Paper Of Pins) Jockey #17 / Best Seller #22 / Top 100 #23 from the Marilyn Monroe film *Bus Stop*	Columbia 40736
2/02/57	**9**	15	**7. Who Needs You** Jockey #9 / Best Seller #13 / Top 100 #14 / Juke Box #17	Columbia 40811
5/20/57	**17**	4	8. I Just Don't Know Jockey #17 / Top 100 #22	Columbia 40914
12/09/57+	**8**	9	**9. Put A Light In The Window** Jockey #8 / Top 100 #35 / Best Seller #39	Columbia 41058
4/07/58	**10**	7	**10. There's Only One Of You** Jockey #10 / Top 100 #41 / Best Seller #43	Columbia 41136
7/14/58	**12**	6	11. Enchanted Island Jockey #12 / Hot 100 #29 / Best Seller #32 from the Jane Powell film of the same title; orchestra directed by Ray Ellis on all of above	Columbia 41194
11/24/58	**32**	3	12. The Mocking Bird [R] new version of their 1952 (POS 23) and 1956 (POS 67) hits	Columbia 41266
			FOUR PREPS, The Vocal group formed while at Hollywood High School: Bruce Belland, Glen Larson, Ed Cobb and Marvin Ingraham. Belland was later in duo with Dave Somerville of the Diamonds.	
1/20/58	**2**(3)	14	**1. 26 Miles (Santa Catalina)** Jockey #2 / Top 100 #4 / Best Seller #5	Capitol 3845
5/05/58	**3**	14	**2. Big Man** Jockey #3 / Top 100 #5 / Best Seller #6	Capitol 3960
9/01/58	**21**	6	3. Lazy Summer Night Hot 100 #21 / Best Seller #34 from the film *Andy Hardy Comes Home*	Capitol 4023
1/11/60	**13**	11	4. Down By The Station new version of tune written in 1948	Capitol 4312
5/16/60	**24**	3	5. Got A Girl [N]	Capitol 4362
9/11/61	**17**	4	6. More Money For You And Me [N] Mr. Blue/Alley Oop/Smoke Gets In Your Eyes/In This Whole Wide World/A Worried Man/Tom Dooley/A Teenager In Love	Capitol 4599
			4 SEASONS, The Vocal group formed in Newark, New Jersey. In 1955, lead singer Frankie Valli (Francis Castelluccio) formed the Variatones with the brothers Nick and Tommy DeVito, and Hank Majewski. Changed name to The Four Lovers in 1956. Bob Gaudio (of The Royal Teens) joined as keyboardist/songwriter in 1959, replacing Nick DeVito. Nick Massi replaced Majewski, and their 1961 lineup was set: Valli, Gaudio, Massi and Tommy DeVito. Group had been doing session work for their producer Bob Crewe and took their new name from a New Jersey bowling alley, The Four Seasons. In 1965, Nick Massi was replaced by the group's arranger Charlie Callelo and then by Joe Long. In 1971, Tommy DeVito retired, and Gaudio left (as a performer) the following year. Numerous personnel changes from then on. Inducted into the Rock and Roll Hall of Fame in 1990. Also recorded as The Wonder Who?	
9/01/62	**1**(5)	12	**1. Sherry**	Vee-Jay 456
10/27/62	**1**(5)	14	**2. Big Girls Don't Cry**	Vee-Jay 465
12/22/62	**23**	2	3. Santa Claus Is Coming To Town [X] #12 hit for George Hall in 1934	Vee-Jay 478
1/26/63	**1**(3)	12	**4. Walk Like A Man**	Vee-Jay 485
5/04/63	**22**	6	5. Ain't That A Shame!	Vee-Jay 512

DATE	POS	WKS	ARTIST—RECORD TITLE	LABEL & NO.
7/20/63	**3**	10	**6. Candy Girl/**	
8/10/63	**36**	3	7. Marlena	Vee-Jay 539
11/02/63	**36**	2	8. New Mexican Rose	Vee-Jay 562
2/08/64	**3**	11	**9. Dawn (Go Away)**	Philips 40166
3/07/64	**16**	8	10. Stay	Vee-Jay 582
4/18/64	**6**	8	**11. Ronnie**	Philips 40185
6/27/64	**1**(2)	11	● **12. Rag Doll**	Philips 40211
6/27/64	**28**	5	13. Alone	Vee-Jay 597
9/05/64	**10**	6	**14. Save It For Me**	Philips 40225
11/21/64	**20**	5	15. Big Man In Town	Philips 40238
1/30/65	**12**	6	16. Bye, Bye, Baby (Baby Goodbye)	Philips 40260
7/10/65	**30**	3	17. Girl Come Running	Philips 40305
10/30/65	**3**	12	**18. Let's Hang On!**	Philips 40317
11/27/65	**12**	8	19. Don't Think Twice THE WONDER WHO?	Philips 40324
2/12/66	**9**	6	**20. Working My Way Back To You**	Philips 40350
5/28/66	**13**	7	21. Opus 17 (Don't You Worry 'Bout Me)	Philips 40370
9/17/66	**9**	8	**22. I've Got You Under My Skin** there were 2 top 10 versions of this Cole Porter classic in 1936	Philips 40393
12/24/66+	**10**	8	**23. Tell It To The Rain**	Philips 40412
3/18/67	**16**	7	24. Beggin'	Philips 40433
6/17/67	**9**	8	**25. C'mon Marianne**	Philips 40460
11/18/67	**30**	4	26. Watch The Flowers Grow	Philips 40490
3/09/68	**24**	5	27. Will You Love Me Tomorrow all of above 4 Seasons' Phillips records (except "Dawn") labeled as: Featuring the "sound" of Frankie Valli	Philips 40523
9/20/75	**3**	12	**28. Who Loves You**	Warner 8122
1/31/76	**1**(3)	15	● **29. December, 1963 (Oh, What a Night)**	Warner 8168
7/04/76	**38**	2	30. Silver Star lead vocals on above 2 by Gerri Polci	Warner 8203

FOUR TOPS

Native Detroit vocal group formed in 1953 as the Four Aims. Consisted of Levi Stubbs (lead singer), Renaldo "Obie" Benson, Lawrence Payton and Abdul "Duke" Fakir. First recorded for Chess in 1956, then Red Top and Columbia, before signing with Motown in 1963. Group has had no personnel changes since its formation. Stubbs is the voice of Audrey II (the voracious vegetation) in the 1986 film *Little Shop of Horrors*. Group inducted into the Rock and Roll Hall of Fame in 1990.

DATE	POS	WKS	ARTIST—RECORD TITLE	LABEL & NO.
8/29/64	**11**	10	1. Baby I Need Your Loving	Motown 1062
2/20/65	**24**	6	2. Ask The Lonely	Motown 1073
5/22/65	**1**(2)	13	**3. I Can't Help Myself**	Motown 1076
8/07/65	**5**	8	**4. It's The Same Old Song**	Motown 1081
11/20/65	**19**	6	5. Something About You	Motown 1084
3/12/66	**18**	6	6. Shake Me, Wake Me (When It's Over)	Motown 1090
9/17/66	**1**(2)	12	**7. Reach Out I'll Be There**	Motown 1098
12/24/66+	**6**	9	**8. Standing In The Shadows Of Love**	Motown 1102
3/18/67	**4**	8	**9. Bernadette**	Motown 1104
6/03/67	**14**	6	10. 7 Rooms Of Gloom	Motown 1110
9/30/67	**19**	5	11. You Keep Running Away	Motown 1113

DATE	POS	WKS	ARTIST—RECORD TITLE	LABEL & NO.
2/17/68	**14**	6	12. Walk Away Renee	Motown 1119
5/11/68	**20**	6	13. If I Were A Carpenter	Motown 1124
5/30/70	**24**	8	14. It's All In The Game	Motown 1164
9/26/70	**11**	10	15. Still Water (Love)	Motown 1170
12/12/70+	**14**	8	16. River Deep - Mountain High **THE SUPREMES & FOUR TOPS**	Motown 1173
2/27/71	**40**	2	17. Just Seven Numbers (Can Straighten Out My Life)	Motown 1175
10/02/71	**38**	3	18. MacArthur Park (Part II)	Motown 1189
12/02/72+	**10**	9	**19. Keeper Of The Castle**	Dunhill 4330
2/24/73	**4**	12	● **20. Ain't No Woman (Like The One I've Got)**	Dunhill 4339
7/28/73	**15**	8	21. Are You Man Enough from the film *Shaft in Africa*	Dunhill 4354
11/17/73	**33**	3	22. Sweet Understanding Love	Dunhill 4366
9/19/81	**11**	11	23. When She Was My Girl	Casablanca 2338
10/01/88	**35**	2	24. Indestructible tune used by NBC-TV for the 1988 Summer Olympics	Arista 9706
			FOUR VOICES, The	
			Male vocal quartet: Allan Chase (tenor), Frank Fosta (bass), Sal Mayo and Bill McBride (baritone). Mitch Miller signed the group to Columbia after seeing them on "Arthur Godfrey's Talent Scouts" TV show.	
3/17/56	**20**	4	1. Lovely One Best Seller #20 / Top 100 #30 orchestra directed by Ray Conniff	Columbia 40643
			FOX, Samantha	
			British singer born on 4/15/66. Rose to stardom as a topless model for the U.K. *Daily Sun* newspaper.	
12/20/86+	**4**	13	**1. Touch Me (I Want Your Body)**	Jive 1006
4/02/88	**3**	14	**2. Naughty Girls (Need Love Too)**	Jive 1089
12/17/88+	**8**	12	● **3. I Wanna Have Some Fun** above 2 written, arranged and produced by Full Force	Jive 1154
4/29/89	**31**	4	4. I Only Wanna Be With You	Jive 1192
			FOXX, Inez	
			Born on 9/09/42 in Greensboro, North Carolina. Sang with the Gospel Tide Chorus. Accompanied vocally by her brother Charlie Fox (b: 10/23/39).	
8/03/63	**7**	10	**1. Mockingbird**	Symbol 919
			FOXY	
			Miami-based Latino dance band. Four of five members came to Florida with the Cuban emigres of 1959. Lead vocalist/guitarist Ish Ledesma later founded and produced Oxo and Company B.	
8/26/78	**9**	13	**1. Get Off** background vocals: Wildflower	Dash 5046
4/28/79	**21**	9	2. Hot Number	Dash 5050
			FRAMPTON, Peter	
			Born on 4/22/50 in Beckenham, England. Vocalist/guitarist/composer. Joined British band The Herd at age 16, before forming Humble Pie in 1969, which he left in 1971 to form Frampton's Camel. Went solo in 1974. Played Billy Shears in the 1978 film *Sgt. Pepper's Lonely Hearts Club Band.* Near-fatal car crash on 6/29/78 temporarily sidelined his career.	
3/13/76	**6**	14	**1. Show Me The Way**	A&M 1795
7/17/76	**12**	11	2. Baby, I Love Your Way	A&M 1832

DATE	POS	WKS	ARTIST—RECORD TITLE	LABEL & NO.
10/09/76	**10**	10	**3. Do You Feel Like We Do** all of above recorded live at San Francisco's Winterland	A&M 1867
6/11/77	**2**(3)	13	**4. I'm In You**	A&M 1941
9/10/77	**18**	10	5. Signed, Sealed, Delivered (I'm Yours)	A&M 1972
6/09/79	**14**	9	6. I Can't Stand It No More	A&M 2148
			FRANCIS, Connie Born Concetta Rosa Maria Franconero on 12/12/38 in Newark, New Jersey. First recorded for MGM in 1955. From 1961-65, appeared in films *Where the Boys Are*, *Follow the Boys*, *Looking for Love* and *When The Boys Meet the Girls*. Connie stopped performing after she was raped on 11/08/74. Began comeback with a performance on "Dick Clark's Live Wednesday" TV show in 1978. Pop music's #1 female vocalist from the late 1950s to the mid-1960s.	
3/03/58	**4**	15	**1. Who's Sorry Now** Top 100 #4 / Best Seller #5 / Jockey #6 there were 5 top 20 versions of this tune in 1923	MGM 12588
6/09/58	**36**	2	2. I'm Sorry I Made You Cry Top 100 #36 / Best Seller #39 #1 hit for Henry Burr in 1918	MGM 12647
8/04/58	**14**	11	3. Stupid Cupid Best Seller #14 / Hot 100 #17	MGM 12683
11/17/58	**30**	1	4. Fallin' written by Neil Sedaka (also #8 below)	MGM 12713
12/15/58+	**2**(2)	14	**5. My Happiness** there were 5 top 30 versions of this tune in 1948	MGM 12738
3/30/59	**22**	4	6. If I Didn't Care #2 hit for the Ink Spots in 1939	MGM 12769
6/01/59	**5**	12	**7. Lipstick On Your Collar/**	
6/01/59	**9**	11	**8. Frankie**	MGM 12793
9/21/59	**34**	4	9. You're Gonna Miss Me	MGM 12824
12/07/59	**7**	11	**10. Among My Souvenirs/** there were 4 top 20 versions of this song in 1928	
12/21/59	**36**	2	11. God Bless America the Irving Berlin classic, popularized by Kate Smith in 1939	MGM 12841
3/14/60	**8**	9	**12. Mama/**	
3/28/60	**17**	6	13. Teddy written by Paul Anka	MGM 12878
5/16/60	**1**(2)	16	**14. Everybody's Somebody's Fool/**	
6/06/60	**19**	8	15. Jealous Of You (Tango Della Gelosia) [F]	MGM 12899
8/22/60	**1**(2)	14	**16. My Heart Has A Mind Of Its Own**	MGM 12923
11/21/60	**7**	10	**17. Many Tears Ago**	MGM 12964
1/30/61	**4**	12	**18. Where The Boys Are/** from the film of the same title	
2/20/61	**34**	2	19. No One	MGM 12971
4/24/61	**7**	9	**20. Breakin' In A Brand New Broken Heart**	MGM 12995
7/03/61	**6**	9	**21. Together** #1 hit for Paul Whiteman in 1928	MGM 13019
10/09/61	**14**	7	22. (He's My) Dreamboat	MGM 13039
12/04/61+	**10**	9	**23. When The Boy In Your Arms (Is The Boy In Your Heart)/**	
1/06/62+	**26**	1	24. Baby's First Christmas [X]	MGM 13051
2/24/62	**1**(1)	10	**25. Don't Break The Heart That Loves You**	MGM 13059

DATE	POS	WKS	ARTIST—RECORD TITLE	LABEL & NO.
5/19/62	**7**	7	**26. Second Hand Love**	MGM 13074
8/11/62	**9**	6	**27. Vacation**	MGM 13087
11/03/62	**24**	4	28. I Was Such A Fool (To Fall In Love With You)	MGM 13096
1/05/63	**18**	6	29. I'm Gonna' Be Warm This Winter	MGM 13116
3/16/63	**17**	7	30. Follow The Boys from the film of the same title	MGM 13127
6/08/63	**23**	5	31. If My Pillow Could Talk	MGM 13143
8/31/63	**36**	3	32. Drownin' My Sorrows	MGM 13160
11/09/63	**28**	4	33. Your Other Love	MGM 13176
3/07/64	**24**	6	34. Blue Winter	MGM 13214
5/30/64	**25**	5	35. Be Anything (But Be Mine)	MGM 13237
			FRANKE & THE KNOCKOUTS	
			Soft-rock quintet led by vocalist Franke Previte of New Brunswick, New Jersey.	
3/28/81	**10**	14	**1. Sweetheart**	Millennium 11801
8/01/81	**27**	5	2. You're My Girl	Millennium 11808
5/08/82	**24**	7	3. Without You (Not Another Lonely Night)	Millennium 13105
			FRANKIE GOES TO HOLLYWOOD	
			Dance-rock quintet from Liverpool, England — vocals by William "Holly" Johnson and Paul Rutherford. Group's name inspired by publicity recounting Frank Sinatra's move into the film industry.	
2/02/85	**10**	10	● **1. Relax** **[R]** originally charted in 1984 (POS 67)	Island 99805
			FRANKLIN, Aretha	
			Born on 3/25/42 in Memphis and raised in Buffalo and Detroit. Daughter of Rev. Cecil L. Franklin, pastor of New Bethel Church in Detroit. Taught to sing gospel at age 9 by Rev. James Cleveland (d: 2/09/91, age 59). First recorded for JVB/Battle in 1956. Signed to Columbia Records in 1960 by John Hammond, then dramatic turn in style and success after signing with Atlantic and working with producer Jerry Wexler. Appeared in the 1980 film *The Blues Brothers*. Winner of 15 Grammy Awards. In 1987, became the first woman to be inducted into the Rock and Roll Hall of Fame. Won Grammy's Legends Award in 1990. The all-time Queen of Soul Music.	
11/20/61	**37**	2	1. Rock-A-Bye Your Baby With A Dixie Melody #1 hit for Al Jolson in 1918	Columbia 42157
3/18/67	**9**	9	● **2. I Never Loved A Man (The Way I Love You)**	Atlantic 2386
5/06/67	**1**(2)	11	● **3. Respect** written by Otis Redding	Atlantic 2403
8/05/67	**4**	8	● **4. Baby I Love You**	Atlantic 2427
10/07/67	**8**	8	**5. A Natural Woman (You Make Me Feel Like)**	Atlantic 2441
12/16/67+	**2**(2)	11	● **6. Chain Of Fools**	Atlantic 2464
3/02/68	**5**	12	● **7. (Sweet Sweet Baby) Since You've Been Gone/**	
4/13/68	**16**	7	8. Ain't No Way written by Aretha's sister, Carolyn Franklin (d: 4/25/88 [age 43])	Atlantic 2486
5/25/68	**7**	9	● **9. Think**	Atlantic 2518
8/24/68	**6**	8	**10. The House That Jack Built/**	
8/24/68	**10**	10	● **11. I Say A Little Prayer**	Atlantic 2546
11/23/68	**14**	8	● 12. See Saw/	
12/28/68+	**31**	2	13. My Song	Atlantic 2574
3/01/69	**19**	6	14. The Weight	Atlantic 2603

DATE	POS	WKS	ARTIST—RECORD TITLE	LABEL & NO.
4/26/69	**28**	6	15. I Can't See Myself Leaving You	Atlantic 2619
8/09/69	**13**	9	16. Share Your Love With Me	Atlantic 2650
11/15/69	**17**	7	17. Eleanor Rigby	Atlantic 2683
2/28/70	**13**	9	18. Call Me	Atlantic 2706
6/13/70	**23**	5	19. Spirit In The Dark	Atlantic 2731
8/22/70	**11**	8	● 20. Don't Play That Song above 2: with The Dixie Flyers	Atlantic 2751
12/19/70	**37**	2	21. Border Song (Holy Moses)	Atlantic 2772
3/06/71	**19**	7	22. You're All I Need To Get By	Atlantic 2787
4/24/71	**6**	11	● **23. Bridge Over Troubled Water**	Atlantic 2796
8/07/71	**2**(2)	11	● **24. Spanish Harlem**	Atlantic 2817
11/06/71	**9**	8	● **25. Rock Steady**	Atlantic 2838
3/25/72	**5**	11	● **26. Day Dreaming**	Atlantic 2866
6/17/72	**26**	6	27. All The King's Horses	Atlantic 2883
3/10/73	**33**	5	28. Master Of Eyes (The Deepness Of Your Eyes)	Atlantic 2941
7/21/73	**20**	10	29. Angel	Atlantic 2969
12/15/73+	**3**	17	● **30. Until You Come Back To Me (That's What I'm Gonna Do)**	Atlantic 2995
5/04/74	**19**	8	31. I'm In Love all of above Atlantics (except #28 & 29) produced by Jerry Wexler	Atlantic 2999
7/10/76	**28**	6	32. Something He Can Feel	Atlantic 3326
9/11/82	**24**	6	33. Jump To It	Arista 0699
7/06/85	**3**	13	**34. Freeway Of Love**	Arista 9354
10/12/85	**7**	13	**35. Who's Zoomin' Who**	Arista 9410
11/02/85	**18**	8	36. Sisters Are Doin' It For Themselves **EURYTHMICS AND ARETHA FRANKLIN**	RCA 14214
2/15/86	**22**	7	37. Another Night	Arista 9453
10/11/86	**21**	6	38. Jumpin' Jack Flash produced by Keith Richards; from the film *Jumpin' Jack Flash*	Arista 9528
1/24/87	**28**	4	39. Jimmy Lee	Arista 9546
3/07/87	**1**(2)	12	**40. I Knew You Were Waiting (For Me)** **ARETHA FRANKLIN AND GEORGE MICHAEL**	Arista 9559
4/29/89	**16**	7	41. Through The Storm **ARETHA FRANKLIN AND ELTON JOHN**	Arista 9809
			FRASER, Wendy — see SWAYZE, Patrick	
			FREBERG, Stan Born on 8/07/26 in Pasadena, California. Began career doing impersonations on Cliffie Stone's radio show in 1943. Did cartoon voices for the major film studios. His first in a long string of brilliant satirical recordings was "John And Marsha" in 1951. Launched highly successful advertising career in early '60s; winner of 21 Clio awards (outstanding achievement award of the radio & TV ad industry).	
10/22/55	**16**	2	1. The Yellow Rose Of Texas [C] Jockey #16 / Top 100 #47 pre backing by Jud Conlon's Rhythmaires and Billy May's Orchestra; featuring Yankee Snare Drumming by Alvin Stoller	Capitol 3249
4/27/57	**25**	1	2. Banana Boat (Day-O) [C] Best Seller #25 / Top 100 #43 interruptions by Peter Leeds	Capitol 3687

The Dream Academy's first hit, 1986's "Life In A Northern Town," mentioned the Beatles and John F. Kennedy, and was dedicated to English folk artist Nick Drake and classical minimalist Steve Reich. If one must drop names, one supposes those will do.

Bob Dylan's reputation as one of the most inspirational lyricists of our time was further cemented in 1991, when he appeared on *For Our Children*, a Disney album benefitting children with AIDS. Dylan sings the kiddie song "This Old Man."

Ronnie Dyson's chart peak coincided with the zenith of 60s counterculture. He starred on Broadway in *Hair*, had a role in the much-lauded film satire *Putney Swope*, and had a No. 8 hit in 1970 with the mildly controversial "(If You Let Me Make Love To You Then) Why Can't I Touch You?"

Sheena Easton's shift from seeming suburban housewife to exotic temptress is evident when one compares her first No. 1 hit—1981's "Morning Train (Nine To Five)"—with the steamy, Prince-penned "Sugar Walls," which shot to No. 9 in 1985.

Duane Eddy's twangin' guitar style brought him 15 top-40 hits during 1958-1963, with his first, "Rebel-'Rouser," perhaps the most famous. Few would deny that he recorded one of the most unusually-titled hits of the 50s: "'Yep!'" reached No. 30 in 1959 with quotation marks fully intact.

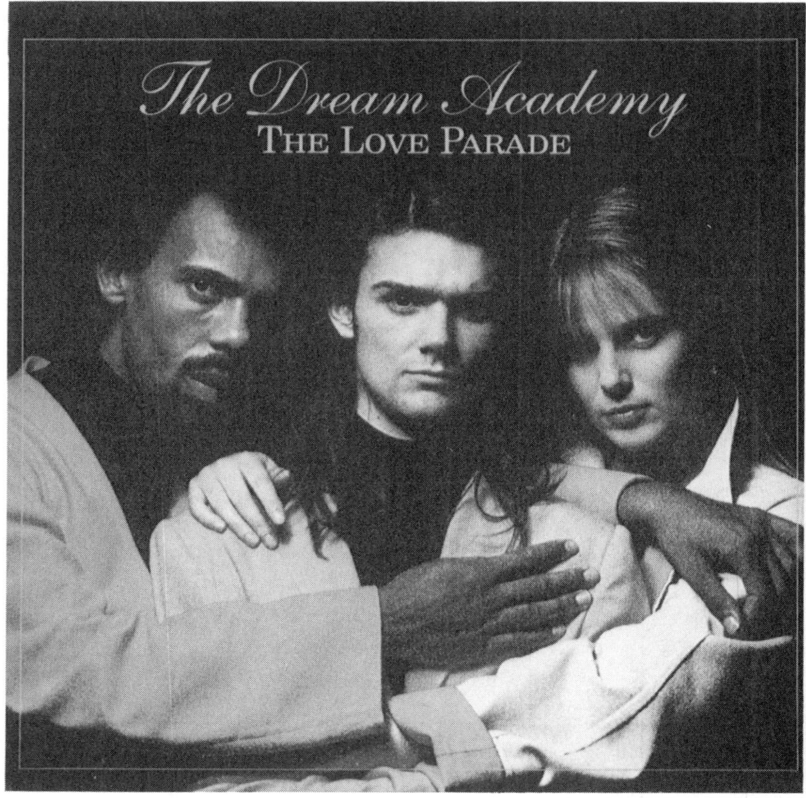

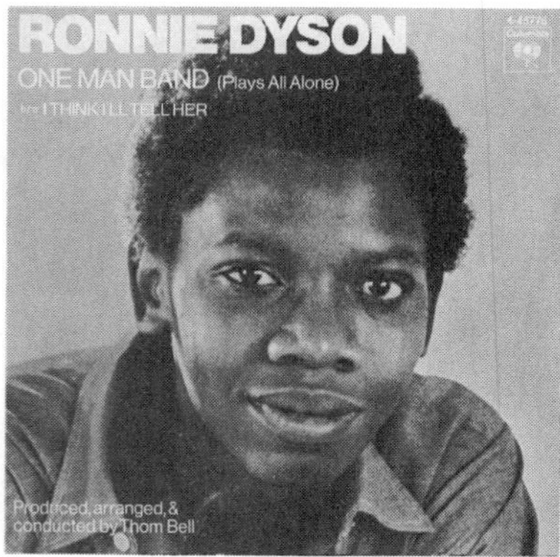

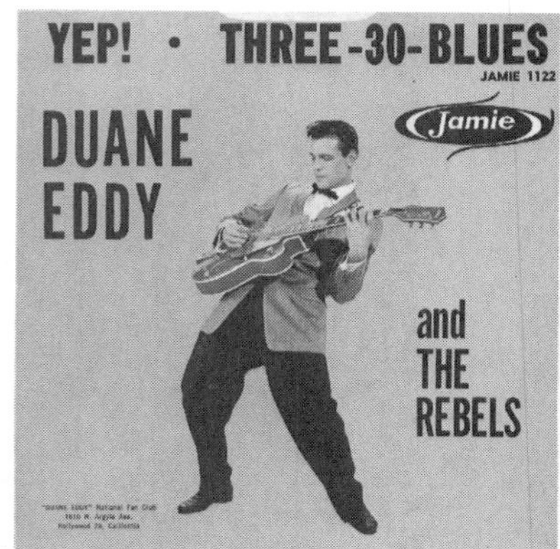

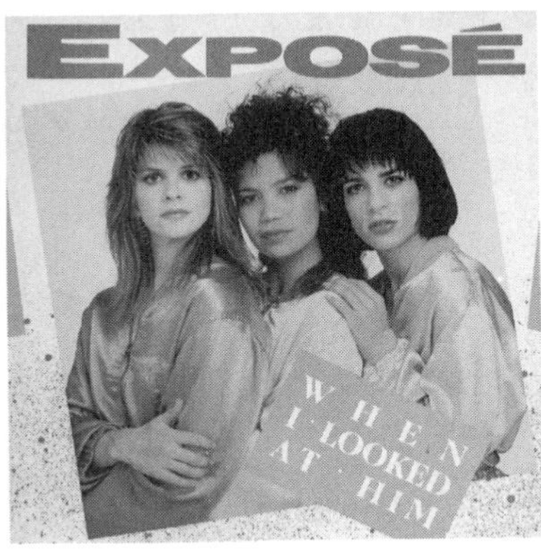

Gloria Estefan & Miami Sound Machine was a transitional name for one of Miami's brightest talents of the 80s. Cuban-born Estefan's band was first billed as Miami Sound Machine for 1985's "Conga," and then Gloria Estefan & Miami Sound Machine for 1987's "Rhythm Is Gonna Get You." By the time of 1989's *Cuts Both Ways* album, Gloria was simply recording albums under her own name.

The Everly Brothers' impact cut across yet another generation in the early 90s when singer Don's daughter Erin was briefly married to Guns N' Roses lead singer Axl Rose.

Every Mothers' Son may have had a No. 6 hit with "Come On Down To My Boat" in 1967, but among those in the burgeoning hippie scene, the New York group's sweater-garbed, preppie image seemed the height of straightness—and, therefore, absurdity.

Expose soared to the top of the pop charts in the late 80s with their commercial brand of catchy dance pop. The Miami-based trio—including Ann Curless, Jeanette Jurado, and Gioia Carmen—had a No. 1 hit with "Seasons Change" and saw six other songs in the Top 10.

Fabian Forte's career as the prototypical teen sensation kicked off in 1959 with his first top-40 hit, "I'm A Man." Seeming species confusion, however, may account for the other animal references in his further hits—like "Tiger" and "Hound Dog Man," both top-10 hits the same year.

DATE	POS	WKS	ARTIST—RECORD TITLE	LABEL & NO.
11/18/57	**32**	3	3. Wun'erful, Wun'erful! (Sides uh-one & uh-two) [C] Best Seller #32 / Top 100 #36 Bubbles In The Wine/Thank You/Louise/Please/ Moonlight & Shadows	Capitol 3815
			FRED, John/His Playboy Band	
			John Fred Gourrier was born on 5/08/41 in Baton Rouge, Louisiana. Formed The Playboys in 1956 as a white band playing R&B music. John played basketball at LSU, and his father, Fred Gourrier, played baseball with the Detroit Tigers.	
12/16/67+	**1**(2)	13	● **1. Judy In Disguise (With Glasses)** a parody of The Beatles' "Lucy In The Sky With Diamonds"	Paula 282
			FREDDIE AND THE DREAMERS	
			Lead singer Freddie Garrity was born on 11/14/40 in Manchester, England. Formed The Dreamers in 1961 with Derek Quinn (lead guitar), Roy Crewsdon (guitar), Peter Birrell (bass) and Bernie Dwyer (drums).	
3/27/65	**1**(2)	8	**1. I'm Telling You Now** first released on Capitol 5053 in 1963	Tower 125
4/24/65	**36**	2	2. I Understand (Just How You Feel)	Mercury 72377
5/15/65	**18**	5	3. Do The Freddie	Mercury 72428
5/15/65	**21**	5	4. You Were Made For Me first released on Capitol 5137 in 1964	Tower 127
			FREE	
			British band formed in 1968: Paul Rodgers (vocals), Paul Kossoff (guitar), Simon Kirke (drums) and Andy Fraser (bass). Kossoff and Fraser left in 1972, replaced by Tetsu Yamauchi (bass, later with Faces) and John "Rabbit" Bundrick (keyboards). Kossoff (d: 3/19/76 of drug-induced heart failure) formed Back Street Crawler. Rodgers and Kirke formed Bad Company in 1974. Rodgers was lead singer of The Firm (1984-85) and The Law (since 1991).	
9/05/70	**4**	13	**1. All Right Now**	A&M 1206
			FREEMAN, Bobby	
			Born on 6/13/40 in San Francisco. R&B singer. Formed vocal group the Romancers, at age 14, and later formed R&B group the Vocaleers.	
5/26/58	**5**	12	**1. Do You Want To Dance** Top 100 #5 / Best Seller #6 / Jockey #11	Josie 835
8/18/58	**37**	1	2. Betty Lou Got A New Pair Of Shoes Hot 100 #37 / Best Seller #40	Josie 841
9/26/60	**37**	3	3. (I Do The) Shimmy Shimmy	King 5373
7/25/64	**5**	10	**4. C'mon And Swim**	Autumn 2
			FREEMAN, Ernie	
			Born on 8/16/22 in Cleveland. Died of a heart attack on 5/16/81. Pianist/ arranger/producer. Prominent sessionman; on recordings by Frank Sinatra, Dean Martin, Sammy Davis, Jr. and Connie Francis. Recorded as "B. Bumble" on all records under that name except "Nut Rocker." Musical director at Reprise Records for 10 years. Retired in the late '70s.	
11/18/57	**4**	12	**1. Raunchy** [I] Jockey #4 / Best Seller #11 / Top 100 #12	Imperial 5474
			FREE MOVEMENT, The	
			Los Angeles-based vocal sextet. Several members formerly with gospel groups.	
9/18/71	**5**	11	**1. I've Found Someone Of My Own**	Decca 32818

DATE	POS	WKS	ARTIST—RECORD TITLE	LABEL & NO.
			FREHLEY, Ace	
			Born on 4/27/51 in the Bronx. Kiss lead guitarist until 1983. Formed own band, Frehley's Comet.	
12/02/78+	**13**	12	1. New York Groove	Casablanca 941
			FREY, Glenn	
			Born on 11/06/48 in Detroit. Singer/songwriter/guitarist. Founding member of the Eagles. Appeared in episodes of TV's "Miami Vice" and "Wiseguy."	
7/17/82	**31**	5	1. I Found Somebody	Asylum 47466
9/11/82	**15**	11	2. The One You Love	Asylum 69974
7/14/84	**20**	9	3. Sexy Girl	MCA 52413
1/19/85	**2**(1)	13	**4. The Heat Is On**	MCA 52512
			from the film *Beverly Hills Cop*	
5/04/85	**12**	11	5. Smuggler's Blues	MCA 52546
9/28/85	**2**(2)	13	**6. You Belong To The City**	MCA 52651
			above 2 from TV's "Miami Vice" soundtrack	
9/10/88	**13**	9	7. True Love	MCA 53363
			FRIDA	
			Born Anni-Frid Lyngstad on 11/15/45 in Narvik, Norway. Member of Abba.	
2/12/83	**13**	12	1. I Know There's Something Going On	Atlantic 89984
			produced by Phil Collins	
			FRIEDMAN, Dean	
			Singer/songwriter from New Jersey.	
5/21/77	**26**	10	1. Ariel	Lifesong 45022
			FRIEND AND LOVER	
			Husband-and-wife duo: James and Cathy Post.	
6/01/68	**10**	11	**1. Reach Out Of The Darkness**	Verve Fore. 5069
			FRIENDS OF DISTINCTION, The	
			Los Angeles-based, soul/MOR group. Original lineup: Floyd Butler, Harry Elston, Jessica Cleaves and Barbara Jean Love. Butler and Elston were in the Hi-Fi's with LaMonte McLemore and Marilyn McCoo (later with The 5th Dimension).	
4/26/69	**3**	13	● **1. Grazing In The Grass**	RCA 0107
10/11/69	**15**	12	● 2. Going In Circles	RCA 0204
3/21/70	**6**	11	**3. Love Or Let Me Be Lonely**	RCA 0319
			FRIJID PINK	
			Rock group formed in Detroit: Kelly Green (lead singer), Gary Thompson (guitar), Tom Beaudry (bass) and Rich Stevens (drums).	
2/21/70	**7**	11	● **1. House Of The Rising Sun**	Parrot 341
			FROST, Max/The Troopers	
			Max Frost is played by movie and TV star Christopher Jones in the film *Wild in the Streets*. Davie Allan & The Arrows are the backing band.	
9/28/68	**22**	9	1. Shape Of Things To Come	Tower 419
			from the film *Wild in the Streets* (starring Chris Jones)	
			FULLER, Bobby, Four	
			Bobby was born on 10/22/43 in Baytown, Texas. Died mysteriously of asphyxiation in Los Angeles on 7/18/66. Band, formed in El Paso, featured Bobby (lead vocals, guitar) and his brother Randy (bass).	
2/12/66	**9**	8	**1. I Fought The Law**	Mustang 3014

DATE	POS	WKS	ARTIST—RECORD TITLE	LABEL & NO.
			first released on Exeter 124 in 1965 as by Bobby Fuller	
5/07/66	**26**	3	2. Love's Made A Fool Of You	Mustang 3016
			written by Buddy Holly	
			FUNKADELIC	
			Funk aggregation formed in 1968. Consisted of The Parliaments plus a backing band. While recording for Westbound, group also recorded for Invictus as Parliament in 1971. Formed corporation "A Parliafunkadelicament Thang" through which they recorded under both names. By 1974, leader/producer George Clinton reorganized the Parliament/Funkadelic corporation to include varying membership. Also see Parliament and The Parliaments.	
11/04/78	**28**	5	• 1. One Nation Under A Groove - Part I	Warner 8618
			FURAY, Richie	
			Born on 5/09/44 in Yello Springs, Ohio. Member of Buffalo Springfield, Poco, and The Souther, Hillman, Furay Band.	
12/15/79	**39**	3	1. I Still Have Dreams	Asylum 46534
			FUZZ, The	
			Black female trio from Washington, D.C.: Sheila Young, Barbara Gilliam and Val Williams. Originally called the Passionettes.	
4/17/71	**21**	8	1. I Love You For All Seasons	Calla 174
			G	
			GABRIEL, Peter	
			Born on 2/13/50 in London. Lead singer of Genesis from 1966-75. Scored films *Birdy* and *The Last Temptation of Christ.* In 1982, financed the World of Music Arts and Dance (WOMAD) festival.	
12/04/82+	**29**	10	1. Shock The Monkey	Geffen 29883
5/31/86	**1**(1)	14	**2. Sledgehammer**	Geffen 28718
9/27/86	**26**	7	3. In Your Eyes	Geffen 28622
1/24/87	**8**	11	**4. Big Time**	Geffen 28503
			GADABOUTS, The	
8/04/56	**39**	1	1. Stranded In The Jungle [N]	Mercury 70898
			GALE, Sunny	
			Singer from Clayton, New Jersey. Began career with Hal McIntyre's band.	
1/08/55	**17**	1	1. Let Me Go, Lover!	RCA 5952
			Jockey #17	
			GALLERY	
			Detroit pop group led by singer/guitarist Jim Gold.	
4/29/72	**4**	13	• **1. Nice To Be With You**	Sussex 232
10/07/72	**22**	8	2. I Believe In Music	Sussex 239
			written by Mac Davis	
2/10/73	**23**	8	3. Big City Miss Ruth Ann	Sussex 248
			GALLOP, Frank	
			Best known as the announcer on Perry Como's TV shows during the 1950s.	
5/07/66	**34**	5	1. The Ballad Of Irving [C]	Kapp 745

DATE	POS	WKS	ARTIST—RECORD TITLE	LABEL & NO.
			GAP BAND, The	
			Soul trio from Tulsa, Oklahoma consisting of brothers Charles, Ronnie and Robert Wilson. Named for three streets in Tulsa: Greenwood, Archer and Pine. Cousins of Bootsy Collins. Charles is part of the Eurythmics' backing band.	
7/03/82	**24**	6	1. Early In The Morning	Total Exp. 8201
9/11/82	**31**	7	2. You Dropped A Bomb On Me	Total Exp. 8203
			GARDNER, Dave	
			Born on 6/11/26 in Jackson, Tennessee. "Brother Dave" had six comedy albums chart in the early 1960s.	
7/22/57	**22**	4	1. White Silver Sands Best Seller #22 / Top 100 #28	OJ 1002
			GARDNER, Don, AND DEE DEE FORD	
			Black vocal duo from Philadelphia. Gardner formed his own group, the Sonotones, in 1952 and recorded for Gotham and Bruce. Ford also plays organ and piano.	
7/07/62	**20**	7	1. I Need Your Loving	Fire 508
			GARFUNKEL, Art	
			Born on 10/13/42 in Queens, New York. Appeared in films *Catch 22, Carnal Knowledge* and *Bad Timing.* Has masters degree in mathematics from Columbia University. Half of Simon & Garfunkel duo.	
			GARFUNKEL:	
10/06/73	**9**	10	**1. All I Know**	Columbia 45926
2/09/74	**38**	1	2. I Shall Sing	Columbia 45983
10/19/74	**34**	3	3. Second Avenue	Columbia 10020
			ART GARFUNKEL:	
9/27/75	**18**	12	4. I Only Have Eyes For You	Columbia 10190
1/31/76	**39**	2	5. Break Away	Columbia 10273
2/11/78	**17**	7	6. (What A) Wonderful World **ART GARFUNKEL with JAMES TAYLOR & PAUL SIMON**	Columbia 10676
			GARI, Frank	
			Born on 4/01/42 in New York City. Appeared in several films in the late '50s.	
2/13/61	**27**	5	1. Utopia	Crusade 1020
5/15/61	**23**	6	2. Lullaby Of Love	Crusade 1021
8/14/61	**30**	3	3. Princess	Crusade 1022
			GARNETT, Gale	
			Born on 7/17/42 in Auckland, New Zealand. Came to the U.S. in 1951. Worked as an actress from age 15. Appeared on many TV shows.	
9/05/64	**4**	13	**1. We'll Sing In The Sunshine**	RCA 8388
			GARRETT, Leif	
			Born on 11/08/61 in Hollywood. Began film career in 1969. Appeared in all three *Walking Tall* films, *Macon County Line, Bob and Carol and Ted and Alice* and *The Outsiders.*	
9/17/77	**20**	8	1. Surfin' USA	Atlantic 3423
12/03/77+	**13**	9	2. Runaround Sue	Atlantic 3440
12/09/78+	**10**	15	**3. I Was Made For Dancin'**	Scotti Br. 403

DATE	POS	WKS	ARTIST—RECORD TITLE	LABEL & NO.
			GATES, David	
			Born on 12/11/40 in Tulsa, Oklahoma. Began career as a session musician, then did songwriting and record producing before becoming the lead singer of Bread. Wrote The Murmaids' hit "Popsicles & Icicles."	
2/15/75	**29**	5	1. Never Let Her Go	Elektra 45223
2/18/78	**15**	12	2. Goodbye Girl	Elektra 45450
			title song from the Neil Simon film	
10/07/78	**30**	5	3. Took The Last Train	Elektra 45500
			GAYE, Marvin	
			Born Marvin Pentz Gay, Jr. on 4/02/39 in Washington, D.C. Sang in his father's Apostolic church. In vocal groups the Rainbows and Marquees. Joined Harvey Fuqua in the re-formed Moonglows. To Detroit in 1960. Session work as a drummer at Motown; married to Berry Gordy's sister Anna, 1961-75. First recorded under own name for Tamla in 1961. In seclusion for several months following the death of Tammi Terrell (b: 1946, Philadelphia; d: 3/16/70). Problems with drugs and the IRS led to his moving to Europe for three years. Fatally shot by his father after a quarrel on 4/01/84 in Los Angeles. Inducted into the Rock and Roll Hall of Fame in 1987.	
3/02/63	**30**	3	1. Hitch Hike	Tamla 54075
6/15/63	**10**	10	**2. Pride And Joy**	Tamla 54079
			backing vocals on above 2 by Martha & The Vandellas	
11/23/63	**22**	10	3. Can I Get A Witness	Tamla 54087
			backing vocals by The Supremes	
3/28/64	**15**	7	4. You're A Wonderful One	Tamla 54093
5/23/64	**19**	6	5. Once Upon A Time/	
6/13/64	**17**	6	6. What's The Matter With You Baby	Motown 1057
			above 2: MARVIN GAYE & MARY WELLS	
6/27/64	**15**	8	7. Try It Baby	Tamla 54095
			backing vocals by The Temptations	
10/10/64	**27**	6	8. Baby Don't You Do It	Tamla 54101
12/12/64+	**6**	11	**9. How Sweet It Is To Be Loved By You**	Tamla 54107
4/10/65	**8**	8	**10. I'll Be Doggone**	Tamla 54112
7/24/65	**25**	5	11. Pretty Little Baby	Tamla 54117
10/23/65	**8**	9	**12. Ain't That Peculiar**	Tamla 54122
3/12/66	**29**	4	13. One More Heartache	Tamla 54129
			10, 12, 13: produced by Smokey Robinson	
2/04/67	**14**	7	14. It Takes Two	Tamla 54141
			MARVIN GAYE & KIM WESTON	
7/22/67	**33**	3	15. Your Unchanging Love	Tamla 54153
2/03/68	**34**	3	16. You	Tamla 54160
10/19/68	**32**	4	17. Chained	Tamla 54170
11/23/68	**1**(7)	15	**18. I Heard It Through The Grapevine**	Tamla 54176
5/10/69	**4**	13	**19. Too Busy Thinking About My Baby**	Tamla 54181
9/13/69	**7**	9	**20. That's The Way Love Is**	Tamla 54185
7/11/70	**40**	2	21. The End Of Our Road	Tamla 54195
3/06/71	**2**(3)	13	**22. What's Going On**	Tamla 54201
7/17/71	**4**	10	**23. Mercy Mercy Me (The Ecology)**	Tamla 54207
10/16/71	**9**	8	**24. Inner City Blues (Make Me Wanna Holler)**	Tamla 54209
12/30/72+	**7**	9	**25. Trouble Man**	Tamla 54228
			from the film of the same title	
7/28/73	**1**(2)	17	**26. Let's Get It On**	Tamla 54234

DATE	POS	WKS	ARTIST—RECORD TITLE	LABEL & NO.
10/13/73	**12**	10	27. You're A Special Part Of Me DIANA ROSS & MARVIN GAYE	Motown 1280
11/17/73	**21**	8	28. Come Get To This	Tamla 54241
3/30/74	**19**	10	29. My Mistake (Was To Love You) DIANA ROSS & MARVIN GAYE	Motown 1269
10/26/74	**28**	3	30. Distant Lover	Tamla 54253
5/08/76	**15**	9	31. I Want You	Tamla 54264
4/23/77	**1**(1)	15	**32. Got To Give It Up (Pt. I)**	Tamla 54280
11/20/82+	**3**	15	● **33. Sexual Healing**	Columbia 03302
			MARVIN GAYE & TAMMI TERRELL:	
6/03/67	**19**	9	34. Ain't No Mountain High Enough	Tamla 54149
9/30/67	**5**	10	**35. Your Precious Love**	Tamla 54156
12/16/67+	**10**	9	**36. If I Could Build My Whole World Around You**	Tamla 54161
4/27/68	**8**	11	**37. Ain't Nothing Like The Real Thing**	Tamla 54163
8/10/68	**7**	10	**38. You're All I Need To Get By**	Tamla 54169
10/19/68	**24**	6	39. Keep On Lovin' Me Honey	Tamla 54173
2/15/69	**30**	4	40. Good Lovin' Ain't Easy To Come By above 4 written and produced by Ashford & Simpson	Tamla 54179
			GAYLE, Crystal	
			Born Brenda Gail Webb on 1/09/51 in Paintsville, Kentucky and raised in Wabash, Indiana. Youngest sister of Loretta Lynn. First country artist to tour China (1979).	
9/24/77	**2**(3)	18	● **1. Don't It Make My Brown Eyes Blue**	United Art. 1016
9/02/78	**18**	11	2. Talking In Your Sleep	United Art. 1214
11/03/79	**15**	10	3. Half The Way	Columbia 11087
11/13/82+	**7**	21	**4. You And I** EDDIE RABBITT with CRYSTAL GAYLE	Elektra 69936
			GAYNOR, Gloria	
			Born on 9/07/49 in Newark, New Jersey. Disco singer. With the Soul Satisfiers in 1971.	
12/07/74+	**9**	10	**1. Never Can Say Goodbye**	MGM 14748
1/20/79	**1**(3)	17	▲ **2. I Will Survive**	Polydor 14508
			G-CLEFS, The	
			Group from Roxbury, Massachusetts: brothers Teddy, Chris, Timmy and Arnold Scott, with Ray Gibson.	
9/15/56	**24**	1	1. Ka-Ding Dong Best Seller #24 / Top 100 #53	Pilgrim 715
10/16/61	**9**	11	**2. I Understand (Just How You Feel)** an adaptation of the "Auld Lang Syne" tune	Terrace 7500
			GEDDES, David	
			While a teenager, formed the group Rock Garden, who recorded for Capitol.	
8/23/75	**4**	9	**1. Run Joey Run**	Big Tree 16044
11/22/75	**18**	6	2. The Last Game Of The Season (A Blind Man In The Bleachers)	Big Tree 16052

DATE	POS	WKS	ARTIST—RECORD TITLE	LABEL & NO.
			GEILS, J., Band	
			Formed in Boston in 1967, guitarist Jerome Geils led rock band consisting of Peter "Wolf" Blankfield (vocals), "Magic Dick" Salwitz (harmonica), Seth Justman (keyboards), Danny Klein (bass) and Stephen Jo Bladd (drums). First recorded for Atlantic in 1969. Wolf left for a solo career in the fall of 1983.	
1/15/72	**39**	2	1. Looking For A Love	Atlantic 2844
5/26/73	**30**	6	2. Give It To Me	Atlantic 2953
11/23/74+	**12**	7	3. Must Of Got Lost	Atlantic 3214
1/20/79	**35**	3	4. One Last Kiss	EMI America 8007
3/08/80	**32**	5	5. Come Back	EMI America 8032
5/24/80	**38**	3	6. Love Stinks	EMI America 8039
11/28/81+	**1**(6)	20	● **7. Centerfold**	EMI America 8102
3/06/82	**4**	12	● **8. Freeze-Frame**	EMI America 8108
7/03/82	**40**	2	9. Angel In Blue	EMI America 8100
12/11/82+	**24**	7	10. I Do	EMI America 8148
			GENE & DEBBE	
			Gene Thomas (b: 12/04/38, Palestine, Texas) and Debbe Nevills.	
3/09/68	**17**	12	1. Playboy	TRX 5006
			GENERAL PUBLIC	
			Fronted by former English Beat vocalists Dave Wakeling and Ranking Roger (Roger Charley). Disbanded in March 1987. Roger recorded solo in 1988, Wakeling in 1991.	
1/26/85	**27**	5	1. Tenderness	I.R.S. 9934
			GENESIS	
			Formed as a progressive-rock group in England in 1967. Consisted of Peter Gabriel (lead vocals), Anthony Phillips (guitar), Tony Banks (keyboards), Michael Rutherford (guitar, bass) and John Mayhew (drums). Phillips and Mayhew left after second album, replaced by Steve Hackett (guitar) and Phil Collins (drums). Gabriel left in June 1975, with Collins replacing him as new lead singer. Hackett went solo in 1977, leaving group as a trio: Collins, Rutherford and Banks. Rutherford also in own group, Mike + The Mechanics, formed in 1985. Hackett later formed group GTR.	
6/03/78	**23**	5	1. Follow You Follow Me	Atlantic 3474
6/21/80	**14**	11	2. Misunderstanding	Atlantic 3662
11/07/81	**29**	6	3. No Reply At All	Atlantic 3858
1/23/82	**26**	6	4. Abacab	Atlantic 3891
5/08/82	**40**	2	5. Man On The Corner	Atlantic 4025
7/24/82	**32**	5	6. Paperlate	Atlantic 4053
12/10/83+	**6**	14	**7. That's All!**	Atlantic 89724
6/07/86	**1**(1)	12	**8. Invisible Touch**	Atlantic 89407
8/23/86	**4**	12	**9. Throwing It All Away**	Atlantic 89372
11/15/86+	**4**	15	**10. Land Of Confusion**	Atlantic 89336
2/21/87	**3**	10	**11. Tonight, Tonight, Tonight**	Atlantic 89290
5/02/87	**3**	12	**12. In Too Deep**	Atlantic 89316
			GENTRY, Bobbie	
			Born Roberta Streeter on 7/27/44 in Chickasaw County, Mississippi; raised in Greenwood, Mississippi. Singer/songwriter. Won the 1967 Best New Artist Grammy Award. Married singer Jim Stafford on 10/15/78.	
8/12/67	**1**(4)	12	● **1. Ode To Billie Joe**	Capitol 5950
3/08/69	**36**	1	2. Let It Be Me	Capitol 2387

DATE	POS	WKS	ARTIST—RECORD TITLE	LABEL & NO.
			BOBBIE GENTRY & GLEN CAMPBELL	
1/31/70	**31**	4	3. Fancy	Capitol 2675
3/14/70	**27**	6	4. All I Have To Do Is Dream **BOBBIE GENTRY & GLEN CAMPBELL**	Capitol 2745
			GENTRYS, The	
			Memphis-based rock band formed in 1963. Group featured Larry Raspberry as lead singer.	
9/25/65	**4**	11	**1. Keep On Dancing**	MGM 13379
			GEORGE, Barbara	
			Born on 8/16/42 in New Orleans. R&B singer/songwriter.	
12/18/61+	**3**	11	**1. I Know (You Don't Love Me No More)** cornet solo: Melvin Lastie	A.F.O. 302
			GEORGIA SATELLITES	
			Rock quartet formed in Atlanta in 1980, led by dual guitarists/vocalists Dan Baird and Rick Richards with bassist Rich Price and drummer Mauro Magellan.	
12/20/86+	**2**(1)	14	**1. Keep Your Hands To Yourself**	Elektra 69502
			GERARDO	
			Rapper/actor. Born Gerardo Mejia III in Guayaquil, Ecuador on 4/16/65. To Glendale, California at age 12. Raps in Spanglish (half Spanish, half English). Appeared in films *Can't Buy Me Love* and *Colors*.	
3/02/91	**7**	10	● **1. Rico Suave**	Interscope 98871#
5/25/91	**16**	6	2. We Want The Funk samples Parliament's "Tear The Roof Off The Sucker (Give Up The Funk)"; produced by Michael Sembello	Interscope 98815#
			GERRY AND THE PACEMAKERS	
			Pop-rock group formed in Liverpool, England in 1959: Gerry Marsden (b: 9/24/42; vocals, guitar), Leslie Maguire (piano), Les Chadwick (bass) and Freddie Marsden (drums). The Marsden brothers had been in skiffle bands; Gerry had own rock band Mars-Bars. Signed in 1962 by The Beatles' manager Brian Epstein.	
6/06/64	**4**	9	**1. Don't Let The Sun Catch You Crying**	Laurie 3251
8/08/64	**9**	7	**2. How Do You Do It?**	Laurie 3261
10/17/64	**17**	6	3. I Like It	Laurie 3271
1/09/65	**14**	5	4. I'll Be There	Laurie 3279
2/13/65	**6**	9	**5. Ferry Cross The Mersey**	Laurie 3284
4/24/65	**23**	5	6. It's Gonna Be Alright above 2 from the film *Ferry Cross the Mersey* (starring Gerry and The Pacemakers)	Laurie 3293
10/08/66	**28**	4	7. Girl On A Swing	Laurie 3354
			GET WET	
			Pop band featuring Sherri Beachfront as lead singer.	
5/23/81	**39**	2	1. Just So Lonely	Boardwalk 02018
			GETZ, Stan	
			Born Stan Gayetzsky on 2/02/27 in Philadelphia. 17-time winner of Down Beat polls as top tenor saxophonist; played with Stan Kenton (1944-45), Jimmy Dorsey (1945-46), Benny Goodman (1946) and Woody Herman (1947-49). Leader of the bossa nova rage of the 1960s. Died of liver cancer on 6/06/91.	
10/27/62	**15**	10	1. Desafinado [I] **STAN GETZ/CHARLIE BYRD**	Verve 10260

DATE	POS	WKS	ARTIST—RECORD TITLE	LABEL & NO.
6/20/64	**5**	10	**2. The Girl From Ipanema**	Verve 10323
			STAN GETZ/ASTRUD GILBERTO	
			above 2 written by Brazilian composer Antonio Carlos Jobim	
			GIANT	
			Rock quartet led by Nashville brothers Dann (vocals) and David (drums) Huff.	
5/05/90	**20**	8	1. I'll See You In My Dreams	A&M 1495#
			GIANT STEPS	
			English duo: vocalist Campsie and multi-instrumentalist George McFarlane. Both initially worked together as members of the British band Grand Hotel, then as Quick.	
10/01/88	**13**	10	1. Another Lover	A&M 1226
			GIBB, Andy	
			Born Andrew Roy Gibb on 3/05/58 in Manchester, England. Moved to Australia when six months old, then back to England at age nine. Youngest brother of Barry, Robin and Maurice Gibb — The Bee Gees. Hosted TV's "Solid Gold" from 1981-82. Died on 3/10/88 of an inflammatory heart virus in Oxford, England.	
5/28/77	**1**(4)	23	● **1. I Just Want To Be Your Everything**	RSO 872
12/10/77+	**1**(2)	22	● **2. (Love Is) Thicker Than Water**	RSO 883
4/22/78	**1**(7)	19	▲ **3. Shadow Dancing**	RSO 893
7/22/78	**5**	13	● **4. An Everlasting Love**	RSO 904
11/04/78	**9**	13	● **5. (Our Love) Don't Throw It All Away**	RSO 911
2/02/80	**4**	12	**6. Desire**	RSO 1019
4/19/80	**12**	8	7. I Can't Help It	RSO 1026
			ANDY GIBB AND OLIVIA NEWTON-JOHN	
12/06/80+	**15**	11	8. Time Is Time	RSO 1059
4/11/81	**40**	1	9. Me (Without You)	RSO 1056
			GIBB, Barry	
			Born on 9/01/46 in Manchester, England. Eldest brother of The Bee Gees. Appeared in *Sgt. Pepper's Lonely Hearts Club Band.*	
			BARBRA STREISAND & BARRY GIBB:	
11/15/80+	**3**	15	● **1. Guilty**	Columbia 11390
2/14/81	**10**	10	**2. What Kind Of Fool**	Columbia 11430
			BARRY GIBB:	
9/29/84	**37**	3	3. Shine Shine	MCA 52443
			GIBB, Robin	
			Born on 12/22/49 in Manchester, England. Twin brother of The Bee Gees' Maurice Gibb.	
8/19/78	**15**	9	1. Oh! Darling	RSO 907
			from the film *Sgt. Pepper's Lonely Hearts Club Band*	
7/07/84	**37**	4	2. Boys Do Fall In Love	Mirage 99743
			GIBBS, Georgia	
			Born Fredda Gibbons on 8/17/20 in Worcester, Massachusetts. Sang on the "Lucky Strike" radio show from 1937-38. With Hudson-DeLange band, then with Frankie Trumbauer (1940) and Artie Shaw (1942). On the "Garry Moore-Jimmy Durante" radio show in the late '40s, where Moore dubbed her "Her Nibs, Miss Gibbs."	
1/29/55	**2**(1)	19	**1. Tweedle Dee**	Mercury 70517
			Jockey #2 / Best Seller #3 / Juke Box #3	

DATE	POS	WKS		ARTIST—RECORD TITLE	LABEL & NO.
3/26/55	**1**(3)	20		**2. Dance With Me Henry (Wallflower)** Juke Box #1 / Best Seller #2 / Jockey #3 revised version of The Midnighters' #1 1954 R&B hit "Work With Me Annie" and Etta James' "The Wallflower"	Mercury 70572
7/09/55	**12**	4		3. Sweet And Gentle Jockey #12	Mercury 70647
9/17/55	**14**	4		4. I Want You To Be My Baby Jockey #14 / Best Seller #22 / Top 100 #48 pre	Mercury 70685
4/14/56	**36**	1		5. Rock Right	Mercury 70811
5/26/56	**30**	4		6. Kiss Me Another	Mercury 70850
8/25/56	**20**	8		7. Happiness Street Jockey #20 / Top 100 #25	Mercury 70920
12/22/56	**24**	1		8. Tra La La Jockey #24 / Top 100 #39	Mercury 70998
10/20/58	**32**	1		9. The Hula Hoop Song Hot 100 #32 / Best Seller #42 end	Roulette 4106
				GIBBS, Terri	
				Born on 6/15/54 in Augusta, Georgia. Country singer/pianist; blind since birth.	
2/28/81	**13**	12		1. Somebody's Knockin'	MCA 41309
				GIBSON, Debbie	
				Singer/songwriter/pianist born on 8/31/70 in Long Island. Playing piano since age five and songwriting since age six.	
6/27/87	**4**	16	●	**1. Only In My Dreams**	Atlantic 89322
10/24/87	**4**	15		**2. Shake Your Love**	Atlantic 89187
2/06/88	**3**	13		**3. Out Of The Blue**	Atlantic 89129
5/07/88	**1**(1)	14		**4. Foolish Beat**	Atlantic 89109
9/03/88	**22**	6		5. Staying Together	Atlantic 89034
1/28/89	**1**(3)	12	●	**6. Lost In Your Eyes**	Atlantic 88970
4/15/89	**11**	8	●	7. Electric Youth	Atlantic 88919
7/08/89	**17**	7		8. No More Rhyme	Atlantic 88885
12/15/90+	**26**	6		9. Anything Is Possible	Atlantic 87793
				GIBSON, Don	
				Born on 4/03/28 in Shelby, North Carolina. Country singer/songwriter/guitarist. Joined the "Grand Ole Opry" in 1958.	
3/31/58	**7**	17		**1. Oh Lonesome Me** Best Seller #7 / Top 100 #8 / Jockey #10	RCA 7133
7/14/58	**20**	8		2. Blue Blue Day Jockey #20 / Best Seller #32 / Top 100 #32	RCA 7010
3/28/60	**29**	6		3. Just One Time	RCA 7690
7/10/61	**21**	8		4. Sea Of Heartbreak	RCA 7890
				GILBERTO, Astrud — see GETZ, Stan	
				GILDER, Nick	
				Born on 11/07/51 in London. Moved to Vancouver, Canada at age 10. Founding member of the rock band Sweeney Todd.	
8/05/78	**1**(1)	18	▲	**1. Hot Child In The City**	Chrysalis 2226

DATE	POS	WKS	ARTIST—RECORD TITLE	LABEL & NO.
			GILKYSON, Terry/The Easy Riders	
			Folk trio: Terry Gilkyson, Rick Dehr and Frank Miller. Terry performed with the legendary Weavers folk group in the early 1950s. Terry's son, Tony, is the bass guitarist of the group X.	
2/09/57	**4**	14	**1. Marianne**	Columbia 40817
			Juke Box #4 / Top 100 #5 / Jockey #5 / Best Seller #6	
			GILL, Johnny	
			Washington, D.C. singer discovered by Stacy Lattisaw. Sang in family group, Wings Of Faith, from age five. Recorded solo at age 16 in 1983. Joined New Edition in 1988.	
5/26/90	**3**	16	● **1. Rub You The Right Way**	Motown 1982
8/18/90	**10**	10	**2. My, My, My**	Motown 919
11/24/90	**28**	6	3. Fairweather Friend	Motown 2049#
			GILLEY, Mickey	
			Born on 3/09/36 in Ferriday, Louisiana. Country singer/pianist. First cousin to both Jerry Lee Lewis and Reverend Jimmy Swaggart. Owner of Gilleys nightclub in Pasadena, Texas. Gilley and the club were featured in the film *Urban Cowboy*.	
6/28/80	**22**	9	1. Stand By Me	Full Moon 46640
			featured in the movie *Urban Cowboy*	
			GILMER, Jimmy — see FIREBALLS	
			GILREATH, James	
			Born on 11/14/39 in Prairie, Mississippi. Singer/guitarist/songwriter.	
4/27/63	**21**	6	1. Little Band Of Gold	Joy 274
			GINO & GINA	
			Aristedes and Irene Giosasi — brother-sister duo from Brooklyn. Aristedes co-wrote "Sorry (I Ran All The Way Home)."	
6/09/58	**20**	1	1. (It's Been A Long Time) Pretty Baby	Mercury 71283
			Jockey #20 / Top 100 #34 / Best Seller #39	
			GIUFFRIA	
			California-based rock quintet led by Gregg Giuffria (keyboardist with Angel) and David Glen Eisley. Gregg and member Chuck Wright joined House Of Lords in 1988.	
1/05/85	**15**	7	1. Call To The Heart	MCA 52497
			GLAHE, Will	
			European accordion player/bandleader.	
11/25/57	**16**	15	1. Liechtensteiner Polka [F]	London 1755
			Best Seller #16 / Jockey #18 / Top 100 #19	
			GLASS BOTTLE, The	
			Pop group featuring lead singer Gary Criss.	
9/18/71	**36**	3	1. I Ain't Got Time Anymore	Avco Emb. 4575
			produced by novelty artist Dickie Goodman	
			GLASS TIGER	
			Canadian rock quintet: Alan Frew (vocals), Sam Reid (keyboards), Al Connelly (guitar), Wayne Parker (bass) and Michael Hanson (drums).	
8/09/86	**2**(1)	14	**1. Don't Forget Me (When I'm Gone)**	Manhattan 50037
11/29/86+	**7**	13	**2. Someday**	Manhattan 50048
3/21/87	**34**	5	3. I Will Be There	Manhattan 50066
5/07/88	**31**	5	4. I'm Still Searching	EMI-Man. 50116

DATE	POS	WKS	ARTIST—RECORD TITLE	LABEL & NO.
			GLAZER, Tom/Do-Re-Mi Children's Chorus	
			Tom (b: 9/03/14 in Philadelphia) is a novelty folk singer. Glazer hosted own ABC radio program, 1945-47. Composed score for 1957 film *A Face in the Crowd.*	
6/15/63	**14**	7	1. On Top Of Spaghetti [N]	Kapp 526
			parody of the tune "On Top Of Old Smokey"	
			GLENCOVES, The	
			Teen folk trio formed at Chaminade High School in Mineola, Long Island, New York in 1961. Singers/ guitarists Don Connors and Bill Byrne with singer Brian Bolger.	
7/27/63	**38**	2	1. Hootenanny	Select 724
			GLITTER, Gary	
			Born Paul Gadd on 5/08/44 in Banbury, England. First recorded as Paul Raven in the early '60s, then as Paul Monday; changed name to Gary Glitter in 1971.	
8/05/72	**7**	9	**1. Rock And Roll Part 2** **[I]**	Bell 45237
12/02/72	**35**	3	2. I Didn't Know I Loved You (Till I Saw You Rock And Roll)	Bell 45276
			GODLEY & CREME	
			Kevin Godley (b: 10/07/45, Manchester, England) and Lol Creme (b: 9/19/47, Manchester, England) formed duo after leaving British group 10cc. Prior to 10cc, both were with Hotlegs.	
8/17/85	**16**	10	1. Cry	Polydor 881786
			GODSPELL	
			The original cast as featured in the Broadway rock musical *Godspell.*	
6/24/72	**13**	9	1. Day By Day	Bell 45210
			lead vocal by original cast member Robin Lamont	
			GO-GO'S	
			Female rock group formed in 1978 in Los Angeles, consisting of Belinda Carlisle (vocals), Jane Wiedlin (guitar), Charlotte Caffey (guitar), Kathy Valentine (bass) and Gina Schock (drums). Disbanded in 1984. Reunion tour in 1990. Caffey formed The Graces in 1989.	
10/24/81	**20**	13	1. Our Lips Are Sealed	I.R.S. 9901
2/13/82	**2**(3)	15	● **2. We Got The Beat**	I.R.S. 9903
7/17/82	**8**	9	**3. Vacation**	I.R.S. 9907
3/31/84	**11**	10	4. Head Over Heels	I.R.S. 9926
7/14/84	**32**	5	5. Turn To You	I.R.S. 9928
			GOLD, Andrew	
			Born on 8/02/51 in Burbank, California. Son of soundtrack composer Ernest Gold (*Exodus*) and singer Marni Nixon. Co-founder of the group Bryndle. Session and arranging work for Linda Ronstadt since early '70s. Member of pop duo Wax, 1986.	
4/16/77	**7**	13	**1. Lonely Boy**	Asylum 45384
3/04/78	**25**	9	2. Thank You For Being A Friend	Asylum 45456
			GOLDEN EARRING	
			Rock band from The Netherlands. Original lineup through 1975: Barry Hay (vocals), George Kooymans (guitars, vocals), Cesar Zuiderwijk (drums) and Rinus Gerritsen (bass, keyboards).	
6/22/74	**13**	10	1. Radar Love	Track 40202
1/22/83	**10**	15	**2. Twilight Zone**	21 Records 103

DATE	POS	WKS	ARTIST—RECORD TITLE	LABEL & NO.
			GOLDSBORO, Bobby	
			Born on 1/18/41 in Marianna, Florida. Singer/songwriter/guitarist. To Dothan, Alabama in 1956. Toured with Roy Orbison, 1962-64. Own syndicated TV show from 1972-75, "The Bobby Goldsboro Show."	
2/15/64	**9**	8	**1. See The Funny Little Clown**	United Art. 672
5/23/64	**39**	2	2. Whenever He Holds You	United Art. 710
2/20/65	**13**	8	3. Little Things	United Art. 810
6/05/65	**27**	6	4. Voodoo Woman	United Art. 862
3/12/66	**23**	5	5. It's Too Late	United Art. 980
1/14/67	**35**	3	6. Blue Autumn	United Art. 50087
3/30/68	**1**(5)	13	● **7. Honey**	United Art. 50283
7/13/68	**19**	7	8. Autumn Of My Life	United Art. 50318
11/30/68	**36**	2	9. The Straight Life	United Art. 50461
1/09/71	**11**	11	10. Watching Scotty Grow	United Art. 50727
10/06/73	**21**	8	11. Summer (The First Time)	United Art. 251
			GOMM, Ian	
			Born on 3/17/47 in Ealing, England. Member of London band Brinsley Schwarz, 1972-75.	
10/06/79	**18**	5	1. Hold On	Stiff/Epic 50747
			GONE ALL STARS	
			Session band arranged by record company mogul George Goldner.	
3/03/58	**30**	4	1. "7-11" [I] Best Seller #30 / Top 100 #31 version of the Perez Prado tune "Mambo No. 5"	Gone 5016
			GONZALEZ	
			British soul/disco band.	
2/10/79	**26**	5	1. Haven't Stopped Dancing Yet	Capitol 4674
			GOODMAN, Benny — see CLOONEY, Rosemary	
			GOODMAN, Dickie	
			Born on 4/19/34 in Hewlett, New York. Dickie and partner Bill Buchanan originated the novelty "break-in" recordings featuring bits of the original versions of Top 40 hits interwoven throughout the recording. Comedy writer for Jackie Mason and head of music department at 20th Century Fox. Died on 11/06/89 of a self-inflicted gunshot. Also see Buchanan & Goodman.	
2/23/74	**33**	4	1. Energy Crisis '74 [N]	Rainy Wed. 206
9/13/75	**4**	7	● **2. Mr. Jaws** **[N]**	Cash 451
			GORDON, Barry	
			Born on 12/21/48 in Brookline, Massachusetts. Many TV appearances. In the Broadway show and film *A Thousand Clowns* (1963).	
12/17/55	**6**	4	**1. Nuttin' For Christmas** **[X-N]** **ART MOONEY AND HIS ORCHESTRA with BARRY GORDON** Best Seller #6 / Top 100 #7 / Juke Box #9 / Jockey #10	MGM 12092
			GORE, Lesley	
			Born on 5/02/46 in New York City; raised in Tenafly, New Jersey. Discovered by Quincy Jones while singing at a hotel in Manhattan. In films *Girls on the Beach*, *Ski Party* and *The T.A.M.I. Show.* Co-wrote two songs on the *Fame* soundtrack with her brother Michael, including "Out Here On My Own."	
5/18/63	**1**(2)	11	**1. It's My Party**	Mercury 72119
7/20/63	**5**	9	**2. Judy's Turn To Cry**	Mercury 72143

DATE	POS	WKS	ARTIST—RECORD TITLE	LABEL & NO.
10/19/63	**5**	11	**3. She's A Fool**	Mercury 72180
1/11/64	**2**(3)	10	**4. You Don't Own Me**	Mercury 72206
4/04/64	**12**	7	5. That's The Way Boys Are	Mercury 72259
6/20/64	**37**	1	6. I Don't Wanna Be A Loser	Mercury 72270
8/15/64	**14**	6	7. Maybe I Know	Mercury 72309
1/23/65	**27**	5	8. Look Of Love	Mercury 72372
7/17/65	**13**	7	9. Sunshine, Lollipops And Rainbows from the film *Ski Party*	Mercury 72433
10/09/65	**32**	3	10. My Town, My Guy And Me all of above produced by Quincy Jones	Mercury 72475
3/04/67	**16**	9	11. California Nights	Mercury 72649
			GORME, Eydie	
			Born on 8/16/31 in New York City. Vocalist with the big bands of Tommy Tucker and Tex Beneke in the late 1940s. Featured on Steve Allen's "Tonight Show" from 1953. Married Steve Lawrence on 12/29/57. Recorded as the duo Parker & Penny in 1979.	
6/16/56	**39**	1	1. Too Close For Comfort from the Broadway musical *Mr. Wonderful*	ABC-Para. 9684
9/01/56	**34**	3	2. Mama, Teach Me To Dance	ABC-Para. 9722
12/30/57	**24**	1	3. Love Me Forever Jockey #24 / Top 100 #86; trumpet solo by Bernie Glow	ABC-Para. 9863
5/26/58	**11**	9	4. You Need Hands Jockey #11 / Best Seller #32 / Top 100 #32	ABC-Para. 9925
2/09/63	**7**	11	**5. Blame It On The Bossa Nova**	Columbia 42661
			STEVE AND EYDIE:	
8/24/63	**28**	5	6. I Want To Stay Here	Columbia 42815
1/25/64	**35**	3	7. I Can't Stop Talking About You	Columbia 42932
			GOULET, Robert	
			Born on 11/26/33 in Lawrence, Massachusetts. Began concert career in Edmonton, Canada. Broadway/film/TV actor. Launched career as Sir Lancelot in the hit Broadway musical *Camelot.* Won the 1962 Best New Artist Grammy Award.	
11/28/64+	**16**	9	1. My Love, Forgive Me (Amore, Scusami)	Columbia 43131
			GO WEST	
			British duo of Peter Cox (vocals) and Richard Drummie (guitar, vocals).	
9/26/87	**39**	2	1. Don't Look Down - The Sequel	Chrysalis 43141
6/23/90	**8**	13	**2. King Of Wishful Thinking** produced by Peter Wolf; from the film *Pretty Woman*	EMI 50307#
			GQ	
			Bronx soul group: Emmanuel Rahiem LeBlanc (lead singer), Keith Crier, Herb Lane and Paul Service. Group became a trio with the departure of Service in 1980.	
4/14/79	**12**	11	● 1. Disco Nights (Rock-Freak)	Arista 0388
8/11/79	**20**	8	2. I Do Love You	Arista 0426
			GRACIE, Charlie	
			Born Charles Graci on 5/14/36 in Philadelphia. Vocalist/guitarist. First recorded for Cadillac in 1951. Regular on "Bandstand" (later: "American Bandstand"), 1952-58.	
2/23/57	**1**(2)	14	**1. Butterfly** Juke Box #1 / Best Seller #3 / Top 100 #7 / Jockey #13	Cameo 105

DATE	POS	WKS	ARTIST—RECORD TITLE	LABEL & NO.
5/20/57	**16**	6	2. Fabulous Best Seller #16 / Top 100 #26	Cameo 107
			GRAHAM, Larry	
			Born on 8/14/46 in Beaumont, Texas. To Oakland at the age of two. Bass player with Sly & The Family Stone from 1966-72. Formed Graham Central Station in 1973. Went solo in 1980.	
9/13/75	**38**	2	1. Your Love	Warner 8105
			GRAHAM CENTRAL STATION	
8/09/80	**9**	9	● **2. One In A Million You**	Warner 49221
			GRAMM, Lou	
			Born on 5/02/50 in Rochester, New York. Lead singer of Foreigner. Member of Black Sheep, 1970-75. Left Foreigner in 1991 to form Shadow King.	
2/28/87	**5**	11	**1. Midnight Blue**	Atlantic 89304
11/18/89+	**6**	14	**2. Just Between You And Me**	Atlantic 88781
3/31/90	**40**	1	3. True Blue Love above 2 produced by Peter Wolf	Atlantic 88768#
			GRAMMER, Billy	
			Born on 8/28/25 in Benton, Illinois. Country singer/guitarist. Performed regularly on "The Jimmy Dean Show," CBS-TV, 1957-58. Prominent session musician in Nashville.	
12/08/58+	**4**	15	**1. Gotta Travel On** based on 19th-century tune that originated in the British Isles	Monument 400
			GRANAHAN, Gerry	
			Born on 6/17/39 in Pittston, Pennsylvania. To New York City at age 17. First recorded for Atco as Jerry Grant. Formed Dicky Doo And The Don'ts and The Fireflies. Formed Caprice Records in 1958 and produced many top hits.	
6/16/58	**23**	8	1. No Chemise, Please Top 100 #23 / Best Seller #25	Sunbeam 102
			GRANATA, Rocco	
			Born in Italy in 1938; moved to Belgium at age 10. Singer/songwriter/accordionist.	
11/23/59	**31**	7	1. Marina [F]	Laurie 3041
			GRAND FUNK RAILROAD	
			Heavy-metal rock group formed in Flint, Michigan in 1968. Consisted of Mark Farner (guitar), Mel Schacher (bass) and Don Brewer (drums). Brewer and Farner had been in Terry Knight & The Pack; Schacher was former bassist with ? & The Mysterians. Knight became producer and manager for Grand Funk, until he was fired in March 1972. Craig Frost (keyboards) added in 1973. Disbanded in 1976. Re-formed in 1981, with Farner, Brewer and Dennis Bellinger (bass). Disbanded again shortly thereafter. Farner recorded Contemporary Christian music.	
9/05/70	**22**	8	1. Closer To Home	Capitol 2877
2/05/72	**29**	5	2. Footstompin' Music	Capitol 3255
11/04/72	**29**	6	3. Rock 'N Roll Soul	Capitol 3363
			GRAND FUNK:	
8/18/73	**1**(1)	13	● **4. We're An American Band**	Capitol 3660
12/29/73+	**19**	6	5. Walk Like A Man	Capitol 3760
3/30/74	**1**(2)	14	● **6. The Loco-Motion**	Capitol 3840
7/20/74	**11**	8	7. Shinin' On above 4 produced by Todd Rundgren	Capitol 3917
12/21/74+	**3**	12	**8. Some Kind Of Wonderful**	Capitol 4002

DATE	POS	WKS	ARTIST—RECORD TITLE	LABEL & NO.
4/19/75	**4**	12	**9. Bad Time**	Capitol 4046
			GRANT, Amy	
			Born on 11/25/60 in Augusta, Georgia. The first lady of contemporary Christian music. Married to singer/songwriter Gary Chapman.	
7/06/85	**29**	6	1. Find A Way	A&M 2734
10/11/86	**1**(1)	15	**2. The Next Time I Fall** **PETER CETERA W/AMY GRANT**	Full Moon 28597
3/09/91	**1**(2)	16	**3. Baby Baby**	A&M 1549
6/22/91	**2**(1)	15	**4. Every Heartbeat**	A&M 1557
			GRANT, Earl	
			Organist/pianist/vocalist born in Oklahoma City in 1931. First recorded for Decca in 1957. In the films *Tender Is the Night, Imitation of Life* and *Tokyo Night.* Died in an automobile accident on 6/10/70.	
9/29/58	**7**	13	**1. The End**	Decca 30719
			GRANT, Eddy	
			Born Edmond Montague Grant on 3/05/48 in Plaisance, Guyana. Moved to London in 1960. Formed group, The Equals in London in 1967. Moved to Barbados in 1982.	
5/21/83	**2**(5)	15	▲ **1. Electric Avenue**	Portrait 03793
6/30/84	**26**	6	2. Romancing The Stone written for, but not included in, the film of the same title; above 2 recorded in St. Phillip, Barbados	Portrait 04433
			GRANT, Gogi	
			Born Audrey Brown on 9/20/24 in Philadelphia. Moved to Los Angeles at age 12. Performed vocals for the film *The Helen Morgan Story.*	
10/01/55	**9**	10	**1. Suddenly There's A Valley** Jockey #9 / Best Seller #14 / Top 100 #14 / Juke Box #19	Era 1003
5/05/56	**1**(8)	22	**2. The Wayward Wind** Jockey #1(8) / Top 100 #1(7) / Best Seller #1(6) / Juke Box #1(4) orchestra conducted by Buddy Bregman on above 2	Era 1013
			GRANT, Janie	
			Singer/songwriter from Paterson, New Jersey. Real name: Rose Marie Cosili. Discovered by recording artist Gerry Granahan.	
5/15/61	**29**	5	1. Triangle	Caprice 104
			GRASS ROOTS, The	
			Rock group formed in San Francisco in 1964 by drummer Joel Larson and lead singer Bill Fulton. Originally called The Bedouins. New group recruited in 1967 by pop producer Lou Adler and songwriters Steve Barri and P.F. Sloan (known as the Fantastic Baggies). Consisted of Rob Grill (lead singer, bass), Warren Entner and Creed Bratton (guitars), and Rick Coonce (drums). New lineup in 1971 included Entner, Grill, guitarists Reed Kailing and Virgil Webber, and Joel Larson (drums).	
7/16/66	**28**	4	1. Where Were You When I Needed You	Dunhill 4029
6/03/67	**8**	9	**2. Let's Live For Today** Rob Grill, lead singer from here on	Dunhill 4084
9/02/67	**23**	4	3. Things I Should Have Said	Dunhill 4094
9/21/68	**5**	12	● **4. Midnight Confessions**	Dunhill 4144
1/11/69	**28**	2	5. Bella Linda	Dunhill 4162
5/17/69	**31**	5	6. The River Is Wide	Dunhill 4187
8/09/69	**15**	10	7. I'd Wait A Million Years	Dunhill 4198
11/22/69	**24**	7	8. Heaven Knows	Dunhill 4217

DATE	POS	WKS	ARTIST—RECORD TITLE	LABEL & NO.
6/13/70	**35**	3	9. Baby Hold On	Dunhill 4237
2/13/71	**15**	11	10. Temptation Eyes	Dunhill 4263
6/19/71	**9**	9	**11. Sooner Or Later**	Dunhill 4279
10/30/71	**16**	8	12. Two Divided By Love	Dunhill 4289
3/18/72	**34**	3	13. Glory Bound	Dunhill 4302
7/22/72	**39**	2	14. The Runway	Dunhill 4316
			GRATEFUL DEAD	
			Legendary psychedelic rock band formed in San Francisco in 1966. Consisted of Jerry Garcia, lead guitar; Bob Weir, rhythm guitar; Ron "Pigpen" McKernan, organ, harmonica; Phil Lesh, bass; and Bill Kreutzmann, drums. Mickey Hart (2nd drummer) and Tom Constanten (keyboards) added in 1968. Constanten left in 1970, Hart in 1971. Keith Godchaux (piano) and his wife Donna (vocals) joined in 1972. Pigpen died of a liver ailment on 3/08/73. Hart returned in 1975. Brent Mydland (keyboards) added in 1979, replacing Keith and Donna Godchaux. Mydland was a member of Silver. Keith Godchaux died on 7/23/80 from injuries suffered in a motorcycle accident. Mydland died on 7/26/90 (age 37) of a drug overdose. Tubes keyboardist Vince Welnick replaced Mydland.	
8/15/87	**9**	9	**1. Touch Of Grey**	Arista 9606
			GRAY, Dobie	
			Born Leonard Victor Ainsworth on 7/26/42 in Brookshire, Texas. Soul vocalist/composer/actor. To Los Angeles in 1960. Worked as an actor on Broadway, and in the L.A. production of *Hair*. Lead singer of Pollution in 1971.	
1/23/65	**13**	7	1. The "In" Crowd	Charger 105
3/31/73	**5**	15	● **2. Drift Away**	Decca 33057
2/10/79	**37**	2	3. You Can Do It	Infinity 50003
			GREAN, Charles Randolph, Sounde	
			Charles (b: 10/01/13 in New York City) is a former artist & repertoire director at RCA and Dot Records. Married singer Betty Johnson.	
7/05/69	**13**	8	1. Quentin's Theme [I] from the TV series "Dark Shadows"	Ranwood 840
			GREAT WHITE	
			Los Angeles hard-rock quintet, led by vocalist Jack Russell and guitarist Mark Kendall. Lineup includes Michael Lardie (keyboards), Audie Desbrow (drums) and Tony Montana (bass).	
6/17/89	**5**	14	● **1. Once Bitten Twice Shy** first released in 1975 on Ian Hunter's self-titled album	Capitol 44366
11/18/89	**30**	4	2. The Angel Song	Capitol 44449
			GREAVES, R.B.	
			Born Ronald Bertram Aloysius Greaves on 11/28/44 at the USAF Base in Georgetown, British Guyana. Half American Indian, raised on a Seminole reservation in California. Nephew of Sam Cooke. To England in 1963, as Sonny Childe & The TNT's.	
10/25/69	2(1)	13	● **1. Take A Letter Maria**	Atco 6714
2/14/70	**27**	5	2. Always Something There To Remind Me	Atco 6726
			GRECCO, Cyndi	
6/12/76	**25**	5	1. Making Our Dreams Come True theme from the TV series "LaVerne & Shirley"	Private S. 45086

DATE	POS	WKS	ARTIST—RECORD TITLE	LABEL & NO.
			GREEN, Al	
			Born on 4/13/46 in Forest City, Arkansas. Soul singer/songwriter. With gospel group the Greene Brothers. To Grand Rapids, Michigan in 1959. First recorded for Fargo in 1960. In group The Creations from 1964-67. Sang with his brother Robert and Lee Virgins in the group Soul Mates from 1967-68. Went solo in 1969. Wrote most of his songs. Returned to gospel music in 1980.	
8/21/71	**11**	15	● 1. Tired Of Being Alone	Hi 2194
12/11/71+	**1**(1)	15	● **2. Let's Stay Together**	Hi 2202
4/08/72	**4**	11	● **3. Look What You Done For Me**	Hi 2211
7/15/72	**3**	11	● **4. I'm Still In Love With You**	Hi 2216
11/04/72	**3**	12	● **5. You Ought To Be With Me**	Hi 2227
3/03/73	**10**	9	● **6. Call Me (Come Back Home)**	Hi 2235
7/21/73	**10**	12	● **7. Here I Am (Come And Take Me)**	Hi 2247
12/22/73+	**19**	8	8. Livin' For You	Hi 2257
5/11/74	**32**	3	9. Let's Get Married	Hi 2262
11/02/74	**7**	11	● **10. Sha-La-La (Make Me Happy)**	Hi 2274
3/22/75	**13**	8	11. L-O-V-E (Love)	Hi 2282
11/29/75	**28**	6	12. Full Of Fire	Hi 2300
12/18/76+	**37**	4	13. Keep Me Cryin'	Hi 2319
			all of above produced by Willie Mitchell	
12/03/88+	**9**	10	**14. Put A Little Love In Your Heart**	A&M 1255
			ANNIE LENNOX & AL GREEN	
			from the film *Scrooged*	
			GREEN, Garland	
			Born Garfield Green, Jr. on 6/24/42 in Leland, Mississippi. Soul singer/pianist.	
10/18/69	**20**	4	1. Jealous Kind Of Fella	Uni 55143
			GREENBAUM, Norman	
			Born on 11/20/42 in Malden, Massachusetts. Moved to the West Coast in 1965 and formed the psychedelic jug band Dr. West's Medicine Show & Junk Band.	
3/07/70	**3**	14	● **1. Spirit In The Sky**	Reprise 0885
			GREENE, Lorne	
			Born on 2/12/14 in Ottawa, Canada; died on 9/11/87 of cardiac arrest. Chief newscaster for CBC radio, 1940-43. Studied acting, appeared in films *The Silver Chalice* and *Tight Spot*; starred in the TV series "Bonanza" and "Battlestar Galactica."	
11/07/64	**1**(1)	10	**1. Ringo** **[S]**	RCA 8444
			GREGG, Bobby/His Friends	
			Bobby's real name is Robert Grego. Jazz drummer from Philadelphia. Performed with Steve Gibson & The Red Caps from 1955-60.	
4/14/62	**29**	5	1. The Jam - Part 1 [I]	Cotton 1003
			featuring Roy Buchanan, guitar	
			GRIFFITH, Andy	
			Born on 6/01/26 in Mount Airy, North Carolina. Screen debut in 1957, *A Face in the Crowd*. Best known as sheriff Andy Taylor on the TV series "The Andy Griffith Show"; currently starring in TV's "Matlock."	
4/02/55	**26**	1	1. Make Yourself Comfortable [C]	Capitol 3057
			Best Seller #26; vocal by Jean Wilson; orchestra conducted by Burt Massengale	

DATE	POS	WKS	ARTIST—RECORD TITLE	LABEL & NO.
			GROCE, Larry	
			Born on 4/22/48 in Dallas. Pop-folk singer/songwriter. Wrote children's songs for Walt Disney Records.	
2/07/76	**9**	9	**1. Junk Food Junkie** [N]	Warner 8165
			recorded live at McCabe's in Santa Monica	
			GROSS, Henry	
			Rock singer from Brooklyn. Original lead guitarist of Sha-Na-Na.	
4/03/76	**6**	13	● **1. Shannon**	Lifesong 45002
8/21/76	**37**	2	2. Springtime Mama	Lifesong 45008
			above 2 produced by Terry Cashman and Tommy West	
			GTR	
			British hard-rock quintet featuring superstar guitarists Steve Hackett (Genesis) and Steve Howe (Yes & Asia), and vocalist Max Bacon.	
5/31/86	**14**	10	1. When The Heart Rules The Mind	Arista 9470
			GUARALDI, Vince, Trio	
			Born on 7/17/32 in San Francisco; died of a heart attack on 2/06/76. Pianist/leader of own jazz trio. Formerly with Woody Herman and Cal Tjader. Wrote the music for the "Charlie Brown" TV specials.	
2/09/63	**22**	6	1. Cast Your Fate To The Wind [I]	Fantasy 563
			GUESS WHO, The	
			Rock group formed in Winnipeg, Canada in 1963. Consisted of Allan "Chad Allan" Kobel (guitar, vocals), Randy Bachman (lead guitar), Garry Peterson (drums), Bob Ashley (piano) and Jim Kale (bass). Recorded as The Reflections, and Chad Allan & The Expressions. Ashley replaced by new lead singer Burton Cummings in 1966. Allan left shortly thereafter. Bachman left in July 1970, to form Bachman-Turner Overdrive; replaced by Kurt Winter and Greg Leskiw. Leskiw and Kale left in 1972, replaced by Don McDougall and Bill Wallace. Domenic Troiano replaced both Winter and McDougall in 1974. Group disbanded in 1975; several reunions since then.	
6/05/65	**22**	7	1. Shakin' All Over	Scepter 1295
			group is actually Chad Allan & The Expressions	
4/26/69	**6**	11	● **2. These Eyes**	RCA 0102
7/26/69	**10**	9	● **3. Laughing/**	
11/08/69	**22**	6	4. Undun	RCA 0195
1/17/70	**5**	10	**5. No Time**	RCA 0300
3/28/70	**1**(3)	14	● **6. American Woman/**	
		14	7. No Sugar Tonight	RCA 0325
			all of above include Randy Bachman before his departure	
8/08/70	**17**	8	8. Hand Me Down World	RCA 0367
11/07/70	**10**	8	**9. Share The Land**	RCA 0388
6/12/71	**29**	4	10. Albert Flasher	RCA 0458
9/04/71	**19**	8	11. Rain Dance	RCA 0522
4/20/74	**39**	1	12. Star Baby	RCA 0217
8/10/74	**6**	11	**13. Clap For The Wolfman**	RCA 0324
			featuring bits of dialogue by Wolfman Jack	
12/14/74+	**28**	4	14. Dancin' Fool	RCA 10075
			all of above (except #1) produced by Jack Richardson	
			GUIDRY, Greg	
			Singer/songwriter/pianist born in 1950 in St. Louis.	
3/20/82	**17**	10	1. Goin' Down	Columbia 02691

DATE	POS	WKS	ARTIST—RECORD TITLE	LABEL & NO.
			GUITAR, Bonnie	
			Born Bonnie Buckingham on 3/25/24 in Seattle. Own group in the early 1950s. Worked as session guitarist in Los Angeles in the mid-1950s. Owner of Dolphin/Dolton Records.	
4/27/57	**6**	10	**1. Dark Moon**	Dot 15550
			Jockey #6 / Top 100 #8 / Best Seller #10 / Juke Box #11	
			GUNHILL ROAD	
			Rock trio: Glen Leopolo, Gil Roman and Steve Goldrich.	
6/02/73	**40**	1	1. Back When My Hair Was Short	Kama Sutra 569
			GUNS N' ROSES	
			Los Angeles-based, hard-rock quintet: lead singer W. Axl Rose (William Bailey) with bassist Michael "Duff" McKagan, guitarists Izzy Stradlin (Jeffrey Isbell) and Slash (Saul Hudson), and drummer Steven Adler. Axl Rose married Erin Everly (daughter of Don Everly of The Everly Brothers) on 4/27/90, divorced three weeks later. Adler left in 1990, replaced by former Cult drummer Matt Sorum. Keyboardist Dizzy Reed joined in 1990.	
7/23/88	**1**(2)	14	● **1. Sweet Child O' Mine**	Geffen 27963
			written by Rose for Erin Everly	
11/05/88	**7**	12	**2. Welcome To The Jungle**	Geffen 27759
1/28/89	**5**	11	**3. Paradise City**	Geffen 27570
4/22/89	**4**	10	● **4. Patience**	Geffen 22996
7/20/91	**29**	8	● 5. You Could Be Mine	Geffen 19039
			from the film *Terminator 2-Judgment Day* (not on soundtrack LP)	
			GUTHRIE, Arlo	
			Born on 7/10/47 in Coney Island, New York. Son of legendary folk singer Woody Guthrie.	
9/09/72	**18**	9	1. The City Of New Orleans	Reprise 1103
			H	
			HAGAR, Sammy	
			Born on 10/13/47 in Monterey, California. Rock singer/songwriter/guitarist. Lead singer of Montrose (1973-75). Replaced David Lee Roth as lead singer of Van Halen in 1985.	
12/25/82+	**13**	13	1. Your Love Is Driving Me Crazy	Geffen 29816
8/18/84	**38**	3	2. Two Sides Of Love	Geffen 29246
10/27/84	**26**	6	3. I Can't Drive 55	Geffen 29173
8/01/87	**23**	7	4. Give To Live	Geffen 28314
			HAGGARD, Merle	
			Born on 4/06/37 in Bakersfield, California. Country singer/songwriter/guitarist. Merle's had 38 #1 singles on the country charts. Appeared in several films (*Bronco Billy*) and TV series.	
1/05/74	**28**	3	1. If We Make It Through December [X]	Capitol 3746
			HAIRCUT ONE HUNDRED	
			British pop-rock sextet founded by vocalist Nick Heyward. Disbanded in 1983.	
7/17/82	**37**	4	1. Love Plus One	Arista 0672

DATE	POS	WKS	ARTIST—RECORD TITLE	LABEL & NO.
			HALEY, Bill/His Comets	
			Born William John Clifton Haley, Jr. on 7/06/25 in Highland Park, Michigan. Began career as a singer with a New England country band, the Down Homers. Formed the Four Aces of Western Swing in 1948. In 1949 formed the Saddlemen, who recorded on various labels before signing with the Essex label (as Bill Haley & The Comets) in 1952; signed with Decca in 1954. The original Comets band who backed Haley on "Rock Around The Clock" were: Danny Cedrone (lead guitar), Joey D'Ambrose (sax), Billy Williamson (steel guitar), Johnny Grande (piano), Marshall Lytle (bass) and Dick Richards (drums). Comets lineup on subsequent recordings included Williamson, Grande, Rudy Pompilli (sax; d: 2/05/76 [age 47]), Al Rex (bass), Ralph Jones (drums) and Frannie Beecher (lead guitar). Bill died of a heart attack in Harlingen, Texas on 2/09/81. Inducted into the Rock and Roll Hall of Fame in 1987. Also see The Kingsmen.	
11/20/54+	**11**	15	1. Dim, Dim The Lights (I Want Some Atmosphere) Best Seller #11 / Jockey #16 / Juke Box #16	Decca 29317
3/05/55	**18**	8	2. Mambo Rock/ Best Seller #18	
3/19/55	**17**	2	3. Birth Of The Boogie Juke Box #17 / Best Seller #26	Decca 29418
5/14/55	**1**(8)	24	**4. (We're Gonna) Rock Around The Clock** Best Seller #1(8)/Juke Box #1(7)/Jockey #1(6)/Top 100 #56 pre recorded on 4/12/54; Grammy Hall of Fame Award winner in 1982; featured in the film *Blackboard Jungle*	Decca 29124
7/23/55	**15**	4	5. Razzle-Dazzle Best Seller #15	Decca 29552
11/19/55	**9**	13	**6. Burn That Candle/** Juke Box #9 / Best Seller #16 / Top 100 #20	
11/19/55	**23**	7	7. Rock-A-Beatin' Boogie Best Seller #23 / Top 100 #41	Decca 29713
1/14/56	**6**	15	**8. See You Later, Alligator** Best Seller #6 / Top 100 #6 / Jockey #6 / Juke Box #6	Decca 29791
4/07/56	**16**	5	9. R-O-C-K/ Juke Box #16 / Best Seller #20 / Top 100 #29 featured in the film *Rock Around the Clock*	
4/07/56	**18**	5	10. The Saints Rock 'N Roll Best Seller #18 / Top 100 #42 rock version of the spiritual "When The Saints Go Marching In"	Decca 29870
9/01/56	**25**	4	11. Rip It Up Best Seller #25 / Top 100 #30	Decca 30028
11/24/56	**34**	3	12. Rudy's Rock [I] sax solo by Rudy Pompilli	Decca 30085
4/21/58	**22**	6	13. Skinny Minnie Top 100 #22 / Best Seller #24	Decca 30592
5/25/74	**39**	1	14. (We're Gonna) Rock Around The Clock [R]	MCA 60025
			HALL, Daryl	
			Born Daryl Franklin Hohl on 10/11/48 in Philadelphia. Half of Hall & Oates duo.	
8/16/86	**5**	11	**1. Dreamtime**	RCA 14387
11/15/86	**33**	5	2. Foolish Pride	RCA 5038

DATE	POS	WKS	ARTIST—RECORD TITLE	LABEL & NO.
			HALL, Daryl, & John Oates	
			Daryl Hall (see previous entry) & John Oates (b: 4/07/49 in New York City) met while students at Temple University in 1967. Hall sang backup for many top soul groups before teaming up with Oates in 1972. In the late 1980s, they passed The Everly Brothers as the #1 charting duo of the rock era.	
4/03/76	**4**	17	● **1. Sara Smile**	RCA 10530
8/14/76	**7**	16	**2. She's Gone** [R] originally charted in 1974 (POS 60)	Atlantic 3332
12/25/76	**39**	3	3. Do What You Want, Be What You Are	RCA 10808
2/05/77	**1**(2)	14	● **4. Rich Girl**	RCA 10860
5/28/77	**28**	4	5. Back Together Again	RCA 10970
9/30/78	**20**	7	6. It's A Laugh	RCA 11371
12/01/79+	**18**	10	7. Wait For Me	RCA 11747
8/30/80	**30**	4	8. How Does It Feel To Be Back	RCA 12048
10/11/80	**12**	14	9. You've Lost That Lovin' Feeling	RCA 12103
2/14/81	**1**(3)	17	● **10. Kiss On My List**	RCA 12142
5/16/81	**5**	14	**11. You Make My Dreams**	RCA 12217
9/12/81	**1**(2)	17	● **12. Private Eyes**	RCA 12296
11/21/81+	**1**(1)	17	● **13. I Can't Go For That (No Can Do)**	RCA 12357
4/03/82	**9**	11	**14. Did It In A Minute**	RCA 13065
7/24/82	**33**	5	15. Your Imagination	RCA 13252
11/06/82	**1**(4)	17	● **16. Maneater**	RCA 13354
2/05/83	**7**	15	**17. One On One**	RCA 13421
5/07/83	**6**	12	**18. Family Man**	RCA 13507
10/29/83	**2**(4)	15	**19. Say It Isn't So**	RCA 13654
2/25/84	**8**	11	**20. Adult Education**	RCA 13714
10/06/84	**1**(2)	16	**21. Out Of Touch**	RCA 13916
1/05/85	**5**	11	**22. Method Of Modern Love**	RCA 13970
3/30/85	**18**	8	23. Some Things Are Better Left Unsaid	RCA 14035
6/15/85	**30**	6	24. Possession Obsession	RCA 14098
9/15/85	**20**	7	25. A Nite At The Apollo Live! The Way You Do The Things You Do/My Girl **DARYL HALL JOHN OATES with DAVID RUFFIN & EDDIE KENDRICK** recorded at the reopening of New York's Apollo Theatre	RCA 14178
4/23/88	**3**	11	**26. Everything Your Heart Desires**	Arista 9684
8/06/88	**29**	5	27. Missed Opportunity	Arista 9727
10/29/88	**31**	3	28. Downtown Life	Arista 9753
10/20/90	**11**	9	29. So Close produced by Jon Bon Jovi and Danny Kortchmar	Arista 2085
			HALL, Jimmy	
			Mobile, Alabama native. Leader of the Southern rock band Wet Willie.	
11/01/80	**27**	4	1. I'm Happy That Love Has Found You	Epic 50931
			HALL, Larry	
			Born on 6/30/41 in Cincinnati.	
12/07/59+	**15**	11	1. Sandy first released on Hot 1 in 1959	Strand 25007

DATE	POS	WKS	ARTIST—RECORD TITLE	LABEL & NO.
			HALL, Tom T.	
			Born on 5/25/36 in Olive Hill, Kentucky. Country music storyteller. Wrote "Harper Valley P.T.A. hit for Jeannie C. Riley. Host of "Pop Goes the Country" TV series.	
1/19/74	**12**	9	1. I Love	Mercury 73436
			HALOS, The	
			New York City R&B group. Backing group on Curtis Lee's "Pretty Little Angel Eyes."	
8/28/61	**25**	4	1. "Nag"	7 Arts 709
			HAMILTON, Bobby	
			Real name: Robert Caristo. Native of Locust Valley, Long Island, New York.	
8/04/58	**40**	1	1. Crazy Eyes For You	Apt 25002
			HAMILTON, George IV	
			Born on 7/19/37 in Winston-Salem, North Carolina. Country-folk-pop singer/songwriter/guitarist. Toured with Buddy Holly, Gene Vincent and The Everly Brothers. Moved to Nashville in 1959 and joined the "Grand Ole Opry." Own TV series on ABC in 1959, and in Canada in the late 1970s.	
11/17/56	**6**	14	**1. A Rose And A Baby Ruth**	ABC-Para. 9765
			Top 100 #6 / Best Seller #7 / Jockey #7 / Juke Box #8 first released on Colonial 420 in 1956	
3/09/57	**33**	4	2. Only One Love	ABC-Para. 9782
12/09/57+	**10**	12	**3. Why Don't They Understand**	ABC-Para. 9862
			Jockey #10 / Top 100 #17 / Best Seller #19	
4/07/58	**25**	1	4. Now And For Always	ABC-Para. 9898
			Jockey #25 / Best Seller #37 / Top 100 #37	
12/15/58+	**29**	5	5. The Teen Commandments [S]	ABC-Para. 9974
			PAUL ANKA-GEO. HAMILTON IV-JOHNNY NASH inspirational talk from above 3 ABC-Paramount artists	
7/20/63	**15**	7	6. Abilene	RCA 8181
			HAMILTON, Roy	
			Born on 4/16/29 in Leesburg, Georgia; died of a stroke on 7/20/69. R&B ballad singer. Moved to Jersey City at age 14. Sang with the Searchlight Gospel Singers in 1948.	
4/23/55	**6**	16	**1. Unchained Melody**	Epic 9102
			Jockey #6 / Juke Box #6 / Best Seller #9 from the film *Unchained*	
1/27/58	**13**	11	2. Don't Let Go	Epic 9257
			Top 100 #13 / Best Seller #14 / Jockey #16	
2/13/61	**12**	7	3. You Can Have Her	Epic 9434
			HAMILTON, Russ	
			Singer/songwriter, born Ronald Hulme in 1934 in Liverpool, England.	
8/05/57	**4**	17	**1. Rainbow**	Kapp 184
			Jockey #4 / Best Seller #7 / Top 100 #7	
			HAMILTON, JOE FRANK & REYNOLDS	
			Dan Hamilton, Joe Frank Carollo and Tommy Reynolds. Trio were members of The T-Bones. Reynolds left group in 1972 and was replaced by Alan Dennison. Although Reynolds had left, group still recorded as Hamilton, Joe Frank & Reynolds until July 1976.	
6/12/71	**4**	11	● **1. Don't Pull Your Love**	Dunhill 4276
7/19/75	**1**(1)	12	● **2. Fallin' In Love**	Playboy 6024
12/13/75+	**21**	8	3. Winners And Losers	Playboy 6054

DATE	POS	WKS	ARTIST—RECORD TITLE	LABEL & NO.
			HAMLISCH, Marvin	
			Born on 6/02/44 in New York City. Pianist/composer/conductor for numerous soundtracks. 1973's Best Song Oscar and Grammy winner for "The Way We Were." Won the 1974 Best New Artist Grammy Award.	
4/20/74	**3**	12	● **1. The Entertainer** [I]	MCA 40174
			written in 1902 by Scott Joplin; featured in film *The Sting*	
			HAMMER, Jan	
			Jazz-rock keyboard virtuoso born in Prague, Czechoslovakia in 1950. Toured with Sarah Vaughan as conductor/keyboardist. Member of Mahavishnu Orchestra until 1973.	
9/21/85	**1**(1)	13	**1. Miami Vice Theme** [I]	MCA 52666
			from the "Miami Vice" TV series	
			HAMMOND, Albert	
			Born on 5/18/42 in London and raised in Gibraltar, Spain. Member of British group Magic Lanterns, 1971.	
11/04/72	**5**	13	● **1. It Never Rains In Southern California**	Mums 6011
4/13/74	**31**	4	2. I'm A Train	Mums 6026
			HAPPENINGS, The	
			Vocal group from Paterson, New Jersey: Bob Miranda (lead), Tom Giuliano (tenor), Ralph DiVito (baritone) and Dave Libert (bass). Bernie LaPorta replaced DiVito in 1968. Originally the Four Graduates, recorded for Rust in 1963.	
7/30/66	**3**	11	**1. See You In September**	B.T. Puppy 520
10/22/66	**12**	5	2. Go Away Little Girl	B.T. Puppy 522
4/29/67	**3**	9	**3. I Got Rhythm**	B.T. Puppy 527
			written in 1930 by George & Ira Gershwin for musical *Girl Crazy*	
7/22/67	**13**	6	4. My Mammy	B.T. Puppy 530
			Al Jolson's theme song; written in 1920	
			HARDCASTLE, Paul	
			Born in London on 12/10/57. Keyboardist/producer. Formed own company, Total Control Records.	
6/22/85	**15**	8	1. 19	Chrysalis 42860
			title refers to the average age of U.S. soldiers in Vietnam	
			HARNELL, Joe	
			Born on 8/02/24 in the Bronx. Conductor/arranger for Frank Sinatra, Peggy Lee and others. Musical director for many TV shows, including "The Mike Douglas Show."	
1/26/63	**14**	8	1. Fly Me To The Moon-Bossa Nova [I]	Kapp 497
			HARNEN, Jimmy — see SYNCH	
			HARPERS BIZARRE	
			Santa Cruz, California quintet led by Ted Templeman, who later produced many albums for The Doobie Brothers and Van Halen.	
3/18/67	**13**	7	1. The 59th Street Bridge Song (Feelin' Groovy)	Warner 5890
			written by Paul Simon; arranged by Leon Russell	
6/17/67	**37**	3	2. Come To The Sunshine	Warner 7028
			HARPO, Slim	
			Blues singer/harmonica player. Born James Moore on 1/11/24 in Lobdell, Louisiana (aka: Harmonica Slim). Died of a heart attack on 1/31/70.	
7/10/61	**34**	2	1. Rainin' In My Heart	Excello 2194
			featuring blues guitarist Lightnin' Slim (Otis Hicks)	

The Fat Boys were a welcome blast of late 80s comic relief both as actors—they starred in the film *Disorderlies*—and nostalgia merchants. Their curious pair of Top 20 records include both "Wipeout," with special guests the Beach Boys, and "The Twist" with Chubby Checker.

Elisa Fiorello's 1987 debut album showed a promising teenage singer in the company of six different producers—and no hit singles. Three years later, a track co-written with Prince—"On The Way Up," one of many he'd characteristically share with young new artists—was a solid top-40 hit.

Dan Fogelberg's long recording career probably reached its chart zenith in 1981, when his album *The Innocent Age* spawned three top-10 singles—including "Same Old Lang Syne," "Hard To Say," and "Leader Of The Band." But "Longer," a No. 2 hit from his previous album, remains his all-time chart high.

Lita Ford's first brush with the charts came in 1975 with near-legendary, all-girl, teenage rock 'n' roll band the Runaways. Though that group never managed a top-40 record, it launched the careers of Ford, singer Joan Jett, and Cherie Currie, who later recorded for Capitol with her twin sister Marie.

The Four Preps had two top-5 hits in 1958, including "26 Miles (Santa Catalina)" and "Big Man," which hit the No. 2 and 3 slots, respectively. Former Prep Ed Cobb would have a colorful future working with punk-rock avatars the Standells in the mid-60s; Cobb later penned "Tainted Love," with which new-wave group Soft Cell would score a hit in 1982.

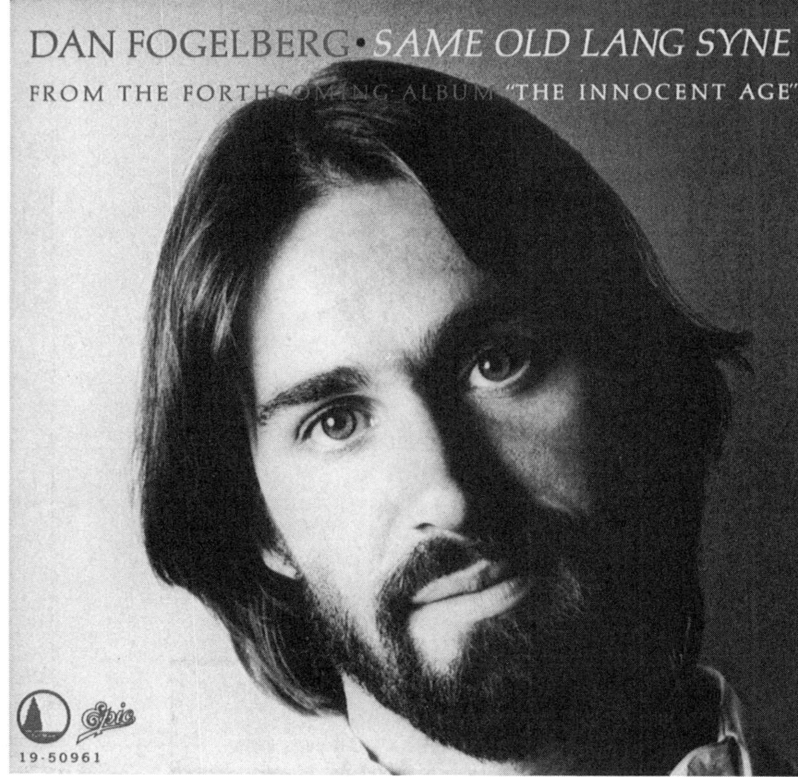

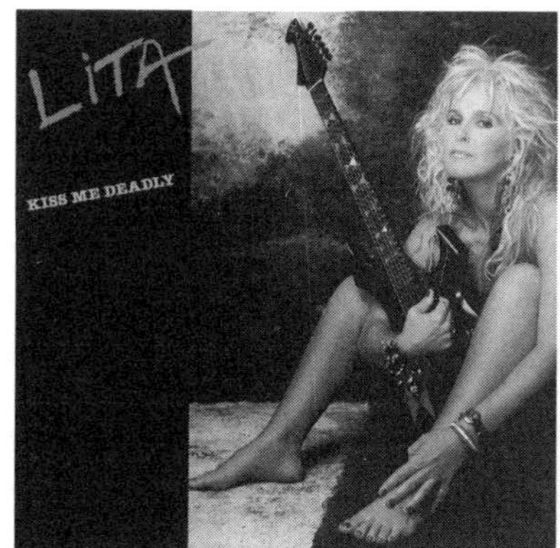

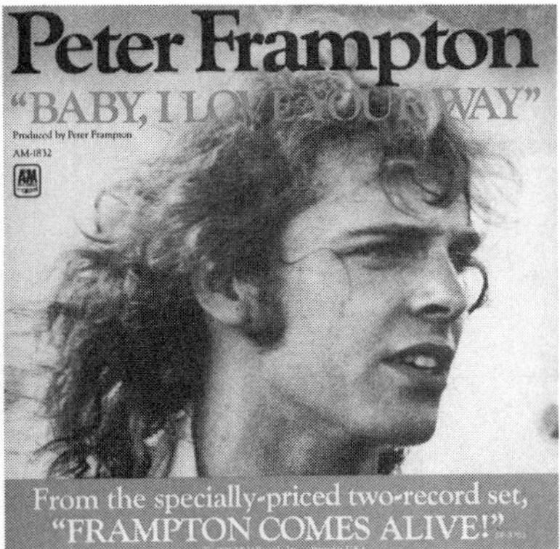

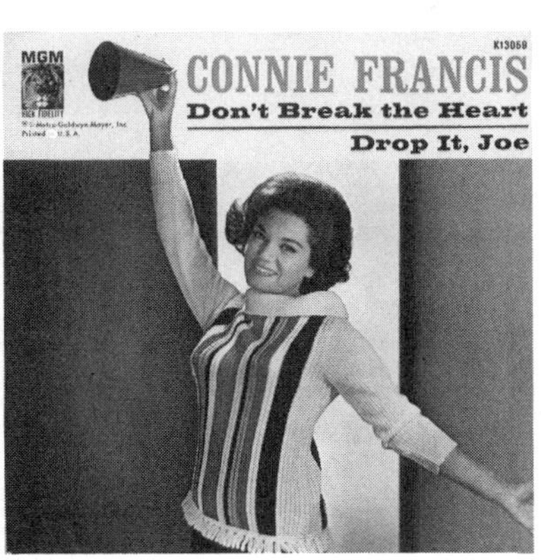

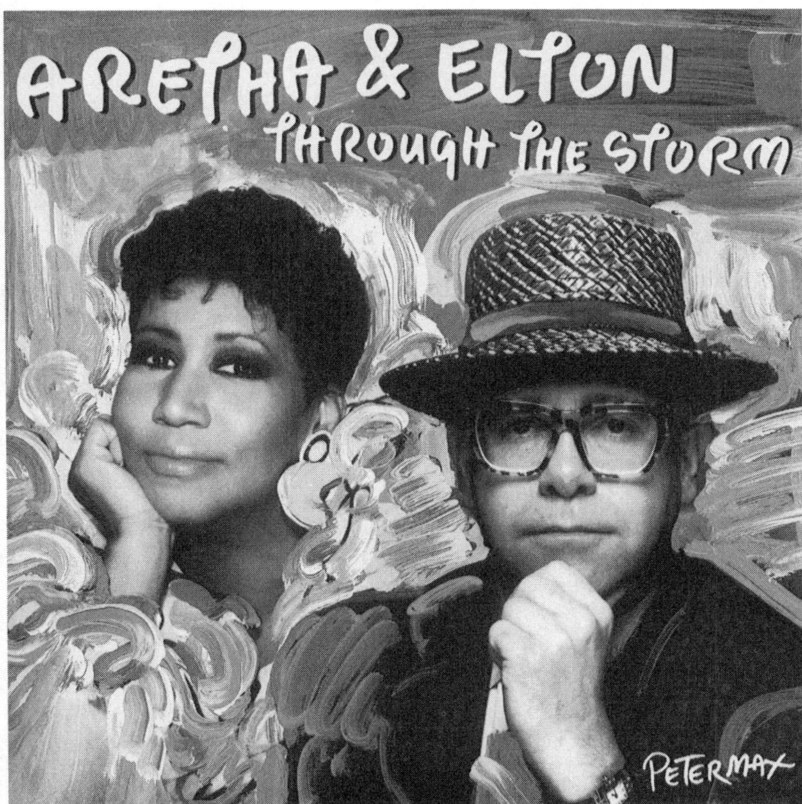

The 4 Seasons were massive hit-makers, with 15 top-10 hits and 15 others also in the Top 40 between 1962 and 1976. At one point viewed by the Beach Boys as their "East Coast competition," Frankie Valli and company matched California's finest in terms of gold singles, too. Each had only two—the Four Seasons with "Rag Doll" and "Who Loves You," and the Beach Boys with "I Get Around" and "Good Vibrations."

Samantha Fox was a British former nude model who charted with such hits as "Touch Me (I Want Your Body)" and "Naughty Girls (Need Love Too)" in the late 80s. Ironically, an American woman with the same name had become famous as a porno actress earlier in the decade.

Peter Frampton's life has taken a bizarre series of twists and turns. A teen star in 60s U.K. group the Herd, he departed to form Humble Pie with former Small Faces member Steve Marriott, left them in 1971 for a solo career that exploded five years later with *Frampton Comes Alive!*, saw that career eventually falter, and, by 1990, was again recording with Marriott.

Connie Francis had a No. 36 hit with "God Bless America" in 1959—effectively beating Whitney Houston's version of the "Star-Spangled Banner" to the patriotic punch by more than 30 years.

Aretha Franklin & Elton John's 1989 hit "Through The Storm" was one of many non-stop collaborations the Queen of Soul undertook in the 80s, and it didn't stop there: In 1991, during a guest shot on "Murphy Brown," Franklin sang her 1967 top-10 hit "A Natural Woman (You Make Me Feel Like)" with a purposely off-key Candice Bergen.

DATE	POS	WKS	ARTIST—RECORD TITLE	LABEL & NO.
3/05/66	**16**	8	2. Baby Scratch My Back [I]	Excello 2273
			HARRIET	
			Harriet Roberts, native of Sheffield, England.	
4/13/91	**39**	1	1. Temple Of Love	East West 98863#
			HARRIS, Betty	
			Born in 1943 in Orlando, Florida. Worked as maid to Big Maybelle, later brought on stage for duets with Maybelle. Worked as road manager for James Carr.	
10/26/63	**23**	6	1. Cry To Me	Jubilee 5456
			HARRIS, Eddie	
			Born on 10/20/36 in Chicago. Jazz tenor saxophonist/vocalist.	
5/29/61	**36**	3	1. Exodus [I] jazz version of the main theme from the film of the same title	Vee-Jay 378
			HARRIS, Emmylou	
			Born on 4/02/47 in Birmingham, Alabama. Contemporary country vocalist. Sang backup with Gram Parsons until his death in 1973. Own band from 1975.	
4/11/81	**37**	3	1. Mister Sandman	Warner 49684
			HARRIS, Major	
			Born on 2/09/47 in Richmond, Virginia. Soul singer. With The Jarmels, Teenagers, and Impacts in the early 1960s. With The Delfonics from 1971-74.	
4/19/75	**5**	14	● **1. Love Won't Let Me Wait**	Atlantic 3248
			HARRIS, Richard	
			Born on 10/01/30 in Limerick, Ireland. Began prolific acting career in 1958. Portrayed King Arthur in the long-running stage production and film version of *Camelot*.	
5/25/68	**2**(1)	10	**1. MacArthur Park**	Dunhill 4134
			HARRIS, Rolf	
			Born in Perth, Australia on 3/30/30. Played piano from age nine. Moved to England in the mid-1950s. Developed his unique "wobble board sound" out of a sheet of masonite. Had own BBC-TV series from 1970.	
6/22/63	**3**	9	**1. Tie Me Kangaroo Down, Sport [N]**	Epic 9596
			HARRIS, Sam	
			Winner of TV's "Star Search" male vocalist category in 1984.	
11/03/84	**36**	3	1. Sugar Don't Bite	Motown 1743
			HARRIS, Thurston	
			Born on 7/11/31 in Indianapolis. First recorded with the Lamplighters in 1953. Died of a heart attack on 4/14/90.	
10/28/57	**6**	13	**1. Little Bitty Pretty One** Best Seller #6 / Top 100 #6 / Jockey #12 vocal backing: The Sharps	Aladdin 3398
			HARRISON, George	
			Born on 2/25/43 in Liverpool, England. Formed his first group, the Rebels, at age 13. Joined John Lennon and Paul McCartney in The Quarrymen in 1958; group later evolved into The Beatles, with Harrison as lead guitarist. Organized the Bangla-Desh benefit concerts at Madison Square Garden in 1971. Member of the 1988 supergroup Traveling Wilburys.	
12/05/70	**1**(4)	13	● **1. My Sweet Lord/**	
		13	2. Isn't It A Pity	Apple 2995

DATE	POS	WKS	ARTIST—RECORD TITLE	LABEL & NO.
3/06/71	**10**	8	**3. What Is Life**	Apple 1828
8/28/71	**23**	5	4. Bangla-Desh	Apple 1836
5/26/73	**1**(1)	11	**5. Give Me Love (Give Me Peace On Earth)**	Apple 1862
12/14/74+	**15**	6	6. Dark Horse	Apple 1877
2/01/75	**36**	2	7. Ding Dong; Ding Dong	Apple 1879
10/11/75	**20**	6	8. You	Apple 1884
12/11/76+	**25**	7	9. This Song	Dark Horse 8294
2/12/77	**19**	7	10. Crackerbox Palace	Dark Horse 8313
3/31/79	**16**	8	11. Blow Away	Dark Horse 8763
5/23/81	**2**(3)	11	**12. All Those Years Ago**	Dark Horse 49725
11/14/87+	**1**(1)	15	**13. Got My Mind Set On You** originally recorded by James Ray in 1962 (Dynamic Sound 503)	Dark Horse 28178
2/27/88	**23**	6	14. When We Was Fab	Dark Horse 28131
			HARRISON, Wilbert R&B singer. Born on 1/05/29 in Charlotte, North Carolina. Plays several instruments as a one-man band. Joined W.C. Baker band. First recorded for Glades in 1952.	
4/27/59	**1**(2)	12	**1. Kansas City**	Fury 1023
1/24/70	**32**	4	2. Let's Work Together (Part 1)	Sue 11
			HART, Corey Born in Montreal, Canada and raised in Spain and Mexico. Singer/songwriter/keyboardist.	
6/23/84	**7**	15	**1. Sunglasses At Night**	EMI America 8203
10/20/84	**17**	9	2. It Ain't Enough	EMI America 8236
6/22/85	**3**	14	**3. Never Surrender**	EMI America 8268
10/05/85	**26**	6	4. Boy In The Box	EMI America 8287
12/28/85+	**30**	7	5. Everything In My Heart	EMI America 8300
10/11/86	**18**	7	6. I Am By Your Side	EMI America 8348
1/31/87	**24**	5	7. Can't Help Falling In Love	EMI America 8368
7/23/88	**38**	2	8. In Your Soul	EMI-Man. 50134
4/21/90	**37**	2	9. A Little Love	EMI 50239#
			HART, Freddie Born Fred Segrest on 12/21/26 in Lochapoka, Alabama. Country singer/songwriter/guitarist.	
9/25/71	**17**	12	● 1. Easy Loving	Capitol 3115
			HARTMAN, Dan Multi-instrumentalist/songwriter/producer from Harrisburg, Pennsylvania. Member of the Edgar Winter Group from 1972-76. Own studio called the Schoolhouse in Westport, Connecticut.	
12/02/78+	**29**	7	● 1. Instant Replay	Blue Sky 2772
6/02/84	**6**	16	**2. I Can Dream About You** from the film *Streets of Fire*	MCA 52378
11/03/84	**25**	9	3. We Are The Young	MCA 52471
3/23/85	**39**	2	4. Second Nature	MCA 52519
			HARVEY & THE MOONGLOWS — see MOONGLOWS	
			HATHAWAY, Donny — see FLACK, Roberta	

DATE	POS	WKS	ARTIST—RECORD TITLE	LABEL & NO.
			HAVENS, Richie	
			Born on 1/21/41 in Brooklyn. Black folk singer/guitarist. Opening act of 1969 Woodstock concert.	
4/24/71	**16**	9	1. Here Comes The Sun	Stormy F. 656
			written by George Harrison (on Beatles' *Abbey Road* album)	
			HAWKINS, Dale	
			Born Delmar Allen Hawkins on 8/22/38 in Goldmine, Louisiana. Rockabilly singer/guitarist. Toured with R&B package shows. Record production work since 1965.	
7/01/57	**27**	5	1. Susie-Q	Checker 863
			Best Seller #27 / Top 100 #29	
10/13/58	**32**	3	2. La-Do-Dada	Checker 900
			Hot 100 #32 / Best Seller #44 end	
			HAWKINS, Edwin, Singers	
			Hawkins (b: August 1943) formed gospel group with Betty Watson in Oakland in 1967 as the Northern California State Youth Choir. Member Dorothy Morrison went on to a solo career.	
5/03/69	**4**	9	• **1. Oh Happy Day**	Pavilion 20001
			THE EDWIN HAWKINS' SINGERS featuring DOROTHY COMBS MORRISON	
5/16/70	**6**	14	**2. Lay Down (Candles In The Rain)**	Buddah 167
			MELANIE with THE EDWIN HAWKINS SINGERS	
			HAWKINS, Ronnie	
			Born on 1/10/35 in Huntsville, Arkansas. Formed The Hawks in 1952. To Canada in 1958. Assembled group later known as The Band.	
9/21/59	**26**	7	1. Mary Lou	Roulette 4177
			HAWLEY, Deane	
7/04/60	**29**	5	1. Look For A Star	Dore 554
			from the film *Circus of Horrors*	
			HAYES, Bill	
			Born on 6/05/26 in Harvey, Illinois. Bill was a regular on Sid Caesar's TV series "Your Show of Shows." Played Doug Williams on the TV soap opera "Days of Our Lives."	
2/26/55	**1**(5)	20	**1. The Ballad Of Davy Crockett**	Cadence 1256
			Best Seller #1(5) / Jockey #1(3) / Juke Box #1(3)	
2/16/57	**33**	3	2. Wringle, Wrangle	ABC-Para. 9785
			from the film *Westward Ho, The Wagons*	
			HAYES, Isaac	
			Born on 8/20/42 in Covington, Tennessee. Soul singer/songwriter/keyboardist/producer/actor. Session musician for Otis Redding and other artists on the Stax label. Teamed with songwriter David Porter to compose "Soul Man," "Hold On! I'm A Comin' " and many others. Composed film scores for *Shaft*, *Tough Guys* and *Truck Turner*.	
9/27/69	**37**	4	1. By The Time I Get To Phoenix/	
10/18/69	**30**	5	2. Walk On By	Enterprise 9003
6/12/71	**22**	5	3. Never Can Say Goodbye	Enterprise 9031
10/23/71	**1**(2)	12	**4. Theme From Shaft**	Enterprise 9038
			from the Richard Roundtree film *Shaft*	
3/25/72	**30**	5	5. Do Your Thing	Enterprise 9042
12/02/72	**38**	2	6. Theme From The Men [I]	Enterprise 9058

DATE	POS	WKS	ARTIST—RECORD TITLE	LABEL & NO.
			from the ABC-TV series "The Men"	
1/12/74	**30**	5	7. Joy - Pt. I	Enterprise 9085
12/08/79+	**18**	12	8. Don't Let Go	Polydor 2011
			HAYMAN, Richard, and JAN AUGUST	
			Hayman: born on 3/27/20 in Cambridge, Massachusetts. Conductor/arranger/harmonica soloist. August: pianist; died on 1/17/76.	
2/11/56	**11**	11	1. A Theme from "The Three Penny Opera" (Moritat) [I]	Mercury 70781
			Jockey #11 / Top 100 #12 / Best Seller #13 / Juke Box #13	
			HAYWOOD, Leon	
			Born on 2/11/42 in Houston. Soul singer/keyboardist. With Big Jay McNeely & Sam Cooke in early '60s.	
11/01/75	**15**	8	1. I Want'a Do Something Freaky To You	20th Century 2228
			HAZLEWOOD, Lee — see SINATRA, Nancy	
			HEAD, Murray	
			British singer/actor. Appeared on the 1970 rock concept LP *Jesus Christ Superstar*. Played juvenile lead in 1971 film *Sunday, Bloody Sunday*.	
5/08/71	**14**	8	1. Superstar	Decca 32603
			with The Trinidad Singers; from *Jesus Christ Superstar-A Rock Opera*	
3/23/85	**3**	13	**2. One Night In Bangkok**	RCA 13988
			from the Tim Rice, Benny Andersson and Bjorn Ulvaeus musical project *Chess*	
			HEAD, Roy	
			Born on 1/09/43 in Three Rivers, Texas. Rock-country singer/guitarist.	
9/18/65	**2**(2)	9	**1. Treat Her Right**	Back Beat 546
			ROY HEAD AND THE TRAITS	
12/04/65	**39**	1	2. Just A Little Bit	Scepter 12116
12/18/65	**32**	2	3. Apple Of My Eye	Back Beat 555
			ROY HEAD AND THE TRAITS	
			HEALEY, Jeff, Band	
			Toronto-based, blues-rock trio: vocalist/guitarist Healey with drummer Tom Stephen and bassist Joe Rockman. Healey, blind since age one and guitarist since three, appeared in the 1989 film *Road House*.	
7/22/89	**5**	13	**1. Angel Eyes**	Arista 9808
			HEART	
			Rock band formed in Seattle in 1973. Originally known as The Army, then White Heart, shortened to Heart in 1974. Group features Ann Wilson (lead singer) and her sister Nancy (guitar, keyboards). Band moved to Vancouver, Canada in 1975 when their manager Mike Fisher was drafted, and signed with the new Mushroom label. When amnesty was declared, group returned to Seattle and signed with the CBS Portrait label in 1976. Band's original guitarist Roger Fisher (brother of Mike) left band in 1979; joined Alias in 1990. In addition to the Wilson sisters, the lineup since 1982 includes guitarist Howard Leese, bassist Mark Andes (ex-Spirit, Jo Jo Gunne and Firefall member) and drummer Denny Carmassi (ex-Gamma).	
5/29/76	**35**	2	1. Crazy On You	Mushroom 7021
			re-charted in 1978 (POS 62)	
9/04/76	**9**	14	**2. Magic Man**	Mushroom 7011
7/02/77	**11**	12	3. Barracuda	Portrait 70004
5/13/78	**24**	7	4. Heartless	Mushroom 7031

DATE	POS	WKS	ARTIST—RECORD TITLE	LABEL & NO.
10/28/78	**15**	10	5. Straight On	Portrait 70020
3/17/79	**34**	3	6. Dog & Butterfly	Portrait 70025
3/15/80	**33**	4	7. Even It Up	Epic 50847
11/29/80+	**8**	11	**8. Tell It Like It Is**	Epic 50950
6/19/82	**33**	4	9. This Man Is Mine	Epic 02925
6/29/85	**10**	12	**10. What About Love?**	Capitol 5481
10/05/85	**4**	14	**11. Never**	Capitol 5512
2/01/86	**1**(1)	13	**12. These Dreams**	Capitol 5541
5/03/86	**10**	10	**13. Nothin' At All**	Capitol 5572
5/23/87	**1**(3)	15	**14. Alone**	Capitol 44002
8/29/87	**7**	11	**15. Who Will You Run To**	Capitol 44040
11/28/87+	**12**	11	16. There's The Girl	Capitol 44089
4/14/90	**2**(2)	13	● **17. All I Wanna Do Is Make Love To You**	Capitol 44507
7/14/90	**23**	7	18. I Didn't Want To Need You	Capitol 44553
10/20/90	**13**	13	19. Stranded	Capitol 44621#
			HEATHERTON, Joey	
			Born on 9/14/44 in Rockville Centre, New York. Movie/TV actress.	
7/15/72	**24**	7	1. Gone	MGM 14387
			HEATWAVE	
			Multinational, interracial group formed in Germany by brothers Johnnie and Keith Wilder of Dayton, Ohio. Johnnie became a paraplegic due to a car accident in 1979.	
8/27/77	**2**(2)	17	▲ **1. Boogie Nights**	Epic 50370
2/04/78	**18**	11	● 2. Always And Forever	Epic 50490
6/03/78	**7**	11	● **3. The Groove Line**	Epic 50524
			HEAVY D. & THE BOYZ	
			Rap quartet from Mt. Vernon, New York: leader Heavy D. (Dwight Meyers), G. Whiz (Glen Parrish), Trouble T-Roy (Troy Dixon) and DJ Eddie F (Edward Ferrell). Dixon died on 7/15/90 (age 22) from an accidental fall in Indianapolis.	
7/20/91	**11**	15	● 1. Now That We Found Love	Uptown 54090#
			HEBB, Bobby	
			Born on 7/26/41 in Nashville. Singer/songwriter/multi-instrumentalist. Featured on the "Grand Ole Opry" at age 12. His brother Hal was a member of the Marigolds.	
7/23/66	**2**(2)	11	● **1. Sunny**	Philips 40365
11/05/66	**39**	1	2. A Satisfied Mind	Philips 40400
			HEFTI, Neal	
			Born on 10/29/22 in Hastings, Nebraska. Trumpeter. Gained fame as arranger for Woody Herman (1944-46), Harry James and Count Basie, then as composer of TV themes.	
3/05/66	**35**	4	1. Batman Theme [I] original theme from the "Batman" TV series	RCA 8755
			HELMS, Bobby	
			Born on 8/15/33 in Bloomington, Indiana. Country singer/guitarist. Appeared on father's local TV show.	
10/14/57	**7**	15	**1. My Special Angel** Best Seller #7 / Top 100 #7 / Jockey #8 with the Anita Kerr Singers	Decca 30423

DATE	POS	WKS	ARTIST—RECORD TITLE	LABEL & NO.
10/14/57	**36**	2	2. Fraulein Top 100 #36 / Best Seller #46	Decca 30194
12/23/57	**6**	4	**3. Jingle Bell Rock** **[X]** Top 100 #6 / Best Seller #7 / Jockey #11	Decca 30513
12/28/58	**35**	1	4. Jingle Bell Rock [X-R]	Decca 30513
12/26/60	**36**	1	5. Jingle Bell Rock [X-R]	Decca 30513
			HENDERSON, Joe	
			R&B singer. Born in 1938 in Como, Mississippi and raised in Gary, Indiana. Moved to Nashville in 1958. With the Fairfield Four gospel group. Died in 1966.	
6/02/62	**8**	10	**1. Snap Your Fingers**	Todd 1072
			HENDERSON, Michael — see CONNORS, Norman	
			HENDRICKS, Bobby	
			Born on 2/22/38 in Columbus, Ohio. R&B vocalist. With the Swallows in 1956. First recorded with the Flyers for Atco in 1957. With The Drifters, 1958, then went solo.	
9/01/58	**25**	4	1. Itchy Twitchy Feeling Hot 100 #25 / Best Seller #35 backing vocals: The Coasters	Sue 706
			HENDRIX, Jimi	
			Born on 11/27/42 in Seattle. Died of a drug overdose in London on 9/18/70. Legendary psychedelic-blues guitarist. Began career as a studio guitarist. In 1965 formed own band, Jimmy James & The Blue Flames. Created The Jimi Hendrix Experience in 1966 with Noel Redding on bass and Mitch Mitchell on drums. Formed new group in 1969, Band of Gypsys, with Buddy Miles on drums and Billy Cox on bass.	
9/28/68	**20**	8	1. All Along The Watchtower **THE JIMI HENDRIX EXPERIENCE** written by Bob Dylan	Reprise 0767
			HENHOUSE FIVE PLUS TOO — see STEVENS, Ray	
			HENLEY, Don	
			Born on 7/22/47 in Gilmer, Texas. Singer/songwriter/drummer. Own band, Shiloh, in the early '70s. Worked with Glenn Frey in Linda Ronstadt's backup band, then the two formed the Eagles with Randy Meisner and Bernie Leadon. Went solo in 1982.	
11/07/81+	**6**	15	**1. Leather And Lace** **STEVIE NICKS with DON HENLEY** written for Waylon Jennings and Jessi Colter	Modern 7341
11/13/82+	**3**	14	● **2. Dirty Laundry**	Asylum 69894
12/08/84+	**5**	14	**3. The Boys Of Summer**	Geffen 29141
3/16/85	**9**	11	**4. All She Wants To Do Is Dance**	Geffen 29065
7/06/85	**34**	5	5. Not Enough Love In The World	Geffen 29012
9/21/85	**22**	8	6. Sunset Grill	Geffen 28906
7/08/89	**8**	12	**7. The End Of The Innocence** co-written and produced by Bruce Hornsby (also on piano)	Geffen 22925
11/11/89	**21**	8	8. The Last Worthless Evening	Geffen 22771
3/24/90	**21**	8	9. The Heart Of The Matter	Geffen 19898#

DATE	POS	WKS	ARTIST—RECORD TITLE	LABEL & NO.
			HENRY, Clarence	
			Born on 3/19/37 in Algiers, Louisiana. R&B vocalist/pianist/trombonist. With Bobby Mitchell's R&B band from 1953-55. Nicknamed "Frogman" from hit "Ain't Got No Home."	
1/12/57	**20**	3	1. Ain't Got No Home [N] Best Seller #20 / Top 100 #30	Argo 5259
3/20/61	**4**	11	**2. But I Do** also titled "I Don't Know Why"	Argo 5378
5/29/61	**12**	7	3. You Always Hurt The One You Love #1 hit in 1944 for The Mills Brothers	Argo 5388
			HENSON, Jim	
			Creator of The Muppets, that famous crew of puppets starring in TV's "Sesame Street" and "The Muppet Show," also in the films *The Muppet Movie* and *The Great Muppet Caper.* Jim (b: 9/24/36 in Greenville, Mississippi) was the voice for both Ernie and Kermit. Died of a sudden virus on 5/16/90.	
8/29/70	**16**	7	1. Rubber Duckie [N] **ERNIE**	Columbia 45207
10/20/79	**25**	7	2. Rainbow Connection **KERMIT** from the original soundtrack of *The Muppet Movie*	Atlantic 3610
			HERMAN'S HERMITS	
			Formed in Manchester, England in 1964. Name derived from cartoon character Sherman of TV's *The Bullwinkle Show.* Consisted of Peter "Herman" Noone (b: 11/05/47; vocals), Derek Leckenby and Keith Hopwood (guitars), Karl Green (bass) and Barry Whitwam (drums). First called The Heartbeats. Noone left in 1972 for a solo career; formed Los Angeles-based group The Tremblers in late '70s. Hosts own show on video musical TV channel VH-1.	
11/14/64	**13**	9	1. I'm Into Something Good	MGM 13280
2/20/65	**2**(2)	11	**2. Can't You Hear My Heartbeat**	MGM 13310
4/17/65	**1**(3)	11	* **3. Mrs. Brown You've Got A Lovely Daughter**	MGM 13341
4/17/65	**5**	10	**4. Silhouettes**	MGM 13332
6/05/65	**4**	8	**5. Wonderful World**	MGM 13354
7/10/65	**1**(1)	8	● **6. I'm Henry VIII, I Am** written in 1911; popularized in England by Harry Champion	MGM 13367
9/25/65	**7**	8	**7. Just A Little Bit Better**	MGM 13398
1/01/66	**8**	8	**8. A Must To Avoid**	MGM 13437
2/26/66	**3**	7	**9. Listen People** from the film *When the Boys Meet the Girls*	MGM 13462
4/16/66	**9**	7	**10. Leaning On The Lamp Post** 8, 10: from the film *Hold On!*	MGM 13500
7/23/66	**12**	5	11. This Door Swings Both Ways	MGM 13548
10/15/66	**5**	8	**12. Dandy** written by Ray Davies of The Kinks	MGM 13603
12/24/66	**27**	5	13. East West	MGM 13639
3/04/67	**4**	9	● **14. There's A Kind Of Hush/**	
3/18/67	**35**	4	15. No Milk Today	MGM 13681
7/08/67	**18**	4	16. Don't Go Out Into The Rain (You're Going To Melt)	MGM 13761
9/16/67	**39**	2	17. Museum	MGM 13787
2/03/68	**22**	6	18. I Can Take Or Leave Your Loving	MGM 13885

DATE	POS	WKS	ARTIST—RECORD TITLE	LABEL & NO.
			all of above: produced by Mickie Most	
			HERNANDEZ, Patrick	
			Rock-disco singer. Born in 1949 in Paris of a Spanish father and Austrian/Italian mother.	
8/04/79	**16**	11	● 1. Born To Be Alive	Columbia 10986
			HESITATIONS, The	
			Soul group from Cleveland. Lead singer George "King" Scott was accidentally killed by a bullet from a gun owned by tenor Fred Deal in February 1968.	
2/17/68	**38**	2	1. Born Free from the film of the same title	Kapp 878
			HEYWOOD, Eddie	
			Born on 12/04/15 in Atlanta; died on 1/02/89. Black jazz pianist/composer/arranger. Played professionally by age 14. Own band in New York City in 1941. Worked with Billie Holiday. To the West Coast in 1947, with own trio. Active into the '70s. Recorded duet with conductor Hugo Winterhalter (b: 8/15/09; d: 9/17/73 of cancer).	
7/21/56	**11**	18	1. Soft Summer Breeze [I] Best Seller #11 / Top 100 #12 / Juke Box #13 / Jockey #14	Mercury 70863
7/28/56	**2**(2)	23	**2. Canadian Sunset** [I] **HUGO WINTERHALTER/EDDIE HEYWOOD** Top 100 #2 / Jockey #2 / Best Seller #3 / Juke Box #3	RCA 6537
			HIBBLER, Al	
			Born on 8/16/15 in Little Rock, Arkansas. Blind since birth, studied voice at Little Rock's Conservatory for the Blind. First recorded with Jay McShann for Decca in 1942. With Duke Ellington, 1943-51. Also recorded with Harry Carney, Tab Smith, Mercer Ellington and Billy Strayhorn.	
4/09/55	**3**	19	**1. Unchained Melody** Jockey #3 / Juke Box #3 / Best Seller #5 from the film *Unchained*	Decca 29441
10/15/55	**4**	22	**2. He** Best Seller #4 / Top 100 #7 / Jockey #7 / Juke Box #8	Decca 29660
2/25/56	**21**	5	3. 11th Hour Melody	Decca 29789
7/14/56	**22**	2	4. Never Turn Back Jockey #22 / Top 100 #48	Decca 29950
8/25/56	**10**	12	**5. After The Lights Go Down Low** Jockey #10 / Juke Box #14 / Top 100 #15 / Best Seller #20	Decca 29982
			HI-FIVE	
			Teen vocal quintet from Waco, Texas and Oklahoma City: Tony Thompson, Roderick Clark, Russell Neal, Marcus Sanders and Toriano Easley (left in late 1990).	
3/16/91	**1**(1)	17	● **1. I Like The Way (The Kissing Game)** written and produced by Teddy Riley of Guy	Jive 1424#
7/13/91	**8**	13	**2. I Can't Wait Another Minute**	Jive 1445#
			HIGGINS, Bertie	
			Singer/songwriter. Born in 1946 in Tarpon Springs, Florida. First recorded for ABC in 1964. Worked as a drummer with the Roemans from 1964-66.	
1/16/82	**8**	17	**1. Key Largo** inspired by the Bogart/Bacall film of the same title	Kat Family 02524

DATE	POS	WKS	ARTIST—RECORD TITLE	LABEL & NO.
			HIGH INERGY	
			Female soul group from Pasadena, California: sisters Barbara and Vernessa Mitchell, Linda Howard and Michelle Rumph. Vernessa left in 1978; group continued as a trio.	
11/19/77	**12**	11	1. You Can't Turn Me Off (In The Middle Of Turning Me On)	Gordy 7155
			HIGHLIGHTS, The	
			Male vocal quintet formed at DePaul University, Chicago: Frank Pizani (lead), Frank Calzaretta and his brother Tony, Bill Melshimer and Jerry Oleski.	
11/10/56	**19**	5	1. City Of Angels Best Seller #19 / Top 100 #30	Bally 1016
			HIGHWAYMEN, The	
			Folk quintet formed at Wesleyan University in Middletown, Connecticut: Dave Fisher, Bob Burnett, Steve Trott, Steve Butts and Chan Daniels (d: 8/02/75).	
7/31/61	**1**(2)	11	**1. Michael** 19th century folk song ("Michael Row The Boat Ashore")	United Art. 258
12/25/61+	**13**	13	2. Cotton Fields traditional American ballad, copyrighted in 1850	United Art. 370
			HILL, Bunker	
			Born David Walker on 5/05/41 in Washington, D.C. Professional boxer. Ex-lead singer of the gospel group Mighty Clouds Of Joy.	
10/13/62	**33**	3	1. Hide & Go Seek, Part I	Mala 451
			HILL, Dan	
			Born on 6/03/54 in Toronto. Author/singer/songwriter.	
12/24/77+	**3**	15	● **1. Sometimes When We Touch**	20th Century 2355
7/25/87	**6**	13	**2. Can't We Try** **DAN HILL with VONDA SHEPPARD**	Columbia 07050
			HILL, Jessie	
			Born on 12/09/32 in New Orleans. R&B singer/drummer/pianist. With Huey Smith to 1958.	
5/09/60	**28**	4	1. Ooh Poo Pah Doo - Part II [I]	Minit 607
			HILLSIDE SINGERS, The	
			Nine-member vocal group assembled by producer/arranger Al Ham.	
12/11/71+	**13**	10	1. I'd Like To Teach The World To Sing (In Perfect Harmony) adapted from a Coca-Cola jingle	Metromedia 231
			HILLTOPPERS, The	
			Quartet formed at Western Kentucky College in Bowling Green, Kentucky in 1952. Group named after the school's nickname. Consisted of Jimmy Sacca (lead singer), Don McGuire, Seymour Spiegelman and Billy Vaughn. Vaughn left in 1955 to become Dot's musical director with a recording career of his own.	
			THE HILLTOPPERS featuring JIMMY SACCA:	
7/30/55	**20**	4	1. The Kentuckian Song Best Seller #20 from the Burt Lancaster film *The Kentuckian*	Dot 15375
11/12/55	**8**	13	**2. Only You (And You Alone)** Jockey #8 / Top 100 #9 / Juke Box #10 / Best Seller #16	Dot 15423
1/21/56	**31**	1	3. My Treasure	Dot 15437

DATE	POS	WKS	ARTIST—RECORD TITLE	LABEL & NO.
10/06/56	**38**	2	4. Ka-Ding-Dong	Dot 15489
2/09/57	**3**	13	**5. Marianne** Juke Box #3 / Jockey #6 / Top 100 #8 / Best Seller #12	Dot 15537
11/25/57	**22**	4	6. The Joker (That's What They Call Me) Jockey #22 / Best Seller #34 / Top 100 #37	Dot 15662
			HINTON, Joe	
			Soul singer, born in 1929; died on 8/13/68 in Boston. With Chosen Gospel Singers. Lead singer of the Spirits Of Memphis gospel group.	
9/05/64	**13**	9	1. Funny	Back Beat 541
			HIPSWAY	
			Scottish quartet led by vocalist Grahame Skinner. Bassist John McElhone (ex-Altered Images) later joined the group Texas.	
3/14/87	**19**	6	1. The Honeythief	Columbia 06579
			HIRT, Al	
			Born Alois Maxwell Hirt on 11/07/22 in New Orleans. Trumpet virtuoso. Toured with Jimmy and Tommy Dorsey, Ray McKinley and Horace Heidt. Formed own Dixieland combo (with Pete Fountain) in the late 1950s.	
1/25/64	**4**	13	**1. Java** **[I]**	RCA 8280
5/02/64	**15**	8	2. Cotton Candy [I]	RCA 8346
8/01/64	**30**	4	3. Sugar Lips [I]	RCA 8391
			HODGES, Eddie	
			Born on 3/05/47 in Hattiesburg, Mississippi. Played Frank Sinatra's son in the film *A Hole in the Head*.	
7/24/61	**12**	8	1. I'm Gonna Knock On Your Door	Cadence 1397
7/07/62	**14**	8	2. (Girls, Girls, Girls) Made To Love written by Phil Everly (of The Everly Brothers)	Cadence 1421
			HOFFS, Susanna	
			Former lead singer of The Bangles. Born on 1/17/57. Starred in 1987 film *The Allnighter*. Her mother is film director Tamara Hoffs.	
3/02/91	**30**	4	1. My Side Of The Bed	Columbia 73529#
			HOLDEN, Ron	
			Born on 8/07/39 in Seattle. R&B vocalist. In group The Playboys in 1957. Worked as emcee at Art Laboe's "Oldies But Goodies" club from 1972-77.	
4/25/60	**7**	13	**1. Love You So** instrumental backing by The Thunderbirds	Donna 1315
			HOLLAND, Amy	
			Daughter of country singer Esmereldy and opera singer Harry Boersma. Married to singer/keyboardist Michael McDonald (The Doobie Brothers).	
9/13/80	**22**	6	1. How Do I Survive produced by Michael McDonald	Capitol 4884
			HOLLAND, Eddie	
			Born on 10/30/39 in Detroit. Singer/songwriter/producer. Member of Motown's hit production trio with brother Brian Holland and Lamont Dozier; wrote many of Motown's greatest hits. Co-founder of the Invictus/Hot Wax label. Holland-Dozier-Holland were inducted into the Rock & Roll Hall of Fame in 1990.	
3/10/62	**30**	4	1. Jamie	Motown 1021

DATE	POS	WKS	ARTIST—RECORD TITLE	LABEL & NO.
			HOLLIDAY, Jennifer	
			Born on 10/19/60 in Riverside, Texas. Won 1982 Tony award for best actress in Broadway's *Dreamgirls.* Also in Broadway's *Your Arm's Too Short to Box with God* (1978) and *Sing, Mahalia Sing* (1985).	
7/31/82	**22**	7	1. And I Am Telling You I'm Not Going	Geffen 29983
			from the original Broadway cast *Dreamgirls*	
			HOLLIES, The	
			Formed in Manchester, England in 1962. Consisted of Allan Clarke (lead vocals), Graham Nash and Tony Hicks (guitars), Eric Haydock (bass) and Don Rathbone (drums). Clarke and Nash had worked as a duo, the Guytones, added other members, became the Fourtones, Deltas, then The Hollies. First recorded for Parlophone in 1963. Rathbone left in 1963, replaced by Bobby Elliott. Haydock left in 1966, replaced by Bernie Calvert (first heard on "Bus Stop"). Nash left in December 1968 to join David Crosby and Stephen Stills in new trio, replaced by Terry Sylvester, formerly in the Swinging Blue Jeans. Shuffling personnel since then. Clarke, Nash, Hicks and Elliott regrouped briefly in 1983.	
1/08/66	**32**	4	1. Look Through Any Window	Imperial 66134
8/20/66	**5**	9	**2. Bus Stop**	Imperial 66186
11/12/66	**7**	7	**3. Stop Stop Stop**	Imperial 66214
4/15/67	**11**	9	4. On A Carousel	Imperial 66231
6/24/67	**28**	3	5. Pay You Back With Interest	Imperial 66240
7/08/67	**9**	10	**6. Carrie-Anne**	Epic 10180
5/18/68	**40**	1	7. Jennifer Eccles	Epic 10298
2/07/70	**7**	11	**8. He Ain't Heavy, He's My Brother**	Epic 10532
7/08/72	**2**(2)	13	• **9. Long Cool Woman (In A Black Dress)**	Epic 10871
12/02/72	**26**	5	10. Long Dark Road	Epic 10920
6/08/74	**6**	11	• **11. The Air That I Breathe**	Epic 11100
			all of above produced by Ron Richards	
7/02/83	**29**	6	12. Stop In The Name Of Love	Atlantic 89819
			HOLLOWAY, Brenda	
			Born on 6/21/46 in Atascadero, California. Soul singer/songwriter. Later a backup singer for Joe Cocker.	
5/23/64	**13**	6	1. Every Little Bit Hurts	Tamla 54094
3/27/65	**25**	5	2. When I'm Gone	Tamla 54111
			written and produced by Smokey Robinson	
11/04/67	**39**	1	3. You've Made Me So Very Happy	Tamla 54155
			HOLLY, Buddy/The Crickets	
			Born Charles Hardin Holley on 9/07/36 in Lubbock, Texas. Began recording western and bop demos with Bob Montgomery in 1954. Signed to Decca label in January 1956 and recorded in Nashville as Buddy Holly & The Three Tunes (Sonny Curtis, lead guitar; Don Guess, bass; and Jerry Ivan Allison, drums). In February 1957, Buddy assembled his backing group, The Crickets (Allison; Niki Sullivan, rhythm guitar; and Joe B. Mauldin, bass) for recordings at Norman Petty's studio in Clovis, New Mexico. Signed to Brunswick and Coral labels (subsidiaries of Decca Records). Because of contract arrangements, all Brunswick records were released as The Crickets and all Coral records were released as Buddy Holly. Holly split from The Crickets in autumn of 1958. Buddy, Ritchie Valens and the Big Bopper were killed in a plane crash near Mason City, Iowa on 2/03/59 (age 22). Holly was inducted into the Rock and Roll Hall of Fame in 1986.	
8/19/57	**1**(1)	16	• **1. That'll Be The Day** *	Brunswick 55009
			Best Seller #1 / Top 100 #3 / Jockey #3 different version released on Decca 30434 in September 1957 as by Buddy Holly And The Three Tunes (recorded July 1956)	

DATE	POS	WKS	ARTIST—RECORD TITLE	LABEL & NO.
11/11/57	**3**	16	**2. Peggy Sue** Best Seller #3 / Top 100 #3 / Jockey #3 first known as "Cindy Lou"; renamed after Allison's girlfriend	Coral 61885
12/02/57+	**10**	13	**3. Oh, Boy!** **THE CRICKETS** Top 100 #10 / Best Seller #11 / Jockey #20	Brunswick 55035
3/10/58	**17**	8	4. Maybe Baby **THE CRICKETS** Jockey #17 / Best Seller #18 / Top 100 #18	Brunswick 55053
6/09/58	**37**	2	5. Rave On Top 100 #37 / Best Seller #41	Coral 61985
8/04/58	**27**	4	6. Think It Over **THE CRICKETS** Hot 100 #27 / Best Seller #38	Brunswick 55072
8/11/58	**32**	4	7. Early In The Morning Hot 100 #32 / Best Seller #45	Coral 62006
3/09/59	**13**	9	8. It Doesn't Matter Anymore written by Paul Anka	Coral 62074
			HOLLYWOOD ARGYLES Gary Paxton recorded "Alley-Oop" as a solo artist; since he was still under contract to Brent Records, where he recorded as Flip of "Skip & Flip," he made up the name of the Hollywood Argyles. After the song was a hit, Gary assembled a Hollywood Argyles group. Formed Garpax Records. Gary is now a gospel artist.	
6/13/60	**1**(1)	12	**1. Alley-Oop** **[N]** written by Dallas Frazier	Lute 5905
			HOLLYWOOD FLAMES Los Angeles-based R&B group formed in 1950 by Bobby Byrd (aka Bobby Day). Known also as The Flames, Four Flames, Hollywood Four Flames, and The Satellites. Earl Nelson was lead singer in 1957.	
12/02/57+	**11**	12	1. Buzz-Buzz-Buzz Top 100 #11 / Best Seller #12 lead vocal: Earl Nelson (of Bob & Earl)	Ebb 119
			HOLMAN, Eddie Born on 6/03/46 in Norfolk, Virginia. Soul singer/songwriter. Recorded for Leopard in the early 1960s.	
1/10/70	**2**(1)	12	● **1. Hey There Lonely Girl** recorded in 1963 by Ruby & The Romantics as "Hey There Lonely Boy"	ABC 11240
			HOLMES, Clint Born on 5/09/46 in Bournemouth, England. Moved to Buffalo, New York as a child.	
5/05/73	**2**(2)	15	● **1. Playground In My Mind** child's vocal is by producer Paul Vance's son, Philip	Epic 10891
			HOLMES, Rupert Born on 2/24/47 in Cheshire, England. Moved to New York at age six. Member of studio group Street People. Wrote and arranged for The Drifters, The Platters and Gene Pitney. Arranged/produced for Barbra Streisand. Wrote The Buoys' hit "Timothy" and the Broadway musical *Drood*.	
11/10/79	**1**(3)	16	● **1. Escape (The Pina Colada Song)**	Infinity 50035
2/09/80	**6**	12	**2. Him**	MCA 41173
6/14/80	**32**	3	3. Answering Machine	MCA 41235

DATE	POS	WKS	ARTIST—RECORD TITLE	LABEL & NO.
			HOMBRES, The	
			Memphis foursome: B.B. Cunningham, Gary Wayne McEwen, Johnny Will Hunter and Jerry Lee Masters. All but Masters were members of Ronny & The Daytonas touring band. Hunter died in 1976. Cunningham's brother, Bill, was a member of The Box Tops.	
10/07/67	**12**	10	1. Let It Out (Let It All Hang Out)	Verve Fore. 5058
			HOMER AND JETHRO	
			Henry "Homer" Haynes (b: 7/29/17, Knoxville, Tennessee; d: 8/07/71; guitar) and Kenneth "Jethro" Burns (b: 3/10/23, Knoxville, Tennessee; mandolin). Country music's foremost comedy duo from the 1940s until Homer's death. Jethro went on to work with popular folk singer Steve Goodman.	
9/14/59	**14**	7	1. The Battle Of Kookamonga [C] a parody of "The Battle Of New Orleans"; produced by Chet Atkins	RCA 7585
			HONDELLS, The	
			Southern California-based quartet led by Ritchie Burns.	
10/03/64	**9**	9	**1. Little Honda** written by Brian Wilson of The Beach Boys	Mercury 72324
			HONEYCOMBS, The	
			English rock quintet featuring Dennis d'Ell (lead singer) and Ann "Honey" Lantree (drums).	
10/10/64	**5**	9	**1. Have I The Right?**	Interphon 7707
			HONEY CONE, The	
			Female soul trio formed in Los Angeles in 1969. Consisted of prominent backup singers; Carolyn Willis (member of The Girlfriends and Bob B. Soxx & The Blue Jeans), Edna Wright (sister of Darlene Love) and Shellie Clark (former Ikette and regular on the TV series "The Jim Nabors Hour" from 1969-70).	
5/01/71	**1**(1)	13	● **1. Want Ads**	Hot Wax 7011
8/21/71	**11**	10	● 2. Stick-Up	Hot Wax 7106
12/11/71+	**15**	8	3. One Monkey Don't Stop No Show Part I	Hot Wax 7110
3/25/72	**23**	6	4. The Day I Found Myself	Hot Wax 7113
			HONEYDRIPPERS, The	
			A rock superstar gathering: vocalist Robert Plant (Led Zeppelin), with guitarists Jimmy Page (The Yardbirds, Led Zeppelin), Jeff Beck (The Yardbirds) and Nile Rodgers (Chic).	
10/27/84+	**3**	14	**1. Sea Of Love**	Es Paranza 99701
1/26/85	**25**	6	2. Rockin' At Midnight recorded by Elvis Presley in 1954 as "Good Rockin' Tonight"	Es Paranza 99686
			HONEYMOON SUITE	
			Rock quintet from Toronto: Johnnie Dee (vocals), Derry Grehan, Rob Preuss, Gary Lalonde and Dave Betts.	
4/26/86	**34**	3	1. Feel It Again	Warner 28779
			HOOTERS	
			Philadelphia rock quintet led by Rob Hyman and Eric Bazilian (arrangers/musicians/backing vocalists on Cyndi Lauper's platinum album *She's So Unusual*). Hooter: nickname of their keyboard-harmonica.	
9/28/85	**21**	8	1. And We Danced	Columbia 05568
2/01/86	**18**	7	2. Day By Day	Columbia 05730
5/24/86	**38**	1	3. Where Do The Children Go	Columbia 05854

DATE	POS	WKS	ARTIST—RECORD TITLE	LABEL & NO.
			HOPKIN, Mary	
			Born on 5/03/50 in Pontardawe, Wales. Discovered by the model Twiggy. Married to producer Tony Visconti (worked with David Bowie) from December 1971 to October 1981.	
10/12/68	**2**(3)	12	● **1. Those Were The Days**	Apple 1801
			melody based on a traditional Russian folk song	
5/03/69	**13**	7	2. Goodbye	Apple 1806
			written by John Lennon and Paul McCartney; above 2 produced by Paul McCartney	
3/28/70	**39**	2	3. Temma Harbour	Apple 1816
			HORNE, Jimmy "Bo"	
			Soul singer/dancer from Miami.	
6/24/78	**38**	1	1. Dance Across The Floor	Sunshine S. 1003
			written and produced by Harry "KC" Casey	
			HORNE, Lena	
			Born on 6/30/17 in Brooklyn. Broadway and movie musical star, long-married to bandleader Lennie Hayton. Her career reached a new peak in the early 1980s with her one-woman Broadway show. Won the Lifetime Achievement Grammy in 1989.	
7/09/55	**19**	1	1. Love Me Or Leave Me	RCA 6073
			Jockey #19; #2 hit for Ruth Etting in 1929	
			HORNSBY, Bruce/The Range	
			Singer/pianist/songwriter/leader of jazz-influenced pop quintet The Range. Born on 11/23/54 in Williamsburg, Virginia. Moved to Los Angeles in 1980. Backing pianist for Sheena Easton's touring band, 1983. Formed The Range in 1984 with Joe Puerta (bass), John Molo (drums), guitarists George Marinelli & David Mansfield (replaced by Peter Harris who left by 1990). Won the 1986 Best New Artist Grammy Award.	
10/18/86	**1**(1)	15	**1. The Way It Is**	RCA 5023
1/31/87	**4**	12	**2. Mandolin Rain**	RCA 5087
5/30/87	**14**	9	3. Every Little Kiss [R]	RCA 5165
			remix of their 1986 hit (POS 72)	
5/14/88	**5**	11	**4. The Valley Road**	RCA 7645
8/27/88	**35**	2	5. Look Out Any Window	RCA 8678
7/21/90	**18**	7	6. Across The River	RCA 2621
			HORTON, Johnny	
			Country singer. Born on 4/30/25 in Los Angeles and raised in Tyler, Texas. Married to Billie Jean Jones, widow of country music superstar Hank Williams. Killed in an auto accident on 11/05/60.	
5/04/59	**1**(6)	18	● **1. The Battle Of New Orleans**	Columbia 41339
			original melody written in celebration of the final battle of the War of 1812	
3/14/60	**3**	13	**2. Sink The Bismarck**	Columbia 41568
			inspired by the film of the same title	
10/17/60	**4**	18	**3. North To Alaska**	Columbia 41782
			from the John Wayne film of the same title	
			HOT	
			Interracial female trio consisting of Gwen Owens, Cathy Carson and Juanita Curiel. First known as Sugar & Spice.	
4/02/77	**6**	19	● **1. Angel In Your Arms**	Big Tree 16085

DATE	POS	WKS	ARTIST—RECORD TITLE	LABEL & NO.
			HOT BUTTER	
			Hot Butter is Moog synthesizer player Stan Free.	
8/19/72	**9**	12	**1. Popcorn** [I]	Musicor 1458
			HOT CHOCOLATE	
			Interracial rock-soul group formed in London by lead singer Errol Brown in 1970. Included Harvey Hinsley (guitar), Larry Ferguson (keyboards), Tony Wilson (bass), Patrick Olive (congas) and Tony Connor (drums). Wilson left in 1975, Olive switched to bass.	
3/08/75	**8**	9	**1. Emma**	Big Tree 16031
7/05/75	**28**	4	2. Disco Queen	Big Tree 16038
12/06/75+	**3**	15	● **3. You Sexy Thing**	Big Tree 16047
8/13/77	**31**	5	4. So You Win Again	Big Tree 16096
12/02/78+	**6**	13	● **5. Every 1's A Winner**	Infinity 50002
			HOTLEGS	
			British trio: Eric Stewart (formerly of The Mindbenders), Kevin Godley and Lol Creme. Graham Gouldman joined the group later on tour. Quartet evolved into 10cc.	
9/05/70	**22**	6	1. Neanderthal Man	Capitol 2886
			HOUSTON, David	
			Born on 12/09/38 in Bossier City, Louisiana. Country singer/songwriter/guitarist. Godson of 1920s pop singer Gene Austin and a descendant of Sam Houston and Robert E. Lee.	
8/27/66	**24**	8	1. Almost Persuaded	Epic 10025
			HOUSTON, Thelma	
			Soul singer/actress from Leland, Mississippi. In films *Norman...Is That You?*, *Death Scream* and *The Seventh Dwarf*.	
1/29/77	**1**(1)	17	**1. Don't Leave Me This Way**	Tamla 54278
5/19/79	**34**	3	2. Saturday Night, Sunday Morning	Tamla 54297
			HOUSTON, Whitney	
			Born on 8/09/63 in Newark, New Jersey. Daughter of Cissy Houston and cousin of Dionne Warwick. Began singing career at age 11 with the gospel group New Hope Baptist Junior Choir. As a teen, worked as a backing vocalist for Chaka Khan and Lou Rawls. Pursued modeling career in 1981, appearing in *Glamour* magazine and the cover of *Seventeen*.	
6/01/85	**3**	13	**1. You Give Good Love**	Arista 9274
8/24/85	**1**(1)	15	**2. Saving All My Love For You**	Arista 9381
12/28/85+	**1**(2)	16	**3. How Will I Know**	Arista 9434
4/05/86	**1**(3)	14	**4. Greatest Love Of All**	Arista 9466
			originally released as the B-side of "You Give Good Love"	
5/16/87	**1**(2)	14	▲ **5. I Wanna Dance With Somebody (Who Loves Me)**	Arista 9598
8/08/87	**1**(2)	13	**6. Didn't We Almost Have It All**	Arista 9616
11/07/87+	**1**(1)	14	**7. So Emotional**	Arista 9642
3/05/88	**1**(2)	13	**8. Where Do Broken Hearts Go**	Arista 9674
7/09/88	**9**	11	**9. Love Will Save The Day**	Arista 9720
9/24/88	**5**	11	**10. One Moment In Time**	Arista 9743
			tune used by NBC-TV for the 1988 Summer Olympics	
10/27/90	**1**(1)	14	● **11. I'm Your Baby Tonight**	Arista 2108
1/05/91	**1**(2)	15	● **12. All The Man That I Need**	Arista 2156
3/09/91	**20**	7	● 13. The Star Spangled Banner	Arista 2207

DATE	POS	WKS	ARTIST—RECORD TITLE	LABEL & NO.
			live recording from the National Anthem Ceremony at Super Bowl XXV	
4/27/91	**9**	9	**14. Miracle**	Arista 2222
			HUDSON BROTHERS	
			Bill, Brett and Mark Hudson from Portland. Own TV variety show during the summer of 1974; also hosted kiddie TV show "The Hudson Brothers Razzle Dazzle Comedy Show." Bill was married to actress Goldie Hawn.	
10/26/74	**21**	5	1. So You Are A Star	Casablanca 0108
8/02/75	**26**	4	2. Rendezvous	Rocket 40417
			HUES CORPORATION, The	
			Black vocal trio formed in Los Angeles in 1969: Bernard Henderson, Fleming Williams and H. Ann Kelley. Williams replaced by Tommy Brown after "Rock The Boat." Brown replaced by Karl Russell in 1975.	
6/15/74	**1**(1)	10	● **1. Rock The Boat**	RCA 0232
10/26/74	**18**	5	2. Rockin' Soul	RCA 10066
			HUGH, Grayson	
			Soul-styled white singer/songwriter/pianist from Connecticut.	
8/05/89	**19**	8	1. Talk It Over	RCA 8802
			HUGHES, Fred	
			Soul singer from Arkansas. To Los Angeles, formed own band, the Creators.	
6/19/65	**23**	6	1. Oo Wee Baby, I Love You	Vee-Jay 684
			HUGHES, Jimmy	
			Soul singer from Florence, Alabama. With Singing Clouds gospel group to 1962. Cousin of Percy Sledge.	
7/11/64	**17**	9	1. Steal Away	Fame 6401
			HUGO & LUIGI	
			Producers/songwriters/label executives Hugo Peretti and Luigi Creatore. Owned record labels Roulette and Avco/Embassy. Hugo died on 5/01/86 (age 68).	
1/04/60	**35**	3	1. Just Come Home	RCA 7639
			HUMAN BEINZ, The	
			Cleveland bar band.	
1/06/68	**8**	11	**1. Nobody But Me**	Capitol 5990
			originally recorded (and written) by The Isley Brothers in 1962	
			HUMAN LEAGUE, The	
			Electro-pop band formed in 1977 in Sheffield, England by synthesists Martyn Ware and Ian Craig Marsh and lead singer/synthesist Philip Oakey. Vocalists Joanne Catherall and Susanne Sulley joined in October 1980 when Ware and Marsh left to form Heaven 17.	
4/10/82	**1**(3)	21	● **1. Don't You Want Me**	A&M 2397
7/02/83	**8**	13	**2. (Keep Feeling) Fascination**	A&M 2547
10/29/83	**30**	5	3. Mirror Man	A&M 2587
9/27/86	**1**(1)	15	**4. Human**	A&M 2861
11/03/90	**32**	3	5. Heart Like A Wheel	Virgin/A&M 1520#

DATE	POS	WKS	ARTIST—RECORD TITLE	LABEL & NO.
			HUMPERDINCK, Engelbert	
			Born Arnold George Dorsey on 5/02/36 in Madras, India. To Leicester, England in 1947. First recorded for Decca in 1958. Met Tom Jones' manager, Gordon Mills, in 1965, who suggested his name change to Engelbert Humperdinck (a famous German opera composer). Starred in his own musical variety TV series in 1970.	
4/29/67	**4**	10	**1. Release Me (And Let Me Love Again)**	Parrot 40011
7/15/67	**20**	4	2. There Goes My Everything	Parrot 40015
10/14/67	**25**	5	3. The Last Waltz	Parrot 40019
1/06/68	**18**	7	4. Am I That Easy To Forget	Parrot 40023
6/01/68	**19**	5	5. A Man Without Love	Parrot 40027
11/23/68	**31**	3	6. Les Bicyclettes De Belsize	Parrot 40032
9/27/69	**38**	1	7. I'm A Better Man	Parrot 40040
1/03/70	**16**	8	8. Winter World Of Love	Parrot 40044
11/20/76+	**8**	14	• **9. After The Lovin'**	Epic 50270
			HUMPHREY, Paul/His Cool Aid Chemists	
			Paul was born on 10/12/35 in Detroit. Black session drummer.	
5/15/71	**29**	7	1. Cool Aid [I]	Lizard 21006
			HUNTER, Ivory Joe	
			Born on 10/10/14 in Kirbyville, Texas; died of lung cancer on 11/08/74. R&B singer/songwriter/pianist. First recorded in 1933 (a cylinder record for the Library of Congress). Own radio shows, KFDM-Beaumont, Texas, early '40s. Own record labels, Ivory and Pacific, 1944. Signed by King Records, 1947; MGM, 1950.	
12/01/56	**12**	15	1. Since I Met You Baby Best Seller #12 / Top 100 #12 / Jockey #14 / Juke Box #14	Atlantic 1111
			HUNTER, John	
			Rock singer/keyboardist from Chicago.	
2/16/85	**39**	2	1. Tragedy	Private I 04643
			HUNTER, Tab	
			Born Arthur Andrew Kelm on 7/11/31 in New York City. Sportsman-turned-actor in 1952. Film/TV actor. Appeared in *Island of Desire*, *Damn Yankees*, *Ride The Wild Surf* and *Lust in the Dust*.	
1/19/57	**1**(6)	17	**1. Young Love** Top 100 #1(6) / Jockey #1(6) / Juke Box #1(5) / Best Seller #1(4)	Dot 15533
3/30/57	**11**	8	2. Ninety-Nine Ways Top 100 #11 / Jockey #11 / Best Seller #12 / Juke Box #17 orchestra conducted by Billy Vaughn on above 2	Dot 15548
2/23/59	**31**	4	3. (I'll Be With You In) Apple Blossom Time #2 hit for Charles Harrison in 1920	Warner 5032
			HUSKY, Ferlin	
			Born on 12/03/25 in Flat River, Missouri. Country singer/songwriter/guitarist. Recorded as Terry Preston in the early 1950s; also did humorous recordings as Simon Crum.	
3/09/57	**4**	19	**1. Gone** Top 100 #4 / Jockey #4 / Juke Box #4 / Best Seller #5 originally recorded by Husky in 1952 as by Terry Preston	Capitol 3628
12/26/60+	**12**	13	2. Wings Of A Dove	Capitol 4406

DATE	POS	WKS	ARTIST—RECORD TITLE	LABEL & NO.
			HYLAND, Brian	
			Born on 11/12/43 in Queens, New York. Own group, the Delphis, at age 12. In production company with Del Shannon in 1970.	
7/11/60	**1**(1)	13	**1. Itsy Bitsy Teenie Weenie Yellow Polkadot Bikini** [N]	Kapp 342
			first released on Leader 805 in 1960; Brian was a high school sophomore at the time of this recording	
9/04/61	**20**	5	2. Let Me Belong To You	ABC-Para. 10236
4/07/62	**21**	6	3. Ginny Come Lately	ABC-Para. 10294
6/30/62	**3**	11	**4. Sealed With A Kiss**	ABC-Para. 10336
10/13/62	**25**	4	5. Warmed Over Kisses (Left Over Love)	ABC-Para. 10359
8/06/66	**20**	8	6. The Joker Went Wild	Philips 40377
11/26/66	**25**	3	7. Run, Run, Look And See	Philips 40405
10/24/70	**3**	13	• **8. Gypsy Woman**	Uni 55240
			produced by Del Shannon	
			HYMAN, Dick	
			Born on 3/08/27 in New York City. Piano playing composer/conductor/arranger who toured Europe with Benny Goodman in 1950. Staff pianist at WMCA and WNBC-New York from 1951-57. Music director of "Arthur Godfrey and His Friends" from 1958-62.	
			THE DICK HYMAN TRIO:	
1/28/56	**8**	15	**1. Moritat (A Theme from "The Three Penny Opera")** [I]	MGM 12149
			Jockey #8 / Top 100 #9 / Best Seller #10 / Juke Box #14	
			DICK HYMAN & HIS ELECTRIC ECLECTICS:	
7/05/69	**38**	2	2. The Minotaur [I]	Command 4126
			I	
			IAN, Janis	
			Born Janis Eddy Fink on 4/07/51 in New York City. Singer/songwriter/pianist/guitarist.	
6/17/67	**14**	8	1. Society's Child (Baby I've Been Thinking)	Verve 5027
7/12/75	**3**	14	**2. At Seventeen**	Columbia 10154
			ICEHOUSE	
			Australian rock quartet led by singer/guitarist Iva Davies. First known as Flowers. "Icehouse" is Australian slang for an insane asylum.	
12/05/87+	**14**	11	1. Crazy	Chrysalis 43156
3/19/88	**7**	13	**2. Electric Blue**	Chrysalis 43201
			co-written by John Oates (of Hall & Oates)	
			ICICLE WORKS	
			Liverpool rock trio: Robert Ian McNabb (vocals), Chris Layhe and Chris Sharrock.	
5/26/84	**37**	4	1. Whisper To A Scream (Birds Fly)	Arista 9155
			IDES OF MARCH, The	
			Rock group formed while classmates at a Chicago high school. Named after a line in Shakespeare's *Julius Caesar.* Lead singer Jim Peterik joined Survivor as keyboardist.	
4/11/70	**2**(1)	10	**1. Vehicle**	Warner 7378

DATE	POS	WKS	ARTIST—RECORD TITLE	LABEL & NO.
			IDOL, Billy	
			Born Willem Wolfe Broad on 11/30/55 in London. Leader of the London punk band Generation X from 1977-81. Suffered serious leg injuries in a motorcycle crash on 2/06/90. Appeared in 1991 film *The Doors*.	
8/07/82	**23**	9	1. Hot In The City	Chrysalis 2605
6/25/83	**36**	3	2. White Wedding originally "Bubbled Under" on 11/27/82 (POS 108)	Chrysalis 42697
5/19/84	**4**	14	**3. Eyes Without A Face**	Chrysalis 42786
9/15/84	**29**	6	4. Flesh For Fantasy	Chrysalis 42809
10/25/86	**6**	13	**5. To Be A Lover**	Chrysalis 43024
2/28/87	**37**	2	6. Don't Need A Gun	Chrysalis 43087
5/30/87	**20**	7	7. Sweet Sixteen	Chrysalis 43114
9/26/87	**1**(1)	12	**8. Mony Mony "Live"** studio version hit Bubbling Under chart on 9/26/81 (POS 107)	Chrysalis 43161
6/02/90	**2**(1)	16	● **9. Cradle Of Love** from the film *The Adventures of Ford Fairlane*	Chrysalis 23509
			IFIELD, Frank	
			Born on 11/30/37 in Coventry, England. Began career as a teenager in Australia with his own radio and TV shows. Signed to Columbia Records in England in 1959.	
9/22/62	**5**	8	**1. I Remember You** #9 hit for Jimmy Dorsey in 1942 (from the film *The Fleet's In*)	Vee-Jay 457
			IGLESIAS, Julio	
			Spanish singer, immensely popular worldwide. Born on 9/23/43 in Madrid. Soccer goalie for the pro Real Madrid team until temporary paralysis from a car crash.	
3/31/84	**5**	12	● **1. To All The Girls I've Loved Before** **JULIO IGLESIAS & WILLIE NELSON**	Columbia 04217
8/04/84	**19**	8	2. All Of You **JULIO IGLESIAS & DIANA ROSS**	Columbia 04507
			IKETTES, The	
			Female R&B trio formed for the Ike & Tina Turner Revue. Atco group consisted of Delores Johnson (lead), Eloise Hester and "Joshie" Jo Armstead. Modern group consisted of Vanetta Fields, Robbie Montgomery and Jessie Smith; later known as The Mirettes.	
2/03/62	**19**	8	1. I'm Blue (The Gong-Gong Song) backing vocal by Tina Turner	Atco 6212
4/10/65	**36**	4	2. Peaches "N" Cream	Modern 1005
			ILLUSION, The	
			Rock quintet led by John Vinci.	
8/23/69	**32**	6	1. Did You See Her Eyes	Steed 718
			IMPALAS, The	
			Pop vocal quartet from Brooklyn: Joe "Speedo" Frazier, Richard Wagner, Lenny Renda and Tony Carlucci. All members, except black lead singer Frazier, are white.	
4/13/59	**2**(2)	11	**1. Sorry (I Ran All the Way Home)**	Cub 9022

DATE	POS	WKS	ARTIST—RECORD TITLE	LABEL & NO.
			IMPRESSIONS, The	
			Soul group formed in Chicago in 1957, originally known as The Roosters. Consisted of Jerry Butler, Curtis Mayfield, Sam Gooden and brothers Arthur and Richard Brooks. Butler left for a solo career in 1958, replaced by Fred Cash. The Brooks brothers left in 1962, leaving Mayfield as the trio's leader. Mayfield left in 1970 for a solo career, replaced by Leroy Hutson. In 1973, Hutson was replaced by Reggie Torian and Ralph Johnson. Johnson joined Mystique in 1976. Group did film soundtrack for *Three the Hard Way* (1974). Butler, Mayfield, Gooden and Cash reunited for a tour in 1983. Group inducted into the Rock and Roll Hall of Fame in 1991.	
6/16/58	**11**	9	1. For Your Precious Love	Falcon 1013
			JERRY BUTLER AND THE IMPRESSIONS Best Seller #11 / Top 100 #11 / Jockey #25 released first on Falcon, then on Abner 1013 (also on Vee-Jay 280 in 1958)	
11/20/61	**20**	8	2. Gypsy Woman	ABC-Para. 10241
10/12/63	**4**	11	**3. It's All Right**	ABC-Para. 10487
1/25/64	**12**	7	4. Talking About My Baby	ABC-Para. 10511
4/18/64	**14**	9	5. I'm So Proud	ABC-Para. 10544
6/27/64	**10**	10	**6. Keep On Pushing**	ABC-Para. 10554
9/19/64	**15**	8	7. You Must Believe Me	ABC-Para. 10581
12/12/64+	**7**	7	**8. Amen**	ABC-Para. 10602
			song featured in the film *Lilies of the Field*	
3/06/65	**14**	5	9. People Get Ready	ABC-Para. 10622
4/24/65	**29**	4	10. Woman's Got Soul	ABC-Para. 10647
1/01/66	**33**	2	11. You've Been Cheatin'	ABC-Para. 10750
2/03/68	**14**	8	12. We're A Winner	ABC 11022
10/05/68	**22**	7	13. Fool For You	Curtom 1932
12/28/68+	**25**	6	14. This Is My Country	Curtom 1934
7/12/69	**21**	9	15. Choice Of Colors	Curtom 1943
6/13/70	**28**	8	16. Check Out Your Mind	Curtom 1951
			all of above (except #1 & 8) written by Curtis Mayfield	
6/29/74	**17**	6	17. Finally Got Myself Together (I'm A Changed Man)	Curtom 1997
			INDECENT OBSESSION	
			Pop band from Brisbane, Australia: David Dixon (vocals), Michael Szumowski, Andrew Coyne and Darryl Simms. Band's name taken from a Colleen McCullough novel.	
9/01/90	**31**	5	1. Tell Me Something	MCA 79029
			INDEPENDENTS, The	
			Soul group consisting of Chuck Jackson, Maurice Jackson, Helen Curry and Eric Thomas. Jackson (no relation to solo singer Chuck Jackson) and Marvin Yancey, Jr. were producers/writers for the group; later teamed in production work, especially for Natalie Cole, to whom Yancey was married for a time.	
4/28/73	**21**	9	● 1. Leaving Me	Wand 11252
			INFORMATION SOCIETY	
			Pop-funk-dance outfit formed in Minneapolis in 1985: songwriter Paul Robb, vocalist Kurt Valaquen, keyboardist Amanda Kramer and bassist James Cassidy. Reduced to a trio in 1990 with departure of Kramer.	
8/27/88	**3**	14	● **1. What's On Your Mind (Pure Energy)**	Tommy B. 27826
1/07/89	**9**	10	**2. Walking Away**	Tommy B. 27736
11/10/90	**28**	5	3. Think	Tommy B. 19591

DATE	POS	WKS	ARTIST—RECORD TITLE	LABEL & NO.
			INGMANN, Jorgen, & His Guitar	
			Born Jorgen Ingmann-Pedersen on 4/26/25 in Copenhagen, Denmark.	
2/20/61	**2**(2)	13	**1. Apache** [I]	Atco 6184
			INGRAM, James	
			R&B vocalist/multi-instrumentalist/composer from Akron, Ohio. To Los Angeles in the late 1970s, with the band Revelation Funk.	
9/19/81	**17**	10	1. Just Once **QUINCY JONES featuring JAMES INGRAM**	A&M 2357
2/13/82	**14**	11	2. One Hundred Ways **QUINCY JONES featuring JAMES INGRAM**	A&M 2387
12/04/82+	**1**(2)	18	● **3. Baby, Come To Me** **PATTI AUSTIN with JAMES INGRAM**	Qwest 50036
1/14/84	**19**	9	4. Yah Mo B There **JAMES INGRAM with Michael McDonald**	Qwest 29394
10/13/84	**15**	9	5. What About Me? **KENNY ROGERS with KIM CARNES and JAMES INGRAM**	RCA 13899
1/24/87	**2**(1)	12	**6. Somewhere Out There** **LINDA RONSTADT AND JAMES INGRAM** from the animated film *An American Tail*	MCA 52973
4/07/90	**31**	4	7. The Secret Garden (Sweet Seduction Suite) **QUINCY JONES/AL B. SURE!/JAMES INGRAM/ EL DeBARGE/BARRY WHITE**	Qwest 19992
9/08/90	**1**(1)	15	**8. I Don't Have The Heart**	Warner 19911
			INGRAM, Luther	
			Born on 11/30/44 in Jackson, Tennessee. Soul singer/songwriter. Sang in gospel group with his brothers. First recorded for Smash in 1965. In the film *Wattstax.*	
6/24/72	**3**	13	**1. (If Loving You Is Wrong) I Don't Want To Be Right**	KoKo 2111
1/20/73	**40**	2	2. I'll Be Your Shelter (In Time Of Storm)	KoKo 2113
			INNOCENCE, The	
			Group is actually the singing/songwriting/producing duo of Pete Anders and Vinnie Poncia. Also recorded as The Trade Winds.	
1/07/67	**34**	3	1. There's Got To Be A Word!	Kama Sutra 214
			INNOCENTS, The	
			Pop trio from Sun Valley, California: James West (lead singer), Al Candelaria (bass) and Darron Stankey (guitar, tenor). Backup vocal group for Kathy Young. First recorded as The Echoes for Andex in 1959.	
9/19/60	**28**	3	1. Honest I Do	Indigo 105
1/09/61	**28**	3	2. Gee Whiz	Indigo 111
			INSTANT FUNK	
			Large funk ensemble formed in Philadelphia in 1977. Led by singer/ percussionist James Carmichael. Former backup band for Bunny Sigler.	
3/31/79	**20**	8	● 1. I Got My Mind Made Up (You Can Get It Girl)	Salsoul 2078
			INTRIGUES, The	
			Soul trio from Philadelphia.	
10/04/69	**31**	4	1. In A Moment	Yew 1001

DATE	POS	WKS	ARTIST—RECORD TITLE	LABEL & NO.
			INTRUDERS, The	
			Soul group formed in Philadelphia in 1960. Consisted of Sam "Little Sonny" Brown, Eugene "Bird" Daughtry, Phil Terry and Robert "Big Sonny" Edwards. First recorded for Gowen in 1961. Not to be confused with the white rock trio of the same name.	
4/06/68	**6**	11	● **1. Cowboys To Girls**	Gamble 214
8/10/68	**26**	4	2. (Love Is Like A) Baseball Game	Gamble 217
6/30/73	**36**	6	3. I'll Always Love My Mama (Part 1)	Gamble 2506
			INXS	
			Rock sextet formed in Sydney, Australia as The Farris Brothers. Members since group's formation in 1977: Michael Hutchence (lead singer), Kirk Pengilly (guitar), Garry Beers (bass), and brothers Tim (guitar), Andy (keyboards, guitar) and Jon Farriss (drums). Hutchence starred in the 1987 film *Dogs in Space* and cofounded the 1989 band Max Q.	
5/14/83	**30**	5	1. The One Thing	Atco 99905
2/15/86	**5**	14	**2. What You Need**	Atlantic 89460
11/21/87+	**1**(1)	17	**3. Need You Tonight**	Atlantic 89188
2/27/88	**2**(2)	12	**4. Devil Inside**	Atlantic 89144
5/28/88	**3**	12	**5. New Sensation**	Atlantic 89080
9/17/88	**7**	11	**6. Never Tear Us Apart**	Atlantic 89038
9/22/90	**9**	9	● **7. Suicide Blonde**	Atlantic 87860
12/22/90+	**8**	12	**8. Disappear**	Atlantic 87784
			IRIS, Donnie	
			Real name: Dominic Ierace. Singer/songwriter/guitarist/lead of the Pittsburgh rock group The Jaggerz. Native of Beaver Falls, Pennsylvania. Toured briefly with the funk group Wild Cherry.	
2/07/81	**29**	6	1. Ah! Leah!	MCA 51025
2/13/82	**37**	2	2. Love Is Like A Rock	MCA 51223
5/01/82	**25**	6	3. My Girl	MCA 52031
			IRISH ROVERS, The	
			Irish-born folk quintet. Group formed in Alberta, Canada in 1964. Brothers Will (vocals) and George Millar, with their cousin Joe Millar and Jimmy Ferguson and Wilcil McDowell.	
4/06/68	**7**	9	**1. The Unicorn**	Decca 32254
4/18/81	**37**	4	2. Wasn't That A Party THE ROVERS	Epic 51007
			IRON BUTTERFLY	
			San Diego heavy-metal band. Consisted of Doug Ingle (vocals, keyboards), Erik Braunn (guitar), Lee Dorman (bass) and Ron Bushy (drums). Braunn left in late 1969, replaced by Mike Pinera (leader of Blues Image) and Larry Reinhardt.	
9/28/68	**30**	7	1. In-A-Gadda-Da-Vida 7" version edited down from original 17-minute album cut	Atco 6606
			IRONHORSE	
			Rock band formed by Bachman-Turner Overdrive founder Randy Bachman.	
4/21/79	**36**	3	1. Sweet Lui-Louise	Scotti Br. 406
			ISAAK, Chris	
			San Francisco-based singer/songwriter/guitarist. Born in Stockton, California on 6/26/56. Attended college in Japan. Cameo appearances in the films *Married to the Mob* and *Silence of the Lambs.*	
1/19/91	**6**	11	● **1. Wicked Game**	Reprise 19704

DATE	POS	WKS	ARTIST—RECORD TITLE	LABEL & NO.
			featured in the David Lynch film *Wild at Heart*	
			IRWIN, Big Dee	
			Real name: Defosca Ervin. R&B vocalist; former lead singer of The Pastels.	
7/13/63	**38**	2	1. Swinging On A Star **BIG DEE IRWIN with LITTLE EVA** #1 hit for Bing Crosby in 1944 (from the film *Going My Way*)	Dimension 1010
			ISLANDERS, The	
			Instrumental duo of Randy Starr (guitar) and Frank Metis (accordion).	
10/19/59	**15**	8	1. The Enchanted Sea [I]	Mayflower 16
			ISLEY BROTHERS, The	
			R&B trio of brothers from Cincinnati. Formed in early 1950s as a gospel group. Consisted of O'Kelly, Ronald and Rudolph Isley. Moved to New York in 1957 and first recorded for Teenage Records. Trio added their younger brothers Ernie (guitar, drums) and Marvin Isley (bass, percussion) and cousin Chris Jasper (keyboards), from 1973-84. Formed own label T-Neck in 1969. Ernie, Chris and Marvin began recording as the trio Isley, Jasper, Isley in 1984. O'Kelly died of a heart attack on 3/31/86 (age 48).	
6/30/62	**17**	11	1. Twist And Shout	Wand 124
3/19/66	**12**	8	2. This Old Heart Of Mine (Is Weak For You)	Tamla 54128
3/29/69	**2**(1)	12	• **3. It's Your Thing**	T-Neck 901
6/21/69	**23**	7	4. I Turned You On	T-Neck 902
7/03/71	**18**	9	5. Love The One You're With	T-Neck 930
8/19/72	**24**	7	6. Pop That Thang	T-Neck 935
8/18/73	**6**	15	• **7. That Lady (Part 1)**	T-Neck 2251
7/12/75	**4**	13	• **8. Fight The Power Part 1**	T-Neck 2256
11/22/75	**22**	9	9. For The Love Of You (Part 1 & 2)	T-Neck 2259
8/06/77	**40**	1	10. Livin' In The Life	T-Neck 2264
5/24/80	**39**	2	11. Don't Say Goodnight (It's Time For Love) (Parts 1 & 2)	T-Neck 2290
4/07/90	**10**	10	**12. This Old Heart Of Mine** **[R]** **ROD STEWART with RONALD ISLEY**	Warner 19983
			IVES, Burl	
			Born on 6/14/09 in Huntington Township, Illinois. Actor/author/singer. Played semi-pro football. Began Broadway career in the late 1930s. Worked in "This Is the Army" service show during World War II. Own CBS network radio show "The Wayfaring Stranger" in 1944. Appeared in many films, including *Our Man in Havana, East of Eden, Smokey, Cat on a Hot Tin Roof* and *The Big Country.* Narrated the kids' TV classic *Rudolph the Red-Nosed Reindeer.* Worked on TV series "The Bold Ones" in the early 1970s.	
1/06/62	**9**	11	**1. A Little Bitty Tear**	Decca 31330
4/21/62	**10**	8	**2. Funny Way Of Laughin'**	Decca 31371
8/11/62	**19**	4	3. Call Me Mr. In-Between	Decca 31405
12/08/62	**39**	1	4. Mary Ann Regrets	Decca 31433
			IVY THREE, The	
			Formed in 1959 at Adelphi College in New York. Consisted of Charles Koppelman (lead), Art Berkowitz and Don Rubin. Koppelman and Rubin did production work for The Turtles and The Lovin' Spoonful. Label executive Koppelman founded SBK Records in 1989, with Rubin as senior vice president.	
8/29/60	**8**	7	**1. Yogi** **[N]** based on a character from TV's "Huckleberry Hound" show	Shell 720

DATE	POS	WKS	ARTIST—RECORD TITLE	LABEL & NO.
			J	
			JACKS, Terry	
			Native of Winnipeg, Canada. Recorded with wife Susan as The Poppy Family.	
2/09/74	**1**(3)	15	● **1. Seasons In The Sun**	Bell 45432
			originally recorded by The Kingston Trio in 1964	
			JACKSON, Chuck	
			Born on 7/22/37 in Latta, South Carolina. R&B singer. Cousin of singer Ann Sexton. Moved to Pittsburgh as a child. Left college in 1957 to work with the Raspberry Singers gospel group. With The Dell-Vikings from 1957-59. First recorded as a solo for Beltone in 1960.	
3/13/61	**36**	2	1. I Don't Want To Cry	Wand 106
6/02/62	**23**	6	2. Any Day Now (My Wild Beautiful Bird)	Wand 122
			JACKSON, Deon	
			Born on 1/26/46 in Ann Arbor, Michigan. Soul singer/clarinetist/drummer.	
2/19/66	**11**	9	1. Love Makes The World Go Round	Carla 2526
			JACKSON, Freddie	
			Soul singer/songwriter. Born on 10/02/56 and raised in Harlem. Backup singer for Melba Moore, Evelyn King and others. Member of Mystic Merlin.	
7/13/85	**18**	8	1. Rock Me Tonight (For Old Times Sake)	Capitol 5459
10/05/85	**12**	11	2. You Are My Lady	Capitol 5495
1/25/86	**25**	6	3. He'll Never Love You (Like I Do)	Capitol 5535
8/15/87	**32**	3	4. Jam Tonight	Capitol 44037
			JACKSON, Janet	
			Born on 5/16/66 in Gary, Indiana. Sister of The Jacksons (youngest of nine children). Debuted at age seven at the MGM Grand in Las Vegas with her brothers. At age 10, she played Penny Gordon Woods in the TV series "Good Times" (1977-79); in the cast of "Diff'rent Strokes" (1981-82) and later "Fame." Married briefly in 1984 to James DeBarge of DeBarge. Signed a $32 million contract with Virgin Records in 1991.	
3/22/86	**4**	13	● **1. What Have You Done For Me Lately**	A&M 2812
6/07/86	**3**	11	● **2. Nasty**	A&M 2830
8/23/86	**1**(2)	13	● **3. When I Think Of You**	A&M 2855
11/22/86+	**5**	13	● **4. Control**	A&M 2877
2/07/87	**2**(1)	11	**5. Let's Wait Awhile**	A&M 2906
6/20/87	**14**	10	6. The Pleasure Principle	A&M 2927
9/09/89	**1**(4)	13	▲ **7. Miss You Much**	A&M 1445
11/18/89+	**2**(2)	12	● **8. Rhythm Nation**	A&M 1455
1/20/90	**1**(3)	15	● **9. Escapade**	A&M 1490
4/14/90	**4**	12	● **10. Alright**	A&M 1479
7/14/90	**2**(2)	11	**11. Come Back To Me**	A&M 1475
9/15/90	**1**(1)	12	● **12. Black Cat**	A&M 1477
			rock mix features Living Colour's Vernon Reid on lead guitar	
12/01/90+	**1**(1)	15	● **13. Love Will Never Do (Without You)**	A&M 1538

Stan Freberg proved that humor, like music, can be timeless, when Capitol Records reissued his album *Stan Freberg Presents the United States of America* on CD in 1990—a full 29 years after its initial release on LP.

The Georgia Satellites hit platinum with their very first album thanks largely to the success of their 1986 No. 2 hit "Keep Your Hands To Yourself," which—for Georgians—wasn't peanuts.

Debbie Gibson has had her share of hits—including No. 1's "Foolish Beat" and "Lost In Your Eyes"—and knows the value of record sales, royalties, and copyrights to a performer's career. She demonstrated as much in late 1991, when testifying at a Congressional hearing about digital recording technology.

Lesley Gore's mid-60s career was boosted with singing roles on two popular television series, including "The Donna Reed Show," where she played herself, and "Batman," in which she was a costumed associate of the Catwoman.

Amy Grant's leap into the pop mainstream came startlingly swift with 1991's "Baby Baby," which held the No. 1 slot for two weeks—and was boosted by a racy video which caused some concern among her longtime Christian fans.

Great White joined the pop crossover brigade in 1989, when the hard-rock band recorded "Once Bitten Twice Shy" —penned by former Mott The Hoople leader Ian Hunter—and hit the Top 5.

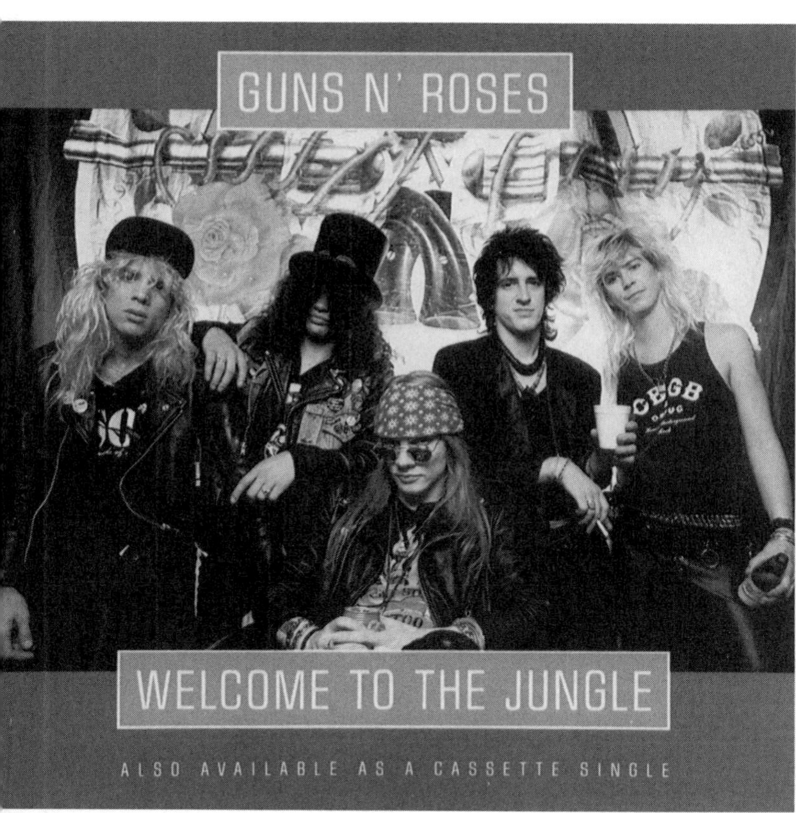

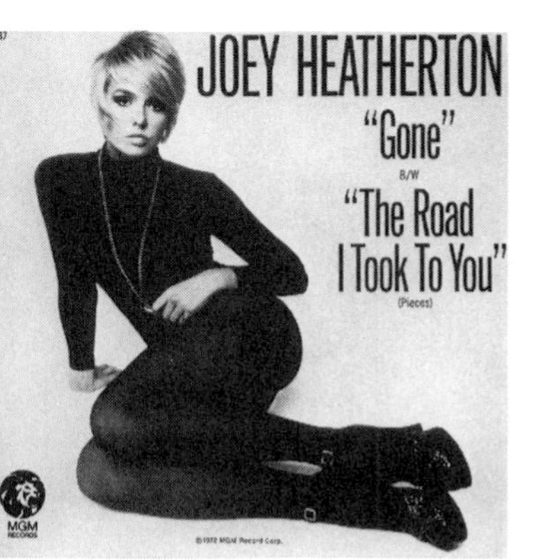

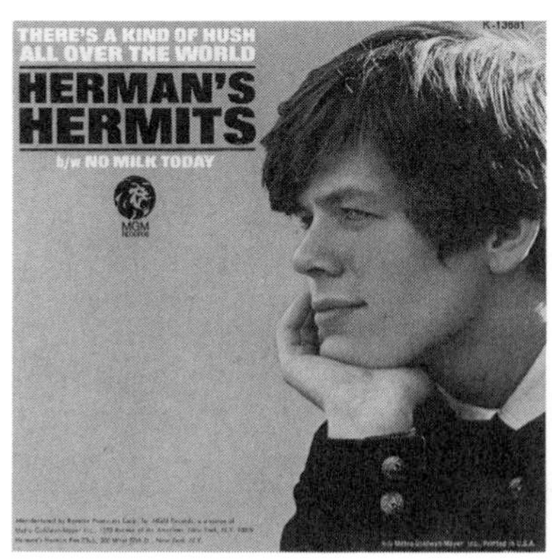

Guns N' Roses were the headline grabbers of 1991 following a concert riot in St. Louis and the huge sales of their second official album, *Use Your Illusion*, which was issued in two separate volumes. Many stores opened at midnight to sell the set on its first day of release.

Sammy Hagar's singles, both with hard-rock group Montrose and as a solo artist, never cracked the Top 10. But with Van Halen, whom he joined in 1985, Sammy did it twice: on 1986's "Why Can't This Be Love" and 1988's "When It's Love."

Corey Hart's first top-10 single had him wearing "Sunglasses At Night" in 1984; after only one more, 1985's "Never Surrender," and a string of decreasing successes, it's likely he now might go unrecognized even without the eyewear.

The Jeff Healey Band's hits have had peculiar personal synchronicity: the blind guitarist's 1989 debut album was titled *See the Light*, and its No. 22 single "Angel Eyes."

Joey Heatherton's "Gone," her sole brush with top-40 success, stayed on the charts for seven weeks in 1972 and was then as good as its name.

Herman's Hermits' string of 18 top-40 hits was topped by "Mrs. Brown You've Got A Lovely Daughter," which was No. 1 for three weeks in 1965 before being pushed aside by the Beatles' "Ticket To Ride"—which only stayed there for one.

DATE	POS	WKS	ARTIST—RECORD TITLE	LABEL & NO.
			JACKSON, Jermaine	
			Born on 12/11/54 in Gary, Indiana. Fourth oldest of the Jackson family. Vocalist/bassist of The Jackson 5 until group left Motown in 1976. Married Hazel Joy Gordy, daughter of Berry Gordy, Jr., on 12/15/73. Rejoined The Jacksons in 1984 for their *Victory* album and tour.	
1/13/73	**9**	13	**1. Daddy's Home**	Motown 1216
5/03/80	**9**	14	**2. Let's Get Serious**	Motown 1469
8/30/80	**34**	4	3. You're Supposed To Keep Your Love For Me above 2 written, produced and arranged by Stevie Wonder	Motown 1490
8/21/82	**18**	7	4. Let Me Tickle Your Fancy backing vocals: Devo	Motown 1628
8/04/84	**15**	10	5. Dynamite	Arista 9190
11/17/84+	**13**	12	6. Do What You Do	Arista 9279
3/15/86	**16**	9	7. I Think It's Love	Arista 9444
			JACKSON, J.J.	
			Born Jerome Louis Jackson on 4/08/41 in Brooklyn. Soul singer/songwriter. Became permanent resident of England in 1969. Not the same person as the MTV VJ.	
11/05/66	**22**	7	1. But It's Alright	Calla 119
			JACKSON, Joe	
			Born on 8/11/55 in Burton-on-Trent, England. Singer/songwriter/pianist, featuring an ever-changing music style. Moved to New York City in 1982.	
7/07/79	**21**	8	1. Is She Really Going Out With Him?	A&M 2132
10/16/82	**6**	15	**2. Steppin' Out**	A&M 2428
2/05/83	**18**	10	3. Breaking Us In Two	A&M 2510
5/05/84	**15**	9	4. You Can't Get What You Want (Till You Know What You Want)	A&M 2628
			JACKSON, Michael	
			Born on 8/29/58 in Gary, Indiana. The seventh of nine children. Became lead singer of his brothers' group, The Jackson 5 (later known as The Jacksons), at age five. Played the Scarecrow in the 1978 movie musical *The Wiz*. His 1982 *Thriller* album, with sales of over 40 million copies, is the best-selling album in history. Starred in the 15-minute film *Captain Eo*, which was shown exclusively at Disneyland/ world. His 1988 autobiography, *Moonwalker*, became a film the same year. Winner of 11 Grammy Awards. Michael signed a $1 billion multimedia contract with Sony Software on 3/20/91.	
11/06/71	**4**	13	**1. Got To Be There**	Motown 1191
3/18/72	**2**(2)	11	**2. Rockin' Robin**	Motown 1197
6/10/72	**16**	9	3. I Wanna Be Where You Are	Motown 1202
9/09/72	**1**(1)	11	**4. Ben** title song from the film about a trained rat	Motown 1207
7/12/75	**23**	6	5. Just A Little Bit Of You	Motown 1349
9/01/79	**1**(1)	12	▲ **6. Don't Stop 'Til You Get Enough**	Epic 50742
11/24/79+	**1**(4)	19	▲ **7. Rock With You**	Epic 50797
2/23/80	**10**	11	● **8. Off The Wall**	Epic 50838
5/10/80	**10**	11	● **9. She's Out Of My Life**	Epic 50871
11/13/82+	**2**(3)	14	● **10. The Girl Is Mine** **MICHAEL JACKSON/PAUL McCARTNEY**	Epic 03288
1/29/83	**1**(7)	17	▲ **11. Billie Jean**	Epic 03509
3/19/83	**1**(3)	18	▲ **12. Beat It** featuring lead guitar work by Eddie Van Halen	Epic 03759

DATE	POS	WKS	ARTIST—RECORD TITLE	LABEL & NO.
6/04/83	**5**	11	**13. Wanna Be Startin' Somethin'**	Epic 03914
7/30/83	**7**	11	**14. Human Nature**	Epic 04026
10/15/83	**1**(6)	18	● **15. Say Say Say** **PAUL McCARTNEY AND MICHAEL JACKSON**	Columbia 04168
10/22/83	**10**	9	**16. P.Y.T. (Pretty Young Thing)**	Epic 04165
2/11/84	**4**	9	▲ **17. Thriller**	Epic 04364
6/23/84	**38**	3	18. Farewell My Summer Love remix of a recording from 8/31/73	Motown 1739
8/08/87	**1**(1)	11	● **19. I Just Can't Stop Loving You** backing vocal by Siedah Garrett	Epic 07253
9/19/87	**1**(2)	11	**20. Bad** organ solo: Jimmy Smith	Epic 07418
11/28/87+	**1**(1)	13	**21. The Way You Make Me Feel**	Epic 07645
2/13/88	**1**(2)	13	**22. Man In The Mirror** background vocals: Siedah Garrett, Winans and Andrae Crouch Choir	Epic 07668
5/14/88	**1**(1)	11	**23. Dirty Diana** featuring Steve Stevens (Billy Idol's guitarist)	Epic 07739
8/06/88	**11**	8	24. Another Part Of Me	Epic 07962
11/26/88+	**7**	11	**25. Smooth Criminal** all of above Epic (and MCA) recordings produced by Quincy Jones	Epic 08044
			JACKSON, Millie Born on 7/15/44 in Thompson, Georgia. Soul singer/songwriter. To Newark, New Jersey in 1958. Worked as a model in New York City. Professional singing debut at Club Zanzibar in Hoboken, New Jersey in 1964. First recorded for MGM in 1970.	
5/13/72	**27**	6	1. Ask Me What You Want	Spring 123
9/29/73	**24**	8	2. Hurts So Good from the film *Cleopatra Jones*	Spring 139
			JACKSON, Rebbie Born Maureen Jackson on 5/29/50 in Gary, Indiana. Eldest of the nine-sibling Jackson family. Worked with The Jacksons from 1974-77, then went solo.	
11/17/84	**24**	8	1. Centipede written and produced by Michael Jackson	Columbia 04547
			JACKSON, Stonewall His real name. Born on 11/06/32 in Tabor City, North Carolina. Country singer/guitarist/pianist. Descended from General Thomas Jonathan "Stonewall" Jackson.	
6/08/59	**4**	12	**1. Waterloo**	Columbia 41393
			JACKSON, Wanda Born on 10/20/37 in Maud, Oklahoma. Country-rockabilly singer/songwriter/guitarist. First recorded for Decca in 1954. Toured with Elvis Presley from 1955-56.	
10/10/60	**37**	1	1. Let's Have A Party backing by Gene Vincent's Blue Caps	Capitol 4397
8/14/61	**29**	3	2. Right Or Wrong	Capitol 4553
11/27/61	**27**	3	3. In The Middle Of A Heartache	Capitol 4635

DATE	POS	WKS	ARTIST—RECORD TITLE	LABEL & NO.
			JACKSON 5/JACKSONS	
			Quintet of brothers formed and managed by their father beginning in 1966 in Gary, Indiana. Consisted of Sigmund "Jackie" (b: 5/04/51), Toriano "Tito" (b: 10/15/53), Jermaine (b: 12/11/54), Marlon (b: 3/12/57) and lead singer Michael (b: 8/29/58). First recorded for Steeltown in 1968. Known as The Jackson 5 from 1968-75. Jermaine replaced by Randy (b: 10/29/61) in 1976. Jermaine re-joined the group for 1984's highly publicized *Victory* album and tour. Marlon left for a solo career in 1987. Their sisters Rebbie, La Toya and Janet backed the group; each had a string of solo hits. Michael and Janet emerged with superstar solo careers in the '80s. Group lineup since 1989: Jackie, Tito, Jermaine and Randy Jackson.	
			THE JACKSON 5:	
12/06/69+	**1**(1)	16	**1. I Want You Back**	Motown 1157
3/21/70	**1**(2)	12	**2. ABC**	Motown 1163
6/06/70	**1**(2)	12	**3. The Love You Save**	Motown 1166
9/19/70	**1**(5)	16	**4. I'll Be There**	Motown 1171
2/06/71	**2**(2)	9	**5. Mama's Pearl**	Motown 1177
4/10/71	**2**(3)	11	**6. Never Can Say Goodbye**	Motown 1179
7/31/71	**20**	6	7. Maybe Tomorrow	Motown 1186
12/25/71+	**10**	8	**8. Sugar Daddy**	Motown 1194
4/29/72	**13**	8	9. Little Bitty Pretty One	Motown 1199
7/29/72	**16**	8	10. Lookin' Through The Windows	Motown 1205
11/18/72	**18**	8	11. Corner Of The Sky from the Broadway musical *Pippin*	Motown 1214
4/14/73	**28**	4	12. Hallelujah Day	Motown 1224
9/22/73	**28**	7	13. Get It Together	Motown 1277
3/30/74	**2**(2)	16	**14. Dancing Machine**	Motown 1286
11/30/74	**38**	2	15. Whatever You Got, I Want	Motown 1308
2/22/75	**15**	7	16. I Am Love (Parts I & II)	Motown 1310
			THE JACKSONS:	
12/11/76+	**6**	15	▲ **17. Enjoy Yourself**	Epic 50289
5/07/77	**28**	3	18. Show You The Way To Go	Epic 50350
3/31/79	**7**	14	▲ **19. Shake Your Body (Down To The Ground)**	Epic 50656
10/11/80	**12**	9	20. Lovely One	Epic 50938
1/10/81	**22**	8	21. Heartbreak Hotel	Epic 50959
6/30/84	**3**	11	• **22. State Of Shock** guest vocalist: Mick Jagger	Epic 04503
8/25/84	**17**	8	23. Torture	Epic 04575
			JACOBS, Dick	
			Born on 3/29/18 in New York City; died in 1988 (age 70) of cancer. Music director of TV's "Your Hit Parade" from 1957-58. A&R director for Coral and Brunswick Records. Author of *Who Wrote That Song?*.	
4/07/56	**22**	7	1. "Main Title" And "Molly-O" Jockey #22 / Top 100 #26 from the Otto Preminger film *The Man with the Golden Arm*	Coral 61606
11/03/56	**16**	9	2. Petticoats Of Portugal Jockey #16 / Top 100 #20 / Juke Box #20 / Best Seller #23	Coral 61724
9/16/57	**17**	4	3. Fascination Jockey #17 / Top 100 #52 from the film *Love in the Afternoon*	Coral 61864

DATE	POS	WKS	ARTIST—RECORD TITLE	LABEL & NO.
			JAGGER, Mick	
			Born Michael Phillip Jagger on 7/26/43 in Dartford, England. Lead singer of The Rolling Stones. Starred in the 1970 film *Ned Kelly.* Married actress/model Jerry Hall on 11/24/90. Also see The Jacksons' "State Of Shock."	
2/16/85	**12**	10	1. Just Another Night	Columbia 04743
5/25/85	**38**	3	2. Lucky In Love	Columbia 04893
9/07/85	**7**	9	**3. Dancing In The Street** **MICK JAGGER/DAVID BOWIE** from the Live-Aid benefit concert	EMI America 8288
10/24/87	**39**	1	4. Let's Work	Columbia 07306
			JAGGERZ, The	
			Rock group formed in Pittsburgh in 1965, featuring lead singer Donnie Iris.	
2/14/70	**2**(1)	11	● **1. The Rapper**	Kama Sutra 502
			JAMES, Etta	
			Born Jamesetta Hawkins on 1/25/38 in Los Angeles. Nicknamed "Miss Peaches." First recorded for Modern in 1954. Recorded duets with Harvey Fuqua of The Moonglows as Etta & Harvey. Frequent bouts with heroin addiction; finally cured in the late '70s. Still active into the '90s.	
6/06/60	**33**	4	1. All I Could Do Was Cry	Argo 5359
11/21/60	**34**	2	2. My Dearest Darling	Argo 5368
4/03/61	**30**	4	3. Trust In Me #5 hit for both Wayne King and Mildred Bailey in 1937	Argo 5385
9/04/61	**39**	2	4. Don't Cry, Baby	Argo 5393
3/31/62	**37**	4	5. Something's Got A Hold On Me	Argo 5409
9/08/62	**34**	2	6. Stop The Wedding	Argo 5418
5/11/63	**25**	6	7. Pushover	Argo 5437
12/30/67+	**23**	7	8. Tell Mama	Cadet 5578
4/06/68	**35**	4	9. Security	Cadet 5594
			JAMES, Joni	
			Born Joan Carmello Babbo on 9/22/30 in Chicago. Worked as a dancer from age 12; model during high school. Toured Canada as a dancer in the late 1940s. First recorded for Sharp in 1952. Married her orchestral arranger/conductor Tony Acquaviva (d: 9/27/86).	
2/19/55	**2**(1)	16	**1. How Important Can It Be?** Jockey #2 / Juke Box #6 / Best Seller #8	MGM 11919
10/22/55	**6**	10	**2. You Are My Love** Jockey #6 / Top 100 #15 / Best Seller #18	MGM 12066
8/11/56	**30**	2	3. Give Us This Day orchestra conducted by David Terry on above 3; by Tony Acquaviva on all below	MGM 12288
10/20/58	**19**	8	4. There Goes My Heart #13 hit for Enric Madriguera in 1934	MGM 12706
2/16/59	**33**	4	5. There Must Be A Way #9 hit for both Johnnie Johnston and Charlie Spivak in 1945	MGM 12746
1/25/60	**35**	3	6. Little Things Mean A Lot #1 hit for Kitty Kallen in 1954	MGM 12849
1/23/61	**38**	1	7. My Last Date (With You)	MGM 12933

DATE	POS	WKS	ARTIST—RECORD TITLE	LABEL & NO.
			JAMES, Rick	
			"Punk funk" singer/songwriter/guitarist. Born James Johnson on 2/01/52 in Buffalo. In Mynah Birds band with Neil Young in the late '60s. To London; formed the band Main Line. Returned to the U.S. and formed Stone City Band; produced Teena Marie, Mary Jane Girls, Eddie Murphy and others.	
8/05/78	**13**	10	1. You And I	Gordy 7156
7/18/81	**40**	2	2. Give It To Me Baby	Gordy 7197
9/05/81	**16**	10	3. Super Freak (Part 1)	Gordy 7205
9/24/83	**40**	1	4. Cold Blooded	Gordy 1687
8/18/84	**36**	3	5. 17	Gordy 1730
			JAMES, Sonny	
			Born James Loden on 5/01/29 in Hackleburg, Alabama. Country singer/songwriter/guitarist. Nicknamed "The Southern Gentleman." Brought to Capitol Records in Nashville by Chet Atkins. In the films *Second Fiddle to a Steel Guitar*, *Nashville Rebel*, *Las Vegas Hillbillies* and *Hillbilly in a Haunted House*.	
1/05/57	**1**(1)	17	**1. Young Love**	Capitol 3602
			Jockey #1 / Best Seller #2 / Top 100 #2 / Juke Box #4	
4/20/57	**25**	1	2. First Date, First Kiss, First Love	Capitol 3674
			Jockey #25 / Top 100 #39	
			JAMES, Tommy/The Shondells	
			Born Thomas Jackson on 4/29/47 in Dayton, Ohio. To Niles, Michigan at age 11. Formed pop group The Shondells at age 12. Recorded "Hanky Panky" on the Snap label in 1963. Tommy relocated to Pittsburgh in 1965 after a DJ there popularized "Hanky Panky." Original master was sold to Roulette, whereupon Tommy recruited Pittsburgh group The Raconteurs to become the official Shondells. Consisted of Mike Vale (bass), Pete Lucia (drums), Eddie Gray (guitar) and Ronnie Rosman (organ). Began recording as a solo artist in 1970.	
6/18/66	**1**(2)	10	**1. Hanky Panky**	Roulette 4686
			first released on Snap 102 in 1963 as by The Shondells; then on Red Fox 110 in 1965 (The Shondells)	
8/20/66	**21**	5	2. Say I Am (What I Am)	Roulette 4695
12/10/66	**31**	4	3. It's Only Love	Roulette 4710
3/11/67	**4**	12	**4. I Think We're Alone Now**	Roulette 4720
5/06/67	**10**	8	**5. Mirage**	Roulette 4736
7/15/67	**25**	5	6. I Like The Way	Roulette 4756
9/02/67	**18**	6	7. Gettin' Together	Roulette 4762
5/04/68	**3**	13	**8. Mony Mony**	Roulette 7008
11/23/68	**38**	2	9. Do Something To Me	Roulette 7024
12/21/68+	**1**(2)	15	**10. Crimson And Clover**	Roulette 7028
4/05/69	**7**	8	**11. Sweet Cherry Wine**	Roulette 7039
6/28/69	**2**(3)	12	**12. Crystal Blue Persuasion**	Roulette 7050
10/25/69	**19**	5	13. Ball Of Fire	Roulette 7060
12/20/69+	**23**	7	14. She	Roulette 7066
			TOMMY JAMES:	
6/26/71	**4**	11	**15. Draggin' The Line**	Roulette 7103
10/23/71	**40**	1	16. I'm Comin' Home	Roulette 7110
			featuring The Stephentown Singers	
2/23/80	**19**	9	17. Three Times In Love	Millennium 11785

DATE	POS	WKS	ARTIST—RECORD TITLE	LABEL & NO.
			JAMIES, The	
			Pop vocal quartet from Dorchester, Massachusetts, led by Tom Jamison and his sister Serena.	
9/15/58	**26**	4	1. Summertime, Summertime	Epic 9281
			Hot 100 #26 / Best Seller #28	
8/04/62	**38**	1	2. Summertime, Summertime [R]	Epic 9281
			JAN & DEAN	
			Jan Berry (b: 4/03/41) and Dean Torrence (b: 3/10/40) formed group called the Barons while attending high school in Los Angeles. Jan & Dean and Barons member Arnie Ginsburg recorded "Jennie Lee" in Jan's garage. Dean left for a six-month Army Reserve stint, whereupon Jan signed with Doris Day's label, Arwin, and the record was released as by Jan & Arnie. Upon Dean's return from the service, Arnie joined the Navy, and Jan & Dean signed with Herb Alpert's Dore label. Jan was critically injured in an auto accident on 4/19/66. Duo made a comeback in 1978, after their biographical film *Dead Man's Curve* aired on TV.	
5/26/58	**8**	11	**1. Jennie Lee**	Arwin 108
			JAN & ARNIE	
			Best Seller #8 / Top 100 #8 / Jockey #17	
8/10/59	**10**	9	**2. Baby Talk**	Dore 522
			originally issued as by Jan & Arnie on Dore 522	
7/10/61	**25**	4	3. Heart And Soul	Challenge 9111
			Larry Clinton hit #1 in 1938 with this Hoagy Carmichael tune	
4/20/63	**28**	5	4. Linda	Liberty 55531
			#1 hit for Ray Noble with Buddy Clark in 1947	
6/22/63	**1**(2)	11	**5. Surf City**	Liberty 55580
			Brian Wilson (Beach Boys) helped on words & vocals for this tune	
9/21/63	**11**	8	6. Honolulu Lulu	Liberty 55613
12/21/63+	**10**	9	**7. Drag City**	Liberty 55641
3/28/64	**8**	11	**8. Dead Man's Curve/**	
4/04/64	**37**	4	9. The New Girl In School	Liberty 55672
7/04/64	**3**	10	**10. The Little Old Lady (From Pasadena)**	Liberty 55704
10/10/64	**16**	5	11. Ride The Wild Surf	Liberty 55724
			from the film of the same title	
11/21/64	**25**	5	12. Sidewalk Surfin'	Liberty 55727
6/26/65	**27**	4	13. You Really Know How To Hurt A Guy	Liberty 55792
11/13/65	**30**	2	14. I Found A Girl	Liberty 55833
6/18/66	**21**	6	15. Popsicle	Liberty 55886
			JANKOWSKI, Horst	
			Born on 1/30/36 in Berlin, Germany. Jazz pianist.	
6/05/65	**12**	9	1. A Walk In The Black Forest [I]	Mercury 72425
			JARMELS, The	
			R&B vocal group from Richmond, Virginia: Nathaniel Ruff, Ray Smith, Paul Burnett, Earl Christian and Tom Eldridge. Named for a street in Harlem.	
8/28/61	**12**	6	1. A Little Bit Of Soap	Laurie 3098
			JARREAU, Al	
			Born on 3/12/40 in Milwaukee. Soul-jazz vocalist. Has masters degree in psychology from the University of Iowa. Worked clubs in San Francisco with George Duke.	
9/12/81	**15**	11	1. We're In This Love Together	Warner 49746

DATE	POS	WKS	ARTIST—RECORD TITLE	LABEL & NO.
4/23/83	**21**	6	2. Mornin' **JARREAU**	Warner 29720
7/04/87	**23**	5	3. Moonlighting theme from the TV series of the same title	MCA 53124
			JAY & THE AMERICANS	
			Group formed in late 1959 by New York University students as the Harbor-Lites: John "Jay" Traynor (formerly with the Mystics), Sandy Yaguda, Kenny Vance (later a Hollywood musical director) and Howie Kane. Guitarist Marty Sanders joined during production of their first album in 1961. Traynor left after their first hit and was replaced by lead singer Jay Black (real name: David Blatt; b: 11/02/38) in 1962.	
4/07/62	**5**	11	**1. She Cried**	United Art. 415
9/21/63	**25**	4	2. Only In America	United Art. 626
10/03/64	**3**	11	**3. Come A Little Bit Closer**	United Art. 759
1/16/65	**11**	7	4. Let's Lock The Door (And Throw Away The Key)	United Art. 805
6/19/65	**4**	11	**5. Cara, Mia** #10 hit for David Whitfield (with Mantovani) in 1954	United Art. 881
9/25/65	**13**	6	6. Some Enchanted Evening there were 6 top 10 versions of this *South Pacific* song in 1949	United Art. 919
12/04/65	**18**	6	7. Sunday And Me Neil Diamond's first major hit as a songwriter	United Art. 948
6/11/66	**25**	4	8. Crying	United Art. 50016
1/25/69	**6**	10	● **9. This Magic Moment**	United Art. 50475
1/17/70	**19**	7	10. Walkin' In The Rain	United Art. 50605
			JAY AND THE TECHNIQUES	
			Interracial R&B-rock group from Allentown, Pennsylvania: Jay Proctor (lead singer), Karl Landis, Ronnie Goosly, John Walsh, George Lloyd, Chuck Crowl and Dante Dancho.	
8/19/67	**6**	11	**1. Apples, Peaches, Pumpkin Pie**	Smash 2086
11/11/67	**14**	9	2. Keep The Ball Rollin'	Smash 2124
2/10/68	**39**	2	3. Strawberry Shortcake	Smash 2142
			JAYE, Jerry	
			Born Jerald Jaye Hatley on 10/19/37 in Manila, Arkansas.	
5/06/67	**29**	6	1. My Girl Josephine	Hi 2120
			JAYHAWKS, The	
			Los Angeles R&B group formed in 1955: James Johnson, Carlton Fisher, Dave Govan and Carver Bunkum. Changed name to The Vibrations in 1960.	
7/28/56	**18**	2	1. Stranded In The Jungle [N] Best Seller #18 / Top 100 #29	Flash 109
			JAYNETTS, The	
			R&B female group from the Bronx, formed by producer/composer/owner of J&S Records Zelma "Zell" Sanders. Her daughter, Johnnie Louise Richardson, was part of Johnnie & Joe duo and a touring member of The Jaynettes. Johnnie died from a stroke on 10/25/88.	
9/07/63	**2**(2)	9	**1. Sally, Go 'Round The Roses**	Tuff 369
			JB's, The	
			James Brown's super-funk backup band led by Fred Wesley.	
6/23/73	**22**	6	● 1. Doing It To Death **FRED WESLEY & THE J.B's** written, produced and arranged by James Brown	People 621

DATE	POS	WKS	ARTIST—RECORD TITLE	LABEL & NO.
			JEFFERSON	
			English vocalist.	
1/24/70	**23**	6	1. Baby Take Me In Your Arms	Janus 106
			JEFFERSON AIRPLANE/STARSHIP	
			Formed as Jefferson Airplane in San Francisco, 1965. Consisted of Marty Balin and Signe Anderson (vocals), Paul Kantner (vocals, guitar), Jorma Kaukonen (guitar), Jack Casady (bass) and Alexander "Skip" Spence (drums). Grace Slick and Spencer Dryden joined in 1966, replacing Anderson and Spence. Slick had been in the Great Society. Spence then formed Moby Grape. Dryden replaced by Joey Covington in 1970. Casady and Kaukonen left by 1974 to go full time with Hot Tuna. Balin left in 1971, rejoined in 1975, by which time group was renamed Jefferson Starship and consisted of Slick, Kantner, Papa John Creach (violin), David Freiberg (bass), Craig Chaquico (pronounced: chuck-ee-so; guitar), Pete Sears (bass) and John Barbata (drums). Slick left group from June 1978 to January 1981 due to personal problems. In 1979, singer Mickey Thomas joined (replaced Balin), along with Aynsley Dunbar who replaced Barbata. Don Baldwin (formerly with Snail) replaced Dunbar (later with Whitesnake) in 1982. Kantner left in 1984, and, due to legal difficulties, band's name was shortened to Starship, whose lineup included Slick, Thomas, Sears, Chaquico and Baldwin. Slick left in early 1988. In 1989, the original 1966 lineup — Balin, Slick, Kantner, Kaukonen and Casady — reunited as Jefferson Airplane with Kenny Aronoff (formerly with John Cougar Mellencamp) replacing Dryden. Continuing as Starship were Thomas, Chaquico, Baldwin, Brett Bloomfield (bass) and Mark Morgan (keyboards). Starship disbanded in 1990.	
			JEFFERSON AIRPLANE:	
5/06/67	**5**	9	**1. Somebody To Love**	RCA 9140
			originally released by the Great Society on North Beach 1001 in 1966, entitled "Someone To Love"	
7/01/67	**8**	9	**2. White Rabbit**	RCA 9248
			JEFFERSON STARSHIP:	
9/13/75	**3**	13	**3. Miracles**	Grunt 10367
8/14/76	**12**	11	4. With Your Love	Grunt 10746
3/25/78	**8**	11	**5. Count On Me**	Grunt 11196
6/24/78	**12**	8	6. Runaway	Grunt 11274
11/24/79+	**14**	10	7. Jane	Grunt 11750
5/02/81	**29**	6	8. Find Your Way Back	Grunt 12211
11/13/82	**28**	6	9. Be My Lady	Grunt 13350
3/19/83	**38**	2	10. Winds Of Change	Grunt 13439
6/09/84	**23**	8	11. No Way Out	Grunt 13811
			STARSHIP:	
9/28/85	**1**(2)	15	● **12. We Built This City**	Grunt 14170
1/18/86	**1**(1)	13	**13. Sara**	Grunt 14253
4/26/86	**26**	6	14. Tomorrow Doesn't Matter Tonight	Grunt 14332
2/14/87	**1**(2)	15	● **15. Nothing's Gonna Stop Us Now**	Grunt 5109
			from the film *Mannequin*	
7/18/87	**9**	10	**16. It's Not Over ('Til It's Over)**	RCA/Grunt 5225
8/26/89	**12**	9	17. It's Not Enough	RCA 9032
			JEFFREY, Joe, Group	
			Joe is an R&B singer/guitarist.	
7/05/69	**14**	8	1. My Pledge Of Love	Wand 11200

DATE	POS	WKS	ARTIST—RECORD TITLE	LABEL & NO.
			JELLYBEAN	
			John "Jellybean" Benitez, native of the Bronx, is a renowned Manhattan club DJ/remixer/producer. Remixing career took off with "Flashdance" and "Maniac" remixes, later to include many of Madonna's hits.	
12/21/85+	**18**	9	1. Sidewalk Talk written by Madonna	EMI America 8297
8/15/87	**16**	8	2. Who Found Who **JELLYBEAN/ELISA FIORILLO**	Chrysalis 43120
			JELLY BEANS, The	
			Quintet from Jersey City: sisters Elyse & Maxine Herbert, Alma Brewer, Diane Taylor and Charles Thomas.	
7/18/64	**9**	7	**1. I Wanna Love Him So Bad**	Red Bird 10003
			JENKINS, Gordon	
			Born on 5/12/10 in Webster Groves, Missouri; died on 5/01/84. Pianist/arranger in the early 1930s with Isham Jones, Benny Goodman and others. Musical director/conductor for Decca Records beginning in 1945.	
12/15/56	**29**	1	1. Blueberry Hill **LOUIS ARMSTRONG AND GORDON JENKINS** recorded in 1949	Decca 30091
			JENNINGS, Waylon	
			Born on 6/15/37 in Littlefield, Texas. While working as a DJ in Lubbock, Texas, Waylon befriended Buddy Holly. Holly produced Waylon's first record "Jole Blon" in 1958. Waylon then joined with Buddy's backing band as bass guitarist on the fateful "Winter Dance Party" tour in 1959. Established himself in the mid-1970s as a leader of the "outlaw" movement in country music. Married to Jessi Colter since 1969. In the films *Nashville Rebel*, *MacKintosh and T.J.* and *Urban Cowboy*.	
3/06/76	**25**	5	1. Good Hearted Woman **WAYLON & WILLIE** (Nelson)	RCA 10529
6/11/77	**25**	7	2. Luckenbach, Texas (Back to the Basics of Love) ending vocal: Willie Nelson	RCA 10924
11/01/80	**21**	10	● 3. Theme From The Dukes Of Hazzard (Good Ol' Boys) **WAYLON** from *The Dukes of Hazzard* TV series	RCA 12067
			JENSEN, Kris	
			Born Peter Jensen on 4/04/42 in New Haven, Connecticut. Pop-country singer/guitarist.	
10/06/62	**20**	6	1. Torture	Hickory 1173
			JESUS JONES	
			Rock-funk-punk quintet from London. Led by vocalist/guitarist Mike Edwards.	
5/25/91	**2**(1)	15	**1. Right Here, Right Now**	SBK 07345#
			JETHRO TULL	
			Progressive rock group formed in 1968 in Blackpool, England. Consisted of Ian Anderson (b: 8/10/47, Edinburgh, Scotland; lead singer, flutist), Mick Abrahams (guitar), Glenn Cornick (bass) and Clive Bunker (drums). Named band after 18th century agriculturist Jethro Tull. Abrahams left in 1968 to form Blodwyn Pig, replaced by Martin Barre. Added keyboardist John Evans in 1970. Cornick replaced by Jeffrey Hammond-Hammond in 1971. Bunker left in late 1971, replaced by Barriemore Barlow, who in turn was replaced by John Glascock (died in 1979). Ian has revamped his lineup several times since then.	
11/25/72+	**11**	10	1. Living In The Past	Chrysalis 2006
11/30/74+	**12**	10	2. Bungle In The Jungle	Chrysalis 2101

DATE	POS	WKS	ARTIST—RECORD TITLE	LABEL & NO.
			JETS, The	
			Minneapolis-based family band consisting of eight brothers and sisters: Leroy, Eddie, Eugene, Haini, Rudy, Kathi, Elizabeth and Moana Wolfgramm. Their parents are from the South Pacific country of Tonga. All members play at least two instruments. Eugene left group and formed duo Boys Club in 1988.	
5/03/86	**3**	13	**1. Crush On You**	MCA 52774
1/17/87	**3**	12	**2. You Got It All**	MCA 52968
6/27/87	**7**	11	**3. Cross My Broken Heart** from the film *Beverly Hills Cop II*	MCA 53123
11/14/87	**20**	6	4. I Do You	MCA 53193
2/13/88	**6**	13	**5. Rocket 2 U**	MCA 53254
5/07/88	**4**	13	**6. Make It Real**	MCA 53311
			JETT, Joan/The Blackhearts	
			Born on 9/22/60 in Philadelphia. Played guitar with the Los Angeles female rock band The Runaways, 1975-78. Formed her backing band The Blackhearts in 1980. Starred in the 1987 film *Light of Day* as the leader of a rock band called The Barbusters.	
2/13/82	**1**(7)	16	▲ **1. I Love Rock 'N Roll**	Boardwalk 135
5/15/82	**7**	10	**2. Crimson And Clover**	Boardwalk 144
8/28/82	**20**	7	3. Do You Wanna Touch Me (Oh Yeah)	Boardwalk 150
7/30/83	**35**	4	4. Fake Friends also released on Blackheart 52256 in 1983	Blackheart 52240
10/15/83	**37**	2	5. Everyday People	Blackheart 52272
3/21/87	**33**	5	6. Light Of Day **THE BARBUSTERS** (name of band in film *Light of Day*); actors Michael J. Fox and Michael McKean are not on the recowritten by Bruce Springsteen	Blackheart 06692
8/13/88	**8**	12	**7. I Hate Myself ForLoving You**	Blackheart 07919
12/10/88+	**19**	10	8. Little Liar	Blackheart 08095
3/03/90	**36**	2	9. Dirty Deeds **JOAN JETT**	Blackheart 73267
			JIGSAW	
			Pop-rock quartet from England: Des Deyer (lead vocals), Clive Scott, Tony Campbell and Barrie Bernard.	
10/11/75	**3**	14	**1. Sky High** from the movie *The Dragon Flies*	Chelsea 3022
3/13/76	**30**	5	2. Love Fire	Chelsea 3037
			JIMENEZ, Jose	
			Real name: Bill Dana. Born William Szarthmary on 10/05/24 in Quincy, Massachusetts. Head writer for TV's "Steve Allen Show." Star of own TV series from 1963-65. Created the Latin American comic character Jose Jimenez for Steve Allen's TV series.	
9/18/61	**19**	4	1. The Astronaut (Parts 1 & 2) [C] interviewed by Don Hinckley	Kapp 409
			JIVE BOMBERS, The	
			New York City quartet: Clarence Palmer, Earl Johnson, Al Tinney and William "Pee Wee" Tinney.	
3/16/57	**36**	1	1. Bad Boy	Savoy 1508

DATE	POS	WKS	ARTIST—RECORD TITLE	LABEL & NO.
			JIVE BUNNY/The Mastermixers	
			British dance outfit: DJ Les Hemstock and mixers John Pickles, Andy Pickles and Ian Morgan.	
11/25/89+	**11**	11	● 1. Swing The Mood	Music Fac. 99140
			includes samplings of these tunes: Let's Twist Again/In The Mood/Rock Around The Clock/Rock-A-Beatin' Boogie/Tutti-Frutti/Wake Up Little Susie/C'mon Everybody/Hound Dog/Shake, Rattle And Roll/All Shook Up/Jailhouse Rock/At The Hop	
			JIVE FIVE, The	
			R&B group formed in Brooklyn in 1959: Eugene Pitt (b: 11/06/37; lead singer; formerly with the Genies), Jerome Hanna and Billy Prophet (tenors), Richard Harris (baritone) and Norman Johnson (bass). After Johnson's death in 1970, group name changed to Jyve Fyve.	
8/14/61	**3**	12	**1. My True Story**	Beltone 1006
9/11/65	**36**	3	2. I'm A Happy Man	United Art. 853
			J.J. FAD	
			Los Angeles female rap trio: M.C.J.B. (Juana Burns), Baby-D (Dania Birks) and Sassy C (Michelle Franklin).	
6/11/88	**30**	4	● 1. Supersonic	Ruthless 99328
			JO, Damita	
			Born Damita Jo DuBlanc in Austin, Texas. Featured singer with Steve Gibson & The Red Caps (married to Gibson), 1951-53 and 1959-60. Regular on Red Foxx's TV variety series in 1977.	
11/07/60	**22**	8	1. I'll Save The Last Dance For You	Mercury 71690
			answer song to The Drifters' "Save The Last Dance For Me"	
7/17/61	**12**	7	2. I'll Be There	Mercury 71840
			answer song to Ben E. King's "Stand By Me"	
			JO, Sami	
			Alabama-bred, country-pop songstress.	
3/23/74	**21**	7	1. Tell Me A Lie	MGM South 7029
			JoBOXERS	
			Pop-rock quintet from England, led by Dig Wayne.	
11/05/83	**36**	4	1. Just Got Lucky	RCA 13601
			JOEL, Billy	
			Born William Martin Joel on 5/09/49 in Hicksville, Long Island, New York. Formed his first band, The Echoes, in 1964, which later became The Lost Souls. Member of Long Island group The Hassles in the late 1960s. Later formed rock duo, Attila, with The Hassles' drummer, Jon Small. Signed solo to Columbia Records in 1973. Involved in a serious motorcycle accident in Long Island in 1982. Married supermodel Christie Brinkley in 1985. Toured and recorded in Russia in 1987. Won Grammy's Legends Award in 1990. Joel composed all of his hits.	
4/06/74	**25**	4	1. Piano Man	Columbia 45963
12/28/74+	**34**	5	2. The Entertainer	Columbia 10064
12/10/77+	**3**	18	● **3. Just The Way You Are**	Columbia 10646
4/15/78	**17**	8	4. Movin' Out (Anthony's Song)	Columbia 10708
6/17/78	**24**	5	5. Only The Good Die Young	Columbia 10750
9/09/78	**17**	9	6. She's Always A Woman	Columbia 10788
11/11/78+	**3**	16	● **7. My Life**	Columbia 10853
3/03/79	**14**	6	8. Big Shot	Columbia 10913
5/12/79	**24**	4	9. Honesty	Columbia 10959

DATE	POS	WKS	ARTIST—RECORD TITLE	LABEL & NO.
3/22/80	**7**	11	**10. You May Be Right**	Columbia 11231
5/24/80	**1**(2)	19	• **11. It's Still Rock And Roll To Me**	Columbia 11276
8/16/80	**19**	9	12. Don't Ask Me Why	Columbia 11331
11/01/80	**36**	3	13. Sometimes A Fantasy	Columbia 11379
9/26/81	**17**	8	14. Say Goodbye To Hollywood	Columbia 02518
12/12/81+	**23**	9	15. She's Got A Way originally released on Family 0900 in 1973	Columbia 02628
10/16/82	**20**	8	16. Pressure	Columbia 03244
12/18/82+	**17**	16	17. Allentown	Columbia 03413
7/30/83	**1**(1)	15	**18. Tell Her About It**	Columbia 04012
10/08/83	**3**	16	• **19. Uptown Girl**	Columbia 04149
1/07/84	**10**	11	**20. An Innocent Man**	Columbia 04259
4/07/84	**14**	11	21. The Longest Time	Columbia 04400
8/04/84	**27**	7	22. Leave A Tender Moment Alone	Columbia 04514
2/09/85	**18**	10	23. Keeping The Faith	Columbia 04681
7/20/85	**9**	11	**24. You're Only Human (Second Wind)**	Columbia 05417
10/26/85	**34**	3	25. The Night Is Still Young	Columbia 05657
6/21/86	**10**	9	**26. Modern Woman** from the film *Ruthless People*	Epic 06118
9/06/86	**10**	10	**27. A Matter Of Trust**	Columbia 06108
12/20/86+	**18**	9	28. This Is The Time all of above (except first two) produced by Phil Ramone	Columbia 06526
10/21/89	**1**(2)	15	• **29. We Didn't Start The Fire**	Columbia 73021
1/27/90	**6**	11	**30. I Go To Extremes**	Columbia 73091
11/24/90	**37**	3	31. And So It Goes originally the B-side of "That's Not Her Style" on Columbia 73442	Columbia 73602#
			JOHN, Elton	
			Born Reginald Kenneth Dwight on 3/25/47 in Pinner, Middlesex, England. Formed his first group Bluesology in 1966. Group backed visiting U.S. soul artists and later became Long John Baldry's backing band. Took the name of Elton John from the first names of Bluesology members Elton Dean and John Baldry. Teamed up with lyricist Bernie Taupin beginning in 1969. Formed Rocket Records in 1973. Played the Pinball Wizard in the film version of *Tommy*. Recorded duet with New York singer Jennifer Rush.	
12/19/70+	**8**	11	**1. Your Song**	Uni 55265
4/10/71	**34**	4	2. Friends from the British film of the same title	Uni 55277
1/01/72	**24**	7	3. Levon	Uni 55314
5/27/72	**6**	12	**4. Rocket Man**	Uni 55328
8/26/72	**8**	7	**5. Honky Cat**	Uni 55343
12/23/72+	**1**(3)	14	• **6. Crocodile Rock**	MCA 40000
4/21/73	**2**(1)	12	**7. Daniel**	MCA 40046
8/11/73	**12**	9	8. Saturday Night's Alright For Fighting	MCA 40105
11/03/73	**2**(3)	14	• **9. Goodbye Yellow Brick Road**	MCA 40148
3/02/74	**1**(1)	16	• **10. Bennie And The Jets**	MCA 40198
7/06/74	**2**(2)	9	• **11. Don't Let The Sun Go Down On Me**	MCA 40259
9/21/74	**4**	9	**12. The Bitch Is Back**	MCA 40297
12/07/74+	**1**(2)	10	• **13. Lucy In The Sky With Diamonds** with the Reggae guitars of Dr. Winston O'Boogie (John Lennon)	MCA 40344

DATE	POS	WKS	ARTIST—RECORD TITLE	LABEL & NO.
3/15/75	1(2)	17	● **14. Philadelphia Freedom** **THE ELTON JOHN BAND**	MCA 40364
7/12/75	**4**	10	● **15. Someone Saved My Life Tonight**	MCA 40421
10/18/75	1(3)	12	● **16. Island Girl**	MCA 40461
1/31/76	**14**	5	17. Grow Some Funk Of Your Own/	
		5	18. I Feel Like A Bullet (In The Gun Of Robert Ford)	MCA 40505
7/17/76	1(4)	15	● **19. Don't Go Breaking My Heart** **ELTON JOHN AND KIKI DEE**	Rocket 40585
11/20/76	**6**	11	● **20. Sorry Seems To Be The Hardest Word**	MCA/Rocket 40645
2/26/77	**28**	3	21. Bite Your Lip (Get up and dance!) all of above produced by Gus Dudgeon	MCA/Rocket 40677
4/29/78	**34**	4	22. Ego	MCA 40892
11/18/78	**22**	7	23. Part-Time Love	MCA 40973
6/23/79	**9**	14	● **24. Mama Can't Buy You Love**	MCA 41042
10/27/79	**31**	4	25. Victim Of Love	MCA 41126
5/10/80	**3**	17	● **26. Little Jeannie**	MCA 41236
9/20/80	**39**	2	27. (Sartorial Eloquence) Don't Ya Wanna Play This Game No More?	MCA 41293
5/30/81	**21**	6	28. Nobody Wins	Geffen 49722
9/05/81	**34**	3	29. Chloe	Geffen 49788
4/17/82	**13**	10	30. Empty Garden (Hey Hey Johnny)	Geffen 50049
8/14/82	**12**	10	31. Blue Eyes	Geffen 29954
5/14/83	**12**	12	32. I'm Still Standing	Geffen 29639
8/20/83	**25**	8	33. Kiss The Bride	Geffen 29568
11/19/83+	**4**	15	**34. I Guess That's Why They Call It The Blues** harmonica solo: Stevie Wonder	Geffen 29460
6/16/84	**5**	13	**35. Sad Songs (Say So Much)**	Geffen 29292
9/15/84	**16**	10	36. Who Wears These Shoes?	Geffen 29189
1/12/85	**38**	3	37. In Neon	Geffen 29111
11/02/85	**20**	10	38. Wrap Her Up	Geffen 28873
11/23/85+	1(4)	17	● **39. That's What Friends Are For** **DIONNE & FRIENDS: Elton John, Gladys Knight and Stevie Wonder**	Arista 9422
2/08/86	**7**	11	**40. Nikita** backing vocal by George Michael	Geffen 28800
7/04/87	**36**	3	41. Flames Of Paradise **JENNIFER RUSH with ELTON JOHN**	Epic 07119
11/28/87+	**6**	12	**42. Candle In The Wind** with The Melbourne Symphony Orchestra; tribute to Marilyn Monroe; tune first recorded for his *Goodbye Yellow Brick Road* LP in 1973	MCA 53196
7/02/88	2(1)	13	**43. I Don't Wanna Go On With You Like That**	MCA 53345
10/15/88	**19**	6	44. A Word In Spanish	MCA 53408
4/29/89	**16**	7	45. Through The Storm **ARETHA FRANKLIN AND ELTON JOHN**	Arista 9809
9/16/89	**13**	9	46. Healing Hands	MCA 53692
2/10/90	**18**	9	47. Sacrifice	MCA 53750
6/09/90	**28**	5	48. Club At The End Of The Street	MCA 79026

DATE	POS	WKS	ARTIST—RECORD TITLE	LABEL & NO.
			JOHN, Little Willie	
			Born William Edgar John on 11/15/37 in Cullendale, Arkansas and raised in Detroit. R&B singer. Brother of Mable John (of The Raeletts). Convicted of manslaughter in 1966; died of a heart attack in Washington State Prison on 5/26/68.	
7/14/56	**24**	9	1. Fever Best Seller #24 / Top 100 #27	King 4935
4/21/58	**20**	7	2. Talk To Me, Talk To Me Top 100 #20 / Best Seller #22	King 5108
7/25/60	**38**	1	3. Heartbreak (It's Hurtin' Me)	King 5356
10/10/60	**13**	10	4. Sleep #1 hit for Fred Waring's Pennsylvanians in 1924	King 5394
			JOHN, Robert	
			Born Robert John Pedrick, Jr. in Brooklyn in 1946. First recorded at age 12 for Big Top Records. In 1963, recorded as lead singer with Bobby & The Consoles.	
1/29/72	**3**	13	● **1. The Lion Sleeps Tonight** adaptation of a South African song (adapted in 1952 as "Wimoweh")	Atlantic 2846
6/30/79	**1**(1)	19	● **2. Sad Eyes**	EMI America 8015
8/23/80	**31**	4	3. Hey There Lonely Girl	EMI America 8049
			JOHN & ERNEST	
			Duo of John Free and Ernest Smith.	
5/12/73	**31**	4	1. Super Fly Meets Shaft [N] break-in song written and produced by Dickie Goodman	Rainy Wed. 201
			JOHNNIE & JOE	
			R&B duo from the Bronx: Johnnie Louise Richardson (d: 10/25/88 from a stroke) and Joe Rivers. Johnnie was the daughter of the late J&S Records owner Zelma "Zell" Sanders and a touring member of The Jaynettes.	
5/27/57	**8**	15	**1. Over The Mountain; Across The Sea** Top 100 #8 / Best Seller #9 / Juke Box #17 end first released on J&S 1664 in 1957	Chess 1654
			JOHNNY AND THE HURRICANES	
			Rock and roll instrumental band formed as the Orbits in Toledo, Ohio in 1958. Consisted of leader John Pocisk "Paris" (saxophone), Paul Tesluk (organ), Dave Yorko (guitar), Lionel "Butch" Mattice (bass) and Tony Kaye (drums; replaced in late 1959 by Bo Savich). First recorded for Twirl in 1959. Paris had own Attila label from 1965-70.	
6/01/59	**23**	6	1. Crossfire [I] first released on Twirl 1001 in 1958	Warwick 502
8/17/59	**5**	13	**2. Red River Rock [I]** rock version of "Red River Valley"	Warwick 509
11/16/59	**25**	6	3. Reveille Rock [I] rock version of the Army bugle call "Reveille"	Warwick 513
2/22/60	**15**	10	4. Beatnik Fly [I] rock version of "Blue Tail Fly"	Warwick 520
			JOHNNY HATES JAZZ	
			U.K.-based trio: Clark Datchler (vocals) and Calvin Hayes (both from England), with American, Mike Nocito. Hayes is the son of pop producer Mickie Most. Datchler left group in late 1988, replaced by producer/ex-Cure member Phil Thornalley.	
4/02/88	**2**(3)	13	**1. Shattered Dreams**	Virgin 99383

DATE	POS	WKS	ARTIST—RECORD TITLE	LABEL & NO.
8/13/88	**31**	5	2. I Don't Want To Be A Hero	Virgin 99304
			JOHNS, Sammy	
			Born on 2/07/46 in Charlotte, North Carolina. Own band, the Devilles, from 1963-73.	
3/01/75	**5**	12	● **1. Chevy Van**	GRC 2046
			JOHNSON — see BROTHERS JOHNSON	
			JOHNSON, Betty	
			Born on 3/16/32 in Charlotte, North Carolina. Married to musical conductor Charles Randolph Grean. Regular on NBC-TV's "Tonight Show" starring Jack Parr.	
12/15/56+	**9**	18	**1. I Dreamed** Jockey #9 / Top 100 #12 / Juke Box #15 / Best Seller #22 featured on an episode of NBC-TV's *Modern Romances*	Bally 1020
6/24/57	**25**	1	2. Little White Lies Jockey #25 / Top 100 #40 #1 hit for Fred Waring's Pennsylvanians in 1930	Bally 1033
2/24/58	**17**	11	3. The Little Blue Man [N] Jockey #17 / Top 100 #19 / Best Seller #20 voice of the Little Blue Man: Hugh Downs (host of TV's "20/20")	Atlantic 1169
6/30/58	**19**	1	4. Dream Jockey #19 / Top 100 #58 #1 hit for the Pied Pipers in 1945; orchestra on above 3 conducted by Betty's husband, Charles Grean	Atlantic 1186
			JOHNSON, Don	
			Born on 12/15/49 in Flatt Creek, Missouri. Actor/singer. Played Sonny Crockett on TV's "Miami Vice." Starred in several films. Remarried his ex-wife, actress Melanie Griffiths, in 1989.	
9/06/86	**5**	10	**1. Heartbeat**	Epic 06285
11/12/88	**25**	5	2. Till I Loved You **BARBRA STREISAND AND DON JOHNSON** love theme from the Broadway musical *Goya*	Columbia 08062
			JOHNSON, Marv	
			Born on 10/15/38 in Detroit. R&B singer/songwriter/pianist. With the Serenaders vocal group, mid-1950s. First recorded for Kudo in 1958. Worked in sales and promotion for Motown in the early '70s.	
4/20/59	**30**	6	1. Come To Me released regionally on Tamla 101; Berry Gordy's first release	United Art. 160
11/16/59+	**10**	16	**2. You Got What It Takes**	United Art. 185
3/21/60	**9**	10	**3. I Love The Way You Love**	United Art. 208
10/10/60	**20**	4	4. (You've Got To) Move Two Mountains all of above: female backing by The Rayber Voices	United Art. 241
			JOHNSON, Michael	
			Born on 7/08/44 in Alamosa, Colorado and raised in Denver. Studied classical guitar in 1966 in Spain. In the Chad Mitchell Trio with John Denver in 1968.	
5/27/78	**12**	10	1. Bluer Than Blue	EMI America 8001
9/23/78	**32**	5	2. Almost Like Being In Love	EMI America 8004
9/29/79	**19**	9	3. This Night Won't Last Forever	EMI America 8019

DATE	POS	WKS	ARTIST—RECORD TITLE	LABEL & NO.
			JOHNSTON, Tom	
			Lead singer/guitarist of The Doobie Brothers from 1971-78. Native of Visalia, California.	
1/12/80	**34**	2	1. Savannah Nights	Warner 49096
			JO JO GUNNE	
			Los Angeles-based rock quartet formed by Jay Ferguson and Mark Andes (former members of Spirit). Named group after the Chuck Berry hit.	
4/15/72	**27**	6	1. Run Run Run	Asylum 11003
			JOLI, France	
			French Canadian singer born in 1963 in Montreal.	
9/29/79	**15**	8	1. Come To Me	Prelude 8001
			JON & ROBIN AND THE IN CROWD	
			Jon Abnor and Robin (who married Jimmy Wright of The Five Americans).	
5/27/67	**18**	6	1. Do It Again A Little Bit Slower	Abnak 119
			JONES, Etta	
			Born on 11/25/28 in Aiken, South Carolina. Jazz singer with Earl Hines' orchestra from 1949-52.	
12/12/60	**36**	1	1. Don't Go To Strangers	Prestige 180
			JONES, Howard	
			Born on 2/23/55 in Southampton, England. Pop singer/songwriter/synth wizard.	
2/25/84	**27**	6	1. New Song	Elektra 69766
6/02/84	**33**	4	2. What Is Love?	Elektra 69737
4/20/85	**5**	14	**3. Things Can Only Get Better**	Elektra 69651
8/03/85	**19**	8	4. Life In One Day	Elektra 69631
5/03/86	**4**	14	**5. No One Is To Blame**	Elektra 69549
11/08/86	**17**	10	6. You Know I Love You...Don't You?	Elektra 69512
4/08/89	**12**	11	7. Everlasting Love	Elektra 69308
8/12/89	**30**	4	8. The Prisoner	Elektra 69288
			JONES, Jack	
			Born on 1/14/38 in Los Angeles. Son of actor/singer Allan Jones, who had the #8 pop hit "The Donkey Serenade" the year Jack was born.	
11/30/63+	**14**	10	1. Wives And Lovers inspired by the film of the same title	Kapp 551
12/26/64+	**30**	5	2. Dear Heart from the film of the same title	Kapp 635
3/20/65	**15**	7	3. The Race Is On	Kapp 651
7/16/66	**35**	4	4. The Impossible Dream (The Quest) from the musical *Man of La Mancha*	Kapp 755
3/25/67	**39**	2	5. Lady	Kapp 800
			JONES, Jimmy	
			Born on 6/02/37 in Birmingham, Alabama. Joined the R&B group Sparks Of Rhythm in New York in 1955. Formed own group, the Savoys (later: Pretenders), in 1956.	
1/18/60	**2**(1)	14	**1. Handy Man**	Cub 9049
5/09/60	**3**	10	**2. Good Timin'**	Cub 9067

DATE	POS	WKS	ARTIST—RECORD TITLE	LABEL & NO.
			JONES, Joe	
			Born on 8/12/26 in New Orleans. Pianist/valet for B.B. King in the early 1950s. First recorded for Capitol in 1954. Produced The Dixie Cups and Alvin Robinson.	
10/10/60	**3**	9	**1. You Talk Too Much**	Roulette 4304
			first released on RIC 972 in 1960	
			JONES, Linda	
			Born on 1/14/44 in Newark, New Jersey; died of diabetes on 3/14/72. R&B singer. First recorded for MGM/Cub as "Linda Lane" in 1963.	
7/22/67	**21**	7	1. Hypnotized	Loma 2070
			JONES, Oran "Juice"	
			Born in Houston in 1959 and raised in Harlem. Soul balladeer singer.	
10/11/86	**9**	9	**1. The Rain**	Def Jam 06209
			JONES, Quincy	
			Born Quincy Delight Jones, Jr. on 3/14/33 in Chicago and raised in Seattle. Composer/producer/conductor/ arranger. Began as a jazz trumpeter with Lionel Hampton, 1950-53. Music director for Mercury Records in 1961, then vice president in 1964. Wrote scores for many films, 1965-73. Scored TV series "Roots" in 1977. Arranger and producer for hundreds of successful singers and orchestras. Produced Michael Jackson's mega-albums *Off the Wall, Thriller* and *Bad.* Established own Qwest label in 1981. Line producer for the film *The Color Purple.* Married for 12 years to actress Peggy Lipton (TV's "Mod Squad." Most nominated artist in Grammy history with 76 nominations and 25 wins. Won the Grammy's Trustees Award in 1989. Won Grammy's Legends Award in 1990. His biographical film *Listen Up: The Lives of Quincy Jones* was released in 1990.	
7/22/78	**21**	7	1. Stuff Like That	A&M 2043
			vocals by Ashford & Simpson and Chaka Khan	
5/09/81	**28**	5	2. Ai No Corrida	A&M 2309
			featuring the vocals of Dune	
9/19/81	**17**	10	3. Just Once	A&M 2357
			QUINCY JONES featuring JAMES INGRAM	
2/13/82	**14**	11	4. One Hundred Ways	A&M 2387
			QUINCY JONES featuring JAMES INGRAM	
12/16/89+	**18**	8	5. I'll Be Good To You	Qwest 22697
			QUINCY JONES featuring RAY CHARLES AND CHAKA KHAN	
4/07/90	**31**	4	• 6. The Secret Garden (Sweet Seduction Suite)	Qwest 19992
			QUINCY JONES/AL B. SURE!/JAMES INGRAM/ EL DeBARGE/BARRY WHITE	
			JONES, Rickie Lee	
			Born on 11/08/54 in Chicago. Pop-jazz-styled singer/songwriter. Moved to Los Angeles in 1977. Won the 1979 Best New Artist Grammy Award.	
5/12/79	**4**	12	**1. Chuck E.'s In Love**	Warner 8825
9/01/79	**40**	1	2. Young Blood	Warner 49018
			JONES, Tom	
			Born Thomas Jones Woodward on 6/07/40 in Pontypridd, South Wales. Worked local clubs as Tommy Scott; formed own trio The Senators in 1963. Began solo career in London in 1964. Won the 1965 Best New Artist Grammy Award. Host of own TV musical variety series from 1969-71.	
5/01/65	**10**	9	**1. It's Not Unusual**	Parrot 9737
7/03/65	**3**	10	**2. What's New Pussycat?**	Parrot 9765
			from the film of the same title	

DATE	POS	WKS	ARTIST—RECORD TITLE	LABEL & NO.
9/18/65	**27**	5	3. With These Hands #7 hit for Eddie Fisher in 1953	Parrot 9787
1/01/66	**25**	6	4. Thunderball from the James Bond film *Thunderball*	Parrot 9801
1/21/67	**11**	7	5. Green, Green Grass Of Home	Parrot 40009
4/01/67	**27**	4	6. Detroit City	Parrot 40012
4/13/68	**15**	11	7. Delilah	Parrot 40025
10/05/68	**35**	2	8. Help Yourself	Parrot 40029
6/07/69	**13**	9	9. Love Me Tonight	Parrot 40038
8/09/69	**6**	14	● **10. I'll Never Fall In Love Again** **[R]** originally charted in 1967 (POS 49)	Parrot 40018
1/03/70	**5**	10	● **11. Without Love (There Is Nothing)**	Parrot 40045
5/09/70	**13**	7	12. Daughter Of Darkness	Parrot 40048
8/29/70	**14**	7	13. I (Who Have Nothing)	Parrot 40051
11/28/70	**25**	7	14. Can't Stop Loving You all of above produced by Peter Sullivan	Parrot 40056
2/20/71	**2**(1)	12	● **15. She's A Lady** written by Paul Anka	Parrot 40058
6/12/71	**26**	6	16. Puppet Man/ written by Neil Sedaka	
7/03/71	**38**	3	17. Resurrection Shuffle	Parrot 40064
2/12/77	**15**	10	18. Say You'll Stay Until Tomorrow	Epic 50308
12/24/88+	**31**	6	19. Kiss **THE ART OF NOISE featuring TOM JONES**	China 871038
			JONES GIRLS, The	
			Detroit soul sister trio: Shirley, Brenda and Valorie Jones. Backup singers for Lou Rawls, Teddy Pendergrass and Aretha Franklin. With Diana Ross from 1975-78. Sang with Le Pamplemousse.	
8/18/79	**38**	1	● 1. You Gonna Make Me Love Somebody Else	Phil. Int. 3680
			JOPLIN, Janis	
			Born on 1/19/43 in Port Arthur, Texas. White blues-rock singer. Nicknamed "Pearl." To San Francisco in 1966, joined Big Brother & The Holding Company. Left band to go solo in 1968. Died of a heroin overdose in Hollywood on 10/04/70. The Bette Midler film *The Rose* was inspired by Joplin's life.	
2/20/71	**1**(2)	12	**1. Me And Bobby McGee**	Columbia 45314
			JOURNEY	
			Rock group formed in San Francisco in 1973. Consisted of Neal Schon, George Tickner (guitars), Gregg Rolie (keyboards, vocals), Ross Valory (bass) and Aynsley Dunbar (drums). Schon and Rolie had been in Santana. Tickner left in 1975. Steve Perry (lead vocals) added in 1978. Dunbar (formerly with Jeff Beck, Frank Zappa and John Mayall) was replaced by Steve Smith in 1979. Jonathan Cain (ex-keyboardist of The Babys) added in 1981, replacing Rolie. In 1986 group pared down to a three-man core: Perry, Schon and Cain. The latter two hooked up with Bad English in 1989. Smith, Valory and Rolie joined Storm in 1991.	
8/25/79	**16**	12	1. Lovin', Touchin', Squeezin'	Columbia 11036
3/29/80	**23**	6	2. Any Way You Want It	Columbia 11213
7/05/80	**32**	4	3. Walks Like A Lady	Columbia 11275
4/04/81	**34**	4	4. The Party's Over (Hopelessly In Love)	Columbia 60505
8/01/81	**4**	14	**5. Who's Crying Now**	Columbia 02241
11/07/81	**9**	13	**6. Don't Stop Believin'**	Columbia 02567

DATE	POS	WKS	ARTIST—RECORD TITLE	LABEL & NO.
1/23/82	**2**(6)	14	**7. Open Arms**	Columbia 02687
6/12/82	**19**	9	8. Still They Ride	Columbia 02883
2/05/83	**8**	16	**9. Separate Ways (Worlds Apart)**	Columbia 03513
4/30/83	**12**	11	10. Faithfully	Columbia 03840
7/23/83	**23**	8	11. After The Fall	Columbia 04004
10/22/83	**23**	7	12. Send Her My Love	Columbia 04151
2/02/85	**9**	11	**13. Only The Young** from the film *Vision Quest*	Geffen 29090
4/19/86	**9**	10	**14. Be Good To Yourself**	Columbia 05869
7/12/86	**17**	7	15. Suzanne	Columbia 06134
9/20/86	**17**	8	16. Girl Can't Help It	Columbia 06302
1/24/87	**14**	9	17. I'll Be Alright Without You	Columbia 06301
			JUMP 'N THE SADDLE	
			Chicago-based band — Peter Quinn, lead singer.	
12/24/83+	**15**	7	1. The Curly Shuffle [N] a Three Stooges parody; first released on Acme 416 in 1983	Atlantic 89718
			JUNIOR	
			Full name: Junior Giscombe. R&B-funk singer/songwriter from England.	
4/10/82	**30**	3	1. Mama Used To Say	Mercury 76132
			JUSTIS, Bill	
			Born on 10/14/26 in Birmingham, Alabama. Died on 7/15/82 in Nashville. Session saxophonist/arranger/ producer. Led house band for Sun Records.	
11/18/57	**2**(1)	14	**1. Raunchy** **[I]** Best Seller #2 / Top 100 #3 / Jockey #5 sax: Bill Justis; guitar: Sid Manker	Phillips 3519
			JUST US	
			Consists of New York City producers Chip Taylor and Al Gorgoni.	
5/07/66	**34**	2	1. I Can't Grow Peaches On A Cherry Tree first released on Minuteman 203 in 1966	Colpix 803
			K	
			KAEMPFERT, Bert	
			Born on 10/16/23 in Hamburg, Germany. Multi-instrumentalist/ bandleader/producer/composer/arranger for Polydor Records in Germany. Produced first Beatles recording session. Died on 6/21/80 in Switzerland.	
11/21/60+	**1**(3)	15	**1. Wonderland By Night** **[I]** trumpet solo by Charly Tabor	Decca 31141
4/10/61	**31**	4	2. Tenderly [I] #17 hit for Rosemary Clooney in 1952	Decca 31236
2/13/65	**11**	10	3. Red Roses For A Blue Lady [I] #3 hit for Vaughn Monroe in 1949	Decca 31722
5/29/65	**33**	3	4. Three O'Clock In The Morning [I] there were 6 top 10 versions of this tune from 1921-30	Decca 31778

DATE	POS	WKS	ARTIST—RECORD TITLE	LABEL & NO.
			KAJAGOOGOO	
			English pop-synth quintet led by Limahl (Chris Hamill), who left in late 1983.	
5/21/83	**5**	12	**1. Too Shy**	EMI America 8161
			KALIN TWINS	
			Herbert and Harold Kalin, born on 2/16/39 in Port Jervis, New York.	
6/30/58	**5**	13	**1. When** Hot 100 #5 / Best Seller #7 / Jockey #8	Decca 30642
10/20/58	**12**	9	2. Forget Me Not	Decca 30745
			KALLEN, Kitty	
			Born on 5/25/22 in Philadelphia. Big band singer with Jack Teagarden, Jimmy Dorsey and Harry James.	
2/11/56	**39**	1	1. Go On With The Wedding **KITTY KALLEN AND GEORGIE SHAW**	Decca 29776
11/09/59	**34**	3	2. If I Give My Heart To You there were 5 top 30 versions of this tune in 1954	Columbia 41473
1/12/63	**18**	6	3. My Coloring Book	RCA 8124
			KANE GANG, The	
			English soul-styled pop trio: vocalists Martin Brammer and Paul Woods with guitarist David Brewis. Band's name derived from the film *Citizen Kane*.	
12/19/87	**36**	3	1. Motortown	Capitol 44062
			KANSAS	
			Progressive rock group formed in Topeka in 1970. Consisted of Steve Walsh (lead vocals, keyboards), Kerry Livgren (guitar, keyboards), Phil Ehart (drums), Robby Steinhardt (violin), Rich Williams (guitar) and Dave Hope (bass). Walsh left in 1981 and was replaced by John Elefante. Livgren became a popular Contemporary Christian artist in the '80s. Revised lineup in 1986: Walsh, Ehart, Williams, Steve Morse (guitarist from Dixie Dregs) and Billy Greer (bass).	
2/05/77	**11**	13	● 1. Carry On Wayward Son	Kirshner 4267
12/17/77+	**28**	6	2. Point Of Know Return	Kirshner 4273
2/18/78	**6**	15	● **3. Dust In The Wind**	Kirshner 4274
6/23/79	**23**	8	4. People Of The South Wind	Kirshner 4284
11/08/80	**40**	1	5. Hold On	Kirshner 4291
5/29/82	**17**	9	6. Play The Game Tonight	Kirshner 02903
11/29/86+	**19**	10	7. All I Wanted	MCA 52958
			KASENETZ-KATZ SINGING ORCHESTRAL CIRCUS	
			Bubblegum rock group assembled by producers Jerry Kasenetz and Jeff Katz. Features members from The 1910 Fruitgum Co./The Ohio Express/The Music Explosion.	
11/09/68	**25**	6	1. Quick Joey Small (Run Joey Run) Joey Levine, lead singer	Buddah 64
			KATRINA AND THE WAVES	
			British-based, pop-rock quartet fronted by Kansas-born Katrina Leskanich, with American Vince de la Cruz (bass) and Britons Alex Cooper (drums) and Kimberley Rew (guitar, former member of the Soft Boys).	
4/20/85	**9**	13	**1. Walking On Sunshine**	Capitol 5466
9/07/85	**37**	2	2. Do You Want Crying	Capitol 5450
8/19/89	**16**	6	3. That's The Way	SBK 07303

DATE	POS	WKS	ARTIST—RECORD TITLE	LABEL & NO.
			KAYE, Sammy	
			Born on 3/13/10 in Rocky River, Ohio; died on 6/02/87 of cancer. Durable leader of popular "sweet" dance band with the slogan "Swing and Sway with Sammy Kaye." Also played clarinet and alto sax.	
5/02/64	**36**	2	1. Charade [I]	Decca 31589
			from the film of the same title	
			KC AND THE SUNSHINE BAND	
			Disco-R&B band formed in Florida in 1973 by lead singer/keyboardist Harry "KC" Casey (b: 1/31/51, Hialeah, Florida) and bassist Richard Finch (b: 1/25/54, Indianapolis). Interracial band contained from seven to 11 members. Casey and Finch wrote, arranged and produced all of their hits.	
8/02/75	**1**(1)	9	**1. Get Down Tonight**	T.K. 1009
11/01/75	**1**(2)	13	**2. That's The Way (I Like It)**	T.K. 1015
7/31/76	**1**(1)	16	**3. (Shake, Shake, Shake) Shake Your Booty**	T.K. 1019
1/29/77	**37**	2	4. I Like To Do It	T.K. 1020
4/02/77	**1**(1)	16	**5. I'm Your Boogie Man**	T.K. 1022
8/13/77	**2**(3)	14	**6. Keep It Comin' Love**	T.K. 1023
3/25/78	**35**	3	7. Boogie Shoes	T.K. 1025
			originally released as the B-side of "Shake Your Booty"	
6/24/78	**35**	2	8. It's The Same Old Song	T.K. 1028
9/29/79+	**1**(1)	18	**9. Please Don't Go**	T.K. 1035
12/22/79+	**2**(2)	16	• **10. Yes, I'm Ready**	Casablanca 2227
			TERI DeSARIO with K.C.	
2/04/84	**18**	10	11. Give It Up	Meca 1001
			KC	
			K-DOE, Ernie	
			Born Ernest Kador, Jr. on 2/22/36 in New Orleans. R&B singer/songwriter. Recorded with the Blue Diamonds on Savoy in 1954. First solo recording for Specialty in 1955.	
4/03/61	**1**(1)	12	**1. Mother-In-Law**	Minit 623
			bass vocal: Benny Spellman	
			KEEDY	
			Kelly Keedy, female dance singer based in Milwaukee. Born on 7/26/65 in Abilene, Texas. Married to her songwriting partner Greg Gerard, leader of the group Gerard.	
4/06/91	**15**	8	1. Save Some Love	Arista 2153
			KEITH	
			Born James Barry Keefer on 5/07/49 in Philadelphia. First recorded as "Keith & The Admirations" on Columbia in 1965.	
11/12/66	**39**	1	1. Ain't Gonna Lie	Mercury 72596
1/07/67	**7**	9	**2. 98.6**	Mercury 72639
			above 2 feature backing vocals by The Tokens	
4/08/67	**37**	2	3. Tell Me To My Face	Mercury 72652
			KELLER, Jerry	
			Born on 6/20/37 in Fort Smith, Arkansas. To Tulsa, Oklahoma at age seven.	
7/20/59	**14**	8	1. Here Comes Summer	Kapp 277
			KELLY, Grace — see CROSBY, Bing	

DATE	POS	WKS	ARTIST—RECORD TITLE	LABEL & NO.
			KELLY, Monty	
			Arranger/conductor from Oakland. Born in 1919. Trumpeter with Paul Whiteman in the early 1940s.	
4/04/60	**30**	3	1. Summer Set [I]	Carlton 527
			KEMP, Johnny	
			Singer/dancer/actor/songwriter. Began performing in nightclubs in his native Nassau, Bahamas, at the age of 13. Moved to Harlem in 1979.	
6/25/88	**10**	11	● **1. Just Got Paid**	Columbia 07744
4/15/89	**36**	3	2. Birthday Suit from the film *Sing*	Columbia 68569
			KEMP, Tara	
			Singer/songwriter/classically trained pianist from the San Francisco Bay area.	
2/09/91	**3**	15	● **1. Hold You Tight**	Giant 19458
6/08/91	**7**	11	**2. Piece Of My Heart**	Giant 19364#
			KENDRICKS, Eddie	
			Born on 12/17/39 in Union Springs, Alabama and raised in Birmingham. Joined R&B group the Primes in Detroit in the late '50s. Group later evolved into The Temptations; Eddie sang lead from 1960-71. Eddie later dropped letter "s" from his last name.	
9/15/73	**1**(2)	16	**1. Keep On Truckin' (Part 1)**	Tamla 54238
1/26/74	**2**(2)	13	**2. Boogie Down**	Tamla 54243
6/01/74	**28**	4	3. Son Of Sagittarius	Tamla 54247
4/05/75	**18**	10	4. Shoeshine Boy	Tamla 54257
3/20/76	**36**	3	5. He's A Friend	Tamla 54266
9/14/85	**20**	7	6. A Nite At The Apollo Live! The Way You Do The Things You Do/My Girl **DARYL HALL JOHN OATES with DAVID RUFFIN & EDDIE KENDRICK**	RCA 14178
			KENNEDY, Joyce — see OSBORNE, Jeffrey	
			KENNER, Chris	
			Born on 12/25/29 in Kenner, Louisiana. Died of a heart attack on 1/28/76. R&B singer/songwriter. First recorded for Baton in 1956.	
7/03/61	**2**(3)	10	**1. I Like It Like That, Part 1** first released on Valiant 3229 in 1961	Instant 3229
			KENNY G	
			Kenny Gorelick; fusion saxophonist from Seattle. With Barry White's Love Unlimited Orchestra at age 17.	
5/16/87	**4**	12	**1. Songbird** **[I]**	Arista 9588
9/26/87	**15**	9	2. Don't Make Me Wait For Love vocal: Lenny Williams (original lead singer for Tower of Power); originally hit Black chart on 12/13/86 (POS 77) on Arista 9544	Arista 9625
11/19/88+	**13**	10	3. Silhouette [I]	Arista 9751
			KENTON, Stan	
			Progressive jazz bandleader/pianist/composer. Born on 2/19/12 in Wichita, Kansas; died in Los Angeles on 8/25/79. Organized his first jazz band in 1941. Third person named to the Jazz Hall of Fame.	
11/17/62	**32**	4	1. Mama Sang A Song [S]	Capitol 4847
			KERMIT — see HENSON, Jim	

DATE	POS	WKS	ARTIST—RECORD TITLE	LABEL & NO.
			KHAN, Chaka	
			Born Yvette Marie Stevens on 3/23/53 in Great Lakes, Illinois. Became lead singer of Rufus in 1972. Recorded solo and with Rufus since 1978. Sister of vocalists Taka Boom and Mark Stevens (Jamaica Boys). Chaka's daughter Milini is a member of Pretty In Pink.	
11/18/78	**21**	8	1. I'm Every Woman	Warner 8683
9/29/84	**3**	17	● **2. I Feel For You**	Warner 29195
			written by Prince; with Grandmaster Melle Mel and Stevie Wonder	
12/16/89	**18**	8	3. I'll Be Good To You	Qwest 22697
			QUINCY JONES featuring RAY CHARLES AND CHAKA KHAN	
			KIHN, Greg, Band	
			Greg is a rock singer/songwriter/guitarist from Baltimore. Formed band in Berkeley, California in 1975.	
7/11/81	**15**	13	1. The Breakup Song (They Don't Write 'Em)	Beserkley 47149
3/05/83	**2**(1)	14	**2. Jeopardy**	Beserkley 69847
			GREG KIHN:	
3/23/85	**30**	4	3. Lucky	EMI America 8255
			KILGORE, Theola	
			Gospel-blues singer from Shreveport, Louisiana and raised in Oakland.	
5/11/63	**21**	8	1. The Love Of My Man	Serock 2004
			KIM, Andy	
			Born Andrew Joachim on 12/05/46 in Montreal, Canada. His parents were from Lebanon. Pop singer/songwriter. Teamed with Jeff Barry to write "Sugar, Sugar."	
6/01/68	**21**	8	1. How'd We Ever Get This Way	Steed 707
10/19/68	**31**	3	2. Shoot'em Up, Baby	Steed 710
6/21/69	**9**	12	● **3. Baby, I Love You**	Steed 716
11/08/69	**36**	1	4. So Good Together	Steed 720
11/28/70	**17**	8	5. Be My Baby	Steed 729
7/20/74	**1**(1)	13	● **6. Rock Me Gently**	Capitol 3895
11/23/74	**28**	4	7. Fire, Baby I'm On Fire	Capitol 3962
			KIMBERLY, Adrian	
			Artist is actually a Don Everly production, recorded on Don's own label.	
7/10/61	**34**	1	1. The Graduation Song...Pomp And Circumstance [I]	Calliope 6501
			written in 1901 for the coronation of King Edward VII	
			KING, B.B.	
			The most famous blues singer/guitarist in the world today. Born Riley B. King on 9/16/25 in Itta Bena, Mississippi. Moved to Memphis in 1946. Own radio show on WDIA-Memphis, 1949-50, where he was dubbed "The Beale Street Blues Boy," later shortened to "Blues Boy," then simply "B.B." First recorded for Bullet in 1949. Inducted into the Rock and Roll Hall of Fame in 1987. Won the Lifetime Achievement Grammy award in 1987. Appeared in the films *Into the Night* (1985) and *Amazon Women on the Moon* (1987).	
6/13/64	**34**	3	1. Rock Me Baby	Kent 393
5/25/68	**39**	1	2. Paying The Cost To Be The Boss	BluesWay 61015
1/31/70	**15**	8	3. The Thrill Is Gone	BluesWay 61032
4/03/71	**40**	1	4. Ask Me No Questions	ABC 11290
9/22/73	**38**	2	5. To Know You Is To Love You	ABC 11373

DATE	POS	WKS	ARTIST—RECORD TITLE	LABEL & NO.
2/09/74	**28**	6	6. I Like To Live The Love	ABC 11406
			KING, Ben E.	
			Born Benjamin Earl Nelson on 9/23/38 in Henderson, North Carolina. To New York in 1947. Worked with The Moonglows for six months while still in high school. Joined the Five Crowns in 1957, who became the new Drifters in 1959. Wrote lyrics to "There Goes My Baby," his first lead performance with The Drifters. Went solo in May 1960.	
1/30/61	**10**	10	**1. Spanish Harlem**	Atco 6185
5/22/61	**4**	11	**2. Stand By Me**	Atco 6194
8/21/61	**18**	5	3. Amor there were 3 top 10 versions of this song in 1944	Atco 6203
5/19/62	**11**	7	4. Don't Play That Song (You Lied)	Atco 6222
8/03/63	**29**	6	5. I (Who Have Nothing)	Atco 6267
3/08/75	**5**	9	**6. Supernatural Thing - Part I**	Atlantic 3241
11/01/86	**9**	13	**7. Stand By Me** [R] featured song in the film of the same title	Atlantic 89361
			KING, Carole	
			Born Carole Klein on 2/09/42 in Brooklyn. Singer/songwriter/pianist. Neil Sedaka wrote his 1959 hit "Oh! Carol" about her. Married lyricist Gerry Goffin in 1958; team wrote four #1 hits: "Will You Love Me Tomorrow," "Go Away Little Girl," "Take Good Care Of My Baby" and "The Loco-Motion." Divorced Goffin in 1968; first solo album in 1970. In 1971, won four Grammys. King and Goffin's daughter, Louise, began a solo career in 1979. One of the most successful female songwriters of the rock era. She and Goffin were inducted as a songwriting team into the Rock and Roll Hall of Fame in 1990.	
9/22/62	**22**	4	1. It Might As Well Rain Until September first released on Companion 2000 in 1962	Dimension 2000
5/22/71	**1**(5)	15	● **2. It's Too Late/**	
		15	3. I Feel The Earth Move	Ode 66015
9/04/71	**14**	9	4. So Far Away	Ode 66019
2/05/72	**9**	8	**5. Sweet Seasons**	Ode 66022
12/09/72+	**24**	7	6. Been To Canaan	Ode 66031
8/11/73	**28**	5	7. Believe In Humanity	Ode 66035
12/08/73	**37**	2	8. Corazon [I]	Ode 66039
9/14/74	**2**(1)	12	**9. Jazzman**	Ode 66101
1/18/75	**9**	8	**10. Nightingale**	Ode 66106
3/06/76	**28**	6	11. Only Love Is Real all of above (except #1) produced by Lou Adler	Ode 66119
8/20/77	**30**	5	12. Hard Rock Cafe	Capitol 4455
6/14/80	**12**	10	13. One Fine Day	Capitol 4864
			KING, Claude	
			Born on 2/05/33 in Shreveport, Louisiana. Country singer/songwriter/guitarist. Acted in the TV miniseries *The Blue and the Gray* in 1982.	
6/16/62	**6**	11	**1. Wolverton Mountain** title is an actual place in Arkansas where Clifton Clowers lived	Columbia 42352
			KING, Evelyn "Champagne"	
			Born on 6/29/60 in the Bronx. To Philadelphia in 1970. Employed as a cleaning woman at Sigma Studios when discovered.	
7/22/78	**9**	10	● **1. Shame**	RCA 11122
3/03/79	**23**	8	● 2. I Don't Know If It's Right	RCA 11386

Honeymoon Suite might well have been called One-Night Stand. The Canadian hard-rockers' sole top-40 hit, 1986's "Feel It Again," peaked at No. 34—and then the honeymoon was over.

Whitney Houston's string of seven consecutive No. 1 records—beginning with 1985's "Saving All My Love For You" and ending with 1988's "Where Do Broken Hearts Go"—was unprecedented in the industry.

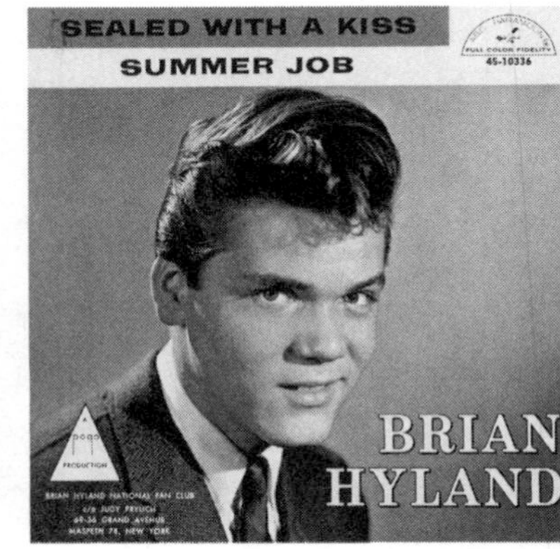

Engelbert Humperdinck entered and exited the charts with a bang. The former Arnold Dorsey opened his top-40 run in 1967 with "Release Me (And Let Me Love Again)," which peaked at No. 4, and closed it in 1976 with the gold single "After The Lovin'."

Brian Hyland's "Itsy Bitsy Teenie Weenie Yellow Polkadot Bikini," his sole No. 1 hit, was pushed aside in August 1960 by Elvis Presley's five-week No. 1 powerhouse, "It's Now Or Never."

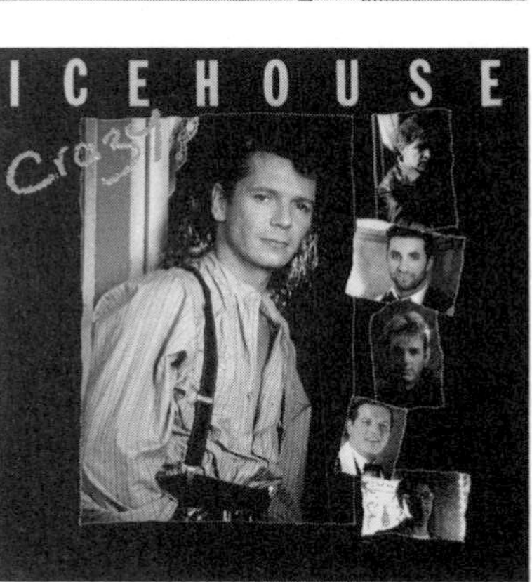

Icehouse, an Australian band formerly called Flowers, had an international hit with their 1982 single "Hey Little Girl"—in seemingly every country but the U.S.A. The group's sole top-10 single in the States came in 1988 with "Electric Blue."

Billy Idol's "Mony Mony" was the former Mr. William Broad's only No. 1 hit—and it was one of 1987's two No. 1 remakes of a Tommy James & The Shondells song. Tiffany scored the other with "I Think We're Alone Now." Ironically, both new versions entered the chart the same week.

INXS's multi-platinum sound was first heard in the U.S. in 1982, when Atco released *Shabooh Shoobah* and called it the Aussie group's "debut album." Shortly thereafter, the label issued two albums the group had recorded in Australia prior to their "debut"—and hasn't looked backward since.

Janet Jackson's 1991 contract with Virgin Records, after an extended stay at A&M, set a new industry high. The overall value of her deal is believed to be a staggering $35 million.

Michael Jackson's 1991 deal with Sony Music was announced a week after his sister Janet signed her huge contract with Virgin. Sony pegged the potential income from the signing—which involved crossover film and video deals, as well as the establishment of Jackson's own label—as "over a billion" dollars.

The Jamies were by no means one-shot wonders: after their 1958 hit "Summertime, Summertime," they scored *again* four years later, with . . . "Summertime, Summertime."

Jan & Dean's only No. 1 hit, "Surf City," topped the charts for two weeks in July 1963. Also hotdogging in the Top 10 at the same time: the Surfaris' classic surf instrumental "Wipe Out."

Rickie Lee Jones's growth as a pop artist since her 1979 No. 4 hit "Chuck E.'s In Love" was ably demonstrated 12 years later by her loving collection of classic crooner ballads and showtunes, *Pop Pop*.

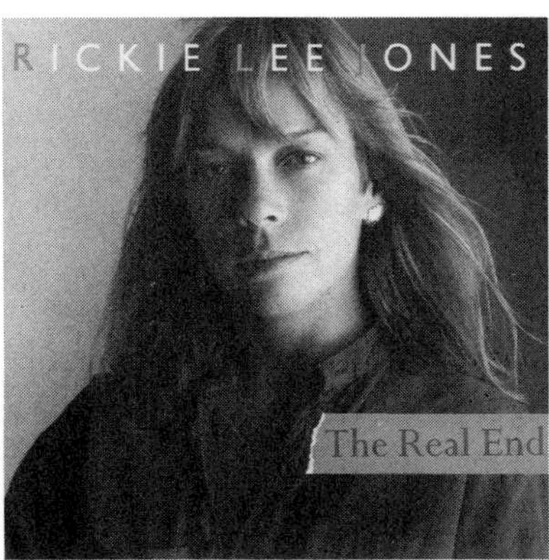

DATE	POS	WKS	ARTIST—RECORD TITLE	LABEL & NO.
			EVELYN KING:	
9/12/81	**40**	2	3. I'm In Love	RCA 12243
10/02/82	**17**	8	4. Love Come Down	RCA 13273
			KING, Freddy	
			Blues vocalist/guitarist. Born Freddie Christian on 9/30/34 in Gilmer, Texas. Moved to Chicago in 1950. Died on 12/28/76 of a hepatitis-related heart attack.	
4/03/61	**29**	4	1. Hide Away [I]	Federal 12401
			titled after Mel's Hide Away Lounge in Chicago	
			KING, Jonathan	
			Born Kenneth King on 12/06/44 in London. Successful singer/songwriter/producer. Formed U.K. Records in 1972. Produced Hedgehoppers Anonymous.	
10/23/65	**17**	7	1. Everyone's Gone To The Moon	Parrot 9774
			KING, Peggy	
			Singer/actress. Regular on TV's "The George Gobel Show," 1954-56. In the 1957 film *Zero Hour.*	
2/05/55	**30**	1	1. Make Yourself Comfortable	Columbia 40363
			Best Seller #30	
			KING, Teddi	
			Born on 9/18/29 in Boston; died on 11/18/77. Jazz-styled vocalist.	
3/03/56	**18**	2	1. Mr. Wonderful	RCA 6392
			Jockey #18 / Top 100 #32 from the Broadway musical of the same title	
			KING CURTIS	
			Born Curtis Ousley on 2/07/34 in Fort Worth, Texas. Stabbed to death on 8/13/71 in New York City. R&B saxophonist. With Lionel Hampton in 1950. Moved to New York City, did session work. First own recording on Gem in 1953. Played on sessions for Bobby Darin, Aretha Franklin, Brook Benton, Nat King Cole, McGuire Sisters, Andy Williams, The Coasters, The Shirelles and hundreds of others.	
4/07/62	**17**	8	1. Soul Twist [I]	Enjoy 1000
			KING CURTIS AND THE NOBLE KNIGHTS	
9/23/67	**33**	4	2. Memphis Soul Stew [I]	Atco 6511
10/07/67	**28**	4	3. Ode To Billie Joe [I]	Atco 6516
			THE KINGPINS	
			KING HARVEST	
			Six-man, pop-rock group.	
1/06/73	**13**	11	1. Dancing In The Moonlight	Perception 515
			KINGPINS, The — see KING CURTIS	
			KINGSMEN, The	
			Group is Bill Haley's band, The Comets (minus Haley).	
9/22/58	**35**	2	1. Week End [I]	East West 115
			Best Seller #35 / Hot 100 #84	

DATE	POS	WKS	ARTIST—RECORD TITLE	LABEL & NO.
			KINGSMEN, The	
			Rock band formed in Portland, Oregon in 1957. Consisted of Jack Ely (lead singer, guitar), Lynn Easton (drums), Mike Mitchell (guitar), Bob Nordby (bass) and Don Gallucci (keyboards). After release of "Louie Louie" (featuring lead vocal by Ely), Easton took over leadership of band and replaced Ely as lead singer. One of America's premier '60s garage bands.	
11/30/63	**2**(6)	13	**1. Louie Louie**	Wand 143
			originally released on Jerden 712 in 1963	
4/04/64	**16**	8	2. Money	Wand 150
1/30/65	**4**	9	**3. The Jolly Green Giant**	Wand 172
			same tune (different lyrics) as The Olympics' "Big Boy Pete"	
			KINGSTON TRIO, The	
			Folk trio formed in San Francisco in 1957: Dave Guard (banjo), Bob Shane and Nick Reynolds (guitars). Big break came at San Francisco's Purple Onion, where they stayed for eight months. Guard left in 1961 to form the Whiskeyhill Singers; John Stewart replaced him. Disbanded in 1968, Shane formed New Kingston Trio. Guard died on 3/22/91 (age 56) of lymphoma. The originators of the folk music craze of the 1960s.	
10/06/58	**1**(1)	18	• **1. Tom Dooley**	Capitol 4049
			traditional American folk song written in 1866 as "Tom Dula"	
3/30/59	**12**	9	2. The Tijuana Jail	Capitol 4167
6/29/59	**15**	6	3. M.T.A.	Capitol 4221
			M.T.A.: Metropolitan Transit Authority of Boston	
9/21/59	**20**	8	4. A Worried Man	Capitol 4271
3/14/60	**32**	5	5. El Matador	Capitol 4338
8/08/60	**37**	2	6. Bad Man Blunder [N]	Capitol 4379
3/03/62	**21**	7	7. Where Have All The Flowers Gone	Capitol 4671
2/23/63	**21**	5	8. Greenback Dollar	Capitol 4898
4/20/63	**8**	8	**9. Reverend Mr. Black**	Capitol 4951
8/31/63	**33**	4	10. Desert Pete	Capitol 5005
			KINKS, The	
			Rock group formed in London in 1963 by Ray Davies (lead singer, guitar) and his brother Dave Davies (lead guitar, vocals). Original lineup also included Peter Quaife (bass) and Mike Avory (drums). Numerous personnel changes during the '70s. Ray appeared in the 1986 film *Absolute Beginners*. 1987 lineup consisted of Ray & Dave Davies, Ian Gibbons (keyboards, left by 1989), Bob Henrit (drums) and Jim Rodford (bass). Henrit and Rodford were members of Argent. Group inducted into the Rock and Roll Hall of Fame in 1990.	
10/24/64	**7**	10	**1. You Really Got Me**	Reprise 0306
1/16/65	**7**	9	**2. All Day And All Of The Night**	Reprise 0334
3/27/65	**6**	8	**3. Tired Of Waiting For You**	Reprise 0347
7/10/65	**23**	4	4. Set Me Free	Reprise 0379
9/04/65	**34**	3	5. Who'll Be The Next In Line	Reprise 0366
1/08/66	**13**	9	6. A Well Respected Man	Reprise 0420
6/18/66	**36**	1	7. Dedicated Follower Of Fashion	Reprise 0471
8/27/66	**14**	7	8. Sunny Afternoon	Reprise 0497
9/12/70	**9**	12	**9. Lola**	Reprise 0930
			live version charted in 1980 (POS 81)	
8/19/78	**30**	5	10. A Rock 'N' Roll Fantasy	Arista 0342
5/28/83	**6**	12	**11. Come Dancing**	Arista 1054
9/17/83	**29**	4	12. Don't Forget To Dance	Arista 9075

DATE	POS	WKS	ARTIST—RECORD TITLE	LABEL & NO.
			KISS	
			Hard-rock band formed in New York City in 1973. Consisted of Gene Simmons (bass), Paul Stanley (guitar), Ace Frehley (lead guitar) and Peter Criss (drums). Noted for elaborate makeup and highly theatrical stage shows. Criss replaced by Eric Carr in 1981. Frehley replaced by Vinnie Vincent in 1982. Group appeared without makeup for the first time in 1983 on album cover *Lick It Up*. Mark St. John replaced Vincent in 1984. Bruce Kulick replaced St. John in 1985. Carr died of cancer on 11/25/91 (age 41).	
11/29/75+	**12**	10	1. Rock And Roll All Nite [R]	Casablanca 850
			live version; original version hit on 5/17/75 (POS 68)	
4/17/76	**31**	4	2. Shout It Out Loud	Casablanca 854
9/25/76	**7**	13	● **3. Beth**	Casablanca 863
1/15/77	**15**	8	4. Hard Luck Woman	Casablanca 873
4/09/77	**16**	8	5. Calling Dr. Love	Casablanca 880
7/30/77	**25**	7	6. Christine Sixteen	Casablanca 889
4/15/78	**39**	2	7. Rocket Ride	Casablanca 915
6/16/79	**11**	11	● 8. I Was Made For Lovin' You	Casablanca 983
2/24/90	**8**	11	**9. Forever**	Mercury 876716
			KISSOON, Mac and Katie	
			Brother and sister from Port-of-Spain, Trinidad. Moved to England in the late '50s.	
9/04/71	**20**	9	1. Chirpy Chirpy Cheep Cheep	ABC 11306
			KIX	
			Hard-rock quintet from Hagerstown, Maryland led by vocalist Steve Whiteman. Includes Ronnie Younkins, Brian Forsythe, Donnie Purnell and Jimmy Chalfant.	
10/21/89	**11**	13	● 1. Don't Close Your Eyes	Atlantic 88902
			KLF, The	
			British duo previously known as The Timelords: Bill Drummond (founding member of Big In Japan/former manager of Echo & The Bunnymen and Teardrop Explodes) & Jimmy Cauty (formerly with Zodiac Mindwarp). KLF stands for Kopyright Liberation Front.	
7/13/91	**5**	12	● **1. 3 A.M. Eternal**	Arista 2230#
			KLYMAXX	
			Black female band founded by drummer/producer Bernadette Cooper in Los Angeles in 1979. Lead vocals by Lorena Porter Shelby and Joyce "Fenderella" Irby. Pared down to a trio of Shelby, Cheryl Cooley (guitar) and Robbin Grider (keyboards) in 1990.	
10/26/85	**5**	17	**1. I Miss You**	Constell. 52606
8/02/86	**15**	8	2. Man Size Love	MCA 52841
			from the film *Running Scared*	
6/20/87	**18**	9	3. I'd Still Say Yes	Constell. 53028
			KNACK, The	
			Rock group formed in Los Angeles in 1978. Consisted of Doug Fieger (lead singer, guitar), Berton Averre (lead guitar), Bruce Gary (drums) and Prescott Niles (bass). Disbanded in 1982. All members but Gary reunited in 1986, replaced by drummer Billy Ward.	
7/21/79	**1**(6)	16	● **1. My Sharona**	Capitol 4731
9/22/79	**11**	11	2. Good Girls Don't	Capitol 4771
3/08/80	**38**	2	3. Baby Talks Dirty	Capitol 4822

DATE	POS	WKS	ARTIST—RECORD TITLE	LABEL & NO.
			KNICKERBOCKERS, The	
			Rock band formed in Bergenfield, New Jersey in 1964 as the Castle Kings. Lead singer, Buddy Randell, was with the Royal Teens. Member Jimmy Walker replaced Bill Medley, for a time, in The Righteous Brothers.	
1/01/66	**20**	9	1. Lies	Challenge 59321
			KNIGHT, Frederick	
			Born on 8/15/44 in Alabama. Soul singer/producer.	
5/27/72	**27**	9	1. I've Been Lonely For So Long	Stax 0117
			KNIGHT, Gladys/The Pips	
			R&B family group from Atlanta, formed in 1952 when lead singer Gladys was eight years old. Consisted of Gladys (b: 5/28/44, Atlanta), her brother Merald "Bubba" Knight and sister Brenda, and cousins William and Eleanor Guest. Named "Pips" for their manager, cousin James "Pip" Woods. First recorded for Brunswick in 1958. Brenda and Eleanor replaced by cousins Edward Patten and Langston George in 1959. Langston left group in 1962 and group has remained a quartet with the same members ever since. Due to legal problems, Gladys could not record with the Pips from 1977-80. Gladys was a cast member of the 1985 TV series "Charlie & Co."	
6/05/61	**6**	10	**1. Every Beat Of My Heart** PIPS	Vee-Jay 386
1/20/62	**19**	6	2. Letter Full Of Tears	Fury 1054
7/04/64	**38**	1	3. Giving Up	Maxx 326
8/19/67	**39**	2	4. Everybody Needs Love	Soul 35034
11/04/67	**2**(3)	14	**5. I Heard It Through The Grapevine**	Soul 35039
2/17/68	**15**	8	6. The End Of Our Road	Soul 35042
7/06/68	**40**	1	7. It Should Have Been Me	Soul 35045
8/09/69	**19**	8	8. The Nitty Gritty	Soul 35063
11/15/69	**17**	10	9. Friendship Train	Soul 35068
4/04/70	**25**	5	10. You Need Love Like I Do (Don't You)	Soul 35071
12/19/70+	**9**	12	**11. If I Were Your Woman**	Soul 35078
6/19/71	**17**	9	12. I Don't Want To Do Wrong	Soul 35083
1/08/72	**27**	5	13. Make Me The Woman That You Go Home To	Soul 35091
4/08/72	**33**	6	14. Help Me Make It Through The Night	Soul 35094
2/17/73	**2**(2)	12	**15. Neither One Of Us (Wants To Be The First To Say Goodbye)**	Soul 35098
6/02/73	**19**	8	16. Daddy Could Swear, I Declare	Soul 35105
7/07/73	**28**	7	17. Where Peaceful Waters Flow	Buddah 363
9/15/73	**1**(2)	16	• **18. Midnight Train To Georgia**	Buddah 383
12/08/73+	**4**	13	• **19. I've Got To Use My Imagination**	Buddah 393
3/09/74	**3**	13	• **20. Best Thing That Ever Happened To Me** 15, 17, 18, 20: written by Jim Weatherly	Buddah 403
6/01/74	**5**	11	• **21. On And On** written and produced by Curtis Mayfield; from the film *Claudine*	Buddah 423
11/16/74	**21**	9	22. I Feel A Song (In My Heart)	Buddah 433
5/24/75	**11**	12	23. The Way We Were/Try To Remember	Buddah 463
11/29/75	**22**	7	24. Part Time Love	Buddah 513
11/23/85+	**1**(4)	17	• **25. That's What Friends Are For** **DIONNE & FRIENDS: Elton John, Gladys Knight and Stevie Wonder**	Arista 9422
1/30/88	**13**	9	26. Love Overboard	MCA 53210

DATE	POS	WKS	ARTIST—RECORD TITLE	LABEL & NO.
			KNIGHT, Jean	
			Born on 1/26/43 in New Orleans. Soul songstress.	
6/19/71	**2**(2)	13	**1. Mr. Big Stuff**	Stax 0088
			KNIGHT, Robert	
			Born on 4/21/45 in Franklin, Tennessee. Soul singer. Recorded for Dot in 1960.	
10/28/67	**13**	8	1. Everlasting Love	Rising Sons 705
			KNIGHT, Sonny	
			Born Joseph C. Smith in 1934 in Maywood, Illinois. R&B singer/songwriter/pianist. Wrote book *The Day the Music Died* in 1981 under real name.	
11/24/56	**17**	9	1. Confidential Juke Box #17 / Best Seller #19 / Top 100 #20 first released on Vita 137 in 1956	Dot 15507
			KNOBLOCK, Fred	
			Born in Jackson, Mississippi. With the rock band Let's Eat in the late 1970s. Member of the country trios Schuyler, Knobloch & Overstreet (SKO) and Schuyler, Knobloch & Bickhardt (SKB).	
7/26/80	**18**	7	1. Why Not Me	Scotti Br. 518
12/27/80+	**28**	9	2. Killin' Time **FRED KNOBLOCK AND SUSAN ANTON**	Scotti Br. 609
			KNOX, Buddy/The Rhythm Orchids	
			Born Buddy Wayne Knox on 7/20/33 in Happy, Texas. Formed The Rhythm Orchids at West Texas State University: Knox (guitar), Jimmy Bowen (bass), Don Lanier (guitar) and Dave "Dicky Doo" Alldred (drums). Formed own record label, Triple-D, named after KDDD radio in Dumas, Texas. Buddy currently lives near Winnipeg, Canada.	
3/02/57	**1**(1)	15	**1. Party Doll** Best Seller #1 / Top 100 #2 / Juke Box #2 / Jockey #5 originally on Triple-D 797 (B-side by Jimmy Bowen)	Roulette 4002
6/03/57	**17**	7	2. Rock Your Little Baby To Sleep Jockey #17 / Best Seller #23 / Top 100 #23	Roulette 4009
9/09/57	**9**	15	**3. Hula Love** Jockey #9 / Top 100 #12 / Best Seller #13	Roulette 4018
8/04/58	**22**	11	4. Somebody Touched Me Hot 100 #22 / Best Seller #32	Roulette 4082
1/09/61	**25**	4	5. Lovey Dovey **BUDDY KNOX**	Liberty 55290
			KOFFMAN, Moe, Quartette	
			Morris was born on 12/28/28 in Toronto. Saxophonist with several U.S. big bands from 1950-55.	
2/10/58	**23**	5	1. The Swingin' Shepherd Blues [I] Jockey #23 / Best Seller #36 / Top 100 #36	Jubilee 5311
			KOKOMO	
			Pianist Jimmy Wisner (b: 12/08/31 in Philadelphia).	
3/06/61	**8**	11	**1. Asia Minor** **[I]** adapted from the Grieg *Piano Concerto*	Felsted 8612

DATE	POS	WKS	ARTIST—RECORD TITLE	LABEL & NO.
			KON KAN	
			Toronto duo: Barry Harris (piano, guitar) and Kevin Wynne (vocals). Became a one-man band when Wynne left in 1989. Name derived from the opposite of Can Con, as in Canadian Content.	
2/04/89	**15**	9	1. I Beg Your Pardon includes several lines from Lynn Anderson's "Rose Garden"	Atlantic 88969
			KOOL & THE GANG	
			R&B group formed in Jersey City, New Jersey in 1964 by bass player Robert "Kool" Bell as the Jazziacs. Session work in New York City, 1964-68. First recorded for De-Lite in 1969. Added lead singer James "J.T." Taylor in 1979. Current lineup consists of brothers Robert and Ronald Bell (sax, keyboards), George Brown (drums), Curtis "Fitz" Williams (keyboards) and Charles Smith (guitar). Taylor left in 1988; replaced by lead singers Gary Brown, Odeen Mays and former Dazz Band lead vocalist Skip Martin.	
10/06/73	**29**	6	1. Funky Stuff	De-Lite 557
1/05/74	**4**	16	● **2. Jungle Boogie**	De-Lite 559
5/18/74	**6**	11	● **3. Hollywood Swinging**	De-Lite 561
10/12/74	**37**	2	4. Higher Plane	De-Lite 1562
6/28/75	**35**	3	5. Spirit Of The Boogie	De-Lite 1567
11/10/79+	**8**	14	● **6. Ladies Night**	De-Lite 801
2/09/80	**5**	13	● **7. Too Hot**	De-Lite 802
11/22/80+	**1**(2)	21	▲ **8. Celebration**	De-Lite 807
6/27/81	**39**	2	9. Jones Vs. Jones	De-Lite 813
11/07/81	**17**	12	10. Take My Heart (You Can Have It If You Want It)	De-Lite 815
4/03/82	**10**	9	● **11. Get Down On It**	De-Lite 818
9/11/82	**21**	7	12. Big Fun	De-Lite 822
12/04/82+	**30**	7	13. Let's Go Dancin' (Ooh La, La, La) above 8 produced by Eumir Deodato	De-Lite 824
12/03/83+	**2**(1)	16	● **14. Joanna**	De-Lite 829
3/17/84	**13**	10	15. Tonight	De-Lite 830
1/05/85	**10**	13	**16. Misled**	De-Lite 880431
4/20/85	**9**	11	**17. Fresh**	De-Lite 880623
7/27/85	**2**(3)	15	● **18. Cherish**	De-Lite 880869
11/23/85	**18**	8	19. Emergency	De-Lite 884199
11/22/86+	**10**	12	**20. Victory**	Mercury 888074
3/14/87	**10**	10	**21. Stone Love**	Mercury 888292
			KORGIS, The	
			British pop duo: James Warren and Andy Davis (both formerly with Stackridge).	
11/08/80	**18**	11	1. Everybody's Got To Learn Sometime	Asylum 47055
			KRAFTWERK	
			Synthesizer band formed in 1970 in Dusseldorf, Germany by Ralf Hutter and Florian Schneider. Kraftwerk is German for power station.	
4/12/75	**25**	5	1. Autobahn [I]	Vertigo 203
			KRAMER, Billy J., with THE DAKOTAS	
			Billy was born William Ashton on 8/19/43 near Liverpool, England. Discovered by The Beatles' manager, Brian Epstein, who teamed him with the group The Dakotas.	
5/02/64	**7**	12	**1. Little Children/**	
6/13/64	**9**	8	**2. Bad To Me**	Imperial 66027

DATE	POS	WKS	ARTIST—RECORD TITLE	LABEL & NO.
			first released on Liberty 55626 and then Liberty 55667	
8/15/64	**30**	3	3. I'll Keep You Satisfied first released on Liberty 55643 in 1964	Imperial 66048
9/19/64	**23**	5	4. From A Window above 3 written by John Lennon and Paul McCartney	Imperial 66051
			KRAVITZ, Lenny	
			Singer/songwriter/multi-instrumentalist raised in New York City and later Los Angeles. Three-year member of the California Boys Choir. Married for a time to actress Lisa Bonet. Son of actress Roxie Roker (played Helen Willis on TV's "The Jeffersons").	
6/22/91	**2**(1)	14	**1. It Ain't Over Til It's Over**	Virgin 98795#
			KRISTOFFERSON, Kris	
			Born on 6/22/36 in Brownsville, Texas. Singer/songwriter/actor. Attended England's Oxford University on a Rhodes scholarship. Married to Rita Coolidge from 1973-80. Wrote "Me And Bobby McGee," "For The Good Times" and "Help Me Make It Through The Night." Has starred in many films since 1972.	
10/02/71	**26**	6	1. Loving Her Was Easier (Than Anything I'll Ever Do Again)	Monument 8525
7/07/73	**16**	19	• 2. Why Me	Monument 8571
			KUBAN, Bob/The In-Men	
			Eight-man, St. Louis pop-rock band formed by drummer Kuban. Lead singer Walter Scott (real name: Walter Notheis, Jr.), disappeared on 12/27/83; his ex-wife and her husband were charged with Scott's murder after his body was found, three years later, with a gunshot wound to the back.	
2/19/66	**12**	7	1. The Cheater	Musicland 20001
			KYPER	
			Born Randall Kyper in Baton Rouge, Louisiana.	
8/04/90	**14**	12	• 1. Tic-Tac-Toe borrows guitar riffs from "Owner Of A Lonely Heart" by Yes	Atlantic 87910#
			L	
			LaBELLE, Patti	
			Born Patricia Holt on 5/24/44 in Philadelphia. Began singing career as leader of the Ordettes which evolved into The Blue Belles. The quartet, formed in Philadelphia in 1962, included Nona Hendryx, Sarah Dash and Cindy Birdsong. Cindy left in 1967 to join The Supremes. Group continued as a trio. In 1971, they shortened their name to LaBelle. In 1977, group disbanded and Patti recorded solo. The Blue-Belles were listed on the label as the artists of "I Sold My Heart To The Junkman," a 1962 hit which was actually recorded by The Starlets.	
			PATTI LaBELLE & THE BLUE BELLES:	
11/02/63	**37**	3	1. Down The Aisle (Wedding Song)	Newtown 5777
2/08/64	**34**	1	2. You'll Never Walk Alone first released on Nicetown 5020 in 1963; from the Rodgers & Hammerstein musical *Carousel*	Parkway 896
			LaBELLE:	
2/01/75	**1**(1)	13	**3. Lady Marmalade**	Epic 50048
			PATTI LaBELLE:	
4/06/85	**17**	9	4. New Attitude	MCA 52517

DATE	POS	WKS	ARTIST—RECORD TITLE	LABEL & NO.
			from the film *Beverly Hills Cop*	
4/19/86	1(3)	15	• **5. On My Own**	MCA 52770
			PATTI LaBELLE AND MICHAEL McDONALD	
8/23/86	**29**	3	6. Oh, People	MCA 52877
			LADD, Cheryl	
			Born Cheryl Stoppelmoor on 7/02/51 in Huron, South Dakota. Played Kris Monroe on the TV series "Charlie's Angels." Married to David Ladd (son of actor Alan Ladd) from 1973-79. Married producer/songwriter Brian Russell (Brian & Brenda) in 1981.	
8/26/78	**34**	3	1. Think It Over	Capitol 4599
			LADY FLASH	
			Barry Manilow's backup singers: Lorraine "Reparata" Mazzola (lead vocals), Monica Burruss and Debra Byrd. Mazzola was in Reparata (Mary Aiese) & The Delrons, 1966-73, then assumed the name "Reparata."	
8/14/76	**27**	6	1. Street Singin'	RSO 852
			written, produced and arranged by Barry Manilow	
			L.A. GUNS	
			Hollywood male hard-rock group led by vocalist Philip Lewis and founded by guitarist Tracii Guns. Includes Mick Cripps, Kelly Nickels and Steve Riley. Guns was also a member of Contraband in 1991.	
6/16/90	**33**	4	1. The Ballad of Jayne	Vertigo 876984#
			LAI, Francis	
			French composer/conductor.	
2/27/71	**31**	4	1. Theme From Love Story [I]	Paramount 0064
			from the film *Love Story*; piano solo: Georges Pludermacher	
			LAID BACK	
			Danish synth-pop duo: Tim Stahl (keyboards) and John Guldberg (guitar). Highly successful in Europe for three years before their U.S. debut.	
4/28/84	**26**	4	1. White Horse	Sire 29346
			LAINE, Frankie	
			Born Frank Paul LoVecchio on 3/30/13 in Chicago. To Los Angeles in the early 1940s. First recorded for Exclusive in 1945. With Johnny Moore's Three Blazers. Signed to Mercury label in 1947. Dynamic style found favor with black and white audiences.	
9/03/55	**17**	3	1. Humming Bird	Columbia 40526
			Juke Box #17	
12/17/55	**19**	10	2. A Woman In Love	Columbia 40583
			Best Seller #19 / Top 100 #24 from the film *Guys And Dolls*	
12/08/56+	**3**	18	**3. Moonlight Gambler**	Columbia 40780
			Top 100 #3 / Juke Box #3 / Jockey #4 / Best Seller #5	
4/20/57	**10**	8	**4. Love Is A Golden Ring**	Columbia 40856
			FRANKIE LAINE with THE EASY RIDERS Jockey #10 / Best Seller #22 / Top 100 #23	
3/04/67	**39**	2	5. I'll Take Care Of Your Cares	ABC 10891
5/06/67	**35**	3	6. Making Memories	ABC 10924
3/01/69	**24**	7	7. You Gave Me A Mountain	ABC 11174
			written by Marty Robbins; produced by Jimmy Bowen	

DATE	POS	WKS	ARTIST—RECORD TITLE	LABEL & NO.
			LaMOND, George	
			Born George Garcia on 2/25/67 in Washington, D.C. and raised in the Bronx. With his cousin Joey Kid, formed New York City club band Loose Touch.	
6/23/90	**25**	6	1. Bad Of The Heart	Columbia 73339
			LANCE, Major	
			Born on 4/04/42 in Chicago. Soul singer. First recorded for Mercury in 1959. Lived in Britain, 1972-74. Had own Osiris label with Al Jackson of the MG's in 1975. In prison for selling cocaine, 1978-81.	
8/10/63	**8**	10	**1. The Monkey Time**	Okeh 7175
11/02/63	**13**	8	2. Hey Little Girl	Okeh 7181
1/11/64	**5**	10	**3. Um, Um, Um, Um, Um, Um**	Okeh 7187
4/11/64	**20**	6	4. The Matador	Okeh 7191
9/19/64	**24**	5	5. Rhythm	Okeh 7203
4/03/65	**40**	1	6. Come See	Okeh 7216
			all of above (except #4) written by Curtis Mayfield	
			LANE, Mickey Lee	
			Born in 1945 in Rochester, New York.	
11/28/64	**38**	1	1. Shaggy Dog	Swan 4183
			LANSON, Snooky	
			Born Roy Landman in Memphis. Star of TV's "Your Hit Parade," 1950-57. Died on 7/02/90 (age 76).	
12/03/55	**20**	6	1. It's Almost Tomorrow	Dot 15424
			Top 100 #20 / Jockey #20 / Juke Box #20	
			LARKS, The	
			Los Angeles R&B group originally named Don Julian & The Meadowlarks: Don Julian (lead singer), Ted Walters and Charles Morrison.	
11/28/64+	**7**	11	**1. The Jerk**	Money 106
			LaROSA, Julius	
			Born on 1/02/30 in Brooklyn. Regular singer on "Arthur Godfrey and His Friends" TV show until he was fired on-the-air on 10/19/53.	
7/23/55	**13**	7	1. Domani (Tomorrow)	Cadence 1265
			Best Seller #13 / Juke Box #13 / Jockey #15	
10/08/55	**20**	5	2. Suddenly There's A Valley	Cadence 1270
			Jockey #20 / Best Seller #22 / Top 100 #29	
2/18/56	**15**	7	3. Lipstick And Candy And Rubbersole Shoes	RCA 6416
			Jockey #15 / Top 100 #21	
6/16/58	**21**	1	4. Torero	RCA 7227
			Jockey #21	
			LARSEN-FEITEN BAND	
			Top session musicians Neil Larsen (keyboards) and Buzz Feiten (guitar). Feiten, a former member of the Paul Butterfield Blues Band and Stevie Wonder's band, joined Mr. Mister in 1989.	
9/13/80	**29**	6	1. Who'll Be The Fool Tonight	Warner 49282
			LARSON, Nicolette	
			Born on 7/17/52 in Helena, Montana and raised in Kansas City. To San Francisco in 1974. Session vocalist with Neil Young, Linda Ronstadt, Van Halen and many others.	
12/23/78+	**8**	14	**1. Lotta Love**	Warner 8664
			written by Neil Young	

DATE	POS	WKS	ARTIST—RECORD TITLE	LABEL & NO.
2/16/80	**35**	3	2. Let Me Go, Love duet with Michael McDonald	Warner 49130
			LaSALLE, Denise	
			Born Denise Craig on 7/16/39 in LeFlore County, Mississippi. Soul singer.	
9/25/71	**13**	9	● 1. Trapped By A Thing Called Love	Westbound 182
			LASLEY, David	
			Born on 8/20/47 in Sault St. Marie, Michigan. Backup singer for James Taylor and others. Member of the studio group Roundtree.	
4/24/82	**36**	3	1. If I Had My Wish Tonight	EMI America 8111
			LAST, James, Band	
			James was born on 4/17/29 in Bremen, Germany. Producer/arranger/conductor of big cabaret band.	
4/26/80	**28**	6	1. The Seduction (Love Theme) [I] from the film *American Gigolo*	Polydor 2071
			LATIMORE	
			Born Benjamin Latimore on 9/07/39 in Charleston, Tennessee. Soul singer. With Steve Alaimo in the '60s.	
11/23/74	**31**	3	1. Let's Straighten It Out	Glades 1722
3/26/77	**37**	2	2. Somethin' 'Bout 'Cha	Glades 1739
			LaTOUR	
			Male solo artist from Chicago.	
5/04/91	**35**	4	1. People Are Still Having Sex	Smash 879666#
			LATTISAW, Stacy	
			Born on 11/25/66 in Washington, D.C. Soul singer. Recorded her first album at age 12. Childhood friend of Johnny Gill.	
10/04/80	**21**	10	1. Let Me Be Your Angel	Cotillion 46001
8/01/81	**26**	7	2. Love On A Two Way Street	Cotillion 46015
10/22/83	**40**	1	3. Miracles	Cotillion 99855
			LAUPER, Cyndi	
			Born on 6/20/53 in Queens, New York. Recorded an album for Polydor Records in 1980 with the group Blue Angel. Supported by The Hooters, 1983-84. Won the 1984 Best New Artist Grammy Award. In the 1988 film *Vibes*.	
1/28/84	**2**(2)	14	▲ **1. Girls Just Want To Have Fun**	Portrait 04120
4/21/84	**1**(2)	14	● **2. Time After Time**	Portrait 04432
7/28/84	**3**	14	● **3. She Bop**	Portrait 04516
10/13/84	**5**	14	**4. All Through The Night**	Portrait 04639
1/12/85	**27**	6	5. Money Changes Everything	Portrait 04737
6/01/85	**10**	9	**6. The Goonies 'R' Good Enough** from the film *The Goonies*	Portrait 04918
9/13/86	**1**(2)	12	**7. True Colors**	Portrait 06247
12/13/86+	**3**	13	**8. Change Of Heart**	Portrait 06431
3/21/87	**12**	10	9. What's Going On	Portrait 06970
5/20/89	**6**	10	**10. I Drove All Night**	Epic 68759
			LAUREN, Rod	
			Born on 3/26/40. Rod was groomed by RCA in 1960 to be a hot new teen idol.	
1/11/60	**31**	5	1. If I Had A Girl	RCA 7645

DATE	POS	WKS	ARTIST—RECORD TITLE	LABEL & NO.
			LAURIE SISTERS, The	
4/16/55	**30**	1	1. Dixie Danny Best Seller #30	Mercury 70548
			LAWRENCE, Eddie	
			Born on 3/02/19 in New York City. Comedian/actor/author/playwright.	
9/01/56	**34**	1	1. The Old Philosopher [C]	Coral 61671
			LAWRENCE, Steve	
			Born Sidney Leibowitz on 7/08/35 in Brooklyn. Regular performer on Steve Allen's "Tonight Show" for five years. First recorded for King in 1953. Married singer Eydie Gorme on 12/29/57. They recorded as Parker & Penny in 1979. Steve and Eydie remain a durable nightclub act.	
1/19/57	**18**	8	1. The Banana Boat Song Jockey #18 / Top 100 #30	Coral 61761
3/09/57	**5**	12	**2. Party Doll** Jockey #5 / Top 100 #10 / Juke Box #11 / Best Seller #12 orchestra directed by Dick Jacobs on above 2	Coral 61792
12/14/59+	**9**	13	**3. Pretty Blue Eyes**	ABC-Para. 10058
3/28/60	**7**	9	**4. Footsteps**	ABC-Para. 10085
4/03/61	**9**	10	**5. Portrait Of My Love**	United Art. 291
12/08/62+	**1**(2)	12	**6. Go Away Little Girl**	Columbia 42601
3/30/63	**26**	6	7. Don't Be Afraid, Little Darlin'	Columbia 42699
6/15/63	**27**	3	8. Poor Little Rich Girl	Columbia 42795
8/24/63	**28**	5	9. I Want To Stay Here **STEVE AND EYDIE**	Columbia 42815
11/09/63	**26**	4	10. Walking Proud	Columbia 42865
1/25/64	**35**	3	11. I Can't Stop Talking About You **STEVE AND EYDIE**	Columbia 42932
			LAWRENCE, Vicki	
			Born on 5/26/49 in Inglewood, California. Regular on Carol Burnett's CBS-TV series from 1967-78. Also starred in TV's "Mama's Family," 1982-83.	
3/17/73	**1**(2)	14	● **1. The Night The Lights Went Out In Georgia** written by Vicki's husband, Bobby Russell	Bell 45303
			LAYNE, Joy	
			Born in Chicago in the late 1930s.	
2/16/57	**20**	5	1. Your Wild Heart Juke Box #20 / Top 100 #30	Mercury 71038
			LEAPY LEE	
			Born Lee Graham on 7/02/42 in Eastbourne, England. Acted on stage and TV in England. Nicknamed "Leapy" in school because "I was always a leaper!"	
11/09/68	**16**	8	1. Little Arrows	Decca 32380
			LEAVES, The	
			Los Angeles garage-rock quintet: John Beck (lead singer), Robert Lee Reiner, Jim Pons, Tom "Ambrose" Ray and Bobby Arlin.	
6/18/66	**31**	4	1. Hey Joe released in 1965 as "Hey Joe, Where You Gonna Go?" on Mira 207	Mira 222

DATE	POS	WKS	ARTIST—RECORD TITLE	LABEL & NO.
			LeBLANC & CARR	
			Lenny LeBlanc and Pete Carr; born on 6/17/51 and 4/22/50, respectively. Lenny (bass) and Pete (lead guitar) were both session musicians at Muscle Shoals, Alabama. Lenny later recorded Christian Contemporary music.	
2/04/78	**13**	10	1. Falling	Big Tree 16100
			LED ZEPPELIN	
			British heavy-metal rock supergroup formed in October 1968. Consisted of Robert Plant (lead singer), Jimmy Page (lead guitar), John Paul Jones (bass, keyboards) and John Bonham (drums). First known as the New Yardbirds. Page had been in the Yardbirds, 1966-68. Plant and Bonham had been in a group called Band Of Joy. Led Zeppelin's U.S. tour in 1973 broke many box office records. Formed own Swan Song label in 1974. Plant seriously injured in an auto accident in Greece on 8/04/75. In concert film *The Song Remains the Same* in 1976. Bonham died on 9/25/80 (age 33) of asphyxiation. Group disbanded in December 1980. Plant and Page formed The Honeydrippers in 1984. "Bonham" is the name of group formed by Jason Bonham, John's son, in 1989. Led Zeppelin's most famous recording, "Stairway To Heaven" (on album *Led Zeppelin IV*), was never released as a single.	
12/06/69+	**4**	13	● **1. Whole Lotta Love**	Atlantic 2690
12/12/70+	**16**	10	2. Immigrant Song	Atlantic 2777
1/15/72	**15**	8	3. Black Dog	Atlantic 2849
11/24/73	**20**	8	4. D'yer Mak'er	Atlantic 2986
5/17/75	**38**	2	5. Trampled Under Foot	Swan Song 70102
1/12/80	**21**	8	6. Fool In The Rain	Swan Song 71003
			LEE, Brenda	
			Born Brenda Mae Tarpley on 12/11/44 in Lithonia, Georgia. Professional singer since age six. Signed to Decca Records in 1956. Became known as "Little Miss Dynamite." Successful country singer since 1971.	
2/15/60	**4**	15	**1. Sweet Nothin's**	Decca 30967
6/06/60	**1**(3)	18	**2. I'm Sorry/**	
6/20/60	**6**	9	**3. That's All You Gotta Do**	Decca 31093
9/19/60	**1**(1)	13	**4. I Want To Be Wanted/**	
10/31/60	**40**	1	5. Just A Little	Decca 31149
12/19/60	**14**	3	6. Rockin' Around The Christmas Tree [X] recorded in 1958	Decca 30776
1/16/61	**7**	9	**7. Emotions/**	
2/06/61	**33**	2	8. I'm Learning About Love	Decca 31195
4/03/61	**6**	10	**9. You Can Depend On Me**	Decca 31231
6/26/61	**4**	10	**10. Dum Dum**	Decca 31272
10/09/61	**3**	12	**11. Fool #1/**	
10/16/61	**31**	3	12. Anybody But Me	Decca 31309
1/20/62	**4**	11	**13. Break It To Me Gently**	Decca 31348
4/28/62	**6**	8	**14. Everybody Loves Me But You**	Decca 31379
7/21/62	**15**	7	15. Heart In Hand/ 10, 15: written by Jackie DeShannon	
7/21/62	**29**	4	16. It Started All Over Again	Decca 31407
10/06/62	**3**	12	**17. All Alone Am I**	Decca 31424
2/16/63	**32**	3	18. Your Used To Be	Decca 31454
4/20/63	**6**	10	**19. Losing You**	Decca 31478
7/27/63	**24**	6	20. My Whole World Is Falling Down/	
7/27/63	**25**	5	21. I Wonder	Decca 31510

DATE	POS	WKS	ARTIST—RECORD TITLE	LABEL & NO.
10/12/63	**17**	5	22. The Grass Is Greener	Decca 31539
12/28/63+	**12**	8	23. As Usual	Decca 31570
3/28/64	**25**	5	24. Think	Decca 31599
10/31/64	**17**	7	25. Is It True	Decca 31690
6/26/65	**13**	8	26. Too Many Rivers	Decca 31792
11/13/65	**33**	3	27. Rusty Bells	Decca 31849
10/29/66	**11**	8	28. Coming On Strong	Decca 32018
2/11/67	**37**	2	29. Ride, Ride, Ride	Decca 32079
			LEE, Curtis	
			Born on 10/28/41 in Yuma, Arizona. Pop singer/songwriter.	
7/17/61	**7**	8	**1. Pretty Little Angel Eyes**	Dunes 2007
			backing vocals by the Halos; produced by Phil Spector	
			LEE, Dickey	
			Born Dickey Lipscomb on 9/21/41 in Memphis. Pop-country singer/songwriter. First recorded for Sun Records in 1957.	
9/08/62	**6**	11	**1. Patches**	Smash 1758
12/29/62+	**14**	8	2. I Saw Linda Yesterday	Smash 1791
6/19/65	**14**	7	3. Laurie (Strange Things Happen)	TCF Hall 102
			LEE, Jackie	
			Earl Nelson, of Bob & Earl, was born on 9/08/28 in Lake Charles, Louisiana. Took name from his wife's middle name, Jackie, and his middle name, Lee. Sang lead on Hollywood Flames' "Buzz-Buzz-Buzz."	
12/18/65+	**14**	9	1. The Duck	Mirwood 5502
			LEE, Johnny	
			Born John Lee Ham on 7/03/46 in Texas City and raised in Alta Loma, Texas. Country singer/songwriter. Married to actress Charlene Tilton from 1982-84.	
8/02/80	**5**	13	● **1. Lookin' For Love**	Full Moon 47004
			from the film *Urban Cowboy*	
			LEE, Laura	
			Born Laura Lee Rundless in 1945 in Chicago. Soul singer.	
10/16/71	**36**	4	1. Women's Love Rights	Hot Wax 7105
			LEE, Leapy — see LEAPY	
			LEE, Peggy	
			Born Norma Jean Egstrom on 5/26/20 in Jamestown, North Dakota. Jazz singer with Jack Wardlow band (1936-40), Will Osborne (1940-41) and Benny Goodman (1941-43). Went solo in March 1943. In films *Mister Music* (1950), *The Jazz Singer* (1953) and *Pete Kelly's Blues* (1955). Co-wrote many songs with husband Dave Barbour (married, 1943-52). Awarded nearly $4 million in court for her singing in the animated film *Lady and the Tramp.*	
3/24/56	**14**	10	1. Mr. Wonderful	Decca 29834
			Jockey #14 / Top 100 #23 / Best Seller #25 from the Broadway musical of the same title	
7/21/58	**8**	13	**2. Fever**	Capitol 3998
			Hot 100 #8 / Best Seller #9 / Jockey #10 end	
10/11/69	**11**	8	3. Is That All There Is	Capitol 2602
			LEFEVRE, Raymond	
			Conductor/pianist/flutist from Paris.	
11/03/58	**30**	5	1. The Day The Rains Came [I]	Kapp 231

DATE	POS	WKS	ARTIST—RECORD TITLE	LABEL & NO.
4/06/68	**37**	5	2. Ame Caline (Soul Coaxing) [I]	Four Corners 147
			LEFT BANKE, The	
			Classical-styled New York rock quintet led by Steve Martin (lead singer) and Mike Brown (keyboards).	
9/24/66	**5**	10	**1. Walk Away Renee**	Smash 2041
2/04/67	**15**	6	2. Pretty Ballerina	Smash 2074
			LEMON PIPERS, The	
			Psychedelic/bubblegum rock quintet from Oxford, Ohio — Ivan Browne, lead singer. Member Bill Bartlett was leader of Ram Jam.	
12/23/67+	**1**(1)	12	● **1. Green Tambourine**	Buddah 23
			LENNON, John	
			Born on 10/09/40 in Liverpool, England. Founding member of The Beatles. Married Cynthia Powell on 8/23/62, had son Julian. Divorced Cynthia on 11/08/68. Met Yoko Ono in 1966 and married her on 3/20/69. Formed Plastic Ono Band in 1969. To New York City in 1971. Fought deportation from the U.S., 1972-76, until he was granted a permanent visa. Lennon was shot to death on 12/08/80 in New York City. Won Grammy's Lifetime Achievement Award in 1991.	
			PLASTIC ONO BAND:	
8/09/69	**14**	6	1. Give Peace A Chance recorded in a hotel suite in Montreal, Canada; new version by the Peace Choir (featuring son, Sean) charted, 1991	Apple 1809
12/13/69+	**30**	7	2. Cold Turkey	Apple 1813
			JOHN LENNON:	
3/07/70	**3**	12	● **3. Instant Karma (We All Shine On)**	Apple 1818
4/10/71	**11**	8	4. Power To The People **JOHN LENNON/PLASTIC ONO BAND; YOKO ONO/PLASTIC ONO BAND**	Apple 1830
10/23/71	**3**	9	**5. Imagine** **JOHN LENNON PLASTIC ONO BAND**	Apple 1840
12/01/73	**18**	8	6. Mind Games	Apple 1868
10/05/74	**1**(1)	11	**7. Whatever Gets You Thru The Night** **JOHN LENNON with THE PLASTIC ONO NUCLEAR BAND** backing vocal: Elton John	Apple 1874
1/11/75	**9**	8	**8. #9 Dream**	Apple 1878
4/05/75	**20**	5	9. Stand By Me	Apple 1881
11/01/80	**1**(5)	19	● **10. (Just Like) Starting Over**	Geffen 49604
1/17/81	**2**(3)	17	● **11. Woman**	Geffen 49644
4/11/81	**10**	10	**12. Watching The Wheels**	Geffen 49695
1/21/84	**5**	11	**13. Nobody Told Me** above 4 recorded in 1980	Polydor 817254
			LENNON, Julian	
			Born John Charles Julian Lennon on 4/08/63. Son of John and Cynthia Lennon. First child to be born to any of The Beatles.	
11/10/84+	**9**	12	**1. Valotte**	Atlantic 89609
2/02/85	**5**	12	**2. Too Late For Goodbyes**	Atlantic 89589
4/27/85	**21**	8	3. Say You're Wrong	Atlantic 89567
4/26/86	**32**	4	4. Stick Around	Atlantic 89437

DATE	POS	WKS	ARTIST—RECORD TITLE	LABEL & NO.
			LENNON SISTERS, The	
			Four sisters from Venice, California: Dianne, Peggy, Kathy and Janet Lennon. TV debut on Lawrence Welk's Christmas Eve show in 1955. Left Welk in 1967.	
9/29/56	**15**	10	1. Tonight You Belong To Me **LAWRENCE WELK with THE LENNON SISTERS** Top 100 #15 / Best Seller #16 / Jockey #16 / Juke Box #17	Coral 61701
			LENNOX, Annie — see GREEN, Al	
			LEONETTI, Tommy	
			Born on 9/10/29 in Bergen, New Jersey; died on 9/15/79. Vocalist with Charlie Spivak and other bands. Featured singer on TV's "Your Hit Parade."	
7/07/56	**23**	2	1. Free Jockey #23 / Top 100 #40	Capitol 3442
			LE ROUX	
			Six-man Louisiana rock band — Jeff Pollard, lead singer.	
3/20/82	**18**	6	1. Nobody Said It Was Easy (Lookin' For The Lights)	RCA 13059
			LESTER, Ketty	
			Born Revoyda Frierson on 8/16/34 in Hope, Arkansas. To Los Angeles in 1955. Acted in several films and TV shows (formerly a cast member of "Days of Our Lives," "Rituals" and "Little House on the Prairie").	
3/10/62	**5**	11	**1. Love Letters** #11 hit for Dick Haymes in 1945	Era 3068
			LETTERMEN, The	
			Harmonic vocal group formed in Los Angeles in 1960. Consisted of Tony Butala (b: 11/20/40), Jim Pike (b: 11/06/38) and Bob Engemann (b: 2/19/36). First recorded for Warner Bros. Engemann replaced by Gary Pike (Jim's brother) in 1968.	
9/25/61	**13**	9	1. The Way You Look Tonight #1 hit for Fred Astaire in 1936	Capitol 4586
12/04/61+	**7**	11	**2. When I Fall In Love** #20 hit for Doris Day in 1952	Capitol 4658
3/10/62	**17**	7	3. Come Back Silly Girl	Capitol 4699
7/17/65	**16**	5	4. Theme From "A Summer Place" from the Sandra Dee/Troy Donahue film *A Summer Place*	Capitol 5437
1/06/68	**7**	11	**5. Goin' Out Of My Head/Can't Take My Eyes Off You**	Capitol 2054
8/16/69	**12**	10	6. Hurt So Bad	Capitol 2482
			LEVEL 42	
			Pop-soul-jazz foursome from Manchester, England: Mark King (lead vocals), Mike Lindup, and brothers Phil and Boon Gould. The brothers left the band in October 1987; replaced by Alan Murphy (guitar) and Gary Husband (drums).	
4/05/86	**7**	14	**1. Something About You**	Polydor 883362
5/16/87	**12**	10	2. Lessons In Love	Polydor 883956
			LEVERT	
			Soul trio from Ohio: Gerald & Sean Levert (sons of the O'Jays' Eddie Levert), and Marc Gordon.	
9/05/87	**5**	12	● **1. Casanova**	Atlantic 89217

DATE	POS	WKS	ARTIST—RECORD TITLE	LABEL & NO.
			LEWIS, Barbara	
			Born on 2/09/43 in South Lyon, Michigan. R&B singer/multi-instrumentalist/ songwriter (since age nine). First recorded in Chicago in 1961. Inactive since the early 1970s.	
5/25/63	**3**	10	**1. Hello Stranger**	Atlantic 2184
			backing vocals: The Dells	
3/14/64	**38**	1	2. Puppy Love	Atlantic 2214
7/17/65	**11**	9	3. Baby, I'm Yours	Atlantic 2283
10/09/65	**11**	8	4. Make Me Your Baby	Atlantic 2300
8/13/66	**28**	4	5. Make Me Belong To You	Atlantic 2346
			LEWIS, Bobby	
			R&B singer. Born on 2/17/33 in Indianapolis. Grew up in an orphanage, adopted by a Detroit family at age 12. First recorded for the Parrot label in 1952.	
5/29/61	**1**(7)	17	**1. Tossin' And Turnin'**	Beltone 1002
9/11/61	**9**	7	**2. One Track Mind**	Beltone 1012
			LEWIS, Gary/The Playboys	
			Leader of pop-rock group The Playboys, formed in Los Angeles in 1964. Consisted of Gary (vocals, drums), Al Ramsey, John West (guitars), David Walker (keyboards) and David Costell (bass). Lewis (b: 7/31/46) is the son of comedian Jerry Lewis. Group worked regularly at Disneyland in 1964. Lewis inducted into the Army on New Year's Day in 1967, resumed career after discharge in 1968.	
1/23/65	**1**(2)	11	● **1. This Diamond Ring**	Liberty 55756
4/17/65	**2**(2)	9	**2. Count Me In**	Liberty 55778
7/17/65	**2**(1)	9	**3. Save Your Heart For Me**	Liberty 55809
10/09/65	**4**	8	**4. Everybody Loves A Clown**	Liberty 55818
12/18/65+	**3**	11	**5. She's Just My Style**	Liberty 55846
3/19/66	**9**	7	**6. Sure Gonna Miss Her**	Liberty 55865
5/21/66	**8**	7	**7. Green Grass**	Liberty 55880
8/13/66	**13**	5	8. My Heart's Symphony	Liberty 55898
10/22/66	**15**	6	9. (You Don't Have To) Paint Me A Picture	Liberty 55914
1/07/67	**21**	6	10. Where Will The Words Come From	Liberty 55933
6/10/67	**39**	2	11. Girls In Love	Liberty 55971
7/27/68	**19**	9	12. Sealed With A Kiss	Liberty 56037
			LEWIS, Huey/The News	
			Born Hugh Cregg, III on 7/05/50 in New York City. Joined the country-rock band Clover in the late '70s. Formed his six-man, pop-rock band, the News, in San Francisco in 1980: Huey (lead singer), Chris Hayes (lead guitar), Mario Cipollina (bass; brother of Quicksilver Messenger Service guitarist John Cipollina), Bill Gibson (drums), Sean Hopper (keyboards) and Johnny Colla (sax, guitar).	
2/20/82	**7**	13	**1. Do You Believe In Love**	Chrysalis 2589
6/12/82	**36**	4	2. Hope You Love Me Like You Say You Do	Chrysalis 2604
10/08/83	**8**	13	**3. Heart And Soul**	Chrysalis 42726
1/28/84	**6**	13	● **4. I Want A New Drug**	Chrysalis 42766
4/28/84	**6**	14	**5. The Heart Of Rock & Roll**	Chrysalis 42782
7/28/84	**6**	13	**6. If This Is It**	Chrysalis 42803
10/27/84	**18**	10	7. Walking On A Thin Line	Chrysalis 42825
7/06/85	**1**(2)	15	● **8. The Power Of Love**	Chrysalis 42876
			from the film *Back to the Future*	

DATE	POS	WKS	ARTIST—RECORD TITLE	LABEL & NO.
8/09/86	**1**(3)	13	**9. Stuck With You**	Chrysalis 43019
10/25/86	**3**	12	**10. Hip To Be Square**	Chrysalis 43065
1/17/87	**1**(1)	12	**11. Jacob's Ladder** written by Bruce Hornsby	Chrysalis 43097
4/11/87	**9**	10	**12. I Know What I Like**	Chrysalis 43108
8/01/87	**6**	11	**13. Doing It All For My Baby**	Chrysalis 43143
7/23/88	**3**	12	**14. Perfect World**	Chrysalis 43265
10/29/88	**25**	6	15. Small World	Chrysalis 43306
5/11/91	**11**	9	16. Couple Days Off	EMI 50346#
			LEWIS, Jerry	
			Comedian/actor. Born Joseph Levitch on 3/16/25 in Newark, New Jersey. Formed comedy duo with Dean Martin in 1946 in Atlantic City that lasted 16 films and 10 years. Film debut in 1949 in *My Friend Irma*. His son Gary was a '60s pop star. National chairman in campaign against muscular dystrophy.	
11/24/56	**10**	15	**1. Rock-A-Bye Your Baby With A Dixie Melody** Best Seller #10 / Top 100 #12 / Juke Box #13 / Jockey #17 #1 hit for Al Jolson in 1918	Decca 30124
			LEWIS, Jerry Lee	
			Born on 9/29/35 in Ferriday, Louisiana. Played piano since age nine, professionally since age 15. First recorded for Sun in 1956. Appeared in the film *Disc Jockey Jamboree* in 1957. Career waned in 1958 after marriage to 13-year-old cousin, Myra Gale Brown, daughter of his bass player. Made comeback in country music beginning in 1968. Nicknamed "The Killer," Lewis has been surrounded by personal tragedies in the past two decades, survived several serious illnesses. Cousin to country singer Mickey Gilley and TV evangelist Jimmy Swaggart. Inducted into the Rock and Roll Hall of Fame in 1986. Jerry's early career is documented in the 1989 film *Great Balls of Fire* starring Dennis Quaid.	
7/15/57	**3**	20	**1. Whole Lot Of Shakin' Going On** Best Seller #3 / Top 100 #3 / Jockey #9	Sun 267
			JERRY LEE LEWIS AND HIS PUMPING PIANO:	
12/02/57+	**2**(4)	13	**2. Great Balls Of Fire** Best Seller #2 / Top 100 #2 / Jockey #9	Sun 281
3/10/58	**7**	9	**3. Breathless** Top 100 #7 / Best Seller #9 / Jockey #23	Sun 288
6/02/58	**21**	8	4. High School Confidential Top 100 #21 / Best Seller #22	Sun 296
4/24/61	**30**	4	5. What'd I Say	Sun 356
			JERRY LEE LEWIS:	
1/15/72	**40**	1	6. Me And Bobby McGee	Mercury 73248
			LEWIS, Ramsey	
			Ramsey (b: 5/27/35, Chicago; piano) formed the Gentlemen Of Swing, a jazz-oriented trio, in 1956 in Chicago. Consisted of Ramsey, Eldee Young (bass) and Isaac "Red" Holt (drums). All had been in The Clefs in the early '50s. First recorded for Chess/Argo in 1956. Disbanded in 1965; Young and Holt then formed the Young-Holt Trio. Lewis re-formed his trio with Cleveland Eaton (bass) and Maurice White (later with Earth, Wind & Fire; drums). Reunited with Young and Holt in 1983.	
			RAMSEY LEWIS TRIO:	
8/21/65	**5**	12	**1. The "In" Crowd** [I]	Argo 5506
11/27/65	**11**	6	2. Hang On Sloopy [I]	Cadet 5522
2/05/66	**29**	4	3. A Hard Day's Night [I]	Cadet 5525

DATE	POS	WKS	ARTIST—RECORD TITLE	LABEL & NO.
			RAMSEY LEWIS:	
8/20/66	**19**	6	4. Wade In The Water [I]	Cadet 5541
			LIGHTFOOT, Gordon	
			Born on 11/17/38 in Orillia, Ontario, Canada. Folk-pop-country singer/songwriter/guitarist. Worked on "Country Hoedown," CBC-TV series. Teamed with Jim Whalen as the Two Tones in the mid-1960s. Wrote hit "Early Mornin' Rain" for Peter, Paul and Mary. First recorded for Chateau in 1965.	
1/23/71	**5**	11	**1. If You Could Read My Mind**	Reprise 0974
5/11/74	**1**(1)	11	● **2. Sundown**	Reprise 1194
10/05/74	**10**	7	**3. Carefree Highway**	Reprise 1309
5/03/75	**26**	4	4. Rainy Day People	Reprise 1328
9/25/76	**2**(2)	13	**5. The Wreck Of The Edmund Fitzgerald** true story of an ore vessel that sunk in Lake Superior on 11/10/75	Reprise 1369
3/25/78	**33**	3	6. The Circle Is Small (I Can See It In Your Eyes)	Warner 8518
			LIGHTHOUSE	
			Rock band from Toronto — Bob McBride, lead singer.	
10/09/71	**24**	8	1. One Fine Morning	Evolution 1048
11/25/72	**34**	5	2. Sunny Days	Evolution 1069
			LIGHTNING SEEDS, The	
			Band with fluctuating lineup spearheaded by U.K. producer/vocalist Ian Broudie. Broudie was a member of Big In Japan and produced Echo & The Bunnymen and others.	
7/07/90	**31**	6	1. Pure	MCA 53816#
			LIMAHL	
			Real name: Chris Hamill (Limahl is an anagram of his last name). Ex-lead singer of Kajagoogoo.	
5/04/85	**17**	9	1. Never Ending Story from the film *The Never Ending Story*	EMI America 8230
			LIND, Bob	
			Born on 11/25/44 in Baltimore. Folk-rock singer/songwriter.	
2/12/66	**5**	9	**1. Elusive Butterfly**	World Pac. 77808
			LINDEN, Kathy	
			Songstress from Moorestown, New Jersey.	
3/31/58	**7**	11	**1. Billy** Jockey #7 / Top 100 #12 / Best Seller #14 #10 hit for Wee Bonnie Baker (of Orrin Tucker's band) in 1939	Felsted 8510
4/27/59	**11**	10	2. Goodbye Jimmy, Goodbye orchestra directed by Joe Leahy on above 2	Felsted 8571
			LINDISFARNE	
			Folk-rock quintet from England — Alan Hull, lead singer. Group's name is an island off of Northumberland, U.K.	
11/25/78	**33**	4	1. Run For Home	Atco 7093
			LINDSAY, Mark	
			Born on 3/09/42 in Cambridge, Idaho. Lead singer/saxophonist of Paul Revere & The Raiders. Also recorded with Raider, Keith Allison, and Steve Alaimo as The Unknowns.	
1/10/70	**10**	11	● **1. Arizona**	Columbia 45037

DATE	POS	WKS	ARTIST—RECORD TITLE	LABEL & NO.
7/11/70	**25**	5	2. Silver Bird	Columbia 45180
			LINEAR	
			Pronounced: lin-EAR. Miami-based male trio: New Yorkers Charlie "Steele" Pennachio (vocals) and Joey Restivo (percussion) with Ecuadoran Wyatt Pauley (guitar).	
3/31/90	**5**	16	● **1. Sending All My Love**	Atlantic 87961
			LIPPS, INC.	
			Pronounced: lip-synch. Funk project from Minneapolis formed by producer/songwriter/multi-instrumentalist Steven Greenberg. Vocals by Miss Black Minnesota U.S.A. of 1976, Cynthia Johnson.	
4/19/80	**1**(4)	15	▲ **1. Funkytown**	Casablanca 2233
			LISA LISA AND CULT JAM	
			Harlem trio: Lisa Velez (lead vocals), Mike Hughes and Alex "Spanador" Moseley. All of their hits were produced by Full Force.	
			LISA LISA AND CULT JAM with FULL FORCE:	
8/03/85	**34**	6	● 1. I Wonder If I Take You Home	Columbia 04886
8/30/86	**8**	13	● **2. All Cried Out**	Columbia 05844
			featuring Paul Anthony & Bow Legged Lou	
			LISA LISA AND CULT JAM:	
5/02/87	**1**(1)	14	● **3. Head To Toe**	Columbia 07008
8/22/87	**1**(1)	13	**4. Lost In Emotion**	Columbia 07267
5/13/89	**29**	4	5. Little Jackie Wants To Be A Star	Columbia 68674
			LITTLE ANTHONY AND THE IMPERIALS	
			R&B group formed in 1957 in Brooklyn. Consisted of Anthony Gourdine (b: 1/08/40), Ernest Wright, Jr., Tracy Lord, Glouster Rogers and Clarence Collins. Anthony first recorded on Winley in 1955 with The DuPonts. Formed The Chesters in 1957, then changed name to The Imperials in 1958. Sammy Strain, who joined group in 1964, left in 1975 to join The O'Jays. Gourdine became an Inspirational artist in 1980.	
8/18/58	**4**	14	**1. Tears On My Pillow**	End 1027
			Hot 100 #4 / Best Seller #5 end also released on End 1027 as The Imperials	
1/18/60	**24**	7	2. Shimmy, Shimmy, Ko-Ko-Bop	End 1060
9/05/64	**15**	8	3. I'm On The Outside (Looking In)	DCP 1104
11/21/64	**6**	12	**4. Goin' Out Of My Head**	DCP 1119
2/13/65	**10**	8	**5. Hurt So Bad**	DCP 1128
7/17/65	**16**	7	6. Take Me Back	DCP 1136
11/06/65	**34**	1	7. I Miss You So	DCP 1149
			with the 101 Strings	
			LITTLE CAESAR/The Romans	
			Los Angeles R&B quintet led by David "Little Caesar" Johnson (b: 6/16/34, Chicago).	
5/29/61	**9**	9	**1. Those Oldies But Goodies (Remind Me Of You)**	Del-Fi 4158
			LITTLE DIPPERS, The	
			Pop quartet organized by producer Buddy Killen: Delores Dinning, Emily Gilmore, Darrell McCall and Hurshel Wigintin.	
2/08/60	**9**	10	**1. Forever**	University 210

DATE	POS	WKS	ARTIST—RECORD TITLE	LABEL & NO.
			LITTLE EVA	
			Born Eva Narcissus Boyd on 6/29/45 in Bellhaven, North Carolina. Discovered by songwriters Carole King and Gerry Goffin while babysitting their daughter Louise.	
7/21/62	**1**(1)	12	**1. The Loco-Motion**	Dimension 1000
11/24/62	**12**	8	2. Keep Your Hands Off My Baby	Dimension 1003
2/23/63	**20**	6	3. Let's Turkey Trot	Dimension 1006
7/13/63	**38**	2	4. Swinging On A Star **BIG DEE IRWIN with LITTLE EVA** #1 hit for Bing Crosby in 1944 (from the film *Going My Way*)	Dimension 1010
			LITTLE JOE & THE THRILLERS	
			R&B vocal group formed in New York City in 1956: Joe Cook (lead), Farris Hill and Richard Frazier (tenors), Donald Burnett (baritone) and Harry Pascle (bass).	
10/07/57	**22**	9	1. Peanuts Best Seller #22 / Top 100 #23	Okeh 7088
			LITTLE JOEY/The Flips	
			R&B quintet from Philadelphia — Joey Hall, lead singer.	
7/14/62	**33**	3	1. Bongo Stomp	Joy 262
			LITTLE MILTON	
			Born Milton Campbell, Jr. on 9/07/34 in Inverness, Mississippi. Blues singer/guitarist. Recorded with Ike Turner at Sun Records, 1953-54. In concert film *Wattstax*, 1972.	
4/24/65	**25**	7	1. We're Gonna Make It	Checker 1105
			LITTLE RICHARD	
			Born Richard Wayne Penniman on 12/05/32 in Macon, Georgia. R&B-rock and roll singer/pianist. Talent contest win led to first recordings for RCA-Victor in 1951. Worked with the Tempo Toppers, 1953-55. Appeared in three early rock and roll films: *Don't Knock the Rock*, *The Girl Can't Help It* and *Mister Rock 'n' Roll* and the 1986 comedy *Down and Out in Beverly Hills.* Earned theology degree in 1961 and was ordained a minister. Left R&B for gospel music, 1959-62 and again in the mid-1970s. One of the key figures in the transition from R&B to rock and roll. Inducted into the Rock and Roll Hall of Fame in 1986.	
1/28/56	**17**	5	1. Tutti-Frutti Juke Box #17 / Best Seller #18 / Top 100 #21	Specialty 561
4/07/56	**6**	12	**2. Long Tall Sally/** Best Seller #6 / Top 100 #13 / Juke Box #14 / Jockey #16	
6/30/56	**33**	1	3. Slippin' And Slidin' (Peepin' And Hidin')	Specialty 572
7/14/56	**17**	7	4. Rip It Up Best Seller #17 / Top 100 #27	Specialty 579
4/06/57	**21**	7	5. Lucille Best Seller #21 / Top 100 #27	Specialty 598
6/24/57	**10**	13	**6. Jenny, Jenny** Best Seller #10 / Top 100 #14	Specialty 606
10/07/57	**8**	12	**7. Keep A Knockin'** Top 100 #8 / Best Seller #9 / Jockey #24 from the film *Mister Rock 'n' Roll*	Specialty 611
2/24/58	**10**	10	**8. Good Golly, Miss Molly** Top 100 #10 / Best Seller #13	Specialty 624
6/23/58	**31**	3	9. Ooh! My Soul Best Seller #31 / Top 100 #35	Specialty 633

DATE	POS	WKS	ARTIST—RECORD TITLE	LABEL & NO.
			LITTLE RIVER BAND	
			Pop-rock group formed in Australia in 1975. Consisted of Glenn Shorrock (lead singer), Rick Formosa, Beeb Birtles and Graham Goble (guitars), Roger McLachlan (bass) and Derek Pellicci (drums). Formosa, McLachlan, replaced by David Briggs (guitar) and George McArdle (bass) after first album. Shorrock replaced by John Farnham in 1983. Numerous personnel changes since 1985. Shorrock replaced Farnham in 1987. 1988 lineup includes: Shorrock, Goble and Pellicci. Band named after a resort town near Melbourne.	
11/06/76	**28**	6	1. It's A Long Way There	Harvest 4318
9/24/77	**14**	11	2. Help Is On Its Way	Harvest 4428
1/21/78	**16**	9	3. Happy Anniversary	Harvest 4524
8/12/78	**3**	14	**4. Reminiscing**	Harvest 4605
1/27/79	**10**	14	**5. Lady**	Harvest 4667
8/04/79	**6**	14	**6. Lonesome Loser**	Capitol 4748
11/10/79+	**10**	13	**7. Cool Change**	Capitol 4789
9/05/81	**6**	14	**8. The Night Owls**	Capitol 5033
12/26/81+	**10**	15	**9. Take It Easy On Me**	Capitol 5057
5/01/82	**14**	8	10. Man On Your Mind	Capitol 5061
12/04/82+	**11**	13	11. The Other Guy	Capitol 5185
5/28/83	**22**	6	12. We Two	Capitol 5231
8/27/83	**35**	3	13. You're Driving Me Out Of My Mind	Capitol 5256
			LITTLE SISTER	
			Female soul trio organized by Sly Stone for his own record label. Consisted of his sister Vanetta Stewart, Mary Rand and Elva Melton.	
3/28/70	**22**	6	1. You're The One-Part I	Stone Flower 9000
1/30/71	**32**	3	2. Somebody's Watching You	Stone Flower 9001
			LIVING COLOUR	
			Black rock quartet from New York City. London-born, Brooklyn-raised lead guitarist/songwriter Vernon Reid, with vocalist Corey Glover (appeared in the film *Platoon*), bassist Muzz Skillings and drummer William Calhoun.	
4/01/89	**13**	9	1. Cult Of Personality	Epic 68611
10/14/89	**31**	3	2. Glamour Boys produced by Mick Jagger	Epic 68548
			LIVING IN A BOX	
			Soul-styled pop trio from England: Richard Darbyshire (vocals), Marcus Vere (keyboards) and Anthony "Tich" Critchlow (drums).	
7/25/87	**17**	7	1. Living In A Box	Chrysalis 43104
			L.L. COOL J	
			Real name: James Todd Smith. Rapper from Queens, New York. Stage name is abbreviation for Ladies Love Cool James. Appeared in the 1985 film *Krush Groove*.	
8/15/87	**14**	8	1. I Need Love	Def Jam 07350
3/26/88	**31**	5	● 2. Going Back To Cali from the film *Less Than Zero*	Def Jam 07679
7/08/89	**15**	8	● 3. I'm That Type Of Guy	Def Jam 68902
1/05/91	**9**	15	● **4. Around The Way Girl**	Def Jam 73609
5/11/91	**17**	9	● 5. Mama Said Knock You Out	Def Jam 73706

DATE	POS	WKS	ARTIST—RECORD TITLE	LABEL & NO.
			LOBO	
			Pop singer/songwriter/guitarist. Born Roland Kent Lavoie on 7/31/43 in Tallahassee, Florida. Played with the Legends in Tampa in 1961. The Legends included Jim Stafford, Gerald Chambers, Gram Parsons and Jon Corneal. Lobo is Spanish for wolf. Lavoie formed own publishing company, Boo Publishing, in 1974.	
4/24/71	**5**	10	**1. Me And You And A Dog Named Boo**	Big Tree 112
10/14/72	**2**(2)	10	● **2. I'd Love You To Want Me**	Big Tree 147
1/13/73	**8**	10	**3. Don't Expect Me To Be Your Friend**	Big Tree 158
5/05/73	**27**	5	4. It Sure Took A Long, Long Time	Big Tree 16001
7/21/73	**22**	8	5. How Can I Tell Her	Big Tree 16004
5/11/74	**37**	2	6. Standing At The End Of The Line	Big Tree 15001
4/26/75	**27**	4	7. Don't Tell Me Goodnight	Big Tree 16033
9/08/79	**23**	8	8. Where Were You When I Was Falling In Love	MCA 41065
			LOCKLIN, Hank	
			Country singer/songwriter/guitarist. Born Lawrence Hankins Locklin on 2/15/18 in McLellan, Florida. Elected mayor of McLellan in the early '60s. Own TV series in Houston and Dallas in the '70s.	
6/13/60	**8**	15	**1. Please Help Me, I'm Falling**	RCA 7692
			LOGGINS, Dave	
			Born on 11/10/47 in Mountain City, Tennessee. Pop-country singer/songwriter. Cousin of Kenny Loggins.	
7/13/74	**5**	10	**1. Please Come To Boston**	Epic 11115
			LOGGINS, Kenny	
			Born on 1/07/47 in Everett, Washington. Pop-rock singer/songwriter/guitarist. Signed as a solo artist with Columbia in 1971 where he met and recorded with Jim Messina from 1972-76.	
8/19/78	**5**	15	**1. Whenever I Call You "Friend"** harmony vocal by Stevie Nicks	Columbia 10794
11/24/79+	**11**	16	2. This Is It	Columbia 11109
4/05/80	**36**	2	3. Keep The Fire	Columbia 11215
8/23/80	**7**	12	**4. I'm Alright** theme from the film *Caddyshack*	Columbia 11317
9/25/82	**17**	6	5. Don't Fight It **KENNY LOGGINS with STEVE PERRY**	Columbia 03192
12/11/82+	**15**	13	6. Heart To Heart	Columbia 03377
4/02/83	**24**	7	7. Welcome To Heartlight inspired by the writings of children from Heartlight School	Columbia 03555
2/11/84	**1**(3)	16	▲ **8. Footloose**	Columbia 04310
6/23/84	**22**	8	9. I'm Free (Heaven Helps The Man) above 2 from the film *Footloose*	Columbia 04452
4/13/85	**29**	4	10. Vox Humana	Columbia 04849
7/20/85	**40**	1	11. Forever	Columbia 04931
6/07/86	**2**(1)	13	**12. Danger Zone** from the film *Top Gun*	Columbia 05893
4/25/87	**11**	12	13. Meet Me Half Way from the Sylvester Stallone film *Over the Top*	Columbia 06690
7/30/88	**8**	11	**14. Nobody's Fool** theme from the film *Caddyshack II*	Columbia 07971

DATE	POS	WKS	ARTIST—RECORD TITLE	LABEL & NO.
			LOGGINS & MESSINA	
			Duo of Kenneth Clarke Loggins (b: 1/07/47, Everett, Washington) and James Messina (b: 12/05/47, Maywood, California). Loggins was raised in Alhambra, California and played guitar from age 13. Worked with Second Helping and Gator Creek and recorded in the late '60s. Wrote "House On Pooh Corner" hit for the Dirt Band. Messina was raised in Harlingen, Texas and played in bands from age 13. Worked as a recording engineer and producer from 1965. Member of Buffalo Springfield and Poco. Duo formed in 1970.	
12/02/72+	**4**	13	● **1. Your Mama Don't Dance** **KENNY LOGGINS AND JIM MESSINA**	Columbia 45719
4/28/73	**18**	8	2. Thinking Of You	Columbia 45815
11/24/73	**16**	8	3. My Music	Columbia 45952
			LOLITA	
			Lolita Ditta from Vienna, Austria.	
11/14/60	**5**	14	**1. Sailor (Your Home Is The Sea)** [F]	Kapp 349
			LONDON, Julie	
			Born on 9/26/26 in Santa Rosa, California. Singer/actress. Played Dixie McCall on the TV series "Emergency." Married to Jack Webb, 1945-53.	
12/03/55	**9**	13	**1. Cry Me A River** Jockey #9 / Top 100 #13 / Juke Box #14 / Best Seller #23	Liberty 55006
			LONDON, Laurie	
			Male vocalist. Born on 1/19/44 in London. Recorded only hit record at age 13.	
3/24/58	**1**(4)	14	● **1. He's Got The Whole World (In His Hands)** Jockey #1 / Best Seller #2 / Top 100 #2 traditional black American gospel song	Capitol 3891
			LONDONBEAT	
			Britain-based soul outfit. Vocal trio of Americans Jimmy Helms and George Chandler with Trinidad native Jimmy Chambers. Backed by British producer/multi-instrumentalist Willy M.	
2/16/91	**1**(1)	14	● **1. I've Been Thinking About You**	Radioact. 54005#
6/08/91	**18**	7	2. A Better Love	Radioact. 54101#
			LONDON SYMPHONY ORCHESTRA — see WILLIAMS, John	
			LONG, Shorty	
			Born Frederick Earl Long on 5/20/40 in Birmingham, Alabama. Soul singer/songwriter. Moved to Detroit in 1959. First recorded for Tri-Phi in 1962. Drowned on 6/29/69 in Ontario, Canada.	
6/15/68	**8**	8	**1. Here Comes The Judge** [N]	Soul 35044
			LOOKING GLASS	
			Rock quartet formed by singer/guitarist Elliot Lurie while at Rutgers University in New Jersey.	
7/01/72	**1**(1)	14	● **1. Brandy (You're A Fine Girl)**	Epic 10874
9/29/73	**33**	3	2. Jimmy Loves Mary-Anne	Epic 11001
			LOPEZ, Denise	
			Dance singer born in Queens, New York. Recorded under the name "Neecy Dee" in 1984.	
8/06/88	**31**	5	1. Sayin' Sorry (Don't Make It Right)	Vendetta 7200

DATE	POS	WKS	ARTIST—RECORD TITLE	LABEL & NO.
			LOPEZ, Trini	
			Born Trinidad Lopez, III on 5/15/37 in Dallas. Pop-folk singer/guitarist. Discovered by Don Costa while performing at PJs nightclub in Los Angeles. Portrayed Pedro Jiminez in the film *The Dirty Dozen*.	
8/10/63	**3**	11	**1. If I Had A Hammer**	Reprise 20198
12/14/63+	**23**	6	2. Kansas City	Reprise 20236
2/06/65	**20**	5	3. Lemon Tree	Reprise 0336
5/07/66	**39**	3	4. I'm Comin' Home, Cindy all of above produced by Don Costa	Reprise 0455
			LORAIN, A'Me	
			Female singer from Simi Valley, California. Twenty-two years old in 1990. Her group The Family Affair features her fiance Victor Indrizzo and her brother Fred Trujillo, Jr.	
2/24/90	**9**	12	**1. Whole Wide World** from the film *True Love*	RCA 9098
			LORBER, Jeff	
			Jazz fusion keyboardist.	
2/07/87	**27**	5	1. Facts Of Love **JEFF LORBER featuring KARYN WHITE**	Warner 28588
			LORING, Gloria	
			Played Liz Curtis on the TV soap "Days of Our Lives." Married to actor Alan Thicke for 14 years.	
8/02/86	**2**(2)	14	**1. Friends And Lovers** **GLORIA LORING & CARL ANDERSON**	USA Carrere 06122
			LOS BRAVOS	
			Rock quintet consisting of four members from Spain and one from Germany — Mike Kogel (Kennedy), leader.	
9/10/66	**4**	8	**1. Black Is Black**	Press 60002
			LOS INDIOS TABAJARAS	
			Brazilian Indian brothers: Natalicio and Antenor Lima.	
10/12/63	**6**	10	**1. Maria Elena** **[I]** #1 hit in 1941 for Jimmy Dorsey & His Orchestra	RCA 8216
			LOS LOBOS	
			Hispanic-American rock quintet formed in East Los Angeles in 1973 by David Hidalgo (lead vocals), Cesar Rosas, Conrad Lozano and Louie Perez. Former Blasters' saxophonist, Steve Berlin, joined in 1983.	
7/18/87	**1**(3)	14	**1. La Bamba** **[F]**	Slash 28336
10/17/87	**21**	7	2. Come On, Let's Go above 2 from the film *La Bamba*	Slash 28186
			LOST GENERATION, The	
			Chicago soul quartet: Lowrell Simon (lead), his brother Fred Simon, Larry Brownlee (of The C.O.D.'s; d: 1978) and Jesse Dean. Disbanded in 1974. Lowrell began recording solo (as Lowrell) in 1978.	
8/01/70	**30**	5	1. The Sly, Slick, And The Wicked	Brunswick 55436
			LOU, Bonnie — see BONNIE	

Kajagoogoo's sole top-10 hit, 1983's "Too Shy" must have been autobiographical: by 1984, they dropped the "googoo" and changed their name to Kaja—perhaps to avoid those embarrassing social introductions.

Kenny G's surprising success as a hitmaker—his instrumental "Songbird" made the Top 5 in 1987—paved the way for a raft of similar-styled saxophonistists, including Richard Elliott, Dave Koz, and Candy Dulfer.

Kiss's bass player Gene Simmons may have looked ghoulish in the full makeup that he and his bandmembers wore as a trademark from 1973-1983—but he was absolutely no relation to the similarly-named 1964 artist who recorded "Haunted House."

Kix's hard-rock fan base, which has consistently grown since the group's first Atlantic album in 1981, has apparently never been bothered that their heroes adopted the name of a breakfast cereal.

Klymaxx, an influential black female band whose "I Miss You" was a top-5 hit in 1985, launched the careers of two singers who'd later do well on their own: Joyce "Fenderella" Irby and Bernadette Cooper.

Buddy Knox's five appearances in the Top 40 during the late 50s and early 60s co-billed his backing band, the Rhythm Orchids, with only one exception: 1961's "Lovey Dovey," which was credited solely to Knox. Future music business executive Jimmy Bowen was one of the three Rhythm Orchids.

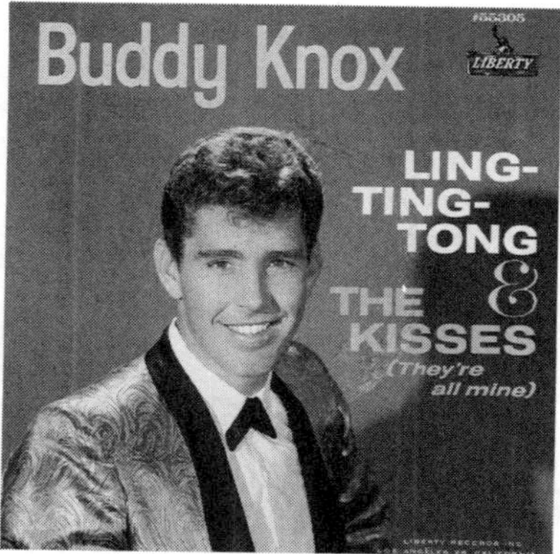

Patti LaBelle's "I Don't Do Duets," a track from her 1991 album *Burnin'*, must have come as a surprise to Michael McDonald. The former Doobie Brother and singer LaBelle had a top-30 hit in 1986 with a duet of their own, "Oh, People."

Major Lance had six top-40 hits in the mid-60s—topped by 1964's No. 5 "Um,Um, Um, Um, Um, Um"—and was later sent to prison for selling cocaine. In 1983, he re-emerged with the Kat Family album *The Major's Back.* Nominally, he was outranked by Chairman Of The Board vocalist General Johnson.

Brenda Lee is one of very few pop artists who have smoothly made the transition from pop—she had 11 top-10 hits between 1960-1963—to country music. In 1991, her album *A Brenda Lee Christmas* kicked things off with a remake of her 1958 classic, "Rockin' Around The Christmas Tree."

The Lemon Pipers had a No. 1 hit with "Green Tambourine" and were considered prime movers in the burgeoning "bubblegum" movement of the late 60s. Others of their ilk—all of whom recorded for the Buddah label—were the Ohio Express and the 1910 Fruitgum Company.

Julian Lennon's 1984 album *Valotte* bore two top-10 hits—the title track and "Too Late For Goodbyes"—and seemed to promise a continuing career in hitmaking. But with only two other, lesser hits to his credit, the famous son of Beatle John Lennon hasn't matched his father chartwise.

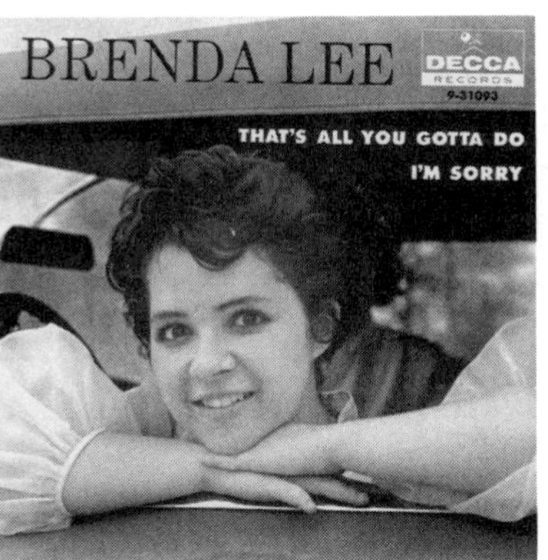

DATE	POS	WKS	ARTIST—RECORD TITLE	LABEL & NO.
			LOUDERMILK, John D.	
			Born on 3/31/34 in Durham, North Carolina. Pop-country singer/songwriter/ multi-instrumentalist. Wrote "Waterloo," "Tobacco Road," "Indian Reservation" and many others. Recorded as "Johnny Dee" and "Ebe Sneezer" in 1956.	
4/06/57	38	1	1. Sittin' In The Balcony	Colonial 430
			JOHNNY DEE	
12/04/61	32	3	2. Language Of Love	RCA 7938
			LOUIE LOUIE	
			Singer/dancer/songwriter Louie Cordero from Southern California. Played Madonna's boyfriend in her "Borderline" video.	
5/26/90	19	8	1. Sittin' In The Lap Of Luxury	WTG 73266
			LOVE	
			Los Angeles-based rock group led by singer/guitarist Arthur Lee (from Memphis).	
9/10/66	33	3	1. 7 And 7 Is	Elektra 45605
			LOVE, Darlene	
			Lead singer of backing group The Blossoms. Sang lead on two songs by The Crystals and with Bob B. Soxx & The Blue Jeans. Starred in the Off-Broadway show *Leader of the Pack.* In the 1987 film *Lethal Weapon.*	
5/11/63	39	1	1. (Today I Met) The Boy I'm Gonna Marry	Philles 111
8/24/63	26	4	2. Wait Til' My Bobby Gets Home	Philles 114
			above 2 produced by Phil Spector	
			LOVE, Monie	
			Simone Wilson, a London-born female rapper based in Brooklyn. Featured on Queen Latifah's single "Ladies First." Nineteen years old in 1990.	
4/20/91	26	6	1. It's A Shame (My Sister)	Warner 19515#
			featuring True Image	
			LOVE AND KISSES	
			Studio group assembled by European disco producer Alec Costandinos. Consisted of vocalists Don Daniels, Elaine Hill, Dianne Brooks and Jean Graham.	
6/24/78	22	6	1. Thank God It's Friday	Casablanca 925
			from the film of the same title	
			LOVE AND ROCKETS	
			British trio: Daniel Ash (guitar, vocals), Kevin Haskins (drums) and David J. (bass). All were members of Bauhaus, 1979-83. Band name taken from the title of an underground comic book. Ash went solo in 1991.	
6/17/89	3	12	**1. So Alive**	RCA 8956
			LOVERBOY	
			Rock quintet formed in Vancouver, Canada in 1978: Mike Reno (lead singer), Paul Dean (lead guitar), Scott Smith (bass), Matt Frenette (drums) and Doug Johnson (keyboards, left by 1989).	
3/21/81	35	6	1. Turn Me Loose	Columbia 11421
1/09/82	29	8	2. Working For The Weekend	Columbia 02589
5/15/82	26	6	3. When It's Over	Columbia 02814
			backing vocals by Nancy Nash	
7/02/83	11	11	4. Hot Girls In Love	Columbia 03941
10/29/83	34	3	5. Queen Of The Broken Hearts	Columbia 04096
9/14/85	9	11	**6. Lovin' Every Minute Of It**	Columbia 05569

DATE	POS	WKS	ARTIST—RECORD TITLE	LABEL & NO.
2/15/86	**10**	10	**7. This Could Be The Night**	Columbia 05765
8/23/86	**12**	11	8. Heaven In Your Eyes from the film *Top Gun*	Columbia 06178
10/10/87	**38**	3	9. Notorious	Columbia 07324
			LOVE UNLIMITED	
			Female soul trio from San Pedro, California: sisters Glodean & Linda James, and Diane Taylor. Barry White, who married Glodean on 7/04/74, was their manager and producer.	
5/06/72	**14**	9	● **1. Walkin' In The Rain With The One I Love** featuring Barry White's voice on the telephone	Uni 55319
1/04/75	**27**	7	2. I Belong To You	20th Century 2141
			LOVE UNLIMITED ORCHESTRA	
			Studio orchestra conducted and arranged by Barry White.	
12/22/73+	**1**(1)	16	● **1. Love's Theme** **[I]**	20th Century 2069
3/15/75	**22**	5	2. Satin Soul [I]	20th Century 2162
			LOVIN' SPOONFUL, The	
			Jug-band rock group formed in New York City in 1965. Consisted of John Sebastian (lead vocals, songwriter, guitarist, harmonica), Zal Yanovsky (lead guitar), Steve Boone (bass) and Joe Butler (drums). Sebastian had been with the Even Dozen Jug Band; did session work at Elektra. Yanovsky and Sebastian were members of the Mugwumps with Cass Elliot and Denny Doherty (later with The Mamas & The Papas). Yanovsky replaced by Jerry Yester (keyboards) in 1967. Disbanded in 1968.	
9/18/65	**9**	8	**1. Do You Believe In Magic**	Kama Sutra 201
12/11/65+	**10**	9	**2. You Didn't Have To Be So Nice**	Kama Sutra 205
3/12/66	**2**(2)	10	**3. Daydream**	Kama Sutra 208
5/14/66	**2**(2)	9	**4. Did You Ever Have To Make Up Your Mind?**	Kama Sutra 209
7/23/66	**1**(3)	10	● **5. Summer In The City**	Kama Sutra 211
10/22/66	**10**	8	**6. Rain On The Roof**	Kama Sutra 216
12/31/66+	**8**	8	**7. Nashville Cats**	Kama Sutra 219
2/25/67	**15**	5	8. Darling Be Home Soon from the Francis Ford Coppola film *You're a Big Boy Now*	Kama Sutra 220
5/20/67	**18**	5	9. Six O'Clock	Kama Sutra 225
11/11/67	**27**	3	10. She Is Still A Mystery	Kama Sutra 239
			LOWE, Jim	
			Born on 5/07/27 in Springfield, Missouri. Disc jockey/vocalist/pianist/composer. DJ in New York City when he recorded "Green Door" in 1956.	
9/29/56	**1**(3)	22	**1. The Green Door** Top 100 #1(3) / Juke Box #1(3) / Best Seller #2 / Jockey #2 piano player: Bob Davie; vocal backing: the High Fives	Dot 15486
5/13/57	**15**	6	2. Four Walls/ Juke Box #15 / Jockey #16 / Best Seller #19 / Top 100 #20	
5/13/57	**15**	5	3. Talkin' To The Blues Juke Box #15 / Jockey #20 / Top 100 #21 from the TV production "Modern Romances"	Dot 15569
			LOWE, Nick	
			Born on 3/25/49 in Woodbridge, Suffolk, England. With Brinsley Schwarz (1970-75) and Rockpile. Married Carlene Carter on 8/18/79. Produced albums for Elvis Costello, Graham Parker & The Rumour and others.	
8/18/79	**12**	10	1. Cruel To Be Kind	Columbia 11018

DATE	POS	WKS	ARTIST—RECORD TITLE	LABEL & NO.
			L.T.D.	
			Ten-man, R&B-funk band from Greensboro, North Carolina — Jeffrey Osborne, lead singer. Osborne left in 1980, replaced by Leslie Wilson and Andre Ray. L.T.D. stands for Love, Togetherness and Devotion.	
11/06/76	**20**	9	1. Love Ballad	A&M 1847
11/12/77	**4**	12	● **2. (Every Time I Turn Around) Back In Love Again**	A&M 1974
1/31/81	**40**	1	3. Shine On	A&M 2283
			LUKE, Robin	
			Born on 3/19/42 in Los Angeles. Recorded "Susie Darlin' " in Hawaii, inspired by his sister, Susie.	
8/18/58	**5**	15	**1. Susie Darlin'** Hot 100 #5 / Best Seller #6 end first released on Bertram International 206 in 1958	Dot 15781
			LULU	
			Born Marie Lawrie on 11/03/48 near Glasgow, Scotland. Married to Maurice Gibb (Bee Gees) from 1969-73. Starred in the 1967 film *To Sir with Love.* Hosted own U.K. TV show in 1968.	
9/23/67	**1**(5)	15	● **1. To Sir With Love** from the film of the same title	Epic 10187
1/06/68	**32**	3	2. Best Of Both Worlds	Epic 10260
2/07/70	**22**	8	3. Oh Me Oh My (I'm A Fool For You Baby)	Atco 6722
8/22/81	**18**	10	4. I Could Never Miss You (More Than I Do)	Alfa 7006
			LUMAN, Bob	
			Country-rockabilly singer/songwriter/guitarist. Born on 4/15/37 in Nacogdoches, Texas; died on 12/27/78.	
9/26/60	**7**	9	**1. Let's Think About Living** **[N]**	Warner 5172
			LUNDBERG, Victor	
			Ex-DJ/newsman born in 1923 in Grand Rapids, Michigan.	
11/25/67	**10**	4	**1. An Open Letter To My Teenage Son** **[S]**	Liberty 55996
			LYMAN, Arthur	
			Arthur was born on the island of Kauai, Hawaii in 1934. Plays vibraphone, guitar, piano and drums. Formerly with the Martin Denny Trio.	
6/12/61	**4**	10	**1. Yellow Bird** **[I]** **ARTHUR LYMAN GROUP**	Hi Fi 5024
			LYMON, Frankie/The Teenagers	
			R&B group formed as The Premiers in the Bronx in 1955. Lead singer Lymon was born on 9/30/42 in New York City; died of a drug overdose on 2/28/68. Other members included Herman Santiago & Jimmy Merchant (tenors), Joe Negroni (baritone; d: 9/05/78) and Sherman Games (bass; d: 2/26/77). Group appeared in the films *Rock, Rock, Rock* and *Mister Rock 'n' Roll.*	
2/18/56	**6**	16	**1. Why Do Fools Fall In Love** **THE TEENAGERS featuring FRANKIE LYMON** Best Seller #6 / Top 100 #7 / Juke Box #8 / Jockey #9	Gee 1002
5/12/56	**13**	11	2. I Want You To Be My Girl Best Seller #13 / Top 100 #17 / Juke Box #20 / Jockey #25	Gee 1012
8/26/57	**20**	7	3. Goody Goody Best Seller #20 / Jockey #21 / Top 100 #22	Gee 1039

DATE	POS	WKS	ARTIST—RECORD TITLE	LABEL & NO.
			LYNN, Barbara	
			Born Barbara Lynn Ozen on 1/16/42 in Beaumont, Texas. R&B singer/songwriter/guitarist.	
7/14/62	**8**	8	**1. You'll Lose A Good Thing**	Jamie 1220
			LYNN, Cheryl	
			Born on 3/11/57 in Los Angeles. Soul singer. Discovered on TV's "Gong Show." Cousin of soul singer D'La Vance.	
1/06/79	**12**	12	● 1. Got To Be Real	Columbia 10808
			LYNNE, Gloria	
			Born on 11/23/31 in New York City. Jazz-styled vocalist.	
2/29/64	**28**	4	1. I Wish You Love	Everest 2036
			LYNYRD SKYNYRD	
			Southern-rock band formed while members were in high school in Jacksonville, Florida in 1965. Named after their gym teacher Leonard Skinner. Band nucleus consisted of Ronnie Van Zant (b: 1/15/49; lead singer), Gary Rossington (guitar) and Allen Collins (guitar). Plane crash on 10/20/77 in Gillsburg, Mississippi killed Van Zant and members Steve and his sister Cassie Gaines. Gary and Allen formed the Rossington Collins Band in 1980; split in 1982. Rossington and vocalist Johnny Van Zant (the younger brother of Ronnie and Donnie [lead singer of 38 Special] Van Zant) regrouped with old and new band members for the 1987 Lynyrd Skynyrd Tribute Tour. Collins (paralyzed in a car accident in 1986) died of pneumonia on 1/23/90 (age 37).	
8/24/74	**8**	11	**1. Sweet Home Alabama**	MCA 40258
1/04/75	**19**	5	2. Free Bird	MCA 40328
7/19/75	**27**	3	3. Saturday Night Special	MCA 40416
1/08/77	**38**	2	4. Free Bird [R] live version of their 1975 hit	MCA 40665
1/07/78	**13**	11	5. What's Your Name	MCA 40819
			M	
			M	
			M is British pop musician Robin Scott.	
8/25/79	**1**(1)	20	● **1. Pop Muzik**	Sire 49033
			MABLEY, Moms	
			Born Loretta Mary Aiken on 3/19/1894 in Brevard, North Carolina; died on 5/23/75. Bawdy comedienne/ actress. Charted 13 comedy albums on *Billboard's* pop albums charts. In the films *Boarding House Blues, Emperor Jones* and *Amazing Grace.*	
7/19/69	**35**	2	1. Abraham, Martin And John	Mercury 72935
			MacGREGOR, Byron	
			Twenty-five-year-old news director at CKLW-Detroit when he did the narration for "Americans." Narration was originally written and delivered as an editorial by Gordon Sinclair for CFRB-Toronto on 6/05/73.	
1/12/74	**4**	9	● **1. Americans** **[S]** backed by instrumental version of "America The Beautiful"	Westbound 222

DATE	POS	WKS	ARTIST—RECORD TITLE	LABEL & NO.
			MacGREGOR, Mary	
			Born on 5/06/48 in St. Paul, Minnesota. Pop singer.	
12/25/76+	1(2)	16	● **1. Torn Between Two Lovers**	Ariola Am. 7638
			written and produced by Peter Yarrow (Peter, Paul & Mary)	
10/06/79	**39**	2	2. Good Friend	RSO 938
			from the film *Meatballs*	
			MACK, Lonnie	
			Born Lonnie McIntosh on 7/18/41 in Aurora, Indiana. Singer/guitarist (since age five). Own country band in 1954. With Troy Seals in the early '60s. Re-discovered in 1968. Retired from music, 1971-85.	
6/22/63	**5**	10	**1. Memphis** **[I]**	Fraternity 906
9/21/63	**24**	4	2. Wham! [I]	Fraternity 912
			MacKENZIE, Gisele	
			Born Gisele LeFleche on 1/10/27 in Winnipeg, Canada. Popular singing star of TV's "Your Hit Parade" (1953-57). Own TV variety show, 1957-58. Regular on The Sid Caesar Show, 1963-64.	
6/04/55	**4**	19	**1. Hard To Get**	X 0137
			Jockey #4 / Best Seller #5 / Juke Box #5 featured on the NBC-TV show *Justice*	
			MacRAE, Gordon	
			Born on 3/12/21 in East Orange, New Jersey; died on 1/24/86. Sang with Horace Heidt (1942-43) and recorded numerous duets with Jo Stafford, late '40s. Starred in the film musicals *Oklahoma* and *Carousel.*	
10/06/58	**18**	6	1. The Secret	Capitol 4033
			orchestra directed by Van Alexander	
			MADDOX, Johnny	
			Born in 1929 in Gallatin, Tennessee. Honky-tonk pianist/bandleader.	
2/05/55	2(7)	20	**1. The Crazy Otto** **[I]**	Dot 15325
			Best Seller #2 / Juke Box #2 / Jockey #7 medley of eight German songs	
			MADIGAN, Betty	
			Singer from Washington, D.C.	
9/08/58	**31**	3	1. Dance Everyone Dance	Coral 62007
			Best Seller #31 / Hot 100 #34 based on the Israeli harvest song "Hava Nagila"	
			MADNESS	
			Septet from North London, England — led by vocalist Graham "Suggs" McPherson. Formed as a ska-pop band in 1978, split up in 1986.	
5/28/83	**7**	13	**1. Our House**	Geffen 29668
9/17/83	**33**	5	2. It Must Be Love	Geffen 29562
			MADONNA	
			Born Madonna Louise Ciccone on 8/16/58 in Bay City, Michigan. To New York in the late '70s; performed with the Alvin Ailey dance troupe. Short-lived member of the Breakfast Club, early '80s. Starred in the films *Desperately Seeking Susan, Shanghai Surprise, Who's That Girl?, Bloodhounds of Broadway* and *Dick Tracy.* Released concert tour documentary film *Truth or Dare* in 1991. Appeared in Broadway's *Speed-The-Plow.* Married to actor Sean Penn from 1985-89.	
12/10/83+	**16**	11	1. Holiday	Sire 29478
4/14/84	**10**	15	**2. Borderline**	Sire 29354
9/01/84	**4**	12	**3. Lucky Star**	Sire 29177

DATE	POS	WKS	ARTIST—RECORD TITLE	LABEL & NO.
11/24/84	**1**(6)	14	● **4. Like A Virgin**	Sire 29210
2/16/85	**2**(2)	12	**5. Material Girl**	Sire 29083
3/16/85	**1**(1)	14	● **6. Crazy For You** from the film *Vision Quest*	Geffen 29051
5/11/85	**5**	12	● **7. Angel** gold certification is for the 12" single	Sire 29008
8/17/85	**5**	11	**8. Dress You Up**	Sire 28919
4/19/86	**1**(1)	13	**9. Live To Tell** from the film *At Close Range*	Sire 28717
7/05/86	**1**(2)	13	**10. Papa Don't Preach**	Sire 28660
10/04/86	**3**	12	**11. True Blue**	Sire 28591
12/13/86+	**1**(1)	14	**12. Open Your Heart**	Sire 28508
3/28/87	**4**	12	**13. La Isla Bonita**	Sire 28425
7/18/87	**1**(1)	11	**14. Who's That Girl**	Sire 28341
9/19/87	**2**(3)	11	**15. Causing A Commotion** above 2 from the film *Who's That Girl*	Sire 28224
3/18/89	**1**(3)	12	▲ **16. Like A Prayer**	Sire 27539
6/10/89	**2**(2)	11	● **17. Express Yourself**	Sire 22948
8/19/89	**2**(2)	12	**18. Cherish**	Sire 22883
11/25/89+	**20**	8	19. Oh Father	Sire 22723
2/17/90	**8**	9	● **20. Keep It Together**	Sire 19986
4/14/90	**1**(3)	16	▲ **21. Vogue**	Sire 19863
6/30/90	**10**	7	● **22. Hanky Panky** above 2 from the *Dick Tracy* soundtrack	Sire 19789
11/24/90+	**1**(2)	13	▲ **23. Justify My Love**	Sire 19485
3/02/91	**9**	6	● **24. Rescue Me**	Sire 19490
			MAESTRO, Johnny	
			Born Johnny Mastrangelo on 5/07/39 in New York City. Lead singer of The Crests and Brooklyn Bridge.	
3/20/61	**20**	5	1. Model Girl	Coed 545
5/22/61	**33**	4	2. What A Surprise	Coed 549
			MAGGARD, Cledus/The Citizen's Band	
			Cledus' real name: Jay Huguely; born in Quick Sand, Kentucky.	
1/24/76	**19**	9	1. The White Knight [N]	Mercury 73751
			MAGIC LANTERNS	
			Rock quintet from Lancashire, England. Albert Hammond was a member in 1971.	
11/30/68	**29**	5	1. Shame, Shame	Atlantic 2560
			MAHARIS, George	
			Born on 9/01/28 in New York City. Film/TV actor. Played Buz Murdock on TV's "Route 66."	
5/26/62	**25**	5	1. Teach Me Tonight there were 5 top 30 versions of this song in 1954	Epic 9504

DATE	POS	WKS	ARTIST—RECORD TITLE	LABEL & NO.
			MAIN INGREDIENT, The	
			New York soul trio, formed as the Poets in 1964. Consisted of Donald McPherson (d: 7/04/71), Luther Simmons, Jr. and Tony Sylvester. First recorded as the Poets for Red Bird in 1965. McPherson replaced by Cuba Gooding in 1971; Gooding's son, Cuba Jr., starred in the 1991 film *Boyz N The Hood.*	
9/02/72	**3**	10	● **1. Everybody Plays The Fool**	RCA 0731
3/16/74	**10**	14	● **2. Just Don't Want To Be Lonely**	RCA 0205
8/10/74	**35**	2	3. Happiness Is Just Around The Bend	RCA 0305
			MAJORS, The	
			Philadelphia R&B group: Ricky Cordo (lead), Eugene Glass, Frank Troutt, Ronald Gathers and Idella Morris. Produced by Jerry Ragavoy.	
9/08/62	**22**	5	1. A Wonderful Dream	Imperial 5855
			MAKEBA, Miriam	
			Born Zensi Miriam Makeba on 3/04/32 in Johannesburg, South Africa. Married five times; husbands included Hugh Masekela (1964-66) and black-power activist Stokeley Carmichael (married in 1968).	
10/28/67	**12**	8	1. Pata Pata [F]	Reprise 0606
			MALO	
			Latin-rock band formed by Jorge Santana (brother of Carlos).	
4/01/72	**18**	8	1. Suavecito	Warner 7559
			MALTBY, Richard	
			Trumpeter/composer/bandleader born on 6/26/14 in Chicago. Attended Northwestern University. Worked with Ethel Merman, Peggy Lee, Dean Martin, Jerry Lewis, Vic Damone and Sarrah Vaughan. Died on 8/19/91. His son, Richard Maltby, Jr., is a Broadway director/lyricist (*Ain't Misbehavin', Miss Saigon*).	
3/31/56	**14**	8	1. Themes From "The Man With The Golden Arm" [I] Top 100 #14 / Best Seller #15 / Juke Box #19 / Jockey #20 from the film *The Man with the Golden Arm*	Vik 0196
			MAMA CASS	
			Born Ellen Naomi Cohen on 9/19/41 in Baltimore. Died of a heart attack on 7/29/74 in London. Cass Elliot of The Mamas & The Papas.	
7/27/68	**12**	8	1. Dream A Little Dream Of Me with The Mamas & The Papas	Dunhill 4145
8/02/69	**30**	7	2. It's Getting Better	Dunhill 4195
11/15/69	**36**	3	3. Make Your Own Kind Of Music **MAMA CASS ELLIOT**	Dunhill 4214
			MAMAS & THE PAPAS, The	
			Quartet formed in New York City in 1963. Consisted of John Phillips (b: 8/30/35, Paris Island, South Carolina); Holly Michelle Gilliam Phillips (b: 6/04/45, Long Beach, California); Dennis Doherty (b: 11/29/41, Halifax, Nova Scotia, Canada) and Cass Elliot. John Phillips had been in the Journeymen, married Michelle Gilliam in 1962. Elliot had been in the Mugwumps with Doherty and future Lovin' Spoonful member Zal Yanovsky. Group moved to Los Angeles in 1964. Disbanded in 1968, reunited briefly in 1971. Michelle Phillips acted in films *Dillinger* and *Valentino*, and is a cast member of TV's "Knots Landing"; married for eight days to actor Dennis Hopper in 1970. New Mamas & Papas group formed in 1982: John and daughter, actress MacKenzie Phillips, Dennis Doherty and Spanky McFarlane of Spanky & Our Gang. Michelle and John's daughter, Chynna, is a member of the trio Wilson Phillips.	
2/05/66	**4**	13	● **1. California Dreamin'**	Dunhill 4020
4/16/66	**1**(3)	10	● **2. Monday, Monday**	Dunhill 4026

DATE	POS	WKS	ARTIST—RECORD TITLE	LABEL & NO.
7/09/66	**5**	8	**3. I Saw Her Again**	Dunhill 4031
11/05/66	**24**	4	4. Look Through My Window	Dunhill 4050
12/17/66+	**5**	9	**5. Words Of Love**	Dunhill 4057
3/04/67	**2**(3)	9	**6. Dedicated To The One I Love**	Dunhill 4077
5/13/67	**5**	7	**7. Creeque Alley**	Dunhill 4083
9/02/67	**20**	5	8. Twelve Thirty (Young Girls Are Coming To The Canyon)	Dunhill 4099
11/04/67	**26**	5	9. Glad To Be Unhappy from the 1936 Rodgers & Hart musical *On Your Toes*; all of above produced by Lou Adler	Dunhill 4107
			MANCHESTER, Melissa Born on 2/15/51 in the Bronx. Vocalist/pianist/composer. Father is a bassoon player with the New York Metropolitan Opera Orchestra. She studied songwriting under Paul Simon at the University School of the Arts in the early '70s. Former backup singer for Bette Midler.	
6/14/75	**6**	11	**1. Midnight Blue**	Arista 0116
10/18/75	**30**	5	2. Just Too Many People	Arista 0146
2/28/76	**27**	4	3. Just You And I	Arista 0168
1/06/79	**10**	14	**4. Don't Cry Out Loud**	Arista 0373
11/24/79	**39**	2	5. Pretty Girls	Arista 0456
4/05/80	**32**	5	6. Fire In The Morning	Arista 0485
7/10/82	**5**	15	**7. You Should Hear How She Talks About You**	Arista 0676
			MANCINI, Henry Born on 4/16/24 in Cleveland and raised in Aliquippa, Pennsylvania. Leading film and TV composer/ arranger/conductor. Staff composer for Universal Pictures, 1952-58. Won more Oscars (four) and Grammys (20) than any other pop artist. Married to Ginny O'Connor, an original member of Mel Torme's Mel-Tones.	
4/18/60	**21**	8	1. Mr. Lucky [I] from the TV series of the same title	RCA 7705
11/13/61	**11**	16	2. Moon River from the film *Breakfast at Tiffany's*; originally charted for 14 weeks; re-entered on 5/19/62 (POS 32)	RCA 7916
3/02/63	**33**	10	3. Days Of Wine And Roses	RCA 8120
1/25/64	**36**	4	4. Charade	RCA 8256
5/09/64	**31**	2	5. The Pink Panther Theme [I]	RCA 8286
5/24/69	**1**(2)	12	● **6. Love Theme From Romeo & Juliet [I]**	RCA 0131
2/06/71	**13**	8	7. Theme From Love Story [I] 3-7: from the films of the same titles	RCA 9927
			MANDELL, Steve — see WEISSBERG, Eric	
			MANDRELL, Barbara Born on 12/25/48 in Houston and raised in Oceanside, California. Country singer. Moved to Nashville in 1971. Host of own TV variety series "Barbara Mandrell & The Mandrell Sisters," 1980-82.	
5/12/79	**31**	5	1. (If Loving You Is Wrong) I Don't Want To Be Right	ABC 12451

DATE	POS	WKS	ARTIST—RECORD TITLE	LABEL & NO.
			MANFRED MANN	
			Rock group formed in England in 1964: Manfred Mann (b: Michael Lubowitz, 10/21/40, Johannesburg, South Africa; keyboards), Paul Jones (vocals), Mike Hugg (drums), Michael Vickers (guitar) and Tom McGuinness (bass). Manfred Mann formed his new Earth Band in 1971, featuring Mick Rogers (vocals), Colin Pattenden (bass) and Chris Slade (drums). Mick replaced by Chris Thompson (vocals, guitar) in 1976. Thompson also recorded with own group Night in 1979. McGuinness left to form McGuinness Flint in 1970.	
9/12/64	**1**(2)	12	**1. Do Wah Diddy Diddy**	Ascot 2157
11/28/64+	**12**	9	2. Sha La La	Ascot 2165
7/23/66	**29**	5	3. Pretty Flamingo	United Art. 50040
3/09/68	**10**	10	**4. Mighty Quinn (Quinn The Eskimo)** written by Bob Dylan	Mercury 72770
			MANFRED MANN'S EARTH BAND:	
12/18/76+	**1**(1)	15	● **5. Blinded By The Light** written by Bruce Springsteen	Warner 8252
6/04/77	**40**	1	6. Spirit In The Night [R] remix of their 1976 hit (POS 97)	Warner 8355
2/18/84	**22**	8	7. Runner	Arista 9143
			MANGIONE, Chuck	
			Born on 11/29/40 in Rochester, New York. Flugelhorn/bandleader/composer. Recorded with older brother Gaspare ("Gap") as The Jazz Brothers for Riverside in 1960. To New York City in 1965; played with Maynard Ferguson, Kai Winding, and Art Blakey's Jazz Messengers.	
3/18/78	**4**	16	**1. Feels So Good [I]**	A&M 2001
2/16/80	**18**	9	2. Give It All You Got [I] featured song by ABC Sports for the 1980 Winter Olympics	A&M 2211
			MANHATTANS, The	
			Soul vocal group from Jersey City, New Jersey. Consisted of George "Smitty" Smith (d: 1970, spinal meningitis; lead vocals), Winfred "Blue" Lovett (bass), Edward "Sonny" Bivins and Kenneth "Wally" Kelly (tenors) and Richard Taylor (baritone). Smith replaced by Gerald Alston in 1971. First recorded for Piney in 1962. Taylor (aka Abdul Rashid Talhah) left in 1976; died on 12/07/87 (age 47) following lengthy illness. Featured female vocalist Regina Belle began solo career in 1987. Alston went solo in 1988.	
2/15/75	**37**	2	1. Don't Take Your Love	Columbia 10045
5/29/76	**1**(2)	17	▲ **2. Kiss And Say Goodbye**	Columbia 10310
5/31/80	**5**	14	● **3. Shining Star**	Columbia 11222
			MANHATTAN TRANSFER, The	
			Versatile vocal harmony quartet formed in New York City in 1972: Tim Hauser, Alan Paul, Janis Siegel and Cheryl Bentyne (replaced by Laurel Masse in 1979).	
11/01/75	**22**	5	1. Operator	Atlantic 3292
5/31/80	**30**	4	2. Twilight Zone/Twilight Tone	Atlantic 3649
6/13/81	**7**	13	**3. Boy From New York City**	Atlantic 3816
11/05/83	**40**	2	4. Spice Of Life	Atlantic 89786

DATE	POS	WKS	ARTIST—RECORD TITLE	LABEL & NO.
			MANILOW, Barry	
			Born Barry Alan Pincus on 6/17/46 in Brooklyn. Vocalist/pianist/composer. Studied at New York's Juilliard School. Music director for the WCBS-TV series "Callback." Worked at New York's Continental Baths bathhouse/nightclub in New York as Bette Midler's accompanist in 1972; later produced her first two albums. First recorded solo as Featherbed. Wrote and sang jingles for Dr. Pepper, Pepsi and McDonald's ("You Deserve A Break Today").	
12/07/74+	**1**(1)	12	● **1. Mandy**	Bell 45613
			formerly charted by Scott English as "Brandy"	
3/29/75	**12**	8	2. It's A Miracle	Arista 0108
7/26/75	**6**	13	**3. Could It Be Magic**	Arista 0126
			first released on Bell 45-133 in 1971 as by Featherbed Featuring Barry Manilow; inspired by Chopin's *Prelude in C Minor*	
11/22/75+	**1**(1)	16	● **4. I Write The Songs**	Arista 0157
			written by the Beach Boys' Bruce Johnston	
4/10/76	**10**	10	**5. Tryin' To Get The Feeling Again**	Arista 0172
10/09/76	**29**	5	6. This One's For You	Arista 0206
12/25/76+	**10**	13	**7. Weekend In New England**	Arista 0212
5/28/77	**1**(1)	13	● **8. Looks Like We Made It**	Arista 0244
10/22/77	**23**	5	9. Daybreak	Arista 0273
2/18/78	**3**	16	● **10. Can't Smile Without You**	Arista 0305
6/10/78	**19**	4	11. Even Now	Arista 0330
7/08/78	**8**	9	● **12. Copacabana (At The Copa)**	Arista 0339
10/07/78	**11**	10	13. Ready To Take A Chance Again	Arista 0357
			above 2 from the film *Foul Play*	
1/06/79	**9**	10	**14. Somewhere In The Night**	Arista 0382
10/20/79	**9**	11	**15. Ships**	Arista 0464
2/02/80	**20**	7	16. When I Wanted You	Arista 0481
5/17/80	**36**	4	17. I Don't Want To Walk Without You	Arista 0501
12/06/80+	**10**	11	**18. I Made It Through The Rain**	Arista 0566
			all of above produced by Manilow and Ron Dante	
10/17/81	**15**	10	19. The Old Songs	Arista 0633
1/23/82	**21**	7	20. Somewhere Down The Road	Arista 0658
4/24/82	**32**	3	21. Let's Hang On	Arista 0675
9/18/82	**38**	2	22. Oh Julie	Arista 0698
1/15/83	**39**	2	23. Memory	Arista 1025
			theme from the musical *Cats*	
4/09/83	**26**	7	24. Some Kind Of Friend	Arista 9003
			also released on Arista 1046 in 1983	
11/26/83+	**18**	10	25. Read 'Em And Weep	Arista 9101
			MANN, Barry	
			Born Barry Iberman on 2/09/39 in Brooklyn. One of pop music's most prolific songwriters. Wrote with wife, Cynthia Weil, "You've Lost That Lovin' Feelin'," "(You're My) Soul & Inspiration," "Kicks," "Hungry," "We Gotta Get Out Of This Place," and many others. Established own publishing company, Dyad Music.	
8/21/61	**7**	9	**1. Who Put The Bomp (In The Bomp, Bomp, Bomp)** [N]	ABC-Para. 10237

DATE	POS	WKS	ARTIST—RECORD TITLE	LABEL & NO.
			MANN, Carl	
			Born on 8/24/42 in Huntingdon, Tennessee. Rockabilly singer/pianist. Toured with Carl Perkins from 1962-64. Left music from 1967-74.	
7/27/59	**25**	6	1. Mona Lisa #1 hit for Nat King Cole in 1950	Phillips 3539
			MANN, Gloria	
			Her son, Bob Rosenberg, is the leader of Will To Power.	
2/12/55	**18**	2	1. Earth Angel (Will You Be Mine) Juke Box #18 / Best Seller #24	Sound 109
12/24/55+	**19**	8	2. Teen Age Prayer Best Seller #19 / Top 100 #21	Sound 126
			MANN, Herbie	
			Born Herbert Jay Solomon on 4/16/30 in Brooklyn. Renowned jazz flutist. First recorded with Mat Mathews Quintet for Brunswick in 1953. First recorded as a solo for Bethlehem in 1954.	
4/26/75	**14**	6	1. Hijack	Atlantic 3246
3/17/79	**26**	6	2. Superman	Atlantic 3547
			MANTOVANI	
			Born Annunzio Paolo Mantovani on 11/15/05 in Venice, Italy; died on 3/29/80. Played classical violin in England before forming his own orchestra in the early 1930s. Had first U.S. chart hit in 1935, "Red Sails In The Sunset" (POS 2). Achieved international fame 20 years later with his 40-piece orchestra and distinctive "cascading strings" sound. Charted 45 albums on *Billboard*'s Top Pop Albums chart.	
7/22/57	**12**	14	1. Around The World [I] Jockey #12 / Best Seller #23 / Top 100 #25 from the film *Around the World in 80 Days*	London 1746
1/23/61	**31**	2	2. Main Theme from Exodus (Ari's Theme) [I] from the film *Exodus*	London 1953
			THE MARATHONS	
			The Olympics' Arvee label needed a new single, but since The Olympics were on tour, they brought in The Vibrations, who were under contract with the Chess/Checker label. The Vibrations recorded "Peanut Butter" and Arvee released it as by The Marathons. Chess discovered the fraud, and stopped the Arvee release, and then released a re-recorded version on their subsidiary label, Argo. Arvee followed up with a new song by The Marathons, recorded by an unknown non-Vibrations group.	
5/22/61	**20**	7	1. Peanut Butter same tune as The Olympics' 1960 hit "(Baby) Hully Gully"; re-recorded on Argo 5389 in 1961 and labeled as: "Vibrations Named By Others As MARATHONS"	Arvee 5027
			MARCELS, The	
			R&B group from Pittsburgh. Consisted of Cornelius "Nini" Harp (lead singer), Ronald "Bingo" Mundy and Gene Bricker (tenors), Richard Knauss (baritone) and Fred Johnson (bass). Knauss replaced by Fred's brother, Allen Johnson, and Bricker replaced by Walt Maddox, mid-1961. Mundy left in late 1961.	
3/20/61	**1**(3)	11	**1. Blue Moon** there were 3 top 10 versions of this Rodgers & Hart tune in 1935	Colpix 186
10/30/61	**7**	8	**2. Heartaches** #12 hit for Guy Lombardo in 1931; #1 hit for Ted Weems in 1947	Colpix 612

DATE	POS	WKS	ARTIST—RECORD TITLE	LABEL & NO.
			MARCH, Little Peggy	
			Born Margaret Battavio on 3/07/48 in Lansdale, Pennsylvania. Lived in Germany from 1969-81. Youngest female singer to have a #1 single on the pop charts.	
4/06/63	**1**(3)	11	**1. I Will Follow Him**	RCA 8139
6/29/63	**32**	3	2. I Wish I Were A Princess	RCA 8189
9/28/63	**26**	4	3. Hello Heartache, Goodbye Love	RCA 8221
			MARCHAN, Bobby	
			Born on 4/30/30 in Youngstown, Ohio. Vocalist with Huey "Piano" Smith & The Clowns.	
7/11/60	**31**	4	1. There's Something On Your Mind, Part 2 [N]	Fire 1022
			MARDONES, Benny	
			Savage, Maryland native.	
7/12/80	**11**	12	1. Into The Night	Polydor 2091
6/03/89	**20**	7	2. Into The Night [R]	Polydor 889368
			newly recorded version released on Curb 10549 in 1989	
			MARESCA, Ernie	
			Born on 4/21/39 in the Bronx. Songwriter/vocalist. Wrote "Runaround Sue" and "The Wanderer."	
4/21/62	**6**	9	**1. Shout! Shout! (Knock Yourself Out)**	Seville 117
			MARIE, Teena	
			White funk singer/composer/keyboardist/guitarist/producer/actress, born Mary Christine Brockert in Santa Monica in 1957; raised in Venice, California.	
1/17/81	**37**	3	1. I Need Your Lovin'	Gordy 7189
2/02/85	**4**	13	**2. Lovergirl**	Epic 04619
			MARK IV, The	
			Chicago-based, pop-rock quartet.	
2/09/59	**24**	7	1. I Got A Wife [N]	Mercury 71403
			MARKETTS, The	
			Hollywood, California instrumental surf quintet.	
2/17/62	**31**	3	1. Surfer's Stomp [I]	Liberty 55401
			first released on Union 501 in 1961	
12/28/63+	**3**	11	**2. Out Of Limits [I]**	Warner 5391
			based on the theme for TV's "The Twilight Zone"	
2/26/66	**17**	5	3. Batman Theme [I]	Warner 5696
			from the hit TV series	
			MAR-KEYS	
			Instrumental group formed in Memphis in 1958. Consisted of Charles Axton (tenor sax), Wayne Jackson (trumpet), Don Nix (baritone sax), Jerry Lee "Smoochie" Smith (keyboards), Steve Cropper (guitar), Donald "Duck" Dunn (bass) and Terry Johnson (drums). Staff musicians at Stax/Volt. Cropper and Dunn later joined Booker T. & The MG's; also backing work for The Blues Brothers.	
7/17/61	**3**	12	**1. Last Night [I]**	Satellite 107
			MARKHAM, Pigmeat	
			Born Dewey Markham in Durham, North Carolina, in 1906; died on 12/13/81. Stage and TV comedian.	
7/06/68	**19**	4	1. Here Comes The Judge [N]	Chess 2049

DATE	POS	WKS	ARTIST—RECORD TITLE	LABEL & NO.
			MARLEY, Ziggy, And The Melody Makers	
			Kingston, Jamaica family reggae group. Children of the late reggae master Bob Marley: David ("Ziggy"), Stephen, Cedella and Sharon Marley.	
7/09/88	**39**	1	1. Tomorrow People	Virgin 99347
			MARLOWE, Marion	
			Ballad singer featured with Frank Parker on "Arthur Godfrey and His Friends" from 1950-55.	
7/16/55	**14**	2	1. The Man In The Raincoat	Cadence 1266
			Jockey #14 / Juke Box #18	
			MARMALADE, The	
			Scottish pop quintet led by vocalist Dean Ford (real name: Thomas McAleese).	
4/04/70	**10**	11	**1. Reflections Of My Life**	London 20058
			M/A/R/R/S	
			U.K.-based, electro-funk group featuring two pairs of brothers: Martyn & Steve Young, with Alex & Rudi Kane. Includes mixers: Chris "CJ" Mackintosh and DJ Dave Dorrell.	
1/16/88	**13**	11	● 1. Pump Up The Volume	4th & B'way 7452
			MARSHALL TUCKER BAND, The	
			Southern-rock band formed in South Carolina in 1971: Doug Gray (lead singer), brothers Toy (lead guitarist) and Tommy Caldwell (bass; d: 4/28/80; replaced by Franklin Wilkie), George McCorkle (rhythm guitar), Paul Riddle (drums) and Jerry Eubanks (sax, flute).	
12/20/75	**38**	2	1. Fire On The Mountain	Capricorn 0244
4/16/77	**14**	13	2. Heard It In A Love Song	Capricorn 0270
			MARTERIE, Ralph	
			Born on 12/24/14 in Naples, Italy (grew up in Chicago); died on 10/08/78. Very popular early '50s bandleader, played trumpet in the '40s for Enric Madriguera and other bands.	
3/30/57	**25**	3	1. Tricky [I]	Mercury 71050
			Jockey #25 / Top 100 #37	
5/13/57	**10**	6	**2. Shish-Kebab [I]**	Mercury 71092
			Jockey #10 / Top 100 #29 same tune as Armenian Jazz Sextet's "Harem Dance"	
			MARTHA & THE VANDELLAS	
			Soul group from Detroit, organized by Martha Reeves (b: 7/18/41, Alabama) in 1962 with Annette Beard and Rosalind Ashford. Reeves had been in The Del-Phis, recorded for Checkmate. Worked at Motown as A&R secretary, sang backup. Vandellas did backup on several of Marvin Gaye's hits. Beard left group in 1964, replaced by Betty Kelly (formerly with The Velvelettes). Group disbanded from 1969-71, re-formed with Martha and sister Lois Reeves, and Sandra Tilley in 1971. Martha Reeves went solo in late 1972.	
5/18/63	**29**	8	1. Come And Get These Memories	Gordy 7014
8/17/63	**4**	11	**2. Heat Wave**	Gordy 7022
12/07/63+	**8**	9	**3. Quicksand**	Gordy 7025
9/05/64	**2**(2)	11	**4. Dancing In The Street**	Gordy 7033
12/26/64+	**34**	4	5. Wild One	Gordy 7036
3/13/65	**8**	8	**6. Nowhere To Run**	Gordy 7039
9/11/65	**36**	2	7. You've Been In Love Too Long	Gordy 7045
2/19/66	**22**	7	8. My Baby Loves Me	Gordy 7048
11/12/66	**9**	7	**9. I'm Ready For Love**	Gordy 7056

DATE	POS	WKS	ARTIST—RECORD TITLE	LABEL & NO.
3/18/67	**10**	10	**10. Jimmy Mack**	Gordy 7058
9/09/67	**25**	6	11. Love Bug Leave My Heart Alone	Gordy 7062
12/02/67	**11**	9	12. Honey Chile	Gordy 7067
			MARTHA REEVES & THE VANDELLAS	
			MARTIKA	
			Nineteen-year-old, Los Angeles-based, Cuban-American singer/writer/actress/dancer born Martika Marrero. Starred in TV program "Kids, Incorporated." Appeared in the 1982 film musical *Annie.*	
0/0/00+	**10**	0	**1. Love . . . Thy Will Be Done**	Columbia 73853
			written by Martika and Prince	
2/18/89	**18**	8	2. More Than You Know	Columbia 08103
6/10/89	**1**(2)	13	● **3. Toy Soldiers**	Columbia 68747
9/30/89	**25**	5	4. I Feel The Earth Move	Columbia 68996
			MARTIN, Bobbi	
			Born Barbara Anne Martin on 11/29/43 in Brooklyn; raised in Baltimore. Toured the Far East with Bob Hope's Christmas Shows.	
1/02/65	**19**	7	1. Don't Forget I Still Love You	Coral 62426
4/11/70	**13**	10	2. For The Love Of Him	United Art. 50602
			MARTIN, Dean	
			Born Dino Crocetti on 6/07/17 in Steubenville, Ohio. Vocalist/actor. To California in 1937, worked local clubs. Teamed with comedian Jerry Lewis in Atlantic City in 1946. First film, *My Friend Irma* in 1949. Team broke up after 16th film *Hollywood or Bust* in 1956. Appeared in many films since then; own TV series from 1965-74.	
12/03/55+	**1**(6)	19	**1. Memories Are Made Of This**	Capitol 3295
			Jockey #1(6) / Best Seller #1(5) / Top 100 #1(5) / Juke Box #1(4) backed by The Easy Riders	
4/07/56	**27**	4	2. Innamorata	Capitol 3352
			from the film *Artists and Models*	
5/26/56	**22**	6	3. Standing On The Corner	Capitol 3414
			Jockey #22 / Top 100 #29 from the musical *The Most Happy Fella*	
4/07/58	**4**	18	**4. Return To Me**	Capitol 3894
			Best Seller #4 / Top 100 #4 / Jockey #4	
8/04/58	**30**	3	5. Angel Baby	Capitol 3988
			Hot 100 #30 / Best Seller #43	
8/11/58	**12**	10	6. Volare (Nel Blu Dipinto Di Blu)	Capitol 4028
			Best Seller #12 / Hot 100 #15	
7/11/64	**1**(1)	13	● **7. Everybody Loves Somebody**	Reprise 0281
10/17/64	**6**	8	**8. The Door Is Still Open To My Heart**	Reprise 0307
1/09/65	**25**	5	9. You're Nobody Till Somebody Loves You	Reprise 0333
3/13/65	**22**	5	10. Send Me The Pillow You Dream On	Reprise 0344
6/12/65	**32**	3	11. (Remember Me) I'm The One Who Loves You	Reprise 0369
8/21/65	**21**	7	12. Houston	Reprise 0393
11/13/65	**10**	8	**13. I Will**	Reprise 0415
3/05/66	**32**	4	14. Somewhere There's A Someone	Reprise 0443
6/11/66	**35**	1	15. Come Running Back	Reprise 0466
7/22/67	**25**	4	16. In The Chapel In The Moonlight	Reprise 0601
9/09/67	**38**	2	17. Little Ole Wine Drinker, Me	Reprise 0608

DATE	POS	WKS	ARTIST—RECORD TITLE	LABEL & NO.
			MARTIN, Marilyn	
			Raised in Louisville. Background vocalist for Stevie Nicks, Tom Petty, Kenny Loggins and Joe Walsh.	
10/12/85	**1**(1)	16	**1. Separate Lives**	Atlantic 89498
			PHIL COLLINS AND MARILYN MARTIN love theme from the film *White Nights*	
2/22/86	**28**	6	2. Night Moves	Atlantic 89465
			MARTIN, Moon	
			Real name: John Martin. Pop-rock singer/songwriter/guitarist from Oklahoma. Wrote Robert Palmer's hit "Bad Case Of Loving You." Moved to Los Angeles in 1968. Lead guitarist of group Southwind.	
9/22/79	**30**	4	1. Rolene	Capitol 4765
			MARTIN, Steve, AND THE TOOT UNCOMMONS	
			Popular TV and film comedian. Born on 6/08/45 in Waco, Texas; raised in California. Comedy writer for the "Smothers Brothers Comedy Hour" TV show and others. Films include *The Jerk, All of Me, Three Amigos, Roxanne, Planes, Trains and Automobiles, Parenthood, My Blue Heaven* and *L.A. Story*. Married actress Victoria Tennant.	
7/08/78	**17**	7	● 1. King Tut [N]	Warner 8577
			MARTIN, Tony	
			Born Alvin Morris, Jr. on 12/25/12 in Oakland. Vocalist/actor. In many films from 1936-57, including *Casbah* in 1948. Married to actress/dancer Cyd Charisse.	
5/26/56	**10**	11	**1. Walk Hand In Hand**	RCA 6493
			Top 100 #10 / Jockey #13 / Juke Box #16 / Best Seller #21	
			MARTIN, Trade	
			Born on 11/19/43 in Union City, New Jersey.	
11/17/62	**28**	4	1. That Stranger Used To Be My Girl	Coed 570
			MARTIN, Vince — see TARRIERS, The	
			MARTINDALE, Wink	
			Born Winston Martindale on 12/04/33 in Jackson, Tennessee. DJ since 1950. Own TV shows starting with "Teenage Dance Party." Host of "Tic Tac Dough," "Gambit" and other TV game shows.	
9/28/59	**7**	12	**1. Deck Of Cards [S]**	Dot 15968
			#2 country hit for T. Texas Tyler in 1948	
			MARTINEZ, Nancy	
			Dance singer/actress born in Quebec, Canada.	
12/06/86	**32**	8	1. For Tonight	Atlantic 89371
			MARTINO, Al	
			Born Alfred Cini on 10/07/27 in Philadelphia. Encouraged by success of boyhood friend, Mario Lanza. Winner on "Arthur Godfrey's Talent Scouts" in 1952. Portrayed singer Johnny Fontane in the 1972 film *The Godfather*.	
5/04/63	**3**	11	**1. I Love You Because**	Capitol 4930
8/17/63	**15**	8	2. Painted, Tainted Rose	Capitol 5000
11/16/63	**22**	6	3. Living A Lie	Capitol 5060
2/15/64	**9**	8	**4. I Love You More And More Every Day**	Capitol 5108
5/30/64	**20**	6	5. Tears And Roses	Capitol 5183
9/12/64	**33**	4	6. Always Together	Capitol 5239
12/18/65+	**15**	9	7. Spanish Eyes	Capitol 5542
4/02/66	**30**	4	8. Think I'll Go Somewhere And Cry Myself To Sleep	Capitol 5598

DATE	POS	WKS	ARTIST—RECORD TITLE	LABEL & NO.
6/17/67	**27**	5	9. Mary In The Morning	Capitol 5904
2/08/75	**17**	8	10. To The Door Of The Sun (Alle Porte Del Sole)	Capitol 3987
12/06/75	**33**	4	11. Volare	Capitol 4134
			MARVELETTES, The	
			R&B group from Inkster High School, Inkster, Michigan. Formed in 1960 by Gladys Horton, with Georgeanna Marie Tillman Gordon (married Billy Gordon of The Contours), Wanda Young (married Bobby Rogers of The Miracles), Katherine Anderson and Juanita Cowart. Young and Horton both sang lead. Cowart left in 1962. Gordon left in 1965; died on 1/06/80 of lupus. Horton left in 1967, replaced by Anne Bogan (later a member of Love, Peace & Happiness and New Birth). Disbanded in 1969.	
10/16/61	**1**(1)	15	**1. Please Mr. Postman**	Tamla 54046
3/03/62	**34**	1	2. Twistin' Postman	Tamla 54054
5/26/62	**7**	11	**3. Playboy**	Tamla 54060
9/01/62	**17**	7	4. Beechwood 4-5789	Tamla 54065
12/05/64+	**25**	8	5. Too Many Fish In The Sea	Tamla 54105
7/03/65	**34**	1	6. I'll Keep Holding On	Tamla 54116
1/29/66	**7**	8	**7. Don't Mess With Bill**	Tamla 54126
2/18/67	**13**	7	8. The Hunter Gets Captured By The Game	Tamla 54143
5/20/67	**23**	5	9. When You're Young And In Love	Tamla 54150
1/06/68	**17**	8	10. My Baby Must Be A Magician 7, 8, 10: written and produced by Smokey Robinson	Tamla 54158
			MARVELOWS, The	
			R&B group from Chicago Heights, Illinois. First known as the Mystics. Included Melvin Mason (lead), Willie "Sonny" Stevenson, Frank Paden and Johnny Paden. Added Jesse Smith in 1964, became The Marvelows.	
7/03/65	**37**	1	1. I Do	ABC-Para. 10629
			MARX, Richard	
			Chicago-bred, pop-rock singer/songwriter. Professional jingle singer since age five. Backing singer for Lionel Richie. Co-wrote Kenny Rogers' hit "What About Me." On 1/08/89, married Cynthia Rhodes, lead singer of Animotion.	
7/11/87	**3**	12	**1. Don't Mean Nothing**	Manhattan 50079
10/17/87	**3**	13	**2. Should've Known Better** backing vocals: Fee Waybill (Tubes) and Timothy B. Schmit	Manhattan 50083
1/30/88	**2**(2)	15	**3. Endless Summer Nights**	EMI-Man. 50113
6/11/88	**1**(1)	14	**4. Hold On To The Nights**	EMI-Man. 50106
5/06/89	**1**(1)	13	**5. Satisfied**	EMI 50189
7/15/89	**1**(3)	13	▲ **6. Right Here Waiting**	EMI 50219
10/21/89	**4**	11	**7. Angelia**	EMI 50218
1/27/90	**12**	9	8. Too Late To Say Goodbye	EMI 50234
5/12/90	**13**	10	9. Children Of The Night tribute to the Los Angeles organization helping child prostitutes	EMI 50288
			MARY JANE GIRLS	
			Female "funk & roll" quartet: Joanne McDuffie, Candice Ghant, Kim Wuletick and Yvette Marina. Formed and produced by Rick James. Marina is the daughter of Patti Brooks.	
4/27/85	**7**	12	**1. In My House**	Gordy 1741

DATE	POS	WKS	ARTIST—RECORD TITLE	LABEL & NO.
			MASEKELA, Hugh	
			Born Hugh Ramapolo Masekela on 4/04/39 in Wilbank, South Africa. Trumpeter/bandleader/arranger. Played trumpet since age 14. To England in 1959; New York City in 1960. Formed own band in 1964. Married to Miriam Makeba from 1964-66.	
6/22/68	**1**(2)	10	● **1. Grazing In The Grass** [I]	Uni 55066
			MASHMAKHAN	
			Montreal rock quartet led by Puerre Senecal, with Brian Edwards, Jerry Mercer (later with April Wine) and Rayburn Blake.	
11/07/70	**31**	4	1. As The Years Go By	Epic 10634
			MASON, Barbara	
			Born on 8/09/47 in Philadelphia. First recorded for Crusader in 1964. Wrote all of her Arctic hits.	
6/12/65	**5**	10	**1. Yes, I'm Ready**	Arctic 105
9/04/65	**27**	5	2. Sad, Sad Girl	Arctic 108
2/24/73	**31**	5	3. Give Me Your Love	Buddah 331
12/28/74+	**28**	4	4. From His Woman To You	Buddah 441
			MASON, Dave	
			Born on 5/10/46 in Worcester, England. Vocalist/composer/guitarist. Original member of Traffic.	
10/08/77	**12**	10	1. We Just Disagree	Columbia 10575
7/08/78	**39**	2	2. Will You Still Love Me Tomorrow	Columbia 10749
			MATHEWS, Tobin, & Co.	
			Guitarist from Calumet City, Illinois.	
11/14/60	**30**	4	1. Ruby Duby Du [I] from the movie *Key Witness*	Chief 7022
			MATHIS, Johnny	
			Born on 9/30/35 in San Francisco. Studied opera from age 13. Track scholarship at the San Francisco State College. Invited to Olympic try-outs, chose singing career instead. Discovered by George Avakian of Columbia Records. To New York City in 1956. Initially recorded as jazz-styled singer. Columbia A&R executive Mitch Miller switched him to singing pop ballads. One of the top album artists of the rock era, Mathis has charted over 60 entries on *Billboard*'s Top Pop Albums chart.	
5/06/57	**14**	20	1. Wonderful! Wonderful! Jockey #14 / Top 100 #17 / Best Seller #18	Columbia 40784
5/20/57	**5**	23	**2. It's Not For Me To Say** Top 100 #5 / Jockey #5 / Best Seller #6 from the film *Lizzie*	Columbia 40851
9/16/57	**1**(1)	22	**3. Chances Are/** Jockey #1 / Best Seller #4 / Top 100 #5	
10/14/57	**9**	14	**4. The Twelfth Of Never** Jockey #9 / Top 100 #51	Columbia 40993
12/16/57	**22**	7	5. Wild Is The Wind/ Jockey #22 / Best Seller #30 / Top 100 #37 from the film of the same title	
1/06/58	**21**	1	6. No Love (But Your Love) Jockey #21 / Best Seller #37 / Top 100 #48 orchestra conducted by Ray Conniff on all of above (except #5)	Columbia 41060
2/10/58	**22**	1	7. Come To Me Jockey #22 / Best Seller #40 / Top 100 #43 from the TV production of the same title	Columbia 41082

DATE	POS	WKS	ARTIST—RECORD TITLE	LABEL & NO.
5/05/58	**21**	7	8. All The Time/ Jockey #21 / Best Seller #30 / Top 100 #42 from the Broadway musical *Oh Captain!*	
5/19/58	**21**	2	9. Teacher, Teacher Jockey #21 / Best Seller #30 / Top 100 #43	Columbia 41152
7/14/58	**14**	11	10. A Certain Smile Jockey #14 / Top 100 #19 / Best Seller #21 from the film of the same title	Columbia 41193
10/20/58	**21**	8	11. Call Me	Columbia 41253
5/04/59	**35**	3	12. Someone 5, 7-12: orchestra conducted by Ray Ellis	Columbia 41355
7/20/59	**20**	8	13. Small World from the Broadway musical *Gypsy*	Columbia 41410
10/19/59	**12**	12	14. Misty the Erroll Garner classic charted at POS 30 in 1954	Columbia 41483
3/28/60	**25**	5	15. Starbright orchestra conducted by Glenn Osser on above 3	Columbia 41583
10/13/62	**6**	9	**16. Gina**	Columbia 42582
2/09/63	**9**	10	**17. What Will Mary Say**	Columbia 42666
6/08/63	**30**	4	18. Every Step Of The Way	Columbia 42799
4/22/78	**1**(1)	11	● **19. Too Much, Too Little, Too Late** **JOHNNY MATHIS/DENIECE WILLIAMS**	Columbia 10693
5/29/82	**38**	3	20. Friends In Love **DIONNE WARWICK AND JOHNNY MATHIS**	Arista 0673
			MATTHEWS, Ian Born Ian Matthew MacDonald in Lincolnshire, England in June 1946. Founder of Fairport Convention and Matthews' Southern Comfort. From 1984-87, in A&R for Island and Windham Hill record labels.	
4/24/71	**23**	9	1. Woodstock **MATTHEWS' SOUTHERN COMFORT**	Decca 32774
12/16/78+	**13**	12	2. Shake It	Mushroom 7039
			MAURIAT, Paul French conductor/arranger; born in 1925. Moved to Paris at age 10. Formed own touring orchestra at 17.	
1/27/68	**1**(5)	15	● **1. Love Is Blue** **[I]**	Philips 40495
			MAXWELL, Robert Born on 4/19/21 in New York City. Jazz harpist/composer. With NBC Symphony under Toscanini at age 17. Also recorded as Mickey Mozart.	
4/18/64	**15**	7	1. Shangri-La [I]	Decca 25622
			MAYER, Nathaniel/The Fabulous Twilights Detroit R&B vocalist.	
5/26/62	**22**	6	1. Village Of Love	Fortune 449

DATE	POS	WKS	ARTIST—RECORD TITLE	LABEL & NO.
			MAYFIELD, Curtis	
			Born on 6/03/42 in Chicago. Soul singer/songwriter/producer. With Jerry Butler in the gospel group Northern Jubilee Singers. Joined The Impressions in 1957. Wrote most of the hits for The Impressions, Jerry Butler and himself. Own labels: Windy C, Mayfield and Curtom. Went solo in 1970. Scored films *Superfly*, *Claudine*, *A Piece of the Action* and *Short Eyes*. Appeared in *Short Eyes*. Paralyzed from the chest down when a stage lighting tower fell on him prior to a concert on 8/13/90.	
1/02/71	**29**	4	1. (Don't Worry) If There's A Hell Below We're All Going To Go	Curtom 1955
9/23/72	**4**	11	● **2. Freddie's Dead (Theme From "Superfly")**	Curtom 1975
11/25/72+	**8**	13	● **3. Superfly**	Curtom 1978
			above 2 from the film *Superfly*	
8/25/73	**39**	2	4. Future Shock	Curtom 1987
8/03/74	**40**	1	5. Kung Fu	Curtom 1999
			McANALLY, Mac	
			Born Lyman McAnally, Jr. in 1957 in Red Bay, Alabama. Session singer/guitarist/songwriter.	
8/13/77	**37**	2	1. It's A Crazy World	Ariola Am. 7665
			McCALL, C.W.	
			Born William Fries on 11/15/28 in Audubon, Iowa. The character "C.W. McCall" was created for the Mertz Bread Company. Fries was their advertising man. Elected mayor of Ouray, Colorado in the early '80s.	
3/22/75	**40**	1	1. Wolf Creek Pass [N]	MGM 14764
12/13/75+	**1**(1)	11	● **2. Convoy [N]**	MGM 14839
			McCANN, Peter	
			Connecticut native; staffwriter with ABC Music. Wrote Jennifer Warnes' hit "Right Time Of The Night."	
5/21/77	**5**	16	● **1. Do You Wanna Make Love**	20th Century 2335
			McCARTNEY, Paul/Wings	
			Born James Paul McCartney on 6/18/42 in Liverpool, England. Writer of over 50 top 10 singles. Founding member/bass guitarist of The Beatles. Married Linda Eastman on 3/12/69. First solo album in 1970. Formed group Wings in 1971 with wife Linda (keyboards, backing vocals), Denny Laine (ex-Moody Blues; guitar) and Denny Seiwell (drums). Henry McCullough (guitar) joined in 1972. Seiwell and McCullough left in 1973. In 1975, Joe English (drums) and ex-Thunderclap Newman guitarist Jimmy McCulloch (d: 9/27/79 [age 26] of heart failure) joined; both left in 1977. Wings officially disbanded in April 1981. McCartney starred in own film *Give My Regards to Broad Street* (1984). Won Lifetime Achievement Grammy in 1990.	
			PAUL McCARTNEY:	
3/13/71	**5**	11	**1. Another Day**	Apple 1829
			PAUL & LINDA McCARTNEY:	
8/21/71	**1**(1)	12	● **2. Uncle Albert/Admiral Halsey**	Apple 1837
			WINGS:	
3/25/72	**21**	6	3. Give Ireland Back To The Irish	Apple 1847
7/08/72	**28**	4	4. Mary Had A Little Lamb	Apple 1851
12/30/72+	**10**	9	**5. Hi, Hi, Hi**	Apple 1857
4/28/73	**1**(4)	15	● **6. My Love**	Apple 1861
			PAUL McCARTNEY & WINGS	
7/21/73	**2**(3)	12	● **7. Live And Let Die**	Apple 1863
			from the James Bond film of the same title	

DATE	POS	WKS	ARTIST—RECORD TITLE	LABEL & NO.
			PAUL McCARTNEY & WINGS:	
12/08/73+	**10**	10	**8. Helen Wheels**	Apple 1869
2/23/74	**7**	10	**9. Jet**	Apple 1871
5/04/74	**1**(1)	13	● **10. Band On The Run**	Apple 1873
11/23/74+	**3**	10	**11. Junior's Farm/**	
12/14/74+	**17**	8	12. Sally G	Apple 1875
			WINGS:	
6/07/75	**1**(1)	11	● **13. Listen To What The Man Said**	Capitol 4091
10/25/75	**39**	2	14. Letting Go	Capitol 4145
11/15/75	**12**	6	15. Venus And Mars Rock Show	Capitol 4175
4/17/76	**1**(5)	15	● **16. Silly Love Songs**	Capitol 4256
7/17/76	**3**	11	● **17. Let 'Em In**	Capitol 4293
2/19/77	**10**	11	**18. Maybe I'm Amazed** live version of song from McCartney's first solo album	Capitol 4385
12/24/77+	**33**	4	19. Girls' School B-side "Mull of Kintyre" is one of England's all-time biggest selling singles (did not chart in U.S.)	Capitol 4504
4/08/78	**1**(2)	12	**20. With A Little Luck**	Capitol 4559
7/15/78	**25**	5	21. I've Had Enough	Capitol 4594
10/14/78	**39**	2	22. London Town	Capitol 4625
3/31/79	**5**	13	● **23. Goodnight Tonight**	Columbia 10939
6/30/79	**20**	6	24. Getting Closer	Columbia 11020
9/22/79	**29**	4	25. Arrow Through Me	Columbia 11070
5/10/80	**1**(3)	16	● **26. Coming Up (Live at Glasgow)** **PAUL McCARTNEY & WINGS**	Columbia 11263
4/10/82	**1**(7)	15	● **27. Ebony And Ivory** **PAUL McCARTNEY with STEVIE WONDER**	Columbia 02860
7/17/82	**10**	11	**28. Take It Away** **PAUL McCARTNEY**	Columbia 03018
			PAUL McCARTNEY AND MICHAEL JACKSON:	
11/13/82+	**2**(3)	14	● **29. The Girl Is Mine**	Epic 03288
10/15/83	**1**(6)	18	● **30. Say Say Say**	Columbia 04168
			PAUL McCARTNEY:	
1/07/84	**23**	8	31. So Bad	Columbia 04296
10/20/84	**6**	14	**32. No More Lonely Nights** from the film *Give My Regards to Broad Street*	Columbia 04581
12/14/85+	**7**	11	**33. Spies Like Us** from the film of the same title	Capitol 5537
8/23/86	**21**	6	34. Press	Capitol 5597
6/17/89	**25**	5	35. My Brave Face co-writer: Elvis Costello	Capitol 44367
			McCLAIN, Alton, & Destiny Black female trio. Destiny: D'Marie Warren and Robyrda Stiger.	
5/19/79	**32**	4	1. It Must Be Love	Polydor 14532
			McCLINTON, Delbert Born on 11/04/40 in Lubbock, Texas. Played harmonica on Bruce Channel's hit "Hey Baby." Leader of the Ron-Dels.	
12/20/80+	**8**	14	**1. Giving It Up For Your Love**	Capitol 4948

DATE	POS	WKS	ARTIST—RECORD TITLE	LABEL & NO.
			McCLURE, Bobby — see BASS, Fontella	
			McCOO, Marilyn, & BILLY DAVIS, JR.	
			Marilyn (b: 9/30/43, Jersey City, New Jersey) and husband Billy (b: 6/26/39, St. Louis) were members of The 5th Dimension. Marilyn co-hosted TV's "Solid Gold" from 1981-84.	
10/23/76+	**1**(1)	18	● **1. You Don't Have To Be A Star (To Be In My Show)**	ABC 12208
4/02/77	**15**	8	2. Your Love	ABC 12262
			McCOY, Van	
			Pianist/producer/songwriter/singer born on 1/06/44 in Washington, D.C.; died on 7/06/79 of a heart attack. Formed own Rock'N label in 1960. A&R man at Scepter/Wand from 1961-64. Own MAXX label, mid-1960s. Produced The Shirelles, Gladys Knight, The Stylistics and Brenda & The Tabulations.	
5/31/75	**1**(1)	12	● **1. The Hustle** [I]	Avco 4653
			with The Soul City Symphony	
			McCOYS, The	
			Rock band formed in Union City, Indiana. Rick Derringer (real name: Zehringer; vocals, guitar), brother Randy Zehringer (drums), Randy Hobbs (bass) and Ronnie Brandon (keyboards). Rick went solo in 1974.	
9/04/65	**1**(1)	11	**1. Hang On Sloopy**	Bang 506
11/27/65	**7**	8	**2. Fever**	Bang 511
5/14/66	**22**	6	3. Come On Let's Go	Bang 522
			McCRACKLIN, Jimmy	
			Born on 8/13/21 in St. Louis. Singer/harmonica player. Settled in Los Angeles. Professional boxer in the mid-1940s. First recorded for Globe in 1945. Own band, the Blues Blasters, in 1949.	
3/03/58	**7**	10	**1. The Walk**	Checker 885
			Top 100 #7 / Best Seller #11 / Jockey #23	
			McCRAE, George	
			Born on 10/19/44 in West Palm Beach, Florida. Duets with wife Gwen McCrae; became her manager.	
6/15/74	**1**(2)	10	**1. Rock Your Baby**	T.K. 1004
3/01/75	**37**	2	2. I Get Lifted	T.K. 1007
			McCRAE, Gwen	
			Born on 12/21/43 in Pensacola, Florida. Married George McCrae, who later became her manager. First recorded with George for Alston in 1969.	
6/21/75	**9**	8	**1. Rockin' Chair**	Cat 1996
			backing vocal: George McCrae	
			McDANIELS, Gene	
			Born Eugene B. McDaniels on 2/12/35 in Kansas City. To Omaha, early 1940s, sang in choirs, attended Omaha Conservatory of Music. Own band, early 50s. Appeared in the film *It's Trad, Dad* in 1962.	
4/03/61	**3**	12	**1. A Hundred Pounds Of Clay**	Liberty 55308
8/07/61	**31**	2	2. A Tear	Liberty 55344
10/16/61	**5**	10	**3. Tower Of Strength**	Liberty 55371
2/10/62	**10**	7	**4. Chip Chip**	Liberty 55405
9/01/62	**21**	5	5. Point Of No Return	Liberty 55480
12/15/62	**31**	2	6. Spanish Lace	Liberty 55510
			with The Johnny Mann Singers on all of above	

DATE	POS	WKS	ARTIST—RECORD TITLE	LABEL & NO.
			McDEVITT, Chas., Skiffle Group	
			British vocal/instrumental group.	
6/10/57	**40**	1	1. Freight Train vocal by Nancy Wiskey	Chic 1008
			McDONALD, Michael	
			Vocalist/keyboardist born in 1952 in St. Louis, Missouri. First recorded for RCA in 1972. Formerly with Steely Dan and The Doobie Brothers. Married to singer Amy Holland. Also see Nicolette Larson.	
8/28/82	**4**	13	**1. I Keep Forgettin' (Every Time You're Near)**	Warner 29933
1/14/84	**19**	9	2. Yah Mo B There **JAMES INGRAM with MICHAEL McDONALD**	Qwest 29394
8/31/85	**34**	4	3. No Lookin' Back	Warner 28960
4/19/86	**1**(3)	15	● **4. On My Own** **PATTI LaBELLE AND MICHAEL McDONALD**	MCA 52770
7/12/86	**7**	13	**5. Sweet Freedom** theme from the film *Running Scared*	MCA 52857
			McDOWELL, Ronnie	
			Country singer/songwriter from Portland, Tennessee. Sang on the soundtrack for the film *Elvis* in 1979.	
9/17/77	**13**	9	● 1. The King Is Gone a tribute to Elvis Presley	Scorpion 135
			McFADDEN, Bob, And Dor	
			Bob is from East Liverpool, Ohio. Began career in 1950 as a singing emcee for a special Navy show called "The Bob McFadden Show." Dor is poet/singer/songwriter/actor Rod McKuen.	
9/14/59	**39**	1	1. The Mummy [N]	Brunswick 55140
			McFADDEN & WHITEHEAD	
			R&B duo of Gene McFadden and John Whitehead from Philadelphia. Wrote songs for many Philadelphia soul acts; defined "The Sound Of Philadelphia." Whitehead recorded solo in 1988.	
6/02/79	**13**	11	▲ 1. Ain't No Stoppin' Us Now	Phil. Int. 3681
			McFERRIN, Bobby	
			Unaccompanied, jazz-styled improvisation vocalist. Born on 3/11/50 in New York. Sang the 1987 "Cosby Show" theme and the Levi's 501 Blues jingle. Father was a baritone with the New York Metropolitan Opera.	
8/13/88	**1**(2)	13	● **1. Don't Worry Be Happy** featured in the film *Cocktail*	EMI-Man. 50146
			McGOVERN, Maureen	
			Born on 7/27/49 in Youngstown, Ohio. Sang theme of TV show "Angie." Cameo roles in *The Towering Inferno* and *Airplane* (as Sister Angelina). Starred in Broadway's *Pirates of Penzance* for 14 months.	
7/14/73	**1**(2)	11	● **1. The Morning After** love theme from the film *The Poseidon Adventure*	20th Century 2010
8/11/79	**18**	9	2. Different Worlds theme from the TV series "Angie"	Warner 8835
			McGRIFF, Jimmy	
			Born on 4/03/36 in Philadelphia. Jazz-R&B organist/multi-instrumentalist.	
10/27/62	**20**	7	1. I've Got A Woman Part I [I]	Sue 770

DATE	POS	WKS	ARTIST—RECORD TITLE	LABEL & NO.
			McGUINN, CLARK & HILLMAN	
			Roger McGuinn (b: 7/13/42; vocals, guitar), Gene Clark (b: 11/17/44; d: 5/24/91; guitar) and Chris Hillman (b: 6/04/42; bass). All are former members of The Byrds.	
4/28/79	**33**	4	1. Don't You Write Her Off	Capitol 4693
			McGUIRE, Barry	
			Born on 10/15/37 in Oklahoma City. Member of The New Christy Minstrels. Currently records Contemporary Christian music.	
8/28/65	**1**(1)	10	**1. Eve Of Destruction**	Dunhill 4009
			backing by the original members of the Grass Roots	
			McGUIRE SISTERS, The	
			Sisters Christine (b: 7/30/29), Dorothy (b: 2/13/30) and Phyllis (b: 2/14/31) from Middletown, Ohio. Replaced the Chordettes on "Arthur Godfrey and His Friends" show in 1953. Phyllis went solo in 1964. Reunited in 1986.	
1/08/55	**1**(10)	21	**1. Sincerely/**	
			Jockey #1(10) / Juke Box #1(7) / Best Seller #1(6)	
1/29/55	**17**	6	2. No More	Coral 61323
			Jockey #17 / Juke Box #17 / Best Seller #23	
3/26/55	**11**	7	3. It May Sound Silly	Coral 61369
			Jockey #11 / Juke Box #14 / Best Seller #23	
6/04/55	**5**	14	**4. Something's Gotta Give**	Coral 61423
			Jockey #5 / Best Seller #6 / Juke Box #6 from the film *Daddy Long Legs*	
10/29/55	**10**	13	**5. He**	Coral 61501
			Juke Box #10 / Best Seller #12 / Top 100 #12 / Jockey #16	
5/19/56	**13**	12	6. Picnic/	
			Top 100 #13 / Jockey #14 / Best Seller #15 / Juke Box #18 from the film of the same title	
6/02/56	**37**	1	7. Delilah Jones	Coral 61627
			from the film *The Man with the Golden Arm*	
8/11/56	**32**	3	8. Weary Blues	Coral 61670
			THE McGUIRE SISTERS AND LAWRENCE WELK	
10/27/56	**37**	3	9. Ev'ry Day Of My Life	Coral 61703
12/22/56+	**32**	3	10. Goodnight My Love, Pleasant Dreams	Coral 61748
1/06/58	**1**(4)	19	**11. Sugartime**	Coral 61924
			Jockey #1 / Top 100 #5 / Best Seller #7	
6/09/58	**25**	1	12. Ding Dong	Coral 61991
			Jockey #25 / Top 100 #43 / Best Seller #44	
1/19/59	**11**	12	13. May You Always	Coral 62059
4/17/61	**20**	7	14. Just For Old Time's Sake	Coral 62249
			M.C. HAMMER	
			Born Stanley Kirk Burrell on 3/30/63 in Oakland. Rapper/producer/founder/leader of The Posse, an eight-member group of dancers, DJs and singers. Burrell was an Oakland A's batboy in the 1970s; his nickname "The Little Hammer" stemmed from his resemblance to baseball great Hank "The Hammer" Aaron. Oaktown's 3-5-7 and Ace Juice are members of The Posse. Dropped the M.C. from his name in mid-1991.	
4/28/90	**8**	13	**1. U Can't Touch This**	Capitol 15571
			music is from Rick James' "Super Freak"; available only as a 12" single	
7/21/90	**4**	12	● **2. Have You Seen Her**	Capitol 44573#
10/06/90	**2**(2)	11	● **3. Pray**	Capitol 44609#

DATE	POS	WKS	ARTIST—RECORD TITLE	LABEL & NO.
			rhythm track is from Prince's "When Doves Cry"	
			McKENZIE, Bob & Doug	
			Canadian comedians Rick Moranis and Dave Thomas of "SCTV." Both featured in the film *Strange Brew.* Moranis later starred in *Ghostbusters, Spaceballs, Honey, I Shrunk the Kids* and many others. Thomas, the brother of singer Ian Thomas, hosts own syndicated TV series.	
2/20/82	**16**	9	1. Take Off [N]	Mercury 76134
			with vocals by Geddy Lee of Rush	
			McKENZIE, Scott	
			Born Philip Blondheim in Jacksonville, Florida on 1/10/39 and raised in Virginia. Sang with John Phillips (Mamas & Papas) in The Journeymen. Co-wrote The Beach Boys' 1988 #1 hit "Kokomo."	
6/10/67	**4**	10	**1. San Francisco (Be Sure To Wear Flowers In Your Hair)**	Ode 103
11/11/67	**24**	3	2. Like An Old Time Movie	Ode 105
			above 2 written and produced by John Phillips	
			McLAIN, Tommy	
			Native of South Louisiana.	
7/23/66	**15**	7	1. Sweet Dreams	MSL 197
			first released on Jin 197 in 1966	
			McLEAN, Don	
			Born on 10/02/45 in New Rochelle, New York. Singer/songwriter/poet. The hit "Killing Me Softly With His Song" was inspired by Don.	
12/04/71+	**1**(4)	17	● **1. American Pie - Parts I & II**	United Art. 50856
			inspired by the death of Buddy Holly	
4/01/72	**12**	10	2. Vincent/	
			a tribute to artist Vincent Van Gogh	
		10	3. Castles In The Air	United Art. 50887
1/20/73	**21**	8	4. Dreidel	United Art. 51100
1/24/81	**5**	15	**5. Crying**	Millennium 11799
5/02/81	**23**	6	6. Since I Don't Have You	Millennium 11804
12/12/81	**36**	5	7. Castles In The Air [R]	Millennium 11819
			new version of Don's 1972 hit	
			McLEAN, Phil	
			Veteran DJ; born in Detroit.	
12/18/61+	**21**	6	1. Small Sad Sam [S-N]	Versatile 107
			a parody of "Big Bad John"	
			McNAMARA, Robin	
			One of the original cast members of *Hair.* Male singer.	
7/18/70	**11**	8	1. Lay A Little Lovin' On Me	Steed 724
			McPHATTER, Clyde	
			Born Clyde Lensley McPhatter on 11/15/32 in Durham, North Carolina. Died on 6/13/72 in New York City (heart attack). Signed by Billy Ward for the Dominoes in 1950. Left the Dominoes in June 1953 to form own group, The Drifters. Drafted in 1954, returned to sing solo. One of the most influential and distinctive male voices of the R&B era. Inducted into the Rock and Roll Hall of Fame in 1987.	
6/09/56	**16**	12	1. Treasure Of Love	Atlantic 1092
			Best Seller #16 / Juke Box #18 / Top 100 #22	
2/23/57	**19**	2	2. Without Love (There Is Nothing)	Atlantic 1117

Levert—or at least two-thirds of the R&B trio—grew up in the music business with famous dad Eddie Levert of the O'Jays. Sons Gerald and Sean Levert and Marc Gordon crossed into pop with the No. 5 "Casanova" in 1987.

Gary Lewis & The Playboys had seven consecutive top-10 singles during 18 months in the mid-60s, and one of the most famous fathers in show biz to boot. A collection of greatest hits issued by EMI in the early 90s sold significantly, and a reconstituted group—including lead singer/drummer Gary—continues to tour.

Huey Lewis & The News had three No. 1 hits to their credit, including 1985's "The Power Of Love" from *Back to the Future*, "Stuck With You," and "Jacob's Ladder." In late 1991, rock promoter Bill Graham was killed in a helicopter crash following a Lewis concert.

Lisa Lisa & Cult Jam's longstanding collaboration with writer/producer team Full Force—resulting in such No. 1 hits as 1987's "Lost In Emotion" and "Head To Toe"—partially ended in 1991 with *Straight Outta Hell's Kitchen*, which featured producers Robert Clivilles and David Cole.

Little Anthony & The Imperials had the original hits and came out ahead of the Lettermen—but only slightly, chartwise. "Goin' Out Of My Head" hit No. 6 in 1964 for Little Anthony and No. 7 four years later for the Lettermen; "Hurt So Bad" likewise hit No. 10 in 1965 for Anthony and No. 12 four years later for the Lettermen.

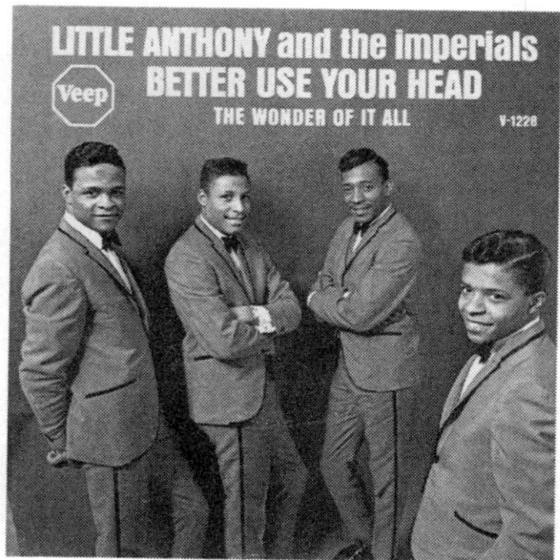

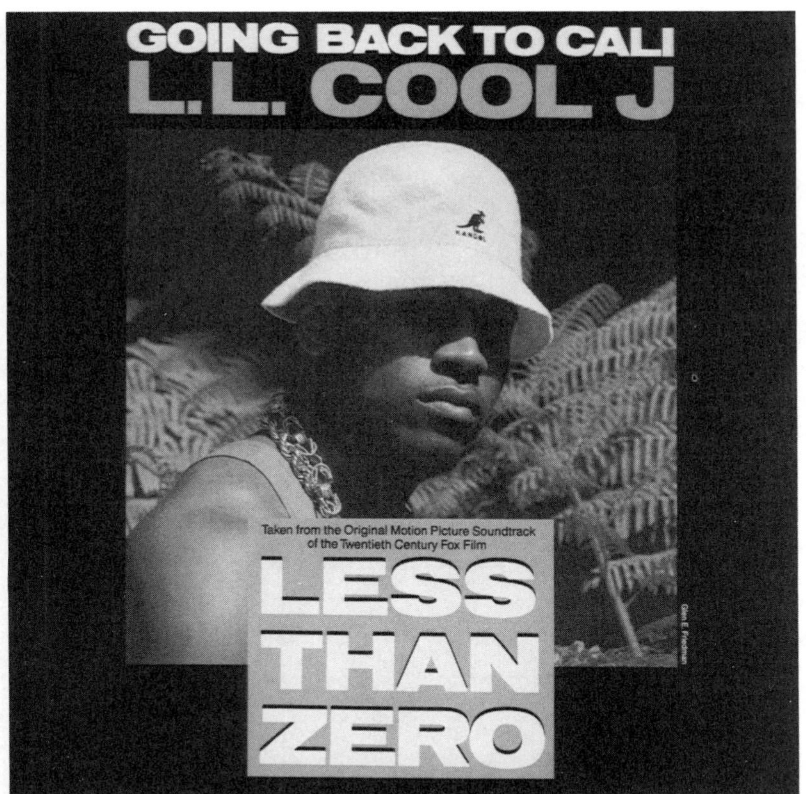

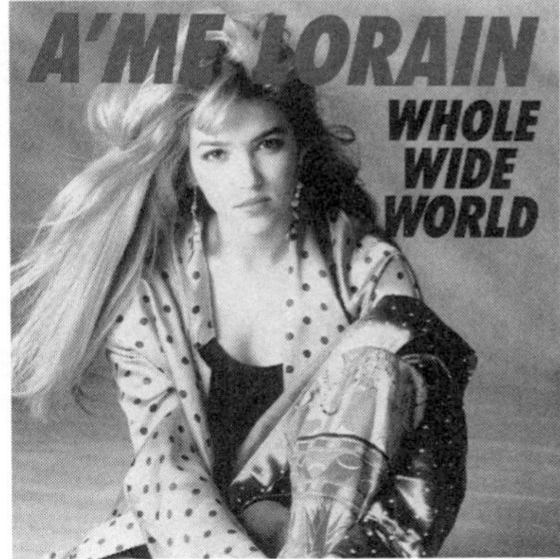

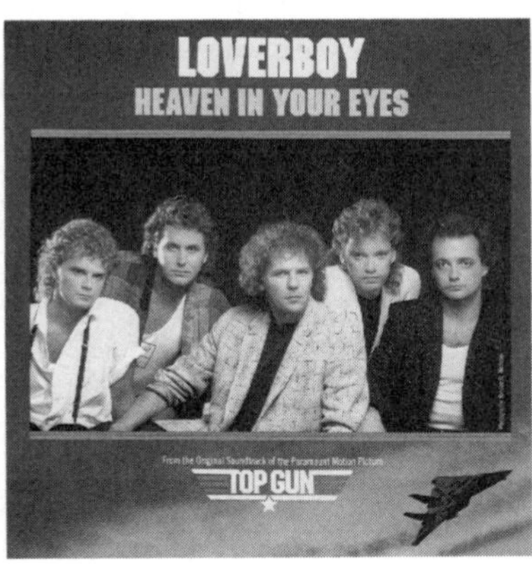

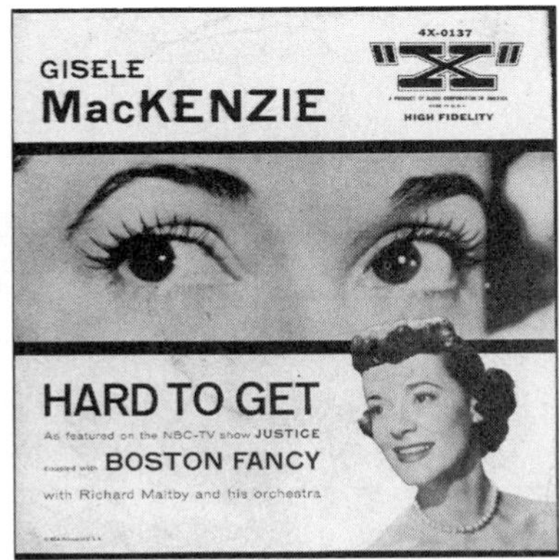

L.L. Cool J, the enormously popular rapper whose name is short for (the quite accurate) Ladies Love Cool James, caused a stir at the 1991 MTV Video Awards by rapping in front of a full band, rather than the sophisticated turntable equipment he favored in the past.

Denise Lopez was one of many female dance divas during the late 80s. Her only top-40 hit came in 1988 with "Sayin' Sorry (Don't Make It Right)" on the A&M-distributed Vendetta label.

A'me Lorain's "Whole Wide World" from the film *True Love* made the Top 10 in April 1990—but wide world or not, that brush with fame has been the artist's sole hit record.

Loverboy's first excursion into the Top 40 came in 1981, when the hard-rock quartet from Vancouver hit No. 35 with "Turn Me Loose." But 22 years earlier, another song with the same name, sung by another loverboy—teen crooner Fabian—peaked at No. 9.

The Lovin' Spoonful's first top-10 single was 1965's "Do You Believe In Magic"—and since it was followed by six more top-10 singles in just 15 months, one presumes the talented group were very much believers.

Gisele MacKenzie's status as a top-10 artist comes via only one song—1955's "Hard To Get." From an early-90s record-collecting standpoint, the fact that the "Your Hit Parade" star's single was released on the little-known X label indicates the accuracy of its title.

DATE	POS	WKS	ARTIST—RECORD TITLE	LABEL & NO.
			Jockey #19 / Top 100 #38	
7/08/57	**26**	3	3. Just To Hold My Hand	Atlantic 1133
			Best Seller #26 / Top 100 #30	
10/20/58+	**6**	20	**4. A Lover's Question**	Atlantic 1199
8/03/59	**38**	2	5. Since You've Been Gone	Atlantic 2028
			written by Neil Sedaka	
8/22/60	**23**	5	6. Ta Ta	Mercury 71660
3/24/62	**7**	10	**7. Lover Please**	Mercury 71941
6/30/62	**25**	5	8. Little Bitty Pretty One	Mercury 71987
			McVIE, Christine	
			Born Christine Perfect on 7/12/43 in Birmingham, England. Vocalist with Fleetwood Mac since 1970. Married to Fleetwood Mac bassist John McVie, 1968-77. Quit touring with group after 1990.	
2/04/84	**10**	11	**1. Got A Hold On Me**	Warner 29372
5/12/84	**30**	6	2. Love Will Show Us How	Warner 29313
			MEAD, Sister Janet	
			Australian nun; born in 1938. Gained prominence through her weekly cathedral rock masses and weekly radio programs.	
3/09/74	**4**	11	● **1. The Lord's Prayer**	A&M 1491
			Biblical text with new music by Arnold Strals	
			MEAT LOAF	
			Born Marvin Lee Aday on 9/27/47 in Dallas. Sang lead vocals on Ted Nugent's 1976 *Free-For-All* LP. Played Eddie in the Los Angeles production and film of *The Rocky Horror Picture Show*. Appeared in films *Americathon* (1979), *Roadie* (1980), *Out of Bounds* (1986) and *The Squeeze* (1987).	
4/29/78	**11**	13	● 1. Two Out Of Three Ain't Bad	Epic 50513
9/16/78	**39**	2	2. Paradise By The Dashboard Light [N]	Epic 50588
			female vocal: Ellen Foley; baseball announcer: Phil Rizzuto	
1/20/79	**39**	1	3. You Took The Words Right Out Of My Mouth	Epic 50634
			above 3 produced by Todd Rundgren	
			MECO	
			Disco producer Meco Monardo; born on 11/29/39 in Johnsonburg, Pennsylvania. Played trombone in Cadet Band at West Point. Later moved to New York and became a session musician and arranger. Co-produced Gloria Gaynor's hit "Never Can Say Goodbye."	
8/27/77	**1**(2)	13	▲ **1. Star Wars Theme/Cantina Band [I]**	Millennium 604
1/21/78	**25**	6	2. Theme From Close Encounters [I]	Millennium 608
10/21/78	**35**	3	3. Themes From The Wizard Of Oz [N]	Millennium 620
7/05/80	**18**	8	4. Empire Strikes Back [I]	RSO 1038
			Darth Vader/Yoda's Theme; all of above inspired by films of the same titles	
4/03/82	**35**	3	5. Pop Goes The Movies Part I [I]	Arista 0660
			20th Century Fox Trademark/Tara's Theme/The Magnificent Seven/The James Bond Theme/Goldfinger/The Good, The Bad And The Ugly/Theme From The Apartment/Theme From The High & The Mighty	
			MEDEIROS, Glenn	
			Born on 6/24/70 and raised in Hawaii. Discovered through a local radio station talent search.	
4/04/87	**12**	13	1. Nothing's Gonna Change My Love For You	Amherst 311
5/26/90	**1**(2)	14	● **2. She Ain't Worth It**	MCA 79047
			GLENN MEDEIROS featuring BOBBY BROWN	

DATE	POS	WKS	ARTIST—RECORD TITLE	LABEL & NO.
9/22/90	**32**	4	3. All I'm Missing Is You **GLENN MEDEIROS featuring RAY PARKER, JR.**	MCA 53886#
			MEDLEY, Bill	
			Born on 9/19/40 in Santa Ana, California. Baritone of The Righteous Brothers duo. Co-owner of a Las Vegas nightclub named Kicks with Paul Revere of The Raiders.	
10/10/87	**1**(1)	15	● **1. (I've Had) The Time Of My Life** **BILL MEDLEY AND JENNIFER WARNES** love theme from the film *Dirty Dancing*	RCA 5224
			MEISNER, Randy	
			Born on 3/08/46 in Scottsbluff, Nebraska. Bassist/vocalist of Poco (1968), Rick Nelson's Stone Canyon Band (1969-71) and the Eagles (1971-77).	
11/08/80	**22**	7	1. Deep Inside My Heart backing vocal by Kim Carnes	Epic 50939
2/07/81	**19**	9	2. Hearts On Fire	Epic 50964
8/28/82	**28**	6	3. Never Been In Love	Epic 03032
			MEL AND TIM	
			Cousins Mel Hardin and Tim McPherson, from Holly Springs, Mississippi.	
11/08/69	**10**	11	● **1. Backfield In Motion**	Bamboo 107
9/16/72	**19**	9	2. Starting All Over Again	Stax 0127
			MELANIE	
			Born Melanie Safka on 2/03/47 in Queens, New York. Neighborhood Records formed by Melanie and her husband/producer Peter Schekeryk.	
5/16/70	**6**	14	**1. Lay Down (Candles In The Rain)** **MELANIE with THE EDWIN HAWKINS SINGERS**	Buddah 167
9/05/70	**32**	4	2. Peace Will Come (According To Plan)	Buddah 186
11/27/71	**1**(3)	14	● **3. Brand New Key**	Neighborhood 4201
2/19/72	**31**	5	4. Ring The Living Bell	Neighborhood 4202
2/26/72	**35**	3	5. The Nickel Song	Buddah 268
4/07/73	**36**	2	6. Bitter Bad	Neighborhood 4210
			MELENDEZ, Lisette	
			Dance singer from East Harlem, New York.	
3/16/91	**35**	4	1. Together Forever	Fever/RAL 73629#
			MELLENCAMP, John Cougar	
			Born on 10/07/51 in Seymour, Indiana. Rock singer/songwriter/producer. Worked outside of music until 1975. Given name Johnny Cougar by David Bowie's manager, Tony DeFries. First recorded for MCA in 1976.	
			JOHN COUGAR:	
11/10/79	**28**	8	1. I Need A Lover	Riva 202
11/08/80	**27**	7	2. This Time	Riva 205
3/14/81	**17**	12	3. Ain't Even Done With The Night	Riva 207
5/22/82	**2**(4)	22	● **4. Hurts So Good**	Riva 209
8/07/82	**1**(4)	17	● **5. Jack & Diane**	Riva 210
11/27/82+	**19**	11	6. Hand To Hold On To	Riva 211
			JOHN COUGAR MELLENCAMP:	
10/22/83	**9**	11	**7. Crumblin' Down**	Riva 214
12/17/83+	**8**	11	**8. Pink Houses**	Riva 215
3/31/84	**15**	9	9. Authority Song	Riva 216

DATE	POS	WKS	ARTIST—RECORD TITLE	LABEL & NO.
8/24/85	**6**	13	**10. Lonely Ol' Night**	Riva 880984
11/16/85	**6**	13	**11. Small Town**	Riva 884202
2/15/86	**2**(1)	11	**12. R.O.C.K. In The U.S.A.** a salute to '60s rock	Riva 884455
5/17/86	**21**	6	13. Rain On The Scarecrow	Riva 884635
8/02/86	**28**	4	14. Rumbleseat	Riva 884856
8/29/87	**9**	10	**15. Paper In Fire**	Mercury 888763
11/14/87+	**8**	12	**16. Cherry Bomb**	Mercury 888934
2/27/88	**14**	9	17. Check It Out	Mercury 870126
5/13/89	**15**	7	18. Pop Singer	Mercury 874012
			MELLO-TONES, The	
5/13/57	**24**	1	1. Rosie Lee Best Seller #24 / Top 100 #60	Gee 1037
			MELLOW MAN ACE	
			Black Hispanic rapper born Ulpiano Sergio Reyez in Cuba on 4/12/67. Moved to the U.S. at age four. Raised in Southgate, California. His brother "Sen Dog" is a member of Cypress Hill.	
6/09/90	**14**	13	● 1. Mentirosa tune samples Santana's "Evil Ways" and "No One To Depend On"	Capitol 44533#
			MELVIN, Harold/The Blue Notes	
			Philadelphia soul group, The Blue Notes, formed in 1954: Harold Melvin, Bernard Williams, Jesse Gillis, Jr., Franklin Peaker and Roosevelt Brodie. First recorded for Josie in 1956. Numerous personnel changes until 1970, when Teddy Pendergrass joined as drummer and lead singer. Pendergrass went solo in 1976, replaced by David Ebo.	
10/28/72	**3**	11	● **1. If You Don't Know Me By Now**	Phil. Int. 3520
10/20/73	**7**	12	● **2. The Love I Lost (Part 1)**	Phil. Int. 3533
5/03/75	**15**	10	3. Bad Luck (Part 1)	Phil. Int. 3562
12/20/75+	**12**	12	4. Wake Up Everybody (Part 1)	Phil. Int. 3579
			MEN AT WORK	
			Melbourne, Australia rock quintet formed in 1979. Colin Hay (lead singer, guitar), Ron Strykert (lead guitar), Greg Ham (sax, keyboards), Jerry Speiser (drums) and John Rees (bass). Won the 1982 Best New Artist Grammy Award. Speiser and Rees left in 1984. Hay went solo as Colin James Hay in 1987.	
8/07/82	**1**(1)	17	**1. Who Can It Be Now?**	Columbia 02888
11/27/82+	**1**(4)	19	● **2. Down Under**	Columbia 03303
4/09/83	**3**	13	**3. Overkill**	Columbia 03795
7/09/83	**6**	12	**4. It's A Mistake**	Columbia 03959
10/08/83	**28**	5	5. Dr. Heckyll & Mr. Jive	Columbia 04111
			MENDES, Sergio/Brasil '66	
			Sergio was born on 2/11/41 in Niteroi, Brazil. Pianist/leader of Latin-styled group originating from Brazil. Member Lani Hall (vocals) married Herb Alpert.	
6/01/68	**4**	11	**1. The Look Of Love** from the film *Casino Royale*	A&M 924
8/24/68	**6**	10	**2. The Fool On The Hill** written by John Lennon and Paul McCartney	A&M 961
12/07/68	**16**	6	3. Scarborough Fair	A&M 986

DATE	POS	WKS	ARTIST—RECORD TITLE	LABEL & NO.
			SERGIO MENDES:	
5/14/83	**4**	16	**4. Never Gonna Let You Go** vocals by Joe Pizzulo and Lez Miller	A&M 2540
7/07/84	**29**	7	5. Alibis vocal by Joe Pizzulo	A&M 2639
			MEN WITHOUT HATS	
			Nucleus of techno-rock band from Montreal, Canada consists of Ivan Doroschuk (singer/songwriter) with his brother Stefan (guitar). Fluctuating personnel included their brother Colin (1983-84).	
7/30/83	**3**	16	**1. The Safety Dance**	Backstreet 52232
12/19/87+	**20**	10	2. Pop Goes The World	Mercury 888859
			MERCY	
			Florida group led by Jack Sigler, Jr.	
5/03/69	**2**(2)	10	● **1. Love (Can Make You Happy)**	Sundi 6811
			MESSINA, Jim — see LOGGINS & MESSINA	
			METALLICA	
			Speed-metal quartet formed by Lars Ulrich (drums) and James Hetfield (vocals) in Los Angeles in 1981. Early rhythm guitarist Dave Mustaine (now the leader of Megadeth) was replaced by Kirk Hammett in 1982. Bassist Cliff Burton was killed in a bus crash in Sweden on 9/27/86 (age 24); replaced by Jason Newsted.	
3/25/89	**35**	4	● 1. One	Elektra 69329
			METERS, The	
			R&B instrumental group formed in New Orleans in 1966 featuring keyboardist Arthur Neville (brother of Aaron Neville). Group disbanded in 1977, when Art, Aaron, and brothers Charles and Cyril formed The Neville Brothers.	
3/22/69	**34**	1	1. Sophisticated Cissy [I]	Josie 1001
5/24/69	**23**	3	2. Cissy Strut [I]	Josie 1005
			METHENY, Pat, Group — see BOWIE, David	
			MFSB	
			Large interracial studio band formed by producers Kenny Gamble and Leon Huff. Also recorded as The James Boys, and Family. Name means "Mothers, Fathers, Sisters, Brothers."	
3/16/74	**1**(2)	14	● **1. TSOP (The Sound Of Philadelphia)** [I] **MFSB featuring THE THREE DEGREES** theme from the TV show "Soul Train"	Phil. Int. 3540
			MIAMI SOUND MACHINE — see ESTEFAN, Gloria	
			MICHAEL, George/WHAM!	
			Born Georgios Kyriacos Panayiotou on 6/26/63 in Bushey, England. Wham!, formed in early 80s, centered around George's vocals and songwriting, and included Andrew Ridgeley (b: 1/26/63, Bushey, England) on guitar. Their association ended in 1986. Ridgeley pursued race car driving, then solo career in 1990.	
10/06/84	**1**(3)	14	● **1. Wake Me Up Before You Go-Go** **WHAM! U.K.**	Columbia 04552
12/22/84+	**1**(3)	17	● **2. Careless Whisper** **WHAM! featuring GEORGE MICHAEL**	Columbia 04691
4/06/85	**1**(2)	14	**3. Everything She Wants** **WHAM! U.K.**	Columbia 04840

DATE	POS	WKS	ARTIST—RECORD TITLE	LABEL & NO.
8/03/85	**3**	12	**4. Freedom** **WHAM! U.K.**	Columbia 05409
12/14/85+	**3**	12	**5. I'm Your Man** **WHAM! U.K.**	Columbia 05721
5/10/86	**7**	10	**6. A Different Corner** **GEORGE MICHAEL**	Columbia 05888
7/19/86	**10**	8	**7. The Edge Of Heaven** **WHAM! U.K.**	Columbia 06182
3/07/87	**1**(2)	12	**8. I Knew You Were Waiting (For Me)** **ARETHA FRANKLIN AND GEORGE MICHAEL**	Arista 9559
			GEORGE MICHAEL:	
6/20/87	**2**(1)	14	▲ **9. I Want Your Sex** from the film *Beverly Hills Cop II*	Columbia 07164
10/31/87	**1**(4)	15	● **10. Faith**	Columbia 07623
1/23/88	**1**(2)	13	**11. Father Figure**	Columbia 07682
4/16/88	**1**(3)	14	● **12. One More Try**	Columbia 07773
7/16/88	**1**(2)	12	**13. Monkey**	Columbia 07941
10/15/88	**5**	10	**14. Kissing A Fool**	Columbia 08050
3/11/89	**5**	0	**15. Heaven Help Me** **DEON ESTUS with GEORGE MICHAEL**	Mika 871538
9/08/90	**1**(1)	10	**16. Praying For Time**	Columbia 73512
11/03/90	**8**	12	● **17. Freedom** different tune than Michael's 1985 Wham! hit	Columbia 73559
2/09/91	**27**	5	18. Waiting For That Day includes the title line from The Rolling Stones' "You Can't Always Get What You Want"	Columbia 73663
			MICHAELS, Lee	
			Born on 11/24/45 in Los Angeles. Rock organist/vocalist.	
9/04/71	**6**	12	**1. Do You Know What I Mean**	A&M 1262
12/25/71	**39**	1	2. Can I Get A Witness	A&M 1303
			MICHEL'LE	
			Michel'le (pronounced: mee-shell-LAY) Toussant is an 18-year-old black singer from Los Angeles. Former backing singer of the World Class Wreckin Cru.	
1/20/90	**7**	15	● **1. No More Lies**	Ruthless 99149#
5/26/90	**29**	5	2. Nicety	Ruthless 98980
3/02/91	**31**	5	3. Something In My Heart	Ruthless 98885#
			MICKEY AND SYLVIA	
			McHouston "Mickey" Baker and Sylvia Vanderpool. Mickey (b: 10/15/25, Louisville) was a prolific session guitarist. Sylvia (b: 3/06/36, New York City) began solo career in 1973, recorded as Sylvia.	
1/12/57	**11**	14	1. Love Is Strange Best Seller #11 / Jockey #11 / Top 100 #13 / Juke Box #17	Groove 0175

DATE	POS	WKS	ARTIST—RECORD TITLE	LABEL & NO.
			MIDLER, Bette	
			Born on 12/01/45 in Paterson, New Jersey. Vocalist/actress. Raised in Hawaii. In the Broadway show *Fiddler on the Roof* for three years. Won the 1973 Best New Artist Grammy Award. Barry Manilow was her arranger/accompanist in early years. Nominated for an Oscar for performance in *The Rose* (1979). Also in films *Down and Out in Beverly Hills, Ruthless People, Outrageous Fortune, Beaches* and others.	
1/20/73	**17**	11	1. Do You Want To Dance?	Atlantic 2928
6/09/73	**8**	11	**2. Boogie Woogie Bugle Boy** #6 hit for The Andrews Sisters in 1941	Atlantic 2964
11/10/73	**40**	1	3. Friends above 2 produced by Barry Manilow	Atlantic 2980
7/07/79	**40**	2	4. Married Men	Atlantic 3582
3/01/80	**35**	3	5. When A Man Loves A Woman	Atlantic 3643
4/26/80	**3**	16	● **6. The Rose** above 2 from the film *The Rose*	Atlantic 3656
1/17/81	**39**	2	7. My Mother's Eyes from the film *Divine Madness*	Atlantic 3771
4/15/89	**1**(1)	15	● **8. Wind Beneath My Wings** from the film *Beaches*	Atlantic 88972
10/20/90	**2**(1)	19	▲ **9. From A Distance**	Atlantic 87820
			MIDNIGHT OIL	
			Australian quintet: Peter Garrett (lead vocals), Peter Gifford, Martin Rotsey, James Moginie and Rob Hirst (replaced by bassist Bones Hillman in 1987). Garrett ran for the Australian Senate in 1984.	
5/21/88	**17**	9	1. Beds Are Burning	Columbia 07433
			MIDNIGHT STAR	
			R&B-funk group formed in 1976 at Kentucky State University. Lead vocals by Belinda Lipscomb. Until 1988, band led by brothers Reginald (trumpet) and Vincent (trombone) Calloway. Reginald and Vincent produced many artists in the mid-1980s; formed own duo Calloway in 1988.	
1/12/85	**18**	8	1. Operator	Solar 69684
			MIKE + THE MECHANICS	
			Rock quintet consisting of bassist Mike Rutherford (Genesis), vocalists Paul Carrack (Ace, Squeeze) and Paul Young (Sad Cafe), drummer Peter Van Hooke (Van Morrison) and keyboardist Adrian Lee.	
1/18/86	**6**	11	**1. Silent Running (On Dangerous Ground)** title track from the movie *On Dangerous Ground*	Atlantic 89488
4/12/86	**5**	12	**2. All I Need Is A Miracle**	Atlantic 89450
8/02/86	**32**	5	3. Taken In	Atlantic 89404
1/21/89	**1**(1)	14	**4. The Living Years**	Atlantic 88964
			MILES, Garry	
			Lead singer of The Statues and Brenda Lee's backing group, The Casuals. Born James Cason on 11/27/39 in Nashville. Also recorded as Buzz Cason. Also see Garry Mills, who is a different artist with another version of the same song.	
7/18/60	**16**	9	1. Look For A Star from the film *Circus of Horrors*	Liberty 55261
			MILES, John	
			Born on 4/23/49 in Jarrow, England. Rock vocalist/guitarist/keyboardist. Guest vocalist with the Alan Parsons Project.	
5/14/77	**34**	5	1. Slowdown	London 20092

DATE	POS	WKS	ARTIST—RECORD TITLE	LABEL & NO.
			MILLER, Chuck	
			Boogie pianist from California.	
6/18/55	**9**	14	**1. The House Of Blue Lights** Best Seller #9 / Jockey #18 / Juke Box #19 #8 hit for Freddie Slack in 1946	Mercury 70627
			MILLER, Jody	
			Pop/country singer. Born in Phoenix on 11/29/41 and raised in Blanchard, Oklahoma.	
5/15/65	**12**	5	1. Queen Of The House answer song to Roger Miller's "King Of The Road"	Capitol 5402
9/25/65	**25**	5	2. Home Of The Brave	Capitol 5483
			MILLER, Mitch	
			Born on 7/04/11 in Rochester, New York. Producer/conductor/arranger. Oboe soloist with the CBS Symphony from 1936-47. A&R executive for both Columbia and Mercury Records. Best known for his sing-along albums and TV show (1961-64).	
8/06/55	**1**(6)	19	**1. The Yellow Rose Of Texas** Best Seller #1(6) / Jockey #1(6) / Juke Box #1(6) / Top 100 #4 pre adaptation of a Civil War campfire song	Columbia 40540
2/18/56	**19**	3	2. Lisbon Antigua (In Old Lisbon) [I] Jockey #19 / Top 100 #30	Columbia 40635
8/11/56	**8**	12	**3. Theme Song from "Song For A Summer Night"** **[I]** Jockey #8 / Best Seller #9 / Top 100 #10 / Juke Box #10 from the "Studio One" TV production "A Song for a Summer Night"	Columbia 40730
1/27/58	**20**	11	4. March From The River Kwai and Colonel Bogey [I] Jockey #20 / Best Seller #21 / Top 100 #21 from the film *The Bridge on the River Kwai*	Columbia 41066
1/26/59	**16**	10	5. The Children's Marching Song from the film *The Inn of the Sixth Happiness*	Columbia 41317
			MILLER, Ned	
			Born Henry Ned Miller on 4/12/25 in Rains, Utah. Country singer/songwriter. To California in 1956. Signed with Fabor in 1956. Wrote the Gale Storm and Bonnie Guitar hit "Dark Moon."	
1/26/63	**6**	8	**1. From A Jack To A King** originally released on Dot 15601 in 1957	Fabor 114
			MILLER, Roger	
			Country vocalist/humorist/guitarist/composer. Born on 1/02/36 in Fort Worth, Texas and raised in Erick, Oklahoma. To Nashville in the mid-1950s, began songwriting career. With Faron Young as writer/drummer in 1962. Won six Grammys in 1965. Own TV show in 1966. Songwriter of 1985's Tony Award-winning Broadway musical *Big River.*	
7/04/64	**7**	8	**1. Dang Me** **[N]**	Smash 1881
10/03/64	**9**	8	**2. Chug-A-Lug** **[N]**	Smash 1926
1/02/65	**31**	3	3. Do-Wacka-Do [N]	Smash 1947
2/06/65	**4**	12	• **4. King Of The Road**	Smash 1965
5/22/65	**7**	7	**5. Engine Engine # 9**	Smash 1983
8/07/65	**34**	2	6. One Dyin' And A Buryin'	Smash 1994
10/02/65	**31**	3	7. Kansas City Star [N]	Smash 1998
11/27/65	**8**	8	**8. England Swings**	Smash 2010

DATE	POS	WKS	ARTIST—RECORD TITLE	LABEL & NO.
3/05/66	**26**	5	9. Husbands And Wives	Smash 2024
7/23/66	**40**	1	10. You Can't Roller Skate In A Buffalo Herd [N]	Smash 2043
5/06/67	**37**	1	11. Walkin' In The Sunshine	Smash 2081
3/16/68	**39**	6	12. Little Green Apples	Smash 2148
			MILLER, Steve, Band	
			Born on 10/05/43 in Milwaukee and raised in Dallas. Blues-rock singer/songwriter/guitarist. Formed band in high school, The Marksmen, which included Boz Scaggs. While at the University of Wisconsin-Madison, Steve led the blues-rock band the Ardells, later known as the Fabulous Night Trains, featuring Scaggs. After graduating, studied literature at the University of Copenhagen. To San Francisco in 1966; formed the Steve Miller Band, which featured a fluctuating lineup.	
11/17/73+	**1**(1)	16	● **1. The Joker**	Capitol 3732
			STEVE MILLER:	
6/05/76	**11**	9	2. Take The Money And Run	Capitol 4260
9/04/76	**1**(1)	14	**3. Rock'n Me**	Capitol 4323
1/08/77	**2**(2)	15	● **4. Fly Like An Eagle**	Capitol 4372
			STEVE MILLER BAND:	
5/14/77	**8**	13	**5. Jet Airliner**	Capitol 4424
9/03/77	**23**	7	6. Jungle Love	Capitol 4466
11/12/77	**17**	9	7. Swingtown	Capitol 4496
11/14/81	**24**	9	8. Heart Like A Wheel	Capitol 5068
6/19/82	**1**(2)	19	● **9. Abracadabra**	Capitol 5126
			MILLI VANILLI	
			Europop act formed in Germany by producer Frank Farian (creator of Boney M and Far Corporation). Milli Vanilli is Turkish for positive energy. Originally thought to be Rob Pilatus (from Germany) and Fabrice Morvan (from France). Stripped of their 1989 Best New Artist Grammy Award when it was revealed that they did not sing on their debut album. Actual vocalists are Charles Shaw, John Davis and Brad Howe.	
2/04/89	**2**(1)	15	▲ **1. Girl You Know It's True**	Arista 9781
5/20/89	**1**(1)	14	● **2. Baby Don't Forget My Number**	Arista 9832
8/12/89	**1**(2)	14	● **3. Girl I'm Gonna Miss You**	Arista 9870
10/21/89	**1**(2)	14	▲ **4. Blame It On The Rain**	Arista 9904
1/13/90	**4**	10	**5. All Or Nothing**	Arista 9923#
			MILLS, Frank	
			Pianist/composer/producer/arranger. Born in Toronto in 1943.	
3/03/79	**3**	12	● **1. Music Box Dancer** [I]	Polydor 14517
			MILLS, Garry	
			British singer. Also see Garry Miles.	
7/04/60	**26**	6	1. Look For A Star - Part I from the film *Circus of Horrors*	Imperial 5674
			MILLS, Hayley	
			Born on 4/18/46 in London. Daughter of English actor John Mills. Disney teen film star of *Pollyana, The Parent Trap, In Search of the Castaways* and others.	
9/18/61	**8**	11	**1. Let's Get Together** from the film *The Parent Trap*	Vista 385
4/14/62	**21**	6	2. Johnny Jingo	Vista 395

DATE	POS	WKS	ARTIST—RECORD TITLE	LABEL & NO.
			MILLS, Stephanie	
			Born in 1957 in Brooklyn. In 1967, appeared for four weeks at the Apollo Theater with The Isley Brothers. At age 15, won starring role of Dorothy in the hit Broadway musical *The Wiz*. Played role for four years. Briefly married to Jeffrey Daniels of Shalamar in 1980.	
9/01/79	**22**	6	1. What Cha Gonna Do With My Lovin'	20th Century 2403
8/30/80	**6**	16	● **2. Never Knew Love Like This Before**	20th Century 2460
7/04/81	**40**	2	3. Two Hearts **STEPHANIE MILLS featuring TEDDY PENDERGRASS**	20th Century 2492
			MILLS BROTHERS, The	
			Smooth family vocal group from Piqua, Ohio. Consisted of John, Jr. (b: 1911; d: 1936), Herbert (b: 1912; d: 4/12/89 [age 77]), Harry (b: 1913; d: 6/28/82 [age 68]) and Donald (b: 1915). Originally featured unusual vocal style of imitating instruments. Achieved national fame via radio broadcasts and appearances in films. Father, John, Sr., joined group in 1936, replacing John, Jr.; remained in group until 1956 (d: 12/08/67). Group continued as a trio until 1982. Donald and his son John, III continued singing as a duo.	
6/17/57	**39**	1	1. Queen Of The Senior Prom	Decca 30299
3/03/58	**21**	2	2. Get A Job Jockey #21	Dot 15695
3/02/68	**23**	10	3. Cab Driver	Dot 17041
			MILSAP, Ronnie	
			Born on 1/16/46 in Robbinsville, North Carolina. Country singer/pianist/guitarist. Blind since birth; multi-instrumentalist by age 12. With J.J. Cale band; own band from 1965.	
8/27/77	**16**	10	1. It Was Almost Like A Song	RCA 10976
1/24/81	**24**	9	2. Smoky Mountain Rain	RCA 12084
7/11/81	**5**	15	**3. (There's) No Gettin' Over Me**	RCA 12264
11/28/81+	**20**	11	4. I Wouldn't Have Missed It For The World	RCA 12342
5/29/82	**14**	9	5. Any Day Now	RCA 13216
4/23/83	**23**	8	6. Stranger In My House	RCA 13470
			MIMMS, Garnet	
			Born Garrett Mimms on 11/16/33 in Ashland, West Virginia. Sang in gospel groups the Evening Stars, Norfolk Four, Harmonizing Four. Formed group the Gainors in 1958. The Enchanters (Zola Pearnell, Sam Bell and Charles Boyer) were formed in 1961.	
			GARNET MIMMS & THE ENCHANTERS:	
9/07/63	**4**	11	**1. Cry Baby**	United Art. 629
12/07/63+	**26**	5	2. For Your Precious Love/	
12/07/63	**30**	4	3. Baby Don't You Weep	United Art. 658
			GARNET MIMMS:	
5/07/66	**30**	3	4. I'll Take Good Care Of You	United Art. 995
			MINDBENDERS, The	
			Rock group from Manchester, England: Wayne Fontana (born Glyn Geoffrey Ellis on 10/28/45; lead singer), Eric Stewart (lead guitar, vocals), Bob Lang (bass) and Ric Rothwell (drums). Fontana left in October 1965. Graham Gouldman joined in 1968. Stewart and Gouldman were later members of Hotlegs and 10cc.	
3/27/65	**1**(1)	10	**1. Game Of Love** **WAYNE FONTANA & THE MINDBENDERS** first released on Fontana 1503 in 1964	Fontana 1509
4/30/66	**2**(2)	10	**2. A Groovy Kind Of Love**	Fontana 1541

DATE	POS	WKS	ARTIST—RECORD TITLE	LABEL & NO.
			MINEO, Sal	
			Broadway/Hollywood actor. Born on 1/10/39 in New York; stabbed to death on 2/12/76 in Los Angeles. Broadway credits include *The Rose Tattoo*, *The King & I* and others. Appeared in films *Rebel Without A Cause*, *Rock Pretty Baby* and others.	
5/20/57	**9**	13	**1. Start Movin' (In My Direction)** Best Seller #9 / Top 100 #10 / Jockey #16 / Juke Box #18 end	Epic 9216
9/23/57	**27**	3	2. Lasting Love Best Seller #27 / Top 100 #35	Epic 9227
			MINOGUE, Kylie	
			Singer/actress from Melbourne, Australia born on 5/28/68. Began TV acting career at age 11. Was a longtime cast member of the popular Australian soap "Neighbours."	
7/02/88	**28**	4	1. I Should Be So Lucky	Geffen 27922
9/17/88	**3**	13	**2. The Loco-Motion**	Geffen 27752
2/04/89	**37**	2	3. It's No Secret	Geffen 27651
			MIRACLES, The	
			R&B group formed at Northern High School in Detroit in 1955. Consisted of William "Smokey" Robinson (lead), Emerson and Bobby Rogers (tenors), Ronnie White (baritone) and Warren "Pete" Moore (bass). Emerson left in 1956 for U.S. Army, replaced by Claudette Rogers Robinson, Smokey's future wife. First recorded for End in 1958. Claudette retired in 1964. Bobby married Wanda Young of The Marvelettes. Smokey wrote many hit songs for the group and other Motown artists. Smokey went solo in 1972, replaced by William Griffin.	
12/31/60+	**2**(1)	13	**1. Shop Around**	Tamla 54034
2/17/62	**35**	2	2. What's So Good About Good-By	Tamla 54053
6/30/62	**39**	1	3. I'll Try Something New	Tamla 54059
1/12/63	**8**	10	**4. You've Really Got A Hold On Me**	Tamla 54073
5/04/63	**31**	3	5. A Love She Can Count On	Tamla 54078
8/31/63	**8**	9	**6. Mickey's Monkey**	Tamla 54083
1/04/64	**35**	3	7. I Gotta Dance To Keep From Crying	Tamla 54089
7/25/64	**27**	4	8. I Like It Like That	Tamla 54098
10/10/64	**35**	1	9. That's What Love Is Made Of	Tamla 54102
4/17/65	**16**	7	10. Ooo Baby Baby	Tamla 54113
8/07/65	**16**	8	11. The Tracks Of My Tears	Tamla 54118
11/06/65	**14**	6	12. My Girl Has Gone	Tamla 54123
1/22/66	**11**	7	13. Going To A Go-Go	Tamla 54127
11/26/66	**17**	6	14. (Come 'Round Here) I'm The One You Need	Tamla 54140
			SMOKEY ROBINSON & THE MIRACLES:	
3/11/67	**20**	7	15. The Love I Saw In You Was Just A Mirage	Tamla 54145
7/08/67	**23**	8	16. More Love	Tamla 54152
11/25/67	**4**	12	**17. I Second That Emotion**	Tamla 54159
3/09/68	**11**	10	18. If You Can Want	Tamla 54162
6/29/68	**31**	3	19. Yester Love	Tamla 54167
8/31/68	**26**	6	20. Special Occasion	Tamla 54172
1/25/69	**8**	11	**21. Baby, Baby Don't Cry**	Tamla 54178
7/19/69	**33**	2	22. Abraham, Martin And John	Tamla 54184
7/26/69	**32**	4	23. Doggone Right/	
10/04/69	**37**	3	24. Here I Go Again	Tamla 54183

DATE	POS	WKS	ARTIST—RECORD TITLE	LABEL & NO.
12/27/69+	**37**	4	25. Point It Out	Tamla 54189
10/31/70	**1**(2)	14	**26. The Tears Of A Clown**	Tamla 54199
4/17/71	**18**	8	27. I Don't Blame You At All	Tamla 54205
			THE MIRACLES:	
9/14/74	**13**	9	28. Do It Baby	Tamla 54248
12/13/75+	**1**(1)	19	**29. Love Machine (Part 1)**	Tamla 54262
			MR. MISTER	
			Los Angeles-based, pop-rock quartet: Richard Page (vocals), Steve George, Pat Mastelotto and Steve Farris (left in 1989; replaced by Buzz Feiten, ex-guitarist of Paul Butterfield Blues Band, Stevie Wonder's band, and the Larsen-Feiten Band).	
10/19/85	**1**(2)	15	**1. Broken Wings**	RCA 14136
1/11/86	**1**(2)	13	**2. Kyrie**	RCA 14258
4/12/86	**8**	11	**3. Is It Love**	RCA 14313
9/19/87	**29**	5	4. Something Real (Inside Me/Inside You)	RCA 5273
			MITCHELL, Guy	
			Born Al Cernik on 2/27/27 in Detroit. Sang briefly with Carmen Cavallaro's orchestra in the late '40s. Appearances in several films and TV series. In the films *Those Red Heads from Seattle* (1953) and *Red Garters* (1954).	
2/25/56	**23**	4	1. Ninety Nine Years (Dead Or Alive)	Columbia 40631
11/03/56	**1**(10)	22	**2. Singing The Blues** Juke Box #1(10) / Best Seller #1(9) / Top 100 #1(9) / Jockey #1(9)	Columbia 40769
2/02/57	**16**	8	3. Knee Deep In The Blues Top 100 #16 / Juke Box #16 / Jockey #17 / Best Seller #21 orchestra directed by Ray Conniff on above 2	Columbia 40820
4/13/57	**10**	12	**4. Rock-A-Billy** Best Seller #10 / Top 100 #13 / Juke Box #14 / Jockey #15	Columbia 40877
10/19/59	**1**(2)	16	**5. Heartaches By The Number**	Columbia 41476
			MITCHELL, Joni	
			Born Roberta Joan Anderson on 11/07/43 in Fort McLeod, Alberta, Canada and raised in Saskatoon, Saskatchewan. Singer/songwriter/guitarist/pianist. Moved to New York in 1966. Wrote the hits "Both Sides Now" and "Woodstock." Married her producer/bassist, Larry Klein, in 1982.	
12/30/72+	**25**	8	1. You Turn Me On, I'm A Radio	Asylum 11010
4/20/74	**7**	11	**2. Help Me**	Asylum 11034
8/24/74	**22**	7	3. Free Man In Paris	Asylum 11041
1/25/75	**24**	4	4. Big Yellow Taxi [R] live version of Joni's 1970 studio hit (POS 67)	Asylum 45221
			MITCHELL, Willie	
			Born in Ashland, Mississippi in 1928. Trumpeter/keyboardist/composer/arranger/producer. To Memphis at an early age. With Tuff Green and Al Jackson in the early '50s. Formed own band in 1954, became house band at Home Of The Blues and Hi Records. Eventually became president of Hi Records.	
10/03/64	**31**	5	1. 20-75 [I] title refers to the record's label number	Hi 2075
4/13/68	**23**	10	2. Soul Serenade [I]	Hi 2140

DATE	POS	WKS	ARTIST—RECORD TITLE	LABEL & NO.
			MOCEDADES	
			Sextet from Bilbao, Spain, featuring the Amezaga sisters, Amaya and Izaskum.	
2/16/74	**9**	11	**1. Eres Tu (Touch The Wind)** [F]	Tara 100
			B-side is sung in English	
			MODELS	
			Pop-rock quintet from Melbourne, Australia. Led by vocalists/guitarists James Freud and Sean Kelly.	
6/07/86	**37**	4	1. Out Of Mind Out Of Sight	Geffen 28762
			MODUGNO, Domenico	
			Born on 1/09/28 in Polignano a Mare, Italy. Singer/actor.	
8/04/58	**1**(5)	13	**1. Nel Blu Dipinto Di Blu (Volare)** [F]	Decca 30677
			Hot 100 #1(5) / Best Seller #1(5)	
			MOJO MEN, The	
			San Francisco-based rock quartet: Jimmy Alaimo, Paul Curcio, Don Metchick and Dennis DeCarr. Originally known as Sly and the Mojo Men, led by Sylvester "Sly Stone" Stewart (not on any of their recordings).	
3/18/67	**36**	3	1. Sit Down, I Think I Love You	Reprise 0539
			MOMENTS, The	
			Soul trio from Hackensack, New Jersey featuring Mark Greene (falsetto lead). Greene left after first record, replaced by William Brown (lead) and Al Goodman. Harry Ray joined after "Love On A Two-Way Street" in 1970. Became Ray, Goodman & Brown in 1978.	
4/18/70	**3**	14	● **1. Love On A Two-Way Street**	Stang 5012
			produced by Sylvia (Robinson)	
2/02/74	**17**	9	2. Sexy Mama	Stang 5052
8/02/75	**39**	3	3. Look At Me (I'm In Love)	Stang 5060
2/16/80	**5**	14	**4. Special Lady**	Polydor 2033
			RAY, GOODMAN & BROWN	
			MONEY, Eddie	
			Born Edward Mahoney on 3/02/49 in Brooklyn, New York. Rock singer discovered and subsequently managed by West Coast promoter Bill Graham. Formerly an officer with the New York Police Department.	
4/08/78	**11**	11	1. Baby Hold On	Columbia 10663
7/29/78	**22**	8	2. Two Tickets To Paradise	Columbia 10765
2/24/79	**22**	8	3. Maybe I'm A Fool	Columbia 10900
7/24/82	**16**	12	4. Think I'm In Love	Columbia 02964
9/27/86	**4**	12	**5. Take Me Home Tonight**	Columbia 06231
			Ronnie Spector sings the lead line from "Be My Baby"	
1/24/87	**14**	10	6. I Wanna Go Back	Columbia 06569
5/30/87	**21**	7	7. Endless Nights	Columbia 07035
10/22/88	**9**	13	**8. Walk On Water**	Columbia 08060
2/11/89	**24**	7	9. The Love In Your Eyes	Columbia 68532
12/23/89+	**11**	9	10. Peace In Our Time	Columbia 73047

DATE	POS	WKS	ARTIST—RECORD TITLE	LABEL & NO.
			MONKEES, The	
			Formed in Los Angeles in 1965. Chosen from over 400 applicants for new Columbia TV series. Consisted of Davy Jones (b: 12/30/45, Manchester, England; vocals), Michael Nesmith (b: 12/30/42, Houston; guitar, vocals), Peter Tork (b: 2/13/44, Washington, D.C.; bass, vocals) and Micky Dolenz (b: 3/08/45, Tarzana, California; drums, vocals). Dolenz had appeared in TV series "Circus Boy," using the name Mickey Braddock in 1956. Jones had been a racehorse jockey, and appeared in London musicals *Oliver* and *Pickwick*. Tork had been in the Phoenix Singers; Nesmith had done session work for Stax/Volt. Group starred in the film *Head* (1968). TV show dropped after 58 episodes, 1966-68. Tork left in 1968. Group disbanded in 1969; re-formed (minus Nesmith) in 1986.	
9/24/66	**1**(1)	12	● **1. Last Train To Clarksville**	Colgems 1001
12/17/66	**1**(7)	13	● **2. I'm A Believer/**	
12/31/66+	**20**	6	3. (I'm Not Your) Steppin' Stone	Colgems 1002
3/25/67	**2**(1)	10	● **4. A Little Bit Me, A Little Bit You/** 2, 4: written by Neil Diamond	
4/15/67	**39**	1	5. The Girl I Knew Somewhere	Colgems 1004
7/29/67	**3**	9	● **6. Pleasant Valley Sunday/**	
8/05/67	**11**	7	7. Words	Colgems 1007
11/18/67	**1**(4)	12	● **8. Daydream Believer**	Colgems 1012
3/09/68	**3**	7	● **9. Valleri/**	
3/30/68	**34**	1	10. Tapioca Tundra	Colgems 1019
6/22/68	**19**	6	11. D. W. Washburn	Colgems 1023
8/02/86	**20**	7	12. That Was Then, This Is Now **MICKY DOLENZ AND PETER TORK OF THE MONKEES**	Arista 9505
			MONOTONES, The	
			Doo-wop group from Newark, New Jersey. Charles Patrick, lead singer.	
4/07/58	**5**	12	**1. Book Of Love** Top 100 #5 / Best Seller #6 / Jockey #9 first released on Mascot 124 in 1957	Argo 5290
			MONRO, Matt	
			Born Terrence Parsons on 12/01/32 in London; died of liver cancer on 2/07/85. Sang with Cyril Stapleton's Orchestra before going solo.	
6/26/61	**18**	9	1. My Kind Of Girl	Warwick 636
12/26/64+	**23**	5	2. Walk Away	Liberty 55745
			MONROE, Vaughn	
			Born on 10/07/11 in Akron, Ohio; died on 5/21/73. Big-voiced baritone/trumpeter/bandleader. Very popular on radio, and featured in several movies.	
11/12/55	**38**	1	1. Black Denim Trousers And Motorcycle Boots	RCA 6260
2/18/56	**38**	1	2. Don't Go To Strangers	RCA 6358
9/08/56	**11**	8	3. In The Middle Of The House [N] Jockey #11 / Top 100 #21	RCA 6619
			MONTE, Lou	
			Born on 4/02/17 in Lyndhurst, New Jersey. Vocalist/guitarist.	
3/17/58	**12**	11	1. Lazy Mary [F] Best Seller #12 / Top 100 #12 / Jockey #22	RCA 7160
12/15/62+	**5**	9	**2. Pepino The Italian Mouse** [N]	Reprise 20106

DATE	POS	WKS	ARTIST—RECORD TITLE	LABEL & NO.
			MONTENEGRO, Hugo	
			Born in 1925 and raised in New York City; died on 2/06/81. Conductor/composer. Composed and conducted the film soundtrack of *Hurry Sundown*.	
4/06/68	**2**(1)	14	**1. The Good, The Bad And The Ugly** [I]	RCA 9423
			from the film of the same title	
			MONTEZ, Chris	
			Born Christopher Montanez on 1/17/43 in Los Angeles. Protege of Ritchie Valens.	
9/08/62	**4**	9	**1. Let's Dance**	Monogram 505
2/12/66	**22**	5	2. Call Me	A&M 780
5/28/66	**16**	7	3. The More I See You	A&M 796
9/10/66	**33**	2	4. There Will Never Be Another You	A&M 810
12/03/66	**36**	2	5. Time After Time	A&M 822
			2, 3, 5: produced by Herb Alpert	
			MONTGOMERY, Melba	
			Country singer/guitarist/fiddler. Born on 10/14/38 in Iron City, Tennessee; raised in Florence, Alabama.	
6/08/74	**39**	1	1. No Charge [N]	Elektra 45883
			MOODY BLUES, The	
			Formed in Birmingham, England in 1964. Consisted of Denny Laine (guitar, vocals), Ray Thomas (flute, vocals), Mike Pinder (keyboards, vocals), Clint Warwick (bass) and Graeme Edge (drums). Laine and Warwick left in the summer of 1966, replaced by Justin Hayward (lead vocals, lead guitar) and John Lodge (vocals, bass). Laine joined Wings in 1971. Switzerland-born Patrick Moraz (former keyboardist of Yes) replaced Pinder in 1978.	
3/27/65	**10**	8	**1. Go Now!**	London 9726
			Denny Laine (Wings), lead singer	
8/24/68	**24**	6	2. Tuesday Afternoon (Forever Afternoon)	Deram 85028
5/30/70	**21**	8	3. Question	Threshold 67004
9/04/71	**23**	7	4. The Story In Your Eyes	Threshold 67006
5/13/72	**29**	7	5. Isn't Life Strange	Threshold 67009
9/02/72	**2**(2)	14	● **6. Nights In White Satin**	Deram 85023
			released from their 1968 album *Days of Future Passed*	
2/17/73	**12**	8	7. I'm Just A Singer (In A Rock And Roll Band)	Threshold 67012
9/02/78	**39**	2	8. Steppin' In A Slide Zone	London 270
6/13/81	**12**	9	9. Gemini Dream	Threshold 601
8/15/81	**15**	11	10. The Voice	Threshold 602
9/17/83	**27**	6	11. Sitting At The Wheel	Threshold 604
5/24/86	**9**	12	**12. Your Wildest Dreams**	Polydor 883906
7/23/88	**30**	4	13. I Know You're Out There Somewhere	Polydor 887600
			MOONEY, Art	
			Born in Lowell, Massachusetts. Leader of a Detroit-based dance band from the mid-1930s to 1940s. To New York following WWII service. Biggest hit: "I'm Looking Over A Four Leaf Clover" (POS 1) in 1948.	
4/23/55	**6**	17	**1. Honey-Babe**	MGM 11900
			Best Seller #6 / Juke Box #6 / Jockey #10 from the film *Battle Cry*	
12/17/55	**6**	4	**2. Nuttin' For Christmas** [X-N]	MGM 12092
			ART MOONEY AND HIS ORCHESTRA with BARRY GORDON Best Seller #6 / Top 100 #7 / Juke Box #9 / Jockey #10	

DATE	POS	WKS	ARTIST—RECORD TITLE	LABEL & NO.
			MOONGLOWS, The	
			R&B group from Louisville. Consisted of lead singers Bobby Lester (d: 10/15/80 of cancer [age 50]) and Harvey Fuqua, with Alexander "Pete" Graves, Prentiss Barnes and Billy Johnson.	
3/26/55	**20**	1	1. Sincerely Juke Box #20	Chess 1581
10/13/56	**25**	1	2. See Saw Best Seller #25 / Top 100 #28	Chess 1629
10/20/58	**22**	4	3. Ten Commandments Of Love **HARVEY AND THE MOONGLOWS**	Chess 1705
			MOORE, Bob	
			Born on 11/30/32 in Nashville. Top session bass player. Led the band on Roy Orbison's sessions for Monument Records. Also worked as sideman for Elvis Presley, Brenda Lee, Pat Boone and others.	
9/11/61	**7**	10	**1. Mexico** [I]	Monument 446
			MOORE, Bobby/The Rhythm Aces	
			Formed in Montgomery, Alabama in 1961. Fronted by Bobby Moore (tenor sax) & Chico Jenkins (vocals).	
7/30/66	**27**	4	1. Searching For My Love	Checker 1129
			MOORE, Dorothy	
			Born in Jackson, Mississippi in 1946. Lead singer of The Poppies. Also a popular gospel artist.	
4/10/76	**3**	16	**1. Misty Blue**	Malaco 1029
9/10/77	**27**	7	2. I Believe You	Malaco 1042
			MOORE, Jackie	
			R&B singer from Jacksonville, Florida.	
1/23/71	**30**	7	● 1. Precious, Precious	Atlantic 2681
			MORALES, Michael	
			Born on 4/25/63. Native of San Antonio, Texas.	
6/10/89	**15**	10	1. Who Do You Give Your Love To?	Wing 887743
9/09/89	**28**	6	2. What I Like About You	Wing 889678#
			MORGAN, Jane	
			Born Jane Currier in Boston and raised in Florida. Popular singer in France before achieving U.S. fame via TV and nightclub entertaining.	
9/09/57	**7**	21	**1. Fascination** Jockey #7 / Top 100 #11 / Best Seller #12 instrumental intro by The Troubadors; from the film *Love in the Afternoon*	Kapp 191
10/13/58	**21**	10	2. The Day The Rains Came	Kapp 235
8/31/59	**39**	1	3. With Open Arms	Kapp 284
			MORGAN, Jaye P.	
			Born Mary Margaret Morgan in Mancos, Colorado on 12/03/31. Sang with Frank DeVol's band from 1950-53. Featured on many TV game shows from the 1950s-'70s. Sister of recording group The Morgan Brothers.	
11/27/54+	**3**	21	**1. That's All I Want From You** Jockey #3 / Best Seller #5 / Juke Box #5	RCA 5896
3/12/55	**12**	8	2. Danger! Heartbreak Ahead Jockey #12 / Juke Box #13 / Best Seller #18	RCA 6016

DATE	POS	WKS	ARTIST—RECORD TITLE	LABEL & NO.
			PERRY COMO AND JAYE P. MORGAN:	
6/11/55	**12**	5	3. Chee Chee-Oo-Chee (Sang the Little Bird)/ Jockey #12 / Juke Box #14 / Best Seller #24	
6/25/55	**18**	1	4. Two Lost Souls Jockey #18; from the Broadway musical *Damn Yankees*	RCA 6137
			PERRY COMO:	
8/20/55	**6**	14	**5. The Longest Walk** Jockey #6 / Juke Box #7 / Best Seller #13 / Top 100 #19 pre	RCA 6182
11/12/55	**14**	8	6. Pepper-Hot Baby/ Juke Box #14 / Top 100 #21	
12/03/55	**12**	3	7. If You Don't Want My Love Juke Box #12 / Top 100 #40 orchestra conducted by Hugo Winterhalter on all of above (except #3, 4 & 6)	RCA 6282
			MORGAN, Russ Born on 4/29/04 in Scranton, Pennsylvania; died on 8/08/69. Trombonist/pianist/popular sweet-band leader. Biggest hit: "Cruising Down The River" in 1949.	
11/12/55	**30**	4	1. Dogface Soldier from the movie *To Hell and Back*	Decca 29703
3/17/56	**19**	3	2. The Poor People Of Paris [I] Juke Box #19 / Jockey #23 / Top 100 #26	Decca 29835
			MORMON TABERNACLE CHOIR, The Three hundred and seventy-five-voice choir directed by Richard P. Condie (died on 12/22/85).	
9/21/59	**13**	11	1. Battle Hymn Of The Republic with the Philadelphia Orchestra, Eugene Ormandy, conductor; written in 1862; a #1 hit for The Columbia Stellar Quartet in 1918	Columbia 41459
			MORODER, Giorgio Born on 4/26/40 in Ortisel, Italy. Electronic composer/conductor/producer for numerous soundtracks. Produced seven of Donna Summer's albums.	
3/10/79	**33**	4	1. Chase [I] from the film *Midnight Express*	Casablanca 956
			MORRISON, Van Born George Ivan on 8/31/45 in Belfast, Ireland. Blue-eyed soul singer/songwriter. Leader of Them. Wrote the classic hit "Gloria."	
8/19/67	**10**	10	**1. Brown Eyed Girl**	Bang 545
4/25/70	**39**	2	2. Come Running	Warner 7383
12/05/70+	**9**	9	**3. Domino**	Warner 7434
3/06/71	**23**	8	4. Blue Money	Warner 7462
11/20/71	**28**	4	5. Wild Night all of above written by Morrison	Warner 7518
			MOTELS, The Los Angeles-based quintet led by vocalist Martha Davis. Formed in Berkeley. To Los Angeles in the early '70s. Re-formed in 1978, signed to Capitol in 1979. Disbanded in 1987.	
5/29/82	**9**	15	**1. Only The Lonely**	Capitol 5114
9/17/83	**9**	13	**2. Suddenly Last Summer**	Capitol 5271
1/14/84	**36**	3	3. Remember The Nights	Capitol 5246
8/10/85	**21**	7	4. Shame	Capitol 5497

DATE	POS	WKS	ARTIST—RECORD TITLE	LABEL & NO.
			MOTHERLODE	
			Canadian pop quartet led by keyboardist William "Smitty" Smith.	
9/13/69	**18**	7	1. When I Die	Buddah 131
			MOTLEY CRUE	
			Los Angeles-based, hard-rock band: "Vince Neil" Wharton (lead vocals), Mick Mars (real name: Bob Deal; guitar), Nikki Sixx (Frank Ferranno; bass) & "Tommy Lee" Bass (drums; married actress Heather Locklear).	
8/03/85	**16**	9	1. Smokin' In The Boys Room	Elektra 69625
6/13/87	**12**	9	2. Girls, Girls, Girls	Elektra 69465
9/23/89	**6**	9	● **3. Dr. Feelgood**	Elektra 69271
1/06/90	**27**	6	4. Kickstart My Heart	Elektra 69248
3/17/90	**8**	10	**5. Without You**	Elektra 64985
6/30/90	**19**	7	6. Don't Go Away Mad (Just Go Away)	Elektra 64962#
			MOTT THE HOOPLE	
			British glitter-rock group led by vocalist Ian Hunter. Group name taken from a Willard Manus novel. Various personnel included guitarist Mick Ralphs (left in 1973 to form Bad Company). Hunter left in 1976; members Pete "Overend" Watts, Morgan Fisher and Dale "Buffin" Griffin formed the British Lions.	
11/04/72	**37**	3	1. All The Young Dudes written, produced and arranged by David Bowie	Columbia 45673
			MOUNTAIN	
			New York power-rock group led by Leslie West (b: Leslie Weinstein, 10/22/45, New York City) and Felix Pappalardi (b: 1939, the Bronx; fatally shot on 4/17/83 [age 44] in New York City).	
6/13/70	**21**	9	1. Mississippi Queen	Windfall 532
			MOUTH & MACNEAL	
			Dutch duo: Willem Duyn and Maggie Macneal (real name: Sjoukje Van't Spijker).	
6/17/72	**8**	12	● **1. How Do You Do?**	Philips 40715
			MOVING PICTURES	
			Australian six-man pop group led by Alex Smith (vocals). Member Garry Frost later formed the group 1927.	
11/27/82+	**29**	13	1. What About Me re-charted in 1989 at POS 46	Network 69952
			MOYET, Alison	
			Born Genevieve Alison-Jane "Alf" Moyet on 6/18/61 in Basildon, Essex, England. Female vocalist of Yaz.	
5/04/85	**31**	6	1. Invisible	Columbia 04781
			MOZART, Mickey, Quintet	
			Mickey Mozart is a pseudonym for jazz harpist/composer Robert Maxwell.	
6/08/59	**30**	6	1. Little Dipper [I]	Roulette 4148
			MULDAUR, Maria	
			Born Maria D'Amato on 9/12/43 in New York City. Member of Jim Kweskin's Jug Band with former husband Geoff Muldaur (divorced in 1972). Maria later became an Inspirational recording artist.	
4/13/74	**6**	14	**1. Midnight At The Oasis**	Reprise 1183
1/25/75	**12**	8	2. I'm A Woman	Reprise 1319

DATE	POS	WKS	ARTIST—RECORD TITLE	LABEL & NO.
			MUNGO JERRY	
			British skiffle quartet: Ray Dorset (lead vocals), Colin Earl, Paul King and Mike Cole.	
7/25/70	**3**	11	● **1. In The Summertime**	Janus 125
			MURDOCK, Shirley	
			Former gospel singer from Toledo. Discovered by Roger Troutman (aka Roger) who hired her as backup singer for his family funk group, Zapp.	
2/28/87	**23**	7	1. As We Lay	Elektra 69518
			MURMAIDS, The	
			Los Angeles teenage trio: sisters Carol and Terry Fischer, with Sally Gordon.	
12/07/63+	**3**	11	**1. Popsicles And Icicles**	Chattahoochee 628
			written by David Gates of Bread	
			MURPHEY, Michael	
			Born Michael Martin Murphey in Dallas. Progressive country singer/songwriter. Toured as Travis Lewis of The Lewis & Clarke Expedition in 1967. Worked as a staff writer for Screen Gems. Appeared in the films *Take This Job and Shove It* and *Hard Country.*	
10/07/72	**37**	2	1. Geronimo's Cadillac	A&M 1368
5/03/75	**3**	13	● **2. Wildfire**	Epic 50084
9/13/75	**21**	7	3. Carolina In The Pines	Epic 50131
2/21/76	**39**	2	4. Renegade	Epic 50184
8/28/82	**19**	11	5. What's Forever For	Liberty 1466
			MURPHY, Eddie	
			Born on 4/03/61 in Hempstead, New York. Comedian/actor. Former cast member of TV's "Saturday Night Live." Starred in the films *Beverly Hills Cop (I & II), Trading Places, Best Defense, 48 Hrs., The Golden Child, Coming to America, Harlem Nights* and *Another 48 Hrs.*	
11/09/85	**2**(3)	14	● **1. Party All The Time**	Columbia 05609
			written, produced and arranged by Rick James	
8/19/89	**27**	4	2. Put Your Mouth On Me	Columbia 68897
			MURPHY, Walter/The Big Apple Band	
			Walter was born in 1952 in New York City. Studied classical and jazz piano at Manhattan School of Music. Former arranger for Doc Severinsen and "The Tonight Show" orchestra.	
7/04/76	**1**(1)	22	● **1. A Fifth Of Beethoven** [I]	Private S. 45073
			based on Beethoven's "Fifth Symphony"	
			MURRAY, Anne	
			Born Morna Anne Murray on 6/20/45 in Springhill, Nova Scotia. High school teacher for one year after college. With CBC-TV show "Sing Along Jubilee." First recorded for ARC in 1969. Regular on Glen Campbell's "Goodtime Hour" TV series. Currently resides in Toronto.	
8/22/70	**8**	11	● **1. Snowbird**	Capitol 2738
2/10/73	**7**	13	**2. Danny's Song**	Capitol 3481
			written by Kenny Loggins for his nephew (also wrote #3 below)	
1/19/74	**12**	10	3. Love Song	Capitol 3776
5/25/74	**8**	10	**4. You Won't See Me**	Capitol 3867
			written by John Lennon & Paul McCartney	
8/19/78	**1**(1)	17	● **5. You Needed Me**	Capitol 4574
2/10/79	**12**	12	6. I Just Fall In Love Again	Capitol 4675
6/23/79	**25**	7	7. Shadows In The Moonlight	Capitol 4716

DATE	POS	WKS	ARTIST—RECORD TITLE	LABEL & NO.
10/20/79	**12**	11	8. Broken Hearted Me	Capitol 4773
1/19/80	**12**	11	9. Daydream Believer	Capitol 4813
10/18/80	**33**	4	10. Could I Have This Dance from the film *Urban Cowboy*	Capitol 4920
5/02/81	**34**	4	11. Blessed Are The Believers	Capitol 4987
			MUSICAL YOUTH Five schoolboys (ages 11 to 16 in 1983) from Birmingham, England: Dennis Seaton (lead), with brothers Kelvin (guitar) & Michael (keyboards) Grant, and Patrick (bass) & Junior (drums) Waite.	
1/15/83	**10**	10	**1. Pass The Dutchie** clean version of the Jamaican hit "Pass The Kouchie" which means "pass the joint"; a dutchie is a Jamaican cooking pot	MCA 52149
			MUSIC EXPLOSION, The Jamie Lyons, lead singer of quintet from Mansfield, Ohio. Produced by Jerry Kasenetz and Jeff Katz.	
5/27/67	**2**(2)	13	● **1. Little Bit O'Soul**	Laurie 3380
			MUSIC MACHINE, The Los Angeles rock quintet — Sean Bonniwell, lead singer/songwriter.	
12/10/66+	**15**	8	1. Talk Talk	Original Sound 61
			MYLES, Alannah Rock singer born in Toronto and raised in Buckhorn, Canada.	
2/03/90	**1**(2)	15	● **1. Black Velvet**	Atlantic 88742
6/16/90	**36**	4	2. Love Is	Atlantic 87945
			MYLES, Billy New York singer/songwriter. Wrote the Mello-Kings' pop hit "Tonite, Tonite."	
11/25/57	**25**	6	1. The Joker (That's What They Call Me) Best Seller #25 / Top 100 #30	Ember 1026
			MYSTICS, The Quintet from Brooklyn: Phil Cracolici (lead), Bob Ferrante & George Galfo (tenors), Albee Cracolici (baritone) and Allie Contrera (bass).	
6/15/59	**20**	9	1. Hushabye	Laurie 3028
			N	
			NAKED EYES English duo: Pete Byrne (vocals) and Rob Fisher (keyboards, synthesizer). Split in 1984. Fisher later in duo Climie Fisher.	
4/23/83	**8**	13	**1. Always Something There To Remind Me**	EMI America 8155
8/13/83	**11**	12	2. Promises, Promises	EMI America 8170
12/17/83	**37**	3	3. When The Lights Go Out	EMI America 8183
9/29/84	**39**	2	4. (What) In The Name Of Love	EMI America 8219
			NAPOLEON XIV Napoleon is Jerry Samuels, a recording engineer/composer from New York.	
7/30/66	**3**	5	**1. They're Coming To Take Me Away, Ha-Haaa!** [N]	Warner 5831

DATE	POS	WKS	ARTIST—RECORD TITLE	LABEL & NO.
			NASH, Graham	
			Born on 2/02/42 in Blackpool, England. Co-founding member/guitarist of The Hollies. Formed Crosby, Stills & Nash in 1970.	
7/10/71	**35**	4	1. Chicago	Atlantic 2804
6/10/72	**36**	4	2. Immigration Man **GRAHAM NASH & DAVID CROSBY**	Atlantic 2873
			NASH, Johnny	
			Born on 8/19/40 in Houston. Vocalist/guitarist/actor. Appeared on local TV from age 13. With Arthur Godfrey's TV and radio shows from 1956-63. In the film *Take a Giant Step* in 1959. Own JoDa label in 1965. Began recording in Jamaica in the late '60s.	
2/03/58	**23**	1	1. A Very Special Love Jockey #23 / Best Seller #45 / Top 100 #46	ABC-Para. 9874
12/15/58+	**29**	5	2. The Teen Commandments [S] **PAUL ANKA-GEO. HAMILTON IV-JOHNNY NASH** inspirational talk from above 3 ABC-Paramount artists	ABC-Para. 9974
10/05/68	**5**	12	**3. Hold Me Tight**	JAD 207
1/24/70	**39**	1	4. Cupid originally released as the B-side of #3 above	JAD 220
10/07/72	**1**(4)	14	● **5. I Can See Clearly Now**	Epic 10902
3/03/73	**12**	10	6. Stir It Up written by Bob Marley	Epic 10949
			NASHVILLE TEENS, The	
			British rock sextet — Arthur Sharp, lead singer. Drummer Barry Jenkins joined The Animals in 1966.	
10/10/64	**14**	6	1. Tobacco Road	London 9689
			NATURAL FOUR	
			Soul group led by Chris James, formed in 1967 in San Francisco.	
2/09/74	**31**	4	1. Can This Be Real	Curtom 1990
			NAUGHTON, David	
			Singer/dancer/actor. Starred in the 1981 film *An American Werewolf in London* and TV shows "Makin' It" and "My Sister Sam."	
5/12/79	**5**	16	● **1. Makin' It** from the film *Meatballs*	RSO 916
			NAZARETH	
			Hard-rock group formed in Scotland in 1969: Dan McCafferty (lead singer), Manny Charlton (lead guitar), Pete Agnew (bass) and Darrell Sweet (drums). Billy Rankin (lead guitar) and John Locke (keyboards) added in 1981.	
1/03/76	**8**	14	● **1. Love Hurts**	A&M 1671
			NEELY, Sam	
			Born on 8/22/48 in Cuero, Texas. Performing since age 11. Played clubs in Corpus Christi, especially at The Rogue, in the late '60s. Long residency at the Electric Eel in Corpus Christi in the late '70s.	
10/07/72	**29**	6	1. Loving You Just Crossed My Mind	Capitol 3381
11/09/74	**34**	2	2. You Can Have Her	A&M 1612
			NEIGHBORHOOD, The	
8/08/70	**29**	4	1. Big Yellow Taxi	Big Tree 102

DATE	POS	WKS	ARTIST—RECORD TITLE	LABEL & NO.
			NELSON	
			Gunnar (vocals, bass) and Matthew Nelson (vocals, rhythm guitar), the identical twin sons (b: 9/20/67) of the late Ricky Nelson. Their sister is actress Tracy Nelson of TV's "Father Dowling Mysteries."	
8/11/90	**1**(1)	14	● **1. (Can't Live Without Your) Love And Affection**	DGC 19689
12/01/90+	**6**	14	**2. After The Rain**	DGC 19667
4/06/91	**14**	9	3. More Than Ever	DGC 19002
7/27/91	**28**	5	4. Only Time Will Tell	DGC 19014
			NELSON, Ricky	
			Born Eric Hilliard Nelson on 5/08/40 in Teaneck, New Jersey. Died on 12/31/85 in a plane crash in DeKalb, Texas. Son of bandleader Ozzie Nelson and vocalist Harriet Hilliard. Rick and brother David appeared on Nelson's radio show from March 1949, later on TV, 1952-66. Formed own Stone Canyon Band in 1969. In films *Rio Bravo*, *Wackiest Ship in the Army* and *Love and Kisses*. Married Kristin Harmon (sister of actor Mark Harmon) in 1963; divorced in 1982. Their daughter Tracy is a film/TV actress. Their twin sons began recording as Nelson in 1990. Ricky was one of the first teen idols of the rock era. Inducted into the Rock and Roll Hall of Fame in 1987.	
5/06/57	**4**	15	**1. I'm Walking/** Best Seller #4 / Juke Box #16 / Top 100 #17	
5/13/57	**2**(1)	15	**2. A Teenager's Romance** Best Seller #2 / Top 100 #8 / Jockey #8 / Juke Box #12	Verve 10047
9/16/57	**14**	7	3. You're My One And Only Love Best Seller #14 / Top 100 #16 orchestra conducted by Barney Kessel on above 3	Verve 10070
10/07/57	**3**	18	**4. Be-Bop Baby/** Best Seller #3 / Top 100 #5 / Jockey #10	
10/28/57	**29**	3	5. Have I Told You Lately That I Love You? #24 hit for Bing Crosby & The Andrews Sisters in 1950	Imperial 5463
12/30/57+	**2**(3)	14	**6. Stood Up/** Best Seller #2 / Top 100 #5 / Jockey #5	
12/30/57+	**18**	9	7. Waitin' In School Top 100 #18 / Jockey #24	Imperial 5483
4/07/58	**4**	10	**8. Believe What You Say/** Best Seller #4 / Top 100 #8 / Jockey #20	
4/07/58	**12**	10	9. My Bucket's Got A Hole In It Best Seller #12 / Top 100 #18 / Jockey #25	Imperial 5503
7/07/58	**1**(2)	15	**10. Poor Little Fool** Hot 100 #1(2) / Best Seller #1(2) / Jockey #2 end	Imperial 5528
10/20/58	**7**	16	**11. Lonesome Town/**	
10/20/58	**10**	13	**12. I Got A Feeling**	Imperial 5545
3/09/59	**6**	12	**13. Never Be Anyone Else But You/**	
3/16/59	**9**	10	**14. It's Late**	Imperial 5565
7/13/59	**9**	9	**15. Just A Little Too Much/** 7, 8, 14, 15: written by Johnny and/or Dorsey Burnette	
7/13/59	**9**	8	**16. Sweeter Than You**	Imperial 5595
12/07/59	**20**	8	17. I Wanna Be Loved/	
12/21/59	**38**	1	18. Mighty Good	Imperial 5614
5/09/60	**12**	9	19. Young Emotions	Imperial 5663
9/19/60	**27**	4	20. I'm Not Afraid/	
9/26/60	**34**	2	21. Yes Sir, That's My Baby #1 hit for Gene Austin in 1925	Imperial 5685

DATE	POS	WKS	ARTIST—RECORD TITLE	LABEL & NO.
1/09/61	**25**	4	22. You Are The Only One	Imperial 5707
5/01/61	**1**(2)	15	● **23. Travelin' Man/**	
5/08/61	**9**	13	**24. Hello Mary Lou** written by Gene Pitney	Imperial 5741
			RICK NELSON:	
10/09/61	**11**	9	25. A Wonder Like You/	
10/09/61	**16**	8	26. Everlovin'	Imperial 5770
3/17/62	**5**	10	**27. Young World**	Imperial 5805
8/25/62	**5**	9	**28. Teen Age Idol**	Imperial 5864
12/29/62+	**6**	9	**29. It's Up To You**	Imperial 5901
6/15/63	**25**	5	30. String Along	Decca 31495
10/05/63	**12**	9	31. Fools Rush In #1 hit for Glenn Miller in 1940	Decca 31533
1/11/64	**6**	9	**32. For You** #9 hit for John Boles in 1930	Decca 31574
5/09/64	**26**	5	33. The Very Thought Of You #1 hit for Ray Noble in 1934	Decca 31612
			RICK NELSON & THE STONE CANYON BAND:	
1/03/70	**33**	6	34. She Belongs To Me written by Bob Dylan	Decca 32550
9/16/72	**6**	12	● **35. Garden Party**	Decca 32980
			NELSON, Sandy	
			Born Sander Nelson on 12/01/38 in Santa Monica, California. Rock 'n' roll drummer. Became prominent studio musician. Heard on "Alley Oop," "To Know Him Is To Love Him," "A Thousand Stars" and many others. Lost portion of right leg in a motorcycle accident in 1963. Returned to performing in 1964.	
9/14/59	**4**	12	**1. Teen Beat** [I]	Original Sound 5
11/20/61	**7**	12	**2. Let There Be Drums** [I]	Imperial 5775
3/03/62	**29**	4	3. Drums Are My Beat [I]	Imperial 5809
			NELSON, Willie	
			Born on 4/30/33 in Ft. Worth, Texas; raised in Abbott, Texas. Prolific country singer/songwriter (writer of Patsy Cline's "Crazy" and Faron Young's "Hello Walls"). Played bass for Ray Price. Moved to Nashville in 1960. Moved back to Texas in 1970. Pioneered the "outlaw" country movement. Appeared in several films including *The Electric Horseman* (1979), *Honeysuckle Rose* (1980) and *Barbarosa* (1982). Won Grammy's Living Legends Award in 1989.	
10/11/75	**21**	9	1. Blue Eyes Crying In The Rain	Columbia 10176
3/06/76	**25**	5	2. Good Hearted Woman **WAYLON & WILLIE**	RCA 10529
9/27/80	**20**	10	3. On The Road Again from the film *Honeysuckle Rose*	Columbia 11351
4/10/82	**5**	15	**4. Always On My Mind**	Columbia 02741
9/18/82	**40**	3	5. Let It Be Me	Columbia 03073
3/31/84	**5**	12	● **6. To All The Girls I've Loved Before** **JULIO IGLESIAS & WILLIE NELSON**	Columbia 04217
			NENA	
			Gabriele "Nena" Kerner (b: 3/26/60) with four-member backup group from Hagen, Germany.	
1/21/84	**2**(1)	13	● **1. 99 Luftballons** [F]	Epic 04108

DATE	POS	WKS	ARTIST—RECORD TITLE	LABEL & NO.
			nuclear protest song	
			NEON PHILHARMONIC, The	
			Chamber-sized orchestra of Nashville Symphony Orchestra musicians. Project headed by Tupper Saussy (composer) and Don Gant (vocals). Gant died on 3/06/87 (age 44).	
5/10/69	**17**	7	1. Morning Girl	Warner 7261
			NERO, Peter	
			Born on 5/22/34 in Brooklyn. Pop-jazz-classical pianist. Won the 1961 Best New Artist Grammy Award.	
11/20/71	**21**	8	1. Theme From "Summer Of '42" [I]	Columbia 45399
			from the film of the same title	
			NERVOUS NORVUS	
			Born Jimmy Drake in 1912; died in 1968 (age 56). Prior to recording, worked as a truck driver in Oakland, California.	
6/09/56	**8**	9	**1. Transfusion** **[N]**	Dot 15470
			Best Seller #8 / Top 100 #13 / Jockey #14 / Juke Box #18	
8/11/56	**24**	4	2. Ape Call [N]	Dot 15485
			Best Seller #24 / Top 100 #28 ape calls by Red Blanchard	
			NESMITH, Michael/The First National Band	
			Born on 12/30/43 in Houston. Michael was a professional musician before joining The Monkees. Wrote Linda Ronstadt's hit "Different Drum." Formed own video production company, Pacific Arts, in 1977; produced *Elephant Parts*, *Repo Man* and others.	
9/05/70	**21**	7	1. Joanne	RCA 0368
			NEVIL, Robbie	
			Pop singer/songwriter/guitarist from Los Angeles.	
11/15/86+	**2**(2)	16	**1. C'est La Vie**	Manhattan 50047
3/14/87	**14**	9	2. Dominoes	Manhattan 50053
6/27/87	**10**	9	**3. Wot's It To Ya**	Manhattan 50075
1/07/89	**34**	3	4. Back On Holiday	EMI 50152
			NEVILLE, Aaron	
			Born on 1/24/41 in New Orleans. Member of the New Orleans R&B family group The Neville Brothers. Brother Art was keyboardist of The Meters. His son Ivan began recording career in 1988.	
12/17/66+	**2**(1)	11	**1. Tell It Like It Is**	Par-Lo 101
			LINDA RONSTADT featuring AARON NEVILLE:	
10/28/89	**2**(2)	16	**2. Don't Know Much**	Elektra 69261
2/24/90	**11**	9	3. All My Life	Elektra 64987
			NEVILLE, Ivan	
			New Orleans bassist, son of singer Aaron Neville (of The Neville Brothers). Formerly with Bonnie Raitt's band. Played on The Rolling Stones' *Dirty Work* album.	
11/12/88	**26**	6	1. Not Just Another Girl	Polydor 887814
			NEWBEATS, The	
			Pop trio: Larry Henley (b: 6/30/41, Arp, Texas; lead singer) with brothers Dean and Marc Mathis (b: Hahira, Georgia on 3/17/39 and 2/09/42, respectively).	
8/22/64	**2**(2)	11	**1. Bread And Butter**	Hickory 1269
11/07/64	**16**	7	2. Everything's Alright	Hickory 1282

DATE	POS	WKS	ARTIST—RECORD TITLE	LABEL & NO.
2/20/65	**40**	1	3. Break Away (From That Boy)	Hickory 1290
10/30/65	**12**	9	4. Run, Baby Run (Back Into My Arms)	Hickory 1332
			NEW BIRTH, The	
			R&B vocal group portion of New Birth, Inc. (see Nite-Liters). Original group consisted of vocalists Londee Loren, Bobby Downs, Melvin Wilson, Leslie Wilson, Ann Bogan and soloist Alan Frye, with instrumental backing by The Nite-Liters. Melvin, Leslie and Ann recorded as Love, Peace & Happiness in 1972. Ann was also a member of The Marvelettes and in duo, Harvey & Ann, with Harvey Fuqua.	
5/05/73	**35**	4	1. I Can Understand It	RCA 0912
8/23/75	**36**	2	2. Dream Merchant	Buddah 470
			NEWBURY, Mickey	
			Born Milton S. Newbury, Jr. on 5/19/40 in Houston. Moved to Nashville in 1963, worked as staff writer for Acuff-Rose. Wrote "Just Dropped In (To See What Condition My Condition Was In)."	
12/04/71+	**26**	7	1. An American Trilogy Dixie/Battle Hymn Of The Republic/All My Trials	Elektra 45750
			NEW CHRISTY MINSTRELS, The	
			Folk/balladeer troupe named after the Christy Minstrels (formed in 1842 by Edwin "Pop" Christy). Group founded and led by Randy Sparks — Barry McGuire, lead singer.	
7/27/63	**14**	7	1. Green, Green	Columbia 42805
11/16/63	**29**	3	2. Saturday Night	Columbia 42887
5/16/64	**17**	9	3. Today from the film *Advance to the Rear*	Columbia 43000
			NEW COLONY SIX, The	
			Soft-rock group from Chicago: Patrick McBride, Ronnie Rice, Gerry Van Kollenburg, Les Kummel, Chuck Jobes and William Herman. Ray Graffia joined in 1969.	
5/11/68	**22**	6	1. I Will Always Think About You	Mercury 72775
2/15/69	**16**	9	2. Things I'd Like To Say	Mercury 72858
			NEW EDITION	
			Boston R&B teen vocal quintet (ages 13 to 15 in 1983): Ralph Tresvant, Ronald DeVoe, Michael Bivins, Ricky Bell and Bobby Brown. Formed in 1982 by future New Kids On The Block and Perfect Gentlemen producer, Maurice Starr. Brown left for solo career in 1986; replaced by Johnny Gill in 1988. Bell, Bivins and DeVoe recorded as Bell Biv DeVoe in 1990. Tresvant and Gill recorded solo in the '90s.	
10/27/84+	**4**	14	● **1. Cool It Now**	MCA 52455
1/26/85	**12**	8	2. Mr. Telephone Man written and produced by Ray Parker, Jr.	MCA 52484
4/27/85	**35**	4	3. Lost In Love	MCA 52553
4/12/86	**38**	2	4. A Little Bit Of Love (Is All It Takes)	MCA 52768
9/20/86	**21**	6	5. Earth Angel featured in the film *The Karate Kid Part II*	MCA 52905
7/30/88	**7**	13	**6. If It Isn't Love**	MCA 53264
			NEW ENGLAND	
			East Coast melodic rock quartet: John Fannon, Jimmy Waldo, Hirsh Gardner and Gary Shea.	
6/16/79	**40**	1	1. Don't Ever Wanna Lose Ya	Infinity 50013

Madonna, the top female pop artist of the 80s, has had such an astounding string of chart successes that her "failures" may actually be more interesting. Her only such chart "failure" is the No. 16 peak position of her earliest single "Holiday"—after which would come an incomparable run in the Top 10.

Henry Mancini's memorable instrumentals of the 60s reached their singles chart peak with 1969's "Love Theme From Romeo & Juliet," a No. 1 record for two weeks. Two of his LPs—1959's *The Music of Peter Gunn* and 1961's *Breakfast at Tiffany's*—reached the same top spot on the album charts.

The Marcels' "Blue Moon" entered the Hot 100 the same week another group's version did in 1961. But while Herb Lance & The Classics' version peaked at No. 50, the Marcels went on to claim the No. 1. slot for two consecutive weeks.

Ziggy Marley & The Melody Makers were the center of much U.S. media attention when their first Virgin album, 1988's *Conscious Party* went gold. Yet few pop fans realized that young Ziggy—son of reggae legend Bob Marley—had already released several major-label albums in this country already.

Martha & The Vandellas' rich legacy of 60s smashes sadly fails to include even one No. 1. hit. The closest the group ever came was "Dancing In The Street"—which held the No. 2 position for two full weeks in 1964, but couldn't beat Manfred Mann's memorable "Do Wah Diddy Diddy."

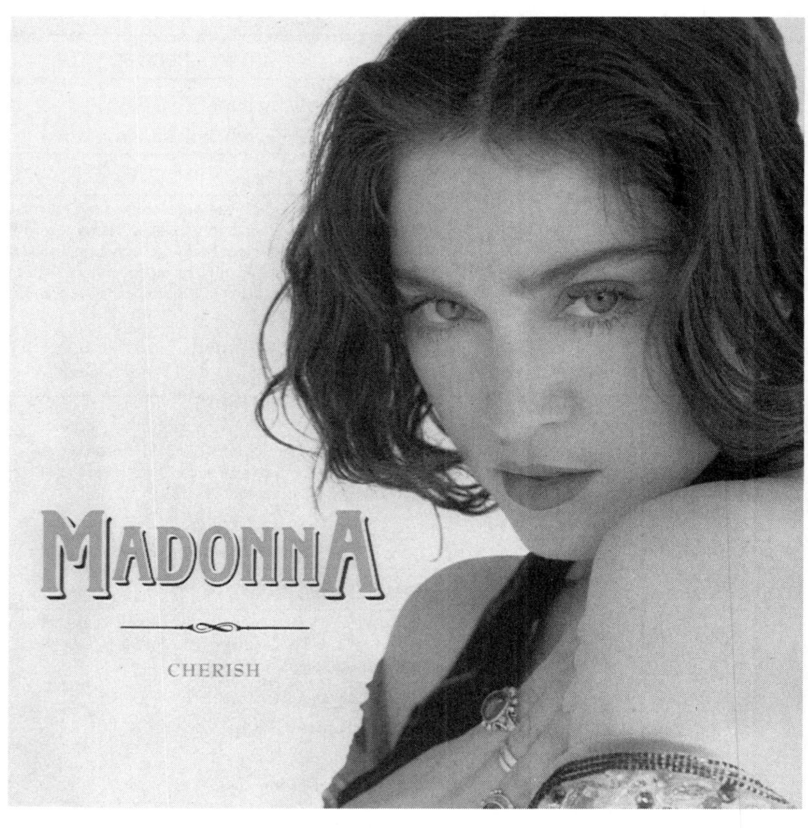

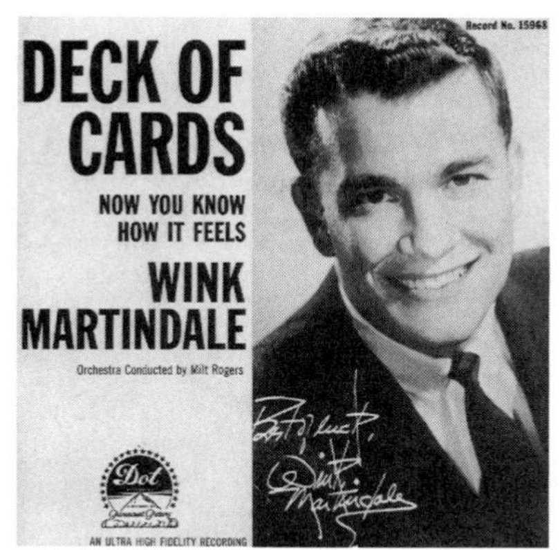

Martika's 1991 hit "Love . . . Thy Will Be Done," co-written with the ever-prolific Prince, dropped out of the Top 10 the same week Prince & The New Power Generation's "Cream" entered—and went on to become the Purple One's fifth No. 1 hit.

Wink Martindale had a top-10 hit with "Deck Of Cards" in 1959—and, by the luck of the draw, soon opted to drop his musical career to pursue a more stable life of TV-gameshow hosting.

The Marvelettes' legacy extended far beyond such top-10 hits as 1961's "Please Mr. Postman" and 1966's "Don't Mess With Bill." British rock idol Morrissey has told rock journalists that Marvelettes singer Gladys Horton is one of his all-time favorites.

Richard Marx launched his 1991 album *Rush Street* in unprecedented style: on the same day, the popular rocker played five dates in five different cities—including New York, Baltimore, Chicago, Cleveland, and Los Angeles—by hopping aboard a chartered jet between each performance.

Johnny Mathis's two No. 1 songs came 21 years apart from each other. But "Chances Are" (his 1957 hit) he wasn't critiquing his own chart performance in his duet with Deniece Williams—"Too Much, Too Little, Too Late."

Bobby McFerrin's 1988 hit from *Cocktail*, "Don't Worry, Be Happy," not only crossed over several radio formats; when various politicians began using (and misusing) its title, it virtually entered the public domain.

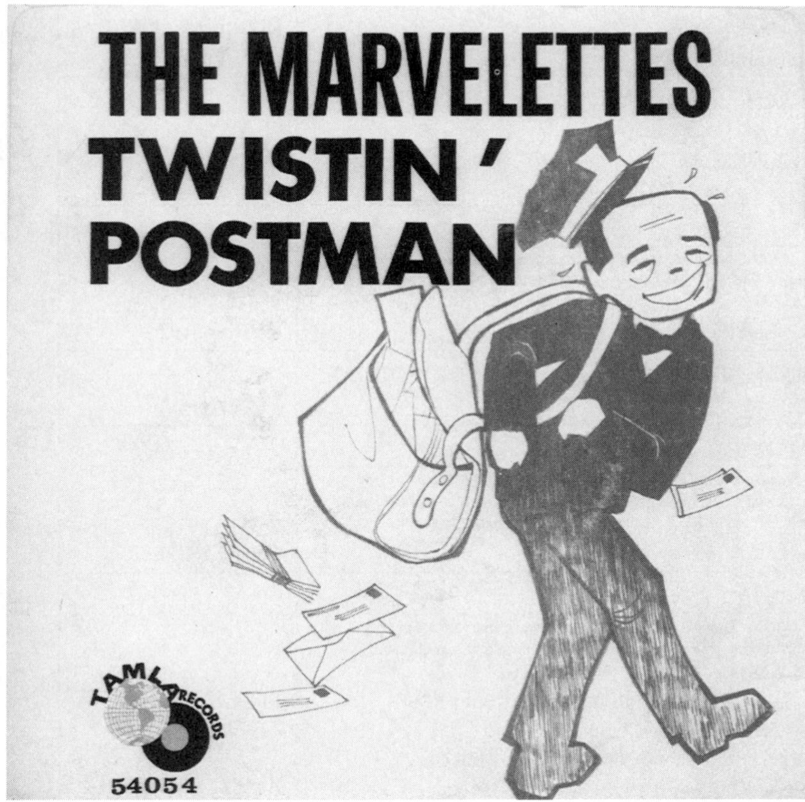

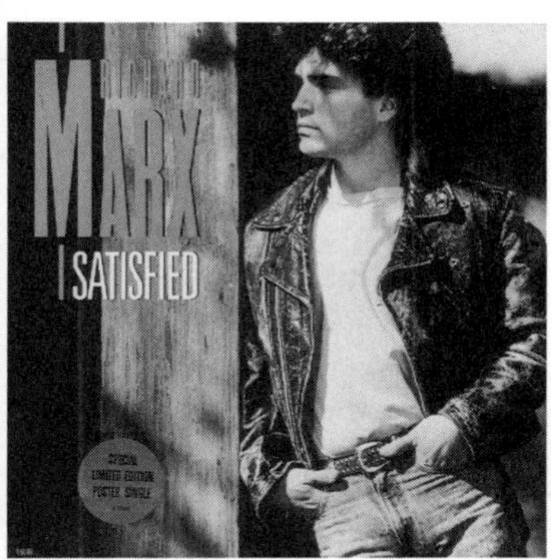

DATE	POS	WKS	ARTIST—RECORD TITLE	LABEL & NO.
			NEW KIDS ON THE BLOCK	
			Boston teen vocal quintet: Joe McIntyre (b: 12/31/72), Donny Wahlberg (b: 8/17/69), Danny Wood (b: 5/14/69), and brothers Jordan (b: 5/17/70) and Jon Knight (b: 11/29/68). Formed in the summer of 1984 by New Edition's founder/producer, Maurice Starr. Also see Tommy Page.	
8/13/88	**10**	12	**1. Please Don't Go Girl**	Columbia 07700
1/14/89	**3**	13	● **2. You Got It (The Right Stuff)**	Columbia 08092
4/22/89	**1**(1)	14	● **3. I'll Be Loving You (Forever)**	Columbia 68671
7/22/89	**1**(1)	12	▲ **4. Hangin' Tough**	Columbia 68960
9/23/89	**2**(1)	10	● **5. Cover Girl**	Columbia 69088
9/30/89	**8**	10	**6. Didn't I (Blow Your Mind)**	Columbia 68960
11/25/89+	**7**	10	● **7. This One's For The Children** [X]	Columbia 73064
5/26/90	**1**(3)	11	▲ **8. Step By Step**	Columbia 73343
8/04/90	**7**	8	**9. Tonight**	Columbia 73461
			NEWMAN, Jimmy	
			Born on 8/27/27 in Big Mamou, Louisiana. Cajun-country singer/guitarist.	
7/22/57	**23**	1	1. A Fallen Star Jockey #23 / Top 100 #42	Dot 15574
			NEWMAN, Randy	
			Born on 11/28/43 in New Orleans. Singer/composer/pianist. Nephew of composers Alfred, Emil and Lionel Newman. Scored the films *Ragtime*, *The Natural* and *Avalon*.	
12/10/77+	**2**(3)	13	● **1. Short People** [N]	Warner 8492
			NEWMAN, Thunderclap — see THUNDERCLAP NEWMAN	
			NEW ORDER	
			Techno-dance group from Manchester, England, formerly known as Joy Division. Lineup since 1986: Bernard Sumner, Stephen Morris, Peter Hook and Gillian Gilbert. In 1990, Sumner was with the group Electronic.	
12/05/87	**32**	8	1. True Faith	Qwest 28271
			NEW SEEKERS, The	
			British-Australian group formed by former Seekers' member Keith Potger after disbandment of The Seekers in 1969. Consisted of Eve Graham, Lyn Paul, Peter Doyle, Marty Kristian and Paul Layton.	
9/19/70	**14**	9	1. Look What They've Done To My Song Ma written by Melanie	Elektra 45699
12/18/71+	**7**	9	● **2. I'd Like To Teach The World To Sing (In Perfect Harmony)**	Elektra 45762
4/14/73	**29**	4	3. Pinball Wizard/See Me, Feel Me from the rock opera *Tommy*	Verve 10709
			NEWTON, Juice	
			Born Judy Kay Newton on 2/18/52 in New Jersey; raised in Virginia Beach. Performed folk music from age 13. Moved to Los Angeles with own Silver Spur band in 1974; recorded for RCA in 1975. Group disbanded in 1978. Juice is an accomplished equestrian.	
3/07/81	**4**	16	● **1. Angel Of The Morning**	Capitol 4976
6/20/81	**2**(2)	19	● **2. Queen Of Hearts**	Capitol 4997
11/07/81+	**7**	18	**3. The Sweetest Thing (I've Ever Known)**	Capitol 5046
5/22/82	**7**	13	**4. Love's Been A Little Bit Hard On Me**	Capitol 5120
9/11/82	**11**	10	5. Break It To Me Gently	Capitol 5148

DATE	POS	WKS	ARTIST—RECORD TITLE	LABEL & NO.
12/18/82+	**25**	10	6. Heart Of The Night	Capitol 5192
9/03/83	**27**	5	7. Tell Her No	Capitol 5265
			NEWTON, Wayne	
			Born on 4/03/42 in Roanoke, Virginia. Singer/multi-instrumentalist. Top Las Vegas entertainer. Began singing career with regular appearances on Jackie Gleason's TV variety show in 1962. Appeared in the 1990 film *The Adventures of Ford Fairlane.*	
8/03/63	**13**	8	1. Danke Schoen with Wayne's brother, Jerry	Capitol 4989
3/27/65	**23**	5	2. Red Roses For A Blue Lady	Capitol 5366
6/10/72	**4**	13	● **3. Daddy Don't You Walk So Fast**	Chelsea 0100
3/22/80	**35**	3	4. Years	Aries II 108
			NEWTON-JOHN, Olivia	
			Born on 9/26/48 in Cambridge, England. To Australia in 1953. At age 16, won talent contest trip to England; sang with Pat Carroll as Pat & Olivia. With the group Toomorrow, in a British film of the same name. Granddaughter of Nobel Prize-winning German physicist Max Born. In films *Grease* (1978), *Xanadu* (1980) and *Two of a Kind* (1983). Married actor Matt Lattanzi in 1984. Opened own chain of clothing boutiques (Koala Blue) in 1984.	
7/17/71	**25**	10	1. If Not For You written by Bob Dylan	Uni 55281
12/15/73+	**6**	14	● **2. Let Me Be There**	MCA 40101
5/11/74	**5**	12	● **3. If You Love Me (Let Me Know)**	MCA 40209
8/24/74	**1**(2)	10	● **4. I Honestly Love You**	MCA 40280
2/08/75	**1**(1)	11	● **5. Have You Never Been Mellow**	MCA 40349
6/21/75	**3**	12	● **6. Please Mr. Please**	MCA 40418
10/11/75	**13**	7	7. Something Better To Do	MCA 40459
1/03/76	**30**	4	8. Let It Shine	MCA 40495
4/17/76	**23**	6	9. Come On Over written by Barry and Robin Gibb	MCA 40525
9/04/76	**33**	4	10. Don't Stop Believin'	MCA 40600
2/19/77	**20**	9	11. Sam	MCA 40670
4/08/78	**1**(1)	16	▲ **12. You're The One That I Want** **JOHN TRAVOLTA AND OLIVIA NEWTON-JOHN**	RSO 891
7/22/78	**3**	15	● **13. Hopelessly Devoted To You**	RSO 903
8/19/78	**5**	12	● **14. Summer Nights** **JOHN TRAVOLTA AND OLIVIA NEWTON-JOHN** above 3 from the film *Grease*	RSO 906
12/09/78+	**3**	17	● **15. A Little More Love**	MCA 40975
5/05/79	**11**	8	16. Deeper Than The Night	MCA 41009
4/19/80	**12**	8	17. I Can't Help It **ANDY GIBB AND OLIVIA NEWTON-JOHN**	RSO 1026
6/14/80	**1**(4)	16	● **18. Magic**	MCA 41247
8/30/80	**8**	10	**19. Xanadu** **OLIVIA NEWTON-JOHN/ELECTRIC LIGHT ORCHESTRA**	MCA 41285
11/22/80+	**20**	11	20. Suddenly **OLIVIA NEWTON-JOHN AND CLIFF RICHARD** above 3 from the film *Xanadu*	MCA 51007
10/17/81	**1**(10)	21	▲ **21. Physical**	MCA 51182
2/27/82	**5**	10	● **22. Make A Move On Me**	MCA 52000
9/25/82	**3**	13	**23. Heart Attack**	MCA 52100

DATE	POS	WKS	ARTIST—RECORD TITLE	LABEL & NO.
2/19/83	**38**	3	24. Tied Up	MCA 52155
11/12/83+	**5**	14	**25. Twist Of Fate**	MCA 52284
2/25/84	**31**	5	26. Livin' In Desperate Times above 2 from the film *Two Of A Kind*	MCA 52341
10/26/85	**20**	7	27. Soul Kiss all of above (except #14, 17, 19, 25, 26) produced by John Farrar	MCA 52686
			NEW VAUDEVILLE BAND, The Creation of British composer/record producer Geoff Stephens (b: 10/01/34, London).	
11/05/66	**1**(3)	13	● **1. Winchester Cathedral**	Fontana 1562
			NEW YORK CITY New York City R&B quartet: Tim McQueen, John Brown, Ed Shell and Claude Johnston. First recorded for Buddah as Triboro Exchange. Name changed in 1972.	
4/28/73	**17**	12	1. I'm Doin' Fine Now	Chelsea 0113
			NICHOLAS, Paul Born Paul Beuselinck on 12/03/45 in Peterborough, England. British theater/film actor. Played Billy Shears' brother in the 1978 film *Sgt. Pepper's Lonely Hearts Club Band.*	
9/17/77	**6**	16	● **1. Heaven On The 7th Floor**	RSO 878
			NICKS, Stevie Born Stephanie Nicks on 5/26/48 in Phoenix; raised in California. Became vocalist of Bay-area group Fritz and subsequently met guitarist Lindsey Buckingham. Teamed up and recorded album *Buckingham-Nicks* in 1973. Vocalist with Fleetwood Mac since January 1975. Quit touring with band after 1990.	
8/01/81	**3**	15	**1. Stop Draggin' My Heart Around** **STEVIE NICKS with TOM PETTY & THE HEARTBREAKERS**	Modern 7336
11/07/81+	**6**	15	**2. Leather And Lace** **STEVIE NICKS with DON HENLEY** written for Waylon Jennings and Jessi Colter	Modern 7341
3/06/82	**11**	10	3. Edge Of Seventeen (Just Like The White Winged Dove)	Modern 7401
6/12/82	**32**	4	4. After The Glitter Fades	Modern 7405
6/18/83	**5**	14	**5. Stand Back**	Modern 99863
9/24/83	**14**	9	6. If Anyone Falls	Modern 99832
1/21/84	**33**	4	7. Nightbird **STEVIE NICKS with SANDY STEWART**	Modern 99799
11/30/85+	**4**	13	**8. Talk To Me**	Modern 99582
3/01/86	**37**	2	9. Needles And Pins **TOM PETTY AND THE HEARTBREAKERS with STEVIE NICKS**	MCA 52772
3/08/86	**16**	8	10. I Can't Wait all of above produced by Jimmy Iovine	Modern 99565
6/03/89	**16**	7	11. Rooms On Fire	Modern 99216
			NIELSEN/PEARSON Sacramento pop quartet fronted by lead vocalists/guitarists Reed Nielsen and Mark Pearson.	
11/15/80	**38**	2	1. If You Should Sail	Capitol 4910

DATE	POS	WKS	ARTIST—RECORD TITLE	LABEL & NO.
			NIGHT	
			Sextet led by female vocalist Stevie Lange and Chris Thompson, lead singer/guitarist of Manfred Mann's Earth Band.	
8/04/79	**18**	8	1. Hot Summer Nights	Planet 45903
10/20/79	**17**	8	2. If You Remember Me **CHRIS THOMPSON & NIGHT** first released on Planet 45904 in 1979 as by Chris Thompson; from the film *The Champ*	Planet 45909
			NIGHTINGALE, Maxine	
			Born on 11/02/52 in Wembly, England. First recorded in 1968. In productions of *Hair*, *Jesus Christ Superstar*, *Godspell* and *Savages* in the early '70s.	
3/13/76	**2**(2)	15	● **1. Right Back Where We Started From**	United Art. 752
7/07/79	**5**	14	● **2. Lead Me On**	Windsong 11530
			NIGHT RANGER	
			Rock group from California: lead singers Kelly Keagy (drums) and Jack Blades (bass), with guitarists Jeff Watson and Brad Gillis, and keyboardist Alan "Fitz" Gerald. Blades and Gillis were members of Rubicon. Gerald left in 1988; band split up in early 1989. Blades joined supergroup Damn Yankees.	
2/26/83	**40**	3	1. Don't Tell Me You Love Me	Boardwalk 171
4/21/84	**5**	12	**2. Sister Christian**	MCA/Camel 52350
8/04/84	**14**	11	3. When You Close Your Eyes	MCA/Camel 52420
6/08/85	**8**	11	**4. Sentimental Street**	MCA/Camel 52591
9/21/85	**19**	6	5. Four In The Morning (I Can't Take Any More)	MCA/Camel 52661
12/07/85+	**17**	10	6. Goodbye all of above (except #2) written by Jack Blades	MCA/Camel 52729
			NIKKI	
			Twenty-one-year-old American male singer/multi-instrumentalist born in Okinawa, Japan and raised in Dayton, Ohio. Backing member of the soul-funk group Sun. Jingle writer of TV commercials.	
6/09/90	**21**	6	1. Notice Me	Geffen 19946#
			NILSSON	
			Born Harry Edward Nelson, III on 6/15/41 in Brooklyn. Wrote Three Dog Night's hit "One"; scored the film *Skidoo* and TV's "The Courtship of Eddie's Father." Close friend of John Lennon and Ringo Starr.	
9/06/69	**6**	9	**1. Everybody's Talkin'** theme song from the film *Midnight Cowboy*	RCA 0161
11/29/69	**34**	2	2. I Guess The Lord Must Be In New York City	RCA 0261
5/08/71	**34**	4	3. Me And My Arrow	RCA 0443
1/15/72	**1**(4)	14	● **4. Without You** written by Badfinger's Pete Ham and Tom Evans	RCA 0604
4/08/72	**27**	6	5. Jump Into The Fire	RCA 0673
7/08/72	**8**	10	**6. Coconut**	RCA 0718
10/14/72	**23**	6	7. Spaceman	RCA 0788
5/25/74	**39**	2	8. Daybreak from the film *Son of Dracula*	RCA 0246
			1910 FRUITGUM CO.	
			New Jersey bubblegum quintet: Mark Gutkowski, Floyd Marcus, Pat Karwan, Steve Mortkowitz and Frank Jeckell. Produced by The Music Explosion and Ohio Express producers Jerry Kasenetz and Jeff Katz.	
2/10/68	**4**	11	● **1. Simon Says**	Buddah 24

DATE	POS	WKS	ARTIST—RECORD TITLE	LABEL & NO.
8/10/68	**5**	11	• **2. 1, 2, 3, Red Light**	Buddah 54
12/07/68	**37**	3	3. Goody Goody Gumdrops	Buddah 71
2/08/69	**5**	11	• **4. Indian Giver**	Buddah 91
6/14/69	**38**	2	5. Special Delivery	Buddah 114
			NITEFLYTE	
			Disco group led by Howard Johnson and Sandy Torano.	
11/24/79	**37**	2	1. If You Want It	Ariola 7747
			NITE-LITERS, The	
			R&B band formed in Louisville in 1963 by Harvey Fuqua and Tony Churchill. Expanded to 17 members with two vocal groups and band. Renamed New Birth, Inc., with The Nite-Liters making up the instrumental section. Also see New Birth.	
9/11/71	**39**	1	1. K-Jee [I]	RCA 0461
			NITTY GRITTY DIRT BAND	
			Country-folk-rock group from Long Beach, California. Led by Jeff Hanna (b: 7/11/47; vocals, guitar) and John McEuen (b: 12/19/45; banjo, mandolin). Changed name to Dirt Band in 1976 when Hanna left the group. Resumed using Nitty Gritty Dirt Band name in 1982. Various members included ex-Eagle Bernie Leadon who replaced McEuen briefly in early 1987. Revamped quartet since late 1987: Hanna, Jimmy Ibbotson, Bob Carpenter and Jimmie Fadden. In the films *For Singles Only* and *Paint Your Wagon*.	
1/02/71	**9**	13	**1. Mr. Bojangles** prologue: Uncle Charlie And His Dog Teddy	Liberty 56197
			THE DIRT BAND:	
1/12/80	**13**	11	2. An American Dream harmony vocal by Linda Ronstadt	United Art. 1330
7/12/80	**25**	9	3. Make A Little Magic backing vocal by Nicolette Larson	United Art. 1356
			NITZSCHE, Jack	
			Born Bernard Nitzsche on 4/22/37 in Chicago. Arranger/producer/composer/keyboardist. Arranger for many of Phil Spector's productions. Wrote "Needles And Pins" and scored the films *One Flew Over the Cuckoo's Nest* and *An Officer and a Gentleman*. Married to Buffy Sainte-Marie.	
9/07/63	**39**	2	1. The Lonely Surfer [I]	Reprise 20202
			NOBLE, Nick	
			Born Nicholas Valkan on 6/21/36 in Chicago. Attended Loyola University.	
8/20/55	**22**	3	1. The Bible Tells Me So Best Seller #22 / Top 100 #61 pre	Wing 90003
3/24/56	**27**	6	2. To You, My Love first released on Wing 90045 in 1955	Mercury 70821
7/15/57	**20**	1	3. A Fallen Star Jockey #20 first released on Mercury 71117 in 1957	Mercury 71124
9/30/57	**37**	1	4. Moonlight Swim	Mercury 71169
			NOBLES, Cliff, & Co.	
			Cliff was born in Mobile, Alabama in 1944. Soul bandleader/singer. Moved to Philadelphia in 1965.	
6/08/68	**2**(3)	12	• **1. The Horse** [I]	Phil-L.A. 313

DATE	POS	WKS	ARTIST—RECORD TITLE	LABEL & NO.
			NOGUEZ, Jacky	
			Popular European society bandleader from Paris.	
7/27/59	**24**	5	1. Ciao, Ciao Bambina [I]	Jamie 1127
			NOLAN, Kenny	
			Los Angeles-based singer/songwriter. Wrote "My Eyes Adored You," "Lady Marmalade" and "Get Dancin'." Fronted studio group The Eleventh Hour.	
12/11/76+	**3**	20	● **1. I Like Dreamin'**	20th Century 2287
5/07/77	**20**	11	2. Love's Grown Deep	20th Century 2331
			NORMAN, Chris — see QUATRO, Suzi	
			NORTH, Freddie	
			Black vocalist from Nashville. Worked in sales and promotion for Nashboro Records. DJ on "Night Train", WLAC-Nashville.	
11/27/71	**39**	1	1. She's All I Got	Mankind 12004
			NOVA, Aldo	
			Born Aldo Scarporuscio in Montreal. Rock singer/songwriter/guitarist/keyboardist.	
5/01/82	**23**	7	1. Fantasy	Portrait 02799
			NUGENT, Ted	
			Born on 12/13/48 in Detroit. Heavy-metal rock guitarist; leader of The Amboy Dukes. Currently a member of the supergroup Damn Yankees.	
9/10/77	**30**	6	1. Cat Scratch Fever	Epic 50425
			NUMAN, Gary	
			Synthesized techno-rock artist. Born Gary Webb on 3/08/58 in Hammersmith, England.	
3/29/80	**9**	17	**1. Cars**	Atco 7211
			NU SHOOZ	
			Portland, Oregon group centered around husband-and-wife team of guitarist/songwriter John Smith and lead singer Valerie Day.	
4/05/86	**3**	15	**1. I Can't Wait**	Atlantic 89446
9/06/86	**28**	8	2. Point Of No Return	Atlantic 89392
			NU TORNADOS, The	
			Philadelphia string band: Eddie Dono (leader), Phil Dale, Tom Dell, Mike Perna and Louie Mann.	
12/15/58	**26**	6	1. Philadelphia U.S.A.	Carlton 492
			NUTTY SQUIRRELS, The	
			Creators and voices: Don Elliot (from Sommerville, New Jersey) and Sascha Burland (from New York City).	
11/30/59	**14**	7	1. Uh! Oh! Part 2 [N]	Hanover 4540
			NYLONS, The	
			Canadian a cappella quartet formed in 1979: Marc Connors, Paul Cooper, Claude Morrison and Arnold Robinson. Connors died on 3/25/91 (age 41).	
6/13/87	**12**	10	1. Kiss Him Goodbye	Open Air 0022

DATE	POS	WKS	ARTIST—RECORD TITLE	LABEL & NO.
			O	
			OAK	
			Northeastern pop group — Rick Pinette, lead singer.	
7/12/80	**36**	3	1. King Of The Hill RICK PINETTE AND OAK	Mercury 76049
			OAK RIDGE BOYS	
			Country-pop vocal group formed as a gospel quartet in 1940 in Oak Ridge, Tennessee. Disbanded after World War II; re-formed in 1957. Many personnel changes. Lineup since early 1970s: Duane Allen (lead), Joe Bonsall (tenor), Richard Sterban (bass) and Bill Golden (baritone; left for a solo career in 1987, replaced by the group's guitarist, Steve Sanders).	
6/06/81	**5**	14	▲ **1. Elvira**	MCA 51084
2/13/82	**12**	9	2. Bobbie Sue	MCA 51231
			O'BANION, John	
			Pop singer from Kokomo, Indiana.	
4/18/81	**24**	7	1. Love You Like I Never Loved Before	Elektra 47125
			OCASEK, Ric	
			Born Richard Otcasek in Baltimore. Lead singer/guitarist/songwriter of The Cars. Appeared in the 1987 film *Made in Heaven.* Married supermodel/ actress Paulina Porizkova in 1989. His son Christopher Otcasek is leader of Glamour Camp.	
10/11/86	**15**	8	1. Emotion In Motion	Geffen 28617
			OCEAN	
			Canadian pop quintet: Janice Morgan (vocals), David Tamblyn, Greg Brown, Jeff Jones and Charles Slater.	
3/27/71	**2**(1)	12	● **1. Put Your Hand In The Hand**	Kama Sutra 519
			OCEAN, Billy	
			Born Leslie Sebastian Charles on 1/21/50 in Trinidad. Raised in England, worked as a tailor. Did session work in London. Moved to the U.S. in the late '70s.	
5/01/76	**22**	6	1. Love Really Hurts Without You	Ariola 7621
9/08/84	**1**(2)	15	● **2. Caribbean Queen (No More Love On The Run)**	Jive 9199
12/08/84+	**2**(1)	15	**3. Loverboy**	Jive 9284
4/13/85	**4**	13	**4. Suddenly**	Jive 9323
7/27/85	**24**	8	5. Mystery Lady	Jive 9374
12/21/85+	**2**(1)	14	**6. When The Going Gets Tough, The Tough Get Going** from the film *The Jewel of the Nile*	Jive 9432
5/03/86	**1**(1)	14	**7. There'll Be Sad Songs (To Make You Cry)**	Jive 9465
8/09/86	**10**	11	**8. Love Zone**	Jive 9510
11/15/86	**16**	11	9. Love Is Forever	Jive 9540
2/20/88	**1**(2)	14	**10. Get Outta My Dreams, Get Into My Car**	Jive 9678
6/25/88	**17**	8	11. The Colour Of Love	Jive 9707
11/11/89	**32**	2	12. Licence To Chill	Jive 1283

DATE	POS	WKS	ARTIST—RECORD TITLE	LABEL & NO.
			O'CONNOR, Sinead	
			Pronounced: shin-NAYD. Female singer/songwriter born (1967) and raised in Dublin, Ireland.	
3/24/90	**1**(4)	15	▲ **1. Nothing Compares 2 U**	Ensign 23488
			written by Prince; first recorded by Minneapolis group The Family	
			O'DAY, Alan	
			Born on 10/03/40 in Hollywood. Singer/songwriter/pianist. Wrote Helen Reddy's #1 hit "Angie Baby" and the Righteous Brothers' "Rock And Roll Heaven."	
5/07/77	**1**(1)	17	● **1. Undercover Angel**	Pacific 001
			O'DELL, Kenny	
			Born Kenneth Gist, Jr. in Oklahoma (early 1940s). Singer/songwriter/guitarist. Worked with Duane Eddy and own band, Guys And Dolls. Moved to Nashville in 1969. Wrote Charlie Rich's "Behind Closed Doors."	
12/16/67	**38**	2	1. Beautiful People	Vegas 718
			ODYSSEY	
			New York soul-disco trio: Manila-born Tony Reynolds, and sisters Lillian and Louise Lopez, originally from the Virgin Islands.	
12/17/77+	**21**	12	1. Native New Yorker	RCA 11129
			OHIO EXPRESS	
			Bubblegum group from Mansfield, Ohio. Produced by Jerry Kasenetz and Jeff Katz (worked with The Music Explosion and 1910 Fruitgum Co.). Joey Levine (later with Reunion) was lead singer on most of the hits.	
11/18/67	**29**	5	1. Beg, Borrow And Steal	Cameo 483
			originally released as by The Rare Breed on Attack 1401 in 1966	
5/18/68	**4**	11	● **2. Yummy Yummy Yummy**	Buddah 38
8/31/68	**33**	5	3. Down At Lulu's	Buddah 56
11/02/68	**15**	10	● 4. Chewy Chewy	Buddah 70
4/26/69	**30**	4	5. Mercy	Buddah 102
			above 4 sung and written by Joey Levine	
			OHIO PLAYERS	
			Originally an R&B instrumental group called the Ohio Untouchables, formed in Dayton in 1959. Backup on The Falcons' records. First recorded for Lupine in 1962. Members during prime (1974-79): Marshall Jones, Clarence "Satch" Satchell, Jimmy "Diamond" Williams, Marvin "Merv" Pierce, Billy Beck, Ralph "Pee Wee" Middlebrook and Leroy "Sugarfoot" Bonner.	
4/14/73	**15**	9	● 1. Funky Worm [N]	Westbound 214
9/22/73	**31**	6	2. Ecstasy	Westbound 216
9/14/74	**13**	7	● 3. Skin Tight	Mercury 73609
12/28/74+	**1**(1)	12	● **4. Fire**	Mercury 73643
10/11/75	**33**	3	5. Sweet Sticky Thing	Mercury 73713
11/22/75+	**1**(1)	14	● **6. Love Rollercoaster**	Mercury 73734
3/27/76	**30**	5	7. Fopp	Mercury 73775
7/31/76	**18**	10	8. Who'd She Coo?	Mercury 73814

DATE	POS	WKS	ARTIST—RECORD TITLE	LABEL & NO.
			O'JAYS, The	
			R&B group from Canton, Ohio formed in 1958 as the Triumphs. Consisted of Eddie Levert, Walter Williams, William Powell, Bobby Massey and Bill Isles. Recorded as the Mascots for the King label in 1961. Renamed by Cleveland DJ, Eddie O'Jay. Isles left in 1965. Massey left to become a record producer in 1971; Levert, Williams and Powell continued as a trio. Powell retired from touring due to illness in late 1975 (d: 5/26/77); replaced by Sammy Strain, formerly with Little Anthony & The Imperials. Levert's sons Gerald and Sean, are members of the trio Levert.	
8/12/72	**3**	12	● **1. Back Stabbers**	Phil. Int. 3517
1/27/73	**1**(1)	13	● **2. Love Train**	Phil. Int. 3524
6/30/73	**33**	2	3. Time To Get Down	Phil. Int. 3531
1/12/74	**10**	11	**4. Put Your Hands Together**	Phil. Int. 3535
5/04/74	**9**	10	● **5. For The Love Of Money**	Phil. Int. 3544
11/15/75+	**5**	14	● **6. I Love Music (Part 1)**	Phil. Int. 3577
3/27/76	**20**	6	7. Livin' For The Weekend	Phil. Int. 3587
6/03/78	**4**	11	● **8. Use Ta Be My Girl**	Phil. Int. 3642
1/05/80	**28**	5	9. Forever Mine	Phil. Int. 3727
			all of above written & produced by Kenneth Gamble and Leon Huff	
			O'KAYSIONS, The	
			R&B sextet from Wilson, North Carolina: Donny Weaver (lead singer), Ron Turner, Jim Spidel, Wayne Pittman, Jimmy Hennant and Bruce Joyner. Originally called The Kays.	
9/07/68	**5**	11	● **1. Girl Watcher**	ABC 11094
			first released on North State 1001 in 1968	
			O'KEEFE, Danny	
			Singer/songwriter born in Spokane, Washington.	
9/23/72	**9**	10	**1. Good Time Charlie's Got The Blues**	Signpost 70006
			OLDFIELD, Mike	
			Born on 5/15/53 in Reading, England. Classical rock multi-instrumentalist/composer.	
3/30/74	**7**	10	**1. Tubular Bells** [I]	Virgin 55100
			theme from the film *The Exorcist*	
			OLIVER	
			Born William Oliver Swofford on 2/22/45 in North Wilkesboro, North Carolina.	
6/07/69	**3**	11	**1. Good Morning Starshine**	Jubilee 5659
			from the Broadway musical *Hair*	
8/30/69	**2**(2)	12	● **2. Jean**	Crewe 334
			from the film *The Prime of Miss Jean Brodie*	
12/20/69	**35**	2	3. Sunday Mornin'	Crewe 337
			above 3 produced by Bob Crewe	
			OLLIE & JERRY	
			Duo of Ollie Brown and Jerry Knight (former member of Raydio).	
6/16/84	**9**	11	**1. Breakin' . . . There's No Stopping Us**	Polydor 821708
			from the film *Breakin'*	
			OLSSON, Nigel	
			Drummer for Elton John's band from 1971-76.	
1/27/79	**18**	9	1. Dancin' Shoes	Bang 740
5/19/79	**34**	4	2. Little Bit Of Soap	Bang 4800

DATE	POS	WKS	ARTIST—RECORD TITLE	LABEL & NO.
			OLYMPICS, The	
			R&B group formed at Centennial High School in Compton, California in 1954 as the Challengers. Consisted of Walter Ward (lead), Eddie Lewis (tenor), Charles Fizer (baritone) and Walter Hammond (baritone). Melvin King replaced Fizer in 1958, remained in group as replacement for Hammond when Fizer returned in 1959. Fizer was was killed in Watts rioting.	
8/04/58	**8**	11	**1. Western Movies** Hot 100 #8 / Best Seller #11	Demon 1508
6/08/63	**40**	2	2. The Bounce	Tri Disc 106
			O'NEAL, Alexander	
			Minneapolis-based black vocalist. Born on 11/15/53 in Natchez, Mississippi. Own band, Alexander, in late 1970s. Lead singer of Flyte Tyme which included Jimmy "Jam" Harris, Terry Lewis and Monte Moir and later evolved into The Time. Went solo in 1980. Co-producer of Janet Jackson's hit "Control."	
3/29/86	**26**	6	1. Saturday Love **CHERRELLE with ALEXANDER O'NEAL**	Tabu 05767
9/05/87	**25**	6	2. Fake	Tabu 07100
3/05/88	**28**	6	3. Never Knew Love Like This **CHERRELLE with ALEXANDER O'NEAL**	Tabu 07646
			100 PROOF AGED IN SOUL	
			Soul group from Detroit: Clyde Wilson ("Steve Mancha"; lead), Joe Stubbs and Eddie Anderson ("Eddie Holiday"). Stubbs, brother of Levi Stubbs of the Four Tops, had been in the Contours and The Falcons.	
10/03/70	**8**	10	● **1. Somebody's Been Sleeping**	Hot Wax 7004
			ONE 2 MANY	
			Norwegian trio: keyboardist Dag Kolsrud, guitarist Jan Gisle Ytterdal and female vocalist Camilla Griehsel. Kolsrud was a-ha's world tour musical director.	
5/06/89	**37**	4	1. Downtown	A&M 1272
			OPUS	
			Pop-rock quintet from Austria led by vocalist Herwig Rudisser.	
3/15/86	**32**	5	1. Live Is Life	Polydor 883730
			ORBISON, Roy	
			Born on 4/23/36 in Vernon, Texas. Had own band, the Wink Westerners in 1952. Attended North Texas University with Pat Boone. First recorded for Je-Wel in early 1956 as leader of The Teen Kings. Toured with Sun Records shows to 1958. Toured with The Beatles in 1963. Wife Claudette killed in a motorcycle accident on 6/07/66; two sons died in a fire in 1968. Resurgence in career beginning in 1985. Inducted into the Rock and Roll Hall of Fame in 1987. Member of the supergroup Traveling Wilburys in 1988. Died of a heart attack on 12/06/88 in Madison, Tennessee.	
6/20/60	**2**(1)	15	**1. Only The Lonely (Know How I Feel)**	Monument 421
10/17/60	**9**	8	**2. Blue Angel**	Monument 425
12/31/60+	**27**	3	3. I'm Hurtin'	Monument 433
4/24/61	**1**(1)	15	**4. Running Scared**	Monument 438
8/28/61	**2**(1)	14	**5. Crying/**	
10/09/61	**25**	5	6. Candy Man	Monument 447
3/03/62	**4**	9	**7. Dream Baby (How Long Must I Dream)**	Monument 456
6/23/62	**26**	6	8. The Crowd	Monument 461
10/27/62	**25**	5	9. Leah/	
10/27/62	**33**	4	10. Workin' For The Man	Monument 467

DATE	POS	WKS	ARTIST—RECORD TITLE	LABEL & NO.
			all of above with Bob Moore's Orchestra & Chorus	
2/23/63	**7**	10	**11. In Dreams**	Monument 806
			new version featured in the 1986 film *Blue Velvet*	
6/22/63	**22**	5	12. Falling	Monument 815
9/28/63	**5**	10	**13. Mean Woman Blues/**	
10/12/63	**29**	5	14. Blue Bayou	Monument 824
12/21/63+	**15**	5	15. Pretty Paper [X]	Monument 830
			written by Willie Nelson	
4/25/64	**9**	9	**16. It's Over**	Monument 837
9/05/64	**1**(3)	14	• **17. Oh, Pretty Woman**	Monument 851
			ROY ORBISON AND THE CANDY MEN	
2/20/65	**21**	6	18. Goodnight	Monument 873
8/07/65	**39**	2	19. (Say) You're My Girl	Monument 891
9/18/65	**25**	5	20. Ride Away	MGM 13386
2/12/66	**31**	4	21. Breakin' Up Is Breakin' My Heart	MGM 13446
5/21/66	**39**	2	22. Twinkle Toes	MGM 13498
2/18/89	**9**	11	**23. You Got It**	Virgin 99245
			written by Roy Orbison, Jeff Lynne and Tom Petty	
			ORCHESTRAL MANOEUVRES IN THE DARK	
			English electro-pop quartet: keyboardists/vocalists Paul Humphreys and Andrew McCluskey with drummer Malcolm Holmes and multi-instrumentalist Martin Cooper. Humphreys left band in 1991.	
10/12/85	**26**	7	1. So In Love	A&M 2746
4/05/86	**4**	13	**2. If You Leave**	A&M 2811
			from the film *Pretty in Pink*	
11/01/86	**19**	7	3. (Forever) Live And Die	A&M 2872
4/16/88	**16**	9	4. Dreaming	A&M 3002
			ORIGINAL CASTE, The	
			Canadian quintet — Dixie Lee Innes, lead singer.	
2/07/70	**34**	2	1. One Tin Soldier	T-A 186
			from the film *Billy Jack*	
			ORIGINALS, The	
			Soul group formed in Detroit in 1966. Consisted of Freddie Gorman (bass), Crathman Spencer and Henry Dixon (tenors) and Walter Gaines (baritone). Spencer replaced by Ty Hunter in 1971.	
10/18/69	**14**	13	1. Baby, I'm For Real	Soul 35066
3/07/70	**12**	9	2. The Bells	Soul 35069
			above 2 written and produced by Marvin Gaye	
			ORLANDO, Tony	
			Born Michael Anthony Orlando Cassavitis on 4/03/44 in New York City of Greek/Puerto Rican parents. Discovered by producer Don Kirshner. Lead singer of Dawn, 1970-77. Hosted weekly TV variety show "Tony Orlando & Dawn," 1974-76. Also see Wind.	
5/29/61	**39**	2	1. Halfway To Paradise	Epic 9441
9/04/61	**15**	7	2. Bless You	Epic 9452
			ORLEANS	
			Rock group founded in New York City by John Hall with the Hoppen brothers (Lawrence and Lance), Wells Kelly and Jerry Marotta. Hall and Marotta left in 1977, replaced by Bob Leinbach and R.A. Martin.	
8/30/75	**6**	11	**1. Dance With Me**	Asylum 45261

DATE	POS	WKS	ARTIST—RECORD TITLE	LABEL & NO.
8/14/76	**5**	12	**2. Still The One**	Asylum 45336
4/07/79	**11**	9	3. Love Takes Time	Infinity 50006
			ORLONS, The	
			R&B group from Philadelphia. Consisted of lead Rosetta Hightower (b: 6/23/44), Marlena Davis (b: 10/04/44), Steve Caldwell (b: 11/22/42) and Shirley Brickley (b: 12/09/44; d: 10/13/77 [gunshot]). Davis and Caldwell left in 1964 and were replaced by Audrey Brickley. Disbanded in 1968.	
6/23/62	**2**(2)	11	**1. The Wah Watusi**	Cameo 218
11/03/62	**4**	11	**2. Don't Hang Up**	Cameo 231
3/02/63	**3**	10	**3. South Street**	Cameo 243
7/06/63	**12**	7	4. Not Me	Cameo 257
10/19/63	**19**	5	5. Cross Fire!	Cameo 273
			ORR, Benjamin	
			Born Benjamin Orzechowski in Cleveland. Bassist/vocalist of The Cars.	
1/17/87	**24**	6	1. Stay The Night	Elektra 69506
			ORRALL, Robert Ellis, with CARLENE CARTER	
			Robert is a Boston-born singer/songwriter/pianist. Carlene (b: 9/26/55) is the daughter of country singers June Carter Cash and Carl Smith. Married Nick Lowe on 8/18/79.	
5/07/83	**32**	3	1. I Couldn't Say No	RCA 13431
			OSBORNE, Jeffrey	
			Born on 3/09/48 in Providence, Rhode Island. Soul singer/songwriter/drummer. Lead singer of L.T.D. until 1980.	
8/14/82	**39**	2	1. I Really Don't Need No Light	A&M 2410
11/20/82	**29**	7	2. On The Wings Of Love	A&M 2434
8/20/83	**25**	6	3. Don't You Get So Mad	A&M 2561
12/17/83+	**30**	8	4. Stay With Me Tonight	A&M 2591
10/06/84	**40**	2	5. The Last Time I Made Love **JOYCE KENNEDY & JEFFREY OSBORNE**	A&M 2656
3/02/85	**38**	2	6. The Borderlines all of above (except #5) produced by George Duke	A&M 2695
6/28/86	**13**	11	7. You Should Be Mine (The Woo Woo Song)	A&M 2814
7/25/87	**12**	9	8. Love Power **DIONNE WARWICK & JEFFREY OSBORNE**	Arista 9567
			OSBOURNE, Ozzy	
			Born John Osbourne on 12/03/48 in Birmingham, England. Heavy-metal artist; former lead singer of Black Sabbath. Appeared in the 1986 film *Trick or Treat.*	
4/22/89	**8**	12	● **1. Close My Eyes Forever** **LITA FORD with OZZY OSBOURNE**	RCA 8899
			OSMOND, Donny	
			Born on 12/09/57 in Ogden, Utah. Seventh son of George and Olive Osmond, Donny became a member of The Osmonds in 1963. Owner of production company Night Star. Burst back on to pop charts in March 1989.	
5/01/71	**7**	11	● **1. Sweet And Innocent** recorded in 1958 by Roy Orbison on RCA 7381	MGM 14227
8/21/71	**1**(3)	13	● **2. Go Away Little Girl**	MGM 14285
12/04/71+	**9**	9	● **3. Hey Girl**	MGM 14322
3/04/72	**3**	10	● **4. Puppy Love**	MGM 14367

DATE	POS	WKS	ARTIST—RECORD TITLE	LABEL & NO.
6/17/72	**13**	8	5. Too Young	MGM 14407
9/16/72	**13**	9	6. Why/	
		9	7. Lonely Boy	MGM 14424
3/24/73	**8**	9	• **8. The Twelfth Of Never**	MGM 14503
8/04/73	**23**	7	9. A Million To One/	
8/04/73	**25**	7	10. Young Love	MGM 14583
12/15/73+	**14**	8	11. Are You Lonesome Tonight above 8 produced by Mike Curb & Don Costa	MGM 14677
7/24/76	**38**	3	12. C'mon Marianne	Polydor 14320
4/15/89	**2**(1)	11	**13. Soldier Of Love**	Capitol 44369
7/15/89	**13**	9	14. Sacred Emotion	Capitol 44379
11/03/90	**21**	9	15. My Love Is A Fire	Capitol 44634#
			OSMOND, Donny And Marie	
			Brother and sister co-hosts of own musical/variety TV series from 1976-78. Starred in the film *Goin' Cocoanuts* (1978).	
7/27/74	**4**	10	• **1. I'm Leaving It (All) Up To You**	MGM 14735
12/14/74+	**8**	10	**2. Morning Side Of The Mountain**	MGM 14765
1/24/76	**14**	13	3. Deep Purple	MGM 14840
12/25/76+	**21**	8	4. Ain't Nothing Like The Real Thing	Polydor 14363
1/07/78	**38**	3	5. (You're My) Soul And Inspiration	Polydor 14439
11/18/78	**38**	2	6. On The Shelf	Polydor 14510
			OSMOND, Little Jimmy	
			Born on 4/16/63 in Canoga Park, California. Youngest member of the Osmond family.	
6/03/72	**38**	3	1. Long Haired Lover From Liverpool with The Mike Curb Congregation	MGM 14376
			OSMOND, Marie	
			Born Olive Marie Osmond on 10/13/59 in Ogden, Utah. Began performing in concert with her brothers at age 14. Co-hosted the TV series "Ripley's Believe It or Not" from 1985-86. Emerged as a top country artist in the '80s.	
10/06/73	**5**	12	• **1. Paper Roses**	MGM 14609
4/05/75	**40**	2	2. Who's Sorry Now above 2 produced by Sonny James	MGM 14786
6/04/77	**39**	1	3. This Is The Way That I Feel	Polydor 14385
			OSMONDS, The	
			Family group from Ogden, Utah. Alan (b: 6/22/49), Wayne (b: 8/28/51), Merrill (b: 4/30/53), Jay (b: 3/02/55) and Donny (b: 12/09/57). Began as a quartet in 1959, singing religious and barbershop- quartet songs. Regulars on Andy Williams' TV show from 1962-67. Alan, Wayne, Merrill and Jay turned to country music as The Osmond Brothers in the early '80s.	
1/23/71	**1**(5)	12	• **1. One Bad Apple**	MGM 14193
5/29/71	**14**	7	2. Double Lovin'	MGM 14259
9/18/71	**3**	12	• **3. Yo-Yo**	MGM 14295
1/29/72	**4**	12	• **4. Down By The Lazy River**	MGM 14324
7/08/72	**14**	7	5. Hold Her Tight	MGM 14405
11/11/72	**14**	8	6. Crazy Horses	MGM 14450
7/07/73	**36**	2	7. Goin' Home	MGM 14562
10/06/73	**36**	3	8. Let Me In	MGM 14617
9/21/74	**10**	7	**9. Love Me For A Reason**	MGM 14746

DATE	POS	WKS	ARTIST—RECORD TITLE	LABEL & NO.
8/23/75	**22**	6	10. The Proud One	MGM 14791
			O'SULLIVAN, Gilbert	
			Born Raymond O'Sullivan on 12/01/46 in Waterford, Ireland.	
7/01/72	**1**(6)	15	● **1. Alone Again (Naturally)**	MAM 3619
11/11/72	**2**(2)	14	● **2. Clair**	MAM 3626
4/07/73	**17**	8	3. Out Of The Question	MAM 3628
7/14/73	**7**	11	● **4. Get Down**	MAM 3629
11/10/73	**25**	4	5. Ooh Baby	MAM 3633
			all of above written by O'Sullivan and produced by Gordon Mills	
			OTHER ONES, The	
			Rock sextet consisting of Australian siblings Jayney (lead vocals), Alf and Johnny Klimek, and Germans Andreas Schwarz-Ruszczynski, Stephan Gottwald and, singularly named, Hoffman.	
10/10/87	**29**	4	1. Holiday	Virgin 99428
			OTIS, Johnny, Show	
			Born John Veliotes of Greek parentage on 12/08/21 in Vallejo, California. R&B bandleader/composer. Johnny's R&B Caravan featured the top R&B artists of the 50s.	
6/30/58	**9**	15	**1. Willie And The Hand Jive**	Capitol 3966
			Hot 100 #9 / Best Seller #14 / Jockey #17	
			OTIS & CARLA — see REDDING, Otis, and/or THOMAS, Carla	
			OUTFIELD, The	
			British pop-rock trio: Tony Lewis (lead singer; bass), John Spinks (guitar, keyboards, vocals) and Alan Jackman (drums). Jackman left by 1990; Lewis and Spinks continued as a duo.	
3/22/86	**6**	12	**1. Your Love**	Columbia 05796
7/12/86	**19**	7	2. All The Love In The World	Columbia 05894
7/25/87	**31**	5	3. Since You've Been Gone	Columbia 07170
4/29/89	**25**	6	4. Voices Of Babylon	Columbia 68601
12/01/90+	**21**	9	5. For You	MCA 53935#
			OUTLAWS	
			Southern-rock band formed in Tampa in 1974. Consisted of guitarists Hughie Thomasson, Billy Jones and Henry Paul, with drummer Monte Yoho and bassist Frank O'Keefe (replaced by Harvey Arnold in 1977). Paul, Yoho and Arnold left by 1980.	
10/11/75	**34**	3	1. There Goes Another Love Song	Arista 0150
2/14/81	**31**	4	2. (Ghost) Riders In The Sky	Arista 0582
			#1 hit for 12 weeks by Vaughn Monroe in 1949	
			OUTSIDERS, The	
			Cleveland rock quintet: Sonny Geraci (lead singer), Tom King (guitar), Bill Bruno (lead guitar), Mert Madsen (bass) and Rick Baker (drums). Geraci later led band Climax.	
3/26/66	**5**	10	**1. Time Won't Let Me**	Capitol 5573
6/04/66	**21**	5	2. Girl In Love	Capitol 5646
8/20/66	**15**	6	3. Respectable	Capitol 5701
			written by the Isley Brothers	
12/10/66	**37**	2	4. Help Me Girl	Capitol 5759

DATE	POS	WKS	ARTIST—RECORD TITLE	LABEL & NO.
			OWEN, Reg	
			British bandleader born in February 1928.	
12/22/58+	**10**	13	**1. Manhattan Spiritual** [I]	Palette 5005
			OWENS, Buck	
			Born Alvis Edgar Owens on 8/12/29 in Sherman, Texas. Country singer/guitarist/songwriter. Has charted over 20 #1 country hits. Co-host of TV's "Hee Haw," 1969-86. Backing group: The Buckaroos.	
2/13/65	**25**	5	1. I've Got A Tiger By The Tail	Capitol 5336
			OWENS, Donnie	
			Pop-country singer born on 10/30/38.	
11/03/58	**25**	8	1. Need You backing vocals by The Ben Denton Singers	Guyden 2001
			OXO	
			West Coast pop-rock quartet led by former Foxy member Ish "Angel" Ledesma.	
4/02/83	**28**	6	1. Whirly Girl	Geffen 29765
			OZARK MOUNTAIN DAREDEVILS	
			Country-rock group from Springfield, Missouri. Nucleus: Larry Lee (keyboards, guitar), Steve Cash (harp), John Dillon (guitar) and Michael Granda (bass).	
6/08/74	**25**	5	1. If You Wanna Get To Heaven	A&M 1515
3/22/75	**3**	12	**2. Jackie Blue**	A&M 1654
			P	
			PABLO CRUISE	
			San Francisco pop-rock quartet formed in 1973: Dave Jenkins (vocals, guitar), Bud Cockrell (member of It's A Beautiful Day; vocals, bass), Cory Lerios (keyboards) and Stephen Price (drums). Cockrell replaced by Bruce Day in 1977. John Pierce replaced Day, and guitarist Angelo Rossi joined in 1980.	
6/11/77	**6**	14	**1. Whatcha Gonna Do?**	A&M 1920
7/01/78	**6**	12	**2. Love Will Find A Way**	A&M 2048
10/21/78	**21**	8	3. Don't Want To Live Without It	A&M 2076
11/10/79	**19**	10	4. I Want You Tonight	A&M 2195
7/25/81	**13**	11	5. Cool Love	A&M 2349
			PACIFIC GAS & ELECTRIC	
			West Coast blues-rock quintet — Charles Allen, lead singer (died on 5/07/90 [age 48] in Los Angeles).	
6/20/70	**14**	9	1. Are You Ready? backing vocals by The Blackberries	Columbia 45158

DATE	POS	WKS	ARTIST—RECORD TITLE	LABEL & NO.
			PAGE, Patti	
			Born Clara Ann Fowler on 11/08/27 in Muskogee, Oklahoma. One of 11 children. Raised in Tulsa. On radio KTUL with Al Klauser & His Oklahomans, as "Ann Fowler," late 1940s. Another singer was billed as "Patti Page" for the Page Milk Company show on KTUL. When she left, Fowler took her place and name. With the Jimmy Joy band in 1947. On "Breakfast Club," Chicago radio in 1947; signed by Mercury Records. Used multi-voice effect on records from 1947. Own TV series "The Patti Page Show," 1955-58 and "The Big Record," 1957-58. In the 1960 film *Elmer Gantry*.	
12/18/54+	**8**	7	**1. Let Me Go, Lover!** Jockey #8 / Juke Box #12 / Best Seller #24	Mercury 70511
11/12/55	**16**	8	2. Croce Di Oro (Cross Of Gold) Top 100 #16 / Juke Box #16 / Jockey #17 / Best Seller #20	Mercury 70713
1/14/56	**11**	8	3. Go On With The Wedding Top 100 #11 / Juke Box #12 / Jockey #16 / Best Seller #17 all of above with Jack Rael and His Orchestra	Mercury 70766
6/16/56	**2**(2)	22	**4. Allegheny Moon** Top 100 #2 / Jockey #2 / Juke Box #2 / Best Seller #5	Mercury 70878
11/03/56	**11**	12	5. Mama From The Train Top 100 #11 / Jockey #12 / Juke Box #12 / Best Seller #17	Mercury 70971
3/23/57	**14**	6	6. A Poor Man's Roses (Or A Rich Man's Gold) Jockey #14 / Top 100 #27	Mercury 71059
6/03/57	**3**	17	**7. Old Cape Cod/** Jockey #3 / Top 100 #7 / Best Seller #8	
6/03/57	**12**	5	8. Wondering Jockey #12 / Top 100 #35	Mercury 71101
11/11/57	**23**	3	9. I'll Remember Today Jockey #23 / Best Seller #31 / Top 100 #32	Mercury 71189
2/10/58	**13**	8	10. Belonging To Someone Jockey #13 / Best Seller #32 / Top 100 #34	Mercury 71247
5/05/58	**20**	1	11. Another Time, Another Place Jockey #20 / Top 100 #81 from the film of the same title	Mercury 71294
6/30/58	**9**	10	**12. Left Right Out Of Your Heart (Hi Lee Hi Lo Hi Lup Up Up)** Jockey #9 / Hot 100 #13 / Best Seller #14	Mercury 71331
10/20/58	**39**	1	13. Fibbin' orchestra conducted by Vic Schoen on above 10	Mercury 71355
7/04/60	**31**	5	14. One Of Us (Will Weep Tonight)	Mercury 71639
5/12/62	**27**	4	15. Most People Get Married	Mercury 71950
5/22/65	**8**	9	**16. Hush, Hush, Sweet Charlotte** from the film of the same title	Columbia 43251
			PAGE, Tommy	
			Born on 5/24/69 in West Caldwell, New Jersey.	
4/15/89	**29**	6	1. A Shoulder To Cry On	Sire 27645
2/24/90	**1**(1)	13	● **2. I'll Be Your Everything** backing vocals by 3 members of New Kids On The Block	Sire 19959
			PAIGE, Kevin	
			White soul-pop singer from Memphis.	
10/14/89	**18**	10	1. Don't Shut Me Out	Chrysalis 23389
2/24/90	**29**	5	2. Anything I Want	Chrysalis 23444#

DATE	POS	WKS	ARTIST—RECORD TITLE	LABEL & NO.
			PALMER, Robert	
			Born Alan Palmer on 1/19/49 in Batley, England and raised on the Mediterranean island of Malta. Formed first band, Mandrake Paddle Steamer, in 1969. Lead singer of short-lived supergroup The Power Station.	
5/06/78	**16**	9	1. Every Kinda People	Island 100
8/11/79	**14**	10	2. Bad Case Of Loving You (Doctor, Doctor)	Island 49016
3/08/86	**1**(1)	14	● **3. Addicted To Love**	Island 99570
6/28/86	**33**	5	4. Hyperactive	Island 99545
9/13/86	**2**(1)	13	**5. I Didn't Mean To Turn You On**	Island 99537
			above 3 produced by Bernard Edwards (Chic)	
7/16/88	**2**(2)	14	**6. Simply Irresistible**	EMI-Man. 50133
11/12/88	**19**	9	7. Early In The Morning	EMI-Man. 50157
12/22/90+	**28**	5	8. You're Amazing	EMI 50338#
3/02/91	**16**	10	9. Mercy Mercy Me (The Ecology)/I Want You	EMI 50344#
			PAPER LACE	
			English quintet formed in 1969: Phil Wright (b: 4/09/48; lead singer, drums), Cliff Fish (bass), Michael Vaughan (lead guitar) and Chris Morris (guitar). Morris later replaced by Carlo Santanna.	
7/13/74	**1**(1)	11	● **1. The Night Chicago Died**	Mercury 73492
			PARADE, The	
			Los Angeles pop-rock trio led by Jerry Riopelle, and including Murray MacLeod and Smokey Roberds.	
5/06/67	**20**	5	1. Sunshine Girl	A&M 841
			PARADONS, The	
			R&B vocal group from Bakersfield, California: West Tyler, Chuck Weldon, Billy Myers and William Powers.	
9/26/60	**18**	7	1. Diamonds And Pearls	Milestone 2003
			PARIS SISTERS, The	
			Albeth, Priscilla and Sherrell Paris from San Francisco.	
10/02/61	**5**	11	**1. I Love How You Love Me**	Gregmark 6
3/03/62	**34**	3	2. He Knows I Love Him Too Much	Gregmark 10
			above 2 produced by Phil Spector	
			PARKER, Fess	
			Born on 8/16/27 in Fort Worth. Starred in the movie *Davy Crockett* and TV's "Daniel Boone" (1964-70).	
3/12/55	**5**	17	**1. Ballad Of Davy Crockett**	Columbia 40449
			Best Seller #5 / Jockey #10 from the Disneyland TV and film production of *Davy Crockett*	
2/09/57	**12**	6	2. Wringle Wrangle	Disneyland 43
			Best Seller #12 / Top 100 #21 from the film *Westward Ho the Wagons*	
			PARKER, Graham/The Shot	
			Parker is a pub-rock vocalist/guitarist/songwriter, born in East London in 1950.	
6/15/85	**39**	3	1. Wake Up (Next To You)	Elektra 69654

DATE	POS	WKS	ARTIST—RECORD TITLE	LABEL & NO.
			PARKER, Ray Jr./Raydio	
			Born on 5/01/54 in Detroit. Prominent session guitarist in California; worked with Stevie Wonder, Barry White and others. Formed band Raydio in 1977 with Arnell Carmichael, Jerry Knight, Larry Tolbert, Darren Carmichael and Charles Fearing. Parker went solo in 1982. Knight later recorded in duo Ollie & Jerry.	
			RAYDIO:	
2/11/78	**8**	16	● **1. Jack And Jill**	Arista 0283
6/09/79	**9**	14	**2. You Can't Change That**	Arista 0399
			RAY PARKER JR. & RAYDIO:	
6/07/80	**30**	5	3. Two Places At The Same Time	Arista 0494
4/25/81	**4**	15	**4. A Woman Needs Love (Just Like You Do)**	Arista 0592
8/08/81	**21**	6	5. That Old Song	Arista 0616
			RAY PARKER JR.:	
4/10/82	**4**	14	**6. The Other Woman**	Arista 0669
8/21/82	**38**	3	7. Let Me Go	Arista 0695
1/15/83	**35**	4	8. Bad Boy	Arista 1030
12/10/83+	**12**	11	9. I Still Can't Get Over Loving You	Arista 9116
6/30/84	**1**(3)	14	● **10. Ghostbusters** from 1984's #1 box-office film *Ghostbusters*	Arista 9212
12/01/84+	**14**	11	11. Jamie	Arista 9293
10/26/85	**34**	4	12. Girls Are More Fun all of above written and produced by Parker	Arista 9352
9/22/90	**32**	4	13. All I'm Missing Is You **GLENN MEDEIROS featuring RAY PARKER JR.**	MCA 53886#
			PARKER, Robert	
			Born on 10/14/30 in Crescent City, Louisiana. Saxophonist/vocalist/bandleader. In Professor Longhair's (Roy Byrd) band from 1949. Led house band at Club Tijuana, New Orleans. Prolific session work.	
5/21/66	**7**	9	**1. Barefootin'**	Nola 721
			PARKS, Michael	
			Born on 4/04/38 in Corona, California. Film and TV actor/singer. In films *The Man Who Came to Dinner, Night Must Fall, Wild Seed* and *Back in Town.* Starred in the 1963 TV series "Channing"; portrayed Jim Bronson in the 1969 TV series "Then Came Bronson."	
3/28/70	**20**	8	1. Long Lonesome Highway from the TV series "Then Came Bronson"	MGM 14104
			PARLIAMENT	
			Funk aggregation which evolved from The Parliaments. Spearheaded by George Clinton, part of his "A Parliafunkadelicament Thang" corporation. The group's nearly 40 members also recorded under the names Funkadelic, P. Funk All Stars and Parlet among others.	
6/12/76	**15**	10	● 1. Tear The Roof Off The Sucker (Give Up The Funk)	Casablanca 856
2/25/78	**16**	12	● 2. Flash Light	Casablanca 909
			PARLIAMENTS, The	
			Soul group consisting of George Clinton (lead), Raymond Davis, Calvin Simon, Clarence "Fuzzy" Haskins and Grady Thomas. Later evolved into Parliament/Funkadelic aggregation. In 1977, Haskins, Simon and Thomas split from the aggregation; in 1981 they recorded as Funkadelic for LAX Records.	
8/05/67	**20**	7	1. (I Wanna) Testify	Revilot 207

DATE	POS	WKS	ARTIST—RECORD TITLE	LABEL & NO.
			PARR, John	
			Singer/songwriter, born in Nottingham, England.	
2/02/85	**23**	8	1. Naughty Naughty	Atlantic 89612
7/20/85	**1**(2)	14	**2. St. Elmo's Fire (Man In Motion)**	Atlantic 89541
			from the film of the same title	
			PARSONS, Alan, Project	
			Duo formed in London in 1975. Consisted of producer Alan Parsons (guitar, keyboards) and lyricist Eric Woolfson (vocals, keyboards). Both had worked at the Abbey Road Studios; Parsons was an engineer, Woolfson a songwriter. Parsons engineered Pink Floyd's *Dark Side of the Moon* and The Beatles' *Abbey Road* albums. Project features varying musicians and vocalists.	
9/11/76	**37**	2	1. (The System Of) Doctor Tarr And Professor Fether	20th Century 2297
9/24/77	**36**	3	2. I Wouldn't Want To Be Like You	Arista 0260
			ALAN PARSONS	
11/17/79	**27**	8	3. Damned If I Do	Arista 0454
1/24/81	**16**	10	4. Games People Play	Arista 0573
			vocals on above 2 by Lenny Zakatek	
6/06/81	**15**	12	5. Time	Arista 0598
7/31/82	**3**	17	**6. Eye In The Sky**	Arista 0696
3/24/84	**15**	8	7. Don't Answer Me	Arista 9160
6/23/84	**34**	3	8. Prime Time	Arista 9208
			5-8: vocal by Eric Woolfson; all of above written by Parsons and Woolfson	
			PARSONS, Bill — see BARE, Bobby	
			PARTLAND BROTHERS	
			Canadian duo: Chris (vocals, guitars) and G.P. (vocals, percussion) Partland.	
6/06/87	**27**	5	1. Soul City	Manhattan 50065
			PARTNERS IN KRYME	
			Rap duo from New York: DJ James Alpern and rapper Richard Usher. Met while speech communications majors at Syracuse University. Kryme stands for Keeping Rhythm Your Motivating Energy.	
5/12/90	**13**	8	● 1. Turtle Power!	SBK 07325
			from the film *Teenage Mutant Ninja Turtles*	
			PARTON, Dolly	
			Born on 1/19/46 in Sevier County, Tennessee. Worked on Knoxville radio show at age 11. First recorded for Gold Band in 1957. To Nashville in 1964. Replaced Norma Jean on the Porter Wagoner TV show, 1967-74. Joined the "Grand Ole Opry" in 1969. Starred in the films *9 to 5*, *The Best Little Whorehouse in Texas* and *Steel Magnolias*. Hosted own TV variety show in 1987.	
11/12/77+	**3**	13	● **1. Here You Come Again**	RCA 11123
4/08/78	**19**	8	2. Two Doors Down	RCA 11240
9/23/78	**37**	4	3. Heartbreaker	RCA 11296
1/13/79	**25**	7	4. Baby I'm Burnin'	RCA 11420
5/03/80	**36**	3	5. Starting Over Again	RCA 11926
			written by Donna Summer and her husband Bruce Sudano	
12/20/80+	**1**(2)	18	● **6. 9 To 5**	RCA 12133
			from the film of the same title	
9/10/83	**1**(2)	18	▲ **7. Islands In The Stream**	RCA 13615

DATE	POS	WKS	ARTIST—RECORD TITLE	LABEL & NO.
			KENNY ROGERS & DOLLY PARTON written by the Bee Gees	
			PARTRIDGE FAMILY, The	
			Popularized through "The Partridge Family" TV series, broadcast from 1970-74. Recordings by series stars David Cassidy (lead singer) and real-life stepmother Shirley Jones (backing vocals). David, son of actor Jack Cassidy, was born on 4/12/50 in New York City; raised in California. Shirley, born on 3/31/34 in Smithton, Pennsylvania, starred in the film musicals *Oklahoma* and *The Music Man*; married David's father in 1956.	
			THE PARTRIDGE FAMILY starring SHIRLEY JONES featuring DAVID CASSIDY:	
10/31/70	**1**(3)	16	● **1. I Think I Love You**	Bell 910
2/20/71	**6**	11	● **2. Doesn't Somebody Want To Be Wanted**	Bell 963
5/15/71	**9**	8	**3. I'll Meet You Halfway**	Bell 996
8/21/71	**13**	10	4. I Woke Up In Love This Morning	Bell 45130
1/01/72	**20**	6	5. It's One Of Those Nights (Yes Love)	Bell 45160
7/29/72	**28**	4	6. Breaking Up Is Hard To Do	Bell 45235
1/27/73	**39**	2	7. Looking Through The Eyes Of Love	Bell 45301
			PASTELS, The	
			R&B vocal quartet: lead singer "Big Dee Irwin" (DiFosco Ervin), Richard Travis, Tony Thomas and Jimmy Willingham. Formed at Air Force base in Narsarssuak, Greenland in 1954.	
3/03/58	**24**	3	1. Been So Long Top 100 #24 / Best Seller #25	Argo 5287
			PASTEL SIX, The	
			California pop septet (ages 18-21 in 1962); headlined at the Cinnamon Cinder club in North Hollywood.	
1/19/63	**25**	5	1. The Cinnamon Cinder (It's A Very Nice Dance)	Zen 102
			PATIENCE & PRUDENCE	
			Los Angeles sister duo: Patience & Prudence McIntyre (ages 11 & 14 in 1956).	
8/25/56	**4**	17	**1. Tonight You Belong To Me** Best Seller #4 / Juke Box #4 / Jockey #5 / Top 100 #6	Liberty 55022
12/01/56	**11**	12	2. Gonna Get Along Without Ya Now Jockey #11 / Best Seller #12 / Top 100 #12 / Juke Box #16 above 2 with their father Mack McIntyre's orchestra	Liberty 55040
			PATTON, Robbie	
			English singer/songwriter. Toured with Fleetwood Mac as a guest in 1979.	
8/01/81	**26**	6	1. Don't Give It Up	Liberty 1420
			PATTY & THE EMBLEMS	
			Soul group from Camden, New Jersey — Pat Russell, lead singer.	
8/15/64	**37**	3	1. Mixed-Up, Shook-Up, Girl	Herald 590
			PAUL, Billy	
			Born Paul Williams on 12/01/34 in Philadelphia. Soul singer; sang on Philadelphia radio broadcasts at age 11. First recorded for Jubilee in 1952.	
11/18/72	**1**(3)	14	● **1. Me And Mrs. Jones**	Phil. Int. 3521
4/20/74	**37**	3	2. Thanks For Saving My Life above 2 written and produced by Kenny Gamble and Leon Huff	Phil. Int. 3538

DATE	POS	WKS	ARTIST—RECORD TITLE	LABEL & NO.
			PAUL, Les, and MARY FORD	
			Les was born Lester Polfus on 6/09/16 in Waukesha, Wisconsin. Mary was born Colleen Summer on 7/07/28 in Pasadena; died on 9/30/77. Paul is a self-taught guitarist. Worked local radio stations, then to Chicago, 1932-37. Own trio in 1936. With Fred Waring from 1938-41. Innovator in electric guitar and multi-track recordings. Married vocalist Mary Ford on 12/29/49; divorced in 1963. Les won the Grammy's Trustees Award in 1983 and he was inducted into the Rock and Roll Hall of Fame in 1988.	
7/09/55	**7**	13	**1. Hummingbird** Juke Box #7 / Best Seller #8 / Jockey #8	Capitol 3165
11/12/55	**38**	2	2. Amukiriki (The Lord Willing) Top 100 #38	Capitol 3248
2/23/57	**35**	2	3. Cinco Robles (Five Oaks)	Capitol 3612
9/08/58	**32**	4	4. Put A Ring On My Finger Hot 100 #32 / Best Seller #44	Columbia 41222
7/03/61	**37**	1	5. Jura (I Swear I Love You)	Columbia 41994
			PAUL & PAULA	
			Real names: Ray Hildebrand (b: 12/21/40, Joshua, Texas) and Jill Jackson (b: 5/20/42, McCaney, Texas). Formed duo at Howard Payne College, Brownwood, Texas.	
1/12/63	**1**(3)	12	● **1. Hey Paula** first released on Le Cam 979 as by Jill & Ray in 1962	Philips 40084
3/23/63	**6**	8	**2. Young Lovers**	Philips 40096
6/22/63	**27**	4	3. First Quarrel	Philips 40114
			PAVONE, Rita	
			Pop singer born in Torino, Italy.	
7/04/64	**26**	4	1. Remember Me	RCA 8365
			PAYNE, Freda	
			Born on 9/19/45 in Detroit. Sister of The Supremes' Scherrie Payne. Attended the Institute of Musical Arts. To New York in 1963. Performed with Pearl Bailey, Duke Ellington and Quincy Jones. First recorded for Impulse in 1965. Hosted the syndicated TV talk show "For You, Black Woman" in the early '80s.	
5/30/70	**3**	15	● **1. Band Of Gold**	Invictus 9075
10/10/70	**24**	8	2. Deeper & Deeper	Invictus 9080
6/26/71	**12**	10	● 3. Bring The Boys Home	Invictus 9092
			PEACHES & HERB	
			Soul duo from Washington, D.C.: Herb Fame (born Herbert Feemster, 1942) and Francine Barker (born Francine Hurd, 1947). Fame had been recording solo, Francine sang in vocal group Sweet Things. Marlene Mack filled in for Francine from 1968-69. Re-formed with Fame and Linda Green in 1977.	
2/25/67	**21**	6	1. Let's Fall In Love	Date 1523
4/15/67	**8**	9	**2. Close Your Eyes**	Date 1549
7/08/67	**20**	5	3. For Your Love	Date 1563
10/14/67	**13**	7	4. Love Is Strange	Date 1574
1/13/68	**31**	3	5. Two Little Kids	Date 1586
1/27/79	**5**	13	● **6. Shake Your Groove Thing**	Polydor 14514
3/31/79	**1**(4)	15	▲ **7. Reunited**	Polydor 14547
3/15/80	**19**	8	8. I Pledge My Love	Polydor 2053

DATE	POS	WKS	ARTIST—RECORD TITLE	LABEL & NO.
			PEARL, Leslie	
			Pop singer/songwriter/producer from Pennsylvania. Wrote jingles for Pepsi, Ford, Gillette and others.	
7/10/82	**28**	7	1. If The Love Fits Wear It	RCA 13235
			PEBBLES	
			Born Perri Alette McKissack. Native of Oakland. Nicknamed "Pebbles" by her family for her resemblance to cartoon character Pebbles Flintstone. Worked with Con Funk Shun in the early '80s while still a teenager. Married to singer/songwriter/producer L.A. Reid of The Deele. Her cousin is vocalist Cherrelle.	
2/27/88	**5**	12	**1. Girlfriend**	MCA 53185
5/28/88	**2**(2)	11	**2. Mercedes Boy**	MCA 53279
9/08/90	**4**	13	**3. Giving You The Benefit**	MCA 79079
1/12/91	**13**	9	4. Love Makes Things Happen backing vocals by Babyface	MCA 53973#
			PEEBLES, Ann	
			Born on 4/27/47 in East St. Louis. Sang in family gospel group, the Peebles Choir, from age eight.	
12/22/73	**38**	1	1. I Can't Stand The Rain	Hi 2248
			PEEPLES, Nia	
			Born on 12/10/61. Singer/actress. Played Nicole Chapman for three seasons on the TV series "Fame." Hosted "Top of the Pops" TV show. Married Howard Hewett in 1989. Hostess of own syndicated music video dance TV program.	
7/02/88	**35**	3	1. Trouble	Mercury 870154
			PENDERGRASS, Teddy	
			Born on 3/26/50 in Philadelphia. Worked local clubs, became drummer for Harold Melvin's Blue Notes in 1969; lead singer with same group in 1970. Went solo in 1976. In the 1982 film *Soup for One*. Auto accident on 3/18/82 left him partially paralyzed.	
8/12/78	**25**	6	• 1. Close The Door	Phil. Int. 3648
7/04/81	**40**	2	2. Two Hearts **STEPHANIE MILLS featuring TEDDY PENDERGRASS**	20th Century 2492
			PENGUINS, The	
			R&B vocal group formed in Los Angeles in 1954: Cleveland Duncan (lead), Dexter Tisby (tenor), Bruce Tate (baritone) and Curtis Williams (bass). Group named for trademark on Kool cigarettes.	
12/25/54+	**8**	15	**1. Earth Angel (Will You Be Mine)** Best Seller #8 / Juke Box #10 / Jockey #13 considered to be the top R&B record of all time in terms of continuous popularity; written by Jesse Belvin and Curtis Williams	DooTone 348
			PENN, Michael	
			L.A.-based singer/songwriter. Older brother of actors Sean and Christopher Penn. Son of actor/director Leo Penn and actress Eileen Ryan.	
2/03/90	**13**	10	1. No Myth	RCA 9111
			PEOPLE	
			San Jose, California pop-rock sextet founded by lead guitarist Jeff Levin.	
5/25/68	**14**	10	1. I Love You	Capitol 2078

DATE	POS	WKS	ARTIST—RECORD TITLE	LABEL & NO.
			PEOPLE'S CHOICE	
			Philadelphia soul group formed in 1971: Frankie Brunson (vocals), Stanley Burton, Roger Andrews, Dave Thompson and Leon Lee.	
9/04/71	**38**	2	1. I Likes To Do It [I]	Phil-L.A. 349
9/13/75	**11**	11	● 2. Do It Any Way You Wanna [I]	TSOP 4769
			PEPPERMINT RAINBOW, The	
4/12/69	**32**	5	1. Will You Be Staying After Sunday	Decca 32410
			PERFECT GENTLEMEN	
			Boston teen trio produced by New Edition and New Kids On The Block producer, Maurice Starr: Corey Blakely, Maurice Starr, Jr. (Starr's son) and Tyrone Sutton. All were between the ages of 11-13 years old in 1990.	
4/28/90	**10**	9	**1. Ooh La La (I Can't Get Over You)**	Columbia 73379
			PERICOLI, Emilio	
			Singer/actor, born in 1928 in Cesenatico, Italy.	
6/09/62	**6**	10	**1. Al Di La'** **[F]** from the film *Rome Adventure*	Warner 5259
			PERKINS, Carl	
			Born on 4/09/32 near Tiptonville, Tennessee. Rockabilly singer/guitarist/songwriter. Formed family band consisting of Carl (guitar), brothers Jay B. (guitar) and Clayton (bass), and W.B. Holland (drums). First recorded for Flip/Sun in 1954. Member of Johnny Cash's touring troupe from 1965-75. The Beatles recorded his songs "Matchbox," "Honey Don't" and "Everybody's Trying To Be My Baby." In film *Into the Night* (1985). Inducted into the Rock and Roll Hall of Fame in 1987.	
3/10/56	**2**(4)	17	**1. Blue Suede Shoes** Juke Box #2 / Best Seller #3 / Top 100 #4 / Jockey #5 Grammy Hall of Fame Award winner in 1986	Sun 234
			PERKINS, Tony	
			Born on 4/14/32 in New York City. Movie actor. Best Supporting Oscar nominee for *Friendly Persuasion* in 1956. Most famous for his portrayal of deranged killer Norman Bates in the 1960 film *Psycho*.	
10/07/57	**24**	1	1. Moon-Light Swim Jockey #24 / Top 100 #43	RCA 7020
			PERRY, Steve	
			Born on 1/22/49 in Hanford, California. Lead singer of Journey since 1978.	
9/25/82	**17**	6	1. Don't Fight It **KENNY LOGGINS with STEVE PERRY**	Columbia 03192
4/14/84	**3**	13	**2. Oh Sherrie**	Columbia 04391
7/07/84	**21**	8	3. She's Mine	Columbia 04496
10/27/84	**40**	1	4. Strung Out	Columbia 04598
12/22/84+	**18**	11	5. Foolish Heart	Columbia 04693
			PERSUADERS, The	
			Soul group formed in New York City in 1969. Consisted of lead Douglas "Smokey" Scott, Willie Holland, James "B.J." Barnes and Charles Stodghill.	
9/18/71	**15**	9	● 1. Thin Line Between Love & Hate	Atco 6822
12/08/73	**39**	3	2. Some Guys Have All The Luck	Atco 6943

DATE	POS	WKS	ARTIST—RECORD TITLE	LABEL & NO.
			PETER AND GORDON	
			Pop duo formed in London in 1963: Peter Asher (b: 6/22/44, London) and Gordon Waller (b: 6/04/45, Braemar, Scotland). Peter's sister Jane was Paul McCartney's girlfriend, and Paul wrote their first three chart hits. Toured the U.S. in 1964, appeared on "Shindig," "Hullabaloo" and Ed Sullivan TV shows. Disbanded in 1967. Asher went into production and management, including work with Linda Ronstadt, James Taylor and 10,000 Maniacs.	
5/16/64	**1**(1)	11	**1. A World Without Love** written by Paul McCartney (also #7 below)	Capitol 5175
7/11/64	**12**	6	2. Nobody I Know	Capitol 5211
10/24/64	**16**	6	3. I Don't Want To See You Again above 2 written by John Lennon and Paul McCartney	Capitol 5272
1/23/65	**9**	9	**4. I Go To Pieces** written by Del Shannon	Capitol 5335
5/08/65	**14**	8	5. True Love Ways written by Buddy Holly and Norman Petty	Capitol 5406
7/24/65	**24**	5	6. To Know You Is To Love You	Capitol 5461
3/12/66	**14**	8	7. Woman	Capitol 5579
11/05/66	**6**	10	**8. Lady Godiva**	Capitol 5740
1/14/67	**15**	5	9. Knight In Rusty Armour	Capitol 5808
4/15/67	**31**	3	10. Sunday For Tea	Capitol 5864
			PETER, PAUL & MARY	
			Folk group formed in New York City in 1961. Consisted of Mary Travers (b: 11/07/37, Louisville); Peter Yarrow (b: 5/31/38, New York City); and Paul Stookey (b: 11/30/37, Baltimore). Yarrow had worked the Newport Folk Festival in 1960. Stookey had done TV work, and Travers had been in the Broadway musical *The Next President*. Disbanded in 1971, reunited in 1978.	
6/09/62	**35**	2	1. Lemon Tree	Warner 5274
9/08/62	**10**	8	**2. If I Had A Hammer (The Hammer Song)**	Warner 5296
3/30/63	**2**(1)	11	**3. Puff The Magic Dragon**	Warner 5348
7/13/63	**2**(1)	12	**4. Blowin' In The Wind**	Warner 5368
9/28/63	**9**	8	**5. Don't Think Twice, It's All Right**	Warner 5385
12/28/63	**35**	2	6. Stewball	Warner 5399
4/04/64	**33**	3	7. Tell It On The Mountain	Warner 5418
2/13/65	**30**	4	8. For Lovin' Me written by Gordon Lightfoot	Warner 5496
9/02/67	**9**	8	**9. I Dig Rock And Roll Music**	Warner 7067
12/23/67	**35**	2	10. Too Much Of Nothing 4, 5, 10: written by Bob Dylan	Warner 7092
5/17/69	**21**	7	11. Day Is Done	Warner 7279
11/08/69	**1**(1)	15	● **12. Leaving On A Jet Plane** written by John Denver	Warner 7340
			PETERS, Bernadette	
			Born Bernadette Lazzara on 2/28/44 in Queens, New York. Broadway/TV/film star. Appeared in the films *The Jerk* and *Annie*, and the TV series "All's Fair" (1976-77).	
5/10/80	**31**	5	1. Gee Whiz	MCA 41210

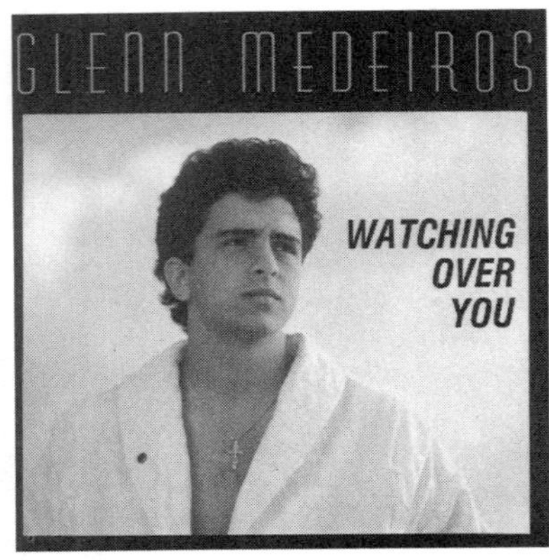

Glenn Medeiros was 16 years old when "Nothing's Gonna Change My Love For You" hit the Top 20 in 1987, so one may safely assume he wasn't singing about puberty. His 1990 hit "She Ain't Worth It" featured Bobby Brown and was No. 1 for two weeks.

Melanie's 1970 hit "Lay Down (Candles In The Rain)" brought the co-billed Edwin Hawkins Singers into the Top 10 for the second time; a year earlier, they'd scored a No. 4 hit (sans Melanie) with "Oh Happy Day."

John Cougar Mellencamp's musical roots were amply on display on his 1976 debut album *Chestnut Street Incident*. Recording as Johnny Cougar, Mellencamp covered Roy Orbison, Elvis Presley, the Doors, and the Lovin' Spoonful—and would later disown the album.

Bette Midler's first No. 1 single, "Wind Beneath My Wings," came 16 years after she began recording for Atlantic Records. The song, taken from the *Beaches* soundtrack, won a Grammy for writer Julie Gold.

Milli Vanilli's final top-10 hit, "All Or Nothing," had an ironic connotation when it was discovered that photogenic duo Rob Pilatus and Fabrice Morvan never actually sang on their records—in all, it seems, they did nothing but look good.

The Miracles' 60s hits inspired cover versions by many of pop's best known artists, including the Beatles ("You've Really Got A Hold On Me") Linda Ronstadt ("Ooh Baby Baby," "Tracks Of My Tears"), and the Captain & Tennille ("Shop Around").

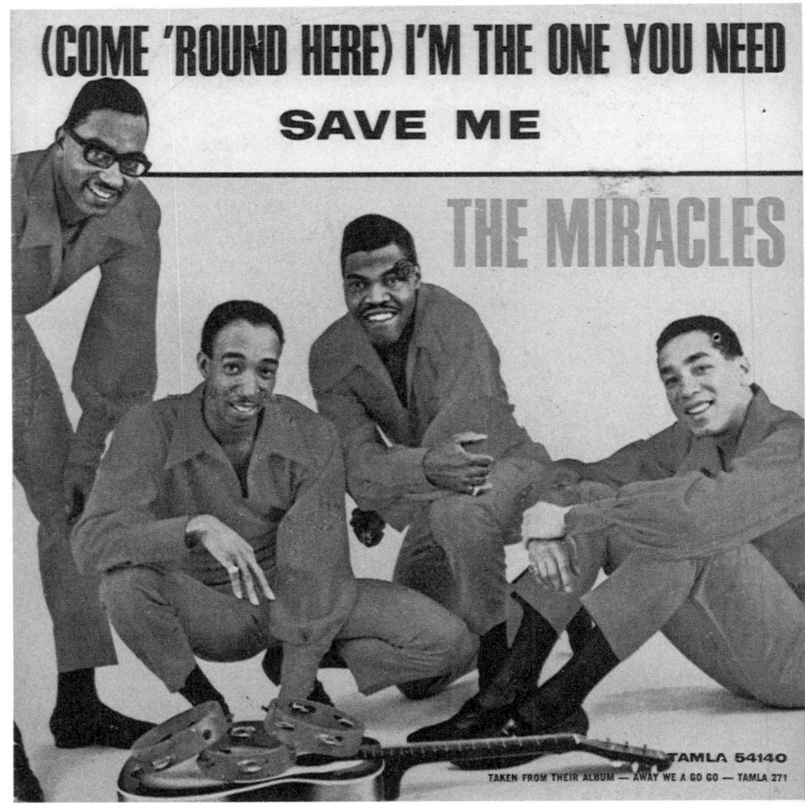

Michael Morales did it, but the Romantics couldn't: "What I Like About You" was a 1989 top-40 hit for Morales, but Detroit rockers the Romantics—who penned the song and included it on their 1980 Nemperor debut album—weren't quite so lucky.

Motley Crue's rise to prominence as one of America's best-known heavy-metal bands was largely credited to their popular 1985 cover version of Brownsville Station's mischievous "Smokin' In The Boys Room." The 1973 original went to No. 3, the Crue's to No. 12.

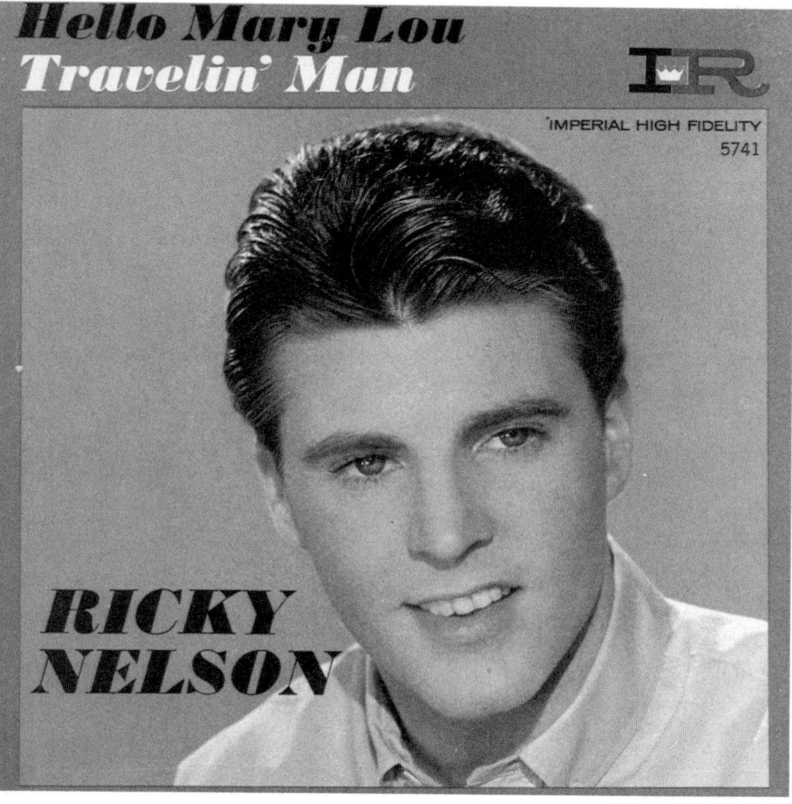

Ricky Nelson's extensive chart performance includes 35 top-40 hits, only two of which—1958's "Poor Little Fool" and 1961's "Travelin' Man"—ever hit No. 1. Nelson's artistic stature has grown since his 1985 death; both EMI and MCA have reissued much of his work on CD.

Robbie Nevil's eponymous 1986 solo album spawned three Top 20 singles, with "C'est La Vie" holding down the No. 2 slot two weeks in a row. Two albums later, he has yet to match his earlier success.

New Edition launched the solid gold careers of Bobby Brown, Ralph Tresvant, and Ricky Bell, Michael Bivins, and Ronald DeVoe—better known as Bell Biv DeVoe. Brown, who left for a solo career and was replaced by Johnny Gill, reunited with the group during the 1990 MTV Video awards show.

New Kids On The Block became a huge pre-teen phenomenon in the early 90s with four multiplatinum albums and a stunning array of colorful merchandising deals. Singer Donny Wahlberg's brother had a No. 1 record of his own in 1991 with his own group, Marky Mark & The Funky Bunch.

DATE	POS	WKS	ARTIST—RECORD TITLE	LABEL & NO.
			PETERSEN, Paul	
			Born on 9/23/45 in Glendale, California. Member of Disney's "Mouseketeers" and played Jeff Stone on TV's "Donna Reed Show" (1958-66). Became a paperback novelist in the '70s.	
3/31/62	**19**	7	1. She Can't Find Her Keys	Colpix 620
12/15/62+	**6**	10	**2. My Dad**	Colpix 663
			PETERSON, Ray	
			Born on 4/23/39 in Denton, Texas. Started singing in his early teens, while being treated for polio at a Texas hospital. Formed own Dunes label in 1961.	
6/15/59	**25**	7	1. The Wonder Of You	RCA 7513
6/27/60	**7**	11	**2. Tell Laura I Love Her**	RCA 7745
12/19/60+	**9**	9	**3. Corinna, Corinna**	Dunes 2002
			produced by Phil Spector	
9/25/61	**29**	3	4. Missing You	Dunes 2006
			PETS, The	
			Member Richard Podolor became a top producer; worked with Three Dog Night and Steppenwolf, among others.	
6/09/58	**34**	1	1. Cha-Hua-Hua [I]	Arwin 109
			Top 100 #34 / Best Seller #38	
			PET SHOP BOYS	
			British duo: Neil Tennant (vocals) and Chris Lowe (keyboards). Tennant was a writer for the British fan magazine *Smash Hits*. In 1989, Tennant was also with the group Electronic.	
3/15/86	**1**(1)	14	**1. West End Girls**	EMI America 8307
6/21/86	**10**	9	**2. Opportunities (Let's Make Lots Of Money)**	EMI America 8330
9/26/87	**9**	10	**3. It's A Sin**	EMI Amer. 43027
12/26/87+	**2**(2)	13	**4. What Have I Done To Deserve This?**	EMI-Man. 50107
			PET SHOP BOYS AND DUSTY SPRINGFIELD	
4/09/88	**4**	10	**5. Always On My Mind**	EMI-Man. 50123
11/05/88	**18**	6	6. Domino Dancing	EMI-Man. 50161
			backing vocals: The Voice In Fashion	
			PETTY, Tom/The Heartbreakers	
			Rock group formed in Los Angeles in 1975. Consisted of Petty (b: 10/20/53, Gainesville, Florida; guitar, vocals), Mike Campbell (guitar), Benmont Tench (keyboards), Ron Blair (bass) and Stan Lynch (drums). Petty, Campbell and Tench had been in Florida group Mudcrutch, early '70s. Backed Stevie Nicks on solo LP *Bella Donna*. Blair left in 1982, replaced by Howard Epstein. Petty appeared in the 1987 film *Made in Heaven*. Member of the supergroup Traveling Wilburys.	
2/18/78	**40**	1	1. Breakdown	Shelter 62008
12/08/79+	**10**	13	**2. Don't Do Me Like That**	Backstreet 41138
2/09/80	**15**	10	3. Refugee	Backstreet 41169
5/16/81	**19**	7	4. The Waiting	Backstreet 51100
8/01/81	**3**	15	**5. Stop Draggin' My Heart Around**	Modern 7336
			STEVIE NICKS with TOM PETTY AND THE HEARTBREAKERS	
12/04/82+	**20**	11	6. You Got Lucky	Backstreet 52144
3/12/83	**21**	7	7. Change Of Heart	Backstreet 52181
4/06/85	**13**	9	8. Don't Come Around Here No More	MCA 52496
3/01/86	**37**	2	9. Needles And Pins	MCA 52772

DATE	POS	WKS	ARTIST—RECORD TITLE	LABEL & NO.
			TOM PETTY AND THE HEARTBREAKERS with STEVIE NICKS	
5/23/87	**18**	6	10. Jammin' Me	MCA 53065
			written by Tom Petty and Bob Dylan	
			TOM PETTY:	
5/27/89	**12**	9	11. I Won't Back Down	MCA 53369
8/26/89	**23**	7	12. Runnin' Down A Dream	MCA 53682
12/02/89+	**7**	12	**13. Free Fallin'**	MCA 53748
			PHILLIPS, Esther	
			Born Esther Mae Jones on 12/23/35 in Galveston, Texas. Vocalist/multi-instrumentalist. Moved to Los Angeles in 1940. One of the first female superstars of R&B. Recorded and toured with The Johnny Otis Orchestra as "Little Esther," 1948-54; scored seven top 10 hits on the R&B charts in 1950. Bouts with drug addiction interrupted her career and led to her death on 8/07/84 (liver, kidney failure).	
11/17/62	**8**	10	**1. Release Me**	Lenox 5555
			re-charted in 1967 at POS 93	
9/20/75	**20**	9	2. What A Diff'rence A Day Makes	Kudu 925
			PHILLIPS, John	
			Born on 8/30/35 in Paris Island, South Carolina. Co-founder of The Mamas & The Papas. Father of actress MacKenzie Phillips and singer Chynna Phillips. Co-wrote The Beach Boys' 1988 #1 hit "Kokomo."	
6/20/70	**32**	7	1. Mississippi	Dunhill 4236
			PHILLIPS, Phil, with The Twilights	
			Born John Phillip Baptiste on 3/14/31. Black vocalist from Lake Charles, Louisiana.	
7/20/59	**2**(2)	14	**1. Sea Of Love**	Mercury 71465
			first released on Khoury's 711 in 1959	
			PHOTOGLO, Jim	
			Pop vocalist from the South Bay area of Los Angeles.	
5/31/80	**31**	4	1. We Were Meant To Be Lovers	20th Century 2446
			PHOTOGLO	
5/30/81	**25**	7	2. Fool In Love With You	20th Century 2487
			PICKETT, Bobby "Boris"/The Crypt-Kickers	
			Born on 2/11/40 in Somerville, Massachusetts. Began recording career in Hollywood while aspiring to be an actor. A member of The Stompers in early 1962. Leon Russell, Johnny MacCrae (Ronny & The Daytonas), Rickie Page (The Bermudas) and Gary Paxton (Hollywood Argyles) were Crypt-Kickers.	
9/15/62	**1**(2)	12	● **1. Monster Mash** **[N]**	Garpax 44167
12/22/62	**30**	4	2. Monsters' Holiday [X-N]	Garpax 44171
6/30/73	**10**	12	**3. Monster Mash** **[N-R]**	Parrot 348
			PICKETT, Wilson	
			Soul singer/songwriter. Born on 3/18/41 in Prattville, Alabama. Sang in local gospel groups. To Detroit in 1955. With the Falcons, 1961-63. Career took off after recording in Memphis with guitarist/producer Steve Cropper. Inducted into the Rock and Roll Hall of Fame in 1991.	
8/14/65	**21**	6	1. In The Midnight Hour	Atlantic 2289
3/05/66	**13**	8	2. 634-5789 (Soulsville, U.S.A.)	Atlantic 2320
8/13/66	**6**	8	**3. Land Of 1000 Dances**	Atlantic 2348
12/10/66	**23**	6	4. Mustang Sally	Atlantic 2365
2/25/67	**29**	3	5. Everybody Needs Somebody To Love	Atlantic 2381

DATE	POS	WKS	ARTIST—RECORD TITLE	LABEL & NO.
4/22/67	**32**	2	6. I Found A Love - Part 1 lead singer of version by The Falcons in 1962 (POS 75)	Atlantic 2394
8/26/67	**8**	9	**7. Funky Broadway**	Atlantic 2430
11/11/67	**22**	5	8. Stag-O-Lee	Atlantic 2448
5/11/68	**15**	6	9. She's Lookin' Good	Atlantic 2504
7/06/68	**24**	4	10. I'm A Midnight Mover written by Bobby Womack	Atlantic 2528
1/04/69	**23**	6	11. Hey Jude	Atlantic 2591
5/23/70	**25**	9	12. Sugar Sugar	Atlantic 2722
10/24/70	**14**	9	13. Engine Number 9	Atlantic 2765
2/06/71	**17**	8	● 14. Don't Let The Green Grass Fool You	Atlantic 2781
5/15/71	**13**	9	● 15. Don't Knock My Love - Pt. 1	Atlantic 2797
1/15/72	**24**	8	16. Fire And Water	Atlantic 2852
			PIERCE, Webb	
			Born on 8/08/21 in West Monroe, Louisiana. Died on 2/24/91 of heart failure. A leading country singer, from 1952-58, had 42 consecutive top 10 hits on *Billboard*'s country charts. In films *Buffalo Guns, Music City USA* and *Road to Nashville.*	
8/31/59	**24**	7	1. I Ain't Never written by Mel Tillis	Decca 30923
			PILOT	
			Scottish trio: David Paton (lead singer, guitar), Bill Lyall (keyboards) and Stuart Tosh (drums).	
5/10/75	**5**	12	● **1. Magic** produced by Alan Parsons	EMI 3992
			PINETTE, Rick — see OAK	
			PINK FLOYD	
			English progressive rock band formed in 1965: David Gilmour (b: 3/06/46; guitar; replaced Syd Barrett in 1968), Roger Waters (b: 9/06/44; bass), Nick Mason (b: 1/27/45; drums) and Rick Wright (b: 7/28/45; keyboards). Wright left in early 1982; Waters went solo in 1984. Band inactive, 1984-86. Gilmour, Mason and Wright re-grouped in 1987. Group name taken from Georgia bluesmen Pink Anderson and Floyd Council.	
6/23/73	**13**	9	1. Money	Harvest 3609
2/09/80	**1**(4)	19	● **2. Another Brick In The Wall (Part II)**	Columbia 11187
			PINK LADY	
			Mei and Kei — Japan's hottest disco duo of the '70s. Hosted own summer TV variety show in U.S., 1979.	
7/21/79	**37**	3	1. Kiss In The Dark	Elektra 46040
			PIPKINS, The	
			British duo: Roger Greenaway and Tony Burrows (low voice).	
6/06/70	**9**	10	**1. Gimme Dat Ding** **[N]** background tune used on TV's "Benny Hill Show"	Capitol 2819
			PIPS — see KNIGHT, Gladys	

DATE	POS	WKS	ARTIST—RECORD TITLE	LABEL & NO.
			PITNEY, Gene	
			Born on 2/17/41 in Hartford, Connecticut and raised in Rockville, Connecticut. Own band at Rockville High School. Recorded for Decca in 1959, with Ginny Arnell as Jamie & Jane. Recorded for Blaze in 1960 as Billy Bryan. First recorded under own name for Festival in 1960. Wrote "Hello Mary Lou," "He's A Rebel" and "Rubber Ball." Recorded with George Jones as George & Gene.	
2/27/61	**39**	1	1. (I Wanna) Love My Life Away	Musicor 1002
12/18/61+	**13**	10	2. Town Without Pity produced by Phil Spector; from the film of the same title	Musicor 1009
5/19/62	**4**	8	**3. (The Man Who Shot) Liberty Valance** inspired by the film of the same title	Musicor 1020
9/29/62	**2**(1)	11	**4. Only Love Can Break A Heart**	Musicor 1022
1/05/63	**12**	8	5. Half Heaven - Half Heartache	Musicor 1026
4/13/63	**12**	7	6. Mecca	Musicor 1028
8/03/63	**21**	6	7. True Love Never Runs Smooth	Musicor 1032
11/16/63	**17**	6	8. Twenty Four Hours From Tulsa 3, 4, 7, 8: written by Burt Bacharach and Hal David	Musicor 1034
8/29/64	**7**	10	**9. It Hurts To Be In Love**	Musicor 1040
11/07/64	**9**	9	**10. I'm Gonna Be Strong**	Musicor 1045
3/20/65	**31**	4	11. I Must Be Seeing Things	Musicor 1070
5/22/65	**13**	7	12. Last Chance To Turn Around	Musicor 1093
8/21/65	**28**	4	13. Looking Through The Eyes Of Love	Musicor 1103
12/18/65	**37**	2	14. Princess In Rags	Musicor 1130
5/14/66	**25**	5	15. Backstage	Musicor 1171
6/15/68	**16**	8	16. She's A Heartbreaker	Musicor 1306
			PIXIES THREE, The	
			White teenage female trio from Hanover, Pennsylvania.	
10/05/63	**40**	1	1. Birthday Party	Mercury 72130
			PLANT, Robert	
			Born on 8/20/48 in West Bromwich, England. Lead singer of Led Zeppelin and The Honeydrippers.	
9/03/83	**20**	9	1. Big Log	Atlantic 99844
12/24/83+	**39**	5	2. In The Mood	Es Paranza 99820
6/15/85	**36**	4	3. Little By Little	Es Paranza 99644
6/04/88	**25**	7	4. Tall Cool One guitar solo: Jimmy Page	Es Paranza 99348
			PLASTIC ONO BAND — see LENNON, John	
			PLATT, Eddie	
			Saxophonist/bandleader from Cleveland.	
3/10/58	**20**	4	1. Tequila [I] Jockey #20 / Best Seller #35 / Top 100 #35	ABC-Para. 9899

DATE	POS	WKS	ARTIST—RECORD TITLE	LABEL & NO.
			PLATTERS, The	
			R&B group formed in Los Angeles in 1953. Consisted of Tony Williams (lead), David Lynch (tenor), Paul Robi (baritone), Herb Reed (bass) and Zola Taylor. Group first recorded for Federal in 1954, with Alex Hodge instead of Robi, and without Zola Taylor. Hit "Only You" was written by manager Buck Ram (d: 1/01/91; age 83) and first recorded for Federal, who did not want to use it. To Mercury in 1955, re-recorded "Only You." Williams left to go solo, replaced by Sonny Turner in 1961. Taylor replaced by Sandra Dawn; Robi replaced by Nate Nelson (formerly in The Flamingos) in 1966. Lynch died of cancer on 1/02/81 (age 61). Robi died of cancer on 2/01/89. Group inducted into the Rock and Roll Hall of Fame in 1990. Several unrelated groups use The Platters' famous name today.	
10/01/55	**5**	20	**1. Only You (And You Alone)** Best Seller #5 / Top 100 #5 / Jockey #5 / Juke Box #5 first released on Federal 12244 in 1954	Mercury 70633
12/24/55+	**1**(2)	19	**2. The Great Pretender** Top 100 #1(2) / Jockey #1(2) / Juke Box #1(1) / Best Seller #2	Mercury 70753
3/31/56	**4**	16	**3. (You've Got) The Magic Touch** Top 100 #4 / Juke Box #4 / Best Seller #5 / Jockey #5	Mercury 70819
7/07/56	**1**(5)	20	**4. My Prayer/** Top 100 #1(5) / Jockey #1(3) / Best Seller #1(2) / Juke Box #1(1) #2 hit for Glenn Miller in 1939	
8/11/56	**39**	1	5. Heaven On Earth	Mercury 70893
10/06/56	**11**	12	6. You'll Never Never Know/ Juke Box #11 / Top 100 #14 / Best Seller #15 / Jockey #18	
10/06/56	**13**	9	7. It Isn't Right Best Seller #13 / Juke Box #13 / Top 100 #23	Mercury 70948
1/12/57	**20**	6	8. On My Word Of Honor/ Juke Box #20 / Best Seller #23 / Top 100 #27	
1/26/57	**20**	2	9. One In A Million Best Seller #20 / Top 100 #31	Mercury 71011
3/23/57	**11**	11	10. I'm Sorry/ Juke Box #11 / Best Seller #14 / Top 100 #19	
4/13/57	**16**	9	11. He's Mine Best Seller #16 / Juke Box #18 / Top 100 #23 / Jockey #24	Mercury 71032
6/10/57	**24**	7	12. My Dream Best Seller #24 / Top 100 #26	Mercury 71093
4/07/58	**1**(1)	14	**13. Twilight Time** Best Seller #1(1) / Top 100 #1(1) / Jockey #1(1) #14 hit for the Three Suns in 1944	Mercury 71289
12/01/58+	**1**(3)	16	**14. Smoke Gets In Your Eyes** #1 hit for Paul Whiteman in 1934	Mercury 71383
4/06/59	**12**	11	15. Enchanted	Mercury 71427
2/15/60	**8**	11	**16. Harbor Lights** there were 5 top 10 versions of this tune in 1950	Mercury 71563
8/22/60	**36**	1	17. Red Sails In The Sunset **THE PLATTERS featuring TONY WILLIAMS** #1 hit for both Bing Crosby and Guy Lombardo in 1935	Mercury 71656
10/24/60	**21**	8	18. To Each His Own there were 3 #1 versions of this tune in 1946	Mercury 71697
1/30/61	**30**	2	19. If I Didn't Care #2 hit for the Ink Spots in 1939	Mercury 71749
8/21/61	**25**	4	20. I'll Never Smile Again #1 hit for Tommy Dorsey in 1940	Mercury 71847

DATE	POS	WKS	ARTIST—RECORD TITLE	LABEL & NO.
6/04/66	**31**	5	21. I Love You 1000 Times	Musicor 1166
3/25/67	**14**	7	22. With This Ring	Musicor 1229
			PLAYER	
			Pop-rock group formed in Los Angeles: Peter Beckett (vocals, guitar), John Crowley (vocals, guitar), Ronn Moss (bass), John Friesen (drums) and Wayne Cooke (keyboards). Moss plays Ridge Forrester on the TV soap "The Bold & The Beautiful." Crowley began solo country career in 1988.	
11/19/77+	**1**(3)	16	● **1. Baby Come Back**	RSO 879
4/01/78	**10**	12	**2. This Time I'm In It For Love**	RSO 890
10/21/78	**27**	3	3. Prisoner Of Your Love	RSO 908
			PLAYMATES, The	
			Donny Conn (b: 3/29/30), Morey Carr (b: 7/31/32) and Chic Hetti (b: 2/26/30) from Waterbury, Connecticut. Solidified act at the University of Connecticut, with more emphasis on comedy than singing.	
1/27/58	**19**	7	1. Jo-Ann Best Seller #19 / Top 100 #20	Roulette 4037
6/09/58	**22**	2	2. Don't Go Home Jockey #22 / Top 100 #36 / Best Seller #38	Roulette 4072
11/10/58	**4**	12	**3. Beep Beep** [N]	Roulette 4115
7/27/59	**15**	9	4. What Is Love?	Roulette 4160
11/21/60	**37**	2	5. Wait For Me	Roulette 4276
			POCO	
			Los Angeles country-rock band formed by Rusty Young and Buffalo Springfield members Richie Furay and Jim Messina. Changing personnel included future Eagles members Randy Meisner and Timothy B. Schmit. 1979 lineup: Paul Cotton, Charlie Harrison, Kim Bullard and Steve Chapman. Disbanded in late 1984. In 1989, Young, Furay, Messina, Meisner and George Grantham reunited as Poco.	
2/10/79	**17**	9	1. Crazy Love	ABC 12439
6/16/79	**20**	7	2. Heart Of The Night	MCA 41023
9/30/89	**18**	8	3. Call It Love	RCA 9038
1/20/90	**39**	1	4. Nothin' To Hide co-written and produced by Richard Marx	RCA 9131
			POINT BLANK	
			Six-man rock band from Texas — Bubba Keith, lead singer (replaced John O'Daniel by 1981).	
8/29/81	**39**	2	1. Nicole	MCA 51132
			POINTER, Bonnie	
			Born on 7/11/51 in East Oakland, California. Member of the Pointer Sisters, 1971-78.	
7/28/79	**11**	15	1. Heaven Must Have Sent You	Motown 1459
2/16/80	**40**	2	2. I Can't Help Myself (Sugar Pie, Honey Bunch)	Motown 1478
			POINTER SISTERS	
			Soul group formed in Oakland in 1971, consisting of sisters Ruth, Anita, Bonnie and June Pointer. Parents were ministers. Group was originally a trio, joined by youngest sister June in the early '70s. First recorded for Atlantic in 1971. Backup work for Cold Blood, Elvin Bishop, Boz Scaggs, Grace Slick and many others. Sang in nostalgic 1940s style, 1973-77. In the 1976 film *Car Wash.* Bonnie went solo in 1978, group continued as trio in new musical style.	
9/08/73	**11**	12	1. Yes We Can Can	Blue Thumb 229

DATE	POS	WKS		ARTIST—RECORD TITLE	LABEL & NO.
11/09/74	**13**	8		2. Fairytale	Blue Thumb 254
8/23/75	**20**	8		3. How Long (Betcha' Got A Chick On The Side)	Blue Thumb 265
12/16/78+	**2**(2)	16	●	**4. Fire** written by Bruce Springsteen	Planet 45901
4/14/79	**30**	4		5. Happiness	Planet 45902
8/30/80	**3**	17	●	**6. He's So Shy**	Planet 47916
6/27/81	**2**(3)	16	●	**7. Slow Hand**	Planet 47929
2/13/82	**13**	10		8. Should I Do It	Planet 47960
7/24/82	**16**	8		9. American Music	Planet 13254
10/30/82	**30**	6		10. I'm So Excited	Planet 13327
2/11/84	**5**	14		**11. Automatic**	Planet 13730
5/12/84	**3**	15		**12. Jump (For My Love)**	Planet 13780
9/08/84	**9**	12		**13. I'm So Excited** **[R]** slightly different mix than #10 above	Planet 13857
12/22/84+	**6**	14		**14. Neutron Dance** from the film *Beverly Hills Cop*	Planet 13951
7/27/85	**11**	13		15. Dare Me	RCA 14126
12/06/86	**33**	3		16. Goldmine	RCA 5062
				POISON Hard-rock quartet formed in Harrisburg, Pennsylvania: Bret Michaels (vocals), Bobby Dall (bass), Rikki Rockett (drums) and CC DeVille (guitar).	
4/11/87	**9**	9		**1. Talk Dirty To Me**	Capitol 5686
10/17/87	**13**	9		2. I Won't Forget You	Enigma 44038
5/21/88	**6**	11		**3. Nothin' But A Good Time**	Enigma 44145
8/27/88	**12**	9		4. Fallen Angel	Enigma 44191
11/12/88	**1**(3)	14	●	**5. Every Rose Has Its Thorn**	Enigma 44203
3/04/89	**10**	10		**6. Your Mama Don't Dance**	Enigma 44293
7/14/90	**3**	14	●	**7. Unskinny Bop**	Enigma 44584
10/20/90	**4**	15	●	**8. Something To Believe In**	Enigma 44617#
3/23/91	**38**	1		9. Ride The Wind	Enigma 44616#
6/29/91	**35**	2		10. Life Goes On	Capitol 44705#
				POLICE, The Rock trio formed in England in 1977: Gordon "Sting" Sumner (b: 10/02/51; vocals, bass), Andy Summers (b: 12/31/42; guitar) and Stewart Copeland (b: 7/16/52; drums). First guitarist was Henri Padovani, replaced by Summers in 1977. Copeland had been with Curved Air. Inactive as a group since appearance at "Amnesty '86." Sting began recording solo in 1985. Copeland formed group Animal Logic in 1989.	
4/07/79	**32**	5		1. Roxanne	A&M 2096
11/22/80+	**10**	13		**2. De Do Do Do, De Da Da Da**	A&M 2275
2/21/81	**10**	13		**3. Don't Stand So Close To Me**	A&M 2301
10/10/81	**3**	15		**4. Every Little Thing She Does Is Magic**	A&M 2371
1/30/82	**11**	10		5. Spirits In The Material World	A&M 2390
6/04/83	**1**(8)	20	●	**6. Every Breath You Take**	A&M 2542
8/27/83	**3**	13		**7. King Of Pain**	A&M 2569
11/19/83	**16**	9		8. Synchronicity II	A&M 2571
1/21/84	**8**	10		**9. Wrapped Around Your Finger** all of above written by Sting	A&M 2614

DATE	POS	WKS	ARTIST—RECORD TITLE	LABEL & NO.
			PONI-TAILS	
			Pop female trio from Brush High School in Lyndhurst, Ohio. Consisted of Toni Cistone (lead), LaVerne Novak (high harmony) and Patti McCabe. First recorded for Point in 1957.	
7/28/58	**7**	12	**1. Born Too Late**	ABC-Para. 9934
			Hot 100 #7 / Best Seller #11	
			POP, Iggy	
			Punk rock pioneer. Real name: James Jewel Osterberg; native of Michigan. Leader of The Stooges from 1969-74. Acted in the film *Cry-Baby.* Adopted nickname Iggy from his first band, The Iguanas.	
1/26/91	**28**	3	1. Candy	Virgin 98900#
			female vocal by Kate Pierson (B-52's)	
			POPPY FAMILY featuring SUSAN JACKS	
			Canadian pop quartet: Susan (vocals) and husband Terry Jacks (guitar, composer), Craig MacCaw (guitar) and Satwan Singh (percussion). Group and marriage broke up in 1973; Susan and Terry began solo careers.	
4/25/70	**2**(2)	13	● **1. Which Way You Goin' Billy?**	London 129
9/19/70	**29**	6	2. That's Where I Went Wrong	London 139
			POSEY, Sandy	
			Born on 6/18/47 in Jasper, Alabama; raised in West Memphis, Arkansas. Worked as a session singer in Nashville and Memphis in the early '60s. Left music from 1968-70. Backup singer on the Nashville Network.	
8/06/66	**12**	12	1. Born A Woman	MGM 13501
12/10/66	**12**	8	2. Single Girl	MGM 13612
4/08/67	**31**	2	3. What A Woman In Love Won't Do	MGM 13702
7/01/67	**12**	8	4. I Take It Back	MGM 13744
			POST, Mike	
			Born on 9/29/44 in Los Angeles. Record producer/composer of numerous TV and film scores. Orchestra leader for two TV variety shows: "The Andy Williams Show" (1969-71) and "The Mac Davis Show" (1974-76).	
6/21/75	**10**	10	**1. The Rockford Files** [I]	MGM 14772
10/03/81	**10**	10	**2. The Theme From Hill Street Blues** [I]	Elektra 47186
			featuring Larry Carlton, guitar	
4/03/82	**25**	7	3. Theme From Magnum P.I. [I]	Elektra 47400
			all of above are theme songs from TV series	
			POURCEL'S, Franck, French Fiddles	
			Frank was born on 1/01/15 in Marseilles, France. String orchestra leader/composer/arranger/violinist.	
4/27/59	**9**	11	**1. Only You** [I]	Capitol 4165
			POWELL, Jane	
			Born Suzanne Burce on 4/01/29 in Portland, Oregon. Star of many movie musicals, mid-1940s through 1950s.	
10/06/56	**15**	9	1. True Love	Verve 2018
			Best Seller #15 / Top 100 #24	
			POWERS, Joey	
			Born in 1939 in Canonsburg, Pennsylvania. Produced "The John Hills Exercise Show" for NBC-TV. Wrestling instructor at Ohio State University.	
12/07/63+	**10**	9	**1. Midnight Mary**	Amy 892

DATE	POS	WKS	ARTIST—RECORD TITLE	LABEL & NO.
			POWER STATION, The	
			Superstar quartet: Robert Palmer (lead singer), Chic's Tony Thompson (drums) and Duran Duran's John Taylor (bass) and Andy Taylor (guitar). Formed as a one-album studio project.	
3/30/85	**6**	12	**1. Some Like It Hot**	Capitol 5444
6/22/85	**9**	10	**2. Get It On**	Capitol 5479
			revival of 1972's "Bang A Gong" by T. Rex (Marc Bolan)	
10/05/85	**34**	3	3. Communication	Capitol 5511
			POZO-SECO SINGERS	
			Native Texan trio: Susan Taylor, Lofton Kline and country star Don Williams (lead singer).	
10/08/66	**32**	6	1. I Can Make It With You	Columbia 43784
1/14/67	**32**	4	2. Look What You've Done	Columbia 43927
			PRADO, Perez	
			Born Damaso Perez Prado on 12/11/16 in Mantanzas, Cuba. Bandleader/organist. Moved to Mexico City in 1949 and formed a big band. Toured and worked in the U.S. beginning in 1954. In the film *Underwater!* "The King of Mambo" died on 9/14/89 after suffering a stroke in Colonia del Valle, Mexico.	
3/05/55	**1**(10)	26	**1. Cherry Pink And Apple Blossom White** [I]	RCA 5965
			Best Seller #1(10) / Juke Box #1(8) / Jockey #1(6) trumpet solo: Billy Regis; from the film *Underwater!*	
6/23/58	**1**(1)	17	• **2. Patricia** [I]	RCA 7245
			Top 100 #1(1) / Jockey #1(1) / Best Seller #2	
			PRATT & McCLAIN	
			Truett Pratt and Jerry McClain, with backing group Brother Love.	
4/24/76	**5**	10	**1. Happy Days**	Reprise 1351
			from the TV series of the same title	
			PRELUDE	
			English folk-based trio: Ian Vardy with Brian and Irene Hume (husband & wife).	
11/02/74	**22**	5	1. After The Goldrush	Island 002
			written by Neil Young	
			PREMIERS, The	
			Latin-rock band from San Gabriel, California.	
7/04/64	**19**	6	1. Farmer John	Warner 5443
			recorded live at The Rhythm Room in Fullerton, California	
			PRESIDENTS, The	
			East Coast soul group consisting of Archie Powell, Bill Shorter and Tony Boyd.	
11/14/70	**11**	9	1. 5-10-15-20 (25-30 Years Of Love)	Sussex 207

DATE	POS	WKS	ARTIST—RECORD TITLE	LABEL & NO.
			PRESLEY, Elvis	
			"The King of Rock & Roll." Born on 1/08/35 in Tupelo, Mississippi. Died in Memphis on 8/16/77 (age 42) of heart failure caused by prescription drug abuse. Won talent contest at age eight, singing "Old Shep." First played guitar at age 11. Moved to Memphis in 1948. Sang in high school shows. Worked as an usher and truck driver after graduation. First recorded for Sun in 1954. Signed to RCA Records on 11/22/55. First film: *Love Me Tender* in 1956. In U.S. Army from 3/24/58 to 3/05/60. In many films thereafter. NBC-TV special in 1968. Married Priscilla Beaulieu on 5/01/67; divorced on 10/11/73. Priscilla pursued acting in the 1980s beginning with a role on TV's "Dallas." Their only child Lisa Marie was born on 2/01/68. Elvis' last live performance was in Indianapolis on 6/26/77. Won the Lifetime Achievement Grammy in 1971. Inducted into the Rock and Roll Hall of Fame in 1986.	
3/10/56	**1**(8)	22	**1. Heartbreak Hotel/** Best Seller #1(8) / Juke Box #1(8) / Top 100 #1(7) / Jockey #1(3)	
3/17/56	**19**	10	2. I Was The One Jockey #19 / Top 100 #23	RCA 47-6420
4/28/56	**20**	5	3. Blue Suede Shoes Best Seller #20 / Top 100 #24 / Jockey #24 from the E.P. *Elvis Presley*	RCA EPA-747
6/02/56	**1**(1)	19	**4. I Want You, I Need You, I Love You/** Best Seller #1 / Top 100 #3 / Juke Box #3 / Jockey #6	
6/09/56	**31**	3	5. My Baby Left Me written and recorded on RCA by Arthur "Big Boy" Crudup in 1950	RCA 47-6540
8/04/56	**1**(11)	24	**6. Don't Be Cruel/** Best Seller #1(11)/Juke Box #1(11)/Jockey #1(8)/Top 100 #1(7)	
8/04/56	**1**(11)	24	**7. Hound Dog** Best Seller #1(11)/Juke Box #1(11)/Top 100 #2/Jockey #4 Grammy Hall Of Fame Award winner in 1988; #1 R&B hit (7 weeks) for Big Mama Thornton in 1953	RCA 47-6604
10/20/56	**1**(5)	19	**8. Love Me Tender/** Best Seller #1(5) / Jockey #1(5) / Top 100 #1(4) / Juke Box #1(1) from Elvis' first movie; tune adapted from "Aura Lee" of 1861	
11/10/56	**20**	4	9. Anyway You Want Me (That's How I Will Be) Jockey #20 / Top 100 #27	RCA 47-6643
11/24/56+	**2**(2)	14	**10. Love Me/** Jockey #2 / Top 100 #6 / Best Seller #7 / Juke Box #8	
12/29/56	**19**	4	11. When My Blue Moon Turns To Gold Jockey #19 / Top 100 #27 above 2 from the E.P. *Elvis*	Again RCA EPA-992
1/05/57	**24**	3	12. Poor Boy Jockey #24 / Top 100 #35 from the film and the E.P. *Love Me Tender*	RCA EPA-4006
1/26/57	**1**(3)	14	**13. Too Much/** Best Seller #1(3) / Juke Box #1(1) / Top 100 #2 / Jockey #2	
2/09/57	**21**	4	14. Playing For Keeps Jockey #21 / Top 100 #34	RCA 47-6800
4/06/57	**1**(9)	22	**15. All Shook Up** Juke Box #1(9) end/Best Seller #1(8)/Top 100 #1(8)/Jockey #1(7)	RCA 47-6870
4/29/57	**25**	1	16. (There'll Be) Peace In The Valley (For Me) Best Seller #25 / Top 100 #39 from the E.P. *Peace in the Valley*	RCA EPA-4054
6/24/57	**1**(7)	18	**17. (Let Me Be Your) Teddy Bear/** Best Seller #1(7) / Top 100 #1(7) / Jockey #1(3)	

DATE	POS	WKS	ARTIST—RECORD TITLE	LABEL & NO.
7/08/57	**20**	13	18. Loving You Jockey #20 / Top 100 #28 above 2 are from the film *Loving You*	RCA 47-7000
10/14/57	1(7)	19	**19. Jailhouse Rock/** Best Seller #1(7) / Top 100 #1(6) / Jockey #1(2)	
10/21/57	**18**	6	20. Treat Me Nice Jockey #18 / Top 100 #27 above 2 are from the film *Jailhouse Rock*	RCA 47-7035
1/27/58	1(5)	16	• **21. Don't/** Best Seller #1(5) / Top 100 #1(1) / Jockey #1(1)	
2/03/58	**8**	7	**22. I Beg Of You** Top 100 #8 / Jockey #11	RCA 47-7150
4/21/58	2(1)	13	• **23. Wear My Ring Around Your Neck/** Best Seller #2 / Top 100 #3 / Jockey #3	
5/05/58	**15**	2	24. Doncha' Think It's Time Jockey #15 / Top 100 #21	RCA 47-7240
6/30/58	1(2)	14	• **25. Hard Headed Woman/** Best Seller #1(2) / Jockey #1(1) / Top 100 #2	
7/14/58	**25**	4	26. Don't Ask Me Why Jockey #25 / Top 100 #28 above 2 are from the film *King Creole*	RCA 47-7280
11/10/58	**4**	14	**27. One Night/** #11 R&B hit for Smiley Lewis in 1956	
11/10/58	**8**	12	• **28. I Got Stung**	RCA 47-7410
3/30/59	2(1)	11	• **29. (Now and Then There's) A Fool Such As I/** #4 country hit for Hank Snow in 1953	
3/30/59	**4**	10	**30. I Need Your Love Tonight**	RCA 47-7506
7/13/59	1(2)	10	**31. A Big Hunk O' Love/** above 4 are Elvis' only new recordings during his Army hitch	
7/13/59	**12**	10	32. My Wish Came True written by Ivory Joe Hunter	RCA 47-7600
4/11/60	1(4)	13	**33. Stuck On You/**	
4/25/60	**17**	7	34. Fame And Fortune above 2 recorded 15 days after his Army discharge	RCA 47-7740
7/25/60	1(5)	16	• **35. It's Now Or Never/** adapted from the Italian song "O Sole Mio" of 1899	
8/01/60	**32**	2	36. A Mess Of Blues	RCA 47-7777
11/14/60	1(6)	14	• **37. Are You Lonesome To-night?/** #4 hit for Vaughn Deleath in 1927	
11/28/60	**20**	8	38. I Gotta Know	RCA 47-7810
2/20/61	1(2)	11	**39. Surrender/** adapted from the Italian song "Come Back To Sorrento"	
3/13/61	**32**	2	40. Lonely Man from the film *Wild in the Country*	RCA 47-7850
4/24/61	**14**	5	41. Flaming Star from the film of the same title and the E.P. *Elvis By Request*	RCA LPC-128
5/22/61	**5**	7	**42. I Feel So Bad/** #8 R&B hit for Chuck Willis in 1954	
6/19/61	**26**	2	43. Wild In The Country from the film of the same title	RCA 47-7880
8/28/61	**5**	10	**44. Little Sister/**	

DATE	POS	WKS	ARTIST—RECORD TITLE	LABEL & NO.
9/04/61	**4**	7	**45. (Marie's the Name) His Latest Flame**	RCA 47-7908
12/18/61+	**2**(1)	12	● **46. Can't Help Falling In Love/**	
12/18/61+	**23**	5	47. Rock-A-Hula Baby above 2 are from the film *Blue Hawaii*	RCA 47-7968
3/24/62	**1**(2)	11	**48. Good Luck Charm/**	
4/07/62	**31**	5	49. Anything That's Part Of You	RCA 47-7992
5/19/62	**15**	7	50. Follow That Dream from the film and the E.P. of the same title	RCA EPA-4368
8/11/62	**5**	9	**51. She's Not You**	RCA 47-8041
10/06/62	**30**	4	52. King Of The Whole Wide World from the film and E.P. *Kid Galahad*	RCA EPA-4371
10/27/62	**2**(5)	14	● **53. Return To Sender** from the film *Girls! Girls! Girls!*	RCA 47-8100
2/23/63	**11**	7	54. One Broken Heart For Sale from the film *It Happened at the World's Fair*	RCA 47-8134
7/13/63	**3**	8	**55. (You're the) Devil In Disguise**	RCA 47-8188
11/02/63	**8**	7	**56. Bossa Nova Baby/** from the film *Fun in Acapulco*	
11/09/63	**32**	3	57. Witchcraft #5 R&B hit for The Spiders in 1956	RCA 47-8243
3/07/64	**12**	7	58. Kissin' Cousins/ from the film of the same title	
3/14/64	**29**	4	59. It Hurts Me	RCA 47-8307
5/23/64	**34**	2	60. Kiss Me Quick recorded on 6/25/61 (on the album *Pot Luck*)	RCA 447-0639
5/30/64	**21**	5	61. What'd I Say/	
5/30/64	**29**	4	62. Viva Las Vegas above 2 from the film *Viva Las Vegas*	RCA 47-8360
8/08/64	**16**	6	63. Such A Night recorded on 4/04/60 (on the album *Elvis Is Back!*)	RCA 47-8400
10/24/64	**12**	8	64. Ask Me/	
10/24/64	**16**	8	65. Ain't That Loving You Baby recorded June 10, 1958	RCA 47-8440
3/13/65	**21**	6	66. Do The Clam from the film *Girl Happy*	RCA 47-8500
5/08/65	**3**	11	● **67. Crying In The Chapel** recorded on 10/31/60	RCA 447-0643
7/03/65	**11**	6	68. (Such An) Easy Question recorded on March 18, 1962 (on the *Pot Luck* LP); from the film *Tickle Me*	RCA 47-8585
9/18/65	**11**	7	69. I'm Yours recorded on June 26, 1961 (on the album *Pot Luck*)	RCA 47-8657
12/04/65	**14**	6	70. Puppet On A String from the film *Girl Happy*	RCA 447-0650
1/22/66	**33**	3	71. Tell Me Why recorded on January 12, 1957	RCA 47-8740
4/09/66	**25**	5	72. Frankie And Johnny version of classic song written around 1850; from the film of the same title	RCA 47-8780
7/09/66	**19**	5	73. Love Letters	RCA 47-8870

DATE	POS	WKS	ARTIST—RECORD TITLE	LABEL & NO.
			#11 hit for Dick Haymes in 1945	
11/05/66	**40**	2	74. Spinout	RCA 47-8941
			from the film of the same title	
2/18/67	**33**	4	75. Indescribably Blue	RCA 47-9056
11/04/67	**38**	2	76. Big Boss Man	RCA 47-9341
4/20/68	**28**	4	77. U.S. Male	RCA 47-9465
			written and originally recorded by Jerry Reed; vocal group on nearly all of above titles: The Jordanaires	
12/14/68+	**12**	11	78. If I Can Dream	RCA 47-9670
4/12/69	**35**	2	79. Memories	RCA 47-9731
			from the NBC-TV special *Elvis*	
5/17/69	**3**	11	● **80. In The Ghetto**	RCA 47-9741
8/02/69	**35**	4	81. Clean Up Your Own Back Yard	RCA 47-9747
			from the film *The Trouble with Girls* (and how to get into it)	
9/20/69	**1**(1)	13	● **82. Suspicious Minds**	RCA 47-9764
12/13/69+	**6**	11	● **83. Don't Cry Daddy**	RCA 47-9768
2/21/70	**16**	8	84. Kentucky Rain	RCA 47-9791
			written by Eddie Rabbitt	
5/23/70	**9**	11	● **85. The Wonder Of You**	RCA 47-9835
			recorded live at Las Vegas	
8/22/70	**32**	3	86. I've Lost You/	
		3	87. The Next Step Is Love	RCA 47-9873
11/07/70	**11**	8	88. You Don't Have To Say You Love Me	RCA 47-9916
1/02/71	**21**	8	89. I Really Don't Want To Know/	
			#11 hit for Les Paul & Mary Ford in 1954	
		8	90. There Goes My Everything	RCA 47-9960
3/27/71	**33**	4	91. Where Did They Go, Lord/	
		4	92. Rags To Riches	RCA 47-9980
			#1 hit (8 weeks) for Tony Bennett in 1953	
8/14/71	**36**	2	93. I'm Leavin'	RCA 47-9998
3/11/72	**40**	1	94. Until It's Time For You To Go	RCA 74-0619
			written by Buffy Sainte-Marie	
9/09/72	**2**(1)	12	● **95. Burning Love**	RCA 74-0769
12/23/72+	**20**	8	96. Separate Ways	RCA 74-0815
			featured in the film *Elvis on Tour*	
5/05/73	**17**	7	97. Steamroller Blues	RCA 74-0910
			recorded live in Hawaii (written by James Taylor in 1970)	
3/23/74	**39**	2	98. I've Got A Thing About You Baby	RCA APBO-0196
6/29/74	**17**	7	99. If You Talk In Your Sleep	RCA APBO-0280
11/09/74	**14**	9	100. Promised Land	RCA PB-10074
2/15/75	**20**	6	101. My Boy	RCA PB-10191
6/07/75	**35**	3	102. T-R-O-U-B-L-E	RCA PB-10278
5/01/76	**28**	5	103. Hurt	RCA PB-10601
2/05/77	**31**	5	104. Moody Blue	RCA PB-10857
7/16/77	**18**	12	● 105. Way Down	RCA PB-10998
12/03/77	**22**	7	● 106. My Way	RCA PB-11165
			recorded live from Elvis' tour; written by Paul Anka in 1969	
2/28/81	**28**	5	107. Guitar Man [R]	RCA PB-12158
			remix by Felton Jarvis (d: 1/03/81) of Elvis' 1968 hit	

DATE	POS	WKS	ARTIST—RECORD TITLE	LABEL & NO.
			PRESTON, Billy	
			Born on 9/09/46 in Houston. R&B vocalist/keyboardist. To Los Angeles at an early age. With Mahalia Jackson in 1956. Played piano in film *St. Louis Blues*, 1958. Regular on "Shindig" TV show. Recorded with The Beatles on "Get Back" and "Let It Be"; worked Concert For Bangladesh in 1969. Prominent session man, played on Sly & The Family Stone hits. With The Rolling Stones U.S. tour in 1975.	
5/13/72	**2**(1)	14	● **1. Outa-Space** [I]	A&M 1320
5/19/73	**1**(2)	14	● **2. Will It Go Round In Circles**	A&M 1411
10/13/73	**4**	13	● **3. Space Race** [I]	A&M 1463
8/03/74	**1**(1)	14	● **4. Nothing From Nothing**	A&M 1544
1/04/75	**22**	6	5. Struttin' [I] B-side is tune Preston wrote, "You Are So Beautiful"	A&M 1644
3/01/80	**4**	15	**6. With You I'm Born Again** **BILLY PRESTON & SYREETA** Syreeta (Wright) was married to Stevie Wonder	Motown 1477
			PRESTON, Johnny	
			Born John Preston Courville on 8/18/39 in Port Arthur, Texas. Discovered by J.P. "Big Bopper" Richardson at the Twilight Club in Port Neches, Texas.	
12/21/59+	**1**(3)	14	**1. Running Bear** Indian sounds by the Big Bopper and George Jones; written by the Big Bopper (J.P. Richardson)	Mercury 71474
4/04/60	**7**	12	**2. Cradle Of Love**	Mercury 71598
7/25/60	**14**	7	3. Feel So Fine Shirley & Lee's version "Feel So Good" hit POS 2-R&B in 1955	Mercury 71651
			PRETENDERS, The	
			Rock quartet featuring lead singer/songwriter/guitarist Chrissie Hynde (b: 9/07/51, Akron, Ohio). Formed in 1978, early British lineup included guitarist James Honeyman-Scott (d: 6/16/82; replaced by Robbie MacIntosh), bassist Pete Farndon (d: 4/14/83; replaced in 1982 by Malcolm Foster) and drummer Martin Chambers. Hynde married Jim Kerr of Simple Minds in 1984. With the exception of Hynde, numerous personnel changes since 1985. Also see UB40.	
4/12/80	**14**	12	1. Brass In Pocket (I'm Special)	Sire 49181
1/29/83	**5**	14	**2. Back On The Chain Gang** from the film *The King of Comedy*	Sire 29840
1/07/84	**19**	9	3. Middle Of The Road	Sire 29444
4/07/84	**28**	6	4. Show Me	Sire 29317
11/01/86	**10**	13	**5. Don't Get Me Wrong**	Sire 28630
			PRETTY POISON	
			Philadelphia dance band founded by Camden, New Jersey natives Jade Starling (vocals) and Whey Cooler.	
10/31/87	**8**	14	● **1. Catch Me (I'm Falling)** from the film *Hiding Out*	Virgin 99416
5/07/88	**36**	4	2. Nightime [R] remake of Svengali 8403 (hit R&B charts on 10/27/84 [POS 82])	Virgin 99350

DATE	POS	WKS	ARTIST—RECORD TITLE	LABEL & NO.
			PRICE, Lloyd	
			Born on 3/09/33 in Kenner, Louisiana. R&B vocalist/pianist/composer. First recording was the #1 R&B hit "Lawdy Miss Clawdy" on Specialty in 1952. In U.S. Army, 1953-56. Formed own record company, KRC, in 1957; leased "Just Because" to ABC Records. Signed to ABC in 1958. Formed Double-L label in 1963. In later years has continued in music, production, and booking agency work.	
4/06/57	**29**	6	1. Just Because	ABC-Para. 9792
1/05/59	**1**(4)	15	**2. Stagger Lee**	ABC-Para. 9972
3/30/59	**23**	4	3. Where Were You (On Our Wedding Day)?	ABC-Para. 9997
5/11/59	**2**(3)	14	**4. Personality**	ABC-Para. 10018
8/17/59	**3**	12	**5. I'm Gonna Get Married**	ABC-Para. 10032
11/23/59	**20**	9	6. Come Into My Heart	ABC-Para. 10062
2/15/60	**14**	9	7. Lady Luck	ABC-Para. 10075
5/30/60	**40**	1	8. No If's - No And's	ABC-Para. 10102
7/18/60	**19**	7	9. Question	ABC-Para. 10123
10/26/63	**21**	6	10. Misty	Double-L 722
			PRICE, Ray	
			Country singer, born on 1/12/26 in Perryville, Texas and raised in Dallas. Ray charted over 80 top 40 singles on *Billboard's* country charts. Known as "The Cherokee Cowboy."	
11/07/70+	**11**	14	1. For The Good Times written by Kris Kristofferson	Columbia 45178
			PRIDE, Charley	
			Born on 3/18/38 in Sledge, Mississippi. Discovered by Red Sovine in 1963. The most successful black country performer. Charley has charted 29 #1 singles on the country charts.	
12/18/71+	**21**	11	• 1. Kiss An Angel Good Mornin'	RCA 0550
			PRIEST, Maxi	
			Reggae singer born and raised in England.	
12/10/88+	**25**	7	1. Wild World	Virgin 99269
8/11/90	**1**(1)	17	• **2. Close To You**	Charisma 98951#
			PRIMA, Louis, & KEELY SMITH	
			Jazz trumpeter/singer/composer/bandleader. Prima (b: 12/07/11, New Orleans; d: 8/24/78) married jazz- styled vocalist Dorothy Keely Smith (b: 3/09/32, Norfolk, Virginia) in 1952; divorced in 1961. First appeared with Prima in 1948.	
11/24/58	**18**	7	1. That Old Black Magic with Sam Butera and The Witnesses; from the film *Senior Prom*	Capitol 4063
12/12/60+	**15**	8	2. Wonderland By Night [I] **LOUIS PRIMA**	Dot 16151

DATE	POS	WKS	ARTIST—RECORD TITLE	LABEL & NO.
			PRINCE	
			Born Prince Roger Nelson on 6/07/58 in Minneapolis. Vocalist/multi-instrumentalist/composer/producer/ actor. Named for the Prince Roger Trio, led by his father. Self-taught musician; own band, Grand Central, in junior high school. Self-produced first album in 1978. Starred in the films *Purple Rain* (1984), *Under the Cherry Moon* (1986), *Sign 'o' the Times* (1987) and *Graffiti Bridge* (1990). Founded own label, Paisley Park. The Revolution featured Lisa Coleman (keyboards), Wendy Melvoin (guitar; twin sister of The Family's vocalist, Susannah), Bobby Z (percussion), Matt "Dr." Fink (keyboards), Eric Leeds (saxophone) and Andre Cymone (bass; replaced by Brownmark in 1981). In 1986, Brownmark founded Mazarati (who also backed Prince). Leeds formed Madhouse in 1987. Coleman and Melvoin recorded as Wendy & Lisa in 1988. Sheila E. (drums) joined Prince's band in 1986. Prince's sister Tyka Nelson began recording in 1988. Prince formed new band, New Power Generation (named for the oldest Prince fan club in Britain), in 1990, featuring Levi Seacer, Jr. (guitar), Sonny T. (bass), Tommy Barbarella (keyboard), dancer/percussionists Kirk Johnson and Damon Dickson, Michael Bland (drums), rapper Tony M. and Rosie Gaines (keyboards, vocals).	
12/08/79+	**11**	12	● 1. I Wanna Be Your Lover	Warner 49050
3/19/83	**6**	15	**2. Little Red Corvette**	Warner 29746
6/18/83	**12**	10	3. 1999	Warner 29896
9/17/83	**8**	11	**4. Delirious**	Warner 29503
6/09/84	**1**(5)	16	▲ **5. When Doves Cry**	Warner 29286
			PRINCE AND THE REVOLUTION:	
8/11/84	**1**(2)	14	● **6. Let's Go Crazy**	Warner 29216
10/06/84	**2**(2)	11	● **7. Purple Rain**	Warner 29174
12/22/84+	**8**	10	**8. I Would Die 4 U**	Warner 29121
3/02/85	**25**	6	9. Take Me With U	Warner 29079
			female vocals: Apollonia; above 5 from the film *Purple Rain*	
5/18/85	**2**(1)	14	**10. Raspberry Beret**	Paisley P. 28972
8/03/85	**7**	10	**11. Pop Life**	Paisley P. 28998
3/08/86	**1**(2)	13	● **12. Kiss**	Paisley P. 28751
6/14/86	**23**	6	13. Mountains	Paisley P. 28711
			above 2 from the film *Under the Cherry Moon*	
			PRINCE:	
3/14/87	**3**	11	**14. Sign 'O' The Times**	Paisley P. 28399
8/29/87	**2**(1)	13	**15. U Got The Look**	Paisley P. 28289
			backing vocal by Sheena Easton	
12/05/87+	**10**	12	**16. I Could Never Take The Place Of Your Man**	Paisley P. 28288
5/14/88	**8**	9	**17. Alphabet St.**	Paisley P. 27900
7/01/89	**1**(1)	11	▲ **18. Batdance**	Warner 22924
			includes snippets of dialog from the film *Batman*	
9/02/89	**18**	7	● 19. Partyman	Warner 22814
12/02/89	**36**	3	20. The Arms Of Orion	Warner 22757
			PRINCE with SHEENA EASTON	
			above 2 from the film *Batman*	
8/11/90	**6**	9	● **21. Thieves In The Temple**	Paisley P. 19751
			from the film *Graffiti Bridge*	
			PRISM	
			Canadian rock group — Ron Tabak, lead singer (replaced by Henry Small in 1981).	
3/13/82	**39**	2	1. Don't Let Him Know	Capitol 5082

DATE	POS	WKS	ARTIST—RECORD TITLE	LABEL & NO.
			PROBY, P.J.	
			Born James Marcus Smith on 11/06/38 in Houston. Achieved greater popularity in England than U.S.	
2/25/67	**23**	5	1. Niki Hoeky	Liberty 55936
			PROCOL HARUM	
			British rock group led by Gary Brooker (vocals, piano). Guitarist Robin Trower was a member from 1968-71. Translation of Latin group name: "beyond these things."	
7/01/67	**5**	10	**1. A Whiter Shade Of Pale**	Deram 7507
			melody based on the Bach cantata *Sleepers Awake*	
11/11/67	**34**	2	2. Homburg	A&M 885
6/24/72	**16**	8	3. Conquistador	A&M 1347
			PRUETT, Jeanne	
			Country singer/songwriter, born Norma Jean Bowman on 1/30/37 in Pell City, Alabama. Moved to Nashville in 1956 with husband Jack Pruett (guitarist for Marty Robbins). Songwriter for Marty Robbins since 1963.	
6/23/73	**28**	5	1. Satin Sheets	MCA 40015
			PSEUDO ECHO	
			Techno-rock quartet from Melbourne, Australia — Brian Canham, lead singer.	
6/06/87	**6**	10	**1. Funky Town**	RCA 5217
			PSYCHEDELIC FURS	
			U.S.-based, British techno-rock group formed in 1979. Consists of brothers Richard (vocals) and Tim Butler (bass), with John Ashton (guitar) and Vince Ely (drums).	
5/02/87	**26**	5	1. Heartbreak Beat	Columbia 06420
			PUCKETT, Gary/The Union Gap	
			Singer/guitarist Puckett (b: 10/17/42, Hibbing, Minnesota) formed The Union Gap in San Diego in 1967; named after the town of Union Gap, Washington. Included Kerry Chater (bass), Paul Whitebread (drums), Dwight Bement (sax) and Gary Withem (keyboards).	
			THE UNION GAP featuring GARY PUCKETT:	
12/02/67+	**4**	15	● **1. Woman, Woman**	Columbia 44297
3/16/68	**2**(3)	13	● **2. Young Girl**	Columbia 44450
			GARY PUCKETT AND THE UNION GAP:	
6/22/68	**2**(2)	11	● **3. Lady Willpower**	Columbia 44547
9/28/68	**7**	10	● **4. Over You**	Columbia 44644
3/22/69	**15**	8	5. Don't Give In To Him	Columbia 44788
9/06/69	**9**	9	**6. This Girl Is A Woman Now**	Columbia 44967
			PURE PRAIRIE LEAGUE	
			Country-rock group formed in Cincinnati in 1971. Numerous personnel changes. Country singer Vince Gill was lead singer from 1980-83.	
4/12/75	**27**	3	1. Amie	RCA 10184
5/24/80	**10**	11	**2. Let Me Love You Tonight**	Casablanca 2266
10/04/80	**34**	4	3. I'm Almost Ready	Casablanca 2294
5/23/81	**28**	7	4. Still Right Here In My Heart	Casablanca 2332

DATE	POS	WKS	ARTIST—RECORD TITLE	LABEL & NO.
			PURIFY, James & Bobby	
			R&B duo: cousins James Purify (b: 5/12/44, Pensacola, Florida) and Robert Lee Dickey (b: 9/02/39, Tallahassee, Florida). Dickey left in the late 60s. Purify worked solo until 1974, when Ben Moore became "Bobby Purify."	
10/22/66	**6**	10	**1. I'm Your Puppet**	Bell 648
2/25/67	**38**	1	2. Wish You Didn't Have To Go	Bell 660
5/13/67	**25**	5	3. Shake A Tail Feather	Bell 669
10/07/67	**23**	5	4. Let Love Come Between Us	Bell 685
			PURSELL, Bill	
			Pianist from Tulare, California. Appeared with the Nashville Symphony Orchestra. Taught musical composition at Vanderbilt University.	
2/16/63	**9**	10	**1. Our Winter Love** [I]	Columbia 42619
			PYRAMIDS, The	
			Surf band from Long Beach, California: Skip Mercer, Willie Glover, Steve Leonard, Ron McMullen and Tom Pittman.	
2/22/64	**18**	6	1. Penetration [I] also released on Best 102 in 1964	Best 13002
			Q	
4/09/77	**23**	7	1. Dancin' Man	Epic 50335
			QUAKER CITY BOYS	
			Philadelphia string band — Tommy Reilly, leader.	
1/26/59	**39**	1	1. Teasin'	Swan 4023
			QUARTERFLASH	
			Rock group from Portland, Oregon led by the husband-and-wife team of Marv (guitar) and Rindy (vocals, saxophone) Ross. Originally known as Seafood Mama.	
11/07/81+	**3**	19	**1. Harden My Heart** originally released as by Seafood Mama on Whitefire in 1980	Geffen 49824
3/13/82	**16**	7	2. Find Another Fool	Geffen 50006
7/02/83	**14**	11	3. Take Me To Heart	Geffen 29603
			QUATRO, Suzi	
			Rock singer born on 6/03/50 in Detroit. Moved to England in 1970, signed with Mickie Most's RAK label. Played Leather Tuscadero on TV's "Happy Days" in 1977. Her older sister Patti was a bassist with Fanny.	
2/24/79	**4**	15	● **1. Stumblin' In** **SUZI QUATRO AND CHRIS NORMAN** (lead singer of Smokie)	RSO 917
			QUEEN	
			Rock group formed in England in 1972: Freddie Mercury (born Fred Bulsara on 9/05/46 in Zanzibar; d:11/24/91 of AIDS; vocals), Brian May (guitar), John Deacon (bass) and Roger Taylor (drums). May and Taylor had been in the group Smile. Mercury had recorded as Larry Lurex. Wrote soundtrack for the film *Flash Gordon* in 1980.	
3/29/75	**12**	11	1. Killer Queen	Elektra 45226
2/07/76	**9**	17	● **2. Bohemian Rhapsody**	Elektra 45297

DATE	POS	WKS	ARTIST—RECORD TITLE	LABEL & NO.
6/12/76	**16**	11	3. You're My Best Friend	Elektra 45318
12/04/76+	**13**	12	4. Somebody To Love	Elektra 45362
11/26/77+	**4**	17	▲ **5. We Are The Champions/**	
			6. We Will Rock You although *Billboard* did not chart this B-side, it received extensive airplay because the B- and A-sides were segued together on the album *News of the World*	Elektra 45441
12/09/78+	**24**	6	7. Bicycle Race/	
		6	8. Fat Bottomed Girls	Elektra 45541
1/12/80	**1**(4)	17	● **9. Crazy Little Thing Called Love**	Elektra 46579
8/30/80	**1**(3)	21	▲ **10. Another One Bites The Dust**	Elektra 47031
12/05/81+	**29**	8	11. Under Pressure **QUEEN & DAVID BOWIE**	Elektra 47235
5/15/82	**11**	8	12. Body Language	Elektra 47452
3/03/84	**16**	8	13. Radio Ga-Ga	Capitol 5317
			QUEENSRYCHE Heavy-metal quintet formed in 1981, in Bellevue, Washington, by high school classmates: Geoff Tate (vocals), Chris DeGarmo, Michael Wilton, Eddie Jackson and Scott Rockenfield.	
4/13/91	**9**	11	**1. Silent Lucidity**	EMI 50345#
			? (QUESTION MARK) & THE MYSTERIANS Early-punk rock quintet. Lead singer Rudy Martinez was born in Mexico and raised in Saginaw, Michigan.	
9/17/66	**1**(1)	12	● **1. 96 Tears** first released on Pa-Go-Go 102 in 1966	Cameo 428
12/10/66	**22**	6	2. I Need Somebody	Cameo 441
			QUIET RIOT Heavy-metal rock quartet from Los Angeles: Kevin DuBrow (lead singer), Carlos Cavazo (guitar), Frankie Banali (drums) and Rudy Sarzo (bass; replaced by Chuck Wright in 1985). DuBrow and Wright left group in 1987; replaced by Paul Shortino (vocals) and Sean McNabb (bass).	
10/15/83	**5**	14	● **1. Cum On Feel The Noize**	Pasha 04005
1/28/84	**31**	4	2. Bang Your Head (Metal Health)	Pasha 04267
			QUIN-TONES, The York, Pennysylvania group consisting of Roberta Haymon (lead singer), Phyllis Carr, Carolyn Holmes, Kenny Sexton, Jeannie Crist and Ronnie Scott (pianist).	
9/08/58	**18**	6	1. Down The Aisle Of Love Best Seller #18 / Hot 100 #20	Hunt 321
			R	
			RABBITT, Eddie Born Edward Thomas Rabbitt on 11/27/44 in Brooklyn; raised in East Orange, New Jersey. Country singer/songwriter/guitarist. First recorded for 20th Century in 1964. Moved to Nashville in 1968. Became established after Elvis Presley recorded his song "Kentucky Rain."	
3/03/79	**30**	4	1. Every Which Way But Loose from the film of the same title	Elektra 45554

DATE	POS	WKS	ARTIST—RECORD TITLE	LABEL & NO.
7/14/79	**13**	10	2. Suspicions	Elektra 46053
7/26/80	**5**	15	● **3. Drivin' My Life Away** from the film *Roadie*	Elektra 46656
12/06/80+	**1**(2)	18	● **4. I Love A Rainy Night**	Elektra 47066
8/08/81	**5**	15	**5. Step By Step**	Elektra 47174
12/05/81+	**15**	10	6. Someone Could Lose A Heart Tonight	Elektra 47239
5/22/82	**35**	4	7. I Don't Know Where To Start	Elektra 47435
11/13/82+	**7**	21	**8. You And I** **EDDIE RABBITT with CRYSTAL GAYLE**	Elektra 69936
			RAFFERTY, Gerry	
			Born on 4/16/47 in Paisley, Scotland. Singer/songwriter/guitarist. Co-leader of Stealers Wheel.	
5/13/78	**2**(6)	15	● **1. Baker Street** sax solo: Raphael Ravenscroft	United Art. 1192
8/26/78	**12**	10	2. Right Down The Line	United Art. 1233
1/06/79	**28**	6	3. Home And Dry	United Art. 1266
6/16/79	**17**	7	4. Days Gone Down (Still Got The Light In Your Eyes)	United Art. 1298
9/08/79	**21**	8	5. Get It Right Next Time	United Art. 1316
			RAIDERS, The — see REVERE, Paul	
			RAINBOW	
			Hard-rock band led by British guitarist Ritchie Blackmore and bassist Roger Glover, both members of Deep Purple. Fluctuating lineup included vocalists Ronnie James Dio and Joe Lynn Turner, keyboardist Tony Carey and drummer Cozy Powell. Group split up upon re-formation of Deep Purple in 1984. Turner joined Deep Purple in 1990.	
6/19/82	**40**	1	1. Stone Cold	Mercury 76146
			RAINDROPS, The	
			Songwriting team of Ellie Greenwich (b: 10/23/40) and husband Jeff Barry (b: 4/03/38). Divorced in 1965, but continued to work together. Barry wrote "Tell Laura I Love Her"; team wrote "Be My Baby," "Da Doo Ron Ron," "Chapel Of Love," "River Deep-Mountain High," "Hanky Panky," "Leader of The Pack" and many more.	
8/31/63	**17**	7	1. The Kind Of Boy You Can't Forget	Jubilee 5455
			RAINWATER, Marvin	
			Born Marvin Karlton Percy on 7/02/25 in Wichita, Kansas. Rockabilly singer of Cherokee Indian heritage. Worked on Arthur Godfrey's TV show in 1955.	
6/10/57	**18**	12	1. Gonna Find Me A Bluebird Juke Box #18 end / Best Seller #19 / Top 100 #22	MGM 12412
			RAMBEAU, Eddie	
			Born Edward Flurie on 6/30/43 in Hazleton, Pennsylvania. Pop singer/songwriter.	
6/05/65	**35**	2	1. Concrete And Clay	DynoVoice 204
			RAM JAM	
			East Coast rock quartet led by Bill Bartlett (lead guitarist of The Lemon Pipers). Member Howie Blauvelt played bass in Billy Joel's group, The Hassles.	
7/23/77	**18**	8	1. Black Betty written by legendary black folksinger Hudie Ledbetter (Leadbelly)	Epic 50357

DATE	POS	WKS	ARTIST—RECORD TITLE	LABEL & NO.
			RAMRODS	
			Instrumental rock quartet from Conncecticut: Vincent Bell Lee (lead guitar) and his cousin Eugene Morrow, Richard Lane and his sister Claire. Lee recorded solo as Vincent Bell.	
2/20/61	**30**	1	1. (Ghost) Riders In The Sky [I]	Amy 813
			RAN-DELLS, The	
			Brothers Steve and Robert Rappaport, and cousin John Spirt from Villas, New Jersey.	
8/31/63	**16**	8	1. Martian Hop [N]	Chairman 4403
			RANDOLPH, Boots	
			Born Homer Louis Randolph, III in Paducah, Kentucky. Premier Nashville session saxophonist.	
3/30/63	**35**	3	1. Yakety Sax [I]	Monument 804
			RANDY & THE RAINBOWS	
			Pop group from Queens, New York, originally called Jr. And The Counts. Consisted of Dominick "Randy" Safuto (lead) and brother Frank Safuto, brothers Mike and Sal Zero, and Ken Arcipowski.	
7/27/63	**10**	10	**1. Denise**	Rust 5059
			RARE EARTH	
			Nucleus of Detroit rock group: Gil Bridges (saxophone, flute), John Persh (trombone, bass) and Pete Rivera (drums). Worked as the Sunliners in the '60s. In 1970, added Ed Guzman (percussion) and Ray Monette (replaced guitarist Rob Richards). Mark Olson replaced Kenneth James (keyboards) in 1971. Many changes thereafter.	
4/04/70	**4**	17	**1. Get Ready**	Rare Earth 5012
8/22/70	**7**	11	**2. (I Know) I'm Losing You**	Rare Earth 5017
1/02/71	**17**	8	3. Born To Wander	Rare Earth 5021
8/07/71	**7**	10	**4. I Just Want To Celebrate**	Rare Earth 5031
12/18/71+	**19**	7	5. Hey Big Brother	Rare Earth 5038
6/17/78	**39**	2	6. Warm Ride written by the Bee Gees	Prodigal 0640
			RASCALS, The	
			Blue-eyed, soul-pop quartet formed in New York City in 1964. Consisted of Felix Cavaliere, Dino Danelli, Eddie Brigati and Gene Cornish. All except Danelli had been in Joey Dee's Starliters. Brigati and Cornish left in 1971, replaced by Robert Popwell, Buzzy Feiten and Ann Sutton. Group disbanded in 1972. Cavaliere, Cornish and Danelli reunited in June 1988.	
			THE YOUNG RASCALS:	
3/26/66	**1**(1)	12	**1. Good Lovin'**	Atlantic 2321
7/09/66	**20**	4	2. You Better Run	Atlantic 2338
2/25/67	**16**	9	3. I've Been Lonely Too Long	Atlantic 2377
5/06/67	**1**(4)	11	● **4. Groovin'**	Atlantic 2401
7/22/67	**10**	8	**5. A Girl Like You**	Atlantic 2424
9/23/67	**4**	9	**6. How Can I Be Sure**	Atlantic 2438
12/23/67+	**20**	5	7. It's Wonderful	Atlantic 2463
			THE RASCALS:	
4/20/68	**3**	11	● **8. A Beautiful Morning**	Atlantic 2493
7/27/68	**1**(5)	13	● **9. People Got To Be Free**	Atlantic 2537
12/14/68+	**24**	6	10. A Ray Of Hope	Atlantic 2584
3/01/69	**39**	2	11. Heaven	Atlantic 2599

DATE	POS	WKS	ARTIST—RECORD TITLE	LABEL & NO.
6/07/69	**27**	5	12. See	Atlantic 2634
9/20/69	**26**	6	13. Carry Me Back	Atlantic 2664
			RASPBERRIES	
			Pop-rock band formed in Mentor, Ohio in 1971: Eric Carmen (lead singer, guitar), Wally Bryson (lead guitar), David Smalley (bass) and Jim Bonfanti (drums). Smalley and Bonfanti replaced by Scott McCarl and Michael McBride in 1974. Carmen went solo in 1975.	
8/19/72	**5**	11	• **1. Go All The Way**	Capitol 3348
12/09/72+	**16**	9	2. I Wanna Be With You	Capitol 3473
5/12/73	**35**	7	3. Let's Pretend	Capitol 3546
10/12/74	**18**	6	4. Overnight Sensation (Hit Record)	Capitol 3946
			RATT	
			Hard-rock quintet from Los Angeles: Stephen Pearcy (lead singer), Warren DeMartini (guitar), Robbin Crosby (guitar), Juan Croucier (bass) and Bobby Blotzer (drums; also a member of Contraband in 1991).	
7/14/84	**12**	10	1. Round And Round	Atlantic 89693
8/17/85	**40**	1	2. Lay It Down	Atlantic 89546
			RAWLS, Lou	
			Born on 12/01/35 in Chicago. With the Pilgrim Travelers gospel group, 1957-59. Summer replacement TV show "Lou Rawls & The Golddiggers" in 1969. In films *Angel Angel, Down We Go* and *Believe in Me.* Voice of many Budweiser beer ads and featured singer in the "Garfield" TV specials.	
10/15/66	**13**	8	1. Love Is A Hurtin' Thing	Capitol 5709
5/06/67	**29**	4	2. Dead End Street the first 1:27 of this tune is a monologue by Rawls	Capitol 5869
8/30/69	**18**	8	3. Your Good Thing (Is About To End)	Capitol 2550
10/16/71	**17**	11	4. A Natural Man	MGM 14262
7/10/76	**2**(2)	13	• **5. You'll Never Find Another Love Like Mine**	Phil. Int. 3592
2/25/78	**24**	8	6. Lady Love	Phil. Int. 3634
			RAY, Diane	
			Born on 9/01/42 in Gastonia, North Carolina.	
9/07/63	**31**	3	1. Please Don't Talk To The Lifeguard	Mercury 72117
			RAY, James	
			R&B singer, born in 1941 in Washington, D.C.	
12/25/61+	**22**	7	1. If You Gotta Make A Fool Of Somebody with the Hutch Davie Orchestra	Caprice 110
			RAY, Johnnie	
			Born on 1/10/27 in Dallas, Oregon. Wore hearing aid since age 14. First recorded for Okeh in 1951. Famous for emotion-packed delivery, with R&B influences. Appeared in three films. Died on 2/25/90 of liver failure.	
9/08/56	**2**(1)	23	**1. Just Walking In The Rain** Top 100 #2 / Juke Box #2 / Best Seller #3 / Jockey #3	Columbia 40729
1/19/57	**10**	10	**2. You Don't Owe Me A Thing/** Best Seller #10 / Top 100 #10 / Jockey #10 / Juke Box #12 written by Marty Robbins	
2/02/57	**36**	2	3. Look Homeward, Angel	Columbia 40803
5/06/57	**12**	5	4. Yes Tonight, Josephine Jockey #12 / Top 100 #18 all of above with Ray Conniff's Orchestra and Chorus	Columbia 40893

DATE	POS	WKS	ARTIST—RECORD TITLE	LABEL & NO.
			RAYBURN, Margie	
			Born in Madera, California. Member of The Sunnysiders; also sang with Ray Anthony's Orchestra. Married Norman Milkin of The Sunnysiders.	
11/11/57	**9**	13	**1. I'm Available**	Liberty 55102
			Jockey #9 / Best Seller #15 / Top 100 #16	
			RAYDIO — see PARKER, Ray Jr.	
			RAY, GOODMAN & BROWN — see MOMENTS, The	
			RAYS, The	
			R&B group formed in New York City in 1955: Harold Miller (lead), Walter Ford and David Jones (tenors) and Harry James (baritone). First recorded for Chess in 1955.	
10/21/57	**3**	17	**1. Silhouettes**	Cameo 117
			Top 100 #3 / Best Seller #4 / Jockey #5 first released on XYZ 102 in 1957	
			REA, Chris	
			Born on 3/04/51 in Middlesborough, England. Pop singer/songwriter.	
7/29/78	**12**	10	1. Fool (If You Think It's Over)	United Art. 1198
			READY FOR THE WORLD	
			Black sextet from Flint, Michigan, formed in 1982: Melvin Riley, Jr. (lead singer), Gordon Strozier, Gregory Potts, Willie Triplett, John Eaton and Gerald Valentine.	
8/24/85	**1**(1)	13	**1. Oh Sheila**	MCA 52636
1/25/86	**21**	6	2. Digital Display	MCA 52734
12/27/86+	**9**	12	**3. Love You Down**	MCA 52947
			REAL LIFE	
			Australian quartet — David Sterry, lead singer.	
1/14/84	**29**	6	1. Send Me An Angel	Curb 52287
5/05/84	**40**	1	2. Catch Me I'm Falling	Curb 52362
6/10/89	**26**	8	3. Send Me An Angel '89 [R]	Curb 10531
			REBELS, The	
			Buffalo DJ Tom Shannon and producer Phil Todaro (Shan-Todd label) recruited the Buffalo group, The Rebels (aka: The Rockin' Rebels) to record Shannon's theme song "Wild Weekend." Consisted of twins Mickey & Jim Kipler, Paul Balon and Tom Gorman. Later Swan recordings, which were billed as The Rockin' Rebels, were by a different group that recorded as the Hot-Toddys in 1959.	
1/26/63	**8**	12	**1. Wild Weekend** [I]	Swan 4125
			first released on Mar-Lee 0094 in 1960	
			REDBONE	
			American Indian "swamp rock" group formed in Los Angeles in 1968. Consisted of brothers Lolly (lead vocals, guitar) and Pat Vegas (lead vocals, bass), Anthony Bellamy (guitar) and Peter De Poe (drums). The Vegas brothers had been session musicians and worked the "Shindig" TV show.	
1/08/72	**21**	7	1. The Witch Queen Of New Orleans	Epic 10749
2/09/74	**5**	18	• **2. Come And Get Your Love**	Epic 11035
			REDDING, Gene	
			Born in Anderson, Indiana in 1945. Discovered by Etta James at a USO Club in Anchorage, Alaska.	
7/06/74	**24**	5	1. This Heart	Haven 7000

DATE	POS	WKS	ARTIST—RECORD TITLE	LABEL & NO.
			REDDING, Otis	
			Born on 9/09/41 in Dawson, Georgia. Killed in a plane crash in Lake Monona in Madison, Wisconsin on on 12/10/67. Soul singer/songwriter/producer/pianist. First recorded with Johnny Jenkins & The Pinetoppers on Confederate in 1960. Own label, Jotis. Plane crash also killed four members of the Bar-Kays. Otis was inducted into the Rock and Roll Hall of Fame in 1989. Sang duets with Carla Thomas (Otis & Carla).	
6/19/65	**21**	6	1. I've Been Loving You Too Long (To Stop Now)	Volt 126
10/23/65	**35**	3	2. Respect	Volt 128
4/02/66	**31**	3	3. Satisfaction	Volt 132
10/29/66	**29**	4	4. Fa-Fa-Fa-Fa-Fa (Sad Song)	Volt 138
12/31/66+	**25**	6	5. Try A Little Tenderness	Volt 141
6/03/67	**26**	4	6. Tramp OTIS & CARLA	Stax 216
9/23/67	**30**	2	7. Knock On Wood OTIS & CARLA	Stax 228
2/10/68	**1**(4)	14	● **8. (Sittin' On) The Dock Of The Bay** recorded 3 days before his death	Volt 157
5/11/68	**25**	5	9. The Happy Song (Dum-Dum)	Volt 163
7/27/68	**36**	1	10. Amen	Atco 6592
12/14/68+	**21**	5	11. Papa's Got A Brand New Bag	Atco 6636
			REDDY, Helen	
			Born on 10/25/42 in Melbourne, Australia. Family was in show business; Helen made stage debut at age four. Own TV series in the early '60s. Migrated to New York in 1966. To Los Angeles in 1968. Acted in the films *Airport 1975* (1974), *Pete's Dragon* (1977) and *Sgt. Pepper's Lonely Hearts Club Band* (1978).	
5/08/71	**13**	9	1. I Don't Know How To Love Him from the rock opera *Jesus Christ Superstar*	Capitol 3027
10/14/72	**1**(1)	14	● **2. I Am Woman** from the film *Stand Up and Be Counted*	Capitol 3350
3/10/73	**12**	10	3. Peaceful	Capitol 3527
7/28/73	**1**(1)	14	● **4. Delta Dawn**	Capitol 3645
11/17/73	**3**	13	● **5. Leave Me Alone (Ruby Red Dress)**	Capitol 3768
3/30/74	**15**	9	6. Keep On Singing	Capitol 3845
7/20/74	**9**	12	**7. You And Me Against The World**	Capitol 3897
11/02/74	**1**(1)	13	● **8. Angie Baby**	Capitol 3972
3/01/75	**22**	5	9. Emotion	Capitol 4021
7/26/75	**35**	2	10. Bluebird written by Leon Russell	Capitol 4108
8/30/75	**8**	9	**11. Ain't No Way To Treat A Lady**	Capitol 4128
12/27/75+	**19**	9	12. Somewhere In The Night	Capitol 4192
8/21/76	**29**	5	13. I Can't Hear You No More	Capitol 4312
6/11/77	**18**	12	14. You're My World	Capitol 4418
			REDEYE	
			Rock quartet led by Dave Hodgkins and Douglas "Red" Mark.	
12/26/70+	**27**	7	1. Games	Pentagram 204
			REED, Dan, Network	
			Portland-based, funk-rock quintet led by singer/composer Dan Reed.	
4/30/88	**38**	2	1. Ritual	Mercury 870183

Night Ranger managed two top-10 singles in the mid-80s—"Sister Christian" and "Sentimental Street"—and eventually disbanded in 1989. Bassist Jack Blades went on to form hard-rock band Damn Yankees with Ted Nugent and Styx's Tommy Shaw.

Ric Ocasek's first brush with platinum success came with Boston-based group the Cars in the late 70s, but in 1972, both he and Cars bassist Ben Orr—then known as Richard Otcasek and Benjamin Orzechowski—were members of Paramount Records group Milkwood.

Billy Ocean's first hit, 1976's "Love Really Hurts Without You," came eight years prior to his hot streak on Arista—and on another label, Ariola. Trend-watchers note: of his 11 top-40 hits, a total of six have the word "love" in their title.

Roy Orbison's legend was busily renewing itself when the much-loved singer died of a heart attack in 1988. He had a posthumous hit with 1989's "You Got It," and was not replaced when his supergroup the Traveling Wilburys recorded their second album.

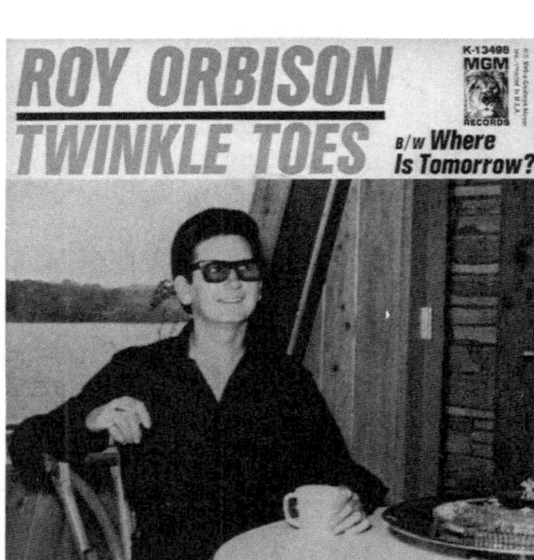

Tommy Page sprang from suburban New Jersey in 1988 and, at 18 years of age, was being compared by his label to young dance pop performers like Tiffany and Debbie Gibson. His second album, *Paintings in My Mind*, spawned the No. 1 hit "I'll Be Your Everything."

Kevin Paige's eponymous Chrysalis solo debut featured the Memphis-born performer playing and singing almost every note on the album. His 1989 hit: "Don't Shut Me Out."

Peaches & Herb's 13-year sporadic string of hits is tempered by one irony: though Herb Fame was involved in each and every one, there have been three "Peaches" since 1967's "Close Your Eyes," a No. 8 hit.

Pebbles is no rocker, but the possible Flintstones fan has got dance-pop down cold. Her first album, *Pebbles*, provided dual top-10 hits in 1988 with "Girlfriend" and "Mercedes Boy."

Peter & Gordon's string of mid-60s hits like "A World Without Love" and "I Go To Pieces" were highlights of the original British Invasion. Peter Asher is now a renowned artists manager; Gordon Waller's 1972 solo album *. . . And Gordon* now fetches top dollar from record collectors.

Ray Peterson's "The Wonder Of You" reached No. 25 in 1959—and then, three top-10 hits later, returned to the charts in April 1964 for three weeks, peaking at No. 70.

Gene Pitney's 1961 hit "Town Without Pity," taken from the film of the same name, was colorfully recast as an energetic instrumental by guitarist Ronnie Montrose on his 1978 album *Open Fire*.

The Pixies Three's "Birthday Party" spent one week (Oct. 5, 1963) ensconced in the Top 40 before the Pennsylvania trio's magic failed . . . and the party was over.

DATE	POS	WKS	ARTIST—RECORD TITLE	LABEL & NO.
			REED, Jerry	
			Born Jerry Reed Hubbard on 3/20/37 in Atlanta. Country singer/guitarist/songwriter/actor. Among his many films, co-starred in *Gator* and *Smokey & The Bandit I* and *II*. Own TV series "Concrete Cowboys." Elvis Presley recorded two of Reed's songs: "U.S. Male" and "Guitar Man."	
1/09/71	**8**	14	● **1. Amos Moses** [N]	RCA 9904
5/29/71	**9**	9	**2. When You're Hot, You're Hot** [N]	RCA 9976
			REED, Jimmy	
			Born Mathis James Reed on 9/06/25 in Dunleith, Mississippi; died from an epileptic seizure on 8/29/76. R&B vocalist/guitarist/harmonica player/songwriter. Taught guitar by Eddie Taylor at age seven. First recorded for Chance in 1953. Afflicted with epilepsy since 1957. Distinctive and influential blues singer, active until death. Inducted into the Rock and Roll Hall of Fame in 1991. His nephew is singer Dezi Phillips.	
11/04/57	**32**	3	1. Honest I Do Top 100 #32 / Best Seller #36	Vee-Jay 253
2/29/60	**37**	2	2. Baby What You Want Me To Do	Vee-Jay 333
			REED, Lou	
			Born Louis Firbank on 3/02/42 in Freeport, Long Island, New York. Lead singer/songwriter of the New York seminal rock band, Velvet Underground. Appeared in the film *One Trick Pony*.	
3/31/73	**16**	8	1. Walk On The Wild Side produced by David Bowie and Mick Ronson	RCA 0887
			REESE, Della	
			Born Delloreese Patricia Early on 7/06/31 in Detroit. With Mahalia Jackson gospel troupe from 1945-49, and Erskine Hawkins in the early '50s. Solo since 1957. Actress/singer on many TV shows. Appeared in the 1958 film *Let's Rock* and the 1989 film *Harlem Nights*. Own series "Della" in 1970. Played "Della Rogers" on the TV series "Chico & The Man" from 1976-78. On TV's "The Royal Family" in 1991.	
9/09/57	**12**	13	1. And That Reminds Me Jockey #12 / Best Seller #23 / Top 100 #29 originally charted on the Best Sellers for 1 week; re-entered the Best Sellers chart for 3 weeks on 11/11/57 (POS 33)	Jubilee 5292
10/05/59	**2**(1)	15	**2. Don't You Know**	RCA 7591
12/28/59+	**16**	8	3. Not One Minute More	RCA 7644
			REEVES, Jim	
			Born James Travis Reeves on 8/20/24 in Panola County, Texas. Killed in a plane crash on 7/31/64 in Nashville. Aspirations of a professional baseball career cut short by an ankle injury. DJ at KWKH-Shreveport, Louisiana, home of the "Louisiana Hayride," early '50s. First recorded for Macy's in 1950. Joined "Hayride" cast following first country hit "Mexican Joe" in 1953. Joined the "Grand Ole Opry" in 1955. Own ABC-TV series in 1957. In the 1963 film *Kimberley Jim*. Posthumously, he continued to have many country hits into the 80s.	
5/06/57	**11**	14	1. Four Walls Jockey #11 / Top 100 #12 / Juke Box #13 / Best Seller #14	RCA 6874
1/11/60	**2**(3)	20	**2. He'll Have To Go**	RCA 7643
7/11/60	**37**	1	3. I'm Gettin' Better	RCA 7756
11/28/60	**31**	4	4. Am I Losing You	RCA 7800
			REEVES, Martha — see MARTHA & THE VANDELLAS	

DATE	POS	WKS	ARTIST—RECORD TITLE	LABEL & NO.
			REFLECTIONS, The	
			Detroit pop-rock quartet: Tony Micale (lead vocals), Dan Bennie, Phil Castrodale and John Dean.	
5/02/64	**6**	9	**1. (Just Like) Romeo & Juliet**	Golden World 9
			RE-FLEX	
			British techno-rock quartet founded by computer keyboardist Paul Fishman.	
2/18/84	**24**	5	1. The Politics Of Dancing	Capitol 5301
			REGENTS, The	
			Bronx vocal group formed as the Desires in 1958. Consisted of Guy Villari (lead), Sal Cuomo, Charles Fassert, Don Jacobucci and Tony "Hot Rod" Gravagna. "Barbara-Ann," written for Fassert's sister, was first recorded as a demo in 1958. Group had disbanded by the time "Barbara-Ann" was released.	
5/22/61	**13**	7	1. Barbara-Ann	Gee 1065
			first released on Cousins 1002 in 1961	
7/31/61	**28**	4	2. Runaround	Gee 1071
			REGINA	
			New York native, Regina Richards.	
7/19/86	**10**	12	**1. Baby Love**	Atlantic 89417
			REID, Clarence	
			Born on 2/14/45 in Cochran, Georgia. Soul singer/composer/arranger/producer. With the Miami vocal group, the Delmiros, in the early '60s. Also recorded as "Blowfly."	
9/13/69	**40**	2	1. Nobody But You Babe	Alston 4574
			R.E.M.	
			Athens, Georgia rock quartet formed in 1980: Michael Stipe (vocals), Peter Buck (guitar), Mike Mills (bass) and Bill Berry (drums). Buck, Mills and Berry joined with Warren Zevon in the Hindu Love Gods.	
10/17/87	**9**	10	**1. The One I Love**	I.R.S. 53171
2/25/89	**6**	11	**2. Stand**	Warner 27688
4/20/91	**4**	14	● **3. Losing My Religion**	Warner 19392
			REMBRANDTS, The	
			Duo of Danny Wilde and Phil Solem. Both were members of the L.A. pop band Great Buildings.	
3/16/91	**14**	9	1. Just The Way It Is, Baby	Atco 98874#
			RENAY, Diane	
			Philadelphian Renee Diane Kushner.	
2/15/64	**6**	8	**1. Navy Blue**	20th Century 456
4/25/64	**29**	4	2. Kiss Me Sailor	20th Century 477
			RENE & RENE	
			Mexican-American duo from Laredo, Texas: Rene Ornelas and Rene Herrera.	
12/14/68+	**14**	9	1. Lo Mucho Que Te Quiero (The More I Love You)	White Whale 287
			RENO, Mike, and ANN WILSON	
			Lead singers of Loverboy and Heart, respectively.	
5/19/84	**7**	13	**1. Almost Paradise . . . Love Theme From Footloose**	Columbia 04418
			from the film *Footloose*	

DATE	POS	WKS	ARTIST—RECORD TITLE	LABEL & NO.
			REO SPEEDWAGON	
			Rock quintet from Champaign, Illinois: Kevin Cronin (lead vocals, rhythm guitar), Gary Richrath (lead guitar), Neal Doughty (keyboards), Bruce Hall (bass) and Alan Gratzer (drums). Gratzer left in 1988, replaced by former Santana drummer Graham Lear. 1990 lineup: Cronin, Doughty and Hall joined by new members Bryan Hitt, Dave Amato and Jesse Harms (left by 1991). Group named after a 1911 fire truck.	
12/27/80+	**1**(1)	20	▲ **1. Keep On Loving You**	Epic 50953
3/28/81	**5**	15	● **2. Take It On The Run**	Epic 01054
7/04/81	**24**	6	3. Don't Let Him Go	Epic 02127
8/29/81	**20**	7	4. In Your Letter	Epic 02457
6/19/82	**7**	13	**5. Keep The Fire Burnin'**	Epic 02967
10/02/82	**26**	6	6. Sweet Time	Epic 03175
11/17/84	**29**	5	7. I Do'wanna Know	Epic 04659
1/26/85	**1**(3)	14	● **8. Can't Fight This Feeling**	Epic 04713
4/20/85	**19**	9	9. One Lonely Night	Epic 04848
8/17/85	**34**	3	10. Live Every Moment	Epic 05412
2/28/87	**16**	7	11. That Ain't Love	Epic 06656
9/19/87	**19**	8	12. In My Dreams	Epic 07255
7/30/88	**20**	9	13. Here With Me	Epic 07901
			RESTLESS HEART	
			Nashville country-rock quintet consisting of former session musicians Larry Stewart (vocals), David Innis, Greg Jennings, Paul Gregg and John Dittrich.	
5/30/87	**33**	5	1. I'll Still Be Loving You	RCA 5065
			REUNION	
			RCA studio group — Joey Levine (Ohio Express), lead singer.	
9/28/74	**8**	10	**1. Life Is A Rock (But The Radio Rolled Me)** [N]	RCA 10056
			REVELS, The	
			Philadelphia group formed in high school, led by John Kelly.	
11/23/59	**35**	2	1. Midnight Stroll originally released as "Dead Man's Stroll"	Norgolde 103
			REVERE, Paul/The Raiders	
			Leader of pop-rock group The Raiders, formed in Portland, Oregon in 1960. Group featured Paul Revere (b: 1/07/42, Boise, Idaho; keyboards) and Mark Lindsay (lead singer). To Los Angeles in 1965. On daily ABC-TV show "Where the Action Is" in 1965. Own TV show "Happening" in 1968. Lindsay and Raider member, Keith Allison, recorded with Steve Alaimo as The Unknowns. Group had many personnel changes.	
4/17/61	**38**	1	1. Like, Long Hair [I]	Gardena 116
12/25/65+	**11**	11	2. Just Like Me	Columbia 43461
3/26/66	**4**	12	**3. Kicks**	Columbia 43556
7/09/66	**6**	7	**4. Hungry**	Columbia 43678
10/15/66	**20**	5	5. The Great Airplane Strike	Columbia 43810
12/17/66+	**4**	10	**6. Good Thing**	Columbia 43907
3/04/67	**22**	6	7. Ups And Downs	Columbia 44018
5/06/67	**5**	8	**8. Him Or Me - What's It Gonna Be?**	Columbia 44094
9/02/67	**17**	5	9. I Had A Dream	Columbia 44227
2/24/68	**19**	6	10. Too Much Talk	Columbia 44444
7/13/68	**27**	6	11. Don't Take It So Hard	Columbia 44553

DATE	POS	WKS	ARTIST—RECORD TITLE	LABEL & NO.
3/08/69	**18**	9	12. Mr. Sun, Mr. Moon	Columbia 44744
6/14/69	**20**	8	13. Let Me	Columbia 44854
			RAIDERS:	
5/29/71	**1**(1)	15	● **14. Indian Reservation (The Lament Of The Cherokee Reservation Indian)**	Columbia 45332
10/02/71	**23**	6	15. Birds Of A Feather	Columbia 45453
			REYNOLDS, Debbie	
			Born Mary Reynolds on 4/01/32 in El Paso, Texas. Leading lady of '50s musicals and later in comedies. Married Eddie Fisher on 9/26/55; divorced by 1959. Mother of actress Carrie Fisher.	
7/22/57	**1**(5)	23	**1. Tammy** Top 100 #1(5) / Jockey #1(5) / Best Seller #1(3) from the film *Tammy and the Bachelor*	Coral 61851
1/20/58	**20**	1	2. A Very Special Love Jockey #20 / Top 100 #83	Coral 61897
2/22/60	**25**	8	3. Am I That Easy To Forget	Dot 15985
			REYNOLDS, Jody	
			Rockabilly singer/guitarist from Yuma, Arizona. Born on 12/03/38 in Denver.	
5/26/58	**5**	14	**1. Endless Sleep** Best Seller #5 / Top 100 #5 / Jockey #7	Demon 1507
			REYNOLDS, Lawrence	
			Singer from Mobile, Alabama.	
10/11/69	**28**	6	1. Jesus Is A Soul Man	Warner 7322
			RHYTHM HERITAGE	
			Los Angeles studio group assembled by prolific producers Steve Barri and Michael Omartian (keyboards). Vocals by Oren and Luther Waters.	
1/10/76	**1**(1)	12	● **1. Theme From S.W.A.T.** [I] from the ABC-TV series "S.W.A.T."	ABC 12135
5/08/76	**20**	8	2. Barretta's Theme ("Keep Your Eye On The Sparrow") from the Robert Blake TV series "Baretta"	ABC 12177
			RICH, Charlie	
			Born on 12/14/32 in Colt, Arkansas. Rockabilly-country singer/pianist/songwriter. First played jazz and blues. Own jazz group, the Velvetones, mid-'50s, while in U.S. Air Force. Session work with Sun Records in 1958. Known as the "Silver Fox."	
5/02/60	**22**	9	1. Lonely Weekends	Phillips 3552
9/25/65	**21**	7	2. Mohair Sam	Smash 1993
6/09/73	**15**	12	● 3. Behind Closed Doors	Epic 10950
10/27/73	**1**(2)	17	● **4. The Most Beautiful Girl**	Epic 11040
2/23/74	**18**	8	5. There Won't Be Anymore	RCA 0195
3/09/74	**11**	9	6. A Very Special Love Song	Epic 11091
8/24/74	**24**	7	7. I Love My Friend	Epic 20006
6/28/75	**19**	6	8. Every Time You Touch Me (I Get High)	Epic 50103

DATE	POS	WKS	ARTIST—RECORD TITLE	LABEL & NO.
			RICHARD, Cliff	
			Born Harry Rodger Webb on 10/14/40 in Lucknow, India, of British parentage. Vocalist/actor/guitarist. To England in 1948. Worked in skiffle groups, mid-1950s. Backing band: The Drifters (later: The Shadows). Cliff also recorded Inspirational music since 1967. The Shadows disbanded in 1969. Superstar in England, with over 80 charted hits, including 10 #1 singles. British films *Expresso Bongo*, *The Young Ones*, *Summer Holiday* and *Wonderful Life*.	
11/02/59	**30**	4	1. Living Doll **CLIFF RICHARD AND THE DRIFTERS** from the film *Serious Charge*	ABC-Para. 10042
1/18/64	**25**	7	2. It's All In The Game	Epic 9633
8/14/76	**6**	12	● **3. Devil Woman**	Rocket 40574
11/17/79+	**7**	14	**4. We Don't Talk Anymore**	EMI America 8025
4/05/80	**34**	3	5. Carrie	EMI America 8035
9/27/80	**10**	13	**6. Dreaming**	EMI America 8057
11/22/80+	**20**	11	7. Suddenly **OLIVIA NEWTON-JOHN AND CLIFF RICHARD** from the film *Xanadu*	MCA 51007
1/24/81	**17**	11	8. A Little In Love	EMI America 8068
2/06/82	**23**	8	9. Daddy's Home	EMI America 8103
			RICHIE, Lionel	
			Born on 6/20/49 in Tuskegee, Alabama. Grew up on the campus of Tuskegee Institute where his grandfather worked. Former lead singer of the Commodores. Appeared in the film *Thank God It's Friday* (1978).	
7/18/81	**1**(9)	19	▲ **1. Endless Love** **DIANA ROSS & LIONEL RICHIE** from the film of the same title	Motown 1519
10/23/82	**1**(2)	13	● **2. Truly**	Motown 1644
1/22/83	**4**	16	**3. You Are**	Motown 1657
4/16/83	**5**	12	**4. My Love**	Motown 1677
10/01/83	**1**(4)	17	● **5. All Night Long (All Night)**	Motown 1698
12/03/83+	**7**	14	**6. Running With The Night**	Motown 1710
3/10/84	**1**(2)	17	● **7. Hello**	Motown 1722
7/07/84	**3**	14	**8. Stuck On You**	Motown 1746
10/13/84	**8**	13	**9. Penny Lover**	Motown 1762
11/09/85	**1**(4)	16	● **10. Say You, Say Me** title song from the film *White Nights*	Motown 1819
7/19/86	**2**(2)	14	**11. Dancing On The Ceiling**	Motown 1843
10/18/86	**9**	10	**12. Love Will Conquer All**	Motown 1866
1/10/87	**7**	10	**13. Ballerina Girl**	Motown 1873
4/18/87	**20**	7	14. Se La	Motown 1883
			RIDDLE, Nelson	
			Born on 6/01/21 in Oradell, New Jersey; died on 10/06/85. Trombonist/arranger with Charlie Spivak and Tommy Dorsey in the 40s. One of the most in-demand of all arranger-conductors for many top artists, including Frank Sinatra (several classic '50s albums), Nat King Cole, Ella Mae Morse, and more recently, Linda Ronstadt; also arranger/musical director for many films.	
12/31/55+	**1**(4)	24	**1. Lisbon Antigua** [I] Best Seller #1(4) / Jockey #1(2) / Top 100 #2 / Juke Box #2	Capitol 3287
3/31/56	**20**	4	2. Port Au Prince [I]	Capitol 3374

DATE	POS	WKS	ARTIST—RECORD TITLE	LABEL & NO.
			Jockey #20 / Top 100 #32	
8/04/56	**39**	2	3. Theme From "The Proud Ones" [I]	Capitol 3472
			from the film *The Proud Ones*	
8/04/62	**30**	3	4. Route 66 Theme [I]	Capitol 4741
			from the CBS-TV series "Route 66"	
			RIFF	
			Male vocal quintet from Paterson, New Jersey formed at Eastside High School. Appeared as themselves (singing the alma mater) in the 1989 film *Lean On Me*, which was based on their school. Kenny Kelly, Steven Capers, Jr., Anthony Fuller, Dwayne Jones and Michael Best.	
4/27/91	**25**	6	1. My Heart Is Failing Me	SBK 07342#
			RIGHTEOUS BROTHERS, The	
			Blue-eyed soul duo: Bill Medley (b: 9/19/40, Santa Ana, California; baritone) and Bobby Hatfield (b: 8/10/40, Beaver Dam, Wisconsin; tenor). Formed duo in 1962. First recorded as the Paramours for Smash in 1962. On "Hullabaloo" and "Shindig" TV shows. Split up from 1968-74. Medley went solo, replaced by Jimmy Walker; rejoined Hatfield in 1974.	
12/26/64+	**1**(2)	13	**1. You've Lost That Lovin' Feelin'**	Philles 124
4/17/65	**9**	10	**2. Just Once In My Life**	Philles 127
7/31/65	**4**	11	**3. Unchained Melody**	Philles 129
12/11/65+	**5**	8	**4. Ebb Tide**	Philles 130
			all of above produced by Phil Spector	
3/19/66	**1**(3)	11	● **5. (You're My) Soul And Inspiration**	Verve 10383
6/18/66	**18**	5	6. He	Verve 10406
8/27/66	**30**	3	7. Go Ahead And Cry	Verve 10430
6/15/74	**3**	10	**8. Rock And Roll Heaven**	Haven 7002
10/05/74	**20**	4	9. Give It To The People	Haven 7004
12/07/74	**32**	3	10. Dream On	Haven 7006
9/08/90	**13**	11	11. Unchained Melody [R]	Verve F. 871882
			featured in the film *Ghost*; available only on vinyl	
10/13/90	**19**	12	▲ 12. Unchained Melody [R]	Curb 76842#
			newly recorded 1990 version; available only on cassette	
			RILEY, Cheryl Pepsii	
			Black singer, native of Brooklyn. Discovered by the group Full Force.	
12/10/88	**32**	5	1. Thanks For My Child	Columbia 07996
			written, produced and arranged by Full Force	
			RILEY, Jeannie C.	
			Born Jeanne Carolyn Stephenson on 10/19/45 in Anson, Texas. Country singer.	
8/31/68	**1**(1)	12	● **1. Harper Valley P.T.A.**	Plantation 3
			written by Tom T. Hall	
			RINKY-DINKS, The — see DARIN, Bobby	
			RIOS, Miguel	
			Born in Granada, Spain in 1944.	
6/20/70	**14**	8	1. A Song Of Joy	A&M 1193
			based on the last movement of Beethoven's Ninth Symphony; Waldo de los Rios, conductor	

DATE	POS	WKS	ARTIST—RECORD TITLE	LABEL & NO.
			RIP CHORDS, The	
			California group featuring the duo of Terry Melcher (Doris Day's son — produced The Byrds, Paul Revere & The Raiders) and Bruce Johnston (Beach Boys). Touring group featured a different foursome.	
1/04/64	**4**	11	**1. Hey Little Cobra**	Columbia 42921
5/23/64	**28**	5	2. Three Window Coupe	Columbia 43035
			RIPERTON, Minnie	
			Born on 11/08/47 in Chicago; died of cancer on 7/12/79 in Los Angeles. Recorded as "Andrea Davis" on Chess in 1966. Lead singer of the rock-R&B sextet Rotary Connection from 1967-70. In Stevie Wonder's backup group Wonderlove in 1973.	
2/15/75	**1**(1)	13	● **1. Lovin' You**	Epic 50057
			RITCHIE FAMILY, The	
			Philadelphia disco group named for arranger/producer Ritchie Rome. Group featured various session singers and musicians.	
9/06/75	**11**	12	1. Brazil [I]	20th Century 2218
10/02/76	**17**	11	2. The Best Disco In Town	Marlin 3306
			RITENOUR, Lee	
			Born on 1/11/52 in Los Angeles. Guitarist/composer/arranger. Top session guitarist, has appeared on more than 200 albums. Nicknamed "Captain Fingers." Joined jazz quartet Fourplay in 1991.	
5/23/81	**15**	9	1. Is It You vocal: Eric Tagg	Elektra 47124
			RITTER, Tex	
			Born Maurice Woodward Ritter on 1/12/05 near Murvaul, Texas; died of a heart attack on 1/03/74. Country singer/actor. Starred in over 80 Hollywood westerns from 1935-45. Elected to the Country Music Hall of Fame in 1964. His son, Jonathan Southworth "John" Ritter, starred in the TV series "Three's Company" and "Hooperman," plus many films.	
7/07/56	**28**	6	1. The Wayward Wind	Capitol 3430
8/14/61	**20**	4	2. I Dreamed Of A Hill-Billy Heaven [S]	Capitol 4567
			RIVERS, Johnny	
			Born John Ramistella on 11/07/42 in New York City; raised in Baton Rouge. Rock and roll singer/guitarist/ songwriter/producer. Recorded with the Spades for Suede in 1956. Named Johnny Rivers by DJ Alan Freed in 1958. To Los Angeles in 1961. Began own Soul City label in 1966.	
6/13/64	**2**(2)	10	**1. Memphis**	Imperial 66032
8/22/64	**12**	7	2. Maybelline above 2 tunes written by Chuck Berry	Imperial 66056
11/14/64	**9**	9	**3. Mountain Of Love**	Imperial 66075
2/27/65	**20**	4	4. Midnight Special	Imperial 66087
6/19/65	**7**	8	**5. Seventh Son** written by blues great, Willie Dixon	Imperial 66112
10/30/65	**26**	4	6. Where Have All The Flowers Gone	Imperial 66133
1/15/66	**35**	3	7. Under Your Spell Again	Imperial 66144
3/26/66	**3**	10	**8. Secret Agent Man** from the TV series of the same title	Imperial 66159
6/25/66	**19**	6	9. (I Washed My Hands In) Muddy Water	Imperial 66175
10/08/66	**1**(1)	12	**10. Poor Side Of Town**	Imperial 66205
2/18/67	**3**	8	**11. Baby I Need Your Lovin'**	Imperial 66227
6/17/67	**10**	6	**12. The Tracks Of My Tears**	Imperial 66244

DATE	POS	WKS	ARTIST—RECORD TITLE	LABEL & NO.
12/02/67+	**14**	8	13. Summer Rain	Imperial 66267
11/11/72+	**6**	14	● **14. Rockin' Pneumonia - Boogie Woogie Flu**	United Art. 50960
5/05/73	**38**	2	15. Blue Suede Shoes	United Art. 198
8/09/75	**22**	5	16. Help Me Rhonda	Epic 50121
7/30/77	**10**	15	● **17. Swayin' To The Music (Slow Dancin')**	Big Tree 16094
			RIVIERAS, The	
			Teenage rock and roll band. Evolved from a South Bend, Indiana high school group known as The Playmates. Lead singer, Marty Fortson, left for Marines after recording "California Sun." Band's manager, Bill Dobslaw, was the lead singer on recordings of subsequent hits.	
2/01/64	**5**	9	**1. California Sun**	Riviera 1401
			ROACHFORD	
			British-based, soul-rock band: Andrew Roachford (vocals, keyboards), Hawi Gondwe (guitar), Derrick Taylor (bass) and Chris Taylor (drums).	
5/27/89	**25**	5	1. Cuddly Toy (Feel For Me)	Epic 68549
			ROAD APPLES, The	
12/27/75+	**35**	4	1. Let's Live Together	Polydor 14285
			ROB BASE & D.J. E-Z ROCK	
			Harlem rap duo: Robert Ginyard with DJ Rodney "Skip" Bryce.	
10/15/88	**36**	3	▲ 1. It Takes Two includes sampling of Lyn Collins' 1972 hit "Think (About It)"	Profile 5186
			ROBBINS, Marty	
			Born Martin David Robinson on 9/26/25 in Glendale, Arizona; died of a heart attack on 12/08/82. Country singer/guitarist/songwriter. Own radio show with K-Bar Cowboys, late 1940s. Own TV show, "Western Caravan," KPHO-Phoenix, 1951. First recorded for Columbia in 1952. Regular on the "Grand Ole Opry" since 1953. Own Robbins label in 1958. Raced stock cars. Films *Road to Nashville* and *Guns of a Stranger.*	
11/24/56	**17**	7	1. Singing The Blues Juke Box #17 / Top 100 #26	Columbia 21545
4/27/57	**2**(1)	21	**2. A White Sport Coat (And A Pink Carnation)** Best Seller #2 / Top 100 #3 / Jockey #4 / Juke Box #4 end	Columbia 40864
12/09/57+	**15**	9	3. The Story Of My Life Jockey #15 / Top 100 #30 / Best Seller #31	Columbia 41013
5/05/58	**26**	5	4. Just Married Best Seller #26 / Top 100 #35	Columbia 41143
8/25/58	**27**	5	5. She Was Only Seventeen (He Was One Year More)	Columbia 41208
3/16/59	**38**	3	6. The Hanging Tree from the film of the same title; above 5 with Ray Conniff & His Orchestra	Columbia 41325
11/30/59+	**1**(2)	16	**7. El Paso**	Columbia 41511
4/11/60	**26**	4	8. Big Iron	Columbia 41589
8/01/60	**31**	3	9. Is There Any Chance	Columbia 41686
12/05/60	**34**	5	10. Ballad Of The Alamo from the film *The Alamo*	Columbia 41809
2/13/61	**3**	12	**11. Don't Worry**	Columbia 41922
8/18/62	**16**	7	12. Devil Woman	Columbia 42486
12/08/62	**18**	5	13. Ruby Ann	Columbia 42614

DATE	POS	WKS	ARTIST—RECORD TITLE	LABEL & NO.
			ROBERT & JOHNNY	
			Bronx R&B duo: Robert Carr and Johnny Mitchell.	
3/03/58	**32**	6	1. We Belong Together	Old Town 1047
			Best Seller #32 / Top 100 #33	
			ROBERTS, Austin	
			Born on 9/19/45 in Newport News, Virginia. Collaborator on cartoon series "Scooby Doo" and "Josie & The Pussycats."	
11/11/72	**12**	10	1. Something's Wrong With Me	Chelsea 0101
8/30/75	**9**	9	**2. Rocky**	Private S. 45020
			ROBERTS, Kane	
			Boston rock singer/guitarist. Guitar work with Alice Cooper, Rod Stewart and Berlin.	
6/22/91	**38**	2	1. Does Anybody Really Fall In Love Anymore?	DGC 19009#
			songwriters include Jon Bon Jovi and Richie Sambora	
			ROBERTSON, Don	
			Born on 12/05/22 in Peking, China; moved to Chicago at age four. Pianist/composer. Created the Nashville piano style. Wrote several of Elvis Presley's hits.	
5/05/56	**6**	14	**1. The Happy Whistler** [I]	Capitol 3391
			Jockey #6 / Best Seller #9 / Top 100 #9 / Juke Box #12	
			ROBIC, Ivo	
			Pronounced: eevo robish. Born near Zagreb, Yugoslavia in 1927.	
8/31/59	**13**	11	1. Morgen [F]	Laurie 3033
			ROBINSON, Floyd	
			Born in 1937 in Nashville. Singer/guitarist/composer. Worked on local radio with his high school band, the Eagle Rangers, at age 12. Own programs on WLAC and WSM-Nashville.	
8/03/59	**20**	12	1. Makin' Love	RCA 7529
			ROBINSON, Smokey	
			Born William Robinson on 2/19/40 in Detroit. Formed The Miracles (then called the Matadors) at Northern High School in 1955. First recorded for End in 1958. Married Miracles' member Claudette Rogers in 1963. Left The Miracles on 1/29/72. Wrote dozens of hit songs for Motown artists. Vice President of Motown Records until 1988. Inducted into the Rock and Roll Hall of Fame in 1987. Won Grammy's Living Legends Award in 1989.	
1/19/74	**27**	6	1. Baby Come Close	Tamla 54239
5/31/75	**26**	6	2. Baby That's Backatcha	Tamla 54258
10/18/75	**36**	3	3. The Agony And The Ecstasy	Tamla 54261
11/17/79+	**4**	17	**4. Cruisin'**	Tamla 54306
5/03/80	**31**	4	5. Let Me Be The Clock	Tamla 54311
3/21/81	**2**(3)	16	● **6. Being With You**	Tamla 54321
2/27/82	**33**	5	7. Tell Me Tomorrow - Part I	Tamla 1601
5/09/87	**8**	12	**8. Just To See Her**	Motown 1877
8/15/87	**10**	11	**9. One Heartbeat**	Motown 1897
			ROBINSON, Vicki Sue	
			Born in Philadelphia in 1955. Disco vocalist. Appeared in the original Broadway productions of *Hair* and *Jesus Christ Superstar*.	
6/19/76	**10**	13	**1. Turn The Beat Around**	RCA 10562

DATE	POS	WKS	ARTIST—RECORD TITLE	LABEL & NO.
			ROCHELL AND THE CANDLES	
			Los Angeles R&B group consisting of lead Johnny Wyatt (b: 1938; d: 1983), Rochell Henderson, Melvin Sasso and T.C. Henderson.	
3/27/61	**26**	4	1. Once Upon A Time	Swingin' 623
			ROCK-A-TEENS	
			New York City-based rock and roll teen sextet from Virginia led by Vic Mizelle.	
10/12/59	**16**	9	1. Woo-Hoo [I] first released on Doran 3515 in 1959	Roulette 4192
			ROCKETS	
			Detroit rock band led by David Gilbert (vocals), Jim McCarty (guitar) and John Badanjek (drums).	
8/11/79	**30**	6	1. Oh Well	RSO 935
			ROCKWELL	
			Born Kennedy Gordy on 3/15/64 in Detroit. Son of Motown chairman, Berry Gordy, Jr.	
2/11/84	**2**(3)	14	● **1. Somebody's Watching Me** backing vocal by Michael Jackson	Motown 1702
6/23/84	**35**	2	2. Obscene Phone Caller	Motown 1731
			ROCKY FELLERS, The	
			Consists of a father and his four sons (Eddie, Albert, Tony and Junior Feller) from Manila, Philippines.	
4/27/63	**16**	8	1. Killer Joe	Scepter 1246
			RODGERS, Eileen	
			Born in Pittsburgh in 1933. Featured vocalist in Charlie Spivak's band, 1954-56.	
9/08/56	**18**	10	1. Miracle Of Love Jockey #18 / Top 100 #19 / Best Seller #23	Columbia 40708
9/29/58	**26**	4	2. Treasure Of Your Love	Columbia 41214
			RODGERS, Jimmie	
			Born James Frederick Rodgers on 9/18/33 in Camas, Washington. Vocalist/guitarist/pianist. Formed first group while in the Air Force. Own NBC-TV variety series in 1959. Career hampered following mysterious assault on the San Diego Freeway on 12/20/67, which left him with a fractured skull. Returned to per- forming a year later. Starred in films: *The Little Shepherd from Kingdom Come* and *Back Door to Hell.*	
8/19/57	**1**(4)	23	**1. Honeycomb** Jockey #1(4) / Best Seller #1(2) / Top 100 #1(2)	Roulette 4015
11/18/57	**3**	14	**2. Kisses Sweeter Than Wine** Jockey #3 / Top 100 #7 / Best Seller #8	Roulette 4031
2/24/58	**7**	9	**3. Oh-Oh, I'm Falling In Love Again** Jockey #7 / Top 100 #22 / Best Seller #23	Roulette 4045
5/19/58	**3**	15	**4. Secretly/** Best Seller #3 / Jockey #3 / Top 100 #4	
5/26/58	**16**	1	5. Make Me A Miracle Jockey #16 / Top 100 #54	Roulette 4070
8/11/58	**10**	10	**6. Are You Really Mine** Hot 100 #10 / Best Seller #10	Roulette 4090
12/01/58	**11**	10	7. Bimbombey	Roulette 4116
3/30/59	**36**	3	8. I'm Never Gonna Tell	Roulette 4129

DATE	POS	WKS	ARTIST—RECORD TITLE	LABEL & NO.
			all of above with Hugo Peretti & His Orchestra	
6/15/59	**32**	4	9. Ring-A-Ling-A-Lario/	
7/06/59	**40**	1	10. Wonderful You	Roulette 4158
10/12/59	**32**	3	11. Tucumcari	Roulette 4191
2/01/60	**24**	5	12. T.L.C. Tender Love And Care	Roulette 4218
			above 4 with Joe Reisman's Orchestra	
6/18/66	**37**	2	13. It's Over	Dot 16861
10/14/67	**31**	4	14. Child Of Clay	A&M 871
			ROE, Tommy	
			Pop-rock singer/guitarist/composer. Born on 5/09/42 in Atlanta. Formed band The Satins at Brown High School, worked local dances in the late 1950s. Group recorded for Judd in 1960. Moved to Britain in the mid-1960s, returned in 1969.	
8/11/62	**1**(2)	11	● **1. Sheila**	ABC-Para. 10329
			first released on Judd 1022 in 1962	
11/03/62	**35**	2	2. Susie Darlin'	ABC-Para. 10362
10/26/63	**3**	11	**3. Everybody**	ABC-Para. 10478
			above 3 produced by Felton Jarvis	
2/08/64	**36**	4	4. Come On	ABC-Para. 10515
7/02/66	**8**	10	● **5. Sweet Pea**	ABC-Para. 10762
10/01/66	**6**	11	**6. Hooray For Hazel**	ABC 10852
1/28/67	**23**	5	7. It's Now Winters Day	ABC 10888
2/15/69	**1**(4)	13	● **8. Dizzy**	ABC 11164
5/17/69	**29**	3	9. Heather Honey	ABC 11211
12/06/69+	**8**	11	● **10. Jam Up Jelly Tight**	ABC 11247
9/25/71	**25**	7	11. Stagger Lee	ABC 11307
			above 4 produced by Steve Barri	
			ROGER	
			Born Roger Troutman from Hamilton, Ohio. Leader of the family group Zapp. Worked with Sly Stone and George Clinton. Father of male singer, Lynch.	
12/12/87+	**3**	13	**1. I Want To Be Your Man**	Reprise 28229
			ROGERS, Julie	
			Born Julie Rolls on 4/06/43 in London.	
12/05/64+	**10**	9	**1. The Wedding**	Mercury 72332
			ROGERS, Kenny/First Edition	
			Born Kenneth Donald Rogers on 8/21/38 in Houston. With high school band the Scholars in 1958. Bass player of jazz group the Bobby Doyle Trio, recorded for Columbia. In Kirby Stone Four and The New Christy Minstrels, mid-1960s. Formed and fronted The First Edition in 1967. Original lineup included Thelma Camacho, Mike Settle, Terry Williams and Mickey Jones. All but Jones were members of The New Christy Minstrels. Group hosted own syndicated TV variety show "Rollin" in 1972. Rogers split from group in 1973. Starred in films *The Gambler*, *The Gambler II*, *Gambler III*, *Coward of the County* and *Six Pack*.	
			THE FIRST EDITION:	
2/24/68	**5**	8	**1. Just Dropped In (To See What Condition My Condition Was In)**	Reprise 0655
2/08/69	**19**	8	2. But You Know I Love You	Reprise 0799
			KENNY ROGERS AND THE FIRST EDITION:	
7/05/69	**6**	9	**3. Ruby, Don't Take Your Love To Town**	Reprise 0829
			written by Mel Tillis	

DATE	POS	WKS	ARTIST—RECORD TITLE	LABEL & NO.
10/25/69	**26**	6	4. Ruben James title also shown as "Reuben James"	Reprise 0854
3/14/70	**11**	12	5. Something's Burning written by Mac Davis	Reprise 0888
7/25/70	**17**	8	6. Tell It All Brother	Reprise 0923
11/14/70	**33**	5	7. Heed The Call	Reprise 0953
			KENNY ROGERS:	
4/23/77	**5**	13	● **8. Lucille**	United Art. 929
9/10/77	**28**	4	9. Daytime Friends	United Art. 1027
7/15/78	**32**	3	10. Love Or Something Like It	United Art. 1210
12/23/78+	**16**	13	11. The Gambler	United Art. 1250
5/12/79	**5**	13	● **12. She Believes In Me**	United Art. 1273
9/22/79	**7**	12	**13. You Decorated My Life**	United Art. 1315
12/01/79+	**3**	15	● **14. Coward Of The County**	United Art. 1327
4/12/80	**4**	14	**15. Don't Fall In Love With A Dreamer** **KENNY ROGERS with KIM CARNES**	United Art. 1345
6/28/80	**14**	8	16. Love The World Away from the film *Urban Cowboy*; above 9 produced by Larry Butler	United Art. 1359
10/04/80	**1**(6)	19	● **17. Lady** written by Lionel Richie	Liberty 1380
4/25/81	**14**	12	18. What Are We Doin' In Love **DOTTIE WEST with KENNY ROGERS**	Liberty 1404
6/13/81	**3**	14	**19. I Don't Need You**	Liberty 1415
9/12/81	**14**	10	20. Share Your Love With Me	Liberty 1430
1/16/82	**13**	11	21. Through The Years above 5 (except #18) produced by Lionel Richie	Liberty 1444
7/24/82	**13**	10	22. Love Will Turn You Around from the film *Six Pack*, starring Kenny Rogers	Liberty 1471
1/29/83	**6**	15	**23. We've Got Tonight** **KENNY ROGERS AND SHEENA EASTON**	Liberty 1492
5/28/83	**37**	3	24. All My Life	Liberty 1495
9/10/83	**1**(2)	18	▲ **25. Islands In The Stream** **KENNY ROGERS with DOLLY PARTON**	RCA 13615
2/04/84	**23**	6	26. This Woman above 2 feature writing and production work by the Bee Gees	RCA 13710
10/13/84	**15**	9	27. What About Me? **KENNY ROGERS with KIM CARNES and JAMES INGRAM**	RCA 13899
			ROGERS, Timmie "Oh Yeah!" Born on 7/04/15 in Detroit. Black vaudeville and nightclub comedian.	
11/04/57	**36**	4	1. Back To School Again Top 100 #36 / Best Seller #37	Cameo 116

DATE	POS	WKS	ARTIST—RECORD TITLE	LABEL & NO.
			ROLLING STONES, The	
			British R&B-influenced rock group formed in London in January 1963. Consisted of Mick Jagger (b: 7/26/43; vocals), Keith Richards (b: 12/18/43; lead guitar), Brian Jones (b: 2/28/42; guitar), Bill Wyman (b: 10/24/36; bass) and Charlie Watts (b: 6/02/41; drums). Jagger was the lead singer of Blues, Inc. Group took name from a Muddy Waters song. Promoted as the bad boys in contrast to The Beatles. First UK tour, with Ronettes, in 1964. Jones left group shortly before drowning on 7/03/69. Replaced by Mick Taylor (b: 1/17/48). In 1975, Ron Wood (ex-Jeff Beck Group, ex-Faces) replaced Taylor. Film *Gimme Shelter* is a documentary of their controversial Altamont concert on 12/06/69 at which a concertgoer was murdered by a member of the Hell's Angels. Won Lifetime Achievement Grammy in 1986. Inducted into the Rock and Roll Hall of Fame in 1989. Considered by many as the world's all-time greatest rock band.	
8/01/64	**24**	5	1. Tell Me (You're Coming Back)	London 9682
8/22/64	**26**	6	2. It's All Over Now	London 9687
11/07/64	**6**	9	**3. Time Is On My Side**	London 9708
1/30/65	**19**	5	4. Heart Of Stone	London 9725
4/10/65	**9**	8	**5. The Last Time**	London 9741
6/19/65	**1**(4)	12	● **6. (I Can't Get No) Satisfaction**	London 9766
10/16/65	**1**(2)	11	**7. Get Off Of My Cloud**	London 9792
1/08/66	**6**	6	**8. As Tears Go By**	London 9808
3/05/66	**2**(3)	9	**9. 19th Nervous Breakdown**	London 9823
5/21/66	**1**(2)	10	**10. Paint It, Black**	London 901
7/16/66	**8**	8	**11. Mothers Little Helper/**	
8/06/66	**24**	4	12. Lady Jane	London 902
10/08/66	**9**	6	**13. Have You Seen Your Mother, Baby, Standing In The Shadow?**	London 903
2/04/67	**1**(1)	9	● **14. Ruby Tuesday**	London 904
9/23/67	**14**	6	15. Dandelion	London 905
			all of above produced by Andrew Loog Oldham	
1/13/68	**25**	4	16. She's A Rainbow	London 906
6/15/68	**3**	11	**17. Jumpin' Jack Flash**	London 908
7/26/69	**1**(4)	14	● **18. Honky Tonk Women**	London 910
5/01/71	**1**(2)	12	**19. Brown Sugar**	Rolling S. 19100
7/03/71	**28**	5	20. Wild Horses	Rolling S. 19101
5/06/72	**7**	9	**21. Tumbling Dice**	Rolling S. 19103
7/29/72	**22**	4	22. Happy	Rolling S. 19104
9/22/73	**1**(1)	13	● **23. Angie**	Rolling S. 19105
2/02/74	**15**	6	24. Doo Doo Doo Doo Doo (Heartbreaker)	Rolling S. 19109
			above 8 produced by Jimmy Miller	
8/17/74	**16**	7	25. It's Only Rock 'N Roll (But I Like It)	Rolling S. 19301
11/16/74	**17**	7	26. Ain't Too Proud To Beg	Rolling S. 19302
5/08/76	**10**	7	**27. Fool To Cry**	Rolling S. 19304
6/10/78	**1**(1)	16	● **28. Miss You**	Rolling S. 19307
9/23/78	**8**	9	**29. Beast Of Burden**	Rolling S. 19309
1/13/79	**31**	4	30. Shattered	Rolling S. 19310
7/05/80	**3**	14	**31. Emotional Rescue**	Rolling S. 20001
10/18/80	**26**	5	32. She's So Cold	Rolling S. 21001
8/29/81	**2**(3)	19	**33. Start Me Up**	Rolling S. 21003
12/12/81+	**13**	12	34. Waiting On A Friend	Rolling S. 21004

DATE	POS	WKS	ARTIST—RECORD TITLE	LABEL & NO.
4/10/82	**20**	6	35. Hang Fire	Rolling S. 21300
7/03/82	**25**	5	36. Going To A Go-Go	Rolling S. 21301
11/19/83	**9**	10	**37. Undercover Of The Night**	Rolling S. 99813
3/22/86	**5**	10	**38. Harlem Shuffle**	Rolling S. 05802
6/14/86	**28**	4	39. One Hit (To The Body)	Rolling S. 05906
9/09/89	**5**	9	**40. Mixed Emotions**	Rolling S. 69008
11/25/89	**23**	8	41. Rock And A Hard Place	Rolling S. 73057
			above 17 produced by The Glimmer Twins	
			ROMANTICS, The	
			Rock quartet from Detroit formed in 1977. Original lineup: Wally Palmar (lead singer, guitar), Mike Skill (lead guitar), Richard Cole (bass) and Jimmy Marinos (drums).	
12/03/83+	**3**	15	**1. Talking In Your Sleep**	Nemperor 04135
3/31/84	**37**	3	2. One In A Million	Nemperor 04373
			ROMEO VOID	
			San Francisco new-wave quintet formed in 1979 — Debora Iyall, lead singer.	
10/20/84	**35**	2	1. A Girl In Trouble (Is A Temporary Thing)	Columbia 04534
			RONALD AND RUBY	
			Ronald Gumby and Beverly "Ruby" Ross (b: 1939). The New Jersey-born Ross wrote "Dim, Dim The Lights," "Lollipop," "Judy's Turn To Cry," "Remember When" and "Candy Man."	
3/24/58	**20**	3	1. Lollipop	RCA 7174
			Jockey #20 / Top 100 #39 / Best Seller #40	
			RONDO, Don	
			Baritone singer from New York City. Sang on TV/radio commercials.	
11/03/56	**11**	12	1. Two Different Worlds	Jubilee 5256
			Jockey #11 / Top 100 #19 / Best Seller #23	
7/29/57	**7**	15	**2. White Silver Sands**	Jubilee 5288
			Jockey #7 / Best Seller #9 / Top 100 #10	
			RONETTES, The	
			Formed in New York City as the Darling Sisters in 1958. Consisted of Veronica "Ronnie" Bennett Spector (b: 8/10/45), sister Estelle Bennett Vann (b: 7/22/44) and cousin Nedra Talley Ross (b: 1/27/46). Sang professionally since junior high school. Backup work for Phil Spector in 1962. Group disbanded in 1966. Veronica married to Phil Spector, 1968-74.	
9/14/63	**2**(3)	10	**1. Be My Baby**	Philles 116
1/11/64	**24**	6	2. Baby, I Love You	Philles 118
5/16/64	**39**	1	3. (The Best Part Of) Breakin' Up	Philles 120
7/18/64	**34**	4	4. Do I Love You?	Philles 121
11/21/64	**23**	7	5. Walking In The Rain	Philles 123
			all of above produced by Phil Spector	
			RONNIE AND THE HI-LITES	
			R&B vocal quintet from Jersey City. Lead singer Ronnie Goodson died of a brain tumor on 11/04/80.	
4/21/62	**16**	8	1. I Wish That We Were Married	Joy 260

DATE	POS	WKS	ARTIST—RECORD TITLE	LABEL & NO.
			RONNY & THE DAYTONAS	
			Nashville group specializing in hot-rod music. Ronny is John "Bucky" Wilkin (b: 4/26/46, Tulsa; vocals). Backed on recordings by well-known sessionmen Bobby Russell (wrote "Little Green Apples"), Chips Moman (prolific producer) and Johnny MacRae (member of Bobby "Boris" Pickett's Crypt-Kickers), among others. The touring group, which featured an entirely different lineup, later charted as The Hombres.	
8/22/64	**4**	10	**1. G.T.O.**	Mala 481
1/08/66	**27**	5	2. Sandy	Mala 513
			RONSTADT, Linda	
			Born on 7/15/46 in Tucson, Arizona. While in high school formed folk trio The Three Ronstadts (with sister and brother). To Los Angeles in 1964. Formed the Stone Poneys with Bobby Kimmel (guitar) and Ken Edwards (keyboards); recorded for Sidewalk in 1965. Went solo in 1968. In 1971 formed backing band with Glenn Frey, Don Henley, Randy Meisner and Bernie Leadon (later became the Eagles). In *Pirates of Penzance* operetta in New York City in 1980, also in film of same name in 1983. Also see Nitty Gritty Dirt Band.	
12/09/67+	**13**	13	1. Different Drum **STONE PONEYS featuring LINDA RONSTADT**	Capitol 2004
9/12/70	**25**	7	2. Long Long Time	Capitol 2846
1/04/75	**1**(1)	10	**3. You're No Good**	Capitol 3990
4/26/75	**2**(2)	13	**4. When Will I Be Loved**	Capitol 4050
10/04/75	**5**	10	**5. Heat Wave**	Asylum 45282
1/24/76	**25**	6	6. Tracks Of My Tears	Asylum 45295
9/04/76	**11**	11	7. That'll Be The Day	Asylum 45340
10/08/77	**3**	16	▲ **8. Blue Bayou**	Asylum 45431
10/29/77	**5**	12	**9. It's So Easy**	Asylum 45438
2/25/78	**31**	3	10. Poor Poor Pitiful Me	Asylum 45462
5/20/78	**32**	3	11. Tumbling Dice	Asylum 45479
9/09/78	**16**	8	12. Back In The U.S.A.	Asylum 45519
11/18/78+	**7**	13	**13. Ooh Baby Baby**	Asylum 45546
2/09/80	**10**	12	**14. How Do I Make You**	Asylum 46602
4/19/80	**8**	11	**15. Hurt So Bad**	Asylum 46624
7/19/80	**31**	4	16. I Can't Let Go	Asylum 46654
10/23/82	**29**	5	17. Get Closer	Asylum 69948
1/29/83	**37**	3	18. I Knew You When	Asylum 69853
1/24/87	**2**(1)	12	**19. Somewhere Out There** **LINDA RONSTADT AND JAMES INGRAM** from the animated film *An American Tail*	MCA 52973
			LINDA RONSTADT featuring AARON NEVILLE:	
10/28/89	**2**(2)	16	● **20. Don't Know Much** tune also known as "All I Need To Know"	Elektra 69261
2/24/90	**11**	9	21. All My Life written by Karla Bonoff; all of above (except first 2) produced by Peter Asher	Elektra 64987
			ROOFTOP SINGERS, The	
			Folk trio from New York City: Erik Darling, Willard Svanoe and Lynne Taylor (d: 1982). Disbanded in 1967. Darling was a member of The Tarriers in 1956 and The Weavers, 1958-62. Taylor was a vocalist with Benny Goodman and Buddy Rich.	
1/12/63	**1**(2)	11	**1. Walk Right In**	Vanguard 35017
4/20/63	**20**	5	2. Tom Cat	Vanguard 35019

DATE	POS	WKS	ARTIST—RECORD TITLE	LABEL & NO.
			ROSE, David	
			Born on 6/15/10 in London; moved to Chicago at an early age. Conductor/composer/arranger for numerous films. Scored many TV series, such as "The Red Skelton Show," "Bonanza" and "Little House on the Prairie." Married to Martha Raye (1938-41) and Judy Garland (1941-43). Died on 8/23/90 of heart disease.	
6/02/62	**1**(1)	13	**1. The Stripper** [I]	MGM 13064
			ROSE GARDEN, The	
			West Virginia quintet: Diana Di Rose (lead singer), Johnny Noreen (lead guitar), James Groshong (guitar), William Fleming (bass/piano) and Bruce Boudin (drums).	
12/09/67	**17**	7	1. Next Plane To London	Atco 6510
			ROSE ROYCE	
			Eight-member backing band formed in Los Angeles in early '70s. Backed Edwin Starr as Total Concept Unlimited in 1973. Backed The Temptations, became regular band for Undisputed Truth. Lead vocalist Gwen Dickey added, name changed to Rose Royce in 1976. Did soundtrack for the film *Car Wash*.	
12/11/76+	**1**(1)	14	▲ **1. Car Wash**	MCA 40615
3/19/77	**10**	10	**2. I Wanna Get Next To You**	MCA 40662
			above 2 from the film *Car Wash*	
10/22/77	**39**	2	3. Do Your Dance - Part 1	Whitfield 8440
1/13/79	**32**	4	4. Love Don't Live Here Anymore	Whitfield 8712
			all of above produced and arranged by Norman Whitfield	
			ROSIE AND THE ORIGINALS	
			San Diego group — Rosalie Hamlin, lead singer.	
12/12/60+	**5**	12	**1. Angel Baby**	Highland 1011
			ROSS, Diana	
			Born Diane Earle on 3/26/44 in Detroit. In vocal group The Primettes, first recorded for LuPine in 1960. Lead singer of The Supremes from 1961-69. Went solo in late 1969. Oscar nominee for the 1972 film *Lady Sings the Blues*. Appeared in the films *Mahogany* and *The Wiz*. Own Broadway show *An Evening with Diana Ross*, 1976.	
5/02/70	**20**	8	1. Reach Out And Touch (Somebody's Hand)	Motown 1165
8/15/70	**1**(3)	13	**2. Ain't No Mountain High Enough**	Motown 1169
1/09/71	**16**	8	3. Remember Me	Motown 1176
5/15/71	**29**	5	4. Reach Out I'll Be There	Motown 1184
9/11/71	**38**	3	5. Surrender	Motown 1188
3/03/73	**34**	4	6. Good Morning Heartache	Motown 1211
			from the film *Lady Sings The Blues*, starring Diana Ross	
7/07/73	**1**(1)	16	**7. Touch Me In The Morning**	Motown 1239
10/13/73	**12**	10	8. You're A Special Part Of Me	Motown 1280
			DIANA ROSS & MARVIN GAYE	
1/26/74	**14**	8	9. Last Time I Saw Him	Motown 1278
3/30/74	**19**	10	10. My Mistake (Was To Love You)	Motown 1269
			DIANA ROSS & MARVIN GAYE	
11/22/75+	**1**(1)	13	**11. Theme From Mahogany (Do You Know Where You're Going To)**	Motown 1377
			from the film *Mahogany*, starring Diana Ross	
4/24/76	**1**(2)	13	**12. Love Hangover**	Motown 1392
8/21/76	**25**	8	13. One Love In My Lifetime	Motown 1398

DATE	POS	WKS	ARTIST—RECORD TITLE	LABEL & NO.
12/03/77+	**27**	7	14. Gettin' Ready For Love	Motown 1427
8/18/79	**19**	9	15. The Boss	Motown 1462
8/09/80	**1**(4)	17	● **16. Upside Down**	Motown 1494
10/04/80	**5**	14	**17. I'm Coming Out**	Motown 1491
11/15/80+	**9**	15	**18. It's My Turn** from the film of the same title	Motown 1496
7/18/81	**1**(9)	19	▲ **19. Endless Love** **DIANA ROSS & LIONEL RICHIE** from the film of the same title	Motown 1519
10/24/81	**7**	14	**20. Why Do Fools Fall In Love**	RCA 12349
1/30/82	**8**	10	**21. Mirror, Mirror**	RCA 13021
10/16/82	**10**	10	**22. Muscles** written and produced by Michael Jackson	RCA 13348
3/19/83	**40**	2	23. So Close	RCA 13424
7/23/83	**31**	3	24. Pieces Of Ice	RCA 13549
8/04/84	**19**	8	25. All Of You **JULIO IGLESIAS & DIANA ROSS**	Columbia 04507
9/22/84	**19**	8	26. Swept Away written and produced by Daryl Hall	RCA 13864
3/09/85	**10**	9	**27. Missing You** dedicated to Marvin Gaye; produced and written by Lionel Richie	RCA 13966
			ROSS, Jack	
			West Coast nightclub entertainer/trumpet player. Died on 12/16/82 (age 66).	
4/07/62	**16**	6	1. Cinderella [C]	Dot 16333
			ROSS, Jackie	
			Born on 1/30/46 in St. Louis. Sang gospel on her parent's radio show at age three. Moved to Chicago in 1954. First recorded for Sar in 1962.	
8/15/64	**11**	8	1. Selfish One	Chess 1903
			ROSS, Spencer	
			Arranger/orchestra leader. Composed arrangements for Gordon Jenkin's orchestra. Arranging work for Big Top and Columbia Records.	
1/18/60	**13**	10	1. Tracy's Theme [I] from the TV show "Philadelphia Story"; sax: Jimmy Abato	Columbia 41532
			ROTH, David Lee	
			Born on 10/10/55 in Bloomington, Indiana. Former lead singer of Van Halen.	
1/26/85	**3**	11	**1. California Girls**	Warner 29102
4/20/85	**12**	10	2. Just A Gigolo/I Ain't Got Nobody "Just A Gigolo": #1 hit for Ted Lewis in 1931; "I Ain't Got Nobody": #3 hit for Marion Harris in 1921	Warner 29040
7/26/86	**16**	8	3. Yankee Rose	Warner 28656
1/30/88	**6**	11	**4. Just Like Paradise**	Warner 28119
			ROUTERS, The	
			Rock and roll instrumental quintet led by Mike Gordon.	
11/24/62	**19**	7	1. Let's Go [I]	Warner 5283
			ROVER BOYS, The	
			Vocal quartet featuring Brooklyn native, lead singer Billy Albert. Remaining three members from Toronto.	
5/19/56	**16**	7	1. Graduation Day	ABC-Para. 9700

DATE	POS	WKS	ARTIST—RECORD TITLE	LABEL & NO.
			Jockey #16 / Best Seller #19 / Top 100 #20	
			ROVERS — see IRISH ROVERS	
			ROXETTE	
			Male/female Swedish duo: Marie Fredriksson (vocals) and Per Gessle (songwriter).	
2/25/89	**1**(1)	13	● **1. The Look**	EMI 50190
6/24/89	**14**	9	2. Dressed For Success	EMI 50204
9/09/89	**1**(1)	14	**3. Listen To Your Heart**	EMI 50223#
1/06/90	**2**(2)	14	**4. Dangerous**	EMI 50233#
4/21/90	**1**(2)	17	● **5. It Must Have Been Love** from the film *Pretty Woman*	EMI 50283#
3/16/91	**1**(1)	13	**6. Joyride**	EMI 50342#
6/29/91	**2**(1)	13	**7. Fading Like A Flower (Every Time You Leave)**	EMI 50355#
			ROXY MUSIC	
			English art-rock band. Nucleus consisted of Bryan Ferry (vocals, keyboards), Phil Manzanera (guitar) and Andy Mackay (horns).	
2/21/76	**30**	5	1. Love Is The Drug	Atco 7042
			ROYAL, Billy Joe	
			Born on 4/03/42 in Valdosta, Georgia; raised in Marietta, Georgia. Guitarist/pianist/drummer. Own band, the Corvettes, while in high school. First recorded in 1962. Moved to Cincinnati in 1963.	
7/31/65	**9**	8	**1. Down In The Boondocks**	Columbia 43305
10/09/65	**14**	8	2. I Knew You When	Columbia 43390
1/15/66	**38**	1	3. I've Got To Be Somebody above 3 written and produced by Joe South	Columbia 43465
11/01/69	**15**	10	4. Cherry Hill Park	Columbia 44902
			ROYAL GUARDSMEN, The	
			Novelty-pop sextet from Ocala, Florida. Consisted of Barry Winslow (vocals, guitar), Chris Nunley (vocals), Tom Richards (lead guitar), Bill Balough (bass) and Billy Taylor (organ).	
12/17/66	**2**(4)	11	● **1. Snoopy Vs. The Red Baron** **[N]**	Laurie 3366
3/11/67	**15**	5	2. The Return Of The Red Baron [N]	Laurie 3379
1/04/69	**35**	5	3. Baby Let's Wait first released on Laurie 3359 in 1966	Laurie 3461
			ROYAL PHILHARMONIC ORCHESTRA, The	
			British — Louis Clark, conductor (born in Birmingham, England; arranger for ELO).	
11/28/81+	**10**	12	**1. Hooked On Classics** [I] Tchaikovsky Piano Concerto No. 1/Flight of the Bumble Bee/ Mozart Symphony No. 40 in G Minor/Rhapsody In Blue/Karelia Suite/The Marriage of Figaro/Romeo & Juliet/Trumpet Voluntary/Hallelujah Chorus/Grieg Piano Concerto in A Minor/March of the Toreadors	RCA 12304
			ROYAL SCOTS DRAGOON GUARDS, The	
			The Pipes and Drums and The Military Band of Scotland's armored regiment. Led by Pipe Major Tony Crease.	
5/27/72	**11**	8	1. Amazing Grace [I] bagpipes solo: Pipe Major Tony Crease	RCA 0709

DATE	POS	WKS	ARTIST—RECORD TITLE	LABEL & NO.
			ROYAL TEENS	
			Quartet from Fort Lee, New Jersey. Consisted of Bob Gaudio, Bill Crandall, Billy Dalton and Tom Austin. Crandall was replaced by Larry Qualiano, and Joseph "Joe Villa" Francavilla joined as vocalist in late 1958. In 1960, Gaudio joined The 4 Seasons. Al Kooper joined the group for a short time in 1959.	
2/03/58	**3**	12	**1. Short Shorts** Top 100 #3 / Best Seller #4 / Jockey #6 first released on Power 215 in 1957	ABC-Para. 9882
11/16/59	**26**	6	2. Believe Me	Capitol 4261
			ROYALTONES, The	
			Rock and roll instrumental group from Dearborn, Michigan. Formed in 1957 as the Paragons. Featuring tenor saxophonist George Katsakis.	
11/10/58	**17**	10	1. Poor Boy [I]	Jubilee 5338
			RUBETTES, The	
			British quintet featuring Paul DaVinci, lead singer.	
8/31/74	**37**	2	1. Sugar Baby Love	Polydor 15089
			RUBICON	
			Bay area septet led by horn player Jerry Martini (member of Sly & The Family Stone, 1966-76). Group included Jack Blades and Brad Gillis of Night Ranger.	
4/08/78	**28**	3	1. I'm Gonna Take Care Of Everything	20th Century 2362
			RUBY AND THE ROMANTICS	
			Akron, Ohio R&B quintet: Ruby Nash Curtis (b: 11/12/39, New York City; lead), Ed Roberts & George Lee (tenors), Ronald Mosley (baritone) and Leroy Fann (bass; d: 1973).	
2/23/63	**1**(1)	10	**1. Our Day Will Come**	Kapp 501
6/15/63	**16**	6	2. My Summer Love	Kapp 525
8/31/63	**27**	5	3. Hey There Lonely Boy	Kapp 544
			RUDE BOYS	
			Cleveland vocal quartet: Larry Marcus, Melvin Sephus, and brothers Edward Lee "Buddy" Banks and Joe'l Little III. Marcus is the cousin of B.B. King. Group discovered by Levert.	
3/30/91	**16**	12	1. Written All Over Your Face	Atlantic 87805#
			RUFFIN, David	
			Born Davis Eli Ruffin on 1/18/41 in Meridian, Mississippi. Brother of Jimmy Ruffin. With the Dixie Nightingales gospel group. Recorded for Anna in 1960. Co-lead singer of The Temptations from 1963-68. Died of a drug overdose on 6/01/91.	
2/22/69	**9**	9	**1. My Whole World Ended (The Moment You Left Me)**	Motown 1140
11/29/75+	**9**	11	**2. Walk Away From Love**	Motown 1376
9/14/85	**20**	7	3. A Nite At The Apollo Live! The Way You Do The Things You Do/My Girl **DARYL HALL JOHN OATES with DAVID RUFFIN & EDDIE KENDRICK**	RCA 14178
			RUFFIN, Jimmy	
			Born on 5/07/39 in Collinsville, Mississippi. Brother of David Ruffin. Backup work at Motown in the early '60s. First recorded for Miracle in 1961.	
9/10/66	**7**	14	**1. What Becomes Of The Brokenhearted**	Soul 35022
12/24/66+	**17**	8	2. I've Passed This Way Before	Soul 35027

DATE	POS	WKS	ARTIST—RECORD TITLE	LABEL & NO.
4/08/67	**29**	3	3. Gonna Give Her All The Love I've Got	Soul 35032
3/22/80	**10**	9	**4. Hold On To My Love**	RSO 1021
			written and produced by Robin Gibb	
			RUFUS featuring CHAKA KHAN	
			Soul group from Chicago. First known as Smoke, then Ask Rufus. Varying membership included Chaka Khan (vocals), Tony Maiden (guitar), Nate Morgan, Kevin Murphy (keyboards), Bobby Watson (bass), Andre Fischer (drums; ex-American Breed and later married to Natalie Cole) and Moon Calhoun. Khan has been recording solo and with Rufus since 1978. After 1978, Maiden and David Wolinski also sang lead.	
7/13/74	**3**	12	● **1. Tell Me Something Good**	ABC 11427
			RUFUS	
			written by Stevie Wonder	
11/02/74	**11**	11	2. You Got The Love	ABC 12032
3/08/75	**10**	7	**3. Once You Get Started**	ABC 12066
2/14/76	**5**	12	● **4. Sweet Thing**	ABC 12149
6/12/76	**39**	1	5. Dance Wit Me	ABC 12179
3/12/77	**30**	6	6. At Midnight (My Love Will Lift You Up)	ABC 12239
6/04/77	**32**	3	7. Hollywood	ABC 12269
			RUFUS AND CHAKA KHAN:	
5/27/78	**38**	3	8. Stay	ABC 12349
1/19/80	**30**	4	9. Do You Love What You Feel	MCA 41131
11/12/83	**22**	8	10. Ain't Nobody	Warner 29555
			RUGBYS, The	
			Steve McNichol (guitar), Mike Mornei (bass), Ed Vernon (keyboards) and Glenn Howerton (drums).	
9/20/69	**24**	7	1. You, I	Amazon 1
			RUNDGREN, Todd	
			Born on 6/22/48 in Upper Darby, Pennsylvania. Virtuoso musician/songwriter/producer/engineer. Leader of groups Nazz and Utopia. Produced Meat Loaf's *Bat Out of Hell* album and produced albums for Badfinger, Grand Funk Railroad, The Tubes, XTC, Patti Smith and many others.	
12/26/70+	**20**	9	1. We Gotta Get You A Woman	Ampex 31001
			RUNT	
5/06/72	**16**	9	2. I Saw The Light	Bearsville 0003
11/10/73	**5**	12	**3. Hello It's Me**	Bearsville 0009
			original version by Nazz charted in 1969 (POS 66)	
6/26/76	**34**	3	4. Good Vibrations	Bearsville 0309
7/08/78	**29**	5	5. Can We Still Be Friends	Bearsville 0324
			all of above (except #4) written and produced by Rundgren	
			RUN-D.M.C.	
			Rap trio from Queens, New York: rappers Joseph Simmons (Run), Darryl McDaniels (DMC), with DJ Jason Mizell (Jam Master Jay). In films *Krush Groove* and *Tougher Than Leather.*	
8/16/86	**4**	10	**1. Walk This Way**	Profile 5112
			with Aerosmith's Steve Tyler (vocals) and Joe Perry (guitar)	
11/29/86	**29**	7	2. You Be Illin'	Profile 5119

DATE	POS	WKS	ARTIST—RECORD TITLE	LABEL & NO.
			RUSH	
			Canadian power-rock trio: Geddy Lee (b: 7/29/53; vocals, bass), Alex Lifeson (b: 8/27/53; guitar) and Neil Peart (b: 9/12/52; drums). Also see Bob & Doug McKenzie.	
10/09/82	**21**	6	1. New World Man	Mercury 76179
			RUSH, Jennifer	
			Native of Queens, New York.	
7/04/87	**36**	3	1. Flames Of Paradise **JENNIFER RUSH with ELTON JOHN**	Epic 07119
			RUSH, Merrilee/The Turnabouts	
			From Seattle, Washington. Discovered by fellow Northwesterners, Paul Revere & The Raiders.	
6/01/68	**7**	12	**1. Angel Of The Morning**	Bell 705
			RUSHEN, Patrice	
			Born on 9/30/54 in Los Angeles. Jazz-soul vocalist/pianist/songwriter. Much session work with Jean Luc-Ponty, Lee Ritenour and Stanley Turrentine.	
6/05/82	**23**	7	1. Forget Me Nots	Elektra 47427
			RUSSELL, Bobby	
			Born on 4/19/41 in Nashville. Wrote "The Night The Lights Went Out In Georgia," "Honey," "Little Green Apples" and "The Joker Went Wild."	
11/23/68	**36**	2	1. 1432 Franklin Pike Circle Hero	Elf 90020
8/28/71	**28**	7	2. Saturday Morning Confusion [N]	United Art. 50788
			RUSSELL, Brenda	
			Soul singer/keyboardist/composer, born Brenda Gordon in Brooklyn. To Toronto at age 12. Recorded as duo, Brian & Brenda, with former husband Brian Russell in 1978; co-hosted the Canadian TV series "Music Machine." Session work for Barbra Streisand, Elton John, Bette Midler and many others.	
10/13/79	**30**	6	1. So Good, So Right	Horizon 123
4/02/88	**6**	13	**2. Piano In The Dark** featuring vocalist Joe Esposito (Brooklyn Dreams)	A&M 3003
			RUSSELL, Leon	
			Born on 4/02/41 in Lawton, Oklahoma. Vocalist/songwriter/top multi-instrumentalist sessionman. Early in session career known as Russell Bridges. Regular with Phil Spector's "Wall of Sound" session group. Formed Shelter Records with British producer Denny Cordell in 1970. Recorded as Hank Wilson in 1973. Married Mary McCreary (vocalist with Little Sister, part of Sly Stone's "family") in 1976. Formed Paradise label in 1976. Wrote "Superstar" and "This Masquerade." Also see Joe Cocker.	
9/23/72	**11**	7	1. Tight Rope	Shelter 7325
9/13/75	**14**	10	2. Lady Blue	Shelter 40378
			RYAN, Charlie/The Timberline Riders	
			Born in Graceville, Minnesota; raised in Montana. Country singer.	
8/08/60	**33**	4	1. Hot Rod Lincoln [S-N]	4 Star 1733
			RYDELL, Bobby	
			Born Robert Ridarelli on 4/26/42 in Philadelphia. Regular on Paul Whiteman's amateur TV show, 1951-54. Drummer with Rocco & His Saints, which included Frankie Avalon on trumpet in 1956. First recorded for Veko in 1957. In films *Bye Bye Birdie* and *That Lady from Peking.*	
8/10/59	**11**	9	1. Kissin' Time	Cameo 167
10/26/59	**6**	14	**2. We Got Love**	Cameo 169

DATE	POS	WKS	ARTIST—RECORD TITLE	LABEL & NO.
2/08/60	**2**(1)	13	**3. Wild One/**	
2/22/60	**19**	10	4. Little Bitty Girl	Cameo 171
5/16/60	**5**	8	**5. Swingin' School/** from the film *Because They're Young*	
5/16/60	**18**	8	6. Ding-A-Ling	Cameo 175
8/01/60	**4**	11	**7. Volare**	Cameo 179
11/14/60	**14**	10	8. Sway	Cameo 182
2/06/61	**11**	8	9. Good Time Baby	Cameo 186
5/08/61	**21**	5	10. That Old Black Magic #1 hit for Glenn Miller in 1943	Cameo 190
7/10/61	**25**	5	11. The Fish	Cameo 192
11/06/61	**21**	6	12. I Wanna Thank You	Cameo 201
12/25/61	**21**	3	13. Jingle Bell Rock [X]	Cameo 205
			BOBBY RYDELL/CHUBBY CHECKER	
3/10/62	**18**	7	14. I've Got Bonnie	Cameo 209
6/23/62	**14**	7	15. I'll Never Dance Again	Cameo 217
10/27/62	**10**	8	**16. The Cha-Cha-Cha**	Cameo 228
2/23/63	**23**	6	17. Butterfly Baby	Cameo 242
6/01/63	**17**	5	18. Wildwood Days many of above hits written by Kal Mann, Bernie Lowe, Dave Appell	Cameo 252
12/07/63+	**4**	12	**19. Forget Him**	Cameo 280
			RYDER, Mitch/The Detroit Wheels	
			Born William Levise, Jr. on 2/26/45 in Detroit. Leader of white soul-rock group The Detroit Wheels. Group was originally known as Billy Lee & The Rivieras. Renamed by their producer Bob Crewe. Ryder went solo in 1967. Formed new rock group, Detroit, in 1971.	
1/08/66	**10**	8	**1. Jenny Take A Ride!** medley: Little Richard's "Jenny, Jenny"/Chuck Willis' "C.C. Rider"	New Voice 806
3/26/66	**17**	6	2. Little Latin Lupe Lu	New Voice 808
10/22/66	**4**	14	**3. Devil With A Blue Dress On & Good Golly Miss Molly**	New Voice 817
2/18/67	**6**	9	**4. Sock It To Me-Baby!**	New Voice 820
5/13/67	**24**	4	5. Too Many Fish In The Sea & Three Little Fishes	New Voice 822
			MITCH RYDER:	
9/30/67	**30**	4	6. What Now My Love all of above produced by Bob Crewe	DynoVoice 901
			RYTHM SYNDICATE	
			R&B band from Connecticut: Evan Rogers (vocals), Carl Sturken (keyboards), John Nevin, Rob Mingrino, Mike McDonald and Kevin Cloud. Evan & Carl produced Donny Osmond's "Soldier Of Love" & "Sacred Emotion."	
6/15/91	**2**(2)	13	**1. P.A.S.S.I.O.N.**	Impact 54046#

DATE	POS	WKS	ARTIST—RECORD TITLE	LABEL & NO.
			S	
			SADE	
			Born Helen Folasade Adu on 1/16/59 in Ibadan, Nigeria; moved to London at age four. Name pronounced: SHAW-day. Appeared in the 1986 film *Absolute Beginners*. Former designer of menswear. Won the 1985 Best New Artist Grammy Award.	
3/30/85	**5**	13	**1. Smooth Operator**	Portrait 04807
12/28/85+	**5**	13	**2. The Sweetest Taboo**	Portrait 05713
4/19/86	**20**	7	3. Never As Good As The First Time	Portrait 05846
6/11/88	**16**	8	4. Paradise	Epic 07904
			SADLER, SSgt Barry	
			Born in New Mexico in 1940. Staff Sergeant of U.S. Army Special Forces (aka Green Berets). Served in Vietnam until injuring leg in booby trap. Shot in the head during a 1988 robbery attempt at his Guatemala home; suffered brain damage. Died of heart failure on 11/05/89 (age 49) in Tennessee.	
2/19/66	**1**(5)	11	● **1. The Ballad Of The Green Berets**	RCA 8739
5/14/66	**28**	4	2. The "A" Team	RCA 8804
			SAFARIS	
			Los Angeles-born pop quartet formed in 1959. Jim Stephens (lead singer), Richard Clasky, Marvin Rosenberg and Shelly Briar.	
7/11/60	**6**	11	**1. Image Of A Girl** with The Phantom's Band	Eldo 101
			SA-FIRE	
			Latin American dance singer from New York City.	
3/18/89	**12**	12	1. Thinking Of You	Cutting 872502
			SAGA	
			Canadian rock quintet: Michael Sadler, brothers Jim and Ian Crichton, Jim Gilmour and Steve Negus.	
1/29/83	**26**	8	1. On The Loose	Portrait 03359
			SAGER, Carole Bayer	
			Born on 3/08/46 in New York City. Prolific pop lyricist. Married Burt Bacharach in 1982. Collaborated in writing "A Groovy Kind Of Love," "Midnight Blue," "Nobody Does It Better," "When I Need You" and many others. Wrote lyrics for many film scores.	
6/13/81	**30**	7	1. Stronger Than Before	Boardwalk 02054
			SAILCAT	
			Country-rock duo: Court Pickett and John Wyker.	
7/15/72	**12**	10	1. Motorcycle Mama	Elektra 45782
			SAINTE-MARIE, Buffy	
			Born on 2/20/41 of Cree Indian parents on Piapot Reserve, Saskatchewan, Canada. Folk singer/songwriter. Co-writer of "Up Where We Belong." Married to Jack Nitzsche.	
4/29/72	**38**	2	1. Mister Can't You See	Vanguard 35151
			ST. PETERS, Crispian	
			Born Peter Smith on 4/05/44 in Swanley, Kent, England. Pop singer/guitarist.	
7/09/66	**4**	8	**1. The Pied Piper**	Jamie 1320

DATE	POS	WKS	ARTIST—RECORD TITLE	LABEL & NO.
7/22/67	**36**	2	2. You Were On My Mind	Jamie 1310
			SAKAMOTO, Kyu	
			Native of Kawasaki, Japan. Kyu (pronounced: cue) was one of 520 people killed in the crash of the Japan Airlines 747 near Tokyo on 8/12/85 (age 43).	
5/25/63	**1**(3)	12	**1. Sukiyaki** **[F]** released in Japan as "Ue O Muite Aruko" (I Look Up When I Walk)	Capitol 4945
			SALSOUL ORCHESTRA	
			Disco orchestra conducted by Philadelphia producer/arranger Vincent Montana, Jr. Vocalists included Phyllis Rhodes, Ronni Tyson, Carl Helm and Philip Hurt.	
2/14/76	**18**	9	1. Tangerine [I] #1 hit for Jimmy Dorsey in 1942	Salsoul 2004
10/30/76	**30**	5	2. Nice 'N' Naasty	Salsoul 2011
			SALT-N-PEPA	
			Queens-based female rap trio: Cheryl "Salt" James, Sandy "Pepa" Denton (from Kingston, Jamaica) and Dee Dee "DJ Spinderella LaToya" Roper.	
12/26/87+	**19**	13	▲ 1. Push It	Next Plat. 315
4/21/90	**26**	8	▲ 2. Expression	Next Plat. 329#
5/11/91	**21**	14	● 3. Do You Want Me featuring Hurby Luv Bug	Next Plat. 331#
			SALVO, Sammy	
			Pop vocalist from Birmingham, Alabama.	
3/03/58	**23**	1	1. Oh Julie Jockey #23 / Top 100 #78	RCA 7097
			SAM & DAVE	
			Samuel Moore (b: 10/12/35, Miami) and David Prater (b: 5/09/37, Ocilla, Georgia). Sam had been with the Melionaires gospel group, and Dave was a solo artist prior to their meeting in Miami in 1961. First recorded for Alston in 1962. Duo produced by Isaac Hayes and David Porter. Dave was killed in a car crash on 4/09/88.	
6/04/66	**21**	7	1. Hold On! I'm A Comin'	Stax 189
9/30/67	**2**(3)	11	● **2. Soul Man**	Stax 231
2/17/68	**9**	9	**3. I Thank You**	Stax 242
			SAM THE SHAM AND THE PHAROAHS	
			Dallas rock & roll group formed in the early 1960s, featuring lead singer Domingo "Sam" Samudio (b: 1940, Dallas). Included Ray Stinnet, David Martin, Jerry Patterson and Butch Gibson. First recorded for Dingo in 1965. Samudio went solo in 1970. Formed new band in 1974. On the 1982 film soundtrack *The Border.* Sam later became a street preacher in Memphis.	
5/01/65	**2**(2)	14	● **1. Wooly Bully** originally released on XL 906 in 1964	MGM 13322
8/21/65	**26**	4	2. Ju Ju Hand	MGM 13364
11/13/65	**33**	3	3. Ring Dang Doo	MGM 13397
7/02/66	**2**(2)	11	● **4. Lil' Red Riding Hood**	MGM 13506
10/15/66	**22**	5	5. The Hair On My Chinny Chin Chin	MGM 13581
1/21/67	**27**	4	6. How Do You Catch A Girl	MGM 13649

Poison's remake of "Your Mama Don't Dance" gave them a No. 10 hit in 1988—just six slots less than the original 1972 version by Loggins & Messina managed. But unlike that duo, the group also scored a No. 1 hit—with "Every Rose Has Its Thorn," released the same year.

Elvis Presley may have died in 1977, but you wouldn't know it in the 90s. As RCA Records continues to release previously-unissued Presley material on CD, groups like England's The Wonder Stuff release albums called *Never Loved Elvis*. And I.R.S. Records signs Dread Zeppelin, who are fronted by an Elvis impersonator and play Led Zeppelin music reggae-style.

Maxi Priest's first charting single was 1988's reggae cover of Cat Stevens's "Wild World." Born in the U.K., the singer shared a top-10 duet with Roberta Flack on 1991's "Set The Night To Music."

Prince & The Revolution soared to the top of the charts beginning with 1984's "Let's Go Crazy." When the Minneapolis superstar disbanded the group in 1986, various members pursued solo careers, including Wendy & Lisa, Eric Leeds, and Brownmark.

The Psychedelic Furs' track "Pretty In Pink," from their 1981 album *Talk Talk Talk*, inspired the 1986 John Hughes film of the same name. The Brit group's reward: a newly-recorded version was included on the film's A&M soundtack, which would go platinum.

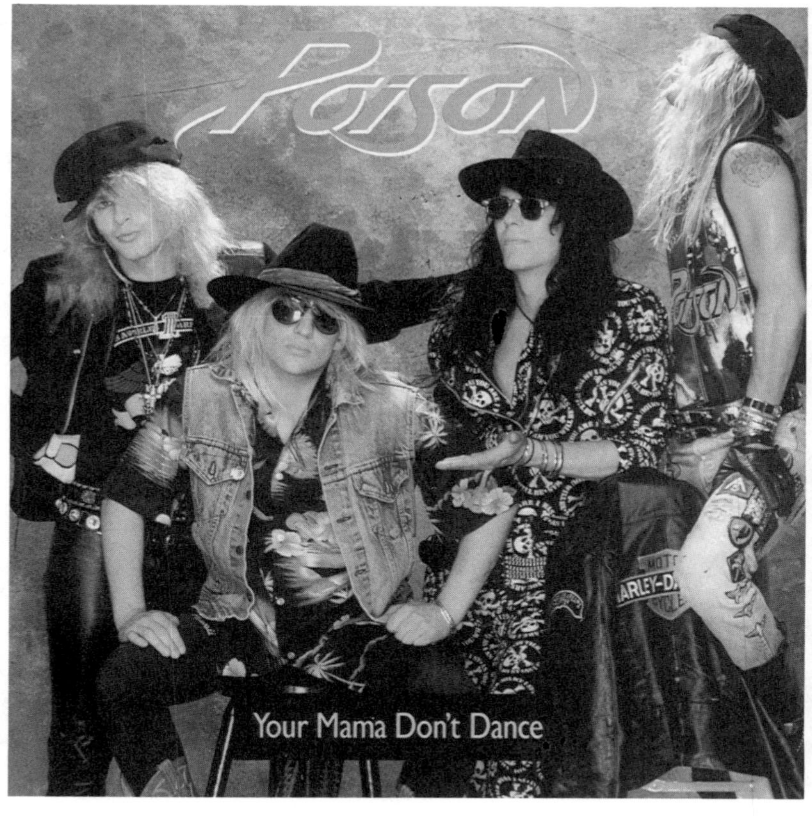

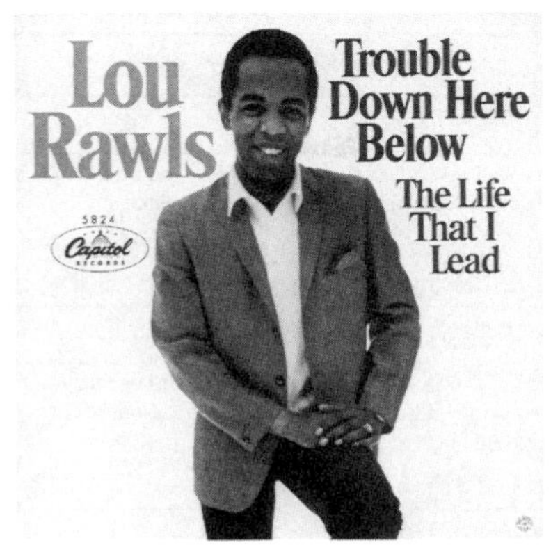

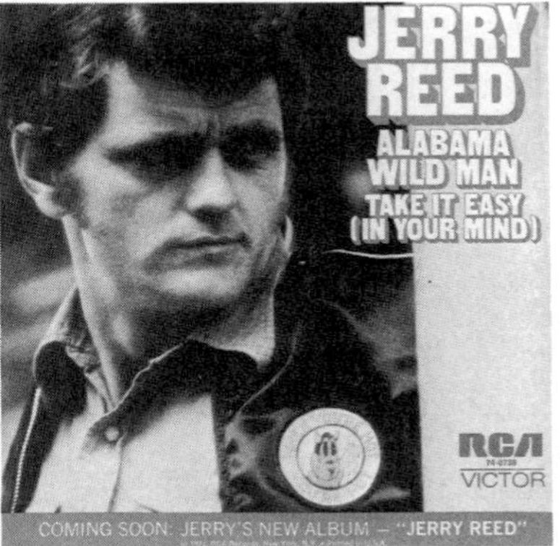

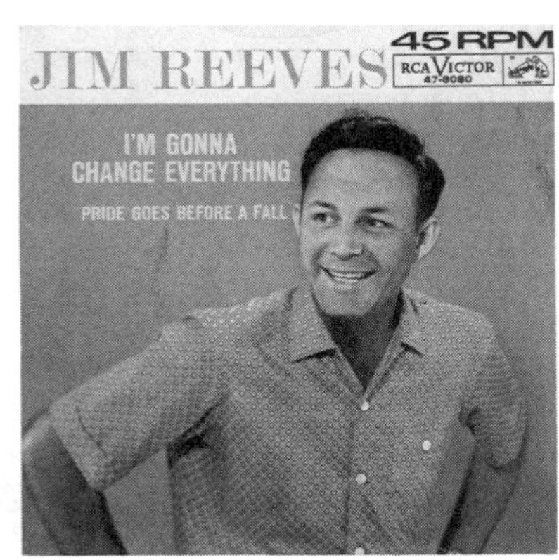

The (Young) Rascals' legacy as blue-eyed soul progenitors continues to prosper through the 90s. 1991's *Live at the Beacon* by the New York Rock And Soul Revue features former Rascal Eddie Brigati and new versions of Rascal hits "Groovin'" and "People Got To Be Free."

Lou Rawls made a surprising label change in 1989 when the "blues and soul" singer signed to jazz label Blue Note. *At Last*, Lou's first album for the label—which at the time was celebrating its 50th anniversary—was the 58th album in his long career.

Diane Ray scored her top-40 hit "Please Don't Talk To The Lifeguard" in 1963—the same year that Robin Ward's "Wonderful Summer" and the Beach Boys' "Surfin U.S.A." pointed America beachward.

Jerry Reed's major contributions to 70s culture were two-fold and equally ubiquitous: he starred in *Smokey & The Bandit* and, via his 1971 hit, helped popularize the catchphrase "When You're Hot, You're Hot."

Jim Reeves' all-time classic hit "He'll Have To Go" was No. 2 for two weeks in March 1960. Two months later, Jeanne Black's answer song "He'll Have To Stay" hit the No. 4 slot.

Regina's 1986 hit "Baby Love" was not the Holland-Dozier-Holland classic; among its writers, however, was Breakfast Club member Steven Bray, who wrote many of Madonna's hits.

DATE	POS	WKS	ARTIST—RECORD TITLE	LABEL & NO.
			SANDERS, Felicia	
			Born in New York City; raised in California. Died on 2/07/75. Vocalist on Percy Faith's 1953 #1 hit "Song From Moulin Rouge."	
5/28/55	**29**	3	1. Blue Star	Columbia 40508
			Best Seller #29; theme from the mid-1950s "Medic" TV series	
			SANDPEBBLES, The	
			Consisted of Calvin White, Andrea Bolden and Lonzine Wright. White had been lead singer of the Gospel Wonders. Group name changed to C & The Shells in 1968.	
1/06/68	**22**	6	1. Love Power	Calla 141
			SANDPIPERS, The	
			Los Angeles-based trio: Jim Brady (b: 8/24/44), Michael Piano (b: 10/26/44) and Richard Shoff (b: 4/30/44); met while in the Mitchell Boys Choir.	
8/13/66	**9**	9	**1. Guantanamera** **[F]**	A&M 806
11/12/66	**30**	4	2. Louie, Louie [F]	A&M 819
5/02/70	**17**	8	3. Come Saturday Morning	A&M 1134
			from the film *The Sterile Cuckoo*	
			SANDS, Jodie	
			Philadelphia pop songstress.	
6/10/57	**15**	9	1. With All My Heart	Chancellor 1003
			Jockey #15 / Top 100 #20 / Best Seller #21	
			SANDS, Tommy	
			Born on 8/27/37 in Chicago. Pop singer/actor. Mother was a vocalist with Art Kassel's band. Married Nancy Sinatra in 1960; divorced in 1965. In the films *Sing Boy Sing, Mardi Gras, Babes in Toyland* and *The Longest Day.*	
2/23/57	**2**(2)	12	**1. Teen-Age Crush**	Capitol 3639
			Best Seller #2 / Top 100 #3 / Jockey #4 / Juke Box #7 from the 1957 TV play *The Singing Idol* (starring Sands)	
5/27/57	**16**	8	2. Goin' Steady	Capitol 3723
			Jockey #16 / Best Seller #18 / Top 100 #19 #2 country hit for Faron Young in 1953	
2/24/58	**24**	2	3. Sing Boy Sing	Capitol 3867
			Jockey #24 / Best Seller #46 / Top 100 #46 from the film of the same title	
			SANFORD/TOWNSEND BAND, The	
			Los Angeles-based rock band led by Ed Sanford and John Townsend.	
7/16/77	**9**	12	**1. Smoke From A Distant Fire**	Warner 8370
			SANG, Samantha	
			Born Cheryl Gray on 8/05/53 in Melbourne, Australia. Began career on Melbourne radio at age eight.	
1/07/78	**3**	17	▲ **1. Emotion**	Private S. 45178
			backing vocal by Barry Gibb; written by Barry and Robin Gibb	
			SAN REMO GOLDEN STRINGS	
			Group of master violinists.	
10/09/65	**27**	5	1. Hungry For Love [I]	Ric-Tic 104
			SANTA ESMERALDA	
			Spanish-flavored disco studio project produced by Nicolas Skorsky and Jean-Manuel de Scarano.	
12/10/77+	**15**	12	1. Don't Let Me Be Misunderstood	Casablanca 902
			vocal by Leroy Gomez	

DATE	POS	WKS	ARTIST—RECORD TITLE	LABEL & NO.
			SANTAMARIA, Mongo	
			Born Ramon Santamaria on 4/07/22 in Havana, Cuba. Bandleader/conga, bongo and percussion player. Member of bands led by Perez Prado, Tito Puente and Cal Tjader. Own group from 1961. In the film *Made in Paris* in 1966.	
4/13/63	**10**	6	**1. Watermelon Man** [I] written by Herbie Hancock	Battle 45909
3/08/69	**32**	2	2. Cloud Nine [I]	Columbia 44740
			SANTANA	
			Latin-rock group formed in San Francisco in 1966. Consisted of Carlos Santana (b: 7/20/47, Autlan de Navarro, Mexico; vocals, guitar), Gregg Rolie (keyboards) and David Brown (bass). Added percussionists Michael Carabello, Jose Chepitos Areas and Michael Shrieve in 1969. Worked Fillmore West and Woodstock in 1969. Neal Schon (guitar) added in 1971. Santana began solo work in 1972. Schon and Rolie formed Journey in 1973. Shrieve left in 1975 to form Automatic Man.	
2/07/70	**9**	11	**1. Evil Ways**	Columbia 45069
11/21/70+	**4**	12	**2. Black Magic Woman**	Columbia 45270
3/06/71	**13**	8	3. Oye Como Va [F]	Columbia 45330
10/30/71	**12**	8	4. Everybody's Everything	Columbia 45472
3/11/72	**36**	4	5. No One To Depend On	Columbia 45552
11/19/77	**27**	5	6. She's Not There	Columbia 10616
2/17/79	**32**	3	7. Stormy	Columbia 10873
1/19/80	**35**	3	8. You Know That I Love You	Columbia 11144
5/16/81	**17**	11	9. Winning	Columbia 01050
8/28/82	**15**	10	10. Hold On	Columbia 03160
			SANTO & JOHNNY	
			Brooklyn-born guitar duo: Santo Farina (b: 10/24/37; steel guitar) and his brother Johnny (b: 4/30/41; rhythm guitar). Sister Ann Farina helped with songwriting.	
8/17/59	**1**(2)	13	**1. Sleep Walk** [I]	Canadian A. 103
12/14/59	**23**	7	2. Tear Drop [I]	Canadian A. 107
			SANTOS, Larry	
			Born on 6/02/41 in Oneonto, New York.	
4/03/76	**36**	2	1. We Can't Hide It Anymore	Casablanca 844
			SAPPHIRES, The	
			Philadelphia R&B trio: Carol Jackson (lead singer), George Gainer and Joe Livingston.	
2/22/64	**25**	5	1. Who Do You Love	Swan 4162
			SAYER, Leo	
			Born Gerard Sayer on 5/21/48 in Shoreham, England. With Patches in the early '70s. Songwriting team with David Courtney, 1972-75. Own British TV show in 1978 and again in 1983.	
3/22/75	**9**	9	**1. Long Tall Glasses (I Can Dance)**	Warner 8043
11/06/76+	**1**(1)	17	• **2. You Make Me Feel Like Dancing**	Warner 8283
3/26/77	**1**(1)	14	• **3. When I Need You**	Warner 8332
7/23/77	**17**	10	4. How Much Love	Warner 8319
11/05/77	**38**	2	5. Thunder In My Heart	Warner 8465
1/28/78	**36**	2	6. Easy To Love	Warner 8502
10/18/80	**2**(5)	15	• **7. More Than I Can Say**	Warner 49565

DATE	POS	WKS	ARTIST—RECORD TITLE	LABEL & NO.
2/14/81	**23**	6	8. Living In A Fantasy	Warner 49657
			SCAGGS, Boz	
			Born William Royce Scaggs on 6/08/44 in Ohio; raised in Texas. Joined Steve Miller's band, The Marksmen, in 1959 in Dallas. Hooked up with Miller at UW-Madison in The Ardells, later known as The Fabulous Night Trains. Joined R&B band The Wigs in 1963. To Europe in 1964, toured as a folk singer. Re-joined Miller in 1967, solo since 1969. Retired from music and opened a restaurant in San Francisco, 1983-87. Made comeback in 1988.	
5/22/76	**38**	3	1. It's Over	Columbia 10319
8/07/76	**3**	15	• **2. Lowdown**	Columbia 10367
3/19/77	**11**	12	3. Lido Shuffle	Columbia 10491
4/19/80	**15**	9	4. Breakdown Dead Ahead	Columbia 11241
7/12/80	**17**	9	5. JoJo	Columbia 11281
9/06/80	**14**	10	6. Look What You've Done To Me	Columbia 11349
12/27/80+	**14**	9	7. Miss Sun backing vocal by Lisa Dal Bello	Columbia 11406
6/11/88	**35**	4	8. Heart Of Mine	Columbia 07780
			SCANDAL featuring PATTY SMYTH	
			New York-based rock band led by Patty Smyth and Zack Smith.	
7/21/84	**7**	15	**1. The Warrior**	Columbia 04424
			SCARBURY, Joey	
			Born on 6/07/55 in Ontario, California. Session singer for producer Mike Post.	
6/13/81	**2**(2)	18	• **1. Theme From "Greatest American Hero" (Believe It or Not)** from the "Greatest American Hero" TV series	Elektra 47147
			SCARLETT & BLACK	
			Keyboardist/singer/songwriter Robin Hild and songwriter Sue West (former backing vocalist for Doctor & The Medics).	
3/12/88	**20**	8	1. You Don't Know	Virgin 99405
			SCHILLING, Peter	
			Born on 1/28/56 in Stuttgart, Germany. Pop singer/songwriter.	
11/12/83	**14**	10	1. Major Tom (Coming Home)	Elektra 69811
			SCHMIT, Timothy B.	
			Born on 10/30/47 in Sacramento. Member of Poco, 1970-77, and the Eagles, 1977-82.	
10/24/87	**25**	5	1. Boys Night Out	MCA 53137
			SCHNEIDER, John	
			Born on 4/08/54 in Mount Kisco, New York. Moved to Atlanta at age 14. Country singer/actor. Played "Bo Duke" on TV's "The Dukes of Hazzard." Appeared in many TV films. Scriptwriter/director.	
6/27/81	**14**	11	1. It's Now Or Never	Scotti Br. 02105
			SCHUMANN, Walter, The Voices of	
			Leader of own choral group.	
4/09/55	**14**	6	1. The Ballad Of Davy Crockett Jockey #14 / Best Seller #29 from the Disney TV series "Davy Crockett"	RCA 6041

DATE	POS	WKS	ARTIST—RECORD TITLE	LABEL & NO.
			SCHWARTZ, Eddie	
			Canadian singer/songwriter. Wrote Pat Benatar's "Hit Me With Your Best Shot."	
1/16/82	**28**	7	1. All Our Tomorrows	Atco 7342
			SCORPIONS	
			German heavy-metal rock quintet: Rudolf Schenker (Michael Schenker's brother; lead guitar), Klaus Meine (lead singer), Matthias Jabs (guitar), Francis Buchholz (bass) and Herman Rarebell (drums).	
4/28/84	**25**	7	1. Rock You Like A Hurricane	Mercury 818440
6/29/91	**4**	16	● **2. Wind Of Change**	Mercury 868180
			SCOTT, Bobby	
			Born on 1/29/37 in Mount Pleasant, New York. Jazz pianist/vocalist/ composer/arranger. Wrote Herb Alpert's hit "Taste Of Honey." Production work for Aretha Franklin and Johnny Mathis. Died on 11/05/90 of lung cancer.	
1/21/56	**13**	10	1. Chain Gang Jockey #13 / Juke Box #13 / Top 100 #15 / Best Seller #17	ABC-Para. 9658
			SCOTT, Freddie	
			Born on 4/24/33 in Providence, Rhode Island. Recorded first hit while working as a songwriter for Columbia Music.	
8/10/63	**10**	9	**1. Hey, Girl**	Colpix 692
2/18/67	**39**	2	2. Are You Lonely For Me	Shout 207
			SCOTT, Jack	
			Born Jack Scafone, Jr. on 1/28/36 in Windsor, Ontario, Canada. Rock and roll-ballad singer/songwriter/ guitarist. Moved to Hazel Park, Michigan in 1946. First recorded for ABC-Paramount in 1957.	
6/16/58	**11**	18	1. Leroy/ Best Seller #11 / Top 100 #25	
7/07/58	**3**	16	**2. My True Love** Hot 100 #3 / Best Seller #7 / Jockey #13 end	Carlton 462
10/20/58	**28**	4	3. With Your Love	Carlton 483
12/28/58+	**8**	13	**4. Goodbye Baby**	Carlton 493
8/03/59	**35**	4	5. The Way I Walk	Carlton 514
1/18/60	**5**	13	**6. What In The World's Come Over You**	Top Rank 2028
5/09/60	**3**	12	**7. Burning Bridges/**	
5/30/60	**34**	2	8. Oh, Little One	Top Rank 2041
9/05/60	**38**	2	9. It Only Happened Yesterday backing vocals on all of above by The Chantones	Top Rank 2055
			SCOTT, Linda	
			Born Linda Joy Sampson on 6/01/45 in Queens, New York. Moved to Teaneck, New Jersey at age 11. Vocalist on Arthur Godfrey's CBS radio show, late 1950s. Co-host of TV's "Where the Action Is." Joined Army, 1970-72. Later earned a degree in Theology and is currently a music teacher/director at the Christian Academy in New York.	
4/03/61	**3**	10	**1. I've Told Every Little Star** from the 1932 stage production *Music in the Air*	Canadian A. 123
7/24/61	**9**	10	**2. Don't Bet Money Honey**	Canadian A. 127
11/27/61	**12**	8	3. I Don't Know Why #2 hit for Wayne King in 1931	Canadian A. 129

DATE	POS	WKS	ARTIST—RECORD TITLE	LABEL & NO.
			SCOTT, Peggy, & JO JO BENSON	
			Soul duo; Jo Jo formerly sang with Chuck Willis and The Blue Notes.	
7/06/68	**31**	7	1. Lover's Holiday	SSS Int'l. 736
11/30/68	**27**	4	2. Pickin' Wild Mountain Berries	SSS Int'l. 748
2/15/69	**37**	3	3. Soulshake	SSS Int'l. 761
			SCRITTI POLITTI	
			British trio: Green Gartside (vocals), Fred Maher (drums) and David Gamson (keyboards). Italian name means "political writing."	
10/26/85	**11**	13	1. Perfect Way	Warner 28949
			SEA, Johnny	
			Born on 7/15/40 in Gulfport, Mississippi. Joined the "Louisiana Hayride" while still in high school. Real last name: Seay.	
6/25/66	**35**	2	1. Day For Decision [S]	Warner 5820
			patriotic answer to "Eve Of Destruction"	
			SEAL	
			Male singer. Born Sealhenry Samuel in Paddington, England of Nigerian/Brazilian descent.	
7/13/91	**7**	13	**1. Crazy**	Sire 19298
			SEALS & CROFTS	
			Pop duo: Jim Seals (b: 10/17/41, Sidney, Texas; guitar, fiddle, saxophone) and Dash Crofts (b: 8/14/40, Cisco, Texas; drums, mandolin, keyboards, guitar). With Dean Beard, recorded for Edmoral and Atlantic in 1957. To Los Angeles in 1958. With the Champs from 1958-65. Own group, the Dawnbreakers, in the late 1960s; entire band converted to Baha'i faith in 1969.	
10/21/72	**6**	11	**1. Summer Breeze**	Warner 7606
2/17/73	**20**	9	2. Hummingbird	Warner 7671
6/16/73	**6**	12	**3. Diamond Girl**	Warner 7708
10/13/73	**21**	8	4. We May Never Pass This Way (Again)	Warner 7740
5/17/75	**18**	8	5. I'll Play For You	Warner 8075
6/05/76	**6**	15	**6. Get Closer**	Warner 8190
			featuring Carolyn Willis (Honey Cone/Bob B. Soxx & The Blue Jeans)	
10/22/77	**28**	5	7. My Fair Share	Warner 8405
			love theme from the film *One on One*	
5/27/78	**18**	7	8. You're The Love	Warner 8551
			all of above produced by Louie Shelton	
			SEARCHERS, The	
			Liverpool, England rock quartet formed in 1960: Mike Pender and John McNally (vocals, guitars), Tony Jackson (vocals, bass) and Chris Curtis (drums). Worked as backup band for Johnny Sandon; toured England and worked Star Club in Hamburg, Germany. Left Sandon in 1962. Jackson replaced by Frank Allen in 1965. Curtis replaced by Billy Adamson in 1969.	
3/21/64	**13**	8	1. Needles And Pins	Kapp 577
6/20/64	**16**	8	2. Don't Throw Your Love Away	Kapp 593
9/12/64	**34**	3	3. Some Day We're Gonna Love Again	Kapp 609
11/14/64	**35**	2	4. When You Walk In The Room	Kapp 618
			written by Jackie DeShannon	
12/19/64+	**3**	11	**5. Love Potion Number Nine**	Kapp 27
2/20/65	**29**	3	6. What Have They Done To The Rain	Kapp 644

DATE	POS	WKS	ARTIST—RECORD TITLE	LABEL & NO.
4/10/65	**21**	4	7. Bumble Bee	Kapp 49
			SEBASTIAN, John	
			Born on 3/17/44 in New York City. Played with the Even Dozen Jug Band as "John Benson" in 1964. Did session work for Elektra Records and toured with Mississippi John Hurt. Formed The Lovin' Spoonful in 1965. Went solo in 1968. Continues to write and perform into the '90s.	
4/10/76	**1**(1)	11	● **1. Welcome Back**	Reprise 1349
			from the ABC-TV series "Welcome Back Kotter"	
			SECRETS, The	
			Cleveland female quartet: Kragen Gray, Josie Allen, Carole Raymont and Pat Miller.	
12/07/63	**18**	6	1. The Boy Next Door	Philips 40146
			SEDAKA, Neil	
			Born on 3/13/39 in Brooklyn. Pop singer/songwriter/pianist. Studied piano since elementary school. Formed songwriting team with lyricist Howard Greenfield while attending Lincoln High School (partnership lasted over 20 years). Recorded with The Tokens on Melba in 1956. Attended Juilliard School for classical piano. Prolific hit songwriter. Career revived in 1974 after signing with Elton John's new Rocket label.	
12/28/58+	**14**	9	1. The Diary	RCA 7408
10/26/59	**9**	13	**2. Oh! Carol**	RCA 7595
			written for singer/songwriter Carole King	
4/18/60	**9**	9	**3. Stairway To Heaven**	RCA 7709
8/29/60	**17**	9	4. You Mean Everything To Me/	
10/03/60	**28**	3	5. Run Samson Run	RCA 7781
12/31/60+	**4**	12	**6. Calendar Girl**	RCA 7829
5/08/61	**11**	7	7. Little Devil	RCA 7874
11/27/61+	**6**	11	**8. Happy Birthday, Sweet Sixteen**	RCA 7957
7/07/62	**1**(2)	12	**9. Breaking Up Is Hard To Do**	RCA 8046
10/20/62	**5**	9	**10. Next Door To An Angel**	RCA 8086
2/16/63	**17**	7	11. Alice In Wonderland	RCA 8137
5/18/63	**26**	5	12. Let's Go Steady Again	RCA 8169
12/07/63	**33**	4	13. Bad Girl	RCA 8254
			all of above produced by Al Nevins and Don Kirshner	
11/16/74+	**1**(1)	15	**14. Laughter In The Rain**	Rocket 40313
4/26/75	**22**	5	15. The Immigrant	Rocket 40370
8/02/75	**27**	4	16. That's When The Music Takes Me	Rocket 40426
9/20/75	**1**(3)	12	● **17. Bad Blood**	Rocket 40460
			backing vocal by Elton John	
12/27/75+	**8**	11	**18. Breaking Up Is Hard To Do** [R]	Rocket 40500
			slow version of Neil's 1962 hit	
5/01/76	**16**	7	19. Love In The Shadows	Rocket 40543
7/24/76	**36**	2	20. Steppin' Out	Rocket 40582
5/10/80	**19**	10	21. Should've Never Let You Go	Elektra 46615
			NEIL SEDAKA AND DARA SEDAKA (Neil's daughter)	
			SEDUCTION	
			Female vocal trio from New York: Idalis Leon (b: 6/15/66), April Harris (b: 3/25/67) and Michelle Visage (b: 9/20/68). Leon left in 1990, replaced by Sinoa Loren (b: 12/06/66).	
9/02/89	**23**	8	1. You're My One And Only (True Love)	Vendetta 1433

DATE	POS	WKS	ARTIST—RECORD TITLE	LABEL & NO.
			uncredited lead vocals by Martha Wash of The Weather Girls	
12/09/89+	**2**(2)	14	● **2. Two To Make It Right**	Vendetta 1464
			samples The Art Of Noise/Tom Jones' version of "Kiss"	
3/17/90	**13**	10	3. Heartbeat	Vendetta 1473
7/07/90	**11**	10	4. Could This Be Love	Vendetta 1509#
			SEEDS, The	
			Los Angeles garage-rock quartet: Sky Saxon (b: Richard Marsh; lead singer, bass), Jan Savage (guitar), Rick Aldridge (drums) and Daryl Hooper (keyboards).	
2/11/67	**36**	3	1. Pushin' Too Hard	GNP Cresc. 372
			SEEKERS, The	
			Pop-folk, Australian-born quartet: Judith Durham (b: 7/03/43; lead singer), Keith Potger (guitar), Bruce Woodley (Spanish guitar) and Athol Guy (standup bass). Potger formed the New Seekers in 1970.	
4/10/65	**4**	10	**1. I'll Never Find Another You**	Capitol 5383
6/26/65	**19**	7	2. A World Of Our Own	Capitol 5430
12/31/66+	**2**(2)	12	● **3. Georgy Girl**	Capitol 5756
			from the film of the same title	
			SEGER, Bob	
			Born on 5/06/45 in Dearborn, Michigan and raised in Detroit. Rock singer/songwriter/guitarist. First recorded in 1966, formed the System in 1968. Left music to attend college in 1969, returned in 1970. Formed own backing group The Silver Bullet Band in 1976: Alto Reed (horns), Robyn Robbins (keyboards), Drew Abbott (guitar), Chris Campbell (bass) and Charlie Allen Martin (drums). Various personnel changes since then; Campbell is the only remaining original member.	
1/25/69	**17**	9	1. Ramblin' Gamblin' Man	Capitol 2297
			BOB SEGER SYSTEM	
1/15/77	**4**	13	**2. Night Moves**	Capitol 4369
5/14/77	**24**	4	3. Mainstreet	Capitol 4422
			BOB SEGER & THE SILVER BULLET BAND:	
6/03/78	**4**	11	**4. Still The Same**	Capitol 4581
8/19/78	**12**	10	5. Hollywood Nights	Capitol 4618
11/25/78+	**13**	11	6. We've Got Tonite	Capitol 4653
5/05/79	**28**	5	7. Old Time Rock & Roll	Capitol 4702
			BOB SEGER:	
3/01/80	**6**	12	**8. Fire Lake**	Capitol 4836
5/10/80	**5**	11	**9. Against The Wind**	Capitol 4863
8/16/80	**14**	9	10. You'll Accomp'ny Me	Capitol 4904
9/26/81	**5**	12	**11. Tryin' To Live My Life Without You**	Capitol 5042
			BOB SEGER & THE SILVER BULLET BAND:	
12/18/82+	**2**(4)	19	**12. Shame On The Moon**	Capitol 5187
3/26/83	**12**	9	13. Even Now	Capitol 5213
6/11/83	**27**	6	14. Roll Me Away	Capitol 5235
12/01/84+	**17**	8	15. Understanding	Capitol 5413
			from the film *Teachers*	
3/29/86	**13**	9	16. American Storm	Capitol 5532
5/31/86	**12**	9	17. Like A Rock	Capitol 5592
			BOB SEGER:	
5/30/87	**1**(1)	14	**18. Shakedown**	MCA 53094

DATE	POS	WKS	ARTIST—RECORD TITLE	LABEL & NO.
			from the film *Beverly Hills Cop II*	
			SELLARS, Marilyn	
			Country singer from Northfield, Minnesota. Worked as an airline stewardess.	
9/28/74	**37**	2	1. One Day At A Time	Mega 1205
			SEMBELLO, Michael	
			Born on 4/17/54 in Philadelphia. Session guitarist/producer/composer/arranger/vocalist. Guitarist on Stevie Wonder's albums from 1974-79.	
7/02/83	**1**(2)	16	**1. Maniac**	Casabl. 812516
			from the film *Flashdance*	
10/29/83	**34**	2	2. Automatic Man	Warner 29485
			SENATOR BOBBY	
			Senator Bobby is Bill Minkin of a comedy troupe called The Hardly-Worthit Players. Another of the members is talkshow host Dennis Wholey.	
1/21/67	**20**	4	1. Wild Thing [C]	Parkway 127
			SENSATIONS, The	
			Philadelphia R&B vocal quartet: Yvonne Mills Baker (lead), Sam Armstrong (baritone), Richard Curtain (tenor) and Alphonso Howell (bass).	
2/10/62	**4**	12	**1. Let Me In**	Argo 5405
			SERENDIPITY SINGERS, The	
			Large pop-folk group organized at the University of Colorado.	
3/21/64	**6**	11	**1. Don't Let The Rain Come Down (Crooked Little Man)**	Philips 40175
6/13/64	**30**	5	2. Beans In My Ears [N]	Philips 40198
			SEVILLE, David	
			Born Ross Bagdasarian on 1/27/19 in Fresno, California; died on 1/16/72. To Los Angeles in 1950. Appeared in the films *Viva Zapata*, *Stalag 17* and *Rear Window*. Wrote "Come On-a My House." Creator of The Chipmunks.	
4/14/58	**1**(3)	18	**1. Witch Doctor [N]**	Liberty 55132
			Top 100 #1(3) / Best Seller #1(2) / Jockey #2	
7/14/58	**34**	2	2. The Bird On My Head [N]	Liberty 55140
			Best Seller #34 / Top 100 #36	
			SEXTON, Charlie	
			Austin, Texas rock singer/guitarist. Lead guitarist for Joe Ely's band at age 13 in 1982.	
2/08/86	**17**	10	1. Beat's So Lonely	MCA 52715
			SEYMOUR, Phil	
			Vocalist/drummer; formerly with the Dwight Twilley Band. Originally from Tulsa, Oklahoma.	
2/21/81	**22**	7	1. Precious To Me	Boardwalk 5703
			SHADES OF BLUE	
			Three-man, one-woman group, from Detroit, discovered by Edwin Starr.	
5/28/66	**12**	8	1. Oh How Happy	Impact 1007
			SHADOWS OF KNIGHT, The	
			Chicago-area "garage band": Jim Sohns (lead singer), Joe Kelley (lead guitarist), Warren Rogers (bass), Jerry McGeorge (rhythm guitar) and Tom Schiffour (drums).	
4/16/66	**10**	8	**1. Gloria**	Dunwich 116

DATE	POS	WKS	ARTIST—RECORD TITLE	LABEL & NO.
			written by Van Morrison	
7/02/66	**39**	1	2. Oh Yeah	Dunwich 122
			SHALAMAR	
			Black vocal trio formed in 1978 by Don Cornelius, the producer/host of TV's "Soul Train." Consisted of vocalists/dancers Jody Watley and Jeffrey Daniels with Gerald Brown. Howard Hewett replaced Brown in early 1979. Watley and Daniels (former husband of Stephanie Mills) pursued solo careers in 1984; replaced by Delisa Davis (former Miss Teenage Georgia and Miss Tennessee State) and Micki Free. Hewett left in 1985, replaced by Sydney Justin (former football defensive back with the L.A. Rams).	
4/16/77	**25**	8	1. Uptown Festival (Part 1)	Soul Train 10885
			recorded by anonymous session singers prior to formation of actual group Going To A Go-Go/I Can't Help Myself (Sugar Pie, Honey Bunch)/Uptight (Everything's Alright)/Stop! In The Name Of Love/It's The Same Old Song	
2/02/80	**8**	13	• **2. The Second Time Around**	Solar 11709
8/06/83	**22**	10	3. Dead Giveaway	Solar 69819
4/14/84	**17**	10	4. Dancing In The Sheets	Columbia 04372
			from the film *Footloose*	
			SHANA	
			Shana Petrone - born on 5/08/72 in Parkridge, Illinois and raised in Ft. Lauderdale, Florida.	
1/13/90	**40**	1	1. I Want You	Vision 4511
			SHANGRI-LAS, The	
			"Girl group" formed at Andrew Jackson High School in Queens, New York. Consisted of two sets of sisters: Mary (lead singer) & Betty Weiss and twins Mary Ann & Marge Ganser. Mary Ann died of encephalitis in 1971 and Marge died of a drug overdose.	
9/05/64	**5**	9	**1. Remember (Walkin' in the Sand)**	Red Bird 008
10/24/64	**1**(1)	10	**2. Leader Of The Pack**	Red Bird 014
1/16/65	**18**	5	3. Give Him A Great Big Kiss	Red Bird 018
6/19/65	**29**	4	4. Give Us Your Blessings	Red Bird 030
11/20/65	**6**	8	**5. I Can Never Go Home Anymore**	Red Bird 043
2/26/66	**33**	2	6. Long Live Our Love	Red Bird 048
			above 5 produced by George "Shadow" Morton	
			SHANNON	
			Brenda Shannon Greene from Washington, D.C. Began singing career at York University.	
1/07/84	**8**	12	• **1. Let The Music Play**	Mirage 99810
			SHANNON, Del	
			Born Charles Westover on 12/30/39 in Coopersville, Michigan. With U.S. Army "Get Up and Go" radio show in Germany. Discovered by Ann Arbor D.J./producer Ollie McLaughlin. Formed own Berlee label in 1963. Wrote "I Go To Pieces" for Peter & Gordon. To Los Angeles in 1966; production work. Died on 2/08/90 of a self-inflicted gunshot wound.	
3/27/61	**1**(4)	12	**1. Runaway**	Big Top 3067
			electric organ (musitron) solo by co-writer Max Crook	
6/19/61	**5**	11	**2. Hats Off To Larry**	Big Top 3075
10/09/61	**28**	5	3. So Long Baby	Big Top 3083
1/06/62	**38**	2	4. Hey! Little Girl	Big Top 3091
1/26/63	**12**	7	5. Little Town Flirt	Big Top 3131
7/25/64	**22**	7	6. Handy Man	Amy 905

DATE	POS	WKS	ARTIST—RECORD TITLE	LABEL & NO.
12/19/64+	**9**	10	**7. Keep Searchin' (We'll Follow The Sun)**	Amy 915
3/13/65	**30**	4	8. Stranger In Town	Amy 919
1/23/82	**33**	4	9. Sea Of Love produced by Tom Petty	Network 47951
			SHARP, Dee Dee	
			Born Dione LaRue on 9/09/45 in Philadelphia. Backing vocalist at Cameo Records in 1961. Married record producer Kenny Gamble in 1967, recorded as Dee Dee Sharp Gamble. Also see Chubby Checker.	
3/17/62	**2**(2)	15	**1. Mashed Potato Time**	Cameo 212
6/23/62	**9**	9	**2. Gravy (For My Mashed Potatoes)**	Cameo 219
11/10/62	**5**	9	**3. Ride!**	Cameo 230
3/09/63	**10**	9	**4. Do The Bird**	Cameo 244
11/02/63	**33**	5	5. Wild!	Cameo 274
			SHAW, Georgie	
			Pop singer styled after Eddie Fisher.	
11/12/55	**23**	6	1. No Arms Can Ever Hold You (Like These Arms Of Mine) Top 100 #23 / Best Seller #25	Decca 29679
2/11/56	**39**	1	2. Go On With The Wedding **KITTY KALLEN AND GEORGIE SHAW**	Decca 29776
			SHAW, Tommy	
			Born in Montgomery, Alabama. Lead guitarist of Styx, 1976-84. Joined superstar rock group, Damn Yankees, in 1990.	
11/03/84	**33**	3	1. Girls With Guns	A&M 2676
			SHEILA E.	
			Born Sheila Escovedo on 12/12/59 in San Francisco. Singer/percussionist. With father Pete Escovedo in the band Azteca in the mid-1970s. Toured with Lionel Richie; since 1986, toured and recorded with Prince. Brother Peto was in Con Funk Shun. Uncle Coke Escovedo is a noted percussionist.	
7/21/84	**7**	16	**1. The Glamorous Life**	Warner 29285
12/08/84	**34**	5	2. The Belle Of St. Mark	Warner 29180
12/28/85+	**11**	12	3. A Love Bizarre from the film *Krush Groove*; backing vocal by Prince	Paisley P. 28890
			SHELLS, The	
			Brooklyn R&B vocal quintet: Nathaniel "Little Nate" Bouknight (lead), Gus Geter (baritone), Bobby Nurse and Randy Alston (tenors) and Danny Small (bass).	
12/31/60+	**21**	5	1. Baby Oh Baby	Johnson 104
			SHEP AND THE LIMELITES	
			R&B vocal trio from New York City: James "Shep" Sheppard, lead (formerly with the Heartbeats) and tenors Clarence Bassett and Charles Baskerville (formerly in the Videos). Group disbanded after Sheppard's death in 1970.	
4/10/61	**2**(1)	11	**1. Daddy's Home** answer to the Heartbeats' "A Thousand Miles Away"	Hull 740
			SHEPHERD SISTERS	
			New York-based family quartet from Middletown, Ohio: Martha, Mary Lou, Gayle and Judy.	
11/04/57	**18**	7	1. Alone (Why Must I Be Alone) Best Seller #18 / Top 100 #20 / Jockey #22	Lance 125

DATE	POS	WKS	ARTIST—RECORD TITLE	LABEL & NO.
			SHEPPARD, T.G.	
			Born William Browder on 7/20/42 in Humboldt, Tennessee. Country singer. Moved to Memphis in 1960. Worked as backup singer with Travis Wammack's band.	
5/16/81	**37**	2	1. I Loved 'Em Every One	Warner 49690
			SHEPPARD, Vonda — see HILL, Dan	
			SHERIFF	
			Canadian rock quintet — Freddy Curci, lead singer. Disbanded in 1983. Members Wolf Hassell and Arnold Lanni are now the duo Frozen Ghost. Bandmates Curci and Steve DeMarchi formed Alias in 1990.	
12/17/88+	**1**(1)	13	● **1. When I'm With You** **[R]** originally charted in 1983 (POS 61)	Capitol 44302
			SHERMAN, Allan	
			Born Allan Copelon on 11/30/24 in Chicago; died on 11/21/73. Began as a professional comedy writer for Jackie Gleason, Joe E. Lewis and others. Creator/producer of TV's "I've Got a Secret."	
8/10/63	**2**(3)	8	**1. Hello Mudduh, Hello Fadduh! (A Letter From Camp)** **[C]** adaptation of Ponchielli's *Dance of the Hours*	Warner 5378
5/08/65	**40**	1	2. Crazy Downtown [C] parody of Petula Clark's "Downtown"	Warner 5614
			SHERMAN, Bobby	
			Born on 7/18/43 in Santa Monica, California. Regular on TV's "Shindig"; played Jeremy Bolt on TV's "Here Come the Brides." Currently involved in TV production.	
9/06/69	**3**	11	● **1. Little Woman**	Metromedia 121
12/06/69+	**9**	9	● **2. La La La (If I Had You)**	Metromedia 150
2/28/70	**9**	11	● **3. Easy Come, Easy Go**	Metromedia 177
6/06/70	**24**	5	4. Hey, Mister Sun	Metromedia 188
8/15/70	**5**	13	● **5. Julie, Do Ya Love Me**	Metromedia 194
2/27/71	**16**	7	6. Cried Like A Baby	Metromedia 206
5/15/71	**29**	5	7. The Drum	Metromedia 217
			SHERRYS, The	
			Female R&B group from Philadelphia. Formed by Joe Cook, included his daughters Dinell (lead) and Delphine. Cook had own hit in 1957, "Peanuts," as "Little Joe."	
11/10/62	**35**	2	1. Pop Pop Pop-Pie	Guyden 2068
			SHIELDS, The	
			R&B group formed by Los Angeles producer George Motola solely to record "You Cheated." Frankie Ervin (lead), Jesse Belvin (falsetto), Johnny "Guitar" Watson, Mel Williams and Buster Williams.	
9/15/58	**12**	9	1. You Cheated Best Seller #12 end / Hot 100 #15 first released on Tender 513 in 1958	Dot 15805
			SHIRELLES, The	
			R&B "girl group" from Passaic, New Jersey. Consisted of Shirley Owens Alston (b: 6/10/41), Beverly Lee (b: 8/03/41), Doris Kenner (b: 8/02/41) and Addie "Micki" Harris (b: 1/22/40; d: 6/10/82). Formed in junior high school as the Poquellos. First recorded for Tiara in 1958. Kenner left group in 1968; returned in 1975. Alston left for solo career in 1975, recorded as "Lady Rose."	
10/17/60	**39**	3	1. Tonights The Night	Scepter 1208

DATE	POS	WKS	ARTIST—RECORD TITLE	LABEL & NO.
12/12/60+	1(2)	15	**2. Will You Love Me Tomorrow** first released on Scepter 1211 as simply "Tomorrow"	Scepter 1211
2/06/61	3	14	**3. Dedicated To The One I Love** [R] originally charted in 1959 (POS 83)	Scepter 1203
5/01/61	4	8	**4. Mama Said**	Scepter 1217
10/23/61	21	5	5. Big John	Scepter 1223
1/06/62	8	11	**6. Baby It's You**	Scepter 1227
3/31/62	1(3)	13	**7. Soldier Boy**	Scepter 1228
7/07/62	22	6	8. Welcome Home Baby	Scepter 1234
10/06/62	36	3	9. Stop The Music	Scepter 1237
12/15/62+	19	9	10. Everybody Loves A Lover	Scepter 1243
4/20/63	4	9	**11. Foolish Little Girl**	Scepter 1248
7/13/63	26	4	12. Don't Say Goodnight And Mean Goodbye	Scepter 1255
			SHIRLEY, Don Pianist/organist. Born in Kingston, Jamaica on 1/27/27.	
10/09/61	40	1	1. Water Boy [I] **DON SHIRLEY TRIO**	Cadence 1392
			SHIRLEY AND COMPANY Shirley Goodman (formerly of Shirley & Lee), and a group of studio musicians. Included Kenny Jeremiah of the Soul Survivors.	
2/22/75	12	8	1. Shame, Shame, Shame male vocal: Jesus Alvarez; written and produced by Sylvia Robinson (Mickey & Sylvia)	Vibration 532
			SHIRLEY & LEE New Orleans R&B duo formed in the early 1950s. Shirley Goodman (b: 6/19/36) and Leonard Lee (b: 6/29/36; d: 10/23/76). First recorded for Aladdin in 1952. Billed as "The Sweethearts of the Blues"; recorded together until 1963.	
9/08/56	20	9	1. Let The Good Times Roll Best Seller #20 / Top 100 #27	Aladdin 3325
1/05/57	38	1	2. I Feel Good	Aladdin 3338
			SHOCKING BLUE, The Dutch rock quartet: Mariska Veres (lead singer), Robbie van Leeuwen (guitar), Cor van Beek (drums) and Klaasje van der Wal (bass). Disbanded in 1974.	
12/20/69+	1(1)	13	● **1. Venus**	Colossus 108
			SHONDELL, Troy Born on 5/14/44 in Fort Wayne, Indiana. Pop-country singer/songwriter.	
9/25/61	6	12	**1. This Time** first released on Gaye 2010 (as Troy Shundell) and then on Goldcrest 161 in 1961	Liberty 55353
			SHORE, Dinah Born Frances Shore on 3/01/17 in Winchester, Tennessee. One of the most popular female vocalists of the 1940 to mid-1950s era. Own TV variety show, 1951-62; own morning talk show "Dinah's Place," 1970-74. Married to actor George Montgomery from 1943-62.	
5/21/55	12	2	1. Whatever Lola Wants (Lola Gets) Jockey #12 / Best Seller #28 from the Broadway musical *Damn Yankees*	RCA 6077
12/10/55	20	1	2. Love And Marriage	RCA 6266

DATE	POS	WKS	ARTIST—RECORD TITLE	LABEL & NO.
			Jockey #20 / Top 100 #42	
2/23/57	**19**	10	3. Chantez-Chantez (Shan-Tay, "Sing")	RCA 6792
			Jockey #19 / Top 100 #27	
9/09/57	**15**	7	4. Fascination	RCA 6980
			Jockey #15 / Top 100 #98 from the film *Love in the Afternoon*	
12/02/57	**24**	1	5. I'll Never Say "Never Again" Again	RCA 7056
			Jockey #24; #4 hit for Ozzie Nelson in 1935	
			SIGLER, Bunny	
			Born Walter Sigler on 3/27/41 in Philadelphia. R&B vocalist/multi-instrumentalist/composer/producer. First recorded for V-Tone in 1959.	
7/22/67	**22**	7	1. Let The Good Times Roll & Feel So Good	Parkway 153
			SILHOUETTES, The	
			Philadelphia R&B doo-wop group formed as the Tornadoes by William Horton (lead), Richard Lewis (tenor), Earl Beal (baritone) and Raymond Edwards (bass).	
1/20/58	**1**(2)	13	**1. Get A Job**	Ember 1029
			Top 100 #1 / Best Seller #2 / Jockey #3 first released on Junior 391 in 1957	
			SILKIE, The	
			Folk quartet formed in 1963 at Hull University in Hull, England — Silvia Tatler, lead singer.	
11/06/65	**10**	7	**1. You've Got To Hide Your Love Away**	Fontana 1525
			Beatles contributed musical accompaniment & production assistance	
			SILVER	
			Country-rock quintet led by John Batdorf (of Batdorf & Rodney). Included organist Brent Mydland, who later joined the Grateful Dead (died on 7/26/90 of a drug overdose at the age of 37).	
8/07/76	**16**	12	1. Wham Bam	Arista 0189
			title also shown as "Wham Bam Shang-A-Lang"	
			SILVER CONDOR	
			Rock quintet led by Joe Cerisano and Earl Slick (Phantom, Rocker & Slick).	
8/29/81	**32**	4	1. You Could Take My Heart Away	Columbia 02268
			SILVER CONVENTION	
			German studio disco act assembled by producer Michael Kunze and writer/arranger Silvester Levay. Female vocal trio formed in 1976 consisting of Penny McLean, Ramona Wolf and Linda Thompson.	
10/25/75	**1**(3)	13	● **1. Fly, Robin, Fly** [I]	Midland I. 10339
4/17/76	**2**(3)	15	● **2. Get Up And Boogie (That's Right)**	Midland I. 10571
			SILVETTI	
			Argentinian Bebu Silvetti.	
3/19/77	**39**	3	1. Spring Rain [I]	Salsoul 2014
			SIMEONE, Harry, Chorale	
			Harry was born on 5/09/11 in Newark, New Jersey. Arranger/conductor for film and TV shows. Began career in 1939 as an arranger for Fred Waring.	
12/28/58	**13**	6	1. The Little Drummer Boy [X]	20th Fox 121
12/28/59	**15**	3	2. The Little Drummer Boy [X-R]	20th Fox 121
12/19/60	**24**	3	3. The Little Drummer Boy [X-R]	20th Fox 121

DATE	POS	WKS	ARTIST—RECORD TITLE	LABEL & NO.
12/25/61	**22**	2	4. The Little Drummer Boy [X-R]	20th Fox 121
12/15/62	**28**	3	5. The Little Drummer Boy [X-R]	20th Fox 121
			SIMMONS, Gene	
			Born in Tupelo, Mississippi in 1933. Nicknamed "Jumpin' Gene."	
8/29/64	**11**	8	1. Haunted House	Hi 2076
			SIMMONS, Patrick	
			Born on 1/23/50 in Aberdeen, Washington; raised in San Jose, California. Vocalist/guitarist. Original member of The Doobie Brothers; wrote their hit "Black Water."	
4/16/83	**30**	5	1. So Wrong	Elektra 69839
			SIMON, Carly	
			Born on 6/25/45 in New York City. Pop vocalist/songwriter. Father is co-founder of Simon & Schuster publishing. Folk duo with sister Lucy (The Simon Sisters), mid-1960s. Won the 1971 Best New Artist Grammy Award. Married James Taylor on 11/03/72; separated in 1982 and divorced a few years later.	
6/05/71	**10**	10	**1. That's The Way I've Always Heard It Should Be**	Elektra 45724
1/01/72	**13**	10	2. Anticipation	Elektra 45759
12/16/72+	**1**(3)	14	● **3. You're So Vain**	Elektra 45824
			backing vocal by Mick Jagger	
4/21/73	**17**	9	4. The Right Thing To Do	Elektra 45843
2/16/74	**5**	13	● **5. Mockingbird**	Elektra 45880
			CARLY SIMON AND JAMES TAYLOR	
6/01/74	**14**	6	6. Haven't Got Time For The Pain	Elektra 45887
5/24/75	**21**	5	7. Attitude Dancing	Elektra 45246
8/27/77	**2**(3)	15	● **8. Nobody Does It Better**	Elektra 45413
			from the film *The Spy Who Loved Me*	
5/06/78	**6**	11	**9. You Belong To Me**	Elektra 45477
9/23/78	**36**	3	10. Devoted To You	Elektra 45506
			CARLY SIMON AND JAMES TAYLOR	
8/23/80	**11**	13	● 11. Jesse	Warner 49518
12/06/86+	**18**	9	12. Coming Around Again	Arista 9525
			from the film *Heartburn*	
			SIMON, Joe	
			Born on 9/02/43 in Simmesport, Louisiana. Moved to Oakland in 1959. First recorded with vocal group, the Golden Tones, for Hush in 1960.	
6/08/68	**25**	7	1. (You Keep Me) Hangin' On	Sound Stage 2608
3/29/69	**13**	11	● 2. The Chokin' Kind	Sound Stage 2628
2/06/71	**40**	3	3. Your Time To Cry	Spring 108
12/11/71+	**11**	11	● 4. Drowning In The Sea Of Love	Spring 120
8/19/72	**11**	8	● 5. Power Of Love	Spring 128
4/14/73	**37**	2	6. Step By Step	Spring 133
8/25/73	**18**	8	7. Theme From Cleopatra Jones	Spring 138
			featuring The Mainstreeters; from the film of the same title	
5/10/75	**8**	11	**8. Get Down, Get Down (Get On The Floor)**	Spring 156

DATE	POS	WKS	ARTIST—RECORD TITLE	LABEL & NO.
			SIMON, Paul	
			Born on 11/05/41 in Newark, New Jersey; raised in Queens, New York. Vocalist/composer/guitarist. Met Art Garfunkel in high school, recorded together as Tom & Jerry in 1957. Worked as Jerry Landis, Paul Kane, Harrison Gregory and True Taylor in the early '60s. To England from 1963-64. Returned to the U.S. and recorded first album with Garfunkel in 1965. Went solo in 1971. Married to actress Carrie Fisher from 1983-85. In the films *Annie Hall* and *One-Trick Pony.*	
2/19/72	**4**	11	**1. Mother And Child Reunion**	Columbia 45547
4/22/72	**22**	8	2. Me And Julio Down By The Schoolyard	Columbia 45585
6/02/73	**2**(2)	11	**3. Kodachrome**	Columbia 45859
8/18/73	**2**(1)	14	● **4. Loves Me Like A Rock** vocal backing by The Dixie Hummingbirds	Columbia 45907
1/05/74	**35**	3	5. American Tune	Columbia 45900
9/06/75	**23**	6	6. Gone At Last **PAUL SIMON/PHOEBE SNOW and THE JESSY DIXON SINGERS**	Columbia 10197
1/03/76	**1**(3)	13	● **7. 50 Ways To Leave Your Lover**	Columbia 10270
5/29/76	**40**	2	8. Still Crazy After All These Years	Columbia 10332
11/05/77+	**5**	14	**9. Slip Slidin' Away**	Columbia 10630
2/11/78	**17**	7	10. (What A) Wonderful World **ART GARFUNKEL with JAMES TAYLOR & PAUL SIMON**	Columbia 10676
8/16/80	**6**	12	**11. Late In The Evening**	Warner 49511
11/22/80	**40**	2	12. One-Trick Pony above 2 from the film *One-Trick Pony*	Warner 49601
4/25/87	**23**	7	13. You Can Call Me Al	Warner 28667
			SIMON & GARFUNKEL	
			Folk-rock duo from New York City: Paul Simon and Art Garfunkel. Recorded as Tom & Jerry in 1957. Duo split in 1964; Simon was working solo in England, Garfunkel was in graduate school. They re-formed in 1965 and stayed together until 1971. Reunited briefly in 1981 for national tour. Inducted into the Rock and Roll Hall of Fame in 1990.	
12/04/65+	**1**(2)	12	● **1. The Sounds Of Silence**	Columbia 43396
2/26/66	**5**	10	**2. Homeward Bound**	Columbia 43511
5/14/66	**3**	10	**3. I Am A Rock**	Columbia 43617
8/27/66	**25**	4	4. The Dangling Conversation	Columbia 43728
11/19/66	**13**	6	5. A Hazy Shade Of Winter	Columbia 43873
4/01/67	**16**	7	6. At The Zoo	Columbia 44046
8/12/67	**23**	5	7. Fakin' It	Columbia 44232
3/16/68	**11**	9	8. Scarborough Fair (/Canticle) song also known as "Parsley, Sage, Rosemary And Thyme"	Columbia 44465
5/04/68	**1**(3)	12	● **9. Mrs. Robinson** above 2 from the film *The Graduate*	Columbia 44511
4/19/69	**7**	9	**10. The Boxer**	Columbia 44785
2/14/70	**1**(6)	13	● **11. Bridge Over Troubled Water**	Columbia 45079
4/18/70	**4**	12	● **12. Cecilia**	Columbia 45133
9/26/70	**18**	8	13. El Condor Pasa	Columbia 45237
11/01/75	**9**	9	**14. My Little Town** all of above written by Paul Simon	Columbia 10230
5/01/82	**27**	6	15. Wake Up Little Susie recorded live in New York's Central Park on 9/19/81	Warner 50053

DATE	POS	WKS	ARTIST—RECORD TITLE	LABEL & NO.
			SIMONE, Nina	
			Born Eunice Waymon on 2/21/33 in Tryon, South Carolina. Jazz-influenced vocalist/pianist/composer. Attended Juilliard School of Music in New York City. Devoted more time to political activism in the '70s, infrequent recording.	
8/24/59	**18**	11	1. I Loves You, Porgy from the film *Porgy and Bess*	Bethlehem 11021
			SIMPLE MINDS	
			Scottish rock group. Nucleus of band: Jim Kerr (lead singer; formerly married to Chrissie Hynde of The Pretenders), Michael MacNeil (keyboards), Charles Burchill (guitar), Mel Gaynor (drums) and John Giblin (bass). MacNeil left in 1989.	
3/23/85	**1**(1)	14	**1. Don't You (Forget About Me)** from the film *The Breakfast Club*	A&M 2703
10/26/85	**3**	16	**2. Alive & Kicking**	A&M 2783
2/08/86	**14**	9	3. Sanctify Yourself	A&M 2810
5/03/86	**28**	6	4. All The Things She Said	A&M 2828
6/29/91	**40**	1	5. See The Lights	Virgin 1553#
			SIMPLY RED	
			Manchester, England group: vocalist Mick "Red" Hucknall (b: 6/08/60), keyboardists Fritz McIntyre & Tim Kellett, Tony Bowers (bass), Chris Joyce (drums) & Sylvan Richardson (guitar). 1991 lineup: Hucknall, McIntyre, Kellett, saxophonist Ian Kirkham, Brazilian guitarist Heitor T.P. & Japanese drummer Gota.	
5/10/86	**1**(1)	14	**1. Holding Back The Years**	Elektra 69564
8/30/86	**28**	6	2. Money$ Too Tight (To Mention) originally released in 1985 on Elektra 69607	Elektra 69528
4/18/87	**27**	6	3. The Right Thing	Elektra 69487
5/27/89	**1**(1)	15	● **4. If You Don't Know Me By Now**	Elektra 69297
			SINATRA, Frank	
			Born Francis Albert Sinatra on 12/12/15 in Hoboken, New Jersey. With Harry James from 1939-40, first recorded for Brunswick in 1939; with Tommy Dorsey, 1940-42. Went solo in late 1942 and charted 40 top 10 hits through 1954. Appeared in many films from 1941 on. Won an Oscar for the film *From Here to Eternity* in 1953. Own TV show in 1957. Own Reprise record company in 1961, sold to Warner Bros. in 1963. Won the Lifetime Achievement Grammy in 1965. Announced his retirement in 1970, but made comeback in 1973. Regarded by many as the greatest popular singer of the 20th century.	
1/22/55	**19**	4	1. Melody Of Love **FRANK SINATRA AND RAY ANTHONY** Jockey #19	Capitol 3018
5/07/55	**1**(2)	21	**2. Learnin' The Blues** Jockey #1 / Best Seller #2 / Juke Box #2	Capitol 3102
9/24/55	**13**	5	3. Same Old Saturday Night Jockey #13 / Top 100 #65 pre	Capitol 3218
11/05/55	**5**	15	**4. Love And Marriage** Top 100 #5 / Jockey #5 / Best Seller #6 / Juke Box #7 from the TV production *Our Town*	Capitol 3260
12/17/55+	**7**	9	**5. (Love Is) The Tender Trap** Jockey #7 / Top 100 #23 / Best Seller #24 from the film *The Tender Trap*	Capitol 3290
3/24/56	**21**	3	6. Flowers Mean Forgiveness Jockey #21 / Top 100 #35	Capitol 3350
6/02/56	**13**	6	7. (How Little It Matters) How Little We Know	Capitol 3423

DATE	POS	WKS	ARTIST—RECORD TITLE	LABEL & NO.
			Jockey #13 / Top 100 #30	
11/03/56+	**3**	17	**8. Hey! Jealous Lover** Jockey #3 / Top 100 #6 / Juke Box #7 / Best Seller #8	Capitol 3552
2/09/57	**15**	6	9. Can I Steal A Little Love Jockey #15 / Top 100 #20 from the film *Rock Pretty Baby*	Capitol 3608
7/22/57	**25**	1	10. You're Cheatin' Yourself (If You're Cheatin' On Me) Jockey #25	Capitol 3744
10/28/57+	**2**(1)	17	**11. All The Way** Jockey #2 / Best Seller #15 / Top 100 #15 from the film *The Joker Is Wild*	Capitol 3793
1/20/58	**6**	14	**12. Witchcraft** Jockey #6 / Best Seller #20 / Top 100 #20	Capitol 3859
5/12/58	**22**	1	13. How Are Ya' Fixed For Love? **FRANK SINATRA AND KEELY SMITH** Jockey #22 / Top 100 #97	Capitol 3952
9/07/59	**30**	1	14. High Hopes from the film *A Hole in the Head*	Capitol 4214
11/16/59	**38**	3	15. Talk To Me	Capitol 4284
11/28/60	**25**	2	16. Ol' MacDonald all of above (except #1 & 13) with Nelson Riddle & His Orchestra	Capitol 4466
1/20/62	**34**	3	17. Pocketful Of Miracles from the film of the same title	Reprise 20040
10/10/64	**27**	6	18. Softly, As I Leave You	Reprise 0301
1/30/65	**32**	3	19. Somewhere In Your Heart	Reprise 0332
1/15/66	**28**	4	20. It Was A Very Good Year	Reprise 0429
5/28/66	**1**(1)	11	**21. Strangers In The Night** from the film *A Man Could Get Killed*	Reprise 0470
9/17/66	**25**	5	22. Summer Wind	Reprise 0509
12/03/66	**4**	9	**23. That's Life**	Reprise 0531
3/25/67	**1**(4)	11	• **24. Somethin' Stupid** **NANCY SINATRA & FRANK SINATRA**	Reprise 0561
8/26/67	**30**	4	25. The World We Knew (Over And Over)	Reprise 0610
11/16/68	**23**	5	26. Cycles	Reprise 0764
4/12/69	**27**	6	27. My Way written by Paul Anka	Reprise 0817
5/31/80	**32**	6	28. Theme From New York, New York from the film *New York, New York*	Reprise 49233
			SINATRA, Nancy	
			Born on 6/08/40 in Jersey City, New Jersey. First child of Frank and Nancy Sinatra. Moved to Los Angeles while a child. Made national TV debut with father and Elvis Presley in 1959. Married to Tommy Sands, 1960-65. Appeared on "Hullabaloo," "American Bandstand," and own specials, mid-'60s. In films *For Those Who Think Young, Get Yourself a College Girl, The Oscar* and *Speedway.*	
2/05/66	**1**(1)	12	• **1. These Boots Are Made For Walkin'**	Reprise 0432
4/30/66	**7**	7	**2. How Does That Grab You, Darlin'?**	Reprise 0461
7/30/66	**36**	2	3. Friday's Child	Reprise 0491
12/10/66	**5**	9	• **4. Sugar Town**	Reprise 0527
3/25/67	**1**(4)	11	• **5. Somethin' Stupid** **NANCY SINATRA & FRANK SINATRA**	Reprise 0561

DATE	POS	WKS	ARTIST—RECORD TITLE	LABEL & NO.
4/08/67	**15**	5	6. Love Eyes	Reprise 0559
7/08/67	**14**	7	7. Jackson	Reprise 0595
			NANCY SINATRA & LEE HAZLEWOOD	
10/07/67	**24**	4	8. Lightning's Girl	Reprise 0620
			NANCY SINATRA & LEE HAZLEWOOD:	
11/04/67	**20**	4	9. Lady Bird	Reprise 0629
1/27/68	**26**	5	10. Some Velvet Morning	Reprise 0651
			all of above (except 5, 7) produced & written by Lee Hazlewood	
			SINCLAIR, Gordon	
			Born on 6/03/1900 in Toronto; died on 5/17/84. Canadian broadcaster/author.	
1/26/74	**24**	4	1. The Americans (A Canadian's Opinion) [S]	Avco 4628
			originally broadcast as an editorial on 6/05/73 on CFRB-Toronto	
			SINGING DOGS, The	
			An actual recording of dogs barking, produced by Don Charles in Copenhagen.	
12/17/55	**22**	2	1. Oh! Susanna [N]	RCA 6344
			Best Seller #22 / Top 100 #37 written in 1848 by Stephen Foster; DJ copies labeled as "Dolly's Oh! Susanna" (Dogs: Dolly, Pearl, Caesar & King)	
			SINGING NUN, The	
			Sister Luc-Gabrielle (real name: Jeanine Deckers) from the Fichermont, Belgium convent. Recorded under the name Soeur Sourire ("Sister Smile"). Committed suicide on 3/31/85 (age 52).	
11/16/63	**1**(4)	12	**1. Dominique [F]**	Philips 40152
			SIR DOUGLAS QUINTET	
			Tex-Mex rock band led by Doug Sahm (b: 11/06/41) from San Antonio. Co-founded by country singer Augie Meyers.	
4/17/65	**13**	9	1. She's About A Mover	Tribe 8308
3/05/66	**31**	5	2. The Rains Came	Tribe 8314
3/15/69	**27**	6	3. Mendocino	Smash 2191
			SISTER SLEDGE	
			Sisters Debra, Joan, Kim and Kathie Sledge from North Philadelphia. First recorded as Sisters Sledge for Money Back label in 1971. Worked as backup vocalists.	
3/10/79	**9**	13	**1. He's The Greatest Dancer**	Cotillion 44245
5/12/79	**2**(2)	11	● **2. We Are Family**	Cotillion 44251
3/06/82	**23**	6	3. My Guy	Cotillion 47000
			SIX TEENS, The	
			Los Angeles R&B sextet: Trudy Williams and Ed Wells (leads), Richard Owens, Darryl Lewis, Beverly Pecot and Louise Williams. In 1956, members ranged in age from 14 to 19.	
9/01/56	**25**	1	1. A Casual Look	Flip 315
			Best Seller #25 / Top 100 #48	
			SKID ROW	
			New York hard-rock quintet: Toronto native Sebastian "Bach" Bierk (vocals), Rachel Bolan (bass), Dave Sabo (guitar), Scott Hill (guitar) and Rob Affuso (drums).	
7/29/89	**4**	13	● **1. 18 And Life**	Atlantic 88883
12/09/89+	**6**	13	**2. I Remember You**	Atlantic 88886

DATE	POS	WKS	ARTIST—RECORD TITLE	LABEL & NO.
			SKIP & FLIP	
			Gary "Flip" Paxton and Clyde "Skip" Battin. Met at the University of Arizona, and appeared on "Arizona Jubilee" in 1958 as the Rockabillies. Paxton formed The Hollywood Argyles, and later started own Garpax record label.	
7/27/59	**11**	9	1. It Was I	Brent 7002
4/25/60	**11**	10	2. Cherry Pie	Brent 7010
			SKYLARK	
			Group from Vancouver: lead singers Donny Gerrard and B.J. (Bonnie Jean) Cook, with David Foster, Duris Maxwell, Norman McPherson, Steven Pugsley and Carl Graves. Keyboardist Foster later joined Attitudes; recorded solo in the mid-1980s.	
3/31/73	**9**	14	**1. Wildflower**	Capitol 3511
			SKYLINERS, The	
			Pittsburgh vocal quintet: Jimmy Beaumont (b: 10/21/40; lead), Janet Vogel (d: 2/21/80, suicide) and Wally Lester (tenors), Joe VerScharen (baritone) and Jackie Taylor (bass voice, guitarist).	
3/23/59	**12**	10	1. Since I Don't Have You	Calico 103
6/15/59	**26**	7	2. This I Swear	Calico 106
6/20/60	**24**	6	3. Pennies From Heaven #1 hit for Bing Crosby in 1936	Calico 117
			SKYY	
			Brooklyn R&B-pop-funk octet. Vocals by sisters Denise, Delores and Bonnie Dunning. Organized by Randy Muller, former leader of Brass Construction.	
2/20/82	**26**	4	1. Call Me	Salsoul 2152
			SLADE	
			English hard-rock quartet: Noddy Holder (b: 6/15/50; lead singer), David Hill (guitar), Jim Lea (bass, keyboards) and Don Powell (drums).	
5/05/84	**20**	8	1. Run Runaway	CBS Assoc. 04398
8/11/84	**37**	3	2. My Oh My	CBS Assoc. 04528
			SLAUGHTER	
			Las Vegas hard-rock quartet led by vocalist Mark Slaughter, who, with bandmate Dana Strum (bass), was a member of the Vinnie Vincent Invasion.	
6/02/90	**27**	6	1. Up All Night	Chrysalis 23486#
9/22/90	**19**	8	2. Fly To The Angels	Chrysalis 23527
2/16/91	**39**	1	3. Spend My Life	Chrysalis 23605#
			SLAVE	
			Funk band from Dayton, Ohio formed by Steve Washington (trumpet) in 1975. Studio vocalist Steve Arrington was a member from 1978-82. Numerous personnel changes.	
7/23/77	**32**	6	1. Slide [I]	Cotillion 44218
			SLEDGE, Percy	
			Born in 1941 in Leighton, Alabama. Worked local clubs with Esquires Combo until going solo.	
4/30/66	**1**(2)	10	● **1. When A Man Loves A Woman**	Atlantic 2326
8/06/66	**17**	6	2. Warm And Tender Love	Atlantic 2342
11/19/66	**20**	7	3. It Tears Me Up	Atlantic 2358
7/22/67	**40**	1	4. Love Me Tender	Atlantic 2414
4/06/68	**11**	11	5. Take Time To Know Her	Atlantic 2490

DATE	POS	WKS	ARTIST—RECORD TITLE	LABEL & NO.
			SLY & THE FAMILY STONE	
			San Francisco interracial "psychedelic soul" group formed by Sylvester "Sly Stone" Stewart (b: 3/15/44, Dallas; lead singer, keyboards), Sly's brother Freddie Stone (guitar), Cynthia Robinson (trumpet), Jerry Martini (saxophone), Sly's sister Rosie Stone (piano, vocals), Larry Graham (bass) and Gregg Errico (drums). Sly recorded gospel at age four. Producer and writer for Bobby Freeman, the Mojo Men, the Beau Brummels. Formed own groups, The Stoners in 1966 and the Family Stone in 1967. Worked Woodstock Festival in 1969. Career waned in the mid-1970s. Worked with George Clinton in 1982. Graham formed Graham Central Station in 1973.	
3/02/68	**8**	12	**1. Dance To The Music**	Epic 10256
1/04/69	**1**(4)	14	● **2. Everyday People**	Epic 10407
4/26/69	**22**	6	3. Stand!	Epic 10450
8/30/69	**2**(2)	13	**4. Hot Fun In The Summertime**	Epic 10497
1/10/70	**1**(2)	12	● **5. Thank You (Falettinme Be Mice Elf Agin)/**	
		12	6. Everybody Is A Star	Epic 10555
6/20/70	**38**	3	7. I Want To Take You Higher [R] originally charted in 1969 (POS 60)	Epic 10450
11/13/71	**1**(3)	13	● **8. Family Affair**	Epic 10805
2/26/72	**23**	6	9. Runnin' Away	Epic 10829
7/14/73	**12**	13	● 10. If You Want Me To Stay	Epic 11017
8/17/74	**32**	3	11. Time For Livin' all of above written and produced by Sly Stone	Epic 11140
			SLY FOX	
			Black-and-white duo: Gary "Mudbone" Cooper (P-Funk) and Michael Camacho.	
2/15/86	**7**	14	**1. Let's Go All The Way** originally released on Capitol 5463; based on the same groove as the Boogie Boys' "Fly Girl"	Capitol 5552
			SMALL, Millie	
			Born Millicent Smith on 10/06/46 in Jamaica. Nicknamed "The Blue Beat Girl."	
6/06/64	**2**(1)	9	**1. My Boy Lollipop**	Smash 1893
9/05/64	**40**	2	2. Sweet William	Smash 1920
			SMALL FACES	
			British rock quartet: Steve Marriott (guitar), Ronnie Lane (bass), Ian McLagen (organ) and Kenney Jones (drums). In 1968, Marriott formed Humble Pie. Remaining members evolved into Faces in 1969; disbanded in 1975. Jones joined The Who in 1978, formed The Law in 1991. Marriott died in a fire on 4/20/91 (age 44).	
1/13/68	**16**	8	1. Itchycoo Park	Immediate 501
			SMITH	
			Los Angeles-based rock quintet fronted by St. Louis blues rocker Gayle McCormick.	
10/04/69	**5**	11	**1. Baby It's You**	Dunhill 4206
			SMITH, Frankie	
			Philadelphia native. Wrote and produced for Philadelphia Int'l. in the late 1970s, and later for WMOT.	
7/11/81	**30**	7	● 1. Double Dutch Bus based on the double-dutch jump rope game; certified gold for both 7" and 12" singles	WMOT 5356

DATE	POS	WKS	ARTIST—RECORD TITLE	LABEL & NO.
			SMITH, Huey (Piano)/The Clowns	
			Huey was born on 1/26/34 in New Orleans. With Earl King in the early 1950s. Recorded with Eddie "Guitar Slim" Jones' band from 1951-54. Much session work in New Orleans. Own band, The Clowns, in 1957 with Bobby Marchan (vocals). Marchan left in 1960, replaced by Curly Smith. Also see Frankie Ford.	
3/31/58	**9**	9	**1. Don't You Just Know It** Top 100 #9 / Best Seller #13	Ace 545
			SMITH, Hurricane	
			Born Norman Smith in northern England in 1923. Vocalist/producer/engineer/ session musician. Produced early Pink Floyd albums and did some engineering for The Beatles.	
12/23/72+	**3**	12	**1. Oh, Babe, What Would You Say?**	Capitol 3383
			SMITH, Jimmy	
			Born on 12/08/25 in Norristown, Pennsylvania. Pioneer jazz organist. Won Major Bowes Amateur Show in 1934. With father (James, Sr.) in song-and-dance team, 1942. With Don Gardner & The Sonotones, recorded for Bruce in 1953. Smith first recorded with own trio for Blue Note in 1956. Began doing vocals in 1966.	
6/09/62	**21**	7	1. Walk On The Wild Side - Part 1 [I] from the film of the same title	Verve 10255
			SMITH, Keely — see PRIMA, Louis, and SINATRA, Frank	
			SMITH, Michael W.	
			Contemporary Christian singer/keyboardist/songwriter from Kenova, West Virginia. To Nashville in 1978. Touring keyboardist for Amy Grant in 1982. Wrote Amy Grant's hits "Find A Way" and "Stay For Awhile."	
6/08/91	**6**	11	**1. Place In This World** co-written by Amy Grant	Reunion 19019
			SMITH, O.C.	
			Born Ocie Lee Smith on 6/21/36 in Mansfield, Louisiana. To Los Angeles in 1939. Sang while in U.S. Air Force from 1953-57. First recorded for Cadence in 1956. With Count Basie from 1961-63.	
4/20/68	**40**	2	1. The Son Of Hickory Holler's Tramp	Columbia 44425
9/21/68	**2**(1)	12	● **2. Little Green Apples**	Columbia 44616
9/20/69	**34**	2	3. Daddy's Little Man	Columbia 44948
			SMITH, Patti, Group	
			Patti was born on 12/31/46 in Chicago; raised in New Jersey. Poet-turned-punk rocker. Married Fred "Sonic" Smith of the MC5.	
5/13/78	**13**	9	1. Because The Night written by Smith and Bruce Springsteen	Arista 0318
			SMITH, Ray	
			Born on 10/31/34 in Melber, Kentucky; committed suicide on 11/29/79.	
2/01/60	**22**	8	1. Rockin' Little Angel	Judd 1016
			SMITH, Rex	
			Born on 9/19/56 in Jacksonville, Florida. Vocalist/Actor. Starred in several Broadway musicals and in TV film *Sooner or Later.* Appeared in the films *The Pirates of Penzance* and *Streethawk.* Recorded duet with rock singer Rachel Sweet (b: 1963, Akron, Ohio).	
5/12/79	**10**	10	● **1. You Take My Breath Away** from the TV movie *Sooner or Later*	Columbia 10908

DATE	POS	WKS	ARTIST—RECORD TITLE	LABEL & NO.
8/08/81	**32**	4	2. Everlasting Love **REX SMITH/RACHEL SWEET**	Columbia 02169
			SMITH, Sammi	
			Born on 8/05/43 in Orange, California and raised in Oklahoma. Country singer. Moved to Nashville in 1967.	
2/20/71	**8**	11	● **1. Help Me Make It Through The Night** written by Kris Kristofferson	Mega 0015
			SMITH, Somethin'/The Redheads	
			Trio from UCLA: Smith (vocals, guitar), Saul Striks (piano) and Major Short (violin).	
4/02/55	**7**	23	**1. It's A Sin To Tell A Lie** Best Seller #7 / Juke Box #8 / Jockey #9 #1 hit for Fats Waller in 1936	Epic 9093
7/14/56	**27**	3	2. In A Shanty In Old Shanty Town #1 hit for Ted Lewis in 1932	Epic 9168
			SMITH, Verdelle	
			Black songstress from St. Petersburg, Florida.	
8/13/66	**38**	2	1. Tar And Cement	Capitol 5632
			SMITH, Whistling Jack	
			Studio session production featuring the Mike Sammes Singers. Billy Moeller (b: 2/02/46, Liverpool, England) was later hired to tour as Whistling Jack Smith.	
5/13/67	**20**	5	1. I Was Kaiser Bill's Batman [I]	Deram 85005
			SMITHEREENS, The	
			New Jersey pop quartet formed in 1980: Pat DiNizio (vocals), Jim Babjak, Dennis Diken and Mike Mesaros.	
3/10/90	**38**	2	1. A Girl Like You	Enigma 44480#
			SMOKIE	
			British pop-rock quartet: Chris Norman (lead singer), Alan Silson (guitar), Terry Utley (bass) and Pete Spencer (drums). Also see Suzi Quatro.	
1/22/77	**25**	8	1. Living Next Door To Alice	RSO 860
			SNAP!	
			Male/female dance duo from Pittsburgh. London-based rapper Turbo B with his cousin Jackie Harris, replaced in 1991 by Penny Ford (a backing singer for the Gap Band).	
6/02/90	**2**(1)	16	▲ **1. The Power**	Arista 2013
10/13/90	**35**	2	● 2. Ooops Up	Arista 2060
			SNEAKER	
			Los Angeles-based, pop-rock sextet.	
12/19/81+	**34**	6	1. More Than Just The Two Of Us	Handshake 02557
			SNIFF 'n' the TEARS	
			British rock group led by Paul Roberts (vocals) and Loz Netto (guitar).	
8/18/79	**15**	9	1. Driver's Seat	Atlantic 3604
			SNOW, Phoebe	
			Born Phoebe Laub on 7/17/52 in New York City; raised in New Jersey. Vocalist/guitarist/songwriter. Began performing in Greenwich Village in the early '70s.	
2/08/75	**5**	11	**1. Poetry Man**	Shelter 40353

DATE	POS	WKS	ARTIST—RECORD TITLE	LABEL & NO.
9/06/75	**23**	6	2. Gone At Last **PAUL SIMON/PHOEBE SNOW and THE JESSY DIXON SINGERS**	Columbia 10197
			SOFT CELL	
			British electro-rock duo: Marc Almond (vocals) and David Ball (synthesizer). Almond began solo career in late 1988.	
5/22/82	**8**	15	**1. Tainted Love**	Sire 49855
			SOHO	
			London-based trio of guitarist Timothy Brinkhurst (b: 11/20/60) and vocalists/twin sisters Jacqueline and Pauline Cuff (b: 11/25/62) — both are psychiatric nurses.	
10/20/90	**14**	9	● 1. Hippychick samples a riff from The Smiths' "How Soon Is Now"	Sav./Atco 98908
			SOMMERS, Joanie	
			Born on 2/24/41 in Buffalo, moved to California, 1954. Sang Pepsi-Cola jingles in the early & mid-1960s.	
6/16/62	**7**	11	**1. Johnny Get Angry**	Warner 5275
			SONNY	
			Born Salvatore Bono on 2/16/35 in Detroit. Sonny Bono of Sonny & Cher. With Specialty Records as A&R man and writer from 1957-59. Co-wrote The Searchers' hit "Needles And Pins." Elected mayor of Palm Springs, California on 4/12/88. Appeared in the 1988 film *Hairspray*.	
9/04/65	**10**	8	**1. Laugh At Me**	Atco 6369
			SONNY & CHER	
			Husband-and-wife duo: Sonny and Cher Bono. Session singers for Phil Spector. First recorded as Caesar & Cleo for Vault in 1963. Married in 1963; divorced in 1974. In the films *Good Times* (1966) and *Chastity* (1968). Own CBS-TV variety series from 1971-74. Brief TV reunion in 1975. Each recorded solo.	
7/31/65	**1**(3)	10	● **1. I Got You Babe**	Atco 6359
9/11/65	**8**	9	**2. Baby Don't Go**	Reprise 0309
9/25/65	**20**	4	3. Just You	Atco 6345
10/23/65	**15**	6	4. But You're Mine	Atco 6381
2/12/66	**14**	6	5. What Now My Love	Atco 6395
10/15/66	**21**	4	6. Little Man	Atco 6440
1/28/67	**6**	8	**7. The Beat Goes On**	Atco 6461
11/13/71	**7**	11	**8. All I Ever Need Is You**	Kapp 2151
3/11/72	**8**	11	**9. A Cowboys Work Is Never Done**	Kapp 2163
8/05/72	**32**	5	10. When You Say Love adapted from a Budweiser jingle	Kapp 2176
			SOPWITH "CAMEL", The	
			San Francisco quintet — Peter Kraemer, lead singer.	
1/28/67	**26**	4	1. Hello Hello	Kama Sutra 217
			S.O.S. BAND, The	
			Funk-R&B band from Atlanta. Lead singer/keyboardist Mary Davis went solo in 1986, various personnel changes since. Name means "Sounds Of Success."	
6/28/80	**3**	14	▲ **1. Take Your Time (Do It Right) Part 1**	Tabu 5522

DATE	POS	WKS	ARTIST—RECORD TITLE	LABEL & NO.
			SOUL, David	
			Born David Solberg on 8/28/43 in Chicago. Ken Hutchinson of TV's "Starsky & Hutch" (1975-79). Began career as a folk singer and appeared several times on "The Merv Griffin Show" as "The Covered Man" (wore a ski mask).	
2/19/77	**1**(1)	13	● **1. Don't Give Up On Us**	Private S. 45129
			SOUL, Jimmy	
			Born James McCleese in New York City in 1942; raised in North Carolina and Portsmouth, Virginia. Worked with gospel groups, including the Nightingales, billed as "The Wonder Boy."	
5/05/62	**22**	8	1. Twistin' Matilda	S.P.Q.R. 3300
4/20/63	**1**(2)	11	**2. If You Wanna Be Happy**	S.P.Q.R. 3305
			SOUL CHILDREN, The	
			Group formed by songwriters Isaac Hayes and David Porter. Consisted of Anita Louis, Shelbra Bennett, John Colbert and Norman West. Colbert later recorded as J. Blackfoot.	
3/23/74	**36**	2	1. I'll Be The Other Woman	Stax 0182
			SOUL SURVIVORS	
			White-soul band from New York City and Philadelphia. Formed by the Ingui brothers, Charles & Richard, and Kenny Jeremiah. Re-formed by the Inguis in 1972. Jeremiah was later in Shirley And Company.	
9/23/67	**4**	12	**1. Expressway To Your Heart**	Crimson 1010
1/20/68	**33**	3	2. Explosion In Your Soul	Crimson 1012
			SOUL II SOUL	
			South London soul outfit led by the duo of Beresford "Jazzie B." Romeo and Nellee Hooper. Features female vocalists Caron Wheeler, Do'Reen and Rose Windross and musical backing by the Reggae Philharmonic Orchestra. Wheeler left in 1990.	
7/29/89	**11**	10	▲ 1. Keep On Movin'	Virgin 99205
10/14/89	**4**	18	▲ **2. Back To Life (However Do You Want Me)**	Virgin 99171
			SOUNDS OF SUNSHINE	
7/24/71	**39**	2	1. Love Means (You Never Have To Say You're Sorry)	Ranwood 896
			SOUNDS ORCHESTRAL	
			British studio project produced by John Schroeder. Included arranger/producer Johnny Pearson on piano.	
4/10/65	**10**	11	**1. Cast Your Fate To The Wind** [I]	Parkway 942
			SOUTH, Joe	
			Born Joe Souter on 2/28/40 in Atlanta. Successful Nashville session guitarist and songwriter in the mid-1960s. Wrote "Down In The Boondocks," "Hush" and "Rose Garden."	
2/01/69	**12**	9	1. Games People Play	Capitol 2248
1/17/70	**12**	9	2. Walk A Mile In My Shoes **JOE SOUTH AND THE BELIEVERS**	Capitol 2704
			SOUTHER, J.D.	
			John David Souther, born in Detroit and raised in Amarillo, Texas. Formed Longbranch Pennywhistle with Glenn Frey. Teamed with Chris Hillman and Richie Furay as The Souther, Hillman, Furay Band in 1974.	
10/20/79	**7**	13	**1. You're Only Lonely**	Columbia 11079
3/14/81	**11**	10	2. Her Town Too **JAMES TAYLOR AND J.D. SOUTHER**	Columbia 60514

R.E.M.'s odd single B-sides—and there have been many—were compiled by I.R.S. records in 1987 for the compilation *Dead Letter Office*. Among the strangest choices: their version of Roger Miller's 1965 hit "King Of The Road."

REO Speedwagon's first album was released in 1971—but it took the Illinois-based group nine full years to get a record in the Top 40. "Keep On Loving You" was a gold No. 1 single, which might have helped ease their pain somewhat.

Paul Revere & The Raiders' classic Columbia pop singles were admirably collected in the 1990 collection *The Legend of Paul Revere*. Included on the set was their 1961 Gardena Records single "Like, Long Hair," which peaked at No. 38.

Cliff Richard's phenomenal status in his British homeland is hardly reflected by his respectable—but comparatively low-key—U.S. chart showing. His three biggest hits, all in the Top 10: "Devil Woman" (1976), "We Don't Talk Anymore" (1979), and "Dreaming" (1980).

Lionel Richie played a key role in four of the 10 best chart-performing Motown singles in the label's history: 1981's "Endless Love" with Diana Ross, 1983's "All Night Long (All Night)," 1978's "Three Times A Lady" with the Commodores," and 1984's "Hello."

The Righteous Brothers' appeal is apparently timeless. When the duo's 1965 hit version of "Unchained Melody" appeared in the 1990 film *Ghost*, their 1967 greatest-hits album swiftly reentered the *Billboard* charts. The set continues to dominate the Top Pop Catalog Albums chart.

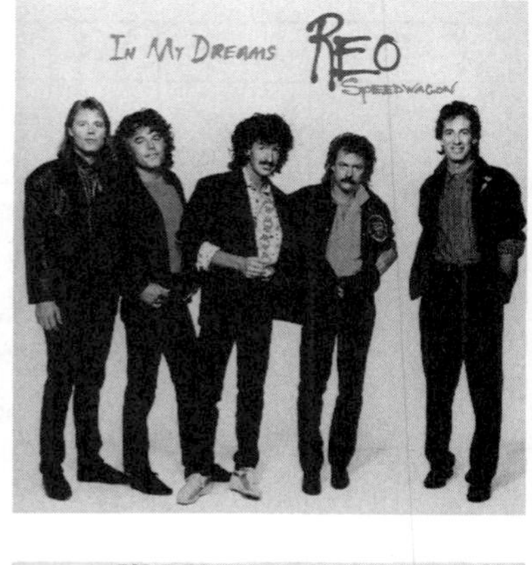

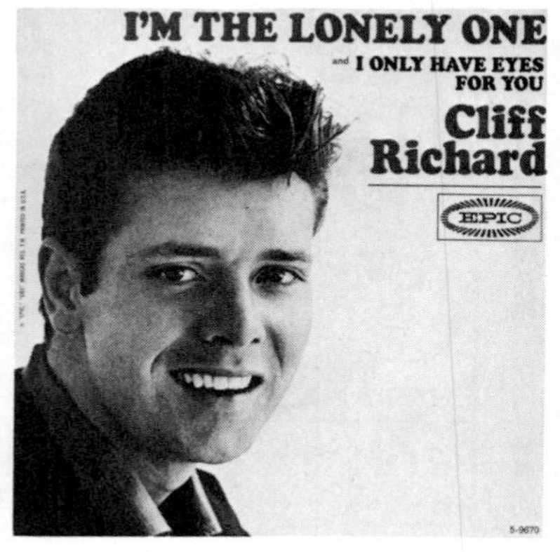

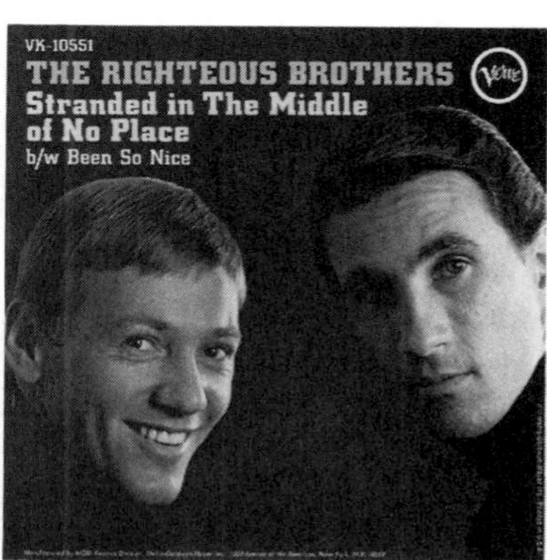

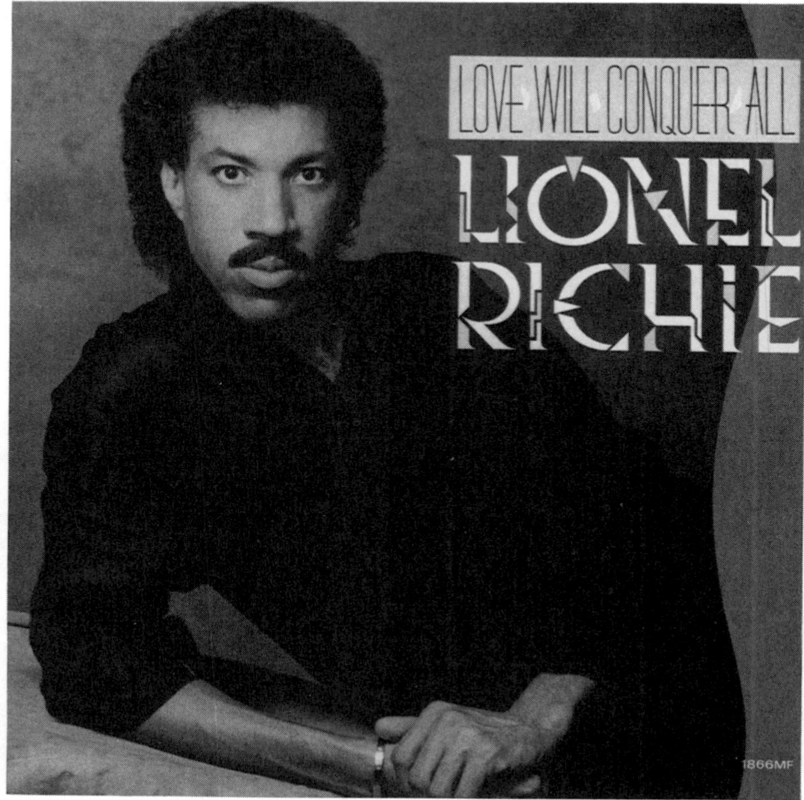

Cheryl Pepsii Riley, discovered by writer/producer team Full Force, hit the Top 40 with her 1988 single "Thanks For My Child." She continued the collaboration with 1991's *Chapters* album—and on it covered Burt Bacharach & Hal David's "A House Is Not A Home."

Johnny Rivers' 17 top-40 hits were dominated by cover versions and remakes of past hits like Chuck Berry's "Memphis," the Four Tops' "Baby, I Need Your Lovin'," and even the Beach Boys' "Help Me, Rhonda." His only No. 1 hit was 1966's "Poor Side Of Town"—a cover version of which he would co-produce for singer Al Wilson three years later.

Rob Base & D.J. E-Z Rock's "It Takes Two" demonstrated the resurgence independent labels would enjoy with rap in the 80s. The Profile Records hit reached No. 36 in 1988 and eventually went gold.

Marty Robbins's second biggest hit, "A White Sport Coat (And A Pink Carnation)," held the No. 2 position for two weeks in 1957. Its title was somewhat appropriated 16 years later for Jimmy Buffett's Dunhill album *A White Sport Coat and a Pink Crustacean*.

Smokey Robinson's recording history has been an integral part of Motown Records' history—on both business and artistic levels. The singer surprised many when he finally departed from Motown in the early 90s to sign with SBK Records—and had a hit with "Double Good Everything."

Roger's 1987 single "I Want To Be Your Man" was his first top-10 hit. The writer/producer/performer, whose last name is Troutman, never managed a similar feat while a part of his early 80s group Zapp.

JOHNNY RIVERS
UNDER YOUR SPELL AGAIN
and LONG TIME MAN
#66144

DATE	POS	WKS	ARTIST—RECORD TITLE	LABEL & NO.
			SOUTHER, HILLMAN, FURAY BAND, The	
			Country-rock sextet formed as a supergroup featuring J.D. Souther, Chris Hillman and Richie Furay.	
9/21/74	**27**	4	1. Fallin' In Love	Asylum 45201
			SOVINE, Red	
			Born Woodrow Wilson Sovine on 7/17/18 in Charleston, West Virginia; died of a heart attack on 4/14/80. Country singer/songwriter/guitarist.	
8/28/76	**40**	1	● 1. Teddy Bear [S]	Starday 142
			SPANDAU BALLET	
			English quintet: Tony Hadley (lead singer), Steve Norman (sax), John Keeble (drums) and brothers Gary (guitar) and Martin (bass) Kemp. The Kemps starred in the 1990 film *The Krays*.	
8/27/83	**4**	13	**1. True**	Chrysalis 42720
12/17/83+	**29**	6	2. Gold	Chrysalis 42743
9/01/84	**34**	4	3. Only When You Leave	Chrysalis 42792
			SPANKY AND OUR GANG	
			Folk-pop group formed in Chicago in 1966 featuring lead singer Elaine "Spanky" McFarlane (b: 6/19/42, Peoria, Illinois). Included Malcolm Hale, Kenny Hodges, Lefty Baker, Nigel Pickering and John Seiter. Spanky became lead singer of the new Mamas & The Papas, early '80s.	
6/03/67	**9**	5	**1. Sunday Will Never Be The Same**	Mercury 72679
9/16/67	**31**	2	2. Making Every Minute Count	Mercury 72714
10/28/67	**14**	9	3. Lazy Day	Mercury 72732
2/03/68	**30**	4	4. Sunday Mornin'	Mercury 72765
5/18/68	**17**	7	5. Like To Get To Know You	Mercury 72795
			SPENCE, Judson	
			Singer/songwriter/multi-instrumentalist born in Pascagoula, Mississippi.	
11/26/88	**32**	4	1. Yeah, Yeah, Yeah	Atlantic 88999
			SPENCER, Tracie	
			Native of Waterloo, Iowa. Twelve years old at time of first hit in 1988. Won the singing competition on TV's "Star Search" in 1986.	
11/19/88	**38**	3	1. Symptoms Of True Love	Capitol 44140
1/26/91	**3**	14	**2. This House**	Capitol 44652#
			SPIDER	
			New York-based rock quintet: South African native Amanda Blue (vocals), Holly Knight, Anton Fig, Keith Lentin and Jimmy Lowell. Keyboardist Knight, a prolific songwriter, later joined Device and then went solo. Drummer Fig joined house band of TV's "Late Night with David Letterman."	
6/07/80	**39**	2	1. New Romance (It's A Mystery)	Dreamland 100
			SPINNERS	
			R&B vocal group from Ferndale High School near Detroit, originally known as the Domingoes. Discovered by producer/lead singer of The Moonglows, Harvey Fuqua, and became the Spinners in 1961. First recorded on Fuqua's Tri-Phi label. Many personnel changes. G.C. Cameron was lead singer from 1968-72. 1972 hit lineup included Phillippe Wynne (tenor; d: 7/14/84), Bobbie Smith (tenor), Billy Henderson (tenor), Henry Fambrough (baritone) and Pervis Jackson (bass). Wynne left group in 1977 and toured with Parliament/Funkadelic; replaced by John Edwards.	
7/17/61	**27**	5	1. That's What Girls Are Made For lead vocal by Harvey Fuqua	Tri-Phi 1001
8/14/65	**35**	2	2. I'll Always Love You	Motown 1078

DATE	POS	WKS	ARTIST—RECORD TITLE	LABEL & NO.
8/22/70	**14**	10	3. It's A Shame written and produced by Stevie Wonder	V.I.P. 25057
10/07/72	**3**	11	● **4. I'll Be Around**	Atlantic 2904
1/20/73	**4**	12	● **5. Could It Be I'm Falling In Love**	Atlantic 2927
5/19/73	**11**	11	● 6. One Of A Kind (Love Affair)	Atlantic 2962
9/08/73	**29**	3	7. Ghetto Child	Atlantic 2973
2/23/74	**20**	8	8. Mighty Love - Pt. 1	Atlantic 3006
6/08/74	**18**	6	9. I'm Coming Home	Atlantic 3027
8/03/74	**1**(1)	15	● **10. Then Came You** **DIONNE WARWICKE AND SPINNERS**	Atlantic 3202
10/26/74	**15**	5	11. Love Don't Love Nobody - Pt. I	Atlantic 3206
4/05/75	**37**	2	12. Living A Little, Laughing A Little	Atlantic 3252
8/30/75	**5**	13	● **13. They Just Can't Stop It the (Games People Play)**	Atlantic 3284
1/24/76	**36**	3	14. Love Or Leave	Atlantic 3309
10/02/76	**2**(3)	17	● **15. The Rubberband Man** all of above Atlantic's produced and arranged by Thom Bell	Atlantic 3355
1/26/80	**2**(2)	16	● **16. Working My Way Back To You/Forgive Me, Girl**	Atlantic 3637
5/24/80	**4**	14	**17. Cupid/I've Loved You For A Long Time**	Atlantic 3664
			SPIRAL STARECASE Sacramento pop-rock quintet: Pat Upton (lead), Harvey Kaplan, Dick Lopes, Bobby Raymond & Vinny Parello.	
5/03/69	**12**	11	1. More Today Than Yesterday	Columbia 44741
			SPIRIT Los Angeles eclectic rock group: Jay Ferguson (lead singer), Mark Andes (bass), Ed Cassidy (drums), Randy California (guitar) and John Locke (keyboards). Ferguson and Andes left to form Jo Jo Gunne in mid-1971. Andes became an original member of Firefall in 1975 and later joined Heart in 1983.	
3/08/69	**25**	5	1. I Got A Line On You	Ode 115
			SPOKESMEN, The Johnny Madara, Dave White and Roy Gilmore. White was with Danny & The Juniors.	
10/09/65	**36**	3	1. The Dawn Of Correction answer song to "Eve Of Destruction"	Decca 31844
			SPRINGFIELD, Dusty Born Mary O'Brien on 4/16/39 in London. Vocalist/guitarist. In The Lana Sisters vocal group. With brother Tom Springfield and Tim Feild in folk trio, The Springfields, 1960-63. Didn't record from 1973-78 except for backup work for Anne Murray in 1975. Began recording again in 1978.	
2/15/64	**12**	7	1. I Only Want To Be With You	Philips 40162
5/02/64	**38**	2	2. Stay Awhile	Philips 40180
7/11/64	**6**	10	**3. Wishin' And Hopin'**	Philips 40207
6/04/66	**4**	10	**4. You Don't Have To Say You Love Me**	Philips 40371
10/01/66	**20**	5	5. All I See Is You	Philips 40396
4/22/67	**40**	2	6. I'll Try Anything	Philips 40439
10/14/67	**22**	5	7. The Look Of Love from the film *Casino Royale*	Philips 40465
12/14/68+	**10**	10	**8. Son-Of-A Preacher Man**	Atlantic 2580
5/24/69	**31**	4	9. The Windmills Of Your Mind	Atlantic 2623

DATE	POS	WKS	ARTIST—RECORD TITLE	LABEL & NO.
11/29/69	**24**	9	10. A Brand New Me	Atlantic 2685
12/26/87+	**2**(2)	13	**11. What Have I Done To Deserve This?** PET SHOP BOYS AND DUSTY SPRINGFIELD	EMI-Man. 50107
			SPRINGFIELD, Rick	
			Born on 8/23/49 in Sydney, Australia. Singer/actor/songwriter. With top Australian teen-idol band Zoot before going solo in 1972. Turned to acting in the late '70s, played Noah Drake on the TV soap opera "General Hospital" in the early '80s. Starred in the film *Hard to Hold* in 1984.	
9/02/72	**14**	9	1. Speak To The Sky	Capitol 3340
5/09/81	**1**(2)	22	● **2. Jessie's Girl**	RCA 12201
9/12/81	**8**	12	**3. I've Done Everything For You** written by Sammy Hagar	RCA 12166
12/26/81+	**20**	10	4. Love Is Alright Tonite	RCA 13008
3/13/82	**2**(4)	16	**5. Don't Talk To Strangers**	RCA 13070
6/19/82	**21**	9	6. What Kind Of Fool Am I	RCA 13245
10/09/82	**32**	5	7. I Get Excited	RCA 13303
4/23/83	**9**	13	**8. Affair Of The Heart**	RCA 13497
7/23/83	**18**	11	9. Human Touch	RCA 13576
11/12/83	**23**	6	10. Souls	RCA 13650
3/17/84	**5**	12	**11. Love Somebody**	RCA 13738
6/09/84	**26**	6	12. Don't Walk Away	RCA 13813
9/08/84	**20**	9	13. Bop 'Til You Drop above 3 from the film *Hard to Hold*	RCA 13861
12/15/84+	**27**	6	14. Bruce [N] recorded in 1978; an autobiographical song about Springfield being mistaken for Bruce Springsteen	Mercury 880405
4/20/85	**26**	6	15. Celebrate Youth	RCA 14047
7/13/85	**22**	8	16. State Of The Heart	RCA 14120
3/05/88	**22**	6	17. Rock Of Life all of above (except #3) written by Springfield	RCA 6853
			SPRINGFIELDS, The	
			English folk trio: Dusty and brother Tom Springfield and Tim Feild.	
9/01/62	**20**	6	1. Silver Threads And Golden Needles	Philips 40038
			SPRINGSTEEN, Bruce	
			Born on 9/23/49 in Freehold, New Jersey. Rock singer/songwriter/guitarist. Worked local clubs in New Jersey and Greenwich Village, mid-1960s. Own E-Street Band in 1973, consisted of Clarence Clemons (saxophone), David Sancious and Danny Federici (keyboards), Gary Tallent (bass) and Vini Lopez (drums). Sancious and Lopez replaced by Roy Bittan and Max Weinberg. Miami Steve Van Zandt (guitar) joined group in 1975. Wrote Earth Band's "Blinded By The Light" and the Pointer Sisters' "Fire." After *Born to Run*, a court injunction prevented the release of any new albums until 1978. Married to model/actress Julianne Phillips from 1985-89. Appeared in the 1987 film *Hail! Hail! Rock 'N' Roll*. Split from the E-Street Band in November 1989. Married Patti Scialfa, former singer with the E-Street Band, on 6/08/91.	
10/11/75	**23**	5	1. Born To Run	Columbia 10209
7/15/78	**33**	2	2. Prove It All Night	Columbia 10763
11/08/80	**5**	14	**3. Hungry Heart**	Columbia 11391
2/21/81	**20**	6	4. Fade Away	Columbia 11431
5/26/84	**2**(4)	15	**5. Dancing In The Dark**	Columbia 04463
8/18/84	**7**	13	**6. Cover Me**	Columbia 04561

DATE	POS	WKS	ARTIST—RECORD TITLE	LABEL & NO.
11/24/84+	**9**	11	**7. Born In The U.S.A.**	Columbia 04680
3/02/85	**6**	12	**8. I'm On Fire**	Columbia 04772
6/08/85	**5**	13	**9. Glory Days**	Columbia 04924
9/14/85	**9**	9	**10. I'm Goin' Down**	Columbia 05603
12/21/85+	**6**	9	**11. My Hometown**	Columbia 05728
			above 7 from the album *Born in the U.S.A.*	
11/29/86	**8**	9	**12. War**	Columbia 06432
			BRUCE SPRINGSTEEN & THE E STREET BAND	
10/03/87	**5**	11	**13. Brilliant Disguise**	Columbia 07595
12/19/87+	**9**	11	**14. Tunnel Of Love**	Columbia 07663
3/19/88	**13**	8	15. One Step Up	Columbia 07726
			all of above (except #12) written by Springsteen	
			SPYRO GYRA	
			Jazz-pop band formed in 1975 in Buffalo, New York. Led by saxophonist Jay Beckenstein (b: 5/14/51).	
7/28/79	**24**	8	1. Morning Dance [I]	Infinity 50011
			SQUEEZE	
			English pop-rock group led by Chris Difford and Glenn Tilbrook. Originally known as UK Squeeze due to confusion with American band Tight Squeeze. Paul Carrack (Ace, Mike + The Mechanics) was lead singer of fluctuating lineup in 1981.	
10/17/87	**15**	10	1. Hourglass	A&M 2967
1/23/88	**32**	5	2. 853-5937	A&M 2994
			SQUIER, Billy	
			Born on 5/12/50 in Wellesley Hills, Massachusetts. Hard-rock singer/songwriter/guitarist.	
6/20/81	**17**	11	1. The Stroke	Capitol 5005
10/17/81	**35**	3	2. In The Dark	Capitol 5040
11/27/82	**32**	6	3. Everybody Wants You	Capitol 5163
7/14/84	**15**	12	4. Rock Me Tonite	Capitol 5370
			STACEY Q	
			Dance singer from Los Angeles. Real name: Stacey Swain.	
8/16/86	**3**	13	**1. Two Of Hearts**	Atlantic 89381
2/21/87	**35**	4	2. We Connect	Atlantic 89331
			STAFFORD, Jim	
			Born on 1/16/44 in Eloise, Florida. Singer/songwriter/guitarist. Moved to Nashville after high school graduation. Own summer variety TV show in 1975, and co-host of "Those Amazing Animals" from 1980-81. Married Bobbie Gentry in 1978.	
7/14/73	**39**	1	1. Swamp Witch	MGM 14496
12/29/73+	**3**	15	● **2. Spiders & Snakes**	MGM 14648
5/04/74	**12**	9	3. My Girl Bill [N]	MGM 14718
7/20/74	**7**	11	**4. Wildwood Weed [N]**	MGM 14737
1/18/75	**24**	5	5. Your Bulldog Drinks Champagne [N]	MGM 14775
9/27/75	**37**	2	6. I Got Stoned And I Missed It [N]	MGM 14819
			all of above produced by Lobo and Phil Gernhard	

DATE	POS	WKS	ARTIST—RECORD TITLE	LABEL & NO.
			STAFFORD, Jo	
			Born on 11/12/20 in Coalinga, California. Member of Tommy Dorsey's vocal group the Pied Pipers, 1940-42. Married to orchestra leader Paul Weston.	
10/15/55	**13**	7	1. Suddenly There's A Valley	Columbia 40559
			Jockey #13 / Top 100 #16 / Juke Box #18 / Best Seller #21 vocal backing by the Norman Luboff Choir	
12/03/55+	**14**	14	2. It's Almost Tomorrow	Columbia 40595
			Juke Box #14 / Top 100 #19 / Jockey #20 / Best Seller #25	
12/22/56	**38**	1	3. On London Bridge	Columbia 40782
			above 3 with Paul Weston & His Music From Hollywood	
			STAFFORD, Terry	
			Born in Hollis, Oklahoma and raised in Amarillo, Texas. Elvis Presley sound-alike. Moved to California in 1960. Appeared in the film *Wild Wheels.*	
3/21/64	**3**	10	**1. Suspicion**	Crusader 101
			first recorded in 1962 by Elvis Presley for his *Pot Luck* album	
6/06/64	**25**	6	2. I'll Touch A Star	Crusader 105
			STALLION	
			Denver-based quintet — Buddy Stephens, lead singer.	
4/23/77	**37**	2	1. Old Fashioned Boy (You're The One)	Casablanca 877
			STALLONE, Frank	
			Philadelphia singer/actor. Brother of actor Sylvester Stallone.	
8/20/83	**10**	10	**1. Far From Over**	RSO 815023
			from the film *Staying Alive*	
			STAMPEDERS	
			Pop-rock trio from Calgary, Canada: Rick Dodson, Ronnie King and Kim Berly.	
9/11/71	**8**	10	**1. Sweet City Woman**	Bell 45120
4/03/76	**40**	2	2. Hit The Road Jack	Quality 501
			featuring a telephone conversation with Wolfman Jack	
			STAMPLEY, Joe	
			Born on 6/06/43 in Springhill, Louisiana. Country singer. Leader of The Uniques.	
3/03/73	**37**	3	1. Soul Song	Dot 17442
			STANDELLS, The	
			Los Angeles-area, punk-rock quartet: Dick Dodd (lead singer, drums), Larry Tamblyn and Tony Valentino (guitars) and Gary Lane (bass). Dodd was an original Mouseketeer.	
6/11/66	**11**	9	1. Dirty Water	Tower 185
			written and produced by Ed Cobb (Four Preps)	
			STANLEY, Michael, Band	
			Cleveland rock group: Michael Stanley (vocals, guitar), Kevin Raleigh (vocals, keyboards), Bob Pelander (keyboards), Tommy Dobeck (drums), Michael Gismondi (bass), Rick Bell (sax) and Gary Markashy (lead guitar; replaced by Danny Powers in 1983). Raleigh recorded solo in 1988.	
1/10/81	**33**	5	1. He Can't Love You	EMI America 8063
11/12/83	**39**	1	2. My Town	EMI America 8178

DATE	POS	WKS	ARTIST—RECORD TITLE	LABEL & NO.
			STANSFIELD, Lisa	
			Lead singer of Blue Zone from Roachdale, England. Vocalist on Coldcut's 1989 club hit "People Hold On."	
2/24/90	**3**	14	▲ **1. All Around The World**	Arista 9928
6/16/90	**14**	8	2. You Can't Deny It	Arista 2024
9/08/90	**21**	7	3. This Is The Right Time	Arista 2049
			STAPLE SINGERS, The	
			Family soul group consisting of Roebuck "Pop" Staples (b: 12/28/15, Winoma, Mississippi), with his son Pervis (who left in 1971) and daughters Cleotha, Yvonne and lead singer Mavis Staples. Roebuck was a blues guitarist in his teens, later with the Golden Trumpets gospel group. Moved to Chicago in 1935. Formed own gospel group in early '50s. First recorded for United in 1953. Mavis recorded solo in 1970.	
3/20/71	**27**	5	1. Heavy Makes You Happy (Sha-Na-Boom Boom)	Stax 0083
11/13/71	**12**	10	2. Respect Yourself	Stax 0104
4/15/72	**1**(1)	14	**3. I'll Take You There**	Stax 0125
8/26/72	**38**	3	4. This World	Stax 0137
4/14/73	**33**	3	5. Oh La De Da	Stax 0156
11/10/73	**9**	11	● **6. If You're Ready (Come Go With Me)**	Stax 0179
3/23/74	**23**	7	7. Touch A Hand, Make A Friend all of above produced by Al Bell	Stax 0196
11/01/75	**1**(1)	12	● **8. Let's Do It Again** from the film of the same title	Curtom 0109
			STAPLETON, Cyril	
			Born on 12/31/14 in Nottingham, England; died on 2/25/74. British bandleader.	
9/29/56	**25**	2	1. The Italian Theme [I]	London 1672
1/19/59	**13**	10	2. The Children's Marching Song (Nick Nack Taddy Whack) with the children from the film *The Inn of the Sixth Happiness*	London 1851
			STARBUCK	
			Atlanta pop-rock septet — Bruce Blackman, lead singer.	
5/29/76	**3**	14	**1. Moonlight Feels Right**	Private S. 45039
5/21/77	**38**	2	2. Everybody Be Dancin'	Private S. 45144
			STARCHER, Buddy	
			Born on 3/16/10 in Ripley, West Virginia. Worked on WFBR-Baltimore in 1928. Worked as a DJ on WCAU, WIBG-Philadelphia. Own band from 1937. Managed KWBA-Bayton, Texas in the early 1970s.	
5/14/66	**39**	1	1. History Repeats Itself [S]	Boone 1038
			STARGARD	
			Disco trio: Rochelle Runnells, Debra Anderson and Janice Williams. Appeared as The Diamonds in film *Sgt. Pepper's Lonely Hearts Club Band.*	
3/04/78	**21**	7	1. Theme Song From "Which Way Is Up" from the film *Which Way Is Up*	MCA 40825
			STARLAND VOCAL BAND	
			Washington, D.C.-based pop quartet: Bill and wife Taffy Danoff, John Carroll and future wife Margot Chapman. Bill and Taffy had fronted the folk quintet Fat City. Bill co-wrote "Take Me Home, Country Roads" with friend John Denver. Denver owned Windsong record label. Won the 1976 Best New Artist Grammy.	
6/05/76	**1**(2)	14	● **1. Afternoon Delight**	Windsong 10588

DATE	POS	WKS	ARTIST—RECORD TITLE	LABEL & NO.
			STARLETS, The	
			Female R&B vocal group from Chicago: Dynetta Boone (aka Liz Walker) (lead), Jane Hall, Maxine Edwards (sister of Earl Edwards of The Dukays), Mickey McKinney, Jeanette Miles and Bernice Williams. While under contract to Pam Records, The Starlets recorded "I Sold My Heart To The Junkman" on the Newtown label. Newtown listed one of their artists, The Blue-Belles (Patti LaBelle's group), on the label.	
6/12/61	**38**	2	1. Better Tell Him No	PAM 1003
5/12/62	**15**	7	2. I Sold My Heart To The Junkman **THE BLUE-BELLES**	Newtown 5000
			STARPOINT	
			Black sextet from Maryland: brothers Ernesto, George, Orlando and Gregory Phillips, with Renee Diggs and Kayode Adeyemo. Formed as Lycindiana, did session work for Motown and All-Platinum Records.	
11/16/85	**25**	9	1. Object Of My Desire	Elektra 69621
			STARR, Brenda K.	
			Real name: Brenda Kaplan. Born on 10/15/66 in Manhattan. Singer/film actress from New York City of Puerto Rican heritage. Daughter of Harvey Kaplan (of Spiral Starecase).	
5/07/88	**13**	12	1. I Still Believe	MCA 53288
9/03/88	**24**	7	2. What You See Is What You Get	MCA 53367
			STARR, Edwin	
			Born Charles Hatcher on 1/21/42 in Nashville and raised in Cleveland. In vocal group, the Futuretones; recorded for Tress in 1957. With Bill Doggett Combo from 1963-65. Recorded duets with Sandra "Blinky" Williams in 1969.	
9/04/65	**21**	6	1. Agent Double-O-Soul	Ric-Tic 103
3/22/69	**6**	9	**2. Twenty-Five Miles**	Gordy 7083
7/25/70	**1**(3)	13	**3. War**	Gordy 7101
1/02/71	**26**	4	4. Stop The War Now	Gordy 7104
			STARR, Kay	
			Born Katherine Starks on 7/21/22 in Dougherty, Oklahoma and raised in Dallas and Memphis. With Joe Venuti's orchestra at age 15, and sang briefly with Glenn Miller, Charlie Barnet and Bob Crosby before launching solo career in 1945. In the films *Make Believe Ballroom* and *When You're Smiling.*	
8/06/55	**17**	1	1. Good And Lonesome Juke Box #17	RCA 6146
1/07/56	**1**(6)	20	**2. Rock And Roll Waltz** Juke Box #1(6) / Top 100 #1(4) / Best Seller #1(1) / Jockey #1(1)	RCA 6359
6/30/56	**40**	1	3. Second Fiddle	RCA 6541
9/16/57	**9**	10	**4. My Heart Reminds Me** Jockey #9 / Top 100 #53	RCA 6981
			STARR, Randy	
			Born Warren Nadel on 7/02/30 in New York City. Pop singer/songwriter/guitarist. Dentist since 1956. Wrote many tunes for Elvis Presley's soundtracks. Formed instrumental duo, The Islanders, with Frank Metis.	
5/06/57	**32**	2	1. After School with "Bugs" Bower's Orchestra	Dale 100

DATE	POS	WKS	ARTIST—RECORD TITLE	LABEL & NO.
			STARR, Ringo	
			Born Richard Starkey on 7/07/40 in Liverpool, England. Ringo joined The Beatles following ousting of drummer Pete Best in 1962. First solo album in 1970. Films *Candy* (made in 1967, released in 1969), *The Magic Christian, 200 Motels, Born to Boogie, Blindman, That'll Be the Day, Cave Man* and Paul McCartney's *Give My Regards to Broad Street.* Married actress Barbara Bach in 1981.	
5/08/71	**4**	11	● **1. It Don't Come Easy**	Apple 1831
4/15/72	**9**	7	**2. Back Off Boogaloo**	Apple 1849
			above 2 produced by George Harrison	
10/20/73	**1**(1)	12	● **3. Photograph**	Apple 1865
12/29/73+	**1**(1)	12	● **4. You're Sixteen**	Apple 1870
3/23/74	**5**	11	**5. Oh My My**	Apple 1872
11/30/74+	**6**	10	**6. Only You**	Apple 1876
2/22/75	**3**	10	**7. No No Song**	Apple 1880
7/05/75	**31**	3	8. It's All Down To Goodnight Vienna	Apple 1882
			written by John Lennon	
10/16/76	**26**	6	9. A Dose Of Rock 'N' Roll	Atlantic 3361
12/05/81	**38**	2	10. Wrack My Brain	Boardwalk 130
			written and produced by George Harrison	
			STARSHIP — see JEFFERSON STARSHIP	
			STARS on 45	
			Dutch session vocalists and musicians assembled by producer Jaap Eggermont. The John Lennon vocals by Bas Muys.	
5/02/81	**1**(1)	14	● **1. Stars on 45**	Radio 3810
			Venus/Sugar Sugar/No Reply/I'll Be Back/Drive My Car/Do You Want To Know A Secret/We Can Work It Out/I Should Have Known Better/Nowhere Man/You're Going To Lose That Girl	
4/17/82	**28**	5	2. Stars on 45 III	Radio 4019
			Uptight Everything's All Right/My Cherie Amour/Yester Me, Yester You/Master Blaster/You Are The Sunshine Of My Life/Isn't She Lovely/Sir Duke/I Wish/I Was Made To Love Her/Superstition/Fingertips	
			STARZ	
			New York-based rock quintet: Michael Lee Smith (lead singer; brother of Rex Smith), Peter Sweval (bassist), Richie Ranno (guitar), Brenden Harkin (guitar) and Joe X. Dube (drums).	
4/30/77	**33**	2	1. Cherry Baby	Capitol 4399
			STATLER BROTHERS, The	
			Country vocal quartet from Staunton, Virginia. Consisted of brothers Harold & Don Reid, Phil Balsley and Lew DeWitt. In 1983, Jimmy Fortune replaced DeWitt who died from Crohn's disease on 8/15/90 (age 52).	
12/11/65+	**4**	9	**1. Flowers On The Wall**	Columbia 43315
			STATON, Candi	
			Born in Hanceville, Alabama. Sang with the Jewel Gospel Trio from age 10. Went solo in 1968. Married for a time to Clarence Carter.	
10/03/70	**24**	9	1. Stand By Your Man	Fame 1472
6/26/76	**20**	11	2. Young Hearts Run Free	Warner 8181

DATE	POS	WKS	ARTIST—RECORD TITLE	LABEL & NO.
			STATUS QUO, The	
			English rock quintet: Francis Michael Rossi, Rick Parfitt, Roy Lynes, John Coghlan and Alan Lancaster. Immensely popular in England, where they've charted over 35 hits, 20 of which went top 10.	
6/29/68	**12**	11	1. Pictures Of Matchstick Men	Cadet Con. 7001
			STEALERS WHEEL	
			Scottish group led by Gerry Rafferty (vocals, guitar) and Joe Egan (vocals, keyboards).	
3/31/73	**6**	13	**1. Stuck In The Middle With You**	A&M 1416
3/09/74	**29**	3	2. Star	A&M 1483
			STEAM	
			New York City studio group assembled by producer Paul Leka.	
11/08/69	**1**(2)	13	• **1. Na Na Hey Hey Kiss Him Goodbye**	Fontana 1667
			STEEL BREEZE	
			Ric Jacobs, lead singer of six-man pop band from California.	
9/18/82	**16**	11	1. You Don't Want Me Anymore	RCA 13283
2/19/83	**30**	6	2. Dreamin' Is Easy	RCA 13427
			STEELHEART	
			Hard-rock quintet from Norwalk, Connecticut led by vocalist Michael Matijevic.	
6/01/91	**23**	9	1. I'll Never Let You Go (Angel Eyes)	MCA 53801#
			STEELY DAN	
			Los Angeles-based, pop/jazz-styled group formed by Donald Fagen (b: 1/10/48, Passaic, New Jersey; keyboards, vocals) and Walter Becker (b: 2/20/50, New York City; bass, vocals). Group, primarily known as a studio unit, featured Fagen and Becker with various studio musicians. Duo went their separate ways in 1981. Drummer Jimmy Hodder drowned on 6/05/90 (age 42).	
12/30/72+	**6**	11	**1. Do It Again**	ABC 11338
4/07/73	**11**	11	2. Reeling In The Years	ABC 11352
6/08/74	**4**	11	**3. Rikki Don't Lose That Number**	ABC 11439
6/21/75	**37**	2	4. Black Friday	ABC 12101
1/07/78	**11**	11	5. Peg	ABC 12320
5/06/78	**19**	8	6. Deacon Blues	ABC 12355
7/01/78	**22**	5	7. FM (No Static At All) from the film *FM*	MCA 40894
9/23/78	**26**	5	8. Josie	ABC 12404
12/13/80+	**10**	13	**9. Hey Nineteen**	MCA 51036
3/28/81	**22**	7	10. Time Out Of Mind all of above written by Fagen & Becker and produced by Gary Katz	MCA 51082
			STEIN, Lou	
			Born on 4/22/22 in Philadelphia. Pianist with Ray McKinley, 1941-42 and 1946-47. Studio and free-lance musician into the '70s.	
3/30/57	**31**	3	1. Almost Paradise [I] with Bill Fontaine's orchestra	RKO Unique 385

DATE	POS	WKS	ARTIST—RECORD TITLE	LABEL & NO.
			STEINMAN, Jim	
			Born in New York City. Wrote and arranged all cuts on Meat Loaf's *Bat Out of Hell* album.	
7/18/81	**32**	6	1. Rock And Roll Dreams Come Through featured vocal: Rory Dodd	Epic 02111
			STEPHENSON, Van	
			Pop singer/songwriter from Nashville.	
5/12/84	**22**	10	1. Modern Day Delilah	MCA 52376
			STEPPENWOLF	
			Hard-rock quintet formed in Los Angeles in 1967. Original lineup: John Kay (born Joachim Krauledat on 4/12/44 in Tilsit, East Germany; vocals, guitar) Michael Monarch (guitar), Goldy McJohn (keyboards), Nick St. Nicholas (bass), Mars Bonfire (born Dennis Edmonton; guitar) and brother Jerry Edmonton (drums). All but Monarch were members of Canadian group Sparrow. Many personnel changes except for Kay.	
7/20/68	**2**(3)	12	● **1. Born To Be Wild**	Dunhill 4138
10/26/68	**3**	13	● **2. Magic Carpet Ride**	Dunhill 4161
3/15/69	**10**	8	**3. Rock Me**	Dunhill 4182
9/06/69	**31**	5	4. Move Over	Dunhill 4205
2/07/70	**39**	1	5. Monster	Dunhill 4221
5/09/70	**35**	3	6. Hey Lawdy Mama all of above produced by Gabriel Mekler	Dunhill 4234
10/05/74	**29**	3	7. Straight Shootin' Woman	Mums 6031
			STEREO MC'S	
			Trio of remixers from GEE Street Records based in East London: Rob Birch, Nick "The Head" Hallam and Owen "If" Rossiter. Features touring/video vocalist Cath Coffey.	
7/20/91	**39**	1	1. Elevate My Mind	4th & B'way 447519#
			STEREOS, The	
			R&B quintet from Steubenville, Ohio. Originally called the Buckeyes. Consisted of Bruce Robinson (lead), Nathaniel Hicks, Sam Profit, George Otis and Ronnie Collins.	
10/16/61	**29**	3	1. I Really Love You	Cub 9095
			STEVE & EYDIE — see LAWRENCE, Steve, and/or GORME, Eydie	
			STEVENS, April — see TEMPO, Nino	
			STEVENS, Cat	
			Born Steven Georgiou on 7/21/47 in London. Began career playing folk music at Hammersmith College in 1966. Contracted tuberculosis in 1968 and spent over a year recuperating. Adopted new style when he re-emerged. Lived in Brazil in the mid-'70s. Converted to Muslim religion in 1979, took name Yusef Islam.	
3/06/71	**11**	10	1. Wild World	A&M 1231
7/10/71	**30**	7	2. Moon Shadow	A&M 1265
10/09/71	**7**	10	**3. Peace Train**	A&M 1291
4/22/72	**6**	11	**4. Morning Has Broken**	A&M 1335
12/02/72+	**16**	9	5. Sitting	A&M 1396
8/04/73	**31**	5	6. The Hurt	A&M 1418
4/20/74	**10**	11	**7. Oh Very Young**	A&M 1503
8/24/74	**6**	9	**8. Another Saturday Night**	A&M 1602

DATE	POS	WKS	ARTIST—RECORD TITLE	LABEL & NO.
1/11/75	**26**	4	9. Ready	A&M 1645
8/16/75	**33**	4	10. Two Fine People	A&M 1700
7/23/77	**33**	3	11. (Remember The Days Of The) Old Schoolyard	A&M 1948
			STEVENS, Connie	
			Born Concetta Ingolia on 4/08/38 in Brooklyn. Played Cricket Blake on TV's "Hawaiian Eye" from 1959-63. Appeared in the films *Eighteen and Anxious, Rockabye Baby, Parrish, Never Too Late, Grease 2, Back to the Beach* and others. Married for a time to Eddie Fisher; singer Tricia Leigh Fisher is their daughter.	
4/27/59	**4**	11	**1. Kookie, Kookie (Lend Me Your Comb)** [N] **EDWARD BYRNES AND CONNIE STEVENS**	Warner 5047
3/14/60	**3**	17	**2. Sixteen Reasons**	Warner 5137
			STEVENS, Dodie	
			Born Geraldine Ann Pasquale on 2/17/46 in Chicago and raised in California. Discovered while singing on Art Linkletter's "House Party" TV show at age 8. First recorded as Geri Pace on Gold Star in 1954.	
3/09/59	**3**	14	**1. Pink Shoe Laces**	Crystalette 724
			STEVENS, Ray	
			Born Ray Ragsdale on 1/24/39 in Clarkdale, Georgia. Attended Georgia State University, studied music theory and composition. Production work in the mid-'60s. Numerous appearances on Andy Williams' TV show in the late '60s. Own TV show in summer of 1970. Featured on "Music Country" TV show, 1973-74. The #1 novelty recording artist of the past 30 years.	
9/18/61	**35**	1	1. Jeremiah Peabody's Poly Unsaturated Quick Dissolving Fast Acting Pleasant Tasting Green And Purple Pills [N]	Mercury 71843
7/14/62	**5**	9	**2. Ahab, The Arab** **[N]**	Mercury 71966
6/29/63	**17**	6	3. Harry The Hairy Ape [N]	Mercury 72125
8/31/68	**28**	3	4. Mr. Businessman	Monument 1083
4/26/69	**8**	10	● **5. Gitarzan** **[N]**	Monument 1131
7/26/69	**27**	4	6. Along Came Jones [N]	Monument 1150
4/18/70	**1**(2)	13	● **7. Everything Is Beautiful**	Barnaby 2011
4/27/74	**1**(3)	12	● **8. The Streak** **[N]**	Barnaby 600
5/24/75	**14**	10	9. Misty	Barnaby 614
2/05/77	**40**	1	10. In The Mood [N] **HENHOUSE FIVE PLUS TOO**	Warner 8301
			STEVENSON, B.W.	
			Born Louis Stevenson on 10/05/49 in Dallas; died on 4/28/88 after heart surgery.	
8/25/73	**9**	12	**1. My Maria**	RCA 0030
			STEVIE B	
			Miami-born Steven B. Hill. Singer/self-taught musician. In high school band with Howard Johnson.	
4/08/89	**32**	5	1. I Wanna Be The One	LMR 74003
7/29/89	**37**	2	2. In My Eyes	LMR 74004
3/10/90	**29**	5	3. Love Me For Life	LMR 84006#
7/28/90	**15**	8	4. Love And Emotion	LMR 2645
10/27/90	**1**(4)	16	● **5. Because I Love You (The Postman Song)**	LMR 2724
2/23/91	**12**	9	6. I'll Be By Your Side	LMR 2758
			STEVIE V — see ADVENTURES OF	

DATE	POS	WKS	ARTIST—RECORD TITLE	LABEL & NO.
			STEWART, Al	
			Born on 9/05/45 in Glasgow, Scotland. Pop-rock singer/composer/guitarist.	
1/22/77	**8**	10	**1. Year Of The Cat**	Janus 266
			written about British comedian Tony Hancock	
10/21/78	**7**	13	**2. Time Passages**	Arista 0362
2/17/79	**29**	4	3. Song On The Radio	Arista 0389
			above 3 produced by Alan Parsons	
9/27/80	**24**	6	4. Midnight Rocks	Arista 0552
			STEWART, Amii	
			Born in Washington, D.C. in 1956. Disco singer/dancer/actress. In the Broadway musical *Bubbling Brown Sugar.* Her niece is singer Sinitta.	
2/24/79	**1**(1)	14	▲ **1. Knock On Wood**	Ariola 7736
			STEWART, Billy	
			Born on 3/24/37 in Washington, D.C.; died in an auto accident on 1/17/70. R&B vocalist/composer/ keyboardist. Discovered by Bo Diddley in 1956. First recorded for Chess/Argo in 1956. Did not record from 1957-62. Nicknamed "Fat Boy."	
5/01/65	**26**	4	1. I Do Love You	Chess 1922
7/10/65	**24**	5	2. Sitting In The Park	Chess 1932
8/06/66	**10**	7	**3. Summertime**	Chess 1966
			from the musical *Porgy & Bess*	
11/05/66	**29**	5	4. Secret Love	Chess 1978
			#1 hit for Doris Day in 1954	
			STEWART, David A.	
			Born on 9/09/52 in England. Half of the Eurythmics duo. Multi-instrumentalist/composer/producer. Married Siobhan Fahey of Bananarama on 8/01/87.	
6/08/91	**11**	9	1. Lily Was Here [I]	Arista 2187
			DAVID A. STEWART introducing CANDY DULFER (saxophonist from Amsterdam); from the Dutch film *Lily Was Here*	
			STEWART, Jermaine	
			Chicago-bred singer. Dancer on TV's "Soul Train." Worked as backup vocalist for Shalamar and Boy George.	
6/28/86	**5**	13	**1. We Don't Have To Take Our Clothes Off**	Arista 9424
4/16/88	**27**	5	2. Say It Again	Arista 9636
			STEWART, John	
			Born on 9/05/39 in San Diego. Member of The Kingston Trio from 1961-67. Wrote "Daydream Believer."	
6/02/79	**5**	13	**1. Gold**	RSO 931
9/29/79	**28**	5	2. Midnight Wind	RSO 1000
			backing vocals on above 2 by Stevie Nicks and Lindsey Buckingham	
1/26/80	**34**	4	3. Lost Her In The Sun	RSO 1016

DATE	POS	WKS	ARTIST—RECORD TITLE	LABEL & NO.
			STEWART, Rod	
			Born Roderick Stewart on 1/10/45 in London. Worked as a folksinger in Europe in the early '60s. Recorded for English Decca in 1964. With the Hoochie Coochie Men, Steampacket and Shotgun Express. Joined Jeff Beck Group, 1967-69. With Faces from 1969-75, also recorded solo during this time. Left Faces in December 1975. Won Grammy's Living Legends Award in 1989. Married to actress Alana Hamilton from 1979-84. Married supermodel Rachel Hunter on 12/15/90.	
8/28/71	**1**(5)	15	● **1. Maggie May**	Mercury 73224
11/27/71	**24**	6	2. (I Know) I'm Losing You **ROD STEWART with FACES**	Mercury 73244
9/16/72	**13**	7	3. You Wear It Well	Mercury 73330
12/16/72	**40**	1	4. Angel written by Jimi Hendrix	Mercury 73344
10/23/76	**1**(8)	17	● **5. Tonight's The Night (Gonna Be Alright)**	Warner 8262
2/26/77	**21**	9	6. The First Cut Is The Deepest written by Cat Stevens	Warner 8321
7/02/77	**30**	4	7. The Killing Of Georgie (Part I And II)	Warner 8396
11/26/77+	**4**	15	● **8. You're In My Heart (The Final Acclaim)**	Warner 8475
3/11/78	**28**	4	9. Hot Legs	Warner 8535
5/27/78	**22**	6	10. I Was Only Joking	Warner 8568
12/23/78+	**1**(4)	18	▲ **11. Da Ya Think I'm Sexy?**	Warner 8724
5/12/79	**22**	6	12. Ain't Love A Bitch	Warner 8810
11/29/80+	**5**	17	**13. Passion**	Warner 49617
10/31/81	**5**	15	**14. Young Turks**	Warner 49843
2/13/82	**20**	8	15. Tonight I'm Yours (Don't Hurt Me)	Warner 49886
6/11/83	**14**	9	16. Baby Jane	Warner 29608
10/01/83	**35**	3	17. What Am I Gonna Do (I'm So In Love With You)	Warner 29564
6/02/84	**6**	13	**18. Infatuation**	Warner 29256
9/15/84	**10**	10	**19. Some Guys Have All The Luck**	Warner 29215
6/14/86	**6**	12	**20. Love Touch** theme from the film *Legal Eagles*	Warner 28668
6/04/88	**12**	9	21. Lost In You	Warner 27927
9/10/88	**12**	10	22. Forever Young	Warner 27796
1/28/89	**4**	13	**23. My Heart Can't Tell You No**	Warner 27729
6/10/89	**11**	10	24. Crazy About Her	Warner 27657
12/02/89+	**3**	14	**25. Downtown Train**	Warner 22685
4/07/90	**10**	10	**26. This Old Heart Of Mine** **[R]** **ROD STEWART with RONALD ISLEY** solo version by Rod charted in 1976 (POS 83)	Warner 19983
3/23/91	**5**	14	**27. Rhythm Of My Heart**	Warner 19366
7/27/91	**10**	11	**28. The Motown Song** backing vocals by The Temptations	Warner 19322
			STEWART, Sandy	
			Born Sandra Galitz on 7/10/37 in Philadelphia. Regular on the Eddie Fisher and Perry Como TV shows.	
1/12/63	**20**	5	1. My Coloring Book	Colpix 669

DATE	POS	WKS	ARTIST—RECORD TITLE	LABEL & NO.
			STILLS, Stephen	
			Born on 1/03/45 in Dallas. Member of Buffalo Springfield and Crosby, Stills & Nash.	
12/19/70+	**14**	10	1. Love The One You're With	Atlantic 2778
3/27/71	**37**	2	2. Sit Yourself Down	Atlantic 2790
			STING	
			Born Gordon Sumner on 10/02/51 in Wallsend, England. Lead singer/bass guitarist of The Police. In the films *Quadrophenia, Dune, The Bride, Plenty* and others. Nicknamed "Sting" because of a yellow and black jersey he liked to wear.	
6/15/85	**3**	14	**1. If You Love Somebody Set Them Free**	A&M 2738
9/07/85	**8**	11	**2. Fortress Around Your Heart**	A&M 2767
11/23/85	**17**	9	3. Love Is The Seventh Wave	A&M 2787
2/01/86	**16**	8	4. Russians	A&M 2799
10/24/87	**7**	12	**5. We'll Be Together**	A&M 2983
2/06/88	**15**	8	6. Be Still My Beating Heart	A&M 2992
2/02/91	**5**	9	**7. All This Time**	A&M 1541
			STITES, Gary	
			Born on 7/23/40 in Denver. Pop singer/songwriter/guitarist.	
5/18/59	**24**	5	1. Lonely For You	Carlton 508
			STOLOFF, Morris	
			Born on 8/01/1898 in Philadelphia; died on 4/16/80. Composer/conductor/violinist. Became musical director for Columbia Pictures in 1936. Winner of three Academy Awards.	
4/21/56	**1**(3)	22	**1. Moonglow and Theme From "Picnic"** [I] Jockey #1 / Best Seller #2 / Top 100 #2 / Juke Box #4 with The Columbia Pictures Orchestra; from the film *Picnic*; four top 10 versions of "Moonglow" charted in 1934	Decca 29888
			STONE, Cliffie	
			Born Clifford Snyder on 3/01/17 in Burbank, California. Bass player/orchestra/square-dance bandleader. Worked with the Anson Weeks and Freddie Slack bands in the late 1930s. Became a country DJ in the mid-1940s. Wrote many country songs.	
8/13/55	**14**	4	1. The Popcorn Song [N] Juke Box #14 / Best Seller #25; vocal by Bob Roubian	Capitol 3131
			STONE, Kirby, Four	
			Kirby was born on 4/27/18 in New York City. His quartet includes: Eddie Hall, Larry Foster and Mike Gardner. Kirby was musical director for various TV shows.	
7/28/58	**25**	1	1. Baubles, Bangles And Beads Jockey #25 end / Hot 100 #50 with Jimmy Carroll's Orchestra; from Broadway's *Kismet*	Columbia 41183
			STONEBOLT	
			Pop-rock quintet from Vancouver, Canada — David Wills, lead singer.	
9/30/78	**29**	5	1. I Will Still Love You	Parachute 512
			STONE PONEYS — see RONSTADT, Linda	
			STOOKEY, Paul	
			Born on 11/30/37 in Baltimore. Paul of Peter, Paul & Mary.	
9/04/71	**24**	9	1. Wedding Song (There Is Love)	Warner 7511

DATE	POS	WKS	ARTIST—RECORD TITLE	LABEL & NO.
			STORIES	
			New York rock quartet: Ian Lloyd (lead singer, bass), Michael Brown (keyboards; founding member of Left Banke), Steve Love (guitar) and Bryan Madey (drums). Brown left group in 1973, replaced by Ken Aaronson (bass; later with Hagar, Schon, Aaronson, Shrieve) and Ken Bichel (keyboards).	
7/14/73	**1**(2)	15	● **1. Brother Louie**	Kama Sutra 577
			STORM, Billy	
			Born on 6/29/38 in Dayton, Ohio. Lead singer of The Valiants and The Alley Cats.	
5/18/59	**28**	6	1. I've Come Of Age with Frank DeVol and his Orchestra	Columbia 41356
			STORM, Gale	
			Born Josephine Cottle on 4/05/22 in Bloomington, Texas. Moved to Hollywood in 1939, leading lady in films during the '40s and early '50s. Own TV series "My Little Margie" from 1952-55, also "The Gale Storm Show," 1956-62.	
10/22/55	**2**(3)	17	**1. I Hear You Knocking** Top 100 #2 / Juke Box #2 / Best Seller #3 / Jockey #4	Dot 15412
12/24/55+	**6**	12	**2. Teen Age Prayer/** Jockey #6 / Juke Box #6 / Top 100 #9 / Best Seller #13	
12/31/55+	**5**	9	**3. Memories Are Made Of This** Jockey #5 / Top 100 #16	Dot 15436
3/03/56	**9**	14	**4. Why Do Fools Fall In Love** Jockey #9 / Juke Box #14 / Best Seller #15 / Top 100 #15	Dot 15448
5/05/56	**6**	14	**5. Ivory Tower** Jockey #6 / Juke Box #6 / Top 100 #10 / Best Seller #15	Dot 15458
4/29/57	**4**	18	**6. Dark Moon** Juke Box #4 end / Top 100 #5 / Best Seller #6 / Jockey #6 orchestra conducted by Billy Vaughn	Dot 15558
			STRANGELOVES, The	
			Writers/producers Bob Feldman, Jerry Goldstein and Richard Gottehrer. Team wrote and produced The Angels' "My Boyfriend's Back," produced The McCoys' "Hang On Sloopy", and charted as The Sheep. Gottehrer became a partner in Sire Records and produced the Go-Go's' first two albums and Blondie's debut album.	
7/10/65	**11**	8	1. I Want Candy	Bang 501
10/23/65	**39**	1	2. Cara-Lin	Bang 508
2/05/66	**30**	4	3. Night Time	Bang 514
			STRAWBERRY ALARM CLOCK	
			West Coast psychedelic rock sextet: Ed King (lead guitar), Mark Weitz (keyboards), Lee Freeman (guitar), Gary Lovetro (bass), George Bunnel (bass) and Randy Seol (drums). King joined Lynyrd Skynyrd, 1973-75. Originally known as the Sixpence.	
10/14/67	**1**(1)	14	● **1. Incense And Peppermints** lead vocal by Greg Munford (16-year-old leader of L.A. band, the Shapes); originally released on All-American 373 in 1967	Uni 55018
1/27/68	**23**	6	2. Tomorrow	Uni 55046

DATE	POS	WKS	ARTIST—RECORD TITLE	LABEL & NO.
			STRAY CATS	
			Long Island, New York rockabilly trio: Brian Setzer (b: 4/10/60; lead singer, guitar), Lee Rocker (born Leon Drucher; string bass) and Slim Jim Phantom (born Jim McDonell; drums). Recorded two albums in Britain in 1981 and 1982. Group disbanded in 1984; reunited in 1988. Phantom and Rocker formed trio Phantom, Rocker & Slick in 1985, also the year Phantom married actress Britt Ekland. Setzer portrayed Eddie Cochran in the film *La Bamba.* Phantom portrayed Charlie Parker's drummer in the film *Bird.*	
10/23/82	**9**	13	**1. Rock This Town**	EMI America 8132
1/08/83	**3**	14	**2. Stray Cat Strut** originally "Bubbled Under" for 6 weeks beginning 7/17/82	EMI America 8122
8/20/83	**5**	12	**3. (She's) Sexy + 17**	EMI America 8168
12/03/83	**35**	3	4. I Won't Stand In Your Way all of above written by Brian Setzer and produced by Dave Edmunds	EMI America 8185
			STREET PEOPLE	
			Studio group — Rupert Holmes, member.	
2/21/70	**36**	5	1. Jennifer Tomkins	Musicor 1365
			STREISAND, Barbra	
			Born Barbara Joan Streisand on 4/24/42 in Brooklyn. Made Broadway debut in *I Can Get It For You Wholesale*, 1962. Lead role in Broadway's *Funny Girl*, 1964. Film debut in *Funny Girl* in 1968 (tied with Katharine Hepburn for Best Actress Oscar); also starred in *A Star Is Born, Hello Dolly, Funny Lady, The Way We Were* and many others. Produced/directed/starred in/co-wrote the 1983 film *Yentl.* Married for a time to actor Elliott Gould.	
5/23/64	**5**	12	**1. People** from the Broadway musical *Funny Girl*	Columbia 42965
1/22/66	**32**	3	2. Second Hand Rose	Columbia 43469
12/12/70+	**6**	12	**3. Stoney End**	Columbia 45236
8/28/71	**40**	1	4. Where You Lead	Columbia 45414
8/12/72	**37**	4	5. Sweet Inspiration/Where You Lead	Columbia 45626
12/22/73+	**1**(3)	17	● **6. The Way We Were** from the film of the same title	Columbia 45944
1/08/77	**1**(3)	18	● **7. Love Theme From "A Star Is Born" (Evergreen)** love theme from the film *A Star Is Born*	Columbia 10450
5/28/77	**4**	14	**8. My Heart Belongs To Me**	Columbia 10555
7/01/78	**25**	5	9. Songbird	Columbia 10756
8/26/78	**21**	6	10. Love Theme From "Eyes of Laura Mars" (Prisoner) from the film *Eyes of Laura Mars*	Columbia 10777
11/04/78	**1**(2)	15	● **11. You Don't Bring Me Flowers** **BARBRA & NEIL** (Diamond)	Columbia 10840
7/07/79	**3**	13	● **12. The Main Event/Fight** from the film *The Main Event*	Columbia 11008
10/27/79	**1**(2)	13	● **13. No More Tears (Enough Is Enough)** **BARBRA STREISAND/DONNA SUMMER** 12" single available on Casablanca 20199	Columbia 11125
2/23/80	**37**	3	14. Kiss Me In The Rain	Columbia 11179
9/13/80	**1**(3)	19	● **15. Woman In Love**	Columbia 11364
11/15/80+	**3**	15	● **16. Guilty** **BARBRA STREISAND & BARRY GIBB**	Columbia 11390
2/14/81	**10**	10	**17. What Kind Of Fool**	Columbia 11430

DATE	POS	WKS	ARTIST—RECORD TITLE	LABEL & NO.
			BARBRA STREISAND & BARRY GIBB	
			above 3 written and produced by Barry Gibb (Bee Gees)	
11/28/81+	**11**	11	18. Comin' In And Out Of Your Life	Columbia 02621
12/10/83	**40**	2	19. The Way He Makes Me Feel	Columbia 04177
			from the film *Yentl*	
11/12/88	**25**	5	20. Till I Loved You	Columbia 08062
			BARBRA STREISAND AND DON JOHNSON	
			love theme from the Broadway musical *Goya*	
			STRING-A-LONGS, The	
			Instrumental quintet: Keith McCormack, Aubrey Lee de Cordova, Richard Stephens and Jimmy Torres (guitars) and Don Allen (drums).	
1/23/61	**3**	13	**1. Wheels** [I]	Warwick 603
4/17/61	**35**	2	2. Brass Buttons [I]	Warwick 625
			STRONG, Barrett	
			Born on 2/05/41 in Mississippi. R&B singer/songwriter. Wrote many of The Temptations' hits with Norman Whitfield, including "Just My Imagination," "Papa Was A Rollin' Stone" and "Ball Of Confusion."	
3/21/60	**23**	8	1. Money (That's what I want)	Anna 1111
			also released on Tamla 54027 and 54029 in 1960	
			STRUNK, Jud	
			Born Justin Strunk, Jr. on 6/11/36 in Jamestown, New York and raised in Farmington, Maine. Killed in a plane crash on 10/15/81. Regular on TV's "Laugh In."	
3/24/73	**14**	10	1. Daisy A Day	MGM 14463
			STRYPER	
			Christian heavy-metal band from Orange County, California: Michael Sweet (vocals), Robert Sweet (drums), Oz Fox (guitar) and Tim Gaines (bass).	
12/26/87+	**23**	8	1. Honestly	Enigma 75009
			STYLE COUNCIL, The	
			English duo: Paul Weller (ex-vocalist of The Jam) and Mick Talbot (keyboards). Expanded to a trio in 1988 with the addition of female vocalist Dee C. Lee.	
5/12/84	**29**	6	1. My Ever Changing Moods	Geffen 29359
			STYLISTICS, The	
			Soul group from Philadelphia formed in 1968. Consisted of Russell Thompkins, Jr. (b: 3/21/51; lead), Airron Love, James Smith, James Dunn and Herbie Murrell. Thompkins, Love and Smith sang with the Percussions; Murrell and Dunn with the Monarchs from 1965-68. First recorded for Sebring in 1969.	
7/17/71	**39**	1	1. Stop, Look, Listen (To Your Heart)	Avco Emb. 4572
11/27/71+	**9**	13	● **2. You Are Everything**	Avco 4581
3/11/72	**3**	14	● **3. Betcha By Golly, Wow**	Avco 4591
7/01/72	**25**	6	4. People Make The World Go Round	Avco 4595
11/11/72	**10**	8	● **5. I'm Stone In Love With You**	Avco 4603
3/03/73	**5**	9	● **6. Break Up To Make Up**	Avco 4611
6/09/73	**23**	5	7. You'll Never Get To Heaven (If You Break My Heart)	Avco 4618
11/17/73	**14**	11	8. Rockin' Roll Baby	Avco 4625
4/13/74	**2**(2)	14	● **9. You Make Me Feel Brand New**	Avco 4634
			all of above produced by Thom Bell	
8/17/74	**18**	7	10. Let's Put It All Together	Avco 4640

DATE	POS	WKS	ARTIST—RECORD TITLE	LABEL & NO.
			STYX	
			Chicago-based rock quintet: Dennis DeYoung (vocals, keyboards), Tommy Shaw (lead guitar), James Young (guitar), and twin brothers John (drums) and Chuck Panozzo (bass). Band earlier known as TW4. Shaw replaced John Curulewski in 1976. Most songs written by Dennis DeYoung and/or Tommy Shaw. Band broke up when DeYoung and Shaw went solo in 1984. Reunited in 1990 with guitarist Glen Burtnick replacing Shaw, who joined the Damn Yankees.	
1/18/75	**6**	11	**1. Lady**	Wooden N. 10102
3/27/76	**27**	5	2. Lorelei	A&M 1786
12/18/76	**36**	3	3. Mademoiselle	A&M 1877
10/29/77+	**8**	15	**4. Come Sail Away**	A&M 1977
4/01/78	**29**	4	5. Fooling Yourself (The Angry Young Man)	A&M 2007
10/21/78	**21**	7	6. Blue Collar Man (Long Nights)	A&M 2087
4/07/79	**16**	13	7. Renegade	A&M 2110
10/20/79	**1**(2)	14	● **8. Babe**	A&M 2188
1/19/80	**26**	5	9. Why Me	A&M 2206
1/24/81	**3**	15	**10. The Best Of Times**	A&M 2300
3/28/81	**9**	13	**11. Too Much Time On My Hands**	A&M 2323
2/12/83	**3**	16	● **12. Mr. Roboto**	A&M 2525
4/30/83	**6**	13	**13. Don't Let It End**	A&M 2543
6/02/84	**40**	2	14. Music Time	A&M 2625
1/26/91	**3**	12	**15. Show Me The Way**	A&M 1536#
5/18/91	**25**	6	16. Love At First Sight	A&M 1548#
			SUAVE	
			Los Angeles native, born on 2/22/66. Son of Waymond Anderson, Sr. (member of GQ).	
4/23/88	**20**	7	1. My Girl	Capitol 44124
			SUGARHILL GANG	
			New York rap trio formed in Harlem. Consisted of Michael "Wonder Mike" Wright, Guy "Master Gee" O'Brien and Henry "Big Bank Hank" Jackson. One of the first commercially successful rap acts.	
1/05/80	**36**	2	1. Rapper's Delight rhythm track taken from Chic's "Good Times"; issued commercially only as a 12" single	Sugar Hill 542
			SUGARLOAF	
			Rock quartet from Denver: Jerry Corbetta (lead singer, keyboards), Bob Webber (guitar), Bob Raymond (bass) and Bob MacVittie (drums). Robert Yeazel (guitar, vocals) joined in 1971. By 1974, Myron Pollock replaced MacVittie, and Yeazel had left.	
9/19/70	**3**	12	**1. Green-Eyed Lady**	Liberty 56183
2/01/75	**9**	11	**2. Don't Call Us, We'll Call You** **SUGARLOAF/JERRY CORBETTA** features brief snippet of The Beatles' "I Feel Fine"	Claridge 402
			SUMMER, Donna	
			Born Adrian Donna Gaines on 12/31/48 in Boston. With group Crow, played local clubs. In German production of *Hair*, European productions of *Godspell*, *The Me Nobody Knows* and *Porgy and Bess*. Settled in Germany, where she recorded "Love To Love You Baby." In the film *Thank God It's Friday* in 1979. Married Bruce Sudano (Alive & Kicking and Brooklyn Dreams) in 1980. Dubbed "The Queen of Disco."	
12/20/75+	**2**(2)	14	● **1. Love To Love You Baby**	Oasis 401

DATE	POS	WKS	ARTIST—RECORD TITLE	LABEL & NO.
9/03/77	**6**	14	● **2. I Feel Love**	Casablanca 884
1/28/78	**37**	3	3. I Love You	Casablanca 907
6/03/78	**3**	14	● **4. Last Dance** from the film *Thank God It's Friday*	Casablanca 926
9/30/78	**1**(3)	15	● **5. MacArthur Park**	Casablanca 939
1/20/79	**4**	14	● **6. Heaven Knows** **DONNA SUMMER with BROOKLYN DREAMS**	Casablanca 959
4/28/79	**1**(3)	17	▲ **7. Hot Stuff**	Casablanca 978
6/09/79	**1**(5)	15	▲ **8. Bad Girls**	Casablanca 988
9/15/79	**2**(2)	14	● **9. Dim All The Lights**	Casablanca 2201
10/27/79	**1**(2)	13	● **10. No More Tears (Enough Is Enough)** **BARBRA STREISAND/DONNA SUMMER** 12" single available on Casablanca 20199	Columbia 11125
1/26/80	**5**	12	● **11. On The Radio**	Casablanca 2236
9/27/80	**3**	13	● **12. The Wanderer**	Geffen 49563
10/11/80	**36**	3	13. Walk Away	Casablanca 2300
1/10/81	**33**	3	14. Cold Love	Geffen 49634
3/28/81	**40**	2	15. Who Do You Think You're Foolin'	Geffen 49664
7/17/82	**10**	11	**16. Love Is In Control (Finger On The Trigger)**	Geffen 29982
2/05/83	**33**	6	17. The Woman In Me	Geffen 29805
6/18/83	**3**	17	**18. She Works Hard For The Money**	Mercury 812370
9/01/84	**21**	8	19. There Goes My Baby	Geffen 29291
5/20/89	**7**	10	● **20. This Time I Know It's For Real**	Atlantic 88899
			SUMMER, Henry Lee Rock singer from Brazil, Indiana. Received full college basketball scholarship.	
4/02/88	**20**	7	1. I Wish I Had A Girl	CBS Assoc. 07720
7/01/89	**18**	8	2. Hey Baby	CBS Assoc. 68891
			SUNNY & THE SUNGLOWS Group from San Antonio, Texas, formed in 1959. Group led by Sunny Ozuna, with Jesse, Oscar and Ray Villanueva, Tony Tostado, Gilbert Fernandez and Alfred Luna.	
9/28/63	**11**	9	1. Talk To Me originally released on Sunglow in 1963 as by The Sunglows	Tear Drop 3014
			SUNNYSIDERS, The Vocal/instrumental group: Freddy Morgan (banjo; d: 1970), Jad Paul and Margie Rayburn (who later recorded solo). Morgan was a member of Spike Jones & The City Slickers, 1947-58.	
5/21/55	**12**	10	1. Hey, Mr. Banjo Juke Box #12 / Jockey #19 / Best Seller #20	Kapp 113
			SUNSHINE COMPANY, The Southern California pop quintet featuring lead singer Mary Nance.	
11/18/67	**36**	3	1. Back On The Street Again	Imperial 66260
			SUPERTRAMP British rock quintet: Roger Hodgson (vocals, guitar), Rick Davies (vocals, keyboards), John Helliwell (sax), Dougie Thomson (bass) and Bob Siebenberg (drums). Hodgson went solo in 1983.	
5/17/75	**35**	2	1. Bloody Well Right	A&M 1660
7/02/77	**15**	11	2. Give A Little Bit	A&M 1938

DATE	POS	WKS	ARTIST—RECORD TITLE	LABEL & NO.
4/28/79	**6**	13	**3. The Logical Song**	A&M 2128
8/04/79	**15**	8	4. Goodbye Stranger	A&M 2162
11/03/79	**10**	11	**5. Take The Long Way Home**	A&M 2193
10/04/80	**15**	8	6. Dreamer	A&M 2269
			from their 1974 album *Crime of the Century*	
10/30/82	**11**	11	7. It's Raining Again	A&M 2502
2/26/83	**31**	5	8. My Kind Of Lady	A&M 2517
6/08/85	**28**	7	9. Cannonball	A&M 2731
			SUPREMES, The	
			R&B vocal group from Detroit, formed as the Primettes in 1959. Consisted of lead singer Diana Ross (b: 3/26/44), Mary Wilson (b: 3/06/44), Florence Ballard (b: 6/30/43; d: 2/22/76 of cardiac arrest) and Barbara Martin. Recorded for LuPine in 1960. Signed to Motown's Tamla label in 1960. Changed name to The Supremes in 1961; Martin left shortly thereafter. Worked as backing vocalists for Motown until 1964. Backed Marvin Gaye on "Can I Get A Witness." Ballard discharged from group in 1967, replaced by Cindy Birdsong, formerly with Patti LaBelle's Blue Belles. Ross left in 1969 for solo career, replaced by Jean Terrell. Birdsong left in 1972, replaced by Lynda Lawrence. Terrell and Lawrence left in 1973. Mary Wilson re-formed group with Scherrie Payne (sister of Freda Payne) and Cindy Birdsong. Birdsong left again in 1976, replaced by Susaye Greene. In 1978, Wilson toured England with Karen Ragland and Karen Jackson, but lost rights to the name "Supremes" thereafter. Inducted into the Rock and Roll Hall of Fame in 1988.	
12/28/63+	**23**	7	1. When The Lovelight Starts Shining Through His Eyes	Motown 1051
7/18/64	**1(2)**	13	**2. Where Did Our Love Go**	Motown 1060
10/10/64	**1(4)**	12	**3. Baby Love**	Motown 1066
11/21/64	**1(2)**	13	**4. Come See About Me**	Motown 1068
3/06/65	**1(2)**	10	**5. Stop! In The Name Of Love**	Motown 1074
5/08/65	**1(1)**	10	**6. Back In My Arms Again**	Motown 1075
8/14/65	**11**	7	7. Nothing But Heartaches	Motown 1080
10/30/65	**1(2)**	10	**8. I Hear A Symphony**	Motown 1083
1/29/66	**5**	8	**9. My World Is Empty Without You**	Motown 1089
5/07/66	**9**	7	**10. Love Is Like An Itching In My Heart**	Motown 1094
8/20/66	**1(2)**	11	**11. You Can't Hurry Love**	Motown 1097
11/05/66	**1(2)**	10	**12. You Keep Me Hangin' On**	Motown 1101
2/04/67	**1(1)**	10	**13. Love Is Here And Now You're Gone**	Motown 1103
4/15/67	**1(1)**	10	**14. The Happening**	Motown 1107
			from the film of the same title	
			DIANA ROSS AND THE SUPREMES:	
8/19/67	**2(2)**	10	**15. Reflections**	Motown 1111
11/25/67	**9**	6	**16. In And Out Of Love**	Motown 1116
4/06/68	**28**	5	17. Forever Came Today	Motown 1122
			all of above written by Eddie Holland, Lamont Dozier and Brian Holland	
7/06/68	**30**	3	18. Some Things You Never Get Used To	Motown 1126
10/26/68	**1(2)**	15	**19. Love Child**	Motown 1135
12/14/68+	**2(2)**	12	**20. I'm Gonna Make You Love Me**	Motown 1137
			DIANA ROSS AND THE SUPREMES & THE TEMPTATIONS	
2/01/69	**10**	7	**21. I'm Livin' In Shame**	Motown 1139
3/22/69	**25**	6	22. I'll Try Something New	Motown 1142

DATE	POS	WKS	ARTIST—RECORD TITLE	LABEL & NO.
			DIANA ROSS AND THE SUPREMES & THE TEMPTATIONS	
4/26/69	**27**	5	23. The Composer	Motown 1146
6/14/69	**31**	4	24. No Matter What Sign You Are	Motown 1148
11/15/69	**1**(1)	15	**25. Someday We'll Be Together**	Motown 1156
			THE SUPREMES:	
3/14/70	**10**	10	**26. Up The Ladder To The Roof**	Motown 1162
8/01/70	**21**	8	27. Everybody's Got The Right To Love	Motown 1167
11/21/70	**7**	12	**28. Stoned Love**	Motown 1172
12/12/70+	**14**	8	29. River Deep - Mountain High	Motown 1173
			THE SUPREMES & FOUR TOPS	
5/22/71	**16**	8	30. Nathan Jones	Motown 1182
1/29/72	**16**	9	31. Floy Joy	Motown 1195
6/03/72	**37**	3	32. Automatically Sunshine	Motown 1200
8/07/76	**40**	1	33. I'm Gonna Let My Heart Do The Walking	Motown 1391
			SURFACE	
			Soul trio from New Jersey: Bernard Jackson (lead singer), David Townsend (son of producer/songwriter Ed Townsend) and Dave Conley (former horn player with Mandrill).	
6/20/87	**20**	8	1. Happy	Columbia 06611
7/29/89	**5**	11	● **2. Shower Me With Your Love**	Columbia 68746
11/24/90+	**1**(2)	18	● **3. The First Time**	Columbia 73502
6/01/91	**17**	8	4. Never Gonna Let You Down	Columbia 73643
			SURFARIS, The	
			Teenage surf band from Glendora, California: Ron Wilson (drummer), Jim Fuller (lead guitar), Bob Berryhill (rhythm guitar), Pat Connolly (bass) and Jim Pash (sax, clarinet).	
7/06/63	**2**(1)	10	**1. Wipe Out** [I] originally released on DFS 12 and then on Princess 50 in 1963	Dot 16479
8/27/66	**16**	10	2. Wipe Out [I-R]	Dot 144
			SURVIVOR	
			Midwest rock group: Dave Bickler (lead singer), Jim Peterik (keyboards; former lead singer of Ides Of March), Frankie Sullivan (guitar), Gary Smith (drums) and Dennis Johnson (bass). Smith and Johnson replaced by Marc Droubay and Stephan Ellis in 1981. Bickler replaced by Jimi Jamison in 1984. Droubay and Ellis left in 1988.	
11/21/81	**33**	4	1. Poor Man's Son	Scotti Br. 02560
6/26/82	**1**(6)	18	▲ **2. Eye Of The Tiger** from the film *Rocky III*	Scotti Br. 02912
10/16/82	**17**	7	3. American Heartbeat	Scotti Br. 03213
10/20/84	**13**	13	4. I Can't Hold Back	Scotti Br. 04603
2/09/85	**8**	11	**5. High On You**	Scotti Br. 04685
5/11/85	**4**	14	**6. The Search Is Over**	Scotti Br. 04871
11/23/85+	**2**(2)	16	**7. Burning Heart** from the film *Rocky IV*	Scotti Br. 05663
11/15/86+	**9**	13	**8. Is This Love**	Scotti Br. 06381

DATE	POS	WKS	ARTIST—RECORD TITLE	LABEL & NO.
			SWAN, Billy	
			Born on 5/12/42 in Cape Girardeau, Missouri. Singer/songwriter/keyboardist/guitarist. Wrote "Lover Please" for Clyde McPhatter. Produced Tony Joe White's first three albums. Toured with Kris Kristofferson from the early '70s. Formed band Black Tie with Randy Meisner in 1986.	
10/26/74	**1**(2)	12	● **1. I Can Help**	Monument 8621
			SWANN, Bettye	
			Born Betty Jean Champion on 10/24/44 in Shreveport, Louisiana. Moved to Los Angeles in the late 1950s. In vocal group the Fawns, recorded for Money in 1964.	
7/01/67	**21**	7	1. Make Me Yours	Money 126
4/19/69	**38**	2	2. Don't Touch Me	Capitol 2382
			SWAYZE, Patrick (featuring WENDY FRASER)	
			Film actor Swayze was born on 8/18/52 in Houston, Texas. Starred in *Red Dawn*, *Dirty Dancing*, *Road House*, *Ghost* and others.	
1/16/88	**3**	13	**1. She's Like The Wind** from the film *Dirty Dancing*	RCA 5363
			SWEAT, Keith	
			Soul singer/songwriter born and raised in Harlem.	
2/06/88	**5**	13	● **1. I Want Her**	Vintertn. 69431
6/30/90	**14**	12	● 2. Make You Sweat	Vintertn. 64961
12/22/90+	**7**	12	**3. I'll Give All My Love To You**	Vintertn. 64915#
			SWEATHOG	
			Rock quartet: Lenny Lee Goldsmith, Frosty, Dave Johnson and B.J.	
12/11/71	**33**	4	1. Hallelujah	Columbia 45492
			SWEET	
			English rock band: Brian Connolly (lead singer), Steve Priest (bass, vocals), Andy Scott (guitar, keyboards) and Mick Tucker (drums).	
3/17/73	**3**	15	● **1. Little Willy**	Bell 45251
8/02/75	**5**	14	**2. Ballroom Blitz**	Capitol 4055
11/22/75+	**5**	11	● **3. Fox On The Run**	Capitol 4157
3/06/76	**20**	7	4. Action	Capitol 4220
4/15/78	**8**	14	**5. Love Is Like Oxygen**	Capitol 4549
			SWEET, Rachel — see SMITH, Rex	
			SWEET INSPIRATIONS, The	
			R&B vocal quartet: Cissy Houston, Estelle Brown, Sylvia Shemwell and Myrna Smith. Spent nearly six years as studio group, primarily for Atlantic. Work included backing Aretha Franklin and Elvis Presley. Cissy, mother of Whitney Houston, recorded solo in 1970.	
3/30/68	**18**	10	1. Sweet Inspiration	Atlantic 2476
			SWEET SENSATION	
			Eight-member soul group from Manchester, England led by Marcel King (vocals), with additional vocals by St. Clair Palmer, Vincent James and Junior Daye.	
2/15/75	**14**	8	1. Sad Sweet Dreamer	Pye 71002
			SWEET SENSATION	
			Female trio from New York City: Betty LeBron, and sisters Margie and Mari Fernandez. Mari replaced in 1989 by Sheila Bega.	
3/25/89	**14**	8	1. Sincerely Yours	Atco 99246

DATE	POS	WKS	ARTIST—RECORD TITLE	LABEL & NO.
			featuring a short rap break by Romeo J.D.	
7/15/89	**23**	7	2. Hooked On You [R]	Atco 99210
			remix of their 1987 hit (POS 64)	
3/31/90	**13**	10	3. Love Child	Atco 98983
7/07/90	**1**(1)	13	**4. If Wishes Came True**	Atco 98953
			SWINGING BLUE JEANS, The	
			Liverpool, England rock quartet: Ray Ennis and Ralph Ellis (guitars), Norman Kuhlke (drums) and Les Braid (bass).	
3/28/64	**24**	5	1. Hippy Hippy Shake	Imperial 66021
			SWINGIN' MEDALLIONS	
			Eight-man rock and roll band from Greenwood, South Carolina led by John McElrath.	
6/04/66	**17**	6	1. Double Shot (Of My Baby's Love)	Smash 2033
			originally released on 4 Sale 002 in 1965	
			SWING OUT SISTER	
			British jazz-pop trio: Corinne Drewery (vocals), Andy Connell and Martin Jackson. Drewery was a fashion designer. Reduced to a duo in 1989 with departure of Jackson.	
9/26/87	**6**	11	**1. Breakout**	Mercury 888016
2/20/88	**31**	3	2. Twilight World	Mercury 888484
			SWITCH	
			Soul-funk sextet from Mansfield, Ohio: Bobby DeBarge, Phillip Ingram (lead vocals), Greg Williams, Tommy DeBarge, Eddie Fluellen and Jody Sims. Discovered by Jermaine Jackson. Brothers Bobby and Tommy DeBarge were later in family group DeBarge.	
12/02/78	**36**	3	1. There'll Never Be	Gordy 7159
			SYBIL	
			Sybil Lynch from Paterson, New Jersey.	
11/04/89	**20**	9	● 1. Don't Make Me Over	Next Plat. 325#
			SYLVERS, Foster	
			Born on 2/25/62 in Memphis. Youngest member of The Sylvers family group. Production work on Janet Jackson's first album.	
6/30/73	**22**	8	1. Misdemeanor	MGM 14580
			first released on Pride 1031 in 1973	
			SYLVERS, The	
			Memphis family of 10 brothers and sisters: Olympia-Ann, Leon, Charmaine, James, Edmund, Ricky, Angelia, Pat, Jonathon and Foster Sylvers. Leon formed the group Dynasty in 1979.	
3/13/76	**1**(1)	15	● **1. Boogie Fever**	Capitol 4179
11/13/76+	**5**	17	● **2. Hot Line**	Capitol 4336
5/21/77	**17**	10	3. High School Dance	Capitol 4405
			SYLVESTER	
			Born Sylvester James in Los Angeles. Moved to San Francisco in 1967. With vocal group the Cockettes. In film *The Rose*. Backing vocals by Martha Wash, Izora Rhodes (later known as Two Tons O' Fun and The Weather Girls) and Jeanie Tracy. Died on 12/16/88 (age 41) of AIDS-related complications.	
9/30/78	**19**	10	1. Dance (Disco Heat)	Fantasy 827
2/17/79	**36**	3	2. You Make Me Feel (Mighty Real)	Fantasy 846
5/05/79	**40**	2	3. I (Who Have Nothing)	Fantasy 855

DATE	POS	WKS	ARTIST—RECORD TITLE	LABEL & NO.
			SYLVIA	
			Born Sylvia Vanderpool on 5/06/36 in New York City. Singer/songwriter/producer. First recorded with Hot Lips Page for Columbia in 1950, as Little Sylvia. Half of Mickey & Sylvia duo. Married Joe Robinson, owner of All-Platinum/Vibration Records (later known as Sugar Hill). Their son Joey was leader of West Street Mob.	
4/21/73	**3**	13	● **1. Pillow Talk**	Vibration 521
			SYLVIA	
			Country singer Sylvia Kirby Allen, born on 12/09/56 in Kokomo, Indiana. Moved to Nashville in 1975. Worked as a secretary for producer Tom Collins. Solo debut in 1979.	
10/09/82	**15**	9	● 1. Nobody	RCA 13223
			SYMS, Sylvia	
			Nightclub singer from the Bronx.	
6/16/56	**20**	2	1. I Could Have Danced All Night Jockey #20 / Top 100 #35 from the musical *My Fair Lady*	Decca 29903
9/01/56	**21**	3	2. English Muffins And Irish Stew Jockey #21 / Top 100 #51 orchestra directed by Jack Pleis on above 2	Decca 29969
			SYNCH	
			Pop-rock sextet from Wilkes-Barre, Pennsylvania — Jimmy Harnen, lead singer.	
4/22/89	**10**	11	**1. Where Are You Now?** [R] **JIMMY HARNEN W/SYNCH** originally charted on 3/01/86 (POS 77)	WTG 68625
			SYNDICATE OF SOUND	
			San Jose garage-rock quintet: Don Baskin (lead singer), Jim Sawyers (guitar), Bob Gonzalez (bass), John Sharkey (rhythm guitar) and John Duckworth (drums).	
6/25/66	**8**	6	**1. Little Girl** first released on Hush 228 in 1966	Bell 640
			SYREETA — see PRESTON, Billy	
			SYSTEM, The	
			New York City-based, techno-funk duo: Mic Murphy (b: Raleigh, North Carolina; vocals, guitar) and David Frank (b: Dayton, Ohio; synthesizer).	
5/16/87	**4**	13	**1. Don't Disturb This Groove**	Atlantic 89320
			T	
			TACO	
			Born Taco Ockerse in 1955 to Dutch parents in Jaharta, Indonesia. German-based singer.	
7/23/83	**4**	14	● **1. Puttin' On The Ritz** written in 1929 by Irving Berlin; #1 hit for Harry Richman in 1930	RCA 13574

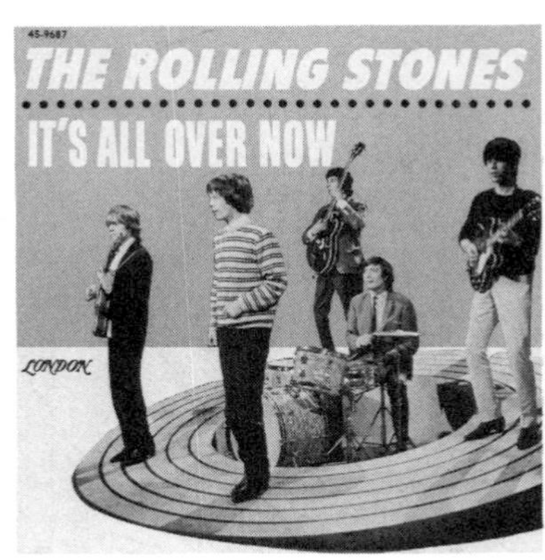

Kenny Rogers's first top-10 single, the slightly psychedelic "Just Dropped In (To See What Condition My Condition Was In)," came via his group the First Edition in 1967. At the time, Rogers' brother Lelan headed up Texas's International Artists label, now a favorite of many record collectors.

The Rolling Stones' nearly 30 years in rock 'n' roll have consistently brought the group hit records—but only a handful of those actually reached No. 1. The biggest of their eight chart-toppers were 1965's "(I Can't Get No) Satisfaction" and 1969's "Honky Tonk Women," each which held the top slot for four weeks.

The Rooftop Singers' hit "Walk Right In" rushed to the top of the charts in early 1963 and pushed Steve Lawrence's memorable "Go Away Little Girl" out of the picture. The group had one more top-40 hit and disbanded four years later.

Diana Ross's all-time highest charting record was not recorded solo or even with the Supremes: "Endless Love," No. 1 for nine weeks in 1981, was a duet with Lionel Richie.

David Lee Roth's 1985 cover of "California Girls" reached the same position as did the Beach Boys' original version 20 years earlier. Ironically, Roth's stayed in the Top 40 two weeks longer.

Ruby & The Romantics' classic "Our Day Will Come" was the Ohio-based quintet's sole No. 1 record. "Young Wings Can Fly (Higher Than You Know)," another single written by the "Our Day" composing team Hilliard-Garson, peaked at No. 47 eight months later.

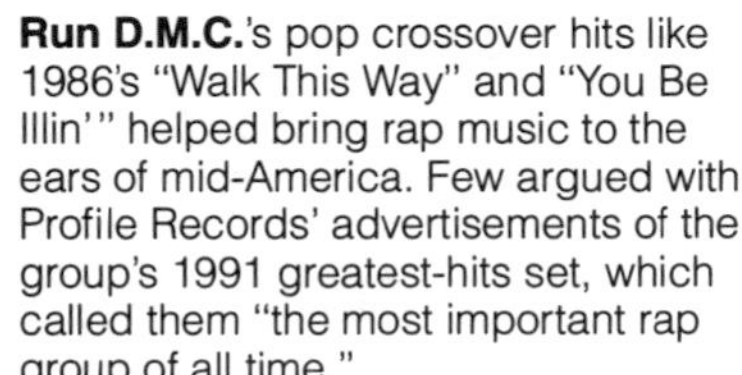

Run D.M.C.'s pop crossover hits like 1986's "Walk This Way" and "You Be Illin'" helped bring rap music to the ears of mid-America. Few argued with Profile Records' advertisements of the group's 1991 greatest-hits set, which called them "the most important rap group of all time."

Patrice Rushen's brand of crossover jazz/R&B brought her three albums that charted in the Top 40 during the early 80s. The young keyboardist/singer managed the feat only once on the singles chart: her "Forget Me Nots" reached No. 23 in 1982.

Bobby Rydell's last top-10 hit, "Forget Him," started its inevitable trek back down the chart a week prior to the Beatles' first U.S. No. 1, "I Want To Hold Your Hand." And the British Invasion had begun . . .

Sade, born in Nigeria as Helen Folasade Adu, has scored platinum with each of her three albums; 1985's *Promise*, which contains the Top 5 single "The Sweetest Taboo," held the No. 1 slot for two weeks. Sade is also the name of her band.

Ssgt. Barry Sadler's two top-40 hits of 1966 have Hollywood associations: "The Ballad Of The Green Berets," No. 1 for five weeks, helped inspire the John Wayne film of the same name; "The 'A' Team," which peaked at No. 28, was later the name of a top-rated 80s TV show starring Mr. T.

Sa-Fire's late-80s success on an independent label brought the New York-based, dance-oriented singer to Mercury Records—where she released her debut album *I Wasn't Born Yesterday* in early 1991.

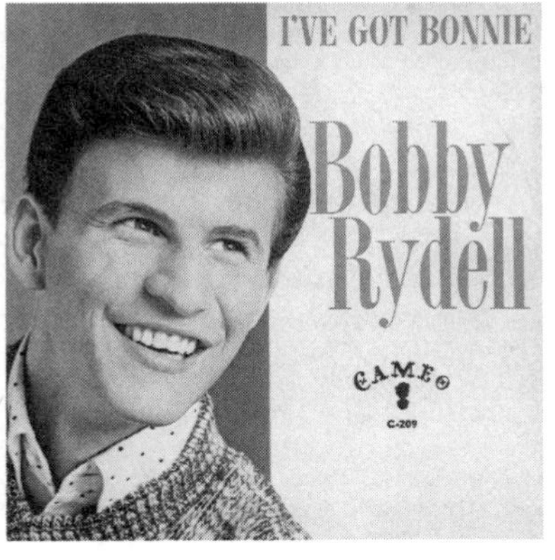

DATE	POS	WKS	ARTIST—RECORD TITLE	LABEL & NO.
			TALKING HEADS	
			New York City-based new wave quartet: David Byrne (lead singer, guitar), Jerry Harrison (keyboards, guitar), Tina Weymouth (bass) and husband Chris Frantz (drums). Formed as a trio of Byrne, Weymouth and Frantz at the Rhode Island School of Design. Harrison was a member of The Modern Lovers. Also see Tom Tom Club.	
12/23/78+	**26**	9	1. Take Me To The River	Sire 1032
9/03/83	**9**	11	**2. Burning Down The House**	Sire 29565
11/08/86	**25**	7	3. Wild Wild Life	Sire 28629
			TALK TALK	
			British rock band — Mark Hollis, lead singer.	
4/21/84	**31**	6	1. It's My Life	EMI America 8195
			TA MARA & THE SEEN	
			Minneapolis quintet led by Margaret Cox, a veteran Minneapolis night club singer. Group includes guitarist Oliver Leiber, son of songwriter Jerry Leiber (of Leiber & Stoller).	
11/30/85+	**24**	10	1. Everybody Dance	A&M 2768
			TAMS, The	
			Atlanta R&B quintet: brothers Charles and Joseph (lead singer) Pope, with Robert Smith, Floyd Ashton and Horace Key. First recorded for Swan in 1960.	
1/18/64	**9**	9	**1. What Kind Of Fool (Do You Think I Am)**	ABC-Para. 10502
			TANEGA, Norma	
			Born on 1/30/39 in Vallejo, California. Singer/songwriter/pianist/guitarist.	
3/19/66	**22**	6	1. Walkin' My Cat Named Dog	New Voice 807
			TARRIERS, The	
			Folk trio: Erik Darling (tenor, banjo), Bob Carey (bass, guitar) and movie actor Alan Arkin (baritone, guitar). Darling became a member of The Rooftop Singers.	
10/13/56	**9**	15	**1. Cindy, Oh Cindy** **VINCE MARTIN with THE TARRIERS** Juke Box #9 / Best Seller #12 / Top 100 #12 / Jockey #12	Glory 247
12/22/56+	**4**	16	**2. The Banana Boat Song** Juke Box #4 / Best Seller #5 / Top 100 #6 / Jockey #6	Glory 249
			TASTE OF HONEY, A	
			Soul-disco quartet, formed in Los Angeles in 1972. Consisted of Janice Marie Johnson (vocals, guitar), Hazel Payne (vocals, bass), Perry Kimble (keyboards) and Donald Johnson (drums). Re-formed in 1980 with Janice Johnson and Hazel Payne. Won the 1978 Best New Artist Grammy Award.	
7/22/78	**1**(3)	17	▲ **1. Boogie Oogie Oogie**	Capitol 4565
4/11/81	**3**	16	● **2. Sukiyaki**	Capitol 4953
			TAVARES	
			Family R&B group from New Bedford, Massachusetts. Consisted of brothers Ralph, Antone "Chubby," Feliciano "Butch," Arthur "Pooch" and Perry Lee "Tiny" Tavares. Worked as Chubby & The Turnpikes from 1964-69. Butch was married to Lola Falana.	
11/03/73	**35**	3	1. Check It Out	Capitol 3674
5/17/75	**25**	5	2. Remember What I Told You To Forget	Capitol 4010
8/23/75	**10**	13	**3. It Only Takes A Minute**	Capitol 4111
7/10/76	**15**	12	● 4. Heaven Must Be Missing An Angel (Part 1)	Capitol 4270
12/11/76	**34**	2	5. Don't Take Away The Music	Capitol 4348

DATE	POS	WKS	ARTIST—RECORD TITLE	LABEL & NO.
4/23/77	**22**	7	6. Whodunit	Capitol 4398
4/15/78	**32**	4	7. More Than A Woman from the film *Saturday Night Fever*	Capitol 4500
11/20/82	**33**	9	8. A Penny For Your Thoughts	RCA 13292
			TAYLOR, Andy	
			Born on 2/16/61 in Dolver-Hampton, England. Lead guitarist of Duran Duran and The Power Station.	
7/05/86	**24**	7	1. Take It Easy from the film *American Anthem*	Atlantic 89414
			TAYLOR, Bobby/The Vancouvers	
			Interracial sextet based in Vancouver, Canada. Included guitarist Tommy Chong (of Cheech & Chong fame), Wes Henderson, Robbie King, Ted Lewis and Eddie Patterson. Bobby Taylor discovered The Jackson 5.	
5/18/68	**29**	5	1. Does Your Mama Know About Me	Gordy 7069
			TAYLOR, James	
			Born on 3/12/48 in Boston. Singer/songwriter/guitarist. With older brother Alex in the Fabulous Corsairs in 1964. In New York group The Flying Machine in 1967, with friend Danny Kortchmar. Moved to England in 1968, recorded for Peter Asher. Married Carly Simon on 11/03/72; filed for divorce in 1982. In film *Two Lane Blacktop* with Dennis Wilson in 1973. Sister Kate and brothers Alex and Livingston also recorded.	
9/26/70	**3**	14	**1. Fire And Rain**	Warner 7423
3/20/71	**37**	1	2. Country Road	Warner 7460
6/19/71	**1**(1)	12	● **3. You've Got A Friend**	Warner 7498
10/16/71	**31**	5	4. Long Ago And Far Away backing vocal on above 2 by Joni Mitchell	Warner 7521
12/16/72+	**14**	9	5. Don't Let Me Be Lonely Tonight	Warner 7655
2/16/74	**5**	13	● **6. Mockingbird** **CARLY SIMON AND JAMES TAYLOR**	Elektra 45880
7/19/75	**5**	10	**7. How Sweet It Is (To Be Loved By You)**	Warner 8109
8/07/76	**22**	8	8. Shower The People	Warner 8222
7/09/77	**4**	13	**9. Handy Man**	Columbia 10557
11/05/77	**20**	9	10. Your Smiling Face	Columbia 10602
2/11/78	**17**	7	11. (What A) Wonderful World **ART GARFUNKEL with JAMES TAYLOR & PAUL SIMON**	Columbia 10676
9/23/78	**36**	3	12. Devoted To You **CARLY SIMON AND JAMES TAYLOR**	Elektra 45506
6/30/79	**28**	5	13. Up On The Roof	Columbia 11005
3/14/81	**11**	10	14. Her Town Too **JAMES TAYLOR AND J.D. SOUTHER**	Columbia 60514
			TAYLOR, John	
			Born on 6/20/60 in Birmingham, England. Bass guitarist of Duran Duran and The Power Station.	
4/05/86	**23**	6	1. I Do What I Do . . . theme from the film *9 1/2 Weeks*; backing vocal by Jonathan Elias	Capitol 5551

DATE	POS	WKS	ARTIST—RECORD TITLE	LABEL & NO.
			TAYLOR, Johnnie	
			Born on 5/05/38 in Crawfordsville, Arkansas. With gospel group the Highway QC's in Chicago, early 1950s. In vocal group the Five Echoes, recorded for Sabre in 1954. In the Soul Stirrers gospel group before going solo. First solo recording for Sar in 1961. Known as "The Soul Philosopher."	
11/02/68	**5**	13	● **1. Who's Making Love**	Stax 0009
1/25/69	**20**	8	2. Take Care Of Your Homework	Stax 0023
5/31/69	**36**	5	3. Testify (I Wonna)	Stax 0033
7/18/70	**37**	2	4. Steal Away	Stax 0068
11/14/70	**39**	2	5. I Am Somebody Part II	Stax 0078
2/13/71	**28**	5	6. Jody's Got Your Girl And Gone	Stax 0085
7/14/73	**11**	12	● 7. I Believe In You (You Believe In Me)	Stax 0161
10/27/73	**15**	8	8. Cheaper To Keep Her	Stax 0176
3/16/74	**34**	2	9. We're Getting Careless With Our Love	Stax 0193
3/06/76	**1**(4)	13	▲ **10. Disco Lady** first single certified platinum by R.I.A.A.	Columbia 10281
6/26/76	**33**	3	11. Somebody's Gettin' It all of above produced by Don Davis	Columbia 10334
			TAYLOR, Little Johnny	
			Born Johnny Young on 2/11/43 in Memphis. Blues singer/harmonica player. To Los Angeles in 1950. With Mighty Clouds Of Joy and Stars Of Bethel gospel groups. Duets with Ted Taylor (no relation) in the '70s.	
9/14/63	**19**	8	1. Part Time Love	Galaxy 722
			TAYLOR, Livingston	
			Born on 11/21/50 in Boston. James Taylor's younger brother.	
12/16/78+	**30**	5	1. I Will Be In Love With You	Epic 50604
9/13/80	**38**	2	2. First Time Love	Epic 50894
			TAYLOR, R. Dean	
			Born in Toronto in 1939. First recorded for Parry in 1960. Co-wrote The Supremes' hit "Love Child."	
9/19/70	**5**	13	**1. Indiana Wants Me**	Rare Earth 5013
			T-BONES, The	
			A Joe Saraceno studio production. Also see Hamilton, Joe Frank & Reynolds.	
12/25/65+	**3**	11	**1. No Matter What Shape (Your Stomach's In)** [I] tune is from an Alka Seltzer jingle	Liberty 55836
			TCHAIKOVSKY, Bram — see BRAM	
			TEARS FOR FEARS	
			British duo: Roland Orzabal (b: 8/22/61; vocals, guitar, keyboards) and Curt Smith (b: 6/24/61; vocals, bass). Adopted name from Arthur Janev's book *Prisoners of Pain.*	
4/13/85	**1**(2)	14	**1. Everybody Wants To Rule The World**	Mercury 880659
6/29/85	**1**(3)	13	● **2. Shout**	Mercury 880294
9/21/85	**3**	12	**3. Head Over Heels**	Mercury 880899
5/03/86	**27**	6	4. Mothers Talk	Mercury 884638
9/09/89	**2**(1)	12	**5. Sowing The Seeds Of Love**	Fontana 874710
1/27/90	**36**	2	6. Woman In Chains female vocal by Oleta Adams	Fontana 876248

DATE	POS	WKS	ARTIST—RECORD TITLE	LABEL & NO.
			TECHNIQUES	
11/25/57	**29**	2	1. Hey! Little Girl Best Seller #29 / Top 100 #33 first released on Stars 551 in 1957	Roulette 4030
			TECHNOTRONIC	
			Dance outfit created by Belgian DJ/producer Jo "Thomas DeQuincy" Bogaert and 17-year-old rapper Manuella "Ya Kid K" Komosi. Includes London rapper MC Eric. Non-vocalist Felly, a model, fronted the group for videos. Komosi and Felly are from Zaire.	
11/11/89+	**2**(2)	16	▲ **1. Pump Up The Jam** **TECHNOTRONIC featuring FELLY**	SBK 07311
2/17/90	**7**	12	● **2. Get Up! (Before The Night Is Over)**	SBK 07315
			TEDDY BEARS, The	
			Los Angeles trio: Phil Spector (b: 12/26/40 in the Bronx), Carol Connors (lead singer; real name: Annette Kleinbard) and Marshall Leib. Spector became a well-known writer and producer; owner of Philles Records. He was inducted into the Rock and Roll Hall of Fame in 1989.	
10/13/58	**1**(3)	18	**1. To Know Him, Is To Love Him**	Dore 503
			TEEGARDEN & VAN WINKLE	
			David Teegarden (drums) and Skip Knape (keyboards). Teegarden later joined Bob Seger's band, 1978-81.	
10/17/70	**22**	5	1. God, Love And Rock & Roll	Westbound 170
			TEENAGERS, The — see LYMON, Frankie	
			TEEN QUEENS, The	
			R&B duo formed in Los Angeles in 1955 by Betty and Rosie Collins, sisters of Aaron Collins of the Cadets/Jacks.	
3/10/56	**14**	8	1. Eddie My Love Best Seller #14 / Juke Box #16 / Top 100 #22	RPM 453
			TEE SET, The	
			Dutch quintet: Peter Tetteroo (vocals), Hans Van Eijck, Dill Bennink, Franklin Madjid and Joop Blom.	
2/07/70	**5**	10	**1. Ma Belle Amie**	Colossus 107
			TEMPO, Nino, & APRIL STEVENS	
			Nino (b: Antonio Lo Tempio on 1/06/35) and sister April (b: Carol Lo Tempio on 4/29/36) from Niagara Falls, New York. Prior to teaming up, Nino was a session saxophonist and April had recorded solo.	
10/05/63	**1**(1)	12	**1. Deep Purple** #1 hit for Larry Clinton & His Orchestra in 1939	Atco 6273
12/28/63+	**11**	7	2. Whispering #1 hit for Paul Whiteman & His Orchestra in 1920	Atco 6281
3/14/64	**32**	3	3. Stardust #1 hit for Isham Jones & His Orchestra in 1931	Atco 6286
10/01/66	**26**	5	4. All Strung Out	White Whale 236
			TEMPOS, The	
			Pittsburgh vocal quartet: Mike Lazo, Gene Schachter, Jim Drake and Tom Minoto.	
8/10/59	**23**	6	1. See You In September	Climax 102

DATE	POS	WKS	ARTIST—RECORD TITLE	LABEL & NO.
			TEMPTATIONS, The	
			White quartet from Flushing, New York: Neil Stevens, Larry Curtis, Artie Sands and Artie Marin.	
5/09/60	**29**	3	1. Barbara	Goldisc 3001
			TEMPTATIONS, The	
			Soul group formed in Detroit in 1960. Consisted of Eddie Kendricks, Paul Williams (d: 8/17/73), Melvin Franklin, Otis Williams and Elbridge Bryant, who was replaced by David Ruffin in 1964. Originally called the Primes and Elgins, first recorded for Miracle in 1961. Ruffin (d: 6/01/91 of drug overdose at age 50; cousin of Billy Stewart) replaced by Dennis Edwards (ex-Contours) in 1968. Kendricks and Paul Williams left in 1971, replaced by Ricky Owens (ex-Vibrations) and Richard Street. Owens was replaced by Damon Harris. Harris left in 1975, replaced by Glenn Leonard. Edwards left group, 1977-79, replaced by Louis Price. Ali Ollie Woodson replaced Edwards from 1984-87. 1988 lineup: Williams, Franklin, Street, Edwards and Ron Tyson. Recognized as America's all-time favorite soul group. Inducted into the Rock and Roll Hall of Fame in 1989.	
3/21/64	**11**	8	1. The Way You Do The Things You Do	Gordy 7028
7/04/64	**33**	4	2. I'll Be In Trouble	Gordy 7032
9/26/64	**26**	6	3. Girl (Why You Wanna Make Me Blue)	Gordy 7035
1/30/65	**1**(1)	11	**4. My Girl**	Gordy 7038
4/17/65	**18**	7	5. It's Growing	Gordy 7040
8/07/65	**17**	7	6. Since I Lost My Baby	Gordy 7043
11/06/65	**13**	6	7. My Baby	Gordy 7047
3/26/66	**29**	3	8. Get Ready	Gordy 7049
			all of above (except #3) written and produced by Smokey Robinson	
6/11/66	**13**	10	9. Ain't Too Proud To Beg	Gordy 7054
9/03/66	**3**	9	**10. Beauty Is Only Skin Deep**	Gordy 7055
12/03/66	**8**	8	**11. (I Know) I'm Losing You**	Gordy 7057
5/13/67	**8**	8	**12. All I Need**	Gordy 7061
8/12/67	**6**	9	**13. You're My Everything**	Gordy 7063
10/21/67	**14**	8	14. (Loneliness Made Me Realize) It's You That I Need	Gordy 7065
1/27/68	**4**	11	**15. I Wish It Would Rain**	Gordy 7068
5/18/68	**13**	8	16. I Could Never Love Another (After Loving You)	Gordy 7072
8/17/68	**26**	5	17. Please Return Your Love To Me	Gordy 7074
11/23/68+	**6**	11	**18. Cloud Nine**	Gordy 7081
12/14/68+	**2**(2)	12	**19. I'm Gonna Make You Love Me**	Motown 1137
			DIANA ROSS AND THE SUPREMES & THE TEMPTATIONS	
2/22/69	**6**	11	**20. Run Away Child, Running Wild**	Gordy 7084
3/22/69	**25**	6	21. I'll Try Something New	Motown 1142
			DIANA ROSS AND THE SUPREMES & THE TEMPTATIONS	
5/31/69	**20**	6	22. Don't Let The Joneses Get You Down	Gordy 7086
8/30/69	**1**(2)	15	**23. I Can't Get Next To You**	Gordy 7093
1/24/70	**7**	10	**24. Psychedelic Shack**	Gordy 7096
6/06/70	**3**	13	**25. Ball Of Confusion (That's What The World Is Today)**	Gordy 7099
10/17/70	**33**	4	26. Ungena Za Ulimwengu (Unite The World)	Gordy 7102
2/20/71	**1**(2)	13	**27. Just My Imagination (Running Away With Me)**	Gordy 7105
11/20/71	**18**	8	28. Superstar (Remember How You Got Where You Are)	Gordy 7111

DATE	POS	WKS	ARTIST—RECORD TITLE	LABEL & NO.
3/18/72	**30**	4	29. Take A Look Around	Gordy 7115
10/28/72	**1**(1)	12	**30. Papa Was A Rollin' Stone**	Gordy 7121
3/10/73	**7**	11	**31. Masterpiece**	Gordy 7126
7/07/73	**40**	2	32. The Plastic Man	Gordy 7129
9/08/73	**35**	4	33. Hey Girl (I Like Your Style)	Gordy 7131
1/12/74	**27**	4	34. Let Your Hair Down	Gordy 7133
2/01/75	**40**	1	35. Happy People co-written by Lionel Richie	Gordy 7138
4/19/75	**26**	9	36. Shakey Ground	Gordy 7142
8/23/75	**37**	2	37. Glasshouse	Gordy 7144
			10cc	
			English art-rock group which evolved from Hotlegs. Consisted of Eric Stewart (guitar), Graham Gouldman (bass), Lol Creme (guitar, keyboards) and Kevin Godley (drums). Stewart and Gouldman were members of The Mindbenders. Godley and Creme left in 1976, replaced by drummer Paul Burgess. Added members Rick Fenn, Stuart Tosh and Duncan MacKay in 1978. Gouldman later in duo, Wax. Also see Godley & Creme.	
6/14/75	**2**(3)	11	**1. I'm Not In Love**	Mercury 73678
1/29/77	**5**	14	● **2. The Things We Do For Love**	Mercury 73875
6/25/77	**40**	1	3. People In Love	Mercury 73917
			TEN YEARS AFTER	
			British blues-rock quartet formed in 1967: Alvin Lee (b: 12/19/44, Nottingham, England; vocals, guitar), Leo Lyons (bass), Chick Churchill (keyboards) and Ric Lee (drums). Inactive as band from 1975-87.	
11/20/71	**40**	2	1. I'd Love To Change The World	Columbia 45457
			TEPPER, Robert	
			Native of Baylor, New Jersey.	
3/01/86	**22**	7	1. No Easy Way Out from the film *Rocky IV*	Scotti Br. 05750
			TERRELL, Tammi — see GAYE, Marvin	
			TESLA	
			Sacramento hard-rock quintet: Jeff Keith (vocals), Frank Hannon, Tommy Skeoch, Brian Wheat and Troy Luccketta. Band named after the inventor of radio, Nikola Tesla.	
11/11/89+	**10**	16	● **1. Love Song**	Geffen 22856
2/09/91	**8**	13	**2. Signs**	Geffen 19653#
			TEX, Joe	
			Born Joseph Arrington, Jr. on 8/08/33 in Rogers, Texas; died of a heart attack on 8/13/82. Sang with local gospel groups. Won recording contract at Apollo Theater talent contest in 1954. First recorded for King in 1955. Became a convert to the Muslim faith, changed name to "Joseph Hazziez" in July 1972.	
1/02/65	**5**	8	**1. Hold What You've Got**	Dial 4001
10/16/65	**23**	5	2. I Want To (Do Everything For You)	Dial 4016
1/01/66	**29**	4	3. A Sweet Woman Like You	Dial 4022
6/18/66	**39**	1	4. S.Y.S.L.J.F.M. (The Letter Song)	Dial 4028
4/08/67	**35**	3	5. Show Me	Dial 4055
11/25/67	**10**	10	● **6. Skinny Legs And All**	Dial 4063
3/02/68	**33**	3	7. Men Are Gettin' Scarce	Dial 4069
2/26/72	**2**(2)	16	● **8. I Gotcha**	Dial 1010

DATE	POS	WKS	ARTIST—RECORD TITLE	LABEL & NO.
			all of above written by Joe Tex	
4/23/77	**12**	10	● 9. Ain't Gonna Bump No More (With No Big Fat Woman)	Epic 50313
			all of above produced by Buddy Killen	
			THEM	
			Belfast, Northern Ireland rock quintet: Van Morrison (lead singer), Billy Harrison, Alan Henderson, John McAuley and Peter Bardens. Disbanded in late 1966. Morrison went on to a highly successful solo career. Bardens formed Camel in 1972; recorded solo in 1987.	
6/26/65	**24**	6	1. Here Comes The Night	Parrot 9749
12/04/65	**33**	2	2. Mystic Eyes [I]	Parrot 9796
			THINK	
			Studio group assembled by producers Lou Stallman and Bobby Susser.	
1/01/72	**23**	5	1. Once You Understand	Laurie 3583
			featuring dialogue between a teenager and his parents	
			THIN LIZZY	
			Dublin, Ireland rock quartet led by Phil Lynott (b: 8/20/51, Dublin, d: 1/04/86; vocals, bass). Gary Moore (lead guitarist, 1978-79) hit the pop charts as a solo act in 1991.	
6/05/76	**12**	9	1. The Boys Are Back In Town	Mercury 73786
			38 SPECIAL	
			Florida Southern-rock sextet: Donnie Van Zant (younger brother of Lynyrd Skynyrd's Ronnie Van Zant; lead singer), Don Barnes, Jeff Carlisi, Steve Brookins, Jack Grondin and Larry Jungstrom (replaced Ken Lyons in 1979). By 1988, Barnes and Brookins replaced by Danny Chauncey and Max Carl.	
4/18/81	**27**	6	1. Hold On Loosely	A&M 2316
5/22/82	**10**	12	**2. Caught Up In You**	A&M 2412
10/02/82	**38**	2	3. You Keep Runnin' Away	A&M 2431
12/03/83+	**19**	9	4. If I'd Been The One	A&M 2594
2/18/84	**20**	8	5. Back Where You Belong	A&M 2615
10/27/84	**25**	5	6. Teacher Teacher	Capitol 5405
			from the film *Teachers*	
5/24/86	**14**	9	7. Like No Other Night	A&M 2831
			THIRTY EIGHT SPECIAL:	
3/11/89	**6**	14	**8. Second Chance**	A&M 1273
			THOMAS, B.J.	
			Born Billy Joe Thomas on 8/07/42 in Hugo, Oklahoma; raised in Rosenberg, Texas. Sang in church choir as a teenager. Joined band, the Triumphs, while in high school. B.J. has featured gospel music since 1976.	
3/12/66	**8**	10	**1. I'm So Lonesome I Could Cry**	Scepter 12129
			B.J. THOMAS AND THE TRIUMPHS	
6/04/66	**22**	5	2. Mama	Scepter 12139
7/23/66	**34**	4	3. Billy And Sue	Hickory 1395
			B.J. THOMAS AND THE TRIUMPHS	
			first released on Bragg 103 and then on Warner 5491 in 1964	
8/03/68	**28**	7	4. The Eyes Of A New York Woman	Scepter 12219
12/14/68+	**5**	12	● **5. Hooked On A Feeling**	Scepter 12230
11/22/69+	**1**(4)	19	● **6. Raindrops Keep Fallin' On My Head**	Scepter 12265
			from the film *Butch Cassidy and the Sundance Kid*	
4/11/70	**26**	6	7. Everybody's Out Of Town	Scepter 12277

DATE	POS	WKS	ARTIST—RECORD TITLE	LABEL & NO.
7/11/70	**9**	10	**8. I Just Can't Help Believing**	Scepter 12283
1/09/71	**38**	3	9. Most Of All	Scepter 12299
3/13/71	**16**	9	10. No Love At All	Scepter 12307
8/14/71	**34**	3	11. Mighty Clouds Of Joy	Scepter 12320
2/26/72	**15**	9	12. Rock And Roll Lullaby featuring Duane Eddy (guitar) and The Blossoms (backing vocals)	Scepter 12344
3/01/75	**1**(1)	14	● **13. (Hey Won't You Play) Another Somebody Done Somebody Wrong Song**	ABC 12054
8/06/77	**17**	10	14. Don't Worry Baby	MCA 40735
			THOMAS, Carla	
			Born on 12/21/42 in Memphis. Daughter of Rufus Thomas. Sang with the Teentown Singers at age 10. First recorded with Rufus for Satellite in 1960. Also recorded duets with Otis Redding.	
2/20/61	**10**	10	**1. Gee Whiz (Look At His Eyes)**	Atlantic 2086
9/24/66	**14**	10	2. B-A-B-Y	Stax 195
			OTIS & CARLA:	
6/03/67	**26**	4	3. Tramp	Stax 216
9/23/67	**30**	2	4. Knock On Wood	Stax 228
			THOMAS, Ian	
			Canadian singer/songwriter. Brother of SCTV comedian Dave Thomas, aka Bob McKenzie.	
12/29/73+	**34**	3	1. Painted Ladies	Janus 224
			THOMAS, Irma	
			Born Irma Lee on 2/18/41 in Ponchatoula, Louisiana. The Soul Queen of New Orleans. Discovered by New Orleans bandleader Tommy Ridgley.	
4/25/64	**17**	7	1. Wish Someone Would Care	Imperial 66013
			THOMAS, Rufus	
			Born on 3/26/17 in Cayce, Mississippi and raised in Memphis. R&B singer/songwriter/choreographer. Father of singers Carla and Vaneese Thomas. First recorded for Talent in 1950. DJ at WDIA-Memphis from 1953-74. Recorded for Alligator Records in the late '80s.	
11/02/63	**10**	9	**1. Walking The Dog**	Stax 140
2/28/70	**28**	8	2. Do The Funky Chicken	Stax 0059
1/23/71	**25**	8	3. (Do The) Push And Pull Part I	Stax 0079
9/18/71	**31**	4	4. The Breakdown (Part I)	Stax 0098
			THOMAS, Timmy	
			Born on 11/13/44 in Evansville, Indiana. Soul singer/songwriter/keyboardist. Studio musician at Gold Wax Records in Memphis. Moved to Miami in 1970. Session work for Betty Wright and KC & The Sunshine Band.	
12/23/72+	**3**	11	**1. Why Can't We Live Together**	Glades 1703
			THOMPSON, Chris — see NIGHT	
			THOMPSON, Kay	
			Born on 11/09/13 in St. Louis. Wrote "Eloise" series of children's books. In the film musical *Funny Face*, 1956.	
3/17/56	**39**	2	1. Eloise [N]	Cadence 1286

DATE	POS	WKS	ARTIST—RECORD TITLE	LABEL & NO.
			THOMPSON, Sue	
			Born Eva Sue McKee on 7/19/26 in Nevada, Missouri and raised in San Jose, California. Became a popular country singer in the '70s.	
9/25/61	**5**	11	**1. Sad Movies (Make Me Cry)**	Hickory 1153
1/13/62	**3**	11	**2. Norman**	Hickory 1159
7/21/62	**31**	5	3. Have A Good Time	Hickory 1174
10/20/62	**17**	6	4. James (Hold The Ladder Steady)	Hickory 1183
2/06/65	**23**	4	5. Paper Tiger	Hickory 1284
			1, 2, 4, 5: written by John D. Loudermilk	
			THOMPSON TWINS	
			British trio: Tom Bailey (b: 1/18/56, England; lead singer, synthesizer), Alannah Currie (b: 9/28/57, New Zealand; xylophone, percussion) and Joe Leeway (b: 11/15/57, London; conga, synthesizer). Leeway left in 1986.	
3/12/83	**30**	5	1. Lies	Arista 1024
2/25/84	**3**	15	**2. Hold Me Now**	Arista 9164
6/09/84	**11**	9	3. Doctor! Doctor!	Arista 9209
10/05/85	**6**	14	**4. Lay Your Hands On Me**	Arista 9396
1/25/86	**8**	11	**5. King For A Day**	Arista 9450
4/25/87	**31**	5	6. Get That Love	Arista 9577
10/28/89	**28**	4	7. Sugar Daddy	Warner 22819
			THOMSON, Ali	
			Singer/songwriter from Glasgow, Scotland. Younger brother of Supertramp's Dougie Thomson.	
7/12/80	**15**	9	1. Take A Little Rhythm	A&M 2243
			THREE DEGREES, The	
			Philadelphia R&B trio discovered by Richard Barrett. Originally consisted of Fayette Pinkney, Linda Turner and Shirley Porter. Turner and Porter replaced by Sheila Ferguson and Valerie Holiday in 1966.	
7/25/70	**29**	4	1. Maybe	Roulette 7079
3/16/74	**1**(2)	14	● **2. TSOP (The Sound Of Philadelphia)** [I]	Phil. Int. 3540
			MFSB featuring THE THREE DEGREES	
			theme from the TV show "Soul Train"	
10/19/74	**2**(1)	13	● **3. When Will I See You Again**	Phil. Int. 3550
			THREE DOG NIGHT	
			Los Angeles pop-rock group formed in 1968 featuring lead singers Danny Hutton (b: 9/10/42), Cory Wells (b: 2/05/42) and Chuck Negron (b: 6/08/42). Disbanded in the mid-1970s. Re-formed in the mid-1980s.	
3/29/69	**29**	4	1. Try A Little Tenderness	Dunhill 4177
5/31/69	**5**	12	● **2. One**	Dunhill 4191
			written by Nilsson	
8/16/69	**4**	12	**3. Easy To Be Hard**	Dunhill 4203
			from the Broadway Rock Musical *Hair*	
11/08/69	**10**	12	**4. Eli's Coming**	Dunhill 4215
			written by Laura Nyro	
3/07/70	**15**	8	5. Celebrate	Dunhill 4229
			all of above produced by Gabriel Mekler	
6/06/70	**1**(2)	13	● **6. Mama Told Me (Not To Come)**	Dunhill 4239
			written by Randy Newman	
9/12/70	**15**	8	7. Out In The Country	Dunhill 4250
12/05/70+	**19**	9	8. One Man Band	Dunhill 4262

DATE	POS	WKS	ARTIST—RECORD TITLE	LABEL & NO.
3/27/71	**1**(6)	15	● **9. Joy To The World**	Dunhill 4272
7/17/71	**7**	11	**10. Liar**	Dunhill 4282
			written by Russ Ballard	
11/20/71	**4**	10	● **11. An Old Fashioned Love Song**	Dunhill 4294
1/08/72	**5**	10	**12. Never Been To Spain**	Dunhill 4299
4/01/72	**12**	8	13. The Family Of Man	Dunhill 4306
8/26/72	**1**(1)	9	● **14. Black & White**	Dunhill 4317
12/09/72+	**19**	9	15. Pieces Of April	Dunhill 4331
6/02/73	**3**	10	● **16. Shambala**	Dunhill 4352
11/17/73	**17**	6	17. Let Me Serenade You	Dunhill 4370
			above 12 produced by Richard Podolor	
4/13/74	**4**	12	● **18. The Show Must Go On**	Dunhill 4382
7/13/74	**16**	8	19. Sure As I'm Sittin' Here	Dunhill 15001
11/02/74	**33**	3	20. Play Something Sweet (Brickyard Blues)	Dunhill 15013
8/09/75	**32**	3	21. Til The World Ends	ABC 12114
			THUNDER, Johnny	
			Born Gil Hamilton on 8/15/41 in Leesburg, Florida. R&B singer discovered by producer Teddy Vann.	
1/05/63	**4**	9	**1. Loop De Loop**	Diamond 129
			THUNDERCLAP NEWMAN	
			British trio: Andy Newman (keyboards), John "Speedy" Keen (vocals) and Jimmy McCulloch (guitarist with Wings, 1975-77; died on 9/27/79 [age 26]). Group put together by Pete Townshend.	
10/25/69	**37**	2	1. Something In The Air	Track 2656
			from the film *The Magic Christian*; "Bubbled Under" on 10/24/70 on Track 2769	
			TIERRA	
			East Los Angeles group formed in 1972. Band led by the Salas brothers: Steve (trombone, timbales) and Rudy (guitar); both formerly with El Chicano.	
12/13/80+	**18**	15	1. Together	Boardwalk 5702
			TIFFANY	
			Tiffany Darwisch, born on 10/02/71. California pop singer, originally from Oklahoma.	
9/26/87	**1**(2)	13	**1. I Think We're Alone Now**	MCA 53167
12/12/87+	**1**(2)	14	**2. Could've Been**	MCA 53231
3/12/88	**7**	9	**3. I Saw Him Standing There**	MCA 53285
			female version of The Beatles' "I Saw Her Standing There"	
12/03/88+	**6**	14	**4. All This Time**	MCA 53371
4/01/89	**35**	1	5. Radio Romance	MCA 53623
			TIJUANA BRASS, The — see ALPERT, Herb	
			TILLOTSON, Johnny	
			Born on 4/20/39 in Jacksonville, Florida; raised in Palatka, Florida. On local radio "Young Folks Revue" from age nine. DJ on WWPF. Appeared on the "Toby Dowdy" TV show in Jacksonville, then own show. Signed by Cadence Records in 1958. In the film *Just for Fun*.	
10/24/60	**2**(1)	12	**1. Poetry In Motion**	Cadence 1384
2/06/61	**25**	5	2. Jimmy's Girl	Cadence 1391
8/28/61	**7**	8	**3. Without You**	Cadence 1404
1/20/62	**35**	1	4. Dreamy Eyes [R]	Cadence 1409

DATE	POS	WKS	ARTIST—RECORD TITLE	LABEL & NO.
			originally charted in 1958 (POS 63)	
5/19/62	**3**	12	**5. It Keeps Right On A-Hurtin'**	Cadence 1418
8/25/62	**17**	6	6. Send Me The Pillow You Dream On	Cadence 1424
11/17/62	**24**	5	7. I Can't Help It (If I'm Still In Love With You)	Cadence 1432
			classic country hit by Hank Williams	
3/23/63	**24**	6	8. Out Of My Mind	Cadence 1434
8/24/63	**18**	7	9. You Can Never Stop Me Loving You	Cadence 1437
11/30/63+	**7**	10	**10. Talk Back Trembling Lips**	MGM 13181
3/14/64	**37**	2	11. Worried Guy	MGM 13193
6/06/64	**36**	2	12. I Rise, I Fall	MGM 13232
11/28/64	**31**	6	13. She Understands Me	MGM 13284
10/02/65	**35**	2	14. Heartaches By The Number	MGM 13376
			'TIL TUESDAY	
			Boston pop quartet: Aimee Mann (lead singer, bass), Michael Hausmann (drums), Robert Holmes (guitar) and Joey Pesce (keyboards; replaced by Michael Montes in 1988).	
5/18/85	**8**	13	**1. Voices Carry**	Epic 04795
11/01/86	**26**	5	2. What About Love	Epic 06289
			TIMBUK 3	
			Austin-based, husband-and-wife duo: Pat and Barbara Kooyman MacDonald. Met while Barbara was attending the University of Wisconsin in 1978.	
11/22/86	**19**	9	1. The Future's So Bright, I Gotta Wear Shades	I.R.S. 52940
			TIME, The	
			Funk group formed in Minneapolis by Prince and Morris Day in 1981. Original lineup: Morris Day (lead singer), Terry Lewis, Jimmy "Jam" Harris, Monte Moir, Jesse Johnson and Jellybean Johnson. Lewis, Harris and Moir left prior to band's featured role in film *Purple Rain*. Paul "St. Paul" Peterson and Lewis' brother, Jerome Benton, joined in 1984; group disbanded later that year. Day and Jesse Johnson went solo; Lewis and Harris became a highly successful songwriting/producing team. Lewis married Karyn White. Original lineup plus Benton re-grouped in 1990.	
1/05/85	**20**	10	1. Jungle Love	Warner 29181
4/13/85	**36**	2	2. The Bird	Warner 29094
			above 2 from the film *Purple Rain*	
7/14/90	**9**	11	● **3. Jerk-Out**	Paisley P. 19750
			TIMES TWO	
			Male duo of vocalists/keyboardists from Pt. Reyes, California: Shanti Jones and Johnny Dollar.	
4/23/88	**21**	8	1. Strange But True	Reprise 27998
			TIMEX SOCIAL CLUB	
			Berkeley, California rap group led by vocalist Michael Marshall; produced by Jay King, who later formed and fronted Club Nouveau.	
7/12/86	**8**	12	**1. Rumors**	Jay 7001
			TIMMY -T-	
			Timmy Torres — native of Fresno, California.	
5/05/90	**40**	1	1. Time After Time	Jam City 5003#
1/19/91	**1**(1)	16	▲ **2. One More Try**	Quality 15114

DATE	POS	WKS	ARTIST—RECORD TITLE	LABEL & NO.
			TIN TIN	
			Australian duo: Steve Kipner (keyboards) and Steve Groves (guitar). Disbanded in 1973. Kipner later co-wrote Chicago's "Hard Habit To Break" and Olivia Newton-John's "Physical" and "Twist Of Fate."	
5/08/71	**20**	6	1. Toast And Marmalade For Tea	Atco 6794
			produced by Maurice Gibb of the Bee Gees	
			TINY TIM	
			Born Herbert Khaury on 4/12/30 in New York City. Novelty singer/ukulele player. National phenomenon when he married "Miss Vicki" on "The Tonight Show" on 12/18/69; divorced in 1977.	
6/08/68	**17**	6	1. Tip-Toe Thru' The Tulips With Me [N]	Reprise 0679
			#1 hit (10 weeks) for Nick Lucas in 1929	
			TOBY BEAU	
			Texas pop quintet: Balde Silva (vocals), Danny McKenna, Rob Young, Steve Zipper and Ron Rose.	
7/01/78	**13**	12	1. My Angel Baby	RCA 11250
			TODD, Art and Dotty	
			Pop duo consisting of Arthur W. Todd (b: 3/11/20) and Dotty Todd (b: 6/22/23), both from Elizabeth, New Jersey. Married in 1941.	
4/21/58	**6**	11	**1. Chanson d'Amour (Song Of Love)**	Era 1064
			Jockey #6 / Best Seller #13 / Top 100 #13	
			TODD, Nick	
			Pat Boone's younger brother. Born Nicholas Boone on 6/01/35 in Jacksonville, Florida.	
2/10/58	**21**	2	1. At The Hop	Dot 15675
			Jockey #21 / Top 100 #70 orchestra directed by Billy Vaughn	
			TOKENS, The	
			Vocal group originally formed as the Linc-Tones at Lincoln High School in Brooklyn in 1955. Consisted of Hank Medress, Neil Sedaka, Eddie Rabkin and Cynthia Zolitin. First recorded for Melba in 1956. Rabkin replaced by Jay Siegel in 1956. Zolitin and Sedaka left in 1958. Medress then formed Darrell & The Oxfords, 1958-59, then re-formed The Tokens with brothers Phil and Mitch Margo and recorded for Warwick in 1960. Formed own label, B.T. Puppy, in 1964. Medress produced Tony Orlando & Dawn, and then left The Tokens, who continued as a trio and recorded as Cross Country in 1973.	
4/24/61	**15**	6	1. Tonight I Fell In Love	Warwick 615
11/27/61	**1**(3)	13	• **2. The Lion Sleeps Tonight**	RCA 7954
			also known as "Wimoweh"; a South African Zulu song	
4/09/66	**30**	5	3. I Hear Trumpets Blow	B.T. Puppy 518
5/20/67	**36**	2	4. Portrait Of My Love	Warner 5900
			TOMMY TUTONE	
			San Francisco rock band led by Tommy Heath (vocals) and Jim Keller (lead guitar).	
6/21/80	**38**	2	1. Angel Say No	Columbia 11278
3/13/82	**4**	16	**2. 867-5309/Jenny**	Columbia 02646
			TOM TOM CLUB	
			Studio project formed by Talking Heads' members Chris Frantz and wife Tina Weymouth. Much production work for Ziggy Marley & The Melody Makers.	
4/10/82	**31**	4	1. Genius Of Love	Sire 49882

DATE	POS	WKS	ARTIST—RECORD TITLE	LABEL & NO.
			TONE LOC	
			L.A.-based rapper, Anthony Smith. Stage name derived from his Spanish nickname "Antonio Loco."	
12/24/88+	**2**(1)	14	▲ **1. Wild Thing**	Delicious 102
3/18/89	**3**	11	▲ **2. Funky Cold Medina**	Delicious 104
			TONEY, Oscar, Jr.	
			Born on 5/26/39 in Selma, Alabama and raised in Columbus, Georgia. R&B singer.	
6/17/67	**23**	5	1. For Your Precious Love	Bell 672
			TONY AND JOE	
			Tony Savonne and Joe Saraceno. Also see The T-Bones.	
8/04/58	**33**	1	1. The Freeze Hot 100 #33 / Best Seller #39	Era 1075
			TONY! TONI! TONE!	
			R&B-funk band from Oakland, California. Nucleus of group: brothers Dwayne and Raphael Wiggins, with cousin Timothy Christian.	
9/22/90	**9**	17	● **1. Feels Good**	Wing 877436
2/02/91	**34**	4	2. It Never Rains (In Southern California)	Wing 879068
			TORME, Mel	
			Born Melvin Howard on 9/13/25 in Chicago. Jazz singer/songwriter/pianist/drummer/actor. Wrote Nat King Cole's "The Christmas Song." Frequently appears as himself on TV's "Night Court."	
12/15/62	**36**	3	1. Comin' Home Baby	Atlantic 2165
			TORNADOES, The	
			English surf-rock instrumental quintet organized by producer Joe Meek in 1962. Original lineup: Alan Caddy (lead guitar), George Bellamy, Roger LaVerne Jackson, Heinz Burt and Clem Cattini. Meek committed suicide on 2/03/67.	
11/17/62	**1**(3)	13	**1. Telstar** [I]	London 9561
			TOROK, Mitchell	
			Born on 10/28/29 in Houston. Singer/songwriter/guitarist. First recorded in 1948.	
4/29/57	**25**	3	1. Pledge Of Love Best Seller #25 / Top 100 #26	Decca 30230
8/31/59	**27**	6	2. Caribbean [R] same version charted in 1953 (POS 26) on Abbott 140	Guyden 2018
			TOTO	
			Pop-rock group formed in Los Angeles in 1978. Consisted of Bobby Kimball (born Robert Toteaux; vocals), Steve Lukather (guitar), David Paich and Steve Porcaro (keyboards), David Hungate (bass) and Jeff Porcaro (drums). Prominent session musicians, most notably behind Boz Scaggs in the late '70s. Hungate was replaced by Mike Porcaro in 1983. (The Porcaros are brothers.) Kimball replaced by Fergie Frederiksen in 1984; Frederiksen replaced by Joseph Williams (conductor John's son) in 1986. Steve Porcaro left in 1988. Paich and his father, Marty, won an Emmy for writing the theme to the TV series "Ironside."	
11/11/78+	**5**	14	● **1. Hold The Line**	Columbia 10830
2/09/80	**26**	8	2. 99	Columbia 11173
5/08/82	**2**(5)	18	**3. Rosanna**	Columbia 02811
9/11/82	**30**	5	4. Make Believe	Columbia 03143
11/20/82+	**1**(1)	16	**5. Africa**	Columbia 03335

DATE	POS	WKS	ARTIST—RECORD TITLE	LABEL & NO.
3/26/83	**10**	12	**6. I Won't Hold You Back**	Columbia 03597
11/24/84	**30**	6	7. Stranger In Town	Columbia 04672
9/27/86	**11**	12	8. I'll Be Over You	Columbia 06280
2/07/87	**38**	2	9. Without Your Love	Columbia 06570
3/26/88	**22**	8	10. Pamela	Columbia 07715
			TOWER OF POWER	
			Interracial Oakland-based, R&B-funk band formed by sax player Emilio "Mimi" Castillo in the late '60s. Lenny Williams sang lead from 1972-75. Originally known as the Motowns.	
8/26/72	**29**	5	1. You're Still A Young Man	Warner 7612
6/16/73	**17**	11	2. So Very Hard To Go	Warner 7687
8/24/74	**26**	4	3. Don't Change Horses (In The Middle Of A Stream)	Warner 7828
			TOWNSEND, Ed	
			Born on 4/16/29 in Fayetteville, Tennessee. R&B singer/songwriter. His son David is a member of Surface. Wrote Marvin Gaye's "Let's Get It On."	
4/28/58	**13**	13	1. For Your Love Jockey #13 / Best Seller #15 / Top 100 #15	Capitol 3926
			TOWNSHEND, Pete	
			Born on 5/19/45 in London. Lead guitarist/songwriter of The Who. First solo album *Who Came First*, 1972. Own publishing house, Eel Pie Press, mid-1970s. Currently plagued by a significant hearing loss.	
7/05/80	**9**	12	**1. Let My Love Open The Door**	Atco 7217
12/21/85+	**26**	7	2. Face The Face	Atco 99590
			TOYS, The	
			Soul trio from Woodrow Wilson High School, Jamaica, New York: Barbara Harris, June Montiero and Barbara Parritt. Appearances on "Shindig" TV show in 1965. In film *The Girl in Daddy's Bikini.*	
10/02/65	**2**(3)	11	● **1. A Lover's Concerto** adapted from Bach's *Minuet in G*	DynoVoice 209
1/01/66	**18**	6	2. Attack	DynoVoice 214
			T'PAU	
			Group from Shrewsbury, England — Carol Decker, lead singer. Band named after a Vulcan Princess in an episode of the TV series "Star Trek."	
6/06/87	**4**	16	**1. Heart And Soul**	Virgin 99466
			TRADE WINDS, The	
			New York City pop singing/songwriting/production duo: Pete Anders (Andreoli) and Vinnie Poncia. First recorded with group, The Videls. Also recorded as The Innocence. Poncia produced several albums for Ringo Starr and Melissa Manchester.	
2/27/65	**32**	4	1. New York's A Lonely Town	Red Bird 020
			TRAMMPS, The	
			Philadelphia disco group. Key members: Jimmy Ellis (lead tenor), Earl Young (lead bass), Harold and Stanley Wade (tenors) and Robert Upchurch (baritone). Own Golden Fleece label in 1973.	
2/21/76	**35**	4	1. Hold Back The Night	Buddah 507
6/05/76	**27**	5	2. That's Where The Happy People Go	Atlantic 3306
3/25/78	**11**	13	3. Disco Inferno in the film *Saturday Night Fever*	Atlantic 3389

DATE	POS	WKS	ARTIST—RECORD TITLE	LABEL & NO.
			TRASHMEN, The	
			Minneapolis/St. Paul surf-rock quartet: Tony Andreason, Dal Winslow, Bob Reed and Steve Wahrer. Both hits taken from tunes by The Rivingtons: "Papa-Oom-Mow-Mow" and "The Bird's The Word." Wahrer died of throat cancer on 1/21/89 (age 47).	
12/28/63+	**4**	10	**1. Surfin' Bird**	Garrett 4002
2/29/64	**30**	4	2. Bird Dance Beat	Garrett 4003
			TRAVIS & BOB	
			Travis Pritchett and Bob Weaver from Jackson, Alabama.	
4/06/59	**8**	9	**1. Tell Him No**	Sandy 1017
			TRAVOLTA, John	
			Born on 2/18/54 in Englewood, New Jersey. Vinnie Barbarino on the TV series "Welcome Back Kotter." Starred in the films *Saturday Night Fever*, *Grease*, *Urban Cowboy*, *Look Who's Talking* and others. Married actress Kelly Preston on 9/05/91.	
6/12/76	**10**	10	**1. Let Her In**	Midland I. 10623
11/27/76	**38**	2	2. Whenever I'm Away From You	Midland I. 10780
3/19/77	**34**	3	3. All Strung Out On You	Midland I. 10907
			JOHN TRAVOLTA AND OLIVIA NEWTON-JOHN:	
4/08/78	**1**(1)	16	▲ **4. You're The One That I Want**	RSO 891
8/19/78	**5**	12	● **5. Summer Nights**	RSO 906
			above 2 from the film *Grease*	
			TREMELOES, The	
			British pop-rock quartet: Alan Blakely, Dave Munden, Ricky West and Len "Chip" Hawkes. Group originally formed by Brian Poole (b: 11/03/41 in England). Alan was the brother of Mike Blakely of Christie. Hawkes is the father of singer Chesney Hawkes.	
5/06/67	**13**	8	1. Here Comes My Baby	Epic 10139
			written by Cat Stevens	
7/15/67	**11**	10	2. Silence Is Golden	Epic 10184
10/21/67	**36**	4	3. Even The Bad Times Are Good	Epic 10233
			TRESVANT, Ralph	
			Member of New Edition. Born on 5/16/68 and raised in Roxbury, Massachusetts.	
11/17/90+	**4**	16	● **1. Sensitivity**	MCA 53932#
4/06/91	**34**	3	2. Stone Cold Gentleman	MCA 54043#
			guest rapper: Bobby Brown	
			T. REX	
			British rock group led by Marc Bolan (born Marc Feld on 7/30/47 in London; killed in an auto accident on 9/16/77).	
1/29/72	**10**	11	**1. Bang A Gong (Get It On)**	Reprise 1032
			TRIPLETS, The	
			Triplet sisters Diana, Sylvia and Vicky Villegas, born on 4/18/65, seven minutes apart. Raised in Mexico by their American mother and Mexican father. Gained recognition after winning an MTV Basement Contest in 1986.	
4/06/91	**14**	10	1. You Don't Have To Go Home Tonight	Mercury 878864

DATE	POS	WKS	ARTIST—RECORD TITLE	LABEL & NO.
			TRIUMPH	
			Canadian hard-rock trio formed in Toronto in 1975. Consisted of Rik Emmett (guitar, vocals), Gil Moore (drums, vocals) and Mike Levine (keyboards, bass). Emmett went solo in 1988.	
8/25/79	**38**	3	1. Hold On	RCA 11569
10/18/86	**27**	5	2. Somebody's Out There	MCA 52898
			TRIUMPHS, The — see THOMAS, B.J.	
			TROGGS, The	
			British rock quartet from Andover, England: Reg Presley (real name: Reg Ball; lead singer), Chris Britton (guitar), Pete Staples (bass) and Ronnie Bond (drums).	
7/09/66	**1**(2)	9	**1. Wild Thing**	Fontana 1548
9/03/66	**29**	2	2. With A Girl Like You	Fontana 1552
			above 2 released simultaneously as a single on Atco 6415	
3/23/68	**7**	12	**3. Love Is All Around**	Fontana 1607
			TROY, Doris	
			Born Doris Payne on 1/06/37 in New York City. R&B vocalist/songwriter. Backing vocalist on Pink Floyd's album *Dark Side of the Moon.*	
7/06/63	**10**	8	**1. Just One Look**	Atlantic 2188
			TRUE, Andrea, Connection	
			Disco act led by white Nashville-born vocalist Andrea True. Andrea moved to New York in 1968 and wrote commercials for radio and TV. Her break came while singing at the Riverboat in the Empire State Building in 1974.	
4/24/76	**4**	16	● **1. More, More, More Pt. 1**	Buddah 515
3/26/77	**27**	5	2. N.Y., You Got Me Dancing	Buddah 564
			TUBES, The	
			San Francisco theatre-rock troupe led by vocalist Fee Waybill (born John Waldo on 9/17/50 in Omaha, Nebraska). Group appeared in musical *Xanadu* with Olivia Newton-John in 1980.	
8/01/81	**35**	3	1. Don't Want To Wait Anymore	Capitol 5007
5/07/83	**10**	12	**2. She's A Beauty**	Capitol 5217
			TUCKER, Tanya	
			Born on 10/10/58 in Seminole, Texas and raised in Wilcox, Arizona. Prominent country singer. Bit part in the film *Jeremiah Johnson* in 1972.	
6/07/75	**37**	2	1. Lizzie And The Rainman	MCA 40402
			TUCKER, Tommy	
			Born Robert Higginbotham on 3/05/39 in Springfield, Ohio. R&B vocalist/pianist. First recorded for Hi in 1959. Died of poisoning on 1/22/82.	
2/29/64	**11**	8	1. Hi-Heel Sneakers	Checker 1067
			TUNE WEAVERS, The	
			Boston R&B quartet consisting of Margo Sylvia (lead), husband John Sylvia (bass), Gilbert Lopez (Margo's brother; tenor) and Charlotte Davis (Margo's cousin).	
9/23/57	**5**	14	**1. Happy, Happy Birthday Baby**	Checker 872
			Top 100 #5 / Best Seller #8 / Jockey #12 first released on Casa Grande 4037 in 1957	
			TURBANS, The	
			Philadelphia R&B quartet: Al Banks (lead), Matthew Platt (tenor), Charles Williams (baritone) and Andrew "Chet" Jones (bass). Disbanded in 1961.	
1/14/56	**33**	1	1. When You Dance	Herald 458

DATE	POS	WKS	ARTIST—RECORD TITLE	LABEL & NO.
			TURNER, Ike & Tina	
			Husband-and-wife duo: guitarist Ike Turner (b: 11/05/31 in Clarksdale, Mississippi) and vocalist Tina (born Anna Mae Bullock on 11/26/38 in Brownsville, Tennessee). Married from 1958-76. At age 11, Ike was backing pianist for bluesmen Sonny Boy Williamson (Aleck Ford) and Robert Nighthawk (of the Nighthawks). Formed own band, the Kings of Rhythm, while in high school; backed Jackie Brenston's hit "Rocket '88'." Prolific session, production and guitar work during the 1950s. In 1960, developed a dynamic stage show around Tina; "The Ike & Tina Turner Revue" featuring her backing vocalists, The Ikettes, and Ike's Kings Of Rhythm. Disbanded in 1974. In the mid-1980s, Tina emerged as a successful solo artist. Duet inducted into the Rock and Roll Hall of Fame in 1991.	
10/03/60	**27**	6	1. A Fool In Love	Sue 730
9/04/61	**14**	5	2. It's Gonna Work Out Fine backing vocals by Mickey & Sylvia	Sue 749
1/13/62	**38**	2	3. Poor Fool	Sue 753
8/08/70	**34**	6	4. I Want To Take You Higher **IKE & TINA TURNER & THE IKETTES**	Liberty 56177
2/13/71	**4**	11	● **5. Proud Mary**	Liberty 56216
10/27/73	**22**	6	6. Nutbush City Limits	United Art. 298
			TURNER, Jesse Lee	
			Rockabilly singer from Bowling, Texas.	
1/26/59	**20**	6	1. The Little Space Girl [N]	Carlton 496
			TURNER, Sammy	
			Born Samuel Black on 6/02/32 in Paterson, New Jersey. Tommy Edwards-styled vocalist.	
7/06/59	**3**	14	**1. Lavender-Blue** originally released on Pacific 3016 in 1958	Big Top 3016
11/16/59	**19**	7	2. Always 4 versions hit the top 10 in 1926	Big Top 3029
			TURNER, Spyder	
			Born Dwight D. Turner in 1947 in Beckley, West Virginia. Soul vocalist.	
1/14/67	**12**	8	1. Stand By Me [N] vocal impressions of Jackie Wilson, David Ruffin, Billy Stewart, Smokey Robinson and Chuck Jackson	MGM 13617
			TURNER, Tina	
			Born Anna Mae Bullock on 11/26/38 in Brownsville, Tennessee. R&B-rock vocalist/actress. Half of Ike & Tina Turner duo, when married to Ike from 1958-76. In films *Tommy* (1975; cast as the Acid Queen) and *Mad Max-Beyond Thunderdome* (1985). With Ike, inducted into the Rock And Roll Hall of Fame in 1991.	
2/18/84	**26**	7	1. Let's Stay Together	Capitol 5322
6/23/84	**1**(3)	18	● **2. What's Love Got To Do With It**	Capitol 5354
10/06/84	**5**	13	**3. Better Be Good To Me**	Capitol 5387
1/26/85	**7**	12	**4. Private Dancer**	Capitol 5433
5/18/85	**37**	3	5. Show Some Respect	Capitol 5461
7/20/85	**2**(1)	12	**6. We Don't Need Another Hero (Thunderdome)**	Capitol 5491
10/12/85	**15**	10	7. One Of The Living above 2 from the film *Mad Max-Beyond Thunderdome*	Capitol 5518
12/07/85+	**15**	9	8. It's Only Love **BRYAN ADAMS/TINA TURNER**	A&M 2791
9/06/86	**2**(3)	12	**9. Typical Male**	Capitol 5615

DATE	POS	WKS	ARTIST—RECORD TITLE	LABEL & NO.
12/20/86+	**30**	6	10. Two People	Capitol 5644
3/07/87	**13**	7	11. What You Get Is What You See	Capitol 5668
9/23/89	**15**	8	12. The Best sax solo: Edgar Winter	Capitol 44442
1/06/90	**39**	1	13. Steamy Windows	Capitol 44473
			TURTLES, The Pop-folk-rock group formed at Westchester High School in Los Angeles in 1961. Led by Mark Volman (b: 4/19/47, Los Angeles) and Howard Kaylan (born Howard Kaplan on 6/22/47, New York City). First called the Nightriders; then the Crossfires. Recorded for Capco in 1963. Name changed to The Turtles in 1965. Many personnel changes except for Volman and Kaylan. Group disbanded in 1970. Volman and Kaylan joined the Mothers Of Invention. Went out as a duo in 1972 and recorded as Phlorescent Leech & Eddie and later as Flo & Eddie. Did soundtrack for the film *Strawberry Shortcake*. Toured again as The Turtles in 1985.	
8/21/65	**8**	8	**1. It Ain't Me Babe** written by Bob Dylan	White Whale 222
11/20/65	**29**	4	2. Let Me Be	White Whale 224
2/19/66	**20**	9	3. You Baby	White Whale 227
3/04/67	**1**(3)	12	• **4. Happy Together**	White Whale 244
5/27/67	**3**	8	**5. She'd Rather Be With Me**	White Whale 249
8/26/67	**12**	7	6. You Know What I Mean	White Whale 254
12/02/67	**14**	7	7. She's My Girl	White Whale 260
10/12/68	**6**	9	**8. Elenore**	White Whale 276
1/25/69	**6**	9	**9. You Showed Me**	White Whale 292
			TUXEDO JUNCTION Female disco studio group assembled by producers W. Michael Lewis and Lauren Rinder.	
7/01/78	**32**	2	1. Chattanooga Choo Choo #1 hit for Glenn Miller in 1941	Butterfly 1205
			TWILLEY, Dwight Born on 6/06/51 in Tulsa, Oklahoma. Rock singer/songwriter/pianist. Formed the Dwight Twilley Band with Phil Seymour (bass, drums) in 1974.	
6/21/75	**16**	8	1. I'm On Fire **DWIGHT TWILLEY BAND**	Shelter 40380
3/03/84	**16**	10	2. Girls	EMI America 8196
			TWISTED SISTER Long Island, New York heavy-metal quintet led by Dee Snider (b: 3/15/55, Massapequa, Long Island, New York). Included Jay French (guitar), Eddie Ojeda (guitar), Mark Mendosa (bass) and A.J. Pero (drums). Pero replaced by Joey Franco in 1987. Disbanded in late 1987.	
8/18/84	**21**	7	1. We're Not Gonna Take It	Atlantic 89641
			TWITTY, Conway Born Harold Lloyd Jenkins on 9/01/33 in Friars Point, Mississippi and raised in Helena, Arkansas. Superstar country singer. Conway has charted over 30 #1 solo country hits. Formed own group, the Phillips County Ramblers, at age 10. Offered a professional career with the Philadelphia Phillies when drafted. With service band, Cimmarons, in Japan, early 1950s. Changed his name in 1957 and first recorded for Sun (unissued recordings). In the films *Sexpot Goes to College* and *College Confidential.* Switched from pop to country music in 1965. Moved to Nashville in 1968. Owns tourist complex, Twitty City, in Hendersonville, Tennessee.	
9/29/58	**1**(2)	17	**1. It's Only Make Believe**	MGM 12677

DATE	POS	WKS	ARTIST—RECORD TITLE	LABEL & NO.
2/16/59	**28**	7	2. The Story Of My Love	MGM 12748
8/24/59	**29**	3	3. Mona Lisa #1 hit for Nat King Cole in 1950	MGM 12804
10/12/59	**10**	13	**4. Danny Boy** based on traditional Irish song "Londonderry Air" of 1855	MGM 12826
1/18/60	**6**	10	**5. Lonely Blue Boy** originally recorded (unreleased) by Elvis Presley as "Danny" for the film *King Creole*	MGM 12857
4/25/60	**26**	5	6. What Am I Living For	MGM 12886
7/11/60	**35**	5	7. Is A Blue Bird Blue	MGM 12911
1/16/61	**22**	5	8. C'est Si Bon (It's So Good) #21 hit for Danny Kaye in 1950	MGM 12969
9/15/73	**22**	7	9. You've Never Been This Far Before	MCA 40094
			2 IN A ROOM Dance duo from Washington Heights, New York: rapper Rafael "Dose" Vargas and remixer Roger "Rog Nice" Pauletta.	
11/10/90	**15**	12	● 1. Wiggle It	Cutting 98887#
			2 LIVE CREW, The Miami-based rap quartet: David "Mr. Mix" Hobbs, Chris "Fresh Kid-Ice" Won Wong, "Brother Marquis" Ross and Luther "Luke Skyywalker" Campbell (owner of Luke Records). Group's obscenity arrests sparked national censorship controversy in 1990.	
10/21/89	**26**	9	● 1. Me So Horny	Skyywalker 130#
8/04/90	**20**	7	● 2. Banned In The U.S.A. **LUKE Featuring THE 2 LIVE CREW** tune based on Bruce Springsteen's "Born In The U.S.A."	Luke 98915
			TYCOON New York-based, pop-rock sextet — Norman Mershon, lead singer.	
4/28/79	**26**	5	1. Such A Woman	Arista 0398
			TYLER, Bonnie Born Gaynor Hopkins on 6/08/53 in Swansea, Wales. Worked local clubs until the mid-1970s. Distinctive raspy vocals caused by operation to remove throat nodules in 1976.	
4/22/78	**3**	15	● **1. It's A Heartache**	RCA 11249
8/13/83	**1**(4)	18	● **2. Total Eclipse Of The Heart**	Columbia 03906
4/07/84	**34**	4	3. Holding Out For A Hero from the film *Footloose*	Columbia 04370
			TYMES, The Soul group formed in Philadelphia in 1956. Consisted of George Williams (lead), George Hilliard, Donald Banks, Albert Berry and Norman Burnett. First called the Latineers. Berry and Hilliard were replaced by female singers Terri Gonzalez and Melanie Moore in the early '70s.	
6/22/63	**1**(1)	12	**1. So Much In Love** originally titled "So In Love"	Parkway 871
8/31/63	**7**	8	**2. Wonderful! Wonderful!**	Parkway 884
1/04/64	**19**	6	3. Somewhere	Parkway 891
12/28/68	**39**	1	4. People from the film *Funny Girl*	Columbia 44630
9/07/74	**12**	8	5. You Little Trustmaker	RCA 10022

DATE	POS	WKS	ARTIST—RECORD TITLE	LABEL & NO.
			U	
			UB40	
			British interracial reggae octet formed in 1978 — Ali Campbell (b: 2/15/59, Birmingham, England), lead singer. Took name from a British unemployment benefit form.	
3/17/84	**34**	4	1. Red Red Wine	A&M 2600
9/07/85	**28**	4	2. I Got You Babe UB40 WITH CHRISSIE HYNDE	A&M 2758
9/03/88	**1**(1)	12	● **3. Red Red Wine** **[R]**	A&M 1244
10/27/90	**6**	15	● **4. The Way You Do The Things You Do**	Virgin 98978#
5/18/91	**7**	12	**5. Here I Am (Come And Take Me)**	Virgin 99141#
			U-KREW, The	
			Rap quintet from Portland, Oregon formed as The Untouchable Krew in October 1984. Led by drum programmer Larry Bell with lead vocals by Kevin Morse.	
3/24/90	**24**	7	1. If U Were Mine	Enigma 75051#
			ULLMAN, Tracy	
			Born on 12/30/59 in Buckinghamshire, England. Actress/singer/comedienne. Own variety-style TV show on Fox Broadcasting network, 1987-90. In films *I Love You to Death*, *Plenty* and *Give My Regards to Broad Street*.	
3/17/84	**8**	11	**1. They Don't Know**	MCA 52347
			UNDERGROUND SUNSHINE	
			Rock quartet: Chris Connors and Jane Little (both from Wisconsin), with Frank and Betty Kohl (from Germany).	
8/23/69	**26**	5	1. Birthday written by John Lennon and Paul McCartney	Intrepid 75002
			UNDISPUTED TRUTH, The	
			Soul group consisting of Joe Harris, Billie Calvin and Brenda Evans. Many personnel changes thereafter.	
7/31/71	**3**	13	**1. Smiling Faces Sometimes**	Gordy 7108
			UNIFICS, The	
			Soul vocal group formed at Howard University in Washington, D.C. — Al Johnson, lead singer. Member Hal Worthington shot to death on 2/20/90 (age 42).	
10/19/68	**25**	5	1. Court Of Love	Kapp 935
1/18/69	**36**	4	2. The Beginning Of My End	Kapp 957
			UNION GAP, The — see PUCKETT, Gary	
			UNIT FOUR PLUS TWO	
			English pop-rock sextet — Tommy Moeller, lead singer.	
5/29/65	**28**	4	1. Concrete And Clay	London 9751
			UPCHURCH, Philip, Combo	
			Philip was born on 7/19/41 in Chicago. R&B guitarist. Session player for George Benson, Quincy Jones, The Jacksons and many others.	
6/26/61	**29**	3	1. You Can't Sit Down Part 2 [I]	Boyd 3398

DATE	POS	WKS	ARTIST—RECORD TITLE	LABEL & NO.
			URBAN DANCE SQUAD	
			Amsterdam, Holland-based interracial, rap-metal crew. Rapper Patrick "Rude Boy" Remington backed by the rhythm section of Magic Stick, DNA, Silly Sil and Tres Manos.	
2/02/91	**21**	7	1. Deeper Shade Of Soul	Arista 2026
			URIAH HEEP	
			British hard-rock band. Key members: David Byron (lead singer), Mick Box (lead guitar) and Ken Hensley (keyboards; later with Blackfoot).	
9/16/72	**39**	3	1. Easy Livin	Mercury 73307
			USA for AFRICA	
			USA: United Support of Artists — a collection of 46 major artists formed to help the suffering people of Africa and the U.S.	
3/23/85	**1**(4)	12	▲ **1. We Are The World**	Columbia 04839
			soloists (in order): Lionel Richie, Stevie Wonder, Paul Simon, Kenny Rogers, James Ingram, Tina Turner, Billy Joel, Michael Jackson, Diana Ross, Dionne Warwick, Willie Nelson, Al Jarreau, Bruce Springsteen, Kenny Loggins, Steve Perry, Daryl Hall, Huey Lewis, Cyndi Lauper, Kim Carnes, Bob Dylan, and Ray Charles; written by Michael Jackson and Lionel Richie	
			UTOPIA	
			Veteran pop-rock group: Todd Rundgren (guitar), Kasim Sulton (bass), Roger Powell (keyboards) and Willie Wilcox (drums). Built own recording studio near Woodstock, New York.	
3/29/80	**27**	5	1. Set Me Free	Bearsville 49180
			U2	
			Rock band formed in Dublin, Ireland in 1976. Consists of Paul "Bono" Hewson (vocals), Dave "The Edge" Evans (guitar), Adam Clayton (bass) and Larry Mullen, Jr. (drums). Emerged in 1987 as a leading rock act. Released concert tour documentary film *Rattle and Hum* in 1988.	
12/01/84	**33**	5	1. Pride (In The Name Of Love)	Island 99704
4/04/87	**1**(3)	13	**2. With Or Without You**	Island 99469
6/20/87	**1**(2)	13	**3. I Still Haven't Found What I'm Looking For**	Island 99430
10/03/87	**13**	9	4. Where The Streets Have No Name	Island 99408
			above 3 later released simultaneously on Island 99453, 99431 and 99407, respectively, for juke boxes	
10/08/88	**3**	13	● **5. Desire**	Island 99250
1/14/89	**14**	8	6. Angel Of Harlem	Island 99254
			a tribute to Billie Holiday; above 2 from the U2 concert tour film *Rattle and Hum*	
			V	
			VALE, Jerry	
			Born Genero Vitaliano on 7/08/32 in the Bronx. Pop ballad singer.	
3/24/56	**30**	5	1. Innamorata (Sweetheart)	Columbia 40634
			from the film *Artists & Models*	
7/28/56	**14**	17	2. You Don't Know Me	Columbia 40710
			Best Seller #14 / Top 100 #14 / Juke Box #14 / Jockey #15 orchestra directed by Percy Faith on above 2	
1/23/65	**24**	4	3. Have You Looked Into Your Heart	Columbia 43181

DATE	POS	WKS	ARTIST—RECORD TITLE	LABEL & NO.
			VALENS, Ritchie	
			Born Richard Valenzuela on 5/13/41 in Pacoima, California. Latin rock and roll singer/songwriter/ guitarist. Killed in the plane crash that also took the lives of Buddy Holly and the Big Bopper on 2/03/59. In the film *Go Johnny Go*. The 1987 film *La Bamba* was based on his life.	
12/15/58+	**2**(2)	18	**1. Donna/**	
1/19/59	**22**	8	2. La Bamba [F]	Del-Fi 4110
			VALENTE, Caterina	
			Born on 1/14/31 in Paris of Italian parentage. Popular European singer/dancer. Sings in six languages.	
4/09/55	**8**	14	**1. The Breeze And I** Jockey #8 / Best Seller #13; #1 hit for Jimmy Dorsey in 1940	Decca 29467
			VALENTI, John	
			Blue-eyed soul singer from Chicago.	
10/30/76	**37**	2	1. Anything You Want	Ariola Am. 7625
			VALENTINO, Mark	
			Born Anthony Busillo on 3/12/42 in Philadelphia.	
12/08/62	**27**	3	1. The Push And Kick	Swan 4121
			VALINO, Joe	
10/27/56	**12**	14	1. Garden Of Eden Top 100 #12 / Jockey #12 / Best Seller #13 / Juke Box #13	Vik 0226
			VALJEAN	
			Born Valjean Johns on 11/19/34 in Shattuck, Oklahoma. Pianist.	
6/16/62	**28**	4	1. Theme From Ben Casey [I] from the TV series "Ben Casey"	Carlton 573
			VALLI, Frankie	
			Born Francis Castellucio on 5/03/37 in Newark, New Jersey. Recorded his first solo single in 1953 as Frank Valley on the Corona label. Formed own group, the Variatones, in 1955 and changed their name to the Four Lovers in 1956, which evolved into The 4 Seasons by 1961. Began solo work in 1965. Suffered from a disease which caused hearing loss in the late 1970s, corrected by surgery.	
2/12/66	**39**	1	1. (You're Gonna) Hurt Yourself	Smash 2015
6/03/67	**2**(1)	14	● **2. Can't Take My Eyes Off You**	Philips 40446
9/16/67	**18**	5	3. I Make A Fool Of Myself	Philips 40484
1/20/68	**29**	4	4. To Give (The Reason I Live)	Philips 40510
1/18/75	**1**(1)	14	● **5. My Eyes Adored You**	Private S. 45003
6/14/75	**6**	9	**6. Swearin' To God** all of above produced by Bob Crewe	Private S. 45021
11/08/75	**11**	8	7. Our Day Will Come	Private S. 45043
5/08/76	**36**	2	8. Fallen Angel	Private S. 45074
6/17/78	**1**(2)	15	▲ **9. Grease** from the film of the same title	RSO 897
			JUNE VALLI	
			Born on 6/30/30 in the Bronx. Married to Chicago DJ Howard Miller.	
5/14/55	**29**	1	1. Unchained Melody Best Seller #29; from the film *Unchained*	RCA 6078
4/18/60	**29**	4	2. Apple Green	Mercury 71588

DATE	POS	WKS	ARTIST—RECORD TITLE	LABEL & NO.
			VANDENBERG	
			Dutch hard-rock band: led by Adrian Vandenberg (guitar, keyboards; joined Whitesnake in 1989), Bert Heerink (lead singer), Dick Kemper (bass) and Jos Zoomer (drums).	
3/12/83	**39**	2	1. Burning Heart	Atco 99947
			VANDROSS, Luther	
			Born on 4/20/51 in New York City. Soul singer/producer/songwriter. Commercial jingle singer, then a top session vocalist/arranger. Sang lead on a few of Change's early albums.	
11/14/81	**33**	4	1. Never Too Much	Epic 02409
10/29/83	**27**	5	2. How Many Times Can We Say Goodbye **DIONNE WARWICK AND LUTHER VANDROSS**	Arista 9073
4/27/85	**29**	6	3. 'Til My Baby Comes Home organ solo: Billy Preston	Epic 04760
12/27/86+	**15**	11	4. Stop To Love	Epic 06523
3/04/89	**30**	4	5. She Won't Talk To Me	Epic 08513
2/10/90	**6**	15	● **6. Here And Now**	Epic 73029
5/11/91	**4**	12	**7. Power Of Love/Love Power** backing vocals: Cissy Houston, Darlene Love, Lisa Fischer & others	Epic 73778
			VAN DYKE, Leroy	
			Born on 10/04/29 in Spring Fork, Missouri. Worked as a newspaper reporter. Served in U.S. Army in the early 1950s. Former livestock auctioneer. In the film *What Am I Bid?* in 1967.	
12/08/56+	**19**	7	1. Auctioneer [N] Juke Box #19 / Best Seller #21 / Top 100 #29	Dot 15503
11/20/61	**5**	12	**2. Walk On By**	Mercury 71834
3/31/62	**35**	2	3. If A Woman Answers (Hang Up The Phone)	Mercury 71926
			VANGELIS	
			Born Evangelos Papathanassiou on 3/29/43 in Valos, Greece. Keyboardist/composer. Moved to Paris during the late 1960s, then to London in the mid-1970s. Formed rock band Aphrodite's Child in France with Demis Roussos, 1968-early 1970s.	
2/20/82	**1**(1)	15	**1. Chariots Of Fire - Titles** [I] from the Academy Award-winning film *Chariots of Fire*	Polydor 2189
			VAN HALEN	
			Hard-rock band formed in Pasadena, California in 1974. Consisted of David Lee Roth (b: 10/10/55; vocals), Eddie Van Halen (b: 1/26/57; guitar), Michael Anthony (b: 6/20/55; bass) and Alex Van Halen (b: 5/08/55; drums). The Van Halen brothers were born in Nijmegen, The Netherlands, and moved to Pasadena in 1968. Sammy Hagar replaced Roth as lead singer in 1985. Eddie married actress Valerie Bertinelli on 4/11/81.	
3/11/78	**36**	3	1. You Really Got Me	Warner 8515
5/26/79	**15**	9	2. Dance The Night Away	Warner 8823
3/13/82	**12**	9	3. (Oh) Pretty Woman first released on Warner 50003 as simply "Pretty Woman"	Warner 50003
6/26/82	**38**	3	4. Dancing In The Street	Warner 29986
1/21/84	**1**(5)	15	● **5. Jump**	Warner 29384
4/21/84	**13**	10	6. I'll Wait	Warner 29307
6/30/84	**13**	10	7. Panama all of above produced by Ted Templeman	Warner 29250
3/29/86	**3**	11	**8. Why Can't This Be Love**	Warner 28740

DATE	POS	WKS	ARTIST—RECORD TITLE	LABEL & NO.
6/14/86	**22**	7	9. Dreams	Warner 28702
8/30/86	**22**	9	10. Love Walks In	Warner 28626
6/18/88	**34**	2	11. Black And Blue	Warner 27891
7/23/88	**5**	12	**12. When It's Love**	Warner 27827
11/05/88	**13**	10	13. Finish What Ya Started	Warner 27746
3/11/89	**35**	3	14. Feels So Good	Warner 27565
			VANILLA FUDGE	
			Psychedelic rock quartet formed in New York in 1966. Consisted of Mark Stein (lead singer, keyboards), Vinnie Martell (guitar), Tim Bogert (bassist with Cactus, Rod Stewart and Jeff Beck) and Carmine Appice (drummer with Cactus, Jeff Beck, Rod Stewart, KGB and Blue Murder).	
8/03/68	**6**	9	**1. You Keep Me Hangin' On** [R] originally charted in 1967 (POS 67)	Atco 6590
10/26/68	**38**	4	2. Take Me For A Little While	Atco 6616
			VANILLA ICE	
			White Dallas-based rapper born Robert Van Winkle on 10/31/68 in Miami Lakes, Florida.	
9/22/90	**1**(1)	15	▲ **1. Ice Ice Baby** bass line sampled from "Under Pressure" by Queen & David Bowie	SBK 07335#
12/15/90+	**4**	12	● **2. Play That Funky Music**	SBK 07339#
			VANITY FARE	
			British pop quintet: Trevor Brice (vocals), Dick Allix, Tony Jarrett, Tony Goulden and Barry Landeman.	
12/20/69+	**12**	9	1. Early In The Morning	Page One 21027
5/16/70	**5**	14	● **2. Hitchin' A Ride**	Page One 21029
			VANNELLI, Gino	
			Born on 6/16/52 in Montreal, Canada. Pop/soul-styled singer/songwriter.	
10/26/74	**22**	5	1. People Gotta Move	A&M 1614
10/14/78	**4**	13	**2. I Just Wanna Stop**	A&M 2072
4/04/81	**6**	14	**3. Living Inside Myself**	Arista 0588
			VANWARMER, Randy	
			Born Randall Van Wormer on 3/30/55 in Indian Hills, Colorado. Singer/songwriter/guitarist. Moved to England at age 12; returned to U.S. in 1979. Charted two country hits in 1988.	
4/21/79	**4**	14	● **1. Just When I Needed You Most**	Bearsville 0334
			VAPORS, The	
			British pub-rock quartet — David Fenton, lead singer.	
11/15/80	**36**	3	1. Turning Japanese also released on United Artists 1364 in 1980	Liberty 1364
			VAUGHAN, Frankie	
			Born Frank Abelson on 2/03/28 in Liverpool. Popular entertainer in England. In film *Let's Make Love* (1960). In London cast of *42nd Street* in 1985.	
7/28/58	**22**	1	1. Judy Jockey #22 / Top 100 #100	Epic 9273

Sam The Sham & The Pharoahs' hits of the mid-60s had a certain "wild" consistency—at least in terms of animal themes and nursery tales. Aside from "Wooly Bully" and "Lil' Red Riding Hood," which both peaked at No. 2, the bearded group also offered "The Hair On My Chinny Chin Chin," which reached No. 22 in 1966.

Santana's longtime American fans were delighted when Sony Music issued the group's 1974 Japanese-only live album, *Lotus*, domestically. The group's long association with Columbia/Sony has brought them only two top-10 hits—1970's "Evil Ways" and "Black Magic Woman"—in over two decades.

Boz Scaggs's hits have been plenty—when the respected singer/songwriter decides to make records. Since his 1988 hit "Heart Of Mine," which reached No. 35, Scaggs has maintained a low profile and appeared only briefly on 1991's *Live at the Beacon* by the New York Rock And Soul Revue.

Scandal, led by Patty Smyth and Zack Smith, recorded a 1983 debut effort for Columbia that became the best-selling EP in the label's history. Though its two hits—"Goodbye To You" and "Love's Got A Line On You"—didn't make the Top 40, the title track from the group's 1984 debut album *The Warrior* reached No. 7.

Peter Schilling's 1983 single "Major Tom (Coming Home)," which reached No. 14, was unusual for two reasons: it was a sequel to someone else's song—David Bowie's "Space Oddity"—and Bowie had already written his own sequel earlier, with 1980's "Ashes To Ashes."

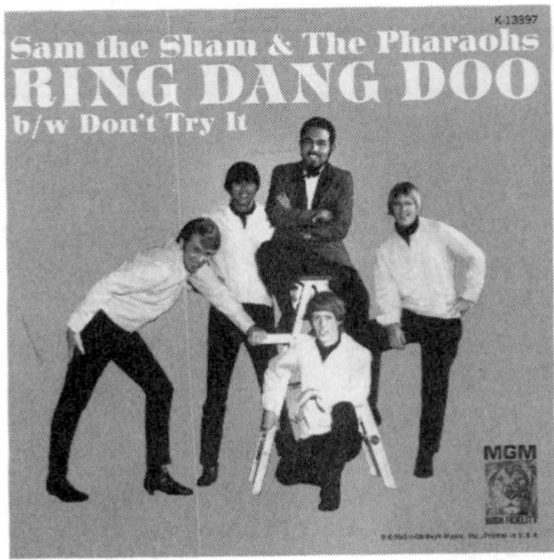

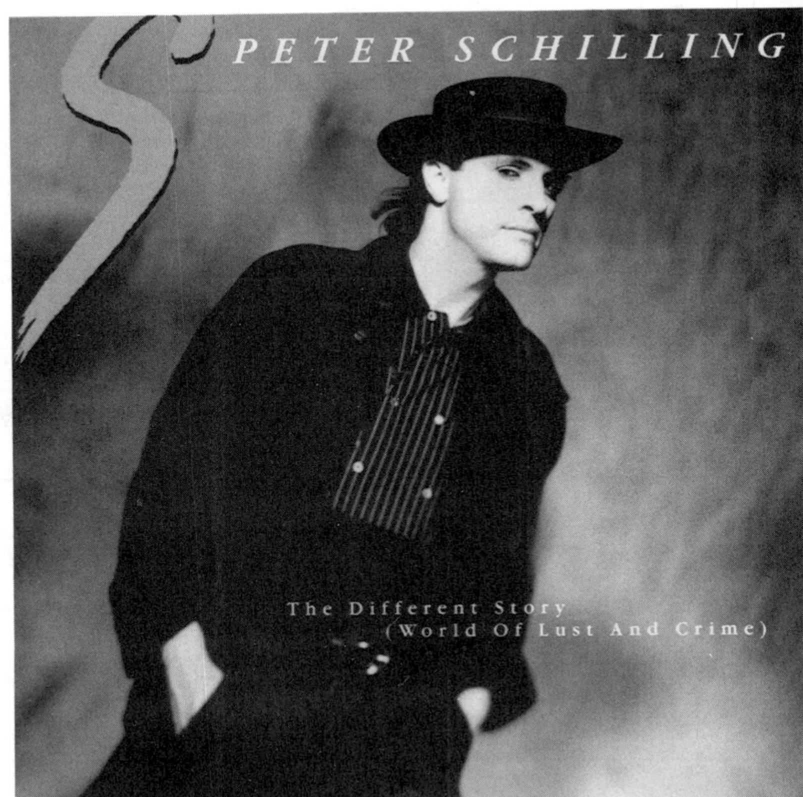

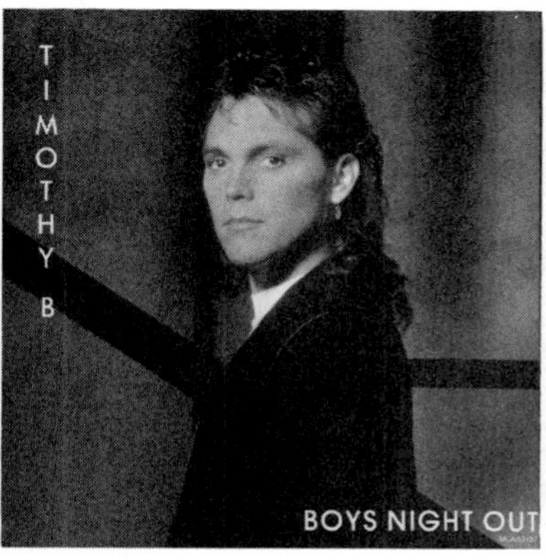

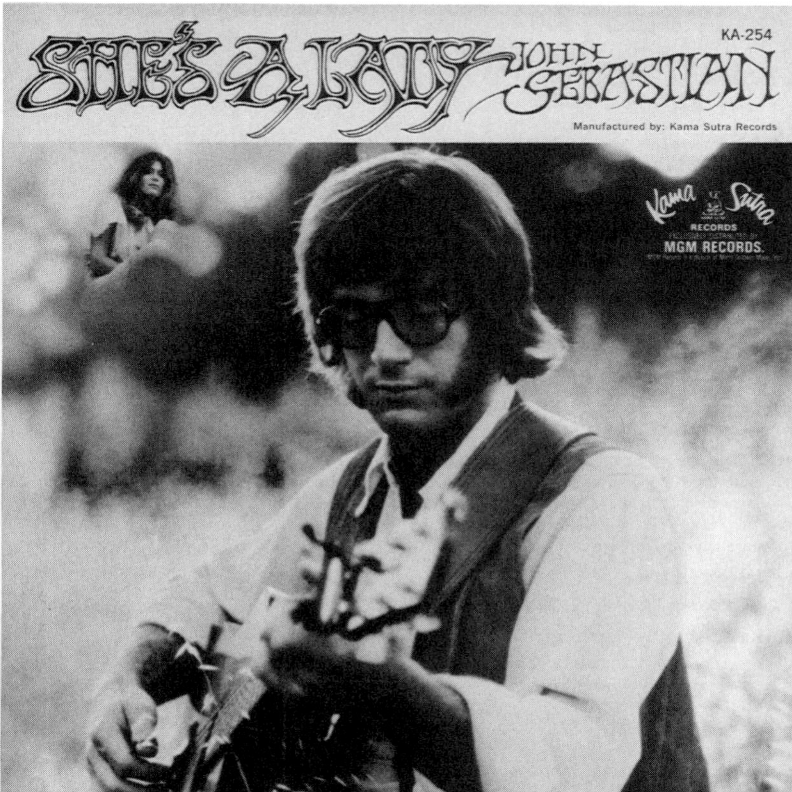

Timothy B (Schmit), formerly a member of pop combos Glad, Poco, and the Eagles, hit the Top 40 on his own in 1987 with "Boys Night Out." His cover version of the Tymes hit "So Much In Love" was prominently featured in the soundtrack to 1982's *Fast Times at Ridgemont High.*

The Scorpions, Germany's best-known heavy-metal export for close to two decades, once counted renowned guitarist Michael Schenker among its members. Longtime album rockers, the group has had only one hit single: 1984's "Rock You Like A Hurricane," which hit No. 25.

Jack Scott's two years on the small Carlton and Top Rank labels brought him three top-10 hits and six others in the Top 40. Ironically, when Capitol Records bought out his contract in 1961, the hits stopped.

John Sebastian's solo career was in its eighth year when the former Lovin' Spoonful leader hit No. 1 again with "Welcome Back," the theme from ABC-TV's "Welcome Back, Kotter." His other No. 1 hit was 1966's "Summer In The City" with the Spoonful.

Neil Sedaka met top-10 success with two versions of the same song. "Breaking Up Is Hard To Do" was No. 1 for two weeks in 1962; a slower version, recorded for Elton John's Rocket Records label, reached No. 8 in 1976.

The Seeds' 1967 hit "Pushin' Too Hard" was the psychedelic group's only hit, reaching No. 37. The L.A. band's spacey material—typified by such album tracks as "March Of The Flower Children" and "Flower Lady And Her Assistant"—may well have been too "far-out" for radio at the time.

DATE	POS	WKS	ARTIST—RECORD TITLE	LABEL & NO.
			VAUGHAN, Sarah	
			Born on 3/27/24 in Newark, New Jersey. Jazz singer. Dubbed "The Divine One." Studied piano from 1931-39. Won amateur contest at the Apollo Theater in 1942, which led to her joining Earl Hines' band as vocalist/second pianist. First recorded solo for Continental in 1944. With Billy Eckstine from 1944-45. Married manager/trumpeter George Treadwell in 1947. Later husbands included pro football player Clyde Atkins and trumpeter Waymon Reed. Performed into the '80s. Won the Lifetime Achievement Grammy in 1989. Died of lung cancer on 4/03/90.	
11/27/54+	**6**	15	**1. Make Yourself Comfortable** Jockey #6 / Best Seller #8 / Juke Box #8	Mercury 70469
2/26/55	**12**	9	2. How Important Can It Be? Jockey #12 / Best Seller #18 / Juke Box #20	Mercury 70534
4/23/55	**6**	11	**3. Whatever Lola Wants** Jockey #6 / Juke Box #9 / Best Seller #12 from the Broadway musical *Damn Yankees*	Mercury 70595
7/16/55	**14**	1	4. Experience Unnecessary Jockey #14	Mercury 70646
12/03/55	**11**	7	5. C'est La Vie Jockey #11 / Top 100 #22	Mercury 70727
3/03/56	**13**	7	6. Mr. Wonderful Jockey #13 / Top 100 #38	Mercury 70777
7/21/56	**19**	6	7. Fabulous Character Jockey #19 / Top 100 #27 orchestra conducted by Hugo Peretti on all of above	Mercury 70885
1/12/57	**19**	5	8. The Banana Boat Song Jockey #19 / Top 100 #31	Mercury 71020
8/17/59	**7**	11	**9. Broken-Hearted Melody**	Mercury 71477
			VAUGHN, Billy	
			Born Richard Vaughn on 4/12/19 in Glasgow, Kentucky. Died on 9/26/91 of cancer. Organized the Hilltoppers vocal group in 1952. Music director for Dot Records. Arranger/conductor for Pat Boone, Gale Storm, The Fontane Sisters and many other Dot artists. Billy had more pop hits than any other orchestra leader during the rock era.	
12/11/54+	**2**(1)	27	**1. Melody Of Love** **[I]** Best Seller #2 / Jockey #2 / Juke Box #3; written in 1903	Dot 15247
9/24/55	**5**	15	**2. The Shifting Whispering Sands (Parts 1 & 2)** **[S]** Best Seller #5 / Top 100 #5 pre / Jockey #5 / Juke Box #10 narration by Ken Nordine	Dot 15409
2/25/56	**37**	2	3. A Theme From (The Three Penny Opera) "Moritat" [I] written in 1928; later known as "Mack The Knife"	Dot 15444
9/08/56	**18**	6	4. When The White Lilacs Bloom Again [I] Juke Box #18 / Jockey #21 / Top 100 #22	Dot 15491
12/16/57	**10**	7	**5. Raunchy/** **[I]** Jockey #10 / Best Seller #25 / Top 100 #33	
1/13/58	**5**	18	**6. Sail Along Silvery Moon** **[I]** Best Seller #5 / Top 100 #5 / Jockey #6 #4 hit for Bing Crosby in 1937	Dot 15661
4/14/58	**30**	4	7. Tumbling Tumbleweeds [I] Best Seller #30 / Top 100 #35 #13 hit for the Sons of The Pioneers in 1934	Dot 15710
8/25/58	**20**	8	8. La Paloma [I] Best Seller #20 / Hot 100 #26; Spanish tango written in 1864	Dot 15795

DATE	POS	WKS	ARTIST—RECORD TITLE	LABEL & NO.
2/02/59	**37**	1	9. Blue Hawaii [I] #5 hit for Bing Crosby in 1937	Dot 15879
7/18/60	**19**	7	10. Look For A Star [I] from the film *Circus of Horrors*	Dot 16106
3/06/61	**28**	3	11. Wheels [I]	Dot 16174
8/11/62	**13**	8	12. A Swingin' Safari [I] written by Bert Kaempfert	Dot 16374
			VEE, Bobby Born Robert Velline on 4/30/43 in Fargo, North Dakota. Formed The Shadows with his brother and a friend in 1959. After Buddy Holly's death in a plane crash, The Shadows filled in on Buddy's next scheduled show in Fargo. First recorded for Soma in 1959. In the films *Swingin' Along, It's Trad, Dad, Play It Cool, C'mon Let's Live a Little* and *Just for Fun.* Still performing on oldies tours.	
9/05/60	**6**	13	**1. Devil Or Angel**	Liberty 55270
12/12/60+	**6**	11	**2. Rubber Ball** co-written by Gene Pitney	Liberty 55287
2/27/61	**33**	3	3. Stayin' In	Liberty 55296
8/21/61	**1**(3)	11	**4. Take Good Care Of My Baby**	Liberty 55354
11/20/61	**2**(1)	13	**5. Run To Him**	Liberty 55388
3/17/62	**15**	6	6. Please Don't Ask About Barbara	Liberty 55419
6/09/62	**15**	6	7. Sharing You	Liberty 55451
9/15/62	**20**	6	8. Punish Her	Liberty 55479
12/22/62+	**3**	11	**9. The Night Has A Thousand Eyes**	Liberty 55521
4/13/63	**13**	7	10. Charms	Liberty 55530
7/20/63	**34**	2	11. Be True To Yourself with The Johnny Mann Singers	Liberty 55581
8/12/67	**3**	13	● **12. Come Back When You Grow Up** **BOBBY VEE AND THE STRANGERS**	Liberty 55964
12/16/67	**37**	2	13. Beautiful People **BOBBY VEE AND THE STRANGERS**	Liberty 56009
5/18/68	**35**	4	14. My Girl/Hey Girl	Liberty 56033
			VEGA, Suzanne New York vocalist/acoustic guitarist/songwriter.	
7/04/87	**3**	12	**1. Luka**	A&M 2937
11/03/90	**5**	14	● **2. Tom's Diner** **D.N.A. featuring SUZANNE VEGA** remix of *a capella* B-side of her "Solitude Standing" single; remixed by D.N.A. (two DJs from Bristol, England)	A&M 1529#
			VELVETS, The R&B doo-wop quintet from Odessa, Texas — Virgil Johnson, lead singer.	
6/26/61	**26**	4	1. Tonight (Could Be The Night)	Monument 441

DATE	POS	WKS	ARTIST—RECORD TITLE		LABEL & NO.
			VENTURES, The		
			Guitar-based instrumental rock and roll band formed in the Seattle/Tacoma, Washington area. Consisted of guitarists Nokie Edwards (bass; b: 5/09/39), Bob Bogle (lead; b: 1/16/37) and Don Wilson (rhythm; b: 2/10/ 37), and drummer Howie Johnson (d: 1988). First recorded for own Blue Horizon label in 1959. Johnson was injured in an auto accident and was replaced by Mel Taylor in 1961. Taylor formed Mel Taylor & The Dynamics in 1973, returned in 1978. Edwards left in 1967, replaced by Gerry McGee. Edwards returned in 1972 and then left again in 1985. Added keyboardist John Durrill in 1969. Latest recordings feature Bogle, Wilson, Taylor and McGee. Group still active into the '90s; extremely popular in Japan.		
7/25/60	**2**(1)	14	**1. Walk—Don't Run** first released on Blue Horizon 101 in 1959	**[I]**	Dolton 25
11/14/60	**15**	10	2. Perfidia 5 versions hit the top 15 in 1941	[I]	Dolton 28
2/13/61	**29**	5	3. Ram-Bunk-Shush	[I]	Dolton 32
8/01/64	**8**	7	**4. Walk-Don't Run '64** new version of their 1960 hit	**[I-R]**	Dolton 96
11/21/64	**35**	3	5. Slaughter On Tenth Avenue written by Richard Rodgers in 1936	[I]	Dolton 300
4/12/69	**4**	9	**6. Hawaii Five-O** from the TV series of the same title	**[I]**	Liberty 56068
			VENUS, Vik		
7/26/69	**38**	3	1. Moonflight a Dickie Goodman-type recording	[N]	Buddah 118
			VERA, Billy		
			Born William McCord, Jr. on 5/28/44 in Riverside, California and raised in Westchester County, New York. Wrote hit songs for many pop, R&B and country artists. In the film *Buckaroo Banzai* (1984) and the HBO movie *Baja Oklahoma* (1988). Formed The Beaters (an R&B-based, 10-piece band) in Los Angeles in 1979.		
3/23/68	**36**	1	1. Country Girl - City Man **BILLY VERA & JUDY CLAY**		Atlantic 2480
6/06/81	**39**	2	2. I Can Take Care Of Myself **BILLY & THE BEATERS**		Alfa 7002
12/06/86+	**1**(2)	15	● **3. At This Moment** **BILLY VERA & THE BEATERS** originally charted in 1981 (POS 79); re-charted due to play on TV's "Family Ties"	**[R]**	Rhino 74403
			VERNE, Larry		
			Born on 2/08/36 in Minneapolis. Photo studio worker-turned-singer by coincidence. A trio of California songwriters (see below) who worked in Verne's building selected him to record "Mr. Custer" because of his Southern drawl.		
9/05/60	**1**(1)	10	**1. Mr. Custer**	**[N]**	Era 3024
			VIBRATIONS, The		
			Los Angeles R&B vocal group. Originally recorded as The Jayhawks. Consisted of James Johnson, Carlton Fisher, Richard Owens, Dave Govan and Don Bradley. Also recorded as The Marathons. Owens joined The Temptations for a short time in 1971.		
3/13/61	**25**	4	1. The Watusi		Checker 969
4/25/64	**26**	5	2. My Girl Sloopy		Atlantic 2221

DATE	POS	WKS	ARTIST—RECORD TITLE	LABEL & NO.
			VILLAGE PEOPLE	
			Campy New York disco group formed by French producer Jacques Morali. (d. 11/15/91 [age 44] of AIDS) Consisted of Victor Willis (lead singer), Randy Jones, David Hodo, Felipe Rose, Glenn Hughes and Alexander Briley. Willis replaced by Ray Simpson (brother of Valerie Simpson of Ashford & Simpson) in late 1979. Group appeared in the film *Can't Stop the Music* (1980).	
7/29/78	**25**	6	● 1. Macho Man	Casablanca 922
11/11/78+	**2**(3)	20	▲ **2. Y.M.C.A.**	Casablanca 945
3/31/79	**3**	13	● **3. In The Navy**	Casablanca 973
			VILLAGE STOMPERS, The	
			Greenwich Village, New York Dixieland-styled band.	
10/05/63	**2**(1)	12	**1. Washington Square** [I]	Epic 9617
			VINCENT, Gene/His Blue Caps	
			Born Vincent Eugene Craddock on 2/11/35 in Norfolk, Virginia; died from an ulcer hemorrhage on 10/12/71. Innovative rock and roll singer/songwriter/ guitarist. Injured left leg in motorcycle accident in 1953, had to wear steel brace thereafter. Formed the Blue Caps in Norfolk in 1956. Appeared in films *The Girl Can't Help It* and *Hot Rod Gang*. To England from 1960-67. Injured in car crash that killed Eddie Cochran in England in 1960.	
6/23/56	**7**	15	**1. Be-Bop-A-Lula** Best Seller #7 / Top 100 #9 / Juke Box #10 / Jockey #11	Capitol 3450
9/16/57	**13**	12	2. Lotta Lovin' Best Seller #13 / Top 100 #14 / Jockey #18	Capitol 3763
1/13/58	**23**	1	3. Dance To The Bop Jockey #23 / Top 100 #43 / Best Seller #44	Capitol 3839
			VINTON, Bobby	
			Born Stanley Robert Vinton on 4/16/35 in Canonsburg, Pennsylvania. Father was a bandleader. Formed own band while in high school; toured as backing band for Dick Clark's "Caravan of Stars" in 1960. Left band for a singing career in 1962. Own musical variety TV series from 1975-78.	
6/16/62	**1**(4)	13	● **1. Roses Are Red (My Love)**	Epic 9509
9/15/62	**12**	7	2. Rain Rain Go Away	Epic 9532
9/22/62	**38**	2	3. I Love You The Way You Are	Diamond 121
1/05/63	**33**	3	4. Trouble Is My Middle Name/	
1/12/63	**38**	2	5. Let's Kiss And Make Up	Epic 9561
3/30/63	**21**	6	6. Over The Mountain (Across The Sea)	Epic 9577
6/01/63	**3**	10	**7. Blue On Blue**	Epic 9593
8/24/63	**1**(3)	12	**8. Blue Velvet** #16 hit for Tony Bennett in 1951	Epic 9614
12/07/63+	**1**(4)	12	**9. There! I've Said It Again** #1 hit for Vaughn Monroe in 1945	Epic 9638
3/07/64	**9**	8	**10. My Heart Belongs To Only You** #22 hit for June Christy in 1953	Epic 9662
5/30/64	**13**	6	11. Tell Me Why #2 hit for The Four Aces in 1952	Epic 9687
8/22/64	**17**	6	12. Clinging Vine	Epic 9705
11/07/64	**1**(1)	14	**13. Mr. Lonely**	Epic 9730
3/20/65	**17**	5	14. Long Lonely Nights	Epic 9768
5/22/65	**22**	6	15. L-O-N-E-L-Y	Epic 9791
10/16/65	**38**	1	16. What Color (Is A Man)	Epic 9846
12/25/65+	**23**	6	17. Satin Pillows	Epic 9869

DATE	POS	WKS	ARTIST—RECORD TITLE	LABEL & NO.
5/28/66	**40**	1	18. Dum-De-Da tune also known as "She Understands Me"	Epic 10014
12/17/66+	**11**	8	19. Coming Home Soldier	Epic 10090
10/14/67	**6**	11	**20. Please Love Me Forever**	Epic 10228
1/27/68	**24**	4	21. Just As Much As Ever	Epic 10266
4/13/68	**33**	6	22. Take Good Care Of My Baby	Epic 10305
8/03/68	**23**	5	23. Halfway To Paradise	Epic 10350
11/16/68	**9**	12	● **24. I Love How You Love Me**	Epic 10397
5/03/69	**34**	2	25. To Know You Is To Love You	Epic 10461
7/12/69	**34**	2	26. The Days Of Sand And Shovels	Epic 10485
3/18/72	**24**	8	27. Every Day Of My Life	Epic 10822
7/08/72	**19**	10	28. Sealed With A Kiss	Epic 10861
10/12/74	**3**	11	● **29. My Melody Of Love**	ABC 12022
4/19/75	**33**	2	30. Beer Barrel Polka #1 hit for Will Glahe in 1939	ABC 12056
			VIRTUES, The Philadelphia rock and roll instrumental trio led by Frank ("Virtue") Virtuoso.	
3/23/59	**5**	12	**1. Guitar Boogie Shuffle** [I] first released on Sure 501 in 1958	Hunt 324
			VISCOUNTS, The New Jersey instrumental quintet: Harry Haller (tenor saxophone), brothers Bobby (guitar) and Joe Spievak (bass), Larry Vecchio (organ) and Clark Smith (drums).	
1/01/66	**39**	1	1. Harlem Nocturne [I-R] originally charted in 1959 (POS 52)	Amy 940
			VIXEN Los Angeles-based, female heavy-metal quartet: Janet Kuehnemund, Janet Gardner (vocals), Roxy Petrucci and Share Pedersen (who was part of Contraband in 1991).	
10/29/88	**26**	5	1. Edge Of A Broken Heart written, produced and arranged by Richard Marx	EMI-Man. 50141
2/25/89	**22**	6	2. Cryin'	EMI-Man. 50167
			VOGUES, The Vocal group formed in Turtle Creek, Pennsylvania in 1960. Consisted of Bill Burkette (lead), Hugh Geyer and Chuck Blasko (tenors) and Don Miller (baritone). Met in high school.	
10/09/65	**4**	9	**1. You're The One** first released on Blue Star 229 in 1965	Co & Ce 229
12/11/65+	**4**	12	**2. Five O'Clock World**	Co & Ce 232
3/19/66	**21**	6	3. Magic Town	Co & Ce 234
6/25/66	**29**	4	4. The Land Of Milk And Honey	Co & Ce 238
7/13/68	**7**	11	● **5. Turn Around, Look At Me**	Reprise 0686
9/21/68	**7**	8	**6. My Special Angel**	Reprise 0766
12/07/68	**27**	4	7. Till	Reprise 0788
3/29/69	**34**	2	8. No, Not Much	Reprise 0803

DATE	POS	WKS	ARTIST—RECORD TITLE	LABEL & NO.
			VOICES THAT CARE	
			Benefit spearheaded by David Foster and his fiancee Linda Thompson Jenner (ex-wife of Olympian Bruce Jenner) supporting the Persian Gulf allied troops and their families. Among superstar choir: Kevin Costner, Meryl Streep, Billy Crystal, Richard Gere, Gloria Estefan, Wayne Gretzky and many others.	
3/30/91	**11**	11	● 1. Voices That Care	Giant 19350
			lead vocals: Ralph Tresvant, Randy Travis, Celine Dion, Peter Cetera, Bobby Brown, Brenda Russell, Warrant, Luther Vandross, Garth Brooks, Kathy Mattea, Nelson, Michael Bolton, Little Richard, Pointer Sisters, Fresh Prince, Mark Knopfler, Kenny G and Warren Wiebe; co-written by Cetera, Foster and Jenner	
			VOLUME'S, The	
			Detroit R&B quintet featuring lead singer Ed Union.	
6/02/62	**22**	6	1. I Love You	Chex 1002
			VOUDOURIS, Roger	
			Born on 12/29/54 in Sacramento, California. Pop singer/songwriter/guitarist.	
4/28/79	**21**	10	1. Get Used To It	Warner 8762
			VOXPOPPERS, The	
			New York City group.	
5/05/58	**18**	1	1. Wishing For Your Love	Mercury 71282
			Jockey #18 / Best Seller #41 / Top 100 #44 first released on Amp 3 1004 in 1958	
			W	
			WADE, Adam	
			Born on 3/17/37 in Pittsburgh. Attended Virginia State College and worked as lab assistant with Dr. Jonas Salk team. TV actor/host of the 1976 game show "Musical Chairs." Worked in *Guys & Dolls* musical in Las Vegas in 1978. TV talkshow host in Los Angeles in the '80s.	
3/27/61	**7**	10	**1. Take Good Care Of Her**	Coed 546
5/29/61	**5**	9	**2. The Writing On The Wall**	Coed 550
8/07/61	**10**	7	**3. As If I Didn't Know**	Coed 553
			all of above with George Paxton & His Orchestra	
			WADSWORTH MANSION	
			Rock quartet: Steve Jablecki (lead vocals), Wayne Gagnon, John Poole and Mike Jablecki.	
2/13/71	**7**	7	**1. Sweet Mary**	Sussex 209
			WAGNER, Jack	
			Born and raised in Washington, Missouri. Plays Frisco Jones on the TV soap opera "General Hospital."	
11/24/84+	**2**(2)	12	**1. All I Need**	Qwest 29238
			WAIKIKIS, The	
			Belgian instrumental group.	
1/09/65	**33**	3	1. Hawaii Tattoo [I]	Kapp 30

DATE	POS	WKS	ARTIST—RECORD TITLE	LABEL & NO.
			WAILERS, The	
			Teenage rock and roll instrumental quintet from Tacoma, Washington formed in 1958 by rhythm guitarist John Greek. Original lineup also included Rich Dangel, Mark Marush, Kent Morrill and Mike Burk.	
6/01/59	**36**	2	1. Tall Cool One [I]	Golden Crest 518
5/30/64	**38**	1	2. Tall Cool One [I-R]	Golden Crest 518
			WAINWRIGHT, Loudon III	
			Born on 9/05/46 in Chapel Hill, North Carolina. Satirical folk singer/songwriter. Acted in three episodes of "M*A*S*H" as Capt. Calvin Spaulding. Appeared in films *The Slugger's Wife* and *Jacknife*.	
2/24/73	**16**	9	1. Dead Skunk [N]	Columbia 45726
			WAITE, John	
			Born on 7/04/55 in England. Lead singer of The Babys and Bad English.	
7/21/84	**1**(1)	16	**1. Missing You**	EMI America 8212
11/10/84	**37**	4	2. Tears	EMI America 8238
8/31/85	**25**	6	3. Every Step Of The Way	EMI America 8282
			WAKELIN, Johnny/The Kinshasa Band	
			British group led by singer/songwriter Wakelin.	
8/16/75	**21**	6	1. Black Superman - "Muhammad Ali" [N]	Pye 71012
			WALKER, Jr./The All Stars	
			R&B group formed in South Bend, Indiana by Walker (born Autry DeWalt II in Blythesville, Arkansas, 1942). Included Walker (sax, vocals), Willie Woods (guitar), Vic Thomas (organ) and James Graves (drums). First recorded for Harvey in 1962. Most recent group included son Autry DeWalt, Jr. on drums.	
3/06/65	**4**	10	**1. Shotgun**	Soul 35008
7/03/65	**36**	2	2. Do The Boomerang	Soul 35012
8/21/65	**29**	5	3. Shake And Fingerpop	Soul 35013
5/21/66	**20**	6	4. (I'm A) Road Runner	Soul 35015
9/03/66	**18**	5	5. How Sweet It Is (To Be Loved By You)	Soul 35024
3/11/67	**31**	4	6. Pucker Up Buttercup	Soul 35030
12/23/67+	**24**	6	7. Come See About Me	Soul 35041
9/14/68	**31**	6	8. Hip City - Pt. 2	Soul 35048
6/21/69	**4**	11	**9. What Does It Take (To Win Your Love)**	Soul 35062
11/22/69	**16**	9	10. These Eyes	Soul 35067
2/28/70	**21**	9	11. Gotta Hold On To This Feeling	Soul 35070
8/01/70	**32**	4	12. Do You See My Love (For You Growing)	Soul 35073
			WALKER BROS., The	
			Los Angeles pop trio: Scott Engel, Gary Leeds and John Maus. More popular in England than the U.S. (charted 10 hits in the U.K.).	
11/13/65	**16**	6	1. Make It Easy On Yourself first released on Smash 2000 in 1965	Smash 2009
4/30/66	**13**	7	2. The Sun Ain't Gonna Shine (Anymore)	Smash 2032
			WALLACE, Jerry	
			Born on 12/15/28 in Guilford, Missouri and raised in Glendale, Arizona. Pop-country singer/guitarist. First recorded for Allied in 1951. Appeared on the TV shows "Night Gallery" and "Hec Ramsey."	
9/15/58	**11**	9	1. How The Time Flies Hot 100 #11 / Best Seller #33 end	Challenge 59013
9/07/59	**8**	15	**2. Primrose Lane**	Challenge 59047

DATE	POS	WKS	ARTIST—RECORD TITLE	LABEL & NO.
			JERRY WALLACE with THE JEWELS theme song for Henry Fonda's TV show "The Smith Family"	
2/01/60	**36**	2	3. Little Coco Palm	Challenge 59060
1/09/61	**26**	4	4. There She Goes	Challenge 59098
12/22/62+	**24**	7	5. Shutters And Boards written by movie star, Audie Murphy	Challenge 9171
8/22/64	**19**	7	6. In The Misty Moonlight	Challenge 59246
9/30/72	**38**	2	7. If You Leave Me Tonight I'll Cry from TV's "Night Gallery: The Tune In Dan's Cafe"	Decca 32989
			WALSH, Joe	
			Born on 11/20/47 in Wichita, Kansas. Rock singer/songwriter/guitarist. Member of The James Gang (1969-71) and the Eagles (1975-82).	
9/22/73	**23**	7	1. Rocky Mountain Way	Dunhill 4361
7/01/78	**12**	9	2. Life's Been Good	Asylum 45493
6/14/80	**19**	8	3. All Night Long from the film *Urban Cowboy*	Full Moon 46639
6/27/81	**34**	4	4. A Life Of Illusion	Asylum 47144
			WAMMACK, Travis	
			Muscle Shoals' session guitarist.	
8/09/75	**38**	2	1. (Shu-Doo-Pa-Poo-Poop) Love Being Your Fool	Capricorn 0239
			WANDERLEY, Walter	
			Brazilian organist/pianist/composer. Died of cancer on 9/04/86 (age 55).	
10/01/66	**26**	4	1. Summer Samba (So Nice) [I]	Verve 10421
			WANG CHUNG	
			British pop-rock group: Jack Hues (lead singer, guitar, keyboards), Nick Feldman (bass, keyboards) and Darren Costin (drums). Costin left in 1985.	
3/10/84	**38**	3	1. Don't Let Go	Geffen 29377
5/26/84	**16**	10	2. Dance Hall Days	Geffen 29310
10/25/86	**2**(2)	15	**3. Everybody Have Fun Tonight**	Geffen 28562
2/14/87	**9**	11	**4. Let's Go!**	Geffen 28531
7/25/87	**36**	2	5. Hypnotize Me from the film *Innerspace*	Geffen 28359
			WAR	
			Band formed in Long Beach, California in 1969. Consisted of Leroy "Lonnie" Jordan (keyboards), Howard Scott (guitar), Charles Miller (saxophone; murdered in 1980), Morris "B.B." Dickerson (bass), Harold Brown and Thomas "Papa Dee" Allen (percussion) and Lee Oskar (harmonica). Eric Burdon's backup band until 1971. Dickerson was replaced by Luther Rabb. Lee Oskar recorded solo, beginning in 1976. Alice Tweed Smyth (vocals) added in 1978. Pat Rizzo (horns) and Ron Hammond (former member of Aalon; percussion) added in 1979. Smyth left group in 1982.	
7/11/70	**3**	13	● **1. Spill The Wine** **ERIC BURDON AND WAR**	MGM 14118
9/25/71	**35**	2	2. All Day Music	United Art. 50815
4/01/72	**16**	10	● 3. Slippin' Into Darkness	United Art. 50867
12/30/72+	**7**	9	● **4. The World Is A Ghetto**	United Art. 50975
3/24/73	**2**(2)	12	● **5. The Cisco Kid**	United Art. 163
8/04/73	**8**	10	**6. Gypsy Man**	United Art. 281
12/08/73+	**15**	10	7. Me And Baby Brother	United Art. 350
7/13/74	**33**	2	8. Ballero [I]	United Art. 432

DATE	POS	WKS	ARTIST—RECORD TITLE	LABEL & NO.
6/14/75	**6**	13	• **9. Why Can't We Be Friends?**	United Art. 629
10/11/75	**7**	11	**10. Low Rider**	United Art. 706
7/31/76	**7**	12	• **11. Summer**	United Art. 834
2/11/78	**39**	2	12. Galaxy all of above produced by Jerry Goldstein	MCA 40820
			WARD, Anita	
			Born on 12/20/57 in Memphis. R&B-disco vocalist. Toured in Rust College female quartet.	
5/26/79	**1**(2)	15	**1. Ring My Bell** written and produced by Frederick Knight	Juana 3422
			WARD, Billy/His Dominoes	
			R&B group formed as The Dominoes in New York in 1950 by Ward (b: Los Angeles) and talent agent Rose Marks. Consisted of Ward (piano), Clyde McPhatter (lead), Charlie White (tenor), Joe Lamont (baritone) and Bill Brown (bass). Signed by King/Federal in 1950. Lead singers, at various times: Clyde McPhatter (1950-53), Jackie Wilson (1953-57) and Eugene Mumford.	
9/15/56	**13**	6	1. St. Therese Of The Roses Jockey #13 / Best Seller #20 / Top 100 #27 Jackie Wilson, lead singer	Decca 29933
7/15/57	**12**	17	2. Star Dust Jockey #12 / Top 100 #13 / Best Seller #14 there have been 19 charted versions of this Hoagy Carmichael tune	Liberty 55071
10/07/57	**20**	8	3. Deep Purple Best Seller #20 / Top 100 #22 3 versions of this tune hit the top 10 in 1939	Liberty 55099
			WARD, Dale	
			Pop-country vocalist. Dale was not a member of The Crescendos, as rumored.	
2/01/64	**25**	5	1. Letter From Sherry Dale's version of "Oh Julie" is on the B-side	Dot 16520
			WARD, Joe	
			Eight-year-old boy from Cincinnati.	
12/24/55	**20**	3	1. Nuttin For Xmas [N-X] Juke Box #20 / Best Seller #22 / Top 100 #22	King 4854
			WARD, Robin	
			Real name: Jackie Ward. Pop female singer originally from Nebraska. Also see Pat Boone.	
11/16/63	**14**	7	1. Wonderful Summer	Dot 16530
			WARNES, Jennifer	
			Born in Seattle and raised in Orange County, California. Pop/MOR-styled vocalist. Lead actress in the Los Angeles production of *Hair*.	
2/26/77	**6**	14	**1. Right Time Of The Night**	Arista 0223
9/22/79	**19**	8	2. I Know A Heartache When I See One	Arista 0430
10/02/82	**1**(3)	15	▲ **3. Up Where We Belong** **JOE COCKER AND JENNIFER WARNES** love theme from the film *An Officer and a Gentleman*	Island 99996
10/10/87	**1**(1)	15	• **4. (I've Had) The Time Of My Life** **BILL MEDLEY AND JENNIFER WARNES** love theme from the film *Dirty Dancing*	RCA 5224

DATE	POS	WKS	ARTIST—RECORD TITLE	LABEL & NO.
			WARRANT	
			Los Angeles, male hard-rock band: Jani Lane (vocals), Erik Turner (guitar), Joey Allen (guitar), Jerry Dixon (bass) and Steven Sweet (drums). Lane married Bobbie Brown, spokesmodel champion on TV's "Star Search," on 7/27/91.	
6/10/89	**27**	6	1. Down Boys	Columbia 68606
8/05/89	2(2)	14	● **2. Heaven**	Columbia 68985
2/03/90	**20**	9	3. Sometimes She Cries	Columbia 73300
9/29/90	**10**	9	**4. Cherry Pie**	Columbia 73510
1/05/91	**10**	11	**5. I Saw Red**	Columbia 73597
			WARWICK, Dionne	
			Born Marie Dionne Warwick on 12/12/40 in East Orange, New Jersey. In church choir from age six. With the Drinkard Singers gospel group. Formed trio, the Gospelaires, with sister Dee Dee and their aunt Cissy Houston. Attended Hartt College Of Music, Hartford, Connecticut. Much backup studio work in New York during the late '50s. Added an "e" to her last name for a time in the early '70s. She was Burt Bacharach and Hal David's main "voice" for the songs they composed. Co-hosted TV's "Solid Gold" 1980-81, 1985-86.	
1/05/63	**21**	7	1. Don't Make Me Over	Scepter 1239
1/04/64	**8**	9	**2. Anyone Who Had A Heart**	Scepter 1262
5/09/64	**6**	11	**3. Walk On By**	Scepter 1274
9/19/64	**34**	3	4. You'll Never Get To Heaven (If You Break My Heart)	Scepter 1282
11/07/64	**20**	6	5. Reach Out For Me	Scepter 1285
1/22/66	**39**	1	6. Are You There (With Another Girl)	Scepter 12122
4/23/66	**8**	8	**7. Message To Michael**	Scepter 12133
7/16/66	**22**	5	8. Trains And Boats And Planes	Scepter 12153
10/22/66	**26**	5	9. I Just Don't Know What To Do With Myself	Scepter 12167
5/27/67	**15**	9	10. Alfie written for (but not included in) the film *Alfie*	Scepter 12187
8/26/67	**32**	3	11. The Windows Of The World	Scepter 12196
11/04/67	**4**	10	● **12. I Say A Little Prayer/**	
2/03/68	2(4)	11	**13. (Theme From) Valley Of The Dolls** from the film *Valley of the Dolls*	Scepter 12203
4/27/68	**10**	9	**14. Do You Know The Way To San Jose**	Scepter 12216
9/21/68	**33**	4	15. Who Is Gonna Love Me?	Scepter 12226
11/23/68	**19**	6	16. Promises, Promises from the Broadway musical of the same title (also #20 below)	Scepter 12231
2/08/69	**7**	11	**17. This Girl's In Love With You**	Scepter 12241
6/07/69	**37**	3	18. The April Fools	Scepter 12249
10/11/69	**16**	7	19. You've Lost That Lovin' Feeling	Scepter 12262
1/03/70	**6**	10	**20. I'll Never Fall In Love Again**	Scepter 12273
5/09/70	**32**	3	21. Let Me Go To Him	Scepter 12276
10/31/70	**37**	2	22. Make It Easy On Yourself all of above produced by Burt Bacharach and Hal David; all of above (except #13 & 19) written by Bacharach & David	Scepter 12294
8/03/74	1(1)	15	● **23. Then Came You** DIONNE WARWICKE AND SPINNERS	Atlantic 3202
7/28/79	**5**	17	● **24. I'll Never Love This Way Again**	Arista 0419
12/15/79+	**15**	11	25. Deja Vu	Arista 0459

DATE	POS	WKS	ARTIST—RECORD TITLE	LABEL & NO.
			above 2 produced by Barry Manilow	
9/06/80	**23**	6	26. No Night So Long	Arista 0527
5/29/82	**38**	3	27. Friends In Love **DIONNE WARWICK AND JOHNNY MATHIS**	Arista 0673
11/06/82+	**10**	13	**28. Heartbreaker** backing vocal: Barry Gibb	Arista 1015
10/29/83	**27**	5	29. How Many Times Can We Say Goodbye **DIONNE WARWICK AND LUTHER VANDROSS**	Arista 9073
11/23/85+	**1**(4)	17	• **30. That's What Friends Are For** **DIONNE & FRIENDS: Elton John, Gladys Knight and Stevie Wonder**	Arista 9422
7/25/87	**12**	9	31. Love Power **DIONNE WARWICK & JEFFREY OSBORNE**	Arista 9567
			WASHINGTON, Baby	
			Born Justine Washington (aka: Jeanette Washington) on 11/13/40 in Bamberg, South Carolina and raised in Harlem. R&B vocalist/pianist. Sang in '50s vocal group, The Hearts. First recorded solo for J&S in 1957.	
6/01/63	**40**	1	1. That's How Heartaches Are Made	Sue 783
			WASHINGTON, Dinah	
			Born Ruth Lee Jones on 8/29/24 in Tuscaloosa, Alabama; died on 12/14/63 (overdose of alcohol and pills). Jazz-blues vocalist/pianist. Moved to Chicago in 1927. With Sallie Martin Gospel Singers, 1940-41; local club work in Chicago, 1941-43. With Lionel Hampton, 1943-46. First recorded for Keynote in 1943. Solo touring from 1946. Married seven times, once to singer Eddie Chamblee.	
6/22/59	**8**	14	**1. What A Diff'rence A Day Makes** #5 hit for the Dorsey Brothers in 1934	Mercury 71435
10/26/59	**17**	8	2. Unforgettable #12 hit for Nat King Cole in 1952	Mercury 71508
2/08/60	**5**	12	**3. Baby (You've Got What It Takes)** **DINAH WASHINGTON & BROOK BENTON**	Mercury 71565
6/06/60	**7**	10	**4. A Rockin' Good Way (To Mess Around And Fall In Love)** **DINAH WASHINGTON & BROOK BENTON**	Mercury 71629
7/18/60	**24**	6	5. This Bitter Earth	Mercury 71635
11/07/60	**30**	2	6. Love Walked In 3 versions of this Gershwin tune hit the top 10 in 1938	Mercury 71696
11/06/61	**23**	6	7. September In The Rain #1 hit for Guy Lombardo in 1937	Mercury 71876
6/23/62	**36**	3	8. Where Are You #5 hit for Mildred Bailey in 1937	Roulette 4424
			WASHINGTON, Grover, Jr.	
			Jazz-R&B saxophonist Washington was born on 12/12/43 in Buffalo. Prolific session artist in Philadelphia. Withers had several solo hits.	
3/07/81	**2**(3)	16	**1. Just The Two Of Us** **GROVER WASHINGTON, JR./BILL WITHERS**	Elektra 47103
			WASHINGTON, Keith	
			Detroit native. Supporting vocalist while a teen for The Dramatics. Former backing vocalist for the Jacksons and Miki Howard.	
7/13/91	**40**	1	1. Kissing You	Qwest 19414

DATE	POS	WKS	ARTIST—RECORD TITLE	LABEL & NO.
			WAS (NOT WAS)	
			Detroit rock-funk ensemble fronted by composer/bassist Don Fagenson and lyricist/flutist David Weiss. Includes vocalists Sweet Pea Atkinson and Sir Harry Bowens. Group appeared in the film *The Freshman.*	
11/05/88	**16**	10	1. Spy In The House Of Love	Chrysalis 43266
2/18/89	**7**	9	**2. Walk The Dinosaur**	Chrysalis 43331
			WATERFRONT	
			Male duo of singer Chris Duffy and guitarist Phil Cilia from Cardiff, Wales. Band name derived from the Marlon Brando film *On the Waterfront.*	
5/06/89	**10**	10	**1. Cry**	Polydor 871110
			WATERS, Crystal	
			Female singer from South New Jersey. Majored in computer science at Howard University. Her father is jazz musician Jr. Waters; her aunt is Ethel Waters.	
6/01/91	**8**	9	● **1. Gypsy Woman (She's Homeless)**	Mercury 868208
			WATLEY, Jody	
			Born on 1/30/59 in Chicago. Female vocalist of Shalamar (1977-84) and former dancer on TV's "Soul Train." Her godfather was Jackie Wilson. Won the 1987 Best New Artist Grammy Award.	
3/21/87	**2**(4)	14	**1. Looking For A New Love**	MCA 52956
10/24/87	**6**	14	**2. Don't You Want Me**	MCA 53162
2/27/88	**10**	10	**3. Some Kind Of Lover**	MCA 53235
4/01/89	**2**(2)	12	● **4. Real Love**	MCA 53484
7/08/89	**9**	11	**5. Friends** JODY WATLEY with ERIC B. & RAKIM	MCA 53660
11/18/89+	**4**	14	**6. Everything**	MCA 53714
			WATTS 103rd STREET RHYTHM BAND — see WRIGHT, Charles	
			WA WA NEE	
			Australian-based dance band. Includes Australians Steve Williams and brothers Mark and Paul Gray, plus Chris Sweeney (from the U.S.) and Phil Witchett (from New Zealand).	
10/31/87	**35**	3	1. Sugar Free	Epic 07283
			WAYLON & WILLIE — see JENNINGS, Waylon, and/or NELSON, Willie	
			WAYNE, Thomas, with THE DeLONS	
			Born Thomas Wayne Perkins on 7/22/40 in Battsville, Mississippi. Killed in an auto accident on 8/15/71. Brother of guitarist Luther Perkins of Johnny Cash's band.	
2/16/59	**5**	13	**1. Tragedy** produced by Scotty Moore (Elvis' former guitarist)	Fernwood 109
			WEATHERLY, Jim	
			Pop-country songwriter/singer born on 3/17/43 in Pontotoc, Mississippi. Wrote Gladys Knight's hits "Neither One Of Us," "Midnight Train To Georgia" and "Best Thing That Ever Happened To Me."	
10/12/74	**11**	8	1. The Need To Be	Buddah 420
			WEBER, Joan	
			Born in 1936 and raised in Paulsboro, New Jersey; died on 5/13/81 (age 45).	
12/04/54+	**1**(4)	16	**1. Let Me Go Lover**	Columbia 40366

DATE	POS	WKS	ARTIST—RECORD TITLE	LABEL & NO.
			Jockey #1(4) / Juke Box #1(4) / Best Seller #1(2) heard six times on the 11/15/54 "Studio One" CBS-TV production	
			WEDNESDAY	
			Pop quartet: Mike O'Neil (vocals), Randy Begg, John Dufek and Paul Andrew Smith.	
2/16/74	**34**	4	1. Last Kiss	Sussex 507
			WE FIVE	
			California pop quintet: Beverly Bivens (lead singer), Mike Stewart (brother of John Stewart), Pete Fullerton, Bob Jones and Jerry Burgan.	
8/07/65	**3**	13	**1. You Were On My Mind**	A&M 770
12/25/65	**31**	2	2. Let's Get Together	A&M 784
			WEISBERG, Tim — see FOGELBERG, Dan	
			WEISSBERG, Eric, & STEVE MANDELL	
			Prominent session musicians. Both had worked with Judy Collins and John Denver.	
2/03/73	**2**(4)	11	• **1. Dueling Banjos** [I] tune written in 1955; featured in the film *Deliverance*	Warner 7659
			WELCH, Bob	
			Born on 7/31/46 in Los Angeles. Guitarist/vocalist with Fleetwood Mac (1971-74). Formed the British rock group Paris in 1976. His father, Robert L. Welch, was a major film/TV producer.	
11/19/77+	**8**	11	**1. Sentimental Lady** backing vocals by Christine McVie and Lindsey Buckingham	Capitol 4479
2/25/78	**14**	10	2. Ebony Eyes	Capitol 4543
7/01/78	**31**	3	3. Hot Love, Cold World	Capitol 4588
3/17/79	**19**	8	4. Precious Love	Capitol 4685
			WELCH, Lenny	
			Born on 5/15/38 in Asbury Park, New Jersey. Black MOR vocalist.	
11/23/63	**4**	12	**1. Since I Fell For You** #20 hit for Paul Gayten in 1947	Cadence 1439
4/11/64	**25**	5	2. Ebb Tide featured in the film *Sweet Bird of Youth*; both Frank Chacksfield & Vic Damone had top 10 versions in 1953	Cadence 1422
2/14/70	**34**	4	3. Breaking Up Is Hard To Do	Common. U. 3004
			WELK, Lawrence	
			Born on 3/11/03 in Strasburg, North Dakota. Accordionist and polka/sweet bandleader since the mid-1920s. Band's style labeled as "champagne music." Own national TV musical variety show began on 7/02/55 and ran on ABC until 9/04/71. New episodes in syndication from 1971 to 1982.	
3/03/56	**17**	2	1. Moritat (A Theme From "The Threepenny Opera") [I] Juke Box #17 / Top 100 #31	Coral 61574
4/07/56	**17**	2	2. The Poor People Of Paris [I] Juke Box #17 / Top 100 #45	Coral 61592
8/11/56	**32**	3	3. Weary Blues **THE McGUIRE SISTERS AND LAWRENCE WELK**	Coral 61670
9/29/56	**15**	10	4. Tonight You Belong To Me **LAWRENCE WELK with THE LENNON SISTERS** Top 100 #15 / Best Seller #16 / Jockey #16 / Juke Box #17	Coral 61701
12/05/60	**21**	3	5. Last Date [I]	Dot 16145

DATE	POS	WKS	ARTIST—RECORD TITLE	LABEL & NO.
12/31/60+	1(2)	13	● **6. Calcutta** [I] above 2 feature Frank Scott (on piano & harpsichord, respectively)	Dot 16161
			WELLS, Mary	
			R&B vocalist born on 5/13/43 in Detroit. At age 17, presented "Bye Bye Baby," a tune she had written for Jackie Wilson, to Wilson's producer, Berry Gordy, Jr. Gordy signed her to his newly formed label, Motown. Wells was the first to have a top 10 and #1 single for that label. Married for a time to Cecil Womack (brother of Bobby Womack). Diagnosed with throat cancer, August 1990.	
8/21/61	**33**	3	1. I Don't Want To Take A Chance	Motown 1011
5/05/62	**8**	10	**2. The One Who Really Loves You**	Motown 1024
8/25/62	**9**	9	**3. You Beat Me To The Punch**	Motown 1032
12/15/62+	**7**	10	**4. Two Lovers**	Motown 1035
3/09/63	**15**	6	5. Laughing Boy	Motown 1039
7/06/63	**40**	1	6. Your Old Stand By	Motown 1042
10/12/63	**22**	7	7. You Lost The Sweetest Boy/	
1/25/64	**29**	6	8. What's Easy For Two Is So Hard	For One Motown 1048
4/11/64	1(2)	13	**9. My Guy** above 8 (except #7) written and produced by Smokey Robinson	Motown 1056
5/23/64	**19**	6	10. Once Upon A Time/ **MARVIN GAYE & MARY WELLS**	
6/13/64	**17**	6	11. What's The Matter With You Baby **MARVIN GAYE & MARY WELLS**	Motown 1057
1/30/65	**34**	2	12. Use Your Head	20th Century 555
			WESLEY, Fred — see JB's	
			WEST, Dottie	
			Born Dorothy Marsh on 10/11/32 in McMinnville, Tennessee. Died on 9/04/91 from injuries suffered in a car accident. Country singer.	
4/25/81	**14**	12	1. What Are We Doin' In Love **DOTTIE WEST with KENNY ROGERS**	Liberty 1404
			WEST COAST RAP ALL-STARS, The	
			Rap benefit for inner city youth: Above The Law, Body & Soul, Def Jef, Digital Underground, Eazy-E, Ice-T, J.J. Fad, King Tee, M.C. Hammer, Michel'le, N.W.A., Oaktown's 3-5-7, Tone Loc and Young M.C.	
8/11/90	**35**	3	● 1. We're All In The Same Gang produced by Andre "Dr. Dre" Young of N.W.A.	Warner 19819#
			WESTON, Kim	
			Born Agatha Natalie Weston in Detroit. R&B vocalist, previously sang in gospel groups.	
2/04/67	**14**	7	1. It Takes Two **MARVIN GAYE & KIM WESTON**	Tamla 54141
			WET WILLIE	
			Mobile, Alabama rock band led by brothers Jimmy (vocals) and Jack Hall (bass).	
7/06/74	**10**	11	**1. Keep On Smilin'**	Capricorn 0043
1/28/78	**30**	4	2. Street Corner Serenade	Epic 50478
6/30/79	**29**	5	3. Weekend	Epic 50714
			WHAM! — see MICHAEL, George	

DATE	POS	WKS	ARTIST—RECORD TITLE	LABEL & NO.
			WHEN IN ROME	
			U.K.-based trio: Clive Farrington (vocals), Michael Floreale (keyboards) and Andrew Mann (vocals).	
10/22/88	**11**	13	1. The Promise	Virgin 99323
			WHISPERS, The	
			Los Angeles soul group formed in 1964. Consisted of Gordy Harmon, twin brothers Walter and Wallace "Scotty" Scott, Marcus Hutson and Nicholas Caldwell. First recorded for Dore in 1964. Harmon replaced in 1973 by Leaveil Degree who was briefly a member of Friends Of Distinction.	
3/15/80	**19**	8	● 1. And The Beat Goes On	Solar 11894
5/24/80	**28**	4	2. Lady	Solar 11928
3/28/81	**28**	5	3. It's A Love Thing	Solar 12154
7/11/87	**7**	12	**4. Rock Steady**	Solar 70006
			WHISTLE	
			Formed as a Brooklyn rap trio in 1985 with Garvin Dublin, Brian Faust and Rickford Bennett. By late 1988, Kerry "Kraze" Hodge was added and Dublin left, replaced by Tarek Stevens; group pursued R&B format.	
5/19/90	**35**	4	1. Always And Forever	Select 2014#
			WHITCOMB, Ian	
			Born on 7/10/41 in Woking, England. Pop singer/songwriter/author. Currently resides in California.	
6/19/65	**8**	8	**1. You Turn Me On (Turn On Song)** IAN WHITCOMB AND BLUESVILLE	Tower 134
			WHITE, Barry	
			Born on 9/12/44 in Galveston, Texas and raised in Los Angeles. Soul singer/songwriter/keyboardist/ producer/arranger. With Upfronts vocal group, recorded for Lummtone in 1960. A&R man for Mustang/Bronco, 1966-67. Formed Love Unlimited in 1969, which included future wife Glodean James. Leader of 40-piece Love Unlimited Orchestra.	
5/05/73	**3**	12	● **1. I'm Gonna Love You Just A Little More Baby**	20th Century 2018
9/01/73	**32**	6	2. I've Got So Much To Give	20th Century 2042
11/17/73+	**7**	15	● **3. Never, Never Gonna Give Ya Up**	20th Century 2058
8/10/74	**1**(1)	9	● **4. Can't Get Enough Of Your Love, Babe**	20th Century 2120
11/16/74+	**2**(2)	12	● **5. You're The First, The Last, My Everything**	20th Century 2133
3/22/75	**8**	7	**6. What Am I Gonna Do With You**	20th Century 2177
6/21/75	**40**	2	7. I'll Do For You Anything You Want Me To	20th Century 2208
1/24/76	**32**	4	8. Let The Music Play	20th Century 2265
10/01/77	**4**	12	● **9. It's Ecstasy When You Lay Down Next To Me**	20th Century 2350
5/27/78	**24**	5	10. Oh What A Night For Dancing all of above written (except #9) and produced by Barry White	20th Century 2365
4/07/90	**31**	4	11. The Secret Garden (Sweet Seduction Suite) QUINCY JONES/AL B. SURE!/JAMES INGRAM/ EL DeBARGE/BARRY WHITE	Qwest 19992
			WHITE, Karyn	
			Prominent session singer from Los Angeles. Touring vocalist with O'Bryan in 1984. Recorded with jazz-fusion keyboardist Jeff Lorber in 1986. Married to superproducer Terry Lewis (member of The Time).	
2/07/87	**27**	5	1. Facts Of Love JEFF LORBER featuring KARYN WHITE	Warner 28588
11/26/88+	**7**	14	● **2. The Way You Love Me**	Warner 27773
2/25/89	**8**	10	● **3. Superwoman**	Warner 27783

DATE	POS	WKS	ARTIST—RECORD TITLE	LABEL & NO.
7/01/89	**6**	12	**4. Secret Rendezvous**	Warner 27863
			WHITE, Tony Joe	
			Born on 7/23/43 in Oak Grove, Louisiana. Bayou rock singer/songwriter. Wrote Brook Benton's hit "Rainy Night In Georgia."	
7/26/69	**8**	8	**1. Polk Salad Annie**	Monument 1104
			produced by Billy Swan	
			WHITE LION	
			New York-based rock band: Mike Tramp (vocals), James Lomenzo, Vito Bratta and Greg D'Angelo (a founding member of Anthrax). Tramp is a native of Denmark.	
4/09/88	**8**	11	**1. Wait**	Atlantic 89126
12/17/88+	**3**	12	**2. When The Children Cry**	Atlantic 89015
			WHITE PLAINS	
			English studio group featuring Tony Burrows (vocals), who was also with The Brotherhood Of Man, Edison Lighthouse, First Class and The Pipkins.	
5/23/70	**13**	10	1. My Baby Loves Lovin'	Deram 85058
			WHITESNAKE	
			British heavy-metal band. Lead singer David Coverdale recorded solo under the name Whitesnake in the late 1970s. Recruited band members after first two Whitesnake albums. Coverdale and early Whitesnake members Jon Lord and Ian Paice were members of Deep Purple. 1987 lineup: Coverdale, John Sykes (guitar), Neil Murray (bass) and Aynsley Dunbar (former Jefferson Starship drummer). Sykes left in 1988 to form Blue Murder. Coverdale fronted new lineup in 1989: Steve Vai (David Lee Roth's former guitarist), Adrian Vandenberg (former guitarist of Vandenberg), Rudy Sarzo (bass) and Tommy Aldridge (drums).	
8/08/87	**1**(1)	14	**1. Here I Go Again**	Geffen 28339
11/07/87	**2**(1)	13	**2. Is This Love**	Geffen 28233
12/16/89	**37**	3	3. Fool For Your Loving [R]	Geffen 22715#
2/17/90	**28**	6	4. The Deeper The Love	Geffen 19951
			WHITING, Margaret	
			Born on 7/22/24 in Detroit and raised in Hollywood. Daughter of popular composer Richard Whiting ("Till We Meet Again"). Very popular from 1946-54, she had over 40 charted hits.	
12/08/56	**20**	5	1. The Money Tree	Capitol 3586
			Jockey #20 / Top 100 #49	
11/19/66	**26**	5	2. The Wheel Of Hurt	London 101
			WHITTAKER, Roger	
			Born on 3/22/36 in Nairobi, Kenya. British adult-contemporary singer.	
5/10/75	**19**	9	1. The Last Farewell	RCA 50030

DATE	POS	WKS	ARTIST—RECORD TITLE	LABEL & NO.
			WHO, The	
			Rock group formed in London in 1964. Consisted of Roger Daltrey (b: 3/01/44, lead singer), Pete Townshend (b: 5/19/45; guitar, vocals), John Entwistle (b: 10/09/44; bass) and Keith Moon (b: 8/23/47; drums). Originally known as the High Numbers in 1964. All but Moon had been in The Detours. Developed stage antics of destroying their instruments. 1969 rock opera album *Tommy* became a film in 1975. Solo work by members began in 1972. Moon died of a drug overdose on 9/07/78, replaced by Kenney Jones (formerly with Small Faces). 1973 rock opera album *Quadrophenia* became a film in 1979. The Who's biographical film *The Kids Are Alright* was released in 1979. Eleven fans trampled to death at their concert in Cincinnati on 12/03/79. Disbanded in 1982. Regrouped at "Live Aid" in 1986. Daltrey, Townshend and Entwistle reunited with an ensemble of 15 for a U.S. tour in 1989. Jones formed The Law with Paul Rodgers in 1991. Inducted into the Rock and Roll Hall of Fame in 1990.	
5/20/67	**24**	4	1. Happy Jack	Decca 32114
10/28/67	**9**	9	**2. I Can See For Miles**	Decca 32206
5/04/68	**40**	2	3. Call Me Lightning	Decca 32288
8/31/68	**25**	6	4. Magic Bus	Decca 32362
5/03/69	**19**	5	5. Pinball Wizard	Decca 32465
8/23/69	**37**	2	6. I'm Free	Decca 32519
8/01/70	**27**	6	7. Summertime Blues	Decca 32708
10/17/70	**12**	9	8. See Me, Feel Me	Decca 32729
8/07/71	**15**	10	9. Won't Get Fooled Again from the film *Lifehouse*	Decca 32846
12/04/71	**34**	5	10. Behind Blue Eyes	Decca 32888
8/05/72	**17**	8	11. Join Together	Decca 32983
1/13/73	**39**	2	12. The Relay	Track 33041
1/03/76	**16**	10	13. Squeeze Box	MCA 40475
9/16/78	**14**	9	14. Who Are You	MCA 40948
4/04/81	**18**	10	15. You Better You Bet	Warner 49698
10/09/82	**28**	6	16. Athena all of above (except #7) written by Pete Townshend	Warner 29905
			WIEDLIN, Jane	
			Born on 5/20/58 in Oconomowoc, Wisconsin and raised in California. Rhythm guitarist of the Go-Go's.	
6/11/88	**9**	10	**1. Rush Hour**	EMI-Man. 50118
			WILCOX, Harlow/The Oakies	
			Harlow is a top session guitarist from Norman, Oklahoma.	
11/22/69	**30**	6	1. Groovy Grubworm [I]	Plantation 28
			WILD CHERRY	
			White funk band formed in Steubenville, Ohio in the early '70s. Consisted of Bob Parissi (lead vocals, guitar), Bryan Bassett (guitar), Mark Avsec (keyboards), Allen Wentz (bass) and Ron Beitle (drums).	
7/31/76	**1**(3)	18	▲ **1. Play That Funky Music**	Epic 50225
			WILDE, Kim	
			Born Kim Smith on 11/18/60 in Chiswick, England. Pop-rock singer. Daughter of singer Marty Wilde.	
7/17/82	**25**	8	1. Kids In America	EMI America 8110
4/18/87	**1**(1)	13	**2. You Keep Me Hangin' On**	MCA 53024

DATE	POS	WKS	ARTIST—RECORD TITLE	LABEL & NO.
			WILDER, Matthew	
			Born and raised in Manhattan; moved to Los Angeles in the late '70s. Singer/songwriter/keyboardist. Session singer for Rickie Lee Jones and Bette Midler.	
11/26/83+	**5**	14	**1. Break My Stride**	Private I 04113
3/24/84	**33**	4	2. The Kid's American	Private I 04363
			WILLIAMS, Andy	
			Born Howard Andrew Williams on 12/03/28 in Wall Lake, Iowa. Formed quartet with his brothers and eventually moved to Los Angeles. With Bing Crosby on hit "Swingin' On A Star," 1944. With comedienne Kay Thompson in the mid-'40s. Went solo in 1952. On Steve Allen's "Tonight Show" from 1952-55. Own NBC-TV variety series from 1962-67, 1969-71. Appeared in the film *I'd Rather Be Rich* in 1964. Formerly married to singer/actress Claudine Longet. One of America's greatest pop-MOR singers.	
8/18/56	**7**	17	**1. Canadian Sunset** Jockey #7 / Top 100 #8 / Juke Box #9 / Best Seller #10	Cadence 1297
12/22/56	**33**	3	2. Baby Doll from the film of the same title	Cadence 1303
3/02/57	**1**(3)	14	**3. Butterfly** Top 100 #1(3) / Jockey #1(2) / Juke Box #2 / Best Seller #4	Cadence 1308
6/03/57	**8**	14	**4. I Like Your Kind Of Love** Jockey #8 / Top 100 #9 / Best Seller #10 / Juke Box #19 end female vocal: Peggy Powers	Cadence 1323
10/14/57	**17**	3	5. Lips Of Wine Jockey #17 / Top 100 #39	Cadence 1336
2/24/58	**3**	14	**6. Are You Sincere** Jockey #3 / Top 100 #10 / Best Seller #11	Cadence 1340
9/22/58	**17**	6	7. Promise Me, Love	Cadence 1351
1/12/59	**11**	15	8. The Hawaiian Wedding Song song written in 1926, with new lyrics added	Cadence 1358
9/28/59	**5**	11	**9. Lonely Street**	Cadence 1370
12/28/59+	**7**	9	**10. The Village Of St. Bernadette**	Cadence 1374
6/05/61	**37**	2	11. The Bilbao Song	Cadence 1398
7/14/62	**38**	1	12. Stranger On The Shore	Columbia 42451
11/03/62	**39**	1	13. Don't You Believe It	Columbia 42523
3/23/63	**2**(4)	12	**14. Can't Get Used To Losing You/**	
4/13/63	**26**	7	15. Days Of Wine And Roses from the film of the same title	Columbia 42674
7/06/63	**13**	8	16. Hopeless	Columbia 42784
1/25/64	**13**	8	17. A Fool Never Learns	Columbia 42950
5/16/64	**34**	4	18. Wrong For Each Other	Columbia 43015
10/03/64	**28**	5	19. On The Street Where You Live from the Broadway musical *My Fair Lady*	Columbia 43128
12/19/64+	**24**	7	20. Dear Heart from the film of the same title	Columbia 43180
4/24/65	**36**	3	21. And Roses And Roses	Columbia 43257
10/16/65	**40**	1	22. Ain't It True all of above Columbia's produced by Robert Mersey	Columbia 43358
4/22/67	**34**	3	23. Music To Watch Girls By	Columbia 44065
11/30/68	**33**	4	24. Battle Hymn Of The Republic with the St. Charles Borromeo Choir; recorded at St. Patrick's Cathedral on 6/08/68 as a eulogy to Senator Robert F. Kennedy	Columbia 44650

DATE	POS	WKS	ARTIST—RECORD TITLE	LABEL & NO.
5/03/69	**22**	7	25. Happy Heart	Columbia 44818
2/27/71	**9**	10	**26. (Where Do I Begin) Love Story** from the film *Love Story*	Columbia 45317
5/20/72	**34**	4	27. Love Theme From "The Godfather" (Speak Softly Love) from the film *The Godfather*	Columbia 45579
			WILLIAMS, Billy	
			Born on 12/28/10 in Waco, Texas; died on 10/17/72 in Chicago. Lead singer of The Charioteers from 1930-50. Formed own Billy Williams Quartet with Eugene Dixon, Claude Riddick and John Ball in 1950. Many appearances on TV, especially "Your Show of Shows" with Sid Caesar. By early '60s, had lost voice due to diabetes. Moved to Chicago and worked as a social worker until his death.	
6/17/57	**3**	18	**1. I'm Gonna Sit Right Down And Write Myself A Letter** Jockey #3 / Top 100 #6 / Best Seller #7 #5 hit for Fats Waller in 1935	Coral 61830
2/16/59	**39**	3	2. Nola #3 instrumental hit for bandleader Vincent Lopez in 1922; above 2 conducted by Dick Jacobs	Coral 62069
			WILLIAMS, Danny	
			Born on 1/07/42 in Port Elizabeth, South Africa. Moved to England in 1960.	
4/04/64	**9**	10	**1. White On White**	United Art. 685
			WILLIAMS, Deniece	
			Born Deniece Chandler on 6/03/51 in Gary, Indiana. Soul vocalist/songwriter. Recorded for Toddlin' Town, early 1960s. Member of Wonderlove, Stevie Wonder's backup group, from 1972-75. Also a popular Inspirational artist.	
3/05/77	**25**	7	1. Free	Columbia 10429
4/22/78	**1**(1)	11	● **2. Too Much, Too Little, Too Late** **JOHNNY MATHIS/DENIECE WILLIAMS**	Columbia 10693
5/01/82	**10**	9	**3. It's Gonna Take A Miracle**	ARC 02812
4/14/84	**1**(2)	14	● **4. Let's Hear It For The Boy** from the film *Footloose*	Columbia 04417
			WILLIAMS, Don	
			Born on 5/27/39 in Floydada, Texas. Country singer/songwriter/guitarist. Charted over 15 #1 country hits. Leader of the Pozo-Seco Singers. In films *W.W. & The Dixie Dancekings* and *Smokey & The Bandit 2.*	
11/15/80	**24**	9	1. I Believe In You	MCA 41304
			WILLIAMS, John	
			Born on 2/08/32 in New York City. Noted composer/conductor of many top box-office film hits. Succeeded Arthur Fiedler as conductor of the Boston Pops in 1980. Winner of 15 Grammys. Williams' son, Joseph, became a member of Toto in 1986.	
9/13/75	**32**	4	1. Main Title (Theme From "Jaws") [I]	MCA 40439
8/13/77	**10**	7	**2. Star Wars (Main Title)** **[I]** performed by The London Symphony Orchestra	20th Century 2345
1/21/78	**13**	8	3. Theme From "Close Encounters Of The Third Kind" [I] all of above from soundtracks composed by Williams	Arista 0300

DATE	POS	WKS	ARTIST—RECORD TITLE	LABEL & NO.
			WILLIAMS, Larry	
			Born on 5/10/35 in New Orleans; committed suicide on 1/07/80 in Los Angeles. R&B-rock and roll singer/songwriter/pianist. With Lloyd Price in the early 1950s. Convicted of narcotics dealing in 1960; jail term interrupted his career.	
7/08/57	**5**	17	**1. Short Fat Fannie** Best Seller #5 / Top 100 #6 / Jockey #15	Specialty 608
11/11/57	**14**	14	2. Bony Moronie Best Seller #14 / Top 100 #18	Specialty 615
			WILLIAMS, Mason	
			Born on 8/24/38 in Abilene, Texas. Folk guitarist/songwriter/author/photographer/TV comedy writer ("The Smothers Brothers Comedy Hour," 1967-69; "Saturday Night Live," 1980).	
7/13/68	**2**(2)	11	**1. Classical Gas** [I]	Warner 7190
			WILLIAMS, Maurice/The Zodiacs	
			R&B vocal group from Lancaster, South Carolina, led by pianist/songwriter Maurice Williams. Originally recorded as The Gladiolas; became The Zodiacs in 1959. Williams re-formed group with Wiley Bennett, Henry Gaston, Charles Thomas, Albert Hill and Little Willie Morrow in 1960.	
10/10/60	**1**(1)	14	**1. Stay**	Herald 552
			WILLIAMS, Otis — see CHARMS, The	
			WILLIAMS, Roger	
			Born Louis Weertz in 1925 in Omaha. Learned to play the piano by age three. Educated at Drake University, Idaho State University, and Juilliard School of Music. Took lessons from Lenny Tristano and Teddy Wilson. Win on the TV show "Arthur Godfrey's Talent Scouts" led to recording contract.	
8/20/55	**1**(4)	26	**1. Autumn Leaves** [I] Best Seller #1 / Top 100 #2 pre / Juke Box #2 / Jockey #3	Kapp 116
1/14/56	**38**	1	2. Wanting You [I] from the 1928 musical *The New Moon*	Kapp 127
3/24/56	**37**	1	3. La Mer (Beyond The Sea) [I] #26 hit for Benny Goodman in 1948	Kapp 138
3/16/57	**15**	10	4. Almost Paradise [I] Jockey #15 / Best Seller #22 / Top 100 #26	Kapp 175
11/11/57	**22**	7	5. Till Jockey #22 / Top 100 #27 / Best Seller #28	Kapp 197
9/08/58	**10**	11	**6. Near You** [I] Hot 100 #10 / Best Seller #16 end #1 hit (17 weeks) for Francis Craig in 1947	Kapp 233
10/15/66	**7**	14	**7. Born Free** from the film of the same title	Kapp 767
			WILLIAMS, Vanessa	
			Singer/actress, born in Tarrytown, New York. In 1983, became the first black woman to win Miss America pageant; relinquished crown after *Penthouse* magazine scandal. Began hosting *Soul of VH-1* on video music TV channel in 1991.	
2/11/89	**8**	11	**1. Dreamin'**	Wing 871078

DATE	POS	WKS	ARTIST—RECORD TITLE	LABEL & NO.
			WILLIS, Bruce	
			Born on 3/19/55 in Penns Grove, New Jersey. Played David Addison on the TV series "Moonlighting." Married actress Demi Moore on 11/21/87. Appeared in the films *Blind Date* (1987), *Die Hard* (1988) and *Die Hard II* (1990). Child's voice in films *Look Who's Talking* and *Look Who's Talking Too.*	
1/31/87	**5**	10	**1. Respect Yourself**	Motown 1876
			WILLIS, Chuck	
			Born on 1/31/28 in Atlanta; died on 4/10/58 (peritonitis). R&B singer/songwriter.	
5/13/57	**12**	8	1. C. C. Rider Top 100 #12 / Best Seller #13; inspired the "Stroll" dance craze	Atlantic 1130
3/10/58	**33**	3	2. Betty And Dupree Best Seller #33 / Top 100 #33	Atlantic 1168
5/12/58	**9**	17	**3. What Am I Living For/** Jockey #9 / Best Seller #15 / Top 100 #15	
5/26/58	**24**	2	4. Hang Up My Rock And Roll Shoes	Atlantic 1179
			WILL TO POWER	
			Florida-based trio formed and fronted by producer Bob Rosenberg with Dr. J. and Maria Mendez. Rosenberg is the son of singer Gloria Mann. By 1990, reduced to a duo of Rosenberg and Elin Michaels. Group name taken from the work of 19th-century German philosopher Frederich Nietzsche.	
10/15/88	**1**(1)	15	● **1. Baby, I Love Your Way/Freebird Medley (Free Baby)**	Epic 08034
12/08/90+	**7**	12	**2. I'm Not In Love**	Epic 73636
			WILSON, Al	
			Born on 6/19/39 in Meridian, Mississippi. Soul singer/drummer. Moved to San Bernadino, California in the late '50s. Member of The Rollers from 1960-62.	
9/21/68	**27**	5	1. The Snake produced by Johnny Rivers (owned Soul City Records)	Soul City 767
11/24/73+	**1**(1)	16	● **2. Show And Tell**	Rocky Road 30073
11/09/74	**30**	3	3. La La Peace Song	Rocky Road 30200
5/01/76	**29**	4	4. I've Got A Feeling (We'll Be Seeing Each Other Again)	Playboy 6062
			WILSON, Ann	
			Born on 6/19/51 in San Diego. Lead singer of the rock group Heart.	
5/19/84	**7**	13	**1. Almost Paradise...Love Theme From Footloose** **MIKE RENO AND ANN WILSON** from the film *Footloose*	Columbia 04418
1/21/89	**6**	10	**2. Surrender To Me** **ANN WILSON AND ROBIN ZANDER** from the film *Tequila Sunrise*; Robin is leader of Cheap Trick	Capitol 44288
			WILSON, Brian	
			Born on 6/20/42 in Hawthorne, California. Leader/bassist/composer/producer of the legendary surf-rock group, The Beach Boys. Due to nervous exhaustion, he quit touring in late 1965, but continued to produce much of the group's material until the early 1970s. In semi-retirement until 1987. His daughters, Carnie and Wendy, formed the trio Wilson Phillips with Chynna Phillips in 1989.	
4/23/66	**32**	3	1. Caroline, No	Capitol 5610
			WILSON, Danny — see DANNY	

DATE	POS	WKS	ARTIST—RECORD TITLE	LABEL & NO.
			WILSON, J. Frank/The Cavaliers	
			J. Frank was born on 12/11/41 in Lufkin, Texas. Band formed in San Angelo, Texas. The Cavaliers: Phil Trunzo, Jerry Graham, Bobby Woods and George Croyle.	
9/26/64	**2**(1)	12	**1. Last Kiss**	Josie 923
			first released on Le Cam 722 and then on Tamara 761 in 1964	
			WILSON, Jackie	
			Born on 6/09/34 in Detroit; died on 1/21/84. Sang with local gospel groups; became an amateur boxer. Worked as a solo singer until 1953, then joined Billy Ward's Dominoes as Clyde McPhatter's replacement. Solo since 1957. Godfather of Jody Watley. Cousin of Hubert Johnson of The Contours. Jackie collapsed from a stroke, on stage, at the Latin Casino in Camden, New Jersey on 9/25/75; spent rest of his life in hospitals. Inducted into the Rock and Roll Hall of Fame in 1987.	
4/21/58	**22**	10	1. To Be Loved	Brunswick 55052
			Top 100 #22 / Best Seller #23	
12/08/58+	**7**	16	**2. Lonely Teardrops**	Brunswick 55105
4/13/59	**13**	9	3. That's Why (I Love You So)	Brunswick 55121
7/06/59	**20**	6	4. I'll Be Satisfied	Brunswick 55136
10/12/59	**37**	1	5. You Better Know It	Brunswick 55149
			from the film *Go Johnny Go*	
1/04/60	**34**	3	6. Talk That Talk	Brunswick 55165
4/11/60	**4**	12	**7. Night/**	
			based on Saint-Saens *Samson & Delilah* aria "My Heart At Thy Sweet Voice"	
4/25/60	**15**	9	8. Doggin' Around	Brunswick 55166
8/01/60	**12**	9	9. (You Were Made For) All My Love/	
8/01/60	**15**	8	10. A Woman, A Lover, A Friend	Brunswick 55167
10/24/60	**8**	12	**11. Alone At Last/**	
			based on Tchaikovsky's Piano Concerto in B Flat	
11/28/60	**32**	2	12. Am I The Man	Brunswick 55170
1/16/61	**9**	6	**13. My Empty Arms**	Brunswick 55201
3/27/61	**20**	5	14. Please Tell Me Why/	
3/27/61	**40**	1	15. Your One And Only Love	Brunswick 55208
6/26/61	**19**	5	16. I'm Comin' On Back To You	Brunswick 55216
9/11/61	**37**	2	17. Years From Now	Brunswick 55219
2/03/62	**34**	4	18. The Greatest Hurt	Brunswick 55221
3/23/63	**5**	9	**19. Baby Workout**	Brunswick 55239
			orchestra directed by Dick Jacobs on all of above (except #1, 18)	
8/10/63	**33**	1	20. Shake! Shake! Shake!	Brunswick 55246
11/19/66	**11**	8	21. Whispers (Gettin' Louder)	Brunswick 55300
9/02/67	**6**	9	**22. (Your Love Keeps Lifting Me) Higher And Higher**	Brunswick 55336
12/16/67	**32**	2	23. Since You Showed Me How To Be Happy	Brunswick 55354
8/31/68	**34**	2	24. I Get The Sweetest Feeling	Brunswick 55381
			WILSON, Meri	
			Born in Japan and raised in Marietta, Georgia.	
7/02/77	**18**	10	● 1. Telephone Man [N]	GRT 127
			produced by Boomer Castleman and Jim Rutledge (of Bloodrock)	

DATE	POS	WKS	ARTIST—RECORD TITLE	LABEL & NO.
			WILSON, Nancy	
			Born on 2/20/37 in Chillicothe, Ohio and raised in Columbus, Ohio. Jazz stylist with Rusty Bryant's Carolyn Club Band in Columbus. First recorded for Dot in 1956. Moved to New York City in 1959.	
7/18/64	**11**	7	1. (You Don't Know) How Glad I Am	Capitol 5198
6/15/68	**29**	9	2. Face It Girl, It's Over	Capitol 2136
			WILSON PHILLIPS	
			Vocal/songwriting trio of sisters Carnie and Wendy Wilson, with Chynna Phillips. Carnie and Wendy's father is Brian Wilson (The Beach Boys). Chynna, the daughter of John and Michelle Phillips (The Mamas & The Papas), acted in the film *Caddyshack II.*	
4/07/90	**1**(1)	18	● **1. Hold On**	SBK 07322
7/21/90	**1**(2)	15	● **2. Release Me**	SBK 07327#
10/27/90	**4**	15	**3. Impulsive**	SBK 07337#
2/23/91	**1**(1)	14	**4. You're In Love**	SBK 07343#
6/15/91	**12**	9	5. The Dream Is Still Alive	SBK 07356#
			WILTON PLACE STREET BAND	
			Los Angeles studio project produced and arranged by Trevor Lawrence (resided on Wilton Place in L.A.).	
3/12/77	**24**	7	1. Disco Lucy (I Love Lucy Theme) [I] discofied theme from the TV series "I Love Lucy"	Island 078
			WINCHESTER, Jesse	
			Born on 5/17/44 in Shreveport, Louisiana. Pop-MOR singer/songwriter/guitarist. Moved to Canada in 1967 to avoid the draft; became a Canadian citizen in 1973.	
5/30/81	**32**	5	1. Say What	Bearsville 49711
			WIND	
			New York studio group featuring Tony Orlando as lead singer.	
10/04/69	**28**	4	1. Make Believe B-side "Groovin With Mr. Bloe" charted in 1970 as by Cool Heat	Life 200
			WINDING, Kai	
			Born on 5/18/22 in Aarhus, Denmark; died on 5/06/83. Jazz trombonist. Moved to U.S. in 1934. With Benny Goodman and Stan Kenton in the mid-1940s.	
7/27/63	**8**	9	**1. More** [I] theme from the film *Mondo Cane*	Verve 10295
			WING AND A PRAYER FIFE & DRUM CORPS., The	
			Studio group from New York City; vocals by Linda November, Vivian Cherry, Arlene Martell & Helen Miles.	
12/20/75+	**14**	12	1. Baby Face 4 versions hit the top 10 in 1926	Wing & Prayer 103
			WINGER	
			Hard-rock quartet formed in New York City in 1986: Kip Winger (vocals, bass), Reb Beach (guitar), Rod Morgenstein (drums) and Paul Taylor (keyboards). Golden, Colorado native Kip was a member of Alice Cooper's band.	
4/08/89	**26**	6	1. Seventeen	Atlantic 88958
7/08/89	**19**	9	2. Headed For A Heartbreak	Atlantic 88922
11/17/90+	**12**	12	3. Miles Away	Atlantic 87824#

DATE	POS	WKS	ARTIST—RECORD TITLE	LABEL & NO.
			WINGFIELD, Pete	
			Keyboardist from England; born on 5/07/48. Worked with Freddy King, Jimmy Witherspoon and Van Morrison. In Olympic Runners band. Turned to production work in the '80s.	
10/25/75	**15**	8	1. Eighteen With A Bullet hit #18 with a bullet on the 11/22/75 "Hot 100" chart	Island 026
			WINGS — see McCARTNEY, Paul	
			WINSTONS, The	
			Washington, D.C. soul septet: Richard Spencer (lead), Ray Maritano, Quincy Mattison, Phil Tolotta, Sonny Peckrol and G.C. Coleman. Toured as backup band for The Impressions.	
6/14/69	**7**	10	● **1. Color Him Father**	Metromedia 117
			WINTER, Edgar, Group	
			Edgar was born on 12/28/46 in Beaumont, Texas. Albino rock singer/keyboardist/saxophonist. Younger brother of rock guitarist Johnny Winter. Group included Rick Derringer and Dan Hartman, 1972-75.	
4/21/73	**1**(1)	14	● **1. Frankenstein** [I] featuring lead guitar work by Ronnie Montrose	Epic 10967
9/08/73	**14**	9	2. Free Ride	Epic 11024
8/10/74	**33**	2	3. River's Risin' **EDGAR WINTER** above 3 produced by Rick Derringer	Epic 11143
			WINTERHALTER, Hugo	
			Born on 8/15/09 in Wilkes-Barre, Pennsylvania; died on 9/17/73 (cancer). Conductor/arranger for RCA Records from 1950-63.	
7/28/56	**2**(2)	23	**1. Canadian Sunset** [I] **HUGO WINTERHALTER/EDDIE HEYWOOD** Top 100 #2 / Jockey #2 / Best Seller #3 / Juke Box #3	RCA 6537
			WINWOOD, Steve	
			Born on 5/12/48 in Birmingham, England. Rock singer/keyboardist/guitarist. Lead singer of rock bands: Spencer Davis Group, Blind Faith and Traffic.	
2/28/81	**7**	12	**1. While You See A Chance**	Island 49656
7/05/86	**1**(1)	14	**2. Higher Love**	Island 28710
10/25/86	**20**	7	3. Freedom Overspill	Island 28595
3/14/87	**8**	12	**4. The Finer Things**	Island 28498
7/04/87	**13**	10	5. Back In The High Life Again	Island 28472
11/07/87	**9**	12	**6. Valerie** [R] remix of his 1982 hit (POS 70)	Island 28231
6/18/88	**1**(4)	14	**7. Roll With It**	Virgin 99326
9/10/88	**6**	11	**8. Don't You Know What The Night Can Do?**	Virgin 99290
12/10/88+	**11**	11	9. Holding On	Virgin 99261
11/17/90	**18**	9	10. One And Only Man	Virgin 98892
			WITHERS, Bill	
			Born on 7/04/38 in Slab Fork, West Virginia. Soul vocalist/guitarist/composer. Moved to California in 1967 and made demo records of his songs. First recorded for Sussex in 1970, produced by Booker T. Jones. Married to actress Denise Nicholas.	
8/14/71	**3**	12	● **1. Ain't No Sunshine** produced by Booker T. Jones	Sussex 219
5/27/72	**1**(3)	14	● **2. Lean On Me**	Sussex 235

Bob Seger's 25-year career has seen his more recent albums coming out at a very slow pace. Between 1986's *Like a Rock* and 1991's *The Fire Inside*, however, the Detroit-based singer had a No. 1 single with "Shakedown" from *Beverly Hills Cop II*.

Tommy Shaw's lengthy stay in Styx brought him six top-10 singles with the group between 1976 and 1984. A solo A&M album provided the singer/guitarist with the No. 33 hit "Girls With Guns" in 1984; since then, he joined forces with Ted Nugent and Night Ranger's Jack Blades and saw platinum once again with Damn Yankees.

Sheila E.'s 1984 hit "The Glamorous Life" was by no means the singer/percussionist's initial foray into recording. She performed with her father Pete Escovedo in San Franciscan band Azteca and later made a record with him—using her full last name.

Sheriff's unusual success story was much discussed at radio in the late 80s. Due to heavy airplay in 1988, the group had a No. 1 hit with "When I'm With You"—despite having broken up five years earlier. Members of the Canadian group later went on to form Frozen Ghost.

Allan Sherman produced three No. 1 albums for Warner Bros. between 1962 and 1963. The last, *My Son, The Nut*, contained his biggest hit single "Hello Mudduh, Hello Fadduh! (A Letter From Camp)," which stayed at No. 2 for three weeks.

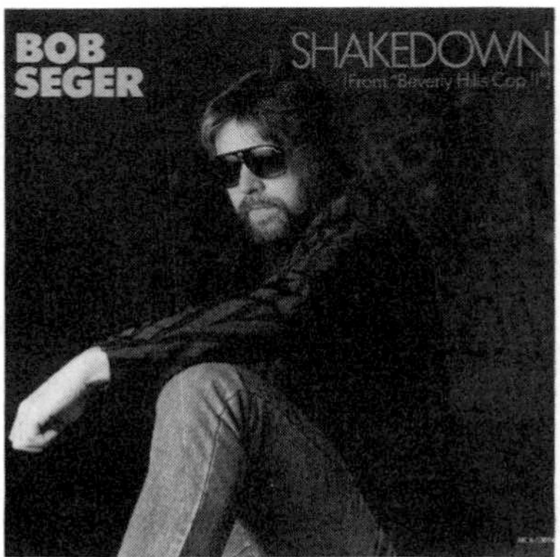

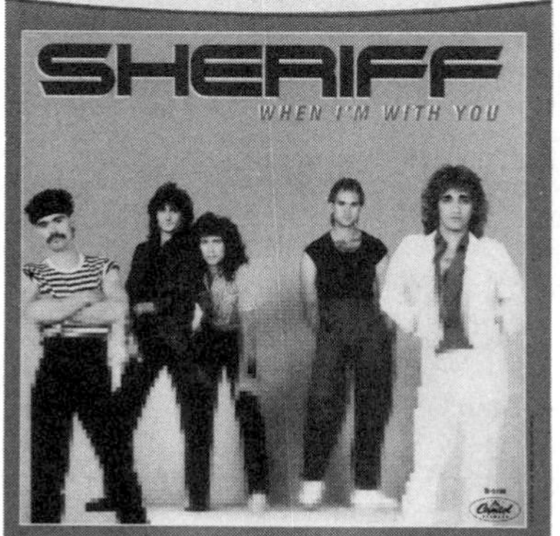

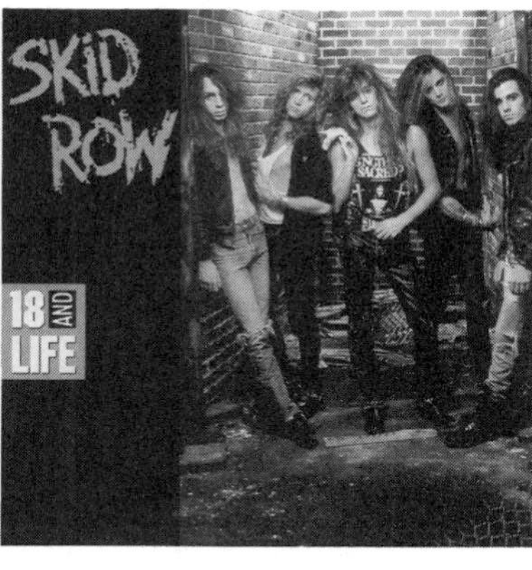

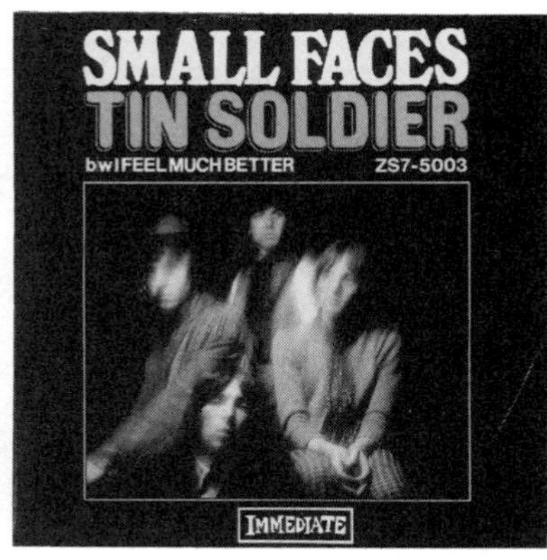

Skid Row's eponymous debut album gave the hard-rocking quintet two top-10 singles in 1989: "18 And Life" and "I Remember You." Another hard-rock group from Ireland took the same name 20 years earlier—and though that Skid Row had no U.S. hits, it did introduce the world to stellar guitarist Gary Moore.

The Small Faces were huge hitmakers in England, but barely known here. Along with their sole hit, 1968's "Itchycoo Park," the group is probably best known for spawning 70s hard-rockers Humble Pie. Steve Marriott, singer for both groups, died in a tragic fire in 1991.

Sonny & Cher's five top-10 singles are highlighted by 1965's "I Got You Babe," which topped the charts for three weeks in 1965 before being nudged off by the Beatles' "Help!" Atlantic issued a deluxe Sonny & Cher hits collection in 1991.

Judson Spence's only top-40 hit—1988's "Yeah, Yeah, Yeah," which reached No. 38—featured a musical cast including organist Billy Preston and guitarist Mick Jones of Foreigner.

Tracie Spencer's first hit, "Symptoms Of True Love," came when the young artist was only 12 years old. Signed to Capitol during a period when other "youngish" singers like Tiffany and Debbie Gibson were enjoying hits, Tracie later had a top-10 hit with "This House" in 1991.

Dusty Springfield's highest-charting record came, remarkably, 23 years after her first hit. Despite solid top-10 hits in the 60s with "Wishin' And Hopin'," "You Don't Have To Say You Love Me," and "Son-Of-A-Preacher Man," her 1987 duet with the Pet Shop Boys beat them all—and stayed at No. 2 for two weeks.

DATE	POS	WKS	ARTIST—RECORD TITLE	LABEL & NO.
9/09/72	**2**(2)	10	● **3. Use Me**	Sussex 241
3/03/73	**31**	5	4. Kissing My Love	Sussex 250
1/21/78	**30**	4	5. Lovely Day all of above written by Withers	Columbia 10627
3/07/81	**2**(3)	16	**6. Just The Two Of Us** **GROVER WASHINGTON, JR./BILL WITHERS**	Elektra 47103
			WOLF, Peter	
			Born Peter Blankfield on 3/07/46 in the Bronx. Lead singer of The J. Geils Band until 1983. Produced hits for Lou Gramm, Kenny Loggins and Go West. Married actress Faye Dunaway on 8/07/74, divorced in 1979.	
7/28/84	**12**	10	1. Lights Out	EMI America 8208
11/17/84	**36**	2	2. I Need You Tonight	EMI America 8241
3/21/87	**15**	9	3. Come As You Are	EMI America 8350
			WOLFMAN JACK — see GUESS WHO and STAMPEDERS	
			WOMACK, Bobby	
			Born on 3/04/44 in Cleveland. Soul vocalist/guitarist/songwriter. Sang in family gospel group the Womack Brothers. Group recorded for Sar as The Valentinos and The Lovers, 1962-64. Toured as guitarist with Sam Cooke. Solo recording for Him label in 1965. Backup guitarist on many sessions, including Wilson Pickett, The Box Tops, Joe Tex, Aretha Franklin and Janis Joplin. Married for a time to Sam Cooke's widow. Nicknamed "The Preacher."	
1/08/72	**27**	7	1. That's The Way I Feel About Cha	United Art. 50847
1/13/73	**31**	6	● 2. Harry Hippie above two with backing group, Peace	United Art. 50946
8/11/73	**29**	6	3. Nobody Wants You When You're Down And Out	United Art. 255
3/09/74	**10**	11	● **4. Lookin' For A Love**	United Art. 375
			WONDER, Stevie	
			Born Steveland Morris on 5/13/50 in Saginaw, Michigan. Singer/songwriter/multi-instrumentalist/ producer. Blind since birth. Signed to Motown in 1960, did backup work. First recorded in 1962, renamed "Little Stevie Wonder" by Berry Gordy, Jr. Married to Syreeta Wright from 1970-72. Near-fatal auto accident on 8/16/73. Winner of 17 Grammy Awards. In the films *Bikini Beach* and *Muscle Beach Party*. Inducted into the Rock and Roll Hall of Fame in 1989.	
7/06/63	**1**(3)	12	**1. Fingertips - Pt 2** **LITTLE STEVIE WONDER**	Tamla 54080
10/19/63	**33**	4	2. Workout Stevie, Workout **LITTLE STEVIE WONDER**	Tamla 54086
7/11/64	**29**	4	3. Hey Harmonica Man	Tamla 54096
1/22/66	**3**	9	**4. Uptight (Everything's Alright)**	Tamla 54124
5/07/66	**20**	4	5. Nothing's Too Good For My Baby	Tamla 54130
7/30/66	**9**	8	**6. Blowin In The Wind**	Tamla 54136
11/26/66	**9**	8	**7. A Place In The Sun**	Tamla 54139
4/01/67	**32**	3	8. Travlin' Man	Tamla 54147
6/24/67	**2**(2)	12	**9. I Was Made To Love Her**	Tamla 54151
10/21/67	**12**	5	10. I'm Wondering	Tamla 54157
4/27/68	**9**	9	**11. Shoo-Be-Doo-Be-Doo-Da-Day**	Tamla 54165
8/17/68	**35**	3	12. You Met Your Match	Tamla 54168
11/09/68	**2**(2)	11	**13. For Once In My Life**	Tamla 54174

DATE	POS	WKS	ARTIST—RECORD TITLE	LABEL & NO.
3/22/69	**39**	1	14. I Don't Know Why/	
6/21/69	**4**	11	**15. My Cherie Amour**	Tamla 54180
11/01/69	**7**	12	**16. Yester-Me, Yester-You, Yesterday**	Tamla 54188
2/21/70	**26**	5	17. Never Had A Dream Come True	Tamla 54191
7/04/70	**3**	13	**18. Signed, Sealed, Delivered I'm Yours**	Tamla 54196
10/31/70	**9**	8	**19. Heaven Help Us All**	Tamla 54200
3/27/71	**13**	9	20. We Can Work It Out	Tamla 54202
9/04/71	**8**	11	**21. If You Really Love Me**	Tamla 54208
6/24/72	**33**	5	22. Superwoman (Where Were You When I Needed You)	Tamla 54216
12/09/72+	**1**(1)	13	**23. Superstition**	Tamla 54226
3/31/73	**1**(1)	13	**24. You Are The Sunshine Of My Life**	Tamla 54232
9/01/73	**4**	12	**25. Higher Ground**	Tamla 54235
11/24/73+	**8**	14	**26. Living For The City**	Tamla 54242
4/27/74	**16**	9	27. Don't You Worry 'Bout A Thing	Tamla 54245
8/17/74	**1**(1)	14	**28. You Haven't Done Nothin** backing vocals by The Jackson 5	Tamla 54252
11/30/74+	**3**	14	**29. Boogie On Reggae Woman**	Tamla 54254
12/04/76+	**1**(1)	15	**30. I Wish**	Tamla 54274
4/16/77	**1**(3)	13	**31. Sir Duke** a tribute to Duke Ellington	Tamla 54281
9/17/77	**32**	4	32. Another Star	Tamla 54286
12/03/77+	**36**	5	33. As	Tamla 54291
11/10/79	**4**	14	**34. Send One Your Love**	Tamla 54303
10/04/80	**5**	16	**35. Master Blaster (Jammin')**	Tamla 54317
1/17/81	**11**	11	36. I Ain't Gonna Stand For It	Tamla 54320
1/30/82	**4**	13	**37. That Girl**	Tamla 1602
4/10/82	**1**(7)	15	● **38. Ebony And Ivory** **PAUL McCARTNEY with STEVIE WONDER**	Columbia 02860
6/19/82	**13**	9	39. Do I Do	Tamla 1612
9/01/84	**1**(3)	15	● **40. I Just Called To Say I Love You**	Motown 1745
12/15/84+	**17**	10	41. Love Light In Flight above 2 from the film *The Woman in Red*	Motown 1769
9/14/85	**1**(1)	14	**42. Part-Time Lover**	Tamla 1808
11/23/85+	**1**(4)	17	● **43. That's What Friends Are For** **DIONNE & FRIENDS: Elton John, Gladys Knight and Stevie Wonder**	Arista 9422
12/14/85+	**10**	11	**44. Go Home**	Tamla 1817
3/22/86	**24**	6	45. Overjoyed	Tamla 1832
11/07/87	**19**	7	46. Skeletons	Motown 1907
			WONDER WHO? — see 4 SEASONS	
			WOOD, Brenton Born Alfred Smith on 7/26/41 in Shreveport and raised in San Pedro, California. Soul singer/songwriter/ pianist. First recorded with Little Freddy & The Rockets in 1958.	
6/24/67	**34**	1	1. The Oogum Boogum Song	Double Shot 111
9/09/67	**9**	10	**2. Gimme Little Sign**	Double Shot 116
12/16/67	**34**	3	3. Baby You Got It	Double Shot 121

DATE	POS	WKS	ARTIST—RECORD TITLE	LABEL & NO.
			WOOD, Lauren	
			Pop singer/songwriter/keyboardist; originally from Pittsburgh.	
10/27/79	**24**	6	1. Please Don't Leave	Warner 49043
			harmony vocal: Michael McDonald	
			WOODS, Stevie	
			Black vocalist based in Los Angeles. Originally from Columbus, Ohio.	
11/14/81	**25**	10	1. Steal The Night	Cotillion 46016
3/20/82	**38**	3	2. Just Can't Win 'Em All	Cotillion 46030
			WOOLEY, Sheb	
			Born Shelby F. Wooley on 4/10/21 near Erick, Oklahoma. Singer/songwriter/actor. Played Pete Nolan in the TV series "Rawhide." Also made comical recordings under pseudonym Ben Colder. Appeared in the films *High Noon*, *Rocky Mountain*, *Giant* and *Hoosiers*. Wrote "Hee Haw"'s theme song.	
6/02/58	**1**(6)	14	**1. The Purple People Eater** [N]	MGM 12651
			Best Seller #1(6) / Top 100 #1(6) / Jockey #1(4)	
			WORLD PARTY	
			London-based group featuring keyboardist/vocalist/producer/engineer Karl Wallinger from North Wales (formerly of The Waterboys).	
4/04/87	**27**	5	1. Ship Of Fools (Save Me From Tomorrow)	Chrysalis 43052
			WRAY, Link/His Ray Men	
			Link was born on 5/02/35 in Dunn, North Carolina. Rock and roll guitarist. Part American Indian. Joined family band the Palomino Ranch Gang in the early 1950s. First recorded as "Lucky" Wray for Starday in 1956. Recorded album with rockabilly singer Robert Gordon in 1977.	
5/12/58	**16**	10	1. Rumble [I]	Cadence 1347
			Best Seller #16 / Top 100 #16	
3/16/59	**23**	3	2. Raw-Hide [I]	Epic 9300
			WRIGHT, Betty	
			Born on 12/21/53 in Miami. Soul singer. In family gospel group, Echoes Of Joy, from 1956. First recorded for Deep City in 1966. Hostess of TV talk shows in Miami.	
9/07/68	**33**	2	1. Girls Can't Do What The Guys Do	Alston 4569
12/11/71+	**6**	12	● **2. Clean Up Woman**	Alston 4601
5/06/78	**8**	14	**3. Dance With Me**	Drive 6269
			PETER BROWN with BETTY WRIGHT	
			WRIGHT, Charles/The Watts 103rd Street Rhythm Band	
			Charles was born in 1942 in Clarksdale, Mississippi. Vocalist/pianist/guitarist/producer/leader of an eight-man, soul-funk band from the Watts section of Los Angeles. Evolved from the Soul Runners. Big break came through assistance by comedian Bill Cosby.	
3/22/69	**11**	10	1. Do Your Thing	Warner 7250
			THE WATTS 103RD STREET RHYTHM BAND	
5/30/70	**16**	10	2. Love Land	Warner 7365
9/12/70	**12**	10	3. Express Yourself	Warner 7417
			WRIGHT, Dale	
			Rockabilly singer. Born Harlan Dale Riffe on 2/04/38 in Middletown, Ohio. Worked as a DJ in Midwest.	
2/24/58	**38**	2	1. She's Neat	Fraternity 792

DATE	POS	WKS	ARTIST—RECORD TITLE	LABEL & NO.
			DALE WRIGHT with THE ROCK-ITS Best Seller #38 / Top 100 #39	
			WRIGHT, Gary	
			Born on 4/26/43 in Creskill, New Jersey. Pop-rock singer/songwriter/keyboardist. Appeared in "Captain Video" TV series at age seven. In the Broadway play *Fanny*. Co-leader of the rock group Spooky Tooth.	
1/31/76	**2**(3)	14	● **1. Dream Weaver**	Warner 8167
5/15/76	**2**(2)	18	**2. Love Is Alive**	Warner 8143
8/01/81	**16**	10	3. Really Wanna Know You	Warner 49769
			WRIGHT, Priscilla	
			Fourteen-year-old. Her father, Don Wright, was leader of a choir in London, Ontario.	
6/25/55	**16**	9	1. The Man In The Raincoat Jockey #16 / Best Seller #18 / Juke Box #20 backing vocals by Don Wright and The Septette	Unique 303
			WYNETTE, Tammy	
			Born Virginia Wynette Pugh on 5/05/42 in Itawamba County, Mississippi. With over 15 #1 country hits, dubbed "The First Lady of Country Music." Discovered by producer Billy Sherrill. Married to country star George Jones from 1969-75.	
12/28/68+	**19**	9	1. Stand By Your Man	Epic 10398
			Y	
			YANKOVIC, "Weird Al"	
			Los Angeles novelty singer/accordionist. Specializes in song parodies. Starred in the 1989 film *UHF*.	
3/17/84	**12**	7	● 1. Eat It [N] parody of Michael Jackson's "Beat It"; guitar: Rick Derringer	Rock 'n' R. 04374
			YARBROUGH, Glenn	
			Born on 1/12/30 in Milwaukee. Lead singer of The Limeliters (1959-63).	
4/17/65	**12**	9	1. Baby The Rain Must Fall from the film of the same title	RCA 8498
			YARBROUGH & PEOPLES	
			Dallas soul duo: Cavin Yarbrough and Alisa Peoples. Discovered by The Gap Band.	
3/14/81	**19**	7	● 1. Don't Stop The Music	Mercury 76085
			YARDBIRDS, The	
			Legendary rock group formed in Surrey, England in 1963. Consisted of Keith Relf (d: 5/14/76; vocals, harmonica), Anthony "Top" Topham and Chris Dreja (guitars), Paul "Sam" Samwell-Smith (bass, keyboards) and Jim McCarty (drums). Formed as the Metropolitan Blues Quartet at Kingston Art School. Topham replaced by Eric Clapton in 1963. Clapton replaced by Jeff Beck in 1965. Samwell-Smith left in 1966, Dreja switched to bass and Jimmy Page (guitar) was added. Beck left in December 1966. Group disbanded in July 1968. Page formed the New Yardbirds in October 1968, which evolved into Led Zeppelin. Relf and McCarty formed Renaissance in 1969. Keith Relf later in Armageddon, 1975; McCarty in Illusion, 1977.	
6/05/65	**6**	9	**1. For Your Love**	Epic 9790
8/21/65	**9**	8	**2. Heart Full Of Soul**	Epic 9823

DATE	POS	WKS	ARTIST—RECORD TITLE	LABEL & NO.
			above 2 written by Graham Gouldman (10cc)	
11/20/65	**17**	7	3. I'm A Man	Epic 9857
4/09/66	**11**	8	4. Shapes Of Things	Epic 10006
			first released on Epic 9891 in 1966	
7/16/66	**13**	7	5. Over Under Sideways Down	Epic 10035
12/24/66	**30**	4	6. Happenings Ten Years Time Ago	Epic 10094
			YELLOW BALLOON, The	
			Quintet from Oregon and Arizona, formed by Don Grady (Robbie Douglas of "My Three Sons") — Alex Valdez, lead singer.	
4/29/67	**25**	5	1. Yellow Balloon	Canterbury 508
			YES	
			Progressive rock group formed in London in 1968. Consisted of Jon Anderson (vocals), Peter Banks (guitar), Tony Kaye (keyboards), Chris Squire (bass) and Bill Bruford (drums). Banks replaced by Steve Howe in 1971. Kaye (joined Badfinger in 1978) replaced by Rick Wakeman in 1971. Bruford left to join King Crimson, replaced by Alan White in late 1972. Wakeman replaced by Patrick Moraz in 1974, rejoined in 1976 when Moraz left. Wakeman and Anderson left in 1980, replaced by The Buggles' Trevor Horne (guitar) and Geoff Downes (keyboards). Group disbanded in 1980. Howe and Downes joined Asia. Re-formed in 1983 with Anderson, Kaye, Squire, White and South African guitarist Trevor Rabin. Anderson left group in 1988. Anderson, Bruford, Wakeman and Howe formed self-named group in early 1989. Yes reunited in 1991 with Anderson, Bruford, Wakeman, Howe, Kaye, Squire, White and Rabin.	
12/04/71	**40**	2	1. Your Move	Atlantic 2819
3/04/72	**13**	10	2. Roundabout	Atlantic 2854
11/19/83+	**1**(2)	17	**3. Owner Of A Lonely Heart**	Atco 99817
3/24/84	**24**	7	4. Leave It	Atco 99787
10/31/87	**30**	6	5. Love Will Find A Way	Atco 99449
2/06/88	**40**	1	6. Rhythm Of Love	Atco 99419
			YOST, Dennis — see CLASSICS IV	
			YOUNG, Barry	
12/04/65+	**13**	7	1. One Has My Name (The Other Has My Heart)	Dot 16756
			YOUNG, Faron	
			Born on 2/25/32 in Shreveport, Louisiana. Country singer/guitarist. Charted over 30 top 10 country hits. In films *The Young Sheriff*, *Daniel Boone* and *Hidden Guns*. Founder and one-time publisher of the *Music City News* magazine in Nashville.	
5/01/61	**12**	11	1. Hello Walls	Capitol 4533
			written by Willie Nelson	
			YOUNG, John Paul	
			Born in Glasgow, Scotland in 1953 and raised in Australia. Pop singer/songwriter/pianist.	
8/05/78	**7**	15	**1. Love Is In The Air**	Scotti Br. 402
			YOUNG, Kathy, with THE INNOCENTS	
			Kathy was born on 10/21/45 in Santa Ana, California. Pop singer. Married for a time to a member of The Walker Bros. Also see The Innocents.	
10/31/60	**3**	15	**1. A Thousand Stars**	Indigo 108
3/06/61	**30**	6	2. Happy Birthday Blues	Indigo 115

DATE	POS	WKS	ARTIST—RECORD TITLE	LABEL & NO.
			YOUNG, Neil	
			Born on 11/12/45 in Toronto. Rock singer/songwriter/guitarist. Formed rock band the Mynah Birds, featuring lead singer Rick James, early '60s. Moved to Los Angeles in 1966 and formed Buffalo Springfield. Went solo in 1969 with backing band Crazy Horse. Joined with Crosby, Stills & Nash, 1970-71. Appeared in the 1987 film *Made in Heaven.* Reunited with Crosby, Stills & Nash in 1988 to record the *American Dream* album.	
12/05/70	**33**	3	1. Only Love Can Break Your Heart	Reprise 0958
2/12/72	**1**(1)	13	• **2. Heart Of Gold** backing vocals: Linda Ronstadt and James Taylor	Reprise 1065
5/20/72	**31**	4	3. Old Man	Reprise 1084
			YOUNG, Paul	
			Born on 1/17/56 in Bedfordshire, England. Pop-rock vocalist/guitarist.	
3/03/84	**22**	8	1. Come Back And Stay	Columbia 04313
6/01/85	**1**(1)	15	• **2. Everytime You Go Away** written by Daryl Hall	Columbia 04867
9/21/85	**13**	9	3. I'm Gonna Tear Your Playhouse Down	Columbia 05577
8/18/90	**8**	11	**4. Oh Girl**	Columbia 73377#
			YOUNG, Victor	
			Born on 8/08/1900 in Chicago; died on 11/11/56. Conductor/composer/violinist.	
7/08/57	**13**	9	1. (Main Theme) Around The World [I] Jockey #13 / Best Seller #20 / Top 100 #26 from the film *Around the World in 80 Days*; B-side is Bing Crosby's charted vocal version	Decca 30262
			YOUNGBLOODS, The	
			Folk-rock group led by vocalist Jesse Colin Young (born Perry Miller on 11/11/44). Band formed in New York City in late 1965, moved to California in late 1967.	
8/02/69	**5**	12	• **1. Get Together** **[R]** re-popularized as theme for National Council of Christians & Jews; originally charted in 1967 (POS 62)	RCA 9752
			YOUNG-HOLT UNLIMITED	
			Chicago instrumental soul group: Eldee Young (bass), Isaac "Red" Holt (drums; both of the Ramsey Lewis Trio) and Don Walker (piano). Walker left by 1968.	
1/21/67	**40**	2	1. Wack Wack [I] **THE YOUNG HOLT TRIO**	Brunswick 55305
12/07/68+	**3**	12	• **2. Soulful Strut** **[I]** instrumental track used for Barbara Acklin's "Am I The Same Girl"	Brunswick 55391
			YOUNG MC	
			Rapper. Born Marvin Young on 5/10/67 in England and raised in Queens, New York. Co-writer of Tone Loc's "Wild Thing" and "Funky Cold Medina." Graduated with economics degree from University of Southern California.	
8/26/89	**7**	20	▲ **1. Bust A Move**	Delicious 105
1/06/90	**33**	3	2. Principal's Office	Delicious 99137
			YOUNG RASCALS — see RASCALS	

DATE	POS	WKS	ARTIST—RECORD TITLE	LABEL & NO.
			YO-YO	
			Yolanda Whitaker, female rapper from Los Angeles. In 1991, 19 years old. Member of Ice Cube's posse.	
6/29/91	**36**	3	1. You Can't Play With My Yo-Yo written by James Brown and Ice Cube	East West 98831#
			YURO, Timi	
			Born Rosemarie Timothy Aurro Yuro on 8/04/40 in Chicago. Moved to Los Angeles in 1952. First recorded for Liberty in 1959. Lost voice in 1980 and underwent three throat operations.	
7/31/61	**4**	10	**1. Hurt**	Liberty 55343
8/11/62	**12**	6	2. What's A Matter Baby (Is It Hurting You)	Liberty 55469
8/10/63	**24**	7	3. Make The World Go Away	Liberty 55587
			Z	
			ZACHARIAS, Helmut/His Magic Violins	
			German violinist.	
9/08/56	**12**	7	1. When The White Lilacs Bloom Again [I] Jockey #12 / Top 100 #16 / Best Seller #19 / Juke Box #19	Decca 30039
			ZACHERLE, John, "The Cool Ghoul"	
			Born on 9/26/18 in Philadelphia. Hosted horror movies on WCAU-TV in Philadelphia during the late 1950s.	
3/10/58	**6**	7	**1. Dinner With Drac Part 1 [N]** Top 100 #6 / Best Seller #8	Cameo 130
			ZADORA, Pia	
			Born Pia Schipani in 1955 in New York City. (Derived Zadora from her mother's maiden name: Zadorowski.) Stage and film actress/singer. In the films *Butterfly*, *The Lonely Lady* and *Hairspray*.	
2/12/83	**36**	3	1. The Clapping Song	Elektra 69889
			ZAGER, Michael, Band	
			Disco studio group led by keyboardist/writer/arranger Michael Zager (b: 1943 in Jersey City, New Jersey). Member of Ten Wheel Drive from 1968-73.	
4/29/78	**36**	4	1. Let's All Chant [I]	Private S. 45184
			ZAGER & EVANS	
			Lincoln, Nebraska duo: Denny Zager and Rick Evans.	
6/28/69	**1**(6)	12	● **1. In The Year 2525 (Exordium & Terminus)** released regionally in 1968 on Truth 8082	RCA 0174
			ZAHND, Ricky/The Blue Jeaners	
			Born on 7/22/46 in New York City. Lawyer since 1972. From 1979-86, was vice president of the New York Knicks basketball team and the New York Rangers hockey team. Partner in New York City's Morrison & Foerster law firm since 1986.	
12/24/55	**21**	2	1. (I'm Gettin') Nuttin' For Christmas [N-X] Best Seller #21 / Top 100 #40	Columbia 40576
			ZANDER, Robin — see WILSON, Ann	

DATE	POS	WKS	ARTIST—RECORD TITLE	LABEL & NO.
			ZAPPA, Frank	
			Born on 12/21/40 in Baltimore, Maryland. Singer/songwriter/guitarist. Rock music's leading satirist. Formed The Mothers Of Invention in 1965. In the films *200 Motels* and *Baby Snakes*. Father of Dweezil and Moon Unit Zappa (both performed in the 1991 Peace Choir, "Give Peace A Chance").	
9/04/82	**32**	3	1. Valley Girl [N]	Barking P. 02972
			featuring Frank's daughter, Moon Unit Zappa	
			ZEVON, Warren	
			Singer/songwriter/pianist. Born on 1/24/47 in Chicago. Parents were Russian immigrants. Recorded with female vocalist Tule Livingston as the duo Lyme & Cybelle in 1966. Worked as the keyboardist/bandleader for The Everly Brothers, shortly before their breakup. Wrote Linda Ronstadt's "Poor Poor Pitiful Me." Recorded with three R.E.M. members as the Hindu Love Gods in 1990.	
4/22/78	**21**	6	1. Werewolves Of London	Asylum 45472
			ZODIACS, The — see WILLIAMS, Maurice	
			ZOMBIES, The	
			British rock quintet: Rod Argent (keyboards), Colin Blunstone (vocals), Paul Atkinson (guitar), Chris White (bass) and Hugh Grundy (drums). Group disbanded in late 1967. Rod formed Argent in 1969.	
11/07/64	**2**(1)	12	**1. She's Not There**	Parrot 9695
1/30/65	**6**	8	**2. Tell Her No**	Parrot 9723
2/22/69	**3**	11	● **3. Time Of The Season**	Date 1628
			recorded in 1967	
			ZZ TOP	
			Boogie-rock trio formed in Houston in 1969. Consists of Billy Gibbons (vocals, guitar), Dusty Hill (vocals, bass) and Frank Beard (drums). All were born in 1949 in Texas. Gibbons had been lead guitarist in Moving Sidewalks, a Houston psychedelic rock band. Hill and Beard had played in American Blues, based in Dallas. Inactive from 1977-79. Group appeared in the film *Back to the Future III*.	
8/16/75	**20**	4	1. Tush	London 220
3/01/80	**34**	3	2. I Thank You	Warner 49163
5/07/83	**37**	3	3. Gimme All Your Lovin	Warner 29693
6/02/84	**8**	12	**4. Legs**	Warner 29272
10/26/85	**8**	13	**5. Sleeping Bag**	Warner 28884
2/08/86	**21**	7	6. Stages	Warner 28810
4/19/86	**22**	7	7. Rough Boy	Warner 28733
8/30/86	**35**	3	8. Velcro Fly	Warner 28650
			all of above produced by Bill Ham	

THE SONGS

THE SONGS

This section lists, alphabetically, all titles in the artist section. The artist's name is listed next to each title along with the highest position attained and year of peak popularity. Some titles show the letter F as a positon, indicating the title was listed as a flip side and did not chart on its own.

A song with more than one charted version is listed once, with the artists' names listed below the title in chronological order. Many songs that have the same title, but are different tunes, are listed separately, with the most popular title listed first. This will make it easy to determine which songs are the same composition, the number of charted versions of a particular song, and which of these were the most popular.

Cross references have been used throughout to aid in finding a title. Please keep the following in mind when using this listing: titles beginning with a contraction follow titles that begin with a similar non-contracted word ("Can't" follows "Can"). Titles such "I.O.U.," "D.O.A.," and "SOS" will be found at the beginning of their respective letters; however, titles such as "T-R-O-U-B-L-E" and "D-I-V-O-R-C-E," which are spellings of works, are listed with their regular spellings. Two-word titles which have the exact same spelling as one-word titles are listed together alphabetically ("Break Out" is listed directly before "Breakout"). Titles which are identical, except for an apostrophized word in one of the titles, are shown together ("Lovin' You" appears immediately above "Loving You").

POS/YR	RECORD TITLE/ARTIST

A

POS/YR	RECORD TITLE/ARTIST
28/66	**"A" Team** . . . SSgt Barry Sadler
1/70	**ABC** . . . Jackson 5
26/82	**Abacab** . . . Genesis
16/64	**Abigail Beecher** . . . Freddy Cannon
15/63	**Abilene** . . . George Hamilton IV
31/60	**About This Thing Called Love** . . . Fabian
32/74	**Abra-Ca-Dabra** . . . DeFranco Family
1/82	**Abracadabra** . . . Steve Miller Band
	Abraham, Martin And John
4/68	Dion
33/69	Miracles
35/69	Moms Mabley
8/71	Tom Clay (medley)
26/71	**Absolutely Right** . . . Five Man Electrical Band
18/90	**Across The River** . . . Bruce Hornsby & The Range
13/65	**Action** . . . Freddy Cannon
20/76	**Action** . . . Sweet
1/86	**Addicted To Love** . . . Robert Palmer
	Admiral Halsey ..see: Uncle Albert
8/84	**Adult Education** . . . Daryl Hall - John Oates
9/83	**Affair Of The Heart** . . . Rick Springfield
16/57	**Affair To Remember (Our Love Affair)** . . . Vic Damone
1/83	**Africa** . . . Toto
6/89	**After All** . . . Cher & Peter Cetera
18/70	**After Midnight** . . . Eric Clapton
32/57	**After School** . . . Randy Starr
23/83	**After The Fall** . . . Journey
32/82	**After The Glitter Fades** . . . Stevie Nicks
22/74	**After The Goldrush** . . . Prelude
10/56	**After The Lights Go Down Low** . . . Al Hibbler
2/79	**After The Love Has Gone** . . . Earth, Wind & Fire
8/77	**After The Lovin'** . . . Engelbert Humperdinck
6/91	**After The Rain** . . . Nelson
1/76	**Afternoon Delight** . . . Starland Vocal Band
1/84	**Against All Odds (Take A Look At Me Now)** . . . Phil Collins

POS/YR	RECORD TITLE/ARTIST
5/80	**Against The Wind** . . . Bob Seger
21/65	**Agent Double-O-Soul** . . . Edwin Starr
36/75	**Agony And The Ecstasy** . . . Smokey Robinson
29/81	**Ah! Leah!** . . . Donnie Iris
5/62	**Ahab, The Arab** . . . Ray Stevens
28/81	**Ai No Corrida** . . . Quincy Jones
17/81	**Ain't Even Done With The Night** . . . John Cougar
12/77	**Ain't Gonna Bump No More (With No Big Fat Woman)** . . . Joe Tex
39/66	**Ain't Gonna Lie** . . . Keith
20/57	**Ain't Got No Home** . . . Clarence Henry
24/70	**Ain't It Funky Now** . . . James Brown
40/65	**Ain't It True** . . . Andy Williams
22/79	**Ain't Love A Bitch** . . . Rod Stewart
	Ain't No Mountain High Enough
19/67	Marvin Gaye & Tammi Terrell
1/70	Diana Ross
13/79	**Ain't No Stoppin' Us Now** . . . McFadden & Whitehead
3/71	**Ain't No Sunshine** . . . Bill Withers
16/68	**Ain't No Way** . . . Aretha Franklin
8/75	**Ain't No Way To Treat A Lady** . . . Helen Reddy
4/73	**Ain't No Woman (Like The One I've Got)** . . . Four Tops
22/83	**Ain't Nobody** . . . Rufus & Chaka Khan
	Ain't Nothing Like The Real Thing
8/68	Marvin Gaye & Tammi Terrell
21/77	Donny & Marie Osmond
20/64	**Ain't Nothing You Can Do** . . . Bobby Bland
19/64	**Ain't She Sweet** . . . Beatles
	Ain't That A Shame
1/55	Pat Boone
10/55	Fats Domino
22/63	4 Seasons
35/79	Cheap Trick
33/61	**Ain't That Just Like A Woman** . . . Fats Domino
16/64	**Ain't That Loving You Baby** . . . Elvis Presley
8/65	**Ain't That Peculiar** . . . Marvin Gaye
	Ain't Too Proud To Beg
13/66	Temptations
17/74	Rolling Stones
21/72	**Ain't Understanding Mellow** . . . Jerry Butler & Brenda Lee Eager
6/74	**Air That I Breathe** . . . Hollies

POS/YR	RECORD TITLE/ARTIST
31/70	**Airport Love Theme** . . . Vincent Bell
	Al Di La'
6/62	Emilio Pericoli
29/64	Ray Charles Singers
14/55	**Alabama Jubilee** . . . Ferko String Band
	Alamo ..see: Ballad Of The
29/71	**Albert Flasher** . . . Guess Who
	Alfie
32/66	Cher
15/67	Dionne Warwick
29/84	**Alibis** . . . Sergio Mendes
17/63	**Alice In Wonderland** . . . Neil Sedaka
27/68	**Alice Long (You're Still My Favorite Girlfriend)** . . . Tommy Boyce & Bobby Hart
29/81	**Alien** . . . Atlanta Rhythm Section
34/72	**Alive** . . . Bee Gees
3/85	**Alive & Kicking** . . . Simple Minds
14/78	**Alive Again** . . . Chicago
35/67	**All** . . . James Darren
3/62	**All Alone Am I** . . . Brenda Lee
20/68	**All Along The Watchtower** . . . Jimi Hendrix Experience
2/59	**All American Boy** . . . Bill Parsons
3/90	**All Around The World** . . . Lisa Stansfield
11/56	**All At Once You Love Her** . . . Perry Como
2/76	**All By Myself** . . . Eric Carmen
8/86	**All Cried Out** . . . Lisa Lisa & Cult Jam
7/65	**All Day And All Of The Night** . . . Kinks
35/71	**All Day Music** . . . War
19/88	**All Fired Up** . . . Pat Benatar
33/60	**All I Could Do Was Cry** . . . Etta James
7/71	**All I Ever Need Is You** . . . Sonny & Cher
	All I Have To Do Is Dream
1/58	Everly Brothers
14/63	Richard Chamberlain
27/70	Bobbie Gentry & Glen Campbell
9/73	**All I Know** . . . Garfunkel
2/85	**All I Need** . . . Jack Wagner
8/67	**All I Need** . . . Temptations
5/86	**All I Need Is A Miracle** . . . Mike + The Mechanics
	All I Really Want To Do
15/65	Cher
40/65	Byrds
20/66	**All I See Is You** . . . Dusty Springfield
2/90	**All I Wanna Do Is Make Love To You** . . . Heart
19/87	**All I Wanted** . . . Kansas
32/90	**All I'm Missing Is You** . . . Glenn Medeiros Feat. Ray Parker, Jr.
19/61	**All In My Mind** . . . Maxine Brown
11/90	**All My Life** . . . Linda Ronstadt/Aaron Neville
37/83	**All My Life** . . . Kenny Rogers
	All My Love ..see: (You Were Made For)
19/80	**All Night Long** . . . Joe Walsh
1/83	**All Night Long (All Night)** . . . Lionel Richie
	(All of a Sudden) My Heart Sings
15/59	Paul Anka
38/65	Mel Carter
19/84	**All Of You** . . . Julio Iglesias & Diana Ross
4/90	**All Or Nothing** . . . Milli Vanilli
28/82	**All Our Tomorrows** . . . Eddie Schwartz
2/80	**All Out Of Love** . . . Air Supply
38/58	**All Over Again** . . . Johnny Cash
13/80	**All Over The World** . . . Electric Light Orchestra
12/83	**All Right** . . . Christopher Cross
	(also see: Alright)
4/70	**All Right Now** . . . Free
22/89	**All She Wants Is** . . . Duranduran
9/85	**All She Wants To Do Is Dance** . . . Don Henley
1/57	**All Shook Up** . . . Elvis Presley
	All Strung Out
26/66	Nino Tempo & April Stevens
34/77	John Travolta
26/72	**All The King's Horses** . . . Aretha Franklin
19/86	**All The Love In The World** . . . Outfield
1/91	**All The Man That I Need** . . . Whitney Houston
28/86	**All The Things She Said** . . . Simple Minds
21/58	**All The Time** . . . Johnny Mathis
2/58	**All The Way** . . . Frank Sinatra
37/72	**All The Young Dudes** . . . Mott The Hoople
17/83	**All This Love** . . . DeBarge
5/91	**All This Time** . . . Sting
6/89	**All This Time** . . . Tiffany
2/81	**All Those Years Ago** . . . George Harrison
5/84	**All Through The Night** . . . Cyndi Lauper
36/83	**All Time High** . . . Rita Coolidge
35/77	**All You Get From Love Is A Love Song** . . . Carpenters
1/67	**All You Need Is Love** . . . Beatles
2/56	**Allegheny Moon** . . . Patti Page

POS/YR	RECORD TITLE/ARTIST
17/83	**Allentown** . . . Billy Joel
7/62	**Alley Cat** . . . Bent Fabric
	Alley-Oop
1/60	Hollywood Argyles
15/60	Dante & the Evergreens
32/59	**Almost Grown** . . . Chuck Berry
32/78	**Almost Like Being In Love** . . . Michael Johnson
25/84	**Almost Over You** . . . Sheena Easton
	Almost Paradise
15/57	Roger Williams
31/57	Lou Stein
7/84	**Almost Paradise...Love Theme From Footloose** . . . Mike Reno & Ann Wilson
24/66	**Almost Persuaded** . . . David Houston
28/78	**Almost Summer** . . . Celebration featuring Mike Love
1/87	**Alone** . . . Heart
1/72	**Alone Again (Naturally)** . . . Gilbert O'Sullivan
8/60	**Alone At Last** . . . Jackie Wilson
	Alone (Why Must I Be Alone)
18/57	Shepherd Sisters
28/64	Four Seasons
	Along Came Jones
9/59	Coasters
27/69	Ray Stevens
14/85	**Along Comes A Woman** . . . Chicago
7/66	**Along Comes Mary** . . . Association
8/88	**Alphabet St.** . . . Prince
32/74	**Already Gone** . . . Eagles
4/90	**Alright** . . . Janet Jackson
	(also see: All Right)
2/73	**Also Sprach Zarathustra (2001)** . . . Deodato
40/62	**Alvin Twist** . . . Chipmunks
3/59	**Alvin's Harmonica** . . . Chipmunks
33/60	**Alvin's Orchestra** . . . Chipmunks
1/87	**Always** . . . Atlantic Starr
19/59	**Always** . . . Sammy Turner
	Always And Forever
18/78	Heatwave
35/90	Whistle
	Always On My Mind
5/82	Willie Nelson
4/88	Pet Shop Boys
	Always Something There To Remind Me ..see: (There's)
18/68	**Always Together** . . . Dells

POS/YR	RECORD TITLE/ARTIST
33/64	**Always Together** . . . Al Martino
31/60	**Am I Losing You** . . . Jim Reeves
	Am I That Easy To Forget
25/60	Debbie Reynolds
18/68	Engelbert Humperdinck
32/60	**Am I The Man** . . . Jackie Wilson
1/86	**Amanda** . . . Boston
	Amazing Grace
15/71	Judy Collins
11/72	Royal Scots Dragoon Guards
37/68	**Ame Caline (Soul Coaxing)** . . . Raymond Lefevre
	Amen
7/65	Impressions
36/68	Otis Redding
8/81	**America** . . . Neil Diamond
27/72	**American City Suite** . . . Cashman & West
13/80	**American Dream** . . . Dirt Band
17/82	**American Heartbeat** . . . Survivor
16/82	**American Music** . . . Pointer Sisters
1/72	**American Pie** . . . Don McLean
13/86	**American Storm** . . . Bob Seger
26/72	**American Trilogy** . . . Mickey Newbury
35/74	**American Tune** . . . Paul Simon
1/70	**American Woman** . . . Guess Who
	Americans
4/74	Byron MacGregor
24/74	Gordon Sinclair
27/75	**Amie** . . . Pure Prairie League
7/59	**Among My Souvenirs** . . . Connie Francis
18/61	**Amor** . . . Ben E. King
	(Amos & Andy Song) ..see: Like A Sunday In Salem
8/71	**Amos Moses** . . . Jerry Reed
38/55	**Amukiriki (The Lord Willing)** . . . Les Paul & Mary Ford
37/57	**Anastasia** . . . Pat Boone
22/67	**And Get Away** . . . Esquires
22/82	**And I Am Telling You I'm Not Going** . . . Jennifer Holliday
12/64	**And I Love Her** . . . Beatles
29/73	**And I Love You So** . . . Perry Como
36/65	**And Roses And Roses** . . . Andy Williams
37/90	**And So It Goes** . . . Billy Joel
	And That Reminds Me
9/57	Kay Starr
12/57	Della Reese
19/80	**And The Beat Goes On** . . . Whispers
21/85	**And We Danced** . . . Hooters

POS/YR	RECORD TITLE/ARTIST
2/69	**And When I Die** . . . Blood, Sweat & Tears
3/88	**Angel** . . . Aerosmith
5/85	**Angel** . . . Madonna
20/73	**Angel** . . . Aretha Franklin
40/72	**Angel** . . . Rod Stewart
5/61	**Angel Baby** . . . Rosie & The Originals
30/58	**Angel Baby** . . . Dean Martin
5/89	**Angel Eyes** . . . Jeff Healey Band
	(also see: I'll Never Let You Go)
40/82	**Angel In Blue** . . . J. Geils Band
6/77	**Angel In Your Arms** . . . Hot
14/89	**Angel Of Harlem** . . . U2
	Angel Of The Morning
7/68	Merrilee Rush
4/81	Juice Newton
22/61	**Angel On My Shoulder** . . . Shelby Flint
38/80	**Angel Say No** . . . Tommy Tutone
33/58	**Angel Smile** . . . Nat "King" Cole
30/89	**Angel Song** . . . Great White
27/60	**Angela Jones** . . . Johnny Ferguson
4/89	**Angelia** . . . Richard Marx
11/56	**Angels In The Sky** . . . Crew Cuts
22/59	**Angels Listened In** . . . Crests
1/73	**Angie** . . . Rolling Stones
	(also see: Different Worlds)
1/74	**Angie Baby** . . . Helen Reddy
	(Angry Young Man) ..see: Fooling Yourself
19/87	**Animal** . . . Def Leppard
1/74	**Annie's Song** . . . John Denver
1/80	**Another Brick In The Wall (Part II)** . . . Pink Floyd
5/71	**Another Day** . . . Paul McCartney
1/89	**Another Day In Paradise** . . . Phil Collins
13/88	**Another Lover** . . . Giant Steps
22/86	**Another Night** . . . Aretha Franklin
1/80	**Another One Bites The Dust** . . . Queen
32/74	**Another Park, Another Sunday** . . . Doobie Brothers
11/88	**Another Part Of Me** . . . Michael Jackson
32/76	**Another Rainy Day In New York City** . . . Chicago
	Another Saturday Night
10/63	Sam Cooke
6/74	Cat Stevens
22/60	**Another Sleepless Night** . . . Jimmy Clanton
	Another Somebody Done Somebody Wrong Song ..see: (Hey Won't You Play)
32/77	**Another Star** . . . Stevie Wonder
20/58	**Another Time, Another Place** . . . Patti Page
32/80	**Answering Machine** . . . Rupert Holmes
	(Anthony's Song) ..see: Movin' Out
13/72	**Anticipation** . . . Carly Simon
	Any Day Now
23/62	Chuck Jackson
14/82	Ronnie Milsap
	Any Other Way ..see: (If There Was)
14/65	**Any Way You Want It** . . . Dave Clark Five
23/80	**Any Way You Want It** . . . Journey
31/61	**Anybody But Me** . . . Brenda Lee
31/60	**Anymore** . . . Teresa Brewer
8/64	**Anyone Who Had A Heart** . . . Dionne Warwick
1/88	**Anything For You** . . . Gloria Estefan & Miami Sound Machine
29/90	**Anything I Want** . . . Kevin Paige
26/91	**Anything Is Possible** . . . Debbie Gibson
31/62	**Anything That's Part Of You** . . . Elvis Presley
37/76	**Anything You Want** . . . John Valenti
33/76	**Anytime (I'll Be There)** . . . Paul Anka
20/56	**Anyway You Want Me (That's How I Will Be)** . . . Elvis Presley
2/61	**Apache** . . . Jorgen Ingmann
	Apartment ..see: Theme From The
24/56	**Ape Call** . . . Nervous Norvus
	Apple Blossom Time ..see: (I'll Be With You In)
29/60	**Apple Green** . . . June Valli
32/65	**Apple Of My Eye** . . . Roy Head
6/67	**Apples, Peaches, Pumpkin Pie** . . . Jay & The Techniques
37/69	**April Fools** . . . Dionne Warwick
28/56	**April In Paris** . . . Count Basie
1/57	**April Love** . . . Pat Boone
1/69	**Aquarius/Let The Sunshine In** . . . 5th Dimension
15/84	**Are We Ourselves?** . . . Fixx
39/69	**Are You Happy** . . . Jerry Butler
39/67	**Are You Lonely For Me** . . . Freddy Scott
	Are You Lonesome To-night?
1/60	Elvis Presley
14/74	Donny Osmond

POS/YR	RECORD TITLE/ARTIST
15/73	**Are You Man Enough** . . . Four Tops
14/70	**Are You Ready?** . . . Pacific Gas & Electric
10/58	**Are You Really Mine** . . . Jimmie Rodgers
11/56	**Are You Satisfied?** . . . Rusty Draper
3/58	**Are You Sincere** . . . Andy Williams
39/66	**Are You There (With Another Girl)** . . . Dionne Warwick
26/77	**Ariel** . . . Dean Friedman
10/70	**Arizona** . . . Mark Lindsay
3/89	**Armageddon It** . . . Def Leppard
28/73	**Armed And Extremely Dangerous** . . . First Choice
36/89	**Arms Of Orion** . . . Prince with Sheena Easton
9/91	**Around The Way Girl** . . . L.L. Cool J
	Around The World In 80 Days
12/57	Mantovani
13/57	Victor Young
25/57	Bing Crosby
29/79	**Arrow Through Me** . . . Wings
1/81	**Arthur's Theme (Best That You Can Do)** . . . Christopher Cross
20/60	**Artificial Flowers** . . . Bobby Darin
36/78	**As** . . . Stevie Wonder
10/61	**As If I Didn't Know** . . . Adam Wade
	As Tears Go By
22/65	Marianne Faithfull
6/66	Rolling Stones
31/70	**As The Years Go By** . . . Mashmakhan
12/64	**As Usual** . . . Brenda Lee
23/87	**As We Lay** . . . Shirley Murdock
37/80	**Ashes By Now** . . . Rodney Crowell
8/61	**Asia Minor** . . . Kokomo
12/64	**Ask Me** . . . Elvis Presley
18/56	**Ask Me** . . . Nat "King" Cole
40/71	**Ask Me No Questions** . . . B.B. King
27/72	**Ask Me What You Want** . . . Millie Jackson
24/65	**Ask The Lonely** . . . Four Tops
19/61	**Astronaut, The** . . . Jose Jimenez
30/77	**At Midnight (My Love Will Lift You Up)** . . . Rufus Featuring Chaka Khan
	At My Front Door
7/55	Pat Boone
17/55	El Dorados
3/75	**At Seventeen** . . . Janis Ian
	(At The Copa) ..see: Copacabana
	At The Hop
1/58	Danny & The Juniors
21/58	Nick Todd

POS/YR	RECORD TITLE/ARTIST
18/66	**At The Scene** . . . Dave Clark Five
16/67	**At The Zoo** . . . Simon & Garfunkel
1/87	**At This Moment** . . . Billy Vera & The Beaters
28/82	**Athena** . . . Who
27/81	**Atlanta Lady (Something About Your Love)** . . . Marty Balin
7/69	**Atlantis** . . . Donovan
39/80	**Atomic** . . . Blondie
18/66	**Attack** . . . Toys
21/75	**Attitude Dancing** . . . Carly Simon
15/73	**Aubrey** . . . Bread
19/57	**Auctioneer** . . . Leroy VanDyke
15/84	**Authority Song** . . . John Cougar Mellencamp
25/75	**Autobahn** . . . Kraftwerk
5/84	**Automatic** . . . Pointer Sisters
34/83	**Automatic Man** . . . Michael Sembello
37/72	**Automatically Sunshine** . . . Supremes
	Autumn Leaves
1/55	Roger Williams
35/55	Steve Allen with George Cates
19/68	**Autumn Of My Life** . . . Bobby Goldsboro
18/56	**Autumn Waltz** . . . Tony Bennett
3/85	**Axel F** . . . Harold Faltermeyer

POS/YR	RECORD TITLE/ARTIST
26/90	**B.B.D. (I Thought It Was Me)?** . . . Bell Biv DeVoe
1/79	**Babe** . . . Styx
14/66	**B-A-B-Y** . . . Carla Thomas
1/91	**Baby Baby** . . . Amy Grant
8/69	**Baby, Baby Don't Cry** . . . Miracles
12/61	**Baby Blue** . . . Echoes
14/72	**Baby Blue** . . . Badfinger
1/78	**Baby Come Back** . . . Player
32/68	**Baby, Come Back** . . . Equals
27/74	**Baby Come Close** . . . Smokey Robinson
1/83	**Baby, Come To Me** . . . Patti Austin with James Ingram
33/56	**Baby Doll** . . . Andy Williams

POS/YR	RECORD TITLE/ARTIST
1/89	**Baby Don't Forget My Number** . . . Milli Vanilli
1/72	**Baby Don't Get Hooked On Me** . . . Mac Davis
8/65	**Baby Don't Go** . . . Sonny & Cher
39/64	**Baby, Don't You Cry** . . . Ray Charles
27/64	**Baby Don't You Do It** . . . Marvin Gaye
30/63	**Baby Don't You Weep** . . . Garnet Mimms & The Enchanters
14/76	**Baby Face** . . . Wing & A Prayer Fife & Drum Corps.
11/78	**Baby Hold On** . . . Eddie Money
35/70	**Baby Hold On** . . . Grass Roots
26/84	**Baby I Lied** . . . Deborah Allen
4/67	**Baby I Love You** . . . Aretha Franklin
	Baby, I Love You
24/64	Ronettes
9/69	Andy Kim
	Baby, I Love Your Way
12/76	Peter Frampton
1/88	Will To Power (medley)
	Baby I Need Your Loving
11/64	Four Tops
3/67	Johnny Rivers
3/71	**Baby I'm-A Want You** . . . Bread
25/79	**Baby I'm Burnin'** . . . Dolly Parton
14/69	**Baby, I'm For Real** . . . Originals
11/65	**Baby, I'm Yours** . . . Barbara Lewis
16/90	**Baby, It's Tonight** . . . Jude Cole
	Baby It's You
8/62	Shirelles
5/69	Smith
14/83	**Baby Jane** . . . Rod Stewart
29/71	**Baby Let Me Kiss You** . . . King Floyd
24/72	**Baby Let Me Take You (In My Arms)** . . . Detroit Emeralds
35/69	**Baby Let's Wait** . . . Royal Guardsmen
1/64	**Baby Love** . . . Supremes
10/86	**Baby Love** . . . Regina
25/82	**Baby Makes Her Blue Jeans Talk** . . . Dr. Hook
11/68	**Baby, Now That I've Found You** . . . Foundations
21/61	**Baby Oh Baby** . . . Shells
16/66	**Baby Scratch My Back** . . . Slim Harpo
6/61	**Baby Sittin' Boogie** . . . Buzz Clifford
23/70	**Baby Take Me In Your Arms** . . . Jefferson
10/59	**Baby Talk** . . . Jan & Dean
38/80	**Baby Talks Dirty** . . . Knack

POS/YR	RECORD TITLE/ARTIST
26/75	**Baby That's Backatcha** . . . Smokey Robinson
12/65	**Baby The Rain Must Fall** . . . Glenn Yarbrough
4/77	**Baby, What A Big Surprise** . . . Chicago
37/60	**Baby What You Want Me To Do** . . . Jimmy Reed
5/63	**Baby Workout** . . . Jackie Wilson
34/67	**Baby You Got It** . . . Brenton Wood
34/67	**Baby You're A Rich Man** . . . Beatles
5/60	**Baby (You've Got What It Takes)** . . . Dinah Washington & Brook Benton
26/61	**Baby's First Christmas** . . . Connie Francis
5/74	**Back Home Again** . . . John Denver
37/81	**Back In Black** . . . AC/DC
	Back In Love Again ..see: (Every Time I Turn Around)
1/65	**Back In My Arms Again** . . . Supremes
13/87	**Back In The High Life Again** . . . Steve Winwood
38/77	**Back In The Saddle** . . . Aerosmith
	Back In The U.S.A.
37/59	Chuck Berry
16/78	Linda Ronstadt
9/72	**Back Off Boogaloo** . . . Ringo Starr
34/89	**Back On Holiday** . . . Robbie Nevil
33/80	**Back On My Feet Again** . . . Babys
5/83	**Back On The Chain Gang** . . . Pretenders
36/67	**Back On The Street Again** . . . Sunshine Company
3/72	**Back Stabbers** . . . O'Jays
4/89	**Back To Life (However Do You Want Me)** . . . Soul II Soul
36/57	**Back To School Again** . . . Timmie "Oh Yeah!" Rogers
28/77	**Back Together Again** . . . Daryl Hall & John Oates
40/73	**Back When My Hair Was Short** . . . Gunhill Road
20/84	**Back Where You Belong** . . . 38 Special
10/69	**Backfield In Motion** . . . Mel & Tim
25/66	**Backstage** . . . Gene Pitney
1/87	**Bad** . . . Michael Jackson
1/73	**Bad, Bad Leroy Brown** . . . Jim Croce
1/75	**Bad Blood** . . . Neil Sedaka
8/86	**Bad Boy** . . . Miami Sound Machine
35/83	**Bad Boy** . . . Ray Parker Jr.
36/57	**Bad Boy** . . . Jive Bombers

POS/YR	RECORD TITLE/ARTIST
14/79	**Bad Case Of Loving You (Doctor, Doctor)** . . . Robert Palmer
33/63	**Bad Girl** . . . Neil Sedaka
1/79	**Bad Girls** . . . Donna Summer
15/75	**Bad Luck** . . . Harold Melvin & The Bluenotes
37/60	**Bad Man Blunder** . . . Kingston Trio
1/88	**Bad Medicine** . . . Bon Jovi
2/69	**Bad Moon Rising** . . . Creedence Clearwater Revival
25/90	**Bad Of The Heart** . . . George LaMond
4/75	**Bad Time** . . . Grand Funk
9/64	**Bad To Me** . . . Billy J. Kramer
2/78	**Baker Street** . . . Gerry Rafferty
3/70	**Ball Of Confusion (That's What The World Is Today)** . . . Temptations
19/69	**Ball Of Fire** . . . Tommy James & The Shondells
14/58	**Ballad Of A Teenage Queen** . . . Johnny Cash
7/68	**Ballad Of Bonnie And Clyde** . . . Georgie Fame
	Ballad Of Davy Crockett
1/55	Bill Hayes
5/55	"Tennessee" Ernie Ford
5/55	Fess Parker
14/55	Voices of Walter Schumann
34/66	**Ballad Of Irving** . . . Frank Gallop
33/90	**Ballad of Jayne** . . . L.A. Guns
8/69	**Ballad Of John And Yoko** . . . Beatles
33/62	**Ballad Of Paladin** . . . Duane Eddy
34/60	**Ballad Of The Alamo** . . . Marty Robbins
1/66	**Ballad Of The Green Berets** . . . SSgt Barry Sadler
18/57	**Ballerina** . . . Nat "King" Cole
7/87	**Ballerina Girl** . . . Lionel Richie
33/74	**Ballero** . . . War
5/75	**Ballroom Blitz** . . . Sweet
	Banana Boat (Day-O)
5/57	Harry Belafonte
25/57	Stan Freberg
	Banana Boat Song
4/57	Tarriers
13/57	Fontane Sisters
18/57	Steve Lawrence
19/57	Sarah Vaughan
3/70	**Band Of Gold** . . . Freda Payne
	Band Of Gold
4/56	Don Cherry
11/56	Kit Carson

POS/YR	RECORD TITLE/ARTIST
32/66	Mel Carter
1/74	**Band On The Run** . . . Paul McCartney
35/67	**Banda, A** . . . Herb Alpert
18/55	**Bandit (O'Cangaceiro)** . . . Eddie Barclay
	Bang A Gong (Get It On)
10/72	T. Rex
9/85	Power Station
2/66	**Bang Bang (My Baby Shot Me Down)** . . . Cher
22/68	**Bang-Shang-A-Lang** . . . Archies
31/84	**Bang Your Head** . . . Quiet Riot
23/71	**Bangla-Desh** . . . George Harrison
15/55	**Banjo's Back In Town** . . . Teresa Brewer
20/90	**Banned In The U.S.A.** . . . Luke Feat. 2 Live Crew
29/60	**Barbara** . . . Temptations
	Barbara-Ann
13/61	Regents
2/66	Beach Boys
7/66	**Barefootin'** . . . Robert Parker
20/76	**Barretta's Theme ("Keep Your Eye On The Sparrow")** . . . Rhythm Heritage
11/77	**Barracuda** . . . Heart
	Baseball Game ..see: (Love Is Like A)
15/73	**Basketball Jones Featuring Tyrone Shoelaces** . . . Cheech & Chong
	(also see: Love Jones)
1/89	**Batdance** . . . Prince
	Batman Theme
17/66	Marketts
35/66	Neal Hefti
37/71	**Battle Hymn Of Lt. Calley** . . . C Company Featuring Terry Nelson
	Battle Hymn Of The Republic
13/59	Mormon Tabernacle Choir
33/68	Andy Williams
14/59	**Battle Of Kookamonga** . . . Homer & Jethro
1/59	**Battle Of New Orleans** . . . Johnny Horton
25/58	**Baubles, Bangles And Beads** . . . Kirby Stone Four
34/73	**Be** . . . Neil Diamond
25/64	**Be Anything (But Be Mine)** . . . Connie Francis
7/56	**Be-Bop-A-Lula** . . . Gene Vincent
3/57	**Be-Bop Baby** . . . Ricky Nelson
31/63	**Be Careful Of Stones That You Throw** . . . Dion
9/86	**Be Good To Yourself** . . . Journey

POS/YR	RECORD TITLE/ARTIST
35/82	**Be Mine Tonight** . . . Neil Diamond
	Be My Baby
2/63	Ronettes
17/70	Andy Kim
8/59	**Be My Guest** . . . Fats Domino
28/82	**Be My Lady** . . . Jefferson Starship
9/85	**Be Near Me** . . . ABC
15/88	**Be Still My Beating Heart** . . . Sting
4/74	**Be Thankful For What You Got** . . . William DeVaughn
6/63	**Be True To Your School** . . . Beach Boys
34/63	**Be True To Yourself** . . . Bobby Vee
30/89	**Be With You** . . . Bangles
4/74	**Beach Baby** . . . First Class
12/81	**Beach Boys Medley** . . . Beach Boys
30/64	**Beans In My Ears** . . . Serendipity Singers
8/78	**Beast Of Burden** . . . Rolling Stones
6/67	**Beat Goes On** . . . Sonny & Cher
1/83	**Beat It** . . . Michael Jackson **(also see: Eat It)**
17/86	**Beat's So Lonely** . . . Charlie Sexton
12/82	**Beatles' Movie Medley** . . . Beatles
15/60	**Beatnik Fly** . . . Johnny & The Hurricanes
3/68	**Beautiful Morning** . . . Rascals
	Beautiful People
37/67	Bobby Vee
38/67	Kenny O'Dell
15/72	**Beautiful Sunday** . . . Daniel Boone
3/66	**Beauty Is Only Skin Deep** . . . Temptations
3/64	**Because** . . . Dave Clark Five
1/90	**Because I Love You (The Postman Song)** . . . Stevie B
27/88	**Because Of You** . . . Cover Girls
13/78	**Because The Night** . . . Patti Smith Group
4/60	**Because They're Young** . . . Duane Eddy
17/88	**Beds Are Burning** . . . Midnight Oil
17/62	**Beechwood 4-5789** . . . Marvelettes
24/58	**Been So Long** . . . Pastels
24/73	**Been To Canaan** . . . Carole King
4/58	**Beep Beep** . . . Playmates
33/75	**Beer Barrel Polka** . . . Bobby Vinton
17/65	**Before And After** . . . Chad & Jeremy
23/78	**Before My Heart Finds Out** . . . Gene Cotton
1/75	**Before The Next Teardrop Falls** . . . Freddy Fender
29/67	**Beg, Borrow And Steal** . . . Ohio Express
16/67	**Beggin'** . . . 4 Seasons

POS/YR	RECORD TITLE/ARTIST
36/69	**Beginning Of My End** . . . Unifics
7/71	**Beginnings** . . . Chicago
34/71	**Behind Blue Eyes** . . . Who
15/73	**Behind Closed Doors** . . . Charlie Rich
2/81	**Being With You** . . . Smokey Robinson
28/73	**Believe In Humanity** . . . Carole King
26/59	**Believe Me** . . . Royal Teens
4/58	**Believe What You Say** . . . Ricky Nelson
28/69	**Bella Linda** . . . Grassroots
34/84	**Belle Of St. Mark** . . . Sheila E.
12/70	**Bells, The** . . . Originals
13/58	**Belonging To Someone** . . . Patti Page
1/72	**Ben** . . . Michael Jackson
	Ben Casey ..see: Theme From
5/68	**Bend Me, Shape Me** . . . American Breed
1/74	**Bennie And The Jets** . . . Elton John
4/67	**Bernadette** . . . Four Tops
14/57	**Bernardine** . . . Pat Boone
16/75	**Bertha Butt Boogie** . . . Jimmy Castor Bunch
15/89	**Best, The** . . . Tina Turner
17/76	**Best Disco In Town** . . . Ritchie Family
32/68	**Best Of Both Worlds** . . . Lulu
1/77	**Best Of My Love** . . . Emotions
1/75	**Best Of My Love** . . . Eagles
3/81	**Best Of Times** . . . Styx
39/64	**(Best Part Of) Breakin' Up** . . . Ronettes
3/74	**Best Thing That Ever Happened To Me** . . . Gladys Knight & The Pips
3/72	**Betcha By Golly, Wow** . . . Stylistics
	(Betcha Got A Chick On The Side) ..see: How Long
36/87	**Betcha Say That** . . . Gloria Estefan & Miami Sound Machine
7/76	**Beth** . . . Kiss
1/81	**Bette Davis Eyes** . . . Kim Carnes
5/84	**Better Be Good To Me** . . . Tina Turner
18/91	**Better Love** . . . Londonbeat
12/80	**Better Love Next Time** . . . Dr. Hook
38/61	**Better Tell Him No** . . . Starlets
33/58	**Betty And Dupree** . . . Chuck Willis
37/58	**Betty Lou Got A New Pair Of Shoes** . . . Bobby Freeman
40/61	**Bewildered** . . . James Brown
	Beyond The Sea
37/56	Roger Williams
6/60	Bobby Darin

POS/YR	RECORD TITLE/ARTIST
	Bible Tells Me So
7/55	Don Cornell
22/55	Nick Noble
24/79	**Bicycle Race** . . . Queen
1/61	**Big Bad John** . . . Jimmy Dean
26/58	**Big Beat** . . . Fats Domino
38/58	**Big Bopper's Wedding** . . . Big Bopper
38/67	**Big Boss Man** . . . Elvis Presley
23/73	**Big City Miss Ruth Ann** . . . Gallery
19/61	**Big Cold Wind** . . . Pat Boone
21/82	**Big Fun** . . . Kool & The Gang
1/62	**Big Girls Don't Cry** . . . 4 Seasons
1/59	**Big Hunk O' Love** . . . Elvis Presley
3/59	**Big Hurt** . . . Miss Toni Fisher
26/60	**Big Iron** . . . Marty Robbins
21/61	**Big John** . . . Shirelles
20/83	**Big Log** . . . Robert Plant
5/87	**Big Love** . . . Fleetwood Mac
3/58	**Big Man** . . . Four Preps
20/64	**Big Man In Town** . . . 4 Seasons
14/79	**Big Shot** . . . Billy Joel
8/87	**Big Time** . . . Peter Gabriel
	Big Yellow Taxi
29/70	Neighborhood
24/75	Joni Mitchell
3/80	**Biggest Part Of Me** . . . Ambrosia
37/61	**Bilbao Song** . . . Andy Williams
1/83	**Billie Jean** . . . Michael Jackson
7/58	**Billy** . . . Kathy Linden
34/66	**Billy And Sue** . . . B.J. Thomas
1/74	**Billy, Don't Be A Hero** . . . Bo Donaldson & The Heywoods
	Billy Jack ..see: One Tin Soldier
11/58	**Bimbombey** . . . Jimmie Rodgers
36/85	**Bird, The** . . . Time
	(also see: Do The)
30/64	**Bird Dance Beat** . . . Trashmen
1/58	**Bird Dog** . . . Everly Brothers
34/58	**Bird On My Head** . . . David Seville
12/63	**Birdland** . . . Chubby Checker
3/65	**Birds And The Bees** . . . Jewel Akens
23/71	**Birds Of A Feather** . . . Raiders
17/55	**Birth Of The Boogie** . . . Bill Haley
26/69	**Birthday** . . . Underground Sunshine
40/63	**Birthday Party** . . . Pixies Three
36/89	**Birthday Suit** . . . Johnny Kemp
4/74	**Bitch Is Back** . . . Elton John

POS/YR	RECORD TITLE/ARTIST
28/77	**Bite Your Lip (Get up and dance!)** . . . Elton John
4/64	**Bits And Pieces** . . . Dave Clark Five
36/73	**Bitter Bad** . . . Melanie
34/88	**Black And Blue** . . . Van Halen
1/72	**Black & White** . . . Three Dog Night
18/77	**Black Betty** . . . Ram Jam
1/90	**Black Cat** . . . Janet Jackson
	Black Denim Trousers
6/55	Cheers
38/55	Vaughn Monroe
15/72	**Black Dog** . . . Led Zeppelin
37/75	**Black Friday** . . . Steely Dan
4/66	**Black Is Black** . . . Los Bravos
4/71	**Black Magic Woman** . . . Santana
13/69	**Black Pearl** . . . Checkmates, Ltd.
17/57	**Black Slacks** . . . Joe Bennett
21/75	**Black Superman - "Muhammad Ali"** . . . Johnny Wakelin
1/90	**Black Velvet** . . . Alannah Myles
1/75	**Black Water** . . . Doobie Brothers
7/63	**Blame It On The Bossa Nova** . . . Eydie Gorme
1/89	**Blame It On The Rain** . . . Milli Vanilli
1/90	**Blaze Of Glory** . . . Jon Bon Jovi
39/64	**Bless Our Love** . . . Gene Chandler
15/61	**Bless You** . . . Tony Orlando
34/81	**Blessed Are The Believers** . . . Anne Murray
	(Blind Man In The Bleachers) ..see: Last Game Of The Season
1/77	**Blinded By The Light** . . . Manfred Mann's Earth Band
33/58	**Blob, The** . . . Five Blobs
35/75	**Bloody Well Right** . . . Supertramp
2/55	**Blossom Fell** . . . Nat "King" Cole
16/79	**Blow Away** . . . George Harrison
	Blowin' In The Wind
2/63	Peter, Paul & Mary
9/66	Stevie Wonder
21/70	**Blowing Away** . . . 5th Dimension
9/60	**Blue Angel** . . . Roy Orbison
35/67	**Blue Autumn** . . . Bobby Goldsboro
	Blue Bayou
29/63	Roy Orbison
3/77	Linda Ronstadt
20/58	**Blue Blue Day** . . . Don Gibson
21/78	**Blue Collar Man (Long Nights)** . . . Styx

POS/YR	RECORD TITLE/ARTIST
12/82	**Blue Eyes** . . . Elton John
21/75	**Blue Eyes Crying In The Rain** . . . Willie Nelson
37/59	**Blue Hawaii** . . . Billy Vaughn
8/84	**Blue Jean** . . . David Bowie
5/57	**Blue Monday** . . . Fats Domino
23/71	**Blue Money** . . . Van Morrison
1/61	**Blue Moon** . . . Marcels
15/79	**Blue Morning, Blue Day** . . . Foreigner
3/63	**Blue On Blue** . . . Bobby Vinton
29/55	**Blue Star** . . . Felicia Sanders
	Blue Suede Shoes
2/56	Carl Perkins
20/56	Elvis Presley
38/73	Johnny Rivers
16/60	**Blue Tango** . . . Bill Black's Combo
1/63	**Blue Velvet** . . . Bobby Vinton
24/64	**Blue Winter** . . . Connie Francis
	Blueberry Hill
29/56	Louis Armstrong & Gordon Jenkins
2/57	Fats Domino
35/75	**Bluebird** . . . Helen Reddy
12/78	**Bluer Than Blue** . . . Michael Johnson
36/62	**Blues (Stay Away From Me)** . . . Ace Cannon
37/67	**Blue's Theme** . . . Davie Allan & The Arrows
	Bo Weevil
17/56	Teresa Brewer
35/56	Fats Domino
	(also see: Boll Weevil)
12/82	**Bobbie Sue** . . . Oak Ridge Boys
8/59	**Bobby Sox To Stockings** . . . Frankie Avalon
3/62	**Bobby's Girl** . . . Marcie Blane
11/82	**Body Language** . . . Queen
9/76	**Bohemian Rhapsody** . . . Queen
2/61	**Boll Weevil Song** . . . Brook Benton
19/61	**Bonanza** . . . Al Caiola
14/59	**Bongo Rock** . . . Preston Epps
33/62	**Bongo Stomp** . . . Little Joey & The Flips
	Bonnie And Clyde ..see: Ballad Of
26/60	**Bonnie Came Back** . . . Duane Eddy
	(also see: My Bonnie)
14/57	**Bony Moronie** . . . Larry Williams
7/67	**Boogaloo Down Broadway** . . . Fantastic Johnny C
12/77	**Boogie Child** . . . Bee Gees

POS/YR	RECORD TITLE/ARTIST
2/74	**Boogie Down** . . . Eddie Kendricks
1/76	**Boogie Fever** . . . Sylvers
2/77	**Boogie Nights** . . . Heatwave
3/75	**Boogie On Reggae Woman** . . . Stevie Wonder
1/78	**Boogie Oogie Oogie** . . . Taste Of Honey
35/78	**Boogie Shoes** . . . KC & The Sunshine Band
6/79	**Boogie Wonderland** . . . Earth, Wind & Fire with The Emotions
8/73	**Boogie Woogie Bugle Boy** . . . Bette Midler
5/58	**Book Of Love** . . . Monotones
17/55	**Boom Boom Boomerang** . . . DeCastro Sisters
	Boomerang ..see: Do The
36/71	**Booty Butt** . . . Ray Charles
20/84	**Bop 'Til You Drop** . . . Rick Springfield
33/83	**Border, The** . . . America
37/70	**Border Song** . . . Aretha Franklin
10/84	**Borderline** . . . Madonna
38/85	**Borderlines** . . . Jeffrey Osborne
12/66	**Born A Woman** . . . Sandy Posey
	Born Free
7/66	Roger Williams
38/68	Hesitations
9/85	**Born In The U.S.A.** . . . Bruce Springsteen
	(also see: Banned In The U.S.A.)
16/79	**Born To Be Alive** . . . Patrick Hernandez
3/89	**Born To Be My Baby** . . . Bon Jovi
2/68	**Born To Be Wild** . . . Steppenwolf
5/56	**Born To Be With You** . . . Chordettes
23/75	**Born To Run** . . . Bruce Springsteen
17/71	**Born To Wander** . . . Rare Earth
7/58	**Born Too Late** . . . Poni-Tails
19/79	**Boss, The** . . . Diana Ross
28/63	**Boss Guitar** . . . Duane Eddy
	Bossa Nova ..see: Fly Me To The Moon
8/63	**Bossa Nova Baby** . . . Elvis Presley
8/68	**Both Sides Now** . . . Judy Collins
9/68	**Bottle Of Wine** . . . Fireballs
19/80	**Boulevard** . . . Jackson Browne
40/63	**Bounce, The** . . . Olympics
40/67	**Bowling Green** . . . Everly Brothers
7/69	**Boxer, The** . . . Simon & Garfunkel
	Boy From New York City
8/65	Ad Libs
7/81	Manhattan Transfer
	Boy I'm Gonna Marry ..see: (Today I Met)

POS/YR	RECORD TITLE/ARTIST
26/85	**Boy In The Box** . . . Corey Hart
2/69	**Boy Named Sue** . . . Johnny Cash
18/63	**Boy Next Door** . . . Secrets
10/59	**Boy Without A Girl** . . . Frankie Avalon
12/76	**Boys Are Back In Town** . . . Thin Lizzy
37/84	**Boys Do Fall In Love** . . . Robin Gibb
25/87	**Boys Night Out** . . . Timothy B. Schmit
5/85	**Boys Of Summer** . . . Don Henley
1/71	**Brand New Key** . . . Melanie
15/87	**Brand New Lover** . . . Dead Or Alive
24/69	**Brand New Me** . . . Dusty Springfield
1/72	**Brandy (You're A Fine Girl)** . . . Looking Glass
35/61	**Brass Buttons** . . . String-A-Longs
14/80	**Brass In Pocket (I'm Special)** . . . Pretenders
11/75	**Brazil** . . . Ritchie Family
2/64	**Bread And Butter** . . . Newbeats
39/76	**Break Away** . . . Art Garfunkel
40/65	**Break Away (From That Boy)** . . . Newbeats
	Break It To Me Gently
4/62	Brenda Lee
11/82	Juice Newton
26/82	**Break It Up** . . . Foreigner
5/84	**Break My Stride** . . . Matthew Wilder
5/73	**Break Up To Make Up** . . . Stylistics
35/68	**Break Your Promise** . . . Delfonics
8/84	**Breakdance** . . . Irene Cara
31/71	**Breakdown, The** . . . Rufus Thomas
40/78	**Breakdown** . . . Tom Petty
15/80	**Breakdown Dead Ahead** . . . Boz Scaggs
7/61	**Breakin' In A Brand New Broken Heart** . . . Connie Francis
9/84	**Breakin'...There's No Stopping Us** . . . Ollie & Jerry
	Breakin' Up ..see: (Best Part Of)
31/66	**Breakin' Up Is Breakin' My Heart** . . . Roy Orbison
22/81	**Breaking Away** . . . Balance
	Breaking Up Is Hard To Do
1/62	Neil Sedaka
34/70	Lenny Welch
28/72	Partridge Family
8/76	Neil Sedaka
18/83	**Breaking Us In Two** . . . Joe Jackson
6/87	**Breakout** . . . Swing Out Sister

POS/YR	RECORD TITLE/ARTIST
15/81	**Breakup Song (They Don't Write 'Em)** . . . Greg Kihn Band
7/58	**Breathless** . . . Jerry Lee Lewis
8/55	**Breeze And I** . . . Caterina Valente
5/77	**Brick House** . . . Commodores
	Bridge Over Troubled Water
1/70	Simon & Garfunkel
6/71	Aretha Franklin
5/87	**Brilliant Disguise** . . . Bruce Springsteen
	Bring It On Home To Me
13/62	Sam Cooke
32/65	Animals
17/68	Eddie Floyd
29/67	**Bring It Up** . . . James Brown
12/71	**Bring The Boys Home** . . . Freda Payne
2/61	**Bristol Stomp** . . . Dovells
27/62	**Bristol Twistin' Annie** . . . Dovells
12/79	**Broken Hearted Me** . . . Anne Murray
7/59	**Broken-Hearted Melody** . . . Sarah Vaughan
1/85	**Broken Wings** . . . Mr. Mister
1/73	**Brother Louie** . . . Stories
22/69	**Brother Love's Travelling Salvation Show** . . . Neil Diamond
32/70	**Brother Rapp** . . . James Brown
10/67	**Brown Eyed Girl** . . . Van Morrison
1/71	**Brown Sugar** . . . Rolling Stones
27/85	**Bruce** . . . Rick Springfield
3/89	**Buffalo Stance** . . . Neneh Cherry
3/69	**Build Me Up Buttercup** . . . Foundations
24/60	**Bulldog** . . . Fireballs
21/65	**Bumble Bee** . . . Searchers
21/61	**Bumble Boogie** . . . B. Bumble & The Stingers
12/75	**Bungle In The Jungle** . . . Jethro Tull
9/55	**Burn That Candle** . . . Bill Haley
40/81	**Burnin' For You** . . . Blue Oyster Cult
3/60	**Burning Bridges** . . . Jack Scott
34/71	**Burning Bridges** . . . Mike Curb Congregation
9/83	**Burning Down The House** . . . Talking Heads
2/86	**Burning Heart** . . . Survivor
39/83	**Burning Heart** . . . Vandenberg
2/72	**Burning Love** . . . Elvis Presley
5/66	**Bus Stop** . . . Hollies
17/56	**Bus Stop Song (A Paper Of Pins)** . . . Four Lads

POS/YR	RECORD TITLE/ARTIST
7/89	**Bust A Move** . . . Young MC
25/63	**Bust Out** . . . Busters
4/63	**Busted** . . . Ray Charles
34/79	**Bustin' Loose** . . . Chuck Brown
4/61	**But I Do** . . . Clarence Henry
22/66	**But It's Alright** . . . J.J. Jackson
19/69	**But You Know I Love You** . . . First Edition
15/65	**But You're Mine** . . . Sonny & Cher
29/75	**Butter Boy** . . . Fanny
	Butterfly
1/57	Charlie Gracie
1/57	Andy Williams
23/63	**Butterfly Baby** . . . Bobby Rydell
11/58	**Buzz-Buzz-Buzz** . . . Hollywood Flames
	By The Time I Get To Phoenix
26/67	Glen Campbell
37/69	Isaac Hayes
12/65	**Bye, Bye, Baby (Baby Goodbye)** . . . 4 Seasons
2/57	**Bye Bye Love** . . . Everly Brothers

POS/YR	RECORD TITLE/ARTIST
	C.C. Rider
12/57	Chuck Willis
34/63	LaVern Baker
10/66	Animals
	(also see: Jenny Take A Ride!)
2/87	**C'est La Vie** . . . Robbie Nevil
11/55	**C'est La Vie** . . . Sarah Vaughan
22/61	**C'est Si Bon (It's So Good)** . . . Conway Twitty
22/57	**Ca, C'est L'amour** . . . Tony Bennett
23/68	**Cab Driver** . . . Mills Brothers
22/62	**Cajun Queen** . . . Jimmy Dean
1/61	**Calcutta** . . . Lawrence Welk
4/61	**Calendar Girl** . . . Neil Sedaka
4/66	**California Dreamin'** . . . Mama's & The Papa's
	California Girls
3/65	Beach Boys
3/85	David Lee Roth
16/67	**California Nights** . . . Lesley Gore
25/69	**California Soul** . . . 5th Dimension

POS/YR	RECORD TITLE/ARTIST
5/64	**California Sun** . . . Rivieras
18/89	**Call It Love** . . . Poco
1/80	**Call Me** . . . Blondie
13/70	**Call Me** . . . Aretha Franklin
21/58	**Call Me** . . . Johnny Mathis
22/66	**Call Me** . . . Chris Montez
26/82	**Call Me** . . . Skyy
10/73	**Call Me (Come Back Home)** . . . Al Green
40/68	**Call Me Lightning** . . . Who
19/62	**Call Me Mr. In-Between** . . . Burl Ives
6/74	**Call On Me** . . . Chicago
22/63	**Call On Me** . . . Bobby Bland
15/85	**Call To The Heart** . . . Giuffria
18/86	**Calling America** . . . Electric Light Orchestra
16/77	**Calling Dr. Love** . . . Kiss
32/77	**Calling Occupants Of Interplanetary Craft** . . . Carpenters
2/75	**Calypso** . . . John Denver
5/69	**Can I Change My Mind** . . . Tyrone Davis
	Can I Get A Witness
22/63	Marvin Gaye
39/71	Lee Michaels
15/57	**Can I Steal A Little Love** . . . Frank Sinatra
31/74	**Can This Be Real** . . . Natural Four
29/78	**Can We Still Be Friends** . . . Todd Rundgren
16/56	**Can You Find It In Your Heart** . . . Tony Bennett
38/78	**Can You Fool** . . . Glen Campbell
1/64	**Can't Buy Me Love** . . . Beatles
1/85	**Can't Fight This Feeling** . . . REO Speedwagon
5/74	**Can't Get Enough** . . . Bad Company
1/74	**Can't Get Enough Of Your Love, Babe** . . . Barry White
9/75	**Can't Get It Out Of My Head** . . . Electric Light Orchestra
2/63	**Can't Get Used To Losing You** . . . Andy Williams
	Can't Help Falling In Love
2/62	Elvis Presley
24/87	Corey Hart
39/76	**Can't Hide Love** . . . Earth, Wind & Fire
1/90	**(Can't Live Without Your) Love And Affection** . . . Nelson
29/83	**Can't Shake Loose** . . . Agnetha Faltskog
3/78	**Can't Smile Without You** . . . Barry Manilow

Bruce Springsteen's long-running career was largely based on album sales prior to his 1984 LP *Born in the U.S.A.* Before then, he'd had only one top-10 hit, with 1980's "Hungry Heart." With *U.S.A.*, Bruce managed to score an amazing total of seven top-10 hits, including the No. 2 smash "Dancing In The Dark."

Frank Stallone's 1983 hit "Far From Over" came from the film *Staying Alive*—which featured actor John Travolta instad of Frank's brother Sylvester. Double irony: Travolta has a brother named Joey who also records.

Lisa Stansfield's former group Blue Zone U.K. featured the singer along with musicians Ian Devaney and Andy Morris. Though that group has disbanded, and Stansfield scored a platinum album with 1990's *Affection*, she continued to work with her former bandmates on 1991's *Real Love.*

Starpoint's first top-40 single, 1985's aptly-named "Object Of My Desire," reached No. 25 on the Hot 100. A sextet featuring four brothers, the group has worked with popular producers Teddy Riley and Gene Griffin.

Brenda K. Starr has contributed to the Top 40 on two fronts: with her own 1988 hits "I Still Believe" and "What You See Is What You Get," and via her one-time backup singer, Mariah Carey.

Ringo Starr's last top-10 hit may have been in 1975, but the former Beatle has certainly been busy. In 1989, he launched a highly successful "all-star" tour (from which a live record was issued), and in 1991, he signed a new recording contract with Private Music.

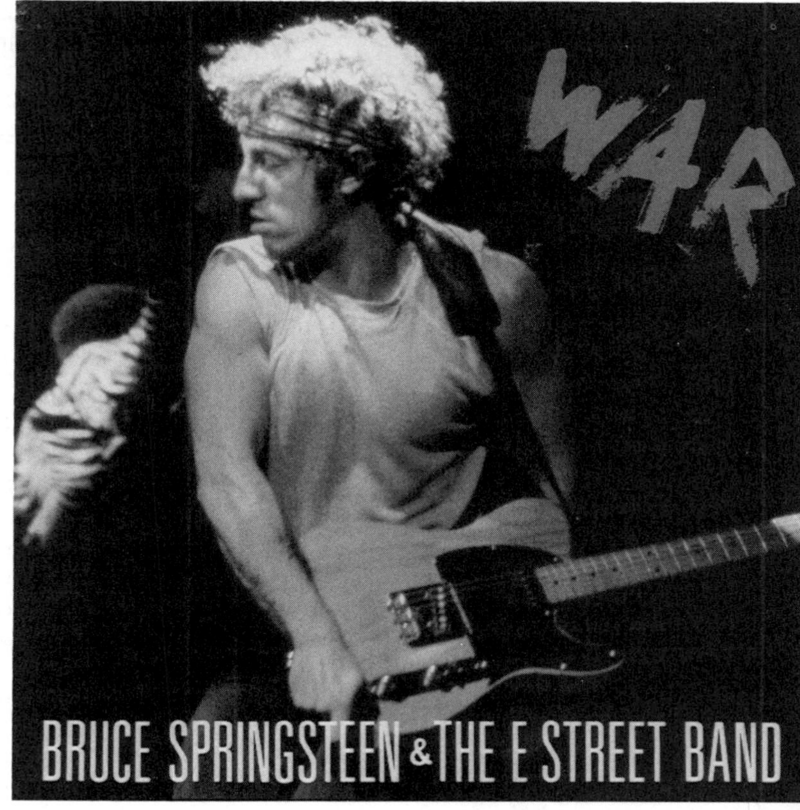

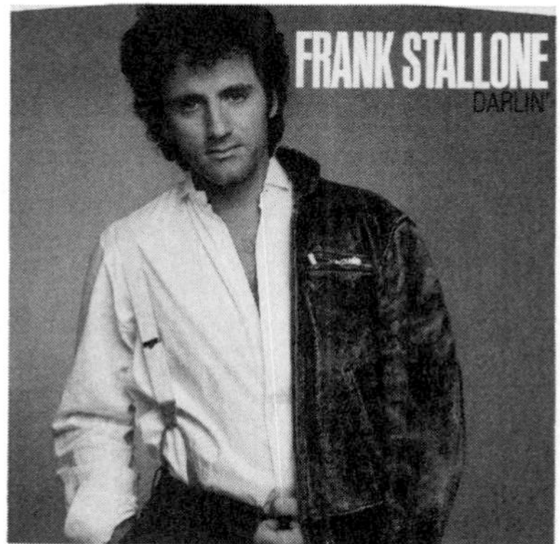

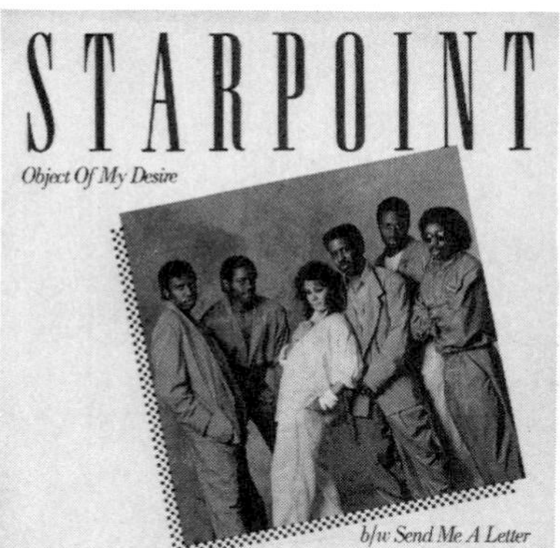

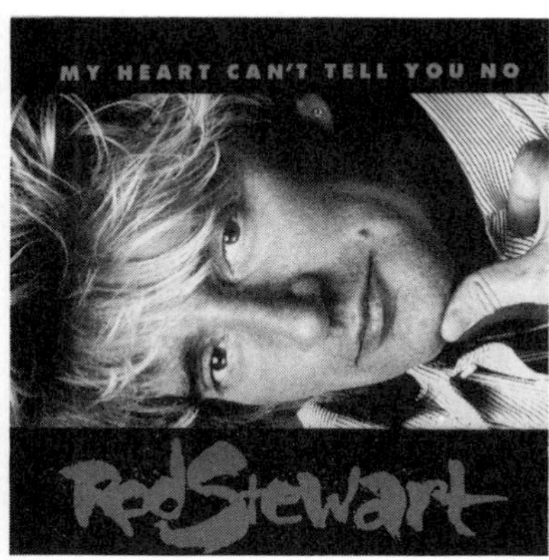

Rod Stewart's lengthy recording career has found him on the Mercury and Warner Brothers labels, but never on Motown. He did give the label a plug, though, with his 1991 hit "The Motown Song," which peaked at No. 10.

Stephen Stills's biggest solo hit, 1970's "Love The One You're With," took its title from a line Stills once heard keyboardist Billy Preston say at a party. That hit plus others by Crosby, Stills, Nash & Young (both as a group and individually) were included in a 1991 Atlantic Records tribute boxed set.

Sting, born Gordon Sumner, played in a jazz-rock group prior to the formation of the Police in 1977. Since then, with them and on his own, he's enjoyed nine top-10 singles—and seen the Blue Note label devote a 1991 jazz anthology to his compositions.

Barbra Streisand & Don Johnson's "Till I Loved You," the love theme from *Goya*, reached No. 25 in 1988. The record was Streisand's 20th top-40 hit, and Johnson's second. The "Miami Vice" actor's "Heartbeat" hit No. 5 in 1986.

Stryper's chances for a top-40 single might have been doubly hindered by their status as a Christian heavy-metal band—but the 1987 single "Honestly" ascended to No. 23 nonetheless.

Patrick Swayze's 1988 hit "She's Like The Wind" was one of three top-10 hits from the *Dirty Dancing* soundtrack. Others included "(I've Had) The Time Of My Life" by Bill Medley and Jennifer Warnes and "Hungry Eyes" by Eric Carmen.

POS/YR	RECORD TITLE/ARTIST
6/88	**Can't Stay Away From You** . . . Gloria Estefan & Miami Sound Machine
6/90	**Can't Stop** . . . After 7
13/77	**Can't Stop Dancin'** . . . Captain & Tennille
12/90	**Can't Stop Fallin' Into Love** . . . Cheap Trick
25/70	**Can't Stop Loving You** . . . Tom Jones
	Can't Take My Eyes Off You
2/67	Frankie Valli
7/68	Lettermen (medley)
6/87	**Can't We Try** . . . Dan Hill/Vonda Sheppard
2/65	**Can't You Hear My Heartbeat** . . . Herman's Hermits
4/64	**Can't You See That She's Mine** . . . Dave Clark Five
20/87	**Can'tcha Say (You Believe In Me)/Still In Love** . . . Boston
	Canadian Sunset
2/56	Hugo Winterhalter/Eddie Heywood
7/56	Andy Williams
3/70	**Candida** . . . Dawn
6/88	**Candle In The Wind** . . . Elton John
	(Candles In The Rain) ..see: Lay Down
21/87	**Candy** . . . Cameo
28/91	**Candy** . . . Iggy Pop
3/63	**Candy Girl** . . . Four Seasons
1/72	**Candy Man** . . . Sammy Davis, Jr.
25/61	**Candy Man** . . . Roy Orbison
15/58	**Cannonball** . . . Duane Eddy
28/85	**Cannonball** . . . Supertramp
16/86	**Captain Of Her Heart** . . . Double
1/77	**Car Wash** . . . Rose Royce
39/65	**Cara-Lin** . . . Strangeloves
4/65	**Cara, Mia** . . . Jay & The Americans
10/74	**Carefree Highway** . . . Gordon Lightfoot
1/85	**Careless Whisper** . . . Wham!/George Michael
27/59	**Caribbean** . . . Mitchell Torok
1/84	**Caribbean Queen (No More Love On The Run)** . . . Billy Ocean
18/58	**Carol** . . . Chuck Berry
21/75	**Carolina In The Pines** . . . Michael Murphey
32/66	**Caroline, No** . . . Brian Wilson
29/68	**Carpet Man** . . . 5th Dimension
3/87	**Carrie** . . . Europe
34/80	**Carrie** . . . Cliff Richard

POS/YR	RECORD TITLE/ARTIST
9/67	**Carrie-Anne** . . . Hollies
26/69	**Carry Me Back** . . . Rascals
11/77	**Carry On Wayward Son** . . . Kansas
9/80	**Cars** . . . Gary Numan
5/87	**Casanova** . . . Levert
27/67	**Casino Royale** . . . Herb Alpert
	Cast Your Fate To The Wind
22/63	Vince Guaraldi Trio
10/65	Sounds Orchestral
	Castles In The Air
F/72	Don McLean
36/81	Don McLean
25/56	**Casual Look** . . . Six Teens
26/67	**Cat In The Window (The Bird In The Sky)** . . . Petula Clark
30/77	**Cat Scratch Fever** . . . Ted Nugent
1/74	**Cat's In The Cradle** . . . Harry Chapin
1/58	**Catch A Falling Star** . . . Perry Como
8/87	**Catch Me (I'm Falling)** . . . Pretty Poison
40/84	**Catch Me I'm Falling** . . . Real Life
23/65	**Catch The Wind** . . . Donovan
4/65	**Catch Us If You Can** . . . Dave Clark Five
23/62	**Caterina** . . . Perry Como
1/60	**Cathy's Clown** . . . Everly Brothers
37/87	**Caught Up In The Rapture** . . . Anita Baker
10/82	**Caught Up In You** . . . 38 Special
2/87	**Causing A Commotion** . . . Madonna
	(Cave Man) ..see: Troglodyte
4/70	**Cecilia** . . . Simon & Garfunkel
15/70	**Celebrate** . . . Three Dog Night
26/85	**Celebrate Youth** . . . Rick Springfield
1/81	**Celebration** . . . Kool & The Gang
1/82	**Centerfold** . . . J. Geils Band
24/84	**Centipede** . . . Rebbie Jackson
14/58	**Certain Smile** . . . Johnny Mathis
23/58	**Cerveza** . . . Boots Brown
10/62	**Cha-Cha-Cha** . . . Bobby Rydell
34/58	**Cha-Hua-Hua** . . . Pets
2/60	**Chain Gang** . . . Sam Cooke
13/56	**Chain Gang** . . . Bobby Scott
2/68	**Chain Of Fools** . . . Aretha Franklin
32/68	**Chained** . . . Marvin Gaye
17/62	**Chains** . . . Cookies
10/56	**Chains Of Love** . . . Pat Boone
12/88	**Chains Of Love** . . . Erasure
1/57	**Chances Are** . . . Johnny Mathis
31/65	**Change Is Gonna Come** . . . Sam Cooke

POS/YR	RECORD TITLE/ARTIST
3/87	**Change Of Heart** . . . Cyndi Lauper
19/78	**Change Of Heart** . . . Eric Carmen
21/83	**Change Of Heart** . . . Tom Petty
37/77	**Changes In Latitudes, Changes In Attitudes** . . . Jimmy Buffett
	Chanson d'Amour (Song Of Love)
6/58	Art & Dotty Todd
12/58	Fontane Sisters
19/57	**Chantez-Chantez** . . . Dinah Shore
6/58	**Chantilly Lace** . . . Big Bopper
	Chapel In The Moonlight
32/65	Bachelors
25/67	Dean Martin
1/64	**Chapel Of Love** . . . Dixie Cups
	Charade
36/64	Sammy Kaye
36/64	Henry Mancini
1/82	**Chariots Of Fire - Titles** . . . Vangelis
40/71	**Charity Ball** . . . Fanny
2/59	**Charlie Brown** . . . Coasters
13/63	**Charms** . . . Bobby Vee
33/79	**Chase** . . . Giorgio Moroder
39/91	**Chasin' The Wind** . . . Chicago
	Chattanooga Choo Choo
36/62	Floyd Cramer
32/78	Tuxedo Junction
34/60	**Chattanooga Shoe Shine Boy** . . . Freddy Cannon
15/73	**Cheaper To Keep Her** . . . Johnnie Taylor
12/66	**Cheater, The** . . . Bob Kuban
14/88	**Check It Out** . . . John Cougar Mellencamp
35/73	**Check It Out** . . . Tavares
28/70	**Check Out Your Mind** . . . Impressions
12/55	**Chee Chee-Oo-Chee (Sang the Little Bird)** . . . Perry Como & Jaye P. Morgan
32/78	**Cheeseburger In Paradise** . . . Jimmy Buffett
	Cherchez La Femme ..see: Whispering
	Cherish
1/66	Association
9/71	David Cassidy
2/85	**Cherish** . . . Kool & The Gang
2/89	**Cherish** . . . Madonna
33/77	**Cherry Baby** . . . Starz
8/88	**Cherry Bomb** . . . John Cougar Mellencamp
	Cherry, Cherry
6/66	Neil Diamond
31/73	Neil Diamond
15/69	**Cherry Hill Park** . . . Billy Joe Royal

POS/YR	RECORD TITLE/ARTIST
10/90	**Cherry Pie** . . . Warrant
11/60	**Cherry Pie** . . . Skip & Flip
	Cherry Pink And Apple Blossom White
1/55	Perez "Prez" Prado
14/55	Alan Dale
5/75	**Chevy Van** . . . Sammy Johns
15/68	**Chewy Chewy** . . . Ohio Express
35/71	**Chicago** . . . Graham Nash
9/71	**Chick-A-Boom (Don't Ya Jes' Love It)** . . . Daddy Dewdrop
31/67	**Child Of Clay** . . . Jimmie Rodgers
13/90	**Children Of The Night** . . . Richard Marx
	Children's Marching Song
13/59	Cyril Stapleton
16/59	Mitch Miller
38/60	**China Doll** . . . Ames Brothers
10/83	**China Girl** . . . David Bowie
15/73	**China Grove** . . . Doobie Brothers
10/62	**Chip Chip** . . . Gene McDaniels
	Chipmunk Song
1/58	Chipmunks
39/61	Chipmunks
40/62	Chipmunks
29/80	**Chiquitita** . . . Abba
20/71	**Chirpy Chirpy Cheep Cheep** . . . Mac & Katie Kissoon
34/81	**Chloe** . . . Elton John
21/69	**Choice Of Colors** . . . Impressions
13/69	**Chokin' Kind** . . . Joe Simon
26/68	**Choo Choo Train** . . . Box Tops
25/77	**Christine Sixteen** . . . Kiss
4/79	**Chuck E.'s In Love** . . . Rickie Lee Jones
9/64	**Chug-A-Lug** . . . Roger Miller
14/56	**Church Bells May Ring** . . . Diamonds
10/83	**Church Of The Poison Mind** . . . Culture Club
24/59	**Ciao, Ciao Bambina** . . . Jacky Noguez
	Cinco Robles (Five Oaks)
22/57	Russell Arms
35/57	Les Paul & Mary Ford
16/62	**Cinderella** . . . Jack Ross
34/77	**Cinderella** . . . Firefall
	Cindy, Oh Cindy
9/56	Tarriers
10/56	Eddie Fisher
8/62	**Cindy's Birthday** . . . Johnny Crawford
11/69	**Cinnamon** . . . Derek
25/63	**Cinnamon Cinder (It's A Very Nice Dance)** . . . Pastel Six

POS/YR	RECORD TITLE/ARTIST
7/88	**Circle In The Sand** . . . Belinda Carlisle
33/78	**Circle Is Small (I Can See It In Your Eyes)** . . . Gordon Lightfoot
38/82	**Circles** . . . Atlantic Starr
2/73	**Cisco Kid** . . . War
23/69	**Cissy Strut** . . . Meters
18/85	**C-I-T-Y** . . . John Cafferty
19/56	**City Of Angels** . . . Highlights
18/72	**City Of New Orleans** . . . Arlo Guthrie
2/72	**Clair** . . . Gilbert O'Sullivan
	Clam ..see: Do The
6/74	**Clap For The Wolfman** . . . Guess Who
	Clapping Song (Clap Pat Clap Slap)
8/65	Shirley Ellis
36/83	Pia Zadora
38/59	**Class, The** . . . Chubby Checker
2/68	**Classical Gas** . . . Mason Williams
30/58	**Claudette** . . . Everly Brothers
6/72	**Clean Up Woman** . . . Betty Wright
35/69	**Clean Up Your Own Back Yard** . . . Elvis Presley
21/60	**Clementine** . . . Bobby Darin
	Cleopatra Jones ..see: Theme From
28/58	**Click-Clack** . . . Dickey Doo & The Don'ts
17/64	**Clinging Vine** . . . Bobby Vinton
40/80	**Clones (We're All)** . . . Alice Cooper
	Close Encounters ..see: Theme From
8/89	**Close My Eyes Forever** . . . Lita Ford/Ozzy Osbourne
25/78	**Close The Door** . . . Teddy Pendergrass
12/62	**Close To Cathy** . . . Mike Clifford
1/90	**Close To You** . . . Maxi Priest
	(also see: They Long To Be)
8/67	**Close Your Eyes** . . . Peaches & Herb
37/73	**Close Your Eyes** . . . Edward Bear
2/78	**Closer I Get To You** . . . Roberta Flack with Donny Hathaway
22/70	**Closer To Home** . . . Grand Funk Railroad
38/83	**Closer You Get** . . . Alabama
	Cloud Nine
6/69	Temptations
32/69	Mongo Santamaria
28/90	**Club At The End Of The Street** . . . Elton John
	C'mon ..see: Come On
F/80	**Cocaine** . . . Eric Clapton
25/57	**Cocoanut Woman** . . . Harry Belafonte
8/72	**Coconut** . . . Nilsson

POS/YR	RECORD TITLE/ARTIST
6/77	**Cold As Ice** . . . Foreigner
40/83	**Cold Blooded** . . . Rick James
1/89	**Cold Hearted** . . . Paula Abdul
33/81	**Cold Love** . . . Donna Summer
7/67	**Cold Sweat** . . . James Brown
30/70	**Cold Turkey** . . . Plastic Ono Band
	Colonel Bogey ..see: March From The River Kwai
7/69	**Color Him Father** . . . Winstons
16/67	**Color My World** . . . Petula Clark
F/71	**Colour My World** . . . Chicago
17/88	**Colour Of Love** . . . Billy Ocean
3/64	**Come A Little Bit Closer** . . . Jay & The Americans
7/70	**Come And Get It** . . . Badfinger
29/63	**Come And Get These Memories** . . . Martha & The Vandellas
5/74	**Come And Get Your Love** . . . Redbone
26/65	**Come And Stay With Me** . . . Marianne Faithfull
15/87	**Come As You Are** . . . Peter Wolf
32/80	**Come Back** . . . J. Geils Band
22/84	**Come Back And Stay** . . . Paul Young
17/62	**Come Back Silly Girl** . . . Lettermen
2/90	**Come Back To Me** . . . Janet Jackson
3/67	**Come Back When You Grow Up** . . . Bobby Vee
38/58	**Come Closer To Me** . . . Nat "King" Cole
6/83	**Come Dancing** . . . Kinks
21/73	**Come Get To This** . . . Marvin Gaye
	Come Go With Me
4/57	Dell-Vikings
18/82	Beach Boys
5/87	**Come Go With Me** . . . Expose
14/65	**Come Home** . . . Dave Clark Five
20/59	**Come Into My Heart** . . . Lloyd Price
30/74	**Come Monday** . . . Jimmy Buffett
36/64	**Come On** . . . Tommy Roe
29/59	**Come On And Get Me** . . . Fabian
10/90	**C'mon And Get My Love** . . . D-Mob
5/64	**C'mon And Swim** . . . Bobby Freeman
6/67	**Come On Down To My Boat** . . . Every Mothers' Son
1/83	**Come On Eileen** . . . Dexys Midnight Runners
35/59	**C'mon Everybody** . . . Eddie Cochran
	Come On Let's Go
22/66	McCoys

POS/YR	RECORD TITLE/ARTIST
21/87	Los Lobos
28/62	**Come On Little Angel** . . . Belmonts
	C'mon Marianne
9/67	4 Seasons
38/76	Donny Osmond
23/76	**Come On Over** . . . Olivia Newton-John
17/66	**(Come 'Round Here) I'm The One You Need** . . . Miracles
39/70	**Come Running** . . . Van Morrison
35/66	**Come Running Back** . . . Dean Martin
8/78	**Come Sail Away** . . . Styx
17/70	**Come Saturday Morning** . . . Sandpipers
40/65	**Come See** . . . Major Lance
	Come See About Me
1/64	Supremes
24/68	Jr. Walker & The All Stars
1/59	**Come Softly To Me** . . . Fleetwoods
15/79	**Come To Me** . . . France Joli
22/58	**Come To Me** . . . Johnny Mathis
30/59	**Come To Me** . . . Marv Johnson
37/67	**Come To The Sunshine** . . . Harpers Bizarre
	Come Together
1/69	Beatles
23/78	Aerosmith
36/62	**Comin' Home Baby** . . . Mel Torme
11/82	**Comin' In And Out Of Your Life** . . . Barbra Streisand
18/87	**Coming Around Again** . . . Carly Simon
20/89	**Coming Home** . . . Cinderella
11/67	**Coming Home Soldier** . . . Bobby Vinton
11/66	**Coming On Strong** . . . Brenda Lee
1/91	**Coming Out Of The Dark** . . . Gloria Estefan
1/80	**Coming Up** . . . Paul McCartney
30/69	**Commotion** . . . Creedence Clearwater Revival
34/85	**Communication** . . . Power Station
27/69	**Composer, The** . . . Supremes
	Concrete And Clay
28/65	Unit Four plus Two
35/65	Eddie Rambeau
17/56	**Confidential** . . . Sonny Knight
37/79	**Confusion** . . . Electric Light Orchestra
10/86	**Conga** . . . Miami Sound Machine
16/72	**Conquistador** . . . Procol Harum
11/62	**Conscience** . . . James Darren
33/61	**Continental Walk** . . . Hank Ballard

POS/YR	RECORD TITLE/ARTIST
	(also see: Do The & Do The New)
5/87	**Control** . . . Janet Jackson
8/72	**Convention '72** . . . Delegates
1/76	**Convoy** . . . C.W. McCall
32/73	**Cook With Honey** . . . Judy Collins
29/71	**Cool Aid** . . . Paul Humphrey
10/80	**Cool Change** . . . Little River Band
4/85	**Cool It Now** . . . New Edition
7/66	**Cool Jerk** . . . Capitols
13/81	**Cool Love** . . . Pablo Cruise
11/82	**Cool Night** . . . Paul Davis
12/57	**Cool Shake** . . . Del Vikings
8/78	**Copacabana (At The Copa)** . . . Barry Manilow
37/73	**Corazon** . . . Carole King
9/61	**Corinna, Corinna** . . . Ray Peterson
18/72	**Corner Of The Sky** . . . Jackson 5
15/64	**Cotton Candy** . . . Al Hirt
13/62	**Cotton Fields** . . . Highwaymen
33/80	**Could I Have This Dance** . . . Anne Murray
37/72	**Could It Be Forever** . . . David Cassidy
4/73	**Could It Be I'm Falling In Love** . . . Spinners
6/75	**Could It Be Magic** . . . Barry Manilow
11/90	**Could This Be Love** . . . Seduction
23/57	**Could This Be Magic** . . . Dubs
1/88	**Could've Been** . . . Tiffany
3/77	**Couldn't Get It Right** . . . Climax Blues Band
35/61	**Count Every Star** . . . Donnie & The Dreamers
2/65	**Count Me In** . . . Gary Lewis & The Playboys
8/78	**Count On Me** . . . Jefferson Starship
25/60	**Country Boy** . . . Fats Domino
11/76	**Country Boy (You Got Your Feet In L.A.)** . . . Glen Campbell
36/68	**Country Girl - City Man** . . . Billy Vera & Judy Clay
37/71	**Country Road** . . . James Taylor
11/91	**Couple Days Off** . . . Huey Lewis & the News
25/68	**Court Of Love** . . . Unifics
31/64	**Cousin Of Mine** . . . Sam Cooke
2/89	**Cover Girl** . . . New Kids On The Block
7/84	**Cover Me** . . . Bruce Springsteen
31/89	**Cover Of Love** . . . Michael Damian

POS/YR	RECORD TITLE/ARTIST
6/73	**Cover Of "Rolling Stone"** . . . Dr. Hook
3/80	**Coward Of The County** . . . Kenny Rogers
6/68	**Cowboys To Girls** . . . Intruders
8/72	**Cowboys Work Is Never Done** . . . Sonny & Cher
19/77	**Crackerbox Palace** . . . George Harrison
1/70	**Cracklin' Rosie** . . . Neil Diamond
2/90	**Cradle Of Love** . . . Billy Idol
7/60	**Cradle Of Love** . . . Johnny Preston
7/91	**Crazy** . . . Seal
9/61	**Crazy** . . . Patsy Cline
14/88	**Crazy** . . . Icehouse
29/90	**Crazy** . . . Boys
11/89	**Crazy About Her** . . . Rod Stewart
36/60	**Crazy Arms** . . . Bob Beckham
	Crazy Downtown ..see: Downtown
40/58	**Crazy Eyes For You** . . . Bobby Hamilton
1/85	**Crazy For You** . . . Madonna
14/72	**Crazy Horses** . . . Osmonds
15/85	**Crazy In The Night (Barking At Airplanes)** . . . Kim Carnes
	Crazy Little Mama ..see: At My Front Door
1/80	**Crazy Little Thing Called Love** . . . Queen
15/58	**Crazy Love** . . . Paul Anka
17/79	**Crazy Love** . . . Poco
29/79	**Crazy Love** . . . Allman Brothers Band
22/72	**Crazy Mama** . . . J.J. Cale
35/76	**Crazy On You** . . . Heart
2/55	**Crazy Otto (medley)** . . . Johnny Maddox
5/67	**Creeque Alley** . . . Mamas & The Papas
16/71	**Cried Like A Baby** . . . Bobby Sherman
	Crimson And Clover
1/69	Tommy James & The Shondells
7/82	Joan Jett
16/55	**Croce Di Oro (Cross Of Gold)** . . . Patti Page
1/73	**Crocodile Rock** . . . Elton John
	(Crooked Little Man) ..see: Don't Let The Rain Come Down
19/63	**Cross Fire!** . . . Orlons
23/59	**Crossfire** . . . Johnny & The Hurricanes
7/87	**Cross My Broken Heart** . . . Jets
	Cross Of Gold ..see: Croce Di Oro
28/69	**Crossroads** . . . Cream
26/62	**Crowd, The** . . . Roy Orbison
9/84	**Cruel Summer** . . . Bananarama

POS/YR	RECORD TITLE/ARTIST
12/79	**Cruel To Be Kind** . . . Nick Lowe
4/80	**Cruisin'** . . . Smokey Robinson
29/90	**Cruising For Bruising** . . . Basia
9/83	**Crumblin' Down** . . . John Cougar Mellencamp
3/86	**Crush On You** . . . Jets
10/89	**Cry** . . . Waterfront
16/85	**Cry** . . . Godley & Creme
18/66	**Cry** . . . Ronnie Dove
4/63	**Cry Baby** . . . Garnet Mimms & The Enchanters
18/56	**Cry Baby** . . . Bonnie Sisters
38/62	**Cry Baby Cry** . . . Angels
7/91	**Cry For Help** . . . Rick Astley
2/68	**Cry Like A Baby** . . . Box Tops
	Cry Me A River
9/55	Julie London
11/70	Joe Cocker
23/63	**Cry To Me** . . . Betty Harris
22/89	**Cryin'** . . . Vixen
	Crying
2/61	Roy Orbison
25/66	Jay & The Americans
5/81	Don McLean
3/65	**Crying In The Chapel** . . . Elvis Presley
6/62	**Crying In The Rain** . . . Everly Brothers
6/66	**Crying Time** . . . Ray Charles
2/69	**Crystal Blue Persuasion** . . . Tommy James & The Shondells
25/89	**Cuddly Toy (Feel For Me)** . . . Roachford
13/89	**Cult Of Personality** . . . Living Colour
5/83	**Cum On Feel The Noize** . . . Quiet Riot
	Cupid
17/61	Sam Cooke
39/70	Johnny Nash
22/76	Dawn
4/80	Spinners (medley)
	Curious Mind ..see: Um, Um, Um, Um, Um, Um
15/84	**Curly Shuffle** . . . Jump 'N The Saddle
10/75	**Cut The Cake** . . . AWB
15/83	**Cuts Like A Knife** . . . Bryan Adams
23/68	**Cycles** . . . Frank Sinatra

POS/YR	RECORD TITLE/ARTIST
	D
36/71	**D.O.A.** . . . Bloodrock
19/68	**D. W. Washburn** . . . Monkees
20/73	**D'yer Mak'er** . . . Led Zeppelin
	Da Doo Ron Ron
3/63	Crystals
1/77	Shaun Cassidy
1/79	**Da Ya Think I'm Sexy?** . . . Rod Stewart
35/88	**Da'Butt** . . . E.U.
19/73	**Daddy Could Swear, I Declare** . . . Gladys Knight & The Pips
4/72	**Daddy Don't You Walk So Fast** . . . Wayne Newton
	Daddy-O
11/55	Fontane Sisters
14/55	Bonnie Lou
	Daddy's Home
2/61	Shep & The Limelites
9/73	Jermaine Jackson
23/82	Cliff Richard
34/69	**Daddy's Little Man** . . . O.C. Smith
14/73	**Daisy A Day** . . . Jud Strunk
20/75	**Daisy Jane** . . . America
15/64	**Daisy Petal Pickin'** . . . Jimmy Gilmer/Fireballs
27/79	**Damned If I Do** . . . Alan Parsons Project
38/78	**Dance Across The Floor** . . . Jimmy "Bo" Horne
8/64	**Dance, Dance, Dance** . . . Beach Boys
6/78	**Dance, Dance, Dance (Yowsah, Yowsah, Yowsah)** . . . Chic
19/78	**Dance (Disco Heat)** . . . Sylvester
31/58	**Dance Everyone Dance** . . . Betty Madigan
16/84	**Dance Hall Days** . . . Wang Chung
30/88	**Dance Little Sister** . . . Terence Trent D'Arby
10/61	**Dance On Little Girl** . . . Paul Anka
19/58	**Dance Only With Me** . . . Perry Como
24/61	**Dance The Mess Around** . . . Chubby Checker
15/79	**Dance The Night Away** . . . Van Halen
23/58	**Dance To The Bop** . . . Gene Vincent
8/68	**Dance To The Music** . . . Sly & The Family Stone

POS/YR	RECORD TITLE/ARTIST
39/76	**Dance Wit Me** . . . Rufus Featuring Chaka Khan
6/75	**Dance With Me** . . . Orleans
8/78	**Dance With Me** . . . Peter Brown/Betty Wright
15/59	**Dance With Me** . . . Drifters
1/55	**Dance With Me Henry (Wallflower)** . . . Georgia Gibbs
12/62	**(Dance With The) Guitar Man** . . . Duane Eddy
28/75	**Dancin' Fool** . . . Guess Who
23/77	**Dancin' Man** . . . Q
12/62	**Dancin' Party** . . . Chubby Checker
18/79	**Dancin' Shoes** . . . Nigel Olsson
2/84	**Dancing In The Dark** . . . Bruce Springsteen
13/73	**Dancing In The Moonlight** . . . King Harvest
17/84	**Dancing In The Sheets** . . . Shalamar
	Dancing In The Street
2/64	Martha & The Vandellas
38/82	Van Halen
7/85	Mick Jagger/David Bowie
2/74	**Dancing Machine** . . . Jackson 5
2/86	**Dancing On The Ceiling** . . . Lionel Richie
1/77	**Dancing Queen** . . . Abba
14/67	**Dandelion** . . . Rolling Stones
5/66	**Dandy** . . . Herman's Hermits
7/64	**Dang Me** . . . Roger Miller
12/55	**Danger! Heartbreak Ahead** . . . Jaye P. Morgan
2/86	**Danger Zone** . . . Kenny Loggins
2/90	**Dangerous** . . . Roxette
25/66	**Dangling Conversation** . . . Simon & Garfunkel
	Dangling On A String ..see: (You've Got Me)
2/73	**Daniel** . . . Elton John
13/63	**Danke Schoen** . . . Wayne Newton
10/59	**Danny Boy** . . . Conway Twitty
7/73	**Danny's Song** . . . Anne Murray
11/85	**Dare Me** . . . Pointer Sisters
32/90	**Dare To Fall In Love** . . . Brent Bourgeois
15/75	**Dark Horse** . . . George Harrison
1/74	**Dark Lady** . . . Cher
	Dark Moon
4/57	Gale Storm
6/57	Bonnie Guitar
19/68	**Darlin'** . . . Beach Boys

POS/YR	RECORD TITLE/ARTIST
15/67	**Darling Be Home Soon** . . . Lovin' Spoonful
7/55	**Darling Je Vous Aime Beaucoup** . . . Nat "King" Cole
13/70	**Daughter Of Darkness** . . . Tom Jones
	Davy Crockett ..see: Ballad Of
3/64	**Dawn (Go Away)** . . . Four Seasons
36/65	**Dawn Of Correction** . . . Spokesmen
4/72	**Day After Day** . . . Badfinger
13/72	**Day By Day** . . . Godspell
18/86	**Day By Day** . . . Hooters
5/72	**Day Dreaming** . . . Aretha Franklin
35/66	**Day For Decision** . . . Johnny Sea
23/72	**Day I Found Myself** . . . Honey Cone
21/87	**Day-In Day-Out** . . . David Bowie
21/69	**Day Is Done** . . . Peter, Paul & Mary
	Day-O ..see: Banana Boat
	Day The Rains Came
21/58	Jane Morgan
30/58	Raymond Lefevre
5/66	**Day Tripper** . . . Beatles
23/77	**Daybreak** . . . Barry Manilow
39/74	**Daybreak** . . . Nilsson
2/66	**Daydream** . . . Lovin' Spoonful
	Daydream Believer
1/67	Monkees
12/80	Anne Murray
17/79	**Days Gone Down (Still Got The Light In Your Eyes)** . . . Gerry Rafferty
34/69	**Days Of Sand And Shovels** . . . Bobby Vinton
	Days Of Wine And Roses
26/63	Andy Williams
33/63	Henry Mancini
28/77	**Daytime Friends** . . . Kenny Rogers
3/77	**Dazz** . . . Brick
10/81	**De Do Do Do, De Da Da Da** . . . Police
19/78	**Deacon Blues** . . . Steely Dan
29/67	**Dead End Street** . . . Lou Rawls
22/83	**Dead Giveaway** . . . Shalamar
8/64	**Dead Man's Curve** . . . Jan & Dean
16/73	**Dead Skunk** . . . Loudon Wainwright III
30/90	**Deadbeat Club** . . . B-52's
	Dear Heart
24/65	Andy Williams
30/65	Jack Jones
24/62	**Dear Ivan** . . . Jimmy Dean
9/62	**Dear Lady Twist** . . . Gary (U.S.) Bonds

POS/YR	RECORD TITLE/ARTIST
13/62	**Dear Lonely Hearts** . . . Nat "King" Cole
11/62	**Dear One** . . . Larry Finnegan
1/76	**December, 1963 (Oh, What a Night)** . . . Four Seasons
7/59	**Deck Of Cards** . . . Wink Martindale
7/58	**Dede Dinah** . . . Frankie Avalon
36/66	**Dedicated Follower Of Fashion** . . . Kinks
	Dedicated To The One I Love
3/61	Shirelles
2/67	Mamas & The Papas
22/80	**Deep Inside My Heart** . . . Randy Meisner
	Deep Purple
20/57	Billy Ward & His Dominoes
1/63	Nino Tempo & April Stevens
14/76	Donny & Marie Osmond
24/70	**Deeper & Deeper** . . . Freda Payne
21/91	**Deeper Shade Of Soul** . . . Urban Dance Squad
11/79	**Deeper Than The Night** . . . Olivia Newton-John
28/90	**Deeper The Love** . . . Whitesnake
15/80	**Deja Vu** . . . Dionne Warwick
22/60	**Delaware** . . . Perry Como
40/58	**Delicious!** . . . Jim Bakus & Friend
15/68	**Delilah** . . . Tom Jones
	Delilah Jones ..see: Man With The Golden Arm
8/83	**Delirious** . . . Prince
1/73	**Delta Dawn** . . . Helen Reddy
10/63	**Denise** . . . Randy & The Rainbows
25/79	**Dependin' On You** . . . Doobie Brothers
5/83	**Der Kommissar** . . . After The Fire
15/62	**Desafinado** . . . Stan Getz/Charlie Byrd
10/84	**Desert Moon** . . . Dennis DeYoung
33/63	**Desert Pete** . . . Kingston Trio
8/71	**Desiderata** . . . Les Crane
3/88	**Desire** . . . U2
4/80	**Desire** . . . Andy Gibb
16/78	**Desiree** . . . Neil Diamond
	Detroit City
16/63	Bobby Bare
27/67	Tom Jones
	Devil In Disguise ..see: (You're the)
2/88	**Devil Inside** . . . INXS
6/60	**Devil Or Angel** . . . Bobby Vee
3/79	**Devil Went Down To Georgia** . . . Charlie Daniels Band

POS/YR	RECORD TITLE/ARTIST
4/66	**Devil With A Blue Dress On (medley)** . . . Mitch Ryder
6/76	**Devil Woman** . . . Cliff Richard
16/62	**Devil Woman** . . . Marty Robbins
36/77	**Devil's Gun** . . . C.J. & Co.
	Devoted To You
10/58	Everly Brothers
36/78	Carly Simon & James Taylor
33/74	**Devotion** . . . Earth, Wind & Fire
13/89	**Dial My Heart** . . . Boys
24/72	**Dialogue** . . . Chicago
6/73	**Diamond Girl** . . . Seals & Crofts
5/87	**Diamonds** . . . Herb Alpert
18/60	**Diamonds And Pearls** . . . Paradons
35/75	**Diamonds And Rust** . . . Joan Baez
1/57	**Diana** . . . Paul Anka
10/64	**Diane** . . . Bachelors
14/59	**Diary, The** . . . Neil Sedaka
15/72	**Diary** . . . Bread
9/82	**Did It In A Minute** . . . Daryl Hall & John Oates
29/76	**Did You Boogie (With Your Baby)** . . . Flash Cadillac & The Continental Kids
2/66	**Did You Ever Have To Make Up Your Mind?** . . . Lovin' Spoonful
32/69	**Did You See Her Eyes** . . . Illusion
	Didn't I (Blow Your Mind This Time)
10/70	Delfonics
8/89	New Kids On The Block
1/87	**Didn't We Almost Have It All** . . . Whitney Houston
	Died In Your Arms ..see: (I Just)
7/86	**Different Corner** . . . George Michael
13/68	**Different Drum** . . . Stone Poneys/Linda Ronstadt
18/79	**Different Worlds** . . . Maureen McGovern
14/86	**Digging Your Scene** . . . Blow Monkeys
21/86	**Digital Display** . . . Ready For The World
2/79	**Dim All The Lights** . . . Donna Summer
11/55	**Dim, Dim The Lights (I Want Some Atmosphere)** . . . Bill Haley
18/60	**Ding-A-Ling** . . . Bobby Rydell
25/58	**Ding Dong** . . . McGuire Sisters
36/75	**Ding Dong; Ding Dong** . . . George Harrison
11/67	**Ding Dong! The Witch Is Dead** . . . Fifth Estate
6/58	**Dinner With Drac** . . . John Zacherle

POS/YR	RECORD TITLE/ARTIST
25/90	**Dirty Cash (Money Talks)** . . . Adventures Of Stevie V
36/90	**Dirty Deeds** . . . Joan Jett
1/88	**Dirty Diana** . . . Michael Jackson
3/83	**Dirty Laundry** . . . Don Henley
11/66	**Dirty Water** . . . Standells
12/79	**Dirty White Boy** . . . Foreigner
36/67	**Dis-Advantages Of You** . . . Brass Ring
8/91	**Disappear** . . . INXS
1/76	**Disco Duck** . . . Rick Dees
11/78	**Disco Inferno** . . . Trammps
1/76	**Disco Lady** . . . Johnnie Taylor
24/77	**Disco Lucy (I Love Lucy Theme)** . . . Wilton Place Street Band
12/79	**Disco Nights (Rock-Freak)** . . . G.Q.
28/75	**Disco Queen** . . . Hot Chocolate
	(Disco 'Round) ..see: I Love The Nightlife
28/74	**Distant Lover** . . . Marvin Gaye
30/66	**Distant Shores** . . . Chad & Jeremy
	Dixie ..see: Theme From
30/55	**Dixie Danny** . . . Laurie Sisters
1/69	**Dizzy** . . . Tommy Roe
	Do ..also see: Doo
13/82	**Do I Do** . . . Stevie Wonder
34/64	**Do I Love You?** . . . Ronettes
36/70	**Do It** . . . Neil Diamond
6/73	**Do It Again** . . . Steely Dan
20/68	**Do It Again** . . . Beach Boys
18/67	**Do It Again A Little Bit Slower** . . . Jon & Robin & The In Crowd
11/75	**Do It Any Way You Wanna** . . . Peoples Choice
13/74	**Do It Baby** . . . Miracles
29/85	**Do It For Love** . . . Sheena Easton
19/79	**Do It Or Die** . . . Atlanta Rhythm Section
2/74	**Do It ('Til You're Satisfied)** . . . B.T. Express
3/90	**Do Me!** . . . Bell Biv DeVoe
27/62	**Do-Re-Mi** . . . Lee Dorsey
23/80	**Do Right** . . . Paul Davis
38/68	**Do Something To Me** . . . Tommy James & The Shondells
1/80	**Do That To Me One More Time** . . . Captain & Tennille
10/63	**Do The Bird** . . . Dee Dee Sharp
36/65	**Do The Boomerang** . . . Jr. Walker & The All Stars
21/65	**Do The Clam** . . . Elvis Presley

POS/YR	RECORD TITLE/ARTIST
18/65	**Do The Freddie** . . . Freddie & The Dreamers
	(also see: Let's Do The Freddie)
28/70	**Do The Funky Chicken** . . . Rufus Thomas
37/62	**Do The New Continental** . . . Dovells
25/71	**(Do The) Push And Pull** . . . Rufus Thomas
13/85	**Do They Know It's Christmas?** . . . Band Aid
31/65	**Do-Wacka-Do** . . . Roger Miller
1/64	**Do Wah Diddy Diddy** . . . Manfred Mann
13/85	**Do What You Do** . . . Jermaine Jackson
37/70	**Do What You Wanna Do** . . . Five Flights Up
39/76	**Do What You Want, Be What You Are** . . . Daryl Hall & John Oates
24/77	**Do Ya** . . . Electric Light Orchestra
	Do Ya Think I'm Sexy? ..see: Da Ya
18/77	**Do Ya Wanna Get Funky With Me** . . . Peter Brown
7/82	**Do You Believe In Love** . . . Huey Lewis & the News
	Do You Believe In Magic
9/65	Lovin' Spoonful
31/78	Shaun Cassidy
10/76	**Do You Feel Like We Do** . . . Peter Frampton
10/68	**Do You Know The Way To San Jose** . . . Dionne Warwick
6/71	**Do You Know What I Mean** . . . Lee Michaels
	Do You Know Where You're Going To ..see: Theme From Mahogany
	Do You Love Me
3/62	Contours
11/64	Dave Clark Five
11/88	Contours
30/80	**Do You Love What You Feel** . . . Rufus & Chaka
2/83	**Do You Really Want To Hurt Me** . . . Culture Club
4/90	**Do You Remember?** . . . Phil Collins
32/70	**Do You See My Love (For You Growing)** . . . Jr. Walker & The All Stars
5/77	**Do You Wanna Make Love** . . . Peter McCann
20/82	**Do You Wanna Touch Me (Oh Yeah)** . . . Joan Jett
37/85	**Do You Want Crying** . . . Katrina & The Waves
21/91	**Do You Want Me** . . . Salt-N-Pepa

POS/YR	RECORD TITLE/ARTIST
	Do You Want To Dance
5/58	Bobby Freeman
12/65	Beach Boys
17/73	Bette Midler
2/64	**Do You Want To Know A Secret** . . . Beatles
39/77	**Do Your Dance** . . . Rose Royce
11/69	**Do Your Thing** . . . Watts 103rd Street Rhythm Band
30/72	**Do Your Thing** . . . Isaac Hayes
	Dock Of The Bay ..see: (Sittin' On)
9/89	**Doctor, The** . . . Doobie Brothers
11/84	**Doctor! Doctor!** . . . Thompson Twins
	(also see: Bad Case Of Loving You)
6/89	**Dr. Feelgood** . . . Motley Crue
28/83	**Dr. Heckyll & Mr. Jive** . . . Men At Work
	Doctor Kildare ..see: Theme From
8/72	**Doctor My Eyes** . . . Jackson Browne
	Doctor Tarr ..see: (System Of)
	Dr. Zhivago ..see: Somewhere My Love
11/75	**Doctor's Orders** . . . Carol Douglas
38/69	**Does Anybody Know I'm Here** . . . Dells
38/91	**Does Anybody Really Fall In Love Anymore?** . . . Kane Roberts
7/71	**Does Anybody Really Know What Time It Is?** . . . Chicago
36/83	**Does It Make You Remember** . . . Kim Carnes
34/91	**Does She Love That Man?** . . . Breathe featuring David Glasper
5/61	**Does Your Chewing Gum Lose Its Flavor (On The Bedpost Over Night)** . . . Lonnie Donegan
29/68	**Does Your Mama Know About Me** . . . Bobby Taylor
19/79	**Does Your Mother Know** . . . Abba
6/71	**Doesn't Somebody Want To Be Wanted** . . . Partridge Family
34/79	**Dog & Butterfly** . . . Heart
30/55	**Dogface Soldier** . . . Russ Morgan
15/60	**Doggin' Around** . . . Jackie Wilson
32/69	**Doggone Right** . . . Miracles
6/87	**Doing It All For My Baby** . . . Huey Lewis & the News
22/73	**Doing It To Death** . . . JB's
31/60	**Doll House** . . . Donnie Brooks
13/55	**Domani (Tomorrow)** . . . Julius LaRosa
1/63	**Dominique** . . . Singing Nun
9/71	**Domino** . . . Van Morrison

POS/YR	RECORD TITLE/ARTIST
18/88	**Domino Dancing** . . . Pet Shop Boys
14/87	**Dominoes** . . . Robbie Nevil
1/58	**Don't** . . . Elvis Presley
15/84	**Don't Answer Me** . . . Alan Parsons Project
19/80	**Don't Ask Me Why** . . . Billy Joel
25/58	**Don't Ask Me Why** . . . Elvis Presley
40/89	**Don't Ask Me Why** . . . Eurythmics
26/63	**Don't Be Afraid, Little Darlin'** . . . Steve Lawrence
	Don't Be Angry
14/55	Crew-Cuts
25/55	Nappy Brown
	Don't Be Cruel
1/56	Elvis Presley
11/60	Bill Black's Combo
4/88	Cheap Trick
8/88	**Don't Be Cruel** . . . Bobby Brown
9/61	**Don't Bet Money Honey** . . . Linda Scott
20/61	**Don't Blame Me** . . . Everly Brothers
37/67	**Don't Blame The Children** . . . Sammy Davis, Jr.
1/62	**Don't Break The Heart That Loves You** . . . Connie Francis
4/79	**Don't Bring Me Down** . . . Electric Light Orchestra
12/66	**Don't Bring Me Down** . . . Animals
9/75	**Don't Call Us, We'll Call You** . . . Sugarloaf
	Don't Cha ..see: Doncha'
26/74	**Don't Change Horses (In The Middle Of A Stream)** . . . Tower Of Power
36/71	**Don't Change On Me** . . . Ray Charles
11/89	**Don't Close Your Eyes** . . . Kix
13/85	**Don't Come Around Here No More** . . . Tom Petty
21/60	**Don't Come Knockin'** . . . Fats Domino
35/73	**Don't Cross The River** . . . America
10/83	**Don't Cry** . . . Asia
39/61	**Don't Cry, Baby** . . . Etta James
6/70	**Don't Cry Daddy** . . . Elvis Presley
10/79	**Don't Cry Out Loud** . . . Melissa Manchester
4/87	**Don't Disturb This Groove** . . . System
34/72	**Don't Do It** . . . Band
10/80	**Don't Do Me Like That** . . . Tom Petty
2/87	**Don't Dream It's Over** . . . Crowded House
23/72	**Don't Ever Be Lonely (A Poor Little Fool Like Me)** . . . Cornelius Brothers & Sister Rose

POS/YR	RECORD TITLE/ARTIST
40/79	**Don't Ever Wanna Lose Ya** . . . New England
8/73	**Don't Expect Me To Be Your Friend** . . . Lobo
4/80	**Don't Fall In Love With A Dreamer** . . . Kenny Rogers with Kim Carnes
12/76	**(Don't Fear) The Reaper** . . . Blue Oyster Cult
17/82	**Don't Fight It** . . . Kenny Loggins/Steve Perry
1/57	**Don't Forbid Me** . . . Pat Boone
19/65	**Don't Forget I Still Love You** . . . Bobbi Martin
2/86	**Don't Forget Me (When I'm Gone)** . . . Glass Tiger
29/83	**Don't Forget To Dance** . . . Kinks
10/86	**Don't Get Me Wrong** . . . Pretenders
15/69	**Don't Give In To Him** . . . Gary Puckett & The Union Gap
26/81	**Don't Give It Up** . . . Robbie Patton
37/68	**Don't Give Up** . . . Petula Clark
1/77	**Don't Give Up On Us** . . . David Soul
19/90	**Don't Go Away Mad (Just Go Away)** . . . Motley Crue
1/76	**Don't Go Breaking My Heart** . . . Elton John & Kiki Dee
22/58	**Don't Go Home** . . . Playmates
17/62	**Don't Go Near The Indians** . . . Rex Allen
18/67	**Don't Go Out Into The Rain (You're Going To Melt)** . . . Herman's Hermits
	Don't Go To Strangers
38/56	Vaughn Monroe
36/60	Etta Jones
4/62	**Don't Hang Up** . . . Orlons
21/79	**Don't Hold Back** . . . Chanson
2/77	**Don't It Make My Brown Eyes Blue** . . . Crystal Gayle
8/65	**Don't Just Stand There** . . . Patty Duke
13/71	**Don't Knock My Love** . . . Wilson Pickett
2/89	**Don't Know Much** . . . Linda Ronstadt/Aaron Neville
12/88	**Don't Know What You Got (Till It's Gone)** . . . Cinderella
	Don't Leave Me This Way
1/77	Thelma Houston
40/87	Communards
	Don't Let Go
13/58	Roy Hamilton
18/80	Isaac Hayes

POS/YR	RECORD TITLE/ARTIST
38/84	**Don't Let Go** . . . Wang Chung
24/81	**Don't Let Him Go** . . . REO Speedwagon
39/82	**Don't Let Him Know** . . . Prism
6/83	**Don't Let It End** . . . Styx
14/73	**Don't Let Me Be Lonely Tonight** . . . James Taylor
	Don't Let Me Be Misunderstood
15/65	Animals
15/78	Santa Esmeralda
35/69	**Don't Let Me Down** . . . Beatles with Billy Preston
17/71	**Don't Let The Green Grass Fool You** . . . Wilson Pickett
20/69	**Don't Let The Joneses Get You Down** . . . Temptations
6/64	**Don't Let The Rain Come Down (Crooked Little Man)** . . . Serendipity Singers
39/67	**Don't Let The Rain Fall Down On Me** . . . Critters
4/64	**Don't Let The Sun Catch You Crying** . . . Gerry & The Pacemakers
2/74	**Don't Let The Sun Go Down On Me** . . . Elton John
4/78	**Don't Look Back** . . . Boston
11/89	**Don't Look Back** . . . Fine Young Cannibals
39/87	**Don't Look Down - The Sequel** . . . Go West
4/85	**Don't Lose My Number** . . . Phil Collins
	Don't Make Me Over
21/63	Dionne Warwick
20/89	Sybil
15/87	**Don't Make Me Wait For Love** . . . Kenny G
3/87	**Don't Mean Nothing** . . . Richard Marx
33/65	**Don't Mess Up A Good Thing** . . . Fontella Bass & Bobby McClure
7/66	**Don't Mess With Bill** . . . Marvelettes
37/87	**Don't Need A Gun** . . . Billy Idol
34/83	**Don't Pay The Ferryman** . . . Chris DeBurgh
40/59	**Don't Pity Me** . . . Dion & The Belmonts
	Don't Play That Song
11/62	Ben E. King
11/70	Aretha Franklin
	Don't Pull Your Love
4/71	Hamilton, Joe Frank & Reynolds
27/76	Glen Campbell (medley)
2/89	**Don't Rush Me** . . . Taylor Dayne

POS/YR	RECORD TITLE/ARTIST
26/63	**Don't Say Goodnight And Mean Goodbye** . . . Shirelles
39/80	**Don't Say Goodnight (It's Time For Love)** . . . Isley Brothers
7/63	**Don't Say Nothin' Bad (About My Baby)** . . . Cookies
15/72	**Don't Say You Don't Remember** . . . Beverly Bremers
20/63	**Don't Set Me Free** . . . Ray Charles
9/88	**Don't Shed A Tear** . . . Paul Carrack
18/89	**Don't Shut Me Out** . . . Kevin Paige
5/67	**Don't Sleep In The Subway** . . . Petula Clark
10/81	**Don't Stand So Close To Me** . . . Police
3/77	**Don't Stop** . . . Fleetwood Mac
9/81	**Don't Stop Believin'** . . . Journey
33/76	**Don't Stop Believin'** . . . Olivia Newton-John
19/81	**Don't Stop The Music** . . . Yarbrough & Peoples
1/79	**Don't Stop 'Til You Get Enough** . . . Michael Jackson
34/76	**Don't Take Away The Music** . . . Tavares
27/68	**Don't Take It So Hard** . . . Paul Revere & The Raiders
32/59	**Don't Take Your Guns To Town** . . . Johnny Cash
37/75	**Don't Take Your Love** . . . Manhattans
2/82	**Don't Talk To Strangers** . . . Rick Springfield
27/75	**Don't Tell Me Goodnight** . . . Lobo
10/89	**Don't Tell Me Lies** . . . Breathe
40/83	**Don't Tell Me You Love Me** . . . Night Ranger
	Don't Think Twice, It's All Right
9/63	Peter, Paul & Mary
12/65	Wonder Who?
22/60	**Don't Throw Away All Those Teardrops** . . . Frankie Avalon
	Don't Throw It All Away ..see: (Our Love)
16/64	**Don't Throw Your Love Away** . . . Searchers
38/69	**Don't Touch Me** . . . Bettye Swann
19/91	**Don't Treat Me Bad** . . . Firehouse
26/84	**Don't Walk Away** . . . Rick Springfield
2/90	**Don't Wanna Fall In Love** . . . Jane Child
1/89	**Don't Wanna Lose You** . . . Gloria Estefan
21/78	**Don't Want To Live Without It** . . . Pablo Cruise

POS/YR	RECORD TITLE/ARTIST
35/81	**Don't Want To Wait Anymore** . . . Tubes
3/61	**Don't Worry** . . . Marty Robbins
	Don't Worry Baby
24/64	Beach Boys
17/77	B.J. Thomas
1/88	**Don't Worry Be Happy** . . . Bobby McFerrin
29/71	**(Don't Worry) If There's A Hell Below We're All Going To Go** . . . Curtis Mayfield
	Don't Ya Wanna Play This Game No More ..see: (Sartorial Eloquence)
	Don't You ..also see: Doncha'
39/62	**Don't You Believe It** . . . Andy Williams
6/67	**Don't You Care** . . . Buckinghams
1/85	**Don't You (Forget About Me)** . . . Simple Minds
	Don't You Forget It ..see: (I Love You)
25/83	**Don't You Get So Mad** . . . Jeffrey Osborne
9/58	**Don't You Just Know It** . . . Huey (Piano) Smith
2/59	**Don't You Know** . . . Della Reese
6/88	**Don't You Know What The Night Can Do?** . . . Steve Winwood
1/82	**Don't You Want Me** . . . Human League
6/87	**Don't You Want Me** . . . Jody Watley
16/74	**Don't You Worry 'Bout A Thing** . . . Stevie Wonder
	(Don't You Worry 'Bout Me) ..see: Opus 17
33/79	**Don't You Write Her Off** . . . McGuinn, Clark & Hillman
15/58	**Doncha' Think It's Time** . . . Elvis Presley
2/59	**Donna** . . . Ritchie Valens
6/63	**Donna The Prima Donna** . . . Dion
15/74	**Doo Doo Doo Doo Doo (Heartbreaker)** . . . Rolling Stones
6/64	**Door Is Still Open To My Heart** . . . Dean Martin
35/74	**Doraville** . . . Atlanta Rhythm Section
26/76	**Dose Of Rock 'N' Roll** . . . Ringo Starr
39/58	**Dottie** . . . Danny & The Juniors
22/71	**Double Barrel** . . . Dave & Ansil Collins
30/81	**Double Dutch Bus** . . . Frankie Smith
14/71	**Double Lovin'** . . . Osmonds
17/66	**Double Shot (Of My Baby's Love)** . . . Swingin' Medallions
2/78	**Double Vision** . . . Foreigner
33/68	**Down At Lulu's** . . . Ohio Express
9/63	**(Down At) Papa Joe's** . . . Dixiebelles

POS/YR	RECORD TITLE/ARTIST
27/89	**Down Boys** . . . Warrant
4/72	**Down By The Lazy River** . . . Osmonds
13/60	**Down By The Station** . . . Four Preps
9/65	**Down In The Boondocks** . . . Billy Joe Royal
3/69	**Down On The Corner** . . . Creedence Clearwater Revival
18/58	**Down The Aisle Of Love** . . . Quin-Tones
37/63	**Down The Aisle (Wedding Song)** . . . Patti LaBelle & The Blue Belles
1/83	**Down Under** . . . Men At Work
	Downtown
1/65	Petula Clark
40/65	Allan Sherman (Crazy Downtown)
37/89	**Downtown** . . . One 2 Many
31/88	**Downtown Life** . . . Daryl Hall John Oates
3/90	**Downtown Train** . . . Rod Stewart
	Dr. ..see: Doctor
10/64	**Drag City** . . . Jan & Dean
4/71	**Draggin' The Line** . . . Tommy James
28/81	**Draw Of The Cards** . . . Kim Carnes
19/58	**Dream** . . . Betty Johnson
12/68	**Dream A Little Dream Of Me** . . . Mama Cass
	Dream Baby (How Long Must I Dream)
4/62	Roy Orbison
31/71	Glen Campbell
37/84	**Dream (Hold On To Your Dream)** . . . Irene Cara
12/91	**Dream Is Still Alive** . . . Wilson Phillips
2/59	**Dream Lover** . . . Bobby Darin
	Dream Merchant
38/67	Jerry Butler
36/75	New Birth
6/76	**Dream On** . . . Aerosmith
32/74	**Dream On** . . . Righteous Brothers
25/65	**Dream On Little Dreamer** . . . Perry Como
26/79	**Dream Police** . . . Cheap Trick
2/76	**Dream Weaver** . . . Gary Wright
	Dreamboat ..see: (He's My)
15/80	**Dreamer** . . . Supertramp
8/89	**Dreamin'** . . . Vanessa Williams
11/60	**Dreamin'** . . . Johnny Burnette
10/80	**Dreaming** . . . Cliff Richard
16/88	**Dreaming** . . . Orchestral Manoeuvres In The Dark
27/79	**Dreaming** . . . Blondie
30/83	**Dreamin' Is Easy** . . . Steel Breeze

POS/YR	RECORD TITLE/ARTIST
1/77	**Dreams** . . . Fleetwood Mac
22/86	**Dreams** . . . Van Halen
32/68	**Dreams Of The Everyday Housewife** . . . Glen Campbell
5/86	**Dreamtime** . . . Daryl Hall
35/62	**Dreamy Eyes** . . . Johnny Tillotson
21/73	**Dreidel** . . . Don McLean
5/85	**Dress You Up** . . . Madonna
14/89	**Dressed For Success** . . . Roxette
5/73	**Drift Away** . . . Dobie Gray
6/63	**Drip Drop** . . . Dion
3/84	**Drive** . . . Cars
15/79	**Driver's Seat** . . . Sniff 'n' the Tears
5/80	**Drivin' My Life Away** . . . Eddie Rabbitt
34/77	**Drivin' Wheel** . . . Foghat
36/63	**Drownin' My Sorrows** . . . Connie Francis
11/72	**Drowning In The Sea Of Love** . . . Joe Simon
29/71	**Drum, The** . . . Bobby Sherman
29/62	**Drums Are My Beat** . . . Sandy Nelson
20/67	**Dry Your Eyes** . . . Brenda & The Tabulations
14/66	**Duck, The** . . . Jackie Lee
14/87	**Dude (Looks Like A Lady)** . . . Aerosmith
2/73	**Dueling Banjos** . . . Eric Weissberg & Steve Mandell
1/62	**Duke Of Earl** . . . Gene Chandler
	Dukes Of Hazzard ..see: Theme From The
	Dum-De-Da ..see: She Understands Me
4/61	**Dum Dum** . . . Brenda Lee
	(also see: Happy Song)
7/56	**Dungaree Doll** . . . Eddie Fisher
18/77	**Dusic** . . . Brick
6/78	**Dust In The Wind** . . . Kansas
30/60	**Dutchman's Gold** . . . Walter Brennan/Billy Vaughn
15/84	**Dynamite** . . . Jermaine Jackson
10/75	**Dynomite** . . . Bazuka

E

POS/YR	RECORD TITLE/ARTIST
9/74	**Earache My Eye Featuring Alice Bowie** . . . Cheech & Chong
12/70	**Early In The Morning** . . . Vanity Fare
	Early In The Morning
24/58	Rinky-Dinks
32/58	Buddy Holly
	Early In The Morning
24/82	Gap Band
19/88	Robert Palmer
	Earth Angel
3/55	Crew-Cuts
8/55	Penguins
18/55	Gloria Mann
21/86	New Edition
1/63	**Easier Said Than Done** . . . Essex
27/66	**East West** . . . Herman's Hermits
4/77	**Easy** . . . Commodores
9/70	**Easy Come, Easy Go** . . . Bobby Sherman
39/72	**Easy Livin** . . . Uriah Heep
2/85	**Easy Lover** . . . Philip Bailey/Phil Collins
17/71	**Easy Loving** . . . Freddie Hart
	Easy Question ..see: (Such An)
4/69	**Easy To Be Hard** . . . Three Dog Night
36/78	**Easy To Love** . . . Leo Sayer
12/84	**Eat It** . . . Weird Al Yankovic
	Ebb Tide
25/64	Lenny Welch
5/66	Righteous Brothers
1/82	**Ebony And Ivory** . . . Paul McCartney & Stevie Wonder
8/61	**Ebony Eyes** . . . Everly Brothers
14/78	**Ebony Eyes** . . . Bob Welch
40/69	**Echo Park** . . . Keith Barbour
31/73	**Ecstasy** . . . Ohio Players
	Eddie My Love
11/56	Fontane Sisters
14/56	Chordettes
14/56	Teen Queens
26/88	**Edge Of A Broken Heart** . . . Vixen
10/86	**Edge Of Heaven** . . . Wham!
11/82	**Edge Of Seventeen (Just Like The White Winged Dove)** . . . Stevie Nicks
26/77	**Edge Of The Universe** . . . Bee Gees
34/78	**Ego** . . . Elton John
1/65	**Eight Days A Week** . . . Beatles
32/88	**853-5937** . . . Squeeze
14/66	**Eight Miles High** . . . Byrds
4/82	**867-5309/Jenny** . . . Tommy Tutone
21/71	**Eighteen** . . . Alice Cooper
4/89	**18 And Life** . . . Skid Row
15/75	**Eighteen With A Bullet** . . . Pete Wingfield

POS/YR	RECORD TITLE/ARTIST
10/63	**18 Yellow Roses** . . . Bobby Darin
	Ein Schiff Wird Kommen ..see: Never On Sunday
18/70	**El Condor Pasa** . . . Simon & Garfunkel
32/60	**El Matador** . . . Kingston Trio
1/60	**El Paso** . . . Marty Robbins
30/58	**El Rancho Rock** . . . Champs
17/63	**El Watusi** . . . Ray Barretto
	(also see: Wah Watusi & Watusi)
	Eleanor Rigby
11/66	Beatles
35/68	Ray Charles
17/69	Aretha Franklin
26/72	**Elected** . . . Alice Cooper
6/85	**Election Day** . . . Arcadia
2/83	**Electric Avenue** . . . Eddy Grant
7/88	**Electric Blue** . . . Icehouse
11/89	**Electric Youth** . . . Debbie Gibson
6/68	**Elenore** . . . Turtles
39/91	**Elevate My Mind** . . . Stereo MC's
	11th Hour Melody
21/56	Al Hibbler
35/56	Lou Busch
10/69	**Eli's Coming** . . . Three Dog Night
39/56	**Eloise** . . . Kay Thompson
5/66	**Elusive Butterfly** . . . Bob Lind
5/81	**Elvira** . . . Oak Ridge Boys
18/85	**Emergency** . . . Kool & The Gang
8/75	**Emma** . . . Hot Chocolate
3/78	**Emotion** . . . Samantha Sang
22/75	**Emotion** . . . Helen Reddy
15/86	**Emotion In Motion** . . . Ric Ocasek
3/80	**Emotional Rescue** . . . Rolling Stones
7/61	**Emotions** . . . Brenda Lee
18/80	**Empire Strikes Back (medley)** . . . Meco
13/57	**Empty Arms** . . . Teresa Brewer
13/82	**Empty Garden (Hey Hey Johnny)** . . . Elton John
12/59	**Enchanted** . . . Platters
12/58	**Enchanted Island** . . . Four Lads
	Enchanted Sea
15/59	Islanders
28/59	Martin Denny
7/58	**End, The** . . . Earl Grant
	End Of Our Road
15/68	Gladys Knight & The Pips
40/70	Marvin Gaye
8/89	**End Of The Innocence** . . . Don Henley

POS/YR	RECORD TITLE/ARTIST
2/63	**End Of The World** . . . Skeeter Davis
1/81	**Endless Love** . . . Diana Ross & Lionel Richie
21/87	**Endless Nights** . . . Eddie Money
5/58	**Endless Sleep** . . . Jody Reynolds
2/88	**Endless Summer Nights** . . . Richard Marx
12/59	**Endlessly** . . . Brook Benton
33/74	**Energy Crisis '74** . . . Dickie Goodman
7/65	**Engine Engine # 9** . . . Roger Miller
14/70	**Engine Number 9** . . . Wilson Pickett
8/65	**England Swings** . . . Roger Miller
21/56	**English Muffins And Irish Stew** . . . Sylvia Syms
8/90	**Enjoy The Silence** . . . Depeche Mode
6/77	**Enjoy Yourself** . . . Jacksons
	(Enough Is Enough) ..see: No More Tears
3/74	**Entertainer, The** . . . Marvin Hamlisch
31/65	**Entertainer, The** . . . Tony Clarke
34/75	**Entertainer, The** . . . Billy Joel
9/90	**Epic** . . . Faith No More
19/67	**Epistle To Dippy** . . . Donovan
9/74	**Eres Tu (Touch The Wind)** . . . Mocedades
1/90	**Escapade** . . . Janet Jackson
1/79	**Escape (The Pina Colada Song)** . . . Rupert Holmes
35/71	**Escape-ism** . . . James Brown
19/62	**Eso Beso (That Kiss!)** . . . Paul Anka
1/89	**Eternal Flame** . . . Bangles
1/65	**Eve Of Destruction** . . . Barry McGuire
33/80	**Even It Up** . . . Heart
12/83	**Even Now** . . . Bob Seger
19/78	**Even Now** . . . Barry Manilow
36/67	**Even The Bad Times Are Good** . . . Tremeloes
5/82	**Even The Nights Are Better** . . . Air Supply
	Evergreen ..see: Love Theme From A Star Is Born
5/78	**Everlasting Love** . . . Andy Gibb
	Everlasting Love
13/67	Robert Knight
6/74	Carl Carlton
32/81	Rex Smith/Rachel Sweet
12/89	**Everlasting Love** . . . Howard Jones
16/61	**Everlovin'** . . . Rick Nelson
6/61	**Every Beat Of My Heart** . . . Pips
1/83	**Every Breath You Take** . . . Police
	Every Day ..also see: Everyday

POS/YR	RECORD TITLE/ARTIST
	Every Day Of My Life
37/56	McGuire Sisters
24/72	Bobby Vinton
2/91	**Every Heartbeat** . . . Amy Grant
16/78	**Every Kinda People** . . . Robert Palmer
13/64	**Every Little Bit Hurts** . . . Brenda Holloway
14/87	**Every Little Kiss** . . . Bruce Hornsby & The Range
3/89	**Every Little Step** . . . Bobby Brown
3/81	**Every Little Thing She Does Is Magic** . . . Police
39/58	**Every Night (I Pray)** . . . Chantels
1/88	**Every Rose Has Its Thorn** . . . Poison
25/85	**Every Step Of The Way** . . . John Waite
30/63	**Every Step Of The Way** . . . Johnny Mathis
	Every Time ..also see: Everytime
13/79	**Every Time I Think Of You** . . . Babys
4/77	**(Every Time I Turn Around) Back In Love Again** . . . L.T.D.
19/75	**Every Time You Touch Me (I Get High)** . . . Charlie Rich
30/79	**Every Which Way But Loose** . . . Eddie Rabbitt
5/81	**Every Woman In The World** . . . Air Supply
3/63	**Everybody** . . . Tommy Roe
38/77	**Everybody Be Dancin'** . . . Starbuck
24/86	**Everybody Dance** . . . Ta Mara & The Seen
38/78	**Everybody Dance** . . . Chic
8/90	**Everybody Everybody** . . . Black Box
2/86	**Everybody Have Fun Tonight** . . . Wang Chung
F/70	**Everybody Is A Star** . . . Sly & The Family Stone
15/64	**Everybody Knows (I Still Love You)** . . . Dave Clark Five
31/59	**Everybody Likes To Cha Cha Cha** . . . Sam Cooke
4/65	**Everybody Loves A Clown** . . . Gary Lewis & The Playboys
	Everybody Loves A Lover
6/58	Doris Day
19/63	Shirelles
6/62	**Everybody Loves Me But You** . . . Brenda Lee
1/64	**Everybody Loves Somebody** . . . Dean Martin
32/78	**Everybody Needs Love** . . . Stephen Bishop

POS/YR	RECORD TITLE/ARTIST
39/67	**Everybody Needs Love** . . . Gladys Knight & The Pips
29/67	**Everybody Needs Somebody To Love** . . . Wilson Pickett
3/72	**Everybody Plays The Fool** . . . Main Ingredient
1/85	**Everybody Wants To Rule The World** . . . Tears For Fears
32/82	**Everybody Wants You** . . . Billy Squier
12/71	**Everybody's Everything** . . . Santana
20/55	**Everybody's Got A Home But Me** . . . Eddie Fisher
21/70	**Everybody's Got The Right To Love** . . . Supremes
18/80	**Everybody's Got To Learn Sometime** . . . Korgis
26/70	**Everybody's Out Of Town** . . . B.J. Thomas
1/60	**Everybody's Somebody's Fool** . . . Connie Francis
6/69	**Everybody's Talkin'** . . . Nilsson
36/83	**Everyday I Write The Book** . . . Elvis Costello
	Everyday People
1/69	Sly & The Family Stone
37/83	Joan Jett
19/69	**Everyday With You Girl** . . . Classics IV
6/79	**Every 1's A Winner** . . . Hot Chocolate
17/65	**Everyone's Gone To The Moon** . . . Jonathan King
4/90	**Everything** . . . Jody Watley
1/91	**(Everything I Do) I Do It For You** . . . Bryan Adams
5/72	**Everything I Own** . . . Bread
30/86	**Everything In My Heart** . . . Corey Hart
1/70	**Everything Is Beautiful** . . . Ray Stevens
1/85	**Everything She Wants** . . . Wham!
10/68	**Everything That Touches You** . . . Association
3/88	**Everything Your Heart Desires** . . . Daryl Hall John Oates
16/64	**Everything's Alright** . . . Newbeats
38/70	**Everything's Tuesday** . . . Chairman Of The Board
1/85	**Everytime You Go Away** . . . Paul Young
14/88	**Everywhere** . . . Fleetwood Mac
9/70	**Evil Ways** . . . Santana
10/76	**Evil Woman** . . . Electric Light Orchestra
19/70	**Evil Woman Don't Play Your Games With Me** . . . Crow

POS/YR	RECORD TITLE/ARTIST
	Exodus
2/61	Ferrante & Teicher
31/61	Mantovani
36/61	Eddie Harris
	Exorcist, Theme From ..see: Tubular Bells
14/55	**Experience Unnecessary** . . . Sarah Vaughan
33/68	**Explosion In Your Soul** . . . Soul Survivors
4/75	**Express** . . . B.T. Express
2/89	**Express Yourself** . . . Madonna
12/70	**Express Yourself** . . . Charles Wright
26/90	**Expression** . . . Salt-N-Pepa
4/67	**Expressway To Your Heart** . . . Soul Survivors
3/82	**Eye In The Sky** . . . Alan Parsons Project
1/82	**Eye Of The Tiger** . . . Survivor
28/68	**Eyes Of A New York Woman** . . . B.J. Thomas
	Eyes Of Laura Mars ..see: Love Theme From
4/84	**Eyes Without A Face** . . . Billy Idol

F

POS/YR	RECORD TITLE/ARTIST
22/78	**FM (No Static At All)** . . . Steely Dan
29/66	**Fa-Fa-Fa-Fa-Fa (Sad Song)** . . . Otis Redding
16/57	**Fabulous** . . . Charlie Gracie
19/56	**Fabulous Character** . . . Sarah Vaughan
29/68	**Face It Girl, It's Over** . . . Nancy Wilson
26/86	**Face The Face** . . . Pete Townshend
27/87	**Facts Of Love** . . . Jeff Lorber/Karyn White
20/81	**Fade Away** . . . Bruce Springsteen
2/91	**Fading Like A Flower (Every Time You Leave)** . . . Roxette
28/90	**Fairweather Friend** . . . Johnny Gill
13/74	**Fairytale** . . . Pointer Sisters
1/87	**Faith** . . . George Michael
12/83	**Faithfully** . . . Journey
25/87	**Fake** . . . Alexander O'Neal
35/83	**Fake Friends** . . . Joan Jett
23/67	**Fakin' It** . . . Simon & Garfunkel
17/83	**Fall In Love With Me** . . . Earth, Wind & Fire

POS/YR	RECORD TITLE/ARTIST
12/88	**Fallen Angel** . . . Poison
36/76	**Fallen Angel** . . . Frankie Valli
	Fallen Star
20/57	Nick Noble
23/57	Jimmy Newman
30/58	**Fallin'** . . . Connie Francis
13/78	**Falling** . . . LeBlanc & Carr
22/63	**Falling** . . . Roy Orbison
1/75	**Fallin' In Love** . . . Hamilton, Joe Frank & Reynolds
27/74	**Fallin' In Love** . . . Souther, Hillman, Furay Band
25/87	**Falling In Love (Uh-Oh)** . . . Miami Sound Machine
1/75	**Fame** . . . David Bowie
4/80	**Fame** . . . Irene Cara
17/60	**Fame And Fortune** . . . Elvis Presley
1/71	**Family Affair** . . . Sly & The Family Stone
6/83	**Family Man** . . . Daryl Hall & John Oates
12/72	**Family Of Man** . . . Three Dog Night
31/70	**Fancy** . . . Bobbie Gentry
39/77	**Fancy Dancer** . . . Commodores
38/60	**Fannie Mae** . . . Buster Brown
12/76	**Fanny (Be Tender With My Love)** . . . Bee Gees
23/82	**Fantasy** . . . Aldo Nova
32/78	**Fantasy** . . . Earth, Wind & Fire
10/83	**Far From Over** . . . Frank Stallone
38/84	**Farewell My Summer Love** . . . Michael Jackson
19/64	**Farmer John** . . . Premiers
21/87	**Fascinated** . . . Company B
	Fascination
7/57	Jane Morgan
15/57	Dinah Shore
17/57	Dick Jacobs
	(also see: Keep Feeling)
6/88	**Fast Car** . . . Tracy Chapman
F/79	**Fat Bottomed Girls** . . . Queen
1/88	**Father Figure** . . . George Michael
34/86	**Feel It Again** . . . Honeymoon Suite
1/74	**Feel Like Makin' Love** . . . Roberta Flack
10/75	**Feel Like Makin' Love** . . . Bad Company
	Feel So Fine
14/60	Johnny Preston
22/67	Bunny Sigler (medley)
	Feelin' Groovy ..see: 59th Street Bridge
10/73	**Feelin' Stronger Every Day** . . . Chicago

POS/YR	RECORD TITLE/ARTIST
33/72	**Feeling Alright** . . . Joe Cocker
6/75	**Feelings** . . . Morris Albert
9/90	**Feels Good** . . . Tony! Toni! Tone!
4/77	**Feels Like The First Time** . . . Foreigner
4/78	**Feels So Good** . . . Chuck Mangione
35/89	**Feels So Good** . . . Van Halen
20/81	**Feels So Right** . . . Alabama
32/61	**Fell In Love On Monday** . . . Fats Domino
13/76	**Fernando** . . . Abba
6/65	**Ferry Cross The Mersey** . . . Gerry & The Pacemakers
	Fever
24/56	Little Willie John
8/58	Peggy Lee
7/65	McCoys
23/78	**Ffun** . . . Con Funk Shun
39/58	**Fibbin'** . . . Patti Page
1/76	**Fifth Of Beethoven** . . . Walter Murphy
1/76	**50 Ways To Leave Your Lover** . . . Paul Simon
13/67	**59th Street Bridge Song (Feelin' Groovy)** . . . Harpers Bizarre
	Fight ..see: Main Event
	Fight For Your Right ..see: (You Gotta)
4/75	**Fight The Power** . . . Isley Brothers
	(Final Acclaim) ..see: You're In My Heart
8/87	**Final Countdown** . . . Europe
17/74	**Finally Got Myself Together (I'm A Changed Man)** . . . Impressions
29/85	**Find A Way** . . . Amy Grant
16/82	**Find Another Fool** . . . Quarterflash
27/61	**Find Another Girl** . . . Jerry Butler
29/81	**Find Your Way Back** . . . Jefferson Starship
22/84	**Fine Fine Day** . . . Tony Carey
8/87	**Finer Things** . . . Steve Winwood
7/60	**Finger Poppin' Time** . . . Hank Ballard
1/63	**Fingertips** . . . Little Stevie Wonder
13/88	**Finish What Ya Started** . . . Van Halen
35/79	**Fins** . . . Jimmy Buffett
1/75	**Fire** . . . Ohio Players
2/68	**Fire** . . . Crazy World Of Arthur Brown
2/79	**Fire** . . . Pointer Sisters
17/81	**Fire And Ice** . . . Pat Benatar
3/70	**Fire And Rain** . . . James Taylor
24/72	**Fire And Water** . . . Wilson Pickett
28/74	**Fire, Baby I'm On Fire** . . . Andy Kim
32/80	**Fire In The Morning** . . . Melissa Manchester

POS/YR	RECORD TITLE/ARTIST
6/80	**Fire Lake** . . . Bob Seger
38/75	**Fire On The Mountain** . . . Marshall Tucker Band
20/58	**Firefly** . . . Tony Bennett
21/77	**First Cut Is The Deepest** . . . Rod Stewart
25/57	**First Date, First Kiss, First Love** . . . Sonny James
33/84	**First Day Of Summer** . . . Tony Carey
20/60	**First Name Initial** . . . Annette
37/69	**First Of May** . . . Bee Gees
27/63	**First Quarrel** . . . Paul & Paula
1/91	**First Time** . . . Surface
1/72	**First Time Ever I Saw Your Face** . . . Roberta Flack
	(First Time I Was A Fool) ..see: Third Time Lucky
38/80	**First Time Love** . . . Livingston Taylor
25/61	**Fish, The** . . . Bobby Rydell
26/74	**Fish Ain't Bitin'** . . . Lamont Dozier
23/88	**Fishnet** . . . Morris Day
10/63	**500 Miles Away From Home** . . . Bobby Bare
4/66	**Five O'Clock World** . . . Vogues
	(Five Oaks) ..see: Cinco Robles
27/78	**5.7.0.5.** . . . City Boy
11/70	**5-10-15-20 (25-30 Years Of Love)** . . . Presidents
1/88	**Flame, The** . . . Cheap Trick
36/87	**Flames Of Paradise** . . . Jennifer Rush/Elton John
14/61	**Flaming Star** . . . Elvis Presley
28/66	**Flamingo** . . . Herb Alpert
16/78	**Flash Light** . . . Parliament
1/83	**Flashdance...What A Feeling** . . . Irene Cara
29/84	**Flesh For Fantasy** . . . Billy Idol
2/77	**Float On** . . . Floaters
21/56	**Flowers Mean Forgiveness** . . . Frank Sinatra
4/66	**Flowers On The Wall** . . . Statler Brothers
16/72	**Floy Joy** . . . Supremes
7/61	**Fly, The** . . . Chubby Checker
13/76	**Fly Away** . . . John Denver
2/77	**Fly Like An Eagle** . . . Steve Miller
14/63	**Fly Me To The Moon-Bossa Nova** . . . Joe Harnell
1/75	**Fly, Robin, Fly** . . . Silver Convention
19/90	**Fly To The Angels** . . . Slaughter

POS/YR	RECORD TITLE/ARTIST
38/78	**Flying High** . . . Commodores
3/56	**Flying Saucer** . . . Buchanan & Goodman
18/57	**Flying Saucer The 2nd** . . . Buchanan & Goodman
15/62	**Follow That Dream** . . . Elvis Presley
17/63	**Follow The Boys** . . . Connie Francis
23/78	**Follow You Follow Me** . . . Genesis
32/68	**Folsom Prison Blues** . . . Johnny Cash
7/56	**Fool, The** . . . Sanford Clark
22/68	**Fool For You** . . . Impressions
37/89	**Fool For Your Loving** . . . Whitesnake
12/78	**Fool (If You Think It's Over)** . . . Chris Rea
27/60	**Fool In Love** . . . Ike & Tina Turner
25/81	**Fool In Love With You** . . . Jim Photoglo
21/80	**Fool In The Rain** . . . Led Zeppelin
13/64	**Fool Never Learns** . . . Andy Williams
3/61	**Fool #1** . . . Brenda Lee
6/68	**Fool On The Hill** . . . Sergio Mendes & Brasil '66
2/59	**Fool Such As I** . . . Elvis Presley
10/76	**Fool To Cry** . . . Rolling Stones
20/55	**Fooled** . . . Perry Como
3/76	**Fooled Around And Fell In Love** . . . Elvin Bishop
28/83	**Foolin'** . . . Def Leppard
29/78	**Fooling Yourself (The Angry Young Man)** . . . Styx
1/88	**Foolish Beat** . . . Debbie Gibson
18/85	**Foolish Heart** . . . Steve Perry
4/63	**Foolish Little Girl** . . . Shirelles
33/86	**Foolish Pride** . . . Daryl Hall
29/59	**Fools Hall Of Fame** . . . Pat Boone
	Fools Rush In
24/60	Brook Benton
12/63	Rick Nelson
25/61	**Foot Stomping** . . . Flares
1/84	**Footloose** . . . Kenny Loggins
7/60	**Footsteps** . . . Steve Lawrence
29/72	**Footstompin' Music** . . . Grand Funk Railroad
30/76	**Fopp** . . . Ohio Players
23/59	**For A Penny** . . . Pat Boone
3/71	**For All We Know** . . . Carpenters
30/86	**For America** . . . Jackson Browne
26/71	**(For God's Sake) Give More Power To The People** . . . Chi-Lites
30/65	**For Lovin' Me** . . . Peter, Paul & Mary
28/61	**For My Baby** . . . Brook Benton

POS/YR	RECORD TITLE/ARTIST
23/58	**For My Good Fortune** . . . Pat Boone
2/68	**For Once In My Life** . . . Stevie Wonder
	For Sentimental Reasons ..see: (I Love You)
11/71	**For The Good Times** . . . Ray Price
13/70	**For The Love Of Him** . . . Bobbi Martin
9/74	**For The Love Of Money** . . . O'Jays
22/75	**For The Love Of You** . . . Isley Brothers
32/86	**For Tonight** . . . Nancy Martinez
7/67	**For What It's Worth** . . . Buffalo Springfield
6/64	**For You** . . . Rick Nelson
21/91	**For You** . . . Outfield
4/81	**For Your Eyes Only** . . . Sheena Easton
6/65	**For Your Love** . . . Yardbirds
	For Your Love
13/58	Ed Townsend
20/67	Peaches & Herb
	For Your Precious Love
11/58	Jerry Butler & The Impressions
26/64	Garnet Mimms & The Enchanters
23/67	Oscar Toney, Jr.
8/90	**Forever** . . . Kiss
	Forever
9/60	Little Dippers
25/64	Pete Drake
	(also see: I'll Be Loving You)
40/85	**Forever** . . . Kenny Loggins
28/68	**Forever Came Today** . . . Supremes
35/56	**Forever Darling** . . . Ames Brothers
20/79	**Forever In Blue Jeans** . . . Neil Diamond
19/86	**(Forever) Live And Die** . . . Orchestral Manoeuvres In The Dark
26/85	**Forever Man** . . . Eric Clapton
28/80	**Forever Mine** . . . O'Jays
12/88	**Forever Young** . . . Rod Stewart
1/89	**Forever Your Girl** . . . Paula Abdul
4/64	**Forget Him** . . . Bobby Rydell
12/58	**Forget Me Not** . . . Kalin Twins
23/82	**Forget Me Nots** . . . Patrice Rushen
2/80	**Forgive Me, Girl (medley)** . . . Spinners
13/55	**Forgive My Heart** . . . Nat "King" Cole
8/85	**Fortress Around Your Heart** . . . Sting
14/69	**Fortunate Son** . . . Creedence Clearwater Revival
9/59	**Forty Miles Of Bad Road** . . . Duane Eddy
36/79	**Found A Cure** . . . Ashford & Simpson
19/85	**Four In The Morning (I Can't Take Any More)** . . . Night Ranger

POS/YR	RECORD TITLE/ARTIST
	Four Walls
11/57	Jim Reeves
15/57	Jim Lowe
36/68	**1432 Franklin Pike Circle Hero** . . . Bobby Russell
5/76	**Fox On The Run** . . . Sweet
1/73	**Frankenstein** . . . Edgar Winter Group
9/59	**Frankie** . . . Connie Francis
	Frankie And Johnny
20/61	Brook Benton
14/63	Sam Cooke
25/66	Elvis Presley
36/57	**Fraulein** . . . Bobby Helms
4/72	**Freddie's Dead** . . . Curtis Mayfield
20/71	**Free** . . . Chicago
23/56	**Free** . . . Tommy Leonetti
25/77	**Free** . . . Deniece Williams
	Free Bird
19/75	Lynyrd Skynyrd
38/77	Lynyrd Skynyrd (Live)
1/88	Will To Power (medley)
7/90	**Free Fallin'** . . . Tom Petty
22/74	**Free Man In Paris** . . . Joni Mitchell
14/73	**Free Ride** . . . Edgar Winter Group
	Freedom
3/85	Wham!
8/90	George Michael
20/86	**Freedom Overspill** . . . Steve Winwood
3/85	**Freeway Of Love** . . . Aretha Franklin
33/58	**Freeze, The** . . . Tony & Joe
4/82	**Freeze-Frame** . . . J. Geils Band
	Freight Train
6/57	Rusty Draper
40/57	Chas. McDevitt Skiffle Group
9/85	**Fresh** . . . Kool & The Gang
	(Friday Night) ..see: Livin' It Up
16/67	**Friday On My Mind** . . . Easybeats
36/66	**Friday's Child** . . . Nancy Sinatra
5/56	**Friendly Persuasion (Thee I Love)** . . . Pat Boone
9/89	**Friends** . . . Jody Watley With Eric B. & Rakim
34/71	**Friends** . . . Elton John
40/73	**Friends** . . . Bette Midler
2/86	**Friends And Lovers** . . . Gloria Loring & Carl Anderson
38/82	**Friends In Love** . . . Dionne Warwick & Johnny Mathis

POS/YR	RECORD TITLE/ARTIST
17/69	**Friendship Train** . . . Gladys Knight & The Pips
32/61	**Frogg** . . . Brothers Four
2/90	**From A Distance** . . . Bette Midler
6/63	**From A Jack To A King** . . . Ned Miller
23/64	**From A Window** . . . Billy J. Kramer
28/75	**From His Woman To You** . . . Barbara Mason
39/72	**From The Beginning** . . . Emerson, Lake & Palmer
11/56	**From The Candy Store On The Corner To The Chapel On The Hill** . . . Tony Bennett
28/75	**Full Of Fire** . . . Al Green
	Fun ..also see: Ffun
5/64	**Fun, Fun, Fun** . . . Beach Boys
8/67	**Funky Broadway** . . . Wilson Pickett
3/89	**Funky Cold Medina** . . . Tone Loc
39/68	**Funky Judge** . . . Bull & The Matadors
15/71	**Funky Nassau** . . . Beginning Of The End
14/68	**Funky Street** . . . Arthur Conley
29/73	**Funky Stuff** . . . Kool & The Gang
15/73	**Funky Worm** . . . Ohio Players
	Funkytown
1/80	Lipps, Inc.
6/87	Pseudo Echo
25/61	**Funny** . . . Maxine Brown
5/73	**Funny Face** . . . Donna Fargo
	Funny How Time Slips Away
22/62	Jimmy Elledge
13/64	Joe Hinton
10/62	**Funny Way Of Laughin'** . . . Burl Ives
39/73	**Future Shock** . . . Curtis Mayfield
19/86	**Future's So Bright, I Gotta Wear Shades** . . . Timbuk 3

POS/YR	RECORD TITLE/ARTIST
4/64	**G.T.O.** . . . Ronny & The Daytonas
39/78	**Galaxy** . . . War
29/67	**Gallant Men** . . . Senator Everett McKinley Dirksen
4/69	**Galveston** . . . Glen Campbell
16/79	**Gambler, The** . . . Kenny Rogers

POS/YR	RECORD TITLE/ARTIST
1/65	**Game Of Love** . . . Wayne Fontana & The Mindbenders
27/71	**Games** . . . Redeye
12/69	**Games People Play** . . . Joe South
	(also see: They Just Can't Stop It)
16/81	**Games People Play** . . . Alan Parsons Project
12/56	**Garden Of Eden** . . . Joe Valino
6/72	**Garden Party** . . . Rick Nelson
21/58	**Gee, But It's Lonely** . . . Pat Boone
19/56	**Gee Whittakers!** . . . Pat Boone
28/61	**Gee Whiz** . . . Innocents
	Gee Whiz (Look At His Eyes)
10/61	Carla Thomas
31/80	Bernadette Peters
12/81	**Gemini Dream** . . . Moody Blues
33/81	**General Hospi-Tale** . . . Afternoon Delights
31/82	**Genius Of Love** . . . Tom Tom Club
31/91	**Gentle** . . . Dino
39/68	**Gentle On My Mind** . . . Glen Campbell
33/72	**George Jackson** . . . Bob Dylan
	Georgia On My Mind
1/60	Ray Charles
36/90	Michael Bolton
2/67	**Georgy Girl** . . . Seekers
37/72	**Geronimo's Cadillac** . . . Michael Murphey
	Get A Job
1/58	Silhouettes
21/58	Mills Brothers
1/69	**Get Back** . . . Beatles with Billy Preston
6/76	**Get Closer** . . . Seals & Crofts
29/82	**Get Closer** . . . Linda Ronstadt
10/75	**Get Dancin'** . . . Disco-Tex & The Sex-O-Lettes
7/73	**Get Down** . . . Gilbert O'Sullivan
8/75	**Get Down, Get Down (Get On The Floor)** . . . Joe Simon
10/82	**Get Down On It** . . . Kool & The Gang
1/75	**Get Down Tonight** . . . K.C. & The Sunshine Band
5/91	**Get Here** . . . Oleta Adams
24/71	**Get It On** . . . Chase
	(also see: Bang A Gong)
21/79	**Get It Right Next Time** . . . Gerry Rafferty
28/73	**Get It Together** . . . Jackson 5
40/67	**Get It Together** . . . James Brown
27/67	**Get Me To The World On Time** . . . Electric Prunes

POS/YR	RECORD TITLE/ARTIST
9/78	**Get Off** . . . Foxy
1/65	**Get Off Of My Cloud** . . . Rolling Stones
18/72	**Get On The Good Foot** . . . James Brown
11/67	**Get On Up** . . . Esquires
11/89	**Get On Your Feet** . . . Gloria Estefan
1/88	**Get Outta My Dreams, Get Into My Car** . . . Billy Ocean
	Get Ready
29/66	Temptations
4/70	Rare Earth
31/87	**Get That Love** . . . Thompson Twins
30/76	**Get The Funk Out Ma Face** . . . Brothers Johnson
	Get Together
31/65	We Five
5/69	Youngbloods
2/76	**Get Up And Boogie (That's Right)** . . . Silver Convention
	(Get up and dance!) ..see: Bite Your Lip
7/90	**Get Up! (Before The Night Is Over)** . . . Technotronic
34/71	**Get Up, Get Into It, Get Involved** . . . James Brown
	Get Up I Feel Like Being A Sex Machine ..see: Sex Machine
21/79	**Get Used To It** . . . Roger Voudouris
12/76	**Getaway** . . . Earth, Wind & Fire
26/85	**Getcha Back** . . . Beach Boys
27/78	**Gettin' Ready For Love** . . . Diana Ross
18/67	**Gettin' Together** . . . Tommy James & The Shondells
38/90	**Getting Away With It** . . . Electronic
20/79	**Getting Closer** . . . Wings
29/73	**Ghetto Child** . . . Spinners
	(Ghost) Riders In The Sky
30/61	Ramrods
31/81	Outlaws
22/56	**Ghost Town** . . . Don Cherry
33/88	**Ghost Town** . . . Cheap Trick
1/84	**Ghostbusters** . . . Ray Parker Jr.
37/83	**Gimme All Your Lovin** . . . ZZ Top
9/70	**Gimme Dat Ding** . . . Pipkins
12/69	**Gimme Gimme Good Lovin'** . . . Crazy Elephant
9/67	**Gimme Little Sign** . . . Brenton Wood
	Gimme Some Lovin'
7/67	Spencer Davis Group
18/80	Blues Brothers
6/62	**Gina** . . . Johnny Mathis

POS/YR	RECORD TITLE/ARTIST
9/58	**Ginger Bread** . . . Frankie Avalon
38/61	**Ginnie Bell** . . . Paul Dino
21/62	**Ginny Come Lately** . . . Brian Hyland
17/86	**Girl Can't Help It** . . . Journey
30/65	**Girl Come Running** . . . 4 Seasons
5/64	**Girl From Ipanema** . . . Stan Getz/Astrud Gilberto
39/67	**Girl I Knew Somewhere** . . . Monkees
27/90	**Girl I Used To Know** . . . Brother Beyond
1/89	**Girl I'm Gonna Miss You** . . . Milli Vanilli
21/66	**Girl In Love** . . . Outsiders
35/84	**Girl In Trouble (Is A Temporary Thing)** . . . Romeo Void
2/83	**Girl Is Mine** . . . Michael Jackson/Paul McCartney
10/67	**Girl Like You** . . . Young Rascals
38/90	**Girl Like You** . . . Smithereens
19/61	**Girl Of My Best Friend** . . . Ral Donner
37/79	**Girl Of My Dreams** . . . Bram Tchaikovsky
28/66	**Girl On A Swing** . . . Gerry & The Pacemakers
5/68	**Girl Watcher** . . . O'Kaysions
26/64	**Girl (Why You Wanna Make Me Blue)** . . . Temptations
13/57	**Girl With The Golden Braids** . . . Perry Como
2/89	**Girl You Know It's True** . . . Milli Vanilli
10/67	**Girl, You'll Be A Woman Soon** . . . Neil Diamond
5/88	**Girlfriend** . . . Pebbles
16/84	**Girls** . . . Dwight Twilley
34/85	**Girls Are More Fun** . . . Ray Parker Jr.
34/80	**Girls Can Get It** . . . Dr. Hook
33/68	**Girls Can't Do What The Guys Do** . . . Betty Wright
12/87	**Girls, Girls, Girls** . . . Motley Crue
14/62	**(Girls, Girls, Girls) Made To Love** . . . Eddie Hodges
33/64	**Girls Grow Up Faster Than Boys** . . . Cookies
39/67	**Girls In Love** . . . Gary Lewis & The Playboys
2/84	**Girls Just Want To Have Fun** . . . Cyndi Lauper
6/90	**Girls Nite Out** . . . Tyler Collins
33/78	**Girls' School** . . . Wings
33/84	**Girls With Guns** . . . Tommy Shaw
8/69	**Gitarzan** . . . Ray Stevens

POS/YR	RECORD TITLE/ARTIST
15/77	**Give A Little Bit** . . . Supertramp
18/65	**Give Him A Great Big Kiss** . . . Shangri-Las
21/72	**Give Ireland Back To The Irish** . . . Wings
18/80	**Give It All You Got** . . . Chuck Mangione
30/73	**Give It To Me** . . . J. Geils Band
40/81	**Give It To Me Baby** . . . Rick James
20/74	**Give It To The People** . . . Righteous Brothers
18/84	**Give It Up** . . . KC
15/69	**Give It Up Or Turnit A Loose** . . . James Brown
38/76	**Give It Up (Turn It Loose)** . . . Tyrone Davis
40/75	**Give It What You Got** . . . B.T. Express
	Give Me ..also see: Gimme
3/70	**Give Me Just A Little More Time** . . . Chairmen Of The Board
1/73	**Give Me Love - (Give Me Peace On Earth)** . . . George Harrison
4/80	**Give Me The Night** . . . George Benson
31/73	**Give Me Your Love** . . . Barbara Mason
	Give More Power To The People ..see: (For God's Sake)
14/69	**Give Peace A Chance** . . . Plastic Ono Band
23/87	**Give To Live** . . . Sammy Hagar
30/56	**Give Us This Day** . . . Joni James
29/65	**Give Us Your Blessings** . . . Shangri-Las
34/73	**Give Your Baby A Standing Ovation** . . . Dells
8/81	**Giving It Up For Your Love** . . . Delbert McClinton
38/64	**Giving Up** . . . Gladys Knight & The Pips
38/89	**Giving Up On Love** . . . Rick Astley
4/90	**Giving You The Benefit** . . . Pebbles
3/88	**Giving You The Best That I Got** . . . Anita Baker
6/64	**Glad All Over** . . . Dave Clark Five
19/55	**Glad Rag Doll** . . . Crazy Otto
26/67	**Glad To Be Unhappy** . . . Mamas & The Papas
7/84	**Glamorous Life** . . . Sheila E.
31/89	**Glamour Boys** . . . Living Colour
37/75	**Glasshouse** . . . Temptations
8/56	**Glendora** . . . Perry Como
2/82	**Gloria** . . . Laura Branigan
10/66	**Gloria** . . . Shadows Of Knight
25/77	**Gloria** . . . Enchantment

POS/YR	RECORD TITLE/ARTIST
34/72	**Glory Bound** . . . Grass Roots
5/85	**Glory Days** . . . Bruce Springsteen
1/86	**Glory Of Love** . . . Peter Cetera
30/66	**Go Ahead And Cry** . . . Righteous Brothers
5/72	**Go All The Way** . . . Raspberries
	Go Away Little Girl
1/63	Steve Lawrence
12/66	Happenings
1/71	Donny Osmond
36/70	**Go Back** . . . Crabby Appleton
32/71	**Go Down Gamblin'** . . . Blood, Sweat & Tears
10/86	**Go Home** . . . Stevie Wonder
23/84	**Go Insane** . . . Lindsey Buckingham
5/60	**Go, Jimmy, Go** . . . Jimmy Clanton
10/65	**Go Now!** . . . Moody Blues
	Go On With The Wedding
11/56	Patti Page
39/56	Kitty Kallen & Georgie Shaw
16/67	**Go Where You Wanna Go** . . . 5th Dimension
10/77	**Go Your Own Way** . . . Fleetwood Mac
36/59	**God Bless America** . . . Connie Francis
18/61	**God, Country And My Baby** . . . Johnny Burnette
22/70	**God, Love And Rock & Roll** . . . Teegarden & Van Winkle
39/66	**God Only Knows** . . . Beach Boys
	Godfather ..see: Love Theme From The
17/82	**Goin' Down** . . . Greg Guidry
36/73	**Goin' Home** . . . Osmonds
	Goin' Out Of My Head
6/64	Little Anthony & The Imperials
7/68	Lettermen (medley)
16/57	**Goin' Steady** . . . Tommy Sands
31/88	**Going Back To Cali** . . . L.L. Cool J
35/64	**Going Going Gone** . . . Brook Benton
15/69	**Going In Circles** . . . Friends Of Distinction
	Going To A Go-Go
11/66	Miracles
25/82	Rolling Stones
11/69	**Going Up The Country** . . . Canned Heat
5/79	**Gold** . . . John Stewart
29/84	**Gold** . . . Spandau Ballet
10/76	**Golden Years** . . . David Bowie
8/65	**Goldfinger** . . . Shirley Bassey
33/86	**Goldmine** . . . Pointer Sisters
	Gone
4/57	Ferlin Husky

POS/YR	RECORD TITLE/ARTIST
24/72	Joey Heatherton
23/75	**Gone At Last** . . . Paul Simon/Phoebe Snow
31/64	**Gone, Gone, Gone** . . . Everly Brothers
23/77	**Gone Too Far** . . . England Dan & John Ford Coley
	(Gong-Gong Song) ..see: I'm Blue
18/57	**Gonna Find Me A Bluebird** . . . Marvin Rainwater
	Gonna Fly Now (Theme From 'Rocky')
1/77	Bill Conti
28/77	Maynard Ferguson
11/56	**Gonna Get Along Without Ya Now** . . . Patience & Prudence
29/67	**Gonna Give Her All The Love I've Got** . . . Jimmy Ruffin
1/91	**Gonna Make You Sweat (Everybody Dance Now)** . . . C & C Music Factory
36/69	**Goo Goo Barabajagal (Love Is Hot)** . . . Donovan
17/55	**Good And Lonesome** . . . Kay Starr
	Good Foot ..see: Get On The
39/79	**Good Friend** . . . Mary MacGregor
11/79	**Good Girls Don't** . . . Knack
	Good Golly, Miss Molly
10/58	Little Richard
4/76	Mitch Ryder (medley)
25/76	**Good Hearted Woman** . . . Waylon & Willie
18/63	**Good Life** . . . Tony Bennett
1/66	**Good Lovin'** . . . Young Rascals
30/69	**Good Lovin' Ain't Easy To Come By** . . . Marvin Gaye & Tammi Terrell
36/75	**Good Lovin' Gone Bad** . . . Bad Company
1/62	**Good Luck Charm** . . . Elvis Presley
34/73	**Good Morning Heartache** . . . Diana Ross
3/69	**Good Morning Starshine** . . . Oliver
11/64	**Good News** . . . Sam Cooke
21/69	**Good Old Rock 'N Roll (medley)** . . . Cat Mother & the All Night News Boys
2/68	**Good, The Bad And The Ugly** . . . Hugo Montenegro
1/89	**Good Thing** . . . Fine Young Cannibals
4/67	**Good Thing** . . . Paul Revere & The Raiders
11/61	**Good Time Baby** . . . Bobby Rydell
9/72	**Good Time Charlie's Got The Blues** . . . Danny O'Keefe
1/79	**Good Times** . . . Chic
11/64	**Good Times** . . . Sam Cooke
3/60	**Good Timin'** . . . Jimmy Jones

POS/YR	RECORD TITLE/ARTIST
40/79	**Good Timin'** . . . Beach Boys
	Good Vibrations
1/66	Beach Boys
34/76	Todd Rundgren
13/69	**Goodbye** . . . Mary Hopkin
17/86	**Goodbye** . . . Night Ranger
8/59	**Goodbye Baby** . . . Jack Scott
33/64	**Goodbye Baby (Baby Goodbye)** . . . Solomon Burke
3/61	**Goodbye Cruel World** . . . James Darren
15/78	**Goodbye Girl** . . . David Gates
33/86	**Goodbye Is Forever** . . . Arcadia
11/59	**Goodbye Jimmy, Goodbye** . . . Kathy Linden
31/68	**Goodbye My Love** . . . James Brown
15/79	**Goodbye Stranger** . . . Supertramp
7/72	**Goodbye To Love** . . . Carpenters
2/73	**Goodbye Yellow Brick Road** . . . Elton John
21/65	**Goodnight** . . . Roy Orbison
	Goodnight My Love
32/57	McGuire Sisters
32/63	Fleetwoods
27/69	Paul Anka
5/79	**Goodnight Tonight** . . . Wings
20/57	**Goody Goody** . . . Frankie Lymon & his Teenagers
37/68	**Goody Goody Gumdrops** . . . 1910 Fruitgum Co.
12/83	**Goody Two Shoes** . . . Adam Ant
10/85	**Goonies 'R' Good Enough** . . . Cyndi Lauper
24/60	**Got A Girl** . . . Four Preps
10/84	**Got A Hold On Me** . . . Christine McVie
39/58	**Got A Match?** . . . Daddy-O's
1/88	**Got My Mind Set On You** . . . George Harrison
12/79	**Got To Be Real** . . . Cheryl Lynn
4/71	**Got To Be There** . . . Michael Jackson
	Got To Get You Into My Life
7/76	Beatles
9/78	Earth, Wind & Fire
22/65	**Got To Get You Off My Mind** . . . Solomon Burke
1/77	**Got To Give It Up** . . . Marvin Gaye
21/70	**Gotta Hold On To This Feeling** . . . Jr. Walker & The All Stars
24/79	**Gotta Serve Somebody** . . . Bob Dylan
4/59	**Gotta Travel On** . . . Billy Grammer

POS/YR	RECORD TITLE/ARTIST
	Graduation Day
16/56	Rover Boys
17/56	Four Freshmen
34/61	**Graduation Song . . . Pomp And Circumstance** . . . Adrian Kimberly
39/59	**Graduation's Here** . . . Fleetwoods
17/63	**Grass Is Greener** . . . Brenda Lee
9/62	**Gravy (For My Mashed Potatoes)** . . . Dee Dee Sharp
	Grazing In The Grass
1/68	Hugh Masekela
3/69	Friends Of Distinction
1/78	**Grease** . . . Frankie Valli
20/66	**Great Airplane Strike** . . . Paul Revere & The Raiders
2/58	**Great Balls Of Fire** . . . Jerry Lee Lewis
	Great Imposter ..see: (He's) The
1/56	**Great Pretender** . . . Platters
	Greatest American Hero ..see: Theme From
34/62	**Greatest Hurt** . . . Jackie Wilson
	Greatest Love Of All
24/77	George Benson
1/86	Whitney Houston
	Green Berets ..see: Ballad Of
1/56	**Green Door** . . . Jim Lowe
3/70	**Green-Eyed Lady** . . . Sugarloaf
8/66	**Green Grass** . . . Gary Lewis & The Playboys
14/63	**Green, Green** . . . New Christy Minstrels
11/67	**Green, Green Grass Of Home** . . . Tom Jones
39/68	**Green Light** . . . American Breed
3/62	**Green Onions** . . . Booker T. & The MG's
2/69	**Green River** . . . Creedence Clearwater Revival
1/68	**Green Tambourine** . . . Lemon Pipers
21/63	**Greenback Dollar** . . . Kingston Trio
2/60	**Greenfields** . . . Brothers Four
4/90	**Groove Is In The Heart** . . . Deee-Lite
7/78	**Groove Line** . . . Heatwave
6/71	**Groove Me** . . . King Floyd
	Groovin'
1/67	Young Rascals
21/67	Booker T. & The M.G.'s
30/69	**Groovy Grubworm** . . . Harlow Wilcox
	Groovy Kind Of Love
2/66	Mindbenders
1/88	Phil Collins

POS/YR	RECORD TITLE/ARTIST
12/70	**Groovy Situation** . . . Gene Chandler
14/76	**Grow Some Funk Of Your Own** . . . Elton John
9/66	**Guantanamera** . . . Sandpipers
11/58	**Guess Things Happen That Way** . . . Johnny Cash
31/59	**Guess Who** . . . Jesse Belvin
3/81	**Guilty** . . . Barbra Streisand & Barry Gibb
5/59	**Guitar Boogie Shuffle** . . . Virtues
11/72	**Guitar Man** . . . Bread
	(also see: Dance With The)
28/81	**Guitar Man** . . . Elvis Presley
10/55	**Gum Drop** . . . Crew-Cuts
12/82	**Gypsy** . . . Fleetwood Mac
24/63	**Gypsy Cried** . . . Lou Christie
8/73	**Gypsy Man** . . . War
	Gypsy Woman
20/61	Impressions
3/70	Brian Hyland
8/91	**Gypsy Woman (She's Homeless)** . . . Crystal Waters
1/71	**Gypsys, Tramps & Thieves** . . . Cher

H

POS/YR	RECORD TITLE/ARTIST
2/69	**Hair** . . . Cowsills
22/66	**Hair On My Chinny Chin Chin** . . . Sam The Sham & The Pharoahs
1/73	**Half-Breed** . . . Cher
12/63	**Half Heaven - Half Heartache** . . . Gene Pitney
15/79	**Half The Way** . . . Crystal Gayle
	Halfway To Paradise
39/61	Tony Orlando
23/68	Bobby Vinton
33/71	**Hallelujah** . . . Sweathog
28/73	**Hallelujah Day** . . . Jackson 5
	Hand Jive ..see: Willie And The Hand Jive
17/70	**Hand Me Down World** . . . Guess Who
19/83	**Hand To Hold On To** . . . John Cougar
2/88	**Hands To Heaven** . . . Breathe
	Handy Man
2/60	Jimmy Jones
22/64	Del Shannon

POS/YR	RECORD TITLE/ARTIST
4/77	James Taylor
9/69	**Hang 'Em High** . . . Booker T. & The MG's
20/82	**Hang Fire** . . . Rolling Stones
23/91	**Hang In Long Enough** . . . Phil Collins
8/74	**Hang On In There Baby** . . . Johnny Bristol
	Hang On Sloopy
26/64	Vibrations (My Girl)
1/65	McCoys
11/65	Ramsey Lewis Trio
24/58	**Hang Up My Rock And Roll Shoes** . . . Chuck Willis
	Hangin' On ..see: (You Keep Me)
1/89	**Hangin' Tough** . . . New Kids On The Block
35/86	**Hanging On A Heart Attack** . . . Device
38/59	**Hanging Tree** . . . Marty Robbins
1/66	**Hanky Panky** . . . Tommy James & The Shondells
10/90	**Hanky Panky** . . . Madonna
	Happening, The
1/67	Supremes
32/67	Herb Alpert
30/66	**Happenings Ten Years Time Ago** . . . Yardbirds
11/72	**Happiest Girl In The Whole U.S.A.** . . . Donna Fargo
30/79	**Happiness** . . . Pointer Sisters
35/74	**Happiness Is Just Around The Bend** . . . Main Ingredient
	Happiness Street
20/56	Georgia Gibbs
38/56	Tony Bennett
20/87	**Happy** . . . Surface
22/72	**Happy** . . . Rolling Stones
16/78	**Happy Anniversary** . . . Little River Band
30/61	**Happy Birthday Blues** . . . Kathy Young with The Innocents
6/62	**Happy Birthday, Sweet Sixteen** . . . Neil Sedaka
5/76	**Happy Days** . . . Pratt & McClain
10/60	**Happy-Go-Lucky-Me** . . . Paul Evans
5/57	**Happy, Happy Birthday Baby** . . . Tune Weavers
22/69	**Happy Heart** . . . Andy Williams
24/67	**Happy Jack** . . . Who
19/76	**Happy Music** . . . Blackbyrds
1/59	**Happy Organ** . . . Dave 'Baby' Cortez
40/75	**Happy People** . . . Temptations

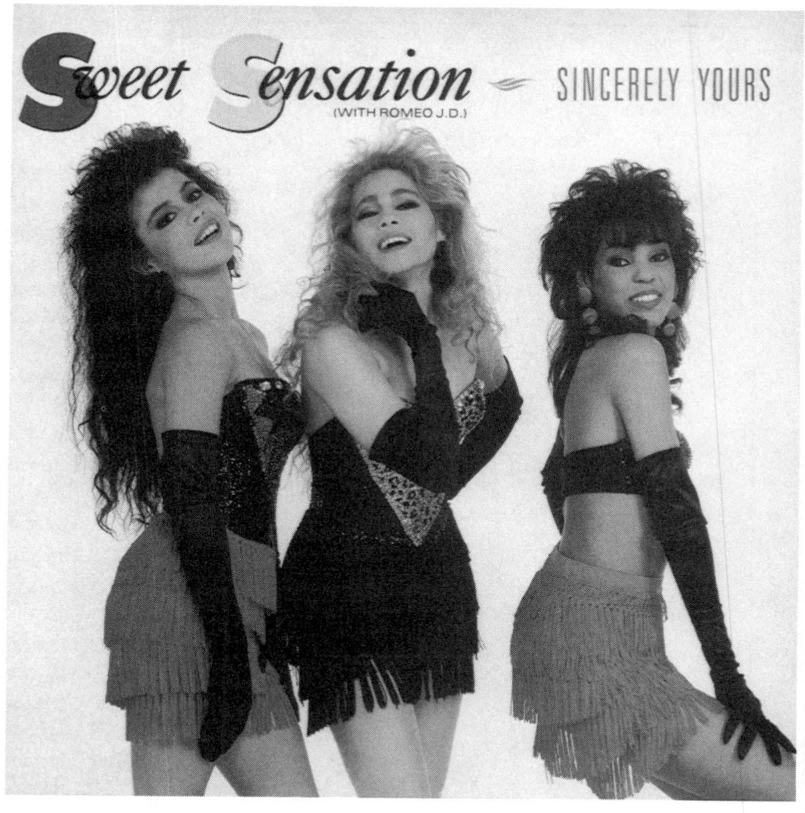

Keith Sweat's two platinum albums spawned many hits, of which one—1990's "Make You Sweat"—may have been the artist's favorite for its title alone.

Sweet Sensation's 1990 single "If Wishes Came True" was the first No. 1 hit for the revitalized Atco label since Yes's 1984 smash "Owner Of A Lonely Heart." Another group with the same name had a top-40 hit in 1975.

Ta-Mara & The Seen's "Everybody Dance" was viewed by many as part of Prince's mid-80s talent invasion. Produced by Jesse Johnson, formerly of the Time, the Minneapolis group featured guitarist Oliver Leiber—who later produced Paula Abdul with great success.

Technotronic featuring Felly, a truly international dance outfit, featured Belgian producer Jo Bogaert and two Zairean rappers, among others. The group's first single, 1990's "Pump Up The Jam," provided new label SBK with its first-ever gold record.

The Temptations' track record for soul hits can barely be topped. Among their 37 top-40 singles, 15 made the Top 10 and four reached No. 1—including 1965's "My Girl," 1969's "I Can't Get Next To You," 1971's "Just My Imagination (Running Away With Me)," and 1972's "Papa Was A Rollin' Stone." Former Tempts vocalist David Ruffin died in 1991.

10cc's highest-charting hit, 1975's "I'm Not In Love," was their very first—under that name. Five years earlier, three-fourths of the quartet scored the No. 22 hit "Neanderthal Man" as Hotlegs.

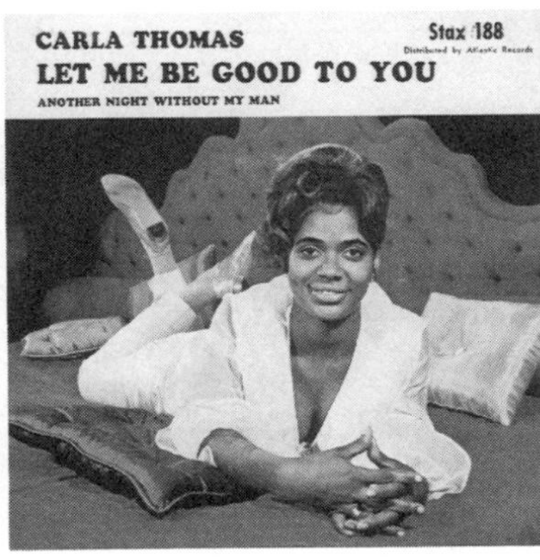

Carla Thomas's 1961 single "Gee Whiz (Look At His Eyes,)" her first top-10 hit, is one of the highlights of the nine-volume Stax/Volt boxed set issued by Atlantic in 1991. Atlantic also reissued her classic *King & Queen* album, made with Otis Redding, the same year.

Tiffany proved that teen music could span two decades in the late 80s with two interesting covers: "I Think We're Alone Now," her No. 1 version of the Tommy James classic, and "I Saw Him Standing There," her take on the Beatles' 1964 hit.

The Tokens' all-time greatest hit, "The Lion Sleeps Tonight"—their version of the South African song "Wimoweh"—stayed at No. 1 for three weeks in late 1961. Members of the group released an Atco album under the name of Cross Country in 1973.

Tina Turner's enormous commercial comeback of the mid-80s—she had five top-10 records in two years—is superbly documented on Capitol Records' 1991 compilation *Simply the Best*. One highlight: Phil Spector's specially-remastered version of Ike & Tina's classic non-hit, "River Deep—Mountain High."

The Turtles helped introduce folk-rock to the 60s pop music scene. Appropriately, their first top-10 single, 1965's "It Ain't Me, Babe," was penned by Bob Dylan, and their last, 1969's "You Showed Me," by Jim McGuinn and Gene Clark—of fellow folk-rockers the Byrds.

Frankie Valli, the Four Seasons' perpetual falsetto, departed the Top 10 in typical cool style. His last hit—"Grease," from the film of the same name—held the No. 1 spot for two weeks in 1978. Other solo top-10 hits included 1967's "Can't Take My Eyes Off You" and 1975's "My Eyes Adored You."

THE TURTLES
She'd Rather Be With Me
WHITE WHALE

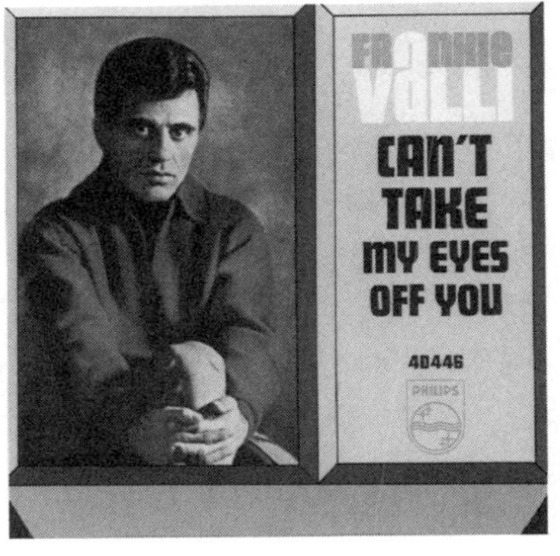

POS/YR	RECORD TITLE/ARTIST
34/59	**Happy Reindeer** . . . Dancer, Prancer & Nervous
25/68	**Happy Song (Dum-Dum)** . . . Otis Redding
27/66	**Happy Summer Days** . . . Ronnie Dove
1/67	**Happy Together** . . . Turtles
6/56	**Happy Whistler** . . . Don Robertson
8/60	**Harbor Lights** . . . Platters
	Hard Day's Night
1/64	Beatles
29/66	Ramsey Lewis Trio
3/84	**Hard Habit To Break** . . . Chicago
1/58	**Hard Headed Woman** . . . Elvis Presley
15/77	**Hard Luck Woman** . . . Kiss
30/77	**Hard Rock Cafe** . . . Carole King
4/55	**Hard To Get** . . . Gisele MacKenzie
26/91	**Hard To Handle** . . . Black Crowes
7/81	**Hard To Say** . . . Dan Fogelberg
1/82	**Hard To Say I'm Sorry** . . . Chicago
3/82	**Harden My Heart** . . . Quarterflash
39/66	**Harlem Nocturne** . . . Viscounts
5/86	**Harlem Shuffle** . . . Rolling Stones
1/68	**Harper Valley P.T.A.** . . . Jeannie C. Riley
31/73	**Harry Hippie** . . . Bobby Womack
17/63	**Harry The Hairy Ape** . . . Ray Stevens
13/75	**Harry Truman** . . . Chicago
5/61	**Hats Off To Larry** . . . Del Shannon
11/64	**Haunted House** . . . Gene Simmons
31/62	**Have A Good Time** . . . Sue Thompson
5/64	**Have I The Right?** . . . Honeycombs
29/57	**Have I Told You Lately That I Love You?** . . . Ricky Nelson
8/71	**Have You Ever Seen The Rain** . . . Creedence Clearwater Revival
18/63	**Have You Heard** . . . Duprees
24/65	**Have You Looked Into Your Heart** . . . Jerry Vale
1/75	**Have You Never Been Mellow** . . . Olivia Newton-John
	Have You Seen Her
3/71	Chi-Lites
4/90	M.C. Hammer
	(Have You Seen My Wife Mr. Jones) ..see: New York Mining Disaster 1941
9/66	**Have You Seen Your Mother, Baby, Standing In The Shadow?** . . . Rolling Stones
14/74	**Haven't Got Time For The Pain** . . . Carly Simon
26/79	**Haven't Stopped Dancing Yet** . . . Gonzalez
17/62	**Having A Party** . . . Sam Cooke
	Having My Baby ..see: (You're)
4/69	**Hawaii Five-O** . . . Ventures
33/65	**Hawaii Tattoo** . . . Waikikis
11/59	**Hawaiian Wedding Song** . . . Andy Williams
	Hazy Shade Of Winter
13/66	Simon & Garfunkel
2/88	Bangles
	He
4/55	Al Hibbler
10/55	McGuire Sisters
18/66	Righteous Brothers
	He Ain't Heavy, He's My Brother
7/70	Hollies
20/70	Neil Diamond
33/81	**He Can't Love You** . . . Michael Stanley Band
	He Don't Love You (Like I Love You)
7/60	Jerry Butler
1/75	Tony Orlando & Dawn
34/62	**He Knows I Love Him Too Much** . . . Paris Sisters
	He Will Break Your Heart ..see: He Don't Love You
	He'll Have To Go (Stay)
2/60	Jim Reeves
4/60	Jeanne Black
25/86	**He'll Never Love You (Like I Do)** . . . Freddie Jackson
36/76	**He's A Friend** . . . Eddie Kendricks
30/81	**He's A Liar** . . . Bee Gees
1/62	**He's A Rebel** . . . Crystals
1/58	**He's Got The Whole World (In His Hands)** . . . Laurie London
16/57	**He's Mine** . . . Platters
14/61	**(He's My) Dreamboat** . . . Connie Francis
1/63	**He's So Fine** . . . Chiffons
3/80	**He's So Shy** . . . Pointer Sisters
11/63	**He's Sure The Boy I Love** . . . Crystals
30/61	**(He's) The Great Impostor** . . . Fleetwoods
9/79	**He's The Greatest Dancer** . . . Sister Sledge
14/79	**Head Games** . . . Foreigner
3/85	**Head Over Heels** . . . Tears For Fears
11/84	**Head Over Heels** . . . go-go's
1/87	**Head To Toe** . . . Lisa Lisa & Cult Jam
35/80	**Headed For A Fall** . . . Firefall

POS/YR	RECORD TITLE/ARTIST
19/89	**Headed For A Heartbreak** . . . Winger
13/89	**Healing Hands** . . . Elton John
14/77	**Heard It In A Love Song** . . . Marshall Tucker Band
	Heart
6/55	Eddie Fisher
13/55	Four Aces
4/87	**Heart And Soul** . . . T'Pau
8/83	**Heart And Soul** . . . Huey Lewis & the News
	Heart And Soul
18/61	Cleftones
25/61	Jan & Dean
3/82	**Heart Attack** . . . Olivia Newton-John
9/65	**Heart Full Of Soul** . . . Yardbirds
21/80	**Heart Hotels** . . . Dan Fogelberg
15/62	**Heart In Hand** . . . Brenda Lee
24/81	**Heart Like A Wheel** . . . Steve Miller Band
32/90	**Heart Like A Wheel** . . . Human League
1/79	**Heart Of Glass** . . . Blondie
1/72	**Heart Of Gold** . . . Neil Young
35/88	**Heart Of Mine** . . . Boz Scaggs
6/84	**Heart Of Rock & Roll** . . . Huey Lewis & the News
12/90	**Heart Of Stone** . . . Taylor Dayne
19/65	**Heart Of Stone** . . . Rolling Stones
20/90	**Heart Of Stone** . . . Cher
21/90	**Heart Of The Matter** . . . Don Henley
20/79	**Heart Of The Night** . . . Poco
25/83	**Heart Of The Night** . . . Juice Newton
15/83	**Heart To Heart** . . . Kenny Loggins
1/79	**Heartache Tonight** . . . Eagles
7/61	**Heartaches** . . . Marcels
	Heartaches By The Number
1/59	Guy Mitchell
35/65	Johnny Tillotson
5/86	**Heartbeat** . . . Don Johnson
13/90	**Heartbeat** . . . Seduction
3/73	**Heartbeat - It's A Lovebeat** . . . DeFranco Family
26/87	**Heartbreak Beat** . . . Psychedelic Furs
1/56	**Heartbreak Hotel** . . . Elvis Presley
22/81	**Heartbreak Hotel** . . . Jacksons
38/60	**Heartbreak (It's Hurtin' Me)** . . . Little Willie John
39/74	**Heartbreak Kid** . . . Bo Donaldson & The Heywoods
10/83	**Heartbreaker** . . . Dionne Warwick

POS/YR	RECORD TITLE/ARTIST
	(also see: Doo Doo Doo Doo)
23/80	**Heartbreaker** . . . Pat Benatar
37/78	**Heartbreaker** . . . Dolly Parton
24/78	**Heartless** . . . Heart
5/82	**Heartlight** . . . Neil Diamond
8/81	**Hearts** . . . Marty Balin
	Hearts Of Stone
1/55	Fontane Sisters
15/55	Charms
20/61	Bill Black's Combo
37/73	Blue Ridge Rangers
19/81	**Hearts On Fire** . . . Randy Meisner
26/87	**Hearts On Fire** . . . Bryan Adams
2/85	**Heat Is On** . . . Glenn Frey
4/82	**Heat Of The Moment** . . . Asia
19/91	**Heat Of The Moment** . . . After 7
6/87	**Heat Of The Night** . . . Bryan Adams
	Heat Wave
4/63	Martha & The Vandellas
5/75	Linda Ronstadt
29/69	**Heather Honey** . . . Tommy Roe
1/85	**Heaven** . . . Bryan Adams
2/89	**Heaven** . . . Warrant
39/69	**Heaven** . . . Rascals
5/89	**Heaven Help Me** . . . Deon Estus/George Michael
9/70	**Heaven Help Us All** . . . Stevie Wonder
12/86	**Heaven In Your Eyes** . . . Loverboy
1/87	**Heaven Is A Place On Earth** . . . Belinda Carlisle
4/79	**Heaven Knows** . . . Donna Summer
24/69	**Heaven Knows** . . . Grass Roots
15/76	**Heaven Must Be Missing An Angel** . . . Tavares
11/79	**Heaven Must Have Sent You** . . . Bonnie Pointer
39/56	**Heaven On Earth** . . . Platters
6/77	**Heaven On The 7th Floor** . . . Paul Nicholas
40/59	**Heavenly Lover** . . . Teresa Brewer
27/71	**Heavy Makes You Happy (Sha-Na-Boom Boom)** . . . Staple Singers
33/70	**Heed The Call** . . . Kenny Rogers & The First Edition
10/74	**Helen Wheels** . . . Paul McCartney
1/84	**Hello** . . . Lionel Richie
6/81	**Hello Again** . . . Neil Diamond
20/84	**Hello Again** . . . Cars

POS/YR	RECORD TITLE/ARTIST
1/64	**Hello, Dolly!** . . . Louis Armstrong
1/67	**Hello Goodbye** . . . Beatles
26/63	**Hello Heartache, Goodbye Love** . . . Little Peggy March
26/67	**Hello Hello** . . . Sopwith "Camel"
35/73	**Hello Hurray** . . . Alice Cooper
1/68	**Hello, I Love You** . . . Doors
5/73	**Hello It's Me** . . . Todd Rundgren
9/61	**Hello Mary Lou** . . . Ricky Nelson
2/63	**Hello Mudduh, Hello Fadduh! (A Letter From Camp)** . . . Allan Sherman
24/76	**Hello Old Friend** . . . Eric Clapton
	Hello Stranger
3/63	Barbara Lewis
15/77	Yvonne Elliman
12/61	**Hello Walls** . . . Faron Young
23/60	**Hello Young Lovers** . . . Paul Anka
1/65	**Help!** . . . Beatles
14/77	**Help Is On Its Way** . . . Little River Band
7/74	**Help Me** . . . Joni Mitchell
	Help Me Girl
29/66	Animals
37/66	Outsiders
	Help Me Make It Through The Night
8/71	Sammi Smith
33/72	Gladys Knight & The Pips
	Help Me, Rhonda
1/65	Beach Boys
22/75	Johnny Rivers
35/68	**Help Yourself** . . . Tom Jones
6/62	**Her Royal Majesty** . . . James Darren
11/81	**Her Town Too** . . . James Taylor & J.D. Souther
6/90	**Here And Now** . . . Luther Vandross
23/77	**Here Come Those Tears Again** . . . Jackson Browne
13/67	**Here Comes My Baby** . . . Tremeloes
14/59	**Here Comes Summer** . . . Jerry Keller
15/71	**Here Comes That Rainy Day Feeling Again** . . . Fortunes
	Here Comes The Judge
8/68	Shorty Long
19/68	Pigmeat Markham
24/65	**Here Comes The Night** . . . Them
4/84	**Here Comes The Rain Again** . . . Eurythmics
16/71	**Here Comes The Sun** . . . Richie Havens
	Here I Am (Come And Take Me)
10/73	Al Green
7/91	UB40
5/81	**Here I Am (Just When I Thought I Was Over You)** . . . Air Supply
1/87	**Here I Go Again** . . . Whitesnake
37/69	**Here I Go Again** . . . Miracles
27/65	**Here It Comes Again** . . . Fortunes
6/90	**Here We Are** . . . Gloria Estefan
3/91	**Here We Go** . . . C & C Music Factory
15/67	**Here We Go Again** . . . Ray Charles
20/88	**Here With Me** . . . REO Speedwagon
3/78	**Here You Come Again** . . . Dolly Parton
12/67	**Heroes And Villains** . . . Beach Boys
1/62	**Hey! Baby** . . . Bruce Channel
18/89	**Hey Baby** . . . Henry Lee Summer
12/67	**Hey Baby (They're Playing Our Song)** . . . Buckinghams
19/72	**Hey Big Brother** . . . Rare Earth
23/64	**Hey, Bobba Needle** . . . Chubby Checker
7/78	**Hey Deanie** . . . Shaun Cassidy
	Hey, Girl
10/63	Freddie Scott
35/68	Bobby Vee (medley)
9/72	Donny Osmond
35/73	**Hey Girl (I Like Your Style)** . . . Temptations
29/64	**Hey Harmonica Man** . . . Stevie Wonder
3/57	**Hey! Jealous Lover** . . . Frank Sinatra
32/64	**Hey Jean, Hey Dean** . . . Dean & Jean
31/66	**Hey Joe** . . . Leaves
	Hey Jude
1/68	Beatles
23/69	Wilson Pickett
36/89	**Hey Ladies** . . . Beastie Boys
35/70	**Hey Lawdy Mama** . . . Steppenwolf
31/67	**Hey, Leroy, Your Mama's Callin' You** . . . Jimmy Castor
20/62	**Hey, Let's Twist** . . . Joey Dee & The Starliters
4/64	**Hey Little Cobra** . . . Rip Chords
13/63	**Hey Little Girl** . . . Major Lance
20/59	**Hey Little Girl** . . . Dee Clark
29/57	**Hey! Little Girl** . . . Techniques
38/62	**Hey! Little Girl** . . . Del Shannon
12/55	**Hey, Mr. Banjo** . . . Sunnysiders
24/70	**Hey, Mister Sun** . . . Bobby Sherman
10/81	**Hey Nineteen** . . . Steely Dan
1/63	**Hey Paula** . . . Paul & Paula

POS/YR	RECORD TITLE/ARTIST
	Hey There Lonely Girl (Boy)
27/63	Ruby & The Romantics
2/70	Eddie Holman
31/80	Robert John
16/68	**Hey, Western Union Man** . . . Jerry Butler
1/75	**(Hey Won't You Play) Another Somebody Done Somebody Wrong Song** . . . B.J. Thomas
21/75	**Hey You** . . . Bachman-Turner Overdrive
14/70	**Hi-De-Ho** . . . Blood, Sweat & Tears
	Hi-Heel Sneakers
11/64	Tommy Tucker
25/68	Jose Feliciano
10/73	**Hi, Hi, Hi** . . . Wings
33/62	**Hide & Go Seek** . . . Bunker Hill
29/61	**Hide Away** . . . Freddy King
21/58	**Hideaway** . . . Four Esquires
20/62	**Hide 'Nor Hair** . . . Ray Charles
3/91	**High Enough** . . . Damn Yankees
	High-Heel ..see: Hi-Heel
30/59	**High Hopes** . . . Frank Sinatra
8/85	**High On You** . . . Survivor
21/58	**High School Confidential** . . . Jerry Lee Lewis
17/77	**High School Dance** . . . Sylvers
28/59	**High School U.S.A.** . . . Tommy Facenda
37/58	**High Sign** . . . Diamonds
22/71	**High Time We Went** . . . Joe Cocker
	Higher & Higher ..see: (Your Love Keeps Lifting Me)
4/73	**Higher Ground** . . . Stevie Wonder
1/86	**Higher Love** . . . Steve Winwood
37/74	**Higher Plane** . . . Kool & The Gang
26/79	**Highway Song** . . . Blackfoot
14/75	**Hijack** . . . Herbie Mann
	Hill Street Blues ..see: Theme From
6/80	**Him** . . . Rupert Holmes
5/67	**Him Or Me - What's It Gonna Be?** . . . Paul Revere & The Raiders
31/68	**Hip City** . . . Jr. Walker & The All Stars
37/67	**Hip Hug-Her** . . . Booker T. & The M.G.'s
3/86	**Hip To Be Square** . . . Huey Lewis & the News
24/64	**Hippy Hippy Shake** . . . Swinging Blue Jeans
14/90	**Hippychick** . . . Soho
	His Latest Flame ..see: (Marie's the Name)
39/66	**History Repeats Itself** . . . Buddy Starcher

POS/YR	RECORD TITLE/ARTIST
9/80	**Hit Me With Your Best Shot** . . . Pat Benatar
	(Hit Record) ..see: Overnight Sensation
	Hit The Road Jack
1/61	Ray Charles
40/76	Stampeders
30/63	**Hitch Hike** . . . Marvin Gaye
34/68	**Hitch It To The Horse** . . . Fantastic Johnny C
5/70	**Hitchin' A Ride** . . . Vanity Fare
9/73	**Hocus Pocus** . . . Focus
35/76	**Hold Back The Night** . . . Trammps
14/72	**Hold Her Tight** . . . Osmonds
4/82	**Hold Me** . . . Fleetwood Mac
3/84	**Hold Me Now** . . . Thompson Twins
8/65	**Hold Me, Thrill Me, Kiss Me** . . . Mel Carter
5/68	**Hold Me Tight** . . . Johnny Nash
40/83	**Hold Me 'Til The Mornin' Comes** . . . Paul Anka
1/90	**Hold On** . . . Wilson Phillips
2/90	**Hold On** . . . En Vogue
15/82	**Hold On** . . . Santana
18/79	**Hold On** . . . Ian Gomm
38/79	**Hold On** . . . Triumph
40/80	**Hold On** . . . Kansas
21/66	**Hold On! I'm A Comin'** . . . Sam & Dave
27/81	**Hold On Loosely** . . . .38 Special
10/81	**Hold On Tight** . . . ELO
10/80	**Hold On To My Love** . . . Jimmy Ruffin
1/88	**Hold On To The Nights** . . . Richard Marx
5/79	**Hold The Line** . . . Toto
5/65	**Hold What You've Got** . . . Joe Tex
3/91	**Hold You Tight** . . . Tara Kemp
5/72	**Hold Your Head Up** . . . Argent
37/82	**Holdin' On** . . . Tane Cain
17/75	**Holdin' On To Yesterday** . . . Ambrosia
1/86	**Holding Back The Years** . . . Simply Red
11/89	**Holding On** . . . Steve Winwood
34/84	**Holding Out For A Hero** . . . Bonnie Tyler
16/67	**Holiday** . . . Bee Gees
16/84	**Holiday** . . . Madonna
29/87	**Holiday** . . . Other Ones
6/69	**Holly Holy** . . . Neil Diamond
32/77	**Hollywood** . . . Rufus Featuring Chaka Khan
12/78	**Hollywood Nights** . . . Bob Seger

POS/YR	RECORD TITLE/ARTIST
6/74	**Hollywood Swinging** . . . Kool & The Gang
23/66	**Holy Cow** . . . Lee Dorsey
34/67	**Homburg** . . . Procol Harum
28/79	**Home And Dry** . . . Gerry Rafferty
25/65	**Home Of The Brave** . . . Jody Miller
5/66	**Homeward Bound** . . . Simon & Garfunkel
28/60	**Honest I Do** . . . Innocents
32/57	**Honest I Do** . . . Jimmy Reed
23/88	**Honestly** . . . Stryper
24/79	**Honesty** . . . Billy Joel
1/68	**Honey** . . . Bobby Goldsboro
6/55	**Honey-Babe** . . . Art Mooney
11/67	**Honey Chile** . . . Martha & The Vandellas
19/70	**Honey Come Back** . . . Glen Campbell
27/74	**Honey, Honey** . . . Abba
1/57	**Honeycomb** . . . Jimmie Rodgers
19/87	**Honeythief, The** . . . Hipsway
8/72	**Honky Cat** . . . Elton John
2/56	**Honky Tonk (Parts 1 & 2)** . . . Bill Doggett
1/69	**Honky Tonk Women** . . . Rolling Stones
11/63	**Honolulu Lulu** . . . Jan & Dean
23/61	**Hoochi Coochi Coo** . . . Hank Ballard
17/64	**Hooka Tooka** . . . Chubby Checker
	Hooked On A Feeling
5/69	B.J. Thomas
1/74	Blue Swede
10/82	**Hooked On Classics** . . . Royal Philharmonic Orchestra
31/82	**Hooked On Swing (medley)** . . . Larry Elgart
23/89	**Hooked On You** . . . Sweet Sensation
6/66	**Hooray For Hazel** . . . Tommy Roe
38/63	**Hootenanny** . . . Glencoves
36/82	**Hope You Love Me Like You Say You Do** . . . Huey Lewis & the News
13/63	**Hopeless** . . . Andy Williams
3/78	**Hopelessly Devoted To You** . . . Olivia Newton-John
2/68	**Horse, The** . . . Cliff Nobles & Co.
1/72	**Horse With No Name** . . . America
3/78	**Hot Blooded** . . . Foreigner
1/78	**Hot Child In The City** . . . Nick Gilder
1/56	**Hot Diggity (Dog Ziggity Boom)** . . . Perry Como
2/69	**Hot Fun In The Summertime** . . . Sly & The Family Stone
11/83	**Hot Girls In Love** . . . Loverboy

POS/YR	RECORD TITLE/ARTIST
23/82	**Hot In The City** . . . Billy Idol
28/78	**Hot Legs** . . . Rod Stewart
5/77	**Hot Line** . . . Sylvers
31/78	**Hot Love, Cold World** . . . Bob Welch
21/79	**Hot Number** . . . Foxy
15/71	**Hot Pants** . . . James Brown
11/63	**Hot Pastrami** . . . Dartells
36/63	**Hot Pastrami With Mashed Potatoes** . . . Joey Dee
15/80	**Hot Rod Hearts** . . . Robbie Dupree
	Hot Rod Lincoln
26/60	Johnny Bond
33/60	Charlie Ryan
9/72	Commander Cody
14/69	**Hot Smoke & Sasafrass** . . . Bubble Puppy
1/79	**Hot Stuff** . . . Donna Summer
18/79	**Hot Summer Nights** . . . Night
1/77	**Hotel California** . . . Eagles
3/63	**Hotel Happiness** . . . Brook Benton
1/56	**Hound Dog** . . . Elvis Presley
9/59	**Hound Dog Man** . . . Fabian
15/87	**Hourglass** . . . Squeeze
9/55	**House Of Blue Lights** . . . Chuck Miller
28/90	**House Of Pain** . . . Faster Pussycat
	House Of The Rising Sun
1/64	Animals
7/70	Frijid Pink
6/68	**House That Jack Built** . . . Aretha Franklin
16/56	**House With Love In It** . . . Four Lads
21/65	**Houston** . . . Dean Martin
33/60	**How About That** . . . Dee Clark
	How Am I Supposed To Live Without You
12/83	Laura Branigan
1/90	Michael Bolton
22/58	**How Are Ya' Fixed For Love?** . . . Frank Sinatra & Keely Smith
12/81	**How 'Bout Us** . . . Champaign
	How Can I Be Sure
4/67	Young Rascals
25/72	David Cassidy
11/91	**How Can I Ease The Pain** . . . Lisa Fischer
3/88	**How Can I Fall?** . . . Breathe
22/73	**How Can I Tell Her** . . . Lobo
3/90	**How Can We Be Lovers** . . . Michael Bolton
1/71	**How Can You Mend A Broken Heart** . . . Bee Gees
1/77	**How Deep Is Your Love** . . . Bee Gees
10/80	**How Do I Make You** . . . Linda Ronstadt

POS/YR	RECORD TITLE/ARTIST
22/80	**How Do I Survive** . . . Amy Holland
27/67	**How Do You Catch A Girl** . . . Sam The Sham & The Pharoahs
8/72	**How Do You Do?** . . . Mouth & Macneal
9/64	**How Do You Do It?** . . . Gerry & The Pacemakers
30/80	**How Does It Feel To Be Back** . . . Daryl Hall & John Oates
7/66	**How Does That Grab You, Darlin'?** . . . Nancy Sinatra
	How Glad I Am ..see: (You Don't Know)
	How Important Can It Be?
2/55	Joni James
12/55	Sarah Vaughan
13/56	**(How Little It Matters) How Little We Know** . . . Frank Sinatra
3/75	**How Long** . . . Ace
20/75	**How Long (Betcha' Got A Chick On The Side)** . . . Pointer Sisters
27/83	**How Many Times Can We Say Goodbye** . . . Dionne Warwick & Luther Vandross
3/78	**How Much I Feel** . . . Ambrosia
35/91	**How Much Is Enough** . . . Fixx
17/77	**How Much Love** . . . Leo Sayer
	How Sweet It Is (To Be Loved By You)
6/65	Marvin Gaye
18/66	Jr. Walker & The All Stars
5/75	James Taylor
11/58	**How The Time Flies** . . . Jerry Wallace
20/86	**(How To Be A) Millionaire** . . . ABC
25/91	**How To Dance** . . . Bingoboys Feat. Princessa
1/86	**How Will I Know** . . . Whitney Houston
12/78	**How You Gonna See Me Now** . . . Alice Cooper
21/68	**How'd We Ever Get This Way** . . . Andy Kim
14/60	**Hucklebuck, The** . . . Chubby Checker
	Hula Hoop Song
32/58	Georgia Gibbs
38/58	Teresa Brewer
9/57	**Hula Love** . . . Buddy Knox
25/62	**Hully Gully Baby** . . . Dovells
1/86	**Human** . . . Human League
7/83	**Human Nature** . . . Michael Jackson
18/83	**Human Touch** . . . Rick Springfield
	Hummingbird
7/55	Les Paul & Mary Ford
17/55	Frankie Laine

POS/YR	RECORD TITLE/ARTIST
20/73	**Hummingbird** . . . Seals & Crofts
11/90	**Humpty Dance** . . . Digital Underground
3/61	**Hundred Pounds Of Clay** . . . Gene McDaniels
6/66	**Hungry** . . . Paul Revere & The Raiders
4/88	**Hungry Eyes** . . . Eric Carmen
27/65	**Hungry For Love** . . . San Remo Golden Strings
5/80	**Hungry Heart** . . . Bruce Springsteen
3/83	**Hungry Like The Wolf** . . . Duran Duran
13/67	**Hunter Gets Captured By The Game** . . . Marvelettes
5/68	**Hurdy Gurdy Man** . . . Donovan
33/76	**Hurricane** . . . Bob Dylan
	Hurt
4/61	Timi Yuro
28/76	Elvis Presley
31/73	**Hurt, The** . . . Cat Stevens
	Hurt So Bad
10/65	Little Anthony & The Imperials
12/69	Lettermen
8/80	Linda Ronstadt
	Hurt Yourself ..see: (You're Gonna)
2/72	**Hurting Each Other** . . . Carpenters
2/82	**Hurts So Good** . . . John Cougar
24/73	**Hurts So Good** . . . Millie Jackson
26/66	**Husbands And Wives** . . . Roger Miller
4/68	**Hush** . . . Deep Purple
8/65	**Hush, Hush, Sweet Charlotte** . . . Patti Page
20/59	**Hushabye** . . . Mystics
1/75	**Hustle, The** . . . Van McCoy
33/86	**Hyperactive** . . . Robert Palmer
36/87	**Hypnotize Me** . . . Wang Chung
21/67	**Hypnotized** . . . Linda Jones
10/88	**Hysteria** . . . Def Leppard

I

POS/YR	RECORD TITLE/ARTIST
26/82	**I.G.Y. (What A Beautiful World)** . . . Donald Fagen
35/76	**I.O.U.** . . . Jimmy Dean
25/63	**I Adore Him** . . . Angels

POS/YR	RECORD TITLE/ARTIST
11/81	**I Ain't Gonna Stand For It** . . . Stevie Wonder
	I Ain't Got Nobody ..see: Just A Gigolo
36/71	**I Ain't Got Time Anymore** . . . Glass Bottle
24/59	**I Ain't Never** . . . Webb Pierce
1/56	**I Almost Lost My Mind** . . . Pat Boone
3/66	**I Am A Rock** . . . Simon & Garfunkel
18/86	**I Am By Your Side** . . . Corey Hart
4/71	**I Am...I Said** . . . Neil Diamond
15/75	**I Am Love** . . . Jackson 5
39/70	**I Am Somebody** . . . Johnnie Taylor
1/72	**I Am Woman** . . . Helen Reddy
8/58	**I Beg Of You** . . . Elvis Presley
15/89	**I Beg Your Pardon** . . . Kon Kan
33/64	**I Believe** . . . Bachelors
33/82	**I Believe** . . . Chilliwack
22/72	**I Believe In Music** . . . Gallery
24/80	**I Believe In You** . . . Don Williams
11/73	**I Believe In You (You Believe In Me)** . . . Johnnie Taylor
15/75	**(I Believe) There's Nothing Stronger Than Our Love** . . . Paul Anka/Odia Coates
27/77	**I Believe You** . . . Dorothy Moore
27/75	**I Belong To You** . . . Love Unlimited
	I Can Dance ..see: Long Tall Glasses
6/84	**I Can Dream About You** . . . Dan Hartman
24/69	**I Can Hear Music** . . . Beach Boys
1/74	**I Can Help** . . . Billy Swan
32/66	**I Can Make It With You** . . . Pozo-Seco Singers
6/65	**I Can Never Go Home Anymore** . . . Shangri-Las
1/72	**I Can See Clearly Now** . . . Johnny Nash
9/67	**I Can See For Miles** . . . Who
	(I Can See It In Your Eyes) ..see: Circle Is Small
22/69	**I Can Sing A Rainbow (medley)** . . . Dells
39/81	**I Can Take Care Of Myself** . . . Billy & The Beaters
22/68	**I Can Take Or Leave Your Loving** . . . Herman's Hermits
35/73	**I Can Understand It** . . . New Birth
26/84	**I Can't Drive 55** . . . Sammy Hagar
1/69	**I Can't Get Next To You** . . . Temptations
	(I Can't Get No) Satisfaction
1/65	Rolling Stones
31/66	Otis Redding

POS/YR	RECORD TITLE/ARTIST
1/82	**I Can't Go For That (No Can Do)** . . . Daryl Hall & John Oates
34/66	**I Can't Grow Peaches On A Cherry Tree** . . . Just Us
29/76	**I Can't Hear You No More** . . . Helen Reddy
12/80	**I Can't Help It** . . . Andy Gibb & Olivia Newton-John
24/62	**I Can't Help It (If I'm Still In Love With You)** . . . Johnny Tillotson
	I Can't Help Myself
1/65	Four Tops
22/72	Donnie Elbert
40/80	Bonnie Pointer
39/60	**(I Can't Help You) I'm Falling Too** . . . Skeeter Davis
	(also see: Please Help Me, I'm Falling)
13/84	**I Can't Hold Back** . . . Survivor
31/80	**I Can't Let Go** . . . Linda Ronstadt
22/56	**I Can't Love You Enough** . . . LaVern Baker
28/69	**I Can't See Myself Leaving You** . . . Aretha Franklin
10/81	**I Can't Stand It** . . . Eric Clapton
14/79	**I Can't Stand It No More** . . . Peter Frampton
28/68	**I Can't Stand Myself (When You Touch Me)** . . . James Brown
	I Can't Stand The Rain
38/73	Ann Peebles
18/78	Eruption
7/63	**I Can't Stay Mad At You** . . . Skeeter Davis
9/68	**I Can't Stop Dancing** . . . Archie Bell
1/62	**I Can't Stop Loving You** . . . Ray Charles
35/64	**I Can't Stop Talking About You** . . . Steve & Eydie
8/80	**I Can't Tell You Why** . . . Eagles
37/68	**I Can't Turn You Loose** . . . Chambers Brothers
3/86	**I Can't Wait** . . . Nu Shooz
16/86	**I Can't Wait** . . . Stevie Nicks
8/91	**I Can't Wait Another Minute** . . . Hi-Five
32/66	**I Chose To Sing The Blues** . . . Ray Charles
20/56	**I Could Have Danced All Night** . . . Sylvia Syms
13/68	**I Could Never Love Another (After Loving You)** . . . Temptations
18/81	**I Could Never Miss You (More Than I Do)** . . . Lulu
10/88	**I Could Never Take The Place Of Your Man** . . . Prince

POS/YR	RECORD TITLE/ARTIST
9/66	**I Couldn't Live Without Your Love** . . . Petula Clark
32/83	**I Couldn't Say No** . . . Robert Ellis Orrall with Carlene Carter
17/61	**I Count The Tears** . . . Drifters
6/59	**I Cried A Tear** . . . LaVern Baker
	I Didn't Get To Sleep At All ..see: (Last Night)
35/72	**I Didn't Know I Loved You (Till I Saw You Rock And Roll)** . . . Gary Glitter
2/86	**I Didn't Mean To Turn You On** . . . Robert Palmer
23/90	**I Didn't Want To Need You** . . . Heart
9/67	**I Dig Rock And Roll Music** . . . Peter, Paul & Mary
	I Do
37/65	Marvelows
24/83	J. Geils Band
15/76	**I Do, I Do, I Do, I Do, I Do** . . . Abba
	I Do It For You ..see: (Everything I Do)
	I Do Love You
26/65	Billy Stewart
20/79	GQ
37/60	**(I Do The) Shimmy Shimmy** . . . Bobby Freeman
29/84	**I Do'wanna Know** . . . REO Speedwagon
23/86	**I Do What I Do...** . . . John Taylor
20/87	**I Do You** . . . Jets
18/71	**I Don't Blame You At All** . . . Miracles
39/83	**I Don't Care Anymore** . . . Phil Collins
1/90	**I Don't Have The Heart** . . . James Ingram
23/91	**I Don't Know Anybody Else** . . . Black Box
	I Don't Know How To Love Him
13/71	Helen Reddy
28/71	Yvonne Elliman
23/79	**I Don't Know If It's Right** . . . Evelyn "Champagne" King
35/82	**I Don't Know Where To Start** . . . Eddie Rabbitt
12/61	**I Don't Know Why** . . . Linda Scott
	(also see: But I Do)
39/69	**I Don't Know Why** . . . Stevie Wonder
8/75	**I Don't Like To Sleep Alone** . . . Paul Anka
38/87	**I Don't Mind At All** . . . Bourgeois Tagg
3/81	**I Don't Need You** . . . Kenny Rogers
37/64	**I Don't Wanna Be A Loser** . . . Lesley Gore
1/91	**I Don't Wanna Cry** . . . Mariah Carey
2/88	**I Don't Wanna Go On With You Like That** . . . Elton John

POS/YR	RECORD TITLE/ARTIST
3/88	**I Don't Wanna Live Without Your Love** . . . Chicago
35/65	**I Don't Wanna Lose You Baby** . . . Chad & Jeremy
20/69	**I Don't Want Nobody To Give Me Nothing** . . . James Brown
31/88	**I Don't Want To Be A Hero** . . . Johnny Hates Jazz
22/64	**I Don't Want To Be Hurt Anymore** . . . Nat King Cole
	I Don't Want To Be Right ..see: (If Loving You Is Wrong)
36/61	**I Don't Want To Cry** . . . Chuck Jackson
17/71	**I Don't Want To Do Wrong** . . . Gladys Knight & The Pips
5/88	**I Don't Want To Live Without You** . . . Foreigner
34/64	**I Don't Want To See Tomorrow** . . . Nat King Cole
16/64	**I Don't Want To See You Again** . . . Peter & Gordon
39/65	**I Don't Want To Spoil The Party** . . . Beatles
33/61	**I Don't Want To Take A Chance** . . . Mary Wells
36/80	**I Don't Want To Walk Without You** . . . Barry Manilow
4/88	**I Don't Want Your Love** . . . Duranduran
9/57	**I Dreamed** . . . Betty Johnson
20/61	**I Dreamed Of A Hill-Billy Heaven** . . . Tex Ritter
6/89	**I Drove All Night** . . . Cyndi Lauper
12/61	**I Fall To Pieces** . . . Patsy Cline
21/74	**I Feel A Song (In My Heart)** . . . Gladys Knight & The Pips
1/64	**I Feel Fine** . . . Beatles
3/84	**I Feel For You** . . . Chaka Khan
38/57	**I Feel Good** . . . Shirley & Lee
F/76	**I Feel Like A Bullet (In The Gun Of Robert Ford)** . . . Elton John
6/77	**I Feel Love** . . . Donna Summer
5/61	**I Feel So Bad** . . . Elvis Presley
	I Feel The Earth Move
F/71	Carole King
25/89	Martika
9/66	**I Fought The Law** . . . Bobby Fuller Four
30/65	**I Found A Girl** . . . Jan & Dean
32/67	**I Found A Love** . . . Wilson Pickett
31/82	**I Found Somebody** . . . Glenn Frey

POS/YR	RECORD TITLE/ARTIST
10/88	**I Found Someone** . . . Cher
1/64	**I Get Around** . . . Beach Boys
32/82	**I Get Excited** . . . Rick Springfield
37/75	**I Get Lifted** . . . George McCrae
34/68	**I Get The Sweetest Feeling** . . . Jackie Wilson
2/88	**I Get Weak** . . . Belinda Carlisle
7/78	**I Go Crazy** . . . Paul Davis
6/90	**I Go To Extremes** . . . Billy Joel
9/65	**I Go To Pieces** . . . Peter & Gordon
10/58	**I Got A Feeling** . . . Ricky Nelson
25/69	**I Got A Line On You** . . . Spirit
10/73	**I Got A Name** . . . Jim Croce
24/59	**I Got A Wife** . . . Mark IV
20/62	**I Got A Woman** . . . Jimmy McGriff
27/73	**I Got Ants In My Pants** . . . James Brown
20/79	**I Got My Mind Made Up (You Can Get It Girl)** . . . Instant Funk
3/67	**I Got Rhythm** . . . Happenings
37/75	**I Got Stoned And I Missed It** . . . Jim Stafford
8/58	**I Got Stung** . . . Elvis Presley
6/68	**I Got The Feelin'** . . . James Brown
16/66	**I Got The Feelin' (Oh No No)** . . . Neil Diamond
28/63	**I Got What I Wanted** . . . Brook Benton
	I Got You Babe
1/65	Sonny & Cher
28/85	UB40 With Chrissie Hynde
3/65	**I Got You (I Feel Good)** . . . James Brown
2/72	**I Gotcha** . . . Joe Tex
35/64	**I Gotta Dance To Keep From Crying** . . . Miracles
20/60	**I Gotta Know** . . . Elvis Presley
4/84	**I Guess That's Why They Call It The Blues** . . . Elton John
34/69	**I Guess The Lord Must Be In New York City** . . . Nilsson
17/67	**I Had A Dream** . . . Paul Revere & The Raiders
11/67	**I Had Too Much To Dream (Last Night)** . . . Electric Prunes
8/88	**I Hate Myself For Loving You** . . . Joan Jett
36/64	**I Have A Boyfriend** . . . Chiffons
1/65	**I Hear A Symphony** . . . Supremes
30/66	**I Hear Trumpets Blow** . . . Tokens
	I Hear You Knocking
2/55	Gale Storm

POS/YR	RECORD TITLE/ARTIST
4/71	Dave Edmunds
4/87	**I Heard A Rumour** . . . Bananarama
	I Heard It Through The Grapevine
2/67	Gladys Knight & The Pips
1/68	Marvin Gaye
1/74	**I Honestly Love You** . . . Olivia Newton-John
1/84	**I Just Called To Say I Love You** . . . Stevie Wonder
9/70	**I Just Can't Help Believing** . . . B.J. Thomas
1/87	**I Just Can't Stop Loving You** . . . Michael Jackson
1/87	**(I Just) Died In Your Arms** . . . Cutting Crew
17/57	**I Just Don't Know** . . . Four Lads
26/66	**I Just Don't Know What To Do With Myself** . . . Dionne Warwick
17/61	**I Just Don't Understand** . . . Ann-Margret
12/79	**I Just Fall In Love Again** . . . Anne Murray
4/78	**I Just Wanna Stop** . . . Gino Vannelli
1/77	**I Just Want To Be Your Everything** . . . Andy Gibb
7/71	**I Just Want To Celebrate** . . . Rare Earth
33/77	**I Just Want To Make Love To You** . . . Foghat
4/82	**I Keep Forgettin' (Every Time You're Near)** . . . Michael McDonald
	I Kissed You ..see: ('Til)
1/87	**I Knew You Were Waiting (For Me)** . . . Aretha Franklin & George Michael
	I Knew You When
14/65	Billy Joe Royal
37/83	Linda Ronstadt
19/79	**I Know A Heartache When I See One** . . . Jennifer Warnes
3/65	**I Know A Place** . . . Petula Clark
	(I Know) I'm Losing You
8/66	Temptations
7/70	Rare Earth
24/71	Rod Stewart with Faces
13/83	**I Know There's Something Going On** . . . Frida
9/87	**I Know What I Like** . . . Huey Lewis & the News
3/62	**I Know (You Don't Love Me No More)** . . . Barbara George
30/88	**I Know You're Out There Somewhere** . . . Moody Blues

POS/YR	RECORD TITLE/ARTIST
19/62	**I Left My Heart In San Francisco** . . . Tony Bennett
3/77	**I Like Dreamin'** . . . Kenny Nolan
7/89	**I Like It** . . . Dino
17/64	**I Like It** . . . Gerry & The Pacemakers
31/83	**I Like It** . . . DeBarge
	I Like It Like That
2/61	Chris Kenner
7/65	Dave Clark Five
27/64	**I Like It Like That** . . . Miracles
25/67	**I Like The Way** . . . Tommy James & The Shondells
1/91	**I Like The Way (The Kissing Game)** . . . Hi-Five
37/77	**I Like To Do It** . . . KC & The Sunshine Band
28/74	**I Like To Live The Love** . . . B.B. King
8/57	**I Like Your Kind Of Love** . . . Andy Williams
38/71	**I Likes To Do It** . . . People's Choice
31/89	**I Live By The Groove** . . . Paul Carrack
13/88	**I Live For Your Love** . . . Natalie Cole
12/74	**I Love** . . . Tom T. Hall
1/81	**I Love A Rainy Night** . . . Eddie Rabbitt
	I Love How You Love Me
5/61	Paris Sisters
9/68	Bobby Vinton
	I Love Lucy ..see: Disco Lucy
5/76	**I Love Music** . . . O'Jays
21/57	**I Love My Baby (My Baby Loves Me)** . . . Jill Corey
24/74	**I Love My Friend** . . . Charlie Rich
1/82	**I Love Rock 'N Roll** . . . Joan Jett
5/78	**I Love The Nightlife (Disco 'Round)** . . . Alicia Bridges
9/60	**I Love The Way You Love** . . . Marv Johnson
12/81	**I Love You** . . . Climax Blues Band
14/68	**I Love You** . . . People
22/62	**I Love You** . . . Volume's
37/78	**I Love You** . . . Donna Summer
3/63	**I Love You Because** . . . Al Martino
39/63	**(I Love You) Don't You Forget It** . . . Perry Como
30/66	**I Love You Drops** . . . Vic Dana
21/71	**I Love You For All Seasons** . . . Fuzz
17/58	**(I Love You) For Sentimental Reasons** . . . Sam Cooke

POS/YR	RECORD TITLE/ARTIST
40/60	**I Love You In The Same Old Way** . . . Paul Anka
28/55	**I Love You Madly** . . . Four Coins
9/64	**I Love You More And More Every Day** . . . Al Martino
31/66	**I Love You 1000 Times** . . . Platters
38/62	**I Love You The Way You Are** . . . Bobby Vinton
37/81	**I Loved 'Em Every One** . . . T.G. Sheppard
18/59	**I Loves You, Porgy** . . . Nina Simone
10/81	**I Made It Through The Rain** . . . Barry Manilow
18/67	**I Make A Fool Of Myself** . . . Frankie Valli
37/68	**I Met Her In Church** . . . Box Tops
5/85	**I Miss You** . . . Klymaxx
	I Miss You So
34/57	Chris Connor
33/59	Paul Anka
34/65	Little Anthony & The Imperials
19/81	**I Missed Again** . . . Phil Collins
31/65	**I Must Be Seeing Things** . . . Gene Pitney
28/79	**I Need A Lover** . . . John Cougar
14/87	**I Need Love** . . . L.L. Cool J
22/66	**I Need Somebody** . . . ? & The Mysterians
25/76	**I Need To Be In Love** . . . Carpenters
9/72	**I Need You** . . . America
37/82	**I Need You** . . . Paul Carrack
36/84	**I Need You Tonight** . . . Peter Wolf
4/59	**I Need Your Love Tonight** . . . Elvis Presley
37/81	**I Need Your Lovin'** . . . Teena Marie
20/62	**I Need Your Loving** . . . Don Gardner & Dee Dee Ford
12/77	**I Never Cry** . . . Alice Cooper
9/67	**I Never Loved A Man (The Way I Love You)** . . . Aretha Franklin
	I Only Have Eyes For You
11/59	Flamingos
18/75	Art Garfunkel
22/56	**I Only Know I Love You** . . . Four Aces
	I Only Want To Be With You
12/64	Dusty Springfield
12/76	Bay City Rollers
31/89	Samantha Fox
25/71	**I Play And Sing** . . . Dawn
19/80	**I Pledge My Love** . . . Peaches & Herb
9/82	**I Ran (So Far Away)** . . . Flock Of Seagulls
39/82	**I Really Don't Need No Light** . . . Jeffrey Osborne

POS/YR	RECORD TITLE/ARTIST
	I Really Don't Want To Know
18/60	Tommy Edwards
22/66	Ronnie Dove
21/71	Elvis Presley
29/61	**I Really Love You** . . . Stereos
8/89	**I Remember Holding You** . . . Boys Club
5/62	**I Remember You** . . . Frank Ifield
6/90	**I Remember You** . . . Skid Row
36/64	**I Rise, I Fall** . . . Johnny Tillotson
5/66	**I Saw Her Again** . . . Mamas & The Papas
	I Saw Her (Him) Standing There
14/64	Beatles
7/88	Tiffany
14/63	**I Saw Linda Yesterday** . . . Dickey Lee
10/91	**I Saw Red** . . . Warrant
16/72	**I Saw The Light** . . . Todd Rundgren
	I Say A Little Prayer
4/67	Dionne Warwick
10/68	Aretha Franklin
4/67	**I Second That Emotion** . . . Miracles
26/66	**I See The Light** . . . Five Americans
38/74	**I Shall Sing** . . . Art Garfunkel
1/74	**I Shot The Sheriff** . . . Eric Clapton
28/88	**I Should Be So Lucky** . . . Kylie Minogue
15/62	**I Sold My Heart To The Junkman** . . . Blue-Belles
6/69	**I Started A Joke** . . . Bee Gees
13/88	**I Still Believe** . . . Brenda K. Starr
12/84	**I Still Can't Get Over Loving You** . . . Ray Parker Jr.
39/79	**I Still Have Dreams** . . . Richie Furay
1/87	**I Still Haven't Found What I'm Looking For** . . . U2
12/67	**I Take It Back** . . . Sandy Posey
13/67	**I Thank The Lord For The Night Time** . . . Neil Diamond
	I Thank You
9/68	Sam & Dave
34/80	ZZ Top
1/70	**I Think I Love You** . . . Partridge Family
16/86	**I Think It's Love** . . . Jermaine Jackson
	I Think We're Alone Now
4/67	Tommy James & The Shondells
1/87	Tiffany
4/91	**I Touch Myself** . . . Divinyls
23/69	**I Turned You On** . . . Isley Brothers
	I Understand (Just How You Feel)
9/61	G-Clefs
36/65	Freddie & The Dreamers

POS/YR	RECORD TITLE/ARTIST
33/59	**I Waited Too Long** . . . LaVern Baker
17/56	**I Walk The Line** . . . Johnny Cash
12/86	**I Wanna Be A Cowboy** . . . Boys Don't Cry
14/63	**I Wanna Be Around** . . . Tony Bennett
20/59	**I Wanna Be Loved** . . . Ricky Nelson
2/90	**I Wanna Be Rich** . . . Calloway
32/89	**I Wanna Be The One** . . . Stevie B
16/72	**I Wanna Be Where You Are** . . . Michael Jackson
16/73	**I Wanna Be With You** . . . Raspberries
11/80	**I Wanna Be Your Lover** . . . Prince
23/75	**I Wanna Dance Wit' Choo** . . . Disco Tex & The Sex-O-Lettes
1/87	**I Wanna Dance With Somebody (Who Loves Me)** . . . Whitney Houston
10/77	**I Wanna Get Next To You** . . . Rose Royce
14/87	**I Wanna Go Back** . . . Eddie Money
8/89	**I Wanna Have Some Fun** . . . Samantha Fox
35/85	**I Wanna Hear It From Your Lips** . . . Eric Carmen
36/68	**I Wanna Live** . . . Glen Campbell
9/64	**I Wanna Love Him So Bad** . . . Jelly Beans
39/61	**(I Wanna) Love My Life Away** . . . Gene Pitney
2/91	**I Wanna Sex You Up** . . . Color Me Badd
	(I Wanna) Testify
20/67	Parliaments
36/69	Johnnie Taylor
21/61	**I Wanna Thank You** . . . Bobby Rydell
6/84	**I Want A New Drug** . . . Huey Lewis & the News
11/65	**I Want Candy** . . . Strangeloves
5/88	**I Want Her** . . . Keith Sweat
	I Want To ..also see: I Wanna, & I Want'a
1/60	**I Want To Be Wanted** . . . Brenda Lee
3/88	**I Want To Be Your Man** . . . Roger
23/65	**I Want To (Do Everything For You)** . . . Joe Tex
36/66	**I Want To Go With You** . . . Eddy Arnold
1/64	**I Want To Hold Your Hand** . . . Beatles
1/85	**I Want To Know What Love Is** . . . Foreigner
28/63	**I Want To Stay Here** . . . Steve & Eydie
	I Want To Take You Higher
34/70	Ike & Tina Turner
38/70	Sly & The Family Stone
8/59	**I Want To Walk You Home** . . . Fats Domino

POS/YR	RECORD TITLE/ARTIST
	I Want You
15/76	Marvin Gaye
16/91	Robert Palmer (medley)
20/66	**I Want You** . . . Bob Dylan
40/90	**I Want You** . . . Shana
1/70	**I Want You Back** . . . Jackson 5
37/81	**I Want You, I Need You** . . . Chris Christian
1/56	**I Want You, I Need You, I Love You** . . . Elvis Presley
	I Want You To Be My Baby
14/55	Georgia Gibbs
18/55	Lillian Briggs
13/56	**I Want You To Be My Girl** . . . Frankie Lymon & The Teenagers
32/58	**I Want You To Know** . . . Fats Domino
7/79	**I Want You To Want Me** . . . Cheap Trick
19/79	**I Want You Tonight** . . . Pablo Cruise
7/79	**I Want Your Love** . . . Chic
2/87	**I Want Your Sex** . . . George Michael
15/75	**I Want'a Do Something Freaky To You** . . . Leon Haywood
29/73	**I Was Checkin' Out She Was Checkin' In** . . . Don Covay
20/67	**I Was Kaiser Bill's Batman** . . . Whistling Jack Smith
10/79	**I Was Made For Dancin'** . . . Leif Garrett
11/79	**I Was Made For Lovin' You** . . . Kiss
2/67	**I Was Made To Love Her** . . . Stevie Wonder
22/78	**I Was Only Joking** . . . Rod Stewart
24/62	**I Was Such A Fool (To Fall In Love With You)** . . . Connie Francis
19/56	**I Was The One** . . . Elvis Presley
19/66	**(I Washed My Hands In) Muddy Water** . . . Johnny Rivers
	I (Who Have Nothing)
29/63	Ben E. King
14/70	Tom Jones
40/79	Sylvester
10/65	**I Will** . . . Dean Martin
22/68	**I Will Always Think About You** . . . New Colony Six
30/79	**I Will Be In Love With You** . . . Livingston Taylor
34/87	**I Will Be There** . . . Glass Tiger
1/63	**I Will Follow Him** . . . Little Peggy March
29/78	**I Will Still Love You** . . . Stonebolt
1/79	**I Will Survive** . . . Gloria Gaynor
1/77	**I Wish** . . . Stevie Wonder

POS/YR	RECORD TITLE/ARTIST
20/88	**I Wish I Had A Girl** . . . Henry Lee Summer
32/63	**I Wish I Were A Princess** . . . Little Peggy March
4/68	**I Wish It Would Rain** . . . Temptations
3/90	**I Wish It Would Rain Down** . . . Phil Collins
16/62	**I Wish That We Were Married** . . . Ronnie & The Hi-Lites
28/64	**I Wish You Love** . . . Gloria Lynne
13/71	**I Woke Up In Love This Morning** . . . Partridge Family
12/89	**I Won't Back Down** . . . Tom Petty
13/87	**I Won't Forget You** . . . Poison
10/83	**I Won't Hold You Back** . . . Toto
11/74	**I Won't Last A Day Without You** . . . Carpenters
35/83	**I Won't Stand In Your Way** . . . Stray Cats
25/63	**I Wonder** . . . Brenda Lee
34/85	**I Wonder If I Take You Home** . . . Lisa-Lisa & Cult Jam with Full Force
8/68	**I Wonder What She's Doing Tonite** . . . Tommy Boyce & Bobby Hart
21/63	**I Wonder What She's Doing Tonight** . . . Barry & The Tamerlanes
22/58	**I Wonder Why** . . . Dion & The Belmonts
8/85	**I Would Die 4 U** . . . Prince
20/82	**I Wouldn't Have Missed It For The World** . . . Ronnie Milsap
22/56	**I Wouldn't Know Where To Begin** . . . Eddy Arnold
36/77	**I Wouldn't Want To Be Like You** . . . Alan Parsons
1/76	**I Write The Songs** . . . Barry Manilow
	I'd Like To Teach The World To Sing (In Perfect Harmony)
7/72	New Seekers
13/72	Hillside Singers
40/71	**I'd Love To Change The World** . . . Ten Years After
2/72	**I'd Love You To Want Me** . . . Lobo
38/80	**I'd Rather Leave While I'm In Love** . . . Rita Coolidge
2/76	**I'd Really Love To See You Tonight** . . . England Dan & John Ford Coley
18/87	**I'd Still Say Yes** . . . Klymaxx
15/69	**I'd Wait A Million Years** . . . Grass Roots
36/73	**I'll Always Love My Mama** . . . Intruders

POS/YR	RECORD TITLE/ARTIST
3/88	**I'll Always Love You** . . . Taylor Dayne
35/65	**I'll Always Love You** . . . Spinners
14/87	**I'll Be Alright Without You** . . . Journey
3/72	**I'll Be Around** . . . Spinners
12/91	**I'll Be By Your Side** . . . Stevie B
8/65	**I'll Be Doggone** . . . Marvin Gaye
	I'll Be Good To You
3/76	Brothers Johnson
18/90	Quincy Jones Feat. Ray Charles & Chaka Khan
4/56	**I'll Be Home** . . . Pat Boone
33/64	**I'll Be In Trouble** . . . Temptations
1/89	**I'll Be Loving You (Forever)** . . . New Kids On The Block
11/86	**I'll Be Over You** . . . Toto
20/59	**I'll Be Satisfied** . . . Jackie Wilson
36/74	**I'll Be The Other Woman** . . . Soul Children
1/70	**I'll Be There** . . . Jackson 5
8/91	**I'll Be There** . . . Escape Club
12/61	**I'll Be There** . . . Damita Jo
	(also see: Stand By Me)
14/65	**I'll Be There** . . . Gerry & The Pacemakers
1/89	**I'll Be There For You** . . . Bon Jovi
31/59	**(I'll Be With You In) Apple Blossom Time** . . . Tab Hunter
1/90	**I'll Be Your Everything** . . . Tommy Page
4/90	**I'll Be Your Shelter** . . . Taylor Dayne
40/73	**I'll Be Your Shelter (In Time Of Storm)** . . . Luther Ingram
18/58	**I'll Come Running Back To You** . . . Sam Cooke
25/64	**I'll Cry Instead** . . . Beatles
20/91	**I'll Do 4 U** . . . Father M.C.
40/75	**I'll Do For You Anything You Want Me To** . . . Barry White
7/91	**I'll Give All My Love To You** . . . Keith Sweat
9/74	**I'll Have To Say I Love You In A Song** . . . Jim Croce
34/65	**I'll Keep Holding On** . . . Marvelettes
30/64	**I'll Keep You Satisfied** . . . Billy J. Kramer
21/65	**I'll Make All Your Dreams Come True** . . . Ronnie Dove
9/71	**I'll Meet You Halfway** . . . Partridge Family
14/62	**I'll Never Dance Again** . . . Bobby Rydell
6/69	**I'll Never Fall In Love Again** . . . Tom Jones
6/70	**I'll Never Fall In Love Again** . . . Dionne Warwick
4/65	**I'll Never Find Another You** . . . Seekers
23/91	**I'll Never Let You Go (Angel Eyes)** . . . Steelheart
5/79	**I'll Never Love This Way Again** . . . Dionne Warwick
24/57	**I'll Never Say "Never Again" Again** . . . Dinah Shore
25/61	**I'll Never Smile Again** . . . Platters
13/55	**I'll Never Stop Loving You** . . . Doris Day
18/75	**I'll Play For You** . . . Seals & Crofts
	(I'll Remember) ..see: In The Still Of The Nite
23/57	**I'll Remember Today** . . . Patti Page
34/58	**I'll Remember Tonight** . . . Pat Boone
22/60	**I'll Save The Last Dance For You** . . . Damita Jo
	(also see: Save The Last Dance For Me)
20/90	**I'll See You In My Dreams** . . . Giant
32/62	**I'll See You In My Dreams** . . . Pat Boone
33/87	**I'll Still Be Loving You** . . . Restless Heart
39/67	**I'll Take Care Of Your Cares** . . . Frankie Laine
30/66	**I'll Take Good Care Of You** . . . Garnet Mimms
25/63	**I'll Take You Home** . . . Drifters
1/72	**I'll Take You There** . . . Staple Singers
25/64	**I'll Touch A Star** . . . Terry Stafford
40/67	**I'll Try Anything** . . . Dusty Springfield
	I'll Try Something New
39/62	Miracles
25/69	Supremes & Temptations
9/83	**I'll Tumble 4 Ya** . . . Culture Club
13/84	**I'll Wait** . . . Van Halen
15/58	**I'll Wait For You** . . . Frankie Avalon
1/66	**I'm A Believer** . . . Monkees
38/69	**I'm A Better Man** . . . Engelbert Humperdinck
17/65	**I'm A Fool** . . . Dino, Desi & Billy
24/61	**I'm A Fool To Care** . . . Joe Barry
35/71	**I'm A Greedy Man** . . . James Brown
36/65	**I'm A Happy Man** . . . Jive Five
38/59	**I'm A Hog For You** . . . Coasters
10/67	**I'm A Man** . . . Spencer Davis Group
17/65	**I'm A Man** . . . Yardbirds
31/59	**I'm A Man** . . . Fabian
24/68	**I'm A Midnight Mover** . . . Wilson Pickett

POS/YR	RECORD TITLE/ARTIST
20/66	**(I'm A) Road Runner** . . . Jr. Walker & The All Stars
25/61	**I'm A Telling You** . . . Jerry Butler
31/74	**I'm A Train** . . . Albert Hammond
12/75	**I'm A Woman** . . . Maria Muldaur
16/80	**I'm Alive** . . . Electric Light Orchestra
35/83	**I'm Alive** . . . Neil Diamond
34/80	**I'm Almost Ready** . . . Pure Prairie League
7/80	**I'm Alright** . . . Kenny Loggins
20/55	**(I'm Always Hearing) Wedding Bells** . . . Eddie Fisher
9/57	**I'm Available** . . . Margie Rayburn
19/62	**I'm Blue (The Gong-Gong Song)** . . . Ikettes
40/71	**I'm Comin' Home** . . . Tommy James
18/74	**I'm Coming Home** . . . Spinners
39/66	**I'm Comin' Home, Cindy** . . . Trini Lopez
19/61	**I'm Comin' On Back To You** . . . Jackie Wilson
5/80	**I'm Coming Out** . . . Diana Ross
19/64	**I'm Crying** . . . Animals
17/73	**I'm Doin' Fine Now** . . . New York City
17/76	**I'm Easy** . . . Keith Carradine
21/78	**I'm Every Woman** . . . Chaka Khan
	I'm Falling Too ..see: (I Can't Help You)
37/69	**I'm Free** . . . Who
22/84	**I'm Free (Heaven Helps The Man)** . . . Kenny Loggins
	(I'm Gettin') ..see: Nuttin' For Christmas
37/60	**I'm Gettin' Better** . . . Jim Reeves
9/85	**I'm Goin' Down** . . . Bruce Springsteen
17/59	**I'm Gonna Be A Wheel Some Day** . . . Fats Domino
9/64	**I'm Gonna Be Strong** . . . Gene Pitney
18/63	**I'm Gonna' Be Warm This Winter** . . . Connie Francis
3/59	**I'm Gonna Get Married** . . . Lloyd Price
12/61	**I'm Gonna Knock On Your Door** . . . Eddie Hodges
40/76	**I'm Gonna Let My Heart Do The Walking** . . . Supremes
3/73	**I'm Gonna Love You Just A Little More Baby** . . . Barry White
	I'm Gonna Make You Love Me
26/68	Madeline Bell
2/69	Supremes & Temptations
10/69	**I'm Gonna Make You Mine** . . . Lou Christie
3/57	**I'm Gonna Sit Right Down And Write Myself A Letter** . . . Billy Williams
28/78	**I'm Gonna Take Care Of Everything** . . . Rubicon
13/85	**I'm Gonna Tear Your Playhouse Down** . . . Paul Young
27/80	**I'm Happy That Love Has Found You** . . . Jimmy Hall
1/65	**I'm Henry VIII, I Am** . . . Herman's Hermits
27/61	**I'm Hurtin'** . . . Roy Orbison
19/74	**I'm In Love** . . . Aretha Franklin
40/81	**I'm In Love** . . . Evelyn King
	I'm In Love Again
3/56	Fats Domino
38/56	Fontane Sisters
38/61	**I'm In The Mood For Love** . . . Chimes
2/77	**I'm In You** . . . Peter Frampton
	I'm Into Something Good
13/64	Herman's Hermits
38/64	Earl-Jean
12/73	**I'm Just A Singer (In A Rock And Roll Band)** . . . Moody Blues
33/61	**I'm Learning About Love** . . . Brenda Lee
36/71	**I'm Leavin'** . . . Elvis Presley
	I'm Leaving It Up To You
1/63	Dale & Grace
4/74	Donny & Marie Osmond
10/69	**I'm Livin' In Shame** . . . Supremes
	I'm Losing You ..see: (I Know)
40/59	**I'm Movin' On** . . . Ray Charles
37/73	**I'm Never Gonna Be Alone Anymore** . . . Cornelius Brothers & Sister Rose
36/59	**I'm Never Gonna Tell** . . . Jimmie Rodgers
27/60	**I'm Not Afraid** . . . Ricky Nelson
14/78	**I'm Not Gonna Let It Bother Me Tonight** . . . Atlanta Rhythm Section
	I'm Not In Love
2/75	10cc
7/91	Will To Power
4/75	**I'm Not Lisa** . . . Jessi Colter
34/70	**I'm Not My Brothers Keeper** . . . Flaming Ember
32/86	**I'm Not The One** . . . Cars
20/67	**(I'm Not Your) Steppin' Stone** . . . Monkees
6/85	**I'm On Fire** . . . Bruce Springsteen
16/75	**I'm On Fire** . . . Dwight Twilley Band

POS/YR	RECORD TITLE/ARTIST
26/75	**I'm On Fire** . . . 5000 Volts
15/64	**I'm On The Outside (Looking In)** . . . Little Anthony & The Imperials
16/59	**I'm Ready** . . . Fats Domino
9/66	**I'm Ready For Love** . . . Martha & The Vandellas
	I'm So Excited
30/82	Pointer Sisters
9/84	Pointer Sisters
8/66	**I'm So Lonesome I Could Cry** . . . B.J. Thomas
14/64	**I'm So Proud** . . . Impressions
1/60	**I'm Sorry** . . . Brenda Lee
1/75	**I'm Sorry** . . . John Denver
11/57	**I'm Sorry** . . . Platters
36/58	**I'm Sorry I Made You Cry** . . . Connie Francis
14/57	**I'm Stickin' With You** . . . Jimmy Bowen
3/72	**I'm Still In Love With You** . . . Al Green
31/88	**I'm Still Searching** . . . Glass Tiger
12/83	**I'm Still Standing** . . . Elton John
10/72	**I'm Stone In Love With You** . . . Stylistics
1/65	**I'm Telling You Now** . . . Freddie & The Dreamers
15/89	**I'm That Type Of Guy** . . . L.L. Cool J
38/62	**(I'm The Girl On) Wolverton Mountain** . . . Jo Ann Campbell
	I'm The One Who Loves You ..see: (Remember Me)
	I'm The One You Need ..see: (Come 'Round Here)
27/57	**I'm Waiting Just For You** . . . Pat Boone
	I'm Walkin'
4/57	Fats Domino
4/57	Ricky Nelson
12/67	**I'm Wondering** . . . Stevie Wonder
1/90	**I'm Your Baby Tonight** . . . Whitney Houston
1/77	**I'm Your Boogie Man** . . . KC & The Sunshine Band
3/86	**I'm Your Man** . . . Wham!
6/66	**I'm Your Puppet** . . . James & Bobby Purify
11/65	**I'm Yours** . . . Elvis Presley
33/59	**I've Been Around** . . . Fats Domino
35/69	**I've Been Hurt** . . . Bill Deal
9/87	**I've Been In Love Before** . . . Cutting Crew
27/72	**I've Been Lonely For So Long** . . . Frederick Knight

POS/YR	RECORD TITLE/ARTIST
16/67	**I've Been Lonely Too Long** . . . Young Rascals
21/65	**I've Been Loving You Too Long (To Stop Now)** . . . Otis Redding
9/74	**(I've Been) Searchin' So Long** . . . Chicago
1/91	**I've Been Thinking About You** . . . Londonbeat
34/75	**I've Been This Way Before** . . . Neil Diamond
28/59	**I've Come Of Age** . . . Billy Storm
8/81	**I've Done Everything For You** . . . Rick Springfield
5/71	**I've Found Someone Of My Own** . . . Free Movement
29/76	**I've Got A Feeling (We'll Be Seeing Each Other Again)** . . . Al Wilson
18/83	**I've Got A Rock N' Roll Heart** . . . Eric Clapton
39/74	**I've Got A Thing About You Baby** . . . Elvis Presley
25/65	**I've Got A Tiger By The Tail** . . . Buck Owens
	I've Got A Woman ..see: I Got A Woman
18/62	**I've Got Bonnie** . . . Bobby Rydell
5/77	**I've Got Love On My Mind** . . . Natalie Cole
33/64	**I've Got Sand In My Shoes** . . . Drifters
32/73	**I've Got So Much To Give** . . . Barry White
12/74	**I've Got The Music In Me** . . . Kiki Dee Band
	I've Got To ..also see: I've Gotta
38/66	**I've Got To Be Somebody** . . . Billy Joe Royal
4/74	**I've Got To Use My Imagination** . . . Gladys Knight & The Pips
9/66	**I've Got You Under My Skin** . . . 4 Seasons
11/69	**I've Gotta Be Me** . . . Sammy Davis, Jr.
8/68	**I've Gotta Get A Message To You** . . . Bee Gees
25/78	**I've Had Enough** . . . Wings
6/59	**I've Had It** . . . Bell Notes
1/87	**(I've Had) The Time Of My Life** . . . Bill Medley & Jennifer Warnes
32/70	**I've Lost You** . . . Elvis Presley
4/80	**I've Loved You For A Long Time (medley)** . . . Spinners
3/82	**I've Never Been To Me** . . . Charlene

POS/YR	RECORD TITLE/ARTIST
40/68	**I've Never Found A Girl (To Love Me Like You Do)** . . . Eddie Floyd
17/67	**I've Passed This Way Before** . . . Jimmy Ruffin
3/61	**I've Told Every Little Star** . . . Linda Scott
1/90	**Ice Ice Baby** . . . Vanilla Ice
9/91	**Iesha** . . . Another Bad Creation
4/71	**If** . . . Bread
32/62	**If A Man Answers** . . . Bobby Darin
35/62	**If A Woman Answers (Hang Up The Phone)** . . . Leroy Van Dyke
14/83	**If Anyone Falls** . . . Stevie Nicks
7/58	**If Dreams Came True** . . . Pat Boone
24/78	**If Ever I See You Again** . . . Roberta Flack
10/84	**If Ever You're In My Arms Again** . . . Peabo Bryson
12/69	**If I Can Dream** . . . Elvis Presley
1/78	**If I Can't Have You** . . . Yvonne Elliman
10/68	**If I Could Build My Whole World Around You** . . . Marvin Gaye & Tammi Terrell
10/72	**If I Could Reach You** . . . 5th Dimension
3/89	**If I Could Turn Back Time** . . . Cher
	If I Didn't Care
22/59	Connie Francis
30/61	Platters
39/75	**If I Ever Lose This Heaven** . . . AWB
34/59	**If I Give My Heart To You** . . . Kitty Kallen
31/60	**If I Had A Girl** . . . Rod Lauren
	If I Had A Hammer
10/62	Peter, Paul & Mary
3/63	Trini Lopez
36/82	**If I Had My Wish Tonight** . . . David Lasley
23/65	**If I Loved You** . . . Chad & Jeremy
8/55	**If I May** . . . Nat "King" Cole/Four Knights
34/65	**If I Ruled The World** . . . Tony Bennett
39/79	**If I Said You Have A Beautiful Body Would You Hold It Against Me** . . . Bellamy Brothers
	If I Were A Carpenter
8/66	Bobby Darin
20/68	Four Tops
36/70	Johnny Cash & June Carter
9/71	**If I Were Your Woman** . . . Gladys Knight & The Pips
19/84	**If I'd Been The One** . . . 38 Special
7/88	**If It Isn't Love** . . . New Edition

POS/YR	RECORD TITLE/ARTIST
	(If Loving You Is Wrong) I Don't Want To Be Right
3/72	Luther Ingram
31/79	Barbara Mandrell
23/63	**If My Pillow Could Talk** . . . Connie Francis
25/71	**If Not For You** . . . Olivia Newton-John
29/86	**If She Knew What She Wants** . . . Bangles
17/87	**If She Would Have Been Faithful...** . . . Chicago
28/82	**If The Love Fits Wear It** . . . Leslie Pearl
35/91	**(If There Was) Any Other Way** . . . Celine Dion
	If There's A Hell Below ..see: (Don't Worry)
6/84	**If This Is It** . . . Huey Lewis & the News
24/90	**If U Were Mine** . . . U-Krew
28/74	**If We Make It Through December** . . . Merle Haggard
1/90	**If Wishes Came True** . . . Sweet Sensation
11/68	**If You Can Want** . . . Miracles
5/71	**If You Could Read My Mind** . . . Gordon Lightfoot
33/59	**(If You Cry) True Love, True Love** . . . Drifters
	If You Don't Know Me By Now
3/72	Harold Melvin & The Bluenotes
1/89	Simply Red
12/55	**If You Don't Want My Love** . . . Jaye P. Morgan
22/62	**If You Gotta Make A Fool Of Somebody** . . . James Ray
11/76	**If You Know What I Mean** . . . Neil Diamond
4/86	**If You Leave** . . . Orchestral Manoeuvres In The Dark
1/76	**If You Leave Me Now** . . . Chicago
38/72	**If You Leave Me Tonight I'll Cry** . . . Jerry Wallace
8/70	**(If You Let Me Make Love To You Then) Why Can't I Touch You?** . . . Ronnie Dyson
5/74	**If You Love Me (Let Me Know)** . . . Olivia Newton-John
3/85	**If You Love Somebody Set Them Free** . . . Sting
37/63	**If You Need Me** . . . Solomon Burke
16/91	**If You Needed Somebody** . . . Bad Company
8/71	**If You Really Love Me** . . . Stevie Wonder

POS/YR	RECORD TITLE/ARTIST
17/79	**If You Remember Me** . . . Chris Thompson & Night
38/80	**If You Should Sail** . . . Nielsen/Pearson
17/74	**If You Talk In Your Sleep** . . . Elvis Presley
1/63	**If You Wanna Be Happy** . . . Jimmy Soul
25/74	**If You Wanna Get To Heaven** . . . Ozark Mountain Daredevils
37/79	**If You Want It** . . . Niteflyte
12/73	**If You Want Me To Stay** . . . Sly & The Family Stone
	If You Were Mine ..see: If U
9/73	**If You're Ready (Come Go With Me)** . . . Staple Singers
	Iko Iko
20/65	Dixie Cups
14/89	Belle Stars
6/60	**Image Of A Girl** . . . Safaris
7/78	**Imaginary Lover** . . . Atlanta Rhythm Section
3/71	**Imagine** . . . John Lennon
22/75	**Immigrant, The** . . . Neil Sedaka
16/71	**Immigrant Song** . . . Led Zeppelin
36/72	**Immigration Man** . . . Graham Nash & David Crosby
35/66	**Impossible Dream** . . . Jack Jones
4/90	**Impulsive** . . . Wilson Phillips
17/83	**In A Big Country** . . . Big Country
30/68	**In-A-Gadda-Da-Vida** . . . Iron Butterfly
31/69	**In A Moment** . . . Intrigues
27/56	**In A Shanty In Old Shanty Town** . . . Somethin' Smith & The Redheads
11/80	**In America** . . . Charlie Daniels Band
9/67	**In And Out Of Love** . . . Supremes
	'In' Crowd
5/65	Ramsey Lewis Trio
13/65	Dobie Gray
7/63	**In Dreams** . . . Roy Orbison
19/87	**In My Dreams** . . . REO Speedwagon
37/89	**In My Eyes** . . . Stevie B
7/85	**In My House** . . . Mary Jane Girls
10/60	**In My Little Corner Of The World** . . . Anita Bryant
23/63	**In My Room** . . . Beach Boys
38/85	**In Neon** . . . Elton John
19/81	**In The Air Tonight** . . . Phil Collins
	In The Chapel In The Moonlight ..see: Chapel
35/81	**In The Dark** . . . Billy Squier

POS/YR	RECORD TITLE/ARTIST
3/69	**In The Ghetto** . . . Elvis Presley
33/67	**In The Heat Of The Night** . . . Ray Charles
27/61	**In The Middle Of A Heartache** . . . Wanda Jackson
	In The Middle Of An Island
9/57	Tony Bennett
23/57	Tennessee Ernie Ford
	In The Middle Of The House
11/56	Vaughn Monroe
20/56	Rusty Draper
	In The Midnight Hour
21/65	Wilson Pickett
30/73	Cross Country
19/64	**In The Misty Moonlight** . . . Jerry Wallace
	In The Mood
4/59	Ernie Fields
40/77	Henhouse Five Plus Too
39/84	**In The Mood** . . . Robert Plant
	In The Name Of Love ..see: (What)
3/79	**In The Navy** . . . Village People
5/72	**In The Rain** . . . Dramatics
38/60	**In The Still Of The Night** . . . Dion & The Belmonts
24/56	**In The Still Of The Nite** . . . Five Satins
3/70	**In The Summertime** . . . Mungo Jerry
1/69	**In The Year 2525 (Exordium & Terminus)** . . . Zager & Evans
3/87	**In Too Deep** . . . Genesis
26/86	**In Your Eyes** . . . Peter Gabriel
20/81	**In Your Letter** . . . REO Speedwagon
5/89	**In Your Room** . . . Bangles
38/88	**In Your Soul** . . . Corey Hart
1/67	**Incense And Peppermints** . . . Strawberry Alarm Clock
33/67	**Indescribably Blue** . . . Elvis Presley
35/88	**Indestructible** . . . Four Tops
5/69	**Indian Giver** . . . 1910 Fruitgum Co.
10/68	**Indian Lake** . . . Cowsills
	Indian Reservation
20/68	Don Fardon
1/71	Raiders
5/70	**Indiana Wants Me** . . . R. Dean Taylor
6/84	**Infatuation** . . . Rod Stewart
	Innamorata
27/56	Dean Martin
30/56	Jerry Vale
9/71	**Inner City Blues (Make Me Wanna Holler)** . . . Marvin Gaye
10/84	**Innocent Man** . . . Billy Joel

POS/YR	RECORD TITLE/ARTIST
32/76	**Inseparable** . . . Natalie Cole
34/66	**Inside-Looking Out** . . . Animals
3/70	**Instant Karma** . . . John Ono Lennon
29/79	**Instant Replay** . . . Dan Hartman
	Into The Night
11/80	Benny Mardones
20/89	Benny Mardones
10/85	**Invincible** . . . Pat Benatar
31/85	**Invisible** . . . Alison Moyet
40/83	**Invisible Hands** . . . Kim Carnes
1/86	**Invisible Touch** . . . Genesis
15/62	**Irresistible You** . . . Bobby Darin
	Irving ..see: Ballad Of
35/60	**Is A Blue Bird Blue** . . . Conway Twitty
8/86	**Is It Love** . . . Mr. Mister
34/69	**Is It Something You've Got** . . . Tyrone Davis
17/64	**Is It True** . . . Brenda Lee
15/81	**Is It You** . . . Lee Ritenour
21/79	**Is She Really Going Out With Him?** . . . Joe Jackson
11/69	**Is That All There Is** . . . Peggy Lee
31/60	**Is There Any Chance** . . . Marty Robbins
4/83	**Is There Something I Should Know** . . . Duran Duran
2/87	**Is This Love** . . . Whitesnake
9/87	**Is This Love** . . . Survivor
1/75	**Island Girl** . . . Elton John
30/57	**Island In The Sun** . . . Harry Belafonte
37/82	**Island Of Lost Souls** . . . Blondie
1/83	**Islands In The Stream** . . . Kenny Rogers with Dolly Parton
F/70	**Isn't It A Pity** . . . George Harrison
13/77	**Isn't It Time** . . . Babys
29/72	**Isn't Life Strange** . . . Moody Blues
9/69	**Israelites** . . . Desmond Dekker & The Aces
17/84	**It Ain't Enough** . . . Corey Hart
8/65	**It Ain't Me Babe** . . . Turtles
2/91	**It Ain't Over Til It's Over** . . . Lenny Kravitz
13/59	**It Doesn't Matter Anymore** . . . Buddy Holly
4/71	**It Don't Come Easy** . . . Ringo Starr
10/70	**It Don't Matter To Me** . . . Bread
29/64	**It Hurts Me** . . . Elvis Presley
7/64	**It Hurts To Be In Love** . . . Gene Pitney
13/56	**It Isn't Right** . . . Platters
23/61	**It Keeps Rainin'** . . . Fats Domino

POS/YR	RECORD TITLE/ARTIST
3/62	**It Keeps Right On A-Hurtin'** . . . Johnny Tillotson
37/77	**It Keeps You Runnin'** . . . Doobie Brothers
11/55	**It May Sound Silly** . . . McGuire Sisters
22/62	**It Might As Well Rain Until September** . . . Carole King
25/83	**It Might Be You** . . . Stephen Bishop
3/67	**It Must Be Him** . . . Vikki Carr
32/79	**It Must Be Love** . . . Alton McClain & Destiny
33/83	**It Must Be Love** . . . Madness
1/90	**It Must Have Been Love** . . . Roxette
5/72	**It Never Rains In Southern California** . . . Albert Hammond
34/91	**It Never Rains (In Southern California)** . . . Tony! Toni! Tone!
38/60	**It Only Happened Yesterday** . . . Jack Scott
11/56	**It Only Hurts For A Little While** . . . Ames Brothers
10/75	**It Only Takes A Minute** . . . Tavares
40/68.	**It Should Have Been Me** . . . Gladys Knight & The Pips
29/62	**It Started All Over Again** . . . Brenda Lee
27/73	**It Sure Took A Long, Long Time** . . . Lobo
14/67	**It Takes Two** . . . Marvin Gaye & Kim Weston
36/88	**It Takes Two** . . . Rob Base & D.J. E-Z Rock
20/66	**It Tears Me Up** . . . Percy Sledge
28/66	**It Was A Very Good Year** . . . Frank Sinatra
16/77	**It Was Almost Like A Song** . . . Ronnie Milsap
11/59	**It Was I** . . . Skip & Flip
10/88	**It Would Take A Strong Strong Man** . . . Rick Astley
37/77	**It's A Crazy World** . . . Mac McAnally
3/78	**It's A Heartache** . . . Bonnie Tyler
20/78	**It's A Laugh** . . . Daryl Hall & John Oates
28/76	**It's A Long Way There** . . . Little River Band
28/81	**It's A Love Thing** . . . Whispers
8/66	**It's A Man's Man's Man's World** . . . James Brown
12/75	**It's A Miracle** . . . Barry Manilow
13/84	**It's A Miracle** . . . Culture Club
6/83	**It's A Mistake** . . . Men At Work
32/70	**It's A New Day** . . . James Brown
14/70	**It's A Shame** . . . Spinners
26/91	**It's A Shame (My Sister)** . . . Monie Love

POS/YR	RECORD TITLE/ARTIST
9/87	**It's A Sin** . . . Pet Shop Boys
7/55	**It's A Sin To Tell A Lie** . . . Somethin' Smith & The Redheads
31/75	**It's All Down To Goodnight Vienna** . . . Ringo Starr
	It's All In The Game
1/58	Tommy Edwards
25/64	Cliff Richard
24/70	Four Tops
26/64	**It's All Over Now** . . . Rolling Stones
4/63	**It's All Right** . . . Impressions
	It's Almost Tomorrow
20/55	David Carroll
20/55	Snooky Lanson
7/56	Dream Weavers
14/56	Jo Stafford
31/65	**It's Alright** . . . Adam Faith
20/58	**(It's Been A Long Time) Pretty Baby** . . . Gino & Gina
4/77	**It's Ecstasy When You Lay Down Next To Me** . . . Barry White
30/69	**It's Getting Better** . . . Mama Cass
12/72	**It's Going To Take Some Time** . . . Carpenters
23/65	**It's Gonna Be Alright** . . . Gerry & The Pacemakers
10/82	**It's Gonna Take A Miracle** . . . Deniece Williams
14/61	**It's Gonna Work Out Fine** . . . Ike & Tina Turner
18/65	**It's Growing** . . . Temptations
10/71	**It's Impossible** . . . Perry Como
	It's In His Kiss ..see: Shoop Shoop Song
38/83	**It's Inevitable** . . . Charlie
3/59	**It's Just A Matter Of Time** . . . Brook Benton
3/89	**(It's Just) The Way That You Love Me** . . . Paula Abdul
9/59	**It's Late** . . . Ricky Nelson
23/66	**It's My Life** . . . Animals
31/84	**It's My Life** . . . Talk Talk
1/63	**It's My Party** . . . Lesley Gore
9/81	**It's My Turn** . . . Diana Ross
7/89	**It's No Crime** . . . Babyface
37/89	**It's No Secret** . . . Kylie Minogue
12/89	**It's Not Enough** . . . Starship
5/57	**It's Not For Me To Say** . . . Johnny Mathis
9/87	**It's Not Over ('Til It's Over)** . . . Starship
10/65	**It's Not Unusual** . . . Tom Jones

POS/YR	RECORD TITLE/ARTIST
	It's Now Or Never
1/60	Elvis Presley
14/81	John Schneider
23/67	**It's Now Winters Day** . . . Tommy Roe
29/76	**It's O.K.** . . . Beach Boys
20/72	**It's One Of Those Nights (Yes Love)** . . . Partridge Family
15/86	**It's Only Love** . . . Bryan Adams/Tina Turner
31/66	**It's Only Love** . . . Tommy James & The Shondells
	It's Only Make Believe
1/58	Conway Twitty
10/70	Glen Campbell
16/74	**It's Only Rock 'N Roll (But I Like It)** . . . Rolling Stones
9/64	**It's Over** . . . Roy Orbison
37/66	**It's Over** . . . Jimmie Rodgers
38/76	**It's Over** . . . Boz Scaggs
11/82	**It's Raining Again** . . . Supertramp
21/77	**It's Sad To Belong** . . . England Dan & John Ford Coley
5/77	**It's So Easy** . . . Linda Ronstadt
1/80	**It's Still Rock And Roll To Me** . . . Billy Joel
	It's The Same Old Song
5/65	Four Tops
35/78	KC & The Sunshine Band
4/59	**It's Time To Cry** . . . Paul Anka
1/71	**It's Too Late** . . . Carole King
23/66	**It's Too Late** . . . Bobby Goldsboro
4/58	**It's Too Soon To Know** . . . Pat Boone
6/63	**It's Up To You** . . . Rick Nelson
20/68	**It's Wonderful** . . . Young Rascals
6/57	**It's You I Love** . . . Fats Domino
33/78	**It's You That I Need** . . . Enchantment
	(also see: Loneliness Made Me Realize)
2/69	**It's Your Thing** . . . Isley Brothers
25/56	**Italian Theme** . . . Cyril Stapleton
25/58	**Itchy Twitchy Feeling** . . . Bobby Hendricks
16/68	**Itchycoo Park** . . . Small Faces
1/60	**Itsy Bitsy Teenie Weenie Yellow Polkadot Bikini** . . . Brian Hyland
	Ivory Tower
2/56	Cathy Carr
6/56	Gale Storm
11/56	Charms
18/57	**Ivy Rose** . . . Perry Como

POS/YR	RECORD TITLE/ARTIST
	J
1/82	**Jack & Diane** . . . John Cougar
8/78	**Jack And Jill** . . . Raydio
3/75	**Jackie Blue** . . . Ozark Mountain Daredevils
14/67	**Jackson** . . . Nancy Sinatra & Lee Hazlewood
1/87	**Jacob's Ladder** . . . Huey Lewis & the News
1/57	**Jailhouse Rock** . . . Elvis Presley
29/62	**Jam, The** . . . Bobby Gregg
32/87	**Jam Tonight** . . . Freddie Jackson
8/70	**Jam Up Jelly Tight** . . . Tommy Roe
14/57	**Jamaica Farewell** . . . Harry Belafonte
	Jambalaya (On The Bayou)
30/62	Fats Domino
16/73	Blue Ridge Rangers
17/62	**James (Hold The Ladder Steady)** . . . Sue Thompson
14/85	**Jamie** . . . Ray Parker Jr.
30/62	**Jamie** . . . Eddie Holland
18/87	**Jammin' Me** . . . Tom Petty
14/80	**Jane** . . . Jefferson Starship
4/90	**Janie's Got A Gun** . . . Aerosmith
4/64	**Java** . . . Al Hirt
	Jaws ..see: Theme From & Mr. Jaws
	Jayne ..see: Ballad of
2/74	**Jazzman** . . . Carole King
20/69	**Jealous Kind Of Fella** . . . Garland Green
19/60	**Jealous Of You** . . . Connie Francis
2/69	**Jean** . . . Oliver
17/77	**Jeans On** . . . David Dundas
8/58	**Jennie Lee** . . . Jan & Arnie
40/68	**Jennifer Eccles** . . . Hollies
26/68	**Jennifer Juniper** . . . Donovan
36/70	**Jennifer Tomkins** . . . Street People
	Jenny ..see: 867-5309
10/57	**Jenny, Jenny** . . . Little Richard
10/66	**Jenny Take A Ride!** . . . Mitch Ryder & The Detroit Wheels
2/83	**Jeopardy** . . . Greg Kihn Band
35/61	**Jeremiah Peabody's Poly Unsaturated Pills** . . . Ray Stevens
7/65	**Jerk, The** . . . Larks
9/90	**Jerk-Out** . . . Time

POS/YR	RECORD TITLE/ARTIST
11/80	**Jesse** . . . Carly Simon
30/73	**Jesse** . . . Roberta Flack
1/81	**Jessie's Girl** . . . Rick Springfield
	Jesus Christ Superstar ..see: Superstar
28/69	**Jesus Is A Soul Man** . . . Lawrence Reynolds
35/73	**Jesus Is Just Alright** . . . Doobie Brothers
7/74	**Jet** . . . Paul McCartney
8/77	**Jet Airliner** . . . Steve Miller Band
	Jim Dandy
17/57	LaVern Baker
25/74	Black Oak Arkansas
28/87	**Jimmy Lee** . . . Aretha Franklin
33/73	**Jimmy Loves Mary-Anne** . . . Looking Glass
10/67	**Jimmy Mack** . . . Martha & The Vandellas
25/61	**Jimmy's Girl** . . . Johnny Tillotson
	Jingle Bell Rock
6/57	Bobby Helms
35/58	Bobby Helms
36/60	Bobby Helms
21/61	Bobby Rydell Chubby Checker
10/70	**Jingle Jangle** . . . Archies
1/75	**Jive Talkin'** . . . Bee Gees
19/58	**Jo-Ann** . . . Playmates
17/80	**JoJo** . . . Boz Scaggs
2/84	**Joanna** . . . Kool & The Gang
21/70	**Joanne** . . . Michael Nesmith
28/71	**Jody's Got Your Girl And Gone** . . . Johnnie Taylor
19/90	**Joey** . . . Concrete Blonde
	John And Yoko ..see: Ballad Of
1/62	**Johnny Angel** . . . Shelley Fabares
8/58	**Johnny B. Goode** . . . Chuck Berry
7/62	**Johnny Get Angry** . . . Joanie Sommers
21/62	**Johnny Jingo** . . . Hayley Mills
21/62	**Johnny Loves Me** . . . Shelley Fabares
35/62	**Johnny Will** . . . Pat Boone
17/72	**Join Together** . . . Who
1/74	**Joker, The** . . . Steve Miller Band
	Joker (That's What They Call Me)
22/57	Hilltoppers
25/57	Billy Myles
20/66	**Joker Went Wild** . . . Brian Hyland
4/65	**Jolly Green Giant** . . . Kingsmen
39/81	**Jones Vs. Jones** . . . Kool & The Gang
18/60	**Josephine** . . . Bill Black's Combo
26/78	**Josie** . . . Steely Dan

POS/YR	RECORD TITLE/ARTIST
16/68	**Journey To The Center Of The Mind** . . . Amboy Dukes
6/72	**Joy** . . . Apollo 100 feat. Tom Parker
30/74	**Joy** . . . Isaac Hayes
1/71	**Joy To The World** . . . Three Dog Night
1/91	**Joyride** . . . Roxette
26/65	**Ju Ju Hand** . . . Sam The Sham & the Pharoahs
22/58	**Judy** . . . Frankie Vaughan
	Judy Blue Eyes ..see: Suite
1/68	**Judy In Disguise (With Glasses)** . . . John Fred
33/75	**Judy Mae** . . . Boomer Castleman
5/63	**Judy's Turn To Cry** . . . Lesley Gore
10/56	**Juke Box Baby** . . . Perry Como
26/82	**Juke Box Hero** . . . Foreigner
5/70	**Julie, Do Ya Love Me** . . . Bobby Sherman
1/84	**Jump** . . . Van Halen
3/84	**Jump (For My Love)** . . . Pointer Sisters
27/72	**Jump Into The Fire** . . . Nilsson
28/60	**Jump Over** . . . Freddy Cannon
13/87	**Jump Start** . . . Natalie Cole
24/82	**Jump To It** . . . Aretha Franklin
	Jumpin' Jack Flash
3/68	Rolling Stones
21/86	Aretha Franklin
21/57	**June Night** . . . Jimmy Dorsey
4/74	**Jungle Boogie** . . . Kool & The Gang
8/72	**Jungle Fever** . . . Chakachas
20/85	**Jungle Love** . . . Time
23/77	**Jungle Love** . . . Steve Miller Band
3/75	**Junior's Farm** . . . Paul McCartney
9/76	**Junk Food Junkie** . . . Larry Groce
37/61	**Jura (I Swear I Love You)** . . . Les Paul & Mary Ford
4/58	**Just A Dream** . . . Jimmy Clanton
9/90	**Just A Friend** . . . Biz Markie
12/85	**Just A Gigolo/I Ain't Got Nobody** . . . David Lee Roth
8/65	**Just A Little** . . . Beau Brummels
40/60	**Just A Little** . . . Brenda Lee
39/65	**Just A Little Bit** . . . Roy Head
7/65	**Just A Little Bit Better** . . . Herman's Hermits
23/75	**Just A Little Bit Of You** . . . Michael Jackson
9/59	**Just A Little Too Much** . . . Ricky Nelson

POS/YR	RECORD TITLE/ARTIST
7/77	**Just A Song Before I Go** . . . Crosby, Stills & Nash
9/91	**Just Another Dream** . . . Cathy Dennis
12/85	**Just Another Night** . . . Mick Jagger
19/85	**Just As I Am** . . . Air Supply
	Just As Much As Ever
32/59	Bob Beckham
24/68	Bobby Vinton
7/59	**Just Ask Your Heart** . . . Frankie Avalon
19/64	**Just Be True** . . . Gene Chandler
14/89	**Just Because** . . . Anita Baker
29/57	**Just Because** . . . Lloyd Price
6/90	**Just Between You And Me** . . . Lou Gramm
8/57	**Just Between You And Me** . . . Chordettes
21/81	**Just Between You And Me** . . . April Wine
12/57	**Just Born (To Be Your Baby)** . . . Perry Como
38/82	**Just Can't Win 'Em All** . . . Stevie Woods
35/60	**Just Come Home** . . . Hugo & Luigi
10/74	**Just Don't Want To Be Lonely** . . . Main Ingredient
5/68	**Just Dropped In (To See What Condition My Condition Was In)** . . . First Edition
20/61	**Just For Old Time's Sake** . . . McGuire Sisters
36/83	**Just Got Lucky** . . . JoBoxers
10/88	**Just Got Paid** . . . Johnny Kemp
18/59	**Just Keep It Up** . . . Dee Clark
33/66	**Just Like A Woman** . . . Bob Dylan
40/88	**Just Like Heaven** . . . Cure
8/89	**Just Like Jesse James** . . . Cher
11/66	**Just Like Me** . . . Paul Revere & The Raiders
6/88	**Just Like Paradise** . . . David Lee Roth
6/64	**(Just Like) Romeo & Juliet** . . . Reflections
1/80	**(Just Like) Starting Over** . . . John Lennon
26/58	**Just Married** . . . Marty Robbins
1/71	**Just My Imagination** . . . Temptations
17/81	**Just Once** . . . Quincy Jones/James Ingram
9/65	**Just Once In My Life** . . . Righteous Brothers
10/63	**Just One Look** . . . Doris Troy
29/60	**Just One Time** . . . Don Gibson
24/61	**Just Out Of Reach (Of My Two Open Arms)** . . . Solomon Burke
11/77	**Just Remember I Love You** . . . Firefall
40/71	**Just Seven Numbers (Can Straighten Out My Life)** . . . Four Tops

POS/YR	RECORD TITLE/ARTIST
39/81	**Just So Lonely** . . . Get Wet
2/81	**Just The Two Of Us** . . . Grover Washington, Jr./Bill Withers
14/91	**Just The Way It Is, Baby** . . . Rembrandts
3/78	**Just The Way You Are** . . . Billy Joel
7/76	**Just To Be Close To You** . . . Commodores
26/57	**Just To Hold My Hand** . . . Clyde McPhatter
8/87	**Just To See Her** . . . Smokey Robinson
30/75	**Just Too Many People** . . . Melissa Manchester
2/56	**Just Walking In The Rain** . . . Johnnie Ray
27/78	**Just What I Needed** . . . Cars
4/79	**Just When I Needed You Most** . . . Randy Vanwarmer
20/65	**Just You** . . . Sonny & Cher
27/76	**Just You And I** . . . Melissa Manchester
4/73	**Just You 'N' Me** . . . Chicago
1/91	**Justify My Love** . . . Madonna

K

POS/YR	RECORD TITLE/ARTIST
39/71	**K-Jee** . . . Nite-Liters
	Ka-Ding Dong
24/56	G-Clefs
35/56	Diamonds
38/56	Hilltoppers
	Kansas City
1/59	Wilbert Harrison
23/64	Trini Lopez
31/65	**Kansas City Star** . . . Roger Miller
1/84	**Karma Chameleon** . . . Culture Club
16/58	**Kathy-O** . . . Diamonds
16/69	**Keem-O-Sabe** . . . Electric Indian
8/57	**Keep A Knockin'** . . . Little Richard
8/83	**(Keep Feeling) Fascination** . . . Human League
2/77	**Keep It Comin' Love** . . . KC & The Sunshine Band
8/90	**Keep It Together** . . . Madonna
37/77	**Keep Me Cryin'** . . . Al Green
4/65	**Keep On Dancing** . . . Gentrys
24/68	**Keep On Lovin' Me Honey** . . . Marvin Gaye & Tammi Terrell

POS/YR	RECORD TITLE/ARTIST
1/81	**Keep On Loving You** . . . REO Speedwagon
11/89	**Keep On Movin'** . . . Soul II Soul
10/64	**Keep On Pushing** . . . Impressions
15/74	**Keep On Singing** . . . Helen Reddy
10/74	**Keep On Smilin'** . . . Wet Willie
1/73	**Keep On Truckin'** . . . Eddie Kendricks
9/65	**Keep Searchin'** . . . Del Shannon
14/67	**Keep The Ball Rollin'** . . . Jay & The Techniques
36/80	**Keep The Fire** . . . Kenny Loggins
7/82	**Keep The Fire Burnin'** . . . REO Speedwagon
	Keep Your Eye On The Sparrow ..see: Baretta's Theme
12/62	**Keep Your Hands Off My Baby** . . . Little Eva
2/87	**Keep Your Hands To Yourself** . . . Georgia Satellites
10/73	**Keeper Of The Castle** . . . Four Tops
18/85	**Keeping The Faith** . . . Billy Joel
20/55	**Kentuckian Song** . . . Hilltoppers
16/70	**Kentucky Rain** . . . Elvis Presley
	Kentucky Woman
22/67	Neil Diamond
38/68	Deep Purple
6/58	**Kewpie Doll** . . . Perry Como
8/82	**Key Largo** . . . Bertie Higgins
4/66	**Kicks** . . . Paul Revere & The Raiders
27/90	**Kickstart My Heart** . . . Motley Crue
33/84	**Kid's American** . . . Matthew Wilder
7/60	**Kiddio** . . . Brook Benton
25/82	**Kids In America** . . . Kim Wilde
16/63	**Killer Joe** . . . Rocky Fellers
12/75	**Killer Queen** . . . Queen
28/81	**Killin' Time** . . . Fred Knoblock & Susan Anton
1/73	**Killing Me Softly With His Song** . . . Roberta Flack
30/77	**Killing Of Georgie** . . . Rod Stewart
1/67	**Kind Of A Drag** . . . Buckinghams
17/63	**Kind Of Boy You Can't Forget** . . . Raindrops
8/86	**King For A Day** . . . Thompson Twins
40/72	**King Heroin** . . . James Brown
13/77	**King Is Gone** . . . Ronnie McDowell
3/83	**King Of Pain** . . . Police
36/80	**King Of The Hill** . . . Rick Pinette & Oak

POS/YR	RECORD TITLE/ARTIST
4/65	**King Of The Road** . . . Roger Miller
	(also see: Queen Of The House)
30/62	**King Of The Whole Wide World** . . . Elvis Presley
8/90	**King Of Wishful Thinking** . . . Go West
17/78	**King Tut** . . . Steve Martin
31/74	**Kings Of The Party** . . . Brownsville Station
	Kiss
1/86	Prince
31/89	Art Of Noise/Tom Jones
21/72	**Kiss An Angel Good Mornin'** . . . Charley Pride
1/76	**Kiss And Say Goodbye** . . . Manhattans
31/88	**Kiss And Tell** . . . Bryan Ferry
25/65	**Kiss Away** . . . Ronnie Dove
	Kiss Him Goodbye
1/69	Steam
12/87	Nylons
37/79	**Kiss In The Dark** . . . Pink Lady
30/56	**Kiss Me Another** . . . Georgia Gibbs
12/88	**Kiss Me Deadly** . . . Lita Ford
15/68	**Kiss Me Goodbye** . . . Petula Clark
37/80	**Kiss Me In The Rain** . . . Barbra Streisand
34/64	**Kiss Me Quick** . . . Elvis Presley
29/64	**Kiss Me Sailor** . . . Diane Renay
1/81	**Kiss On My List** . . . Daryl Hall & John Oates
25/83	**Kiss The Bride** . . . Elton John
35/90	**Kiss This Thing Goodbye** . . . del Amitri
1/78	**Kiss You All Over** . . . Exile
8/89	**Kisses On The Wind** . . . Neneh Cherry
3/57	**Kisses Sweeter Than Wine** . . . Jimmie Rodgers
12/64	**Kissin' Cousins** . . . Elvis Presley
35/61	**Kissin' On The Phone** . . . Paul Anka
11/59	**Kissin' Time** . . . Bobby Rydell
5/88	**Kissing A Fool** . . . George Michael
31/73	**Kissing My Love** . . . Bill Withers
40/91	**Kissing You** . . . Keith Washington
16/57	**Knee Deep In The Blues** . . . Guy Mitchell
15/67	**Knight In Rusty Armour** . . . Peter & Gordon
	Knock On Wood
28/66	Eddie Floyd
30/67	Otis & Carla
1/79	Amii Stewart
1/71	**Knock Three Times** . . . Dawn
9/90	**Knockin' Boots** . . . Candyman
12/73	**Knockin' On Heaven's Door** . . . Bob Dylan
14/77	**Knowing Me, Knowing You** . . . Abba
	Ko Ko Mo (I Love You So)
2/55	Perry Como
6/55	Crew-Cuts
2/73	**Kodachrome** . . . Paul Simon
1/88	**Kokomo** . . . Beach Boys
4/59	**Kookie, Kookie (Lend Me Your Comb)** . . . Edward Byrnes & Connie Stevens
40/74	**Kung Fu** . . . Curtis Mayfield
1/74	**Kung Fu Fighting** . . . Carl Douglas
1/86	**Kyrie** . . . Mr. Mister

L

POS/YR	RECORD TITLE/ARTIST
	La Bamba
22/59	Ritchie Valens
1/87	Los Lobos
9/58	**La Dee Dah** . . . Billy & Lillie
32/58	**La-Do-Dada** . . . Dale Hawkins
4/87	**La Isla Bonita** . . . Madonna
9/70	**La La La (If I Had You)** . . . Bobby Sherman
4/68	**La-La Means I Love You** . . . Delfonics
30/74	**La La Peace Song** . . . Al Wilson
	La Mer ..see: Beyond The Sea
20/58	**La Paloma** . . . Billy Vaughn
8/80	**Ladies Night** . . . Kool & The Gang
1/80	**Lady** . . . Kenny Rogers
6/75	**Lady** . . . Styx
10/79	**Lady** . . . Little River Band
28/80	**Lady** . . . Whispers
39/67	**Lady** . . . Jack Jones
20/67	**Lady Bird** . . . Nancy Sinatra & Lee Hazlewood
14/75	**Lady Blue** . . . Leon Russell
6/66	**Lady Godiva** . . . Peter & Gordon
3/87	**Lady In Red** . . . Chris DeBurgh
24/66	**Lady Jane** . . . Rolling Stones
24/78	**Lady Love** . . . Lou Rawls
30/83	**Lady Love Me (One More Time)** . . . George Benson
14/60	**Lady Luck** . . . Lloyd Price

POS/YR	RECORD TITLE/ARTIST
4/68	**Lady Madonna** . . . Beatles
1/75	**Lady Marmalade** . . . LaBelle
2/68	**Lady Willpower** . . . Gary Puckett & The Union Gap
8/81	**Lady (You Bring Me Up)** . . . Commodores
33/68	**Lalena** . . . Donovan
	(Lament Of Cherokee) ..see: Indian Reservation
4/87	**Land Of Confusion** . . . Genesis
29/66	**Land Of Milk And Honey** . . . Vogues
	Land Of 1000 Dances
30/65	Cannibal & The Headhunters
6/66	Wilson Pickett
13/84	**Language Of Love** . . . Dan Fogelberg
32/61	**Language Of Love** . . . John D. Loudermilk
	Lara's Theme ..see: Somewhere My Love
13/65	**Last Chance To Turn Around** . . . Gene Pitney
21/76	**Last Child** . . . Aerosmith
3/78	**Last Dance** . . . Donna Summer
	Last Date
2/60	Floyd Cramer
21/60	Lawrence Welk
	(also see: My Last Date With You)
19/75	**Last Farewell** . . . Roger Whittaker
18/75	**Last Game Of The Season (A Blind Man In The Bleachers)** . . . David Geddes
	Last Kiss
2/64	J. Frank Wilson
34/74	Wednesday
36/89	**Last Mile** . . . Cinderella
3/61	**Last Night** . . . Mar-Keys
8/72	**(Last Night) I Didn't Get To Sleep At All** . . . 5th Dimension
3/73	**Last Song** . . . Edward Bear
9/65	**Last Time** . . . Rolling Stones
40/84	**Last Time I Made Love** . . . Joyce Kennedy & Jeffrey Osborne
14/74	**Last Time I Saw Him** . . . Diana Ross
1/66	**Last Train To Clarksville** . . . Monkees
39/80	**Last Train To London** . . . Electric Light Orchestra
25/67	**Last Waltz** . . . Engelbert Humperdinck
40/66	**Last Word In Lonesome Is Me** . . . Eddy Arnold
21/89	**Last Worthless Evening** . . . Don Henley
27/57	**Lasting Love** . . . Sal Mineo
6/80	**Late In The Evening** . . . Paul Simon
10/65	**Laugh At Me** . . . Sonny

POS/YR	RECORD TITLE/ARTIST
15/65	**Laugh, Laugh** . . . Beau Brummels
10/69	**Laughing** . . . Guess Who
15/63	**Laughing Boy** . . . Mary Wells
1/75	**Laughter In The Rain** . . . Neil Sedaka
14/65	**Laurie (Strange Things Happen)** . . . Dickey Lee
3/59	**Lavender-Blue** . . . Sammy Turner
	LaVerne & Shirley Theme ..see: Making Our Dreams Come True
13/83	**Lawyers In Love** . . . Jackson Browne
11/70	**Lay A Little Lovin' On Me** . . . Robin McNamara
6/70	**Lay Down (Candles In The Rain)** . . . Melanie/Edwin Hawkins Singers
3/78	**Lay Down Sally** . . . Eric Clapton
16/56	**Lay Down Your Arms** . . . Chordettes
40/85	**Lay It Down** . . . Ratt
7/69	**Lay Lady Lay** . . . Bob Dylan
6/85	**Lay Your Hands On Me** . . . Thompson Twins
7/89	**Lay Your Hands On Me** . . . Bon Jovi
10/72	**Layla** . . . Derek & The Dominos
14/67	**Lazy Day** . . . Spanky & Our Gang
40/64	**Lazy Elsie Molly** . . . Chubby Checker
12/58	**Lazy Mary** . . . Lou Monte
14/61	**Lazy River** . . . Bobby Darin
21/58	**Lazy Summer Night** . . . Four Preps
1/78	**Le Freak** . . . Chic
5/79	**Lead Me On** . . . Maxine Nightingale
9/82	**Leader Of The Band** . . . Dan Fogelberg
19/65	**Leader Of The Laundromat** . . . Detergents
1/64	**Leader Of The Pack** . . . Shangri-Las
25/62	**Leah** . . . Roy Orbison
	Lean On Me
1/72	Bill Withers
1/87	Club Nouveau
9/66	**Leaning On The Lamp Post** . . . Herman's Hermits
1/55	**Learnin' The Blues** . . . Frank Sinatra
6/82	**Leather And Lace** . . . Stevie Nicks/Don Henley
11/89	**Leave A Light On** . . . Belinda Carlisle
27/84	**Leave A Tender Moment Alone** . . . Billy Joel
24/84	**Leave It** . . . Yes
3/73	**Leave Me Alone (Ruby Red Dress)** . . . Helen Reddy

Van Halen's albums have steadily reached No. 1 on the album charts since Sammy Hagar replaced lead vocalist David Lee Roth—but the group's only No. 1 single was 1984's "Jump," which prominently featured singer Roth.

Bobby Vee's enviable string of six top-10 hits during the 1960s made him self-conscious of his "pop" roots years later. The man who topped the charts with songs like "Rubber Ball" and "Run To Him" released *Nothin' Like a Sunny Day* in 1972 under his given name Robert Thomas Velline—and it contained a remake of "Take Good Care Of My Baby."

The Ventures remain the preeminent rock instrumental group of all time. For four consecutive years—from 1963-1966—the group placed three albums in the Top 40 each year. Their all-time hit single "Walk Don't Run" reached No. 2 in 1960, and a 1964 remake later climbed to No. 8.

The Village People, a six-man group who wore zany "macho" costumes onstage, may have typified what some felt to be disco music's inherent absurdity. The group's biggest hit was 1978's "Y.M.C.A."

Bobby Vinton's "Blue Velvet" held the No. 1 position for three weeks in 1963—and then took on a whole new meaning in the 80s, when filmmaker David Lynch used the song throughout his classic (and controversial) film of the same name.

Vixen's sole top-40 hit, 1988's "Edge Of A Broken Heart," was penned and produced by prolific hitmaker Richard Marx. One member of the all-female metal group, Roxy Petrucci, earlier recorded with Atlantic's Madame X.

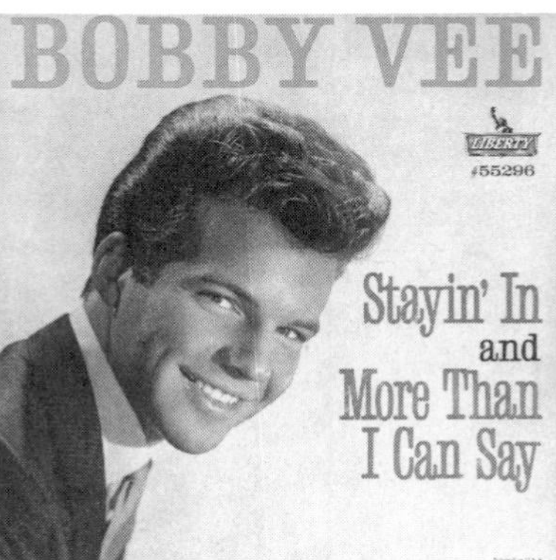

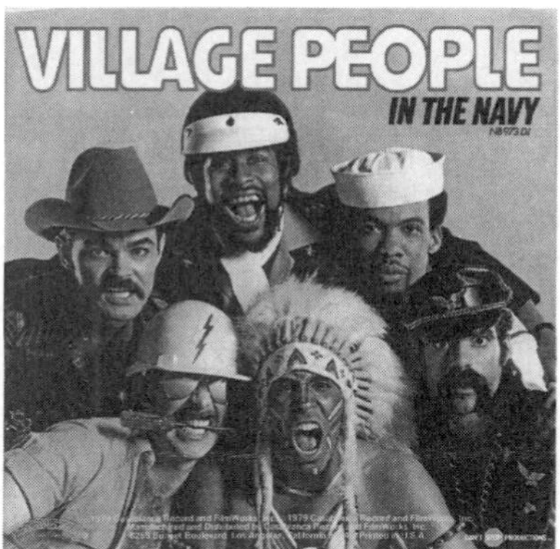

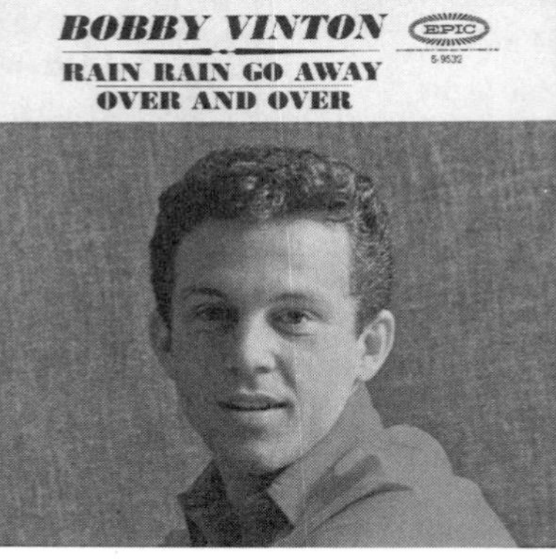

Dionne Warwick's sophisticated approach to pop music has worked for her since 1963's hit "Don't Make Me Over." Surprisingly, she's had only one No. 1 single in her career: 1985's "That's What Friends Are For," sung with Elton John, Stevie Wonder, and Gladys Knight and credited to "Dionne & Friends."

Dinah Washington's first top-10 hit, "What A Diff'rence A Day Makes," reached No. 8 in 1959. Sixteen years later, respected R&B star Esther Phillips took the same song to the Top 20.

Jody Watley helped kick off a trend in late-80s pop music with her 1989 album *You Wanna Dance With Me?* The set—a compilation of her greatest hits in 12" dance mix versions—was one of the first of the "dance remix" albums later offered by the likes of Paula Abdul.

Mary Wells built her reputation as one of Motown's premier female vocalists with hits like 1964's "My Guy." The first artist to record for Motown, she was also among the first to depart in the mid-60s. When it was announced in 1990 that she had throat cancer, several performers rallied to her support.

Karyn White's eponymous debut album featured three top-10 hits; her 1991 *Ritual of Love* promptly shot her single "Romantic" to the first No. 1 pop single of her career. At the helm: multi-platinum producers JImmy Jam and Terry Lewis.

White Lion's 1988 Atlantic debut album offered two singles that roared up the Top 10—"Wait," which reached No. 8, and "When The Children Cry," which hit No. 3. The group's long-haired vocalist carried a name no teenager's mother would love: Mike Tramp.

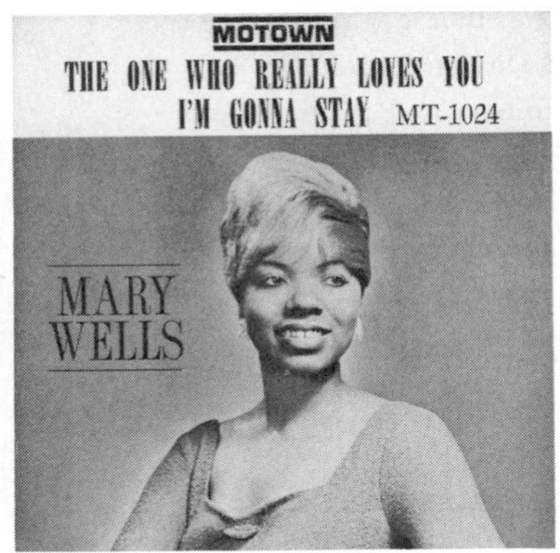

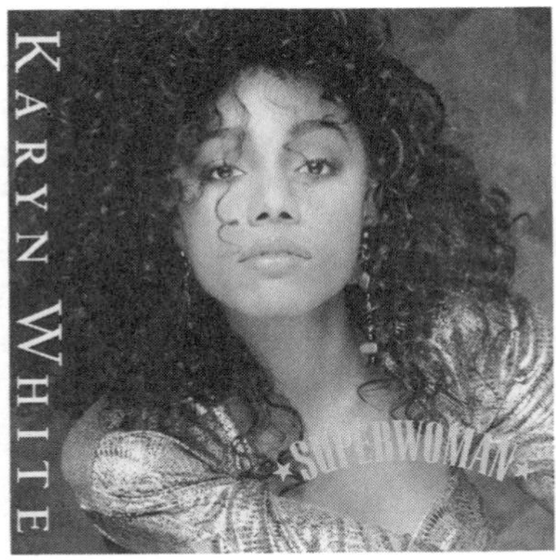

POS/YR	RECORD TITLE/ARTIST
21/73	**Leaving Me** . . . Independents
1/69	**Leaving On A Jet Plane** . . . Peter, Paul & Mary
9/58	**Left Right Out Of Your Heart** . . . Patti Page
	(Legend Of Billy Jack) ..see: One Tin Soldier
31/80	**Legend Of Wooley Swamp** . . . Charlie Daniels Band
8/84	**Legs** . . . ZZ Top
	Lemon Tree
35/62	Peter, Paul & Mary
20/65	Trini Lopez
11/58	**Leroy** . . . Jack Scott
31/68	**Les Bicyclettes De Belsize** . . . Engelbert Humperdinck
34/68	**Lesson, The** . . . Vikki Carr
12/87	**Lessons In Love** . . . Level 42
	Let A Man Come In And Do The Popcorn
21/69	James Brown (Part One)
40/70	James Brown (Part Two)
36/69	**Let A Woman Be A Woman - Let A Man Be A Man** . . . Dyke & The Blazers
3/76	**Let 'Em In** . . . Wings
34/89	**Let Go** . . . Sharon Bryant
10/76	**Let Her In** . . . John Travolta
39/85	**Let Him Go** . . . Animotion
1/70	**Let It Be** . . . Beatles
	Let It Be Me
7/60	Everly Brothers
5/64	Betty Everett & Jerry Butler
36/69	Glen Campbell & Bobbie Gentry
40/82	Willie Nelson
12/67	**Let It Out (Let It All Hang Out)** . . . Hombres
23/74	**Let It Ride** . . . Bachman-Turner Overdrive
30/76	**Let It Shine** . . . Olivia Newton-John
5/82	**Let It Whip** . . . Dazz Band
23/67	**Let Love Come Between Us** . . . James & Bobby Purify
20/69	**Let Me** . . . Paul Revere & The Raiders
29/65	**Let Me Be** . . . Turtles
31/80	**Let Me Be The Clock** . . . Smokey Robinson
7/87	**Let Me Be The One** . . . Expose
6/74	**Let Me Be There** . . . Olivia Newton-John
21/80	**Let Me Be Your Angel** . . . Stacy Lattisaw
1/57	**(Let Me Be Your) Teddy Bear** . . . Elvis Presley

POS/YR	RECORD TITLE/ARTIST
20/61	**Let Me Belong To You** . . . Brian Hyland
38/82	**Let Me Go** . . . Ray Parker Jr.
35/80	**Let Me Go, Love** . . . Nicolette Larson
	Let Me Go, Lover!
1/55	Joan Weber
6/55	Teresa Brewer
8/55	Patti Page
17/55	Sunny Gale
32/70	**Let Me Go To Him** . . . Dionne Warwick
4/62	**Let Me In** . . . Sensations
36/73	**Let Me In** . . . Osmonds
10/80	**Let Me Love You Tonight** . . . Pure Prairie League
17/73	**Let Me Serenade You** . . . Three Dog Night
18/82	**Let Me Tickle Your Fancy** . . . Jermaine Jackson
9/80	**Let My Love Open The Door** . . . Pete Townshend
16/58	**Let The Bells Keep Ringing** . . . Paul Anka
	Let The Four Winds Blow
29/57	Roy Brown
15/61	Fats Domino
	Let The Good Times Roll
20/56	Shirley & Lee
22/67	Bunny Sigler (medley)
7/60	**Let The Little Girl Dance** . . . Billy Bland
8/84	**Let The Music Play** . . . Shannon
32/76	**Let The Music Play** . . . Barry White
	Let The Sunshine In ..see: Aquarius
	Let Them ..see: Let 'Em
7/61	**Let There Be Drums** . . . Sandy Nelson
27/74	**Let Your Hair Down** . . . Temptations
1/76	**Let Your Love Flow** . . . Bellamy Brothers
28/71	**Let Your Love Go** . . . Bread
36/78	**Let's All Chant** . . . Michael Zager Band
1/83	**Let's Dance** . . . David Bowie
4/62	**Let's Dance** . . . Chris Montez
1/75	**Let's Do It Again** . . . Staple Singers
40/65	**Let's Do The Freddie** . . . Chubby Checker **(also see: Do The Freddie)**
21/67	**Let's Fall In Love** . . . Peaches & Herb
1/73	**Let's Get It On** . . . Marvin Gaye
32/74	**Let's Get Married** . . . Al Green
9/80	**Let's Get Serious** . . . Jermaine Jackson
8/61	**Let's Get Together** . . . Hayley Mills **(also see: Get Together)**
9/87	**Let's Go!** . . . Wang Chung
14/79	**Let's Go** . . . Cars

POS/YR	RECORD TITLE/ARTIST
19/62	**Let's Go** . . . Routers
39/61	**Let's Go Again** . . . Hank Ballard
7/86	**Let's Go All The Way** . . . Sly Fox
1/84	**Let's Go Crazy** . . . Prince
30/83	**Let's Go Dancin' (Ooh La, La, La)** . . . Kool & The Gang
31/66	**Let's Go Get Stoned** . . . Ray Charles
6/60	**Let's Go, Let's Go, Let's Go** . . . Hank Ballard
26/63	**Let's Go Steady Again** . . . Neil Sedaka
3/81	**Let's Groove** . . . Earth, Wind & Fire
	Let's Hang On!
3/65	4 Seasons
32/82	Barry Manilow
37/60	**Let's Have A Party** . . . Wanda Jackson
1/84	**Let's Hear It For The Boy** . . . Deniece Williams
38/63	**Let's Kiss And Make Up** . . . Bobby Vinton
20/63	**Let's Limbo Some More** . . . Chubby Checker
8/67	**Let's Live For Today** . . . Grass Roots
35/76	**Let's Live Together** . . . Road Apples
11/65	**Let's Lock The Door** . . . Jay & The Americans
35/73	**Let's Pretend** . . . Raspberries
18/74	**Let's Put It All Together** . . . Stylistics
20/66	**Let's Start All Over Again** . . . Ronnie Dove
	Let's Stay Together
1/72	Al Green
26/84	Tina Turner
31/74	**Let's Straighten It Out** . . . Latimore
7/60	**Let's Think About Living** . . . Bob Luman
20/63	**Let's Turkey Trot** . . . Little Eva
8/61	**Let's Twist Again** . . . Chubby Checker
2/87	**Let's Wait Awhile** . . . Janet Jackson
39/87	**Let's Work** . . . Mick Jagger
	Let's Work Together
26/70	Canned Heat
32/70	Wilbert Harrison
	Letter, The
1/67	Box Tops
20/69	Arbors
7/70	Joe Cocker
25/64	**Letter From Sherry** . . . Dale Ward
19/62	**Letter Full Of Tears** . . . Gladys Knight & The Pips
	Letter Song ..see: S.Y.S.L.J.F.M.
25/58	**Letter To An Angel** . . . Jimmy Clanton

POS/YR	RECORD TITLE/ARTIST
33/73	**Letter To Myself** . . . Chi-Lites
39/75	**Letting Go** . . . Wings
24/72	**Levon** . . . Elton John
7/71	**Liar** . . . Three Dog Night
12/65	**Liar, Liar** . . . Castaways
	Liberty Valance ..see: (Man Who Shot)
32/89	**Licence To Chill** . . . Billy Ocean
14/68	**Licking Stick - Licking Stick** . . . James Brown
11/77	**Lido Shuffle** . . . Boz Scaggs
13/62	**Lie To Me** . . . Brook Benton
16/57	**Liechtensteiner Polka** . . . Will Glahe
20/66	**Lies** . . . Knickerbockers
27/87	**Lies** . . . Jonathan Butler
30/83	**Lies** . . . Thompson Twins
38/90	**Lies** . . . En Vogue
35/91	**Life Goes On** . . . Poison
7/86	**Life In A Northern Town** . . . Dream Academy
19/85	**Life In One Day** . . . Howard Jones
11/77	**Life In The Fast Lane** . . . Eagles
8/74	**Life Is A Rock (But The Radio Rolled Me)** . . . Reunion
34/81	**Life Of Illusion** . . . Joe Walsh
12/78	**Life's Been Good** . . . Joe Walsh
	Light My Fire
1/67	Doors
3/68	Jose Feliciano
33/87	**Light Of Day** . . . Barbusters (Joan Jett)
1/66	**Lightnin' Strikes** . . . Lou Christie
24/67	**Lightning's Girl** . . . Nancy Sinatra
12/84	**Lights Out** . . . Peter Wolf
11/67	**(Lights Went Out In) Massachusetts** . . . Bee Gees
27/66	**Like A Baby** . . . Len Barry
1/89	**Like A Prayer** . . . Madonna
12/86	**Like A Rock** . . . Bob Seger
2/65	**Like A Rolling Stone** . . . Bob Dylan
36/76	**Like A Sad Song** . . . John Denver
40/78	**Like A Sunday In Salem (The Amos & Andy Song)** . . . Gene Cotton
1/84	**Like A Virgin** . . . Madonna
24/67	**Like An Old Time Movie** . . . Scott McKenzie
38/61	**Like, Long Hair** . . . Paul Revere & The Raiders
14/86	**Like No Other Night** . . . 38 Special
22/60	**Like Strangers** . . . Everly Brothers

POS/YR	RECORD TITLE/ARTIST
17/68	**Like To Get To Know You** . . . Spanky & Our Gang
	Lil' ..see: Little
11/91	**Lily Was Here** . . . David A. Stewart & Candy Dulfer
	Limbo Rock
2/62	Chubby Checker
40/62	Champs
28/63	**Linda** . . . Jan & Dean
	Ling, Ting, Tong
26/55	Charms
28/55	Five Keys
	Lion Sleeps Tonight
1/61	Tokens
3/72	Robert John
17/57	**Lips Of Wine** . . . Andy Williams
15/56	**Lipstick And Candy And Rubbersole Shoes** . . . Julius LaRosa
5/59	**Lipstick On Your Collar** . . . Connie Francis
	Lisbon Antigua
1/56	Nelson Riddle
19/56	Mitch Miller
3/66	**Listen People** . . . Herman's Hermits
11/72	**Listen To The Music** . . . Doobie Brothers
1/75	**Listen To What The Man Said** . . . Wings
1/89	**Listen To Your Heart** . . . Roxette
16/68	**Little Arrows** . . . Leapy Lee
21/63	**Little Band Of Gold** . . . James Gilreath
2/67	**Little Bit Me, A Little Bit You** . . . Monkees
11/76	**Little Bit More** . . . Dr. Hook
16/65	**Little Bit Of Heaven** . . . Ronnie Dove
38/86	**Little Bit Of Love (Is All It Takes)** . . . New Edition
	Little Bit Of Soap
12/61	Jarmels
34/79	Nigel Olsson
2/67	**Little Bit O'Soul** . . . Music Explosion
19/60	**Little Bitty Girl** . . . Bobby Rydell
	Little Bitty Pretty One
6/57	Thurston Harris
25/62	Clyde McPhatter
13/72	Jackson 5
9/62	**Little Bitty Tear** . . . Burl Ives
29/62	**Little Black Book** . . . Jimmy Dean
17/58	**Little Blue Man** . . . Betty Johnson
17/61	**Little Boy Sad** . . . Johnny Burnette
36/85	**Little By Little** . . . Robert Plant
7/64	**Little Children** . . . Billy J. Kramer

POS/YR	RECORD TITLE/ARTIST
36/60	**Little Coco Palm** . . . Jerry Wallace
2/57	**Little Darlin'** . . . Diamonds
15/63	**Little Deuce Coupe** . . . Beach Boys
11/61	**Little Devil** . . . Neil Sedaka
8/62	**Little Diane** . . . Dion
30/59	**Little Dipper** . . . Mickey Mozart Quintet
	Little Drummer Boy
13/58	Harry Simeone Chorale
15/59	Harry Simeone Chorale
24/60	Harry Simeone Chorale
22/61	Harry Simeone Chorale
28/62	Harry Simeone Chorale
23/61	**Little Egypt (Ying-Yang)** . . . Coasters
8/66	**Little Girl** . . . Syndicate Of Sound
20/66	**Little Girl I Once Knew** . . . Beach Boys
	Little Green Apples
2/68	O.C. Smith
39/68	Roger Miller
21/70	**Little Green Bag** . . . George Baker Selection
9/64	**Little Honda** . . . Hondells
17/81	**Little In Love** . . . Cliff Richard
29/89	**Little Jackie Wants To Be A Star** . . . Lisa Lisa & Cult Jam
3/80	**Little Jeannie** . . . Elton John
17/66	**Little Latin Lupe Lu** . . . Mitch Ryder & The Detroit Wheels
19/89	**Little Liar** . . . Joan Jett
4/87	**Little Lies** . . . Fleetwood Mac
37/90	**Little Love** . . . Corey Hart
33/56	**Little Love Can Go A Long, Long Way** . . . Dream Weavers
21/66	**Little Man** . . . Sonny & Cher
3/79	**Little More Love** . . . Olivia Newton-John
3/64	**Little Old Lady (From Pasadena)** . . . Jan & Dean
38/67	**Little Old Wine Drinker, Me** . . . Dean Martin
4/67	**Little Ole Man (Uptight-Everything's Alright)** . . . Bill Cosby
6/83	**Little Red Corvette** . . . Prince
23/62	**Little Red Rented Rowboat** . . . Joe Dowell
2/66	**Lil' Red Riding Hood** . . . Sam The Sham & The Pharoahs
11/63	**Little Red Rooster** . . . Sam Cooke
14/89	**Little Respect** . . . Erasure
32/57	**Little Sandy Sleighfoot** . . . Jimmy Dean
5/61	**Little Sister** . . . Elvis Presley
20/59	**Little Space Girl** . . . Jesse Lee Turner

POS/YR	RECORD TITLE/ARTIST
1/58	**Little Star** . . . Elegants
13/65	**Little Things** . . . Bobby Goldsboro
35/60	**Little Things Mean A Lot** . . . Joni James
20/83	**Little Too Late** . . . Pat Benatar
12/63	**Little Town Flirt** . . . Del Shannon
25/57	**Little White Lies** . . . Betty Johnson
3/73	**Little Willy** . . . Sweet
3/69	**Little Woman** . . . Bobby Sherman
	Live And Die ..see: (Forever)
2/73	**Live And Let Die** . . . Wings
34/85	**Live Every Moment** . . . REO Speedwagon
32/86	**Live Is Life** . . . Opus
40/88	**Live My Life** . . . Boy George
1/86	**Live To Tell** . . . Madonna
20/76	**Livin' For The Weekend** . . . O'Jays
19/74	**Livin' For You** . . . Al Green
31/84	**Livin' In Desperate Times** . . . Olivia Newton-John
40/77	**Livin' In The Life** . . . Isley Brothers
15/79	**Livin' It Up (Friday Night)** . . . Bell & James
1/87	**Livin' On A Prayer** . . . Bon Jovi
13/77	**Livin' Thing** . . . Electric Light Orchestra
22/63	**Living A Lie** . . . Al Martino
37/75	**Living A Little, Laughing A Little** . . . Spinners
30/59	**Living Doll** . . . Cliff Richard
8/74	**Living For The City** . . . Stevie Wonder
17/87	**Living In A Box** . . . Living In A Box
23/81	**Living In A Fantasy** . . . Leo Sayer
22/72	**Living In A House Divided** . . . Cher
4/86	**Living In America** . . . James Brown
9/89	**Living In Sin** . . . Bon Jovi
11/73	**Living In The Past** . . . Jethro Tull
6/81	**Living Inside Myself** . . . Gino Vannelli
25/77	**Living Next Door To Alice** . . . Smokie
32/73	**Living Together, Growing Together** . . . 5th Dimension
1/89	**Living Years** . . . Mike & The Mechanics
37/75	**Lizzie And The Rainman** . . . Tanya Tucker
14/69	**Lo Mucho Que Te Quiero** . . . Rene & Rene
F/78	**Load-Out, The** . . . Jackson Browne
	Loco-Motion
1/62	Little Eva
1/74	Grand Funk
3/88	Kylie Minogue
12/63	**Loddy Lo** . . . Chubby Checker

POS/YR	RECORD TITLE/ARTIST
6/79	**Logical Song** . . . Supertramp
9/70	**Lola** . . . Kinks
	Lollipop
2/58	Chordettes
20/58	Ronald & Ruby
39/78	**London Town** . . . Wings
14/67	**(Loneliness Made Me Realize) It's You That I Need** . . . Temptations
22/65	**L-O-N-E-L-Y** . . . Bobby Vinton
6/60	**Lonely Blue Boy** . . . Conway Twitty
	Lonely Boy
1/59	Paul Anka
F/72	Donny Osmond
7/77	**Lonely Boy** . . . Andrew Gold
6/62	**Lonely Bull** . . . Tijuana Brass feat. Herb Alpert
3/71	**Lonely Days** . . . Bee Gees
24/59	**Lonely For You** . . . Gary Stites
26/58	**Lonely Island** . . . Sam Cooke
32/61	**Lonely Man** . . . Elvis Presley
3/76	**Lonely Night (Angel Face)** . . . Captain & Tennille
6/85	**Lonely Ol' Night** . . . John Cougar Mellencamp
23/59	**Lonely One** . . . Duane Eddy
5/75	**Lonely People** . . . America
5/59	**Lonely Street** . . . Andy Williams
39/63	**Lonely Surfer** . . . Jack Nitzsche
7/59	**Lonely Teardrops** . . . Jackie Wilson
12/60	**Lonely Teenager** . . . Dion
22/60	**Lonely Weekends** . . . Charlie Rich
6/79	**Lonesome Loser** . . . Little River Band
7/58	**Lonesome Town** . . . Ricky Nelson
31/71	**Long Ago And Far Away** . . . James Taylor
1/70	**Long And Winding Road** . . . Beatles
2/72	**Long Cool Woman (In A Black Dress)** . . . Hollies
26/72	**Long Dark Road** . . . Hollies
38/72	**Long Haired Lover From Liverpool** . . . Little Jimmy Osmond
33/66	**Long Live Our Love** . . . Shangri-Las
17/65	**Long Lonely Nights** . . . Bobby Vinton
20/70	**Long Lonesome Highway** . . . Michael Parks
25/70	**Long Long Time** . . . Linda Ronstadt
20/78	**Long, Long Way From Home** . . . Foreigner
	(Long Nights) ..see: Blue Collar Man
8/80	**Long Run** . . . Eagles

POS/YR	RECORD TITLE/ARTIST
9/75	**Long Tall Glasses (I Can Dance)** . . . Leo Sayer
	Long Tall Sally
6/56	Little Richard
8/56	Pat Boone
22/77	**Long Time** . . . Boston
8/73	**Long Train Runnin'** . . . Doobie Brothers
2/80	**Longer** . . . Dan Fogelberg
14/84	**Longest Time** . . . Billy Joel
6/55	**Longest Walk** . . . Jaye P. Morgan
5/74	**Longfellow Serenade** . . . Neil Diamond
1/89	**Look, The** . . . Roxette
39/75	**Look At Me (I'm In Love)** . . . Moments
1/88	**Look Away** . . . Chicago
	Look For A Star
16/60	Garry Miles
19/60	Billy Vaughn
26/60	Garry Mills
29/60	Deane Hawley
36/57	**Look Homeward, Angel** . . . Johnnie Ray
14/61	**Look In My Eyes** . . . Chantels
11/75	**Look In My Eyes Pretty Woman** . . . Dawn
18/83	**Look Of Love** . . . ABC
	Look Of Love
22/67	Dusty Springfield
4/68	Sergio Mendes & Brasil '66
27/65	**Look Of Love** . . . Lesley Gore
35/88	**Look Out Any Window** . . . Bruce Hornsby & The Range
32/66	**Look Through Any Window** . . . Hollies
24/66	**Look Through My Window** . . . Mamas & The Papas
14/70	**Look What They've Done To My Song Ma** . . . New Seekers
4/72	**Look What You Done For Me** . . . Al Green
32/67	**Look What You've Done** . . . Pozo Seco Singers
14/80	**Look What You've Done To Me** . . . Boz Scaggs
	Lookin' For A Love
39/72	J. Geils Band
10/74	Bobby Womack
5/80	**Lookin' For Love** . . . Johnny Lee
2/70	**Lookin' Out My Back Door** . . . Creedence Clearwater Revival
16/72	**Lookin' Through The Windows** . . . Jackson 5
5/58	**Looking Back** . . . Nat "King" Cole
2/87	**Looking For A New Love** . . . Jody Watley

POS/YR	RECORD TITLE/ARTIST
39/83	**Looking For A Stranger** . . . Pat Benatar
29/76	**Looking For Space** . . . John Denver
	Looking Through The Eyes Of Love
28/65	Gene Pitney
39/73	Partridge Family
1/77	**Looks Like We Made It** . . . Barry Manilow
4/63	**Loop De Loop** . . . Johnny Thunder
4/74	**Lord's Prayer** . . . Sister Janet Mead
27/76	**Lorelei** . . . Styx
4/91	**Losing My Religion** . . . R.E.M.
6/63	**Losing You** . . . Brenda Lee
34/80	**Lost Her In The Sun** . . . John Stewart
1/87	**Lost In Emotion** . . . Lisa Lisa & Cult Jam
3/80	**Lost In Love** . . . Air Supply
35/85	**Lost In Love** . . . New Edition
12/88	**Lost In You** . . . Rod Stewart
1/89	**Lost In Your Eyes** . . . Debbie Gibson
35/61	**Lost Love** . . . H.B. Barnum
9/77	**Lost Without Your Love** . . . Bread
8/79	**Lotta Love** . . . Nicolette Larson
13/57	**Lotta Lovin'** . . . Gene Vincent
	Louie Louie
2/63	Kingsmen
30/66	Sandpipers
	Love And Affection ..see: (Can't Live Without Your)
15/90	**Love And Emotion** . . . Stevie B
	Love And Marriage
5/55	Frank Sinatra
20/55	Dinah Shore
17/91	**Love And Understanding** . . . Cher
25/91	**Love At First Sight** . . . Styx
	Love Ballad
20/76	L.T.D.
18/79	George Benson
	Love Being Your Fool ..see: (Shu-Doo-Pa-Poo-Poop)
1/88	**Love Bites** . . . Def Leppard
11/86	**Love Bizarre** . . . Sheila E.
25/67	**Love Bug Leave My Heart Alone** . . . Martha & The Vandellas
10/62	**Love Came To Me** . . . Dion
2/69	**Love (Can Make You Happy)** . . . Mercy
23/88	**Love Changes (Everything)** . . . Climie Fisher
	Love Child
1/68	Supremes
13/90	Sweet Sensation
17/82	**Love Come Down** . . . Evelyn King

POS/YR	RECORD TITLE/ARTIST
32/79	**Love Don't Live Here Anymore** . . . Rose Royce
15/74	**Love Don't Love Nobody** . . . Spinners
15/67	**Love Eyes** . . . Nancy Sinatra
30/76	**Love Fire** . . . Jigsaw
5/70	**Love Grows (Where My Rosemary Goes)** . . . Edison Lighthouse
1/76	**Love Hangover** . . . Diana Ross
11/71	**Love Her Madly** . . . Doors
8/76	**Love Hurts** . . . Nazareth
7/73	**Love I Lost** . . . Harold Melvin & The Bluenotes
20/67	**Love I Saw In You Was Just A Mirage** . . . Miracles
5/89	**Love In An Elevator** . . . Aerosmith
36/77	**Love In 'C' Minor** . . . Cerrone
22/83	**Love In Store** . . . Fleetwood Mac
15/82	**Love In The First Degree** . . . Alabama
16/76	**Love In The Shadows** . . . Neil Sedaka
24/89	**Love In Your Eyes** . . . Eddie Money
36/90	**Love Is** . . . Alannah Myles
5/83	**Love Is A Battlefield** . . . Pat Benatar
10/57	**Love Is A Golden Ring** . . . Frankie Laine
13/66	**Love Is A Hurtin' Thing** . . . Lou Rawls
	Love Is A Many-Splendored Thing
1/55	Four Aces
26/55	Don Cornell
23/83	**Love Is A Stranger** . . . Eurythmics
4/91	**Love Is A Wonderful Thing** . . . Michael Bolton
2/76	**Love Is Alive** . . . Gary Wright
7/68	**Love Is All Around** . . . Troggs
15/58	**Love Is All We Need** . . . Tommy Edwards
20/82	**Love Is Alright Tonite** . . . Rick Springfield
	Love Is Blue
1/68	Paul Mauriat
22/69	Dells (medley)
16/86	**Love Is Forever** . . . Billy Ocean
1/67	**Love Is Here And Now You're Gone** . . . Supremes
10/82	**Love Is In Control (Finger On The Trigger)** . . . Donna Summer
7/78	**Love Is In The Air** . . . John Paul Young
26/68	**(Love Is Like A) Baseball Game** . . . Intruders
37/82	**Love Is Like A Rock** . . . Donnie Iris
9/66	**Love Is Like An Itching In My Heart** . . . Supremes

POS/YR	RECORD TITLE/ARTIST
8/78	**Love Is Like Oxygen** . . . Sweet
	Love Is Strange
11/57	Mickey & Sylvia
13/67	Peaches & Herb
10/79	**Love Is The Answer** . . . England Dan & John Ford Coley
30/76	**Love Is The Drug** . . . Roxy Music
17/85	**Love Is The Seventh Wave** . . . Sting
7/56	**(Love Is) The Tender Trap** . . . Frank Sinatra
1/78	**(Love Is) Thicker Than Water** . . . Andy Gibb
16/73	**Love Jones** . . . Brighter Side Of Darkness **(also see: Basketball Jones)**
16/70	**Love Land** . . . Charles Wright
	Love Letters
5/62	Ketty Lester
19/66	Elvis Presley
1/57	**Love Letters In The Sand** . . . Pat Boone
17/85	**Love Light In Flight** . . . Stevie Wonder
13/75	**L-O-V-E (Love)** . . . Al Green
	Love, Love, Love
30/56	Clovers
30/56	Diamonds
1/76	**Love Machine** . . . Miracles
15/68	**Love Makes A Woman** . . . Barbara Acklin
11/66	**Love Makes The World Go Round** . . . Deon Jackson
26/63	**Love (Makes The World Go 'Round)** . . . Paul Anka
33/58	**Love Makes The World Go 'Round** . . . Perry Como
13/91	**Love Makes Things Happen** . . . Pebbles
2/57	**Love Me** . . . Elvis Presley
14/76	**Love Me** . . . Yvonne Elliman
1/64	**Love Me Do** . . . Beatles
10/74	**Love Me For A Reason** . . . Osmonds
29/90	**Love Me For Life** . . . Stevie B
	Love Me Forever
24/57	Eydie Gorme
25/57	Four Esquires
	Love Me Or Leave Me
12/55	Sammy Davis, Jr.
19/55	Lena Horne
	Love Me Tender
1/56	Elvis Presley
21/62	Richard Chamberlain
40/67	Percy Sledge
11/57	**Love Me To Pieces** . . . Jill Corey

POS/YR	RECORD TITLE/ARTIST
22/82	**Love Me Tomorrow** . . . Chicago
13/69	**Love Me Tonight** . . . Tom Jones
25/68	**Love Me Two Times** . . . Doors
12/62	**Love Me Warm And Tender** . . . Paul Anka
	Love Me With All Your Heart
3/64	Ray Charles Singers
38/66	Bachelors
39/71	**Love Means (You Never Have To Say You're Sorry)** . . . Sounds Of Sunshine
	Love My Life Away ..see: (I Wanna)
40/58	**Love Of My Life** . . . Everly Brothers
21/63	**Love Of My Man** . . . Theola Kilgore
	Love On A Two-Way Street
3/70	Moments
26/81	Stacy Lattisaw
2/81	**Love On The Rocks** . . . Neil Diamond
36/76	**Love Or Leave** . . . Spinners
	Love Or Let Me Be Lonely
6/70	Friends Of Distinction
40/82	Paul Davis
32/78	**Love Or Something Like It** . . . Kenny Rogers
13/88	**Love Overboard** . . . Gladys Knight & The Pips
34/79	**Love Pains** . . . Yvonne Elliman
36/86	**Love Parade** . . . Dream Academy
37/82	**Love Plus One** . . . Haircut One Hundred
	Love Potion Number Nine
23/59	Clovers
3/65	Searchers
12/87	**Love Power** . . . Dionne Warwick & Jeffrey Osborne
	Love Power
22/68	Sandpebbles
4/91	Luther Vandross (medley)
22/76	**Love Really Hurts Without You** . . . Billy Ocean
1/76	**Love Rollercoaster** . . . Ohio Players
3/89	**Love Shack** . . . B-52's
31/63	**Love She Can Count On** . . . Miracles
40/63	**Love So Fine** . . . Chiffons
3/76	**Love So Right** . . . Bee Gees
5/84	**Love Somebody** . . . Rick Springfield
2/89	**Love Song** . . . Cure
10/90	**Love Song** . . . Tesla
12/74	**Love Song** . . . Anne Murray
38/80	**Love Stinks** . . . J. Geils Band
	Love Story ..see: Theme From
1/90	**Love Takes Time** . . . Mariah Carey

POS/YR	RECORD TITLE/ARTIST
11/79	**Love Takes Time** . . . Orleans
	Love The One You're With
14/71	Stephen Stills
18/71	Isley Brothers
14/80	**Love The World Away** . . . Kenny Rogers
1/77	**Love Theme From A Star Is Born (Evergreen)** . . . Barbra Streisand
21/78	**Love Theme From Eyes Of Laura Mars (Prisoner)** . . . Barbra Streisand
37/61	**Love Theme From One Eyed Jacks** . . . Ferrante & Teicher
	Love Theme From One On One ..see: My Fair Share
1/69	**Love Theme From Romeo & Juliet** . . . Henry Mancini
15/85	**Love Theme From St. Elmo's Fire** . . . David Foster
34/72	**Love Theme From The Godfather** . . . Andy Williams
2/76	**Love To Love You Baby** . . . Donna Summer
6/86	**Love Touch** . . . Rod Stewart
1/73	**Love Train** . . . O'Jays
30/60	**Love Walked In** . . . Dinah Washington
22/86	**Love Walks In** . . . Van Halen
30/71	**Love We Had (Stays On My Mind)** . . . Dells
9/86	**Love Will Conquer All** . . . Lionel Richie
6/78	**Love Will Find A Way** . . . Pablo Cruise
30/87	**Love Will Find A Way** . . . Yes
40/69	**Love Will Find A Way** . . . Jackie DeShannon
1/75	**Love Will Keep Us Together** . . . Captain & Tennille
1/90	**Love Will Lead You Back** . . . Taylor Dayne
1/91	**Love Will Never Do (Without You)** . . . Janet Jackson
9/88	**Love Will Save The Day** . . . Whitney Houston
30/84	**Love Will Show Us How** . . . Christine McVie
13/82	**Love Will Turn You Around** . . . Kenny Rogers
5/75	**Love Won't Let Me Wait** . . . Major Harris
9/87	**Love You Down** . . . Ready For The World
1/79	**Love You Inside Out** . . . Bee Gees
24/81	**Love You Like I Never Loved Before** . . . John O'Banion
26/58	**Love You Most Of All** . . . Sam Cooke

POS/YR	RECORD TITLE/ARTIST
1/70	**Love You Save** . . . Jackson 5
7/60	**Love You So** . . . Ron Holden
10/86	**Love Zone** . . . Billy Ocean
7/82	**Love's Been A Little Bit Hard On Me** . . . Juice Newton
20/77	**Love's Grown Deep** . . . Kenny Nolan
19/71	**Love's Lines, Angles And Rhymes** . . . 5th Dimension
26/66	**Love's Made A Fool Of You** . . . Bobby Fuller Four
1/74	**Love's Theme** . . . Love Unlimited Orchestra
30/78	**Lovely Day** . . . Bill Withers
12/80	**Lovely One** . . . Jacksons
20/56	**Lovely One** . . . Four Voices
2/89	**Lover In Me** . . . Sheena Easton
7/62	**Lover Please** . . . Clyde McPhatter
2/65	**Lover's Concerto** . . . Toys
31/68	**Lover's Holiday** . . . Peggy Scott & Jo Jo Benson
40/80	**Lover's Holiday** . . . Change
31/61	**Lover's Island** . . . Blue Jays
6/59	**Lover's Question** . . . Clyde McPhatter
2/85	**Loverboy** . . . Billy Ocean
4/85	**Lovergirl** . . . Teena Marie
36/62	**Lovers By Night, Strangers By Day** . . . Fleetwoods
3/62	**Lovers Who Wander** . . . Dion
2/73	**Loves Me Like A Rock** . . . Paul Simon
25/61	**Lovey Dovey** . . . Buddy Knox
9/85	**Lovin' Every Minute Of It** . . . Loverboy
16/79	**Lovin', Touchin', Squeezin'** . . . Journey
1/75	**Lovin' You** . . . Minnie Riperton
32/67	**Lovin' You** . . . Bobby Darin
26/71	**Loving Her Was Easier (Than Anything I'll Ever Do Again)** . . . Kris Kristofferson
20/57	**Loving You** . . . Elvis Presley
29/72	**Loving You Just Crossed My Mind** . . . Sam Neely
7/75	**Low Rider** . . . War
3/76	**Lowdown** . . . Boz Scaggs
35/71	**Lowdown** . . . Chicago
	Lt. Calley ..see: Battle Hymn Of
5/77	**Lucille** . . . Kenny Rogers
	Lucille
21/57	Little Richard
21/60	Everly Brothers
25/77	**Luckenbach, Texas** . . . Waylon Jennings

POS/YR	RECORD TITLE/ARTIST
30/85	**Lucky** . . . Greg Kihn
25/60	**Lucky Devil** . . . Carl Dobkins, Jr.
38/85	**Lucky In Love** . . . Mick Jagger
14/59	**Lucky Ladybug** . . . Billy & Lillie
25/57	**Lucky Lips** . . . Ruth Brown
20/84	**Lucky One** . . . Laura Branigan
4/84	**Lucky Star** . . . Madonna
29/70	**Lucretia Mac Evil** . . . Blood, Sweat & Tears
1/75	**Lucy In The Sky With Diamonds** . . . Elton John
3/87	**Luka** . . . Suzanne Vega
16/56	**Lullaby Of Birdland** . . . Blue Stars
23/61	**Lullaby Of Love** . . . Frank Gari
2/75	**Lyin' Eyes** . . . Eagles
27/90	**Lyin' To Myself** . . . David Cassidy

POS/YR	RECORD TITLE/ARTIST
15/59	**M.T.A.** . . . Kingston Trio
5/70	**Ma Belle Amie** . . . Tee Set
	MacArthur Park
2/68	Richard Harris
38/71	Four Tops
1/78	Donna Summer
22/74	**Machine Gun** . . . Commodores
25/78	**Macho Man** . . . Village People
	Mack The Knife
8/56	Dick Hyman Trio
11/56	Richard Hayman & Jan August
17/56	Lawrence Welk
20/56	Louis Armstrong
37/56	Billy Vaughn
1/59	Bobby Darin
27/60	Ella Fitzgerald
3/86	**Mad About You** . . . Belinda Carlisle
	Made To Love ..see: (Girls, Girls, Girls)
36/76	**Mademoiselle** . . . Styx
23/60	**Madison, The** . . . Al Brown's Tunetoppers
30/60	**Madison Time** . . . Ray Bryant Combo
1/71	**Maggie May** . . . Rod Stewart
1/80	**Magic** . . . Olivia Newton-John
5/75	**Magic** . . . Pilot
12/84	**Magic** . . . Cars
25/68	**Magic Bus** . . . Who

POS/YR	RECORD TITLE/ARTIST
3/68	**Magic Carpet Ride** . . . Steppenwolf
9/76	**Magic Man** . . . Heart
4/58	**Magic Moments** . . . Perry Como
	Magic Touch ..see: (You've Got)
21/66	**Magic Town** . . . Vogues
39/77	**Magical Mystery Tour** . . . Ambrosia
8/78	**Magnet And Steel** . . . Walter Egan
35/61	**Magnificent Seven** . . . Al Caiola
	Magnum P.I. ..see: Theme From
	Mahogany ..see: Theme From
3/79	**Main Event/Fight** . . . Barbra Streisand
	Main Theme From Exodus ..see: Exodus
	Main Title And Molly-O ..see: Man With The Golden Arm
24/77	**Mainstreet** . . . Bob Seger
36/61	**Majestic, The** . . . Dion
14/83	**Major Tom (Coming Home)** . . . Peter Schilling
25/80	**Make A Little Magic** . . . Dirt Band
5/82	**Make A Move On Me** . . . Olivia Newton-John
28/69	**Make Believe** . . . Wind
30/82	**Make Believe** . . . Toto
	Make It Easy On Yourself
20/62	Jerry Butler
16/65	Walker Bros.
37/70	Dionne Warwick
22/71	**Make It Funky** . . . James Brown
4/88	**Make It Real** . . . Jets
1/70	**Make It With You** . . . Bread
29/83	**Make Love Stay** . . . Dan Fogelberg
16/58	**Make Me A Miracle** . . . Jimmie Rodgers
28/66	**Make Me Belong To You** . . . Barbara Lewis
3/88	**Make Me Lose Control** . . . Eric Carmen
9/70	**Make Me Smile** . . . Chicago
27/72	**Make Me The Woman That You Go Home To** . . . Gladys Knight & The Pips
11/65	**Make Me Your Baby** . . . Barbara Lewis
21/67	**Make Me Yours** . . . Bettye Swann
	Make The World Go Away
24/63	Timi Yuro
6/65	Eddy Arnold
14/90	**Make You Sweat** . . . Keith Sweat
36/69	**Make Your Own Kind Of Music** . . . Mama Cass Elliot
	Make Yourself Comfortable
6/55	Sarah Vaughan

POS/YR	RECORD TITLE/ARTIST
26/55	Andy Griffith
30/55	Peggy King
5/79	**Makin' It** . . . David Naughton
20/59	**Makin' Love** . . . Floyd Robinson
13/82	**Making Love** . . . Roberta Flack
31/67	**Making Every Minute Count** . . . Spanky & Our Gang
35/87	**Making Love In The Rain** . . . Herb Alpert
2/83	**Making Love Out Of Nothing At All** . . . Air Supply
35/67	**Making Memories** . . . Frankie Laine
25/76	**Making Our Dreams Come True** . . . Cyndi Grecco
	Mama ..also see: Mamma
8/60	**Mama** . . . Connie Francis
22/66	**Mama** . . . B.J. Thomas
9/79	**Mama Can't Buy You Love** . . . Elton John
14/63	**Mama Didn't Lie** . . . Jan Bradley
11/56	**Mama From The Train** . . . Patti Page
11/57	**Mama Look At Bubu** . . . Harry Belafonte
4/61	**Mama Said** . . . Shirelles
17/91	**Mama Said Knock You Out** . . . L.L. Cool J
	Mama Sang A Song
32/62	Stan Kenton
38/62	Walter Brennan
34/56	**Mama, Teach Me To Dance** . . . Eydie Gorme
1/70	**Mama Told Me (Not To Come)** . . . Three Dog Night
30/82	**Mama Used To Say** . . . Junior
2/71	**Mama's Pearl** . . . Jackson 5
18/55	**Mambo Rock** . . . Bill Haley
19/66	**Mame** . . . Herb Alpert
32/76	**Mamma Mia** . . . Abba
16/55	**Man Chases A Girl** . . . Eddie Fisher
31/79	**Man I'll Never Be** . . . Boston
1/88	**Man In The Mirror** . . . Michael Jackson
	Man In The Raincoat
14/55	Marion Marlowe
16/55	Priscilla Wright
40/82	**Man On The Corner** . . . Genesis
14/82	**Man On Your Mind** . . . Little River Band
15/86	**Man Size Love** . . . Klymaxx
4/62	**(Man Who Shot) Liberty Valance** . . . Gene Pitney
	Man With The Golden Arm (Main Title/Molly-O/Delilah Jones)
14/56	Richard Maltby
16/56	Elmer Bernstein

POS/YR	RECORD TITLE/ARTIST
22/56	Dick Jacobs
37/56	McGuire Sisters
19/68	**Man Without Love** . . . Engelbert Humperdinck
4/87	**Mandolin Rain** . . . Bruce Hornsby & The Range
1/75	**Mandy** . . . Barry Manilow
1/82	**Maneater** . . . Daryl Hall & John Oates
10/57	**Mangos** . . . Rosemary Clooney
10/59	**Manhattan Spiritual** . . . Reg Owen
1/83	**Maniac** . . . Michael Sembello
2/86	**Manic Monday** . . . Bangles
7/60	**Many Tears Ago** . . . Connie Francis
20/58	**March From The River Kwai and Colonel Bogey** . . . Mitch Miller
8/77	**Margaritaville** . . . Jimmy Buffett
6/63	**Maria Elena** . . . Los Indios Tabajaras
	Marianne
3/57	Hilltoppers
4/57	Terry Gilkyson & The Easy Riders
15/65	**Marie** . . . Bachelors
4/61	**(Marie's the Name) His Latest Flame** . . . Elvis Presley
31/59	**Marina** . . . Rocco Granata
36/63	**Marlena** . . . Four Seasons
28/69	**Marrakesh Express** . . . Crosby, Stills & Nash
40/79	**Married Men** . . . Bette Midler
16/63	**Martian Hop** . . . Ran-Dells
39/62	**Mary Ann Regrets** . . . Burl Ives
28/72	**Mary Had A Little Lamb** . . . Wings
27/67	**Mary In The Morning** . . . Al Martino
26/59	**Mary Lou** . . . Ronnie Hawkins
12/56	**Mary's Boy Child** . . . Harry Belafonte
39/62	**Mary's Little Lamb** . . . James Darren
23/87	**Mary's Prayer** . . . Danny Wilson
2/62	**Mashed Potato Time** . . . Dee Dee Sharp
	Massachusetts ..see: (Lights Went Out In)
5/80	**Master Blaster (Jammin')** . . . Stevie Wonder
18/68	**Master Jack** . . . Four Jacks & A Jill
33/73	**Master Of Eyes** . . . Aretha Franklin
7/73	**Masterpiece** . . . Temptations
20/64	**Matador, The** . . . Major Lance
17/64	**Matchbox** . . . Beatles
2/85	**Material Girl** . . . Madonna
10/86	**Matter Of Trust** . . . Billy Joel
39/69	**May I** . . . Bill Deal

POS/YR	RECORD TITLE/ARTIST
15/65	**May The Bird Of Paradise Fly Up Your Nose** . . . "Little" Jimmy Dickens
11/59	**May You Always** . . . McGuire Sisters
	Maybe
15/58	Chantels
29/70	Three Degrees
17/58	**Maybe Baby** . . . Crickets
14/64	**Maybe I Know** . . . Lesley Gore
22/79	**Maybe I'm A Fool** . . . Eddie Money
10/77	**Maybe I'm Amazed** . . . Wings
20/71	**Maybe Tomorrow** . . . Jackson 5
	Maybellene
5/55	Chuck Berry
12/64	Johnny Rivers
15/74	**Me And Baby Brother** . . . War
	Me And Bobby McGee
1/71	Janis Joplin
40/72	Jerry Lee Lewis
22/72	**Me And Julio Down By The Schoolyard** . . . Paul Simon
1/72	**Me And Mrs. Jones** . . . Billy Paul
34/71	**Me And My Arrow** . . . Nilsson
5/71	**Me And You And A Dog Named Boo** . . . Lobo
34/89	**Me Myself And I** . . . De La Soul
26/89	**Me So Horny** . . . 2 Live Crew
40/81	**Me (Without You)** . . . Andy Gibb
5/63	**Mean Woman Blues** . . . Roy Orbison
12/63	**Mecca** . . . Gene Pitney
	"Medic" Theme ..see: Blue Star
22/69	**Medicine Man** . . . Buchanan Brothers
11/87	**Meet Me Half Way** . . . Kenny Loggins
2/66	**Mellow Yellow** . . . Donovan
5/57	**Melodie D'Amour** . . . Ames Brothers
	Melody Of Love
2/55	Billy Vaughn
3/55	Four Aces
8/55	David Carroll
19/55	Frank Sinatra & Ray Anthony
30/55	Leo Diamond
35/69	**Memories** . . . Elvis Presley
	Memories Are Made Of This
1/56	Dean Martin
5/56	Gale Storm
	Memories Of You
22/55	Four Coins
20/56	Benny Goodman Trio/Rosemary Clooney
39/83	**Memory** . . . Barry Manilow

POS/YR	RECORD TITLE/ARTIST
	Memphis
5/63	Lonnie Mack
2/64	Johnny Rivers
33/67	**Memphis Soul Stew** . . . King Curtis
	Men ..see: Theme From The
33/68	**Men Are Gettin' Scarce** . . . Joe Tex
6/66	**Men In My Little Girl's Life** . . . Mike Douglas
27/69	**Mendocino** . . . Sir Douglas Quintet
14/90	**Mentirosa** . . . Mellow Man Ace
2/88	**Mercedes Boy** . . . Pebbles
30/69	**Mercy** . . . Ohio Express
35/64	**Mercy, Mercy** . . . Don Covay
	Mercy Mercy Me (The Ecology)
4/71	Marvin Gaye
16/91	Robert Palmer (medley)
	Mercy, Mercy, Mercy
5/67	Buckinghams
11/67	"Cannonball" Adderley
32/60	**Mess Of Blues** . . . Elvis Presley
8/66	**Message To Michael** . . . Dionne Warwick
5/85	**Method Of Modern Love** . . . Daryl Hall John Oates
16/58	**Mexican Hat Rock** . . . Applejacks
7/61	**Mexico** . . . Bob Moore
1/85	**Miami Vice Theme** . . . Jan Hammer
1/61	**Michael** . . . Highwaymen
18/66	**Michelle** . . . David & Jonathan
1/82	**Mickey** . . . Toni Basil
8/63	**Mickey's Monkey** . . . Miracles
19/84	**Middle Of The Road** . . . Pretenders
6/74	**Midnight At The Oasis** . . . Maria Muldaur
5/87	**Midnight Blue** . . . Lou Gramm
6/75	**Midnight Blue** . . . Melissa Manchester
5/68	**Midnight Confessions** . . . Grass Roots
10/70	**Midnight Cowboy** . . . Ferrante & Teicher
	Midnight Hour ..see: In The
2/62	**Midnight In Moscow** . . . Kenny Ball
10/64	**Midnight Mary** . . . Joey Powers
	Midnight Rider
27/72	Joe Cocker
19/74	Gregg Allman
24/80	**Midnight Rocks** . . . Al Stewart
	Midnight Special
16/60	Paul Evans
20/65	Johnny Rivers
35/59	**Midnight Stroll** . . . Revels

POS/YR	RECORD TITLE/ARTIST
1/73	**Midnight Train To Georgia** . . . Gladys Knight & The Pips
28/79	**Midnight Wind** . . . John Stewart
34/71	**Mighty Clouds Of Joy** . . . B.J. Thomas
38/59	**Mighty Good** . . . Ricky Nelson
20/74	**Mighty Love** . . . Spinners
29/74	**Mighty Mighty** . . . Earth, Wind & Fire
10/68	**Mighty Quinn (Quinn The Eskimo)** . . . Manfred Mann
12/91	**Miles Away** . . . Winger
33/64	**Miller's Cave** . . . Bobby Bare
	Million To One
5/60	Jimmy Charles
23/73	Donny Osmond
	Millionaire ..see: (How To Be A)
26/69	**Mind, Body and Soul** . . . Flaming Ember
18/73	**Mind Games** . . . John Lennon
38/69	**Minotaur, The** . . . Dick Hyman
14/79	**Minute By Minute** . . . Doobie Brothers
9/91	**Miracle** . . . Whitney Houston
12/90	**Miracle** . . . Jon Bon Jovi
18/56	**Miracle Of Love** . . . Eileen Rodgers
3/75	**Miracles** . . . Jefferson Starship
40/83	**Miracles** . . . Stacy Lattisaw
10/67	**Mirage** . . . Tommy James & the Shondells
30/83	**Mirror Man** . . . Human League
8/82	**Mirror, Mirror** . . . Diana Ross
22/73	**Misdemeanor** . . . Foster Sylvers
10/85	**Misled** . . . Kool & The Gang
5/84	**Miss Me Blind** . . . Culture Club
14/81	**Miss Sun** . . . Boz Scaggs
1/78	**Miss You** . . . Rolling Stones
7/89	**Miss You Like Crazy** . . . Natalie Cole
1/89	**Miss You Much** . . . Janet Jackson
29/88	**Missed Opportunity** . . . Daryl Hall John Oates
1/84	**Missing You** . . . John Waite
10/85	**Missing You** . . . Diana Ross
23/82	**Missing You** . . . Dan Fogelberg
29/61	**Missing You** . . . Ray Peterson
7/60	**Mission Bell** . . . Donnie Brooks
14/86	**Missionary Man** . . . Eurythmics
32/70	**Mississippi** . . . John Phillips
21/70	**Mississippi Queen** . . . Mountain
33/85	**Mistake No. 3** . . . Culture Club
	Mister ..see: Mr.

POS/YR	RECORD TITLE/ARTIST
	Misty
12/59	Johnny Mathis
21/63	Lloyd Price
14/75	Ray Stevens
3/76	**Misty Blue** . . . Dorthy Moore
14/80	**Misunderstanding** . . . Genesis
5/89	**Mixed Emotions** . . . Rolling Stones
37/64	**Mixed-Up, Shook-Up, Girl** . . . Patty & The Emblems
32/58	**Mocking Bird, The** . . . Four Lads
	Mockingbird
7/63	Inez Foxx with Charlie Foxx
5/74	Carly Simon & James Taylor
20/61	**Model Girl** . . . Johnny Mastro
22/84	**Modern Day Delilah** . . . Van Stephenson
18/81	**Modern Girl** . . . Sheena Easton
14/83	**Modern Love** . . . David Bowie
10/86	**Modern Woman** . . . Billy Joel
21/65	**Mohair Sam** . . . Charlie Rich
	Molly-O ..see: Man With The Golden Arm
2/55	**Moments To Remember** . . . Four Lads
	Mona Lisa
25/59	Carl Mann
29/59	Conway Twitty
1/66	**Monday, Monday** . . . Mama's & The Papa's
13/73	**Money** . . . Pink Floyd
27/85	**Money Changes Everything** . . . Cyndi Lauper
1/85	**Money For Nothing** . . . Dire Straits
9/76	**Money Honey** . . . Bay City Rollers
	Money (That's what I want)
23/60	Barrett Strong
16/64	Kingsmen
20/56	**Money Tree** . . . Margaret Whiting
28/86	**Money$ Too Tight (To Mention)** . . . Simply Red
23/91	**Moneytalks** . . . AC/DC
	(also see: Dirty Cash)
1/88	**Monkey** . . . George Michael
8/63	**Monkey Time** . . . Major Lance
39/70	**Monster** . . . Steppenwolf
	Monster Mash
1/62	Bobby "Boris" Pickett
10/73	Bobby "Boris" Pickett
30/62	**Monsters' Holiday** . . . Bobby "Boris" Pickett
8/70	**Montego Bay** . . . Bobby Bloom

POS/YR	RECORD TITLE/ARTIST
15/68	**Monterey** . . . Animals
	Mony Mony
3/68	Tommy James & The Shondells
1/87	Billy Idol
31/77	**Moody Blue** . . . Elvis Presley
1/61	**Moody River** . . . Pat Boone
24/69	**Moody Woman** . . . Jerry Butler
	Moon River
11/61	Jerry Butler
11/61	Henry Mancini
30/71	**Moon Shadow** . . . Cat Stevens
28/58	**Moon Talk** . . . Perry Como
38/69	**Moonflight** . . . Vik Venus
	Moonglow and Theme From "Picnic"
1/56	Morris Stoloff
4/56	George Cates
13/56	McGuire Sisters (Picnic)
3/76	**Moonlight Feels Right** . . . Starbuck
3/57	**Moonlight Gambler** . . . Frankie Laine
	Moonlight Swim
24/57	Tony Perkins
37/57	Nick Noble
23/87	**Moonlighting** . . . Al Jarreau
4/56	**More** . . . Perry Como
8/63	**More** . . . Kai Winding
16/66	**More I See You** . . . Chris Montez
	More Love
23/67	Miracles
10/80	Kim Carnes
17/61	**More Money For You And Me** . . . Four Preps
4/76	**More, More, More** . . . Andrea True Connection
5/76	**More Than A Feeling** . . . Boston
32/78	**More Than A Woman** . . . Tavares
14/91	**More Than Ever** . . . Nelson
2/80	**More Than I Can Say** . . . Leo Sayer
34/82	**More Than Just The Two Of Us** . . . Sneaker
1/91	**More Than Words** . . . Extreme
2/90	**More Than Words Can Say** . . . Alias
18/89	**More Than You Know** . . . Martika
12/69	**More Today Than Yesterday** . . . Spiral Starecase
13/59	**Morgen** . . . Ivo Robic
	Moritat ..see: Mack The Knife
21/83	**Mornin'** . . . Jarreau
14/75	**Mornin' Beautiful** . . . Dawn
1/73	**Morning After** . . . Maureen McGovern

POS/YR	RECORD TITLE/ARTIST
24/79	**Morning Dance** . . . Spyro Gyra
17/69	**Morning Girl** . . . Neon Philharmonic
6/72	**Morning Has Broken** . . . Cat Stevens
	Morning Side Of The Mountain
27/59	Tommy Edwards
8/75	Donny & Marie Osmond
1/81	**Morning Train (Nine To Five)** . . . Sheena Easton
1/73	**Most Beautiful Girl** . . . Charlie Rich
14/55	**Most Of All** . . . Don Cornell
38/71	**Most Of All** . . . B.J. Thomas
27/62	**Most People Get Married** . . . Patti Page
31/56	**Mostly Martha** . . . Crew Cuts
4/72	**Mother And Child Reunion** . . . Paul Simon
37/71	**Mother Freedom** . . . Bread
1/61	**Mother-In-Law** . . . Ernie K-Doe
11/69	**Mother Popcorn** . . . James Brown
8/66	**Mothers Little Helper** . . . Rolling Stones
27/86	**Mothers Talk** . . . Tears For Fears
12/72	**Motorcycle Mama** . . . Sailcat
36/87	**Motortown** . . . Kane Gang
10/91	**Motown Song** . . . Rod Stewart
3/91	**Motownphilly** . . . Boyz II Men
	Mountain Of Love
21/60	Harold Dorman
9/64	Johnny Rivers
2/61	**Mountain's High** . . . Dick & DeeDee
23/86	**Mountains** . . . Prince
12/86	**Move Away** . . . Culture Club
31/69	**Move Over** . . . Steppenwolf
	Move Two Mountains ..see: (You've Got To)
14/76	**Movin'** . . . Brass Construction
19/75	**Movin' On** . . . Bad Company
17/78	**Movin' Out (Anthony's Song)** . . . Billy Joel
16/63	**Mr. Bass Man** . . . Johnny Cymbal
2/71	**Mr. Big Stuff** . . . Jean Knight
1/59	**Mr. Blue** . . . Fleetwoods
35/78	**Mr. Blue Sky** . . . Electric Light Orchestra
9/71	**Mr. Bojangles** . . . Nitty Gritty Dirt Band
28/68	**Mr. Businessman** . . . Ray Stevens
38/72	**Mr. Can't You See** . . . Buffy Sainte-Marie
1/60	**Mr. Custer** . . . Larry Verne
17/66	**Mr. Dieingly Sad** . . . Critters
	Mr. Dream Merchant ..see: Dream Merchant

POS/YR	RECORD TITLE/ARTIST
4/75	**Mr. Jaws** . . . Dickie Goodman
6/57	**Mr. Lee** . . . Bobbettes
1/64	**Mr. Lonely** . . . Bobby Vinton
21/60	**Mr. Lucky** . . . Henry Mancini
3/83	**Mr. Roboto** . . . Styx
37/81	**Mr. Sandman** . . . Emmylou Harris
36/66	**Mr. Spaceman** . . . Byrds
18/69	**Mr. Sun, Mr. Moon** . . . Paul Revere & The Raiders
1/65	**Mr. Tambourine Man** . . . Byrds
12/85	**Mr. Telephone Man** . . . New Edition
	Mr. Wonderful
13/56	Sarah Vaughan
14/56	Peggy Lee
18/56	Teddi King
1/65	**Mrs. Brown You've Got A Lovely Daughter** . . . Herman's Hermits
	Mrs. Robinson
1/68	Simon & Garfunkel
37/69	Booker T. & The M.G.'s
	Muddy Water ..see: (I Washed My Hands In)
	Muhammad Ali ..see: Black Superman
5/60	**Mule Skinner Blues** . . . Fendermen
30/62	**Multiplication** . . . Bobby Darin
39/59	**Mummy, The** . . . Bob McFadden & Dor
39/82	**Murphy's Law** . . . Cheri
10/82	**Muscles** . . . Diana Ross
39/67	**Museum** . . . Herman's Hermits
3/79	**Music Box Dancer** . . . Frank Mills
40/84	**Music Time** . . . Styx
	Music To Watch Girls By
15/67	Bob Crewe Generation
34/67	Andy Williams
4/76	**Muskrat Love** . . . Captain & Tennille
12/75	**Must Of Got Lost** . . . J. Geils Band
8/66	**Must To Avoid** . . . Herman's Hermits
23/66	**Mustang Sally** . . . Wilson Pickett
21/56	**Mutual Admiration Society** . . . Teresa Brewer
13/78	**My Angel Baby** . . . Toby Beau
13/65	**My Baby** . . . Temptations
	(My Baby Don't Love Me) ..see: No More
31/56	**My Baby Left Me** . . . Elvis Presley
13/70	**My Baby Loves Lovin'** . . . White Plains
22/66	**My Baby Loves Me** . . . Martha & The Vandellas

POS/YR	RECORD TITLE/ARTIST
17/68	**My Baby Must Be A Magician** . . . Marvelettes
	(My Baby Shot Me Down) ..see: Bang Bang
30/67	**My Back Pages** . . . Byrds
35/78	**My Best Friend's Girl** . . . Cars
19/56	**My Blue Heaven** . . . Fats Domino
26/64	**My Bonnie** . . . Beatles/Tony Sheridan
	(also see: Bonnie Came Back)
11/55	**My Bonnie Lassie** . . . Ames Brothers
21/62	**My Boomerang Won't Come Back** . . . Charlie Drake
20/75	**My Boy** . . . Elvis Presley
	My Boy-Flat Top
16/55	Dorothy Collins
39/55	Boyd Bennett
2/64	**My Boy Lollipop** . . . Millie Small
1/63	**My Boyfriend's Back** . . . Angels
25/89	**My Brave Face** . . . Paul McCartney
12/58	**My Bucket's Got A Hole In It** . . . Ricky Nelson
4/69	**My Cherie Amour** . . . Stevie Wonder
	My Coloring Book
18/63	Kitty Kallen
20/63	Sandy Stewart
8/67	**My Cup Runneth Over** . . . Ed Ames
6/63	**My Dad** . . . Paul Petersen
34/60	**My Dearest Darling** . . . Etta James
1/72	**My Ding-A-Ling** . . . Chuck Berry
	(also see: Ding-A-Ling)
24/57	**My Dream** . . . Platters
9/61	**My Empty Arms** . . . Jackie Wilson
29/84	**My Ever Changing Moods** . . . Style Council
1/75	**My Eyes Adored You** . . . Frankie Valli
28/77	**My Fair Share** . . . Seals & Crofts
	My Girl
1/65	Temptations
35/68	Bobby Vee (medley)
0/85	Hall & Oates/David Ruffin/Eddie Kendrick (medley)
20/88	Suave
25/82	**My Girl** . . . Donnie Iris
12/74	**My Girl Bill** . . . Jim Stafford
22/81	**My Girl (Gone, Gone, Gone)** . . . Chilliwack
14/65	**My Girl Has Gone** . . . Miracles
	My Girl Josephine
14/60	Fats Domino

POS/YR	RECORD TITLE/ARTIST
29/67	Jerry Jaye
	My Girl Sloopy ..see: Hang On Sloopy
	My Guy
1/64	Mary Wells
23/82	Sister Sledge
2/59	**My Happiness** . . . Connie Francis
4/77	**My Heart Belongs To Me** . . . Barbra Streisand
9/64	**My Heart Belongs To Only You** . . . Bobby Vinton
4/89	**My Heart Can't Tell You No** . . . Rod Stewart
38/64	**My Heart Cries For You** . . . Ray Charles
1/60	**My Heart Has A Mind Of Its Own** . . . Connie Francis
3/59	**My Heart Is An Open Book** . . . Carl Dobkins, Jr.
25/91	**My Heart Is Failing Me** . . . Riff
	My Heart Reminds Me ..see: And That Reminds Me
	My Heart Sings ..see: (All Of A Sudden)
38/89	**My Heart Skips A Beat** . . . Cover Girls
13/66	**My Heart's Symphony** . . . Gary Lewis & The Playboys
8/60	**My Home Town** . . . Paul Anka
6/86	**My Hometown** . . . Bruce Springsteen
18/61	**My Kind Of Girl** . . . Matt Monro
31/83	**My Kind Of Lady** . . . Supertramp
30/90	**My Kinda Girl** . . . Babyface
	My Last Date (With You)
26/61	Skeeter Davis
38/61	Joni James
	(also see: Last Date)
3/79	**My Life** . . . Billy Joel
22/56	**My Little Angel** . . . Four Lads
9/75	**My Little Town** . . . Simon & Garfunkel
1/66	**My Love** . . . Petula Clark
1/73	**My Love** . . . Paul McCartney
5/83	**My Love** . . . Lionel Richie
16/65	**My Love, Forgive Me** . . . Robert Goulet
21/90	**My Love Is A Fire** . . . Donny Osmond
13/67	**My Mammy** . . . Happenings
9/73	**My Maria** . . . B.W. Stevenson
26/59	**My Melancholy Baby** . . . Tommy Edwards
3/74	**My Melody Of Love** . . . Bobby Vinton
19/74	**My Mistake (Was To Love You)** . . . Diana Ross & Marvin Gaye
39/81	**My Mother's Eyes** . . . Bette Midler

POS/YR	RECORD TITLE/ARTIST
16/73	**My Music** . . . Loggins & Messina
10/90	**My, My, My** . . . Johnny Gill
37/84	**My Oh My** . . . Slade
	My One Sin
24/55	Nat "King" Cole
28/57	Four Coins
	My Own True Love
33/59	Jimmy Clanton
13/62	Duprees
21/57	**My Personal Possession** . . . Nat "King" Cole/Four Knights
14/69	**My Pledge Of Love** . . . Joe Jeffrey Group
1/56	**My Prayer** . . . Platters
1/89	**My Prerogative** . . . Bobby Brown
1/79	**My Sharona** . . . Knack
30/91	**My Side Of The Bed** . . . Susanna Hoffs
31/69	**My Song** . . . Aretha Franklin
	My Special Angel
7/57	Bobby Helms
7/68	Vogues
16/63	**My Summer Love** . . . Ruby & The Romantics
	My Sweet Lady
17/74	Cliff DeYoung
32/77	John Denver
1/70	**My Sweet Lord** . . . George Harrison
29/74	**My Thang** . . . James Brown
39/83	**My Town** . . . Michael Stanley Band
32/65	**My Town, My Guy And Me** . . . Lesley Gore
31/56	**My Treasure** . . . Hilltoppers
22/63	**My True Confession** . . . Brook Benton
3/58	**My True Love** . . . Jack Scott
3/61	**My True Story** . . . Jive Five
	My Way
27/69	Frank Sinatra
22/77	Elvis Presley
9/69	**My Whole World Ended (The Moment You Left Me)** . . . David Ruffin
24/63	**My Whole World Is Falling Down** . . . Brenda Lee
12/59	**My Wish Came True** . . . Elvis Presley
16/72	**My World** . . . Bee Gees
5/66	**My World Is Empty Without You** . . . Supremes
24/85	**Mystery Lady** . . . Billy Ocean
33/65	**Mystic Eyes** . . . Them

POS/YR	RECORD TITLE/ARTIST
	Na Na Hey Hey Kiss Him Goodbye ..see: Kiss Him Goodbye
8/76	**Nadia's Theme (The Young And The Restless)** . . . Barry DeVorzon & Perry Botkin, Jr.
23/64	**Nadine (Is It You?)** . . . Chuck Berry
25/61	**"Nag"** . . . Halos
3/65	**Name Game** . . . Shirley Ellis
12/78	**Name Of The Game** . . . Abba
8/67	**Nashville Cats** . . . Lovin' Spoonful
3/86	**Nasty** . . . Janet Jackson
16/71	**Nathan Jones** . . . Supremes
21/78	**Native New Yorker** . . . Odyssey
38/60	**Natural Born Lover** . . . Fats Domino
10/73	**Natural High** . . . Bloodstone
17/71	**Natural Man** . . . Lou Rawls
8/67	**Natural Woman** . . . Aretha Franklin
40/68	**Naturally Stoned** . . . Avant-Garde
40/61	**Nature Boy** . . . Bobby Darin
3/88	**Naughty Girls (Need Love Too)** . . . Samantha Fox
	Naughty Lady Of Shady Lane
3/55	Ames Brothers
17/55	Archie Bleyer
23/85	**Naughty Naughty** . . . John Parr
6/64	**Navy Blue** . . . Diane Renay
22/70	**Neanderthal Man** . . . Hotlegs
10/58	**Near You** . . . Roger Williams
40/58	**Nee Nee Na Na Na Na Nu Nu** . . . Dicky Doo & The Don'ts
11/74	**Need To Be** . . . Jim Weatherly
31/64	**Need To Belong** . . . Jerry Butler
25/58	**Need You** . . . Donnie Owens
1/88	**Need You Tonight** . . . INXS
	Needles And Pins
13/64	Searchers
37/86	Tom Petty/Stevie Nicks
2/73	**Neither One Of Us (Wants To Be The First To Say Goodbye)** . . . Gladys Knight & The Pips
	Nel Blu Dipinto Di Blu ..see: Volare
24/67	**Neon Rainbow** . . . Box Tops

POS/YR	RECORD TITLE/ARTIST
6/85	**Neutron Dance** . . . Pointer Sisters
4/85	**Never** . . . Heart
20/86	**Never As Good As The First Time** . . . Sade
6/59	**Never Be Anyone Else But You** . . . Ricky Nelson
15/80	**Never Be The Same** . . . Christopher Cross
28/82	**Never Been In Love** . . . Randy Meisner
5/72	**Never Been To Spain** . . . Three Dog Night
	Never Can Say Goodbye
2/71	Jackson 5
22/71	Isaac Hayes
9/75	Gloria Gaynor
13/71	**Never Ending Song Of Love** . . . Delaney & Bonnie & Friends
17/85	**Never Ending Story** . . . Limahl
20/68	**Never Give You Up** . . . Jerry Butler
11/76	**Never Gonna Fall In Love Again** . . . Eric Carmen
1/88	**Never Gonna Give You Up** . . . Rick Astley
17/91	**Never Gonna Let You Down** . . . Surface
4/83	**Never Gonna Let You Go** . . . Sergio Mendes
26/70	**Never Had A Dream Come True** . . . Stevie Wonder
28/88	**Never Knew Love Like This** . . . Alexander O'Neal/Cherrelle
6/80	**Never Knew Love Like This Before** . . . Stephanie Mills
29/75	**Never Let Her Go** . . . David Gates
27/87	**Never Let Me Down** . . . David Bowie
	Never My Love
2/67	Association
12/71	5th Dimension
7/74	Blue Swede
7/74	**Never, Never Gonna Give Ya Up** . . . Barry White
	Never On Sunday
19/60	Don Costa
13/61	Chordettes
3/85	**Never Surrender** . . . Corey Hart
7/88	**Never Tear Us Apart** . . . INXS
33/81	**Never Too Much** . . . Luther Vandross
22/56	**Never Turn Back** . . . Al Hibbler
17/85	**New Attitude** . . . Patti LaBelle
37/64	**New Girl In School** . . . Jan & Dean
1/77	**New Kid In Town** . . . Eagles
	New Lovers ..see: (Welcome)
36/63	**New Mexican Rose** . . . Four Seasons

POS/YR	RECORD TITLE/ARTIST
10/84	**New Moon On Monday** . . . Duran Duran
6/60	**New Orleans** . . . U.S. Bonds
39/80	**New Romance (It's A Mystery)** . . . Spider
3/88	**New Sensation** . . . INXS
27/84	**New Song** . . . Howard Jones
21/82	**New World Man** . . . Rush
13/79	**New York Groove** . . . Ace Frehley
14/67	**New York Mining Disaster 1941** . . . Bee Gees
	New York, New York ..see: Theme From
27/77	**New York, You Got Me Dancing** . . . Andrea True Connection
32/65	**New York's A Lonely Town** . . . Trade Winds
5/62	**Next Door To An Angel** . . . Neil Sedaka
17/67	**Next Plane To London** . . . Rose Garden
F/70	**Next Step Is Love** . . . Elvis Presley
1/86	**Next Time I Fall** . . . Peter Cetera w/Amy Grant
37/82	**Nice Girls** . . . Eye To Eye
30/76	**Nice 'N' Naasty** . . . Salsoul Orchestra
4/72	**Nice To Be With You** . . . Gallery
29/90	**Nicety** . . . Michel'le
35/72	**Nickel Song** . . . Melanie
39/81	**Nicole** . . . Point Blank
4/60	**Night** . . . Jackie Wilson
1/74	**Night Chicago Died** . . . Paper Lace
1/78	**Night Fever** . . . Bee Gees
3/63	**Night Has A Thousand Eyes** . . . Bobby Vee
34/85	**Night Is Still Young** . . . Billy Joel
11/56	**Night Lights** . . . Nat "King" Cole
4/77	**Night Moves** . . . Bob Seger
28/86	**Night Moves** . . . Marilyn Martin
6/81	**Night Owls** . . . Little River Band
1/73	**Night The Lights Went Out In Georgia** . . . Vicki Lawrence
3/71	**Night They Drove Old Dixie Down** . . . Joan Baez
30/66	**Night Time** . . . Strangeloves
36/88	**Nightime** . . . Pretty Poison
35/62	**Night Train** . . . James Brown
33/84	**Nightbird** . . . Stevie Nicks
9/75	**Nightingale** . . . Carole King
15/88	**Nightmare On My Street** . . . DJ Jazzy Jeff & The Fresh Prince
10/76	**Nights Are Forever Without You** . . . England Dan & John Ford Coley

POS/YR	RECORD TITLE/ARTIST
2/72	**Nights In White Satin** . . . Moody Blues
24/91	**Nights Like This** . . . After 7
7/75	**Nights On Broadway** . . . Bee Gees
3/85	**Nightshift** . . . Commodores
23/67	**Niki Hoeky** . . . P.J. Proby
7/86	**Nikita** . . . Elton John
1/81	**9 To 5** . . . Dolly Parton
15/85	**19** . . . Paul Hardcastle
2/66	**19th Nervous Breakdown** . . . Rolling Stones
1/66	**96 Tears** . . . ? & The Mysterians
7/67	**98.6** . . . Keith
26/80	**99** . . . Toto
2/84	**99 Luftballons** . . . Nena
11/57	**Ninety-Nine Ways** . . . Tab Hunter
23/56	**Ninety Nine Years (Dead Or Alive)** . . . Guy Mitchell
33/71	**1900 Yesterday** . . . Liz Damon's Orient Express
12/83	**1999** . . . Prince
7/88	**Nite And Day** . . . Al B. Sure!
	Nitty Gritty
8/64	Shirley Ellis
19/69	Gladys Knight & The Pips
	No Arms Can Ever Hold You
23/55	Georgie Shaw
26/55	Pat Boone
27/65	Bachelors
39/74	**No Charge** . . . Melba Montgomery
23/58	**No Chemise, Please** . . . Gerry Granahan
22/86	**No Easy Way Out** . . . Robert Tepper
	No Gettin' Over Me ..see: (There's)
40/60	**No If's - No And's** . . . Lloyd Price
34/85	**No Lookin' Back** . . . Michael McDonald
16/71	**No Love At All** . . . B.J. Thomas
21/58	**No Love (But Your Love)** . . . Johnny Mathis
8/70	**No Matter What** . . . Badfinger
3/66	**No Matter What Shape (Your Stomach's In)** . . . T-Bones
31/69	**No Matter What Sign You Are** . . . Supremes
35/67	**No Milk Today** . . . Herman's Hermits
	No More
6/55	DeJohn Sisters
17/55	McGuire Sisters
7/90	**No More Lies** . . . Michel'le
6/84	**No More Lonely Nights** . . . Paul McCartney
25/73	**No More Mr. Nice Guy** . . . Alice Cooper
17/89	**No More Rhyme** . . . Debbie Gibson
1/79	**No More Tears (Enough Is Enough)** . . . Barbra Streisand/Donna Summer
23/84	**No More Words** . . . Berlin
13/90	**No Myth** . . . Michael Penn
23/80	**No Night So Long** . . . Dionne Warwick
3/75	**No No Song** . . . Ringo Starr
	No, Not Much!
2/56	Four Lads
34/69	Vogues
	No One
34/61	Connie Francis
21/63	Ray Charles
4/86	**No One Is To Blame** . . . Howard Jones
19/58	**No One Knows** . . . Dion & The Belmonts
36/72	**No One To Depend On** . . . Santana
	No Other Arms ..also see: No Arms Can Ever Hold You
27/59	**No Other Arms, No Other Lips** . . . Chordettes
10/64	**No Particular Place To Go** . . . Chuck Berry
29/81	**No Reply At All** . . . Genesis
F/70	**No Sugar Tonight** . . . Guess Who
14/79	**No Tell Lover** . . . Chicago
5/70	**No Time** . . . Guess Who
33/83	**No Time For Talk** . . . Christopher Cross
23/84	**No Way Out** . . . Jefferson Starship
15/82	**Nobody** . . . Sylvia
8/68	**Nobody But Me** . . . Human Beinz
21/59	**Nobody But You** . . . Dee Clark
40/69	**Nobody But You Babe** . . . Clarence Reid
2/77	**Nobody Does It Better** . . . Carly Simon
12/64	**Nobody I Know** . . . Peter & Gordon
30/60	**Nobody Loves Me Like You** . . . Flamingos
18/82	**Nobody Said It Was Easy** . . . Le Roux
5/84	**Nobody Told Me** . . . John Lennon
29/73	**Nobody Wants You When You're Down And Out** . . . Bobby Womack
21/81	**Nobody Wins** . . . Elton John
8/88	**Nobody's Fool** . . . Kenny Loggins
13/87	**Nobody's Fool** . . . Cinderella
39/59	**Nola** . . . Billy Williams
3/62	**Norman** . . . Sue Thompson
4/60	**North To Alaska** . . . Johnny Horton
34/85	**Not Enough Love In The World** . . . Don Henley

POS/YR	RECORD TITLE/ARTIST
26/88	**Not Just Another Girl** . . . Ivan Neville
12/63	**Not Me** . . . Orlons
16/60	**Not One Minute More** . . . Della Reese
25/65	**Not The Lovin' Kind** . . . Dino, Desi & Billy
10/86	**Nothin' At All** . . . Heart
6/88	**Nothin' But A Good Time** . . . Poison
39/90	**Nothin' To Hide** . . . Poco
	Nothin' Yet ..see: (We Ain't Got)
34/69	**Nothing But A Heartache** . . . Flirtations
11/65	**Nothing But Heartaches** . . . Supremes
12/62	**Nothing Can Change This Love** . . . Sam Cooke
18/65	**Nothing Can Stop Me** . . . Gene Chandler
1/90	**Nothing Compares 2 U** . . . Sinead O'Connor
	Nothing For Xmas ..see: Nuttin'
1/74	**Nothing From Nothing** . . . Billy Preston
12/87	**Nothing's Gonna Change My Love For You** . . . Glenn Medeiros
1/87	**Nothing's Gonna Stop Us Now** . . . Starship
20/66	**Nothing's Too Good For My Baby** . . . Stevie Wonder
21/90	**Notice Me** . . . Nikki
2/87	**Notorious** . . . Duran Duran
38/87	**Notorious** . . . Loverboy
25/58	**Now And For Always** . . . George Hamilton IV
	(Now And Then There's) A ..see: Fool Such As I
11/91	**Now That We Found Love** . . . Heavy D. & The Boyz
3/66	**Nowhere Man** . . . Beatles
8/65	**Nowhere To Run** . . . Martha & The Vandellas
9/75	**# 9 Dream** . . . John Lennon
22/73	**Nutbush City Limits** . . . Ike & Tina Turner
23/62	**Nutrocker** . . . B. Bumble & The Stingers
	Nuttin' For Christmas
6/55	Art Mooney/Barry Gordon
20/55	Joe Ward
21/55	Ricky Zahnd
36/55	Fontane Sisters

POS/YR	RECORD TITLE/ARTIST

POS/YR	RECORD TITLE/ARTIST
10/60	**O Dio Mio** . . . Annette
25/85	**Object Of My Desire** . . . Starpoint
35/84	**Obscene Phone Caller** . . . Rockwell
6/85	**Obsession** . . . Animotion
	Ode To Billie Joe
1/67	Bobbie Gentry
28/67	Kingpins
10/80	**Off The Wall** . . . Michael Jackson
	Oh ..also see: O
3/73	**Oh, Babe, What Would You Say?** . . . Hurricane Smith
23/64	**Oh Baby Don't You Weep** . . . James Brown
10/58	**Oh, Boy!** . . . Crickets
9/59	**Oh! Carol** . . . Neil Sedaka
15/78	**Oh! Darling** . . . Robin Gibb
20/90	**Oh Father** . . . Madonna
	Oh Girl
1/72	Chi-Lites
8/90	Paul Young
39/85	**Oh Girl** . . . Boy Meets Girl
	Oh Happy Day
4/69	Edwin Hawkins' Singers
40/70	Glen Campbell
12/66	**Oh How Happy** . . . Shades Of Blue
	Oh Julie
5/58	Crescendos
23/58	Sammy Salvo
38/82	**Oh Julie** . . . Barry Manilow
33/73	**Oh La De Da** . . . Staple Singers
34/60	**Oh, Little One** . . . Jack Scott
7/58	**Oh Lonesome Me** . . . Don Gibson
22/70	**Oh Me Oh My (I'm A Fool For You Baby)** . . . Lulu
5/74	**Oh My My** . . . Ringo Starr
4/81	**Oh No** . . . Commodores
24/65	**Oh No Not My Baby** . . . Maxine Brown
7/58	**Oh-Oh, I'm Falling In Love Again** . . . Jimmie Rodgers
29/86	**Oh, People** . . . Patti LaBelle
	Oh, Pretty Woman
1/64	Roy Orbison
12/82	Van Halen
1/85	**Oh Sheila** . . . Ready For The World

POS/YR	RECORD TITLE/ARTIST
3/84	**Oh Sherrie** . . . Steve Perry
22/55	**Oh! Susanna** . . . Singing Dogs
10/74	**Oh Very Young** . . . Cat Stevens
30/79	**Oh Well** . . . Rockets
10/69	**Oh, What A Night** . . . Dells **(also see: December, 1963)**
24/78	**Oh What A Night For Dancing** . . . Barry White
39/66	**Oh Yeah** . . . Shadows Of Knight
14/70	**Ohio** . . . Crosby, Stills, Nash & Young
3/57	**Old Cape Cod** . . . Patti Page
5/75	**Old Days** . . . Chicago
20/80	**Old-Fashion Love** . . . Commodores
37/77	**Old Fashioned Boy (You're The One)** . . . Stallion
4/71	**Old Fashioned Love Song** . . . Three Dog Night
5/60	**Old Lamplighter** . . . Browns
25/60	**Ol' MacDonald** . . . Frank Sinatra
31/72	**Old Man** . . . Neil Young
10/85	**Old Man Down The Road** . . . John Fogerty
34/56	**Old Philosopher** . . . Eddie Lawrence
5/62	**Old Rivers** . . . Walter Brennan
	Old Schoolyard ..see: (Remember The Days Of The)
15/81	**Old Songs** . . . Barry Manilow
28/79	**Old Time Rock & Roll** . . . Bob Seger
25/61	**Ole Buttermilk Sky** . . . Bill Black's Combo
11/67	**On A Carousel** . . . Hollies
5/74	**On And On** . . . Gladys Knight & The Pips
11/77	**On And On** . . . Stephen Bishop
	On Broadway
9/63	Drifters
7/78	George Benson
38/56	**On London Bridge** . . . Jo Stafford
1/86	**On My Own** . . . Patti LaBelle & Michael McDonald
20/57	**On My Word Of Honor** . . . Platters
2/89	**On Our Own** . . . Bobby Brown
7/84	**On The Dark Side** . . . John Cafferty
26/83	**On The Loose** . . . Saga
5/80	**On The Radio** . . . Donna Summer
4/61	**On The Rebound** . . . Floyd Cramer
16/68	**On The Road Again** . . . Canned Heat
20/80	**On The Road Again** . . . Willie Nelson
38/78	**On The Shelf** . . . Donny & Marie Osmond

POS/YR	RECORD TITLE/ARTIST
	On The Street Where You Live
4/56	Vic Damone
18/56	Eddie Fisher
28/64	Andy Williams
27/82	**On The Way To The Sky** . . . Neil Diamond
27/91	**On The Way Up** . . . Elisa Fiorillo
29/82	**On The Wings Of Love** . . . Jeffrey Osborne
14/63	**On Top Of Spaghetti** . . . Tom Glazer
5/89	**Once Bitten Twice Shy** . . . Great White
11/61	**Once In Awhile** . . . Chimes
19/64	**Once Upon A Time** . . . Marvin Gaye & Mary Wells
26/61	**Once Upon A Time** . . . Rochell & The Candles
10/75	**Once You Get Started** . . . Rufus Featuring Chaka Khan
23/72	**Once You Understand** . . . Think
5/69	**One** . . . Three Dog Night
7/89	**One** . . . Bee Gees
35/89	**One** . . . Metallica
18/90	**One And Only Man** . . . Steve Winwood
1/71	**One Bad Apple** . . . Osmonds
11/63	**One Broken Heart For Sale** . . . Elvis Presley
37/74	**One Day At A Time** . . . Marilyn Sellars
34/65	**One Dyin' And A Buryin'** . . . Roger Miller
	One Eyed Jacks ..see: Love Theme From
	One Fine Day
5/63	Chiffons
12/80	Carole King
24/71	**One Fine Morning** . . . Lighthouse
38/87	**One For The Mockingbird** . . . Cutting Crew
28/88	**One Good Reason** . . . Paul Carrack
4/88	**One Good Woman** . . . Peter Cetera
13/66	**One Has My Name (The Other Has My Heart)** . . . Barry Young
10/87	**One Heartbeat** . . . Smokey Robinson
11/74	**One Hell Of A Woman** . . . Mac Davis
28/86	**One Hit (To The Body)** . . . Rolling Stones
14/82	**One Hundred Ways** . . . Quincy Jones/James Ingram
9/87	**One I Love** . . . R.E.M.
20/57	**One In A Million** . . . Platters
37/84	**One In A Million** . . . Romantics
9/80	**One In A Million You** . . . Larry Graham
14/65	**One Kiss For Old Times' Sake** . . . Ronnie Dove

POS/YR	RECORD TITLE/ARTIST
35/79	**One Last Kiss** . . . J. Geils Band
2/70	**One Less Bell To Answer** . . . 5th Dimension
37/73	**One Less Set Of Footsteps** . . . Jim Croce
19/85	**One Lonely Night** . . . REO Speedwagon
25/76	**One Love In My Lifetime** . . . Diana Ross
19/71	**One Man Band** . . . Three Dog Night
28/73	**One Man Band (Plays All Alone)** . . . Ronnie Dyson
7/75	**One Man Woman/One Woman Man** . . . Paul Anka/Odia Coates
8/61	**One Mint Julep** . . . Ray Charles
5/88	**One Moment In Time** . . . Whitney Houston
15/72	**One Monkey Don't Stop No Show** . . . Honey Cone
29/66	**One More Heartache** . . . Marvin Gaye
1/85	**One More Night** . . . Phil Collins
	One More Sunrise ..see: Morgen
32/65	**One More Time** . . . Ray Charles Singers
1/88	**One More Try** . . . George Michael
1/91	**One More Try** . . . Timmy -T-
28/78	**One Nation Under A Groove** . . . Funkadelic
4/58	**One Night** . . . Elvis Presley
3/85	**One Night In Bangkok** . . . Murray Head
13/85	**One Night Love Affair** . . . Bryan Adams
11/73	**One Of A Kind (Love Affair)** . . . Spinners
15/85	**One Of The Living** . . . Tina Turner
1/75	**One Of These Nights** . . . Eagles
31/60	**One Of Us (Will Weep Tonight)** . . . Patti Page
7/83	**One On One** . . . Daryl Hall & John Oates
	One On One, Love Theme From ..see: My Fair Share
29/76	**One Piece At A Time** . . . Johnny Cash
24/81	**One Step Closer** . . . Doobie Brothers
22/86	**One Step Closer To You** . . . Gavin Christopher
13/88	**One Step Up** . . . Bruce Springsteen
	One Summer Night
7/58	Danleers
22/61	Diamonds
1/81	**One That You Love** . . . Air Supply
30/83	**One Thing** . . . INXS
4/83	**One Thing Leads To Another** . . . Fixx
	One Tin Soldier (The Legend Of Billy Jack)
34/70	Original Caste

POS/YR	RECORD TITLE/ARTIST
26/71	Coven
10/71	**One Toke Over The Line** . . . Brewer & Shipley
9/61	**One Track Mind** . . . Bobby Lewis
40/80	**One-Trick Pony** . . . Paul Simon
2/65	**1-2-3** . . . Len Barry
3/88	**1-2-3** . . . Gloria Estefan & Miami Sound Machine
5/68	**1, 2, 3, Red Light** . . . 1910 Fruitgum Company
24/79	**One Way Or Another** . . . Blondie
8/62	**One Who Really Loves You** . . . Mary Wells
15/82	**One You Love** . . . Glenn Frey
36/80	**Only A Lonely Heart Sees** . . . Felix Cavaliere
25/63	**Only In America** . . . Jay & The Americans
4/87	**Only In My Dreams** . . . Debbie Gibson
2/62	**Only Love Can Break A Heart** . . . Gene Pitney
33/70	**Only Love Can Break Your Heart** . . . Neil Young
28/76	**Only Love Is Real** . . . Carole King
33/57	**Only One Love** . . . George Hamilton IV
	Only Sixteen
28/59	Sam Cooke
6/76	Dr. Hook
24/78	**Only The Good Die Young** . . . Billy Joel
2/60	**Only The Lonely** . . . Roy Orbison
9/82	**Only The Lonely** . . . Motels
4/69	**Only The Strong Survive** . . . Jerry Butler
9/85	**Only The Young** . . . Journey
17/82	**Only Time Will Tell** . . . Asia
28/91	**Only Time Will Tell** . . . Nelson
34/84	**Only When You Leave** . . . Spandau Ballet
12/75	**Only Women** . . . Alice Cooper
4/75	**Only Yesterday** . . . Carpenters
	Only You
5/55	Platters
8/55	Hilltoppers
9/59	Franck Pourcel's French Fiddles
6/75	Ringo Starr
20/71	**Only You Know And I Know** . . . Delaney & Bonnie
23/65	**Oo Wee Baby, I Love You** . . . Fred Hughes
34/67	**Oogum Boogum Song** . . . Brenton Wood
25/73	**Ooh Baby** . . . Gilbert O'Sullivan
	Ooh Baby Baby
16/65	Miracles

POS/YR	RECORD TITLE/ARTIST
7/79	Linda Ronstadt
8/70	**O-o-h Child** . . . 5 Stairsteps
10/90	**Ooh La La (I Can't Get Over You)** . . . Perfect Gentlemen
31/58	**Ooh! My Soul** . . . Little Richard
36/85	**Ooh Ooh Song** . . . Pat Benatar
28/60	**Ooh Poo Pah Doo** . . . Jessie Hill
35/90	**Ooops Up** . . . Snap!
2/82	**Open Arms** . . . Journey
10/67	**Open Letter To My Teenage Son** . . . Victor Lundberg
27/66	**Open The Door To Your Heart** . . . Darrell Banks
8/55	**Open Up Your Heart (And Let The Sunshine In)** . . . Cowboy Church Sunday School
1/87	**Open Your Heart** . . . Madonna
18/85	**Operator** . . . Midnight Star
22/75	**Operator** . . . Manhattan Transfer
17/72	**Operator (That's Not the Way it Feels)** . . . Jim Croce
10/86	**Opportunities (Let's Make Lots Of Money)** . . . Pet Shop Boys
1/90	**Opposites Attract** . . . Paula Abdul
13/66	**Opus 17 (Don't You Worry 'Bout Me)** . . . 4 Seasons
24/89	**Orinoco Flow (Sail Away)** . . . Enya
11/83	**Other Guy** . . . Little River Band
31/67	**Other Man's Grass Is Always Greener** . . . Petula Clark
22/90	**Other Side** . . . Aerosmith
4/82	**Other Woman** . . . Ray Parker Jr.
	Our Day Will Come
1/63	Ruby & The Romantics
11/75	Frankie Valli
7/83	**Our House** . . . Madness
30/70	**Our House** . . . Crosby, Stills, Nash & Young
20/81	**Our Lips Are Sealed** . . . Go-Go's
10/78	**Our Love** . . . Natalie Cole
	(Our Love Affair) ..see: Affair To Remember
9/78	**(Our Love) Don't Throw It All Away** . . . Andy Gibb
9/63	**Our Winter Love** . . . Bill Pursell
39/67	**Out & About** . . . Tommy Boyce & Bobby Hart
19/80	**Out Here On My Own** . . . Irene Cara
15/70	**Out In The Country** . . . Three Dog Night

POS/YR	RECORD TITLE/ARTIST
3/64	**Out Of Limits** . . . Marketts
37/86	**Out Of Mind Out Of Sight** . . . Models
24/63	**Out Of My Mind** . . . Johnny Tillotson
24/64	**Out Of Sight** . . . James Brown
23/56	**Out Of Sight, Out Of Mind** . . . Five Keys
3/88	**Out Of The Blue** . . . Debbie Gibson
17/73	**Out Of The Question** . . . Gilbert O'Sullivan
1/84	**Out Of Touch** . . . Daryl Hall John Oates
21/82	**Out Of Work** . . . Gary U.S. Bonds
2/72	**Outa-Space** . . . Billy Preston
28/60	**Outside My Window** . . . Fleetwoods
34/74	**Outside Woman** . . . Bloodstone
1/65	**Over And Over** . . . Dave Clark Five
20/76	**Over My Head** . . . Fleetwood Mac
	Over The Mountain; Across The Sea
8/57	Johnnie & Joe
21/63	Bobby Vinton
16/60	**Over The Rainbow** . . . Demensions
13/66	**Over Under Sideways Down** . . . Yardbirds
7/68	**Over You** . . . Gary Puckett & The Union Gap
24/86	**Overjoyed** . . . Stevie Wonder
3/83	**Overkill** . . . Men At Work
18/74	**Overnight Sensation (Hit Record)** . . . Raspberries
16/70	**Overture From Tommy (A Rock Opera)** . . . Assembled Multitude
1/84	**Owner Of A Lonely Heart** . . . Yes
13/71	**Oye Como Va** . . . Santana

P

POS/YR	RECORD TITLE/ARTIST
10/64	**P.S. I Love You** . . . Beatles
8/62	**P.T. 109** . . . Jimmy Dean
10/83	**P.Y.T. (Pretty Young Thing)** . . . Michael Jackson
9/82	**Pac-Man Fever** . . . Buckner & Garcia
13/58	**Padre** . . . Toni Arden
1/66	**Paint It, Black** . . . Rolling Stones
	Paint Me A Picture ..see: (You Don't Have To)
34/74	**Painted Ladies** . . . Ian Thomas

POS/YR	RECORD TITLE/ARTIST
15/63	**Painted, Tainted Rose** . . . Al Martino
	Paladin ..see: Ballad Of
3/62	**Palisades Park** . . . Freddy Cannon
26/76	**Paloma Blanca** . . . George Baker Selection
22/88	**Pamela** . . . Toto
13/84	**Panama** . . . Van Halen
35/66	**Pandora's Golden Heebie Jeebies** . . . Association
1/86	**Papa Don't Preach** . . . Madonna
31/74	**Papa Don't Take No Mess** . . . James Brown
	Papa Joe's ..see: (Down At)
1/72	**Papa Was A Rollin' Stone** . . . Temptations
	Papa's Got A Brand New Bag
8/65	James Brown
21/69	Otis Redding
34/67	**Paper Cup** . . . 5th Dimension
9/87	**Paper In Fire** . . . John Cougar Mellencamp
	Paper Roses
5/60	Anita Bryant
5/73	Marie Osmond
23/65	**Paper Tiger** . . . Sue Thompson
1/66	**Paperback Writer** . . . Beatles
32/82	**Paperlate** . . . Genesis
16/88	**Paradise** . . . Sade
39/78	**Paradise By The Dashboard Light** . . . Meat Loaf
5/89	**Paradise City** . . . Guns N' Roses
34/86	**Paranoimia** . . . Art Of Noise/Max Headroom
12/88	**Parents Just Don't Understand** . . . D.J. Jazzy Jeff & The Fresh Prince
38/58	**Part Of Me** . . . Jimmy Clanton
31/75	**Part Of The Plan** . . . Dan Fogelberg
19/63	**Part Time Love** . . . Little Johnny Taylor
22/75	**Part Time Love** . . . Gladys Knight & The Pips
22/78	**Part-Time Love** . . . Elton John
1/85	**Part-Time Lover** . . . Stevie Wonder
2/85	**Party All The Time** . . . Eddie Murphy
	Party Doll
1/57	Buddy Knox
5/57	Steve Lawrence
5/62	**Party Lights** . . . Claudine Clark
34/81	**Party's Over (Hopelessly In Love)** . . . Journey
18/89	**Partyman** . . . Prince
10/83	**Pass The Dutchie** . . . Musical Youth

POS/YR	RECORD TITLE/ARTIST
2/91	**P.A.S.S.I.O.N.** . . . Rythm Syndicate
5/81	**Passion** . . . Rod Stewart
12/67	**Pata Pata** . . . Miriam Makeba
4/70	**Patches** . . . Clarence Carter
6/62	**Patches** . . . Dickey Lee
4/89	**Patience** . . . Guns N' Roses
1/58	**Patricia** . . . Perez Prado
13/71	**Pay To The Piper** . . . Chairmen Of The Board
28/67	**Pay You Back With Interest** . . . Hollies
26/74	**Payback, The** . . . James Brown
39/68	**Paying The Cost To Be The Boss** . . . B.B. King
11/90	**Peace In Our Time** . . . Eddie Money
	Peace In The Valley ..see: (There'll Be)
38/77	**Peace Of Mind** . . . Boston
31/75	**Peace Pipe** . . . B.T. Express
7/71	**Peace Train** . . . Cat Stevens
32/70	**Peace Will Come (According To Plan)** . . . Melanie
12/73	**Peaceful** . . . Helen Reddy
22/73	**Peaceful Easy Feeling** . . . Eagles
36/65	**Peaches "N" Cream** . . . Ikettes
20/61	**Peanut Butter** . . . Marathons
22/57	**Peanuts** . . . Little Joe & The Thrillers
28/59	**Peek-A-Boo** . . . Cadillacs
11/78	**Peg** . . . Steely Dan
3/57	**Peggy Sue** . . . Buddy Holly
18/64	**Penetration** . . . Pyramids
24/60	**Pennies From Heaven** . . . Skyliners
33/82	**Penny For Your Thoughts** . . . Tavares
1/67	**Penny Lane** . . . Beatles
8/84	**Penny Lover** . . . Lionel Richie
	People
5/64	Barbra Streisand
39/68	Tymes
13/85	**People Are People** . . . Depeche Mode
35/91	**People Are Still Having Sex** . . . LaTour
12/67	**People Are Strange** . . . Doors
14/65	**People Get Ready** . . . Impressions
1/68	**People Got To Be Free** . . . Rascals
22/74	**People Gotta Move** . . . Gino Vannelli
40/77	**People In Love** . . . 10cc
25/72	**People Make The World Go Round** . . . Stylistics
23/79	**People Of The South Wind** . . . Kansas
12/64	**People Say** . . . Dixie Cups

POS/YR	RECORD TITLE/ARTIST
18/61	**"Pepe"** . . . Duane Eddy
5/63	**Pepino The Italian Mouse** . . . Lou Monte
14/55	**Pepper-Hot Baby** . . . Jaye P. Morgan
1/62	**Peppermint Twist** . . . Joey Dee & the Starliters
10/62	**Percolator** . . . Billy Joe & The Checkmates
11/85	**Perfect Way** . . . Scritti Politti
3/88	**Perfect World** . . . Huey Lewis & The News
15/60	**Perfidia** . . . Ventures
28/90	**Personal Jesus** . . . Depeche Mode
2/59	**Personality** . . . Lloyd Price
19/82	**Personally** . . . Karla Bonoff
	Peter Gunn
8/59	Ray Anthony
27/60	Duane Eddy
5/59	**Petite Fleur** . . . Chris Barber's Jazz Band
16/56	**Petticoats Of Portugal** . . . Dick Jacobs
1/75	**Philadelphia Freedom** . . . Elton John
26/58	**Philadelphia U.S.A.** . . . Nu Tornados
32/66	**Phoenix Love Theme** . . . Brass Ring
1/73	**Photograph** . . . Ringo Starr
12/83	**Photograph** . . . Def Leppard
1/81	**Physical** . . . Olivia Newton-John
6/88	**Piano In The Dark** . . . Brenda Russell
25/74	**Piano Man** . . . Billy Joel
1/75	**Pick Up The Pieces** . . . AWB
27/68	**Pickin' Wild Mountain Berries** . . . Peggy Scott & Jo Jo Benson
	Picnic ..see: Moonglow
12/68	**Pictures Of Matchstick Men** . . . Status Quo
7/91	**Piece Of My Heart** . . . Tara Kemp
12/68	**Piece Of My Heart** . . . Big Brother & The Holding Company
19/73	**Pieces Of April** . . . Three Dog Night
31/83	**Pieces Of Ice** . . . Diana Ross
4/66	**Pied Piper** . . . Crispian St. Peters
3/73	**Pillow Talk** . . . Sylvia
13/80	**Pilot Of The Airwaves** . . . Charlie Dore
	(Pina Colada Song) ..see: Escape
	Pinball Wizard
19/69	Who
29/73	New Seekers (medley)
11/60	**Pineapple Princess** . . . Annette
5/88	**Pink Cadillac** . . . Natalie Cole
8/84	**Pink Houses** . . . John Cougar Mellencamp
31/64	**Pink Panther Theme** . . . Henry Mancini
3/59	**Pink Shoe Laces** . . . Dodie Stevens

POS/YR	RECORD TITLE/ARTIST
	Piove ..see: Ciao, Ciao Bambina
4/63	**Pipeline** . . . Chantay's
9/66	**Place In The Sun** . . . Stevie Wonder
6/91	**Place In This World** . . . Michael W. Smith
38/59	**Plain Jane** . . . Bobby Darin
19/55	**Plantation Boogie** . . . Lenny Dee
40/73	**Plastic Man** . . . Temptations
11/72	**Play Me** . . . Neil Diamond
6/55	**Play Me Hearts And Flowers (I Wanna Cry)** . . . Johnny Desmond
33/74	**Play Something Sweet (Brickyard Blues)** . . . Three Dog Night
	Play That Funky Music
1/76	Wild Cherry
4/91	Vanilla Ice
17/82	**Play The Game Tonight** . . . Kansas
7/62	**Playboy** . . . Marvelettes
17/68	**Playboy** . . . Gene & Debbe
10/91	**Playground** . . . Another Bad Creation
2/73	**Playground In My Mind** . . . Clint Holmes
21/57	**Playing For Keeps** . . . Elvis Presley
3/67	**Pleasant Valley Sunday** . . . Monkees
18/78	**Please Come Home For Christmas** . . . Eagles
5/74	**Please Come To Boston** . . . Dave Loggins
15/62	**Please Don't Ask About Barbara** . . . Bobby Vee
1/80	**Please Don't Go** . . . K.C. & The Sunshine Band
39/61	**Please Don't Go** . . . Ral Donner
10/88	**Please Don't Go Girl** . . . New Kids On The Block
24/79	**Please Don't Leave** . . . Lauren Wood
31/63	**Please Don't Talk To The Lifeguard** . . . Diane Ray
8/60	**Please Help Me, I'm Falling** . . . Hank Locklin
	(also see: I Can't Help You)
	Please Love Me Forever
12/61	Cathy Jean & The Roommates
6/67	Bobby Vinton
3/75	**Please Mr. Please** . . . Olivia Newton-John
	Please Mr. Postman
1/61	Marvelettes
1/75	Carpenters
11/59	**Please Mr. Sun** . . . Tommy Edwards
3/64	**Please Please Me** . . . Beatles
26/68	**Please Return Your Love To Me** . . . Temptations

POS/YR	RECORD TITLE/ARTIST
14/61	**Please Stay** . . . Drifters
20/61	**Please Tell Me Why** . . . Jackie Wilson
28/66	**Please Tell Me Why** . . . Dave Clark Five
14/87	**Pleasure Principle** . . . Janet Jackson
	Pledge Of Love
12/57	Ken Copeland
25/57	Mitchell Torok
	Pledging My Love
17/55	Johnny Ace
17/55	Teresa Brewer
34/62	**Pocketful Of Miracles** . . . Frank Sinatra
2/60	**Poetry In Motion** . . . Johnny Tillotson
5/75	**Poetry Man** . . . Phoebe Snow
37/70	**Point It Out** . . . Miracles
28/78	**Point Of Know Return** . . . Kansas
5/87	**Point Of No Return** . . . Expose
21/62	**Point Of No Return** . . . Gene McDaniels
28/86	**Point Of No Return** . . . Nu Shooz
3/90	**Poison** . . . Bell Biv DeVoe
7/89	**Poison** . . . Alice Cooper
25/83	**Poison Arrow** . . . ABC
7/59	**Poison Ivy** . . . Coasters
15/90	**Policy Of Truth** . . . Depeche Mode
24/84	**Politics Of Dancing** . . . Re-Flex
8/69	**Polk Salad Annie** . . . Tony Joe White
	Pomp & Circumstance ..see: Graduation Song
1/61	**Pony Time** . . . Chubby Checker
17/58	**Poor Boy** . . . Royaltones
24/57	**Poor Boy** . . . Elvis Presley
38/62	**Poor Fool** . . . Ike & Tina Turner
22/59	**Poor Jenny** . . . Everly Brothers
1/58	**Poor Little Fool** . . . Ricky Nelson
27/63	**Poor Little Rich Girl** . . . Steve Lawrence
14/57	**Poor Man's Roses (Or A Rich Man's Gold)** . . . Patti Page
33/81	**Poor Man's Son** . . . Survivor
	Poor People Of Paris
1/56	Les Baxter
17/56	Lawrence Welk
19/56	Russ Morgan
31/78	**Poor Poor Pitiful Me** . . . Linda Ronstadt
1/66	**Poor Side Of Town** . . . Johnny Rivers
35/82	**Pop Goes The Movies** . . . Meco
20/88	**Pop Goes The World** . . . Men Without Hats
7/85	**Pop Life** . . . Prince
1/79	**Pop Muzik** . . . M

POS/YR	RECORD TITLE/ARTIST
35/62	**Pop Pop Pop-Pie** . . . Sherrys
15/89	**Pop Singer** . . . John Cougar Mellencamp
24/72	**Pop That Thang** . . . Isley Brothers
9/72	**Popcorn** . . . Hot Butter
30/69	**Popcorn, The** . . . James Brown
14/55	**Popcorn Song** . . . Cliffie Stone
10/62	**Popeye The Hitchhiker** . . . Chubby Checker
21/66	**Popsicle** . . . Jan & Dean
3/64	**Popsicles And Icicles** . . . Murmaids
20/56	**Port Au Prince** . . . Nelson Riddle
	Portrait Of My Love
9/61	Steve Lawrence
36/67	Tokens
19/56	**Portuguese Washerwomen** . . . Joe "Fingers" Carr
	Poseidon Adventure ..see: Morning After
7/65	**Positively 4th Street** . . . Bob Dylan
21/90	**Possession** . . . Bad English
30/85	**Possession Obsession** . . . Daryl Hall John Oates
2/88	**Pour Some Sugar On Me** . . . Def Leppard
2/90	**Power, The** . . . Snap!
24/78	**Power Of Gold** . . . Dan Fogelberg/Tim Weisberg
1/85	**Power Of Love** . . . Huey Lewis & The News
4/91	**Power Of Love (medley)** . . . Luther Vandross
11/72	**Power Of Love** . . . Joe Simon
26/88	**Power Of Love** . . . Laura Branigan
11/71	**Power To The People** . . . John Lennon
2/90	**Pray** . . . M.C. Hammer
1/90	**Praying For Time** . . . George Michael
3/72	**Precious And Few** . . . Climax
19/79	**Precious Love** . . . Bob Welch
30/71	**Precious, Precious** . . . Jackie Moore
22/81	**Precious To Me** . . . Phil Seymour
21/86	**Press** . . . Paul McCartney
20/82	**Pressure** . . . Billy Joel
	Pretty Baby ..see: (It's Been A Long Time)
15/67	**Pretty Ballerina** . . . Left Banke
9/60	**Pretty Blue Eyes** . . . Steve Lawrence
29/66	**Pretty Flamingo** . . . Manfred Mann
39/79	**Pretty Girls** . . . Melissa Manchester
36/59	**Pretty Girls Everywhere** . . . Eugene Church
7/61	**Pretty Little Angel Eyes** . . . Curtis Lee

Vanessa Williams proved that former Miss Americas—no matter how brief their reign—can extend their rule to the pop charts as well. Her 1989 single "Dreamin'" hit No. 8, and 1991's "Running Back To You" made the Top 20.

Jackie Wilson's fame continues to span the decades. The influential R&B vocalist had six top-10 hits during the 50s and 60s—and had a song written about him by Van Morrison ("Jackie Wilson Said [I'm In Heaven When You Smile]") in the 70s, which was covered by Dexy's Midnight Runners in the 80s.

Nancy Wilson's way with a song has been evident since her Capitol recordings of the 60s and her 1964 hit "(You Don't Know) How Glad I Am." Offering further evidence in 1991 was her Columbia album *With My Lover Beside Me*, which featured music by Barry Manilow and lyrics by Johnny Mercer.

Wilson Phillips, unlike other offspring of the stars, shot to the top and proved they had staying power. In the 60s, the Mamas & the Papas' John and Michelle Phillips and Beach Boy Brian Wilson churned out hits; in 1990, daughters Chyna Phillips and Carnie and Wendy Wilson did the same with No. 1 hits like "Hold On" and "Release Me."

Winger sported their hard-rock pedigree from the first note of their platinum debut album: singer/bassist Kip Winger had played with Alice Cooper, and drummer Rod Morgenstein—much admired by musicians—spent time with the Dixie Dregs.

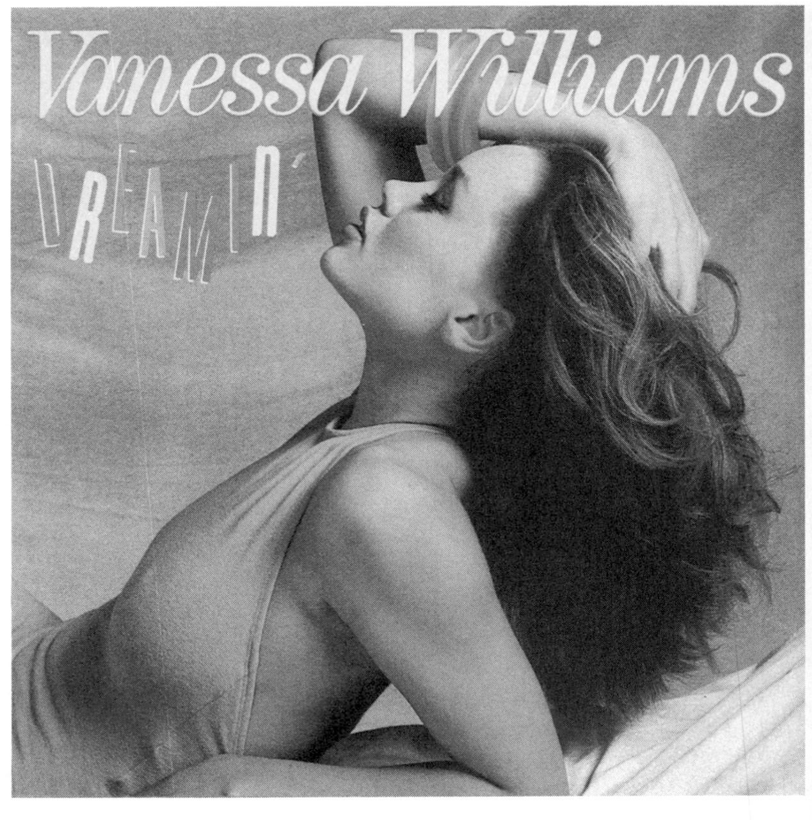

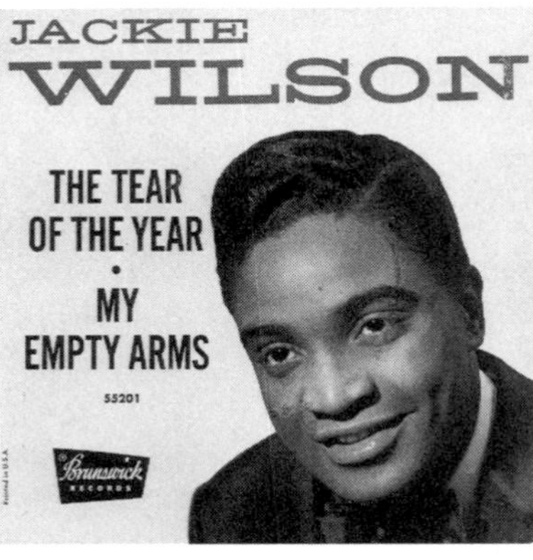

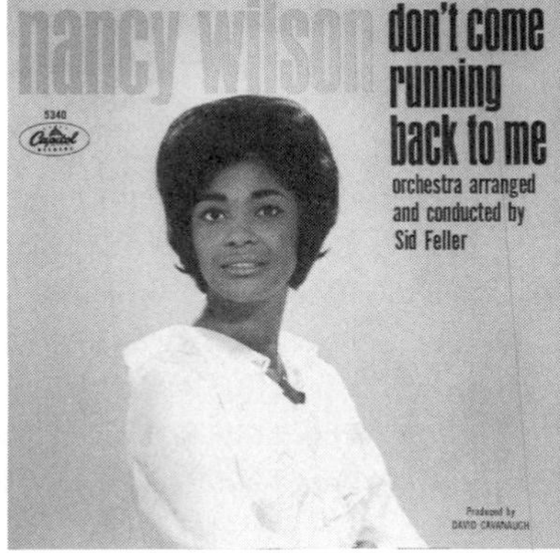

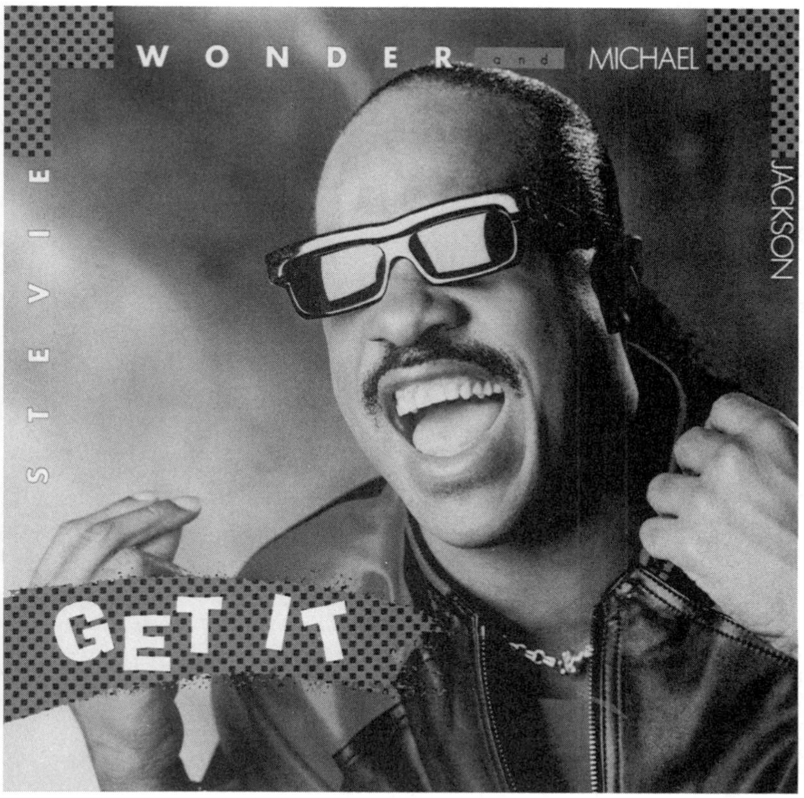

Stevie Wonder & Michael Jackson both scored No. 1 hits when they sang with Paul McCartney on 1982's "Ebony And Ivory" and 1983's "Say Say Say," respectively. Ironically, the pair's own duet—"Get It," from Wonder's 1987 *Characters* album—never even made the Top 40.

Paul Young's penchant for unusual cover versions saw him singing tunes originally done by Marvin Gaye, Joy Division, and Waylon Jennings, among others. But in 1985, Paul topped them all—by recording Hall & Oates' 1980 album track "Everytime You Go Away" and taking it to No. 1.

Young M.C. busted one big move onto the charts in 1989: first by co-writing Tone Loc's smash singles "Wild Thing" and "Funky Cold Medina," then with his own "Bust A Move," which peaked at No. 7. After an extended contractual struggle, he emerged with a new album on Capitol in late 1991.

The Zombies, who with hits "She's Not There" and "Time Of The Season" were one of the most critically-respected of the 60s' British Invasion bands, launched the 70s band Argent and the solo singing career of vocalist Colin Blunstone. Original guitarist Paul Atkinson now serves as an A&R executive at MCA Records.

ZZ Top were the object of special attention from Warner Bros. in 1987, when the label issued six of the group's earlier albums in a special 3-CD set called *The ZZ Top Sixpack*. Included within: their first Top 20 single, 1975's "Tush."

POS/YR	RECORD TITLE/ARTIST
25/65	**Pretty Little Baby** . . . Marvin Gaye
15/64	**Pretty Paper** . . . Roy Orbison
	Pretty Woman ..see: Oh, Pretty Woman
5/90	**Price Of Love** . . . Bad English
10/63	**Pride And Joy** . . . Marvin Gaye
33/84	**Pride (In The Name Of Love)** . . . U2
34/84	**Prime Time** . . . Alan Parsons Project
8/59	**Primrose Lane** . . . Jerry Wallace
30/61	**Princess** . . . Frank Gari
37/65	**Princess In Rags** . . . Gene Pitney
33/90	**Principal's Office** . . . Young M.C.
20/56	**Priscilla** . . . Eddie Cooley
30/89	**Prisoner, The** . . . Howard Jones **(also see: Love Theme From Eyes of Laura Mars)**
18/63	**Prisoner Of Love** . . . James Brown
27/78	**Prisoner Of Your Love** . . . Player
7/85	**Private Dancer** . . . Tina Turner
1/81	**Private Eyes** . . . Daryl Hall & John Oates
2/58	**Problems** . . . Everly Brothers
11/88	**Promise, The** . . . When In Rome
40/88	**Promise Me** . . . Cover Girls
17/58	**Promise Me, Love** . . . Andy Williams
1/91	**Promise Of A New Day** . . . Paula Abdul
14/74	**Promised Land** . . . Elvis Presley
9/79	**Promises** . . . Eric Clapton
38/81	**Promises In The Dark** . . . Pat Benatar
11/83	**Promises, Promises** . . . Naked Eyes
19/68	**Promises, Promises** . . . Dionne Warwick
29/63	**Proud** . . . Johnny Crawford
	Proud Mary
2/69	Creedence Clearwater Revival
4/71	Ike & Tina Turner
22/75	**Proud One** . . . Osmonds
	Proud Ones ..see: Theme From
33/78	**Prove It All Night** . . . Bruce Springsteen
7/88	**Prove Your Love** . . . Taylor Dayne
7/70	**Psychedelic Shack** . . . Temptations
5/66	**Psychotic Reaction** . . . Count Five
31/67	**Pucker Up Buttercup** . . . Jr. Walker & The All Stars
2/63	**Puff The Magic Dragon** . . . Peter, Paul & Mary
2/90	**Pump Up The Jam** . . . Technotronic
13/88	**Pump Up The Volume** . . . M/A/R/R/S
20/62	**Punish Her** . . . Bobby Vee

POS/YR	RECORD TITLE/ARTIST
	Puppet Man
24/70	5th Dimension
26/71	Tom Jones
14/65	**Puppet On A String** . . . Elvis Presley
	Puppy Love
2/60	Paul Anka
3/72	Donny Osmond
38/64	**Puppy Love** . . . Barbara Lewis
31/90	**Pure** . . . Lightning Seeds
1/58	**Purple People Eater** . . . Sheb Wooley
2/84	**Purple Rain** . . . Prince
27/62	**Push And Kick** . . . Mark Valentino
	Push And Pull ..see: (Do The)
19/88	**Push It** . . . Salt-N-Pepa
36/67	**Pushin' Too Hard** . . . Seeds
25/63	**Pushover** . . . Etta James
17/58	**Pussy Cat** . . . Ames Brothers
8/58	**Put A Light In The Window** . . . Four Lads
	Put A Little Love In Your Heart
4/69	Jackie DeShannon
9/89	Annie Lennox & Al Green
32/58	**Put A Ring On My Finger** . . . Les Paul & Mary Ford
40/83	**Put It In A Magazine** . . . Sonny Charles
2/71	**Put Your Hand In The Hand** . . . Ocean
10/74	**Put Your Hands Together** . . . O'Jays
2/59	**Put Your Head On My Shoulder** . . . Paul Anka
27/89	**Put Your Mouth On Me** . . . Eddie Murphy
4/83	**Puttin' On The Ritz** . . . Taco

POS/YR	RECORD TITLE/ARTIST
1/61	**Quarter To Three** . . . U.S. Bonds
2/56	**Que Sera, Sera (Whatever Will Be, Will Be)** . . . Doris Day
2/81	**Queen Of Hearts** . . . Juice Newton
40/76	**Queen Of My Soul** . . . Average White Band
34/83	**Queen Of The Broken Hearts** . . . Loverboy
9/58	**Queen Of The Hop** . . . Bobby Darin
12/65	**Queen Of The House** . . . Jody Miller **(also see: King Of The Road)**

POS/YR	RECORD TITLE/ARTIST
39/57	**Queen Of The Senior Prom** . . . Mills Brothers
13/69	**Quentin's Theme** . . . Charles Randolph Grean Sounde
19/60	**Question** . . . Lloyd Price
21/70	**Question** . . . Moody Blues
37/68	**Question Of Temperature** . . . Balloon Farm
24/71	**Questions 67 And 68** . . . Chicago
25/68	**Quick Joey Small (Run Joey Run)** . . . Kasenetz-Katz Singing Orchestral Circus
8/64	**Quicksand** . . . Martha & The Vandellas
4/59	**Quiet Village** . . . Martin Denny
27/61	**Quite A Party** . . . Fireballs

R

POS/YR	RECORD TITLE/ARTIST
15/65	**Race Is On** . . . Jack Jones
13/74	**Radar Love** . . . Golden Earring
16/84	**Radio Ga-Ga** . . . Queen
35/89	**Radio Romance** . . . Tiffany
28/85	**Radioactive** . . . Firm
1/64	**Rag Doll** . . . 4 Seasons
17/88	**Rag Doll** . . . Aerosmith
F/71	**Rags To Riches** . . . Elvis Presley
16/59	**Ragtime Cowboy Joe** . . . Chipmunks
9/86	**Rain, The** . . . Oran "Juice" Jones
23/66	**Rain** . . . Beatles
19/71	**Rain Dance** . . . Guess Who
10/66	**Rain On The Roof** . . . Lovin' Spoonful
21/86	**Rain On The Scarecrow** . . . John Cougar Mellencamp
12/62	**Rain Rain Go Away** . . . Bobby Vinton
2/67	**Rain, The Park & Other Things** . . . Cowsills
4/57	**Rainbow** . . . Russ Hamilton
25/79	**Rainbow Connection** . . . Kermit (Jim Henson)
2/61	**Raindrops** . . . Dee Clark
	(also see: Cloudy Summer Afternoon)
1/70	**Raindrops Keep Fallin' On My Head** . . . B.J. Thomas
34/61	**Rainin' In My Heart** . . . Slim Harpo
31/66	**Rains Came** . . . Sir Douglas Quintet
26/75	**Rainy Day People** . . . Gordon Lightfoot
2/66	**Rainy Day Women # 12 & 35** . . . Bob Dylan
2/71	**Rainy Days And Mondays** . . . Carpenters
4/70	**Rainy Night In Georgia** . . . Brook Benton
29/61	**Ram-Bunk-Shush** . . . Ventures
21/61	**Rama Lama Ding Dong** . . . Edsels
17/69	**Ramblin' Gamblin' Man** . . . Bob Seger System
2/73	**Ramblin Man** . . . Allman Brothers Band
2/62	**Ramblin' Rose** . . . Nat King Cole
27/58	**Ramrod** . . . Duane Eddy
2/70	**Rapper, The** . . . Jaggerz
36/80	**Rapper's Delight** . . . Sugarhill Gang
1/81	**Rapture** . . . Blondie
2/85	**Raspberry Beret** . . . Prince
	Raunchy
2/57	Bill Justis
4/57	Ernie Freeman
10/57	Billy Vaughn
37/58	**Rave On** . . . Buddy Holly
23/59	**Raw-Hide** . . . Link Wray
24/69	**Ray Of Hope** . . . Rascals
15/55	**Razzle-Dazzle** . . . Bill Haley
20/70	**Reach Out And Touch (Somebody's Hand)** . . . Diana Ross
20/64	**Reach Out For Me** . . . Dionne Warwick
	Reach Out I'll Be There
1/66	Four Tops
29/71	Diana Ross
10/68	**Reach Out Of The Darkness** . . . Friend & Lover
18/84	**Read 'Em And Weep** . . . Barry Manilow
26/75	**Ready** . . . Cat Stevens
7/90	**Ready or Not** . . . After 7
35/69	**Ready Or Not Here I Come (Can't Hide From Love)** . . . Delfonics
11/78	**Ready To Take A Chance Again** . . . Barry Manilow
2/89	**Real Love** . . . Jody Watley
5/80	**Real Love** . . . Doobie Brothers
16/81	**Really Wanna Know You** . . . Gary Wright
	Reaper, The ..see: (Don't Fear)
6/58	**Rebel-'Rouser** . . . Duane Eddy
28/69	**Reconsider Me** . . . Johnny Adams
37/66	**Recovery** . . . Fontella Bass

POS/YR	RECORD TITLE/ARTIST
	Red Red Wine
34/84	UB40
1/88	UB40
5/59	**Red River Rock** . . . Johnny & The Hurricanes
37/59	**Red River Rose** . . . Ames Brothers
	Red Roses For A Blue Lady
10/65	Vic Dana
11/65	Bert Kaempfert
23/65	Wayne Newton
2/66	**Red Rubber Ball** . . . Cyrkle
	Red Sails In The Sunset
36/60	Platters
35/63	Fats Domino
	Reelin' And Rockin'
23/65	Dave Clark Five
27/73	Chuck Berry
11/73	**Reeling In The Years** . . . Steely Dan
2/67	**Reflections** . . . Supremes
10/70	**Reflections Of My Life** . . . Marmalade
1/84	**Reflex, The** . . . Duran Duran
15/80	**Refugee** . . . Tom Petty
10/85	**Relax** . . . Frankie Goes To Hollywood
39/73	**Relay, The** . . . Who
1/90	**Release Me** . . . Wilson Phillips
	Release Me
8/62	Esther Phillips
4/67	Engelbert Humperdinck
39/63	**Remember Diana** . . . Paul Anka
16/71	**Remember Me** . . . Diana Ross
26/64	**Remember Me** . . . Rita Pavone
32/65	**(Remember Me) I'm The One Who Loves You** . . . Dean Martin
33/77	**(Remember The Days Of The) Old Schoolyard** . . . Cat Stevens
36/84	**Remember The Nights** . . . Motels
24/63	**Remember Then** . . . Earls
5/64	**Remember (Walkin' in the Sand)** . . . Shangri-Las
25/75	**Remember What I Told You To Forget** . . . Tavares
6/57	**Remember You're Mine** . . . Pat Boone
3/78	**Reminiscing** . . . Little River Band
26/75	**Rendezvous** . . . Hudson Brothers
16/79	**Renegade** . . . Styx
39/76	**Renegade** . . . Michael Murphey
4/65	**Rescue Me** . . . Fontella Bass
9/91	**Rescue Me** . . . Madonna

POS/YR	RECORD TITLE/ARTIST
	Respect
35/65	Otis Redding
1/67	Aretha Franklin
	Respect Yourself
12/71	Staple Singers
5/87	Bruce Willis
15/66	**Respectable** . . . Outsiders
	Resurrection Shuffle
38/71	Tom Jones
40/71	Ashton, Gardner & Dyke
15/67	**Return Of The Red Baron** . . . Royal Guardsmen
4/58	**Return To Me** . . . Dean Martin
2/62	**Return To Sender** . . . Elvis Presley
	Reuben ..see: Ruben
1/79	**Reunited** . . . Peaches & Herb
25/59	**Reveille Rock** . . . Johnny & The Hurricanes
15/62	**Revenge** . . . Brook Benton
8/63	**Reverend Mr. Black** . . . Kingston Trio
12/68	**Revolution** . . . Beatles
16/66	**Rhapsody In The Rain** . . . Lou Christie
11/76	**Rhiannon (Will You Ever Win)** . . . Fleetwood Mac
1/75	**Rhinestone Cowboy** . . . Glen Campbell
24/64	**Rhythm** . . . Major Lance
5/87	**Rhythm Is Gonna Get You** . . . Gloria Estefan & Miami Sound Machine
2/90	**Rhythm Nation** . . . Janet Jackson
40/88	**Rhythm Of Love** . . . Yes
5/91	**Rhythm Of My Heart** . . . Rod Stewart
3/85	**Rhythm Of The Night** . . . DeBarge
3/63	**Rhythm Of The Rain** . . . Cascades
1/77	**Rich Girl** . . . Daryl Hall & John Oates
7/91	**Rico Suave** . . . Gerardo
5/62	**Ride!** . . . Dee Dee Sharp
25/65	**Ride Away** . . . Roy Orbison
4/70	**Ride Captain Ride** . . . Blues Image
23/75	**Ride 'Em Cowboy** . . . Paul Davis
2/80	**Ride Like The Wind** . . . Christopher Cross
37/67	**Ride, Ride, Ride** . . . Brenda Lee
16/64	**Ride The Wild Surf** . . . Jan & Dean
38/91	**Ride The Wind** . . . Poison
28/65	**Ride Your Pony** . . . Lee Dorsey
	Riders In The Sky ..see: (Ghost)
14/71	**Riders On The Storm** . . . Doors
2/76	**Right Back Where We Started From** . . . Maxine Nightingale

POS/YR	RECORD TITLE/ARTIST
29/84	**Right By Your Side** . . . Eurythmics
12/78	**Right Down The Line** . . . Gerry Rafferty
2/91	**Right Here, Right Now** . . . Jesus Jones
1/89	**Right Here Waiting** . . . Richard Marx
23/71	**Right On The Tip Of My Tongue** . . . Brenda & The Tabulations
7/87	**Right On Track** . . . Breakfast Club
	Right Or Wrong
29/61	Wanda Jackson
14/64	Ronnie Dove
9/73	**Right Place Wrong Time** . . . Dr. John
27/87	**Right Thing** . . . Simply Red
17/73	**Right Thing To Do** . . . Carly Simon
6/77	**Right Time Of The Night** . . . Jennifer Warnes
4/74	**Rikki Don't Lose That Number** . . . Steely Dan
32/59	**Ring-A-Ling-A-Lario** . . . Jimmie Rodgers
33/65	**Ring Dang Doo** . . . Sam The Sham & The Pharoahs
1/79	**Ring My Bell** . . . Anita Ward
17/63	**Ring Of Fire** . . . Johnny Cash
31/72	**Ring The Living Bell** . . . Melanie
1/64	**Ringo** . . . Lorne Greene
17/71	**Rings** . . . Cymarron
10/62	**Rinky Dink** . . . Baby Cortez
14/83	**Rio** . . . Duran Duran
	Rip It Up
17/56	Little Richard
25/56	Bill Haley
36/64	**Rip Van Winkle** . . . Devotions
1/79	**Rise** . . . Herb Alpert
38/88	**Ritual** . . . Dan Reed Network
14/71	**River Deep - Mountain High** . . . Supremes & Four Tops
31/69	**River Is Wide** . . . Grassroots
	River Kwai March ..see: March From
33/74	**River's Risin'** . . . Edgar Winter
30/78	**Rivers Of Babylon** . . . Boney M
	Road Runner ..see: (I'm A)
3/90	**Roam** . . . B-52's
25/59	**Robbin' The Cradle** . . . Tony Bellus
16/56	**R-O-C-K** . . . Bill Haley
23/55	**Rock-A-Beatin' Boogie** . . . Bill Haley
10/57	**Rock-A-Billy** . . . Guy Mitchell
	Rock-A-Bye Your Baby With A Dixie Melody
10/56	Jerry Lewis

POS/YR	RECORD TITLE/ARTIST
37/61	Aretha Franklin
23/62	**Rock-A-Hula Baby** . . . Elvis Presley
23/89	**Rock And A Hard Place** . . . Rolling Stones
	Rock And Roll ..also see: Rock 'N' Roll, & Rockin' Roll
7/72	**Rock And Roll** . . . Gary Glitter
12/76	**Rock And Roll All Nite** . . . Kiss
32/81	**Rock And Roll Dreams Come Through** . . . Jim Steinman
20/85	**Rock And Roll Girls** . . . John Fogerty
3/74	**Rock And Roll Heaven** . . . Righteous Brothers
23/74	**Rock And Roll, Hoochie Koo** . . . Rick Derringer
19/58	**Rock And Roll Is Here To Stay** . . . Danny & The Juniors
28/76	**Rock And Roll Love Letter** . . . Bay City Rollers
15/72	**Rock And Roll Lullaby** . . . B.J. Thomas
	Rock And Roll Music
8/57	Chuck Berry
5/76	Beach Boys
1/56	**Rock And Roll Waltz** . . . Kay Starr
	Rock Around The Clock
1/55	Bill Haley
39/74	Bill Haley
2/86	**R.O.C.K. In The U.S.A.** . . . John Cougar Mellencamp
8/56	**Rock Island Line** . . . Lonnie Donegan
13/55	**Rock Love** . . . Fontane Sisters
10/69	**Rock Me** . . . Steppenwolf
1/86	**Rock Me Amadeus** . . . Falco
34/64	**Rock Me Baby** . . . B.B. King
38/72	**Rock Me Baby** . . . David Cassidy
1/74	**Rock Me Gently** . . . Andy Kim
18/85	**Rock Me Tonight (For Old Times Sake)** . . . Freddie Jackson
15/84	**Rock Me Tonite** . . . Billy Squier
	Rock 'N' Roll ..also see: Rock And Roll, & Rockin' Roll
13/79	**Rock 'N' Roll Fantasy** . . . Bad Company
30/78	**Rock 'N' Roll Fantasy** . . . Kinks
15/75	**Rock N' Roll (I Gave You The Best Years Of My Life)** . . . Mac Davis
19/83	**Rock 'N' Roll Is King** . . . ELO
29/72	**Rock 'N Roll Soul** . . . Grand Funk Railroad
16/83	**Rock Of Ages** . . . Def Leppard
22/88	**Rock Of Life** . . . Rick Springfield

POS/YR	RECORD TITLE/ARTIST
	Rock On
5/74	David Essex
1/89	Michael Damian
36/56	**Rock Right** . . . Georgia Gibbs
7/87	**Rock Steady** . . . Whispers
9/71	**Rock Steady** . . . Aretha Franklin
1/74	**Rock The Boat** . . . Hues Corporation
8/83	**Rock The Casbah** . . . Clash
30/87	**Rock The Night** . . . Europe
9/82	**Rock This Town** . . . Stray Cats
7/89	**Rock Wit'cha** . . . Bobby Brown
1/80	**Rock With You** . . . Michael Jackson
25/84	**Rock You Like A Hurricane** . . . Scorpions
1/74	**Rock Your Baby** . . . George McCrae
17/57	**Rock Your Little Baby To Sleep** . . . Buddy Knox
38/59	**Rocka-Conga** . . . Applejacks
12/89	**Rocket** . . . Def Leppard
6/72	**Rocket Man** . . . Elton John
39/78	**Rocket Ride** . . . Kiss
6/88	**Rocket 2 U** . . . Jets
10/75	**Rockford Files** . . . Mike Post
27/75	**Rockin' All Over The World** . . . John Fogerty
14/60	**Rockin' Around The Christmas Tree** . . . Brenda Lee
25/85	**Rockin' At Midnight** . . . Honeydrippers
9/75	**Rockin' Chair** . . . Gwen McCrae
7/60	**Rockin' Good Way (To Mess Around And Fall In Love)** . . . Dinah Washington & Brook Benton
22/60	**Rockin' Little Angel** . . . Ray Smith
1/76	**Rockin' Me** . . . Steve Miller
6/73	**Rockin' Pneumonia And The Boogie Woogie Flu** . . . Johnny Rivers
	Rockin' Robin
2/58	Bobby Day
2/72	Michael Jackson
	Rockin' Roll ..also see: Rock And Roll, & Rock 'N' Roll
14/73	**Rockin' Roll Baby** . . . Stylistics
18/74	**Rockin' Soul** . . . Hues Corporation
9/75	**Rocky** . . . Austin Roberts
9/73	**Rocky Mountain High** . . . John Denver
23/73	**Rocky Mountain Way** . . . Joe Walsh
	Rocky, Theme From ..see: Gonna Fly Now
30/79	**Rolene** . . . Moon Martin
27/83	**Roll Me Away** . . . Bob Seger

POS/YR	RECORD TITLE/ARTIST
14/75	**Roll On Down The Highway** . . . Bachman-Turner Overdrive
29/56	**Roll Over Beethoven** . . . Chuck Berry
1/88	**Roll With It** . . . Steve Winwood
34/79	**Roller** . . . April Wine
13/55	**Rollin' Stone** . . . Fontane Sisters
26/84	**Romancing The Stone** . . . Eddy Grant
6/90	**Romeo** . . . Dino
	Romeo & Juliet ..see: Love Theme, & (Just Like)
11/80	**Romeo's Tune** . . . Steve Forbert
3/89	**Roni** . . . Bobby Brown
6/64	**Ronnie** . . . 4 Seasons
17/90	**Room At The Top** . . . Adam Ant
9/89	**Room To Move** . . . Animotion
16/89	**Rooms On Fire** . . . Stevie Nicks
2/82	**Rosanna** . . . Toto
3/80	**Rose, The** . . . Bette Midler
6/56	**Rose And A Baby Ruth** . . . George Hamilton IV
3/71	**Rose Garden** . . . Lynn Anderson
	Roses And Roses ..see: And Roses
1/62	**Roses Are Red (My Love)** . . . Bobby Vinton
24/57	**Rosie Lee** . . . Mello-Tones
30/80	**Rotation** . . . Herb Alpert
22/86	**Rough Boy** . . . ZZ Top
1/57	**Round And Round** . . . Perry Como
12/84	**Round And Round** . . . Ratt
12/91	**Round And Round** . . . Tevin Campbell
21/65	**Round Every Corner** . . . Petula Clark
13/72	**Roundabout** . . . Yes
30/62	**Route 66 Theme** . . . Nelson Riddle
37/82	**Route 101** . . . Herb Alpert
32/79	**Roxanne** . . . Police
16/74	**Rub It In** . . . Billy "Crash" Craddock
3/90	**Rub You The Right Way** . . . Johnny Gill
6/61	**Rubber Ball** . . . Bobby Vee
37/79	**Rubber Biscuit** . . . Blues Brothers
16/70	**Rubber Duckie** . . . Ernie (Jim Henson)
2/76	**Rubberband Man** . . . Spinners
26/69	**Ruben James** . . . Kenny Rogers & The First Edition
28/60	**Ruby** . . . Ray Charles
18/62	**Ruby Ann** . . . Marty Robbins
	Ruby Baby
2/63	Dion

POS/YR	RECORD TITLE/ARTIST
33/75	Billy "Crash" Craddock
6/69	**Ruby, Don't Take Your Love To Town** . . . Kenny Rogers & The First Edition
30/60	**Ruby Duby Du** . . . Tobin Mathews & Co.
	(Ruby Red Dress) ..see: Leave Me Alone
1/67	**Ruby Tuesday** . . . Rolling Stones
21/60	**Rudolph The Red Nosed Reindeer** . . . Chipmunks
34/56	**Rudy's Rock** . . . Bill Haley
16/58	**Rumble** . . . Link Wray
28/86	**Rumbleseat** . . . John Cougar Mellencamp
8/86	**Rumors** . . . Timex Social Club
12/62	**Rumors** . . . Johnny Crawford
6/69	**Run Away Child, Running Wild** . . . Temptations
12/65	**Run, Baby Run (Back Into My Arms)** . . . Newbeats
33/78	**Run For Home** . . . Lindisfarne
18/82	**Run For The Roses** . . . Dan Fogelberg
4/75	**Run Joey Run** . . . David Geddes
36/60	**Run Red Run** . . . Coasters
25/66	**Run, Run, Look And See** . . . Brian Hyland
27/72	**Run Run Run** . . . Jo Jo Gunne
20/84	**Run Runaway** . . . Slade
28/60	**Run Samson Run** . . . Neil Sedaka
2/61	**Run To Him** . . . Bobby Vee
16/72	**Run To Me** . . . Bee Gees
6/85	**Run To You** . . . Bryan Adams
23/60	**Runaround** . . . Fleetwoods
28/61	**Runaround** . . . Regents
	Runaround Sue
1/61	Dion
13/78	Leif Garrett
1/61	**Runaway** . . . Del Shannon
12/78	**Runaway** . . . Jefferson Starship
39/84	**Runaway** . . . Bon Jovi
22/84	**Runner** . . . Manfred Mann's Earth Band
23/72	**Runnin' Away** . . . Sly & The Family Stone
23/89	**Runnin' Down A Dream** . . . Tom Petty
1/60	**Running Bear** . . . Johnny Preston
11/78	**Running On Empty** . . . Jackson Browne
1/61	**Running Scared** . . . Roy Orbison
30/85	**Running Up That Hill** . . . Kate Bush
7/84	**Running With The Night** . . . Lionel Richie
39/72	**Runway, The** . . . Grass Roots
9/88	**Rush Hour** . . . Jane Wiedlin

POS/YR	RECORD TITLE/ARTIST
1/91	**Rush, Rush** . . . Paula Abdul
16/86	**Russians** . . . Sting
33/65	**Rusty Bells** . . . Brenda Lee

S

POS/YR	RECORD TITLE/ARTIST
15/75	**S.O.S.** . . . Abba
39/66	**S.Y.S.L.J.F.M. (The Letter Song)** . . . Joe Tex
20/61	**Sacred** . . . Castells
13/89	**Sacred Emotion** . . . Donny Osmond
18/90	**Sacrifice** . . . Elton John
1/79	**Sad Eyes** . . . Robert John
29/60	**Sad Mood** . . . Sam Cooke
5/61	**Sad Movies (Make Me Cry)** . . . Sue Thompson
27/65	**Sad, Sad Girl** . . . Barbara Mason
5/84	**Sad Songs (Say So Much)** . . . Elton John
14/75	**Sad Sweet Dreamer** . . . Sweet Sensation
5/91	**Sadeness** . . . Enigma
3/83	**Safety Dance** . . . Men Without Hats
5/58	**Sail Along Silvery Moon** . . . Billy Vaughn
	(Sail Away) ..see: Orinoco Flow
4/79	**Sail On** . . . Commodores
1/80	**Sailing** . . . Christopher Cross
5/60	**Sailor (Your Home Is The Sea)** . . . Lolita
	Saint ..see: St.
	Saints Rock 'N Roll ..see: When The Saints Go Marchin' In
17/75	**Sally G** . . . Paul McCartney
2/63	**Sally, Go 'Round The Roses** . . . Jaynetts
36/83	**Salt In My Tears** . . . Martin Briley
20/77	**Sam** . . . Olivia Newton-John
9/81	**Same Old Lang Syne** . . . Dan Fogelberg
13/55	**Same Old Saturday Night** . . . Frank Sinatra
16/60	**Same One** . . . Brook Benton
8/61	**San Antonio Rose** . . . Floyd Cramer
9/67	**San Franciscan Nights** . . . Animals
4/67	**San Francisco (Be Sure To Wear Flowers In Your Hair)** . . . Scott McKenzie
14/86	**Sanctify Yourself** . . . Simple Minds
23/55	**Sand And The Sea** . . . Nat "King" Cole
15/60	**Sandy** . . . Larry Hall

POS/YR	RECORD TITLE/ARTIST
21/63	**Sandy** . . . Dion
27/66	**Sandy** . . . Ronny & The Daytonas
32/57	**Santa And The Satellite** . . . Buchanan & Goodman
23/62	**Santa Claus Is Coming To Town** . . . 4 Seasons
1/86	**Sara** . . . Starship
7/80	**Sara** . . . Fleetwood Mac
4/76	**Sara Smile** . . . Daryl Hall & John Oates
39/80	**(Sartorial Eloquence) Don't Ya Wanna Play This Game No More?** . . . Elton John
23/66	**Satin Pillows** . . . Bobby Vinton
28/73	**Satin Sheets** . . . Jeanne Pruett
22/75	**Satin Soul** . . . Love Unlimited Orchestra
	Satisfaction ..see: (I Can't Get No)
1/89	**Satisfied** . . . Richard Marx
39/66	**Satisfied Mind** . . . Bobby Hebb
3/72	**Saturday In The Park** . . . Chicago
26/86	**Saturday Love** . . . Cherrelle with Alexander O'Neal
28/71	**Saturday Morning Confusion** . . . Bobby Russell
1/76	**Saturday Night** . . . Bay City Rollers
29/63	**Saturday Night** . . . New Christy Minstrels
35/79	**Saturdaynight** . . . Herman Brood
21/77	**Saturday Nite** . . . Earth, Wind & Fire
18/64	**Saturday Night At The Movies** . . . Drifters
27/75	**Saturday Night Special** . . . Lynyrd Skynyrd
34/79	**Saturday Night, Sunday Morning** . . . Thelma Houston
12/73	**Saturday Night's Alright For Fighting** . . . Elton John
25/81	**Sausalito Summernight** . . . Diesel
34/80	**Savannah Nights** . . . Tom Johnston
16/85	**Save A Prayer** . . . Duran Duran
22/77	**Save It For A Rainy Day** . . . Stephen Bishop
10/64	**Save It For Me** . . . 4 Seasons
33/90	**Save Me** . . . Fleetwood Mac
15/91	**Save Some Love** . . . Keedy
27/70	**Save The Country** . . . 5th Dimension
	Save The Last Dance For Me
1/60	Drifters
18/74	DeFranco Family
	(also see: I'll Save The Last Dance)

POS/YR	RECORD TITLE/ARTIST
2/65	**Save Your Heart For Me** . . . Gary Lewis & The Playboys
27/76	**Save Your Kisses For Me** . . . Brotherhood Of Man
37/61	**Saved** . . . LaVern Baker
20/83	**Saved By Zero** . . . Fixx
1/85	**Saving All My Love For You** . . . Whitney Houston
21/90	**Say A Prayer** . . . Breathe
17/81	**Say Goodbye To Hollywood** . . . Billy Joel
3/73	**Say, Has Anybody Seen My Sweet Gypsy Rose** . . . Dawn
21/66	**Say I Am (What I Am)** . . . Tommy James & The Shondells
27/88	**Say It Again** . . . Jermaine Stewart
2/83	**Say It Isn't So** . . . Daryl Hall - John Oates
10/68	**Say It Loud - I'm Black And I'm Proud** . . . James Brown
20/59	**Say Man** . . . Bo Diddley
1/83	**Say Say Say** . . . Paul McCartney & Michael Jackson
22/65	**Say Something Funny** . . . Patty Duke
32/81	**Say What** . . . Jesse Winchester
40/64	**Say You** . . . Ronnie Dove
11/76	**Say You Love Me** . . . Fleetwood Mac
1/85	**Say You, Say Me** . . . Lionel Richie
6/88	**Say You Will** . . . Foreigner
20/81	**Say You'll Be Mine** . . . Christopher Cross
15/77	**Say You'll Stay Until Tomorrow** . . . Tom Jones
39/65	**(Say) You're My Girl** . . . Roy Orbison
21/85	**Say You're Wrong** . . . Julian Lennon
31/88	**Sayin' Sorry (Don't Make It Right)** . . . Denise Lopez
	Scarborough Fair
11/68	Simon & Garfunkel
16/68	Sergio Mendes & Brasil '66
13/59	**Scarlet Ribbons (For Her Hair)** . . . Browns
33/75	**School Boy Crush** . . . Average White Band
3/57	**School Day** . . . Chuck Berry
28/61	**School Is In** . . . Gary (U.S.) Bonds
5/61	**School Is Out** . . . Gary (U.S.) Bonds
7/72	**School's Out** . . . Alice Cooper
6/72	**Scorpio** . . . Dennis Coffey
20/87	**Se La** . . . Lionel Richie
	Se Si Bon ..see: Whispering
14/59	**Sea Cruise** . . . Frankie Ford
21/61	**Sea Of Heartbreak** . . . Don Gibson

POS/YR	RECORD TITLE/ARTIST
	Sea Of Love
2/59	Phil Phillips With The Twilights
33/82	Del Shannon
3/85	Honeydrippers
	Sealed With A Kiss
3/62	Brian Hyland
19/68	Gary Lewis & The Playboys
19/72	Bobby Vinton
4/85	**Search Is Over** . . . Survivor
3/57	**Searchin'** . . . Coasters
	Searchin' So Long ..see: (I've Been)
27/66	**Searching For My Love** . . . Bobby Moore
1/88	**Seasons Change** . . . Expose
1/74	**Seasons In The Sun** . . . Terry Jacks
38/69	**Seattle** . . . Perry Como
34/74	**Second Avenue** . . . Garfunkel
6/89	**Second Chance** . . . Thirty Eight Special
40/56	**Second Fiddle** . . . Kay Starr
7/62	**Second Hand Love** . . . Connie Francis
32/66	**Second Hand Rose** . . . Barbra Streisand
39/85	**Second Nature** . . . Dan Hartman
8/80	**Second Time Around** . . . Shalamar
18/58	**Secret, The** . . . Gordon MacRae
3/66	**Secret Agent Man** . . . Johnny Rivers
31/90	**Secret Garden (Sweet Seduction Suite)** . . . Quincy Jones/Al B. Sure!/James Ingram/El DeBarge/Barry White
	Secret Love
29/66	Billy Stewart
20/75	Freddy Fender
3/86	**Secret Lovers** . . . Atlantic Starr
6/89	**Secret Rendezvous** . . . Karyn White
19/86	**Secret Separation** . . . Fixx
3/58	**Secretly** . . . Jimmie Rodgers
35/68	**Security** . . . Etta James
28/80	**Seduction, The** . . . James Last Band
27/69	**See** . . . Rascals
	See Me, Feel Me
12/70	Who
29/73	New Seekers (medley)
25/56	**See Saw** . . . Moonglows
14/68	**See Saw** . . . Aretha Franklin
	See See ..see: C.C.
9/64	**See The Funny Little Clown** . . . Bobby Goldsboro
40/91	**See The Lights** . . . Simple Minds
	See You In September
23/59	Tempos

POS/YR	RECORD TITLE/ARTIST
3/66	Happenings
6/56	**See You Later, Alligator** . . . Bill Haley
4/84	**Self Control** . . . Laura Branigan
11/64	**Selfish One** . . . Jackie Ross
6/57	**Send For Me** . . . Nat "King" Cole
23/83	**Send Her My Love** . . . Journey
	Send In The Clowns
36/75	Judy Collins
19/77	Judy Collins
	Send Me An Angel
29/84	Real Life
26/89	Real Life ('89)
13/63	**Send Me Some Lovin'** . . . Sam Cooke
	Send Me The Pillow You Dream On
17/62	Johnny Tillotson
22/65	Dean Martin
4/79	**Send One Your Love** . . . Stevie Wonder
5/90	**Sending All My Love** . . . Linear
4/91	**Sensitivity** . . . Ralph Tresvant
8/78	**Sentimental Lady** . . . Bob Welch
8/85	**Sentimental Street** . . . Night Ranger
1/85	**Separate Lives** . . . Phil Collins & Marilyn Martin
20/73	**Separate Ways** . . . Elvis Presley
8/83	**Separate Ways (Worlds Apart)** . . . Journey
8/79	**September** . . . Earth, Wind & Fire
23/61	**September In The Rain** . . . Dinah Washington
17/80	**September Morn'** . . . Neil Diamond
23/80	**Sequel** . . . Harry Chapin
21/87	**Serious** . . . Donna Allen
13/78	**Serpentine Fire** . . . Earth, Wind & Fire
23/65	**Set Me Free** . . . Kinks
27/80	**Set Me Free** . . . Utopia
33/66	**7 And 7 Is** . . . Love
21/81	**Seven Bridges Road** . . . Eagles
27/62	**Seven Day Weekend** . . . Gary (US) Bonds
	Seven Days
17/56	Dorothy Collins
18/56	Crew Cuts
30/58	**"7-11" (Mambo No. 5)** . . . Gone All Stars
9/59	**Seven Little Girls Sitting In The Back Seat** . . . Paul Evans
14/67	**7 Rooms Of Gloom** . . . Four Tops
19/87	**Seven Wonders** . . . Fleetwood Mac
22/81	**Seven Year Ache** . . . Rosanne Cash
7/65	**Seventh Son** . . . Johnny Rivers

POS/YR	RECORD TITLE/ARTIST
	Seventeen
3/55	Fontane Sisters
5/55	Boyd Bennett
18/55	Rusty Draper
26/89	**Seventeen** . . . Winger
36/84	**17** . . . Rick James
28/86	**Sex As A Weapon** . . . Pat Benatar
15/70	**Sex Machine** . . . James Brown
3/83	**Sexual Healing** . . . Marvin Gaye
	Sexy + 17 ..see: (She's)
5/80	**Sexy Eyes** . . . Dr. Hook
20/84	**Sexy Girl** . . . Glenn Frey
17/74	**Sexy Mama** . . . Moments
12/65	**Sha La La** . . . Manfred Mann
7/74	**Sha-La-La (Make Me Happy)** . . . Al Green
1/78	**Shadow Dancing** . . . Andy Gibb
25/79	**Shadows In The Moonlight** . . . Anne Murray
13/82	**Shadows Of The Night** . . . Pat Benatar
19/62	**Shadrack** . . . Brook Benton
	Shaft ..see: Theme From
38/64	**Shaggy Dog** . . . Mickey Lee Lane
7/65	**Shake** . . . Sam Cooke
25/67	**Shake A Tail Feather** . . . James & Bobby Purify
29/65	**Shake And Fingerpop** . . . Jr. Walker & The All Stars
28/89	**Shake For The Sheik** . . . Escape Club
13/79	**Shake It** . . . Ian Matthews
4/82	**Shake It Up** . . . Cars
18/66	**Shake Me, Wake Me (When It's Over)** . . . Four Tops
31/67	**Shake, Rattle & Roll** . . . Arthur Conley
33/63	**Shake! Shake! Shake!** . . . Jackie Wilson
1/76	**(Shake, Shake, Shake) Shake Your Booty** . . . KC & The Sunshine Band
1/87	**Shake You Down** . . . Gregory Abbott
7/79	**Shake Your Body (Down To The Ground)** . . . Jacksons
5/79	**Shake Your Groove Thing** . . . Peaches & Herb
4/87	**Shake Your Love** . . . Debbie Gibson
23/77	**Shake Your Rump To The Funk** . . . Bar-Kays
1/87	**Shakedown** . . . Bob Seger
31/79	**Shakedown Cruise** . . . Jay Ferguson
26/75	**Shakey Ground** . . . Temptations
22/65	**Shakin' All Over** . . . Guess Who?

POS/YR	RECORD TITLE/ARTIST
3/73	**Shambala** . . . Three Dog Night
9/78	**Shame** . . . Evelyn "Champagne" King
21/85	**Shame** . . . Motels
23/62	**Shame On Me** . . . Bobby Bare
2/83	**Shame On The Moon** . . . Bob Seger
29/68	**Shame, Shame** . . . Magic Lanterns
12/75	**Shame, Shame, Shame** . . . Shirley & Company
31/82	**Shanghai Breezes** . . . John Denver
	Shangri-La
11/57	Four Coins
15/64	Robert Maxwell
27/64	Vic Dana
6/76	**Shannon** . . . Henry Gross
22/68	**Shape Of Things To Come** . . . Max Frost
11/66	**Shapes Of Things** . . . Yardbirds
10/70	**Share The Land** . . . Guess Who
	Share Your Love With Me
13/69	Aretha Franklin
14/81	Kenny Rogers
6/79	**Sharing The Night Together** . . . Dr. Hook
15/62	**Sharing You** . . . Bobby Vee
31/79	**Shattered** . . . Rolling Stones
2/88	**Shattered Dreams** . . . Johnny Hates Jazz
30/75	**Shaving Cream** . . . Benny Bell
23/70	**She** . . . Tommy James & The Shondells
1/90	**She Ain't Worth It** . . . Glenn Medeiros & Bobby Brown
5/79	**She Believes In Me** . . . Kenny Rogers
33/70	**She Belongs To Me** . . . Rick Nelson
5/83	**She Blinded Me With Science** . . . Thomas Dolby
3/84	**She Bop** . . . Cyndi Lauper
30/70	**She Came In Through The Bathroom Window** . . . Joe Cocker
19/62	**She Can't Find Her Keys** . . . Paul Petersen
	She Comes To Me ..see: (When She Needs Good Lovin')
5/62	**She Cried** . . . Jay & The Americans
23/77	**She Did It** . . . Eric Carmen
1/89	**She Drives Me Crazy** . . . Fine Young Cannibals
27/67	**She Is Still A Mystery** . . . Lovin' Spoonful
1/64	**She Loves You** . . . Beatles
18/59	**She Say (Oom Dooby Doom)** . . . Diamonds
30/91	**She Talks To Angels** . . . Black Crowes

POS/YR	RECORD TITLE/ARTIST
	She Understands Me
31/64	Johnny Tillotson
40/66	Bobby Vinton (Dum-De-Da)
6/89	**She Wants To Dance With Me** . . . Rick Astley
27/58	**She Was Only Seventeen (He Was One Year More)** . . . Marty Robbins
30/89	**She Won't Talk To Me** . . . Luther Vandross
3/83	**She Works Hard For The Money** . . . Donna Summer
3/67	**She'd Rather Be With Me** . . . Turtles
22/81	**She's A Bad Mama Jama (She's Built, She's Stacked)** . . . Carl Carlton
10/83	**She's A Beauty** . . . Tubes
5/63	**She's A Fool** . . . Lesley Gore
16/68	**She's A Heartbreaker** . . . Gene Pitney
2/71	**She's A Lady** . . . Tom Jones
25/68	**She's A Rainbow** . . . Rolling Stones
4/64	**She's A Woman** . . . Beatles
13/65	**She's About A Mover** . . . Sir Douglas Quintet
39/71	**She's All I Got** . . . Freddie North
17/78	**She's Always A Woman** . . . Billy Joel
18/62	**She's Everything (I Wanted You To Be)** . . . Ral Donner
7/76	**She's Gone** . . . Daryl Hall & John Oates
23/82	**She's Got A Way** . . . Billy Joel
14/62	**She's Got You** . . . Patsy Cline
3/66	**She's Just My Style** . . . Gary Lewis & The Playboys
3/88	**She's Like The Wind** . . . Patrick Swayze/Wendy Fraser
15/68	**She's Lookin' Good** . . . Wilson Pickett
21/84	**She's Mine** . . . Steve Perry
14/67	**She's My Girl** . . . Turtles
38/58	**She's Neat** . . . Dale Wright
11/71	**She's Not Just Another Woman** . . . 8th Day
	She's Not There
2/64	Zombies
27/77	Santana
5/62	**She's Not You** . . . Elvis Presley
10/80	**She's Out Of My Life** . . . Michael Jackson
5/83	**(She's) Sexy + 17** . . . Stray Cats
26/80	**She's So Cold** . . . Rolling Stones
33/64	**She's The One** . . . Chartbusters
1/62	**Sheila** . . . Tommy Roe
36/91	**Shelter Me** . . . Cinderella

POS/YR	RECORD TITLE/ARTIST
17/64	**Shelter Of Your Arms** . . . Sammy Davis Jr.
1/62	**Sherry** . . . 4 Seasons
	Shifting, Whispering Sands
3/55	Rusty Draper
5/55	Billy Vaughn
24/70	**Shilo** . . . Neil Diamond
	Shimmy Shimmy ..see: (I Do The)
24/60	**Shimmy, Shimmy, Ko-Ko-Bop** . . . Little Anthony & The Imperials
8/79	**Shine A Little Love** . . . Electric Light Orchestra
40/81	**Shine On** . . . L.T.D.
37/84	**Shine Shine** . . . Barry Gibb
11/74	**Shinin' On** . . . Grand Funk
1/75	**Shining Star** . . . Earth, Wind & Fire
5/80	**Shining Star** . . . Manhattans
27/87	**Ship Of Fools (Save Me From Tomorrow)** . . . World Party
9/79	**Ships** . . . Barry Manilow
10/57	**Shish-Kebab** . . . Ralph Marterie
29/83	**Shock The Monkey** . . . Peter Gabriel
18/75	**Shoeshine Boy** . . . Eddie Kendricks
	Shoo ..also see: Shu
9/68	**Shoo-Be-Doo-Be-Doo-Da-Day** . . . Stevie Wonder
	Shoop Shoop Song (It's In His Kiss)
6/64	Betty Everett
33/91	Cher
31/68	**Shoot'em Up, Baby** . . . Andy Kim
	Shop Around
2/61	Miracles
4/76	Captain & Tennille
5/57	**Short Fat Fannie** . . . Larry Williams
2/78	**Short People** . . . Randy Newman
3/58	**Short Shorts** . . . Royal Teens
4/65	**Shotgun** . . . Jr. Walker & The All Stars
13/82	**Should I Do It** . . . Pointer Sisters
3/87	**Should've Known Better** . . . Richard Marx
19/80	**Should've Never Let You Go** . . . Neil Sedaka & Dara Sedaka
29/89	**Shoulder To Cry On** . . . Tommy Page
1/85	**Shout** . . . Tears For Fears
6/62	**Shout** . . . Joey Dee & The Starliters
31/76	**Shout It Out Loud** . . . Kiss
6/62	**Shout! Shout! (Knock Yourself Out)** . . . Ernie Maresca
1/74	**Show And Tell** . . . Al Wilson
28/84	**Show Me** . . . Pretenders

POS/YR	RECORD TITLE/ARTIST
35/67	**Show Me** . . . Joe Tex
3/91	**Show Me The Way** . . . Styx
6/76	**Show Me The Way** . . . Peter Frampton
4/74	**Show Must Go On** . . . Three Dog Night
37/85	**Show Some Respect** . . . Tina Turner
28/77	**Show You The Way To Go** . . . Jacksons
5/89	**Shower Me With Your Love** . . . Surface
22/76	**Shower The People** . . . James Taylor
38/75	**(Shu-Doo-Pa-Poo-Poop) Love Being Your Fool** . . . Travis Wammack
32/61	**Shu Rah** . . . Fats Domino
23/63	**Shut Down** . . . Beach Boys
24/63	**Shutters And Boards** . . . Jerry Wallace
22/58	**Sick And Tired** . . . Fats Domino
8/74	**Sideshow** . . . Blue Magic
25/64	**Sidewalk Surfin'** . . . Jan & Dean
18/86	**Sidewalk Talk** . . . Jellybean
3/87	**Sign 'O' The Times** . . . Prince
11/66	**Sign Of The Times** . . . Petula Clark
32/84	**Sign Of Fire** . . . Fixx
4/88	**Sign Your Name** . . . Terence Trent D'Arby
	Signed, Sealed, Delivered I'm Yours
3/70	Stevie Wonder
18/77	Peter Frampton
	Signs
3/71	Five Man Electrical Band
8/91	Tesla
11/67	**Silence Is Golden** . . . Tremeloes
9/91	**Silent Lucidity** . . . Queensryche
6/86	**Silent Running (On Dangerous Ground)** . . . Mike + The Mechanics
13/89	**Silhouette** . . . Kenny G
	Silhouettes
3/57	Rays
10/57	Diamonds
5/65	Herman's Hermits
1/76	**Silly Love Songs** . . . Wings
25/70	**Silver Bird** . . . Mark Lindsay
20/55	**Silver Dollar** . . . Teresa Brewer
38/76	**Silver Star** . . . Four Seasons
20/62	**Silver Threads And Golden Needles** . . . Springfields
4/68	**Simon Says** . . . 1910 Fruitgum Co.
2/88	**Simply Irresistible** . . . Robert Palmer
	Since I Don't Have You
12/59	Skyliners
23/81	Don McLean
4/63	**Since I Fell For You** . . . Lenny Welch

POS/YR	RECORD TITLE/ARTIST
17/65	**Since I Lost My Baby** . . . Temptations
	Since I Met You Baby
12/56	Ivory Joe Hunter
34/57	Mindy Carson
32/67	**Since You Showed Me How To Be Happy** . . . Jackie Wilson
31/87	**Since You've Been Gone** . . . Outfield **(also see: Sweet Sweet Baby)**
38/59	**Since You've Been Gone** . . . Clyde McPhatter
	Sincerely
1/55	McGuire Sisters
20/55	Moonglow's
14/89	**Sincerely Yours** . . . Sweet Sensation
3/73	**Sing** . . . Carpenters
5/76	**Sing A Song** . . . Earth, Wind & Fire
24/58	**Sing Boy Sing** . . . Tommy Sands
	Singing The Blues
1/56	Guy Mitchell
17/56	Marty Robbins
12/66	**Single Girl** . . . Sandy Posey
3/60	**Sink The Bismarck** . . . Johnny Horton
1/77	**Sir Duke** . . . Stevie Wonder
5/84	**Sister Christian** . . . Night Ranger
1/75	**Sister Golden Hair** . . . America
24/74	**Sister Mary Elephant (Shudd-Up!)** . . . Cheech & Chong
18/85	**Sisters Are Doin' It For Themselves** . . . Eurythmics & Aretha Franklin
36/67	**Sit Down, I Think I Love You** . . . Mojo Men
37/71	**Sit Yourself Down** . . . Stephen Stills
	Sittin' In The Balcony
18/57	Eddie Cochran
38/57	Johnny Dee
19/90	**Sittin' In The Lap Of Luxury** . . . Louie Louie
	(Sittin' On) The Dock Of The Bay
1/68	Otis Redding
11/88	Michael Bolton
16/73	**Sitting** . . . Cat Stevens
27/83	**Sitting At The Wheel** . . . Moody Blues
24/65	**Sitting In The Park** . . . Billy Stewart
32/63	**Six Days On The Road** . . . Dave Dudley
28/59	**Six Nights A Week** . . . Crests
18/67	**Six O'Clock** . . . Lovin' Spoonful
13/66	**634-5789 (Soulsville, U.S.A.)** . . . Wilson Pickett

POS/YR	RECORD TITLE/ARTIST
	(also see: Beechwood 4-5789)
2/59	**16 Candles** . . . Crests
3/60	**Sixteen Reasons** . . . Connie Stevens
	Sixteen Tons
1/55	Tennessee Ernie Ford
17/55	Johnny Desmond
6/82	**'65 Love Affair** . . . Paul Davis
19/87	**Skeletons** . . . Stevie Wonder
13/74	**Skin Tight** . . . Ohio Players
39/87	**Skin Trade** . . . Duran Duran
10/67	**Skinny Legs And All** . . . Joe Tex
22/58	**Skinny Minnie** . . . Bill Haley
25/68	**Skip A Rope** . . . Henson Cargill
3/75	**Sky High** . . . Jigsaw
14/68	**Sky Pilot** . . . Animals
35/64	**Slaughter On Tenth Avenue** . . . Ventures
1/86	**Sledgehammer** . . . Peter Gabriel
13/60	**Sleep** . . . Little Willie John
1/59	**Sleep Walk** . . . Santo & Johnny
8/85	**Sleeping Bag** . . . ZZ Top
	Sleeping Beauty ..see: To A
32/77	**Slide** . . . Slave
6/68	**Slip Away** . . . Clarence Carter
5/78	**Slip Slidin' Away** . . . Paul Simon
33/56	**Slipin' And Slidin'** . . . Little Richard
19/75	**Slippery When Wet** . . . Commodores
16/72	**Slippin' Into Darkness** . . . War
39/83	**Slipping Away** . . . Dave Edmunds
3/66	**Sloop John B** . . . Beach Boys
20/77	**Slow Dancin' Don't Turn Me On** . . . Addrisi Bros.
10/77	**Slow Dancing (Swayin' To The Music)** . . . Johnny Rivers
25/64	**Slow Down** . . . Beatles
2/81	**Slow Hand** . . . Pointer Sisters
20/76	**Slow Ride** . . . Foghat
3/62	**Slow Twistin'** . . . Chubby Checker
	Slow Walk
17/56	Sil Austin
26/57	Bill Doggett
34/77	**Slowdown** . . . John Miles
30/70	**Sly, Slick, And The Wicked** . . . Lost Generation
29/72	**Small Beginnings** . . . Flash
21/62	**Small Sad Sam** . . . Phil McLean
6/85	**Small Town** . . . John Cougar Mellencamp
20/59	**Small World** . . . Johnny Mathis

POS/YR	RECORD TITLE/ARTIST
25/88	**Small World** . . . Huey Lewis & The News
5/69	**Smile A Little Smile For Me** . . . Flying Machine
34/83	**Smile Has Left Your Eyes** . . . Asia
21/55	**Smiles** . . . Crazy Otto
3/71	**Smiling Faces Sometimes** . . . Undisputed Truth
9/77	**Smoke From A Distant Fire** . . . Sanford/Townsend Band
	Smoke Gets In Your Eyes
1/59	Platters
27/73	Blue Haze
4/73	**Smoke On The Water** . . . Deep Purple
17/60	**Smokie** . . . Bill Black's Combo
	Smokin' In The Boy's Room
3/74	Brownsville Station
16/85	Motley Crue
22/87	**Smoking Gun** . . . Robert Cray Band
24/81	**Smoky Mountain Rain** . . . Ronnie Milsap
12/62	**Smoky Places** . . . Corsairs
7/89	**Smooth Criminal** . . . Michael Jackson
5/85	**Smooth Operator** . . . Sade
12/85	**Smuggler's Blues** . . . Glenn Frey
27/68	**Snake, The** . . . Al Wilson
8/62	**Snap Your Fingers** . . . Joe Henderson
31/69	**Snatching It Back** . . . Clarence Carter
2/66	**Snoopy Vs. The Red Baron** . . . Royal Guardsmen
	(also see: Return Of The Red Baron)
8/70	**Snowbird** . . . Anne Murray
3/89	**So Alive** . . . Love & Rockets
23/84	**So Bad** . . . Paul McCartney
11/90	**So Close** . . . Daryl Hall John Oates
38/59	**So Close** . . . Brook Benton
40/83	**So Close** . . . Diana Ross
1/88	**So Emotional** . . . Whitney Houston
14/71	**So Far Away** . . . Carole King
19/86	**So Far Away** . . . Dire Straits
11/59	**So Fine** . . . Fiestas
30/79	**So Good, So Right** . . . Brenda Russell
36/69	**So Good Together** . . . Andy Kim
39/69	**So I Can Love You** . . . Emotions
26/85	**So In Love** . . . Orchestral Manoeuvres In The Dark
7/77	**So In To You** . . . Atlanta Rhythm Section
28/61	**So Long Baby** . . . Del Shannon
6/59	**So Many Ways** . . . Brook Benton
1/63	**So Much In Love** . . . Tymes

POS/YR	RECORD TITLE/ARTIST
2/57	**So Rare** . . . Jimmy Dorsey
7/60	**So Sad (To Watch Good Love Go Bad)** . . . Everly Brothers
21/62	**So This Is Love** . . . Castells
17/73	**So Very Hard To Go** . . . Tower Of Power
30/83	**So Wrong** . . . Patrick Simmons
21/74	**So You Are A Star** . . . Hudson Brothers
29/67	**So You Want To Be A Rock 'N' Roll Star** . . . Byrds
31/77	**So You Win Again** . . . Hot Chocolate
14/67	**Society's Child (Baby I've Been Thinking)** . . . Janis Ian
6/67	**Sock It To Me-Baby!** . . . Mitch Ryder & The Detroit Wheels
35/57	**Soft** . . . Bill Doggett
	Soft Summer Breeze
11/56	Eddie Heywood
34/56	Diamonds
27/64	**Softly, As I Leave You** . . . Frank Sinatra
29/72	**Softly Whispering I Love You** . . . English Congregation
1/62	**Soldier Boy** . . . Shirelles
	(also see: To A)
2/89	**Soldier Of Love** . . . Donny Osmond
12/85	**Solid** . . . Ashford & Simpson
7/83	**Solitaire** . . . Laura Branigan
17/75	**Solitaire** . . . Carpenters
21/70	**Solitary Man** . . . Neil Diamond
34/64	**Some Day We're Gonna Love Again** . . . Searchers
36/81	**Some Days Are Diamonds (Some Days Are Stone)** . . . John Denver
13/65	**Some Enchanted Evening** . . . Jay & The Americans
	Some Guys Have All The Luck
39/73	Persuaders
10/84	Rod Stewart
37/59	**Some Kind-A Earthquake** . . . Duane Eddy
26/83	**Some Kind Of Friend** . . . Barry Manilow
10/88	**Some Kind Of Lover** . . . Jody Watley
3/75	**Some Kind Of Wonderful** . . . Grand Funk
32/61	**Some Kind Of Wonderful** . . . Drifters
6/85	**Some Like It Hot** . . . Power Station
18/85	**Some Things Are Better Left Unsaid** . . . Daryl Hall John Oates
30/68	**Some Things You Never Get Used To** . . . Supremes
26/68	**Some Velvet Morning** . . . Nancy Sinatra & Lee Hazlewood

POS/YR	RECORD TITLE/ARTIST
11/85	**Somebody** . . . Bryan Adams
5/67	**Somebody To Love** . . . Jefferson Airplane
13/77	**Somebody To Love** . . . Queen
22/58	**Somebody Touched Me** . . . Buddy Knox
18/56	**Somebody Up There Likes Me** . . . Perry Como
7/82	**Somebody's Baby** . . . Jackson Browne
8/70	**Somebody's Been Sleeping** . . . 100 Proof Aged in Soul
33/76	**Somebody's Gettin' It** . . . Johnnie Taylor
13/81	**Somebody's Knockin'** . . . Terri Gibbs
27/86	**Somebody's Out There** . . . Triumph
2/84	**Somebody's Watching Me** . . . Rockwell
32/71	**Somebody's Watching You** . . . Little Sister
	Someday ..also see: Some Day
1/91	**Someday** . . . Mariah Carey
7/87	**Someday** . . . Glass Tiger
25/72	**Someday Never Comes** . . . Creedence Clearwater Revival
36/82	**Someday, Someway** . . . Marshall Crenshaw
1/69	**Someday We'll Be Together** . . . Supremes
35/59	**Someone** . . . Johnny Mathis
15/82	**Someone Could Lose A Heart Tonight** . . . Eddie Rabbitt
4/75	**Someone Saved My Life Tonight** . . . Elton John
21/80	**Someone That I Used To Love** . . . Natalie Cole
13/55	**Someone You Love** . . . Nat "King" Cole
37/77	**Somethin' 'Bout 'Cha** . . . Latimore
1/67	**Somethin' Stupid** . . . Nancy & Frank Sinatra
3/69	**Something** . . . Beatles
7/86	**Something About You** . . . Level 42
19/65	**Something About You** . . . Four Tops
13/75	**Something Better To Do** . . . Olivia Newton-John
4/90	**Something Happened On The Way To Heaven** . . . Phil Collins
28/76	**Something He Can Feel** . . . Aretha Franklin
31/91	**Something In My Heart** . . . Michel'le
37/69	**Something In The Air** . . . Thunderclap Newman
29/87	**Something Real (Inside Me/Inside You)** . . . Mr. Mister
7/87	**Something So Strong** . . . Crowded House

POS/YR	RECORD TITLE/ARTIST
4/90	**Something To Believe In** . . . Poison
11/70	**Something's Burning** . . . Kenny Rogers & The First Edition
37/62	**Something's Got A Hold On Me** . . . Etta James
	Something's Gotta Give
5/55	McGuire Sisters
9/55	Sammy Davis, Jr.
12/72	**Something's Wrong With Me** . . . Austin Roberts
31/77	**Sometimes** . . . Facts Of Life
36/80	**Sometimes A Fantasy** . . . Billy Joel
20/90	**Sometimes She Cries** . . . Warrant
3/78	**Sometimes When We Touch** . . . Dan Hill
19/64	**Somewhere** . . . Tymes
26/66	**Somewhere** . . . Len Barry
21/82	**Somewhere Down The Road** . . . Barry Manilow
	Somewhere In The Night
19/76	Helen Reddy
9/79	Barry Manilow
32/65	**Somewhere In Your Heart** . . . Frank Sinatra
9/66	**Somewhere, My Love** . . . Ray Conniff
2/87	**Somewhere Out There** . . . Linda Ronstadt & James Ingram
32/66	**Somewhere There's A Someone** . . . Dean Martin
10/69	**Son Of A Preacher Man** . . . Dusty Springfield
40/68	**Son Of Hickory Holler's Tramp** . . . O.C. Smith
28/74	**Son Of Sagittarius** . . . Eddie Kendricks
8/56	**Song For A Summer Night** . . . Mitch Miller
14/70	**Song Of Joy** . . . Miguel Rios
	(also see: Joy)
11/55	**Song Of The Dreamer** . . . Eddie Fisher
29/79	**Song On The Radio** . . . Al Stewart
1/72	**Song Sung Blue** . . . Neil Diamond
4/87	**Songbird** . . . Kenny G
25/78	**Songbird** . . . Barbra Streisand
30/70	**Soolaimon (African Trilogy II)** . . . Neil Diamond
9/71	**Sooner Or Later** . . . Grass Roots
34/69	**Sophisticated Cissy** . . . Meters
25/76	**Sophisticated Lady (She's A Different Lady)** . . . Natalie Cole

POS/YR	RECORD TITLE/ARTIST
2/59	**Sorry (I Ran All the Way Home)** . . . Impalas
6/76	**Sorry Seems To Be The Hardest Word** . . . Elton John
	Soul And Inspiration ..see: (You're My)
27/87	**Soul City** . . . Partland Brothers
	Soul Coaxing ..see: Ame Caline
18/69	**Soul Deep** . . . Box Tops
17/67	**Soul Finger** . . . Bar-Kays
20/85	**Soul Kiss** . . . Olivia Newton-John
17/68	**Soul-Limbo** . . . Booker T. & The M.G.'s
35/73	**Soul Makossa** . . . Manu Dibango
	Soul Man
2/67	Sam & Dave
14/79	Blues Brothers
29/71	**Soul Power** . . . James Brown
17/89	**Soul Provider** . . . Michael Bolton
23/68	**Soul Serenade** . . . Willie Mitchell
37/73	**Soul Song** . . . Joe Stampley
17/62	**Soul Twist** . . . King Curtis
3/69	**Soulful Strut** . . . Young-Holt Unlimited
23/83	**Souls** . . . Rick Springfield
37/69	**Soulshake** . . . Peggy Scott & Jo Jo Benson
	(Soulsville, U.S.A.) ..see: 634-5789
36/67	**Sound Of Love** . . . Five Americans
1/66	**Sounds Of Silence** . . . Simon & Garfunkel
3/63	**South Street** . . . Orlons
29/75	**South's Gonna Do It** . . . Charlie Daniels Band
18/82	**Southern Cross** . . . Crosby, Stills & Nash
1/77	**Southern Nights** . . . Glen Campbell
15/64	**Southtown, U.S.A.** . . . Dixiebelles
2/89	**Sowing The Seeds Of Love** . . . Tears For Fears
30/83	**Space Age Love Song** . . . Flock Of Seagulls
15/73	**Space Oddity** . . . David Bowie
4/73	**Space Race** . . . Billy Preston
23/72	**Spaceman** . . . Nilsson
40/85	**Spanish Eddie** . . . Laura Branigan
15/66	**Spanish Eyes** . . . Al Martino
27/66	**Spanish Flea** . . . Herb Alpert
	Spanish Harlem
10/61	Ben E. King
2/71	Aretha Franklin
31/62	**Spanish Lace** . . . Gene McDaniels
	(Speak Softly Love) ..see: Love Theme From The Godfather
14/72	**Speak To The Sky** . . . Rick Springfield

POS/YR	RECORD TITLE/ARTIST
38/69	**Special Delivery** . . . 1910 Fruitgum Co.
5/80	**Special Lady** . . . Ray, Goodman, & Brown
26/68	**Special Occasion** . . . Miracles
17/56	**Speedoo** . . . Cadillacs
6/62	**Speedy Gonzales** . . . Pat Boone
39/91	**Spend My Life** . . . Slaughter
40/83	**Spice Of Life** . . . Manhattan Transfer
3/74	**Spiders & Snakes** . . . Jim Stafford
7/86	**Spies Like Us** . . . Paul McCartney
3/70	**Spill The Wine** . . . Eric Burdon & War
2/69	**Spinning Wheel** . . . Blood, Sweat & Tears
40/66	**Spinout** . . . Elvis Presley
23/70	**Spirit In The Dark** . . . Aretha Franklin
40/77	**Spirit In The Night** . . . Manfred Mann's Earth Band
3/70	**Spirit In The Sky** . . . Norman Greenbaum
35/75	**Spirit Of The Boogie** . . . Kool & The Gang
11/82	**Spirits In The Material World** . . . Police
3/58	**Splish Splash** . . . Bobby Darin
	Spooky
3/68	Classics IV
17/79	Atlanta Rhythm Section
39/77	**Spring Rain** . . . Silvetti
37/76	**Springtime Mama** . . . Henry Gross
16/88	**Spy In The House Of Love** . . . Was (Not Was)
16/76	**Squeeze Box** . . . Who
1/85	**St. Elmo's Fire (Man In Motion)** . . . John Parr
	(also see: Love Theme From)
13/56	**St. Therese Of The Roses** . . . Billy Ward & The Dominoes
21/86	**Stages** . . . ZZ Top
	Stagger Lee
1/59	Lloyd Price
22/67	Wilson Pickett
25/71	Tommy Roe
9/60	**Stairway To Heaven** . . . Neil Sedaka
6/89	**Stand** . . . R.E.M.
22/69	**Stand!** . . . Sly & The Family Stone
5/83	**Stand Back** . . . Stevie Nicks
	Stand By Me
4/61	Ben E. King
12/67	Spyder Turner
20/75	John Lennon
22/80	Mickey Gilley
9/86	Ben E. King
	(also see: I'll Be There)

POS/YR	RECORD TITLE/ARTIST
	Stand By Your Man
19/69	Tammy Wynette
24/70	Candi Staton
10/77	**Stand Tall** . . . Burton Cummings
37/74	**Standing At The End Of The Line** . . . Lobo
6/67	**Standing In The Shadows Of Love** . . . Four Tops
	Standing On The Corner
3/56	Four Lads
22/56	Dean Martin
29/74	**Star** . . . Stealers Wheel
39/74	**Star Baby** . . . Guess Who
	Star Is Born ..see: Love Theme From A
20/91	**Star Spangled Banner** . . . Whitney Houston
	Star Wars Theme
1/77	Meco
10/77	John Williams
25/60	**Starbright** . . . Johnny Mathis
	Stardust
12/57	Billy Ward & His Dominoes
32/64	Nino Tempo & April Stevens
1/81	**Stars on 45** . . . Stars on 45
28/82	**Stars on 45 III** . . . Stars On
2/81	**Start Me Up** . . . Rolling Stones
9/57	**Start Movin' (In My Direction)** . . . Sal Mineo
19/72	**Starting All Over Again** . . . Mel & Tim
	Starting Over ..see: (Just Like)
36/80	**Starting Over Again** . . . Dolly Parton
3/84	**State Of Shock** . . . Jacksons
22/85	**State Of The Heart** . . . Rick Springfield
	Stay
1/60	Maurice Williams
16/64	4 Seasons
20/78	Jackson Browne
38/78	**Stay** . . . Rufus/Chaka Khan
7/71	**Stay Awhile** . . . Bells
38/64	**Stay Awhile** . . . Dusty Springfield
10/68	**Stay In My Corner** . . . Dells
16/84	**Stay The Night** . . . Chicago
24/87	**Stay The Night** . . . Benjamin Orr
17/72	**Stay With Me** . . . Faces
30/84	**Stay With Me Tonight** . . . Jeffrey Osborne
1/78	**Stayin' Alive** . . . Bee Gees
33/61	**Stayin' In** . . . Bobby Vee
22/88	**Staying Together** . . . Debbie Gibson
37/81	**Staying With It** . . . Firefall

POS/YR	RECORD TITLE/ARTIST
	Steal Away
17/64	Jimmy Hughes
37/70	Johnnie Taylor
6/80	**Steal Away** . . . Robbie Dupree
25/81	**Steal The Night** . . . Stevie Woods
17/73	**Steamroller Blues** . . . Elvis Presley
39/90	**Steamy Windows** . . . Tina Turner
13/62	**Steel Guitar And A Glass Of Wine** . . . Paul Anka
1/90	**Step By Step** . . . New Kids On The Block
5/81	**Step By Step** . . . Eddie Rabbitt
14/60	**Step By Step** . . . Crests
37/73	**Step By Step** . . . Joe Simon
24/67	**Step Out Of Your Mind** . . . American Breed
39/78	**Steppin' In A Slide Zone** . . . Moody Blues
6/82	**Steppin' Out** . . . Joe Jackson
36/76	**Steppin' Out** . . . Neil Sedaka
7/74	**Steppin' Out (Gonna Boogie Tonight)** . . . Tony Orlando & Dawn
	Steppin' Stone ..see: (I'm Not Your)
35/63	**Stewball** . . . Peter, Paul & Mary
32/86	**Stick Around** . . . Julian Lennon
25/61	**Stick Shift** . . . Duals
11/71	**Stick-Up** . . . Honey Cone
40/60	**Sticks And Stones** . . . Ray Charles
1/79	**Still** . . . Commodores
8/63	**Still** . . . Bill Anderson
40/76	**Still Crazy After All These Years** . . . Paul Simon
	Still In Love ..see: Can'tcha Say (You Believe In Me)
22/82	**Still In Saigon** . . . Charlie Daniels Band
28/81	**Still Right Here In My Heart** . . . Pure Prairie League
5/76	**Still The One** . . . Orleans
4/78	**Still The Same** . . . Bob Seger
19/82	**Still They Ride** . . . Journey
11/70	**Still Water (Love)** . . . Four Tops
12/73	**Stir It Up** . . . Johnny Nash
7/80	**Stomp!** . . . Brothers Johnson
36/78	**Stone Blue** . . . Foghat
40/82	**Stone Cold** . . . Rainbow
34/91	**Stone Cold Gentleman** . . . Ralph Tresvant
10/87	**Stone Love** . . . Kool & The Gang
7/70	**Stoned Love** . . . Supremes
30/73	**Stoned Out Of My Mind** . . . Chi-Lites
3/68	**Stoned Soul Picnic** . . . 5th Dimension

POS/YR	RECORD TITLE/ARTIST
14/71	**Stones** . . . Neil Diamond
6/71	**Stoney End** . . . Barbra Streisand
2/58	**Stood Up** . . . Ricky Nelson
9/74	**Stop And Smell The Roses** . . . Mac Davis
8/64	**Stop And Think It Over** . . . Dale & Grace
3/81	**Stop Draggin' My Heart Around** . . . Stevie Nicks with Tom Petty
	Stop! In The Name Of Love
1/65	Supremes
29/83	Hollies
39/71	**Stop, Look, Listen (To Your Heart)** . . . Stylistics
7/66	**Stop Stop Stop** . . . Hollies
36/62	**Stop The Music** . . . Shirelles
26/71	**Stop The War Now** . . . Edwin Starr
34/62	**Stop The Wedding** . . . Etta James
15/87	**Stop To Love** . . . Luther Vandross
	Stormy
5/68	Classics IV
32/79	Santana
23/71	**Story In Your Eyes** . . . Moody Blues
15/58	**Story Of My Life** . . . Marty Robbins
16/61	**Story Of My Love** . . . Paul Anka
28/59	**Story Of My Love** . . . Conway Twitty
16/55	**Story Untold** . . . Crew-Cuts
10/83	**Straight From The Heart** . . . Bryan Adams
39/81	**Straight From The Heart** . . . Allman Brothers Band
36/68	**Straight Life** . . . Bobby Goldsboro
15/78	**Straight On** . . . Heart
29/74	**Straight Shootin' Woman** . . . Steppenwolf
1/89	**Straight Up** . . . Paula Abdul
13/90	**Stranded** . . . Heart
	Stranded In The Jungle
15/56	Cadets
18/56	Jayhawks
39/56	Gadabouts
21/88	**Strange But True** . . . Times Two
14/76	**Strange Magic** . . . Electric Light Orchestra
11/78	**Strange Way** . . . Firefall
23/83	**Stranger In My House** . . . Ronnie Milsap
30/65	**Stranger In Town** . . . Del Shannon
30/84	**Stranger In Town** . . . Toto
	Stranger On The Shore
1/62	Mr. Acker Bilk
38/62	Andy Williams
1/66	**Strangers In The Night** . . . Frank Sinatra
8/67	**Strawberry Fields Forever** . . . Beatles

POS/YR	RECORD TITLE/ARTIST
5/77	**Strawberry Letter 23** . . . Brothers Johnson
39/68	**Strawberry Shortcake** . . . Jay & The Techniques
3/83	**Stray Cat Strut** . . . Stray Cats
1/74	**Streak, The** . . . Ray Stevens
30/78	**Street Corner Serenade** . . . Wet Willie
36/79	**Street Life** . . . Crusaders
27/76	**Street Singin'** . . . Lady Flash
8/91	**Strike It Up** . . . Black Box
	String Along
39/60	Fabian
25/63	Rick Nelson
1/62	**Stripper, The** . . . David Rose
17/81	**Stroke** . . . Billy Squier
4/58	**Stroll, The** . . . Diamonds
30/81	**Stronger Than Before** . . . Carole Bayer Sager
40/84	**Strung Out** . . . Steve Perry
7/84	**Strut** . . . Sheena Easton
22/75	**Struttin'** . . . Billy Preston
6/73	**Stuck In The Middle With You** . . . Stealers Wheel
1/60	**Stuck On You** . . . Elvis Presley
3/84	**Stuck On You** . . . Lionel Richie
1/86	**Stuck With You** . . . Huey Lewis & the News
21/78	**Stuff Like That** . . . Quincy Jones
4/79	**Stumblin' In** . . . Suzi Quatro & Chris Norman
14/58	**Stupid Cupid** . . . Connie Francis
18/72	**Suavecito** . . . Malo
39/65	**Subterranean Homesick Blues** . . . Bob Dylan
16/64	**Such A Night** . . . Elvis Presley
26/79	**Such A Woman** . . . Tycoon
11/65	**(Such An) Easy Question** . . . Elvis Presley
4/85	**Suddenly** . . . Billy Ocean
20/81	**Suddenly** . . . Olivia Newton-John & Cliff Richard
9/83	**Suddenly Last Summer** . . . Motels
	Suddenly There's A Valley
9/55	Gogi Grant
13/55	Jo Stafford
20/55	Julius LaRosa
37/74	**Sugar Baby Love** . . . Rubettes
10/72	**Sugar Daddy** . . . Jackson 5
28/89	**Sugar Daddy** . . . Thompson Twins
36/84	**Sugar Don't Bite** . . . Sam Harris

POS/YR	RECORD TITLE/ARTIST
32/65	**Sugar Dumpling** . . . Sam Cooke
35/87	**Sugar Free** . . . Wa Wa Nee
30/64	**Sugar Lips** . . . Al Hirt
5/58	**Sugar Moon** . . . Pat Boone
22/69	**Sugar On Sunday** . . . Clique
1/63	**Sugar Shack** . . . Jimmy Gilmer/Fireballs
	Sugar, Sugar
1/69	Archies
25/70	Wilson Pickett
5/66	**Sugar Town** . . . Nancy Sinatra
9/85	**Sugar Walls** . . . Sheena Easton
1/58	**Sugartime** . . . McGuire Sisters
9/90	**Suicide Blonde** . . . INXS
21/69	**Suite: Judy Blue Eyes** . . . Crosby, Stills & Nash
	Sukiyaki
1/63	Kyu Sakamoto
3/81	Taste Of Honey
4/79	**Sultans Of Swing** . . . Dire Straits
7/76	**Summer** . . . War
6/72	**Summer Breeze** . . . Seals & Crofts
1/66	**Summer In The City** . . . Lovin' Spoonful
	Summer Night ..see: Song For A
5/78	**Summer Nights** . . . John Travolta & Olivia Newton-John
24/65	**Summer Nights** . . . Marianne Faithfull
	Summer Of '42 ..see: Theme From
5/85	**Summer Of '69** . . . Bryan Adams
	Summer Place ..see: Theme From A
14/68	**Summer Rain** . . . Johnny Rivers
30/90	**Summer Rain** . . . Belinda Carlisle
26/66	**Summer Samba (So Nice)** . . . Walter Wanderley
33/71	**Summer Sand** . . . Dawn
30/60	**Summer Set** . . . Monty Kelly
7/64	**Summer Song** . . . Chad & Jeremy
21/73	**Summer (The First Time)** . . . Bobby Goldsboro
25/66	**Summer Wind** . . . Frank Sinatra
11/60	**Summer's Gone** . . . Paul Anka
4/91	**Summertime** . . . D.J. Jazzy Jeff & The Fresh Prince
10/66	**Summertime** . . . Billy Stewart
	Summertime Blues
8/58	Eddie Cochran
14/68	Blue Cheer
27/70	Who

POS/YR	RECORD TITLE/ARTIST
	Summertime, Summertime
26/58	Jamies
38/62	Jamies
13/66	**Sun Ain't Gonna Shine (Anymore)** . . . Walker Bros.
20/86	**Sun Always Shines On T.V.** . . . a-ha
38/85	**Sun City** . . . Artists United Against Apartheid
18/65	**Sunday And Me** . . . Jay & The Americans
31/67	**Sunday For Tea** . . . Peter & Gordon
	Sunday Mornin'
30/68	Spanky & Our Gang
35/69	Oliver
9/67	**Sunday Will Never Be The Same** . . . Spanky & Our Gang
1/74	**Sundown** . . . Gordon Lightfoot
39/77	**Sunflower** . . . Glen Campbell
7/84	**Sunglasses At Night** . . . Corey Hart
2/66	**Sunny** . . . Bobby Hebb
14/66	**Sunny Afternoon** . . . Kinks
34/72	**Sunny Days** . . . Lighthouse
34/76	**Sunrise** . . . Eric Carmen
22/85	**Sunset Grill** . . . Don Henley
4/72	**Sunshine** . . . Jonathan Edwards
23/89	**Sunshine** . . . Dino
20/67	**Sunshine Girl** . . . Parade
13/65	**Sunshine, Lollipops And Rainbows** . . . Lesley Gore
5/68	**Sunshine Of Your Love** . . . Cream
1/74	**Sunshine On My Shoulders** . . . John Denver
1/66	**Sunshine Superman** . . . Donovan
13/70	**Super Bad** . . . James Brown
31/73	**Super Fly Meets Shaft** . . . John & Ernest
16/81	**Super Freak** . . . Rick James
8/73	**Superfly** . . . Curtis Mayfield
	(also see: Freddie's Dead)
26/79	**Superman** . . . Herbie Mann
5/75	**Supernatural Thing** . . . Ben E. King
30/88	**Supersonic** . . . J.J. Fad
2/71	**Superstar** . . . Carpenters
35/76	**Superstar** . . . Paul Davis
14/71	**Superstar - Jesus Christ Superstar** . . . Murray Head
18/71	**Superstar (Remember How You Got Where You Are)** . . . Temptations
1/73	**Superstition** . . . Stevie Wonder
31/88	**Superstitious** . . . Europe

POS/YR	RECORD TITLE/ARTIST
8/89	**Superwoman** . . . Karyn White
33/72	**Superwoman (Where Were You When I Needed You)** . . . Stevie Wonder
16/74	**Sure As I'm Sittin' Here** . . . Three Dog Night
9/66	**Sure Gonna Miss Her** . . . Gary Lewis & The Playboys
1/63	**Surf City** . . . Jan & Dean
7/63	**Surfer Girl** . . . Beach Boys
31/62	**Surfer's Stomp** . . . Mar-Kets
4/64	**Surfin' Bird** . . . Trashmen
14/62	**Surfin' Safari** . . . Beach Boys
	Surfin' U.S.A.
3/63	Beach Boys
36/74	Beach Boys
20/77	Leif Garrett
1/61	**Surrender** . . . Elvis Presley
38/71	**Surrender** . . . Diana Ross
6/89	**Surrender To Me** . . . Ann Wilson & Robin Zander
11/68	**Susan** . . . Buckinghams
	Susie Darlin'
5/58	Robin Luke
35/62	Tommy Roe
3/64	**Suspicion** . . . Terry Stafford
13/79	**Suspicions** . . . Eddie Rabbitt
1/69	**Suspicious Minds** . . . Elvis Presley
1/85	**Sussudio** . . . Phil Collins
17/86	**Suzanne** . . . Journey
	Suzie-Q
27/57	Dale Hawkins
11/68	Creedence Clearwater Revival
39/73	**Swamp Witch** . . . Jim Stafford
34/57	**Swanee River Rock (Talkin' 'Bout That River)** . . . Ray Charles
	S.W.A.T. ..see: Theme From
14/60	**Sway** . . . Bobby Rydell
6/75	**Swearin' To God** . . . Frankie Valli
	Sweet And Gentle
10/55	Alan Dale
12/55	Georgia Gibbs
7/71	**Sweet And Innocent** . . . Donny Osmond
19/81	**Sweet Baby** . . . Stanley Clarke/George Duke
13/68	**Sweet Blindness** . . . 5th Dimension
4/69	**Sweet Caroline (Good Times Never Seemed So Good)** . . . Neil Diamond
7/69	**Sweet Cherry Wine** . . . Tommy James & The Shondells

POS/YR	RECORD TITLE/ARTIST
1/88	**Sweet Child O' Mine** . . . Guns N' Roses
8/71	**Sweet City Woman** . . . Stampeders
28/69	**Sweet Cream Ladies, Forward March** . . . Box Tops
5/82	**Sweet Dreams** . . . Air Supply
15/66	**Sweet Dreams** . . . Tommy McLain
1/83	**Sweet Dreams (Are Made of This)** . . . Eurythmics
36/75	**Sweet Emotion** . . . Aerosmith
7/86	**Sweet Freedom** . . . Michael McDonald
6/71	**Sweet Hitch-Hiker** . . . Creedence Clearwater Revival
8/74	**Sweet Home Alabama** . . . Lynyrd Skynyrd
	Sweet Inspiration
18/68	Sweet Inspirations
37/72	Barbra Streisand (medley)
17/78	**Sweet Life** . . . Paul Davis
2/58	**Sweet Little Sixteen** . . . Chuck Berry
5/76	**Sweet Love** . . . Commodores
8/86	**Sweet Love** . . . Anita Baker
36/79	**Sweet Lui-Louise** . . . Ironhorse
7/71	**Sweet Mary** . . . Wadsworth Mansion
40/75	**Sweet Maxine** . . . Doobie Brothers
4/60	**Sweet Nothin's** . . . Brenda Lee
7/56	**Sweet Old Fashioned Girl** . . . Teresa Brewer
8/66	**Sweet Pea** . . . Tommy Roe
9/72	**Sweet Seasons** . . . Carole King
20/87	**Sweet Sixteen** . . . Billy Idol
2/67	**Sweet Soul Music** . . . Arthur Conley
33/75	**Sweet Sticky Thing** . . . Ohio Players
13/75	**Sweet Surrender** . . . John Denver
15/72	**Sweet Surrender** . . . Bread
5/68	**(Sweet Sweet Baby) Since You've Been Gone** . . . Aretha Franklin
10/66	**Sweet Talkin' Guy** . . . Chiffons
17/78	**Sweet Talkin' Woman** . . . Electric Light Orchestra
5/76	**Sweet Thing** . . . Rufus Featuring Chaka Khan
26/82	**Sweet Time** . . . REO Speedwagon
33/73	**Sweet Understanding Love** . . . Four Tops
40/64	**Sweet William** . . . Millie Small
29/66	**Sweet Woman Like You** . . . Joe Tex
9/59	**Sweeter Than You** . . . Ricky Nelson
5/86	**Sweetest Taboo** . . . Sade
7/82	**Sweetest Thing (I've Ever Known)** . . . Juice Newton

POS/YR	RECORD TITLE/ARTIST
32/67	**Sweetest Thing This Side Of Heaven** . . . Chris Bartley
10/81	**Sweetheart** . . . Franke & The Knockouts
16/61	**Sweets For My Sweet** . . . Drifters
19/84	**Swept Away** . . . Diana Ross
11/90	**Swing The Mood (medley)** . . . Jive Bunny & the Mastermixers
39/60	**Swingin' On A Rainbow** . . . Frankie Avalon
13/62	**Swingin' Safari** . . . Billy Vaughn
5/60	**Swingin' School** . . . Bobby Rydell
23/58	**Swingin' Shepherd Blues** . . . Moe Koffman Quartette
38/63	**Swinging On A Star** . . . Big Dee Irwin/Little Eva
17/77	**Swingtown** . . . Steve Miller Band
26/61	**Switch-A-Roo** . . . Hank Ballard
5/72	**Sylvia's Mother** . . . Dr. Hook
38/88	**Symptoms Of True Love** . . . Tracie Spencer
16/83	**Synchronicity II** . . . Police
37/76	**(System Of) Doctor Tarr And Professor Fether** . . . Alan Parsons Project

T

POS/YR	RECORD TITLE/ARTIST
24/60	**T.L.C. Tender Love And Care** . . . Jimmie Rodgers
1/74	**TSOP (The Sound Of Philadelphia)** . . . MFSB featuring The Three Degrees
23/60	**Ta Ta** . . . Clyde McPhatter
8/82	**Tainted Love** . . . Soft Cell
3/78	**Take A Chance On Me** . . . Abba
2/69	**Take A Letter Maria** . . . R.B. Greaves
15/80	**Take A Little Rhythm** . . . Ali Thomson
30/72	**Take A Look Around** . . . Temptations
16/59	**Take A Message To Mary** . . . Everly Brothers
20/69	**Take Care Of Your Homework** . . . Johnnie Taylor
25/61	**Take Five** . . . Dave Brubeck Quartet
7/61	**Take Good Care Of Her** . . . Adam Wade

POS/YR	RECORD TITLE/ARTIST
	Take Good Care Of My Baby
1/61	Bobby Vee
33/68	Bobby Vinton
10/82	**Take It Away** . . . Paul McCartney
12/72	**Take It Easy** . . . Eagles
24/86	**Take It Easy** . . . Andy Taylor
10/82	**Take It Easy On Me** . . . Little River Band
33/76	**Take It Like A Man** . . . Bachman-Turner Overdrive
5/81	**Take It On The Run** . . . REO Speedwagon
4/76	**Take It To The Limit** . . . Eagles
16/65	**Take Me Back** . . . Little Anthony & The Imperials
18/82	**Take Me Down** . . . Alabama
38/68	**Take Me For A Little While** . . . Vanilla Fudge
7/86	**Take Me Home** . . . Phil Collins
8/79	**Take Me Home** . . . Cher
2/71	**Take Me Home, Country Roads** . . . John Denver
4/86	**Take Me Home Tonight** . . . Eddie Money
11/75	**Take Me In Your Arms (Rock Me)** . . . Doobie Brothers
14/83	**Take Me To Heart** . . . Quarterflash
26/79	**Take Me To The River** . . . Talking Heads
25/85	**Take Me With U** . . . Prince
1/86	**Take My Breath Away** . . . Berlin
17/81	**Take My Heart (You Can Have It If You Want It)** . . . Kool & The Gang
16/82	**Take Off** . . . Bob & Doug McKenzie
1/85	**Take On Me** . . . a-ha
10/79	**Take The Long Way Home** . . . Supertramp
11/76	**Take The Money And Run** . . . Steve Miller
8/63	**Take These Chains From My Heart** . . . Ray Charles
11/68	**Take Time To Know Her** . . . Percy Sledge
3/80	**Take Your Time (Do It Right)** . . . S.O.S. Band
32/86	**Taken In** . . . Mike + The Mechanics
12/74	**Takin' Care Of Business** . . . Bachman-Turner Overdrive
13/76	**Takin' It To The Streets** . . . Doobie Brothers
7/64	**Talk Back Trembling Lips** . . . Johnny Tillotson
9/87	**Talk Dirty To Me** . . . Poison
19/89	**Talk It Over** . . . Grayson Hugh
15/67	**Talk Talk** . . . Music Machine

POS/YR	RECORD TITLE/ARTIST
34/60	**Talk That Talk** . . . Jackie Wilson
4/86	**Talk To Me** . . . Stevie Nicks
21/87	**Talk To Me** . . . Chico DeBarge
38/59	**Talk To Me** . . . Frank Sinatra
	Talk To Me, Talk To Me
20/58	Little Willie John
11/63	Sunny & The Sunglows
15/57	**Talkin' To The Blues** . . . Jim Lowe
12/64	**Talking About My Baby** . . . Impressions
3/84	**Talking In Your Sleep** . . . Romantics
18/78	**Talking In Your Sleep** . . . Crystal Gayle
27/72	**Talking Loud And Saying Nothing** . . . James Brown
25/88	**Tall Cool One** . . . Robert Plant
	Tall Cool One
36/59	Wailers
38/64	Wailers
	Tall Oak Tree ..see: (There Was A)
7/59	**Tall Paul** . . . Annette
6/59	**Tallahassee Lassie** . . . Freddy Cannon
	Tammy
1/57	Debbie Reynolds
5/57	Ames Brothers
18/76	**Tangerine** . . . Salsoul Orchestra
31/75	**Tangled Up In Blue** . . . Bob Dylan
34/68	**Tapioca Tundra** . . . Monkees
38/66	**Tar And Cement** . . . Verdelle Smith
13/86	**Tarzan Boy** . . . Baltimora
7/65	**Taste Of Honey** . . . Herb Alpert
18/72	**Taurus** . . . Dennis Coffey
24/72	**Taxi** . . . Harry Chapin
7/58	**Tea For Two Cha Cha** . . . Tommy Dorsey Orchestra
25/62	**Teach Me Tonight** . . . George Maharis
16/70	**Teach Your Children** . . . Crosby, Stills, Nash & Young
21/58	**Teacher, Teacher** . . . Johnny Mathis
25/84	**Teacher Teacher** . . . 38 Special
31/61	**Tear, A** . . . Gene McDaniels
23/59	**Tear Drop** . . . Santo & Johnny
20/57	**Tear Drops** . . . Lee Andrews & the Hearts
5/56	**Tear Fell** . . . Teresa Brewer
15/76	**Tear The Roof Off The Sucker (Give Up The Funk)** . . . Parliament
37/84	**Tears** . . . John Waite
20/64	**Tears And Roses** . . . Al Martino
1/70	**Tears Of A Clown** . . . Miracles

POS/YR	RECORD TITLE/ARTIST
4/58	**Tears On My Pillow** . . . Little Anthony & The Imperials
39/59	**Teasin'** . . . Quaker City Boys
17/60	**Teddy** . . . Connie Francis
40/76	**Teddy Bear** . . . Red Sovine
	(also see: Let Me Be Your)
32/73	**Teddy Bear Song** . . . Barbara Fairchild
	Teen Age ..also see: Teenage
2/57	**Teen-Age Crush** . . . Tommy Sands
5/62	**Teen Age Idol** . . . Rick Nelson
	Teen Age Prayer
6/56	Gale Storm
19/56	Gloria Mann
1/60	**Teen Angel** . . . Mark Dinning
4/59	**Teen Beat** . . . Sandy Nelson
29/59	**Teen Commandments** . . . Paul Anka-Geo. Hamilton IV-Johnny Nash
	Teenage Queen ..see: Ballad Of
5/59	**Teenager In Love** . . . Dion & The Belmonts
2/57	**Teenager's Romance** . . . Ricky Nelson
9/83	**Telefone (Long Distance Love Affair)** . . . Sheena Easton
7/77	**Telephone Line** . . . Electric Light Orchestra
18/77	**Telephone Man** . . . Meri Wilson
1/83	**Tell Her About It** . . . Billy Joel
	Tell Her No
6/65	Zombies
27/83	Juice Newton
40/73	**Tell Her She's Lovely** . . . El Chicano
4/63	**Tell Him** . . . Exciters
8/59	**Tell Him No** . . . Travis & Bob
17/70	**Tell It All Brother** . . . Kenny Rogers & The First Edition
	Tell It Like It Is
2/67	Aaron Neville
8/81	Heart
33/64	**Tell It On The Mountain** . . . Peter, Paul & Mary
7/88	**Tell It To My Heart** . . . Taylor Dayne
10/67	**Tell It To The Rain** . . . 4 Seasons
7/60	**Tell Laura I Love Her** . . . Ray Peterson
23/68	**Tell Mama** . . . Etta James
22/62	**Tell Me** . . . Dick & DeeDee
21/74	**Tell Me A Lie** . . . Sami Jo
31/90	**Tell Me Something** . . . Indecent Obsession
3/74	**Tell Me Something Good** . . . Rufus
37/67	**Tell Me To My Face** . . . Keith

POS/YR	RECORD TITLE/ARTIST
33/82	**Tell Me Tomorrow** . . . Smokey Robinson
9/90	**Tell Me Why** . . . Expose
13/64	**Tell Me Why** . . . Bobby Vinton
18/61	**Tell Me Why** . . . Belmonts
33/66	**Tell Me Why** . . . Elvis Presley
24/64	**Tell Me (You're Coming Back)** . . . Rolling Stones
1/62	**Telstar** . . . Tornadoes
39/70	**Temma Harbour** . . . Mary Hopkin
39/91	**Temple Of Love** . . . Harriet
6/91	**Temptation** . . . Corina
27/61	**Temptation** . . . Everly Brothers
15/71	**Temptation Eyes** . . . Grass Roots
22/58	**Ten Commandments Of Love** . . . Harvey & The Moonglows
	(also see: Teen Commandments)
38/84	**10-9-8** . . . Face To Face
25/83	**Tender Is The Night** . . . Jackson Browne
10/86	**Tender Love** . . . Force M.D.'s
	Tender, Love and Care ..see: T.L.C.
14/90	**Tender Lover** . . . Babyface
	Tender Trap ..see: (Love Is)
31/85	**Tender Years** . . . John Cafferty
31/61	**Tenderly** . . . Bert Kaempfert
27/85	**Tenderness** . . . General Public
23/70	**Tennessee Bird Walk** . . . Jack Blanchard & Misty Morgan
35/64	**Tennessee Waltz** . . . Sam Cooke
	Tequila
1/58	Champs
20/58	Eddie Platt
	Testify ..see: (I Wanna)
1/75	**Thank God I'm A Country Boy** . . . John Denver
22/78	**Thank God It's Friday** . . . Love & Kisses
1/70	**Thank You (Falettinme Be Mice Elf Agin)** . . . Sly & The Family Stone
25/78	**Thank You For Being A Friend** . . . Andrew Gold
35/64	**Thank You Girl** . . . Beatles
16/59	**Thank You Pretty Baby** . . . Brook Benton
32/88	**Thanks For My Child** . . . Cheryl Pepsii Riley
37/74	**Thanks For Saving My Life** . . . Billy Paul
16/87	**That Ain't Love** . . . REO Speedwagon
4/82	**That Girl** . . . Stevie Wonder
22/80	**That Girl Could Sing** . . . Jackson Browne
	(That Kiss!) ..see: Eso Beso

POS/YR	RECORD TITLE/ARTIST
6/73	**That Lady** . . . Isley Brothers
20/64	**That Lucky Old Sun** . . . Ray Charles
	That Old Black Magic
13/55	Sammy Davis, Jr.
18/58	Louis Prima & Keely Smith
21/61	Bobby Rydell
21/81	**That Old Song** . . . Ray Parker Jr. & Raydio
28/62	**That Stranger Used To Be My Girl** . . . Trade Martin
12/63	**That Sunday, That Summer** . . . Nat King Cole
20/86	**That Was Then, This Is Now** . . . Mickey Dolenz & Peter Tork
12/85	**That Was Yesterday** . . . Foreigner
	That'll Be The Day
1/57	Crickets
11/76	Linda Ronstadt
6/84	**That's All!** . . . Genesis
17/56	**That's All** . . . "Tennessee" Ernie Ford
3/55	**That's All I Want From You** . . . Jaye P. Morgan
16/56	**That's All There Is To That** . . . Nat "King" Cole/Four Knights
6/60	**That's All You Gotta Do** . . . Brenda Lee
40/63	**That's How Heartaches Are Made** . . . Baby Washington
39/58	**That's How Much I Love You** . . . Pat Boone
31/61	**That's It-I Quit-I'm Movin' On** . . . Sam Cooke
4/66	**That's Life** . . . Frank Sinatra
28/83	**That's Love** . . . Jim Capaldi
9/62	**That's Old Fashioned (That's The Way Love Should Be)** . . . Everly Brothers
3/77	**That's Rock 'N' Roll** . . . Shaun Cassidy
16/89	**That's The Way** . . . Katrina & The Waves
12/64	**That's The Way Boys Are** . . . Lesley Gore
27/72	**That's The Way I Feel About Cha** . . . Bobby Womack
1/75	**That's The Way (I Like It)** . . . KC & The Sunshine Band
10/71	**That's The Way I've Always Heard It Should Be** . . . Carly Simon
7/69	**That's The Way Love Is** . . . Marvin Gaye
33/63	**That's The Way Love Is** . . . Bobby Bland
12/75	**That's The Way Of The World** . . . Earth, Wind & Fire
1/86	**That's What Friends Are For** . . . Dionne & Friends

POS/YR	RECORD TITLE/ARTIST
27/61	**That's What Girls Are Made For** . . . Spinners
19/87	**That's What Love Is All About** . . . Michael Bolton
35/64	**That's What Love Is Made Of** . . . Miracles
27/75	**That's When The Music Takes Me** . . . Neil Sedaka
29/70	**That's Where I Went Wrong** . . . Poppy Family
27/76	**That's Where The Happy People Go** . . . Trammps
13/59	**That's Why (I Love You So)** . . . Jackie Wilson
35/60	**Theme For Young Lovers** . . . Percy Faith
	Theme From A Summer Place
1/60	Percy Faith
16/65	Lettermen
28/62	**Theme From Ben Casey** . . . Valjean
18/73	**Theme From Cleopatra Jones** . . . Joe Simon
	Theme From Close Encounters
13/78	John Williams
25/78	Meco
39/61	**Theme From Dixie** . . . Duane Eddy
10/62	**Theme From Dr. Kildare (Three Stars Will Shine Tonight)** . . . Richard Chamberlain
	Theme From Exorcist ..see: Tubular Bells
2/81	**Theme From Greatest American Hero (Believe It Or Not)** . . . Joey Scarbury
10/81	**Theme From Hill Street Blues** . . . Mike Post
32/75	**Theme From Jaws (Main Title)** . . . John Williams
	Theme From Love Story
9/71	Andy Williams (Where Do I Begin)
13/71	Henry Mancini
31/71	Francis Lai
25/82	**Theme From Magnum P.I.** . . . Mike Post
1/76	**Theme From Mahogany (Do You Know Where You're Going To)** . . . Diana Ross
32/80	**Theme From New York, New York** . . . Frank Sinatra
	Theme From Picnic ..see: Moonglow
	Theme From Pink Panther ..see: Pink Panther Theme
	Theme From Rocky ..see: Gonna Fly Now
1/71	**Theme From Shaft** . . . Isaac Hayes
21/71	**Theme From Summer Of '42** . . . Peter Nero

POS/YR	RECORD TITLE/ARTIST
	Theme From Superfly ..see: Freddie's Dead
1/76	**Theme From S.W.A.T.** . . . Rhythm Heritage
10/60	**Theme From The Apartment** . . . Ferrante & Teicher
21/80	**Theme From The Dukes Of Hazzard (Good Ol' Boys)** . . . Waylon Jennings
	Theme From The Man With The Golden Arm ..see: Man With The Golden Arm
38/72	**Theme From The Men** . . . Isaac Hayes
39/56	**Theme From The Proud Ones** . . . Nelson Riddle
	Theme From The Three Penny Opera ..see: Mack The Knife
27/60	**Theme From The Unforgiven (The Need For Love)** . . . Don Costa
2/68	**Theme From Valley Of The Dolls** . . . Dionne Warwick
21/78	**Theme From Which Way Is Up** . . . Stargard
35/78	**Themes From The Wizard Of Oz** . . . Meco
1/74	**Then Came You** . . . Dionne Warwicke & Spinners
6/63	**Then He Kissed Me** . . . Crystals
	Then You Can Tell Me Goodbye
6/67	Casinos
27/76	Glen Campbell (medley)
34/75	**There Goes Another Love Song** . . . Outlaws
	There Goes My Baby
2/59	Drifters
21/84	Donna Summer
	There Goes My Everything
20/67	Engelbert Humperdinck
F/71	Elvis Presley
19/58	**There Goes My Heart** . . . Joni James
1/64	**There! I've Said It Again** . . . Bobby Vinton
20/68	**There Is** . . . Dells
11/67	**There Is A Mountain** . . . Donovan
	(There Is Love) ..see: Wedding Song
32/73	**There It Is** . . . Tyrone Davis
33/59	**There Must Be A Way** . . . Joni James
22/85	**There Must Be An Angel (Playing With My Heart)** . . . Eurythmics
26/61	**There She Goes** . . . Jerry Wallace
23/60	**(There Was A) Tall Oak Tree** . . . Dorsey Burnette
36/68	**There Was A Time** . . . James Brown

POS/YR	RECORD TITLE/ARTIST
33/66	**There Will Never Be Another You** . . . Chris Montez
18/74	**There Won't Be Anymore** . . . Charlie Rich
25/57	**(There'll Be) Peace In The Valley (For Me)** . . . Elvis Presley
1/86	**There'll Be Sad Songs (To Make You Cry)** . . . Billy Ocean
26/69	**There'll Come A Time** . . . Betty Everett
36/78	**There'll Never Be** . . . Switch
14/57	**There's A Gold Mine In The Sky** . . . Pat Boone
	There's A Kind Of Hush (All Over The World)
4/67	Herman's Hermits
12/76	Carpenters
3/61	**There's A Moon Out Tonight** . . . Capris
	(There's) Always Something There To Remind Me
27/70	R.B. Greaves
8/83	Naked Eyes
21/69	**There's Gonna Be A Showdown** . . . Archie Bell
34/67	**There's Got To Be A Word!** . . . Innocence
5/81	**(There's) No Gettin' Over Me** . . . Ronnie Milsap
20/62	**There's No Other (Like My Baby)** . . . Crystals
	There's Nothing Stronger Than Our Love ..see: (I Believe)
10/58	**There's Only One Of You** . . . Four Lads
31/60	**There's Something On Your Mind** . . . Bobby Marchan
12/88	**There's The Girl** . . . Heart
1/66	**These Boots Are Made For Walkin'** . . . Nancy Sinatra
1/86	**These Dreams** . . . Heart
	These Eyes
6/69	Guess Who?
16/69	Jr. Walker & The All Stars
8/84	**They Don't Know** . . . Tracey Ullman
5/75	**They Just Can't Stop It the (Games People Play)** . . . Spinners
1/70	**(They Long To Be) Close To You** . . . Carpenters
3/66	**They're Coming To Take Me Away, Ha-Haaa!** . . . Napoleon XIV
	Thicker Than Water ..see: (Love Is)
6/90	**Thieves In The Temple** . . . Prince
15/71	**Thin Line Between Love & Hate** . . . Persuaders

POS/YR	RECORD TITLE/ARTIST
3/62	**Things** . . . Bobby Darin
5/85	**Things Can Only Get Better** . . . Howard Jones
23/67	**Things I Should Have Said** . . . Grass Roots
16/69	**Things I'd Like To Say** . . . New Colony Six
4/91	**Things That Make You Go Hmmmm...** . . . C & C Music Factory
5/77	**Things We Do For Love** . . . 10 CC
7/68	**Think** . . . Aretha Franklin
25/64	**Think** . . . Brenda Lee
28/90	**Think** . . . Information Society
33/60	**Think** . . . James Brown
20/80	**Think About Me** . . . Fleetwood Mac
30/66	**Think I'll Go Somewhere And Cry Myself To Sleep** . . . Al Martino
16/82	**Think I'm In Love** . . . Eddie Money
27/58	**Think It Over** . . . Crickets
34/78	**Think It Over** . . . Cheryl Ladd
9/84	**Think Of Laura** . . . Christopher Cross
11/61	**Think Twice** . . . Brook Benton
12/89	**Thinking Of You** . . . Sa-Fire
18/73	**Thinking Of You** . . . Loggins & Messina
14/75	**Third Rate Romance** . . . Amazing Rhythm Aces
23/80	**Third Time Lucky (First Time I Was A Fool)** . . . Foghat
24/60	**This Bitter Earth** . . . Dinah Washington
10/86	**This Could Be The Night** . . . Loverboy
1/65	**This Diamond Ring** . . . Gary Lewis & The Playboys
12/66	**This Door Swings Both Ways** . . . Herman's Hermits
12/59	**This Friendly World** . . . Fabian
9/69	**This Girl Is A Woman Now** . . . Gary Puckett & The Union Gap
	This Guy's (Girl's) In Love With You
1/68	Herb Alpert
7/69	Dionne Warwick
24/74	**This Heart** . . . Gene Redding
3/91	**This House** . . . Tracie Spencer
26/59	**This I Swear** . . . Skyliners
11/80	**This Is It** . . . Kenny Loggins
35/78	**This Is Love** . . . Paul Anka
25/69	**This Is My Country** . . . Impressions
3/67	**This Is My Song** . . . Petula Clark

POS/YR	RECORD TITLE/ARTIST
32/85	**This Is Not America** . . . David Bowie/Pat Metheny Group
21/90	**This Is The Right Time** . . . Lisa Stansfield
18/87	**This Is The Time** . . . Billy Joel
39/77	**This Is The Way That I Feel** . . . Marie Osmond
32/65	**This Little Bird** . . . Marianne Faithfull
11/81	**This Little Girl** . . . Gary U.S. Bonds
21/63	**This Little Girl** . . . Dion
26/58	**This Little Girl Of Mine** . . . Everly Brothers
24/58	**This Little Girl's Gone Rockin'** . . . Ruth Brown
	This Magic Moment
16/60	Drifters
6/69	Jay & The Americans
33/82	**This Man Is Mine** . . . Heart
10/76	**This Masquerade** . . . George Benson
19/79	**This Night Won't Last Forever** . . . Michael Johnson
	This Old Heart Of Mine
12/66	Isley Brothers
10/90	Rod Stewart (with Ronald Isley)
7/90	**This One's For The Children** . . . New Kids On The Block
29/76	**This One's For You** . . . Barry Manilow
20/59	**This Should Go On Forever** . . . Rod Bernard
25/77	**This Song** . . . George Harrison
6/61	**This Time** . . . Troy Shondell
24/83	**This Time** . . . Bryan Adams
27/80	**This Time** . . . John Cougar
7/89	**This Time I Know It's For Real** . . . Donna Summer
10/78	**This Time I'm In It For Love** . . . Player
6/75	**This Will Be** . . . Natalie Cole
23/84	**This Woman** . . . Kenny Rogers
38/72	**This World** . . . Staple Singers
6/63	**Those Lazy-Hazy-Crazy Days Of Summer** . . . Nat King Cole
9/61	**Those Oldies But Goodies (Remind Me Of You)** . . . Little Caesar & The Romans
2/68	**Those Were The Days** . . . Mary Hopkin
13/65	**Thou Shalt Not Steal** . . . Dick & DeeDee
3/60	**Thousand Stars** . . . Kathy Young with The Innocents
5/91	**3 A.M. Eternal** . . . KLF
	Three Bells
1/59	Browns

POS/YR	RECORD TITLE/ARTIST
23/59	Dick Flood
35/61	**Three Hearts In A Tangle** . . . Roy Drusky
24/67	**Three Little Fishes (medley)** . . . Mitch Ryder & The Detroit Wheels
15/60	**Three Nights A Week** . . . Fats Domino
33/65	**Three O'Clock In The Morning** . . . Bert Kaempfert
	Three Penny Opera ..see: Mack The Knife
36/74	**Three Ring Circus** . . . Blue Magic
11/59	**Three Stars** . . . Tommy Dee
1/78	**Three Times A Lady** . . . Commodores
19/80	**Three Times In Love** . . . Tommy James
28/64	**Three Window Coupe** . . . Rip Chords
15/70	**Thrill Is Gone** . . . B.B. King
4/84	**Thriller** . . . Michael Jackson
16/89	**Through The Storm** . . . Aretha Franklin & Elton John
13/82	**Through The Years** . . . Kenny Rogers
4/86	**Throwing It All Away** . . . Genesis
17/72	**Thunder And Lightning** . . . Chi Coltrane
38/77	**Thunder In My Heart** . . . Leo Sayer
9/78	**Thunder Island** . . . Jay Ferguson
25/66	**Thunderball** . . . Tom Jones
14/90	**Tic-Tac-Toe** . . . Kyper
1/65	**Ticket To Ride** . . . Beatles
1/81	**Tide Is High** . . . Blondie
1/73	**Tie A Yellow Ribbon Round The Ole Oak Tree** . . . Dawn
3/63	**Tie Me Kangaroo Down, Sport** . . . Rolf Harris
38/83	**Tied Up** . . . Olivia Newton-John
37/60	**Ties That Bind** . . . Brook Benton
3/59	**Tiger** . . . Fabian
11/72	**Tight Rope** . . . Leon Russell
1/68	**Tighten Up** . . . Archie Bell
7/70	**Tighter, Tighter** . . . Alive & Kicking
12/59	**Tijuana Jail** . . . Kingston Trio
38/66	**Tijuana Taxi** . . . Herb Alpert
4/59	**('Til) I Kissed You** . . . Everly Brothers
29/85	**'Til My Baby Comes Home** . . . Luther Vandross
32/75	**Til The World Ends** . . . Three Dog Night
	Till
22/57	Roger Williams
14/62	Angels
27/68	Vogues
26/62	**Till Death Do Us Part** . . . Bob Braun

POS/YR	RECORD TITLE/ARTIST
25/88	**Till I Loved You** . . . Barbra Streisand & Don Johnson
20/63	**Till Then** . . . Classics
30/59	**Till There Was You** . . . Anita Bryant
15/81	**Time** . . . Alan Parsons Project
1/84	**Time After Time** . . . Cyndi Lauper
40/90	**Time After Time** . . . Timmy -T-
36/66	**Time After Time** . . . Chris Montez
30/60	**Time And The River** . . . Nat King Cole
26/88	**Time And Tide** . . . Basia
2/83	**Time (Clock Of The Heart)** . . . Culture Club
32/90	**Time For Letting Go** . . . Jude Cole
32/74	**Time For Livin'** . . . Sly & The Family Stone
39/68	**Time For Livin'** . . . Association
	(Time For Us) ..see: Love Theme From Romeo & Juliet
11/68	**Time Has Come Today** . . . Chambers Brothers
1/73	**Time In A Bottle** . . . Jim Croce
6/64	**Time Is On My Side** . . . Rolling Stones
6/69	**Time Is Tight** . . . Booker T. & The M.G.'s
15/81	**Time Is Time** . . . Andy Gibb
7/91	**Time, Love And Tenderness** . . . Michael Bolton
	Time Of My Life ..see: (I've Had)
3/69	**Time Of The Season** . . . Zombies
22/81	**Time Out Of Mind** . . . Steely Dan
7/78	**Time Passages** . . . Al Stewart
33/73	**Time To Get Down** . . . O'Jays
	Time To Love-A Time To Cry ..see: Petite Fleur
18/84	**Time Will Reveal** . . . DeBarge
5/66	**Time Won't Let Me** . . . Outsiders
7/76	**Times Of Your Life** . . . Paul Anka
17/71	**Timothy** . . . Buoys
4/74	**Tin Man** . . . America
5/55	**Tina Marie** . . . Perry Como
17/68	**Tip-Toe Thru' The Tulips With Me** . . . Tiny Tim
11/71	**Tired Of Being Alone** . . . Al Green
8/80	**Tired Of Toein' The Line** . . . Rocky Burnette
6/65	**Tired Of Waiting For You** . . . Kinks
	To ..also see: Too
26/62	**To A Sleeping Beauty** . . . Jimmy Dean
5/84	**To All The Girls I've Loved Before** . . . Julio Iglesias & Willie Nelson

POS/YR	RECORD TITLE/ARTIST
6/86	**To Be A Lover** . . . Billy Idol
22/58	**To Be Loved** . . . Jackie Wilson
21/60	**To Each His Own** . . . Platters
29/68	**To Give (The Reason I Live)** . . . Frankie Valli
	To Know Him Is To Love Him
1/58	Teddy Bears
24/65	Peter & Gordon
34/69	Bobby Vinton
38/73	**To Know You Is To Love You** . . . B.B. King
17/67	**To Love Somebody** . . . Bee Gees
1/67	**To Sir With Love** . . . Lulu
35/69	**To Susan On The West Coast Waiting** . . . Donovan
25/57	**To The Aisle** . . . Five Satins
17/75	**To The Door Of The Sun (Alle Porte Del Sole)** . . . Al Martino
25/56	**To The Ends Of The Earth** . . . Nat "King" Cole
27/56	**To You, My Love** . . . Nick Noble
20/71	**Toast And Marmalade For Tea** . . . Tin Tin
14/64	**Tobacco Road** . . . Nashville Teens
17/64	**Today** . . . New Christy Minstrels
39/63	**(Today I Met) The Boy I'm Gonna Marry** . . . Darlene Love
23/76	**Today's The Day** . . . America
6/61	**Together** . . . Connie Francis
18/81	**Together** . . . Tierra
19/66	**Together Again** . . . Ray Charles
1/88	**Together Forever** . . . Rick Astley
35/91	**Together Forever** . . . Lisette Melendez
37/72	**Together Let's Find Love** . . . 5th Dimension
26/60	**Togetherness** . . . Frankie Avalon
20/63	**Tom Cat** . . . Rooftop Singers
1/58	**Tom Dooley** . . . Kingston Trio
5/90	**Tom's Diner** . . . D.N.A. Feat. Suzanne Vega
29/59	**Tomboy** . . . Perry Como
23/68	**Tomorrow** . . . Strawberry Alarm Clock
26/86	**Tomorrow Doesn't Matter Tonight** . . . Starship
39/88	**Tomorrow People** . . . Ziggy Marley/Melody Makers
7/90	**Tonight** . . . New Kids On The Block
8/61	**Tonight** . . . Ferrante & Teicher
13/84	**Tonight** . . . Kool & The Gang
26/61	**Tonight (Could Be The Night)** . . . Velvets

POS/YR	RECORD TITLE/ARTIST
16/83	**Tonight, I Celebrate My Love** . . . Peabo Bryson/Roberta Flack
15/61	**Tonight I Fell In Love** . . . Tokens
20/82	**Tonight I'm Yours (Don't Hurt Me)** . . . Rod Stewart
13/61	**Tonight My Love, Tonight** . . . Paul Anka
7/86	**Tonight She Comes** . . . Cars
3/87	**Tonight, Tonight, Tonight** . . . Genesis
	Tonight You Belong To Me
4/56	Patience & Prudence
15/56	Lawrence Welk with The Lennon Sisters
28/65	**Tonight's The Night** . . . Solomon Burke
39/60	**Tonight's The Night** . . . Shirelles
1/76	**Tonight's The Night (Gonna Be Alright)** . . . Rod Stewart
4/69	**Too Busy Thinking About My Baby** . . . Marvin Gaye
39/56	**Too Close For Comfort** . . . Eydie Gorme
5/80	**Too Hot** . . . Kool & The Gang
24/78	**Too Hot Ta Trot** . . . Commodores
5/85	**Too Late For Goodbyes** . . . Julian Lennon
12/90	**Too Late To Say Goodbye** . . . Richard Marx
2/72	**Too Late To Turn Back Now** . . . Cornelius Brothers & Sister Rose
	Too Many Fish In The Sea
25/65	Marvelettes
24/67	Mitch Ryder & The Detroit Wheels (medley)
13/65	**Too Many Rivers** . . . Brenda Lee
8/91	**Too Many Walls** . . . Cathy Dennis
1/57	**Too Much** . . . Elvis Presley
1/79	**Too Much Heaven** . . . Bee Gees
35/67	**Too Much Of Nothing** . . . Peter, Paul & Mary
19/68	**Too Much Talk** . . . Paul Revere & The Raiders
30/60	**Too Much Tequila** . . . Champs
9/81	**Too Much Time On My Hands** . . . Styx
1/78	**Too Much, Too Little, Too Late** . . . Johnny Mathis/Deniece Williams
5/83	**Too Shy** . . . Kajagoogoo
	Too Soon To Know ..see: It's Too Soon
40/81	**Too Tight** . . . Con Funk Shun
13/69	**Too Weak To Fight** . . . Clarence Carter
13/72	**Too Young** . . . Donny Osmond
21/56	**Too Young To Go Steady** . . . Nat "King" Cole
30/78	**Took The Last Train** . . . David Gates

POS/YR	RECORD TITLE/ARTIST
1/73	**Top Of The World** . . . Carpenters
27/58	**Topsy I** . . . Cozy Cole
3/58	**Topsy II** . . . Cozy Cole
	Torero
18/58	Renato Carosone
21/58	Julius LaRosa
1/77	**Torn Between Two Lovers** . . . Mary MacGregor
39/59	**Torquay** . . . Fireballs
17/84	**Torture** . . . Jacksons
20/62	**Torture** . . . Kris Jensen
1/61	**Tossin' And Turnin'** . . . Bobby Lewis
1/83	**Total Eclipse Of The Heart** . . . Bonnie Tyler
23/74	**Touch A Hand, Make A Friend** . . . Staple Singers
37/80	**Touch And Go** . . . Cars
3/69	**Touch Me** . . . Doors
19/74	**Touch Me** . . . Fancy
2/91	**Touch Me (All Night Long)** . . . Cathy Dennis
4/87	**Touch Me (I Want Your Body)** . . . Samantha Fox
1/73	**Touch Me In The Morning** . . . Diana Ross
16/81	**Touch Me When We're Dancing** . . . Carpenters
9/87	**Touch Of Grey** . . . Grateful Dead
	Touch The Wind ..see: Eres Tu
	Tough ..also see: Tuff
22/85	**Tough All Over** . . . John Cafferty
5/61	**Tower Of Strength** . . . Gene McDaniels
13/62	**Town Without Pity** . . . Gene Pitney
1/89	**Toy Soldiers** . . . Martika
24/56	**Tra La La** . . . Georgia Gibbs
35/64	**Tra La La La Suzy** . . . Dean & Jean
2/69	**Traces** . . . Classics IV
	Tracks Of My Tears
16/65	Miracles
10/67	Johnny Rivers
25/76	Linda Ronstadt
9/69	**Tracy** . . . Cuff Links
13/60	**Tracy's Theme** . . . Spencer Ross
1/79	**Tragedy** . . . Bee Gees
	Tragedy
5/59	Thomas Wayne
10/61	Fleetwoods
39/85	**Tragedy** . . . John Hunter
23/80	**Train In Vain (Stand By Me)** . . . Clash

POS/YR	RECORD TITLE/ARTIST
36/60	**Train Of Love** . . . Annette
27/74	**Train Of Thought** . . . Cher
38/79	**Train, Train** . . . Blackfoot
22/66	**Trains And Boats And Planes** . . . Dionne Warwick
26/67	**Tramp** . . . Otis & Carla
38/75	**Trampled Under Foot** . . . Led Zeppelin
8/56	**Transfusion** . . . Nervous Norvus
35/61	**Transistor Sister** . . . Freddy Cannon
13/71	**Trapped By A Thing Called Love** . . . Denise LaSalle
2/70	**Travelin' Band** . . . Creedence Clearwater Revival
1/61	**Travelin' Man** . . . Ricky Nelson
32/67	**Travlin' Man** . . . Stevie Wonder
16/56	**Treasure Of Love** . . . Clyde McPhatter
26/58	**Treasure Of Your Love** . . . Eileen Rodgers
3/71	**Treat Her Like A Lady** . . . Cornelius Brothers & Sister Rose
2/65	**Treat Her Right** . . . Roy Head
18/57	**Treat Me Nice** . . . Elvis Presley
18/81	**Treat Me Right** . . . Pat Benatar
29/61	**Triangle** . . . Janie Grant
25/57	**Tricky** . . . Ralph Marterie
6/72	**Troglodyte (Cave Man)** . . . Jimmy Castor Bunch
9/82	**Trouble** . . . Lindsey Buckingham
35/75	**T-R-O-U-B-L-E** . . . Elvis Presley
35/88	**Trouble** . . . Nia Peeples
20/60	**Trouble In Paradise** . . . Crests
33/63	**Trouble Is My Middle Name** . . . Bobby Vinton
7/73	**Trouble Man** . . . Marvin Gaye
4/83	**True** . . . Spandau Ballet
3/86	**True Blue** . . . Madonna
40/90	**True Blue Love** . . . Lou Gramm
1/86	**True Colors** . . . Cyndi Lauper
32/87	**True Faith** . . . New Order
35/69	**True Grit** . . . Glen Campbell
	True Love
3/56	Bing Crosby & Grace Kelly
15/56	Jane Powell
13/88	**True Love** . . . Glenn Frey
21/63	**True Love Never Runs Smooth** . . . Gene Pitney
	True Love, True Love ..see: (If You Cry)
14/65	**True Love Ways** . . . Peter & Gordon
1/82	**Truly** . . . Lionel Richie

POS/YR	RECORD TITLE/ARTIST
30/61	**Trust In Me** . . . Etta James
23/69	**Try A Little Kindness** . . . Glen Campbell
	Try A Little Tenderness
25/67	Otis Redding
29/69	Three Dog Night
23/83	**Try Again** . . . Champaign
15/64	**Try It Baby** . . . Marvin Gaye
33/58	**Try The Impossible** . . . Lee Andrews & The Hearts
12/66	**Try Too Hard** . . . Dave Clark Five
10/76	**Tryin' To Get The Feeling Again** . . . Barry Manilow
5/81	**Tryin' To Live My Life Without You** . . . Bob Seger
10/77	**Tryin' To Love Two** . . . William Bell
15/74	**Trying To Hold On To My Woman** . . . Lamont Dozier
40/70	**Trying To Make A Fool Of Me** . . . Delfonics
7/74	**Tubular Bells** . . . Mike Oldfield
32/59	**Tucumcari** . . . Jimmie Rodgers
24/68	**Tuesday Afternoon (Forever Afternoon)** . . . Moody Blues
17/62	**Tuff** . . . Ace Cannon
10/86	**Tuff Enuff** . . . Fabulous Thunderbirds
30/80	**Tulsa Time** . . . Eric Clapton
	Tumbling Dice
7/72	Rolling Stones
32/78	Linda Ronstadt
30/58	**Tumbling Tumbleweeds** . . . Billy Vaughn
9/88	**Tunnel Of Love** . . . Bruce Springsteen
27/64	**Turn Around** . . . Dick & DeeDee
7/68	**Turn Around, Look At Me** . . . Vogues
3/70	**Turn Back The Hands Of Time** . . . Tyrone Davis
16/66	**Turn-Down Day** . . . Cyrkle
9/59	**Turn Me Loose** . . . Fabian
35/81	**Turn Me Loose** . . . Loverboy
28/62	**Turn On Your Love Light** . . . Bobby Bland
10/76	**Turn The Beat Around** . . . Vicki Sue Robinson
13/78	**Turn To Stone** . . . Electric Light Orchestra
32/84	**Turn To You** . . . go-go's
1/65	**Turn! Turn! Turn!** . . . Byrds
29/85	**Turn Up The Radio** . . . Autograph
5/82	**Turn Your Love Around** . . . George Benson
36/80	**Turning Japanese** . . . Vapors
13/90	**Turtle Power!** . . . Partners In Kryme

POS/YR	RECORD TITLE/ARTIST
36/58	**Turvy II** . . . Cozy Cole
20/75	**Tush** . . . ZZ Top
8/79	**Tusk** . . . Fleetwood Mac
	Tutti' Frutti
12/56	Pat Boone
17/56	Little Richard
	Tweedlee Dee
2/55	Georgia Gibbs
14/55	LaVern Baker
	Twelfth Of Never
9/57	Johnny Mathis
8/73	Donny Osmond
20/67	**Twelve Thirty (Young Girls Are Coming To The Canyon)** . . . Mamas & The Papas
15/63	**Twenty Miles** . . . Chubby Checker
31/64	**20-75** . . . Willie Mitchell
17/63	**Twenty Four Hours From Tulsa** . . . Gene Pitney
6/69	**Twenty-Five Miles** . . . Edwin Starr
4/70	**25 Or 6 To 4** . . . Chicago
2/58	**26 Miles (Santa Catalina)** . . . Four Preps
38/81	**Twilight** . . . ELO
1/58	**Twilight Time** . . . Platters
31/88	**Twilight World** . . . Swing Out Sister
10/83	**Twilight Zone** . . . Golden Earring
30/80	**Twilight Zone/Twilight Tone** . . . Manhattan Transfer
14/65	**Twine Time** . . . Alvin Cash & The Crawlers
39/66	**Twinkle Toes** . . . Roy Orbison
	Twist, The
1/60	Chubby Checker
28/60	Hank Ballard
1/62	Chubby Checker
16/88	Fat Boys/Chubby Checker (Yo, Twist!)
	Twist And Shout
17/62	Isley Brothers
2/64	Beatles
23/86	Beatles
26/62	**Twist-Her** . . . Bill Black's Combo
25/63	**Twist It Up** . . . Chubby Checker
5/84	**Twist Of Fate** . . . Olivia Newton-John
9/62	**Twist, Twist Senora** . . . Gary "U.S." Bonds
22/62	**Twistin' Matilda** . . . Jimmy Soul
34/62	**Twistin' Postman** . . . Marvelettes
9/62	**Twistin' The Night Away** . . . Sam Cooke
27/60	**Twistin' U.S.A.** . . . Danny & The Juniors
	Twistin' White Silver Sands ..see: White Silver Sands

POS/YR	RECORD TITLE/ARTIST
17/59	**Twixt Twelve And Twenty** . . . Pat Boone
11/56	**Two Different Worlds** . . . Don Rondo
16/71	**Two Divided By Love** . . . Grass Roots
19/78	**Two Doors Down** . . . Dolly Parton
6/63	**Two Faces Have I** . . . Lou Christie
33/75	**Two Fine People** . . . Cat Stevens
1/89	**Two Hearts** . . . Phil Collins
16/55	**Two Hearts** . . . Pat Boone
40/81	**Two Hearts** . . . Stephanie Mills/Teddy Pendergrass
38/83	**Two Less Lonely People In The World** . . . Air Supply
31/68	**Two Little Kids** . . . Peaches & Herb
18/55	**Two Lost Souls** . . . Perry Como & Jaye P. Morgan
7/63	**Two Lovers** . . . Mary Wells
10/88	**Two Occasions** . . . Deele
3/86	**Two Of Hearts** . . . Stacey Q
11/78	**Two Out Of Three Ain't Bad** . . . Meat Loaf
30/87	**Two People** . . . Tina Turner
30/80	**Two Places At The Same Time** . . . Ray Parker Jr. & Raydio
38/84	**Two Sides Of Love** . . . Sammy Hagar
22/78	**Two Tickets To Paradise** . . . Eddie Money
32/63	**Two Tickets To Paradise** . . . Brook Benton
2/90	**Two To Make It Right** . . . Seduction
	2001 Space Odyssey ..see: Also Sprach Zarathustra
2/86	**Typical Male** . . . Tina Turner

POS/YR	RECORD TITLE/ARTIST
	U ..see: You
28/68	**U.S. Male** . . . Elvis Presley
14/59	**Uh! Oh! (Part 2)** . . . Nutty Squirrels
5/64	**Um, Um, Um, Um, Um, Um** . . . Major Lance
1/91	**Unbelievable** . . . EMF
9/62	**Unchain My Heart** . . . Ray Charles
	Unchained Melody
1/55	Les Baxter
3/55	Al Hibbler
6/55	Roy Hamilton
29/55	June Valli
4/65	Righteous Brothers
13/90	Righteous Brothers
19/90	Righteous Brothers
1/71	**Uncle Albert/Admiral Halsey** . . . Paul & Linda McCartney
29/82	**Under Pressure** . . . Queen & David Bowie
4/64	**Under The Boardwalk** . . . Drifters
24/88	**Under The Milky Way** . . . Church
35/66	**Under Your Spell Again** . . . Johnny Rivers
1/77	**Undercover Angel** . . . Alan O'Day
9/83	**Undercover Of The Night** . . . Rolling Stones
35/64	**Understand Your Man** . . . Johnny Cash
17/85	**Understanding** . . . Bob Seger
22/69	**Undun** . . . Guess Who
9/73	**Uneasy Rider** . . . Charlie Daniels
	Unforgettable
17/59	Dinah Washington
14/91	Natalie Cole
	Unforgiven ..see: Theme From The
33/70	**Ungena Za Ulimwengu (Unite The World)** . . . Temptations
7/68	**Unicorn, The** . . . Irish Rovers
24/76	**Union Man** . . . Cate Bros.
3/83	**Union Of The Snake** . . . Duran Duran
13/70	**United We Stand** . . . Brotherhood Of Man
39/68	**Unknown Soldier** . . . Doors
3/90	**Unskinny Bop** . . . Poison
40/72	**Until It's Time For You To Go** . . . Elvis Presley
3/74	**Until You Come Back To Me (That's What I'm Gonna Do)** . . . Aretha Franklin
	Up A Lazy River ..see: Lazy River
27/90	**Up All Night** . . . Slaughter
4/70	**Up Around The Bend** . . . Creedence Clearwater Revival
16/75	**Up In A Puff Of Smoke** . . . Polly Brown
25/70	**Up On Cripple Creek** . . . Band
	Up On The Roof
5/63	Drifters
28/79	James Taylor
10/70	**Up The Ladder To The Roof** . . . Supremes
7/67	**Up-Up And Away** . . . 5th Dimension
1/82	**Up Where We Belong** . . . Joe Cocker & Jennifer Warnes
22/67	**Ups And Downs** . . . Paul Revere & The Raiders
1/80	**Upside Down** . . . Diana Ross

POS/YR	RECORD TITLE/ARTIST
3/66	**Uptight (Everything's Alright)** . . . Stevie Wonder
	(also see: Little Ole Man)
13/62	**Uptown** . . . Crystals
25/77	**Uptown Festival (Motown Medley)** . . . Shalamar
3/83	**Uptown Girl** . . . Billy Joel
4/81	**Urgent** . . . Foreigner
2/72	**Use Me** . . . Bill Withers
4/78	**Use Ta Be My Girl** . . . O'Jays
34/65	**Use Your Head** . . . Mary Wells
27/61	**Utopia** . . . Frank Gari

V

POS/YR	RECORD TITLE/ARTIST
8/82	**Vacation** . . . Go-Go's
9/62	**Vacation** . . . Connie Francis
9/87	**Valerie** . . . Steve Winwood
3/68	**Valleri** . . . Monkees
32/82	**Valley Girl** . . . Frank Zappa
8/57	**Valley Of Tears** . . . Fats Domino
	Valley Of The Dolls ..see: Theme From
5/88	**Valley Road** . . . Bruce Hornsby & The Range
9/85	**Valotte** . . . Julian Lennon
2/70	**Vehicle** . . . Ides Of March
35/86	**Velcro Fly** . . . ZZ Top
8/72	**Ventura Highway** . . . America
1/59	**Venus** . . . Frankie Avalon
	Venus
1/70	Shocking Blue
1/86	Bananarama
12/75	**Venus And Mars Rock Show** . . . Wings
7/62	**Venus In Blue Jeans** . . . Jimmy Clanton
19/89	**Veronica** . . . Elvis Costello
23/58	**Very Precious Love** . . . Ames Brothers
	Very Special Love
20/58	Debbie Reynolds
23/58	Johnny Nash
11/74	**Very Special Love Song** . . . Charlie Rich
26/64	**Very Thought Of You** . . . Rick Nelson
31/79	**Victim Of Love** . . . Elton John
32/87	**Victim Of Love** . . . Bryan Adams
10/87	**Victory** . . . Kool & The Gang
40/79	**Video Killed The Radio Star** . . . Buggles
18/86	**Vienna Calling** . . . Falco
1/85	**View To A Kill** . . . Duran Duran
22/62	**Village Of Love** . . . Nathaniel Mayer
7/60	**Village Of St. Bernadette** . . . Andy Williams
12/72	**Vincent** . . . Don McLean
1/90	**Vision Of Love** . . . Mariah Carey
29/64	**Viva Las Vegas** . . . Elvis Presley
28/70	**Viva Tirado** . . . El Chicano
1/90	**Vogue** . . . Madonna
15/81	**Voice** . . . Moody Blues
32/80	**Voices** . . . Cheap Trick
8/85	**Voices Carry** . . . 'til tuesday
25/89	**Voices Of Babylon** . . . Outfield
11/91	**Voices That Care** . . . Voices That Care
	Volare (Nel Blu Dipinto Di Blu)
1/58	Domenico Modugno
12/58	Dean Martin
4/60	Bobby Rydell
33/75	Al Martino
27/65	**Voodoo Woman** . . . Bobby Goldsboro
29/85	**Vox Humana** . . . Kenny Loggins
29/82	**Voyeur** . . . Kim Carnes

POS/YR	RECORD TITLE/ARTIST
36/74	**WOLD** . . . Harry Chapin
40/67	**Wack Wack** . . . Young Holt Trio
	Wade In The Water
19/66	Ramsey Lewis
37/67	Herb Alpert
2/62	**Wah Watusi** . . . Orlons
	(also see: El Watusi & Watusi)
8/88	**Wait** . . . White Lion
37/61	**Wait A Minute** . . . Coasters
23/57	**Wait And See** . . . Fats Domino
18/80	**Wait For Me** . . . Daryl Hall & John Oates
37/60	**Wait For Me** . . . Playmates
26/63	**Wait Til' My Bobby Gets Home** . . . Darlene Love
18/58	**Waitin' In School** . . . Ricky Nelson

POS/YR	RECORD TITLE/ARTIST
19/81	**Waiting** . . . Tom Petty
2/81	**Waiting For A Girl Like You** . . . Foreigner
5/88	**Waiting For A Star To Fall** . . . Boy Meets Girl
13/91	**Waiting For Love** . . . Alias
27/91	**Waiting For That Day** . . . George Michael
13/82	**Waiting On A Friend** . . . Rolling Stones
1/84	**Wake Me Up Before You Go-Go** . . . Wham!
	Wake The Town And Tell The People
5/55	Les Baxter
13/55	Mindy Carson
12/76	**Wake Up Everybody** . . . Harold Melvin & The Blue Notes
	Wake Up Little Susie
1/57	Everly Brothers
27/82	Simon & Garfunkel
39/85	**Wake Up (Next To You)** . . . Graham Parker
7/58	**Walk, The** . . . Jimmy McCracklin
12/70	**Walk A Mile In My Shoes** . . . Joe South
23/65	**Walk Away** . . . Matt Monro
36/80	**Walk Away** . . . Donna Summer
9/76	**Walk Away From Love** . . . David Ruffin
	Walk Away Renee
5/66	Left Banke
14/68	Four Tops
	Walk Don't Run
2/60	Ventures
8/64	Ventures ('64)
10/56	**Walk Hand In Hand** . . . Tony Martin
12/65	**Walk In The Black Forest** . . . Horst Jankowski
1/63	**Walk Like A Man** . . . 4 Seasons
19/74	**Walk Like A Man** . . . Grand Funk
1/86	**Walk Like An Egyptian** . . . Bangles
7/86	**Walk Of Life** . . . Dire Straits
5/61	**Walk On By** . . . Leroy Van Dyke
	Walk On By
6/64	Dionne Warwick
30/69	Isaac Hayes
16/73	**Walk On The Wild Side** . . . Lou Reed
21/62	**Walk On The Wild Side** . . . Jimmy Smith
9/88	**Walk On Water** . . . Eddie Money
17/72	**Walk On Water** . . . Neil Diamond
7/61	**Walk Right Back** . . . Everly Brothers
1/63	**Walk Right In** . . . Rooftop Singers
7/89	**Walk The Dinosaur** . . . Was (Not Was)
	Walk This Way
10/77	Aerosmith

POS/YR	RECORD TITLE/ARTIST
4/86	Run-D.M.C.
12/57	**Walkin' After Midnight** . . . Patsy Cline
	Walkin' In The Rain
23/64	Ronettes
19/70	Jay & The Americans
14/72	**Walkin' In The Rain With The One I Love** . . . Love Unlimited
	Walkin' In The Sand ..see: Remember
37/67	**Walkin' In The Sunshine** . . . Roger Miller
12/63	**Walkin' Miracle** . . . Essex
22/66	**Walkin' My Cat Named Dog** . . . Norma Tanega
29/58	**Walking Along** . . . Diamonds
9/89	**Walking Away** . . . Information Society
11/87	**Walking Down Your Street** . . . Bangles
13/91	**Walking In Memphis** . . . Marc Cohn
6/75	**Walking In Rhythm** . . . Blackbyrds
18/84	**Walking On A Thin Line** . . . Huey Lewis & the News
9/85	**Walking On Sunshine** . . . Katrina & The Waves
26/63	**Walking Proud** . . . Steve Lawrence
10/63	**Walking The Dog** . . . Rufus Thomas
	Walking The Floor ..see: I'm Walking
6/60	**Walking To New Orleans** . . . Fats Domino
32/80	**Walks Like A Lady** . . . Journey
2/62	**Wanderer, The** . . . Dion
3/80	**Wanderer, The** . . . Donna Summer
5/83	**Wanna Be Startin' Somethin'** . . . Michael Jackson
1/71	**Want Ads** . . . Honey Cone
7/87	**Wanted Dead Or Alive** . . . Bon Jovi
38/56	**Wanting You** . . . Roger Williams
	War
1/70	Edwin Starr
8/86	Bruce Springsteen
17/84	**War Song** . . . Culture Club
17/66	**Warm And Tender Love** . . . Percy Sledge
39/78	**Warm Ride** . . . Rare Earth
25/62	**Warmed Over Kisses (Left Over Love)** . . . Brian Hyland
7/84	**Warrior, The** . . . Scandal
24/90	**Was It Nothing At All** . . . Michael Damian
2/63	**Washington Square** . . . Village Stompers
37/81	**Wasn't That A Party** . . . Rovers
8/75	**Wasted Days And Wasted Nights** . . . Freddy Fender

POS/YR	RECORD TITLE/ARTIST
9/82	**Wasted On The Way** . . . Crosby, Stills & Nash
40/79	**Watch Out For Lucy** . . . Eric Clapton
30/67	**Watch The Flowers Grow** . . . 4 Seasons
11/71	**Watching Scotty Grow** . . . Bobby Goldsboro
10/81	**Watching The Wheels** . . . John Lennon
40/61	**Water Boy** . . . Don Shirley Trio
4/59	**Waterloo** . . . Stonewall Jackson
6/74	**Waterloo** . . . Abba
10/63	**Watermelon Man** . . . Mongo Santamaria Band
25/61	**Watusi, The** . . . Vibrations
	(also see: El Watusi & Wah Watusi)
18/77	**Way Down** . . . Elvis Presley
3/60	**Way Down Yonder In New Orleans** . . . Freddie Cannon
40/83	**Way He Makes Me Feel** . . . Barbra Streisand
24/78	**Way I Feel Tonight** . . . Bay City Rollers
35/59	**Way I Walk** . . . Jack Scott
4/75	**Way I Want To Touch You** . . . Captain & Tennille
1/86	**Way It Is** . . . Bruce Hornsby & The Range
7/72	**Way Of Love** . . . Cher
	Way That You Love Me ..see: (It's Just)
	Way We Were
1/74	Barbra Streisand
11/75	Gladys Knight & The Pips (medley)
	Way You Do The Things You Do
11/64	Temptations
20/78	Rita Coolidge
0/85	Hall & Oates/David Ruffin/Eddie Kendrick (medley)
6/90	UB40
13/61	**Way You Look Tonight** . . . Lettermen
7/89	**Way You Love Me** . . . Karyn White
1/88	**Way You Make Me Feel** . . . Michael Jackson
24/58	**Ways Of A Woman In Love** . . . Johnny Cash
	Wayward Wind
1/56	Gogi Grant
28/56	Tex Ritter
5/67	**(We Ain't Got) Nothin' Yet** . . . Blues Magoos
	(We All Shine On) ..see: Instant Karma
14/88	**We All Sleep Alone** . . . Cher
2/79	**We Are Family** . . . Sister Sledge

POS/YR	RECORD TITLE/ARTIST
4/78	**We Are The Champions** . . . Queen
1/85	**We Are The World** . . . USA for Africa
25/84	**We Are The Young** . . . Dan Hartman
5/85	**We Belong** . . . Pat Benatar
32/58	**We Belong Together** . . . Robert & Johnny
1/85	**We Built This City** . . . Starship
21/68	**We Can Fly** . . . Cowsills
	We Can Work It Out
1/66	Beatles
13/71	Stevie Wonder
8/90	**We Can't Go Wrong** . . . Cover Girls
36/76	**We Can't Hide It Anymore** . . . Larry Santos
35/87	**We Connect** . . . Stacey Q
1/89	**We Didn't Start The Fire** . . . Billy Joel
5/86	**We Don't Have To Take Our Clothes Off** . . . Jermaine Stewart
2/85	**We Don't Need Another Hero (Thunderdome)** . . . Tina Turner
7/80	**We Don't Talk Anymore** . . . Cliff Richard
6/59	**We Got Love** . . . Bobby Rydell
35/69	**We Got More Soul** . . . Dyke & The Blazers
2/82	**We Got The Beat** . . . Go-Go's
13/65	**We Gotta Get Out Of This Place** . . . Animals
20/71	**We Gotta Get You A Woman** . . . Runt (Todd Rundgren)
12/77	**We Just Disagree** . . . Dave Mason
27/80	**We Live For Love** . . . Pat Benatar
39/64	**We Love You Beatles** . . . Carefrees
21/73	**We May Never Pass This Way (Again)** . . . Seals & Crofts
22/83	**We Two** . . . Little River Band
16/91	**We Want The Funk** . . . Gerardo
31/80	**We Were Meant To Be Lovers** . . . Photoglo
F/78	**We Will Rock You** . . . Queen
7/87	**We'll Be Together** . . . Sting
9/78	**We'll Never Have To Say Goodbye Again** . . . England Dan & John Ford Coley
4/64	**We'll Sing In The Sunshine** . . . Gale Garnett
14/68	**We're A Winner** . . . Impressions
7/77	**We're All Alone** . . . Rita Coolidge
35/90	**We're All In The Same Gang** . . . West Coast Rap All-Stars
1/73	**We're An American Band** . . . Grand Funk
40/72	**We're Free** . . . Beverly Bremers

POS/YR	RECORD TITLE/ARTIST
34/74	**We're Getting Careless With Our Love** . . . Johnnie Taylor
	(We're Gonna) ..see: Rock Around The Clock
25/65	**We're Gonna Make It** . . . Little Milton
15/81	**We're In This Love Together** . . . Al Jarreau
21/84	**We're Not Gonna Take It** . . . Twisted Sister
9/87	**We're Ready** . . . Boston
25/72	**We've Got To Get It On Again** . . . Addrisi Brothers
	We've Got Tonite
13/79	Bob Seger
6/83	Kenny Rogers & Sheena Easton
2/70	**We've Only Just Begun** . . . Carpenters
2/58	**Wear My Ring Around Your Neck** . . . Elvis Presley
23/67	**Wear Your Love Like Heaven** . . . Donovan
32/56	**Weary Blues** . . . McGuire Sisters & Lawrence Welk
10/65	**Wedding, The** . . . Julie Rogers
1/69	**Wedding Bell Blues** . . . 5th Dimension
	Wedding Bells ..see: (I'm Always Hearing)
24/71	**Wedding Song (There Is Love)** . . . Paul Stookey
	(also see: Down The Aisle)
35/58	**Week End** . . . Kingsmen
29/79	**Weekend** . . . Wet Willie
10/77	**Weekend In New England** . . . Barry Manilow
19/69	**Weight, The** . . . Aretha Franklin
1/76	**Welcome Back** . . . John Sebastian
22/62	**Welcome Home Baby** . . . Shirelles
18/60	**(Welcome) New Lovers** . . . Pat Boone
24/83	**Welcome To Heartlight** . . . Kenny Loggins
37/86	**Welcome To The Boomtown** . . . David & David
7/88	**Welcome To The Jungle** . . . Guns N' Roses
29/61	**Well, I Told You** . . . Chantels
13/66	**Well Respected Man** . . . Kinks
21/78	**Werewolves Of London** . . . Warren Zevon
1/86	**West End Girls** . . . Pet Shop Boys
37/62	**West Of The Wall** . . . Toni Fisher
24/70	**Westbound # 9** . . . Flaming Ember
8/58	**Western Movies** . . . Olympics
5/67	**Western Union** . . . Five Americans
24/63	**Wham!** . . . Lonnie Mack
16/76	**Wham Bam** . . . Silver

POS/YR	RECORD TITLE/ARTIST
	What A Beautiful World ..see: I.G.Y.
	What A Diff'rence A Day Makes
8/59	Dinah Washington
20/75	Esther Phillips
	What A Feeling ..see: Flashdance
1/79	**What A Fool Believes** . . . Doobie Brothers
22/61	**What A Party** . . . Fats Domino
22/61	**What A Price** . . . Fats Domino
33/61	**What A Surprise** . . . Johnny Maestro
31/67	**What A Woman In Love Won't Do** . . . Sandy Posey
32/88	**What A Wonderful World** . . . Louis Armstrong
	(also see: Wonderful World)
10/85	**What About Love?** . . . Heart
26/86	**What About Love** . . . 'Til Tuesday
15/84	**What About Me?** . . . Kenny Rogers/Kim Carnes/James Ingram
29/83	**What About Me** . . . Moving Pictures
39/72	**What Am I Crying For?** . . . Classics IV
35/83	**What Am I Gonna Do (I'm So In Love With You)** . . . Rod Stewart
8/75	**What Am I Gonna Do With You** . . . Barry White
	What Am I Living For
9/58	Chuck Willis
26/60	Conway Twitty
14/81	**What Are We Doin' In Love** . . . Dottie West with Kenny Rogers
39/71	**What Are You Doing Sunday** . . . Dawn
7/66	**What Becomes Of The Brokenhearted** . . . Jimmy Ruffin
	What Cha ..also see: What You & Whatcha
22/79	**What Cha Gonna Do With My Lovin'** . . . Stephanie Mills
38/65	**What Color (Is A Man)** . . . Bobby Vinton
19/91	**What Comes Naturally** . . . Sheena Easton
4/69	**What Does It Take (To Win Your Love)** . . . Jr. Walker & The All Stars
2/88	**What Have I Done To Deserve This?** . . . Pet Shop Boys/Dusty Springfield
29/65	**What Have They Done To The Rain** . . . Searchers
4/86	**What Have You Done For Me Lately** . . . Janet Jackson
7/89	**What I Am** . . . Edie Brickell & New Bohemians

POS/YR	RECORD TITLE/ARTIST
28/89	**What I Like About You** . . . Michael Morales
39/84	**(What) In The Name Of Love** . . . Naked Eyes
5/60	**What In The World's Come Over You** . . . Jack Scott
10/71	**What Is Life** . . . George Harrison
15/59	**What Is Love?** . . . Playmates
33/84	**What Is Love?** . . . Howard Jones
19/70	**What Is Truth** . . . Johnny Cash
9/90	**What It Takes** . . . Aerosmith
10/81	**What Kind Of Fool** . . . Barbra Streisand & Barry Gibb
17/62	**What Kind Of Fool Am I** . . . Sammy Davis Jr.
21/82	**What Kind Of Fool Am I** . . . Rick Springfield
	What Kind Of Fool Do You Think I Am
9/64	Tams
23/69	Bill Deal
18/62	**What Kind Of Love Is This** . . . Joey Dee & The Starliters
5/90	**What Kind Of Man Would I Be?** . . . Chicago
40/65	**What Now** . . . Gene Chandler
	What Now My Love
14/66	Sonny & Cher
24/66	Herb Alpert
30/67	Mitch Ryder
	What The World Needs Now Is Love
7/65	Jackie DeShannon
8/71	Tom Clay (medley)
9/63	**What Will Mary Say** . . . Johnny Mathis
	What You ..also see: What Cha & Whatcha
8/89	**What You Don't Know** . . . Expose
13/87	**What You Get Is What You See** . . . Tina Turner
5/86	**What You Need** . . . INXS
24/88	**What You See Is What You Get** . . . Brenda K. Starr
9/79	**What You Won't Do For Love** . . . Bobby Caldwell
	What'd I Say
6/59	Ray Charles
30/61	Jerry Lee Lewis
24/62	Bobby Darin
21/64	Elvis Presley
	What's ..also see: Wot's
12/62	**What's A Matter Baby** . . . Timi Yuro
29/64	**What's Easy For Two Is So Hard For One** . . . Mary Wells
19/82	**What's Forever For** . . . Michael Murphey
	What's Going On
2/71	Marvin Gaye
12/87	Cyndi Lauper
1/84	**What's Love Got To Do With It** . . . Tina Turner
3/65	**What's New Pussycat?** . . . Tom Jones
3/88	**What's On Your Mind (Pure Energy)** . . . Information Society
35/62	**What's So Good About Good-By** . . . Miracles
17/64	**What's The Matter With You Baby** . . . Marvin Gaye & Mary Wells
20/69	**What's The Use Of Breaking Up** . . . Jerry Butler
7/62	**What's Your Name** . . . Don & Juan
13/78	**What's Your Name** . . . Lynyrd Skynyrd
	Whatcha ..also see: What Cha & What You
6/77	**Whatcha Gonna Do** . . . Pablo Cruise
9/71	**Whatcha See Is Whatcha Get** . . . Dramatics
1/74	**Whatever Gets You Thru The Night** . . . John Lennon
	Whatever Lola Wants
6/55	Sarah Vaughan
12/55	Dinah Shore
	Whatever Will Be, Will Be ..see: Que Sera, Sera
38/74	**Whatever You Got, I Want** . . . Jackson 5
26/66	**Wheel Of Hurt** . . . Margaret Whiting
	Wheels
3/61	String-A-Longs
28/61	Billy Vaughn
5/58	**When** . . . Kalin Twins
	When A Man (Woman) Loves A Woman (Man)
1/66	Percy Sledge
35/80	Bette Midler
27/82	**When All Is Said And Done** . . . Abba
1/84	**When Doves Cry** . . . Prince
30/82	**When He Shines** . . . Sheena Easton
18/69	**When I Die** . . . Motherlode
7/62	**When I Fall In Love** . . . Lettermen
9/64	**When I Grow Up (To Be A Man)** . . . Beach Boys
10/89	**When I Looked At Him** . . . Expose
1/77	**When I Need You** . . . Leo Sayer

POS/YR	RECORD TITLE/ARTIST
29/57	**When I See You** . . . Fats Domino
1/89	**When I See You Smile** . . . Bad English
1/86	**When I Think Of You** . . . Janet Jackson
20/80	**When I Wanted You** . . . Barry Manilow
15/67	**When I Was Young** . . . Animals
7/90	**When I'm Back On My Feet Again** . . . Michael Bolton
25/65	**When I'm Gone** . . . Brenda Holloway
1/89	**When I'm With You** . . . Sheriff
5/88	**When It's Love** . . . Van Halen
26/82	**When It's Over** . . . Loverboy
18/66	**When Liking Turns To Loving** . . . Ronnie Dove
19/56	**When My Blue Moon Turns To Gold Again** . . . Elvis Presley
14/56	**When My Dreamboat Comes Home** . . . Fats Domino
28/62	**When My Little Girl Is Smiling** . . . Drifters
37/66	**(When She Needs Good Lovin') She Comes To Me** . . . Chicago Loop
11/81	**When She Was My Girl** . . . Four Tops
5/87	**When Smokey Sings** . . . ABC
10/62	**When The Boy In Your Arms (Is The Boy In Your Heart)** . . . Connie Francis
19/58	**When The Boys Talk About The Girls** . . . Valerie Carr
3/89	**When The Children Cry** . . . White Lion
2/86	**When The Going Gets Tough, The Tough Get Going** . . . Billy Ocean
14/86	**When The Heart Rules The Mind** . . . GTR
37/83	**When The Lights Go Out** . . . Naked Eyes
23/64	**When The Lovelight Starts Shining Through His Eyes** . . . Supremes
11/90	**When The Night Comes** . . . Joe Cocker
18/56	**When The Saints Go Marching In** . . . Bill Haley
	When The White Lilacs Bloom Again
12/56	Helmut Zacharias
18/56	Billy Vaughn
10/61	**When We Get Married** . . . Dreamlovers
36/88	**When We Kiss** . . . Bardeux
23/88	**When We Was Fab** . . . George Harrison
	When Will I Be Loved
8/60	Everly Brothers
2/75	Linda Ronstadt
2/74	**When Will I See You Again** . . . Three Degrees
14/84	**When You Close Your Eyes** . . . Night Ranger
33/56	**When You Dance** . . . Turbans
32/72	**When You Say Love** . . . Sonny & Cher
35/64	**When You Walk In The Room** . . . Searchers
30/60	**When You Wish Upon A Star** . . . Dion & The Belmonts
9/71	**When You're Hot, You're Hot** . . . Jerry Reed
6/79	**When You're In Love With A Beautiful Woman** . . . Dr. Hook
23/67	**When You're Young And In Love** . . . Marvelettes
35/85	**When Your Heart Is Weak** . . . Cock Robin
39/64	**Whenever He Holds You** . . . Bobby Goldsboro
5/78	**Whenever I Call You "Friend"** . . . Kenny Loggins
38/76	**Whenever I'm Away From You** . . . John Travolta
32/60	**Where Are You** . . . Frankie Avalon
36/62	**Where Are You** . . . Dinah Washington
10/89	**Where Are You Now?** . . . Jimmy Harnen W/Synch
	Where Did Our Love Go
1/64	Supremes
15/71	Donnie Elbert
33/71	**Where Did They Go, Lord** . . . Elvis Presley
1/88	**Where Do Broken Hearts Go** . . . Whitney Houston
	(Where Do I Begin) ..see: Theme From Love Story
38/86	**Where Do The Children Go** . . . Hooters
25/65	**Where Do You Go** . . . Cher
4/91	**Where Does My Heart Beat Now** . . . Celine Dion
	Where Have All The Flowers Gone
21/62	Kingston Trio
26/65	Johnny Rivers
5/72	**Where Is The Love** . . . Roberta Flack & Donny Hathaway
3/60	**Where Or When** . . . Dion & The Belmonts
28/73	**Where Peaceful Waters Flow** . . . Gladys Knight & The Pips
	Where The Action Is ..see: Action
4/61	**Where The Boys Are** . . . Connie Francis
13/87	**Where The Streets Have No Name** . . . U2

POS/YR	RECORD TITLE/ARTIST
23/59	**Where Were You (On Our Wedding Day)?** . . . Lloyd Price
28/66	**Where Were You When I Needed You** . . . Grass Roots
23/79	**Where Were You When I Was Falling In Love** . . . Lobo
21/67	**Where Will The Words Come From** . . . Gary Lewis & The Playboys
	Where You Lead
40/71	Barbra Streisand
37/72	Barbra Streisand (medley)
26/69	**Where's The Playground Susie** . . . Glen Campbell
	Which Way Is Up ..see: Theme From
2/70	**Which Way You Goin' Billy?** . . . Poppy Family
7/81	**While You See A Chance** . . . Steve Winwood
6/90	**Whip Appeal** . . . Babyface
14/80	**Whip It** . . . Devo
28/83	**Whirly Girl** . . . Oxo
37/84	**Whisper To A Scream (Birds Fly)** . . . Icicle Works
	Whispering
11/64	Nino Tempo & April Stevens
27/77	Dr. Buzzard's Original "Savannah" Band
9/57	**Whispering Bells** . . . Dell-Vikings
11/66	**Whispers (Gettin' Louder)** . . . Jackie Wilson
	White Christmas
7/55	Bing Crosby
34/57	Bing Crosby
26/60	Bing Crosby
12/61	Bing Crosby
38/62	Bing Crosby
26/84	**White Horse** . . . Laid Back
19/76	**White Knight** . . . Cledus Maggard
28/72	**White Lies, Blue Eyes** . . . Bullet
9/64	**White On White** . . . Danny Williams
8/67	**White Rabbit** . . . Jefferson Airplane
6/68	**White Room** . . . Cream
	White Silver Sands
7/57	Don Rondo
18/57	Owen Bradley Quintet
22/57	Dave Gardner
9/60	Bill Black's Combo
2/57	**White Sport Coat (And A Pink Carnation)** . . . Marty Robbins
36/83	**White Wedding** . . . Billy Idol
5/67	**Whiter Shade Of Pale** . . . Procol Harum

POS/YR	RECORD TITLE/ARTIST
21/66	**Who Am I** . . . Petula Clark
14/78	**Who Are You** . . . Who
33/64	**Who Can I Turn To** . . . Tony Bennett
1/82	**Who Can It Be Now?** . . . Men At Work
15/89	**Who Do You Give Your Love To?** . . . Michael Morales
25/64	**Who Do You Love** . . . Sapphires
15/74	**Who Do You Think You Are** . . . Bo Donaldson & The Heywoods
40/81	**Who Do You Think You're Foolin'** . . . Donna Summer
16/87	**Who Found Who** . . . Jellybean/Elisa Fiorillo
33/68	**Who Is Gonna Love Me?** . . . Dionne Warwick
3/75	**Who Loves You** . . . Four Seasons
9/57	**Who Needs You** . . . Four Lads
7/61	**Who Put The Bomp (In The Bomp, Bomp, Bomp)** . . . Barry Mann
16/84	**Who Wears These Shoes?** . . . Elton John
19/68	**Who Will Answer?** . . . Ed Ames
7/87	**Who Will You Run To** . . . Heart
18/76	**Who'd She Coo?** . . . Ohio Players
29/80	**Who'll Be The Fool Tonight** . . . Larsen-Feiten Band
34/65	**Who'll Be The Next In Line** . . . Kinks
F/70	**Who'll Stop The Rain** . . . Creedence Clearwater Revival
4/81	**Who's Crying Now** . . . Journey
6/85	**Who's Holding Donna Now** . . . DeBarge
27/73	**Who's In The Strawberry Patch With Sally** . . . Dawn
3/86	**Who's Johnny** . . . El DeBarge
	Who's Making Love
5/68	Johnnie Taylor
39/81	Blues Brothers
	Who's Sorry Now
4/58	Connie Francis
40/75	Marie Osmond
1/87	**Who's That Girl** . . . Madonna
21/84	**Who's That Girl?** . . . Eurythmics
40/70	**Who's Your Baby?** . . . Archies
7/85	**Who's Zoomin' Who** . . . Aretha Franklin
22/77	**Whodunit** . . . Tavares
3/57	**Whole Lot Of Shakin' Going On** . . . Jerry Lee Lewis
4/70	**Whole Lotta Love** . . . Led Zeppelin
6/59	**Whole Lotta Loving** . . . Fats Domino
9/90	**Whole Wide World** . . . A'Me Lorain

POS/YR	RECORD TITLE/ARTIST
	Why
1/59	Frankie Avalon
13/72	Donny Osmond
5/57	**Why Baby Why** . . . Pat Boone
33/85	**Why Can't I Have You** . . . Cars
	Why Can't I Touch You ..see: (If You Let Me Make Love To You Then)
3/86	**Why Can't This Be Love** . . . Van Halen
6/75	**Why Can't We Be Friends?** . . . War
3/73	**Why Can't We Live Together** . . . Timmy Thomas
	Why Do Fools Fall In Love
6/56	Frankie Lymon & The Teenagers
9/56	Gale Storm
12/56	Diamonds
7/81	Diana Ross
38/63	**Why Do Lovers Break Each Other's Heart?** . . . Bob B. Soxx & The Blue Jeans
10/58	**Why Don't They Understand** . . . George Hamilton IV
37/63	**Why Don't You Believe Me** . . . Duprees
13/83	**Why Me?** . . . Irene Cara
16/73	**Why Me** . . . Kris Kristofferson
26/80	**Why Me** . . . Styx
18/80	**Why Not Me** . . . Fred Knoblock
39/87	**Why You Treat Me So Bad** . . . Club Nouveau
3/69	**Wichita Lineman** . . . Glen Campbell
6/91	**Wicked Game** . . . Chris Isaak
15/90	**Wiggle It** . . . 2 In A Room
22/63	**Wiggle Wobble** . . . Les Cooper
33/63	**Wild!** . . . Dee Dee Sharp
2/84	**Wild Boys** . . . Duran Duran
29/56	**Wild Cherry** . . . Don Cherry
31/67	**Wild Honey** . . . Beach Boys
28/71	**Wild Horses** . . . Rolling Stones
26/61	**Wild In The Country** . . . Elvis Presley
22/57	**Wild Is The Wind** . . . Johnny Mathis
28/71	**Wild Night** . . . Van Morrison
2/60	**Wild One** . . . Bobby Rydell
34/65	**Wild One** . . . Martha & The Vandellas
	Wild Thing
1/66	Troggs
20/67	Senator Bobby
14/74	Fancy
2/89	**Wild Thing** . . . Tone Loc
8/63	**Wild Weekend** . . . Rebels
25/86	**Wild Wild Life** . . . Talking Heads
1/88	**Wild, Wild West** . . . Escape Club

POS/YR	RECORD TITLE/ARTIST
34/90	**Wild Women Do** . . . Natalie Cole
	Wild World
11/71	Cat Stevens
25/89	Maxi Priest
3/75	**Wildfire** . . . Michael Murphey
9/73	**Wildflower** . . . Skylark
17/63	**Wildwood Days** . . . Bobby Rydell
7/74	**Wildwood Weed** . . . Jim Stafford
1/73	**Will It Go Round In Circles** . . . Billy Preston
32/69	**Will You Be Staying After Sunday** . . . Peppermint Rainbow
	Will You Love Me Tomorrow
1/61	Shirelles
24/68	4 Seasons
39/78	Dave Mason
3/87	**Will You Still Love Me?** . . . Chicago
	Willie And The Hand Jive
9/58	Johnny Otis Show
26/74	Eric Clapton
15/65	**Willow Weep For Me** . . . Chad & Jeremy
22/58	**Win Your Love For Me** . . . Sam Cooke
1/66	**Winchester Cathedral** . . . New Vaudeville Band
1/89	**Wind Beneath My Wings** . . . Bette Midler
4/91	**Wind Of Change** . . . Scorpions
31/69	**Windmills Of Your Mind** . . . Dusty Springfield
32/67	**Windows Of The World** . . . Dionne Warwick
38/83	**Winds Of Change** . . . Jefferson Starship
1/67	**Windy** . . . Association
12/61	**Wings Of A Dove** . . . Ferlin Husky
8/81	**Winner Takes It All** . . . Abba
21/76	**Winners And Losers** . . . Hamilton, Joe Frank & Reynolds
17/81	**Winning** . . . Santana
16/70	**Winter World Of Love** . . . Engelbert Humperdinck
	Wipe Out
2/63	Surfaris
16/66	Surfaris
12/87	Fat Boys/Beach Boys
35/57	**Wisdom Of A Fool** . . . Five Keys
17/64	**Wish Someone Would Care** . . . Irma Thomas
38/67	**Wish You Didn't Have To Go** . . . James & Bobby Purify
6/64	**Wishin' And Hopin'** . . . Dusty Springfield

POS/YR	RECORD TITLE/ARTIST
18/58	**Wishing For Your Love** . . . Voxpoppers
26/83	**Wishing (If I Had A Photograph Of You)** . . . Flock Of Seagulls
1/88	**Wishing Well** . . . Terence Trent D'Arby
11/74	**Wishing You Were Here** . . . Chicago
1/58	**Witch Doctor** . . . David Seville
21/72	**Witch Queen Of New Orleans** . . . Redbone
6/58	**Witchcraft** . . . Frank Sinatra
32/63	**Witchcraft** . . . Elvis Presley
9/72	**Witchy Woman** . . . Eagles
29/66	**With A Girl Like You** . . . Troggs
1/78	**With A Little Luck** . . . Wings
15/57	**With All My Heart** . . . Jodie Sands
5/89	**With Every Beat Of My Heart** . . . Taylor Dayne
39/59	**With Open Arms** . . . Jane Morgan
1/87	**With Or Without You** . . . U2
35/69	**With Pen In Hand** . . . Vikki Carr
21/59	**With The Wind And The Rain In Your Hair** . . . Pat Boone
27/65	**With These Hands** . . . Tom Jones
14/67	**With This Ring** . . . Platters
4/80	**With You I'm Born Again** . . . Billy Preston & Syreeta
30/57	**With You On My Mind** . . . Nat "King" Cole
12/76	**With Your Love** . . . Jefferson Starship
28/58	**With Your Love** . . . Jack Scott
	Without Love (There Is Nothing)
19/57	Clyde McPhatter
29/63	Ray Charles
5/70	Tom Jones
1/72	**Without You** . . . Nilsson
	(also see: Love Will Never Do)
7/61	**Without You** . . . Johnny Tillotson
8/90	**Without You** . . . Motley Crue
24/82	**Without You (Not Another Lonely Night)** . . . Franke & The Knockouts
20/80	**Without Your Love** . . . Roger Daltrey
38/87	**Without Your Love** . . . Toto
14/64	**Wives And Lovers** . . . Jack Jones
	Wizard Of Oz ..see: Themes From The
40/75	**Wolf Creek Pass** . . . C.W. McCall
6/62	**Wolverton Mountain** . . . Claude King
	(also see: I'm The Girl On)
2/81	**Woman** . . . John Lennon
14/66	**Woman** . . . Peter & Gordon

POS/YR	RECORD TITLE/ARTIST
15/60	**Woman, A Lover, A Friend** . . . Jackie Wilson
36/90	**Woman In Chains** . . . Tears For Fears
1/80	**Woman In Love** . . . Barbra Streisand
	Woman In Love
14/55	Four Aces
19/55	Frankie Laine
33/83	**Woman In Me** . . . Donna Summer
24/83	**Woman In You** . . . Bee Gees
4/81	**Woman Needs Love (Just Like You Do)** . . . Ray Parker Jr. & Raydio
22/74	**Woman To Woman** . . . Shirley Brown
4/68	**Woman, Woman** . . . Union Gap feat. Gary Puckett
29/65	**Woman's Got Soul** . . . Impressions
36/71	**Women's Love Rights** . . . Laura Lee
15/71	**Won't Get Fooled Again** . . . Who
19/60	**Won't You Come Home Bill Bailey** . . . Bobby Darin
11/61	**Wonder Like You** . . . Rick Nelson
	Wonder Of You
25/59	Ray Peterson
9/70	Elvis Presley
22/62	**Wonderful Dream** . . . Majors
14/63	**Wonderful Summer** . . . Robin Ward
4/58	**Wonderful Time Up There** . . . Pat Boone
16/78	**Wonderful Tonight** . . . Eric Clapton
	Wonderful! Wonderful!
14/57	Johnny Mathis
7/63	Tymes
	(also see: Wun'erful, Wun'erful)
	Wonderful World
12/60	Sam Cooke
4/65	Herman's Hermits
17/78	Art Garfunkel with James Taylor & Paul Simon
	(also see: What A)
25/70	**Wonderful World, Beautiful People** . . . Jimmy Cliff
40/59	**Wonderful You** . . . Jimmie Rodgers
12/57	**Wondering** . . . Patti Page
21/80	**Wondering Where The Lions Are** . . . Bruce Cockburn
25/80	**Wonderland** . . . Commodores
	Wonderland By Night
1/61	Bert Kaempfert
15/61	Louis Prima
18/61	Anita Bryant
16/59	**Woo-Hoo** . . . Rock-A-Teens

POS/YR	RECORD TITLE/ARTIST
	Woo Woo Song ..see: You Should Be Mine
1/61	**Wooden Heart** . . . Joe Dowell
	Woodstock
11/70	Crosby, Stills, Nash & Young
23/71	Matthews' Southern Comfort
2/65	**Wooly Bully** . . . Sam The Sham & the Pharoahs
19/88	**Word In Spanish** . . . Elton John
6/86	**Word Up** . . . Cameo
11/67	**Words** . . . Monkees
15/68	**Words** . . . Bee Gees
5/86	**Words Get In The Way** . . . Miami Sound Machine
5/67	**Words Of Love** . . . Mamas & The Papas
13/57	**Words Of Love** . . . Diamonds
18/66	**Work Song** . . . Herb Alpert
32/74	**Workin' At The Car Wash Blues** . . . Jim Croce
33/62	**Workin' For The Man** . . . Roy Orbison
20/69	**Workin' On A Groovy Thing** . . . 5th Dimension
29/82	**Working For The Weekend** . . . Loverboy
8/66	**Working In The Coal Mine** . . . Lee Dorsey
	Working My Way Back To You
9/66	4 Seasons
2/80	Spinners (medley)
33/63	**Workout Stevie, Workout** . . . Little Stevie Wonder
37/69	**World** . . . James Brown
7/73	**World Is A Ghetto** . . . War
19/65	**World Of Our Own** . . . Seekers
21/58	**World Outside** . . . Four Coins
30/67	**World We Knew (Over And Over)** . . . Frank Sinatra
1/64	**World Without Love** . . . Peter & Gordon
37/64	**Worried Guy** . . . Johnny Tillotson
20/59	**Worried Man** . . . Kingston Trio
3/69	**Worst That Could Happen** . . . Brooklyn Bridge
10/87	**Wot's It To Ya** . . . Robbie Nevil
5/85	**Would I Lie To You?** . . . Eurythmics
8/66	**Wouldn't It Be Nice** . . . Beach Boys
38/81	**Wrack My Brain** . . . Ringo Starr
20/85	**Wrap Her Up** . . . Elton John
8/84	**Wrapped Around Your Finger** . . . Police
2/76	**Wreck Of The Edmund Fitzgerald** . . . Gordon Lightfoot

POS/YR	RECORD TITLE/ARTIST
	Wringle Wrangle
12/57	Fess Parker
33/57	Bill Hayes
5/61	**Writing On The Wall** . . . Adam Wade
16/91	**Written All Over Your Face** . . . Rude Boys
34/64	**Wrong For Each Other** . . . Andy Williams
32/57	**Wun'erful, Wun'erful!** . . . Stan Freberg

POS/YR	RECORD TITLE/ARTIST
8/80	**Xanadu** . . . Olivia Newton-John/Electric Light Orchestra

POS/YR	RECORD TITLE/ARTIST
2/79	**Y.M.C.A.** . . . Village People
7/61	**Ya Ya** . . . Lee Dorsey
19/84	**Yah Mo B There** . . . James Ingram (with Michael McDonald)
35/63	**Yakety Sax** . . . Boots Randolph
1/58	**Yakety Yak** . . . Coasters
16/86	**Yankee Rose** . . . David Lee Roth
32/88	**Yeah, Yeah, Yeah** . . . Judson Spence
8/77	**Year Of The Cat** . . . Al Stewart
35/80	**Years** . . . Wayne Newton
37/61	**Years From Now** . . . Jackie Wilson
21/65	**Yeh, Yeh** . . . Georgie Fame
25/67	**Yellow Balloon** . . . Yellow Balloon
4/61	**Yellow Bird** . . . Arthur Lyman Group
23/70	**Yellow River** . . . Christie
	Yellow Rose Of Texas
1/55	Mitch Miller
3/55	Johnny Desmond
16/55	Stan Freberg
2/66	**Yellow Submarine** . . . Beatles
30/59	**"Yep!"** . . . Duane Eddy
	Yes, I'm Ready
5/65	Barbara Mason
2/80	Teri DeSario with K.C.

POS/YR	RECORD TITLE/ARTIST
34/60	**Yes Sir, That's My Baby** . . . Ricky Nelson
12/57	**Yes Tonight, Josephine** . . . Johnnie Ray
11/73	**Yes We Can Can** . . . Pointer Sisters
31/68	**Yester Love** . . . Miracles
7/69	**Yester-Me, Yester-You, Yesterday** . . . Stevie Wonder
	Yesterday
1/65	Beatles
25/67	Ray Charles
2/73	**Yesterday Once More** . . . Carpenters
19/69	**Yesterday, When I Was Young** . . . Roy Clark
21/64	**Yesterday's Gone** . . . Chad & Jeremy
11/82	**Yesterday's Songs** . . . Neil Diamond
3/71	**Yo-Yo** . . . Osmonds
8/60	**Yogi** . . . Ivy Three
20/75	**You** . . . George Harrison
21/58	**You** . . . Aquatones
25/78	**You** . . . Rita Coolidge
34/68	**You** . . . Marvin Gaye
1/74	**You Ain't Seen Nothing Yet** . . . Bachman-Turner Overdrive
12/61	**You Always Hurt The One You Love** . . . Clarence Henry
7/83	**You And I** . . . Eddie Rabbitt with Crystal Gayle
13/78	**You And I** . . . Rick James
9/77	**You And Me** . . . Alice Cooper
9/74	**You And Me Against The World** . . . Helen Reddy
4/83	**You Are** . . . Lionel Richie
9/72	**You Are Everything** . . . Stylistics
26/62	**You Are Mine** . . . Frankie Avalon
7/58	**You Are My Destiny** . . . Paul Anka
12/85	**You Are My Lady** . . . Freddie Jackson
6/55	**You Are My Love** . . . Joni James
27/76	**You Are My Starship** . . . Norman Connors
7/62	**You Are My Sunshine** . . . Ray Charles
5/75	**You Are So Beautiful** . . . Joe Cocker
17/87	**You Are The Girl** . . . Cars
25/61	**You Are The Only One** . . . Ricky Nelson
1/73	**You Are The Sunshine Of My Life** . . . Stevie Wonder
9/76	**You Are The Woman** . . . Firefall
20/66	**You Baby** . . . Turtles
29/86	**You Be Illin'** . . . Run-D.M.C.
9/62	**You Beat Me To The Punch** . . . Mary Wells
6/78	**You Belong To Me** . . . Carly Simon

POS/YR	RECORD TITLE/ARTIST
7/62	**You Belong To Me** . . . Duprees
2/85	**You Belong To The City** . . . Glenn Frey
37/59	**You Better Know It** . . . Jackie Wilson
24/62	**You Better Move On** . . . Arthur Alexander
20/66	**You Better Run** . . . Young Rascals
9/67	**You Better Sit Down Kids** . . . Cher
18/81	**You Better You Bet** . . . Who
23/87	**You Can Call Me Al** . . . Paul Simon
6/61	**You Can Depend On Me** . . . Brenda Lee
37/79	**You Can Do It** . . . Dobie Gray
8/82	**You Can Do Magic** . . . America
	You Can Have Her
12/61	Roy Hamilton
34/74	Sam Neely
36/58	**You Can Make It If You Try** . . . Gene Allison
18/63	**You Can Never Stop Me Loving You** . . . Johnny Tillotson
9/79	**You Can't Change That** . . . Raydio
14/90	**You Can't Deny It** . . . Lisa Stansfield
15/84	**You Can't Get What You Want (Till You Know What You Want)** . . . Joe Jackson
	You Can't Hurry Love
1/66	Supremes
10/83	Phil Collins
36/91	**You Can't Play With My Yo-Yo** . . . Yo-Yo
40/66	**You Can't Roller Skate In A Buffalo Herd** . . . Roger Miller
20/56	**You Can't Run Away From It** . . . Four Aces
	You Can't Sit Down
29/61	Philip Upchurch Combo
3/63	Dovells
8/90	**U Can't Touch This** . . . M.C. Hammer
12/77	**You Can't Turn Me Off (In The Middle Of Turning Me On)** . . . High Inergy
12/58	**You Cheated** . . . Shields
29/91	**You Could Be Mine** . . . Guns N' Roses
32/72	**You Could Have Been A Lady** . . . April Wine
15/82	**You Could Have Been With Me** . . . Sheena Easton
32/81	**You Could Take My Heart Away** . . . Silver Condor
7/79	**You Decorated My Life** . . . Kenny Rogers
10/66	**You Didn't Have To Be So Nice** . . . Lovin' Spoonful
1/78	**You Don't Bring Me Flowers** . . . Barbra Streisand & Neil Diamond

POS/YR	RECORD TITLE/ARTIST
3/63	**You Don't Have To Be A Baby To Cry** . . . Caravelles
1/77	**You Don't Have To Be A Star** . . . Marilyn McCoo & Billy Davis, Jr.
14/91	**You Don't Have To Go Home Tonight** . . . Triplets
15/66	**(You Don't Have To) Paint Me A Picture** . . . Gary Lewis & The Playboys
	You Don't Have To Say You Love Me
4/66	Dusty Springfield
11/70	Elvis Presley
20/88	**You Don't Know** . . . Scarlett & Black
11/64	**(You Don't Know) How Glad I Am** . . . Nancy Wilson
	You Don't Know Me
14/56	Jerry Vale
2/62	Ray Charles
4/61	**You Don't Know What You've Got (Until You Lose It)** . . . Ral Donner
8/72	**You Don't Mess Around With Jim** . . . Jim Croce
10/57	**You Don't Owe Me A Thing** . . . Johnnie Ray
2/64	**You Don't Own Me** . . . Lesley Gore
16/82	**You Don't Want Me Anymore** . . . Steel Breeze
31/82	**You Dropped A Bomb On Me** . . . Gap Band
24/69	**You Gave Me A Mountain** . . . Frankie Laine
3/85	**You Give Good Love** . . . Whitney Houston
1/86	**You Give Love A Bad Name** . . . Bon Jovi
38/79	**You Gonna Make Me Love Somebody Else** . . . Jones Girls
9/89	**You Got It** . . . Roy Orbison
3/87	**You Got It All** . . . Jets
3/89	**You Got It (The Right Stuff)** . . . New Kids On The Block
20/83	**You Got Lucky** . . . Tom Petty
2/87	**U Got The Look** . . . Prince
11/74	**You Got The Love** . . . Rufus Featuring Chaka Khan
18/67	**You Got To Me** . . . Neil Diamond
	You Got What It Takes
10/60	Marv Johnson
7/67	Dave Clark Five
40/69	**You Got Yours And I'll Get Mine** . . . Delfonics
7/87	**(You Gotta) Fight For Your Right (To Party!)** . . . Beastie Boys

POS/YR	RECORD TITLE/ARTIST
1/74	**You Haven't Done Nothin** . . . Stevie Wonder
24/69	**You, I** . . . Rugbys
	You Keep Me Hangin' On
1/66	Supremes
6/68	Vanilla Fudge
1/87	Kim Wilde
25/68	**(You Keep Me) Hangin' On** . . . Joe Simon
38/82	**You Keep Runnin' Away** . . . 38 Special
19/67	**You Keep Running Away** . . . Four Tops
17/86	**You Know I Love You...Don't You?** . . . Howard Jones
35/80	**You Know That I Love You** . . . Santana
12/67	**You Know What I Mean** . . . Turtles
1/77	**You Light Up My Life** . . . Debby Boone
12/74	**You Little Trustmaker** . . . Tymes
22/63	**You Lost The Sweetest Boy** . . . Mary Wells
10/77	**You Made Me Believe In Magic** . . . Bay City Rollers
9/77	**You Make Loving Fun** . . . Fleetwood Mac
2/74	**You Make Me Feel Brand New** . . . Stylistics
1/77	**You Make Me Feel Like Dancing** . . . Leo Sayer
36/79	**You Make Me Feel (Mighty Real)** . . . Sylvester
5/81	**You Make My Dreams** . . . Daryl Hall & John Oates
7/80	**You May Be Right** . . . Billy Joel
17/60	**You Mean Everything To Me** . . . Neil Sedaka
35/68	**You Met Your Match** . . . Stevie Wonder
7/84	**You Might Think** . . . Cars
15/64	**You Must Believe Me** . . . Impressions
	You Must Have Been A Beautiful Baby
5/61	Bobby Darin
35/67	Dave Clark Five
40/79	**You Need A Woman Tonight** . . . Captain & Tennille
11/58	**You Need Hands** . . . Eydie Gorme
25/70	**You Need Love Like I Do (Don't You)** . . . Gladys Knight & The Pips
1/78	**You Needed Me** . . . Anne Murray
14/64	**You Never Can Tell** . . . Chuck Berry
10/78	**You Never Done It Like That** . . . Captain & Tennille
3/72	**You Ought To Be With Me** . . . Al Green
	You Really Got A Hold On Me ..see: You've Really

POS/YR	RECORD TITLE/ARTIST
	You Really Got Me
7/64	Kinks
36/78	Van Halen
27/65	**You Really Know How To Hurt A Guy** . . . Jan & Dean
37/81	**You Saved My Soul** . . . Burton Cummings
	You Send Me
1/57	Sam Cooke
8/57	Teresa Brewer
3/76	**You Sexy Thing** . . . Hot Chocolate
35/80	**You Shook Me All Night Long** . . . AC/DC
1/76	**You Should Be Dancing** . . . Bee Gees
13/86	**You Should Be Mine (The Woo Woo Song)** . . . Jeffrey Osborne
39/64	**You Should Have Seen The Way He Looked At Me** . . . Dixie Cups
5/82	**You Should Hear How She Talks About You** . . . Melissa Manchester
6/69	**You Showed Me** . . . Turtles
11/85	**You Spin Me Round (Like A Record)** . . . Dead Or Alive
10/79	**You Take My Breath Away** . . . Rex Smith
3/60	**You Talk Too Much** . . . Joe Jones
38/65	**You Tell Me Why** . . . Beau Brummels
40/79	**You Thrill Me** . . . Exile
39/79	**You Took The Words Right Out Of My Mouth** . . . Meat Loaf
8/65	**You Turn Me On** . . . Ian Whitcomb
25/73	**You Turn Me On, I'm A Radio** . . . Joni Mitchell
36/72	**You Want It, You Got It** . . . Detroit Emeralds
13/72	**You Wear It Well** . . . Rod Stewart
12/60	**(You Were Made For) All My Love** . . . Jackie Wilson
21/65	**You Were Made For Me** . . . Freddie & The Dreamers
27/58	**You Were Made For Me** . . . Sam Cooke
21/59	**You Were Mine** . . . Fireflies
	You Were On My Mind
3/65	We Five
36/67	Crispian St. Peters
30/65	**You Were Only Fooling (While I Was Falling In Love)** . . . Vic Damone
22/62	**You Win Again** . . . Fats Domino
8/74	**You Won't See Me** . . . Anne Murray
22/65	**You'd Better Come Home** . . . Petula Clark
14/80	**You'll Accomp'ny Me** . . . Bob Seger

POS/YR	RECORD TITLE/ARTIST
	You'll Lose A Good Thing
8/62	Barbara Lynn
32/76	Freddy Fender
2/76	**You'll Never Find Another Love Like Mine** . . . Lou Rawls
	You'll Never Get To Heaven (If You Break My Heart)
34/64	Dionne Warwick
23/73	Stylistics
11/56	**You'll Never Never Know** . . . Platters
34/64	**You'll Never Walk Alone** . . . Patti LaBelle & Her Blue Belles
	You're ..also see: Your
18/86	**You're A Friend Of Mine** . . . Clarence Clemons & Jackson Browne
36/78	**You're A Part Of Me** . . . Gene Cotton with Kim Carnes
12/73	**You're A Special Part Of Me** . . . Diana Ross & Marvin Gaye
15/64	**You're A Wonderful One** . . . Marvin Gaye
	You're All I Need To Get By
7/68	Marvin Gaye & Tammi Terrell
19/71	Aretha Franklin
34/75	Dawn
28/91	**You're Amazing** . . . Robert Palmer
25/57	**You're Cheatin' Yourself (If You're Cheatin' On Me)** . . . Frank Sinatra
35/83	**You're Driving Me Out Of My Mind** . . . Little River Band
39/66	**(You're Gonna) Hurt Yourself** . . . Frankie Valli
34/59	**You're Gonna Miss Me** . . . Connie Francis
1/74	**(You're) Having My Baby** . . . Paul Anka
1/91	**You're In Love** . . . Wilson Phillips
4/78	**You're In My Heart (The Final Acclaim)** . . . Rod Stewart
16/76	**You're My Best Friend** . . . Queen
6/67	**You're My Everything** . . . Temptations
27/81	**You're My Girl** . . . Franke & The Knockouts
	You're My Girl ..see: (Say)
14/57	**You're My One And Only Love** . . . Ricky Nelson
23/89	**You're My One And Only (True Love)** . . . Seduction
	(You're My) Soul And Inspiration
1/66	Righteous Brothers
38/78	Donny & Marie Osmond
	You're My World
26/64	Cilla Black

POS/YR	RECORD TITLE/ARTIST
18/77	Helen Reddy
1/75	**You're No Good** . . . Linda Ronstadt
25/65	**You're Nobody Till Somebody Loves You** . . . Dean Martin
10/89	**You're Not Alone** . . . Chicago
9/85	**You're Only Human (Second Wind)** . . . Billy Joel
7/79	**You're Only Lonely** . . . J.D. Souther
	You're Sixteen
8/60	Johnny Burnette
1/74	Ringo Starr
17/59	**You're So Fine** . . . Falcons
1/73	**You're So Vain** . . . Carly Simon
29/72	**You're Still A Young Man** . . . Tower Of Power
34/80	**You're Supposed To Keep Your Love For Me** . . . Jermaine Jackson
3/63	**(You're the) Devil In Disguise** . . . Elvis Presley
2/75	**You're The First, The Last, My Everything** . . . Barry White
3/85	**You're The Inspiration** . . . Chicago
18/78	**You're The Love** . . . Seals & Crofts
4/65	**You're The One** . . . Vogues
22/70	**You're The One** . . . Little Sister
1/78	**You're The One That I Want** . . . John Travolta & Olivia Newton-John
	You're The Only Woman (You & I)
13/80	Ambrosia
36/90	Brat Pack
11/61	**You're The Reason** . . . Bobby Edwards
3/63	**You're The Reason I'm Living** . . . Bobby Darin
33/66	**You've Been Cheatin'** . . . Impressions
36/65	**You've Been In Love Too Long** . . . Martha & The Vandellas
	(You've Got) ..see: Personality
	You've Got A Friend
1/71	James Taylor
29/71	Roberta Flack & Donny Hathaway
38/70	**(You've Got Me) Dangling On A String** . . . Chairmen Of The Board
33/77	**You've Got Me Runnin'** . . . Gene Cotton
4/56	**(You've Got) The Magic Touch** . . . Platters
28/71	**You've Got To Crawl (Before You Walk)** . . . 8th Day
10/65	**You've Got To Hide Your Love Away** . . . Silkie

POS/YR	RECORD TITLE/ARTIST
20/60	**(You've Got To) Move Two Mountains** . . . Marv Johnson
	(You've Got What It Takes) ..see: Baby
7/65	**You've Got Your Troubles** . . . Fortunes
	You've Lost That Lovin' Feelin'
1/65	Righteous Brothers
16/69	Dionne Warwick
12/80	Daryl Hall & John Oates
	You've Made Me So Very Happy
39/67	Brenda Holloway
2/69	Blood, Sweat & Tears
22/73	**You've Never Been This Far Before** . . . Conway Twitty
8/63	**You've Really Got A Hold On Me** . . . Miracles
25/55	**Young Abe Lincoln** . . . Don Cornell
28/75	**Young Americans** . . . David Bowie
17/63	**Young And In Love** . . . Dick & DeeDee
	Young And The Restless ..see: Nadia's Theme
23/58	**Young And Warm And Wonderful** . . . Tony Bennett
	Young Blood
8/57	Coasters
20/76	Bad Company
40/79	**Young Blood** . . . Rickie Lee Jones
12/60	**Young Emotions** . . . Ricky Nelson
2/68	**Young Girl** . . . Union Gap feat. Gary Puckett
20/76	**Young Hearts Run Free** . . . Candi Staton
	Young Love
1/57	Tab Hunter
1/57	Sonny James
17/57	Crew-Cuts
25/73	Donny Osmond
38/82	**Young Love** . . . Air Supply
6/63	**Young Lovers** . . . Paul & Paula
	(also see: Theme For)
5/81	**Young Turks** . . . Rod Stewart
5/62	**Young World** . . . Rick Nelson
	Your ..also see: You're
17/90	**Your Baby Never Looked Good In Blue** . . . Expose
24/75	**Your Bulldog Drinks Champagne** . . . Jim Stafford
29/62	**Your Cheating Heart** . . . Ray Charles
34/61	**Your Friends** . . . Dee Clark
18/69	**Your Good Thing (Is About To End)** . . . Lou Rawls

POS/YR	RECORD TITLE/ARTIST
33/82	**Your Imagination** . . . Daryl Hall & John Oates
6/86	**Your Love** . . . Outfield
15/77	**Your Love** . . . Marilyn McCoo & Billy Davis Jr.
38/75	**Your Love** . . . Graham Central Station
13/83	**Your Love Is Driving Me Crazy** . . . Sammy Hagar
	(Your Love Keeps Lifting Me) Higher And Higher
6/67	Jackie Wilson
2/77	Rita Coolidge
24/61	**Your Ma Said You Cried In Your Sleep Last Night** . . . Kenny Dino
	Your Mama Don't Dance
4/73	Loggins & Messina
10/89	Poison
40/71	**Your Move** . . . Yes
14/62	**Your Nose Is Gonna Grow** . . . Johnny Crawford
40/63	**Your Old Stand By** . . . Mary Wells
40/61	**Your One And Only Love** . . . Jackie Wilson
28/63	**Your Other Love** . . . Connie Francis
5/67	**Your Precious Love** . . . Marvin Gaye & Tammi Terrell

POS/YR	RECORD TITLE/ARTIST
	(also see: For Your Precious Love)
20/77	**Your Smiling Face** . . . James Taylor
8/71	**Your Song** . . . Elton John
40/71	**Your Time To Cry** . . . Joe Simon
33/67	**Your Unchanging Love** . . . Marvin Gaye
32/63	**Your Used To Be** . . . Brenda Lee
20/57	**Your Wild Heart** . . . Joy Layne
9/86	**Your Wildest Dreams** . . . Moody Blues
	(Yowsah, Yowsah, Yowsah) ..see: Dance, Dance, Dance
4/68	**Yummy Yummy Yummy** . . . Ohio Express

POS/YR	RECORD TITLE/ARTIST
8/63	**Zip-A-Dee Doo-Dah** . . . Bob B. Soxx & The Blue Jeans
36/67	**Zip Code** . . . Five Americans
16/57	**Zip Zip** . . . Diamonds
11/66	**Zorba The Greek** . . . Herb Alpert
17/58	**Zorro** . . . Chordettes

THE RECORD HOLDERS

TOP ARTIST AND RECORD ACHIEVEMENTS

	WEEKS				THE TOP 100 RECORDS 1955 - 1991*
YR	CHR	T40	T10	#1	TITLE/ARTIST
56	28	24	21	11	1. DON'T BE CRUEL/HOUND DOG...Elvis Presley
55	26	26	20	10	2. CHERRY PINK AND APPLE BLOSSOM WHITE...Perez Prado
55	21	21	18	10	3. SINCERELY...The McGuire Sisters
56	26	22	17	10	4. SINGING THE BLUES...Guy Mitchell
81	26	21	15	10	5. PHYSICAL...Olivia Newton-John
77	25	21	14	10	6. YOU LIGHT UP MY LIFE...Debby Boone
59	26	22	16	9	7. MACK THE KNIFE...Bobby Darin
57	30	22	15	9	8. ALL SHOOK UP...Elvis Presley
81	26	20	14	9	9. BETTE DAVIS EYES...Kim Carnes
68	19	19	14	9	10. HEY JUDE...The Beatles
81	27	19	13	9	11. ENDLESS LOVE...Diana Ross & Lionel Richie
60	21	17	12	9	12. THE THEME FROM "A SUMMER PLACE"...Percy Faith
55	38	25	19	8	13. ROCK AROUND THE CLOCK...Bill Haley & His Comets
56	37	22	16	8	14. THE WAYWARD WIND...Gogi Grant
55	22	19	16	8	15. SIXTEEN TONS...Tennessee Ernie Ford
56	27	22	15	8	16. HEARTBREAK HOTEL...Elvis Presley
83	22	20	13	8	17. EVERY BREATH YOU TAKE...The Police
78	20	18	13	8	18. NIGHT FEVER...Bee Gees
76	23	17	11	8	19. TONIGHT'S THE NIGHT (GONNA BE ALRIGHT)...Rod Stewart
57	34	24	17	7	20. LOVE LETTERS IN THE SAND...Pat Boone
57	27	19	15	7	21. JAILHOUSE ROCK...Elvis Presley
57	25	18	14	7	22. (LET ME BE YOUR) TEDDY BEAR...Elvis Presley
78	25	19	12	7	23. SHADOW DANCING...Andy Gibb
58	21	18	12	7	24. AT THE HOP...Danny & The Juniors
61	23	17	12	7	25. TOSSIN' AND TURNIN'...Bobby Lewis
82	20	16	12	7	26. I LOVE ROCK 'N ROLL...Joan Jett & The Blackhearts
82	19	15	12	7	27. EBONY AND IVORY...Paul McCartney with Stevie Wonder
64	15	14	12	7	28. I WANT TO HOLD YOUR HAND...The Beatles
66	15	13	12	7	29. I'M A BELIEVER...The Monkees
83	24	17	11	7	30. BILLIE JEAN...Michael Jackson
68	15	15	11	7	31. I HEARD IT THROUGH THE GRAPEVINE...Marvin Gaye
91	22	17	10	7	32. (EVERYTHING I DO) I DO IT FOR YOU...Bryan Adams
55	21	21	17	6	33. LOVE IS A MANY-SPLENDORED THING...Four Aces
56	25	20	16	6	34. ROCK AND ROLL WALTZ...Kay Starr
56	24	20	16	6	35. THE POOR PEOPLE OF PARIS...Les Baxter
55	19	19	16	6	36. THE YELLOW ROSE OF TEXAS...Mitch Miller
78	25	19	15	6	37. LE FREAK...Chic
56	24	19	15	6	38. MEMORIES ARE MADE OF THIS...Dean Martin
82	25	18	15	6	39. EYE OF THE TIGER...Survivor
83	25	20	14	6	40. FLASHDANCE...WHAT A FEELING...Irene Cara
57	26	19	14	6	41. APRIL LOVE...Pat Boone
80	25	19	13	6	42. LADY...Kenny Rogers
83	22	18	13	6	43. SAY SAY SAY...Paul McCartney & Michael Jackson
59	21	18	13	6	44. THE BATTLE OF NEW ORLEANS...Johnny Horton
57	21	17	13	6	45. YOUNG LOVE...Tab Hunter
82	25	20	12	6	46. CENTERFOLD...The J. Geils Band

YR	WEEKS CHR	T40	T10	#1	THE TOP 100 RECORDS 1955 - 1991* TITLE/ARTIST
80	25	19	12	6	47. CALL ME...Blondie
58	22	19	12	6	48. IT'S ALL IN THE GAME...Tommy Edwards
79	22	16	12	6	49. MY SHARONA...The Knack
69	17	16	11	6	50. AQUARIUS/LET THE SUNSHINE IN...The 5th Dimension
72	18	15	11	6	51. THE FIRST TIME EVER I SAW YOUR FACE...Roberta Flack
72	18	15	11	6	52. ALONE AGAIN (NATURALLY)...Gilbert O'Sullivan
71	17	15	11	6	53. JOY TO THE WORLD...Three Dog Night
60	16	14	11	6	54. ARE YOU LONESOME TO-NIGHT?...Elvis Presley
58	14	14	10	6	55. THE PURPLE PEOPLE EATER...Sheb Wooley
70	14	13	10	6	56. BRIDGE OVER TROUBLED WATER...Simon & Garfunkel
84	19	14	9	6	57. LIKE A VIRGIN...Madonna
69	13	12	9	6	58. IN THE YEAR 2525 (EXORDIUM & TERMINUS)...Zager & Evans
57	31	23	16	5	59. TAMMY...Debbie Reynolds
55	20	20	16	5	60. THE BALLAD OF DAVY CROCKETT...Bill Hayes
56	23	19	15	5	61. LOVE ME TENDER...Elvis Presley
56	23	20	14	5	62. MY PRAYER...The Platters
80	22	19	14	5	63. (JUST LIKE) STARTING OVER...John Lennon
77	23	17	12	5	64. BEST OF MY LOVE...The Emotions
58	19	16	12	5	65. ALL I HAVE TO DO IS DREAM...The Everly Brothers
84	21	16	11	5	66. WHEN DOVES CRY...Prince
60	20	16	11	5	67. IT'S NOW OR NEVER...Elvis Presley
58	19	16	11	5	68. TEQUILA...The Champs
70	16	16	11	5	69. I'LL BE THERE...The Jackson 5
76	19	15	11	5	70. SILLY LOVE SONGS...Wings
71	17	15	11	5	71. MAGGIE MAY...Rod Stewart
62	18	14	11	5	72. I CAN'T STOP LOVING YOU...Ray Charles
58	20	16	10	5	73. DON'T...Elvis Presley
84	21	15	10	5	74. JUMP...Van Halen
79	20	15	10	5	75. BAD GIRLS...Donna Summer
68	18	15	10	5	76. LOVE IS BLUE...Paul Mauriat
71	17	15	10	5	77. IT'S TOO LATE...Carole King
59	17	14	10	5	78. VENUS...Frankie Avalon
62	16	14	10	5	79. BIG GIRLS DON'T CRY...The 4 Seasons
58	16	13	10	5	80. NEL BLU DIPINTO DI BLU (VOLARE)...Domenico Modugno
61	16	13	10	5	81. BIG BAD JOHN...Jimmy Dean
63	15	13	10	5	82. SUGAR SHACK...Jimmy Gilmer & The Fireballs
68	15	13	10	5	83. HONEY...Bobby Goldsboro
91	19	15	9	5	84. RUSH, RUSH...Paula Abdul
67	17	15	9	5	85. TO SIR WITH LOVE...Lulu
60	17	13	9	5	86. CATHY'S CLOWN...The Everly Brothers
73	16	13	9	5	87. KILLING ME SOFTLY WITH HIS SONG...Roberta Flack
68	14	13	9	5	88. PEOPLE GOT TO BE FREE...The Rascals
71	15	12	9	5	89. ONE BAD APPLE...The Osmonds
69	12	12	9	5	90. GET BACK...The Beatles
66	13	11	9	5	91. THE BALLAD OF THE GREEN BERETS...SSgt Barry Sadler

	WEEKS				THE TOP 100 RECORDS 1955 - 1991*
YR	CHR	T40	T10	#1	TITLE/ARTIST
62	14	12	7	5	92. SHERRY...The 4 Seasons
64	10	9	6	5	93. CAN'T BUY ME LOVE...The Beatles
55	26	26	18	4	94. AUTUMN LEAVES...Roger Williams
56	29	24	17	4	95. LISBON ANTIGUA...Nelson Riddle
77	31	23	16	4	96. I JUST WANT TO BE YOUR EVERYTHING...Andy Gibb
56	23	19	14	4	97. I ALMOST LOST MY MIND...Pat Boone
80	29	17	14	4	98. UPSIDE DOWN...Diana Ross
57	28	23	13	4	99. HONEYCOMB...Jimmie Rodgers
78	27	22	13	4	100. STAYIN' ALIVE...Bee Gees

* : Ranking period includes all #1 hits which peaked prior to August, 1991.
YR : Year record reached its peak position
CHR: Total weeks charted in the Top 100
T40 : Total weeks charted in the Top 40
T10 : Total weeks charted in the Top 10
#1 : Total weeks record held the #1 position

Records are ranked according to the number of weeks they held the #1 position. Ties are broken in the following order:

1. Total weeks in the Top 10
2. Total weeks in the Top 40
3. Total weeks charted in the Top 100

This ranking system is identical to the one used in compiling Record Research's *Top 3000 1955-1987* book. However, the above ranking takes into account all singles from 1955, whereas the *Top 3000* ranking begins on July 9, 1955, the date "Rock Around The Clock" peaked at position #1.

THE TOP 100 ARTISTS 1955 -1991*

	ARTIST	POINTS
	1. ELVIS PRESLEY •	7857
	2. THE BEATLES •	4543
	3. STEVIE WONDER	3691
▲	4. ELTON JOHN	3542
	5. THE ROLLING STONES	3129
	6. PAUL McCARTNEY/WINGS	2970
	7. PAT BOONE	2826
	8. THE SUPREMES •	2735
	9. MARVIN GAYE •	2720
	10. ARETHA FRANKLIN	2713
▲	11. CHICAGO	2526
	12. THE TEMPTATIONS •	2466
	13. BEE GEES	2463
▲	14. MICHAEL JACKSON	2461
	15. RICKY NELSON •	2446
	16. THE BEACH BOYS •	2408
	17. NEIL DIAMOND	2406
▲	18. MADONNA	2386
	19. JAMES BROWN	2345
	20. DARYL HALL & JOHN OATES	2291
	21. CONNIE FRANCIS	2287
	22. THE 4 SEASONS	2241
	23. OLIVIA NEWTON-JOHN	2220
	24. FATS DOMINO	2196
	25. PAUL ANKA	2192
	26. BILLY JOEL	2139
▲	27. ROD STEWART	2116
	28. DIANA ROSS	2069
	29. RAY CHARLES	2029
	30. DIONNE WARWICK	1979
	31. THE EVERLY BROTHERS	1975
	32. BOBBY VINTON	1956
	33. PERRY COMO	1945
	34. KENNY ROGERS/FIRST EDITION	1933
	35. BRENDA LEE	1887
▲	36. GEORGE MICHAEL/WHAM!	1854
	37. FRANK SINATRA	1823
	38. THE JACKSON 5/JACKSONS	1808
	39. GLADYS KNIGHT & THE PIPS	1791
▲	40. PRINCE	1738
	41. THE MIRACLES	1735
	42. DONNA SUMMER	1728
	43. SAM COOKE	1717
	44. CARPENTERS	1691
▲	45. PHIL COLLINS	1687
	46. BARRY MANILOW	1668
	47. ANDY WILLIAMS	1638
	48. BARBRA STREISAND	1603
	49. NAT "KING" COLE •	1586
	50. THE PLATTERS •	1581

* :Ranking includes all records which hit the Top 40 on or before the July 27, 1991 cut-off date.
▲ = Hot Artist (at least five Top 40 hits from 1987 through July, 1991)
• = Deceased (solo artist or key member of a group)

Points are awarded according to the following formula:

1. Each artist's charted singles are given points based on their highest charted position:
   - # 1 = 100 points for its first week at # 1, plus 10 points for each additional week at # 1
   - # 2 = 90 points for its first week at # 2, plus 5 points for each additional week at # 2
   - # 3 = 80 points for its first week at # 3, plus 5 points for each additional week at # 3
   - # 4-5 = 70 points
   - # 6-10 = 60 points
   - # 11-20 = 50 points
   - # 21-30 = 45 points
   - # 31-40 = 40 points
2. Total weeks charted are added in.

When two artists combine for a hit record, such as Aretha Franklin and George Michael, the full point value is given to both artists. Duos such as Simon & Garfunkel, Hall & Oates, and Loggins & Messina are considered regular recording teams, and their points are not shared by either artist individually.

THE TOP 100 ARTISTS 1955 -1991

	ARTIST	POINTS
	51. CHUBBY CHECKER	1580
	52. THREE DOG NIGHT	1577
	53. BOBBY DARIN •	1542
	54. FOUR TOPS	1527
	55. ROY ORBISON •	1522
	56. BROOK BENTON •	1499
	57. LINDA RONSTADT	1487
	58. KOOL & THE GANG	1483
▲	59. WHITNEY HOUSTON	1469
	60. LIONEL RICHIE	1462
	61. NEIL SEDAKA	1446
▲	62. CHER	1445
	63. DION/DION & THE BELMONTS	1444
	64. THE 5TH DIMENSION	1394
▲	65. JANET JACKSON	1341
	66. JACKIE WILSON •	1336
▲	67. HEART	1321
	68. JOHN COUGAR MELLENCAMP	1308
	69. HERMAN'S HERMITS	1305
	70. EAGLES	1290
▲	71. HUEY LEWIS & THE NEWS	1285
	72. FOREIGNER	1280
	73. JOHNNY MATHIS	1271
	74. BOB SEGER	1261
▲	75. FLEETWOOD MAC	1254
	76. COMMODORES	1250
	77. JEFFERSON AIRPLANE/STARSHIP	1241
	78. GLEN CAMPBELL	1237
	79. ELECTRIC LIGHT ORCHESTRA	1211
	80. SPINNERS •	1203
	81. BOBBY RYDELL	1200
	82. TOMMY JAMES/SHONDELLS	1198
	83. SIMON & GARFUNKEL	1192
	84. JOHN DENVER	1170
	85. HERB ALPERT/TIJUANA BRASS	1169
	86. POINTER SISTERS	1166
	87. JOHNNY RIVERS	1161
	88. TOM JONES	1155
	89. RICK SPRINGFIELD	1126
	90. THE DAVE CLARK FIVE	1125
	91. DURAN DURAN	1122
	92. STYX	1119
	93. EARTH, WIND & FIRE	1114
	94. JOURNEY	1103
	95. DEAN MARTIN	1085
	96. JOHN LENNON •	1081
	97. TONY ORLANDO & DAWN	1070
	98. BRUCE SPRINGSTEEN	1068
	99. CREEDENCE CLEARWATER REVIVAL •	1064
▲	100. GLORIA ESTEFAN/ MIAMI SOUND MACHINE	1062

TOP ARTISTS BY DECADE

FIFTIES ('55-'59)

ARTIST	POINTS
1. ELVIS PRESLEY	3216
2. PAT BOONE	2446
3. PERRY COMO	1584
4. FATS DOMINO	1386
5. RICKY NELSON	1358
6. THE PLATTERS	1218
7. NAT "KING" COLE	1149
8. THE EVERLY BROTHERS	1048
9. FRANK SINATRA	1013
10. THE McGUIRE SISTERS	970
11. THE FOUR LADS	905
12. JOHNNY MATHIS	879
13. BILL HALEY & HIS COMETS	876
14. THE DIAMONDS	856
15. PATTI PAGE	838
16. PAUL ANKA	805
17. JIMMIE RODGERS	783
18. TERESA BREWER	718
19. CONNIE FRANCIS	702
20. FRANKIE AVALON	679
21.ANDY WILLIAMS	677
22. THE FONTANE SISTERS	672
23. CHUCK BERRY	630
24. THE AMES BROTHERS	605
25. BILLY VAUGHN	603

SIXTIES ('60-'69)

ARTIST	POINTS
1. THE BEATLES	4119
2. ELVIS PRESLEY	3412
3. THE SUPREMES	2281
4. THE 4 SEASONS	1967
5. BRENDA LEE	1887
6. THE BEACH BOYS	1847
7. RAY CHARLES	1732
8. MARVIN GAYE	1721
9. BOBBY VINTON	1705
10. CONNIE FRANCIS	1585
11. THE TEMPTATIONS	1564
12. THE ROLLING STONES	1493
13. CHUBBY CHECKER	1480
14. ROY ORBISON	1451
15. THE MIRACLES	1331
16. JAMES BROWN	1330
17. HERMAN'S HERMITS	1305
18. DION	1207
19. SAM COOKE	1166
20. ARETHA FRANKLIN	1153
21. DIONNE WARWICK	1138
22. STEVIE WONDER	1126
23. THE DAVE CLARK FIVE	1125
24. BROOK BENTON	1091
25. BOBBY RYDELL	1067

SEVENTIES ('70-'79)

ARTIST	POINTS
1. ELTON JOHN	2011
2. PAUL McCARTNEY/WINGS	2007
3. BEE GEES	1830
4. CARPENTERS	1633
5. THE JACKSON 5/JACKSONS	1537
6. STEVIE WONDER	1466
7. CHICAGO	1462
8. THREE DOG NIGHT	1292
9. OLIVIA NEWTON-JOHN	1257
10. NEIL DIAMOND	1241
11. ELVIS PRESLEY	1179
12. BARRY MANILOW	1145
13. EAGLES	1094
14. JOHN DENVER	1081
15. DIANA ROSS	1080
16. TONY ORLANDO & DAWN	1070
17. DONNA SUMMER	1068
18. GLADYS KNIGHT & THE PIPS	1045
19. HELEN REDDY	1021
20. ROD STEWART	978
21. BARBRA STREISAND	973
22. ARETHA FRANKLIN	954
23. EARTH, WIND & FIRE	938
24. JAMES BROWN	934
25. AL GREEN	920

EIGHTIES ('80-'89)

ARTIST	POINTS
1. MICHAEL JACKSON	1939
2. MADONNA	1867
3. DARYL HALL & JOHN OATES	1796
4. PRINCE	1669
5. GEORGE MICHAEL/WHAM!	1622
6. LIONEL RICHIE	1462
7. BILLY JOEL	1450
8. ELTON JOHN	1422
9. PHIL COLLINS	1379
10. JOHN COUGAR MELLENCAMP	1255
11. HUEY LEWIS & THE NEWS	1226
12. KOOL & THE GANG	1190
13. DURAN DURAN	1122
14. KENNY ROGERS	1119
15. WHITNEY HOUSTON	1104
16. STEVIE WONDER	1099
17. RICK SPRINGFIELD	1067
18. JOURNEY	1041
19. DIANA ROSS	989
20. BRUCE SPRINGSTEEN	976
21. PAUL McCARTNEY	963
22. OLIVIA NEWTON-JOHN	963
23. AIR SUPPLY	952
24. CHICAGO	940
25. BILLY OCEAN	940

TOP ARTIST ACHIEVEMENTS

MOST TOP 40 RECORDS

ARTIST	TOTAL
1. ELVIS PRESLEY	107
2. THE BEATLES	49
3. ELTON JOHN	48
4. STEVIE WONDER	46
5. JAMES BROWN	44
6. THE ROLLING STONES	41
7. ARETHA FRANKLIN	41
8. MARVIN GAYE	40
9. PAT BOONE	38
10. THE TEMPTATIONS	37
11. NEIL DIAMOND	37
12. FATS DOMINO	37
13. PAUL McCARTNEY/WINGS	35
14. CHICAGO	35
15. RICKY NELSON	35
16. THE BEACH BOYS	35
17. CONNIE FRANCIS	35
18. THE SUPREMES	33
19. PAUL ANKA	33
20. RAY CHARLES	33
21. BILLY JOEL	31
22. DIONNE WARWICK	31
23. THE 4 SEASONS	30
24. BOBBY VINTON	30

MOST #1 RECORDS

ARTIST	TOTAL
1. THE BEATLES	20
2. ELVIS PRESLEY	18
3. THE SUPREMES	12
4. MICHAEL JACKSON	11
5. STEVIE WONDER	10
6. PAUL McCARTNEY/WINGS	9
7. BEE GEES	9
8. MADONNA	9
9. GEORGE MICHAEL/WHAM!	9
10. WHITNEY HOUSTON	9
11. THE ROLLING STONES	8
12. ELTON JOHN	7
13. PHIL COLLINS	7
14. PAT BOONE	6
15. DARYL HALL & JOHN OATES	6
16. DIANA ROSS	6
17. PAULA ABDUL	6
18. THE 4 SEASONS	5
19. OLIVIA NEWTON-JOHN	5
20. BARBRA STREISAND	5
21. LIONEL RICHIE	5
22. JANET JACKSON	5
23. EAGLES	5
24. BON JOVI	5
25. KC & THE SUNSHINE BAND	5

MOST TOP 10 RECORDS

ARTIST	TOTAL
1. ELVIS PRESLEY	38
2. THE BEATLES	33
3. STEVIE WONDER	28
4. ELTON JOHN	23
5. THE ROLLING STONES	23
6. PAUL McCARTNEY/WINGS	22
7. MADONNA	22
8. MICHAEL JACKSON	21
9. THE SUPREMES	20
10. CHICAGO	20
11. RICKY NELSON	19
12. PAT BOONE	18
13. MARVIN GAYE	18
14. ARETHA FRANKLIN	17
15. GEORGE MICHAEL/WHAM!	17
16. DARYL HALL & JOHN OATES	16
17. CONNIE FRANCIS	16
18. THE TEMPTATIONS	15
19.BEE GEES	15
20. THE BEACH BOYS	15
21. THE 4 SEASONS	15
22. OLIVIA NEWTON-JOHN	15
23. THE EVERLY BROTHERS	15
24. PRINCE	15

MOST WEEKS HELD #1 POSITION

ARTIST	TOTAL
1. ELVIS PRESLEY	80
2. THE BEATLES	59
3. PAUL McCARTNEY/WINGS	30
4. MICHAEL JACKSON	29
5. BEE GEES	27
6. STEVIE WONDER	25
7. THE SUPREMES	22
8. GEORGE MICHAEL/WHAM!	22
9. PAT BOONE	21
10. LIONEL RICHIE	21
11. MADONNA	20
12. DIANA ROSS	20
13. ELTON JOHN	19
14. THE 4 SEASONS	18
15. OLIVIA NEWTON-JOHN	18
16. THE ROLLING STONES	17
17. ROD STEWART	17
18. WHITNEY HOUSTON	16
19. THE EVERLY BROTHERS	15
20. PHIL COLLINS	15
21. PAULA ABDUL	15
22. DARYL HALL & JOHN OATES	14
23. THE McGUIRE SISTERS	14

TOP RECORDS BY DECADE

YR	WEEKS CHR	T40	T10	#1	TITLE/ARTIST
					FIFTIES ('55-'59)
56	28	24	21	11	1. DON'T BE CRUEL/HOUND DOG...Elvis Presley
55	26	26	20	10	2. CHERRY PINK AND APPLE BLOSSOM WHITE...Perez Prado
55	21	21	18	10	3. SINCERELY...The McGuire Sisters
56	26	22	17	10	4. SINGING THE BLUES...Guy Mitchell
59	26	22	16	9	5. MACK THE KNIFE...Bobby Darin
57	30	22	15	9	6. ALL SHOOK UP...Elvis Presley
55	24	24	19	8	7. ROCK AROUND THE CLOCK...Bill Haley & His Comets
56	28	22	16	8	8. THE WAYWARD WIND...Gogi Grant
55	22	19	16	8	9. SIXTEEN TONS...Tennessee Ernie Ford
56	27	22	15	8	10. HEARTBREAK HOTEL...Elvis Presley
57	34	24	17	7	11. LOVE LETTERS IN THE SAND...Pat Boone
57	27	19	15	7	12. JAILHOUSE ROCK...Elvis Presley
57	25	18	14	7	13. (LET ME BE YOUR) TEDDY BEAR...Elvis Presley
58	21	18	12	7	14. AT THE HOP...Danny & The Juniors
55	21	21	17	6	15. LOVE IS A MANY-SPLENDORED THING...Four Aces
56	25	20	16	6	16. ROCK AND ROLL WALTZ...Kay Starr
56	24	20	16	6	17. THE POOR PEOPLE OF PARIS...Les Baxter
55	19	19	16	6	18. THE YELLOW ROSE OF TEXAS...Mitch Miller
56	24	19	15	6	19. MEMORIES ARE MADE OF THIS...Dean Martin
57	26	19	14	6	20. APRIL LOVE...Pat Boone
59	21	18	13	6	21. THE BATTLE OF NEW ORLEANS...Johnny Horton
57	21	17	13	6	22. YOUNG LOVE...Tab Hunter
58	22	19	12	6	23. IT'S ALL IN THE GAME...Tommy Edwards
58	14	14	10	6	24. THE PURPLE PEOPLE EATER...Sheb Wooley
57	31	23	16	5	25. TAMMY...Debbie Reynolds
					SIXTIES ('60-'69)
68	19	19	14	9	1. HEY JUDE...The Beatles
60	21	17	12	9	2. THE THEME FROM "A SUMMER PLACE"...Percy Faith
61	23	17	12	7	3. TOSSIN' AND TURNIN'...Bobby Lewis
64	15	14	12	7	4. I WANT TO HOLD YOUR HAND...The Beatles
66	15	13	12	7	5. I'M A BELIEVER...The Monkees
68	15	15	11	7	6. I HEARD IT THROUGH THE GRAPEVINE...Marvin Gaye
69	17	16	11	6	7. AQUARIUS/LET THE SUNSHINE IN...The 5th Dimension
60	16	14	11	6	8. ARE YOU LONESOME TO-NIGHT?...Elvis Presley
69	13	12	9	6	9. IN THE YEAR 2525 (EXORDIUM & TERMINUS)...Zager & Evans
60	20	16	11	5	10. IT'S NOW OR NEVER...Elvis Presley
62	18	14	11	5	11. I CAN'T STOP LOVING YOU...Ray Charles
68	18	15	10	5	12. LOVE IS BLUE...Paul Mauriat
62	16	14	10	5	13. BIG GIRLS DON'T CRY...The 4 Seasons
61	16	13	10	5	14. BIG BAD JOHN...Jimmy Dean
63	15	13	10	5	15. SUGAR SHACK...Jimmy Gilmer & The Fireballs
68	15	13	10	5	16. HONEY...Bobby Goldsboro
67	17	15	9	5	17. TO SIR WITH LOVE...Lulu
60	17	13	9	5	18. CATHY'S CLOWN...The Everly Brothers
68	14	13	9	5	19. PEOPLE GOT TO BE FREE...The Rascals
69	12	12	9	5	20. GET BACK...The Beatles
66	13	11	9	5	21. THE BALLAD OF THE GREEN BERETS...SSgt Barry Sadler
62	14	12	7	5	22. SHERRY...The 4 Seasons
64	10	9	6	5	23. CAN'T BUY ME LOVE...The Beatles
69	22	18	12	4	24. SUGAR, SUGAR...The Archies
68	16	14	11	4	25. (SITTIN' ON) THE DOCK OF THE BAY...Otis Redding

TOP RECORDS BY DECADE					
	WEEKS				TITLE/ARTIST
YR	CHR	T40	T10	#1	SEVENTIES ('70-'79)
77	25	21	14	10	1. YOU LIGHT UP MY LIFE...Debby Boone
78	20	18	13	8	2. NIGHT FEVER...Bee Gees
76	23	17	11	8	3. TONIGHT'S THE NIGHT (GONNA BE ALRIGHT)...Rod Stewart
78	25	19	12	7	4. SHADOW DANCING...Andy Gibb
78	25	19	15	6	5. LE FREAK...Chic
79	22	16	12	6	6. MY SHARONA...The Knack
72	18	15	11	6	7. THE FIRST TIME EVER I SAW YOUR FACE...Roberta Flack
72	18	15	11	6	8. ALONE AGAIN (NATURALLY)...Gilbert O'Sullivan
71	17	15	11	6	9. JOY TO THE WORLD...Three Dog Night
70	14	13	10	6	10. BRIDGE OVER TROUBLED WATER...Simon & Garfunkel
77	23	17	12	5	11. BEST OF MY LOVE...The Emotions
70	16	16	11	5	12. I'LL BE THERE...The Jackson 5
76	19	15	11	5	13. SILLY LOVE SONGS...Wings
71	17	15	11	5	14. MAGGIE MAY...Rod Stewart
79	20	15	10	5	15. BAD GIRLS...Donna Summer
71	17	15	10	5	16. IT'S TOO LATE...Carole King
73	16	13	9	5	17. KILLING ME SOFTLY WITH HIS SONG...Roberta Flack
71	15	12	9	5	18. ONE BAD APPLE...The Osmonds
77	31	23	16	4	19. I JUST WANT TO BE YOUR EVERYTHING...Andy Gibb
78	27	22	13	4	20. STAYIN' ALIVE...Bee Gees
70	22	19	13	4	21. RAINDROPS KEEP FALLIN' ON MY HEAD...B.J. Thomas
79	21	18	12	4	22. DA YA THINK I'M SEXY?...Rod Stewart
78	23	17	12	4	23. KISS YOU ALL OVER...Exile
73	23	17	11	4	24. TIE A YELLOW RIBBON ROUND THE OLE OAK TREE ...Dawn featuring Tony Orlando
72	19	17	11	4	25. AMERICAN PIE - Parts I & II...Don McLean
					EIGHTIES ('80-'89)
81	26	21	15	10	1. PHYSICAL...Olivia Newton-John
81	26	20	14	9	2. BETTE DAVIS EYES...Kim Carnes
81	27	19	13	9	3. ENDLESS LOVE...Diana Ross & Lionel Richie
83	22	20	13	8	4. EVERY BREATH YOU TAKE...The Police
82	20	16	12	7	5. I LOVE ROCK 'N ROLL...Joan Jett & The Blackhearts
82	19	15	12	7	6. EBONY AND IVORY...Paul McCartney with Stevie Wonder
83	24	17	11	7	7. BILLIE JEAN...Michael Jackson
82	25	18	15	6	8. EYE OF THE TIGER...Survivor
83	25	20	14	6	9. FLASHDANCE...WHAT A FEELING...Irene Cara
80	25	19	13	6	10. LADY...Kenny Rogers
83	22	18	13	6	11. SAY SAY SAY...Paul McCartney & Michael Jackson
82	25	20	12	6	12. CENTERFOLD...The J. Geils Band
80	25	19	12	6	13. CALL ME...Blondie
84	19	14	9	6	14. LIKE A VIRGIN...Madonna
80	22	19	14	5	15. (JUST LIKE) STARTING OVER...John Lennon
84	21	16	11	5	16. WHEN DOVES CRY...Prince
84	21	15	10	5	17. JUMP...Van Halen
80	29	17	14	4	18. UPSIDE DOWN...Diana Ross
83	24	17	13	4	19. ALL NIGHT LONG (ALL NIGHT)...Lionel Richie
82	23	17	13	4	20. MANEATER...Daryl Hall & John Oates
80	25	19	12	4	21. ANOTHER BRICK IN THE WALL (PART II)...Pink Floyd
80	22	17	12	4	22. CRAZY LITTLE THING CALLED LOVE...Queen
83	29	18	11	4	23. TOTAL ECLIPSE OF THE HEART...Bonnie Tyler
83	25	19	10	4	24. DOWN UNDER...Men At Work
86	23	17	10	4	25. THAT'S WHAT FRIENDS ARE FOR...Dionne & Friends

#1 RECORDS LISTED CHRONOLOGICALLY 1955-1991

For the years 1955 through 1958 (when *Billboard* published more than one weekly pop chart) special columns are used to show the weeks each #1 record spent on each of the various pop charts.

The date shown is the earliest date that a record hit #1 on any of the pop charts. The weeks column (next to date) lists the total weeks at #1, from whichever chart it achieved its highest total. This total is not a combined total from the various pop charts.

Because of the multiple charts used in our research, some dates are duplicated, as certain #1 hits may have peaked on the same week on different charts. *Billboard* also showed ties at #1 on some of these charts, therefore the total weeks for each year may calculate out to more than 52.

Lines are drawn in on the charts column to show when any of the four pop charts were not published.

See the introduction of this book for more details about researching the four pop charts.

DATE: Date record first hit the #1 position
WKS : Total weeks record held the #1 position
* : Consensus #1 record—hit #1 on all pop charts published ('55-'58)
† : Indicates record hit #1, dropped down, then returned to the #1 spot

CHARTS COLUMN:
BS : Best Sellers
JY : Jockeys
JB : Juke Box
TP : Top 100
HT : Hot 100

819 records have hit the #1 position on *Billboard*'s pop charts from 1955 through July 27, 1991. "The Twist," even though it hit #1 in 1960 and again in 1962, is counted only once. There have been 753 #1 records since the Hot 100 chart began in 1958.

Billboard has not published an issue at the end of the year since 1976; therefore, the year's last regular chart is considered frozen and the #1 hit remains the same for the unpublished week. This frozen week is included when calculating total weeks at #1.

DATE	WKS	RECORD TITLE	ARTIST	BS	JY	JB	TP
		1955					
1/01	4	* 1. LET ME GO LOVER	Joan Weber	2	4†	4	—
2/05	3	2. HEARTS OF STONE	The Fontane Sisters	1	—	3	—
2/12	10	* 3. SINCERELY	The McGuire Sisters	6	10	7	—
3/26	5	* 4. THE BALLAD OF DAVY CROCKETT	Bill Hayes	5	3	3	—
4/30	10	* 5. CHERRY PINK AND APPLE BLOSSOM WHITE	Perez Prado	10	6†	8	—
5/14	3	6. DANCE WITH ME HENRY	Georgia Gibbs	—	—	3	—
5/14	2	7. UNCHAINED MELODY	Les Baxter	—	2†	—	—
7/09	8	* 8. ROCK AROUND THE CLOCK	Bill Haley & His Comets	8	6†	7	—
7/09	2	9. LEARNIN' THE BLUES	Frank Sinatra	—	2†	—	—
9/03	6	* 10. THE YELLOW ROSE OF TEXAS	Mitch Miller	6†	6	6	—
9/17	2	11. AIN'T THAT A SHAME	Pat Boone	—	—	2	—
10/08	6	* 12. LOVE IS A MANY-SPLENDORED THING Top 100 chart debuted on 11/12/55	Four Aces	2†	6	3	3
10/29	4	13. AUTUMN LEAVES	Roger Williams	4	—	—	—
11/26	8	* 14. SIXTEEN TONS	Tennessee Ernie Ford	7	6	8	6
		1956					
1/07	6	* 1. MEMORIES ARE MADE OF THIS	Dean Martin	5	6	4	5
2/18	6	* 2. ROCK AND ROLL WALTZ	Kay Starr	1	1	6	4
2/18	2	3. THE GREAT PRETENDER	The Platters	—	2	1	2
2/25	4	4. LISBON ANTIGUA	Nelson Riddle	4	2†	—	—
3/17	6	* 5. THE POOR PEOPLE OF PARIS	Les Baxter	4	6†	3	6
4/21	8	* 6. HEARTBREAK HOTEL	Elvis Presley	8	3	8	7
5/05	1	7. HOT DIGGITY	Perry Como	—	1	—	—

DATE	WKS	RECORD TITLE	ARTIST	CHARTS BS	JY	JB	TP
		1956 CONTINUED		BS	JY	JB	TP
6/02	3	8. MOONGLOW AND THEME FROM "PICNIC"	Morris Stoloff	—	3	—	—
6/16	8	* 9. THE WAYWARD WIND	Gogi Grant	6	8	4	7
7/28	4	10. I ALMOST LOST MY MIND	Pat Boone	—	—	4	2
7/28	1	11. I WANT YOU, I NEED YOU, I LOVE YOU	Elvis Presley	1	—	—	—
8/04	5	* 12. MY PRAYER	The Platters	2	3	1	5
8/18	11	* 13. DON'T BE CRUEL/ 14. HOUND DOG	Elvis Presley	11	8	11	7
11/03	5	* 15. LOVE ME TENDER	Elvis Presley	5	5	1	4†
11/03	3	16. THE GREEN DOOR	Jim Lowe	—	—	3	3
12/08	10	* 17. SINGING THE BLUES	Guy Mitchell	9	9	10	9
		1957					
2/09	3	1. TOO MUCH	Elvis Presley	3	—	1	—
2/09	1	2. DON'T FORBID ME	Pat Boone	—	—	1	1
2/09	1	3. YOUNG LOVE	Sonny James	—	1	—	—
2/16	6	* 4. YOUNG LOVE	Tab Hunter	4	6	5†	6
3/30	3	5. BUTTERFLY	Andy Williams	—	2	—	3
3/30	1	6. PARTY DOLL	Buddy Knox	1	—	—	—
4/06	2	7. ROUND AND ROUND	Perry Como	1	2	—	1
4/06	2	8. BUTTERFLY	Charlie Gracie	—	—	2	—
4/13	9	* 9. ALL SHOOK UP	Elvis Presley	8	7	9	8
6/03	7	* 10. LOVE LETTERS IN THE SAND Juke Box chart terminated on 6/17/57	Pat Boone	5	7	—	5
7/08	7	* 11. (LET ME BE YOUR) TEDDY BEAR	Elvis Presley	7	3		7
8/19	5	* 12. TAMMY	Debbie Reynolds	3†	5		5
9/09	1	13. DIANA	Paul Anka	1	—		—
9/23	4	* 14. HONEYCOMB	Jimmie Rodgers	2	4		2
9/23	1	15. THAT'LL BE THE DAY	The Crickets	1	—		—
10/14	4	* 16. WAKE UP LITTLE SUSIE	The Everly Brothers	1	4		2
10/21	7	* 17. JAILHOUSE ROCK	Elvis Presley	7†	2		6
10/21	1	18. CHANCES ARE	Johnny Mathis	—	1		—
12/02	3	* 19. YOU SEND ME	Sam Cooke	2	1		3
12/16	6	* 20. APRIL LOVE	Pat Boone	2	6		1
		1958					
1/06	7	* 1. AT THE HOP	Danny & The Juniors	5	3		7
2/10	5	* 2. DON'T	Elvis Presley	5	1		1
2/17	4	3. SUGARTIME	The McGuire Sisters	—	4		—
2/24	2	4. GET A JOB	The Silhouettes	—	—		2
3/17	5	* 5. TEQUILA	The Champs	5	2		5
3/24	1	6. CATCH A FALLING STAR	Perry Como	—	1		—
4/14	4	7. HE'S GOT THE WHOLE WORLD (IN HIS HANDS)	Laurie London	—	4		—
4/21	1	* 8. TWILIGHT TIME	The Platters	1	1		1
4/28	3	9. WITCH DOCTOR	David Seville	2	—		3
5/12	5	* 10. ALL I HAVE TO DO IS DREAM	The Everly Brothers	4	5		3
6/09	6	* 11. THE PURPLE PEOPLE EATER	Sheb Wooley	6	4		6
7/21	2	12. HARD HEADED WOMAN	Elvis Presley	2	1		—
7/21	1	13. YAKETY YAK	The Coasters	—	—		1

DATE	WKS	RECORD TITLE	ARTIST	BS	JY	TP	HT
		1958 CONTINUED					
7/28	1	14. PATRICIA Jockeys and Top 100 charts terminated on 7/28/58	Perez Prado	—	1	1	
8/04	2	* 15. POOR LITTLE FOOL Hot 100 chart debuted on 8/4/58	Ricky Nelson	2			2
8/18	5	* 16. NEL BLU DIPINTO DI BLU (VOLARE)	Domenico Modugno	5†			5†
8/25	1	17. LITTLE STAR	The Elegants	—			1
8/25	1	18. BIRD DOG	The Everly Brothers	1			—
9/29	6	* 19. IT'S ALL IN THE GAME Best Sellers chart terminated on 10/13/58 Hot 100 chart used exclusively here on	Tommy Edwards	3			6
11/10	2	20. IT'S ONLY MAKE BELIEVE	Conway Twitty				2†
11/17	1	21. TOM DOOLEY	The Kingston Trio				1
12/01	3	22. TO KNOW HIM, IS TO LOVE HIM	The Teddy Bears				3
12/22	4	23. THE CHIPMUNK SONG	The Chipmunks				4

DATE	WKS	RECORD TITLE	ARTIST
		1959	
1/19	3	1. SMOKE GETS IN YOUR EYES	The Platters
2/09	4	2. STAGGER LEE	Lloyd Price
3/09	5	3. VENUS	Frankie Avalon
4/13	4	4. COME SOFTLY TO ME	The Fleetwoods
5/11	1	5. THE HAPPY ORGAN	Dave 'Baby' Cortez
5/18	2	6. KANSAS CITY	Wilbert Harrison
6/01	6	7. THE BATTLE OF NEW ORLEANS	Johnny Horton
7/13	4	8. LONELY BOY	Paul Anka
8/10	2	9. A BIG HUNK O' LOVE	Elvis Presley
8/24	4	10. THE THREE BELLS	The Browns
9/21	2	11. SLEEP WALK	Santo & Johnny
10/05	9	†12. MACK THE KNIFE	Bobby Darin
11/16	1	13. MR. BLUE	The Fleetwoods
12/14	2	14. HEARTACHES BY THE NUMBER	Guy Mitchell
12/28	1	15. WHY	Frankie Avalon
		1960	
1/04	2	1. EL PASO	Marty Robbins
1/18	3	2. RUNNING BEAR	Johnny Preston
2/08	2	3. TEEN ANGEL	Mark Dinning
2/22	9	4. THE THEME FROM "A SUMMER PLACE"	Percy Faith
4/25	4	5. STUCK ON YOU	Elvis Presley
5/23	5	6. CATHY'S CLOWN	The Everly Brothers
6/27	2	7. EVERYBODY'S SOMEBODY'S FOOL	Connie Francis
7/11	1	8. ALLEY-OOP	Hollywood Argyles
7/18	3	9. I'M SORRY	Brenda Lee
8/08	1	10. ITSY BITSY TEENIE WEENIE YELLOW POLKADOT BIKINI	Brian Hyland
8/15	5	11. IT'S NOW OR NEVER	Elvis Presley
9/19	1	12. THE TWIST re-entered #1 position in 1962 for 2 more weeks	Chubby Checker
9/26	2	13. MY HEART HAS A MIND OF ITS OWN	Connie Francis
10/10	1	14. MR. CUSTER	Larry Verne

DATE	WKS	RECORD TITLE	ARTIST
1960 CONTINUED			
10/17	3	†15. SAVE THE LAST DANCE FOR ME	The Drifters
10/24	1	16. I WANT TO BE WANTED	Brenda Lee
11/14	1	17. GEORGIA ON MY MIND	Ray Charles
11/21	1	18. STAY	Maurice Williams & The Zodiacs
11/28	6	19. ARE YOU LONESOME TO-NIGHT?	Elvis Presley
1961			
1/09	3	1. WONDERLAND BY NIGHT	Bert Kaempfert
1/30	2	2. WILL YOU LOVE ME TOMORROW	The Shirelles
2/13	2	3. CALCUTTA	Lawrence Welk
2/27	3	4. PONY TIME	Chubby Checker
3/20	2	5. SURRENDER	Elvis Presley
4/03	3	6. BLUE MOON	The Marcels
4/24	4	7. RUNAWAY	Del Shannon
5/22	1	8. MOTHER-IN-LAW	Ernie K-Doe
5/29	2	†9. TRAVELIN' MAN	Ricky Nelson
6/05	1	10. RUNNING SCARED	Roy Orbison
6/19	1	11. MOODY RIVER	Pat Boone
6/26	2	12. QUARTER TO THREE	U.S. Bonds
7/10	7	13. TOSSIN' AND TURNIN'	Bobby Lewis
8/28	1	14. WOODEN HEART	Joe Dowell
9/04	2	15. MICHAEL	The Highwaymen
9/18	3	16. TAKE GOOD CARE OF MY BABY	Bobby Vee
10/09	2	17. HIT THE ROAD JACK	Ray Charles
10/23	2	18. RUNAROUND SUE	Dion
11/06	5	19. BIG BAD JOHN	Jimmy Dean
12/11	1	20. PLEASE MR. POSTMAN	The Marvelettes
12/18	3	21. THE LION SLEEPS TONIGHT	The Tokens
1962			
1/13	2	1. THE TWIST first entered #1 position in 1960 for 1 week	Chubby Checker
1/27	3	2. PEPPERMINT TWIST	Joey Dee & The Starliters
2/17	3	3. DUKE OF EARL	Gene Chandler
3/10	3	4. HEY! BABY	Bruce Channel
3/31	1	5. DON'T BREAK THE HEART THAT LOVES YOU	Connie Francis
4/07	2	6. JOHNNY ANGEL	Shelley Fabares
4/21	2	7. GOOD LUCK CHARM	Elvis Presley
5/05	3	8. SOLDIER BOY	The Shirelles
5/26	1	9. STRANGER ON THE SHORE	Mr. Acker Bilk
6/02	5	10. I CAN'T STOP LOVING YOU	Ray Charles
7/07	1	11. THE STRIPPER	David Rose
7/14	4	12. ROSES ARE RED (MY LOVE)	Bobby Vinton
8/11	2	13. BREAKING UP IS HARD TO DO	Neil Sedaka
8/25	1	14. THE LOCO-MOTION	Little Eva
9/01	2	15. SHEILA	Tommy Roe
9/15	5	16. SHERRY	The 4 Seasons
10/20	2	17. MONSTER MASH	Bobby "Boris" Pickett
11/03	2	18. HE'S A REBEL	The Crystals
11/17	5	19. BIG GIRLS DON'T CRY	The 4 Seasons
12/22	3	20. TELSTAR	The Tornadoes

DATE	WKS	RECORD TITLE	ARTIST
1963			
1/12	2	1. GO AWAY LITTLE GIRL	Steve Lawrence
1/26	2	2. WALK RIGHT IN	The Rooftop Singers
2/09	3	3. HEY PAULA	Paul & Paula
3/02	3	4. WALK LIKE A MAN	The 4 Seasons
3/23	1	5. OUR DAY WILL COME	Ruby & The Romantics
3/30	4	6. HE'S SO FINE	The Chiffons
4/27	3	7. I WILL FOLLOW HIM	Little Peggy March
5/18	2	8. IF YOU WANNA BE HAPPY	Jimmy Soul
6/01	2	9. IT'S MY PARTY	Lesley Gore
6/15	3	10. SUKIYAKI	Kyu Sakamoto
7/06	2	11. EASIER SAID THAN DONE	The Essex
7/20	2	12. SURF CITY	Jan & Dean
8/03	1	13. SO MUCH IN LOVE	The Tymes
8/10	3	14. FINGERTIPS - PT 2	Little Stevie Wonder
8/31	3	15. MY BOYFRIEND'S BACK	The Angels
9/21	3	16. BLUE VELVET	Bobby Vinton
10/12	5	17. SUGAR SHACK	Jimmy Gilmer & The Fireballs
11/16	1	18. DEEP PURPLE	Nino Tempo & April Stevens
11/23	2	19. I'M LEAVING IT UP TO YOU	Dale & Grace
12/07	4	20. DOMINIQUE	The Singing Nun
1964			
1/04	4	1. THERE! I'VE SAID IT AGAIN	Bobby Vinton
2/01	7	2. I WANT TO HOLD YOUR HAND	The Beatles
3/21	2	3. SHE LOVES YOU	The Beatles
4/04	5	4. CAN'T BUY ME LOVE	The Beatles
5/09	1	5. HELLO, DOLLY!	Louis Armstrong
5/16	2	6. MY GUY	Mary Wells
5/30	1	7. LOVE ME DO	The Beatles
6/06	3	8. CHAPEL OF LOVE	The Dixie Cups
6/27	1	9. A WORLD WITHOUT LOVE	Peter & Gordon
7/04	2	10. I GET AROUND	The Beach Boys
7/18	2	11. RAG DOLL	The 4 Seasons
8/01	2	12. A HARD DAY'S NIGHT	The Beatles
8/15	1	13. EVERYBODY LOVES SOMEBODY	Dean Martin
8/22	2	14. WHERE DID OUR LOVE GO	The Supremes
9/05	3	15. THE HOUSE OF THE RISING SUN	The Animals
9/26	3	16. OH, PRETTY WOMAN	Roy Orbison
10/17	2	17. DO WAH DIDDY DIDDY	Manfred Mann
10/31	4	18. BABY LOVE	The Supremes
11/28	1	19. LEADER OF THE PACK	The Shangri-Las
12/05	1	20. RINGO	Lorne Greene
12/12	1	21. MR. LONELY	Bobby Vinton
12/19	2	†22. COME SEE ABOUT ME	The Supremes
12/26	3	23. I FEEL FINE	The Beatles

DATE	WKS	RECORD TITLE	ARTIST
1965			
1/23	2	1. DOWNTOWN	Petula Clark
2/06	2	2. YOU'VE LOST THAT LOVIN' FEELIN'	The Righteous Brothers
2/20	2	3. THIS DIAMOND RING	Gary Lewis & The Playboys
3/06	1	4. MY GIRL	The Temptations
3/13	2	5. EIGHT DAYS A WEEK	The Beatles
3/27	2	6. STOP! IN THE NAME OF LOVE	The Supremes
4/10	2	7. I'M TELLING YOU NOW	Freddie & The Dreamers
4/24	1	8. GAME OF LOVE	Wayne Fontana & The Mindbenders
5/01	3	9. MRS. BROWN YOU'VE GOT A LOVELY DAUGHTER	Herman's Hermits
5/22	1	10. TICKET TO RIDE	The Beatles
5/29	2	11. HELP ME, RHONDA	The Beach Boys
6/12	1	12. BACK IN MY ARMS AGAIN	The Supremes
6/19	2	†13. I CAN'T HELP MYSELF	Four Tops
6/26	1	14. MR. TAMBOURINE MAN	The Byrds
7/10	4	15. (I CAN'T GET NO) SATISFACTION	The Rolling Stones
8/07	1	16. I'M HENRY VIII, I AM	Herman's Hermits
8/14	3	17. I GOT YOU BABE	Sonny & Cher
9/04	3	18. HELP!	The Beatles
9/25	1	19. EVE OF DESTRUCTION	Barry McGuire
10/02	1	20. HANG ON SLOOPY	The McCoys
10/09	4	21. YESTERDAY	The Beatles
11/06	2	22. GET OFF OF MY CLOUD	The Rolling Stones
11/20	2	23. I HEAR A SYMPHONY	The Supremes
12/04	3	24. TURN! TURN! TURN!	The Byrds
12/25	1	25. OVER AND OVER	The Dave Clark Five
1966			
1/01	2	†1. THE SOUNDS OF SILENCE	Simon & Garfunkel
1/08	3	†2. WE CAN WORK IT OUT	The Beatles
2/05	2	3. MY LOVE	Petula Clark
2/19	1	4. LIGHTNIN' STRIKES	Lou Christie
2/26	1	5. THESE BOOTS ARE MADE FOR WALKIN'	Nancy Sinatra
3/05	5	6. THE BALLAD OF THE GREEN BERETS	SSgt Barry Sadler
4/09	3	7. (YOU'RE MY) SOUL AND INSPIRATION	The Righteous Brothers
4/30	1	8. GOOD LOVIN'	The Young Rascals
5/07	3	9. MONDAY, MONDAY	The Mamas & The Papas
5/28	2	10. WHEN A MAN LOVES A WOMAN	Percy Sledge
6/11	2	11. PAINT IT, BLACK	The Rolling Stones
6/25	2	†12. PAPERBACK WRITER	The Beatles
7/02	1	13. STRANGERS IN THE NIGHT	Frank Sinatra
7/16	2	14. HANKY PANKY	Tommy James & The Shondells
7/30	2	15. WILD THING	The Troggs
8/13	3	16. SUMMER IN THE CITY	The Lovin' Spoonful
9/03	1	17. SUNSHINE SUPERMAN	Donovan
9/10	2	18. YOU CAN'T HURRY LOVE	The Supremes
9/24	3	19. CHERISH	The Association
10/15	2	20. REACH OUT I'LL BE THERE	Four Tops

DATE	WKS	RECORD TITLE	ARTIST
1966 CONTINUED			
10/29	1	21. 96 TEARS	? & The Mysterians
11/05	1	22. LAST TRAIN TO CLARKSVILLE	The Monkees
11/12	1	23. POOR SIDE OF TOWN	Johnny Rivers
11/19	2	24. YOU KEEP ME HANGIN' ON	The Supremes
12/03	3	†25. WINCHESTER CATHEDRAL	The New Vaudeville Band
12/10	1	26. GOOD VIBRATIONS	The Beach Boys
12/31	7	27. I'M A BELIEVER	The Monkees
1967			
2/18	2	1. KIND OF A DRAG	The Buckinghams
3/04	1	2. RUBY TUESDAY	The Rolling Stones
3/11	1	3. LOVE IS HERE AND NOW YOU'RE GONE	The Supremes
3/18	1	4. PENNY LANE	The Beatles
3/25	3	5. HAPPY TOGETHER	The Turtles
4/15	4	6. SOMETHIN' STUPID	Nancy & Frank Sinatra
5/13	1	7. THE HAPPENING	The Supremes
5/20	4	†8. GROOVIN'	The Young Rascals
6/03	2	9. RESPECT	Aretha Franklin
7/01	4	10. WINDY	The Association
7/29	3	11. LIGHT MY FIRE	The Doors
8/19	1	12. ALL YOU NEED IS LOVE	The Beatles
8/26	4	13. ODE TO BILLIE JOE	Bobbie Gentry
9/23	4	14. THE LETTER	The Box Tops
10/21	5	15. TO SIR WITH LOVE	Lulu
11/25	1	16. INCENSE AND PEPPERMINTS	Strawberry Alarm Clock
12/02	4	17. DAYDREAM BELIEVER	The Monkees
12/30	3	18. HELLO GOODBYE	The Beatles
1968			
1/20	2	1. JUDY IN DISGUISE (WITH GLASSES)	John Fred & His Playboy Band
2/03	1	2. GREEN TAMBOURINE	The Lemon Pipers
2/10	5	3. LOVE IS BLUE	Paul Mauriat
3/16	4	4. (SITTIN' ON) THE DOCK OF THE BAY	Otis Redding
4/13	5	5. HONEY	Bobby Goldsboro
5/18	2	6. TIGHTEN UP	Archie Bell & The Drells
6/01	3	7. MRS. ROBINSON	Simon & Garfunkel
6/22	4	8. THIS GUY'S IN LOVE WITH YOU	Herb Alpert
7/20	2	9. GRAZING IN THE GRASS	Hugh Masekela
8/03	2	10. HELLO, I LOVE YOU	The Doors
8/17	5	11. PEOPLE GOT TO BE FREE	The Rascals
9/21	1	12. HARPER VALLEY P.T.A.	Jeannie C. Riley
9/28	9	13. HEY JUDE	The Beatles
11/30	2	14. LOVE CHILD	Diana Ross & The Supremes
12/14	7	15. I HEARD IT THROUGH THE GRAPEVINE	Marvin Gaye

DATE	WKS	RECORD TITLE	ARTIST
1969			
2/01	2	1. CRIMSON AND CLOVER	Tommy James & The Shondells
2/15	4	2. EVERYDAY PEOPLE	Sly & The Family Stone
3/15	4	3. DIZZY	Tommy Roe
4/12	6	4. AQUARIUS/LET THE SUNSHINE IN	The 5th Dimension
5/24	5	5. GET BACK	The Beatles
6/28	2	6. LOVE THEME FROM ROMEO & JULIET	Henry Mancini
7/12	6	7. IN THE YEAR 2525 (EXORDIUM & TERMINUS)	Zager & Evans
8/23	4	8. HONKY TONK WOMEN	The Rolling Stones
9/20	4	9. SUGAR, SUGAR	The Archies
10/18	2	10. I CAN'T GET NEXT TO YOU	The Temptations
11/01	1	11. SUSPICIOUS MINDS	Elvis Presley
11/08	3	12. WEDDING BELL BLUES	The 5th Dimension
11/29	1	13. COME TOGETHER	The Beatles
12/06	2	14. NA NA HEY HEY KISS HIM GOODBYE	Steam
12/20	1	15. LEAVING ON A JET PLANE	Peter, Paul & Mary
12/27	1	16. SOMEDAY WE'LL BE TOGETHER	Diana Ross & The Supremes
1970			
1/03	4	1. RAINDROPS KEEP FALLIN' ON MY HEAD	B.J. Thomas
1/31	1	2. I WANT YOU BACK	The Jackson 5
2/07	1	3. VENUS	The Shocking Blue
2/14	2	4. THANK YOU (FALETTINME BE MICE ELF AGIN)	Sly & The Family Stone
2/28	6	5. BRIDGE OVER TROUBLED WATER	Simon & Garfunkel
4/11	2	6. LET IT BE	The Beatles
4/25	2	7. ABC	The Jackson 5
5/09	3	8. AMERICAN WOMAN	The Guess Who
5/30	2	9. EVERYTHING IS BEAUTIFUL	Ray Stevens
6/13	2	10. THE LONG AND WINDING ROAD	The Beatles
6/27	2	11. THE LOVE YOU SAVE	The Jackson 5
7/11	2	12. MAMA TOLD ME (NOT TO COME)	Three Dog Night
7/25	4	13. (THEY LONG TO BE) CLOSE TO YOU	Carpenters
8/22	1	14. MAKE IT WITH YOU	Bread
8/29	3	15. WAR	Edwin Starr
9/19	3	16. AIN'T NO MOUNTAIN HIGH ENOUGH	Diana Ross
10/10	1	17. CRACKLIN' ROSIE	Neil Diamond
10/17	5	18. I'LL BE THERE	The Jackson 5
11/21	3	19. I THINK I LOVE YOU	The Partridge Family
12/12	2	20. THE TEARS OF A CLOWN	Smokey Robinson & The Miracles
12/26	4	21. MY SWEET LORD	George Harrison

DATE	WKS	RECORD TITLE	ARTIST
1971			
1/23	3	1. KNOCK THREE TIMES	Dawn
2/13	5	2. ONE BAD APPLE	The Osmonds
3/20	2	3. ME AND BOBBY MCGEE	Janis Joplin
4/03	2	4. JUST MY IMAGINATION (RUNNING AWAY WITH ME)	The Temptations
4/17	6	5. JOY TO THE WORLD	Three Dog Night
5/29	2	6. BROWN SUGAR	The Rolling Stones
6/12	1	7. WANT ADS	The Honey Cone
6/19	5	8. IT'S TOO LATE	Carole King
7/24	1	9. INDIAN RESERVATION	Raiders
7/31	1	10. YOU'VE GOT A FRIEND	James Taylor
8/07	4	11. HOW CAN YOU MEND A BROKEN HEART	The Bee Gees
9/04	1	12. UNCLE ALBERT/ADMIRAL HALSEY	Paul & Linda McCartney
9/11	3	13. GO AWAY LITTLE GIRL	Donny Osmond
10/02	5	14. MAGGIE MAY	Rod Stewart
11/06	2	15. GYPSYS, TRAMPS & THIEVES	Cher
11/20	2	16. THEME FROM SHAFT	Isaac Hayes
12/04	3	17. FAMILY AFFAIR	Sly & The Family Stone
12/25	3	18. BRAND NEW KEY	Melanie
1972			
1/15	4	1. AMERICAN PIE - PARTS I & II	Don McLean
2/12	1	2. LET'S STAY TOGETHER	Al Green
2/19	4	3. WITHOUT YOU	Nilsson
3/18	1	4. HEART OF GOLD	Neil Young
3/25	3	5. A HORSE WITH NO NAME	America
4/15	6	6. THE FIRST TIME EVER I SAW YOUR FACE	Roberta Flack
5/27	1	7. OH GIRL	Chi-Lites
6/03	1	8. I'LL TAKE YOU THERE	The Staple Singers
6/10	3	9. THE CANDY MAN	Sammy Davis, Jr.
7/01	1	10. SONG SUNG BLUE	Neil Diamond
7/08	3	11. LEAN ON ME	Bill Withers
7/29	6	†12. ALONE AGAIN (NATURALLY)	Gilbert O'Sullivan
8/26	1	13. BRANDY (YOU'RE A FINE GIRL)	Looking Glass
9/16	1	14. BLACK & WHITE	Three Dog Night
9/23	3	15. BABY DON'T GET HOOKED ON ME	Mac Davis
10/14	1	16. BEN	Michael Jackson
10/21	2	17. MY DING-A-LING	Chuck Berry
11/04	4	18. I CAN SEE CLEARLY NOW	Johnny Nash
12/02	1	19. PAPA WAS A ROLLIN' STONE	The Temptations
12/09	1	20. I AM WOMAN	Helen Reddy
12/16	3	21. ME AND MRS. JONES	Billy Paul

DATE	WKS	RECORD TITLE	ARTIST
1973			
1/06	3	1. YOU'RE SO VAIN	Carly Simon
1/27	1	2. SUPERSTITION	Stevie Wonder
2/03	3	3. CROCODILE ROCK	Elton John
2/24	5	†4. KILLING ME SOFTLY WITH HIS SONG	Roberta Flack
3/24	1	5. LOVE TRAIN	O'Jays
4/07	2	6. THE NIGHT THE LIGHTS WENT OUT IN GEORGIA	Vicki Lawrence
4/21	4	7. TIE A YELLOW RIBBON ROUND THE OLE OAK TREE	Dawn featuring Tony Orlando
5/19	1	8. YOU ARE THE SUNSHINE OF MY LIFE	Stevie Wonder
5/26	1	9. FRANKENSTEIN	The Edgar Winter Group
6/02	4	10. MY LOVE	Paul McCartney & Wings
6/30	1	11. GIVE ME LOVE (GIVE ME PEACE ON EARTH)	George Harrison
7/07	2	12. WILL IT GO ROUND IN CIRCLES	Billy Preston
7/21	2	13. BAD, BAD LEROY BROWN	Jim Croce
8/04	2	14. THE MORNING AFTER	Maureen McGovern
8/18	1	15. TOUCH ME IN THE MORNING	Diana Ross
8/25	2	16. BROTHER LOUIE	Stories
9/08	2	†17. LET'S GET IT ON	Marvin Gaye
9/15	1	18. DELTA DAWN	Helen Reddy
9/29	1	19. WE'RE AN AMERICAN BAND	Grand Funk
10/06	2	20. HALF-BREED	Cher
10/20	1	21. ANGIE	The Rolling Stones
10/27	2	22. MIDNIGHT TRAIN TO GEORGIA	Gladys Knight & The Pips
11/10	2	23. KEEP ON TRUCKIN'	Eddie Kendricks
11/24	1	24. PHOTOGRAPH	Ringo Starr
12/01	2	25. TOP OF THE WORLD	Carpenters
12/15	2	26. THE MOST BEAUTIFUL GIRL	Charlie Rich
12/29	2	27. TIME IN A BOTTLE	Jim Croce

DATE	WKS	RECORD TITLE	ARTIST
1974			
1/12	1	1. THE JOKER	Steve Miller Band
1/19	1	2. SHOW AND TELL	Al Wilson
1/26	1	3. YOU'RE SIXTEEN	Ringo Starr
2/02	3	†4. THE WAY WE WERE	Barbra Streisand
2/09	1	5. LOVE'S THEME	Love Unlimited Orchestra
3/02	3	6. SEASONS IN THE SUN	Terry Jacks
3/23	1	7. DARK LADY	Cher
3/30	1	8. SUNSHINE ON MY SHOULDERS	John Denver
4/06	1	9. HOOKED ON A FEELING	Blue Swede
4/13	1	10. BENNIE AND THE JETS	Elton John
4/20	2	11. TSOP (THE SOUND OF PHILADELPHIA)	MFSB featuring The Three Degrees
5/04	2	12. THE LOCO-MOTION	Grand Funk
5/18	3	13. THE STREAK	Ray Stevens
6/08	1	14. BAND ON THE RUN	Paul McCartney & Wings
6/15	2	15. BILLY, DON'T BE A HERO	Bo Donaldson & The Heywoods
6/29	1	16. SUNDOWN	Gordon Lightfoot
7/06	1	17. ROCK THE BOAT	The Hues Corporation
7/13	2	18. ROCK YOUR BABY	George McCrae
7/27	2	19. ANNIE'S SONG	John Denver
8/10	1	20. FEEL LIKE MAKIN' LOVE	Roberta Flack
8/17	1	21. THE NIGHT CHICAGO DIED	Paper Lace
8/24	3	22. (YOU'RE) HAVING MY BABY	Paul Anka
9/14	1	23. I SHOT THE SHERIFF	Eric Clapton
9/21	1	24. CAN'T GET ENOUGH OF YOUR LOVE, BABE	Barry White
9/28	1	25. ROCK ME GENTLY	Andy Kim
10/05	2	26. I HONESTLY LOVE YOU	Olivia Newton-John
10/19	1	27. NOTHING FROM NOTHING	Billy Preston
10/26	1	28. THEN CAME YOU	Dionne Warwicke & Spinners
11/02	1	29. YOU HAVEN'T DONE NOTHIN	Stevie Wonder
11/09	1	30. YOU AIN'T SEEN NOTHING YET	Bachman-Turner Overdrive
11/16	1	31. WHATEVER GETS YOU THRU THE NIGHT	John Lennon with The Plastic Ono Nuclear Band
11/23	2	32. I CAN HELP	Billy Swan
12/07	2	33. KUNG FU FIGHTING	Carl Douglas
12/21	1	34. CAT'S IN THE CRADLE	Harry Chapin
12/28	1	35. ANGIE BABY	Helen Reddy

DATE	WKS	RECORD TITLE	ARTIST
1975			
1/04	2	1. LUCY IN THE SKY WITH DIAMONDS	Elton John
1/18	1	2. MANDY	Barry Manilow
1/25	1	3. PLEASE MR. POSTMAN	Carpenters
2/01	1	4. LAUGHTER IN THE RAIN	Neil Sedaka
2/08	1	5. FIRE	Ohio Players
2/15	1	6. YOU'RE NO GOOD	Linda Ronstadt
2/22	1	7. PICK UP THE PIECES	AWB
3/01	1	8. BEST OF MY LOVE	The Eagles
3/08	1	9. HAVE YOU NEVER BEEN MELLOW	Olivia Newton-John
3/15	1	10. BLACK WATER	The Doobie Brothers
3/22	1	11. MY EYES ADORED YOU	Frankie Valli
3/29	1	12. LADY MARMALADE	LaBelle
4/05	1	13. LOVIN' YOU	Minnie Riperton
4/12	2	14. PHILADELPHIA FREEDOM	The Elton John Band
4/26	1	15. (HEY WON'T YOU PLAY) ANOTHER SOMEBODY DONE SOMEBODY WRONG SONG	B.J. Thomas
5/03	3	16. HE DON'T LOVE YOU (LIKE I LOVE YOU)	Tony Orlando & Dawn
5/24	1	17. SHINING STAR	Earth, Wind & Fire
5/31	1	18. BEFORE THE NEXT TEARDROP FALLS	Freddy Fender
6/07	1	19. THANK GOD I'M A COUNTRY BOY	John Denver
6/14	1	20. SISTER GOLDEN HAIR	America
6/21	4	21. LOVE WILL KEEP US TOGETHER	The Captain & Tennille
7/19	1	22. LISTEN TO WHAT THE MAN SAID	Wings
7/26	1	23. THE HUSTLE	Van McCoy
8/02	1	24. ONE OF THESE NIGHTS	Eagles
8/09	2	25. JIVE TALKIN'	Bee Gees
8/23	1	26. FALLIN' IN LOVE	Hamilton, Joe Frank & Reynolds
8/30	1	27. GET DOWN TONIGHT	K.C. & The Sunshine Band
9/06	2	28. RHINESTONE COWBOY	Glen Campbell
9/20	2	†29. FAME	David Bowie
9/27	1	30. I'M SORRY	John Denver
10/11	3	31. BAD BLOOD	Neil Sedaka
11/01	3	32. ISLAND GIRL	Elton John
11/22	2	†33. THAT'S THE WAY (I LIKE IT)	KC & The Sunshine Band
11/29	3	34. FLY, ROBIN, FLY	Silver Convention
12/27	1	35. LET'S DO IT AGAIN	The Staple Singers

DATE	WKS	RECORD TITLE	ARTIST
1976			
1/03	1	1. SATURDAY NIGHT	Bay City Rollers
1/10	1	2. CONVOY	C.W. McCall
1/17	1	3. I WRITE THE SONGS	Barry Manilow
1/24	1	4. THEME FROM MAHOGANY (DO YOU KNOW WHERE YOU'RE GOING TO)	Diana Ross
1/31	1	5. LOVE ROLLERCOASTER	Ohio Players
2/07	3	6. 50 WAYS TO LEAVE YOUR LOVER	Paul Simon
2/28	1	7. THEME FROM S.W.A.T	.Rhythm Heritage
3/06	1	8. LOVE MACHINE (PART 1)	The Miracles
3/13	3	9. DECEMBER, 1963 (OH, WHAT A NIGHT)	The Four Seasons
4/03	4	10. DISCO LADY	Johnnie Taylor
5/01	1	11. LET YOUR LOVE FLOW	Bellamy Brothers
5/08	1	12. WELCOME BACK	John Sebastian
5/15	1	13. BOOGIE FEVER	Sylvers
5/22	5	†14. SILLY LOVE SONGS	Wings
5/29	2	15. LOVE HANGOVER	Diana Ross
7/10	2	16. AFTERNOON DELIGHT	Starland Vocal Band
7/24	2	17. KISS AND SAY GOODBYE	Manhattans
8/07	4	18. DON'T GO BREAKING MY HEART	Elton John & Kiki Dee
9/04	1	19. YOU SHOULD BE DANCING	Bee Gees
9/11	1	20. (SHAKE, SHAKE, SHAKE) SHAKE YOUR BOOTY	KC & The Sunshine Band
9/18	3	21. PLAY THAT FUNKY MUSIC	Wild Cherry
10/09	1	22. A FIFTH OF BEETHOVEN	Walter Murphy & The Big Apple Band
10/16	1	23. DISCO DUCK (PART 1)	Rick Dees & His Cast Of Idiots
10/23	2	24. IF YOU LEAVE ME NOW	Chicago
11/06	1	25. ROCK'N ME	Steve Miller
11/13	8	26. TONIGHT'S THE NIGHT (GONNA BE ALRIGHT)	Rod Stewart
1977			
1/08	1	1. YOU DON'T HAVE TO BE A STAR (TO BE IN MY SHOW)	Marilyn McCoo & Billy Davis, Jr.
1/15	1	2. YOU MAKE ME FEEL LIKE DANCING	Leo Sayer
1/22	1	3. I WISH	Stevie Wonder
1/29	1	4. CAR WASH	Rose Royce
2/05	2	5. TORN BETWEEN TWO LOVERS	Mary MacGregor
2/19	1	6. BLINDED BY THE LIGHT	Manfred Mann's Earth Band
2/26	1	7. NEW KID IN TOWN	Eagles
3/05	3	8. EVERGREEN	Barbra Streisand
3/26	2	9. RICH GIRL	Daryl Hall & John Oates

DATE	WKS	RECORD TITLE	ARTIST
1977 CONTINUED			
4/09	1	10. DANCING QUEEN	Abba
4/16	1	11. DON'T GIVE UP ON US	David Soul
4/23	1	12. DON'T LEAVE ME THIS WAY	Thelma Houston
4/30	1	13. SOUTHERN NIGHTS	Glen Campbell
5/07	1	14. HOTEL CALIFORNIA	Eagles
5/14	1	15. WHEN I NEED YOU	Leo Sayer
5/21	3	16. SIR DUKE	Stevie Wonder
6/11	1	17. I'M YOUR BOOGIE MAN	KC & The Sunshine Band
6/18	1	18. DREAMS	Fleetwood Mac
6/25	1	19. GOT TO GIVE IT UP (PT. I)	Marvin Gaye
7/02	1	20. GONNA FLY NOW	Bill Conti
7/09	1	21. UNDERCOVER ANGEL	Alan O'Day
7/16	1	22. DA DOO RON RON	Shaun Cassidy
7/23	1	23. LOOKS LIKE WE MADE IT	Barry Manilow
7/30	4	†24. I JUST WANT TO BE YOUR EVERYTHING	Andy Gibb
8/20	5	†25. BEST OF MY LOVE	The Emotions
10/01	2	26. STAR WARS THEME/CANTINA BAND	Meco
10/15	10	27. YOU LIGHT UP MY LIFE	Debby Boone
12/24	3	28. HOW DEEP IS YOUR LOVE	Bee Gees
1978			
1/14	3	1. BABY COME BACK	Player
2/04	4	2. STAYIN' ALIVE	Bee Gees
3/04	2	3. (LOVE IS) THICKER THAN WATER	Andy Gibb
3/18	8	4. NIGHT FEVER	Bee Gees
5/13	1	5. IF I CAN'T HAVE YOU	Yvonne Elliman
5/20	2	6. WITH A LITTLE LUCK	Wings
6/03	1	7. TOO MUCH, TOO LITTLE, TOO LATE	Johnny Mathis/ Deniece Williams
6/10	1	8. YOU'RE THE ONE THAT I WANT	John Travolta & Olivia Newton-John
6/17	7	9. SHADOW DANCING	Andy Gibb
8/05	1	10. MISS YOU	The Rolling Stones
8/12	2	11. THREE TIMES A LADY	Commodores
8/26	2	12. GREASE	Frankie Valli
9/09	3	13. BOOGIE OOGIE OOGIE	A Taste Of Honey
9/30	4	14. KISS YOU ALL OVER	Exile
10/28	1	15. HOT CHILD IN THE CITY	Nick Gilder
11/04	1	16. YOU NEEDED ME	Anne Murray
11/11	3	17. MACARTHUR PARK	Donna Summer
12/02	2	†18. YOU DON'T BRING ME FLOWERS	Barbra Streisand & Neil Diamond
12/09	6	†19. LE FREAK	Chic

DATE	WKS	RECORD TITLE	ARTIST
		1979	
1/06	2	1. TOO MUCH HEAVEN	Bee Gees
2/10	4	2. DA YA THINK I'M SEXY?	Rod Stewart
3/10	3	†3. I WILL SURVIVE	Gloria Gaynor
3/24	2	4. TRAGEDY	Bee Gees
4/14	1	5. WHAT A FOOL BELIEVES	The Doobie Brothers
4/21	1	6. KNOCK ON WOOD	Amii Stewart
4/28	1	7. HEART OF GLASS	Blondie
5/05	4	8. REUNITED	Peaches & Herb
6/02	3	†9. HOT STUFF	Donna Summer
6/09	1	10. LOVE YOU INSIDE OUT	Bee Gees
6/30	2	11. RING MY BELL	Anita Ward
7/14	5	12. BAD GIRLS	Donna Summer
8/18	1	13. GOOD TIMES	Chic
8/25	6	14. MY SHARONA	The Knack
10/06	1	15. SAD EYES	Robert John
10/13	1	16. DON'T STOP 'TIL YOU GET ENOUGH	Michael Jackson
10/20	2	17. RISE	Herb Alpert
11/03	1	18. POP MUZIK	M
11/10	1	19. HEARTACHE TONIGHT	Eagles
11/17	1	20. STILL	Commodores
11/24	2	21. NO MORE TEARS (ENOUGH IS ENOUGH)	Barbra Streisand / Donna Summer
12/08	2	22. BABE	Styx
12/22	3	†23. ESCAPE (THE PINA COLADA SONG)	Rupert Holmes
		1980	
1/05	1	1. PLEASE DON'T GO	K.C. & The Sunshine Band
1/19	4	2. ROCK WITH YOU	Michael Jackson
2/16	1	3. DO THAT TO ME ONE MORE TIME	The Captain & Tennille
2/23	4	4. CRAZY LITTLE THING CALLED LOVE	Queen
3/22	4	5. ANOTHER BRICK IN THE WALL (PART II)	Pink Floyd
4/19	6	6. CALL ME	Blondie
5/31	4	7. FUNKYTOWN	Lipps, Inc.
6/28	3	8. COMING UP (LIVE AT GLASGOW)	Paul McCartney & Wings
7/19	2	9. IT'S STILL ROCK AND ROLL TO ME	Billy Joel
8/02	4	10. MAGIC	Olivia Newton-John
8/30	1	11. SAILING	Christopher Cross
9/06	4	12. UPSIDE DOWN	Diana Ross
10/04	3	13. ANOTHER ONE BITES THE DUST	Queen
10/25	3	14. WOMAN IN LOVE	Barbra Streisand
11/15	6	15. LADY	Kenny Rogers
12/27	5	16. (JUST LIKE) STARTING OVER	John Lennon

DATE	WKS	RECORD TITLE	ARTIST
1981			
1/31	1	1. THE TIDE IS HIGH	Blondie
2/07	2	2. CELEBRATION	Kool & The Gang
2/21	2	†3. 9 TO 5	Dolly Parton
2/28	2	4. I LOVE A RAINY NIGHT	Eddie Rabbitt
3/21	1	5. KEEP ON LOVING YOU	REO Speedwagon
3/28	2	6. RAPTURE	Blondie
4/11	3	7. KISS ON MY LIST	Daryl Hall & John Oates
5/02	2	8. MORNING TRAIN (NINE TO FIVE)	Sheena Easton
5/16	9	†9. BETTE DAVIS EYES	Kim Carnes
6/20	1	10. STARS ON 45	Stars on 45
7/25	1	11. THE ONE THAT YOU LOVE	Air Supply
8/01	2	12. JESSIE'S GIRL	Rick Springfield
8/15	9	13. ENDLESS LOVE	Diana Ross & Lionel Richie
10/17	3	14. ARTHUR'S THEME (BEST THAT YOU CAN DO)	Christopher Cross
11/07	2	15. PRIVATE EYES	Daryl Hall & John Oates
11/21	10	16. PHYSICAL	Olivia Newton-John
1982			
1/30	1	1. I CAN'T GO FOR THAT (NO CAN DO)	Daryl Hall & John Oates
2/06	6	2. CENTERFOLD	The J. Geils Band
3/20	7	3. I LOVE ROCK 'N ROLL	Joan Jett & The Blackhearts
5/08	1	4. CHARIOTS OF FIRE - TITLES	Vangelis
5/15	7	5. EBONY AND IVORY	Paul McCartney with Stevie Wonder
7/03	3	6. DON'T YOU WANT ME	The Human League
7/24	6	7. EYE OF THE TIGER	Survivor
9/04	2	†8. ABRACADABRA	The Steve Miller Band
9/11	2	9. HARD TO SAY I'M SORRY	Chicago
10/02	4	10. JACK & DIANE	John Cougar
10/30	1	11. WHO CAN IT BE NOW?	Men At Work
11/06	3	12. UP WHERE WE BELONG	Joe Cocker & Jennifer Warnes
11/27	2	13. TRULY	Lionel Richie
12/11	1	14. MICKEY	Toni Basil
12/18	4	15. MANEATER	Daryl Hall & John Oates

DATE	WKS	RECORD TITLE	ARTIST
1983			
1/15	4	†1. DOWN UNDER	Men At Work
2/05	1	2. AFRICA	Toto
2/19	2	3. BABY, COME TO ME	Patti Austin with James Ingram
3/05	7	4. BILLIE JEAN	Michael Jackson
4/23	1	5. COME ON EILEEN	Dexys Midnight Runners
4/30	3	6. BEAT IT	Michael Jackson
5/21	1	7. LET'S DANCE	David Bowie
5/28	6	8. FLASHDANCE	What A Feeling...Irene Cara
7/09	8	9. EVERY BREATH YOU TAKE	The Police
9/03	1	10. SWEET DREAMS (ARE MADE OF THIS)	Eurythmics
9/10	2	11. MANIAC	Michael Sembello
9/24	1	12. TELL HER ABOUT IT	Billy Joel
10/01	4	13. TOTAL ECLIPSE OF THE HEART	Bonnie Tyler
10/29	2	14. ISLANDS IN THE STREAM	Kenny Rogers & Dolly Parton
11/12	4	15. ALL NIGHT LONG (ALL NIGHT)	Lionel Richie
12/10	6	16. SAY SAY SAY	Paul McCartney & Michael Jackson
1984			
1/21	2	1. OWNER OF A LONELY HEART	Yes
2/04	3	2. KARMA CHAMELEON	Culture Club
2/25	5	3. JUMP	Van Halen
3/31	3	4. FOOTLOOSE	Kenny Loggins
4/21	3	5. AGAINST ALL ODDS (TAKE A LOOK AT ME NOW)	Phil Collins
5/12	2	6. HELLO	Lionel Richie
5/26	2	7. LET'S HEAR IT FOR THE BOY	Deniece Williams
6/09	2	8. TIME AFTER TIME	Cyndi Lauper
6/23	2	9. THE REFLEX	Duran Duran
7/07	5	10. WHEN DOVES CRY	Prince
8/11	3	11. GHOSTBUSTERS	Ray Parker Jr.
9/01	3	12. WHAT'S LOVE GOT TO DO WITH IT	Tina Turner
9/22	1	13. MISSING YOU	John Waite
9/29	2	14. LET'S GO CRAZY	Prince & The Revolution
10/13	3	15. I JUST CALLED TO SAY I LOVE YOU	Stevie Wonder
11/03	2	16. CARIBBEAN QUEEN (NO MORE LOVE ON THE RUN)	Billy Ocean
11/17	3	17. WAKE ME UP BEFORE YOU GO-GO	Wham!
12/08	2	18. OUT OF TOUCH	Daryl Hall John Oates
12/22	6	19. LIKE A VIRGIN	Madonna

DATE	WKS	RECORD TITLE	ARTIST
1985			
2/02	2	1. I WANT TO KNOW WHAT LOVE IS	Foreigner
2/16	3	2. CARELESS WHISPER	Wham! featuring George Michael
3/09	3	3. CAN'T FIGHT THIS FEELING	REO Speedwagon
3/30	2	4. ONE MORE NIGHT	Phil Collins
4/13	4	5. WE ARE THE WORLD	USA for Africa
5/11	1	6. CRAZY FOR YOU	Madonna
5/18	1	7. DON'T YOU (FORGET ABOUT ME)	Simple Minds
5/25	2	8. EVERYTHING SHE WANTS	Wham!
6/08	2	9. EVERYBODY WANTS TO RULE THE WORLD	Tears For Fears
6/22	2	10. HEAVEN	Bryan Adams
7/06	1	11. SUSSUDIO	Phil Collins
7/13	2	12. A VIEW TO A KILL	Duran Duran
7/27	1	13. EVERYTIME YOU GO AWAY	Paul Young
8/03	3	14. SHOUT	Tears For Fears
8/24	2	15. THE POWER OF LOVE	Huey Lewis & The News
9/07	2	16. ST. ELMO'S FIRE (MAN IN MOTION)	John Parr
9/21	3	17. MONEY FOR NOTHING	Dire Straits
10/12	1	18. OH SHEILA	Ready For The World
10/19	1	19. TAKE ON ME	a-ha
10/26	1	20. SAVING ALL MY LOVE FOR YOU	Whitney Houston
11/02	1	21. PART-TIME LOVER	Stevie Wonder
11/09	1	22. MIAMI VICE THEME	Jan Hammer
11/16	2	23. WE BUILT THIS CITY	Starship
11/30	1	24. SEPARATE LIVES	Phil Collins & Marilyn Martin
12/07	2	25. BROKEN WINGS	Mr. Mister
12/21	4	26. SAY YOU, SAY ME	Lionel Richie

DATE	WKS	RECORD TITLE	ARTIST
1986			
1/18	4	1. THAT'S WHAT FRIENDS ARE FOR	Dionne & Friends
2/15	2	2. HOW WILL I KNOW	Whitney Houston
3/01	2	3. KYRIE	Mr. Mister
3/15	1	4. SARA	Starship
3/22	1	5. THESE DREAMS	Heart
3/29	3	6. ROCK ME AMADEUS	Falco
4/19	2	7. KISS	Prince & The Revolution
5/03	1	8. ADDICTED TO LOVE	Robert Palmer
5/10	1	9. WEST END GIRLS	Pet Shop Boys
5/17	3	10. GREATEST LOVE OF ALL	Whitney Houston
6/07	1	11. LIVE TO TELL	Madonna
6/14	3	12. ON MY OWN	Patti LaBelle & Michael McDonald
7/05	1	13. THERE'LL BE SAD SONGS (TO MAKE YOU CRY)	Billy Ocean
7/12	1	14. HOLDING BACK THE YEARS	Simply Red
7/19	1	15. INVISIBLE TOUCH	Genesis
7/26	1	16. SLEDGEHAMMER	Peter Gabriel
8/02	2	17. GLORY OF LOVE	Peter Cetera
8/16	2	18. PAPA DON'T PREACH	Madonna
8/30	1	19. HIGHER LOVE	Steve Winwood
9/06	1	20. VENUS	Bananarama
9/13	1	21. TAKE MY BREATH AWAY	Berlin
9/20	3	22. STUCK WITH YOU	Huey Lewis & The News
10/11	2	23. WHEN I THINK OF YOU	Janet Jackson
10/25	2	24. TRUE COLORS	Cyndi Lauper
11/08	2	25. AMANDA	Boston
11/22	1	26. HUMAN	Human League
11/29	1	27. YOU GIVE LOVE A BAD NAME	Bon Jovi
12/06	1	28. THE NEXT TIME I FALL	Peter Cetera with Amy Grant
12/13	1	29. THE WAY IT IS	Bruce Hornsby & The Range
12/20	4	30. WALK LIKE AN EGYPTIAN	Bangles

DATE	WKS	RECORD TITLE	ARTIST
1987			
1/17	1	1. SHAKE YOU DOWN	Gregory Abbott
1/24	2	2. AT THIS MOMENT	Billy Vera & The Beaters
2/07	1	3. OPEN YOUR HEART	Madonna
2/14	4	4. LIVIN' ON A PRAYER	Bon Jovi
3/14	1	5. JACOB'S LADDER	Huey Lewis & The News
3/21	2	6. LEAN ON ME	Club Nouveau
4/04	2	7. NOTHING'S GONNA STOP US NOW	Starship
4/18	2	8. I KNEW YOU WERE WAITING (FOR ME)	Aretha Franklin & George Michael
5/02	2	9. (I JUST) DIED IN YOUR ARMS	Cutting Crew
5/16	3	10. WITH OR WITHOUT YOU	U2
6/06	1	11. YOU KEEP ME HANGIN' ON	Kim Wilde
6/13	1	12. ALWAYS	Atlantic Starr
6/20	1	13. HEAD TO TOE	Lisa Lisa & Cult Jam
6/27	2	14. I WANNA DANCE WITH SOMEBODY (WHO LOVES ME)	Whitney Houston
7/11	3	15. ALONE	Heart
8/01	1	16. SHAKEDOWN	Bob Seger
8/08	2	17. I STILL HAVEN'T FOUND WHAT I'M LOOKING FOR	U2
8/22	1	18. WHO'S THAT GIRL	Madonna
8/29	3	19. LA BAMBA	Los Lobos
9/19	1	20. I JUST CAN'T STOP LOVING YOU	Michael Jackson
9/26	2	21. DIDN'T WE ALMOST HAVE IT ALL	Whitney Houston
10/10	1	22. HERE I GO AGAIN	Whitesnake
10/17	1	23. LOST IN EMOTION	Lisa Lisa & Cult Jam
10/24	2	24. BAD	Michael Jackson
11/07	2	25. I THINK WE'RE ALONE NOW	Tiffany
11/21	1	26. MONY MONY "LIVE"	Billy Idol
11/28	1	27. (I'VE HAD) THE TIME OF MY LIFE	Bill Medley & Jennifer Warnes
12/05	1	28. HEAVEN IS A PLACE ON EARTH	Belinda Carlisle
12/12	4	29. FAITH	George Michael

DATE	WKS	RECORD TITLE	ARTIST
1988			
1/09	1	1. SO EMOTIONAL	Whitney Houston
1/16	1	2. GOT MY MIND SET ON YOU	George Harrison
1/23	1	3. THE WAY YOU MAKE ME FEEL	Michael Jackson
1/30	1	4. NEED YOU TONIGHT	INXS
2/06	2	5. COULD'VE BEEN	Tiffany
2/20	1	6. SEASONS CHANGE	Expose
2/27	2	7. FATHER FIGURE	George Michael
3/12	2	8. NEVER GONNA GIVE YOU UP	Rick Astley
3/26	2	9. MAN IN THE MIRROR	Michael Jackson
4/09	2	10. GET OUTTA MY DREAMS, GET INTO MY CAR	Billy Ocean
4/23	2	11. WHERE DO BROKEN HEARTS GO	Whitney Houston
5/07	1	12. WISHING WELL	Terence Trent D'Arby
5/14	2	13. ANYTHING FOR YOU	Gloria Estefan & Miami Sound Machine
5/28	3	14. ONE MORE TRY	George Michael
6/18	1	15. TOGETHER FOREVER	Rick Astley
6/25	1	16. FOOLISH BEAT	Debbie Gibson
7/02	1	17. DIRTY DIANA	Michael Jackson
7/09	2	18. THE FLAME	Cheap Trick
7/23	1	19. HOLD ON TO THE NIGHTS	Richard Marx
7/30	4	20. ROLL WITH IT	Steve Winwood
8/27	2	21. MONKEY	George Michael
9/10	2	22. SWEET CHILD O' MINE	Guns N' Roses
9/24	2	23. DON'T WORRY BE HAPPY	Bobby McFerrin
10/08	1	24. LOVE BITES	Def Leppard
10/15	1	25. RED RED WINE	UB40
10/22	2	26. GROOVY KIND OF LOVE	Phil Collins
11/05	1	27. KOKOMO	The Beach Boys
11/12	1	28. WILD, WILD WEST	The Escape Club
11/19	2	29. BAD MEDICINE	Bon Jovi
12/03	1	30. BABY, I LOVE YOUR WAY/FREEBIRD MEDLEY (FREE BABY)	Will To Power
12/10	2	31. LOOK AWAY	Chicago
12/24	3	32. EVERY ROSE HAS ITS THORN	Poison
1989			
1/14	1	1. MY PREROGATIVE	Bobby Brown
1/21	2	2. TWO HEARTS	Phil Collins
2/04	1	3. WHEN I'M WITH YOU	Sheriff
2/11	3	4. STRAIGHT UP	Paula Abdul
3/04	3	5. LOST IN YOUR EYES	Debbie Gibson
3/25	1	6. THE LIVING YEARS	Mike + The Mechanics
4/01	1	7. ETERNAL FLAME	Bangles
4/08	1	8. THE LOOK	Roxette
4/15	1	9. SHE DRIVES ME CRAZY	Fine Young Cannibals
4/22	3	10. LIKE A PRAYER	Madonna
5/13	1	11. I'LL BE THERE FOR YOU	Bon Jovi
5/20	2	12. FOREVER YOUR GIRL	Paula Abdul
6/03	1	13. ROCK ON	Michael Damian
6/10	1	14. WIND BENEATH MY WINGS	Bette Midler
6/17	1	15. I'LL BE LOVING YOU (FOREVER)	New Kids on the Block
6/24	1	16. SATISFIED	Richard Marx

DATE	WKS	RECORD TITLE	ARTIST
1989 (continued)			
7/01	1	17. BABY DON'T FORGET MY NUMBER	Milli Vanilli
7/08	1	18. GOOD THING	Fine Young Cannibals
7/15	1	19. IF YOU DON'T KNOW ME BY NOW	Simply Red
7/22	2	20. TOY SOLDIERS	Martika
8/05	1	21. BATDANCE	Prince
8/12	3	22. RIGHT HERE WAITING	Richard Marx
9/02	1	23. COLD HEARTED	Paula Adbul
9/09	1	24. HANGIN' TOUGH	New Kids on the Block
9/16	1	25. DON'T WANNA LOSE YOU	Gloria Estefan
9/23	2	26. GIRL I'M GONNA MISS YOU	Milli Vanilli
10/07	4	27. MISS YOU MUCH	Janet Jackson
11/04	1	28. LISTEN TO YOUR HEART	Roxette
11/11	2	29. WHEN I SEE YOU SMILE	Bad Engish
11/25	2	30. BLAME IT ON THE RAIN	Milli Vanilli
12/09	2	31. WE DIDN'T START THE FIRE	Billy Joel
12/23	4	32. ANOTHER DAY IN PARADISE	Phil Collins
1990			
1/20	3	1. HOW AM I SUPPOSED TO LIVE WITHOUT YOU	Michael Bolton
2/10	3	2. OPPOSITES ATTRACT	Paula Abdul with The Wild Pair
3/03	3	3. ESCAPADE	Janet Jackson
3/24	2	4. BLACK VELVET	Alannah Myles
4/07	1	5. LOVE WILL LEAD YOU BACK	Taylor Dayne
4/14	1	6. I'LL BE YOUR EVERYTHING	Tommy Page
4/21	4	7. NOTHING COMPARES 2U	Sinead O'Connor
5/19	3	8. VOGUE	Madonna
6/09	1	9. HOLD ON	Wilson Phillips
6/16	2	10. IT MUST HAVE BEEN LOVE	Roxette
6/30	3	11. STEP BY STEP	New Kids on the Block
7/21	2	12. SHE AIN'T WORTH IT	Glenn Medeiros (featuring Bobby Brown)
8/04	4	13. VISION OF LOVE	Mariah Carey
9/01	1	14. IF WISHES CAME TRUE	Sweet Sensation
9/08	1	15. BLAZE OF GLORY	Jon Bon Jovi
9/15	2	16. RELEASE ME	Wilson Phillips
9/29	1	17. (CAN'T LIVE WITHOUT YOUR) LOVE AND AFFECTION	Nelson
10/06	1	18. CLOSE TO YOU	Maxi Priest
10/13	1	19. PRAYING FOR TIME	George Michael
10/20	1	20. I DON'T HAVE THE HEART	James Ingram
10/27	1	21. BLACK CAT	Janet Jackson
11/03	1	22. ICE ICE BABY	Vanilla Ice
11/10	3	23. LOVE TAKES TIME	Mariah Carey
12/01	1	24. I'M YOUR BABY TONIGHT	Whitney Houston
12/08	4	25. BECAUSE I LOVE YOU (THE POSTMAN SONG)	Stevie B

DATE	WKS	RECORD TITLE	ARTIST
1991 (to date)			
1/05	2	1. JUSTIFY MY LOVE	Madonna
1/19	1	2. LOVE WILL NEVER DO WITHOUT YOU	Janet Jackson
1/26	2	3. THE FIRST TIME	Surface
2/09	2	4. GONNA MAKE YOU SWEAT (EVERYBODY DANCE NOW)	C & C Music Factory featuring Freedom Williams
2/23	2	5. ALL THE MAN THAT I NEED	Whitney Houston
3/09	2	6. SOMEDAY	Mariah Carey
3/23	1	7. ONE MORE TRY	Timmy -T-
3/30	2	8. COMING OUT OF THE DARK	Gloria Estefan
4/13	1	9. I'VE BEEN THINKING ABOUT YOU	Londonbeat
4/20	1	10. YOU'RE IN LOVE	Wilson Phillips
4/27	2	11. BABY BABY	Amy Grant
5/11	1	12. JOYRIDE	Roxette
5/18	1	13. I LIKE THE WAY (THE KISSING GAME)	Hi-Five
5/25	2	14. I DON'T WANNA CRY	Mariah Carey
6/08	1	15. MORE THAN WORDS	Extreme
6/15	5	16. RUSH, RUSH	Paula Abdul
7/20	1	17. UNBELIEVABLE	EMF
7/27	7	18. (EVERYTHING I DO) I DO IT FOR YOU	Bryan Adams

The Billboard Charts From Top To Bottom!

Only Joel Whitburn's Record Research Books List Every Record To Ever Appear On Every Major Billboard *Chart.*

When the talk turns to music, more people turn to Joel Whitburn's Record Research Collection than to any other reference source.

That's because these are the only books that get right to the bottom of *Billboard*'s major charts, with complete, fully accurate chart data on every record ever charted. So they're quoted with conflence by DJ's, music show hosts, program directors, collectors and other music enthusiasts worldwide.

Each book lists every record's signifiant chart data, such as peak position, debut date, peak date, weeks charted, label, record number and much more, all conveniently arranged for fast, easy reference. Most books also feature artist biographies, record notes, RIAA Platinum/Gold Record certifiations, top artist and record achievements, all-time artist and record rankings, a chronological listing of all #1 hits, and additional in-depth chart information.

And now, the new large-format *Billboard* Hot 100 Charts book series takes chart research one step further, by actually reproducing weekly "Hot 100" charts by decade.

Joel Whitburn's Record Research Collection. #1 on everyone's hit list.

TOP POP SINGLES
1955–1990
Nearly 20,000 Pop singles—every "Hot 100" hit—arranged by artist. $70.00 Hardcover/$60.00 Softcover.

POP SINGLES ANNUAL
1955–1990
A year-by-year ranking, based on chart performance, of the nearly 20,000 Pop hits. $70.00 Hardcover/$60.00 Softcover.

THE BILLBOARD HOT 100 CHARTS:
THE SIXTIES 1960–1969
THE SEVENTIES 1970–1979
THE EIGHTIES 1980–1989
Three complete collections of the actual weekly "Hot 100" charts from each decade, reproduced in black-and-white at 70% of original size. Deluxe Hardcover. $90.00 each.

TOP POP ALBUMS
1955–1985
The 14,000 LPs that ever appeared on *Billboard*'s Pop albums charts, arranged by artist. $50.00 Softcover.

POP MEMORIES
1890–1954
The only documented chart history of early American popular music, arranged by artist. $60.00 Hardcover/$50.00 Softcover.

TOP COUNTRY SINGLES
1944–1988
An artist-by-artist listing of every "Country" single ever charted. $60.00 Hardcover/$50.00 Softcover.

TOP R&B SINGLES
1942–1988

Every "Soul," "Black," "Urban Contemporary" and "Rhythm & Blues" charted single, listed by artist. $60.00 Hardcover/$50.00 Softcover.

BILLBOARD'S TOP 10 CHARTS
1958–1988

1,550 actual, weekly Top 10 Pop singles charts in the original "Hot 100" chart format. $60.00 Hardcover/$50.00 Softcover.

BUBBLING UNDER THE HOT 100
1959–1981

Over 4,000 big regional hits, one-shot efforts and other semi-popular singles from the "Bubbling Under" Pop charts, arranged by artist. $35.00 Softcover.

BILLBOARD #1 HITS
1950–1991

A week-by-week listing of every #1 single and album from *Billboard*'s Pop, R&B, Country and Adult Contemporary charts. $35.00 Softcover.

BILLBOARD'S TOP 3000+
1955–1990

Every single that ever appeared in the Top 10 of *Billboard*'s Pop charts, ranked by all-time popularity. $25.00 Softcover.

MUSIC YEARBOOKS
1983/1984/1985/1986

The complete story of each year in music, covering *Billboard*'s biggest singles and albums charts. $35.00 each. Softcover.

MUSIC & VIDEO YEARBOOKS
1987/1988/1989/1990

Comprehensive, yearly updates on *Billboard*'s major singles, albums and videocassettes charts. $35.00 each. Softcover.

DAILY #1 HITS
1940–1989

A day-by-day listing of the #1 Pop records of the past 50 years. $25.00 Spiral-bound Softcover.

For complete book descriptions and ordering information, call, write or fax today.

The World's Leading Authority On Recorded Entertainment

RECORD RESEARCH INC.
P.O. Box 200
Menomonee Falls, WI 53052-0200
Phone: 414-251-5408
Fax: 414-251-9452